Principles of Marketing

Pearson

PHILP KOTLER GARY ARMSTRONG LLOYD C. HARRIS NIGEL PIERCY

PRINCIPLES OF Marketing

7TH EUROPEAN EDITION

Harlow, England • London • New York • Boston • San Francisco • Toronto • Sydney • Dubai • Singapore • Hong Kong
Tokyo • Seoul • Taipei • New Delhi • Cape Town • São Paulo • Mexico City • Madrid • Amsterdam • Munich • Paris • Milan

Pearson Education Limited
Edinburgh Gate
Harlow CM20 2JE
United Kingdom
Tel: +44 (0)1279 623623

Web: www.pearson.com/uk

Authorised adaptation from the United States edition, entitled Principles of Marketing, 16th Edition, ISBN 9780133795028 by Armstrong, Gary; Kotler, Philip, published by Pearson Education, Inc, Copyright © 2016.

First European edition published 1996 by Prentice Hall Europe (print)
Second European edition published 1999 (print)
Third European edition published 2001 by Pearson Education (print)
Fourth European edition published 2005 (print)
Fifth European edition published 2008 (print)
Sixth European edition published 2013 (print and electronic)
Seventh European edition published 2017 (print and electronic)

© Prentice Hall Europe 1996, 1999 (print)
© Pearson Education Limited 2013, 2017 (print and electronic)

Pearson Education is not responsible for the content of third-party internet sites.

The screenshots in this book are reprinted by permission of Microsoft Corporation.

ISBN: 978-1-292-09289-8 (print)
         978-1-292-11525-2 (PDF)
         978-1-292-17066-4 (ePub)

British Library Cataloguing-in-Publication Data
A catalogue record for this book is available from the British Library

Library of Congress Cataloguing-in-Publication Data
A catalogue record for this book is available from the Library of Congress

10 9 8 7 6 5 4 3 2
20 19 18

Front cover image: Henrik Sorensen/Getty Images

Typeset in 10/12 pt Sabon MT Pro by Lumina Datamatics, Inc.
Printed and bound by L.E.G.O. S.p.A., Italy

NOTE THAT ANY PAGE CROSS REFERENCES REFER TO THE PRINT EDITION

BRIEF CONTENTS

CONTENTS

Part 2: Understanding the marketplace and consumers

Chapter 3 Analysing the marketing environment

Chapter 4 Managing marketing information to gain customer insights

Chapter 10 Pricing: understanding and capturing customer value

Chapter 11 Pricing strategies: additional consideration

Companion Website

For open-access **student resources** specifically written to complement this textbook and support your learning, please visit **www.pearsoned.co.uk/kotler**

Lecturer Resources

For password-protected online resources tailored to support the use of this textbook in teaching, please visit **www.pearsoned.co.uk/kotler**

PREFACE

The Seventh European Edition of *Principles of Marketing* setting the standard in undergraduate marketing education

Principles of Marketing is the most-trusted source for teaching and learning basic marketing concepts and practices. More than ever, the Seventh European Edition introduces new marketing students to the fascinating world of modern marketing in an innovative, complete and authoritative yet fresh, practical and enjoyable way. In this Seventh European Edition, we've once again added substantial new content and pored over every page, table, figure, fact and example in order to keep this the best text from which to learn about and teach marketing. Enhanced by the Companion Website, which includes, among other resources, videos and questions, the Seventh European Edition of *Principles of Marketing* remains the world standard in introductory and marketing education.

Marketing: creating customer value and engagement in the digital and social age

Top marketers share a common goal: putting the consumer at the heart of marketing. Today's marketing is all about creating customer value and engagement in a fast-changing, increasingly digital and social, marketplace.

Marketing starts with understanding consumer needs and wants, determining which target markets the organisation can serve best, and developing a compelling value proposition by which the organisation can attract and grow valued consumers. Then, more than just making a sale, today's marketers want to *engage* customers and build deep customer relationships that make their brands a meaningful part of consumers' conversations and lives. In this digital age, to go along with their tried-and-true traditional marketing methods, marketers have a dazzling set of new customer relationship-building tools – from the Internet, smartphones and tablets, to online, mobile and social media – for engaging customers any time, any place to shape brand conversations, experiences and community. If marketers do these things well, they will reap the rewards in terms of market share, profits and customer equity. In the Seventh European Edition of *Principles of Marketing*, you'll learn how *customer value* and *customer engagement* drive every good marketing strategy.

What's new in the Seventh European Edition?

- More than any other developments, sweeping new **online, social media, mobile and other digital technologies** are now affecting how marketers, brands and customers engage each other. The new edition features new and revised discussions and examples of the explosive impact of exciting *new digital marketing technologies* shaping marketing strategy and practice – from online, mobile and social media engagement technologies discussed in **Chapters 1**, **5**, **13**, **14**, **15** and **17**, to 'real-time listening' and 'big data' research tools in **Chapter 4**, online influence and brand communities in **Chapter 5**, and location-based marketing in **Chapter 7**; to the use of social media and social selling in business-to-business marketing in **Chapters 6** and **16**; to consumer, web, social media, mobile marketing and other new communications technologies in **Chapters 1**, **5**, **14**, **15**, **17** and throughout the text.
- A new **Chapter 1** section on the digital age (online, mobile and social media marketing) introduces the exciting new developments in digital and social media marketing. A completely revised **Chapter 17** on direct, online, social media and mobile marketing digs deeply into digital marketing tools such as online sites, social media, mobile ads and apps, online video, email, blogs and other digital platforms that engage consumers anywhere, anytime, via their computers, smartphones, tablets, Internet-ready TVs and other digital devices. The new edition is packed with new stories and examples illustrating how companies employ digital technology to gain competitive advantage – from McDonald's to new-age digital competitors such as Google, Amazon, Apple, Netflix, Pinterest and Facebook.
- The new edition features completely new and revised coverage of the emerging trend towards **customer engagement marketing** – building direct and continuous customer involvement in shaping brands, brand conversations, brand experiences and brand community. The burgeoning Internet and social media have created better informed, more connected and more empowered consumers. Thus today's marketers must now *engage* consumers rather than interrupt them. Marketers are augmenting their mass-media marketing efforts with a rich mix of online, mobile and social media marketing that promote deep consumer involvement and a sense of customer community surrounding their brands. Today's **new customer engagement-building tools** include everything from online sites, blogs, in-person events and video sharing to online communities and social media such as Facebook, YouTube, Pinterest, Vine, Twitter or a company's own social networking sites.
- In all, today's more engaged consumers are giving as much as they get in the form of two-way brand relationships. The new edition contains substantial new material on **customer engagement** and related developments such as **consumer empowerment**, **crowd sourcing**, **customer co-creation**, **consumer-generated marketing** and **real-time marketing**. A new **Chapter 1** section on engaging customers introduces customer engagement marketing. This and other related customer engagement topics are presented in **Chapter 1** (new or revised sections on customer engagement and today's digital and social media, and consumer-generated marketing); **Chapter 4** (big data and real-time research to gain deeper customer insights); **Chapter 5** (managing online influence and customer community through digital and social media marketing); **Chapter 13** (online, social media and digitised retailing); **Chapter 9** (crowdsourcing and customer-driven new-product development); **Chapters 14** and **15** (the new, more engaging marketing communications model and content marketing); and Chapter 17 (direct digital, online social media, and mobile marketing).
- The new edition continues to build on and extend the innovative **customer-value framework** from previous editions. The customer value and engagement model presented in the first chapter is fully integrated throughout the remainder of the book. No other marketing text presents such a clear and compelling customer-value approach.
- The new edition provides revised and expanded coverage of developments in the fast-changing area of integrated marketing communications. It tells how marketers are blending traditional media with new digital and social media tools – everything from Internet and mobile marketing to blogs, viral videos and social media – to create more targeted,

personal and engaging customer relationships. Marketers are no longer simply creating integrated promotion programmes; they are practising content marketing in paid, owned, earned and shared media. No other text provides more current or encompassing coverage of these exciting developments.

- New material throughout the new edition highlights the increasing importance of **sustainable marketing**. The discussion begins in **Chapter 1** and ends in **Chapter 20**, which pulls marketing together under a sustainable marketing framework. In between, frequent discussions and examples show how sustainable marketing calls for socially and environmentally responsible actions that meet both the immediate and the future needs of customers, companies and society as a whole.

- The new edition provides new discussions and examples of the growth in **global marketing**. As the world becomes a smaller, more competitive place, marketers face new global marketing challenges and opportunities, especially in fast-growing emerging markets such as China, India, Brazil, Africa, and others. You'll find much new coverage of global marketing throughout the text, starting in **Chapter 1**; the topic is discussed fully in **Chapter 19**.

- The new edition continues its emphasis on **measuring and managing return** on marketing, including many new end-of-chapter financial and quantitative marketing exercises that let students apply analytical thinking to relevant concepts in each chapter and link chapter concepts to the text's innovative and comprehensive **Appendix 2: Marketing by the numbers**.

- The new edition continues to improve on its **innovative learning design**. The text's active and integrative presentation includes learning enhancements such as annotated chapter-opening stories, a chapter-opening objectives outline, and explanatory author comments on major chapter sections and figures. The chapter-opening material helps to preview and position the chapter and its key concepts. Figures annotated with author comments help students to simplify and organise material. End-of-chapter features help to summarise important chapter concepts and highlight important themes, such as **digital and social media marketing**, **marketing ethics** and **financial marketing analysis**. This innovative learning design facilitates student understanding and eases learning.

- The new edition provides 20 new or revised end-of-chapter company cases by which students can apply what they learn to actual company situations. Finally all of the chapter-opening stories are either new or revised to maintain currency

Five major customer value and engagement themes

The Seventh European Edition of *Principles of Marketing* builds on five major value and customer engagement themes.

1. *Creating value for customers in order to capture value from customers in return.* Today's marketers must be good at *creating customer value, engaging customers,* and *managing customer relationships.* Outstanding marketing companies understand the marketplace and customer needs, design value-creating marketing strategies, develop integrated marketing programmes that engage customers and deliver value and satisfaction, and build strong customers in the form of sales, profits and customer equity.

    This innovative *customer-value and engagement framework* is introduced at the start of Chapter 1, in a five-step marketing process model, which details how marketing *creates* customer value and *captures* value in return. The framework is carefully developed in the first two chapters and then fully integrated through the remainder of the text.

2. *Customer engagement and today's digital and social media.* New digital and social media have taken today's marketing by storm, dramatically changing how companies and brands engage consumers, as well as how consumers connect and influence each other's brand behaviours. The new edition introduces and thoroughly explores the contemporary concept of *customer engagement marketing* and the exciting new digital and social media technologies that help

brands to engage customers more deeply and interactively. It starts with two major new **Chapter 1** sections: 'Customer engagement and today's digital and social media' and 'The digital age: online, mobile and social media marketing'. A completely revised **Chapter 17** on 'Direct, online, social media and mobile marketing' summarises the latest developments in digital engagement and relationship-building tools. Everywhere inbetween you'll find revised and expanded coverage of the exploding use of digital and social tools to create customer engagement and build brand community.

3. *Building and managing strong, value-creating brands.* Well-positioned brands with strong brand equity provide the basis on which to build customer value and profitable customer relationships. Today's marketers must position their brands powerfully and manage them well to create valued brand experiences. The new edition provides a deep focus on brands, anchored by a **Chapter 8** section on 'Branding strategy: building strong brands'.

4. *Measuring and managing return on marketing.* Especially in uneven economic times, marketing managers must ensure that their marketing euros are being well spent. in the past, many marketers spent freely on big, expensive marketing programmes, often without thinking carefully about the financial returns on their spending. But all that has changed rapidly. 'Marketing accountability' – measuring and managing marketing return on investment – has now become an important part of strategic marketing decision making. This emphasis on marketing accountability is addressed in **Chapter 2**, **Appendix 2: Marketing by the numbers**, and through the new edition.

5. *Sustainable marketing around the globe.* As technological developments make the world an increasingly smaller and more fragile place, marketers must be good at marketing their brands globally and in sustainable ways. New material through the new edition emphasises the concepts of global marketing and sustainable marketing – meeting the present needs of consumers and businesses while also preserving or enhancing the ability of future generations to meet their needs. The new edition integrates global marketing and sustainability topics throughout the text. It then provides focused coverage on each topic in **Chapters 19** and **20** respectively.

An emphasis on real marketing and bringing marketing to life

Principles of Marketing takes a practical marketing-management approach, providing countless in-depth, real-life examples and stories that engage students with marketing concepts and bring modern marketing to life. In the new edition, every chapter includes an engaging opening story that provides fresh insights into real marketing practices. Learn how:

- Nike's outstanding success results from more than just making and selling good sports gear. It's based on a customer-focused strategy through which Nike creates brand engagement and a close brand community with and among its customers
- At T-shirt and apparel maker Life is Good, engagement and social media are about building meaningful customer engagement, measured by the depth of consumer comment and community that surround the brand.
- Chipotle's sustainability mission isn't an add-on, created just to position the company as 'socially responsible' – doing good is ingrained in everything the company does.
- Sony's dizzying fall from market leadership provides a cautionary tale of what can happen when a company – even a dominant marketing leader – fails to adapt to its changing environment.
- Netflix uses 'big data' to personalise each customer's viewing experience; while Netflix subscribers are busy watching videos, Netflix is busy watching *them* – very, very closely.
- Giant social network Facebook promises to become one of the world's most powerful and profitable digital marketers – but it's just getting started.

- Wildly innovative Google has become an incredibly successful new product 'moonshot' factory, unleashing a seemingly unending flurry of diverse products, most of which are market leaders in their categories.
- Retail giants Walmart and Amazon are fighting it out in a pitched price war for online supremacy.
- Direct marketing insurance giant GEICO has gone from bit player to behemoth thanks to a big-budget advertising campaign featuring a smooth-talking gecko and an enduring '15 minutes could save you 15 per cent' tagline.
- The explosion of the Internet, social media, mobile devices and other technologies has some marketers asking 'Who needs face-to-face selling anymore?'
- Under its 'Conscious consumption' mission, outdoor apparel and gear maker Patagonia takes sustainability to new extremes by telling consumers to buy *less*.

Beyond such features, each chapter is packed with countless real, engaging and timely examples that reinforce key concepts. No other text brings marketing to life like the new edition of *Principles of Marketing*.

Learning aids that create value and engagement

A wealth of chapter-opening, within-chapter and end-of-chapter learning devices help students to learn, link and apply major concepts.

- *Integrated chapter-opening preview sections.* The active and integrative chapter-opening spread in each chapter starts with a 'Chapter preview', which briefly previews chapter concepts, links them with previous chapter concepts, and introduces the chapter-opening story. This leads to a chapter-opening vignette – an engaging, deeply developed, illustrated and annotated marketing story that introduces the chapter material and sparks student interest. Finally an 'Objectives outline' provides a helpful preview of chapter contents and learning objectives, complete with page numbers.
- *Author comments and figure annotations.* Throughout each chapter, author comments ease and enhance student learning by introducing and explaining major text sections and organising figures.
- *Objectives review and key terms.* A summary at the end of each chapter reviews major chapter concepts, chapter objectives and key terms.
- *Discussion questions and critical thinking exercises.* Sections at the end of each chapter help students to keep track of and apply what they've learned in the chapter.
- *Applications and mini-cases.* Brief 'Online, mobile and social media marketing', 'Marketing ethics' and 'Marketing by the numbers' sections at the end of each chapter provide short application cases that facilitate discussion of current issues and company situations in areas such as mobile and social marketing, ethics and financial marketing analysis. End-of chapter Company case sections provide all-new or revised company cases that help students to apply major marketing concepts to real company and brand situations.
- *Marketing plan:* **Appendix 1** contains a sample marketing plan that helps students to apply important marketing planning concepts.
- *Marketing by the numbers.* The innovative **Appendix 2** provides students with a comprehensive introduction to the marketing financial analysis that helps to guide, assess and support marketing decisions. An exercise at the end of each chapter lets students apply analytical and financial thinking to relevant chapter concepts and links the chapter to the Appendix.

More than ever before, the new edition of *Principles of Marketing* creates value and engagement for you – it gives you all you need to know about marketing in an effective and enjoyable total learning package!

ABOUT THE AUTHORS

Philip Kotler is S.C. Johnson & Son Distinguished Professor of International Marketing at the Kellogg School of Management, Northwestern University. He received his master's degree at the University of Chicago and his PhD at MIT, both in economics. Dr Kotler is the author of *Marketing Management* (Pearson), now in its fifteenth edition and the most widely used marketing textbook in graduate schools of business worldwide. He has authored dozens of other successful books and written more than 100 articles in leading journals. He is the only three-time winner of the coveted Alpha Kappa Psi award for the best annual article in the *Journal of Marketing*.

Professor Kotler was named the first recipient of four major awards: the *Distinguished Marketing Educator of the Year Award* and the *William L. Wilkie 'Marketing for a Better World' Award* both given by the American Marketing Association; the *Philip Kotler Award for Excellence in Health Care Marketing* presented by the Academy for Health Care Services Marketing; and the *Sheth Foundation Medal for Exceptional Contribution to Marketing Scholarship and Practice*. His numerous other major honours include the Sales and Marketing Executives International *Marketing Educator of the Year Award*; the European Association of Marketing Consultants and Trainers *Marketing Excellence Award*; the *Charles Coolidge Parlin Marketing Research Award*; and the *Paul D. Converse Award* given by the American Marketing Association to honour 'outstanding contributions to science in marketing'. A recent *Forbes* survey ranks Professor Kotler in the top 10 of the world's most influential business thinkers. And in a recent *Financial Times* poll of 1,000 senior executives across the world, Professor Kotler was ranked as the fourth 'most influential business writer/guru' of the twenty-first century

Dr Kotler has served as chairman of the College of Marketing of the Institute of Management Sciences, a director of the American Marketing Association, and a trustee of the Marketing Science Institute. He has consulted with many major US and international companies in the areas of marketing strategy and planning, marketing organisation and international marketing. He has travelled and lectured extensively throughout Europe, Asia and South America, advising companies and governments about global marketing practices and opportunities.

Gary Armstrong is Crist W. Blackwell Distinguished Professor Emeritus of Undergraduate Education in the Kenan-Flagler Business School at the University of North Carolina at Chapel Hill. He holds undergraduate and master's degrees in business from Wayne State University in Detroit, and he received his PhD in marketing from Northwestern University. Dr Armstrong has contributed numerous articles to leading business journals. As a consultant and researcher, he has worked with many companies on marketing research, sales management and marketing strategy.

But Professor Armstrong's first love has always been teaching. His long-held Blackwell Distinguished Professorship is the only permanent endowed professorship for distinguished undergraduate teaching at the University of North Carolina at Chapel Hill. He has been very active in the teaching and administration of Kenan-Flagler's undergraduate programme. His administrative posts have included Chair of Marketing, Associate Director of the Undergraduate Business Program, Director of the Business Honors Program and many others. Through the years, he has worked closely with business student groups and has received several UNC campus-wide and Business School teaching awards. He is the only repeat recipient of the school's highly regarded Award for Excellence in Undergraduate Teaching, which he received three times. Most recently, Professor Armstrong received the

UNC Board of Governors Award for Excellence in Teaching, the highest teaching honour bestowed by the 16-campus University of North Carolina system.

Lloyd C. Harris is the Head of the Marketing Department and Professor of Marketing at Birmingham Business School, University of Birmingham. After working in retail and service organisations, he received his PhD in Marketing from Cardiff University and his Higher Doctorate (DSc) from the University of Warwick. His research results have been disseminated via a range of marketing strategy, HRM and general management journals. He has written widely in these fields and has published over 100 pieces. He is particularly proud of papers that have been published in the *Journal of Retailing, Journal of the Academy of Marketing Science, Journal of Management Studies, Human Resource Management, Organization Studies* and the *Annals of Tourism Research*. He has consulted and run programmes for many leading private and public organisations, especially focussing on retailing and service organisations.

Nigel Piercy was formerly Associate Dean and Professor of Marketing and Strategy at Warwick Business School, University of Warwick. Earlier he was Professor of Strategic Marketing and Head of the Marketing Group at Cranfield School of Management and before that he was the Sir Julian Hodge Chair in Marketing and Strategy at Cardiff Business School. He has also been a visiting professor at Texas Christian University, the Fuqua School of Business at Duke University in North Carolina, the Columbia Graduate school of Business in New York, the University of California, Berkeley, and the Vienna University of Economics and Business. He has managerial experience in retailing and worked in business planning with Nycomed Amersham plc (now part of GE Healthcare). He has extensive experience as a management workshop speaker with many organisations around the world, specialising in the issues of marketing strategy and implementation, and strategic sales management. He has published more than 300 articles, including pieces in the *Journal of Marketing* and the *Journal of the Academy of Marketing Science*, as well as more than 20 books. He has been awarded many prizes for teaching excellence as well as the distinction of being the first UK academic to be awarded a higher doctorate (Doctor of Letters) for his published research work in strategic marketing. He is now a consultant and management writer with visiting posts at several universities.

ACKNOWLEDGEMENTS

We are grateful to the following for permission to reproduce copyright material:

Figures

Figure 1.5 adapted from Mismanagement of Customer Loyalty, *Harvard Business Review*, p. 93 (Rel-nartz W. and Kumar V. 2002), Harvard Business School Publishing, Reprinted by permission of Harvard Business Review; Figure 2.2 adapted from www.bcg.com/documents/file13904.pdf, The BCG Portfolio Matrix (c) 1970, The Boston Consulting Group; Figure 2.3 from Strategies for Diversification, *Harvard Business Review*, pp. 113-124 (Ansoff H.I. 1957) Copyright ©1957. Reprinted by permission of Harvard Business Review; Figure 2.8 adapted from Return on Marketing: Using Consumer Equity to Focus on Marketing Strategy, *Journal of Marketing*, p.112 (Roland T. Rust, Katherine Lemon and Valerie A. Zeithaml 2004), American Marketing Association (AMA), Reprinted with permission from Journal of Marketing, published by the American Marketing Association; Figure 5.5 adapted from *Consumer Behavior and Marketing Action*, Kent Publishing Company (Assael H. 1987) p. 87, Henry Assael, Reprinted with permission of Henry Assael; Figure 5.7 With the permission of The Free Press, a Division of Simon & Schuster, Inc., from *Diffusion of Innovations* by Rogers E.M. Copyright © 2003 by Rogers E.M. All rights reserved; Figure 11.2 adapted from Pricing and Public Policy: A Research Agenda and Overview of the Special Issue, *Journal of Public Policy and Marketing*, pp.3-10 (Dhruv Grewal and Larry D. Compeau 1999), American Marketing Association (AMA). Reprinted with permission from Journal of Public Policy and Marketing, published by the American Marketing Association (AMA); Figure 20.2 adapted from Innovation, Creative Destruction and Sustainability, *Research Technology Management*, September-October ed., pp. 21-27 (Hart S.L. 2005) © The Industrial Research Institute. Reproduced with permission.

Tables

Table 9.2 from *Marketing Management*, 13 ed., Prentice Hall (Kotler P., Keller K.L. 2009) p. 288, Pearson Education Inc. (NJ), Reproduced by permission of Pearson Education Inc., Upper Saddle River, New Jersey; Table on page 402 from The Major Auchen Businesses, *Business Week* (Matlack, C.), Bloomberg L.P.

Text

Quote on page 40 from State Your Business; Too Many Mission Statements Are Loaded with Fatheaded Jargon. Play It Straight, *Business Week*, p. 80 (Jack Welch), Bloomberg L.P.

Photos

The publisher would like to thank the following for their kind permission to reproduce their photographs:

(Key: b-bottom; c-centre; l-left; r-right; t-top)

123RF.com: p.108, 485, Mark Adams p.22, Paco Ayala p.180, Takashi Honma p.24, Aleksandar Hubenov p.199, Trond Runar Solevaag p.68, Wavebreak Media Ltd. p.157, Cathy Yeulet p.141; **Adidas:** p.117; **Alamy Images:** Acorn 1 p.46, Greg Balfour Evans p.407, Jeffrey Blackler p.380, Alexander Blinov p.25, D. Callcut p.134, Robert Convery p.211, Ashley Cooper p.417, Ian Dagnall p.435, Lev Dolgachov p.375, Julian Eales p.512, EPA European Pressphoto Agency B.V. p.501, Lou-Foto p.39, Gallo Images p.442, Clynt Garnham Food & Drink p.9, Tim Gartside p.252, GBimages p.591, Kevin George p.342, Tim Graham p.317, Russell Hart p.225, Matthew Horwood p.388, Iconic Cornwall p.379, Juice Images p.275, M-dash p.387, MASP Food Photography p.277, Mauritius Images GmbH p.563, Maximimages.com p.215, MBI p.475, Richard McDowell p.443, Music Alan King p.544, NetPhotos p.179, Susan Norwood p.373, Oleksiy Maksymenko Photography p.236, REDA & CO srl p.561, Romantiche p.177, Kumar Sriskandan p.138, Stockbroker p.363, Studiomode p.71, Lynne Sutherland p.595, Tetra Images p.473, Peter Titmuss p.575, René Van den Berg p.547; **Boots.** Courtesy of Boots UK: p.519; **BuyMyFace.com:** p.450; **Climax Portable Machine Tools:** p.472; **CUUSOO System Co. Ltd.** © CUUSOO System 2014: p.265; **Digital Advertising Alliance:** p.522; **European Commission** © European Union, 2016: p.565; **Fotolia.com:** Pabkov p.537; **Getty Images:** Anatolii Babii p.104, Clemens Bilan p.383, Stephen Brashear p.467, Business Wire p.550, Mike Clarke / AFP p.568, Mike Coppola / SodaStream p.535, Simon Dawson / Bloomberg p.84, Eric Feferberg / AFP p.343, Steve Fitchett p.142, Elan Fleisher / LOOK-foto p.14, Shirlaine Forrest / Coca-Cola p.202, Christopher Furlong p.81, Andrew Harrer / Bloomberg p.339, Hannes Hepp / Fuse p.121, Dave J Hogan / Walkers Do Us A Flavour p.410, Christopher Lee / Red Bull p.491t, Brent Lewin / Bloomberg p.355, Dick Loek / Toronto Star p.240, Lonely Planet p.300, Damien Meyer / AFP p.455, Mint Images - Tim Robbins p.474, David Paul Morris / Bloomberg p.261, Roberto Machado Noa / LightRocket p.48, 195, Zhang Peng / LightRocket p.571, Adrian Pope p.315, Steve Sands p.73, Oli Scarff p.393, Alexandre Simoes / Borussia Dortmund p.313, Henrik Sorensen p.iii, Akos Stiller / Bloomberg p.481, Justin Sullivan p.361, Paul Taggart / Bloomberg p.325, Betsie Van der Meer p.227, Lilian WU / AFP p.579; **History of Advertising Trust:** / Hovis Ltd. p.446; **Intuit** p.271; **Marriott Hotels International Limited:** p.76; **Messe München GmbH:** p.491b; **Nike Europe.** Images courtesy of Nike Inc.: p.37; **Patagonia** Property of Patagonia Inc. Used with permission: p.609; **Red Bull Company Ltd.** Courtesy of © Red Bull Media House: p.111; **Reuters:** Stefano Rellandini p.596; **Rex / Shutterstock:** Action Press p.296, Everett Collection p.465, David Hartley p.3, imageBROKER p.415, Stefan Kiefer / imageBROKER p.291, Andy Lauwers p.425; **Shutterstock.com:** p.323, Ysbrand Cosijn p.151, Patryk Kosmider p.7, Monkey Business Images p.468, Tyler Olson p.146, Pressmaster p.55, RDaniel p.198, ScottMurph p.509, Rachata Teyparsit p.145, YanLev p.305, Zurijeta p.389; **Tiger Retail Ltd:** p.103; **Toyota (GB) PLC.** Courtesy of Toyota (GB) Ltd.: p.303; **Vapur:** Kev Steele / kevsteele.com p.610; **Vertu Corporation:** p.302; **Victorinox:** p.266; **Vivago Oy:** p.44; **Volkswagen Group:** p.191; **Jim Whitmer Photography.** Photo by Jim Whitmer: p.319.

Cover images: *Front:* **Getty Images:** Henrik Sorensen

PART ONE

Defining marketing and the marketing process

CHAPTER ONE

Marketing: creating customer value and engagement

Chapter preview

This chapter introduces you to the basic concepts of marketing. We start with the question: what is marketing? Simply put, marketing is engaging customers and managing profitable customer relationships. The aim of marketing is to create value for customers in order to capture value from customers in return. Next we discuss the five steps in the marketing process – from understanding customer needs, to designing customer value-driven marketing strategies and integrated marketing programmes, to building customer relationships and capturing value for the firm. Finally, we discuss the major trends and forces affecting marketing in this new age of digital, mobile and social media. Understanding these basic concepts and forming your own ideas about what they really mean to you will provide a solid foundation for all that follows.

Let's start with a good story about marketing in action with Mini, the iconic British car. The secret to Mini's success? It's really no secret at all. Mini have a deep-down passion for creating customer engagement, value and relationships. You'll see this theme of creating customer value in order to capture value in return repeated throughout this chapter and the remainder of the text.

Objectives outline

➤ **Objective 1** Define marketing and outline the steps in the marketing process.
What is marketing? (pp. 4–5)

➤ **Objective 2** Explain the importance of understanding the marketplace and customers and identify the five core marketplace concepts.
Understanding the marketplace and customer needs (pp. 6–8)

➤ **Objective 3** Identify the key elements of a customer-driven marketing strategy and discuss the marketing management orientations that guide marketing strategy.
Designing a customer-driven marketing strategy (pp. 9–12)

Preparing an integrated marketing plan and programme (p. 13)

➤ **Objective 4** Discuss customer relationship management and identify strategies *for* creating value for customers and capturing value *from* customers in return.
Building customer relationships (pp. 13–18)
Capturing value from customers (pp. 18–20)

➤ **Objective 5** Describe the major trends and forces that are changing the marketing landscape in this age of relationships.
The changing marketing landscape (pp. 21–22)

Mini: Marketing Master?
Kate L. Daunt, Cardiff Business School

The Mini is arguably the most successful British car brand in history. Designed by Sir Alec Issigonis, two models of Mini zoomed into production in the UK in 1959, the Morris Mini Minor and the Austin Seven. The Mini, representing a breakthrough in small car design, offered consumers something different. Priced at £496, the car was affordable, economical to run and, with a 34bhp engine, practical and agile to drive. Safely seating four adults, the Mini was somewhat like Dr Who's Tardis, small on the outside but big on the inside. Mini quickly became the car of choice for housewives running family errands. However, it was the swinging 60s that defined the Mini brand. A collaboration with John Cooper (twice F1 champion constructor) in 1961 resulted in the release of the Mini Cooper model. With its sporty 55bhp engine, iconic two-tone paint (the roof was a different colour to the body of the car) and bonnet stripes, the Mini was made fashionable. The brand now transcended demographics: everyone who was anyone owned a Mini Cooper ranging from the pop band the Beatles, to fashion designer Mary Quant, to royal Prince Charles, to actor Clint Eastwood, to my Dad (!). Mini's connections to Hollywood, celebrities and motorsports shaped a brand personality that was stylish, sporty, fun-loving and a little bit cheeky. This is demonstrated in the 1960s advertising strapline, 'You don't need a big one to be happy. Happiness is Mini shaped'. With the introduction of the super sporty Cooper S and stretched Clubman Estate models it seemed that the Mini brand could do no wrong.

Yet, in spite of Mini's momentous start to life, the 1970s, 1980s and 1990s held a darker picture in terms of customer demand. Mini increasingly no longer held the niche for small cars with competitors including Volkswagen, Ford and Renault not only entering the UK's small car market, but offering customers technological innovations, increased specifications and new body shapes. At the same time, Mini's technology, style and size remained comparatively unchanged. The Mini's adventure appeared all but over; with unsuccessful changes to ownership and management, the last Mini rolled off of the production line in Oxford on 3 October 2000. However, all was not lost. Acquired by BMW (when under the ownership of Rover), the German firm had big plans for the little car's future. Expanding BMW's current product portfolio and offering instant access to the small car sector, in 2001 the BMW Mini was launched. Although markedly larger than its original incarnation, the design and 'go-kart' handling was unmistakably 'Mini' and it proved a huge commercial success. At the heart of this success was an offering that customers valued – the ability to customise and personalise their vehicle. Literally thousands of different colour, exterior and interior trims and technological specification combinations were offered. Thus, the average price paid by the customer for their car far exceeded that of the list price for the vehicle. The basic shape of the car may look like its 60s predecessor but beneath the bonnet the updated design was tailored to the needs of modern consumers. This strategy placed Mini in the previously untapped 'premium' segment of the small car market. Under the management of BMW, Mini's customer service was also taken seriously. Mini salespeople were awarded bonuses based on customer satisfaction ratings not car sales alone, a marked departure from the industry norm.

Mini returned to its quirky roots, presenting a stylish, heritage-founded, and above all fun brand image. Demand for the growing line-up of Mini models grew not only in domestic markets but international markets too. The quintessential British car was coveted by consumers spanning the USA to Australia, with India representing the 100th country in which Mini made a pit stop in 2012. Explaining Mini's marketing strategy, Tom Salkowsky, Mini's USA Head of Marketing, states: 'We do things differently. Win markets but international markets too. The quintessentially British 2001 New Mini was a little quirky. We lean into that. That's not typical, that's not traditional, that's not ordinary, that's not normal. That's Mini.' Indeed, doing things differently appears to underpin Mini's ethos. New car owners are encouraged to personify their car with a formal name (which they can log online). Cost-effective stunts, digital and events marketing are favoured over more traditional methods; Mini appreciates the power of brand experience and that owning a Mini is membership to a club. As such the line between organisationally driven

Mini styles its self as exciting, quirky and downright fun!

Source: David Hartley/REX/ Shutterstock

events and owner-driven activities is somewhat blurred, ranging from Guinness Book of Records attempts for the biggest ever parade of Minis and the most people crammed into a Mini, to web-generated content, to rallies, to a presence at the 2012 British-hosted Olympic games. Here, in addition to holding a starring role in the closing ceremony, smiles were brought to spectators' faces as miniature radio-controlled Minis were used to return javelins, discuses and hammers to competitors in the field events.

Noting changes in the marketing environment, by 2014 the Mini was ready for a facelift and the New Mini was launched on what would have been Sir Issigonis' 107th birthday. Larger than its predecessor, Mini argue that their latest model is more practical, with a 134bhp Cooper engine, improved fuel economy, reduced CO_2 emissions and improved suspension and handling, the Mini is made for the modern driver. Quirky yet practical specifications also include variable suspension settings (comfort or sport), a self-parking function and an assist option that warns drivers of imminent collisions. Recognising consumers' need for easy access, a five-door hatch was also launched. But what does the future hold for Mini? To triumph against the ever growing competition, including the Audi A1 and the Fiat 500, size will once again play a role. Since its re-launch, in addition to special editions, the number of Mini models has risen to eight to include the SUV crossover Countryman, Convertible and Coupé models, and the super sporty and pricey John Cooper Works. Moving forward, Mini is reportedly planning to cut the size of its range to five models in a bid to sharpen its appeal in an increasingly saturated market. Peter Schwarzenbauer, Mini Brand Chief, notes, 'Mini now faces competition in areas where it previously stood alone' and 'less is more … we have to set the right properties and always remember what premium really means: Excellent product substance and a strong, emotionally-appealing brand'. Keeping the fun and quirk in the brand, Schwarzenbauer explains that each model in the new line-up will be recognisable for its own personality and capabilities 'like a superhero'. With trade reports noting future projects including contactless credit card car access and operation and integrated Spotify streaming, may the marvel of Mini continue.[1]

Today's successful companies have one thing in common: like Mini, they are strongly customer focused and heavily committed to marketing. These companies share a passion for understanding and satisfying customer needs in well-defined target markets. They motivate everyone in the organisation to help build lasting customer relationships based on creating value.

Customer relationships and value are especially important today. Facing dramatic technological advances and deep economic, social and environmental challenges, today's customers are relating digitally with companies and each other, spending more carefully, and reassessing how they engage with brands. New digital, mobile and social media developments have revolutionised how consumers shop and interact, in turn calling for new marketing strategies and tactics. In these fast-changing times, it's now more important than ever to build strong customer relationships based on real and enduring customer value.

We'll discuss the exciting new challenges facing both customers and marketers later in the chapter. But first, let's introduce the basics of marketing.

WHAT IS MARKETING?[2]

Author comment

Pause here and think about how you'd answer this question before studying marketing. Then see how your answer changes as you read the chapter.

Marketing, more than any other business function, deals with customers. Although we will soon explore more detailed definitions of marketing, perhaps the simplest definition is this one: *Marketing is engaging customers and managing profitable customer relationships.* The two-fold goal of marketing is to attract new customers by promising superior value and to keep and grow current customers by delivering satisfaction.

For example, Dyson's underlying philosophy of taking everyday products that don't work particularly well and making them more efficient, more effective and simply better has rocketed Dyson to (well-deserved) global success. McDonald's fulfils its 'I'm lovin' it' motto by being 'our customers' favourite place and way to eat' the world over, giving it nearly as much market share as its nearest four competitors combined. Facebook has attracted more than a billion active web and mobile users worldwide by helping them to 'connect and share with the people in their lives'. Virgin Atlantic fulfils its motto to 'embrace the fun spirit and let it fly' through being hugely attractive and responsive to customer needs, wants and demands.

Sound marketing is critical to the success of every organisation. Large for-profit firms, such as Unilever, Nestlé, Shell and Santander use marketing. But so do not-for-profit organisations, such as colleges, hospitals, museums, symphony orchestras and even churches.

You already know a lot about marketing – it's all around you. Marketing comes to you in the good old traditional forms: you see it in the abundance of products at your nearby shopping centre and the ads that fill your TV screen, spice up your magazines or stuff your mailbox. But in recent years, marketers have assembled a host of new marketing approaches, everything from imaginative websites and mobile phone apps to blogs, online videos and social media. These new approaches do more than just blast out messages to the masses. They reach you directly, personally and interactively. Today's marketers want to become a part of your life and enrich your experiences with their brands – to help you *live* their brands.

At home, at school, where you work and where you play, you see marketing in almost everything you do. Yet there is much more to marketing than meets the consumer's casual eye. Behind it all is a massive network of people, technologies and activities competing for your attention and purchases. This book will give you a complete introduction to the basic concepts and practices of today's marketing. In this chapter, we begin by defining marketing and the marketing process.

Marketing defined

What *is* marketing? Many people think of marketing as only selling and advertising. We are bombarded every day with TV commercials, catalogues, spiels from salespeople, and online pitches. However, selling and advertising are only the tip of the marketing iceberg.

Today, marketing must be understood not in the old sense of making a sale – 'telling and selling' – but in the new sense of *satisfying customer needs*. If the marketer engages consumers effectively, understands their needs, develops products that provide superior customer value, and prices, distributes and promotes them well, these products will sell easily. In fact, according to management guru Peter Drucker, 'The aim of marketing is to make selling unnecessary.'[3] Selling and advertising are only part of a larger *marketing mix* – a set of marketing tools that work together to engage customers, satisfy customer needs, and build customer relationships.

Broadly defined, marketing is a social and managerial process by which individuals and organisations obtain what they need and want through creating and exchanging value with others. In a narrower business context, marketing involves building profitable, value-laden exchange relationships with customers. Hence, we define **marketing** as the process by which companies create value for customers and build strong customer relationships in order to capture value from customers in return.[4]

> **Marketing**—The process by which companies create value for customers and build strong customer relationships in order to capture value from customers in return.

The marketing process

Figure 1.1 presents a simple, five-step model of the marketing process for creating and capturing customer value. In the first four steps, companies work to understand consumers, create customer value and build strong customer relationships. In the final step, companies reap the rewards of creating superior customer value. By creating value *for* consumers, they in turn capture value *from* consumers in the form of sales, profits and long-term customer equity.

In this chapter and the next, we will examine the steps of this simple model of marketing. In this chapter, we review each step but focus more on the customer relationship steps – understanding customers, engaging and building relationships with customers, and capturing value from customers. In Chapter 2, we look more deeply into the second and third steps – designing value-creating marketing strategies and constructing marketing programmes.

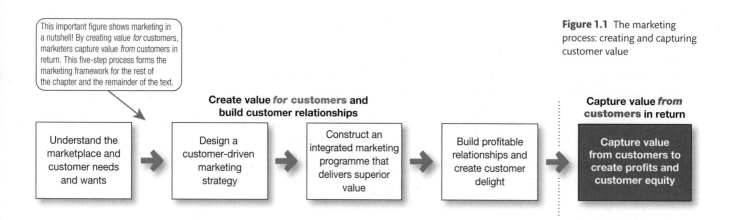

Figure 1.1 The marketing process: creating and capturing customer value

UNDERSTANDING THE MARKETPLACE AND CUSTOMER NEEDS

> **Author comment**
>
> Marketing is all about creating value for customers. So, as the first step in the marketing process, the company must fully understand consumers and the marketplace in which it operates.

As a first step, marketers need to understand customer needs and wants and the marketplace in which they operate. We examine five core customer and marketplace concepts: (1) *needs, wants, and demands*; (2) *market offerings (products, services, and experiences)*; (3) *value and satisfaction*; (4) *exchanges and relationships*; and (5) *markets*.

Customer needs, wants and demands

Needs—States of felt deprivation.

The most basic concept underlying marketing is that of human **needs**. Human needs are states of felt deprivation. They include basic *physical* needs for food, clothing, warmth and safety; *social* needs for belonging and affection; and *individual* needs for knowledge and self-expression. Marketers did not create these needs; they are a basic part of the human make-up.

Wants—The form human needs take as they are shaped by culture and individual personality.

Wants are the form human needs take as they are shaped by culture and individual personality. If you'll excuse the stereotypes – used for illustrative purposes only – a German consumer *needs* food but *wants* a sauerkraut, sausage and beer. A trite example of a person in Papua, New Guinea, *needs* food but *wants* taro, rice, yams and pork. A similarly clichéd Englishman *needs* food but *wants* cucumber sandwiches and gallons of insipid tea. Wants are shaped by one's society and are described in terms of objects that will satisfy those needs. When backed by buying power, wants become **demands**. Given their wants and resources, people demand products and services with benefits that add up to the most value and satisfaction.

Demands—Human wants that are backed by buying power.

Outstanding marketing companies go to great lengths to learn about and understand their customers' needs, wants and demands. They conduct consumer research, analyse mountains of customer data, and observe customers as they shop and interact, offline and online. People at all levels of the company – including top management – stay close to customers. For example, James Averdiek, founder and MC of extraordinarily amazing Gü Chocolate Puds, argues that a core tenet of any successful business is getting close to your customers by finding out what they are doing and taking part in it. At P&G, executives from the chief executive officer down spend time with customers in their homes and on shopping trips. P&G brand managers routinely spend a week or two living on the budget of low-end consumers to gain insights into what they can do to improve customers' lives.[5]

Market offerings – products, services and experiences

Market offerings—Some combination of products, services, information or experiences offered to a market to satisfy a need or want.

Consumers' needs and wants are fulfilled through **market offerings** – some combination of products, services, information or experiences offered to a market to satisfy a need or a want. Market offerings are not limited to physical *products*. They also include *services* – activities or benefits offered for sale that are essentially intangible and do not result in the ownership of anything. Examples include banking, airline, hotel, retailing and home repair services.

More broadly, market offerings also include other entities, such as *persons, places, organisations, information* and *ideas*. For example, Tourism Ireland invites tourists to 'Jump into' Ireland's Wild Atlantic Way, at 2400km the longest defined coastal drive in the world. In late 2014 alone, Tourism Ireland will spend around €11 million to boosting late season travel bookings to Ireland by around 30 per cent. This campaign is tailored to different markets with slightly different campaigns for the UK, North America, mainland Europe and developing markets such as Australia.[6]

Many sellers make the mistake of paying more attention to the specific products they offer than to the benefits and experiences produced by these products. These sellers suffer from **marketing myopia**. They are so taken with their products that they focus only on existing wants and lose sight of underlying customer needs.[7] They forget that a product is only a tool to solve a consumer problem. A manufacturer of quarter-inch drill bits may think that the customer needs a drill bit. But what the customer *really* needs is a quarter-inch hole. These sellers will have trouble if a new product comes along that serves the customer's need better or less expensively. The customer will have the same *need* but will *want* the new product.

Marketing myopia—The mistake of paying more attention to the specific products a company offers than to the benefits and experiences produced by these products.

Smart marketers look beyond the attributes of the products and services they sell. By orchestrating several services and products, they create *brand experiences* for consumers. For example, you don't just watch a Wimbledon tennis tournament; you immerse yourself in the historical home of tennis. Similarly, Ferrari recognises that their cars are much more than just a combustion engine, a collection of wires and electrical components. To the owners of a Ferrari car, their Ferrari is an expression of their status, taste and style.

Similarly, Angry Birds is much more than just a mobile game app. To more than 200 million fans a month in 116 countries, it's a deeply involving experience. As one observer puts it: 'Angry Birds land is a state of mind – a digital immersion in addictively cheerful destruction, a refuge from the boredom of subway commutes and doctors' waiting rooms, where the fine art of sling-shotting tiny brightly hued birds at wooden fortresses to vanquish pigs taking shelter inside makes eminent sense and is immensely satisfying.' So far, in all its forms, Angry Birds has been downloaded more than 2 billion times. The game's creator, Rovio, plans to expand the Angry Birds experience through everything from animated short videos (called *Angry Birds Toons*) and three-dimensional animated movies (the first released in the summer of 2016) to a growing list of new games, licensed toys, apparel, yard art, and even Angry Birds-branded playgrounds, activity parks and theme parks.[8]

Tourism Ireland stresses the breadth of experiences visitors to beautiful Ireland can embrace.
Source: Patryk Kosmider/ Shutterstock.com

Customer value and satisfaction

Consumers usually face a broad array of products and services that might satisfy a given need. How do they choose among these many market offerings? Customers form expectations about the value and satisfaction that various market offerings will deliver and buy accordingly. Satisfied customers buy again and tell others about their good experiences. Dissatisfied customers often switch to competitors and disparage the product to others.

Marketers must be careful to set the right level of expectations. If they set expectations too low, they may satisfy those who buy but fail to attract enough buyers. If they set expectations too high, buyers will be disappointed. Customer value and customer satisfaction are key building blocks for developing and managing customer relationships. We will revisit these core concepts later in the chapter.

Exchanges and relationships

Exchange—The act of obtaining a desired object from someone by offering something in return.

Marketing occurs when people decide to satisfy their needs and wants through exchange relationships. **Exchange** is the act of obtaining a desired object from someone by offering something in return. In the broadest sense, the marketer tries to bring about a response to some market offering. The response may be more than simply buying or trading products and services. A political candidate, for instance, wants votes; a church wants membership; an orchestra wants an audience; and a social action group wants idea acceptance.

Marketing consists of actions taken to create, maintain and grow desirable exchange *relationships* with target audiences involving a product, service, idea or other object. Companies want to build strong relationships by consistently delivering superior customer value. We will expand on the important concept of managing customer relationships later in the chapter.

Markets

Market—The set of all actual and potential buyers of a product or service.

The concepts of exchange and relationships lead to the concept of a market. A **market** is the set of actual and potential buyers of a product or service. These buyers share a particular need or want that can be satisfied through exchange relationships.

Marketing means managing markets to bring about profitable customer relationships. However, creating these relationships takes work. Sellers must search for and engage buyers, identify their needs, design good market offerings, set prices for them, promote them, and store and deliver them. Activities such as consumer research, product development, communication, distribution, pricing and service are core marketing activities.

Although we normally think of marketing as being carried out by sellers, buyers also carry out marketing. Consumers market when they search for products, interact with companies to obtain information, and make their purchases. In fact, today's digital technologies, from online sites and smartphone apps to the explosion of social media, have empowered consumers and made marketing a truly two-way affair. Thus, in addition to customer relationship management, today's marketers must also deal effectively with *customer-managed relationships*. Marketers are no longer asking only 'How can we influence our customers?' but also 'How can our customers influence us?' and even 'How can our customers influence each other?'

Figure 1.2 shows the main elements in a marketing system. Marketing involves serving a market of final consumers in the face of competitors. The company and competitors research the market and interact with consumers to understand their needs. Then they create and exchange market offerings, messages and other marketing content with consumers, either directly or through marketing intermediaries. Each party in the system is affected by major environmental forces (demographic, economic, natural, technological, political and social/cultural).

Figure 1.2 A modern marketing system

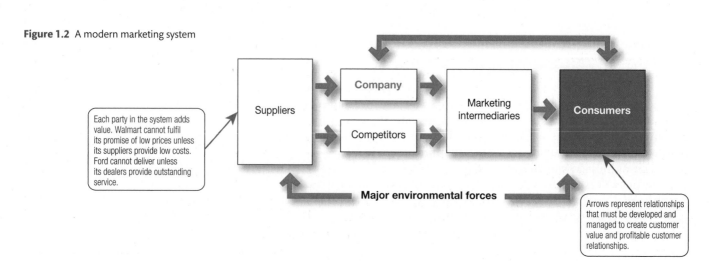

Each party in the system adds value for the next level. The arrows represent relationships that must be developed and managed. Thus, a company's success at engaging customers and building profitable relationships depends not only on its own actions but also on how well the entire system serves the needs of final consumers. Lidl cannot fulfil its promise of low prices unless its suppliers provide merchandise at low costs, while Citroen cannot deliver a high-quality car-ownership experience unless its dealers provide outstanding sales and service.

DESIGNING A CUSTOMER VALUE-DRIVEN MARKETING STRATEGY

Author comment

Once a company fully understands its consumers and the marketplace, it must decide which customers it will serve and how it will bring them value.

Once it fully understands consumers and the marketplace, marketing management can design a customer value-driven marketing strategy. We define **marketing management** as the art and science of choosing target markets and building profitable relationships with them. The marketing manager's aim is to find, engage, keep and grow target customers by creating, delivering and communicating superior customer value.

To design a winning marketing strategy, the marketing manager must answer two important questions: *What customers will we serve (what's our target market)*? and *How can we serve these customers best (what's our value proposition)*? We will discuss these marketing strategy concepts briefly here and then look at them in more detail in Chapters 2 and 6.

Marketing management— The art and science of choosing target markets and building profitable relationships with them.

Selecting customers to serve

The company must first decide *whom* it will serve. It does this by dividing the market into segments of customers (*market segmentation*) and selecting which segments it will go after (*target marketing*). Some people think of marketing management as finding as many customers as possible and increasing demand. But marketing managers know that they cannot serve all customers in every way. By trying to serve all customers, they may not serve any customers well. Instead, the company wants to select only customers that it can serve well and profitably. For example, La Perla (with Headquarters in Italy) profitably targets affluent professionals; Aldi profitably targets families with more modest means.

Ultimately, marketing managers must decide which customers they want to target and on the level, timing and nature of their demand. Simply put, marketing management is *customer management and demand management*.

Value propositions: in tough economic times, companies must emphasise the *value* in their value propositions. Waitrose now has an essential range that they promote as 'Waitrose quality at everyday prices.'
Source: Clynt Garnham Food & Drink/Alamy Images

Choosing a value proposition

The company must also decide how it will serve targeted customers – how it will *differentiate and position* itself in the marketplace. A brand's *value proposition* is the set of benefits or values it promises to deliver to consumers to satisfy their needs. Red Bull Energy Drink 'gives you wiiings' whereas with T-Mobile, family and friends can 'stick together'. Saab cars boast their engineering excellence credentials by being 'born from jets'. The diminutive Smart car suggests that you 'open your mind to the car that challenges the status quo', whereas Infiniti 'makes luxury affordable', and BMW promises 'the ultimate driving machine'. Facebook helps you 'connect and share with the people in your life', whereas YouTube 'provides a place for people to connect, inform, and inspire others across the globe'. And Twitter's Vine app gives you 'the best way to see and share life in motion' through 'short, beautiful, looping videos in a simple and fun way for your friends and family to see'.[9]

Such value propositions differentiate one brand from another. They answer the customer's question, 'Why should I buy your brand rather than a competitor's?' Companies must design strong value propositions that give them the greatest advantage in their target markets. For example, the Smart car is positioned as compact, yet comfortable; agile, yet economical; and safe, yet ecological: 'Sheer automotive genius in a totally fun, efficient package. Smart thinking, indeed.'

Marketing management orientations

Marketing management wants to design strategies that will engage target customers and build profitable relationships with them. But what *philosophy* should guide these marketing strategies? What weight should be given to the interests of customers, the organisation and society? Very often, these interests conflict.

There are five alternative concepts under which organisations design and carry out their marketing strategies: the *production, product, selling, marketing and societal marketing concepts.*

The production concept

Production concept—The idea that consumers will favour products that are available and highly affordable; therefore, the organisation should focus on improving production and distribution efficiency.

The **production concept** holds that consumers will favour products that are available and highly affordable. Therefore, management should focus on improving production and distribution efficiency. This concept is one of the oldest orientations that guides sellers.

The production concept is still a useful philosophy in some situations. For example, both personal computer maker Lenovo and home appliance maker Haier dominate the highly competitive, price-sensitive Chinese market through low labour costs, high production efficiency and mass distribution. However, although useful in some situations, the production concept can lead to marketing myopia. Companies adopting this orientation run a major risk of focusing too narrowly on their own operations and losing sight of the real objective – satisfying customer needs and building customer relationships.

The product concept

Product concept—The idea that consumers will favour products that offer the most quality, performance and features; therefore, the organisation should devote its energy to making continuous product improvements.

The **product concept** holds that consumers will favour products that offer the most in quality, performance and innovative features. Under this concept, marketing strategy focuses on making continuous product improvements.

Product quality and improvement are important parts of most marketing strategies. However, focusing *only* on the company's products can also lead to marketing myopia. For example, some manufacturers believe that if they can 'build a better mousetrap, the world will beat a path to their doors'. But they are often rudely shocked. Buyers may be looking for a better solution to a mouse problem but not necessarily for a better mousetrap. The better solution might be a chemical spray, an exterminating service, a housecat, or something else that suits their needs even better than a mousetrap. Furthermore, a better mousetrap will not sell unless the manufacturer designs, packages and prices it attractively; places it in convenient distribution channels; brings it to the attention of people who need it; and convinces buyers that it is a better product.

The selling concept

Selling concept—The idea that consumers will not buy enough of the firm's products unless the firm undertakes a large-scale selling and promotion effort.

Many companies follow the **selling concept**, which holds that consumers will not buy enough of the firm's products unless it undertakes a large-scale selling and promotion effort. The selling concept is typically practised with unsought goods – those that buyers do not normally think of buying, such as life insurance or blood donations. These industries must be good at tracking down prospects and selling them on a product's benefits.

Such aggressive selling, however, carries high risks. It focuses on creating sales transactions rather than on building long-term, profitable customer relationships. The aim often is to sell what the company makes rather than making what the market wants. It assumes that customers who

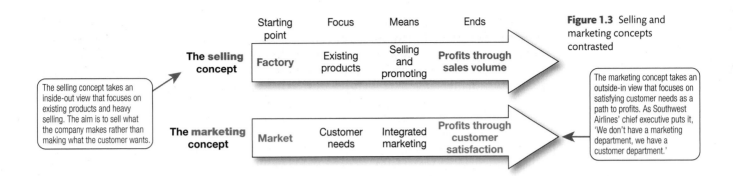

The selling concept takes an inside-out view that focuses on existing products and heavy selling. The aim is to sell what the company makes rather than making what the customer wants.

Figure 1.3 Selling and marketing concepts contrasted

The marketing concept takes an outside-in view that focuses on satisfying customer needs as a path to profits. As Southwest Airlines' chief executive puts it, 'We don't have a marketing department, we have a customer department.'

are coaxed into buying the product will like it. Or, if they don't like it, they will possibly forget their disappointment and buy it again later. These are usually poor assumptions.

The marketing concept

The **marketing concept** holds that achieving organisational goals depends on knowing the needs and wants of target markets and delivering the desired satisfactions better than competitors do. Under the marketing concept, customer focus and value are the *paths* to sales and profits. Instead of a product-centred *make-and-sell* philosophy, the marketing concept is a customer-centred *sense-and-respond* philosophy. The job is not to find the right customers for your product but to find the right products for your customers.

Figure 1.3 contrasts the selling concept and the marketing concept. The selling concept takes an *inside-out* perspective. It starts with the factory, focuses on the company's existing products, and calls for heavy selling and promotion to obtain profitable sales. It focuses primarily on customer conquest – getting short-term sales with little concern about who buys or why.

In contrast, the marketing concept takes an *outside-in* perspective. For example, Liverpool Football Club has a Customer Experience Department whose role is exclusively focused on improving supporters' off-the-pitch experiences. Similarly, O2 proudly proclaim that they are 'putting customers first: it's all about you'! The marketing concept starts with a well-defined market, focuses on customer needs, and integrates all the marketing activities that affect customers. In turn, it yields profits by creating relationships with the right customers based on customer value and satisfaction.

Implementing the marketing concept often means more than simply responding to customers' stated desires and obvious needs. *Customer-driven* companies research customers deeply to learn about their desires, gather new product ideas, and test product improvements. Such customer-driven marketing usually works well when a clear need exists and when customers know what they want.

In many cases, however, customers *don't* know what they want or even what is possible. As Henry Ford once remarked, 'If I'd asked people what they wanted, they would have said faster horses.'[10] For example, even 20 years ago, how many consumers would have thought to ask for now-commonplace products such as tablet computers, smartphones, digital cameras, 24-hour online buying, video sharing services, and GPS systems in their cars and phones? Such situations call for *customer-driving* marketing – understanding customer needs even better than customers themselves do and creating products and services that meet both existing and latent needs, now and in the future. As an executive at 3M put it, 'Our goal is to lead customers where they want to go before *they* know where they want to go.'

The societal marketing concept

The **societal marketing concept** questions whether the pure marketing concept overlooks possible conflicts between consumer *short-run wants* and consumer *long-run welfare*. Is a firm that satisfies the immediate needs and wants of target markets always doing what's best for its consumers

Marketing concept— A philosophy in which achieving organisational goals depends on knowing the needs and wants of target markets and delivering the desired satisfactions better than competitors do.

Societal marketing concept— The idea that a company's marketing decisions should consider consumers' wants, the company's requirements, consumers' long-run interests, and society's long-run interests.

in the long run? The societal marketing concept holds that marketing strategy should deliver value to customers in a way that maintains or improves both the consumer's *and society's* well-being. It calls for *sustainable marketing*, socially and environmentally responsible marketing that meets the present needs of consumers and businesses while also preserving or enhancing the ability of future generations to meet their needs.

Even more broadly, many leading business and marketing thinkers are now preaching the concept of *shared value*, which recognises that societal needs, not just economic needs, define markets.[11] The concept of shared value focuses on creating economic value in a way that also creates value for society. A growing number of companies known for their hard-nosed approaches to business – such as BP, Glaxo-Smith Klein, Siemens, Google, IBM, Intel, Johnson & Johnson, Nestlé, Unilever and Marks & Spencer – are rethinking the interactions between society and corporate performance. They are concerned not just with short-term economic gains, but with the well-being of their customers, the depletion of natural resources vital to their businesses, the viability of key suppliers, and the economic well-being of the communities in which they produce and sell.

One prominent marketer calls this *Marketing 3.0*. 'Marketing 3.0 organisations are values-driven,' he says. 'I'm not talking about being value-driven. I'm talking about "values" plural, where values amount to caring about the state of the world.' Another marketer calls it purpose-driven marketing. 'The future of profit is purpose,' he says.[12]

As Figure 1.4 shows, companies should balance three considerations in setting their marketing strategies: company profits, consumer wants *and* society's interests. British-based cosmetics retailer Lush operates this way:[13]

> Lush is known for 'fresh handmade cosmetics' – premium beauty products made by hand from the freshest possible natural ingredients. It sells products with evocative names such as 'Flying Fox' shower gel, 'Angels on Bareskin' cleanser, and 'Honey I Washed the Kids' soap. But Lush does much more than just make and sell body care products for profit. It also dedicates itself to doing right by customers, employees, the environment, and society. Its do-good mission is spelt out in a seven-point statement titled, 'A Lush life: we believe . . .'. For example, the company believes in inventing and making its own products from fresh organic fruits and vegetables using little or no preservatives or packaging. Lush has strict policy against animal testing and supports Fair Trade and Community Trade efforts. Each year, the company invests heavily in sustainable initiatives and support of grassroots charities. Lush takes care of its employees – 'We believe in happy people making happy soap . . .'. In fact, Lush seems to wish well to everyone, everywhere – 'We believe in long candlelit baths, sharing showers, massage, filling the world with perfume, and the right to make mistakes, lose everything, and start again.' Only in its final belief does Lush mention profits – 'We believe our products are good value, that we should make a profit, and that the customer is always right.' Thanks to its societal mission, Lush is thriving like fresh flowers in springtime. It now operates stores in 50 countries, with e-commerce sites in 27 countries. Its sales have nearly doubled in just the past three years, suggesting that doing good can benefit both the planet and the company.

Figure 1.4 Three considerations underlying the societal marketing concept

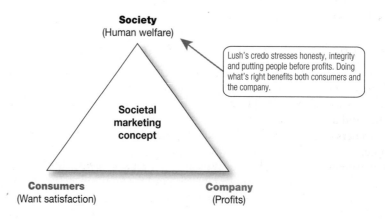

PREPARING AN INTEGRATED MARKETING PLAN AND PROGRAMME

The company's marketing strategy outlines which customers it will serve and how it will create value for these customers. Next, the marketer develops an integrated marketing programme that will actually deliver the intended value to target customers. The marketing programme builds customer relationships by transforming the marketing strategy into action. It consists of the firm's *marketing mix*, the set of marketing tools the firm uses to implement its marketing strategy.

The major marketing mix tools are classified into four broad groups, called the *four Ps* of marketing: product, price, place and promotion. To deliver on its value proposition, the firm must first create a need-satisfying market offering (product). It must then decide how much it will charge for the offering (price) and how it will make the offering available to target consumers (place). Finally, it must engage target consumers, communicate about the offering, and persuade consumers of the offer's merits (promotion). The firm must blend each marketing mix tool into a comprehensive integrated marketing programme that communicates and delivers the intended value to chosen customers. We will explore marketing programmes and the marketing mix in much more detail in later chapters.

Author comment

The customer value-driven marketing strategy discussed in the previous section outlines which customers the company will serve (the target market) and how it will serve them (positioning and the value proposition). Now, the company develops marketing plans and programmes – a marketing mix – that will actually deliver the intended customer value.

BUILDING CUSTOMER RELATIONSHIPS

The first three steps in the marketing process – understanding the marketplace and customer needs, designing a customer value-driven marketing strategy, and constructing a marketing programme – all lead up to the fourth and most important step: building and managing profitable customer relationships. We first discuss the basics of customer relationship management. Then, we examine how companies go about engaging customers on a deeper level in this age of digital and social marketing.

Author comment

Doing a good job with the first three steps in the marketing process sets the stage for step four, building and managing customer relationships.

Customer relationship management

Customer relationship management is perhaps the most important concept of modern marketing. In the broadest sense, **customer relationship management** is the overall process of building and maintaining profitable customer relationships by delivering superior customer value and satisfaction. It deals with all aspects of acquiring, engaging and growing customers.

Customer relationship management—The overall process of building and maintaining profitable customer relationships by delivering superior customer value and satisfaction.

Relationship building blocks: customer value and satisfaction

The key to building lasting customer relationships is to create superior customer value and satisfaction. Satisfied customers are more likely to be loyal customers and give the company a larger share of their business.

Customer value

Attracting and retaining customers can be a difficult task. Customers often face a bewildering array of products and services from which to choose. A customer buys from the firm that offers the highest **customer-perceived value** – the customer's evaluation of the difference between all the benefits and all the costs of a market offering relative to those of competing offers. Importantly, customers often do not judge values and costs 'accurately' or 'objectively'. They act on *perceived* value.

To some consumers, value might mean sensible products at affordable prices. To other consumers, however, value might mean paying more to get more. For example, Renault ZE electric car owners gain a number of benefits. The most obvious benefit is fuel efficiency (especially

Customer-perceived value—The customer's evaluation of the difference between all the benefits and all the costs of a marketing offer relative to those of competing offers.

when oil prices are rising). However, by purchasing a Renault ZE, the owners also may receive some status and image values. Driving a Renault ZE makes owners feel and appear more environmentally responsible. When deciding whether to purchase a Renault ZE, customers will weigh these and other perceived values of owning the car against the money, effort and psychic costs of acquiring it.

Customer satisfaction

Customer satisfaction—The extent to which a product's perceived performance matches a buyer's expectations.

Customer satisfaction depends on the product's perceived performance relative to a buyer's expectations. If the product's performance falls short of expectations, the customer is dissatisfied. If performance matches expectations, the customer is satisfied. If performance exceeds expectations, the customer is highly satisfied or delighted.

Outstanding marketing companies go out of their way to keep important customers satisfied. Most studies show that higher levels of customer satisfaction lead to greater customer loyalty, which in turn results in better company performance. Smart companies aim to delight customers by promising only what they can deliver and then delivering more than they promise. Delighted customers not only make repeat purchases but also become willing marketing partners and 'customer evangelists' who spread the word about their good experiences to others.

For companies interested in delighting customers, exceptional value and service become part of the overall company culture. For example, year after year, Ritz-Carlton ranks at or near the top of the hospitality industry in terms of customer satisfaction. Its passion for satisfying customers is summed up in the company's credo, which promises that its luxury hotels will deliver a truly memorable experience – one that 'enlivens the senses, instils well-being, and fulfils even the unexpressed wishes and needs of our guests.'[14]

Check into any Ritz-Carlton hotel around the world, and you'll be amazed by the company's fervent dedication to anticipating even your slightest need. Without ever asking, they seem to know that

you're allergic to peanuts and want a king-size bed, a non-allergenic pillow, extra body gel, the blinds open when you arrive, and breakfast with decaffeinated coffee in your room. Each day, hotel staffers – from those at the front desk to those in maintenance and housekeeping – discreetly observe and record even the smallest guest preferences. Then, every morning, each hotel reviews the files of all new arrivals who have previously stayed at a Ritz-Carlton and prepares a list of suggested extra touches that might delight each guest. For example, according to one Ritz-Carlton manager, if the chain gets hold of a picture of a guest's pet, it will make a copy, have it framed, and display it in the guest's room in whatever Ritz-Carlton the guest visits.

Once they identify a special customer need, Ritz-Carlton employees go to legendary extremes to meet it. For instance, to serve the needs of a guest whose son had food allergies, a Ritz-Carlton chef in Bali located special eggs and milk in a small grocery store in another country and had them delivered to the hotel. In another case, when a business man attending a conference at the

Customer satisfaction: Ritz-Carlton's passion for satisfying customers is summed up in its credo, which promises a truly memorable experience – one that 'enlivens the senses, instils well-being, and fulfills even the unexpressed wishes and needs of our guests'.

Source: Elan Fleisher/LOOK-foto/ Getty Images

Ritz-Carlton Orlando ordered his favourite soda during a dinner in a hotel ballroom, his banquet server told him that the hotel didn't serve that beverage but he would see what he could do. To no one's surprise, the server quickly returned with the requested beverage, and for the rest of the week he had the drink waiting for the guest. But here's the best part. A year later when the guest returned for the conference, as he sat in the ballroom waiting for dinner the first night, the same server walked up with his favourite drink in hand. As a result of such customer service heroics, an amazing 95 per cent of departing guests report that their stay has been a truly memorable experience. More than 90 per cent of Ritz-Carlton's delighted customers return.

Other companies that have become legendary for customer delight and their service heroics include John Lewis, Virgin Atlantic, Amazon and Singapore Airways. However, a company doesn't need to have over-the-top service to create customer delight. For example, no-frills grocery chain ALDI has highly satisfied customers, even though they have to bag their own groceries and can't use credit cards. ALDI's everyday very low pricing on good-quality products delights customers and keeps them coming back. Thus, customer satisfaction comes not just from service heroics, but from how well a company delivers on its basic value proposition and helps customers solve their buying problems. 'Most customers don't want to be "wowed",' says one marketing consultant. 'They [just] want an effortless experience.'[15]

Although a customer-centred firm seeks to deliver high customer satisfaction relative to competitors, it does not attempt to *maximise* customer satisfaction. A company can always increase customer satisfaction by lowering its prices or increasing its services. But this may result in lower profits. Thus, the purpose of marketing is to generate customer value profitably. This requires a very delicate balance: The marketer must continue to generate more customer value and satisfaction but not 'give away the house'.

Customer relationship levels and tools

Companies can build customer relationships at many levels, depending on the nature of the target market. At one extreme, a company with many low-margin customers may seek to develop *basic relationships* with them. For example, Häagen-Dazs does not phone or call on all of its consumers to get to know them personally. Instead, Häagen-Dazs creates relationships through brand-building advertising, public relations, its newsletter, its website (www.haagendazs.com) and via over 300,000 Facebook followers. At the other extreme, in markets with few customers and high margins, sellers want to create *full partnerships* with key customers. For example, Häagen-Dazs sales representatives work closely with Tesco, Carrefour and other large retailers. In between these two extremes, other levels of customer relationships are appropriate.

Beyond offering consistently high value and satisfaction, marketers can use specific marketing tools to develop stronger bonds with customers. For example, many companies offer *frequency marketing programmes* that reward customers who buy frequently or in large amounts. Airlines offer frequent-flyer programmes, hotels give room upgrades to their frequent guests, and supermarkets give patronage discounts to 'very important customers'. For example, KLM Airways and Air France offer their Flying Blue members frequent-flyer points they can use on any seat on any KLM or Air France flight. Flying Blue promises its members that 'As you travel more and more with us, we reward your loyalty by offering more and more services you can enjoy, to make every trip that much more special. By simply showing your Flying Blue card, you can access countless extra services and make your travels, or even your waiting time at the airport, smoother, easier and more pleasant.'[16]

These days almost every brand has a loyalty rewards programme. However, some innovative loyalty programmes go a step beyond the usual. Other companies sponsor *club marketing programmes* that offer members special benefits and create member communities. For example, BMW sponsors the BMW Car Club, which gives BMW drivers a way to share their driving passion. BMW Car Club membership benefits include a quarterly magazine, discounts on BMW servicing, parts and accessories, the club shop stocks BMW books, clothing, model cars and other BMW merchandise at discount prices. The club also organises track events and BMW festivals.

Engaging customers

Significant changes are occurring in the nature of customer brand relationships. Today's digital technologies – the Internet and the surge in online, mobile and social media – have profoundly changed the ways that people on the planet relate to one another. In turn, these events have had a huge impact on how companies and brands connect with customers, and how customers connect with and influence each other's brand behaviours.

Customer engagement and today's digital and social media

The digital age has spawned a dazzling set of new customer relationship-building tools, from websites, online ads and videos, mobile ads and apps, and blogs to online communities and the major social media, such as Twitter, Facebook, YouTube, Instagram and Pinterest.

Yesterday's companies focused mostly on mass marketing to broad segments of customers at arm's length. By contrast, today's companies are using online, mobile and social media to refine their targeting and to engage customers more deeply and interactively. The *old marketing* involved marketing brands to consumers. *The new marketing* is **customer-engagement marketing** – fostering direct and continuous customer involvement in shaping brand conversations, brand experiences and brand community. Customer-engagement marketing goes beyond just selling a brand to consumers. Its goal is to make the brand a meaningful part of consumers' conversations and lives.

The burgeoning Internet and social media have given a huge boost to customer-engagement marketing. Today's consumers are better informed, more connected and more empowered than ever before. Newly empowered consumers have more information about brands, and they have a wealth of digital platforms for airing and sharing their brand views with others. Thus, marketers are now embracing not only customer relationship management, but also *customer-managed relationships*, in which customers connect with companies and with each other to help forge their own brand experiences.

Greater consumer empowerment means that companies can no longer rely on marketing by *intrusion*. Instead, they must practise marketing by *attraction* – creating market offerings and messages that engage consumers rather than interrupt them. Hence, most marketers now augment their mass-media marketing efforts with a rich mix of online, mobile and social media marketing that promotes brand–consumer engagement and conversation.

For example, companies post their latest ads and videos on social media sites, hoping they'll go viral. They maintain an extensive presence on Twitter, YouTube, Facebook, Google+, Pinterest, Vine, and other social media to create brand buzz. They launch their own blogs, mobile apps, online microsites and consumer-generated review systems, all with the aim of engaging customers on a more personal, interactive level.

Take Twitter, for example. Organisations ranging from FC Barcelona, Santander, Munich Airport, Le Tour de France, Volvo to Howell's School Llandaff have created Twitter pages and promotions. They use 'tweets' to start conversations with and between Twitter's more than 645 million registered users, address customer service issues, research customer reactions, and drive traffic to relevant articles, web and mobile marketing sites, contests, videos and other brand activities.

Similarly, almost every company has something going on Facebook these days. Burberry has around 18 million Facebook 'fans', Converse has around 40 million, Zara has about 25 million, Starbucks has more than 36 million, Coca-Cola has more than 80 million. And every major marketer has a YouTube channel where the brand and its fans post current ads and other entertaining or informative videos. Artful use of social media can get consumers involved with and talking about a brand.

IKEA used a simple but inspired Facebook campaign to promote the opening of a new store in Malmo, Sweden. It opened a Facebook profile for the store's manager, Gordon Gustavsson. Then it uploaded pictures of IKEA showrooms to Gustavsson's Facebook photo album and announced that whoever was first to photo tag a product in the pictures with their name would

Customer-engagement marketing—Making the brand a meaningful part of consumers' conversations and lives by fostering direct and continuous customer involvement in shaping brand conversations, experiences and community.

win it. Thousands of customers rushed to tag items. Word spread quickly to friends, and customers were soon begging for more pictures. More than just looking at an ad with IKEA furniture in it, the Facebook promotion had people poring over the pictures, examining products item by item.[17]

The key to engagement marketing is to find ways to enter consumers' conversations with engaging and relevant brand messages. Simply posting a humorous video, creating a social media page, or hosting a blog isn't enough. Successful engagement marketing means making relevant and genuine contributions to consumers' lives and conversations. According to David Oksman, chief marketer for T-shirt and apparel maker Life is Good, engagement and social media are 'about deep meaningful relationships that go beyond the product you are selling. The real depth of engagement is in the commenting and community that go on [around the brand]'.

Consumer-generated marketing

A growing form of customer-engagement marketing is **consumer-generated marketing**, by which consumers themselves are playing a bigger role in shaping their own brand experiences and those of others. This might happen through uninvited consumer-to-consumer exchanges in blogs, video-sharing sites, social media and other digital forums. But increasingly, companies themselves are inviting consumers to play a more active role in shaping products and brand content.

Consumer-generated marketing—Brand exchanges created by consumers themselves – both invited and uninvited – by which consumers are playing an increasing role in shaping their own brand experiences and those of other consumers.

Some companies ask consumers for new product ideas. For example, McAfee actively seek new product ideas from existing users via their online community site.[18] Ideas regarding new products are solicited, community members are asked to comment, then vote and McAfee staff incorporate good ideas into the product range. Innocent have also generated a range of products through soliciting, listening and responding to customer ideas. For example, Innocent asked customers to send postcards with suggestions. One of the results was the hugely successful 'banana-free smoothie' sold with the tag line, 'You asked, we made it'. Coca-Cola's Vitaminwater brand recently created a Facebook app to obtain consumer suggestions for a new flavour, promising to manufacture and sell the winner ('Vitaminwater was our idea; the next one will be yours'). The new flavour – Connect (black cherry-lime with vitamins and a kick of caffeine) – was a big hit. In the process, Vitaminwater doubled its Facebook fan base to more than 1 million.[19]

Other companies are inviting customers to play an active role in shaping ads. For example, Redrow, T-Mobile, L'Oréal, MasterCard, Unilever, H.J. Heinz, and many other companies have run contests for customer-generated commercials that have been aired on national television. T-Mobile have sponsored and filmed 'flashmob' events at Liverpool Street Station and Trafalgar Square in London that have been viewed over 35 million times online as well as aired on television. Such success inspired T-Mobile to film a spoof Royal Wedding in 2011 during which actors playing the Royal Family (and a surprisingly funky Archbishop of Canterbury) literally danced down the aisle watched by over 30 million online viewers. Similarly, for the past eight years, PepsiCo's Doritos brand has held a 'Crash the Super Bowl' contest in which it invites 30-second ads from consumers and runs the best ones during the game. The consumer-generated ads have been a huge success. Last year, Doritos opened up the contest to people in all 46 countries where Doritos are sold. From more than 5,400 entries, Doritos aired two fan-produced ads during the Super Bowl. Past campaigns have produced numerous top-place finishers in *USA Today's* AdMeter rankings, earning their creators around €1 million in cash prizes from PepsiCo's Frito-Lay division. In the recent campaign, the prizes were instead awarded based on fan votes at Doritos.com. The winner, 'Time Machine' – a witty ad about a man who humours a small kid by taking a ride in his cardboard box time machine, only to be hoodwinked out of his bag of Doritos – earned its amateur creators around €1 million in cash. The homemade commercial cost €200 to make and took just eight hours to shoot.[20]

Despite the successes, however, harnessing consumer-generated content can be a time-consuming and costly process, and companies may find it difficult to glean even a little gold from all the garbage. Indeed, companies all too frequently rush headlong into trying to increase customer involvement in their campaigns without always thinking through the potential downsides, Starbucks unwisely asked +UK customers to tweet messages that used the hashtag #spreadthecheer and (very unwisely) displayed the resulting tweets on a big screen at the National History Museum in London. Very, very, very unwisely, Starbucks forgot to monitor the tweets, some of which derided the company's alleged tax avoidance measures. One read 'Hey #Starbucks PAY YOUR F***ING TAX'. Similarly, British Gas arranged a twitter question and answer session on the same day that they announced a very unpopular 11 per cent price hike. They had over 16,000 angry responses – 145 contained the word 'death' and 88 accused the company of being 'greedy'.[21]

Moreover, because consumers have so much control over social media content, inviting their input can sometimes backfire. For example, Benadryl thought that their interactive pollen count map would allow sufferers to identify (and assumedly avoid) pollen hotspots. However, Benadryl users clearly had a developed sense of humour that was greater than their pollen-avoidance needs. Astute (bored?) users very quickly realised that pins could be dropped to spell out expletives, obscenities or (for the particularly inventive hay fever sufferers with lots of time) draw rude and very amusing pictures.[22]

As consumers become more connected and empowered, and as the boom in digital and social media technologies continues, consumer brand engagement – whether invited by marketers or not – will be an increasingly important marketing force. Through a profusion of consumer-generated videos, shared reviews, blogs, mobile apps and websites, consumers are playing a growing role in shaping their own and other consumers' brand experiences. Engaged consumers are now having a say in everything from product design, usage and packaging to brand messaging, pricing and distribution. Brands must embrace this new consumer empowerment and master the new digital and social media relationship tools or risk being left behind.

Partner relationship management

Partner relationship management—Working closely with partners in other company departments and outside the company to jointly bring greater value to customers.

When it comes to creating customer value and building strong customer relationships, today's marketers know that they can't go it alone. They must work closely with a variety of marketing partners. In addition to being good at *customer relationship management*, marketers must also be good at **partner relationship management** – working closely with others inside and outside the company to jointly engage and bring more value to customers.

Traditionally, marketers have been charged with understanding customers and representing customer needs to different company departments. However, in today's more connected world, every functional area in the organisation can interact with customers. The new thinking is that – no matter what your job is in a company – you must understand marketing and be customer focused. Rather than letting each department go its own way, firms must link all departments in the cause of creating customer value.

Marketers must also partner with suppliers, channel partners, and others outside the company. Marketing channels consist of distributors, retailers, and others who connect the company to its buyers. The *supply chain* describes a longer channel, stretching from raw materials to components to final products that are carried to final buyers. Through *supply chain management*, companies today are strengthening their connections with partners all along the supply chain. They know that their fortunes rest on more than just how well they perform. Success at delivering customer value rests on how well their entire supply chain performs against competitors' supply chains.

CAPTURING VALUE FROM CUSTOMERS

Author comment

Look back at Figure 1.1. In the first four steps of the marketing process, the company creates value for target customers and builds strong relationships with them. If it does that well, it can capture value *from* customers in return, in the form of loyal customers who buy and continue to buy the company's brands.

The first four steps in the marketing process outlined in Figure 1.1 involve building customer relationships by creating and delivering superior customer value. The final step involves capturing value in return in the form of sales, market share and profits. By creating superior customer value, the firm creates highly satisfied customers who stay loyal and buy more. This, in turn, means greater long-run returns for the firm. Here, we discuss the outcomes of creating customer value: customer loyalty and retention, share of market and share of customer and customer equity.

Creating customer loyalty and retention

Good customer relationship management creates customer satisfaction. In turn, satisfied customers remain loyal and talk favourably to others about the company and its products. Studies show big differences in the loyalty of customers who are less satisfied, somewhat satisfied and completely satisfied. Even a slight drop from complete satisfaction can create an enormous drop in loyalty. Thus, the aim of customer relationship management is to create not only customer satisfaction but also customer delight.

Keeping customers loyal makes good economic sense. Loyal customers spend more and stay around longer. Research also shows that it's five times cheaper to keep an old customer than acquire a new one. Conversely, customer defections can be costly. Losing a customer means losing more than a single sale. It means losing the entire stream of purchases that the customer would make over a lifetime of patronage. For example, here is a classic illustration of **customer lifetime value**:[23]

Customer lifetime value— The value of the entire stream of purchases a customer makes over a lifetime of patronage.

Lexus, for example, estimates that a single satisfied and loyal customer is worth more than €800,000 in lifetime sales while the estimated lifetime value of a young mobile phone consumer is €34,000.[24] In fact, a company can lose money on a specific transaction but still benefit greatly from a long-term relationship. This means that companies must aim high in building customer relationships. Customer delight creates an emotional relationship with a brand, not just a rational preference. And that relationship keeps customers coming back.

Growing share of customer

Beyond simply retaining good customers to capture customer lifetime value, effective customer relationship management can help marketers increase their **share of customer** – the share they get of the customer's purchasing in their product categories. Thus, banks want to increase 'share of wallet'. Supermarkets and restaurants want to get more 'share of stomach'. Car companies want to increase 'share of garage', and airlines want greater 'share of travel'.

Share of customer—The portion of the customer's purchasing that a company gets in its product categories.

To increase share of customer, firms can offer greater variety to current customers. Or they can create programmes to cross-sell and up-sell to market more products and services to existing customers. For example, Amazon is highly skilled at leveraging relationships with its 237 million customers to increase its share of each customer's spending budget:[25]

> Once they log onto Amazon, customers often buy more than they intend, and Amazon does all it can to help make that happen. The online giant continues to broaden its merchandise assortment, creating an ideal spot for one-stop shopping. And based on each customer's purchase and search history, the company recommends related products that might be of interest. This recommendation system influences up to 30 per cent of all sales. Amazon's ingenious Amazon Prime two-day shipping programme has also helped boost its share of customers' wallets. For an annual fee, Prime members receive delivery of all their purchases within two days, whether it's a single paperback book or a 60-inch HDTV. According to one analyst, the ingenious Amazon Prime programme 'converts casual shoppers, who gorge on the gratification of having purchases reliably appear two days after the order, into Amazon addicts'. As a result, Amazon's 16.7 million Prime customers now account for around half of its sales. A Prime member is about six times more valuable to Amazon that a non-Prime member.

Building customer equity

We can now see the importance of not only acquiring customers but also keeping and growing them. The value of a company comes from the value of its current and future customers. Customer relationship management takes a long-term view. Companies want not only to create profitable customers but also 'own' them for life, earn a greater share of their purchases, and capture their customer lifetime value.

What is customer equity?

Customer equity—The total combined customer lifetime values of all of the company's customers.

The ultimate aim of customer relationship management is to produce high *customer equity*.[26] **Customer equity** is the total combined customer lifetime values of all of the company's current and potential customers. As such, it's a measure of the future value of the company's customer base. Clearly, the more loyal the firm's profitable customers, the higher its customer equity. Customer equity may be a better measure of a firm's performance than current sales or market share. Whereas sales and market share reflect the past, customer equity suggests the future. Consider Cadillac:[27]

In the 1970s and 1980s, Cadillac had some of the most loyal customers in the industry. To an entire generation of car buyers, the name *Cadillac* defined 'The standard of the world'. Cadillac's share of the luxury car market reached a whopping 51 per cent in 1976, and based on market share and sales, the brand's future looked rosy. However, measures of customer equity would have painted a bleaker picture. Cadillac customers were getting older (average age 60) and average customer lifetime value was falling. Many Cadillac buyers were on their last cars. Thus, although Cadillac's market share was good, its customer equity was not.

Compare this with BMW. Its more youthful and vigorous image didn't win BMW the early market share war. However, it did win BMW younger customers (average age about 40) with higher customer lifetime values. The result: in the years that followed, BMW's market share and profits soared while Cadillac's fortunes eroded badly. BMW overtook Cadillac in the 1980s. In recent years, Cadillac has struggled to make the Caddy cool again with edgier, high-performance designs that target a younger generation of consumers. The brand now bills itself as 'The new standard of the world' with marketing pitches based on 'power, performance and design', attributes that position it more effectively against the likes of BMW and Audi. However, for the past decade, Cadillac's share of the luxury car market has stagnated. The moral: marketers should care not just about current sales and market share. Customer lifetime value and customer equity are the name of the game.

Building the right relationships with the right customers

Companies should manage customer equity carefully. They should view customers as assets that need to be managed and maximised. But not all customers, not even all loyal customers, are good investments. Surprisingly, some loyal customers can be unprofitable, and some disloyal customers can be profitable. Which customers should the company acquire and retain?

The company can classify customers according to their potential profitability and manage its relationships with them accordingly. Figure 1.5 classifies customers into one of four relationship groups, according to their profitability and projected loyalty.[28] Each group requires a different relationship management strategy. *Strangers* show low potential profitability and little projected loyalty. There is little fit between the company's offerings and their needs. The relationship management strategy for these customers is simple: Don't invest anything in them; make money on every transaction.

Butterflies are potentially profitable but not loyal. There is a good fit between the company's offerings and their needs. However, like real butterflies, we can enjoy them for only a short while and then they're gone. An example is stock market investors who trade shares often and in large amounts but who enjoy hunting out the best deals without building a regular relationship with any single brokerage company. Efforts to convert butterflies into loyal customers are rarely successful. Instead, the company should enjoy the butterflies for the moment. It should create satisfying and profitable transactions with them, capturing as much of their business as possible in the short time during which they buy from the company. Then, it should move on and cease investing in them until the next time around.

True friends are both profitable and loyal. There is a strong fit between their needs and the company's offerings. The firm wants to make continuous relationship investments to delight these customers and nurture, retain and grow them. It wants to turn true friends into *true believers*, who come back regularly and tell others about their good experiences with the company.

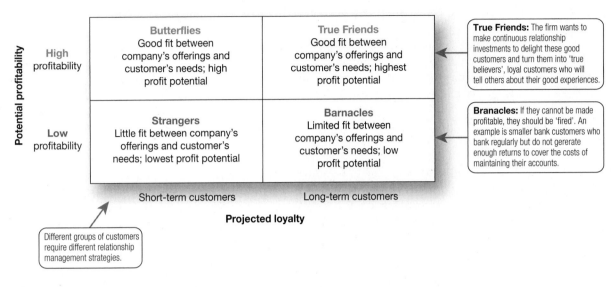

Barnacles are highly loyal but not very profitable. There is a limited fit between their needs and the company's offerings. An example is smaller bank customers who bank regularly but do not generate enough returns to cover the costs of maintaining their accounts. Like barnacles on the hull of a ship, they create drag. Barnacles are perhaps the most problematic customers. The company might be able to improve their profitability by selling them more, raising their fees, or reducing service to them. However, if they cannot be made profitable, they should be 'fired'.

The point here is an important one: different types of customers require different engagement and relationship management strategies. The goal is to build the *right relationships* with the *right customers*.

THE CHANGING MARKETING LANDSCAPE

Every day, dramatic changes are occurring in the marketplace. Richard Love of HP observed, 'The pace of change is so rapid that the ability to change has now become a competitive advantage'. Indeed, Rupert Murdock notes, 'The world is changing very fast. Big will not beat small any more. It will be the fast beating the slow.' As the marketplace changes, so must those who serve it or as Niccolo Machiavelli claims, 'Whosoever desires constant success must change his conduct with the times'.

In this section, we examine the major trends and forces that are changing the marketing landscape and challenging marketing strategy. We look at five major developments: the digital age, the changing economic environment, the growth of not-for-profit marketing, rapid globalisation and the call for more ethics and social responsibility.

The digital age: online, mobile and social media marketing

The explosive growth in digital technology has fundamentally changed the way we live – how we communicate, share information, access entertainment and shop. An estimated 3 billion people – 40 per cent of the world's population – are now online. In Europe, seven countries have Internet usage of more than 90 per cent (Ireland and Norway leading the way with 95 per cent each). More than two-thirds of Europe is now online, Eastern Europe spends most time online (Polish and Russian users both spending an average 4.8 hours online very day). Italy leads mobile Internet usage at 2.2 hours per day. In 2014 Europe boasted around 300 million active social media users (around 40 per cent of the population). In Western Europe Facebook dominates with 232 million active users while in Eastern Europe VKontakte is stronger with 60 million active users.[29]

Author comment

Marketing doesn't take place in a vacuum. Now that we've discussed the five steps in the marketing process, let's look at how the ever-changing marketplace affects both consumers and the marketers who serve them. We'll look more deeply into these and other marketing environment factors in Chapter 3.

Marketers increasingly need to consider the different means with which they can connect with customers.

Source: Mark Adams/123RF.com

Digital and social media marketing—Using digital marketing tools such as websites, social media, mobile apps and ads, online video, email and blogs that engage consumers anywhere, at any time, via their digital devices.

Most consumers are totally smitten with all things digital. For example, according to one study, more than half of Europeans keep their mobile phone next to them when they sleep – they say it's the first thing they touch when they get up in the morning and the last thing they touch at night. Favourite online and mobile destinations include the profusion of websites and social media that have sprung up.

The consumer love affair with digital and mobile technology makes it fertile ground for marketers trying to engage customers. So it's no surprise that the Internet and rapid advances in digital and social media have taken the marketing world by storm. **Digital and social media marketing** involves using digital marketing tools such as websites, social media, mobile ads and apps, online video, email, blogs and other digital platforms that engage consumers anywhere, anytime via their computers, smartphones, tablets, Internet-ready TVs and other digital devices. These days, it seems that every company is reaching out to customers with multiple websites, newsy tweets and Facebook pages, viral ads and videos posted on YouTube, rich-media emails and mobile apps that solve consumer problems and help them shop.

At the most basic level, marketers set up company and brand websites that provide information and promote the company's products. Many of these sites also serve as online brand communities, where customers can congregate and exchange brand-related interests and information. For example, Avia Premiership Rugby Club's website for the Harlequins serves as a hub for the club's super-passionate fans can check out the latest team news, buy tickets, engage with players, learn about the 'Quins', shop for merchandise, link with community programmes and otherwise get the latest teams news and gossip.[30]

Beyond brand websites, most companies are also integrating social and mobile media into their marketing mixes.

Social media marketing

It's hard to find a brand website, or even a traditional media ad, that doesn't feature links to the brand's Facebook, Twitter, Google+, LinkedIn, YouTube, Pinterest, Instagram, or other social media sites. Social media provide exciting opportunities to extend customer engagement and get people talking about a brand. Most European companies are catching on to the merits or using social media as part of their marketing mixes, and the majority have dedicated social marketing teams. By various estimates, social media spending accounts for about 10 per cent of marketing budgets and will rise to an estimated nearly 20 per cent within the next five years.[31]

Some social media are huge – Facebook has more than 1.1 billion members; Twitter has more than 500 million; and Pinterest draws in 70 million. Instagram racks up an estimated 85 million unique monthly visitors. And Reddit, the online social news community, has nearly 70 million unique visitors a month from 174 countries. But more focused social media sites are also thriving, such as CafeMom, an online community of 20 million moms who exchange advice, entertainment and commiseration at the community's online, Facebook, Twitter, Pinterest, YouTube, Google+ and mobile sites. Online social networks provide a digital home where people can connect and share important information and moments in their lives.

Using social media might involve something as simple as a contest or promotion to garner Facebook 'Likes', tweets or YouTube postings. For example, Asos, the online fashion retailer, recently won the prestigious Media Lion in Cannes for its global digital campaign. The company helped drive more than €7 million of sales via the #BestNightEver hashtag. The campaign featured the model Charlotte Free and the singers Ellie Goulding and Azealia Bates who all used their social media networks to post videos and offer fans the chance to win the clothes they were wearing. Asos featured the stars in a number of videos with shoppable technology that showed off Asos's latest products. As the videos were viewed, shoppers could click and buy the clothes they saw directly.[32]

ESPN also won a Media Lion for the best use of social media by creating 'Twitterball'. ESPN created Twitterball for fans to play during the halftime of a Champion's League match between Real Madrid and Borussia Dortmund. The game attached over 75,000 fans and was so successful it was adopted for use during the Fifa Football World Cup.[33]

Mobile marketing

Mobile marketing is perhaps the fastest-growing digital marketing platform. Twenty-nine per cent of smartphone owners use their phones for shopping-related activities – browsing product information through apps or the mobile web, making in-store price comparisons, reading on-line product reviews, finding and redeeming coupons and more.[34] Smartphones are ever-present, always on, finely targeted and highly personal. This makes them ideal for engaging customers any-time, anywhere as they move through the buying process. For example, Costa Coffee customers can use their mobile devices for everything from finding the nearest Costa Coffee and learning about new products to placing and paying for orders.

Marketers use mobile channels to stimulate immediate buying, make shopping easier, enrich the brand experience, or all of these. For example, P&G recently used mobile marketing to boost sampling through vending machines – called Freebies – that it placed in Walmart stores. To get a sample of, say, Tide Pods, customers first used their mobile phones in the store to check into the Tide Pods Facebook site, where they received product information and marketing.

Unilever's Wish-Bone campaign was an innovative new approach to mobile marketing. They wanted to increase brand awareness of their new range of Italian salad dressing. So, the company ran full-page adverts and created content that played up to the most important keywords – zesty, tangy and tasty. The company spurred customer engagement by getting customers to type in keywords associated with the brand in order to unlock content. This innovative approach lifted brand awareness by 122 per cent and purchase intents up by 87 per cent.[35]

Although online, social media and mobile marketing offer huge potential, most marketers are still learning how to use them effectively. The key is to blend the new digital approaches with tra-ditional marketing to create a smoothly integrated marketing strategy and mix. We will examine digital, mobile and social media marketing throughout the text – they touch almost every area of marketing strategy and tactics. Then, after we've covered the marketing basics, we'll look more deeply into digital and direct marketing in Chapter 17.

THE CHANGING ECONOMIC ENVIRONMENT

The Great Recession and its aftermath hit consumers hard. After two decades of overspending, new economic realities forced consumers to bring their consumption back in line with their in-comes and rethink their buying priorities.

In today's post-recession era, consumer incomes and spending are again on the rise. How-ever, even as the economy has strengthened, rather than reverting to their old free-spending ways, Europeans are now showing an enthusiasm for frugality not seen in decades. Sensible con-sumption has made a comeback and it appears to be here to stay. The new consumer spending values emphasise simpler living and more value for the euro. Despite their rebounding means, consumers continue to buy less, clip more coupons, swipe their credit cards less, and put more in the bank.

Many consumers are reconsidering their very definition of the good life. 'People are finding happiness in old-fashioned virtues – thrift, savings, do-it-yourself projects, self-improvement, hard work, faith and community', says one consumer behaviour expert. 'We are moving from mindless to mindful consumption.' The new, more frugal spending values don't mean that people have resigned themselves to lives of deprivation. As the economy has improved, consumers are

Customers are increasingly frugal. Even diamond marketer De Beers has adjusted its long-standing 'a diamond is forever' promise.

Source: Takashi Honma/123RF.com

indulging in luxuries and bigger-ticket purchases again, just more sensibly.

In response, companies in all industries – from discounters such as Lidl and Aldi to luxury brands such as Lexus and Montblanc – have aligned their marketing strategies with the new economic realities. More than ever, marketers are emphasising the *value* in their value propositions. They are focusing on value-for-the-money, practicality and durability in their product offerings and marketing pitches. 'Value is the magic word,' says a marketing executive. These days, 'people are doing the maths in their heads, and they're being much more thoughtful before making purchases. Now, we're going to be even more focused on helping consumers see value.' Similarly, Whitbread customers seek 'value for money', according to the owner of Premier Inn hotels and restaurants including Brewers Fayre and Beefeater. Occupancy at their budget hotels increased to 77 per cent in 2013 with sales up 12.7 per cent.[36]

Even wealthier consumers have joined the trend towards frugality. Conspicuous free spending is no longer so fashionable. As a result, even luxury brands are stressing value. Indeed, even diamond marketer De Beers has adjusted its longstanding, iconic 'a diamond is forever' promise to these more frugal times by cleverly adding, 'Here's to less'.

In adjusting to the new economy, companies may be tempted to cut their marketing budgets and slash prices in an effort to coax more frugal customers into opening their wallets. However, although cutting costs and offering selected discounts can be important marketing tactics, smart marketers understand that making cuts in the wrong places can damage long-term brand images and customer relationships. The challenge is to balance the brand's value proposition with the current times while also enhancing its long-term equity. Thus, rather than slashing prices in uncertain economic times, many marketers hold the line on prices and instead explain why their brands are worth it.

The growth of not-for-profit marketing

In recent years, marketing has also become a major part of the strategies of many not-for-profit organisations, such as colleges, hospitals, museums, zoos, symphony orchestras, foundations, and even churches. The nation's not-for-profits face stiff competition for support and membership. Sound marketing can help them attract membership, funds and support.[37]

Consider the marketing efforts of WaterAid. WaterAid's mission is to 'transform lives by improving access to safe water, hygiene and sanitation in the world's poorest communities'. They argue that this 'enables the world's poorest people to gain access to safe water and sanitation. Together with improved hygiene, these basic human rights underpin health, education and livelihoods, forming the first essential step in overcoming poverty'. To promote their work WaterAid ran emotive television advertisement but also used video blogging from a range of events including the G8 summit and the Glastonbury Music Festival. They were the first international development charity to run a 24-hour 'Australia to Zambia' 'tweetathon' that raised the profile of the charity worldwide. In this way, WaterAid are an excellent example of how charities and other not-for-profit organisations are embracing marketing in all its forms.[38]

Government agencies have also shown an increased interest in marketing. For example, the UK military has a marketing plan to attract recruits to its different services, and various government agencies are now designing *social marketing campaigns* to encourage energy conservation and concern for the environment or discourage smoking, excessive drinking and drug use. Indeed, the UK government has an annual advertising budget of measured in hundreds of millions of pounds.[39]

Rapid globalisation

As they are redefining their customer relationships, marketers are also taking a fresh look at the ways in which they relate with the broader world around them. Today, almost every company, large or small, is touched in some way by global competition. A neighbourhood florist buys its flowers from Egyptian nurseries, and a large Belgian electronics manufacturer competes in its home markets with giant Korean rivals. A fledgling Internet retailer finds itself receiving orders from all over the world at the same time that a European consumer goods producer introduces new products into emerging markets abroad.

The skilful marketing of American and Asian multinationals has challenged European firms at home. Companies such as Toyota, IBM, Chevron and Samsung have often outperformed their European competitors. Similarly, European companies in a wide range of industries have developed truly global operations, making and selling their products worldwide. While 80 per cent of IKEA's sales are in Europe, China and Russia are their fastest growing markets. Today, companies are not only selling more of their locally produced goods in international markets but also buying more supplies and components abroad.

Thus, managers in countries around the world are increasingly taking a global, not just local, view of the company's industry, competitors and opportunities. They are asking: What is global marketing? How does it differ from domestic marketing? How do global competitors and forces affect our business? To what extent should we 'go global'? We will discuss the global marketplace in more detail in Chapter 19.

While 80% of Ikea's sales are in Europe – China and Russia are their fastest growing markets.
Source: Alexander Blinov/Alamy Images

SUSTAINABLE MARKETING – THE CALL FOR MORE ENVIRONMENTAL AND SOCIAL RESPONSIBILITY

Marketers are re-examining their relationships with social values and responsibilities and with the very Earth that sustains us. As the worldwide consumerism and environmentalism movements mature, today's marketers are being called on to develop *sustainable marketing* practices. Corporate ethics and social responsibility have become hot topics for almost every business. And few companies can ignore the renewed and very demanding environmental movement. Every company action can affect customer relationships. Today's customers expect companies to deliver value in a socially and environmentally responsible way.

The social responsibility and environmental movements will place even stricter demands on companies in the future. Some companies resist these movements, budging only when forced by legislation or organised consumer outcries. Forward-looking companies, however, readily accept their responsibilities to the world around them. They view sustainable marketing as an opportunity to do well by doing good. They seek ways to profit by serving immediate needs and the best long-run interests of their customers and communities.

Some companies, such as Statoil, Marks & Spencer, Edison, Grupo Ferrovial and others, practise 'caring capitalism', setting themselves apart by being civic minded and responsible. They build social responsibility and action into their company value and mission statements.

For those in the business of gold, turning green is increasingly important – that is the belief of Michael Kowalski, chief executive and chairman of Tiffany & Co. Mr Kowalski is so convinced of the need to address environmental issues that he has spent ten years developing the company's environmental strategy. 'There is so much work to be done, so much complexity surrounding these issues of environmental responsibility, that our philosophy has always been to work quietly behind the scenes,' says Mr Kowalski. 'So we made a conscious decision to build a record of activity before we spoke out, to have a history to point to.' This is true not only for gold, but for precious gemstones – Tiffany, along with other jewellers such as Cartier, has not sold newly mined rubies since 2002. Similarly, Tiffany stopped selling coral, after discovering that 'there is no such thing as sustainable coral farming', says Mr Kowalski.[40] Hence, the Tiffany & Co. mission is 'to ensure the highest quality diamonds, ethical sourcing, lifetime warranty, affordable price options, and that they'll always be there for you'.[41]

Ben & Jerry's, a division of Unilever, has long prided itself on being a 'values-led business', one that creates 'linked prosperity' for everyone connected to the brand – from suppliers to employees to customers and communities.[42] Under its three-part mission, Ben & Jerry's wants to make fantastic ice cream (product mission), manage the company for sustainable financial growth (economic mission), and use the company 'in innovative ways to make the world a better place' (social mission). Ben & Jerry's backs its mission with actions. For example, the company is committed to using wholesome, natural, non-GMO, Fairtrade-certified ingredients and buys from local farms. It employs business practices 'that respect the earth and the environment', investing in wind energy, solar usage, travel offsets and carbon neutrality. Its 'Caring Dairy' programme helps farmers develop more sustainable practices on the farm ('Caring Dairy means happy cows, happy farmers and a happy planet'). The Ben & Jerry's Foundation awards nearly €2 million annually in grassroots grants to community service organisations and projects in communities across the nation. Ben & Jerry's also operates 14 PartnerShops, scoop shops that are independently owned and operated by community-based not-for-profit organisations. The company waives standard franchise fees for these shops.

Sustainable marketing presents both opportunities and challenges for marketers. We will revisit the topic of sustainable marketing in greater detail in Chapter 20.

SO, WHAT IS MARKETING? PULLING IT ALL TOGETHER

Author comment

Remember Figure 1.1 outlining the marketing process? Now, based on everything we've discussed in this chapter, we'll expand that figure to provide a roadmap for learning marketing throughout the remainder of the text.

At the start of this chapter, Figure 1.1 presented a simple model of the marketing process. Now that we've discussed all the steps in the process, Figure 1.6 presents an expanded model that will help you pull it all together. What is marketing? Simply put, marketing is the process of engaging customers and building profitable customer relationships by creating value for customers and capturing value in return.

The first four steps of the marketing process focus on creating value for customers. The company first gains a full understanding of the marketplace by researching customer needs and managing marketing information. It then designs a customer-driven marketing strategy based on the answers to two simple questions. The first question is 'What consumers will we serve?' (market segmentation and targeting). Good marketing companies know that they cannot serve all customers in every way. Instead, they need to focus their resources on the customers they can serve best and most profitably. The second marketing strategy question is 'How can we best serve targeted customers?' (differentiation and positioning). Here, the marketer outlines a value proposition that spells out what values the company will deliver to win target customers.

With its marketing strategy chosen, the company now constructs an integrated marketing programme – consisting of a blend of the four marketing mix elements, the four Ps – that transforms the marketing strategy into real value for customers. The company develops product offers and creates strong brand identities for them. It prices these offers to create real customer value and distributes the offers to make them available to target consumers. Finally, the company designs promotion programmes that engage target customers, communicate the value proposition, and persuade customers to act on the market offering.

Perhaps the most important step in the marketing process involves building value-laden, profitable relationships with target customers. Throughout the process, marketers practise customer relationship management to create customer satisfaction and delight. They engage customers in the process of creating brand conversations, experiences and community. In creating customer value and relationships, however, the company cannot go it alone. It must work closely with marketing partners both inside the company and throughout its marketing system. Thus, beyond practising good customer relationship management and customer-engagement marketing, firms must also practise good partner relationship management.

The first four steps in the marketing process create value *for* customers. In the final step, the company reaps the rewards of its strong customer relationships by capturing value *from* customers. Delivering superior customer value creates highly satisfied customers who will buy more and buy again. This helps the company capture customer lifetime value and greater share of customer. The result is increased long-term customer equity for the firm.

Finally, in the face of today's changing marketing landscape, companies must take into account three additional factors. In building customer and partner relationships, they must harness marketing technologies in the new digital age, take advantage of global opportunities, and ensure that they act sustainably in an environmentally and socially responsible way.

Figure 1.6 provides a good road map to future chapters of this text. Chapters 1 and 2 introduce the marketing process, with a focus on building customer relationships and capturing value from

Figure 1.6 An expanded model of the marketing process

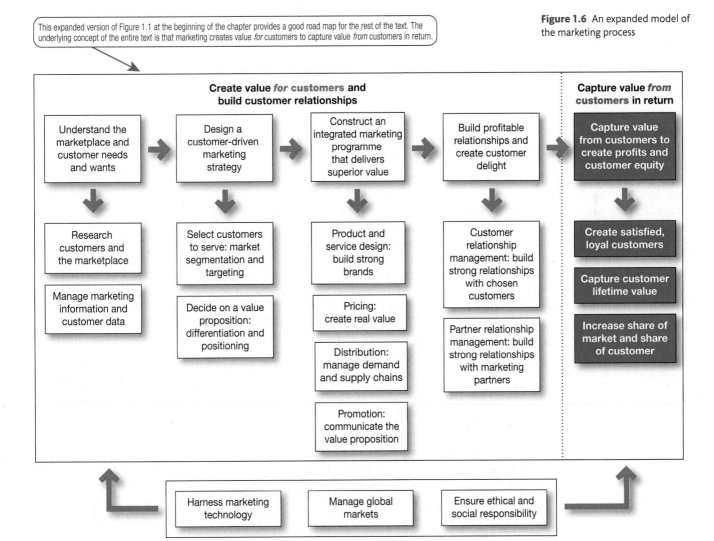

This expanded version of Figure 1.1 at the beginning of the chapter provides a good road map for the rest of the text. The underlying concept of the entire text is that marketing creates value *for* customers to capture value *from* customers in return.

customers. Chapters 3 through 6 address the first step of the marketing process – understanding the marketing environment, managing marketing information, and understanding consumer and business buyer behaviour. In Chapter 7, we look more deeply into the two major marketing strategy decisions: selecting which customers to serve (segmentation and targeting) and determining a value proposition (differentiation and positioning). Chapters 8 through 17 discuss the marketing mix variables, one by one. Chapter 18 sums up customer-driven marketing strategy and creating competitive advantage in the marketplace. The final two chapters examine special marketing considerations: global marketing and sustainable marketing.

OBJECTIVES REVIEW AND KEY TERMS

Today's successful companies – whether large or small, for-profit or not-for-profit, domestic or global – share a strong customer focus and a heavy commitment to marketing. The goal of marketing is to engage customers and manage profitable customer relationships.

OBJECTIVE 1 Define marketing and outline the steps in the marketing process (pp. 4–5)

Marketing is the process by which companies create value for customers and build strong customer relationships in order to capture value from customers in return. The marketing process involves five steps. The first four steps create value *for* customers. First, marketers need to understand the marketplace and customer needs and wants. Next, marketers design a customer-driven marketing strategy with the goal of getting, keeping and growing target customers. In the third step, marketers construct a marketing programme that actually delivers superior value. All of these steps form the basis for the fourth step, building profitable customer relationships and creating customer delight. In the final step, the company reaps the rewards of strong customer relationships by capturing value *from* customers.

OBJECTIVE 2 Explain the importance of understanding the marketplace and customers and identify the five core marketplace concepts (pp. 6–8)

Outstanding marketing companies go to great lengths to learn about and understand their customers' *needs*, *wants* and *demands*. This understanding helps them to design want-satisfying market offerings and build value-laden customer relationships by which they can capture customer *lifetime value* and greater *share of customer*. The result is increased long-term *customer equity* for the firm.

The core marketplace concepts are needs, wants and demands; market offerings (products, services and experiences); value and satisfaction; exchange and relationships; and markets. Wants are the form taken by human needs when shaped by culture and individual personality. When backed by buying power, wants become demands. Companies address needs by putting forth a value proposition, a set of benefits that they promise to consumers to satisfy their needs. The value proposition is fulfilled through a market offering, which delivers customer value and satisfaction, resulting in long-term exchange relationships with customers.

OBJECTIVE 3 Identify the key elements of a customer-driven marketing strategy and discuss the marketing management orientations that guide marketing strategy (pp. 9–12)

To design a winning marketing strategy, the company must first decide whom it will serve. It does this by dividing the market into segments of customers (*market segmentation*) and selecting which segments it will cultivate (*target marketing*). Next, the company must decide *how* it will serve targeted customers (how it will *differentiate and position* itself in the marketplace).

Marketing management can adopt one of five competing market orientations. The *production* concept holds that management's task is to improve production efficiency and bring down prices. The *product concept* holds that consumers favour products that offer the most in quality, performance and innovative features; thus, little promotional effort is required. The *selling* concept holds that consumers will not buy enough of an organisation's products unless it undertakes a large-scale selling and promotion effort. The *marketing concept* holds that achieving organisational goals depends on determining the needs and wants of target markets and delivering the desired satisfactions more effectively and efficiently than competitors do. The *societal marketing* concept holds that generating customer satisfaction *and* long-run societal well-being through sustainable marketing strategies is key to both achieving the company's goals and fulfilling its responsibilities.

OBJECTIVE 4 **Discuss customer relationship management and identify strategies for creating value for customers and capturing value from customers in return (pp. 13–20)**

Broadly defined, *customer relationship management* is the process of building and maintaining profitable customer relationships by delivering superior customer value and satisfaction. *Customer-engagement marketing* aims to make a brand a meaningful part of consumers' conversations and lives through direct and continuous customer involvement in shaping brand conversations, experiences and community. The aim of customer relationship management and customer engagement is to produce high *customer equity*, the total combined customer lifetime values of all of the company's customers. The key to building lasting relationships is the creation of superior *customer value and satisfaction*.

Companies want to not only acquire profitable customers but also build relationships that will keep them and grow 'share of customer'. Different types of customers require different customer relationship management strategies. The marketer's aim is to build the *right relationships* with the *right customers*. In return for creating value *for* targeted customers, the company captures value *from* customers in the form of profits and customer equity.

In building customer relationships, good marketers realise that they cannot go it alone. They must work closely with marketing partners inside and outside the company. In addition to being good at customer relationship management, they must also be good at *partner relationship management*.

OBJECTIVE 5 **Describe the major trends and forces that are changing the marketing landscape in this age of relationships (pp. 21–22)**

Dramatic changes are occurring in the marketing arena. The digital age has created exciting new ways to learn about and relate to individual customers. As a result, advances in digital and social media have taken the marketing world by storm. Online, mobile and social media marketing offer exciting new opportunities to target customers more selectively and engage them more deeply. Although the new digital and social media offer huge potential, most marketers are still learning how to use them effectively. The key is to blend the new digital approaches with traditional marketing to create a smoothly integrated marketing strategy and mix.

The Great Recession hit consumers hard, causing them to rethink their buying priorities and bring their consumption back in line with their incomes. Even as the post-recession economy has strengthened, Europeans are now showing an enthusiasm for frugality not seen in decades. Sensible consumption has made a comeback, and it appears to be here to stay. More than ever, marketers must now emphasise the *value* in their value propositions. The challenge is to balance a brand's value proposition with current times while also enhancing its long-term equity.

In recent years, marketing has become a major part of the strategies for many not-for-profit organisations, such as colleges, hospitals, museums, zoos, symphony orchestras, foundations, and even churches. Also, in an increasingly smaller world, many marketers are now connected *globally* with their customers and marketing partners. Today, almost every company, large or small, is touched in some way by global competition. Finally, today's marketers are also re-examining their ethical and societal responsibilities. Marketers are being called on to take greater responsibility for the social and environmental impacts of their actions.

Pulling it all together, as discussed throughout the chapter, the major new developments in marketing can be summed up in a single concept: *creating and capturing customer value*. Today, marketers of all kinds are taking advantage of new opportunities for building value-laden relationships with their customers, their marketing partners, and the world around them.

NAVIGATING THE KEY TERMS

OBJECTIVE 1
Marketing (p. 5)

OBJECTIVE 2
Needs (p. 6)
Wants (p. 6)
Demands (p. 6)
Market offerings (p. 6)
Marketing myopia (p. 7)
Exchange (p. 8)
Market (p. 8)

OBJECTIVE 3
Marketing management (p. 9)
Production concept (p. 10)
Product concept (p. 10)
Selling concept (p. 10)
Marketing concept (p. 11)
Societal marketing concept (p. 11)

OBJECTIVE 4
Customer relationship
  management (p. 13)

Customer-perceived value (p. 13)
Customer satisfaction (p. 14)
Customer-engagement marketing (p. 16)
Consumer-generated marketing (p. 17)
Partner relationship management (p. 18)
Customer lifetime value (p. 19)
Share of customer (p. 19)
Customer equity (p. 20)

OBJECTIVE 5
Digital and social media marketing (p. 22)

DISCUSSION AND CRITICAL THINKING

Discussion questions

1-1 Define marketing. What is marketing myopia and how can it be avoided? (AACSB: Communication; Reflective thinking)

1-2 Explain the importance of understanding the marketplace and customers and identify the five core marketplace concepts. (AACSB: Communication)

1-3 Describe the key elements of a customer-driven marketing strategy and discuss the marketing management orientations that guide marketing strategy. (AACSB: Communication; Reflective thinking)

1-4 What is customer-engagement marketing? Describe an example of a brand that engages customers well. (AACSB: Communication; Reflective thinking)

1-5 When implementing customer relationship management, why might a business desire fewer customers over more customers? Shouldn't the focus of marketing be to acquire as many customers as possible? (AACSB: Communication; Reflective thinking)

Critical-thinking exercises

1-6 Go to a company's, organisation's or specific brand's website that has a link to Facebook, Google+, YouTube, Twitter and/or Pinterest. Click on the links and describe how that company is using social media to market its products. Evaluate its effectiveness in creating customer engagement. (AACSB: Communication; Use of IT; Reflective thinking)

1-7 Search the Internet for salary information regarding jobs in marketing from a website such as www .simplyhired.com/a/salary/search/q-marketing or a similar site. What is the national average salary for five different jobs in marketing? How do the averages compare in different areas of the country? Write a brief report on your findings. (AACSB: Communication; Use of IT; Reflective thinking)

Mini-cases and applications

Online, mobile and social media marketing: Xbox One

Eight years after the launch of its wildly successful Xbox 360, Microsoft finally launched its new Xbox One in 2013. The company was hoping the new console would turn around its 71 per cent plunge in profits in 2012. The Xbox One touts a Blu-ray video player, voice-activated on-demand movies and TV, Skype calling, and social media integration. Smart TV features customise menus for each player and tailor content for individual users. Xbox Live's 48 million members can interact on social media during special televised events such as the Olympics, Oscars, and other special programming. Games have greater artificial intelligence, enabling players to feel like the virtual athletes are making decisions on their own. Sports data such as daily performance and injury updates feed into online games, mirroring its real-world counterpart. Players can augment live televised games with fantasy football stats that can be shared with friends via Skype and Microsoft's Smart-Glass apps. One thing the Xbox One can't do is play old games. Competitor Sony came out with its PlayStation 4 that has touch-sensors in its controller and allows players to play any game – current or old – instantly over the Internet. Both companies are banking on more digital and social media applications to save them from the fate that competitor Nintendo faced with its failed Wii U console introduced in 2012.

1-8 Debate whether these new features in game consoles are enough to survive against the growth of smartphone and tablet apps that offer free or inexpensive games. (AACSB: Communication; Reflective thinking)

1-9 Brainstorm three new game console features incorporating digital, mobile or social media technology to encourage consumer interaction and engagement with gaming. (AACSB: Communication; Reflective thinking)

Marketing ethics: extreme baby monitoring

Every parents' fear when they put an infant to sleep is Sudden Infant Death Syndrome (SIDS) – the sudden unexplainable death of an otherwise healthy baby. In Europe thousands of infants die each year of SIDS; a leading cause of infant death. For around €199, parents can buy monitors that track babies' vital signs, such as respiration, heart rate, skin temperature, sleeping position and quality of sleep. The Mimo Smart Baby Monitor is a cute clip-on turtle that attaches to a special organic cotton onesie, and the Owlet Baby Monitor is a smart sock that looks like a little toeless boot. If parents don't want to attach these devices on their little ones, they can opt for the SafeToSleep Breathing Monitor sheet with a built in monitor. All of these devices stream data to parents' smartphones. Manufacturers of these devices promote them to parents for 'your baby's health' or 'gives you that extra assurance' to protect against SIDS. However, several government agencies agree that these devices cannot protect a baby from SIDS. But fear sells, and most of these manufacturers cannot keep up with the demand for their products.

1-10 Is it right for marketers to play on parents' fear to sell products that experts conclude are not necessary or effective? (AACSB: Communication; Ethical Reasoning; Reflective thinking)

1-11 Discuss other examples of marketers using emotion to sell products. Are they ethical? (AACSB: Communication; Ethical reasoning)

Marketing by the numbers: consumers rule!

Marketing is expensive! Do you want customers to order your product by phone? That will cost you €5–€10 per order. Do you want a sales representative calling on customers? That's about €70 per sales call, and that's if the rep doesn't have to get on an aeroplane and stay In a hotel, which can be very costly considering some companies have thousands of sales reps calling on thousands of customers. What about the €1 off coupon for Tropicana orange juice that you found in the Sunday newspaper. It costs Tropicana more than €1 when you redeem it at the store. These are all examples of costs of distributing products to buyers, and the costs of all the employees working in marketing.

1. Select a publicly traded company and research how much the company spent on marketing activities in the most recent year of available data. What percentage of sales does marketing expenditures represent? Have these expenditures increased or decreased over the past five years? Write a brief report of your findings. (AACSB Communication; Analytic reasoning)

2. Search the Internet for salary information regarding jobs in marketing. Use www.marketingjobs.brandrepublic.com or a similar website. What is the average for five different jobs in marketing? How do the averages compare between countries? Write a brief report on your findings. (AACSB: Communication; Use of IT; Reflective thinking)

REFERENCES

[1] See Swaraj Baggonkar 'The wind beneath Mini's wings', *Business Standard*, 7 January 2015; Rian Boden, 'BMW offer contactless credit card that can unlock and start hire cars', *NFC World*, 7 January 2015; A. Broderick, P. Maclaran and P.Y. Ma, 'Brand meaning negotiation and the role of online community: a Mini case study' (2003), *Journal of Consumer Behaviour*, 2, 75–103; M. McCarthy,'Mini Cooper's road map to fending off surging rivals', *Advertising Age*, 15 August 2013; T. Lewis, 'BMW's Mini to cut model line-up', *Just-Auto Global News*, 27 November 2014; C.D. Simms and P. Trott, 'The perceptions of the BMW Mini brand: the importance of historical associations and the development of the model' (2006), *Journal of Product and Brand Management*, 15, 4, 228–238; Lucy Nicholson, 'BMW's Mini to limit range in long term to sharpen its premium appeal', *Reuters*, 26 November 2014, http://uk.reuters.com/article/2014/11/26/uk-bmw-mini-idUKKCN0JA18620141126; T. Urquhart, 'BMW introduces Spotify streaming service on ConnectedDrive platform', *IHS Global Insight*, 20 November 2014; L. Wilkinson, 'Bigger and better: BMW reveals all-new Mini', *The Telegraph*, 18 November 2013; L. Wilkinson, 'Mini: a brief history', *The Telegraph*, 18 November 2013; www.Automoz.net/launch-of-the-mini-cooper and www.Mini.co.uk, accessed October 2015.

[2] The authors would like to thank Professors Amelia C. Harris, Heidi Homewood and Holly Bostock for their invaluable help in preparing this chapter.

[3] See Philip Kotler and Kevin Lane Keller, *Marketing Management*, 14th ed. (Upper Saddle River, NJ: Prentice Hall, 2012), p. 5.

[4] The American Marketing Association offers the following definition: 'Marketing is the activity, set of institutions, and processes for creating, communicating, delivering, and exchanging offerings that have value for customers, clients, partners, and society at large.' See www.marketingpower.com/_layouts/Dictionary.aspx?dLetter=M, accessed October 2015.

[5] Jeffrey M. O'Brien, 'Zappos knows how to kick it', *Fortune*, 22 January 2009, accessed at http://money.cnn.com/2009/01/15/news/companies/Zappos_best_companies_obrien.fortune/index.htm; and Roland T. Rust, Christine Moorman and Gaurav Bhalla, 'Rethinking marketing', *Harvard Business Review*, January–February 2010, pp. 94–101.

[6] See http://blog.discoveringireland.com/tourism-ireland-new-campaign-to-promote-the-wild-atlantic-way/, http://tourismireland.com/Home!/Our-Marketing-Overseas/Autumn-Campaign-2014.aspx, accessed October 2015.

[7] See Theodore Levitt's classic article, 'Marketing myopia', *Harvard Business Review*, July–August 1960, pp. 45–56; for more recent discussions, see Minette E. Drumright and Mary C. Gentile, 'The new marketing myopia', *Journal of Public Policy & Marketing*, Spring 2010, pp. 4–11; Roberto Friedmann, 'What business are you in?' *Marketing Management*, Summer 2011, pp. 18–23; and Al Ries, "Marketing myopia' revisited: perhaps a narrow vision is better business', *Advertising Age*, 4 December2013, http://adage.com/print/245511.

[8] See J. J. McCorvey, 'Bird of Pplay', *Fast Company*, December 2012/January 2013, pp. 100–107+; Neil Long, 'Two billion downloads? We're just getting started, says Angry Birds creator Rovio', *Edge*, 23 January2014, www.edge-online.com/features/two-billion-download-swere-just-getting-started-says-angry-birds-creator-rovio/; and www.angrybirds.com, accessed October 2015.

[9] See https://play.google.com/store/apps/details?id=co.vine.androidm, accessed October 2015.

[10] 'The difference in creating companies and categories', *happycustomer*, 4 March, 2014, http://happycustomer.stellaservice.com/2014/03/04/column-the-difference-in-creating-companies-and-categories/.

[11] See Michael E. Porter and Mark R. Kramer, 'Creating shared value', *Harvard Business Review*, January–February 2011, pp. 63–77; Marc Pfitzer, Valerie Bockstette, and Mike Stamp, 'Innovating for shared value', *Harvard Business Review*, September 2013, pp. 100–107; 'About shared

value', *Shared Value Initiative*, http://sharedvalue.org/about-shared-value, accessed October 2015; and 'Shared value', www.fsg.org, accessed October 2015.

12 Michael Krauss, 'Evolution of an academic: Kotler on Marketing 3.0', *Marketing News*, 30 January 2011, p. 12; and Simon Mainwaring, 'Marketing 3.0 will be won by purpose-driven, social brands', *Forbes*, 16 July 2013, www.forbes.com/sites/simonmainwaring/2013/07/16/marketing-3-0-will-be-won-by-purpose-driven-social-brands-infographic/.

13 See Scott Campbell, 'Lush defies the Christmas retail slump', *The Telegraph*, 6 January 2014, www.telegraph.co.uk/finance/newsbysector/retailandconsumer/10554068/Lush-defies-the-Christmas-retail-slump.html; and 'Lush life: we believe', www.lushusa.com/on/demandware.store/Sites-Lush-Site/en_US/AboutUs-OurStoryShow?cid=we-believe, accessed October 2015.

14 Based on information from Michael Bush, 'Why you should be putting on the Ritz', *Advertising Age*, 21 June 2010, p. 1; Julie Barker, 'Power to the people', *Incentive*, February 2008, p. 34; Philip Kotler and Kevin Lane Keller, *Marketing Management*, 14th ed. (Upper Saddle River, NJ: Prentice Hall, 2012), p. 381; http://corporate.ritzcarlton.com/en/About/Awards.htm, accessed October 2015; and 'Stories that stay with you', www.ritzcarlton.com/en/StoriesThatStay.htm, accessed October 2015.

15 'Delighting the customer doesn't pay', *Sales & Marketing Management*, 11 November 2013, http://salesandmarketing.com/content/delighting-customers-doesnt-pay.

16 See www.klm.com, accessed October 2015.

17 See 'Successful IKEA Facebook campaign shows importance of offering deals to consumers on social media', *Illuminea*, 27 November 2009, http://illuminea.com/social-media/ikea-facebook-social-media/; Chris Matyszczyk, 'IKEA's brilliant Facebook Ccampaign', *CNET News*, 24 November 2009, http://news.cnet.com/8301-17852_3-10404937-71.html; and www.youtube.com/watch?v=P_K1ti4RU78&feature=player_embedded, accessed October 2015.

18 See https://community.mcafee.com/docs/DOC-2489, accessed October 2015.

19 Joel Rubenstein, 'Marketers, researchers, and your ears', *Brandweek*, 15 February 2010, p. 34.

20 '2014 USA Today Ad Meter', http://admeter.usatoday.com/, accessed February 2014; and www.doritos.com/, accessed October 2015.

21 See https://econsultancy.com/blog/63901-the-top-16-social-media-fails-of-2013#i.169qyp410jld96, accessed October 2015.

22 See https://econsultancy.com/blog/63901-the-top-16-social-media-fails-of-2013#i.169qyp410jld96, accessed October 2015.

23 Stew Leonard's *Hoover's Company Records*, 15 July 2012, www.hoovers.com; and www.stew-leonards.com/html/about.cfm, accessed September 2014.

24 Graham Brown, 'Mobile youth key statistics', 28 March 2008, www.mobileyouth.org/?s=MobileYouth+Key+Statistics; for interesting discussions on customer lifetime value, see Sunil Gupta *et al.*, 'Modeling customer lifetime value', *Journal of Service Research*, November 2006, pp. 139–146; Nicolas Glady, Bart Baesens and Christophe Croux, 'Modeling churn using customer lifetime value', *European Journal of Operational Research*, 16 August 2009, p. 402; and Jason Q. Zhang, Ashutosh Dixit, and Roberto Friedman, 'Customer loyalty and lifetime value: an empirical investigation of consumer packaged goods', *Journal of Marketing Theory and Practice*, Spring 2010, p. 127.

25 Based on quotes and information from Brad Stone, 'What's in the box? Instant gratification', *Bloomberg Businessweek*, 29 November–5 December 2010, pp. 39–40; Patrick Seitz, 'Amazon Prime is a growing

threat to Netflix', *Investor's Business Daily*, 9 December 2013; and www.amazon.com/gp/prime/ref=footer_prime, accessed October 2015.

26 For more discussions on customer equity, see Roland T. Rust, Valerie A. Zeithaml, and Katherine N. Lemon, *Driving Customer Equity*, New York: Free Press, 2000; Rust, Lemon, and Zeithaml, 'Return on marketing: using customer equity to focus marketing strategy', *Journal of Marketing*, January 2004, pp. 109–127; Christian Gronroos and Pekka Helle, 'Return on relationships: conceptual understanding and measurement of mutual gains from relational business engagements', *Journal of Business & Industrial Marketing*, Vol. 27, No. 5, 2012, pp. 344–359; and Peter C. Verhoef and Katherine N. Lemon, 'Successful customer value management: key lessons and emerging trends', *European Management Journal*, February 2013, p. 1.

27 This example is adapted from information found in Rust, Lemon, and Zeithaml, 'Where should the next marketing dollar go?' *Marketing Management*, September–October 2001, pp. 24–28; with information from Jeff Bennett and Joseph B. White, 'New Cadillac, old dilemma', *Wall Street Journal*, 27 March 2013, p. B1; and Grant McCracken, 'Provocative Cadillac, rescuing the brand from bland', *Harvard Business Review*, 4 March 2014, http://blogs.hbr.org/2014/03/provocative-cadillac-rescuing-the-brand-from-bland/.

28 Based on Werner Reinartz and V. Kumar, 'The mismanagement of customer loyalty', *Harvard Business Review*, July 2002, pp. 86–94'; also see Stanley F. Slater, Jakki J. Mohr, and Sanjit Sengupta, Know your customer', *Marketing Management*, February 2009, pp. 37–44; Crina O. Tarasi *et al.*, 'Balancing risk and return in a customer portfolio', *Journal of Marketing*, May 2011, pp. 1–17; and Chris Lema, 'Not all customers are equal – butterflies and barnacles', 18 April 2013, http://chrislema.com/not-all-customers-are-equal-butterflies-barnacles/.

29 See wearesocial.net/blog/2014/02/social-digital-mobile-europe-2014/, accessed October 2015.

30 See www.quins.co.uk, accessed October 2015.

31 See Stuart Feil, 'How to win friends and influence people', *Adweek*, 12 September 2013, pp. S1–S7; Joe Mandese, 'Carat projects digital at one-fifth of all ad spend, beginning to dominate key markets', *MediaPost News*, 20 March 2013, www.mediapost.com/publications/article/196238/carat-projects-digitalat-one-fifth-of-all-ad-spen.html#axzz2PsYL9uFf; and Julia McCoy, 'A 2014 social media guide: new trends and solutions to live by', *socialmediatoday*, 15 January 2014, http://socialmediatoday.com/expresswriters/2066416/2014-social-media-guide-new-trendsand-solutions-live.

32 See https://blog.twitter.com/2013/asos-drives-ps5m-sales-with-cannes-lions-winning-campaign, accessed October 2015.

33 See www.mediavisioninteractive.com/blog/social-media/five-best-social-media-campaigns-love/, accessed January 2016

34 Michael Applebaum, 'Mobile magnetism', *Adweek*, 25 June 2012, pp. S1–S9; and Bill Briggs, 'M-commerce is saturating the globe', *Internet Retailer*, 20 February 2014, www.internetretailer.com/2014/02/20/m-commerce-saturating-globe.

35 See www.mobilemarketer.com/cms/news/advertising/15918.html, accessed October 2015.

36 Rose Jacobs, 'Value demand helps boost sales at Whitbread', *Financial Times*, London (UK), 15 December 2010, p. 20; www.whitbread.co.uk/media/news-press-releases/Whitbread-Trading-Update-18-June-2013.html, accessed October 2015.

37 For examples and for a good review of non-profit marketing, see Philip Kotler and Alan R. Andreasen, *Strategic Marketing for Nonprofit Organizations*, 7th ed. (Upper Saddle River, NJ: Prentice Hall, 2008);

Philip Kotler and Karen Fox, *Strategic Marketing for Educational Institutions* (Upper Saddle River, NJ: Prentice Hall, 1995); Philip Kotler, John Bowen and James Makens, *Marketing for Hospitality and Tourism*, 4th ed. (Upper Saddle River, NJ: Prentice Hall, 2006); and Philip Kotler and Nancy Lee, *Marketing in the Public Sector: A Roadmap for Improved Performance* (Philadelphia: Wharton School Publishing, 2006).

[38] Example based on data found at http://www.wateraid.org/uk/about_us/vision_and_mission/default.asp, accessed October 2011.

[39] For more on social marketing, see Philip Kotler, Ned Roberto and Nancy R. Lee, *Social Marketing: Improving the Quality of Life*, 2nd ed. (Thousand Oaks, CA: Sage Publications, 2002).

[40] Vanessa Friedman, 'Michael Kowalski: Tiffany parades its voluntary standards', *Financial Times*, 28 May 2008, http://www.ft.com/cms/s/0/69c21434–292e-11dd-96ce-000077b07658.html#axzz1UPifHx5H, accessed October 2015.

[41] See www.tiffany.com, accessed October 2015.

[42] See www.benjerry.com/values, www.benandjerrysfoundation.org/, and www.unilever.com/brands-in-action/detail/ben-and-jerrys/291995/, accessed October 2015.

COMPANY CASE

Pegasus Airlines: delighting a new type of travelling customer

Until 1982, Turkish Airlines was the only airline company operating in Turkey, and it had no domestic competitors. Following deregulation and reduction of government controls across the airline industry, 29 airlines were established, with 22 finding themselves bankrupted a few years later, demonstrating the strong level of both internal and external competition and how the airline industry is affected by economic instability. Over the past 20 years, Turkey has experienced a number of financial crises, as well as political turmoil culminating in a military coup in 1980. Pegasus was created in 1989 as a charter airline partnered with Aer Lingus to create all-inclusive holidays. In 1994, the company was sold to a Turkish investment fund and in 2005 was re-sold to Ali Sabanci (of Sabanci Holding, an influential family-owned business in Turkey), who changed the airline from a charter airline to a low-cost airline. In 2008, Pegasus carried a total 4.4 million passengers in Turkey, more than any other private airline. However, by 2013 passenger traffic had exploded to 16.8 million passengers carried. As of 2015, Pegasus has a fleet of 54 Boeing and Airbus planes with 78 on order. Its major competitors – other than the national carrier, Turkish Airlines – are Onur Air, Fly Air, Sun Express and Atlasjet. Instead of operating from Istanbul's main airport, which is overcrowded, Pegasus Airlines flies from Istanbul's second main hub, Sabiha Gökçen International Airport. Its on-time departure rate is 90 per cent, which is well above the European average of 81 per cent, demonstrating the importance the company attaches to customer service. Recently, Pegasus has been awarded the title of 'fastest growing airline in Europe' among the 25 biggest airline companies in Europe (according to a ranking based on seat capacity data) and was named the cheapest European low-cost airline in both 2013 and 2014.

Truly customer focused

What is the secret to the airline's success? Quite simply, it involves making sure Pegasus is continually developing to meet passenger expectations and priorities. Pegasus has put in place a yield management strategy for ticket pricing, using the strategy of Southwest Airlines of North America as an example. Supply and demand, as well as time, are taken into account in the ticket pricing strategy; for example, if customers book early (60 days) they receive further savings while those who book later pay the maximum current fare offered by competitors. The system is complemented by an electronic ticket policy whereby passengers receive their information via email and SMS. Pegasus has also developed a credit/loyalty card (the Pegasus Plus Card), which offers customers a range of benefits including insurance rate reductions. Although airlines can't often control flight delays, Pegasus has developed a specific customer satisfaction guarantee policy that provides customers with (i) in the case of a delay greater than three hours, a refund of the ticket and (ii) in the case of a delay greater than five hours, a refund and a free ticket. Pegasus also offers a customer service experience at the airport: it provides exclusive allotments for the first 72 hours of parking with a valet parking option, VIP and Business Class lounges, car rental and many hotel partners where customers can get some discount. Unlike many airlines, a one-class interior configuration is operated, but passengers can pay a small extra premium to choose their seats. This is complemented by the Pegasus Flying Café, which offers a range of refreshments and catering options for a small additional charge, allowing customers to pre-order and reserve their inflight meals. Pegasus offers further customer service options, including a 10 per cent discount to passengers on international flights who order their in-flight meals 48 hours in advance. An in-plane bulletin is also available, with a mix of offers and features on certain destinations. This bulletin is free for customers but generates income via advertising. These services are supported by Pegasus' own flight crew training centre and maintenance organisation, Pegasus Technic. Both are fully licensed and are used to train new staff members. Pegasus also provides these training and technical services for other local airlines. Pegasus' innovative customer service recently won the company an award for 'Best Airline Business Price' in 2016. Indeed, the company regularly receives awards and recognition for, among other things, its management strategy; initiatives in website development; and its marketing strategy, which employs a new approach to advertising that includes viral marketing, flash campaigns and mobile campaigns. This strategy has succeeded in making Pegasus the most searched airline in Turkey on Google. Between 2008 and 2012 domestic passenger numbers grew at a compound average growth rate of 36 per cent pa while its scheduled international passenger growth was 43 per cent over the same period. This compares with Turkish Airlines' lowly rates of 10 per cent and 19 per cent respectively.

More than amenities

Although the tangible amenities that Pegasus offers are likely to delight most travellers, General Manager Sertaç Haybat recognises that these practices are not nearly enough to provide a sustainable competitive advantage and that Pegasus must always present its customers with the most economical flight opportunities. Here the importance of the crew training centre remains crucial. Haybat emphasises that a culture that breeds trust is the most crucial factor. It's this personal culture that gives Pegasus' customer service an edge. Indeed, taking care of customers starts as early as a customer's first encounter with the Pegasus brand and website. In 2012, Pegasus was recognised as one of Turkey's top brands and awarded the title of 'Superbrand Turkey'. Pegasus' employees work as a team with their goal being a common understanding of the airline's long-term objective to provide a democratic environment in which everyone shares their ideas freely. Training, as well as continuous development, is provided to ensure regular career progression and high levels of motivation through a solid performance system and regular personal feedback. Early in the process, Pegasus selects the people who best exhibit these values while directing the right person to the right department at the right time. The last tenet of Pegasus' customer-service strategy lies in the regularly scheduled and innovative destinations it offers. Not only does Pegasus share planes with Pegasus Asia and Izair, but it also has charter and scheduled services to around 120 airports in Europe and Asia. Pegasus operates regular flights to Georgia and Lebanon, providing additional destinations outside of Europe, thus maximising Turkey's short flights opportunities. These flights have prompted a strong reaction from the competition. The regular service to Tbilisi (Georgia) has been met by an announcement from Austrian Airlines of the withdrawal of its own regular flight to the same destination.

This prompted speculation in the media about the changing preference of air travellers where low-cost companies are seen as a sustainable substitute to middle- and high-cost traditional carriers. Pegasus has also successfully developed its internal market with over 19 destinations within Turkey.

Love your customers

Customers are the most important aspect of any service industry. Since the global recession, many airlines have seen a drop in passenger numbers, and it is a challenge to achieve and sustain profitability. In the case of Turkey, other factors provide further opportunities for the airline industry. On the one hand, the economy is growing at a faster rate than in the rest of Europe, and on the other hand, as is the case in many emerging countries and in traditional industrial areas of developed economies, a substantial expatriate population exists. New migrants or integrated second- or third-generation migrants usually provide opportunities for travel due to cultural affinities and understanding. Regular holidays or business-related trips 'home' can create a good foundation in terms of overall capacity planning. In terms of weekly seat capacity, Pegasus currently ranks in the top 30 among European airlines. While most airline customers are loyal because of frequent flyer programmes, in the case of Pegasus and Turkey in general, further affinities can be developed and sustained, including a certain sense of nationalist pride or nostalgia. History can also provide potential future markets. Countries such as Azerbaijan, Turkmenistan, Uzbekistan, and others around the Black Sea region are long-term trading partners of Turkey and have been growing rapidly since the breakup of the USSR in 1991. This potential is also opening up opportunities with countries in the Middle East, which have large, young markets both in terms of tourism and business. However, Pegasus customers want more in terms of social network relationships with the brand and, therefore, Pegasus aims to keep up with its customers even when they are not flying. For example, Pegasus has a Facebook page complete with a game entitling customers to win free tickets. The company also has a Twitter account, through which it offers customers special competitions. Furthermore, in association with Vodafone, a special campaign was developed called 'mobile phone fly', whereby consumers accumulated for each SMS an award of 5 per cent towards a Pegasus ticket discount, emulating the 'shop and miles' strategy of traditional airlines. Over time, Pegasus hopes to create a sustainable relationship with its customers while leveraging the possibilities of social networks and other digital technologies. Pegasus' strong word of mouth has also been important in the airline's success and is reflected in the words of customers on a special website titled 'Pegasus listens to you'. Sections of the website encourage customers to generate ideas for service improvement, to debate generic questions and topics relating to the airline's management and services, and to encourage customers to report problems they have encountered. Since its formation in 2005, Pegasus has shown that a low-cost airline can deliver low fares, excellent service and steady profits. It has demonstrated that even in the airline business, entry barriers can be lowered and a powerful brand can be created. Pegasus embodies success in four marketing cornerstones: (i) it ensures successful service through safety, training and its devoted employees, (ii) it employs creative communication with its customers, (iii) it offers great destinations and easy access to international hubs, and (iv) it uses efficient management techniques, delivering low prices with a high-quality service experience. To be successful in the low-cost airline industry, great attention needs to be paid to customers' changing travel patterns and needs. Booking flights, post-purchase evaluation through regular customer relationship management, and intangible value created by a variety of details make Pegasus a formidable brand in the low-cost airline industry.

Questions for discussion

1. Give examples of needs, wants and demands that Pegasus customers demonstrate, differentiating these three concepts. What are the implications of each for Pegasus' practices?
2. Describe in detail all the facets of Pegasus' product. What is being exchanged in a Pegasus transaction?
3. Which of the five marketing management concepts best applies to Pegasus?
4. What value does Pegasus create for its customers?
5. Is Pegasus likely to continue being successful in building customer relationships? Why or why not?

Sources: Özlem Atalık and Melike Arslan, 'Wisdom of domestic customers: an empirical analysis of the Turkish private airline sector', International Journal of Business and Management, Vol. 4 (7), pp. 61–67; N.G. Torlak, M. Sanal, 'David's strategy formulation framework in action: the example of Turkish Airlines on domestic air transportation', I'Óstanbul Ticaret Üniversitesi Fen Bilimleri Dergisi, Vol. 6 (12), pp. 81–114; Ralph Anker, 'Airline capacity at European airports down just 2% in early winter', Airport Business website www.airport-business.com, accessed October 2015; 'Road block receives more than 140,000 clicks in 18 hours', Microsoft Advertising, http://advertising.microsoft.com/home, accessed November 2006; 'Headquarters', Pegasus Airlines website, www.flypgs.com, accessed October 2015; 'Pegasus history', Pegasus Airlines website, www.flypgs.com/en/about-pegasus/pegasus-history.aspx; 'Ryanair: not the cheapest airline?' The Telegraph, www.telegraph.co.uk/travel/travelnews/10393475/Ryanair-not-the-cheapest-airline.html, accessed October 2015; 'Battle of the low-cost airlines: is Ryanair the cheapest?' Which Airline, www.whichairline.com/news/Battle-of-the-low-cost-airlines%3A-is-Ryanair-the-cheapest, accessed October 2015; 'Battle of the low-cost airlines: Ryanair, AirAsia or tigerair? None of them in 2014!' Which Airline, www.whichairline.com/news/Battle-of-the-low-cost-airlines%3A-Ryanair-AirAsia-or-tigerair-None-of-them-in-2014%21, accessed October 2015; 'CAPA Centre for Aviation, Pegasus Airlines: strong 2Q2013 earnings growth for the "low-cost network carrier"', http://centreforaviation.com/analysis/pegasus-airlines-strong-2q2013-earnings-growth-for-the-low-cost-network-carrier-124641, accessed October 2015.

CHAPTER TWO

Company and marketing strategy: partnering to build customer engagement, value and relationships

Chapter preview

In the first chapter, we explored the marketing process by which companies create value for customers to capture value from them in return. In this chapter, we dig deeper into steps two and three of that process: designing customer value-driven marketing strategies and constructing marketing programmes. First, we look at the organisation's overall strategic planning, which guides marketing strategy and planning. Next, we discuss how, guided by the strategic plan, marketers partner closely with others inside and outside the firm to engage customers and create value for them. We then examine marketing strategy and planning — how marketers choose target markets, position their market offerings, develop a marketing mix and manage their marketing programmes. Finally, we look at the important step of measuring and managing marketing return on investment (marketing ROI).

First, let's look at Nike, a good company and a good marketing strategy story. During the past several decades, Nike has built the Nike swoosh into one of the world's best-known brand symbols. Nike's outstanding success results from much more than just making and selling good sports gear. It's based on a customer-focused marketing strategy through which Nike creates valued brand engagement and close brand community with and among its customers.

Objectives outline

➤ **Objective 1** Explain company-wide strategic planning and its four steps.
Company-wide strategic planning: defining marketing's role (pp. 38–41)

➤ **Objective 2** Discuss how to design business portfolios and develop growth strategies.
Designing the business portfolio (pp. 41–44)

➤ **Objective 3** Explain marketing's role in strategic planning and how marketing works with its partners to create and deliver customer value.
Planning marketing: partnering to build customer relationships (pp. 45–47)

➤ **Objective 4** Describe the elements of a customer value-driven marketing strategy and mix and the forces that influence it.
Marketing strategy and the marketing mix (pp. 47–51)

➤ **Objective 5** List the marketing management functions, including the elements of a marketing plan, and discuss the importance of measuring and managing marketing return on investment.
Managing the marketing effort (pp. 51–55)
Measuring and managing marketing return on investment (pp. 55–56)

Nike's customer-driven marketing: building brand engagement and community

The Nike 'swoosh' — it's everywhere! Just for fun, try counting the swooshes whenever you pick up the sports pages or watch a basketball game or tune into a televised soccer match. Over the past nearly 50 years, through innovative marketing, Nike has built the ever-present swoosh into one of the best-known brand symbols on the planet.

Early on, a brash, young Nike revolutionised sports marketing. To build image and market share, the brand lavishly outspent competitors on big-name endorsements, splashy promotional events and big-budget, in-your-face 'Just do it' ads. Whereas competitors stressed technical performance, Nike built customer engagement and relationships. Beyond shoes, apparel and equipment, Nike marketed a way of life, a genuine passion for sports, a 'just-do-it' attitude. Customers didn't just wear their Nikes, they *experienced* them. As the company stated on its web page, 'Nike has always known the truth — it's not so much the shoes but where they take you.'

Nike powered its way through the early years, aggressively adding products in a dozen new sports, including baseball, golf, skateboarding, wall climbing, bicycling and hiking. It seemed that things just couldn't be going any better. In the late 1990s, however, Nike stumbled and its sales slipped. As the company grew larger, its creative juices seemed to run a bit dry and buyers seeking a new look switched to competing brands. Looking back, Nike's biggest obstacle may have been its own incredible success. As sales grew, the swoosh may have become too common to be cool. Instead of being *anti*establishment, Nike *was* the establishment, and its hip, once-hot relationship with customers cooled. Nike needed to rekindle the brand's meaning to consumers.

To turn things around, Nike returned to its roots: new product innovation and a focus on customer relationships. But it set out to forge a new kind of brand–customer connection — a deeper, more personal, more engaging one. This time around, rather than simply outspending competitors on big media ads and celebrity endorsers that talk at customers, Nike shifted toward cutting-edge digital and social media marketing tools that interact *with* customers to build brand connections and community. According to one industry analyst, 'the legendary brand blew up its single-slogan approach and drafted a whole new playbook for the digital era'.

Nike still invests heavily in traditional advertising. But its spending on TV and print media has dropped by a whopping 30 per cent in only three years, even as its global marketing budget has increased steadily. Traditional media now account for only about 20 per cent of the brand's $1 billion US promotion budget. Instead, Nike spends the lion's share of its marketing budget on non-traditional media. Using community-oriented, digital-based social networking tools, Nike is now building communities of customers who talk not just with the company about the brand, but with each other as well.

Nike has mastered social networking, both online and off. Whether customers come to know Nike through ads, in-person events at Niketown stores, a local Nike running club, or at one of the company's profusion of community web and social media sites, more and more people are bonding closely with the Nike brand.

Nike has raced ahead of its industry in the use of today's new social networking tools. In a recent ranking of 42 sportswear companies, digital consultancy L2 crowned Nike 'top genius' in 'digital IQ' for its innovative use of online, mobile and social media. L2 also placed Nike first in creating brand 'tribes' — large groups of highly engaged users — with the help of social media platforms such as Facebook, Twitter, Instagram and Pinterest. For example, the main Nike Facebook page has more than 16.4 million Likes. The Nike Soccer page adds another 21.6 million, Nike Basketball page 5.4 million more, and Nike Running another 1.8 million.

Nike has mastered social networking, both online and off, creating deep engagement and community among customers. Its Nike+ and FuelBand apps and technologies have made Nike a part of the daily fitness routines of millions of customers around the world.

Source: Images courtesy of Nike Inc.

More than just numbers, Nike's social media presence engages customers at a high level and gets them talking with each other about the brand.

Nike excels at cross-media campaigns that integrate the new media with traditional tools to build brand community. For example, Nike's 'Find your greatness' campaign for the Olympics launched two days before the opening ceremonies – not with splashy media ads but with a video posted on YouTube, Nike websites and other digital platforms. The compelling video featured people getting in touch with their inner athlete. Then, on opening day, Nike followed up with big-budget TV ads in 25 countries based on the video. But rather than just running the ads in isolation, the campaign urged customers to share their feelings about the 'Find your greatness' message via Twitter and other digital media using a #findgreatness hashtag. Within a month, the video had been viewed more than 5 million times on Nike's YouTube channel alone.

Nike has also built brand community through groundbreaking mobile apps and technologies. For example, its Nike+ apps have helped Nike become a part of the daily fitness routines of millions of customers around the world. The Nike+ FuelBand, for instance, is an ergonomic work of art. Worn on the wrist, FuelBand converts just about every imaginable physical movement into NikeFuel, Nike's own universal activity metric. According to a recent Nike video called 'Counts', whether your activity is running, jumping, baseball, skating, dancing, stacking sports cups or chasing chickens, it counts for NikeFuel points. 'Life is a sport,' the video concludes. 'Make it count.' Everyday athletes can use NikeFuel to track their personal performance, then share and compare it across sports and geographic locations with others in the global Nike community. The Nike+ FuelBand mobile app lets users watch their progress, get extra motivation on the go, and stay connected with friends.

Nike+ has engaged a huge global brand community. The tickers on nikeplus.com update continuously with numbers in the billions: 85,566,409,830 steps taken, 50,841,842,647 calories burned, and 36,364,639,579 NikeFuel points earned. The site also tracks personal achievements earned and daily goals hit by individuals in the Nike+ community. To date, the millions of Nike+ users worldwide have logged 1,118,434,247 miles. That's 44,914 trips around the world or 4,682 journeys to the moon and back.

Thus, Nike has built a new kinship and sense of community with and between the brand and its customers. Nike's marketing strategy is no longer only about big-budget ads at arm's length and aloof celebrity endorsers. Instead, the brand is connecting directly with customers, whether it's through local running clubs, a performance-tracking wristband, a 30-store billboard that posts fan headlines from Twitter, or videos that debut on YouTube rather than primetime TV. More than just something to buy, the Nike brand has once again become a part of customers' lives and times.

As a result, Nike remains the world's largest sports apparel company, an impressive 26 per cent larger than closest rival Adidas. During the past seven years, even as the faltering economy left most sports apparel and footwear competitors gasping for breath, Nike's global sales and income sprinted ahead nearly 70 per cent.

As in sports competition, the strongest and best-prepared brand has the best chance of winning. With engagement and deep brand–customer relationships comes powerful competitive advantage. And Nike is once again very close to its customers. Notes Nike CEO Mark Parker, 'Connecting used to be, "Here's some product, and here's some advertising. We hope you like it." Connecting today is a dialogue.'[1]

COMPANY-WIDE STRATEGIC PLANNING: DEFINING MARKETING'S ROLE

Each company must find the game plan for long-run survival and growth that makes the most sense given its specific situation, opportunities, objectives and resources. This is the focus of **strategic planning** – the process of developing and maintaining a strategic fit between the organisation's goals and capabilities and its changing marketing opportunities.

Strategic planning sets the stage for the rest of planning in the firm. Companies usually prepare annual plans, long-range plans and strategic plans. The annual and long-range plans deal with the company's current businesses and how to keep them going. In contrast, the strategic plan involves adapting the firm to take advantage of opportunities in its constantly changing environment.

At the corporate level, the company starts the strategic planning process by defining its overall purpose and mission (see Figure 2.1). This mission is then turned into detailed supporting

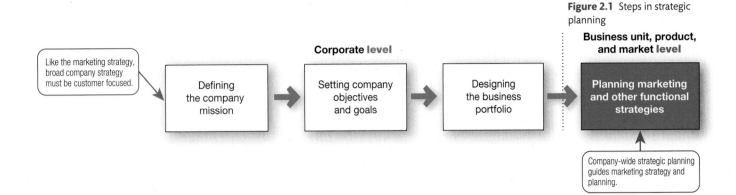

Figure 2.1 Steps in strategic planning

objectives that guide the entire company. Next, headquarters decides what portfolio of businesses and products is best for the company and how much support to give each one. In turn, each business and product develops detailed marketing and other departmental plans that support the company-wide plan. Thus, marketing planning occurs at the business-unit, product, and market levels. It supports company strategic planning with more detailed plans for specific marketing opportunities.

Defining a market-oriented mission

An organisation exists to accomplish something, and this purpose should be clearly stated. Forging a sound mission begins with the following questions: What is our business? Who is the customer? What do consumers value? What *should* our business be? These simple-sounding questions are among the most difficult the company will ever have to answer. Successful companies continuously raise these questions and answer them carefully and completely

Many organisations develop formal **mission statements** that answer these questions. A mission statement is a statement of the organisation's purpose – what it wants to accomplish in the larger environment. A clear mission statement acts as an 'invisible hand' that guides people in the organisation.

Some companies define their missions myopically in product or technology terms ('We make and sell furniture' or 'We are a chemical-processing firm'). But mission statements should be *market oriented* and defined in terms of satisfying basic customer needs. Products and technologies eventually become outdated, but basic market needs may last forever. Virgin Atlantic's mission statement is simply to sell lots of flights but is 'To grow a profitable airline where people love to fly and people love to work.' Similarly, Bosch doesn't talk about selling or making automotive parts and power tools but rather 'BeQIK': Focus on quality (Q), innovation (I), customer orientation (K for the German term '*Kundenorientierung*') and speed.[2] Table 2.1 provides several other examples of product-oriented versus market-oriented business definitions.

Mission statements should be meaningful and specific yet motivating. They should emphasise the company's strengths in the marketplace. Too often, mission statements are

Mission statement—
A statement of the organisation's purpose – what it wants to accomplish in the larger environment.

BeQIK: Focus on quality (Q), innovation (I), customer orientation (K for the German term 'Kundenorientierung') and speed.

Source: Lou-Foto/Alamy Images

Table 2.1 Market-oriented business definitions

Company	Product-oriented definition	Market-oriented definition
Michelin	We make tyres.	We provide service to people and their transportation.
Royal Dutch Shell	We find, extract, refine and sell oil.	We refine and deliver energy solutions in a sustainable way.
Nestlé	We make consumer nutrition and health products.	As the world's leading nutrition, health and wellness company, we are committed to increasing the nutritional value of our products while offering better taste and more pleasure.
B&Q	We sell tools and home repair and improvement items.	We help people to create homes of which they can be proud.
eBay	We hold online auctions.	We provide a global marketplace where practically anyone can trade practically anything.
Revlon	We make cosmetics.	We sell lifestyle and self-expression; success and status; memories, hopes, and dreams.
Ritz-Carlton Hotels & Resorts	We rent rooms.	We create the Ritz-Carlton experience – one that enlivens the senses, instils well-being, and fulfils even the unexpressed wishes and needs of our guests.
easyJet	We sell cheap flights.	To provide our customers with safe, good value, point-to-point air services.

written for public relations (PR) purposes and lack specific, workable guidelines. Says marketing consultant Jack Welch:[3]

> Few leaders actually get the point of forging a mission with real grit and meaning. [Mission statements] have largely devolved into fat-headed jargon. Almost no one can figure out what they mean. [So companies] sort of ignore them or gussy up a vague package deal along the lines of: 'our mission is to be the best fill-in-the-blank company in our industry.' [Instead, Welch advises, CEOs should] make a choice about how your company will win. Don't mince words! Remember Nike's old mission, 'Crush Reebok'? That's directionally correct. And Google's mission statement isn't something namby-pamby like 'To be the world's best search engine'. It's 'To organise the world's information and make it universally accessible and useful'. That's simultaneously inspirational, achievable and completely graspable.

Finally, a company's mission should not be stated as making more sales or profits; profits are only a reward for creating value for customers. Instead, the mission should focus on customers and the customer experience the company seeks to create. Thus, IKEA's mission isn't 'to be the world's best and most profitable furniture retailer'; it's 'to create a better everyday life for the many'. If IKEA accomplishes this market-focused mission, profits will follow.

Setting company objectives and goals

The company needs to turn its mission into detailed supporting objectives for each level of management. Each manager should have objectives and be responsible for reaching them. For example, Kohler makes and markets familiar kitchen and bathroom fixtures – everything from Mira showers, bathtubs and toilets to kitchen sinks. But Kohler also offers a breadth of other products and services, including furniture, tile and stone, and even small engines and backup power systems (in Italy and China). It also owns golf resorts and spas in the United States and Scotland.

Kohler ties this diverse product portfolio together under the mission of 'contributing to a higher level of gracious living for those who are touched by our products and services.'

This broad mission leads to a hierarchy of objectives, including business objectives and marketing objectives. Kohler's overall objective is to build profitable customer relationships by developing efficient yet beautiful products that embrace the 'essence of gracious living' mission. It does this by investing heavily in research and design. Research is expensive and must be funded through improved profit, so improving profits becomes another major objective for Kohler. Profits can be improved by increasing sales or reducing costs. Sales can be increased by improving the company's share of domestic and international markets. These goals then become the company's current marketing objectives.

Marketing strategies and programmes must be developed to support these marketing objectives. To increase its market share, Kohler might increase its products' availability and promotion in existing markets and expand into new markets. For example, Kohler is boosting production capacity in India and China to better serve the Asian market.[4]

These are Kohler's broad marketing strategies. Each broad marketing strategy must then be defined in greater detail. For example, increasing the product's promotion may require more salespeople, advertising and PR efforts; if so, both requirements will need to be spelled out. In this way, the firm's mission is translated into a set of objectives for the current period.

Designing the business portfolio

Guided by the company's mission statement and objectives, management now must plan its business portfolio – the collection of businesses and products that make up the company. The best **business portfolio** is the one that best fits the company's strengths and weaknesses to opportunities in the environment.

Business portfolio—
The collection of businesses and products that make up the company.

Most large companies have complex portfolios of businesses and brands. Strategic and marketing planning for such business portfolios can be a daunting but critical task. For example, GE is a giant €116 billion conglomerate operating in dozens of consumer and business markets, with a broad portfolio of products that 'move, power, build, and cure the world'. Most consumers know GE for its home appliance and lighting products, part of the company's GE Home & Business Solutions unit. But that's just the beginning for GE. Other company units – such as GE Transportation, GE Aviation, GE Energy Management, GE Power & Water, GE Gas & Oil, GE Healthcare, and others – offer products and services ranging from jet engines, diesel-electric locomotives, wind turbines and off-shore drilling solutions to aerospace systems and medical imaging equipment. GE Capital, which accounts for about a third of GE's total revenues, offers a breadth of business and consumer financial products and services. Successfully managing such a broad portfolio takes plenty of management skill and – as GE's long-running corporate slogan suggests – lots of 'Imagination at work'.[5]

Business portfolio planning involves two steps. First, the company must analyse its current business portfolio and determine which businesses should receive more, less, or no investment. Second, it must shape the future portfolio by developing strategies for growth and downsizing.

Analysing the current business portfolio

The major activity in strategic planning is business **portfolio analysis**, whereby management evaluates the products and businesses that make up the company. The company will want to put strong resources into its more profitable businesses and phase down or drop its weaker ones.

Portfolio analysis—
The process by which management evaluates the products and businesses that make up the company.

Management's first step is to identify the key businesses that make up the company, called strategic *business units* (SBUs). An SBU can be a company division, a product line within a division, or sometimes a single product or brand. The company next assesses the attractiveness of its various SBUs and decides how much support each deserves. When designing a business portfolio, it's a good idea to add and support products and businesses that fit closely with the firm's core philosophy and competencies.

The purpose of strategic planning is to find ways in which the company can best use its strengths to take advantage of attractive opportunities in the environment. For this reason, most standard portfolio analysis methods evaluate SBUs on two important dimensions: the attractiveness of the SBU's market or industry and the strength of the SBU's position in that market or industry. The best-known portfolio-planning method was developed by the Boston Consulting Group, a leading management consulting firm.[6]

The Boston Consulting Group approach

Using the now-classic Boston Consulting Group (BCG) approach, a company classifies all its SBUs according to the **growth–share matrix**, as shown in Figure 2.2. On the vertical axis, *market growth rate* provides a measure of market attractiveness. On the horizontal axis, *relative market share* serves as a measure of company strength in the market. The growth–share matrix defines four types of SBUs:

1. *Stars*. Stars are high-growth, high-share businesses or products. They often need heavy investments to finance their rapid growth. Eventually their growth will slow down, and they will turn into cash cows.

2. *Cash cows*. Cash cows are low-growth, high-share businesses or products. These established and successful SBUs need less investment to hold their market share. Thus, they produce a lot of the cash that the company uses to pay its bills and support other SBUs that need investment.

3. *Question marks*. Question marks are low-share business units in high-growth markets. They require a lot of cash to hold their share, let alone increase it. Management has to think hard about which question marks it should try to build into stars and which should be phased out.

4. *Dogs*. Dogs are low-growth, low-share businesses and products. They may generate enough cash to maintain themselves but do not promise to be large sources of cash.

The ten circles in the growth–share matrix represent the company's ten current SBUs. The company has two stars, two cash cows, three question marks and three dogs. The areas of the circles are proportional to the SBU's euro sales. This company is in fair shape, although not in good shape. It wants to invest in the more promising question marks to make them stars and maintain the stars so that they will become cash cows as their markets mature. Fortunately, it has two good-sized cash cows. Income from these cash cows will help finance the company's question marks, stars, and dogs. The company should take some decisive action concerning its dogs and its question marks.

Growth–share matrix—A portfolio-planning method that evaluates a company's SBUs in terms of market growth rate and relative market share.

Figure 2.2 The BCG growth–share matrix
Source: adapted from The BCG Portfolio Matrix © 1970, The Boston Consulting Group

Under the classic BCG portfolio planning approach, the company invests funds from mature, successful products and businesses (cash cows) to support promising products and businesses in faster-growing markets (stars and question marks), hoping to turn them into future cash cows.

The company must decide how much it will invest in each product or business (SBU). For each SBU, it must decide whether to build, hold, harvest or divest.

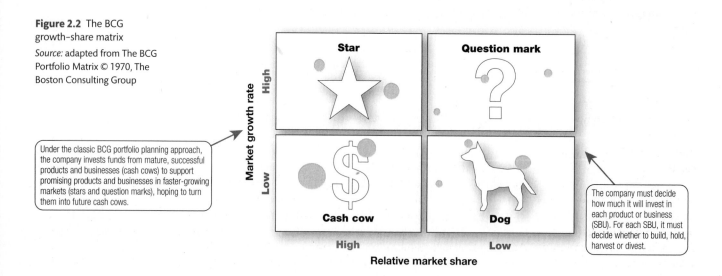

Relative market share

Once it has classified its SBUs, the company must determine what role each will play in the future. It can pursue one of four strategies for each SBU. It can invest more in the business unit to *build* its share. Or it can invest just enough to *hold* the SBU's share at the current level. It can harvest the SBU, milking its short-term cash flow regardless of the long-term effect. Finally, it can *divest* the SBU by selling it or phasing it out and using the resources elsewhere.

As time passes, SBUs change their positions in the growth–share matrix. Many SBUs start out as question marks and move into the star category if they succeed. They later become cash cows as market growth falls, and then finally die off or turn into dogs toward the end of the life cycle. The company needs to add new products and units continuously so that some of them will become stars and, eventually, cash cows that will help finance other SBUs.

Problems with matrix approaches

The BCG and other formal methods revolutionised strategic planning. However, such centralised approaches have limitations. They can be difficult, time-consuming and costly to implement. Management may find it difficult to define SBUs and measure market share and growth. In addition, these approaches focus on classifying current businesses but provide little advice for future planning.

Because of such problems, many companies have dropped formal matrix methods in favour of more customised approaches that better suit their specific situations. Moreover, unlike former strategic planning efforts that rested mostly in the hands of senior managers at company headquarters, today's strategic planning has been decentralised. Increasingly, companies are placing responsibility for strategic planning in the hands of cross-functional teams of divisional managers who are close to their markets.

For example, think about The Walt Disney Company. Most Europeans think of Disney as theme parks and wholesome family entertainment. But in the mid-1980s, Disney set up a powerful, centralised strategic planning group to guide its direction and growth. Over the next two decades, the strategic planning group turned The Walt Disney Company into a huge and diverse collection of media and entertainment businesses. The sprawling company grew to include everything from theme resorts and film studios (Walt Disney Pictures, Touchstone Pictures, Pixar Animation and Marvel Studios) to media networks (ABC Television plus ESPN, Disney Channel, parts of A&E and the History Channel, and a half dozen others) to consumer products (from apparel and toys to interactive games) and a cruise line.

The newly transformed company proved hard to manage and performed unevenly. To improve performance, Disney disbanded the centralised strategic planning unit, decentralising its functions to Disney division managers. As a result, Disney retains its position at the head of the world's media conglomerates. And even through the recently weak economy, Disney's sound strategic management of its broad mix of businesses, plus a touch of the famed Disney magic, has helped it fare better than rival media companies.[7]

Developing strategies for growth and downsizing

Beyond evaluating current businesses, designing the business portfolio involves finding businesses and products the company should consider in the future. Companies need growth if they are to compete more effectively, satisfy their stakeholders and attract top talent. At the same time, a firm must be careful not to make growth itself an objective. The company's objective must be to manage 'profitable growth'.

Marketing has the main responsibility for achieving profitable growth for the company. Marketing needs to identify, evaluate and select market opportunities and establish strategies for capturing them. One useful device for identifying growth opportunities is the **product/market expansion grid**, shown in Figure 2.3.[8] We apply it here to Finnish company Vivago Oy – a healthcare technology company that develops, sells and markets automatic personal security systems monitoring and analysing users' activity levels.[9] Vivago markets the world's

Product/market expansion grid—A portfolio-planning tool for identifying company growth opportunities through market penetration, market development, product development, or diversification.

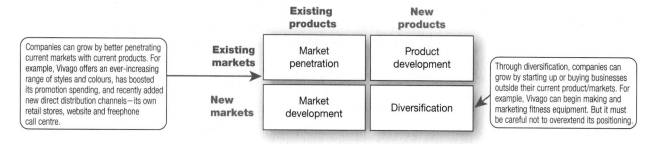

Companies can grow by better penetrating current markets with current products. For example, Vivago offers an ever-increasing range of styles and colours, has boosted its promotion spending, and recently added new direct distribution channels—its own retail stores, website and freephone call centre.

Through diversification, companies can grow by starting up or buying businesses outside their current product/markets. For example, Vivago can begin making and marketing fitness equipment. But it must be careful not to overextend its positioning.

Figure 2.3 The product/market expansion grid

Market penetration— Company growth by increasing sales of current products to current market segments without changing the product.

Market development— Company growth by identifying and developing new market segments for current company products.

Product development— Company growth by offering modified or new products to current market segments.

Diversification—Company growth through starting up or acquiring businesses outside the company's current products and markets.

Downsizing—Reducing the business portfolio by eliminating products or business units that are not profitable or that no longer fit the company's overall strategy.

There are many possible options for Vivago Oy. - a healthcare technology company that develops, sells and markets automatic personal security systems monitoring and analysing users' activity levels.

Source: Vivago Oy

first system that monitors the physiological signals of wearers (including movement, skin conductivity and body temperature) and sends an alarm via the local telephone network if the health of the wearer appears to deteriorate (or if they manually trigger an alarm). Worn on a wristband that also functions as a watch, the Vivago system has won numerous international awards for innovation.

First, Vivago might consider whether the company can achieve deeper **market penetration** – making more sales without changing its original product. It can spur growth through marketing mix improvements – adjustments to its product design, advertising, pricing and distribution efforts. For example, Vivago could offer a broader range of styles, colours and designs for different users. The company could also add direct-to-consumer distribution channels, including its own retail stores, or toll-free call centres.

Second, Vivago might consider possibilities for **market development** – identifying and developing new markets for its current products. Given the global ageing population, various markets could prove fruitful. Japan and the United States of America both have large, affluent ageing populations who could prove to be a profitable long-term market.

Third, Vivago could consider **product development** – offering modified or new products to current markets. Vivago could develop and introduce other wrist- or body-worn physiological monitors for sport and fitness users. Although this would put the company into direct competition with current sports technology providers, it also offers promise for big growth.

Finally, Vivago might consider **diversification** – starting up or buying businesses beyond its current products and markets. For example, it could move into broader security and monitoring businesses. When diversifying, companies must be careful not to overextend their brands' positioning.

Companies must not only develop strategies for *growing* their business portfolios but also strategies for **downsizing** them. There are many reasons that a firm might want to abandon products or markets. The firm may have grown too fast or entered areas where it lacks experience. This can occur when a firm enters too many international markets without the proper research or when a company introduces new products that do not offer superior customer value. The market environment might change, making some products or markets less profitable. For example, in difficult economic times, many firms prune out weaker, less-profitable products and markets to focus their more limited resources on the strongest ones. Finally, some products or business units simply age and die.

When a firm finds brands or businesses that are unprofitable or that no longer fit its overall strategy, it must carefully prune, harvest, or divest them. For example, over the past several years, P&G has sold off all of its big food brands – such as Sunny Delight and Pringles – allowing the company to focus on household care and beauty and grooming products from Gilette to Pampers. And in recent years, GM has pruned several underperforming brands from its portfolio, including Hummer and Saab. Weak businesses usually require a disproportionate amount of management attention. Managers should focus on promising growth opportunities, not fritter away energy trying to salvage fading ones.

PLANNING MARKETING: PARTNERING TO BUILD CUSTOMER RELATIONSHIPS

The company's strategic plan establishes what kinds of businesses the company will operate and its objectives for each. Then, within each business unit, more detailed planning takes place. The major functional departments in each unit – marketing, finance, accounting, purchasing, operations, information systems, human resources and others – must work together to accomplish strategic objectives.

Marketing plays a key role in the company's strategic planning in several ways. First, marketing provides a guiding *philosophy* – the marketing concept – that suggests the company strategy should revolve around creating customer value and building profitable relationships with important consumer groups. Second, marketing provides *inputs* to strategic planners by helping to identify attractive market opportunities and assessing the firm's potential to take advantage of them. Finally, within individual business units, marketing designs *strategies* for reaching the unit's objectives. Once the unit's objectives are set, marketing's task is to help carry them out profitably.

Customer engagement and value are the key ingredients in the marketer's formula for success. However, as noted in Chapter 1, although marketing plays a leading role, it alone cannot produce engagement and superior value for customers. It can be only a partner in attracting, engaging and growing customers. In addition to *customer relationship management*, marketers must also practise *partner relationship management*. They must work closely with partners in other company departments to form an effective internal value chain that serves customers. Moreover, they must partner effectively with other companies in the marketing system to form a competitively superior external value delivery network. We now take a closer look at the concepts of a company value chain and a value delivery network.

Partnering with other company departments

Each company department can be thought of as a link in the company's internal **value chain**.[10] That is, each department carries out value-creating activities to design, produce, market, deliver and support the firm's products. The firm's success depends not only on how well each department performs its work but also on how well the various departments coordinate their activities.

For example, Aldi's goal is to create customer value and satisfaction by providing shoppers with the products they want at the lowest possible prices. Marketers at Aldi play an important role. They learn what customers need and stock the stores' shelves with the desired products at unbeatable low prices. They prepare advertising and merchandising programmes and assist shoppers with customer service. Through these and other activities, Aldi's marketers help deliver value to customers.

However, the marketing department needs help from the company's other departments. Aldi's ability to offer the right products at low prices depends on the purchasing department's skill in developing the needed suppliers and buying from them at low cost. Aldi's information technology (IT) department must provide fast and accurate information about which products are selling in each store. And its operations people must provide effective, low-cost merchandise handling.

A company's value chain is only as strong as its weakest link. Success depends on how well each department performs its work of adding customer value and the activity coordination of various departments. At Aldi, if purchasing can't obtain the lowest prices from suppliers, or if operations can't distribute merchandise at the lowest costs, then marketing can't deliver on its promise of unbeatable low prices – 'Like Aldi, like the price'.

Ideally, then, a company's different functions should work in harmony to produce value for consumers. But, in practice, interdepartmental relations are full of conflicts and misunderstandings. The marketing department takes the consumer's point of view. But when marketing tries to improve customer satisfaction, it can cause other departments to do a poorer job *in their terms*. Marketing department actions can increase purchasing costs, disrupt production schedules, increase inventories and create budget headaches. Thus, other departments may resist the marketing department's efforts.

Author comment

Marketing can't go it alone in creating customer value. Under the company-wide strategic plan, marketing must work closely with other departments to form an effective internal company value chain and with other companies in the marketing system to create an external value delivery network that jointly serves customers.

Value chain—The series of internal departments that carry out value-creating activities to design, produce, market, deliver and support a firm's products.

Yet marketers must find ways to get all departments to 'think consumer' and develop a smoothly functioning value chain. One marketing expert puts it this way: 'True market orientation . . . means that the entire company obsesses over creating value for the customer and views itself as a bundle of processes that profitably define, create, communicate and deliver value to its target customers. . . . Everyone must do marketing regardless of function or department.' Says another, 'Engaging customers today requires commitment from the entire company. We're all marketers now.'[11] Thus, whether you're an accountant, an operations manager, a financial analyst, an IT specialist, or a human resources manager, you need to understand marketing and your role in creating customer value.

Partnering with others in the marketing system

In its quest to create customer value, the firm needs to look beyond its own internal value chain and into the value chains of its suppliers, distributors and, ultimately, its customers. Consider IKEA. People do not swarm to IKEA because they only love the chain's furniture. Consumers flock to the IKEA *network*, not only to its furniture products. Throughout the world, IKEA's finely tuned value delivery network delivers a high standard of quality, service, cleanliness and value. IKEA's is effective only to the extent that it successfully partners with its suppliers and others jointly to create 'a better everyday life' for its customers.

More companies today are partnering with other members of the supply chain – suppliers, distributors and, ultimately, customers – to improve the performance of the customer **value delivery network**. For example, cosmetics maker L'Oréal knows the importance of building close relationships with its extensive network of suppliers, who supply everything from polymers and fats to spray cans and packaging to production equipment and office supplies:[12]

Value delivery network—The network made up of the company, its suppliers, its distributors and, ultimately, its customers who partner with each other to improve the performance of the entire system.

L'Oreal builds long-term supplier relations based on mutual benefit and growth. The aim is to generate respect through respecting others.

Source: Acorn 1/Alamy Images

L'Oréal is the world's largest cosmetics manufacturer, with 25 brands ranging from Maybelline and Kiehl's to Lancôme and Redken. The company's supplier network is crucial to its success. As a result, L'Oréal treats suppliers as respected partners. On the one hand, it expects a lot from suppliers in terms of design innovation, quality and socially responsible actions. The company carefully screens new suppliers and regularly assesses the performance of current suppliers. On the other hand, L'Oréal works closely with suppliers to help them meet its exacting standards. Whereas some companies make unreasonable demands of their suppliers and 'squeeze' them for short-term gains, L'Oréal builds long-term supplier relationships based on mutual benefit and growth. According to the company's supplier website, it treats suppliers with 'fundamental respect for their business, their culture, their growth and the individuals who work there. Each relationship is based on . . . shared efforts aimed at promoting growth and mutual profits that make it possible for suppliers to invest, innovate, and compete'. As a result, more than 75 per cent of L'Oréal's supplier-partners have been working with the company for ten years or more and the majority of them for several decades. Says the company's head of purchasing, 'The CEO wants to make L'Oréal a top performer and one of the world's most respected companies. Being respected also means being respected by our suppliers.'

Increasingly in today's marketplace, competition no longer takes place between individual competitors. Rather, it takes place between the entire value delivery networks created by these competitors. Thus, Citroën's performance against Ford depends on the quality of Citroën's overall value delivery network versus Ford's.

Even if Citroën makes the best cars, it might lose in the marketplace if Ford's dealer network provides more customer-satisfying sales and service.

MARKETING STRATEGY AND THE MARKETING MIX

The strategic plan defines the company's overall mission and objectives. Marketing's role is shown in Figure 2.4, which summarises the major activities involved in managing a customer-driven marketing strategy and the marketing mix.

Consumers are in the centre. The goal is to create value for customers and build profitable customer relationships. Next comes **marketing strategy** – the marketing logic by which the company hopes to create this customer value and achieve these profitable relationships. The company decides which customers it will serve (segmentation and targeting) and how (differentiation and positioning). It identifies the total market and then divides it into smaller segments, selects the most promising segments, and focuses on serving and satisfying the customers in these segments.

Guided by marketing strategy, the company designs an integrated *marketing* mix made up of factors under its control – product, price, place and promotion (the four Ps). To find the best marketing strategy and mix, the company engages in marketing analysis, planning, implementation and control. Through these activities, the company watches and adapts to the actors and forces in the marketing environment. We will now look briefly at each activity. In later chapters, we will discuss each one in more depth.

Customer value-driven marketing strategy

To succeed in today's competitive marketplace, companies must be customer centred. They must win customers from competitors and then engage and grow them by delivering greater value. But before it can satisfy customers, a company must first understand customer needs and wants. Thus, sound marketing requires careful customer analysis.

Author comment

Now that we've set the context in terms of companywide strategy, it's time to discuss customer-driven marketing strategies and programmes.

Marketing strategy—The marketing logic by which the company hopes to create customer value and achieve profitable customer relationships.

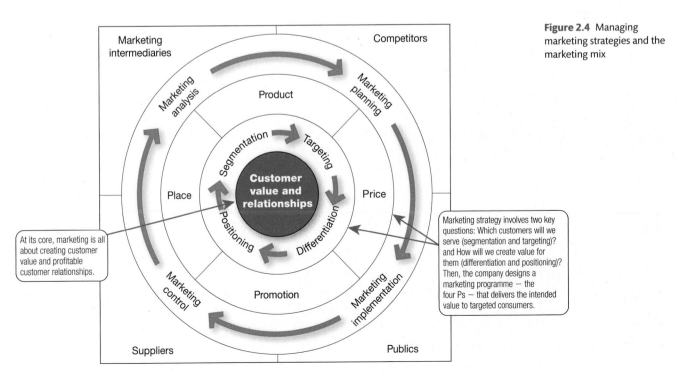

Figure 2.4 Managing marketing strategies and the marketing mix

Marketing intermediaries

Competitors

Marketing analysis

Marketing planning

Product

Segmentation

Targeting

Place

Customer value and relationships

Price

Positioning

Differentiation

Marketing control

Marketing implementation

Promotion

Suppliers

Publics

At its core, marketing is all about creating customer value and profitable customer relationships.

Marketing strategy involves two key questions: Which customers will we serve (segmentation and targeting)? and How will we create value for them (differentiation and positioning)? Then, the company designs a marketing programme — the four Ps — that delivers the intended value to targeted consumers.

Companies know that they cannot profitably serve all consumers in a given market – at least not all consumers in the same way. There are too many different kinds of consumers with too many different kinds of needs. Most companies are in a position to serve some segments better than others. Thus, each company must divide up the total market, choose the best segments, and design strategies for profitably serving chosen segments. This process involves *market segmentation*, *market targeting*, *differentiation* and *positioning*.

Market segmentation

Market segmentation—
Dividing a market into distinct groups of buyers who have different needs, characteristics, or behaviours, and who might require separate products or marketing programmes.

The market consists of many types of customers, products and needs. The marketer must determine which segments offer the best opportunities. Consumers can be grouped and served in various ways based on geographic, demographic, psychographic and behavioural factors. The process of dividing a market into distinct groups of buyers who have different needs, characteristics or behaviours, and who might require separate products or marketing programmes, is called **market segmentation.**

Every market has segments, but not all ways of segmenting a market are equally useful. For example, Tylenol would gain little by distinguishing between low-income and high-income pain-relief users if both respond the same way to marketing efforts. A **market segment** consists of consumers who respond in a similar way to a given set of marketing efforts. In the car market, for example, consumers who want the biggest, most comfortable car regardless of price make up one market segment. Consumers who care mainly about price and operating economy make up another segment. It would be difficult to make one car model that was the first choice of consumers in both segments. Companies are wise to focus their efforts on meeting the distinct needs of individual market segments.

Market segment—A group of consumers who respond in a similar way to a given set of marketing efforts.

Market targeting

Market targeting—The process of evaluating each market segment's attractiveness and selecting one or more segments to enter.

After a company has defined its market segments, it can enter one or many of these segments. **Market targeting** involves evaluating each market segment's attractiveness and selecting one or more segments to enter. A company should target segments in which it can profitably generate the greatest customer value and sustain it over time.

A company with limited resources might decide to serve only one or a few special segments or market niches. Such niches specialise in serving customer segments that major competitors overlook or ignore. For example, Ferrari sells around 670 of its very high-performance cars in the United Kingdom each year but at very high prices – from an eye-opening €252,000 for its Ferrari F458 Spider to an astonishing more than €1.6 million for its F599XX super sports car, which can

Ferrari focus on a niche but lucrative luxury-oriented market.

Source: Roberto Machado Noa/ LightRocket via Getty Images

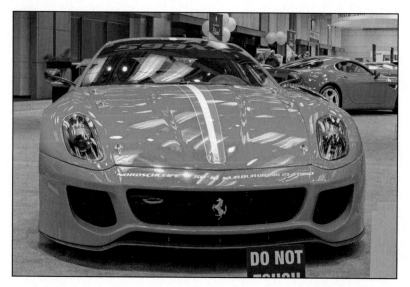

be driven only on race tracks. Most niches aren't quite so exotic. Tetra GmbH manufactures aquarist and pond-related products and with their Tetramin flakes dominates the fish food market.

Alternatively, a company might choose to serve several related segments – perhaps those with different kinds of customers but with the same basic wants. Gap Inc., for example, targets different age, income and lifestyle clothing and accessory segments with six different store and online brands: Gap, Banana Republic, Old Navy, Piperlime, Athleta and INTERMIX. The Gap store brand breaks its segment down into even smaller niches, including Gap, GapKids, babyGap, GapMaternity and GapBody.[13] Or a large company (for example, car companies like Honda and Ford) might decide to offer a complete range of products to serve all market segments.

Most companies enter a new market by serving a single segment; if this proves successful, they add more segments. For example, Nike started with innovative running shoes for serious runners. Large companies eventually seek full market coverage. Nike now makes and sells a broad range of sports products for just about anyone and everyone, in about every sport. It designs different products to meet the special needs of each segment it serves.

Market differentiation and positioning

After a company has decided which market segments to enter, it must determine how to differentiate its market offering for each targeted segment and what positions it wants to occupy in those segments. A product's *position* is the place it occupies relative to competitors' products in consumers' minds. Marketers want to develop unique market positions for their products. If a product is perceived to be exactly like others on the market, consumers would have no reason to buy it.

Positioning is arranging for a product to occupy a clear, distinctive and desirable place relative to competing products in the minds of target consumers. Marketers plan positions that distinguish their products from competing brands and give them the greatest advantage in their target markets.

BMW is 'The ultimate driving machine'. Adidas promises 'Impossible is nothing'. At Philips it is 'Sense and simplicity'. YouTube let's you 'Broadcast yourself'. At McDonald's you'll be saying 'I'm lovin' it', whereas at Burger King you can 'Have it your way'. Such deceptively simple statements form the backbone of a product's marketing strategy. For example, Burger King designs its entire worldwide integrated marketing campaign – from television and print commercials to its websites – around the 'Have it your way' positioning.

In positioning its brand, a company first identifies possible customer value differences that provide competitive advantages on which to build the position. A company can offer greater customer value by either charging lower prices than competitors or offering more benefits to justify higher prices. But if the company *promises* greater value, it must then *deliver* that greater value. Thus, effective positioning begins with **differentiation** – actually *differentiating* the company's market offering so that it gives consumers more value. Once the company has chosen a desired position, it must take strong steps to deliver and communicate that position to target consumers. The company's entire marketing programme should support the chosen positioning strategy.

Developing an integrated marketing mix

After determining its overall marketing strategy, the company is ready to begin planning the details of the marketing mix, one of the major concepts in modern marketing. The **marketing mix** is the set of tactical marketing tools that the firm blends to produce the response it wants in the target market. The marketing mix consists of everything the firm can do to influence the demand for its product. The many possibilities can be collected into four groups of variables – the four Ps. Figure 2.5 shows the marketing tools under each P.

- *Product* means the goods-and-services combination the company offers to the target market. Thus, an Alfa Romeo Mito consists of nuts and bolts, spark plugs, pistons, headlights and thousands of other parts. Alfa Romeo offers dozens of optional Mito features. The car comes fully serviced and with a comprehensive warranty that is as much a part of the product as the exhaust pipe.
- *Price* is the amount of money customers must pay to obtain the product. Alfa Romeo calculates suggested retail prices that its dealers might charge for each Mito. But Alfa Romeo dealers rarely charge the full sticker price. Instead, they negotiate the price with each customer, offering discounts, trade-in allowances and credit terms. These actions adjust prices for the current competitive and economic situations and bring them into line with the buyer's perception of the car's value.

Positioning—Arranging for a product to occupy a clear, distinctive and desirable place relative to competing products in the minds of target consumers.

Differentiation—Actually differentiating the market offering to create superior customer value.

Marketing mix—The set of tactical marketing tools — product, price, place and promotion — that the firm blends to produce the response it wants in the target market.

- *Place* includes company activities that make the product available to target consumers. Alfa Romeo partners with a large body of independently owned dealerships that sell the company's many different models. Alfa Romeo selects its dealers carefully and strongly supports them. The dealers keep an inventory of Alfa Romeo automobiles, demonstrate them to potential buyers, negotiate prices, close sales and service the cars after the sale.

- *Promotion* means activities that communicate the merits of the product and persuade target customers to buy it. Alfa Romeo spends millions of euros each year on advertising to tell consumers about the company and its many products. Dealership salespeople assist potential buyers and persuade them that Alfa Romeo is the best car for them. Alfa Romeo and its dealers offer special promotions – sales, cash rebates and low financing rates – as added purchase incentives.

An effective marketing programme blends the marketing mix elements into an integrated marketing programme designed to achieve the company's marketing objectives by engaging consumers and delivering value to them. The marketing mix constitutes the company's tactical tool kit for establishing strong positioning in target markets.

Some critics think that the four Ps may omit or under-emphasise certain important activities. For example, they ask, 'Where are services? Just because they don't start with a P doesn't justify omitting them.' The answer is that services, such as banking, airline and retailing services, are products too. We might call them *service products*. 'Where is packaging?' the critics might ask. Marketers would answer that they include packaging as one of many product decisions. All said, as Figure 2.5 suggests, many marketing activities that might appear to be left out of the marketing mix are included under one of the four Ps. The issue is not whether there should be four, six or ten Ps so much as what framework is most helpful in designing integrated marketing programmes.

There is another concern, however, that is valid. It holds that the four Ps concept takes the seller's view of the market, not the buyer's view. From the buyer's viewpoint, in this age of customer value and relationships, the four Ps might be better described as the four Cs:[14]

Four Ps	Four Cs
Product	Customer solution
Price	Customer cost
Place	Convenience
Promotion	Communication

Figure 2.5 The four Ps of the marketing mix

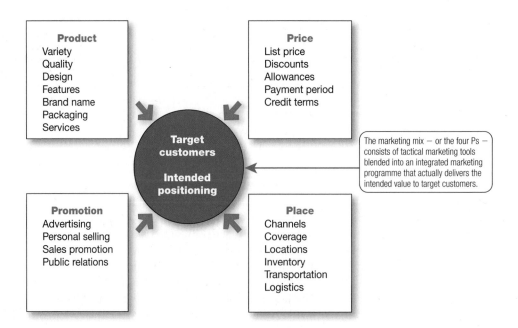

Thus, whereas marketers see themselves as selling products, customers see themselves as buying value or solutions to their problems. And customers are interested in more than just the price; they are interested in the total costs of obtaining, using and disposing of a product. Customers want the product and service to be as conveniently available as possible. Finally, they want two-way communication. Marketers would do well to think through the four Cs first and then build the four Ps on that platform.

MANAGING THE MARKETING EFFORT

In addition to being good at the *marketing* in marketing management, companies also need to pay attention to the *management*. Managing the marketing process requires the five marketing management functions shown in Figure 2.6 – *analysis, planning, implementation, organisation* and *control*. The company first develops company-wide strategic plans and then translates them into marketing and other plans for each division, product and brand. Through implementation and organisation, the company turns the plans into actions. Control consists of measuring and evaluating the results of marketing activities and taking corrective action where needed. Finally, marketing analysis provides the information and evaluations needed for all the other marketing activities.

Author comment

So far we've focused on the marketing in marketing management. Now, let's turn to the *management*.

Marketing analysis

Managing the marketing function begins with a complete analysis of the company's situation. The marketer should conduct a **SWOT analysis**, by which it evaluates the company's overall strengths (S), weaknesses (W), opportunities (O) and threats (T) (see Figure 2.7). Strengths include internal capabilities, resources and positive situational factors that may help the company serve its customers and achieve its objectives. Weaknesses include internal limitations and negative situational factors that may interfere with the company's performance. Opportunities are favourable factors or trends in the external environment that the company may be able to exploit to its advantage. And threats are unfavourable external factors or trends that may present challenges to performance.

SWOT analysis—An overall evaluation of the company's strengths (S), weaknesses (W), opportunities (O) and threats (T).

Figure 2.6 Managing marketing: analysis, planning, implementation and control

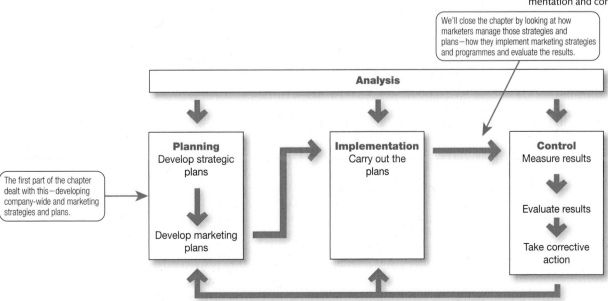

We'll close the chapter by looking at how marketers manage those strategies and plans—how they implement marketing strategies and programmes and evaluate the results.

The first part of the chapter dealt with this—developing company-wide and marketing strategies and plans.

Figure 2.7 SWOT analysis: Strengths (S), Weaknesses (W), Opportunities (O) and Threats (T)

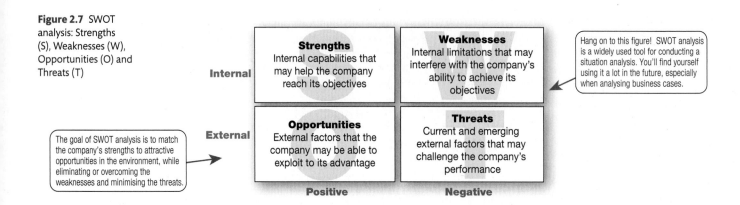

The company should analyse its markets and marketing environment to find attractive opportunities and identify threats. It should analyse company strengths and weaknesses as well as current and possible marketing actions to determine which opportunities it can best pursue. The goal is to match the company's strengths to attractive opportunities in the environment, while simultaneously eliminating or overcoming the weaknesses and minimising the threats. Marketing analysis provides inputs to each of the other marketing management functions. We discuss marketing analysis more fully in Chapter 3.

Marketing planning

Through strategic planning, the company decides what it wants to do with each business unit. Marketing planning involves choosing marketing strategies that will help the company attain its overall strategic objectives. A detailed marketing plan is needed for each business, product or brand. What does a marketing plan look like? Our discussion focuses on product or brand marketing plans.

Table 2.2 outlines the major sections of a typical product or brand marketing plan. (See Appendix 1 for a sample marketing plan.) The plan begins with an executive summary that quickly reviews major assessments, goals and recommendations. The main section of the plan presents a detailed SWOT analysis of the current marketing situation as well as potential threats and opportunities. The plan next states major objectives for the brand and outlines the specifics of a marketing strategy for achieving them.

A *marketing strategy* consists of specific strategies for target markets, positioning, the marketing mix and marketing expenditure levels. It outlines how the company intends to engage target customers and create value in order to capture value in return. In this section, the planner explains how each strategy responds to the threats, opportunities and critical issues spelled out earlier in the plan. Additional sections of the marketing plan lay out an action programme for implementing the marketing strategy along with the details of a supporting *marketing budget*. The last section outlines the controls that will be used to monitor progress, measure return on marketing investment, and take corrective action.

Marketing implementation

Marketing implementation—
Turning marketing strategies and plans into marketing actions to accomplish strategic marketing objectives.

Planning good strategies is only a start toward successful marketing. A brilliant marketing strategy counts for little if the company fails to implement it properly. **Marketing implementation** is the process that turns marketing *plans* into marketing *actions* to accomplish strategic marketing objectives. Whereas marketing planning addresses the *what* and *why* of marketing activities, implementation addresses the *who, where, when and how.*

Many managers think that 'doing things right' (implementation) is as important as, or even more important than, 'doing the right things' (strategy). The fact is that both are critical to success, and companies can gain competitive advantages through effective implementation. One firm

Table 2.2 Contents of a marketing plan

Section	Purpose
Executive summary	Presents a brief summary of the main goals and recommendations of the plan for management review, helping top management find the plan's major points quickly.
Current marketing situation	Describes the target market and the company's position in it, including information about the market, product performance, competition and distribution. This section includes the following: • A *market description* that defines the market and major segments and then reviews customer needs and factors in the marketing environment that may affect customer purchasing. • A *product review* that shows sales, prices and gross margins of the major products in the product line. • A review of *competition* that identifies major competitors and assesses their market positions and strategies for product quality, pricing, distribution and promotion. • A review of *distribution* that evaluates recent sales trends and other developments in major distribution channels.
Threats and opportunities analysis	Assesses major threats and opportunities that the product might face, helping management to anticipate important positive or negative developments that might have an impact on the firm and its strategies.
Objectives and issues	States the marketing objectives that the company would like to attain during the plan's term and discusses key issues that will affect their attainment.
Marketing strategy	Outlines the broad marketing logic by which the business unit hopes to engage customers, create customer value and build customer relationships, plus the specifics of target markets, positioning and marketing expenditure levels. How will the company create value for customers in order to capture value from customers in return? This section also outlines specific strategies for each marketing mix element and explains how each responds to the threats, opportunities and critical issues spelled out earlier in the plan.
Action programmes	Spells out how marketing strategies will be turned into specific action programmes that answer the following questions: *What* will be done? *When* will it be done? Who will do it? How much will it cost?
Budgets	Details a supporting marketing budget that is essentially a projected profit-and-loss statement. It shows expected revenues and expected costs of production, distribution and marketing. The difference is the projected profit. The budget becomes the basis for materials buying, production scheduling, personnel planning and marketing operations.
Controls	Outlines the controls that will be used to monitor progress, allow management to review implementation results, and spot products that are not meeting their goals. It includes measures of return on marketing investment.

can have essentially the same strategy as another, yet win in the marketplace through faster or better execution. Still, implementation is difficult – it is often easier to think up good marketing strategies than it is to carry them out.

In an increasingly connected world, people at all levels of the marketing system must work together to implement marketing strategies and plans. At Mercedes-Benz, for example, marketing implementation for the company's automobile manufacturing requires day-to-day decisions and actions by thousands of people both inside and outside the organisation. Marketing managers make decisions about target segments, branding, product development, pricing, promotion and distribution. They talk with engineering about product design, with manufacturing about production and inventory levels, and with finance about funding and cash flows. They also connect with outside people, such as advertising agencies to plan advertising campaigns and the news media to obtain publicity support. The sales force urges and supports dealers in their efforts to convince customers that choosing a Mercedes-Benz is really a choice between 'The best or nothing'.

Marketing department organisation

The company must design a marketing organisation that can carry out marketing strategies and plans. If the company is very small, one person might do all the research, selling, advertising, customer service and other marketing work. As the company expands, however, a marketing department emerges to plan and carry out marketing activities. In large companies, this department contains many specialists – product and market managers, sales managers and salespeople, market researchers, and advertising and social media experts, among others.

To head up such large marketing organisations, many companies have now created a *chief marketing officer* (or CMO) position. This person heads up the company's entire marketing operation and represents marketing on the company's top management team. The CMO position puts marketing on equal footing with other 'C-level' executives, such as the chief operating officer (COO) and the chief financial officer (CFO). As a member of top management, the CMO's role is to champion the customer's cause – to be the 'chief customer officer'.

Modern marketing departments can be arranged in several ways. The most common form of marketing organisation is the *functional organisation*. Under this organisation, different marketing activities are headed by a functional specialist – a sales manager, an advertising manager, a marketing research manager, a customer service manager, or a new product manager. A company that sells across the country or internationally often uses a *geographic organisation*. Its sales and marketing people are assigned to specific countries, regions and districts. Geographic organisation allows salespeople to settle into a territory, get to know their customers, and work with a minimum of travel time and cost. Companies with many very different products or brands often create a *product management organisation*. Using this approach, a product manager develops and implements a complete strategy and marketing programme for a specific product or brand.

For companies that sell one product line to many different types of markets and customers who have different needs and preferences, a *market* or *customer management organisation* might be best. A market management organisation is similar to the product management organisation. Market managers are responsible for developing marketing strategies and plans for their specific markets or customers. This system's main advantage is that the company is organised around the needs of specific customer segments. Many companies develop special organisations to manage their relationships with large customers. For example, companies such as Unilever have created large teams, or even whole divisions, to serve large customers, such as Edeka, Metro, Carrefour and Tesco.

Large companies that produce many different products flowing into many different geographic and customer markets usually employ some *combination* of the functional, geographic, product and market organisation forms.

Marketing organisation has become an increasingly important issue in recent years. More and more, companies are shifting their brand management focus toward *customer management* – moving away from managing only product or brand profitability and toward managing customer profitability and customer equity. They think of themselves not as managing portfolios of brands but as managing portfolios of customers. And rather than managing the fortunes of a brand, they see themselves as managing customer–brand engagement, experiences and relationships.

Marketing control

Marketing control—
Measuring and evaluating the results of marketing strategies and plans and taking corrective action to ensure that the objectives are achieved.

Because many surprises occur during the implementation of marketing plans, marketers must practise constant **marketing control** – evaluating the results of marketing strategies and plans and taking corrective action to ensure that the objectives are attained. Marketing control involves four steps. Management first sets specific marketing goals. It then measures its performance in the marketplace and evaluates the causes of any differences between expected and actual performance. Finally, management takes corrective action to close the gaps between goals and performance. This may require changing the action programmes or even changing the goals.

Operating control involves checking on-going performance against the annual plan and taking corrective action when necessary. Its purpose is to ensure that the company achieves the sales, profits and other goals set out in its annual plan. It also involves determining the profitability of different products, territories, markets and channels. *Strategic control* involves looking at whether the company's basic strategies are well matched to its opportunities. Marketing strategies and programmes can quickly become out-dated, and each company should periodically reassess its overall approach to the marketplace.

MEASURING AND MANAGING MARKETING RETURN ON INVESTMENT

Marketing managers must ensure that their marketing euros are being well spent. In the past, many marketers spent freely on big, expensive marketing programmes and flashy advertising campaigns, often without thinking carefully about the financial returns on their spending. Their goal was often a general one – to 'build brands and consumer preference'. They believed that marketing produces intangible creative outcomes, which do not lend themselves readily to measures of productivity or return.

In today's leaner economic times, however, all that has changed. The free-spending days have been replaced by a new era of marketing measurement and accountability. More than ever, today's marketers are being held accountable for linking their strategies and tactics to measurable marketing performance outcomes. One important marketing performance measure is **marketing return on investment** (or **marketing ROI**). *Marketing ROI* is the net return from a marketing investment divided by the costs of the marketing investment. It measures the profits generated by investments in marketing activities.

In one recent survey, 64 per cent of senior marketers rated accountability as a top three concern, well ahead of the 50 per cent rating the hot topic of integrated marketing communications as a top concern. However, another survey found that only about a third of chief marketing officers felt able to quantitatively measure the short- or long-term return on their marketing spending. A startling 57 per cent of CMOs don't take ROI measures into account when setting their marketing budgets, and an even more startling 28 per cent said they base their marketing budgets on 'gut instinct'. Clearly, marketers must think more strategically about the marketing performance returns of their marketing spending.[15]

Marketing ROI can be difficult to measure. In measuring financial ROI, both the *R* and the *I* are uniformly measured in euros. For example, when buying a piece of equipment, the productivity gains resulting from the purchase are fairly straightforward. As of yet, however, there is no consistent definition of marketing ROI. For instance, returns such as engagement, advertising and brand-building impact aren't easily put into euro returns.

A company can assess marketing ROI in terms of standard marketing performance measures, such as brand awareness, sales, or market share. Many companies are assembling such measures into *marketing dashboards* – meaningful sets of marketing performance measures in a single display used to monitor strategic marketing performance. Just as automobile dashboards present drivers with details on how their cars are performing, the marketing dashboard gives marketers the detailed measures they need to assess and adjust their marketing strategies.

Increasingly, however, beyond standard performance measures, marketers are using customer-centred measures of marketing impact, such as customer acquisition, customer engagement, customer retention, customer lifetime value and customer equity. These measures capture not

Author comment

Measuring marketing return on investment has become a major emphasis. But it can be difficult. For example, a Champion's League Final ad reaches millions of consumers but may cost millions of euros for 30 seconds of airtime. How do you measure the return on such an investment in terms of sales, profits and building customer engagement and relationships? We'll look at this question again in Chapter 15.

Marketing return on investment (or marketing ROI)—The net return from a marketing investment divided by the costs of the marketing investment.

Many companies assemble marketing dashboards – meaningful sets of marketing performance measures in a unified display.

Source: Pressmaster/Shutterstock.com

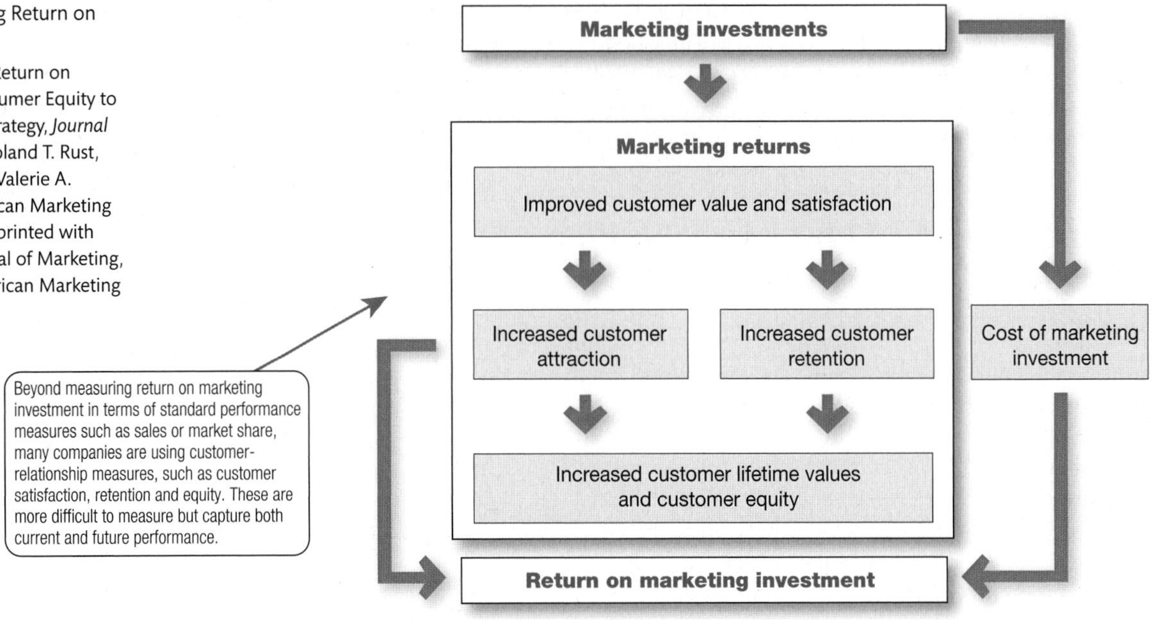

Figure 2.8 Marketing Return on Investment

Source: adapted from Return on Marketing: Using Consumer Equity to Focus on Marketing Strategy, *Journal of Marketing*, p.112 (Roland T. Rust, Katherine Lemon and Valerie A. Zeithaml 2004), American Marketing Association (AMA), Reprinted with permission from Journal of Marketing, published by the American Marketing Association

Beyond measuring return on marketing investment in terms of standard performance measures such as sales or market share, many companies are using customer-relationship measures, such as customer satisfaction, retention and equity. These are more difficult to measure but capture both current and future performance.

only current marketing performance but also future performance resulting from stronger customer relationships. Figure 2.8 views marketing expenditures as investments that produce returns in the form of more profitable customer relationships.[16] Marketing investments result in improved customer value, engagement and satisfaction, which in turn increases customer attraction and retention. This increases individual customer lifetime values and the firm's overall customer equity. Increased customer equity, in relation to the cost of the marketing investments, determines return on marketing investment.

Regardless of how it's defined or measured, the marketing ROI concept is here to stay. In good times or bad, marketers will be increasingly accountable for the performance outcomes of their activities. As one marketer puts it, marketers 'have got to know how to count'.[17]

OBJECTIVES REVIEW AND KEY TERMS

In Chapter 1, we defined marketing and outlined the steps in the marketing process. In this chapter, we examined company-wide strategic planning and marketing's role in the organisation. Then we looked more deeply into marketing strategy and the marketing mix and reviewed the major marketing management functions. So you've now had a pretty good overview of the fundamentals of modern marketing.

OBJECTIVE 1 Explain company-wide strategic planning and its four steps (pp. 38–41)

Strategic planning sets the stage for the rest of the company's planning. Marketing contributes to strategic planning, and the overall plan defines marketing's role in the company.

Strategic planning involves developing a strategy for long-run survival and growth. It consists of four steps: (1) defining the company's

mission, (2) setting objectives and goals, (3) designing a business portfolio, and (4) developing functional plans. The company's mission should be market oriented, realistic, specific, motivating and consistent with the market environment. The mission is then transformed into detailed *supporting goals* and objectives, which in turn guide decisions about the business portfolio. Then each business and product unit must *develop detailed marketing plans* in line with the company-wide plan.

OBJECTIVE 2 Discuss how to design business portfolios and develop growth strategies (pp. 41–44)

Guided by the company's mission statement and objectives, management plans its *business portfolio*, or the collection of businesses and products that make up the company. The firm wants to produce a business portfolio that best fits its strengths and weaknesses to opportunities in the environment. To do this, it must analyse and adjust its current business portfolio and develop *growth* and *downsizing* strategies for adjusting the future portfolio. The company might use a formal portfolio-planning method. But many companies are now designing more customised portfolio-planning approaches that better suit their unique situations.

OBJECTIVE 3 Explain marketing's role in strategic planning and how marketing works with its partners to create and deliver customer value (pp. 45–47)

Under the strategic plan, the major functional departments — marketing, finance, accounting, purchasing, operations, information systems, human resources, and others — must work together to accomplish strategic objectives. Marketing plays a key role in the company's strategic planning by providing a *marketing concept philosophy* and *inputs* regarding attractive market opportunities. Within individual business units, marketing designs *strategies* for reaching the unit's objectives and helps to carry them out profitably.

Marketers alone cannot produce superior value for customers. Marketers must practise *partner relationship management*, working closely with partners in other departments to form an effective *value chain* that serves the customer. And they must also partner effectively with other companies in the marketing system to form a competitively superior *value delivery network*.

OBJECTIVE 4 Describe the elements of a customer value-driven marketing strategy and mix and the forces that influence it (pp. 47–51)

Customer value and relationships are at the centre of marketing strategy and programmes. Through market segmentation, targeting, differentiation and positioning, the company divides the total market into smaller segments, selects segments it can best serve, and decides how it wants to bring value to target consumers in the selected segments. It then designs an *integrated* *marketing* mix to produce the response it wants in the target market. The marketing mix consists of product, price, place and promotion decisions (the four Ps).

OBJECTIVE 5 List the marketing management functions, including the elements of a marketing plan, and discuss the importance of measuring and managing marketing return on investment (pp. 55–56)

To find the best strategy and mix and to put them into action, the company engages in marketing analysis, planning, implementation and control. The main components of a *marketing plan* are the executive summary, the current marketing situation, threats and opportunities, objectives and issues, marketing strategies, action programmes, budgets and controls. Planning good strategies is often easier than carrying them out. To be successful, companies must also be effective at *implementation* — turning marketing strategies into marketing actions.

Marketing departments can be organised in one way or a combination of ways: *functional marketing organisation, geographic organisation, product management organisation* or *market management organisation*. In this age of customer relationships, more and more companies are now changing their organisational focus from product or territory management to customer relationship management. Marketing organisations carry out *marketing con*trol, both operating control and strategic control.

More than ever, marketing accountability is the top marketing concern. Marketing managers must ensure that their marketing euros are being well spent. In a tighter economy, today's marketers face growing pressures to show that they are adding value in line with their costs. In response, marketers are developing better measures of *marketing return on investment*. Increasingly, they are using customer-centred measures of marketing impact as a key input into their strategic decision making.

NAVIGATING THE KEY TERMS

OBJECTIVE 1
Strategic planning (p. 38)
Mission statement (p. 39)

OBJECTIVE 2
Business portfolio (p. 41)
Portfolio analysis (p. 41)
Growth–share matrix (p. 42)
Product/market expansion grid (p. 43)
Market penetration (p. 44)
Market development (p. 44)
Product development (p. 44)

Diversification (p. 44)
Downsizing (p. 44)

OBJECTIVE 3
Value chain (p. 45)
Value delivery network (p. 46)

OBJECTIVE 4
Marketing strategy (p. 47)
Market segmentation (p. 48)
Market segment (p. 48)
Market targeting (p. 48)

Positioning (p. 49)
Differentiation (p. 49)
Marketing mix (p. 49)

OBJECTIVE 5
SWOT analysis (p. 51)
Marketing implementation (p, 52)
Marketing control (p. 54)
Marketing return on investment
 (marketing ROI) (p. 55)

DISCUSSION AND CRITICAL THINKING

Discussion questions

2-1 Explain how marketing plays a key role in an organisation's strategic planning. (AACSB: Communication)

2-2 Name and describe the four product/market expansion grid strategies. Provide an example of a company implementing each strategy. (AACSB: Communication; Reflective thinking)

2-3 What is positioning and what role does differentiation play in implementing it? (AACSB: Communication)

2-4 What are the four Ps of marketing? What insights might a firm gain by considering the four Cs rather than the four Ps? (AACSB: Communication; Reflective thinking)

2-5 What is a marketing dashboard and how is it useful to marketers? What types of performance measures do marketers use to assess marketing performance? (AACSB: Communication)

Critical-thinking exercises

2-6 Form a small group and conduct a SWOT analysis for your school, a group that you are a member of, a publicly traded company, a local business, or a non-profit organisation. Based on your analysis, suggest a strategy from the product/market expansion grid and an appropriate marketing mix to implement that strategy. (AACSB: Communication; Reflective thinking)

2-7 The Boston Consulting Group (BCG) matrix is a useful strategic tool. Another classic portfolio planning method useful to marketers is the GE/McKinsey matrix (see www.quickmba.com/strategy/matrix/ge-mckinsey/). How is the GE/McKinsey matrix similar to and different from the BCG matrix? (AACSB: Communication; Reflective thinking)

2-8 Create a mission statement for a non-profit organisation you would be interested in starting. Have another student evaluate your mission statement while you evaluate the other student's statement, suggesting areas of improvement. (AACSB: Communication; Reflective thinking)

Mini-cases and applications

Online, mobile and social media marketing: the PC-osaurus

In 2011, Hewlett-Packard CEO Leo Apothekar made the strategic decision to exit the personal computer business, but he got fired and incoming CEO Meg Wittman reversed that decision. However, sales of personal computers have plummeted since the introduction of post-PC devices (tablets, e-readers and smartphones). In 2013, total PC shipments fell 10 per cent, and no one felt that more than leading PC-maker HP. PC-makers

dropped prices – some more than 50 per cent – on laptops and some are offering touch screens to compete with tablets and mobile devices in an attempt to gain back market share. HP's former CEO wanted to shift strategic focus more toward offering software to business markets. Maybe he had read the future correctly and was on the right strategic path. With the game-changing introduction of tablets, mobile technology, and social media, the future is not what it used to be. The growth in mobile technology is there; HP just 'missed the boat'.

2-9 Explain which product/market expansion grid strategy PC-makers are currently pursuing to deal with the threat of post-PC mobile devices. Is this a smart strategy? (AACSB: Communication; Reflective thinking)

2-10 Discuss how companies such as HP and other PC-makers can adapt to and capitalise on new online, mobile, or social media technologies. (AACSB: Communication; Reflective Thinking)

Marketing ethics: digital dark side

More than half of the world's population lives under autocratic regimes, limiting access to the Internet. But that is changing, opening new market opportunities for companies specialising in digital monitoring technologies. Everything an oppressive regime needs to build a digital police state is commercially available and is being implemented. Filtering devices manufactured by Blue Coat Systems, a Silicon Valley-based company, are used in Syria to suppress civil unrest. Although Blue Coat Systems acknowledges this, it claims it did not sell the product to the Syrian government. North Korea, China, Libya, and other oppressive states demand data mining software and surveillance cameras as well as cutting-edge technologies that collect, store and analyse biometric information. As social media proliferate in these countries, off-the-shelf facial recognition software and cloud computing can identify people in a matter of seconds, enabling these states to quash dissent. Although the European Union may have sanctions against European-based companies selling products to these governments, others may not, resulting in their country's products, as well European-based products, getting into the hands of oppressive regimes.

2-11 In most cases, it is not illegal to sell such products to governments, oppressive or otherwise. But is it moral? Shouldn't companies be allowed to pursue a market development strategy wherever they find demand? (AACSB: Communication; Ethical reasoning)

2-12 Research the Blue Coat Systems incident and write a report of your findings. Did the company illegally sell surveillance products to Syria? Which element of the marketing mix is most related to this issue? (AACSB: Communication; Reflective thinking)

Marketing by numbers: profitability

Appendix 2: Marketing by the numbers discusses other marketing profitability metrics beyond the marketing ROI measure described in this chapter. Below are the profit-and-loss statements for two businesses. Review Appendix 2 and answer the following questions.

1. Calculate marketing return on sales and marketing ROI for both companies, as described in Appendix 2. (AACSB: Communication; Analytic thinking)

2. Which company is doing better overall and with respect to marketing? Explain. (AACSB: Communication; Analytic reasoning; Reflective thinking)

Business A		
Net sales		€800,000,000
Cost of goods sold		€375,000,000
Gross margin		€425,000,000
Marketing expenses		
Sales expenses	€70,000,000	
Promotion expenses	€30,000,000	
		€100,000,000
General and administrative expenses		
Marketing salaries and expenses	€10,000,000	
Indirect overhead	€80,000,000	
		€90,000,000
Net profit before income tax		€235,000,000

Business B		
Net sales		€900,000,000
Cost of goods sold		€400,000,000
Gross margin		€500,000,000
Marketing expenses		
Sales expenses	€90,000,000	
Promotion expenses	€50,000,000	
		€140,000,000
General and administrative expenses		
Marketing salaries and expenses	€20,000,000	
Indirect overhead	€100,000,000	
		€120,000,000
Net profit before income tax		€240,000,000

REFERENCES

[1] Based on information from Austin Carr, 'Nike: the no. 1 most innovative company of 2013', *Fast Company*, March 2013, pp. 89–93; Mary Lisbeth D'Amico, 'Report sends Nike and Adidas to head of digital marketing class', *Clickz*, 25 September 2012, www.clickz.com /clickz/news/2208172/report-sends-nike-and-adidas-to-head-of-digital-marketing-class; Sebastian Joseph, 'Nike takes social media in-house', *Marketing Week*, 3 January 2013, www.marketingweek. co.uk/sectors/sport/nike-takes-social-media-in-house/4005240.article; John Cashman, 'How Nike is killing it in social media marketing', *Digital Firefly*, 19 October 2013, https://digitalfireflymarketing.com /how-nike-killing-it-social-media-marketing; and http://investors .nikeinc.com/Investors and https://secure-nikeplus.nike.com/plus/, accessed September 2014.

[2] See http://www.bosch-career.com/en/com/bosch_worldwide_1 /corporate_culture/corporate_culture_1.html, accessed October 2015.

[3] Jack and Suzy Welch, 'State your business; too many mission statements are loaded with fatheaded jargon. Play it straight', *BusinessWeek*, 14 January 2008, p. 80; also see Nancy Lublin, 'Do something', *Fast Company*, November 2009, p. 86; and Jack Neff, 'P&G, Walmart, Lever, General Mills are major marketers on a mission', *Advertising Age*, 16 November 2009, pp. 1, 45.

4 See 'Kohler Mulls second manufacturing plant in Guj', *Economic Times*, 18 November 2009; and the Kohler Press Room, '2008 IBS Press Kit', www.us.kohler.com/pr/presskit.jsp?aid=1194383270995, accessed October 2015.

5 See 'General Electric Co.', *Reuters*, www.reuters.com/finance/stocks/companyProfile?symbol=GE.N, accessed October 2015; and www.ge.com/ar2013/pdf/GE_AR13.pdf and www.ge.com/products, accessed October 2015.

6 The following discussion is based in part on information found at www.bcg.com/documents/file13904.pdf, accessed October 2015.

7 See http://corporate.disney.go.com/investors/annual_reports.html, accessed October 2015.

8 H. Igor Ansoff, 'Strategies for diversification', *Harvard Business Review*, September–October 1957, pp. 113–124.

9 See http://www.vivago.com/en.html, accessed October 2015.

10 See Michael E. Porter, *Competitive Advantage: Creating and Sustaining Superior Performance* (New York: Free Press, 1985); and Michael E. Porter, 'What is strategy?', *Harvard Business Review*, November–December 1996, pp. 61–78; also see 'The value chain', www.quickmba.com/strategy/value-chain, accessed October 2015; and Philip Kotler and Kevin Lane Keller, *Marketing Management*, 14th ed. (Upper Saddle River, NJ: Prentice Hall, 2012), pp. 34–35 and pp. 203–204.

11 Nirmalya Kumar, 'The CEO's marketing manifesto', *Marketing Management*, November–December 2008, pp. 24–29; and Tom French and others, 'We're all marketers now', *McKinsey Quarterly*, July 2011, www.mckinseyquarterly.com/Were_all_marketers_now_2834.

12 Rebecca Ellinor, 'Crowd pleaser', *Supply Management*, 13 December 2007, pp. 26–29; and information from www.loreal.com/_en/_ww/html/suppliers/index.aspx, accessed October 2015.

13 See www.gapinc.com/content/gapinc/html/aboutus/ourbrands/gap.html, accessed October 2015.

14 The four Ps classification was first suggested by E. Jerome McCarthy, *Basic Marketing: A Managerial Approach* (Homewood, IL: Irwin, 1960). For the four Cs, other proposed classifications, and more discussion, see Robert Lauterborn, 'New marketing litany: 4P's passé C-words take over', *Advertising Age*, 1 October 1990, p. 26; Richard Ettenson and others, 'Rethinking the 4Ps', *Harvard Business Review*, January–February 2013, p. 26; and Roy McClean, 'Marketing 101–4Cs versus the 4 Ps of marketing', www.customfitfocus.com/marketing-1.htm, accessed October 2015.

15 'Study finds marketers don't practice ROI they preach', *Advertising Age*, 11 March 2012, http://adage.com/article/233243/; 'Accountability remains senior marketers' top concern', *Marketing Charts*, 7 March 2013, www.marketingcharts.com/wp/topics/branding/accountability-remains-senior-marketers-top-concern-27565/; and 'Quantitative proof of marketing spend's ROI still eludes CMOs', *Marketing Charts*, 21 February 2014, www.marketingcharts.com/wp/traditional/quantitative-proof-of-marketing-spends-impact-stilleludes-cmos-40005/.

16 For a full discussion of this model and details on customer-centreed measures of return on marketing investment, see Roland T. Rust, Katherine N. Lemon and Valerie A. Zeithaml, 'Return on marketing: using customer equity to focus marketing strategy', *Journal of Marketing*, January 2004, pp. 109–127; Roland T. Rust, Katherine N. Lemon and Das Narayandas, *Customer Equity Management* (Upper Saddle River, NJ: Prentice Hall, 2005); Roland T. Rust, 'Seeking higher ROI? Base strategy on customer equity', *Advertising Age*, 10 September 2007, pp. 26–27; Andreas Persson and Lynette Ryals, 'Customer assets and customer equity: Management and measurement issues', *Marketing Theory*, December 2010, pp. 417–436; and Kirsten Korosec, 'Tomato, tomäto'? Not exactly', *Marketing News*, 13 January 2012, p. 8.

17 'Marketing strategy: Diageo CMO: 'Workers must be able to count', *Marketing Week*, 3 June 2010, p. 5; also see Art Weinstein and Shane Smith, 'Game plan: how can marketers face the challenge of managing customer metrics?', *Marketing Management*, Fall 2012, pp. 24–32; and Francis Yu, 'Why is it so hard to prove ROI when data and metrics are so abundant?', *Advertising Age*, 15 October 2012, p. 27.

COMPANY CASE

LEGO: one more brick in the wall?

In 1916 the founder of the LEGO dynasty, Ole Kirk Kristiansen, bought a woodworking business and sold furniture to local residents and framers. By the 1930s he switched his attention to children's toys and in 1934 coined the name 'LEGO' for his company. The name 'LEGO' is an abbreviation of the two Danish words '*leg*' and '*godt*', meaning 'play' and 'well'. LEGO claim that this is more than their name; it is their ideal. The early toys made by LEGO were wood-based – it wasn't until 1940 that the firm began making plastic toys that could be deconstructed and re-assembled. In 1953 LEGO began producing the now eponymous LEGO interlocking bricks (actually based on an earlier UK patent by Kiddicraft that LEGO spotted as full of potential and quickly bought). Today, the brand rivals IKEA, the Swedish furniture chain, as a symbol of Scandinavian design and values.

Since its formation to the late 1990s, LEGO experienced steady (if not necessarily spectacular) growth. However, in 1998 the company started losing money – fast. The crisis deepened for LEGO to the extent that in the mid-2000s, sales had dropped by 26 per cent and then a further 20 per cent in the following year. These two years represented the biggest losses in LEGO history. The firm was struggling against a falling dollar, cheap Chinese imported toys and young children's growing fascination with electronic gadgetry such as MP3 players and mobile phones. But yet there was hope – 'During the crisis, people wrote letters to us saying, "Please, for God's sake, save this brand because we love it so much",' Jorgen Vig Knudstorp the current CEO recalls. 'People theorise that it's all going to be "virtual play" in future but kids are always going to want to run after a soccer ball and build things with LEGO bricks.'

Nevertheless, the owners and managers of the firm could see that the strategic mission of the firm was out-dated, the LEGO portfolio was in big trouble, key internal and external partnerships were ineffective and much of the marketing effort wasted.

The crisis reached its head when Kjeld Kirk Kristiansen, the grandson of the founder of the LEGO toy empire, took a brave decision and stepped down as chief executive after forecasting the largest annual loss in the history of the firm. As owner, Kjeld remained deputy chairman but relinquished control of the firm to Jorgen Vig Knudstorp, previously senior vice-president for corporate affairs. Jorgen had been poached by LEGO from McKinsey Management Consultants in 2001. Aged just 36 at the time, he was handpicked by Kjeld, as the first outsider to run the family-owned business.

Jochen's challenge

With remarkable insight, Jochen recognised that the firm needed rapid restructuring, cultural change and re-focused effort if it were to be saved from financial collapse. The company's internal focus on creativity, innovation and superior quality had created high complexity that was far from market or customer oriented. The company had a total of 12,500 stock-keeping units, with more than 100 different colours and more than 11,000 suppliers. LEGO also operated one of the largest injection-moulding operations in the world, with production sites in Denmark and Switzerland, and packing and other facilities in the Czech Republic, the US and South Korea.

The process of planned change began with the company gathering a diverse group of both senior executives and (importantly) outside specialists in a 'war room', where they analysed the company's portfolio, product development, sourcing, manufacturing, marketing and logistics process. These analyses led to a five-year plan called 'Shared Vision' which was fully supported and approved by the board. This plan pivoted on developing and maintaining effective partnerships (both internally and externally) and was supported with a truly market-oriented mission that is to 'inspire and develop the builders of tomorrow', which they further explain is driven by their 'ultimate purpose to inspire and develop children to think creatively, reason systematically and release their potential to shape their own future – experiencing the endless human possibility'.

While Jochen is today viewed as a miracle worker in his native Denmark for saving a cherished national institution, his appointment was a huge gamble. His first challenge as chief executive was winning the support of subordinates left behind in the wake of his meteoric rise to the top of the firm. 'I told them, "I can't do this on my own, you have to work with me",' he recalls. 'Most people realised it was in their interests to help me succeed rather than prove themselves right by showing I couldn't do the job.' Jochen could draw from what he describes as a 'very good LEGO upbringing' as the son of a teacher and an engineer – the kind of middle class northern European

household that has been LEGO's key market for generations. He had a deep understanding of children having spent 18 months as a trainee kindergarten teacher before finally deciding to opt for a career in business. Nevertheless, this teaching experience proved valuable to Jochen, who claims that, 'My dad says that's where I learnt everything I needed to know about leadership,' he says. 'If you can be a leader with kindergarten children, you can be a leader anywhere.'

During the development and implementation of the turna-round five-year plan, Jochen argued that the hardest challenges for him was to get to the truth of what LEGO was doing right and wrong – and crucially to avoid complacency when things were going well. 'It's so easy when you're in a leadership position to think how good you're doing based on all the nice things people say and dismiss the 1 per cent who complain,' he says. 'You have to listen extra hard to that 1 per cent because they usually represent a much bigger proportion of silent unhappiness.' LEGO tries to get at the 'truth' by basing a large proportion of managers' bonuses, including Jochen's, on customer satisfaction surveys of retailers, parents and children rather than sales figures. This approach is designed to ensure that LEGO's long-term corporate health is never sacrificed for short-term financial success. 'Nobody at LEGO is measured on sales because the most important thing is that kids and retailers return for more in future,' Jochen says.

For all his empathy with LEGO's heritage and the paternalism of the Kristiansen family, Jochen did not shy away from hard decisions. He saw that harsh and fast measures were needed to turn LEGO round. In the small town of Billund in the Netherlands (where LEGO was founded), hundreds of workers were made redundant and a some manufacturing shifted to the more cost-effective locations of Mexico and Eastern Europe. While Billund remains LEGO's largest production site with its assembly plant adjoining the corporate headquarters, diversifying assembly to multiple locations has proved both efficient and effective at reducing fixed cost. This process has not affected quality; Jochen proudly claims that, 'We've never had to recall a single LEGO brick,' stressing the importance of quality to the brand. As part of the wider strategy the portfolio was slimmed as the company's flagship LEGOland theme parks were sold (although a minority share was retained) and non-core products scrapped as part of a back-to-basics strategy focused on its classic bricks and mini-figures.

Jochen also recognised that the family nature of the firm had created problems and strategic inertia. 'The family values had made the company too undisciplined,' he recalls. Throughout the process of restructuring he tried to run LEGO like a ruthless private equity firm, focusing solely on the mission of the firm. More recently, he has adopted practices from growth-oriented public companies. As a result, the embryonic family business has grown from a tiny carpentry workshop (that burned down twice) into the world's third biggest toymaker by sales. In many regards, the culture has altered from one of benevolent paternalism to that of a market-driven, professional culture. Yet Jochen argues that family ownership continues to hold important advantages. 'You can think long term but act very fast,' he explains. 'I can talk to shareholders in the morning and have a decision by the evening.' He describes his relationship with the Kristiansen family as 'very open and trusting' but not always smooth. 'Part of getting along is that you can have conflicts and still get along. We have disagreements but they are always resolved behind closed doors.'

Possibly, most crucially Jochen and his team focused on their partnerships of its suppliers, distributors and customers. Through a series of collaborations between different functions in the company, LEGO cut the number of colours by half and reduced the number of stock-keeping units to 6,500. The company also decided to stick to its core functions and to outsource logistics and production. In an effort to better understand what its customers did and did not need and want, the company sought extended meetings with its top 20 clients who represented 70 per cent of LEGO's total business. This process revealed one very important finding: in direct contrast to what the company had assumed, most customers did not need daily or next-day deliveries. This led to LEGO's decision to solicit orders in advance and to deliver to customers just once a week.

As with all plans, implementation was not always easy. In particular, the outsourcing of logistics strained the important relationship with DHL, LEGO's logistics partner. When DHL initially won the contract, it made its revenue calculations based on the existing customer service requirements (daily, which meant many more deliveries than weekly). However, after analysing the real needs of its customers, LEGO required a much lower number of deliveries than DHL had originally forecast. At the same time, the new outsourced logistics facility was the biggest of its kind in Eastern Europe, thus creating huge start-up challenges for DHL. These stresses and strains inevitably caused conflicts that could have derailed the LEGO turnaround. The breakthrough came when two LEGO executives met secretly with their DHL counterparts in a hotel in Prague. They took a 'four musketeers' oath – 'all for one and one for all' – to not discuss the outcome of this meeting with anyone. Instead, they undertook to change their behaviour towards one another to set a good example for the rest of their staff. It seems to have worked and relations have since flourished to genuine mutual respect.

After sorting out these operational issues, streamlining supply and forging a leaner, fitter LEGO the company has continued its core toy production but enhanced its global reputation and profile through a series of film-related and gaming-related link-ups. A quick search for LEGO games finds games for all tastes and ages – (to name but a few) LEGO racing games, LEGO fighting games, LEGO puzzle games, LEGO shooting games, LEGO pre-school games and (of course!) LEGO building games. The firm has also worked a series of very clever (and profitable) links with high-profile film franchises. *The Lord of the Rings* proved especially popular and the three *Hobbit* movies continues the trend. Link-ups with the Batman franchises look set to continue while the hugely successful *LEGO Movie* will be followed up by a sequel in 2018. The sets of collectable LEGO from these movie link-ups prove not only hugely collectable but also massively popular with children and parents alike – parents being especially fond of themed birthdays and Christmas gifts.

The outcomes of change

When Jochen took charge, LEGO was so deeply in the red that it faced genuine questions over its short-term survival in an era of online computer games and ever-increasing digital gadgets. In the mid-2000s industry commentators were predicting further losses and probable collapse – LEGO seemed destined to become yet another crumbled edifice in the face of a virtual world. Today, those doubts have been emphatically answered and the future seems bright (and slightly brick shaped). The most recent results saw revenue increased by 10 per cent to €3,403 million. Operating profit is up to €1,118m while net profit was €820m – a year-on-year increase of 9 per cent. The number of full-time employees rose by 13 per cent – an increase of 1,355 to 11,755 employees.

Sales are now more than twice as high as in those gloomy days in the late 2000s at around €3.41bn, while in 2013 LEGO became the world's second-biggest toy maker after reporting a 13 per cent increase in sales, overtaking US-based rival Hasbro. The fixed cost base had been slashed from a debilitating 75 per cent to highly respectable 33 per cent. Further, LEGO is thinking more about the very long term. Recently, Jochen's big decisions have been positive ones about new investment. In many ways, LEGO has proved relatively immune to global economic turmoil (largely because caring parents keep spending on traditional and educational toys no matter the hardship). The workforce has almost tripled in the past eight years to around 11,755 as recovery in Europe and the US is supplemented by growth in new territories such as Russia. Expansion into other emerging markets such as China, India and Brazil is proving especially good, with recent annual growth of 35 per cent in China alone, driving the need for a new manufacturing facility especially for the Chinese market. However, Jochen rules out diversifying into other products, saying: 'LEGO has been around 80 years and we've never made an acquisition. Companies with single brands, such as Apple and Nintendo, tend to do better than those with several.'

For customers, the outcomes were also good. While customers saw the number of product options reduced and were asked to change their ordering habits, they obtained a substantial improvement in customer service. On-time delivery rose from 62 per cent to 92 per cent. Recently, customers rated LEGO as a 'best in class' supplier and LEGO won a European supply chain excellence award. Those customers were now asking their other suppliers to use LEGO as the benchmark for excellence. LEGO has launched an online club with over 5 million members, customers can design and order their own LEGO designs, the LEGO

Universe MMPG has hundreds of thousands of players, the firm has well over 10 million followers on facebook, over 12.5m (yes 12.5m!) videos on youtube are tagged as 'LEGO'.

Questions for discussion

1. Prior to 2004, was LEGO focused on its products or its marketplace? Why?
2. Using the product/market expansion grid, which approach has LEGO adopted under the leadership of Jochen? Is this different to past approaches?
3. On which internal and external partners did Jochen's approach concentrate? Why?
4. Implementing change is never easy. In implementing their plans, what did LEGO do right and what did they do wrong? How would you have done things differently?

Sources: This case study draws heavily on the excellent case studies and analyses (including quotes and other information) of: Carlos Cordon, Ralf Seifert and Edwin Wellian, 'Case study: LEGO', *Financial Times*, 24 November 2010, http://www.ft.com/cms/s/0/05806aa4-f819-11df-8875-00144feab49a.html#ixzz1ZnO0srvW, accessed October 2015; Clare MacCarthy, 'LEGO suffers as children shun toys', *Financial Times*, 7 April 2005, http://www.ft.com/cms/s/0/716a2a26-a701-11d9-a6df00000e2511c8.html#ixzz1ZnP1b6ce, accessed October 2015; Andrew Ward, 'A brick by brick brand revival', *Financial Times*, 17 July 2011, http://www.ft.com/cms/s/0/0596a1f0-af27-11e0-14e00144fe-abdc0.html#ixzz1ZnPfOHIo, accessed October 2015; http://aboutus.LEGO.com/en-us/group/future.aspx, accessed October 2011; http://aboutus.LEGO.com/en-US/factsfigures/default.aspx (company profile), accessed October 2015; 'LEGO becomes world's second-biggest toy maker' available at http://www.bbc.co.uk/news/business-23968860, accessed October 2015; Katrina Bishop, 'LEGO builds sales with new product launches', available at http://www.cnbc.com/id/101451329#, accessed October 2015; Holly Ellyatt, 'Toymaker LEGO looks to build on success in China', available at http://www.cnbc.com/id/101010443, accessed October 2015; LEGO website http://www.LEGO.com/en-gb/games and http://thelordoftherings.LEGO.com/en-gb/default.aspx, accessed October 2015.

PART TWO

Understanding the marketplace and consumers

CHAPTER THREE

Analysing the marketing environment

Chapter preview

In Part 1, you learned about the basic concepts of marketing and the steps in the marketing process for building profitable relationships with targeted consumers. In Part 2, we'll look deeper into the first step of the marketing process — understanding the marketplace and customer needs and wants. In this chapter, you'll see that marketing operates in a complex and changing environment. Other actors in this environment — suppliers, intermediaries, customers, competitors, publics and others — may work with or against the company. Major environmental forces — demographic, economic, natural, technological, political and cultural — shape marketing opportunities, pose threats and affect the company's ability to build customer relationships. To develop effective marketing strategies, you must first understand the environment in which marketing operates.

To start, let's look at the massive impact of collapse of oil prices across the world in 2015. Even in a digital world of connectivity and Internet-based change, the price of a basic raw material like oil has deep-seated effects for business globally. Successful companies should prepare for change in the environment they face and be flexible in responding, to maintain their ability to engage and satisfy their customers.

Objectives outline

➤ **Objective 1** Describe the environmental forces that affect the company's ability to serve its customers.
The microenvironment (pp. 70–72)
The macroenvironment (pp. 73–74)

➤ **Objective 2** Explain how changes in demographic and economic environments affect marketing decisions.
The demographic environment (pp. 74–81)
The economic environment (pp. 82–84)

➤ **Objective 3** Identify the major trends in the firm's natural and technological environments.
The natural environment (p. 85)
The technological environment (pp. 86–88)

➤ **Objective 4** Explain the key changes in political and cultural environments.
The political and social environment (pp. 88–90)
The cultural environment (pp. 90–92)

➤ **Objective 5** Discuss how companies can react to the marketing environment.
Responding to the marketing environment (pp. 92–93)

Adapting to what cheap oil means for marketing?

In early 2015, the global price of oil halved. A year earlier, the price of oil was $105 a barrel, and now it had dropped to $50. Since then, oil investors expecting a quick recovery have been disappointed. Some say that the price of oil being in three digits will soon be a distant memory. By mid-2015, the slowdown in the Chinese economy saw oil prices dip to as low as $43 a barrel, with analysts fearing a drop to $30 and no recovery in the near term. The oil industry is actually running out of places to store the resulting glut of oil – storage tanks in the US are overflowing. The scale of the current oil shock is difficult to exaggerate.

The price of oil is based on supply and demand. Over the past six years, US domestic production has doubled, reducing its need to buy elsewhere (a US government goal is to be independent of foreign oil supplies). Meanwhile demand in struggling European and developing countries has been weaker as countries use their reserves more efficiently, and demand from China reflects the economic slow-down there.

In the past, if supply outstripped demand, the Organisation of Petroleum Export Countries (OPEC) would cut production to shore up the price. This time some producers refused because they feared that reducing oil availability would encourage users to move to shale gas as a substitute.

The fundamentals persisted throughout 2015 – the number of rigs in the US is rising, there are new pipelines of supply due to come into production, and a lack of economic growth globally is dampening demand for oil.

As long as supply exceeds demand, the price will stay low. The oil industry and business in general has to live with this fundamental change in their environment for the foreseeable future.

Why was it a surprise?

Predicting oil prices is always difficult. With a traded commodity which is bought at spot prices as well as being bought forward, and with speculators gambling on small changes in the price, it is difficult to forecast price with any certainty. But the current situation is extreme, and yet was not expected.

Notwithstanding the steady accumulation of oil stocks around the world for several years, for most of the players in the multi-trillion dollar oil and gas industry, the swift plunge in the price of crude oil has been almost as surprising as it has been costly. In fact, analysts were actually expecting an oil shortage and price spike at this time, resulting from geopolitical tensions in Ukraine and Iraq.

The impact on oil-producing countries

The fall in oil prices has inflicted massive pain on oil-exporting countries, widening budget deficits and weakening currencies around the world. Energy companies have been forced to lay off thousands of workers and scrap investment projects. Venezuela, for example, is facing the greatest economic threat of any of the world's major producers, with shortages of basic goods – from milk to nappies – becoming more acute each day as imports shrink, and social costs are being dramatically cut. Already mired in corruption and mismanagement, Venezuela is struggling to pay its bills.

One estimate is that the oil price fall amounts to a $1.6 trillion shift from the oil-producing countries to the oil-consuming countries. Certainly, Venezuela alone is looking at a $39 billion funding gap on its external debt this year.

The impact on the oil industry

For the oil companies, the global oil glut has reduced prices and cut profits. For example, in July 2015, Shell's profit dropped by a third in one quarter and the company announced plans to cut 6,500 jobs, though still maintaining its Arctic exploration investment. In the UK, BP and BG both applied the brakes sharply to capital investment plans.

The lower oil price has, in fact, galvanised big oil companies to slash costs, shake up their organisations and refashion relations with suppliers and host countries. The challenge for companies like Total in France and Occidental Petroleum is to get back to a position where revenue exceeds costs – but at $50 a barrel instead of $105. Payments to suppliers have to be reduced, which is reflected in job losses in those companies: Schlumberger has cut 20,000 jobs, Baker Hughes 2,500 and Halliburton 9,000. Other oil companies, like BP, are 'recycling' projects to see if they can be delivered cheaper, and favouring countries that offer better terms to attract investment.

At one point shale looked an attractive alternative source of oil for the major players, even though it is a relatively high-cost way of extracting fuel. Low oil prices change the economics. Shale producers now see declining profit, cuts in jobs and investments, and equipment standing idle. Several US shale producers have gone bankrupt, and others are struggling.

Conventional oil companies are pulling back from investments in high-cost exploration areas – they may have made sense economically at $100 a barrel, but not at $50. Most prominent exits have been in Arctic exploration because of the high costs. Statoil in Norway has postponed drilling in the Norwegian Arctic; Chevron in the US has shelved indefinitely plans for the Canadian Arctic; while Statoil, Dong Energy (Denmark) and GDF Suez (France) have all handed back drilling licences in Greenland.

Certainly, the collapse in oil prices was having a chilling effect on North Sea oil, forcing companies such as BP to cut nearly a tenth of its workforce in its Scottish fields. Since oil and gas accounts for roughly a fifth of overall business investment, this is likely to drag down overall investment growth for the UK. In the first quarter of 2015 North Sea oil revenues were down 75 per cent on the previous quarter. The end of the North Sea basin could come much earlier than previously expected – the ageing fields were already seen as a marginal bet by some companies, which are now withdrawing altogether.

The broader impact of crisis in the oil industry is big. In the UK the oil and gas industry accounts for some 450,000 jobs and paid £5 billion in tax in 2013.

The impact on business

For marketers, a shift downward in the global price of oil has major implications for the availability of income for consumers and governments to buy goods. Consumer demand may also shift within product categories – the demand for gas-guzzling 4×4 cars goes up when fuel is cheap and the demand for more economical vehicles goes down. Some businesses look to suffer badly because of low oil prices. Notwithstanding their green credentials, electric cars and biofuels are likely victims – simply because they compete with petrol-fuelled cars which are now cheaper to run.

For companies outside the oil industry, falling oil prices may have a beneficial effect because reduced costs mean higher profit margins. Consumers are unlikely to defer expenditure, expecting lower oil prices in the future, for most retail expenditure. Companies for which oil is a significant raw material stand to gain.

The general view is that the oil price slide will boost global demand. Consumers generally benefit from lower fuel prices. In this sense, for consumers – especially those who drive cars – lower oil prices are a boon. By summer 2015, petrol and diesel prices at the pump were the lowest they had been for five years. Early in 2015, it was estimated that the fall in oil prices over the previous six months had increased by £10 billion the amount UK households had to spend on goods other than petrol.

But not all effects are positive – falling oil prices also raise consumer expectations of lower prices for their goods and services, and some annoyance when they do not always materialise. Airlines are under strong pressure to reduce

Early in 2015 it was estimated that the fall in oil prices over the previous six months had increased the amount UK households had to spend by £10 billion.

Source: Trond Runar Solevaag/ 123RF.com

fares to reflect lower oil prices, even though they are actually burning fuel bought forward at much higher prices. Also, if households in China, Europe and Japan feel any need to save any windfalls they receive, the global demand boost will be severely restricted.

What happens next?

History does not tell us how long the current price fall will last. But it does show that it will not necessarily be short. In the past, price rebounds have taken years to happen. Last time, prices stayed below $60 a barrel from the late 1980s for around a decade.

The message for marketers

The most important lesson for marketers from the evolving oil price saga is that constant vigilance is needed to prepare for major changes in the environment. Beyond simple awareness of potential changes, marketers need to consider carefully how a change in the environment will create new customer opportunities as well as threats to the business. So, for example, will lower oil prices: provide a boost for sales of your products and services; put you under pressure to reduce prices; lose you business with oil companies and oil-producing countries; make some markets less attractive because of their reduced ability to pay; reduce demand because of the unemployment and reduced investment by the oil companies impacting more broadly on other companies; shift demand from some products to others; raise unrealistic consumer expectations for price cuts? Careful study of how changes in the marketing environment will impact on customers and markets at home and abroad is an essential.[1]

A company's **marketing environment** consists of the actors and forces outside marketing that affect marketing management's ability to build and maintain successful relationships with target customers. As shown in looking at the halving of worldwide oil prices, wise companies must constantly watch and adapt to the changing environment and in some cases act to completely re-shape the environment – as technology changes, competitors come out with radical innovations, customer needs and preferences evolve, and other fundamental changes occur, companies must evolve and change as well or risk being left behind.

More than any other group in the company, marketers must be environmental trend trackers and opportunity seekers. Although every manager in an organisation should watch the outside environment, marketers have two special aptitudes. They have disciplined methods – marketing research and marketing intelligence – for collecting information about the marketing environment. They also spend more time in customer and competitor environments. By carefully studying the environment, marketers can adapt their strategies to meet new marketplace challenges and opportunities.

The marketing environment consists of a *microenvironment* and a *macroenvironment*. The **microenvironment** consists of the actors close to the company that affect its ability to serve its customers – the company itself, suppliers, marketing intermediaries, customer markets, competitors and publics. The **macroenvironment** consists of the larger societal forces that affect the microenvironment – demographic, economic, natural, technological, political and cultural forces. We look first at the company's microenvironment.

Marketing environment—The actors and forces outside marketing that affect marketing management's ability to build and maintain successful relationships with target customers.

Microenvironment—The actors close to the company that affect its ability to serve its customers — the company itself, suppliers, marketing intermediaries, customer markets, competitors and publics.

Macroenvironment—The larger societal forces that affect the microenvironment — demographic, economic, natural, technological, political and cultural forces.

THE MICROENVIRONMENT

Author comment

The microenvironment includes all the actors close to the company that affect, positively or negatively, its ability to create value for, and relationships with, its customers.

Marketing management's job is to build relationships with customers by creating customer value and satisfaction. However, marketing managers cannot do this alone. Figure 3.1 shows the major actors in the marketer's microenvironment. Marketing success requires building relationships with other company departments, suppliers, marketing intermediaries, competitors, various publics and customers, which combine to compose the company's value delivery network.

The company

In designing marketing plans, marketing management must take other company groups into account – groups such as top management, finance, research and development (R&D), purchasing, operations and accounting. All of these interrelated groups form the internal environment. Top management sets the company's mission, objectives, broad strategies and policies. Marketing managers make decisions within the strategies and plans created by top management.

As we discussed in Chapter 2, marketing managers must work closely with other company departments. Other departments have an impact on the marketing department's plans and actions. With marketing taking the lead, all departments – from manufacturing and finance to legal and human resources – share the responsibility for understanding customer needs and creating customer value.

Suppliers

Suppliers form an important link in the company's overall customer value delivery network. They provide the resources needed by the company to produce its goods and services. Supplier problems can seriously affect marketing. Marketing managers must watch supply availability and costs. Supply shortages or delays, labour strikes, and other events can cost sales in the short run and damage customer satisfaction in the long run. Rising supply costs may force price increases that can harm the company's sales volume.

Most marketers today treat their suppliers as partners in creating and delivering customer value. For example, French cosmetics maker L'Oréal knows the importance of building close relationships with its extensive network of suppliers, which supply everything from polymers and fats to spray cans and packaging to production equipment and office supplies:[2]

> French company L'Oréal is the world's largest cosmetics maker, with 34 global brands ranging from Maybelline and Kiehl's to Lancôme and The Body Shop. The company's supplier network is crucial to its success. As a result, L'Oréal treats suppliers as respected partners. On the one hand, it expects a lot from suppliers in terms of design innovation, quality and sustainability. On the other hand, L'Oréal works closely with suppliers to help them meet its exacting standards. According to the company's supplier website, L'Oréal treats suppliers with 'fundamental respect for their business, their culture, their growth,

Figure 3.1 Actors in the microenvironment

In creating value for customers, marketers must partner with other firms in the company's value delivery network.

Marketers must work in harmony with other company departments to create customer value and relationships.

Customers are the most important actors in the company's microenvironment. The aim of the entire value delivery system is to serve target customers and create strong relationships with them.

and the individuals who work there'. Each relationship is based on 'dialogue and joint efforts. L'Oréal seeks not only to help its suppliers meet its expectations but also to contribute to their growth, through opportunities for innovation and competitiveness'. As a result, more than 75 per cent of L'Oréal's supplier partners have been working with the company for ten years or more, and the majority of them for several decades. Says the company's head of purchasing, 'The CEO wants to make L'Oréal a top performer and one of the world's most respected companies. Being respected also means being respected by our suppliers.'

French company L'Oréal is the world's largest cosmetics maker. The company's supplier network is crucial to its success.

Source: studiomode/Alamy Images

In the tough times of recovery from recession, many major companies have had to act to repair and protect their supply chains in Europe. For example, companies like Sainsbury's, Rolls-Royce, GlaxoSmith-Klein, Tesco, Vodafone and BT have lent money to suppliers to keep them afloat. In other cases, suppliers dropping out of business has severely limited growth in the UK motor industry, where components suppliers are the vital link in production. Managing supplier relationships closely is a particularly high priority for many industries in the current environment.[3]

Marketing intermediaries

Marketing intermediaries help the company promote, sell and distribute its products to final buyers. They include resellers, physical distribution firms, marketing services agencies and financial intermediaries. *Resellers* are distribution channel firms that help the company find customers or make sales to them. These include wholesalers and retailers who buy and resell merchandise. Selecting and partnering with resellers is not easy. No longer do manufacturers have many small, independent resellers from which to choose. They now face large and growing reseller organisations, such as Tesco in the UK, Walmart in the US, and Carrefour and Metro in Europe. In the UK for example, Tesco alone accounts for nearly one-third of all grocery sales, and the top three retailers dominate almost two-thirds of all food distribution.[4] These organisations frequently have enough power to dictate terms or even shut smaller manufacturers out of large markets.

Physical distribution firms help the company stock and move goods from their points of origin to their destinations. *Marketing services agencies* are the marketing research firms, advertising agencies, media firms and marketing consulting firms that help the company target and promote its products to the right markets. *Financial intermediaries* include banks, credit companies, insurance companies, and other businesses that help finance transactions or insure against the risks associated with the buying and selling of goods.

Like suppliers, marketing intermediaries form an important component of the company's overall value delivery network. In its quest to create satisfying customer relationships, the company must do more than just optimise its own performance. It must partner effectively with marketing intermediaries to optimise the performance of the entire system.

Thus, today's marketers recognise the importance of working with their intermediaries as partners rather than simply as channels through which they sell their products. For example, when Coca-Cola signs on as the exclusive provider for a fast-food chain, such as global chains like McDonald's, as well as smaller chains, it provides much more than just soft drinks. It also pledges powerful marketing support.[5]

Marketing intermediaries— Firms that help the company promote, sell and distribute its goods to final buyers.

Competitors

The marketing concept states that, to be successful, a company must provide greater customer value and satisfaction than its competitors do. Thus, marketers must do more than simply adapt to the needs of target consumers. They also must gain strategic advantage by positioning their offerings strongly against competitors' offerings in the minds of consumers.

No single competitive marketing strategy is best for all companies. Each firm should consider its own size and industry position compared to those of its competitors. Large firms with dominant positions in an industry can use certain strategies that smaller firms cannot afford. But being large is not enough. There are winning strategies for large firms, but there are also losing ones. And small firms can develop strategies that give them better rates of return than large firms enjoy.

Publics

Public—Any group that has an actual or potential interest in, or impact on, an organisation's ability to achieve its objectives.

The company's marketing environment also includes various publics. A **public** is any group that has an actual or potential interest in, or impact on, an organisation's ability to achieve its objectives. We can identify seven types of publics:

- *Financial publics.* This group influences the company's ability to obtain funds. Banks, investment analysts and shareholders are the major financial publics.
- *Media publics.* This group carries news, features and editorial opinion. It includes newspapers, magazines, television and radio stations, and blogs and other social media.
- *Government publics.* Management must take government developments in a country into account, as well as regulatory bodies within international groupings of countries like the European Union. Marketers must often consult the company's lawyers on issues of product safety, truth in advertising, and other matters.
- *Citizen-action publics.* Consumer organisations, environmental groups, minority groups, and others may question a company's marketing decisions. Its public relations department can help it stay in touch with consumer and citizen groups.
- *Local publics.* This group includes neighbourhood residents and community organisations. Large companies usually create departments and programmes that deal with local community issues and provide community support.
- *General public.* A company needs to be concerned about the general public's attitude toward its products and activities. The public's image of the company affects its buying.
- *Internal publics.* This group includes workers, managers, volunteers and the board of directors. Large companies use newsletters, social media, blogs, and other means to inform and motivate their internal publics. When employees feel good about the companies they work for, this positive attitude spills over to the external publics.

A company can prepare marketing plans for these major publics as well as for its customer markets. Suppose the company wants a specific response from a particular public, such as goodwill, favourable word of mouth, or donations of time or money. The company would have to design an offer to this public that is attractive enough to produce the desired response.

Customers

As we have emphasised throughout, customers are the most important actors in the company's microenvironment. The aim of the entire value delivery network is to engage target customers and create strong relationships with them. The company might target any or all five types of customer markets. *Consumer markets* consist of individuals and households that buy goods and services for personal consumption. *Business markets* buy goods and services for further processing or use in their production processes, whereas *reseller markets* buy goods and services to resell at a profit. *Government markets* consist of government agencies that buy goods and services to produce public services or transfer the goods and services to others who need them. Finally, *international markets* consist of these buyers in other countries, including consumers, producers, resellers and governments. Each market type has special characteristics that call for careful study by the seller.

THE MACROENVIRONMENT

Author comment

The macroenvironment consists of broader forces that affect the actors in the microenvironment.

The company and all its other actors operate in a larger macroenvironment of forces that shape opportunities and pose threats to the company. Figure 3.2 shows the six major forces in the company's macroenvironment. Even the most dominant companies can be vulnerable to the often turbulent and changing forces in the marketing environment. Some of these forces are unforeseeable and uncontrollable, such as the collapse in the price of oil, examined at the start of this chapter. Others can be predicted and handled through skilful management. Companies that understand and adapt well to their environments can thrive. Those that don't can face difficult times. One-time dominant market leaders such as Microsoft have learned this lesson the hard way:[6]

At the start of 2000, the total value of Microsoft's stock had hit a record $618.9 billion, making it the most valuable company in history. In those heady days, no company was more relevant than Microsoft. But moving into the new millennium, the high-tech marketing environment took a turn. PC sales growth flattened as the world fell in love with a rush of alluring new digital devices and technologies. These devices are connected and mobile, not stationary standalones like the old PCs.

In this new digitally connected world, Microsoft found itself lagging behind more glamorous competitors such as Google, Apple, Samsung, and even Amazon and Facebook, which seemed to provide all things digital — the smart devices, the connecting technologies, and even the digital destinations. In the year 2000 — due largely to the collapse of the stock market technology bubble — Microsoft's value plummeted by 60 per cent. And whereas other tech stocks recovered, Microsoft's share price and profits languished at 2000's levels for a dozen years or more.

But recently, Microsoft has begun a dramatic transformation in its vision and direction to better align itself with the new digital world order. To make this mission a reality, over the past few years, Microsoft has unleashed a flurry of new, improved, or acquired digital products and services. Over one short span, it introduced a new version of Windows that serves not just computers but also tablets and smartphones; a next-generation Xbox console; a music and movie service to rival iTunes and Google Play; an upgraded version of Skype (acquired in 2011); a SkyDrive cloud storage solution; and even an innovative new tablet – the Microsoft Surface – that it hopes will give it a firmer footing in digital devices. Perhaps Microsoft's biggest about-face is the development of its own hardware devices. Thus, Microsoft's

Perhaps Microsoft's biggest about-face is the development of its own hardware devices.
Source: Steve Sands/Getty Images

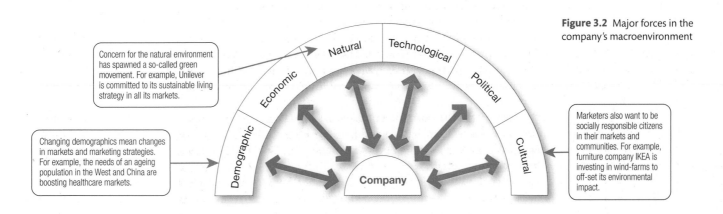

Figure 3.2 Major forces in the company's macroenvironment

Concern for the natural environment has spawned a so-called green movement. For example, Unilever is committed to its sustainable living strategy in all its markets.

Changing demographics mean changes in markets and marketing strategies. For example, the needs of an ageing population in the West and China are boosting healthcare markets.

Marketers also want to be socially responsible citizens in their markets and communities. For example, furniture company IKEA is investing in wind-farms to off-set its environmental impact.

Natural — Technological — Economic — Political — Demographic — Cultural — **Company** sweeping transformation is well under way. The company is putting a whopping $1.5 billion of marketing support behind its revamped mission and all its new software, hardware and services. Still, Microsoft has a long way to go.

In the remaining sections of this chapter, we examine these forces and show how they affect marketing plans.

The demographic environment

Demography is the study of human populations in terms of size, density, location, age, gender, race, occupation, and other statistics. The demographic environment is of major interest to marketers because it involves people, and people are the driving force for markets. The world population has grown at an explosive rate. In 2015, world population reached 7.3 billion and is expected to exceed 8 billion by the year 2030. The most populous countries are: China (1.36 billion); India (1.25 billion); United States (0.32 billion); Indonesia (0.26 billion); and Brazil (0.20 billion). By contrast, the European Union numbers 0.51 billion in population, making this trading area substantially larger than the United States, though much smaller than China and India. The largest EU countries are Germany, the United Kingdom, France and Italy, with the other 24 member states considerably smaller.[7] The world's large and highly diverse population poses both exciting opportunities and major challenges for marketers.

Changes in the world demographic environment have major implications for business. Thus, marketers must keep a close eye on demographic trends and developments in their existing and possible markets throughout the world. They need to analyse changing age and family structures, geographic population shifts, educational characteristics and population diversity. Here, we discuss some of the most important demographic trends influencing markets and marketing throughout the world.

World population growth

World population passed the 6 billion mark in 1998 to reach 7.3 billion in 2015, and is likely to double again by the end of the 21st century. But the likelihood is that only a minority of the world's new inhabitants will be born into the sort of wealth and stability that most of the developed countries take for granted. More than 70 per cent of the world's population increase over the next 40 years is expected to take place outside the world's richest 20 nations.[8]

Ever more population has been supported by economic growth, while improved nutrition, sanitation and medical care have allowed people to live increasingly long lives. Life expectancy globally was around 46 years in 1950. By 2015 it had reached an average of 71, and more than 80 in richer countries. Improvements in life expectancy have been greatest in the low-income developing countries, mainly as a result of improving health care for newborns.[9]

The new inhabitants are likely to be urban, as millions of people across the world are being drawn from rural, agricultural areas to cities, by the promise of work and economic advancement. But creaking infrastructure and overcrowding means the reality of sprawling slums, in cities such as Lagos and Mumbai, is that life there is challenging.

Traditionally high birth rates in the world's poorer countries contrast with lower birth rates and ageing populations in many developed countries, notably Japan, which places a severe strain on the next generation, many of whom will have to work longer to support their parents' retirement. Such is the concern at Russia's low birth rate that some fear its population could soon drop to a level that could destabilise the country. The United States, Europe and China share the common characteristics of ageing populations. Meanwhile, in India, a high birth rate and booming economy are expected to propel the country past China to become the most populous nation on earth by about 2030.

Nonetheless, the example of some emerging markets like Brazil suggests that the correct combination of economic growth and education can bring birth rates down to levels which are lower, but still high enough to support the country's prospects.

The changing age structure of the world's population

Changes in the world demographic environment have major implications for business. Perhaps the single most important demographic trend in the world is the changing age structure of the population. For example, India has one of the youngest population profiles in the world – more than 70 per cent of the population is under 35. By 2020, the median age in India will be 28, compared to 37 in China, 38 in the United States, 45 in western Europe and 49 in Japan.[10] If demography defines destiny, then the next century will belong to India and Africa. This is because their youthful population ensures that they will continue to enjoy a plentiful supply of young workers supporting a relatively small population of elderly people. In demographic terms, their 'dependency ratios' will be favourable. In contrast, European Union countries, the United States and China will all be carrying a growing burden because their populations are ageing and their dependency ratios will be increasingly unfavourable. Countries with unfavourable age structures have concerns about a loss of dynamism and a growing burden on public finances.[11]

Generational differences in the developed world

In the developed world, distinctions are often made between several generational groups. Here, we discuss the following groups – the baby boomers, Generation X, the Millennials and Generation Z – and their impact on today's marketing strategies. Although mainly considered in the developed markets of Europe and the United States, these generational groupings are starting to cut across many national boundaries when marketers start to think about target markets.

The baby boomers

The post-World War II **baby boomers** were born between 1946 and 1964. Over the years, the baby boomers have been one of the most powerful forces shaping the marketing environment. The youngest boomers are now in their fifties; the oldest are in their late sixties with many retiring from work. Maturing boomers are rethinking the purpose and value of their work, responsibilities and relationships.

Baby boomers—People born in the years following World War II until 1964.

After years of prosperity, free spending and saving little, economic downturn and recession hit many baby boomers hard, especially the pre-retirement boomers. A sharp decline in investment values and home values ate into their savings and retirement prospects. Nonetheless, as they reach their peak earning and spending years, the boomers will continue to constitute a lucrative market for financial services, new housing and home improvements, travel and entertainment, eating out, health and fitness products, and just about everything else. Many boomers retiring from work have pension deals which are the envy of the young and will never occur again.

Generation X

The baby boom was followed by a 'birth dearth', creating another, smaller, generation born between 1965 and 1976. Author Douglas Coupland called them **Generation X** because they lie in the shadow of the boomers and lack obvious distinguishing characteristics. Considerably smaller than the boomer generation that precedes them and the Millennials who follow, the Generation Xers are a sometimes overlooked consumer group.

Generation X—People born between 1965 and 1975 in the 'birth dearth' following the post-War baby boom.

The Generation Xers are defined as much by their shared experiences as by their age. Although they seek success, they are less materialistic than the other groups; they prize experience, not acquisition. In the developed countries, increasing parental divorce rates and higher employment for their mothers made them the first generation of latchkey kids (children who return home from school to an empty house because their parents are both at work). They tend to research products before they consider a purchase, prefer quality to quantity, and tend to be less receptive to overt marketing pitches. They were, after all, the first to grow up in the Internet era, so Generation X is a connected generation that embraces the benefits of new technology – most own smartphones and tablets, use the Internet for banking, for researching companies or products, and for making online purchases. Most are active on social media.[12]

Moxy hotels offer stylish, no-frills accommodation. But they feature plenty of the technologies that young Millennials favour.

Source: Marriott Hotels International Limited

Millennials (or Generation Y)– The children of the baby boomers born between 1977 and 2000.

Generation Z–People born after 2000 (although many analysts include people born after 1995) who make up the 'kids, tweens and teens' markets.

Millennials

Both the baby boomers and Generation Xers will one day be passing the reins to the **Millennials** (also called **Generation Y** or the echo boomers). Born between 1977 and 2000, these children of the baby boomers constitute a generation dwarfing the Generation Xers, and larger even than the baby boomer segment. In the post-recession era, the Millennials are the most financially strapped generation. Facing higher unemployment and saddled with more debt, many of these young consumers have little money. Nonetheless, in the US, some suggest that the '23-year-olds will save America' because their numbers will expand the workforce and hence the creation of economic wealth.[13] Also, because of their numbers, the Millennials make up a huge and attractive market, both now and in the future.

One thing that all the Millennials have in common is their utter fluency and comfort with digital technology. They don't just embrace technology; it's a way of life. The Millennials were the first generation to grow up in a world filled with computers, mobile phones, satellite TV, iPods and online social media. As a result, they engage with brands in an entirely new way, such as with mobile or social media. More than sales pitches from marketers, Millennials seek opportunities to shape their own brand experiences and share them with others. Thus, reaching these message-saturated consumers effectively requires highly creative marketing approaches.[14]

For example, in 2103 Marriott launched the new European hotel chain Moxy Hotels. The innovative lifestyle hotel chain targets the fast-emerging market of young Millennial travellers by combining contemporary design, approachable service, high-tech features and – perhaps most important – reasonable prices. Moxy hotels offer stylish, no-frills accommodations to keep prices down. But they feature plenty of the technologies that young Millennials favour, such as checking in via mobile devices, big screen TVs, plenty of built-in USB ports in rooms, free Wi-Fi, and 'plug and meet' common areas furnished with state-of-the-art computers, writing walls and large TV screens for presentations. Marriott is working with a range of operators and owners to grow this brand.[15]

Generation Z

Hard on the heels of the Millennials is **Generation Z**, young people born after 2000 (although many analysts include people born after 1995 in this group). The Gen Zers make up important 'kids, tweens and teens' markets. These young consumers represent tomorrow's markets – they are now forming brand relationships that will affect their buying well into the future.

Even more than the Millennials, the defining characteristic of Gen Zers is their utter fluency and comfort with digital technologies. Generation Z take smartphones, tablets, iPods, Internet-connected game consoles, wireless Internet, and digital and social media for granted – they've always had them – making this group highly mobile, connected and social. 'If they're awake, they're online,' quips one analyst. They have 'digital in their DNA,' says another.[16]

Gen Zers blend the online and offline worlds seamlessly as they socialise and shop. According to recent studies, despite their youth, more than half of all Generation Z tweens and teens do product research before buying a product, or having their parents buy it for them. Of those who shop online, more than half *prefer* shopping online in categories ranging from electronics, books, music, sports equipment and beauty products to clothes, shoes and fashion accessories.

Today's kids are notoriously hard to pin down, and they have short attention spans. The key is to engage these young consumers and let them help to define their brand experiences. Says one expert, 'Today's tweens demand a more personal, more tactile, truly up-close-and-in-person connection to their favourite brands.'[17] Another Generation Z concern involves children's privacy and their vulnerability to marketing pitches. Companies marketing to this group must do so responsibly or risk the wrath of parents and public policy makers.

Generational marketing

Do marketers need to create separate products and marketing programmes for each generation? Some experts warn that marketers need to be careful about turning off one generation each time they craft a product or message that appeals effectively to another. Others caution that each generation spans decades of time and many socioeconomic levels. For example, marketers often split the baby boomers into three smaller groups – leading-edge boomers, core boomers and trailing-edge boomers – each with its own distinctive beliefs and behaviours. Similarly, they split the Millennials into tweens, teens and young adults.

Thus, marketers need to form more precise age-specific segments within each group. More important, defining people by their birth date may be less effective than segmenting them by their lifestyle, life stage, or the common values they seek in the products they buy. We will discuss many other ways to segment markets in Chapter 7.

Changing family structures

The family unit is a basic structure underpinning social and economic behaviour in most societies, and yet is subject to several fundamental changes which challenge traditional assumptions.

New household formats

The traditional Western household consisted of husband, wife and children (and sometimes grandparents). However, in many European countries, married couples with children represent a smaller proportion of total households, while married couples without children represent a substantial group, and single-parent households another. A growing percentage are non-family households – singles living alone or adults of one or both sexes living together. More people are divorcing or separating, choosing not to marry, marrying later, or marrying without intending to have children. Marketers must increasingly consider the special needs of non-traditional households because they are now growing more rapidly than traditional households. Each group has distinctive needs and buying habits.

Social trends are important to marketing planning. Sometimes trends may be surprising. In 2015, for example, there appeared to be a boom in large families in the UK again – homes with four children or more are at the highest level for 45 years. This appears to be the impact of a changing ethnic composition of the British population and more super-rich families opting for large families. Nonetheless, overall family sizes are falling in Britain, as they are across Europe.[18]

Singletons

Euromonitor estimates that the number of people living alone worldwide is increasing dramatically – in 2011 the global population of singletons had reached 277 million and this is expected to rise to 331 million by 2020, or around 16 per cent of all households. In Europe and North America single-person households already stand at 31 per cent and 28 per cent of all households. Driving factors include greater female employment, higher divorce rates, longevity and mass urbanisation, as well as lifestyle choices made by individuals who simply prefer living alone.

Experian divides the demographic of single people into: *Starting Out Singletons* – younger people who own or rent and are reasonably affluent; *Struggling Singletons* – aged 18 to 25 years, the least affluent and unlikely to own a home or car; *Suddenly Singletons* – affluent executives in their early 40s with high incomes, probably divorced, who eat out regularly and have a busy lifestyle; and, *Solus Singletons* – mainly elderly people living on private pensions, who have down-sized to live in small flats. Companies are trying to catch up with the diverse social and shopping habits of the single household, by moving away from family-focused brands and ad campaigns, but have to recognise diversity in needs and buying preferences within the singleton population.[19]

Working women

The number of women in paid employment outside the home has also increased greatly in most European nations. In a seismic shift in the British family structure, the number of mothers who are full-time homemakers has halved, while the number of couples who are both in full-time work has doubled since the 1960s and 1970s.[20] Both husband and wife work in the majority of all married-couple families. Meanwhile, more men are staying home with their children, managing the household while their wives go to work. This trend has been amplified by rising male unemployment in economic recession – economic reality meant for many households that as men coped with unemployment, their wives headed back to work.[21]

The significantly increased number of women in the workforce has spawned the childcare business and increased the consumption of career-oriented women's clothing, financial services, and convenience foods and services. Indeed, it has been pointed out that as a market women represent a bigger opportunity than China and India combined, yet despite their dominant buying power many companies market mainly to men and fail to explore how they might meet women's needs beyond the simplistic and patronising 'make it pink' reaction.[22] Part of the challenge is that as more women balance a job with raising children, they struggle to find free time, so time-saving shopping and buying processes are vital.[23]

Innovative gender-oriented marketing strategies are not restricted to adults. LEGO, manufacturer of the famous plastic bricks for children, is building its growth strategy around selling to girls as well as boys. Female children have the same instinct for building as boys, but favour role-play as well. LEGO Friends introduces new colours and mini-figures and encourages children to create scenarios for storytelling, rather than just create the model pictured on the box. LEGO Friends is the company's most strategic launch in decades.[24]

The youth market

One significant change in family units in many European countries has been that young people are remaining at home with their parents far longer than in the past – in the UK the proportion of 20- to 34-year-olds living at home rose to 26 per cent in 2014, amounting to 3.3 million adults still living with their parents.[25] In most European countries, the real disposable income of people in their 20s has stagnated over the past ten years, and these younger people are unlikely to ever match their parents' living standards.[26]

In fact, demographic change suggests a decline in the size of the youth market in Europe in coming years. Also, harsh economic conditions in many Western countries have seen a dramatic rise of long-term unemployment among young people – the educated and jobless young – associated with driving unrest in the Middle East and undermining society in Europe and the US. The continuing jobs crisis is in danger of creating a 'lost generation' of long-term unemployed across the developed world. In the UK, jobless rates among young people are escalating. Youth unemployment in Africa and the Arab world also risks exporting tensions to Europe – as an ageing, relatively rich and socially conservative region acts as a magnet for young workers, many of them illegal immigrants, from across the Mediterranean.[27]

In the UK, young adults, who for most of the twentieth century enjoyed living standards well above average, have been displaced by the rise of comfortably off pensioners in the most dramatic generational change in decades. The relative living standards of the young and the old have changed places. This is a generation for which education has failed to bring the social mobility achieved by the older generation.[28]

Older consumers and workers

The corollary to a declining youth market is that in the United States and many European countries, people have to continue working beyond what was once considered retirement age. Older people may have failed to plan well, may have earned a lot but saved little, may have suffered financial losses in the economic downturn, or longer lives may have simply depleted savings. In the UK, the number of older workers past traditional retirement age has doubled in 20 years – driven not just by income needs but by the desire for status as employed people.[29]

It is estimated that by 2050 the percentage of population aged over 60 will be 27 per cent in the US, 35 per cent in the UK, and 43 per cent in Japan, reflecting longer life expectancy and falling birth rates – those over 65 will outnumber children under 5 years of age. This demographic shift is creating a new and powerful consumer class, already being called 'the silver economy', with spending power already reaching $15 trillion.[30]

Geographic shifts in population and market diversity

This is a time of considerable migratory movement both between and within countries. For example, in the UK there has been a general shift of population from the North to the South – mainly as people search for work – and the share of England's population living in the North is at its lowest for 200 years.[31] Such population shifts interest marketers because they indicate where their customers are located and their changing needs and buying priorities. However, migration on a global scale, rather than within countries, has even bigger implications for marketers.

Migration

For a variety of reasons, the world's migrant population is rising fast. Currently, about 3 per cent of the world's population live outside the country of their birth. Indeed, economic recession of the late 2000s led to that number falling slightly, as poor economic growth in host countries led some migrants to head home. However, United Nations figures suggest that this amounts to a global population of international migrants of 232 million.[32] Indeed, global migrant flows look set to double by 2050.[33]

The US is the largest destination for migrants (a population of about 46 million people in 2014), while within the EU the countries hardest hit by the recession, such as Greece and Spain, have seen net emigration in recent years, while stronger economies like the UK and Germany have attracted more migrants.[34] Nonetheless, 2014 saw the number of Britons living abroad reach 5 million for the first time, with Australia and the US the biggest draws.[35] Migration impacts both on the location of market demand – where people can be reached – and the nature of demand for products and services – the needs of people in new situations.

Higher migrant flows will partly be a matter of choice – fast-ageing advanced economies face a looming labour shortage of potentially as many as 100 million workers by 2050, and much of that shortfall will probably be met by increased immigration. For example, in the UK, in 2015 around 16 per cent of the workforce – almost 5 million people – was overseas workers, up from 7 per cent in 1997, covering gaps in many areas of employment.[36] But alongside these factors, other issues will push migrants out from developing nations. For example, Africa faces particular challenges – by 2050, the continent's population will have doubled to 1.8 billion, many of whom will struggle to find economic opportunities at home.

Key pressure points for migration include the following:

- **Europe** – geographic proximity and economic pull ensures Europe remains on the frontline of migration flows. To maintain a stable 'dependency ratio' between working and non-working population, Europe may have to admit 1.3 billion migrants by 2050.
- **Russia and the Caucasus** – Russia is the world's second largest migrant destination with up to 15 million incomers propping up its declining population. In averting a demographic crisis, Russia has created an ethnic one, with migrants facing a nationalist backlash. As many as a third of Russia's professional class also want to leave the country.

- **China's periphery** – China's vast population, hunger for resources and willingness to deploy labour in neighbouring countries is causing disquiet around its borders. Russian nationalists fear encroachments from the south by an influx of Chinese.
- **US/Mexico border** – America's southern frontier is one of the world's most militarised borders – $8 billion has been spent on fences, sensors and surveillance drones to stop migrants from the south. Mexico suffers the consequences, with people movement, drugs and criminal violence destabilising many provinces.
- **Sub-Saharan Africa** – About 18 per cent of the world's population live in dry zones. But environmental migrants are more likely to move to poor neighbouring countries, rather than more distant advanced economies. The effect is large flows of people into the countries least able to cope, such as Somali refugees spilling over the border into Kenya.
- **UAE/Middle East** – The desert states of the Middle East top the league of nations most densely populated by migrants. Qatar and the United Arab Emirates both have populations where more than seven in ten are foreign-born – including large, marginalised groups from south Asia.
- **Mega-cities** – Karachi in Pakistan has been dubbed the world's most dangerous city, with its 15 million residents beset by an explosive mixture of poverty, ethnic violence, crime and ineffective governance. The city offers a worrying vision of where other sprawling global mega-cities, such as Kinshasa and Lagos, may be heading.
- **Remittances** – Remittances (cash sent home by migrant workers) are an increasingly important factor in global development, providing emerging markets with vital capital flows. Some nations are increasingly dependent on these flows – in the Philippines, Moldova and Tajikastan, for example, remittances make up nearly half of GDP.[37]

Dramatic moves in migrant worker flows continue. In 2012, because of its underlying economic problems particularly in the property and construction sectors, Spain saw an exodus of workers leaving to work in other countries. As well as relocating in other European countries, larger numbers of Spanish workers headed for Brazil, Africa and the United States. The Spanish exodus includes many skilled professional workers. For the first time since 1990, in 2011 more people left Spain than moved in.[38]

Ethnic diversity in markets

Certainly, population movements create interesting opportunities for marketing specialised products and services to ethnic groups within a country. For example, Mecca Cola, a pro-Muslim alternative to other colas, that capitalises on anti-American sentiment, sold 300,000 litres in its first two weeks on sale in Britain.[39] Mecca Cola sells successfully to its market niche in the Arab world, many European regions and the United States and Canada. In another example, in London, high-end stores, such as Burberry and Christian Dior, and retailers like Marks & Spencer, Primark and H&M all report the benefits of an annual 'Ramadan rush' – gift buying around the Muslim holy month of Ramadan and the Eid al-Fitr celebration. London retailers make particular efforts to appeal to Muslim shoppers during Ramadan and Eid – a season now second only to Christmas in revenues.[40]

More broadly, the UK is seeing the development of 'super-diverse' cities where no single ethnic group will provide the majority. This pluralism encompasses places like Leicester, Birmingham, Slough, Luton and many of the London boroughs. However, it is anticipated that immigrant and ethnic minority populations will not be dominated by the currently strong Afro-Caribbean or Asian communities, but increasing numbers will come from countries scattered across the world.

It is telling that in the United States, the spending power of African American, Asian and most particularly Hispanic consumers has become pivotal for many firms. For example, Procter & Gamble is aiming to turn its Gain cleaning products range into a mega-brand, largely on the basis of the appeal of the heavier scented products to the Hispanic consumer.[41]

For multinational brands, the challenge is transferring brand experiences and lessons about consumer preferences from Mexico and Russia to reach Hispanics in Albuquerque and Russians in Brighton Beach in the US.[42] In 2012, US new births crossed the 'majority-minority' threshold for the first time – whites of European ancestry accounted for less than half of newborn children, marking a demographic tipping point that is already changing the country's economy and workforce.[43]

Interesting new markets are developing which recognise the importance of ethnic and religious differences between consumers, within and across countries. For example, fashion designers in Turkey are leading the way in attempting to convey fashion which does not infringe on Muslim values. *Ala* in Turkey is the first fashion publication for conservative Muslim women. The editor says: 'We are trying to convey international fashion to ladies without infringing on our values.' The magazine and designers concentrate on the needs of affluent women who lack information about Islamic designers, because Muslim fashion has traditionally been a word-of-mouth industry.[44]

Britain's vibrant expatriate Polish community has provided a new market for many sellers.
Source: Christopher Furlong/ Getty Images

Similarly, in the UK, migrant workers, largely from within the European Union, are changing the consumer market rapidly and providing marketers with new opportunities. In 2015, the Oxford University Migration Observatory estimated that one in eight of the UK population were people born overseas, underlining the growing diversity and richness of the British community, and suggesting the emergence of many new market opportunities.[45] For example, the vibrant Polish immigrant community has seen a Polish radio station launched, road signs in Polish, banks like NatWest offering a dedicated account for Polish customers, supermarkets Tesco and Asda stocking wide ranges of Polish delicacies which are advertised in the burgeoning UK-based Polish language media, and estate agents advertising properties for sales and rent in the Polish language.[46]

Recognising other aspects of diversity in markets

Diversity goes beyond ethnic heritage. For example, many major companies explicitly target gay and lesbian consumers. Increasing marketing attention is being paid to the role of the gay buyer in the property market. The gay community provides an attractive target of affluent buyers, often with double-income households, and high property ownership. The gay community is also one of the most enthusiastic about buying holiday homes abroad. Research suggests these trends are developing in most of the liberal Western democracies. As a market segment, there are specialist media such as gay lifestyle magazines offering access to this community.[47]

Another interesting diversity segment is adults with disabilities. In the United States, there are nearly 60 million US adults with disabilities – comprising a market larger than African Americans or Hispanics, and representing more than $200 billion in annual spending power. Most individuals with disabilities are active consumers. For example, one study found that more than two-thirds of adults with disabilities had travelled at least once for business or pleasure during the preceding two years. Thirty-one per cent had booked at least one flight, more than half had stayed in hotels, and 20 per cent had rented a car. More than 75 per cent of people with disabilities dine out at least once a week.[48]

How are companies trying to reach consumers with disabilities? Many marketers now recognise that the worlds of people with disabilities and those without disabilities are one and the same. Marketers such as McDonald's, Nike and Honda have all featured people with disabilities in their mainstream advertising. For instance, Samsung and Nike sign endorsement deals with Paralympic athletes and feature them in advertising.

As the population within an individual country or a region like Europe grows more diverse, successful marketers will continue to diversify their marketing programmes to take advantage of opportunities in fast-growing segments.

Urbanisation of population

In addition to flows of population between nations, there are significant movements within countries. There is, for example, a continued trend towards the movement of people from rural to urban areas. Evidence suggests that 500 million farmers will move to cities over the next 50 years, creating pressure on already teeming cities like Mumbai, Delhi, Dhaka and Shanghai (each expected to be home to more than 20 million people), as well as Kinshasa, Cairo and Lagos (each expected to contain more than 15 million people). In three decades China has been transformed into a mainly urban society by the movement of people from rural areas to the cities.[49]

In most developed countries, the shift in where people live has also often caused a shift in where they work. For example, the migration toward suburban areas has resulted in a rapid increase in the number of people who 'telecommute' – work at home or in a remote office and conduct their business by phone, fax, modem or the Internet. This trend, in turn, has created a booming small office/home office market. An increasing number of people are working from home with the help of electronic conveniences such as PCs, smartphones and broadband Internet access.

Many marketers are actively courting the lucrative telecommuting market. For example, WebEx, the web-conferencing division of Cisco, helps overcome the isolation that often accompanies telecommuting. With WebEx, people can meet and collaborate online via computer or smartphone, no matter what their work location. 'All you need to run effective online meetings is a browser and a phone,' says the company. With WebEx, people working anywhere can interact with other individuals or small groups to make presentations, exchange documents and share desktops, complete with audio and full-motion video.[50]

The economic environment

Markets require buying power as well as people. The **economic environment** consists of economic factors that affect consumer purchasing power and spending patterns. Marketers must pay close attention to major trends and consumer spending patterns both across and within their world markets.

The changing world order

Nations vary greatly in their levels and distribution of income. Some countries have *industrial economies*, which constitute rich markets for many different kinds of goods. At the other extreme are *subsistence economies*; they consume most of their own agricultural and industrial output and may offer few immediate market opportunities. In between are *developing economies* that can offer outstanding marketing opportunities for the right kinds of products.

Incomes, as measured by Gross Domestic Product per capita, show huge variation around the world. The average for the whole world in 2014 calculated by the International Monetary Fund is only just over $15,000. The Western economies are much higher – for example, United States, $54,600, Germany, $45,900, France $40,375, United Kingdom $39,500. The emerging markets are much lower than the West – for example, Russia $24,800, Brazil $16,100, China $12,900 and India $5,900.[51] Obviously, the distribution of income within countries also varies. But income levels and trends are an important factor in assessing market value and attractiveness.

However, it is also important to understand that the economic world order has been subject to important and major changes in the 21st century, particularly regarding the impact of emerging markets like India and China. The term 'BRIC' (Brazil, Russia, India, China) is often used to describe the leading group of newly rich and rapidly expanding countries, but in reality the group is much larger than this and their characteristics are increasingly shared by countries like South Africa, Indonesia, Mexico, and others. Interestingly, the degree of change is illustrated by the fact that there are now more individuals who are dollar-billionaires in the BRIC countries than there are in Europe.[52] Nonetheless, the paradox is that while the BRIC countries contribute more than half the world's growth, relative to population, they remain poor: estimates are that GDP per capita in 2014 in the BRIC countries was around $8,654, compared to $45,780 in the G7 countries.[53]

The impact of economic change at this level should not be underestimated. Recent years have seen an end to Western dominance of the global economy. In 2014, International Monetary Fund figures showed that China had overtaken the US as the world's largest economy, though China was unenthusiastic about revealing this fact.[54] Statistics in 2012 from the Centre for Economics and Business Research in London show Brazil in sixth place had overtaken the UK on that list. The same study suggests that by 2020, no European economy will be in the world top 20.

Interestingly, history repeats itself – the US reign as largest world economic power began a little before 1890, when it supplanted the previous global giant: China. Throughout the 2000s the annual real growth in China's gross domestic product averaged 10.5 per cent compared to 1.7 per cent in the US in the same period, although some economists are sceptical about China's ability to maintain this rate of growth.[55] Nonetheless, by 2010, China was exporting as much every six hours as it did in the whole of 1978.[56] Economic change of this magnitude has clear implications for consumer buying power – millions of Chinese have entered the 'consumer class' for the first time.[57]

For example, it is estimated that the top five grocery markets in the world in order of value are: China, the US, India, Russia and Brazil, with the US showing lower growth than the others. Correspondingly, the five largest worldwide grocery retailers (Walmart, Carrefour, Tesco, CostCo and Metro) – two American and three European companies – have been looking for aggressive growth strategies in these high-growth, expanding markets, while defending their home market position. Nonetheless, these are fiercely competitive markets for international retailers to tackle and success in the home market does not guarantee success in these emerging markets.[58]

In fact, by 2015, there was some disappointment in the economic performance of the BRIC countries, and fears that earlier expectations had been over-optimistic. Brazil and Russia are floundering economically, there are doubts about India's ability to sustain growth, and there has been a dramatic slowdown in the Chinese economy. In 2013, China and India together accounted for half of all economic expansion in the world, but the BRICs are no longer seen as the engine of economic growth. While emerging markets show higher growth rates than most Western economies, they are slowing down compared to previous highs.[59]

Emerging markets outside the BRIC grouping are doing better – countries like Mexico, Nigeria and Thailand are outperforming the BRICs – indeed, the key group may now be the MINTS (Mexico, Indonesia, Nigeria, Turkey).[60]

In 2015, for example, the slowdown in the Chinese economy, and government actions to devalue the currency, reduce interest rates and protect the stock market led to a global panic and drop in share values – a trillion dollars wiped off shares across the world. Shares in companies relying on demand in China fell dramatically – Burberry selling high-end fashion to Chinese consumers, Diageo selling drinks, and miners, all saw shares fall dramatically in value.[61] Economics developments in the new world order are critical to marketing products and services and they may not always be favourable developments.

Nonethless, there is no doubt that the impact of economic change, the shift in the balance of power in the world economy, and new patterns of globalisation are disrupting and reshaping whole industrial sectors. For example, in the car-making sector, long dominated by US and Japanese manufacturers: Fiat from Italy has taken over US car giant Chrysler;[62] Volkswagen in Germany overtook Toyota and General Motors in vehicle sales to lead the sector prior to its emissions scandal;[63] and the world's cheapest car, though not selling well, is the Nano produced by Tata Motors in India, selling for around $2,000 with ambitions to tap into the European and US markets.[64]

Changes in consumer spending

Importantly, economic factors can have a dramatic effect on consumer spending and buying behaviour. For example, until fairly recently, American and European consumers spent freely, fuelled by income growth, easily available credit, a boom in the investment market, rapid increases in house values, and other economic good fortune. They bought and bought, seemingly without caution, amassing record levels of debt. However, the free spending and high expectations of those days were dashed by the economic downturn, credit squeeze and recession of the late 2000s and early 2010s. Having led the way in voluntary reduction of spending deficits, the UK has entered a period of extreme austerity and is looking at a prolonged period of economic near-stagnation and high unemployment numbers.[65]

Budget retailers like Aldi, Lidl, Poundland and Primark have been successful in growing business during economic downturn.

Source: Simon Dawson/ Bloomberg via Getty Images

As a result, as discussed in Chapter 1, consumers have now adopted a back-to-basics frugality in their lifestyles and spending patterns that will most likely persist for years to come. They are buying less and looking for greater value in the things that they do buy. In turn, *value marketing* has become the watchword for many marketers. Marketers in all industries are looking for ways to offer today's more financially cautious buyers greater value – just the right combination of product quality and good service at a fair price.

In many markets in the Western world the new 'normal' for consumers has become one of thrift and caution in spending, and a new 'age of austerity'. Shoppers are suffering from what Bain & Co. are calling 'luxury shame', and feeling guilty about buying indulgences. Add a scepticism and lack of trust in business, and the potential is for long-term shifts in consumer behaviour away from consumption towards austerity.[66] The 'Great Recession' has been followed by the 'New Caution', changing spending habits and lowering future growth.[67]

But some companies have prospered in harsher economic conditions. Budget retailers like Aldi, Lidl, Poundland and Primark have been successful in growing business during economic downturn, with the intention of retaining the new customers they have acquired from more expensive competitors. Successful marketing strategies in this new reality will depend on a deep understanding of how economic conditions have influenced consumer choices.

Income distribution

Marketers should pay attention to *income distribution* as well as income levels. Even within the UK, the richest 10 per cent of households hold 44 per cent of all wealth and the poorest 50 per cent own just 9.5 per cent. The UK has a very high level of income inequality compared to the other developed countries – people in the bottom 10 per cent of the population have an average net income of £8,468, while the top 10 per cent have incomes almost ten times that (£79,042). Income is also spread unevenly across the UK's regions – the average household income in London is considerably higher than that in the North East, for example.[68]

One key to understanding demand in emerging markets like India, Africa and China is the growth of an affluent middle class with high disposable income and the willingness to spend. Nonetheless, while growing affluence characterises the emerging markets and provides important targets, for example for luxury brands like high-end motor cars and fashion clothing, this affluence tends to be concentrated in a relatively small proportion of the population. Across the world it is usual than the poorest half of the population controls less than half of the country's wealth, and deepening income inequality is a particular concern in India and China.[69] There are also major differences between the different emerging markets – for example the poor of China are substantially better off than the poor of India.

The new wealthy in the emerging markets are an attractive target for luxury brands like Versace, LVMH, Cartier and Coach, because these countries have a rapidly growing number of affluent people. Luxury property, furnishings and luxury cars dominate the spending profiles of the new rich. But not only are their purchase priorities different to those of the wealthy in other markets, they are much younger. However, emerging markets also have the largest income gap between rich and poor – it appears that with high economic growth, the rich are getting richer faster than the poor, increasing income inequality.

Unevenness in the distribution of income in a country creates a tiered market. For example, many retail fashion companies – such as Harrods and Harvey Nichols – aggressively target the very affluent. Others – such as Primark and Matalan – target those with more modest means. In fact, budget retailers are now the fastest-growing retailers in the UK. Still other companies tailor their marketing offers across a range of markets, from the affluent to the less affluent. Car-makers like Volkswagen excel in offering low-priced cars (such as under the Skoda brand) and very high priced vehicles (Audi in the mass market and Bentley in the prestige market).

Changes in major economic variables, such as income, cost of living, interest rates, and savings and borrowing patterns have a large impact on the marketplace. Companies watch these variables through economic forecasting. Businesses do not have to be wiped out by an economic downturn or caught short in a boom. With adequate warning, they can take advantage of changes in the economic environment. However, marketers must maintain constant vigilance for significant changes in this turbulent economic environment.

The natural environment

The **natural environment** involves the natural resources that are needed as inputs by marketers or that are affected by marketing activities. At the most basic level, unexpected happenings in the physical environment – anything from weather to natural disasters – can affect companies and their marketing strategies. The damage caused by the recent earthquake and tsunami in Japan had a devastating effect on the ability of Japanese companies such as Sony and Toyota to meet worldwide demand for their products. Although companies can't prevent such natural occurrences, they should prepare contingency plans for dealing with them.

At the broadest level, environmental concerns have grown steadily over the past three decades. In many cities around the world, air and water pollution have reached dangerous levels. World concern continues to mount about the possibilities of global warming, and many environmentalists fear that we soon will be buried in our own rubbish.

Marketers should be aware of several trends in the natural environment. The first involves growing *shortages of raw materials*. Air and water may seem to be infinite resources, but some groups see long-run dangers. Air pollution chokes many of the world's large cities, and water shortages are already a big problem in many parts of the world. By 2030, more than one in three of the world's population will not have enough water to drink.[70]

Renewable resources, such as forests and food, also have to be used wisely. Non-renewable resources, such as oil, coal and various minerals, pose a serious problem. Firms making products that require these scarce resources face large cost increases, even if the materials remain available.

A second environmental trend is *increased pollution*. Industry will almost always damage the quality of the natural environment. Consider the disposal of chemical and nuclear waste; the dangerous mercury levels in the ocean; the quantity of chemical pollutants in the soil and food supply; and the littering of the environment with non-biodegradable bottles, plastics and other packaging materials.

A third trend is *increased government intervention* in natural resource management. The governments of different countries vary in their concern and efforts to promote a clean environment. Some, such as the German government, vigorously pursue environmental quality policies and sanctions. Others, especially many poorer nations, do little about pollution, largely because they lack the needed funds or political will. Even richer nations lack the vast funds and political accord needed to mount a worldwide environmental effort. The general hope is that companies around the world will accept more social responsibility and that less expensive devices can be found to control and reduce pollution.

In many countries business faces increased regulation and pressure from lobby groups to behave more responsibly towards the natural environment. Instead of opposing regulation, marketers should help develop solutions to the material and energy problems facing the world.

Concern for the natural environment has spawned the so-called 'green movement'. Today, enlightened companies go beyond what government regulations dictate at home or abroad. They

Author comment
Today's enlightened companies are developing *environmentally sustainable* strategies in an effort to create a world economy that the planet can support indefinitely.

Natural environment—The physical environment and natural resources that are needed as inputs by marketers or are affected by marketing activities.

Environmental sustainability—Developing strategies and practices that create a world economy that the planet can support indefinitely.

are developing strategies and practices that support **environmental sustainability** – an effort to create a world economy that the planet can support indefinitely. They are responding to consumer demands with more environmentally responsible products. Environmental sustainability means meeting present needs without compromising the ability of future generations to meet their needs.

Many companies are responding to consumer demands with more environmentally responsible products. Others are developing recyclable or biodegradable packaging, recycled materials and components, better pollution controls and more energy-efficient operations. For example, GE is using its 'ecomagination' initiative to create products for a better world – cleaner aircraft engines, cleaner locomotives, cleaner fuel technologies. In the period 2005–2014, on the back of a $15 billion R&D spend on green technology, GE's ecomagination has generated $200 billion in additional revenue, and grown four times faster than the rest of GE. Across customer operations and its own, GE's project has reduced emissions by 31 per cent and fresh water use by 42 per cent, and the initiative is accelerating in the period up to 2020. Green engineering has become a hotly contested competition between GE and rival Siemens in Germany as to which has the greener technology, benefiting the environment and company performance.[71]

Other companies are developing recyclable or biodegradable packaging, recycled materials and components, better pollution controls and more energy-efficient operations. Companies today are looking to do more than just good deeds. More and more, they are recognising the link between a healthy ecology and a healthy economy. They are learning that environmentally responsible actions can also be good business.

But the pivotal issue is the alignment between environmental issues and customer perceptions of value. For example, the car-making business has been under pressure to respond to environmental concerns, and has done so. *Hybrid* vehicles (combining electric and conventional fuel-powered engines) like the Toyota Prius are growing in popularity to some extent but account for less than 3 per cent of the global car market, because of their high price compared to conventional cars. *Electric* vehicles are now being offered by most large car groups – Nissan's new Leaf has been made in Sunderland since 2013 – but carmakers admit their limited ranges and higher prices will restrict sales. *Biofuels* to power cars have lost support because of environmental concerns on how the fuel is produced – though many big carmakers have cars that run on biofuels, and those than run on ethanol are a big market segment in sugar-rich Brazil. *Hydrogen fuel* cells have great future promise because they have zero exhaust emissions and can cover long distances – but there are environmental problems in producing the fuel and refuelling stations are expensive, limiting the number of vehicles likely to be sold. In fact, *engine downsizing* is one of the most cost-effective ways of cutting emissions, though lacking the glamour of new technologies – the UK government supported Ford's recent investment in a new generation of fuel-efficient engines in Britain. Nonetheless, sales of electric cars were so poor, that at one point there were more charging points in the UK than there were electric cars on the road, in spite of a government scheme offering grants towards the purchase of electric cars.[72]

Marketers face the important challenge of developing and implementing environmentally responsible products and ways of doing business, while at the same time focusing on customer needs and preferences. It is important to identify the link between socially responsible business practices and the creation of superior customer value.[73]

The technological environment

Author comment

Technological advances are perhaps the most dramatic forces affecting today's marketing strategies. Just think about the tremendous impact on marketing of digital technologies – which have exploded in only the last dozen years or so. You'll see examples of the fast-growing world of online, mobile and social media marketing throughout every chapter, and we'll discuss them in detail in Chapter 17.

Technological environment—Forces that create new technologies, creating new product and market opportunities.

The **technological environment** is perhaps the most dramatic force now shaping our destiny. Technology has released such wonders as antibiotics, robotic surgery, miniaturised electronics, smartphones and the Internet. It also has released such horrors as nuclear missiles, chemical weapons and assault rifles. It has released such mixed blessings as the motor car, television and credit cards. Our attitude toward technology depends on whether we are more impressed with its wonders or its blunders.

New technologies can offer exciting opportunities for marketers. For example, what would you think about having tiny little transmitters implanted in all the products you buy, which would allow tracking of the products from their point of production through use and disposal? Or how about a bracelet with a chip inserted that would let you make and pay for purchases, receive personalised special offers at the shops, or even track your whereabouts or those of friends? On the one hand, it would provide many advantages to both buyers and sellers. On the other hand, it could be a bit scary. Either way, it's already happening, thanks to radio-frequency identification (RFID) transmitters that can be embedded in the products you buy.

Many firms are already using RFID technology to track products through various points in the distribution channel. For example, in the US Walmart has strongly encouraged suppliers shipping products to its distribution centres to apply RFID tags to their pallets. Other retailers use RFID to manage stock in retail stores – every stocked item carries an RFID tag, which is scanned at the receiving docks as the item goes into stock. When the item is sold, a point-of-sale RFID reader alerts the inventory system and prompts employees to bring a replacement onto the shop floor. Another RFID reader located between the stockroom and the store floor checks to see that this was done. In all, the system creates inventory efficiencies and ensures that the right items are always on the sales floor. Fashion and accessories maker Burberry even uses chips embedded in items and linked to smartphones to provide personalised, interactive experiences for customers in its stores and at runway shows.[74]

And Disney is taking RFID technology to new levels with its cool new MagicBand RFID wristband:[75]

> Wearing a MagicBand at The Walt Disney World Resort opens up a whole new level of Disney's famed magic. After registering for cloud-based MyMagic+ services, with the flick of your wrist you can enter a park or attraction, buy dinner or souvenirs, or even unlock your hotel room. But Disney has only begun to tap the MagicBand's potential for personalising guest experiences. Future applications could be truly magical. Imagine, for example, the wonder of a child who receives a warm hug from Mickey Mouse, or a bow from Prince Charming, who then greets the child by name and wishes her a happy birthday. Imagine animatronics that interact with nearby guests based on personal information supplied in advance. You get separated from family or friends? No problem. A quick scan of your MagicBand at a nearby directory could pinpoint the locations of your entire party. Linked to your Disney phone app, the MagicBand could trigger in-depth information about park features, ride wait times, FastPass check-in alerts, and your reservations schedule. Of course, the MagicBand also offers Disney a potential treasure of digital data on guest activities and movements in minute detail, helping to improve guest logistics, services, and sales. If all this seems too invasive, there will be privacy options — for example, letting parents opt out of things like characters knowing children's names. In all, such digital technologies promise to enrich the Disney experience for both guests and the company.

The technological environment changes rapidly. Think of all of today's common products that were not available until recently. Two hundred years ago, people did not know about motor cars, airplanes, radios or the electric light. A hundred years ago, no one knew about television, aerosol cans, automatic dishwashers, air conditioners, antibiotics or computers. Seventy-five years ago, people did not know about photocopying, synthetic detergents, birth control pills, jet engines or Earth satellites. Fifty years ago, people did not know about PCs, mobile phones, the Internet or Google, and twenty-five years ago no one knew about smartphones or social media.

New technologies create new markets and opportunities. However, every new technology replaces an older technology. Transistors hurt the vacuum-tube industry, digital photography hurt the film and camera business, and digital downloads and streaming are hurting the CD and DVD businesses. When old industries fought or ignored new technologies, their businesses declined. Thus, marketers should watch the technological environment closely. Companies that do not keep up will soon find their products outdated. And they will miss new product and market opportunities.

Today's research usually is carried out by research teams rather than by lone inventors like Thomas Edison or Alexander Graham Bell. Many companies are adding marketing people to R&D teams to try to obtain a stronger marketing orientation. Scientists also speculate on fantasy products, such as flying cars and space colonies. The challenge in each case is not only technical but also commercial – to make *practical*, *affordable* versions of these products. For example, Google runs a radical ideas factory – known as the coolest skunkworks in Silicon Valley – called the Advanced Technology and Projects group to explore ideas as diverse as wearable technology, new forms of virtual reality, artificial intelligence and the secrets of ageing.[76]

Naturally, as products and technology become more complex, the public needs to know that these are safe. Many countries have created agencies and complex regulations to ban potentially unsafe products, and to establish safety standards for consumer products and penalise companies that fail to meet them. This growing regulation has resulted in higher research and development costs and longer times between new product ideas and their introduction. Marketers should be aware of these regulations when applying new technologies and developing new products.

The political and social environment

Marketing decisions are strongly affected by developments in the political environment. The **political environment** consists of laws, government and transnational agencies, and pressure groups that influence or limit various organisations and individuals in a given society.

Legislation regulating business

Even the most liberal advocates of free-market economies agree that the system works best with at least some regulation. Well-conceived regulation can encourage competition and ensure fair markets for goods and services. Thus, governments develop *public policy* to guide commerce – sets of laws and regulations that limit business for the good of society as a whole – and may go further in exerting influence over business actions. Almost every marketing activity is subject to a wide range of laws, regulations and government influence. In Europe much of that regulation now emanates from Brussels, where the European Union imposes an escalating volume of directives and regulation on member states.

Increasing legislation

Legislation affecting business around the world has increased dramatically over the years. Many countries now have a large number of laws covering issues such as competition, fair trade practices, environmental protection, product safety, truth in advertising, consumer privacy, packaging and labeling, pricing and other important areas. For example, the European Commission has been active in establishing a new framework of laws covering competitive behaviour, product standards, product liability and commercial transactions for the nations of the European Union, in addition to those countries' own legislation.

Understanding the public policy implications of a particular marketing activity is not a simple matter. Moreover, regulations are constantly changing – what was allowed last year may now be prohibited, and what was prohibited may now be allowed. Marketers must work hard to keep up with changes in regulations and their interpretations.

Business legislation is enacted for a number of reasons. The first is to *protect companies* from each other. Although business executives may praise competition, they sometimes try to neutralise it when it threatens them. So laws are passed to define and prevent unfair competition.

The second purpose of government regulation is to *protect consumers* from unfair business practices. Some firms, if left alone, would make shoddy products, invade consumer privacy, mislead consumers in their advertising, and deceive consumers through their packaging and pricing. Unfair business practices have been defined and regulations are enforced by various agencies.

The third purpose of government regulation is to *protect the interests of society* against unrestrained business behaviour. Profitable business activity does not always create a better quality of life. Regulation arises to ensure that firms take responsibility for the social costs of their production or products.

Political environment—Laws, government and transnational agencies, and pressure groups that influence and limit various organisations and individuals in a given society.

In other cases, laws exist to pursue and enforce *government policy* – the sanctions against Russia because of its incursions in the Ukraine; the Chinese government's crack-down on bribery and marketing transgressions, and control of Internet access; the Indian government's desire to control inward investment and prevent the take-over of domestic firms by foreigners.

For example, IKEA in Sweden is keen to develop its furnishings business in India. In spite of local political controversy, after much wavering the Indian government has recently decided to allow foreign retailers to enter the country. The potential of the Indian market is attractive to many global retailers, including IKEA. Indeed, Mikael Ohlsson, chief executive of IKEA, told the press he had been dreaming of selling flat-pack furniture to India's rising middle class. However, in spite of New Delhi rapidly moving to open its market to foreign retailers for the first time, IKEA's strategy is stalled. The barrier is India's legal requirements for single-brand retailers to source 30 per cent of their goods from local small and medium sized companies in India.[77]

New laws and their enforcement will continue to increase. International marketers will encounter dozens, or even hundreds, of agencies created to enforce trade policies and regulations. Business executives must watch these developments when planning their products and marketing programmes. Marketers need to know about the major laws protecting competition, consumers and society, or enforcing other government policies. They need to understand these laws at national and international levels. International marketers, in particular, need to stay close to the ways in which foreign governments operate to control and influence business within their borders, and sometimes make hard choices.

Increased emphasis on ethics and socially responsible actions

Written regulations cannot possibly cover all potential marketing abuses, and existing laws are often difficult to enforce. However, beyond written laws and regulations, business is also governed by social codes and rules of professional ethics.

Socially responsible behaviour

Enlightened companies encourage their managers to look beyond what the regulatory system allows and simply 'do the right thing'. These socially responsible firms actively seek out ways to protect the long-run interests of their consumers and the environment.

The recent rash of business scandals and increased concerns about the environment have created fresh interest in the issues of ethics and social responsibility. Almost every aspect of marketing involves such issues. Unfortunately, because these issues usually involve conflicting interests, well-meaning people can honestly disagree about the right course of action in a given situation. Thus, many industrial and professional trade associations have suggested codes of ethics. And more companies are now developing policies, guidelines, and other responses to complex social responsibility issues.

The boom in Internet marketing has created a new set of social and ethical issues. Critics worry most about online privacy issues. There has been an explosion in the amount of personal digital data available. Users, themselves, supply some of it. They voluntarily place highly private information on social media sites, such as Facebook or LinkedIn, or on genealogy sites that are easily searched by anyone with a computer or a smartphone.

However, much of the information is systematically developed by businesses seeking to learn more about their customers, often without consumers realising that they are under the microscope. Legitimate businesses track consumers' online browsing and buying behaviour, and collect, analyse and share digital data from every move consumers make at their online sites. Critics are concerned that companies may now know too much and might use digital data to take unfair advantage of consumers. Although most companies fully disclose their Internet privacy policies and most work to use data to benefit their customers, abuses do occur. As a result, consumer advocates and policymakers are taking action to protect consumer privacy. In Chapters 4 and 20, we discuss these and other societal marketing issues in greater depth.

Cause-related marketing

To exercise their social responsibility and build more positive images, many companies are now linking themselves to worthwhile causes. In fact, some companies are founded entirely on cause-related missions. Under the concept of 'value-led business' or 'caring capitalism', their mission is to use business to make the world a better place.

Cause-related marketing has become a primary form of corporate giving. It lets companies 'do well by doing good' by linking purchases of the company's products or services with fund-raising for worthwhile causes or charitable organisations. Companies now sponsor dozens of cause-related marketing campaigns each year. Many are backed by large budgets and a full complement of marketing activities.

Cause-related marketing has stirred some controversy. Critics worry that cause-related marketing is more a strategy for selling than a strategy for giving – that 'cause-related' marketing is really 'cause-exploitative' marketing. Thus, companies using cause-related marketing might find themselves walking a fine line between increased sales and an improved image and facing charges of exploitation.

However, if handled well, cause-related marketing can greatly benefit both the company and the cause. The company gains an effective marketing tool while building a more positive public image. The charitable organisation or cause gains greater visibility and important new sources of funding and support.

The cultural environment

Author comment

Cultural factors strongly affect how people think and how they consume. So marketers are keenly interested in the cultural environment.

Cultural environment— Institutions and other forces that affect society's basic values, perceptions, preferences and behaviours.

The **cultural environment** consists of institutions and other forces that affect a society's basic values, perceptions, preferences and behaviours. People grow up in a particular society that shapes their basic beliefs and values. They absorb a worldview that defines their relationships with others. The following cultural characteristics can affect marketing decision making.

The persistence of cultural values

People in a given society hold many beliefs and values. Their core beliefs and values have a high degree of persistence. These beliefs shape more specific attitudes and behaviours found in everyday life. *Core* beliefs and values are passed on from parents to children and are reinforced by schools, churches, business and government.

Secondary beliefs and values are more open to change. Believing in marriage is a core belief; believing that people should get married early in life is a secondary belief. Marketers have some chance of changing secondary values but little chance of changing core values. For example, family-planning marketers could argue more effectively that people should get married later in life than not get married at all.

Shifts in secondary cultural values

Although core values are fairly persistent, cultural swings do take place. Consider the impact of popular music groups, film personalities, and other celebrities on young people's hairstyling and clothing norms. Marketers want to predict cultural shifts to spot new opportunities or threats. Several firms offer 'futures' forecasts in this connection. The major cultural values of a society are expressed in people's views of themselves and others, as well as in their views of organisations, society, nature and the universe.

People's views of themselves

People vary in their emphasis on serving themselves versus serving others. Some people seek personal pleasure, wanting fun, change and escape. Others seek self-realisation through religion, recreation, or the avid pursuit of careers or other life goals. Some people see themselves as sharers and joiners; others see themselves as individualists. People use products, brands and services as a means of self-expression, and they buy products and services that match their views of themselves. Marketers can target their products and services based on such self-views.

For example, there are challenges in selling tea to Americans – traditionally a coffee-drinking country. On one hand, ads for Tetley tea focus on taste, appealing to tea drinkers with a more practical view and telling them to 'brew up something brilliant'. Its Classic Blend black tea offers 'a deep amber colour and delicious tea flavour'. By contrast, Yogi Tea Company appeals to tea drinkers with a more transcendent, holistic view of themselves, their lives and their teas. The brand offers more than 100 herbs and botanicals, blended 'for both flavour and purpose'. Yogi's slogan, 'How good can you feel?', suggests that its teas not only taste good but also make your body feel well, both physically and mentally. For example, Yogi Stress Relief tea is 'a delicious, all-natural blend that helps soothe your body and mind'. Yogi Sweet Tangerine Positive Energy tea 'is a harmonising and aromatic blend that energises and elevates mood'. A recent post at the Yogi Community online site invited everyone to have a 'Happy feel-good Friday and a happy Spring!'[78]

People's views of others

People's attitudes towards, and interactions with, others shift over time. In recent years, some analysts have voiced concerns that the Internet age would result in diminished human interaction, as people buried themselves in social media pages or e-mailed and texted rather than interacting personally. Instead, today's digital technologies seem to have launched an era of what one trend watcher calls 'mass mingling'. Rather than interacting less, people are using online social media and mobile communications to connect more than ever. Basically, the more people meet, network, tweet and socialise online, the more likely they are to eventually meet up with friends and followers in the real world.

However, these days, even when people are together, they are often 'alone together'. Groups of people may sit or walk in their own little bubbles, intensely connected to tiny screens and keyboards. One expert describes the latest communication skill as 'maintaining eye contact with someone while you text someone else; it's hard but it can be done', she says. 'Technology-enabled, we are able to be with one another, and also elsewhere, connected to wherever we want to be.'[79] Thus, whether the new technology-driven communication is a blessing or a curse is a matter of much debate.

This new way of interacting strongly affects how companies market their brands and communicate with customers. Consumers increasingly tap digitally into networks of friends and online brand communities to learn about and buy products, and to shape and share brand experiences. As a result, it is important for brands to participate in these networks too.

People's views of organisations

People vary in their attitudes toward corporations, government agencies, trade unions, universities and other organisations. By and large, people are willing to work for major organisations and expect them, in turn, to carry out society's work.

The past two decades have seen a sharp decrease in confidence in and loyalty toward business and political organisations and institutions in many of the developed countries. In the workplace, there has been an overall decline in organisational loyalty. Waves of company downsizings bred cynicism and distrust. In just the last decade, rounds of redundancies resulting from the economic downturn and recession, major corporate scandals, the financial meltdown triggered by bankers' greed and incompetence, and other unsettling activities have resulted in a further loss of confidence in big business. Many people today see work not as a source of satisfaction but as a required chore to earn money to enjoy their non-work hours. This trend suggests that organisations need to find new ways to win consumer and employee confidence. Trust is becoming a key value being promoted in marketing communications from many companies, such as those in the financial services industry.

People's views of nature

People vary in their attitudes toward the natural world; some feel ruled by it, others feel in harmony with it, and still others seek to master it. A long-term trend has been people's growing mastery over nature through technology and the belief that nature is bountiful. More recently, however, people have recognised that nature is finite and fragile; it can be destroyed or spoiled by human activities.

Food producers have found fast-growing markets for natural and organic products. It is interesting that even after severe economic downturn in the UK, research suggests that sales of ethical goods continue to rise – it seems British consumers refuse to sacrifice principle for price or convenience. This growth is sustained in part by the conversion of many brands like Cadbury's chocolate and Nestlé's Kit Kat bars to Fair Trade – guaranteeing minimum price and conditions for producers in emerging markets.[80]

People's views of the universe

Finally, people vary in their beliefs about the origin of the universe and their place in it. Although many people are dropping out of organised religion in the West, it doesn't mean that they are abandoning their faith. Some futurists have noted a renewed interest in spirituality, perhaps as a part of a broader search for a new inner purpose. People have been moving away from materialism and dog-eat-dog ambition to seek more permanent values – family, community, earth, faith – and a more certain grasp of right and wrong. This changing spiritualism affects consumers in everything from the television shows they watch and the books they read to the products and services they buy.

RESPONDING TO THE MARKETING ENVIRONMENT

Someone once observed, 'There are three kinds of companies: those that make things happen, those that watch things happen, and those that wonder what's happened.' Many companies view the marketing environment as an uncontrollable element to which they must react and adapt. They passively accept the marketing environment and do not try to change it. They analyse environmental forces and design strategies that will help the company avoid the threats and take advantage of the opportunities the environment provides.

Other companies take a *proactive* stance toward the marketing environment. Rather than assuming that strategic options are bounded by the current environment, these firms develop strategies to change the environment. Companies and their products often create and shape new industries and their structures – products such as Ford's Model T car, Apple's iPod and iPhone and Google's search engine.

Even more, rather than simply watching and reacting to environmental events, proactive firms take aggressive actions to affect their publics and the important forces in their marketing environment. Such companies hire lobbyists to influence legislation affecting their industries and stage media events to gain favourable press coverage. They run 'advertorials' (ads expressing editorial points of view) and blogs to shape public opinion. They press lawsuits and file complaints with regulators to keep competitors in line, and they form contractual agreements to better control their distribution channels.

Marketing management cannot always control environmental forces. In many cases, it must settle for simply watching and reacting to the environment. For example, a company would have little success trying to influence geographic population shifts, the economic environment, or major cultural values. But whenever possible, smart marketing managers will take a *proactive* rather than *reactive* approach to the marketing environment:[81]

Today's more empowered consumers use the new digital media to share their brand experiences with companies and with each other. The Internet and social media have turned the traditional power relationship between businesses and consumers upside down. All of this back-and-forth helps both the company and its customers. But sometimes, the dialogue can get nasty.

A young creative team at Ford's ad agency in India produced a Ford Figo print ad and released it to the Internet without approval. The ad featured three women – bound, gagged and scantily clad – in the hatch of a Figo, with a caricature of a grinning Silvio Berlusconi (Italy's sex-scandal-plagued ex-prime minister) at the wheel. The ad's tagline: 'Leave your worries behind with Figo's extra-large boot.' Ford quickly pulled the ad, but not before it had gone viral. Within days, millions of people around the world has viewed the ad, causing an online uproar about its tastelessness and giving Ford a global black eye.

But how should companies react to online attacks? The real quandary for targeted companies is figuring out how far they can go to protect their images without fuelling the already raging fire. One point on which all experts seem to agree: Don't try to retaliate in kind. 'It's rarely a good idea to lob bombs at the fire,' says one analyst. In response to its Figo ad fiasco, Ford's chief marketing officer issued a deep public apology, citing that Ford had not approved the ads and that it had since modified its ad review process. Ford's ad agency promptly fired the guilty creatives.

By monitoring and proactively responding to seemingly uncontrollable events in the environment, companies can prevent the negatives from spiralling out of control or even turn them into positives.

OBJECTIVES REVIEW AND KEY TERMS

In this chapter and the next three chapters, you'll examine the environments of marketing and how companies analyse these environments to better understand the marketplace and consumers. Companies must constantly watch and manage the *marketing environment* to seek opportunities and ward off threats. The marketing environment consists of all the actors and forces influencing the company's ability to transact business effectively with its target market.

OBJECTIVE 1 Describe the environmental forces that affect the company's ability to serve its customers (pp. 70–74).

The company's *microenvironment* consists of actors close to the company that combine to form its value delivery network or that affect its ability to serve its customers. It includes the company's *internal environment* – its several departments and management levels – as it influences marketing decision making. *Marketing channel firms* – suppliers and marketing intermediaries, including resellers, physical distribution firms, marketing services agencies and financial intermediaries – cooperate to create customer value. *Competitors* vie with the company in an effort to serve customers better. Various *publics* have an actual or potential interest in, or impact on, the company's ability to meet its objectives. Finally, five types of *customer markets* exist – consumer, business, reseller, government and international markets.

The *macroenvironment* consists of larger societal forces that affect the entire microenvironment. The six forces making up the company's macroenvironment include demographic, economic, natural, technological, political/social and cultural forces. These forces shape opportunities and pose threats to the company.

OBJECTIVE 2 Explain how changes in the demographic and economic environments affect marketing decisions (pp. 74–84).

Demography is the study of the characteristics of human populations. Today's *demographic environment* shows a changing age structure, shifting family profiles, geographic population shifts and increasing diversity. The *economic environment* consists of factors that affect buying power and patterns. The economic environment is characterised by more frugal consumers who are seeking greater value – the right combination of good quality and service at a fair price. The distribution of income also is shifting, leading to tiered markets in many countries.

OBJECTIVE 3 Identify the major trends in the firm's natural and technological environments (pp. 85–88).

The *natural environment* shows three major trends: shortages of certain raw materials, higher pollution levels, and more government intervention in natural resource management. Environmental concerns create marketing opportunities for alert companies. The *technological environment* creates both opportunities and challenges. Companies that fail to keep up with technological change will miss out on new product and marketing opportunities.

OBJECTIVE 4 Explain the key changes in the political and cultural environments (pp. 88–92).

The *political environment* consists of laws, agencies and groups that influence or limit marketing actions. The political environment has undergone changes that affect marketing worldwide: increasing legislation regulating business, strong government enforcement, and greater emphasis on ethics and socially responsible actions. The *cultural environment* consists of institutions and forces that affect a society's values, perceptions, preferences and behaviours. The environment shows trends toward new technology-enabled communication, a lessening trust in institutions, greater appreciation for nature, a changing spiritualism, and the search for more meaningful and enduring values.

OBJECTIVE 5 Discuss how companies can react to the marketing environment (pp. 90–92).

Companies can passively accept the marketing environment as an uncontrollable element to which they must adapt, avoiding threats and taking advantage of opportunities as they arise. Or they can take a *proactive* stance, working to change the environment rather than simply reacting to it. Whenever possible, companies should try to be proactive rather than reactive.

NAVIGATING THE KEY TERMS

OBJECTIVE 1
Marketing environment (p. 69)
Microenvironment (p. 69)
Macroenvironment (p. 69)
Marketing intermediaries (p. 71)
Public (p. 72)

OBJECTIVE 2
Demography (p. 74)
Baby boomers (p. 75)
Generation X (p. 75)

Millennials (Generation Y)
  (p. 76)
Generation Z (p. 76)
Economic environment (p. 82)

OBJECTIVE 3
Natural environment (p. 85)
Environmental sustainability (p. 86)
Technological environment
  (p. 86)

OBJECTIVE 4
Political environment (p. 88)
Cultural environment (p. 90)

DISCUSSION AND CRITICAL THINKING

Discussion questions

3-1 Name and briefly describe the elements of an organisation's microenvironment and discuss how they affect marketing. (AACSB: Communication)

3-2 What is demography and why is it so important for marketers? (AACSB: Communication; Reflective thinking)

3-3 Who are the Millennials and why are they of so much interest to marketers? (AACSB: Communication; Reflective thinking)

3-4 Compare and contrast core beliefs/values and secondary beliefs/values. Provide an example of each and discuss the potential impact marketers have on each. (AACSB: Communication; Reflective thinking)

3-5 How should marketers respond to the changing environment? (AACSB: Communication)

Critical-thinking exercises

3-6 Research a current or emerging change in the legal or regulatory environment in a specific country affecting marketing. Explain its impact on marketing and how companies are reacting to the law or regulation. (AACSB: Communication; Reflective thinking)

3-7 Cause-related marketing has grown considerably over the past ten years. Use Google to identify companies with outstanding cause-related marketing programmes. Present a case study of successful cause-related marketing to your class. (AACSB: Communication; Use of IT)

3-8 Discuss a recent change in the technological environment that impacts marketing. How has it affected buyer behaviour and how has it changed marketing? (AACSB: Communication; Reflective thinking)

Mini-cases and applications

Online, mobile and social media marketing: social data

People throughout the world have been using Twitter's social media platform to tweet short bursts of information in 140 characters or less since 2006 and now average 500 million tweets a day. The full stream of tweets is referred to as Twitter's fire hose. Data from the fire hose are analysed and the information gleaned from that analysis is sold to other companies. Twitter recently purchased Gnip, the world's largest social data provider and one of the few companies that has access to the fire hose. Gnip also mines public data from Facebook, Google+, Tumblr, and other social media platforms. Analysing social data has become a big business because many major companies pay to learn consumers' sentiments toward them. According to the CEO of social-media analysis company BrandWatch, 'We're at the bottom of the foothills in terms of the kind of global demand for social data.' Twitter alone earned more than $70 million last year from licensing its data. Perhaps Mark Twain's character, Mulberry Sellers, summed it up nicely — 'There's gold in them thar hills' — and Twitter and other social media platforms and data analytic companies are mining that gold.

3-9 Discuss the value of social data for marketers. (AACSB: Communication; Reflective thinking)

3-10 'A dark social channel' refers to a private channel or a channel difficult to match with other digital channels. An example of a dark channel is e-mail. However, Google routinely mines its roughly half a billion Gmail users' e-mails. Research how Google scans e-mail data and the fallout from those actions. (AACSB: Communication; Use of IT; Reflective thinking)

Marketing ethics: television isn't what it used to be

Does a company 'publicly perform' a copyrighted television programme if it is distributed to paid subscribers over the Internet? That is the issue in the United States behind the *American Broadcasting Companies, Inc.* v *Aereo, Inc.*, a lawsuit brought before the US Supreme Court. It is illegal to re-transmit copyrighted television programmes in a 'public performance' without paying re-transmission fees to the copyright holder. With the help of technology, however, Aereo seemed to have found a way to circumvent those copyright laws and not pay re-transmission fees to broadcasters. Each customer had a small antenna that provides a 'private performance', thus allowing Aereo to avoid having to pay re-transmission fees to deliver the programming to customers. Viewers in New York, Denver, Boston, Atlanta, Miami, and other major US markets were able to ditch their high-cost cable and satellite television service and receive 24 channels and DVR space to record shows, for as little as $8–$12 per month. Moreover, Aereo could pick up low-power stations not carried by cable and satellite providers, letting advertisers expose their ads to 'eyeballs' they wouldn't normally get. This also helped the smaller broadcasters, because cable and satellite providers do not usually carry these stations. A US judge didn't see it that way, however, and ruled that Aereo's business model is 'indistinguishable from that of a cable company'. The case went all the way to the Supreme Court. One expert says the case was really about old versus new technology, about 'rabbit ears meets the cloud'. Rabbit ears refers to the old television antennas that received broadcast signals over the air

for free (once the only way to receive TV). In fact, the Supreme Court ruled in a 6–3 decision that Aereo's business model was no different than that of a cable television provider, despite the differences in technology. As a result of that decision the company announced that it would immediately suspend its services while consulting with the Court on how to proceed. Aereo's services were suspended in June 2014 and the company filed for Chapter 11 bankruptcy in November 2014, but was later purchased by DVR company TiVo for $1 million in March 2015. TiVo claims to be keeping the Aereo dream alive.

3-11 Learn how Aereo delivered value to customers and how TiVo has now extended the service. Write a report on the TiVo/Aereo value proposition and the four Ps and the potential for replicating the business model in other countries. (AACSB: Communication; Use of IT; Reflective thinking)

3-12 Debate whether or not the TiVo/Aereo business model is unethical or just smart marketing based on an opportunity made available by technology. (AACSB: Communication; Use of IT; Reflective thinking)

Marketing by the numbers: tiny markets

Many marketing decisions boil down to numbers. An important question is this: what is the sales potential in a given market? If the sales potential in a market is not large enough to warrant pursuing that market, then companies will not offer products and services to that market, even though a need may exist. Consider the medical market segment of infants and children. You've probably heard of heart procedures such as angioplasty and stents that are routinely performed on adults. But such heart procedures, devices and related medications are not available for infants and children, despite the fact that thousands of children every year are born with heart defects that often require repair. This is a life or death situation for many young patients, yet doctors must improvise by using devices designed and tested on adults. For instance, doctors use an adult kidney balloon on an infant's heart because it is the appropriate size for a newborn's aortic valve. However, this device is not approved for the procedure. Why are specific devices and medicines developed for the multibillion cardiovascular market not also designed for children? It's a matter of economics — this segment comprising young consumers is just too small. One leading cardiologist attributed the discrepancy to a 'profitability gap' between the children's market and the much more profitable adult market for treating heart disease. While this might make good economic sense for companies, it is little comfort to the parents of these small patients. Certainly there is a need for medical products to save children's lives. Still, companies are not pursuing this market.

3-13 Using the chain ratio method described in Appendix 2: Marketing by the numbers, estimate the market sales potential for heart catheterisation products to meet the needs of the infant and child segment in a country or region of your choice (e.g., the UK or the EU). Assume that of children with heart defects each year, 60 per cent will benefit from these types of products but that only 50 per cent of their families have the financial resources to obtain such treatment (and they are not available free in national healthcare facilities). Also assume the average

price for a device is €1,000. (AACSB: Communication; Analytical reasoning)

3-14 Research the medical devices market and compare the market potential you estimated to the sales of various devices. Are companies justified in not pursuing the infant and child segment? (AACSB: Communication; Reflective thinking)

REFERENCES

[1] Pilita Clark, 'Electric cars and biofuels "likely to be biggest green victims of oil price fall"', *Financial Times*, 19 January 2015, p. 17; Christopher Adams, Michael Kavanagh and Chros Tighe, 'That sinking feeling', *Financial Times*, 26 February 2015, p. 11; Ferdinand Giugliano, 'Why low inflation is not universally welcomed', *Financial Times*, 18 February 2015, p. 3; Richard Milne, Christopher Adams and Ed Crooks, 'Low oil prices leave offshore Arctic wells out in the cold', *Financial Times*, 6 February 2015, p. 17; Brian O'Keefe, 'Oil's new math', *Fortune*, 1 March 2015, pp. 20–27; Ed Crooks, 'US shale industry shows remarkable resilience', *Financial Times*, 16 March 2015, p. 23; Matthew Phillips, 'Too much oil and no place to put it', *Bloomberg BusinessWeek*, 16–22 March 2015, pp. 10–11; Ed Crooks and Christopher Adams, 'Big oil seizes the chance offered by crude crash', *Financial Times*, 28 April 2015, p. 19; Holly Black, 'Oil glut damages returns', *Daily Mail*, 8 August 2015, p. 99; Paul M. Barrett and Ben Eglin, 'The Arctic or bust', *Bloomberg BusinessWeek*, 10 August 2015, pp. 56–63; Andres Schipani, 'We are terrorised by the drop in oil prices', *Financial Times*, 10 August 2015, p. 7; 'Oil could drop below $30', *Daily Mail*, 26 August 2015, p. 61.

[2] See Rebecca Ellinor, 'Crowd pleaser', *Supply Management*, 13 December 2007, pp. 26–29; and information from www.loreal.co.in/_hi/_in/HTML/suppliers/values-partnership/values-mutual-benefits.aspx and www.lorealusa.com/profiles/suppliers.aspx, accessed September 2014.

[3] Rupert Steiner, 'Sainsbury's loan lifeline to suppliers', *Daily Mail*, 1 December 2012, p. 99; Henry Foy, 'Carmakers' suppliers hold the whip hand', *Financial Times*, 19 May 2014; Andy Sharman, 'Shortage of suppliers takes shine off accelerating motor industry', *Financial Times*, 6 April 2015, p. 3.

[4] Andrea Felsted, 'All lined up', *Financial Times*, 6 January 2012, p. 9; James Salmon, 'Discounters gain on top four grocers', *Daily Mail*, 26 August 2015, p. 63.

[5] Information from Robert J. Benes, Abbie Jarman and Ashley Williams, '2007 NRA sets records', www.chefmagazine.com, accessed September 2007; and www.cokesolutions.com, accessed September 2014.

[6] Based on information from Ashley Vance, 'Microsoft sees a new image of itself in Windows 8', *Business Week*, 29 October 2012, pp. 41–42; Spencer Jakab, 'Microsoft holds more than meets the eye', *Wall Street Journal*, 23 January 2013, p. C1; Ashlee Vance and Dina Bass, 'Microsoft's Office 2013 is software for the Cloud', *Bloomberg Businessweek*, 29 January 2013, www.businessweek.com/articles/2013-01-29/microsofts-oldsoftware-comes-with-a-new-image; Ritsuko Ando and Bill Rigby, 'Microsoft swallows Nokia's phone business for $7.2 billion', 3 September 2013, www.reuters.com/article/2013/09/03/usmicrosoft-nokia-idUSBRE98202V20130903; 'Microsoft Board names Satya Nadella as CEO', *Microsoft News Center*, 4 February 2014, www.microsoft.com/en-us/news/press/2014/feb14/02-04newspr.aspx; and annual reports and other information from www.microsoft.com/investor/default.aspx, accessed September 2014.

[7] World POPClock, US Census Bureau, at www.census.gov, accessed August 2015. This website provides continuously updated projections of the US and world populations. Details of European Union population are given at http://europa.eu/about-eu/facts-figures/living/index_en.htm, accessed August 2015.

[8] The comments in this section of based on Robert Orr, 'Growing pains' in 'New Demographics', *Financial Times*, 18 October 2011, p. 3.

[9] Andrew Jack, 'Seven billion and counting', in 'New Demographics', *Financial Times*, 19 October 2011, pp. 8–11; Global Health Observatory Data repository: 'Life expectancy, Geneva, Switzerland: World Health Statistics 2015', World Health Organisation, http://apps.who.int/gho/data/node.main.687?lang=en, accessed August 2015.

[10] James Lamont, 'Tiger, tiger, burning bright', in 'New Demographics', *Financial Times*, 19 October 2011, pp. 13–15.

[11] The comments in this section are based on Gideon Rachman, 'Taking the long view on success', in 'New Demographics', *Financial Times*, 19 October 2011, pp. 6–7.

[12] For more discussion, see Bernadette Turner, 'Generation X . . . let's GO!' *New Pittsburgh Courier*, 2–8 March 2011, p. A11; Leonard Klie, 'Gen X: stuck in the middle', *Customer Relationship Management*, February 2012, pp. 24–29; and Gavin O'Malley, 'Gen X proves boon to marketers', *Online Media Daily*, 25 April 2013, www.mediapost.com/publications/article/198964/gen-x-provesboon-to-marketers.html.

[13] Matthew Philips and Jeanna Smialek, 'The 23-year-olds will save America', *Bloomberg BusinessWeek*, 30 June–6 July 2014, pp. 14–16.

[14] See Greg Petro, 'Millennial engagement and loyalty — make them part of the process', *Forbes*, 21 March 2013, www.forbes.com/sites/gregpetro/2013/03/21/millennial-engagement-and-loyaltymake-them-part-of-the-process/.

[15] See 'Moxy Milan Malpensa set to open in September followed by a further five hotels in Europe by end of 2015', *Marriott New Center*, 3 March 2014, http://news.marriott.com/moxy-hotels/; and www.moxy-hotels.com, accessed September 2014.

[16] See 'GenZ: digital in their DNA', J Walter Thompson International, www.jwt.com/en/worldwide/thinking/genzdigitalintheirdna/, accessed October 2015; and Shannon Bryant, ' "Generation Z" children more tech-savvy; prefer gadgets, not toys', *Marketing Forecast*, 3 April 2013, www.ad-ology.com/tag/tech-savvy-children/#. U5d9avldV8E.

[17] Heather Chaet, 'The tween machine', *Adweek*, 25 June 2012, www.adweek.com/print/141357; and Greg Smith, 'Tweens 'R Shoppers: a look at the tween market & shopping behavior', *POPAI*, March 2013, www.popai.com/store/downloads/POPAIWhitePaper-Tweens-R-Shoppers-2013.pdf.

18 Louise Eccles, 'Migrants and super-rich spark big families boom', *Daily Mail*, 17 August 2015, p. 25.

19 Emma Jacobs, 'Singular behaviour', *Financial Times*, 6 August 2013, p. 10.

20 Becky Barrow, 'A 50-year revolution in British family life', *Daily Mail*, 16 July 2014, p. 18.

21 Diane Brady, 'The reluctant breadwinners', *Bloomberg BusinessWeek*, 27 September–3 October 2010, pp. 15–26.

22 Michael J. Silverstein and Kate Sayre, 'The female economy', *Harvard Business Review*, September 2009, pp. 46–53.

23 Michael J. Silverstein and Kate Sayre, *Women Want More: How to Capture Your Share of the World's Largest, Fastest-Growing Market*, New York: Harper-Collins, 2009.

24 Brad Wieners, 'Lego is for girls', *Bloomberg BusinessWeek*, 19–25 December, 2011, pp. 68–73.

25 Andrew Taylor, 'Cost forces more young men to live with parents', *Financial Times*, 16 April 2009, p. 3, http://www.bbc.co.uk/news/uk-25827061, accessed August 2015.

26 Chris Giles and Sarah Neville, 'Years of struggle for a jinxed generation', *Financial Times*, 17/18 March 2012, p. 1.

27 Daniel Pimlott, 'Business wake-up call on vanishing youth', *Financial Times*, 31 May 2010, p. 3; Stanley Reed, Carol Matlack, Dexter Roberts, Diane Brady and Caroline Winter, 'A message', *Bloomberg BusinessWeek*, 7–14 February 2011, pp. 59–65; Peter Coy, 'The lost generation', *BusinessWeek*, 19 October 2009, pp. 33–35; Gideon Rachman, 'Taking the long view on success', in 'New Demographics', *Financial Times*, 19 October 2011.

28 Chris Giles and Sarah O'Connor, 'No country for young men – the UK's widening generation gap', *Financial Times*, 24 February 2015, p. 1; Sarah O'Connor and Chris Giles, 'Young grapple with lowered expectations', *Financial Times*, 24 February 2015, p.3.

29 Norma Cohen and Brian Groom, 'The number of older workers past retirement age doubles in 20 years', *Financial Times*, 14 June 2012, p. 2.

30 Norma Cohen, 'The silver economy', *Financial Times*, 20 October 2014, p. 9; Henry Foy and Andrew Ward, 'Baby boomers' spending power drives $15tn silver economy', *Financial Times*, 20 October 2014, p. 1.

31 Steve Doughty, 'The new social mobility: now more move down the ladder', *Daily Mail*, 6 November 2014, p. 21.

32 Shawn Donnan, 'The numbers game', *Financial Times*, 2 December 2014, p. 11.

33 James Crabtree, 'Colliding forces', in 'New Demographics', *Financial Times*, 19 October 2011, pp. 40–43.

34 Shawn Donnan, 'The numbers game', *Financial Times*, 2 December 2014, p. 11.

35 Matt Chorley, 'Rise of the expat', *Daily Mail*, 15 July 2014, p. 34.

36 Ian Drury and Louise Eccles, '1 in 6 workers in UK are foreign', *Daily Mail*, 13 August 2015, p. 8; Helen Warrell, 'Toil and trouble', *Financial Times*, 13 August 2015, p. 7.

37 James Crabtree, 'Colliding forces', in 'New Demographics', *Financial Times*, 19 October 2011, p. 42.

38 Richard Boudreaux and Paulo Prada, 'Exodus of European workers reverses continent's patterns', *Wall Street Journal*, 16 January 2012, pp. 12–13.

39 Jack Grimston, 'British Muslims find things go better with Mecca', *The Sunday Times*, 19 January 2003, S1, p.3, http://www.libyacola.biz/, accessed August 2015.

40 Ese Erheriene, '"Ramadan rush" gives U.K. retail a lift', *Wall Street Journal*, 29 July 2014, p. 15.

41 Andrew Edgecliffe Johnson, 'Hispanic dawn breaks for US marketers', *Financial Times*, 21 October 2010, p. 29; Jonathan Birchall, 'P&G taps into popularity of heavier scents', *Financial Times*, 21 October 2010, p. 29.

42 Andrew Edgecliffe-Johnson, 'Not yet wrapped up', *Financial Times*, 8 September 2010, p. 11.

43 Conor Dougherty and Miriam Jordan, 'U.S. births cross the "majority minority" threshold for first time', *Wall Street Journal*, 17 May 2012, p. 7.

44 Sarah A. Topol, 'Muslim style is not a contradiction in terms', *Bloomberg BusinessWeek*, 22–28 April 2013, pp. 14–15.

45 Ian Drury, 'Now number of foreigners in UK passes 8 million', *Daily Mail*, 26 August 2015, p. 4.

46 Robert Gray, 'World of opportunity', *The Marketer*, November 2007, pp. 28–31.

47 Katrina Burroughs, 'The pink niche', *Financial Times Weekend*, 10/11 May 2008, p. 1.

48 Andrew Adam Newman, 'Web marketing to a segment too big to be a niche', *New York Times*, 30 October 2007, p. 9; Kenneth Hein, 'The invisible demographic', *Brandweek*, 3 March 2008, p. 20; and Tanya Mohn, 'Smoothing the way', *New York Times*, 26 April 2010, www.nytimes.com.

49 Gabriel Windau, 'At the turning point', *Financial Times*, 5 May 2015, p. 9.

50 See 'About WebEx', http://www.webex.com/index.html, accessed August 2015;

51 World Economic Outlook Database, April 2015, www.imf.org/external/pubs/ft/weo/2015/01/weodata/weorept.aspx, accessed August 2015.

52 Alan Rappaport, 'Bric's billionaires outnumber Europe's', *Financial Times*, 10 March 2011, p. 5.

53 Alan Beattie, 'Changing faces of power: stars shine bright but fail to transform the world', *Financial Times*, 18 January 2010, p. 8.

54 Hugo Duncan, 'China overtakes U.S. as the world's largest economy', *Daily Mail*, 9 October 2014, p. 2; Jamil Anderlini and David Pilling, 'China fought against data showing economy to take top spot this year', *Financial Times*, 2 May 2014, p. 1.

55 Charles Kenny, 'The case for second place', *Bloomberg BusinessWeek*, 17–23 October 2011. pp. 13–15.

56 Tim Harford, 'China's rise will change the nuts and bolts of British industry', *FT Magazine*, 19/20 June 2010, p. 13.

57 Nicky Burridge, 'A red alert over China's growth', *Daily Mail*, 29 December 2011, p. 73.

58 Andrea Felsted, 'All lined up', *Financial Times*, 6 January 2012, p. 9.

59 Bob David, 'Brics fade as engine of growth', *Wall Street Journal*, 2 January 2013, p.9; Tom Wright, 'Emerging markets hit a growth pivot point', *Wall Street Journal*, 4 November 2013, p. 1; Gideon Rachman, 'Cracks start to show in the Brics', *Financial Times*, 4 November 2014, p. 11; James Kynge and Jonathan Wheatley, 'Emerging markets: the great unravelling', *Financial Times*, 2 April 2015, p. 9.

60 Gideon Rachman, 'The future still belongs to the emerging markets', *Financial Times*, 4 February 2014, p. 11; Alison Smith, 'Non-Bric EM groups undergoing power shift', *Financial Times*, 5 May 2014, p. 21.

61 Hugo Duncan and Jason Groves, 'Great fall of China', *Daily Mail*, 25 August 2015, pp. 1, 6–7.

[62] John Reed, 'Fiat boosts stake in Chrysler after hitting target', *Financial Times*, 6 January 2012, p. 19.

[63] Chris Bryant and John Reed, 'VW overtakes Toyota with record 8m sales', *Financial Times*, 20 January 2012, p. 21.

[64] Paul Beckett and Santanu Choudhury, 'Tata Chairman bemoans early nano sales efforts', *Wall Street Journal*, 6–8 January 2012, p. 21.

[65] Chris Giles and Andrew Bounds, 'Brutal for Britain', *Financial Times*, 16 January 2012, p. 9; Brian Groom, 'Rocky time ahead as joblessness near 2.7m', *Financial Times*, 19 January 2012, p. 3.

[66] Nigel F. Piercy, David W. Cravens and Nikala Lane, 'Marketing out of the recession: recovery is coming, but things will never be the same again', *The Marketing Review*, Vol. 10, No. 1, 2010, pp. 3–23.

[67] Daniel Yergin, 'A crisis in search of a narrative', *Financial Times*, 21 October 2009, p. 13.

[68] See https://www.equalitytrust.org.uk/scale-economic-inequality-uk, accessed August 2015.

[69] See http://reports.weforum.org/outlook-global-agenda-2015/top-10-trends-of-2015/1-deepening-income-inequality/, accessed August 2015.

[70] The 2030 Water Resources Group, www.2030wrg.org, accessed September 2014; and 'The world's water', *Pacific Institute*, www.worldwater.org/data.html, accessed September 2014.

[71] See http://www.ge.com/about-us/ecomagination, accessed August 2015.

[72] John Reed, 'Hydrogen cells move to fast lane', *Financial Times*, 18 January 2012, p. 4; James Gillespie, 'Spark goes out of electric car sales', *The Sunday Times*, 15 January 2012, S1, p. 15.

[73] Nigel F. Piercy and Nikala Lane, 'Corporate social responsibility', *The Marketing Review*, Vol. 9 No. 4, 2009, pp. 335–360; Nigel F. Piercy and Nikala Lane, 'Corporate social responsibility initiatives and strategic marketing perspectives', *Social Business*, Vol. 1, No. 4, 2011, pp. 325–345.

[74] See David Blanchard, 'The five stages of RFID', *Industry Week*, January 2009, p. 50; Mary Hayes Weier, 'Slow and steady progress', *InformationWeek*, 16 November 2009, p. 31; and information at www.autoidlabs.org, accessed August 2015; Maid Napolitano, 'RFID surges ahead', *Materials Handling*, April 2012, pp. S48–S50; 'Burberry introduces smart personalization for shoppers', *Integer*, 25 March 2013, http://shopperculture.integer.com/2013/03/burberry-introduces-smartpersonalization-for-shoppers.html; and Bob Trebilcock, 'RFID: Macy's way', *Modern Materials Handling*, 1 June 2013, www.mmh.com/view/rfid_the_macys_way/inventory.

[75] See 'A $1 billion project to remake the Disney World experience, using RFID', www.fastcodesign.com/1671616/a-1-billion-projectto-remake-the-disney-world-experience-using-rfid#1; and Brooks Barnes, 'At Disney Parks, a bracelet meant to build loyalty (and sales)', *New York Times*, 7 January 2013, p. B1.

[76] Miguel Helft, 'Google does darpa', *Fortune*, 1 September 2014, pp. 40–46.

[77] Megha Bahree and Miguel Bustillo, 'Big retailers retool India plans', *Wall Street Journal*, 12 December 2011, p. 22; James Fontanella-Khan and Andrea Felsted, 'India opens up to foreigners with limited retail reforms', *Financial Times*, 11 January 2012, p. 17; James Lamont, 'Ikea shelves entry to India over rules on local sourcing', *Financial Times*, 23 January 2012, p. 21.

[78] See www.yogiproducts.com/ and www.yogiproducts.com/ourstory/our-story/, accessed September 2014.

[79] Sherry Turkle, 'The flight from conversation', *New York Times*, 22 April 2012, p. SR1.

[80] Andrew Bounds, 'Consumers stick with principle over price', *Financial Times*, 15 December 2011, p. 4.

[81] Brent Snavely, 'Ford marketing chief apologizes for ads', *USA Today*, 27 March 2013; David Angelo, 'CMOs, agencies: it's time to live your brands', *Advertising Age*, 2 October 2013, http:// adage.com/print/244524; and www.youtube.com/watch?v=C5uIH0VTg_o, accessed September 2014.

COMPANY CASE

The era of cheap chic for Primark

Fashion retailer Primark has had a wonderful decade. Way back in 2006, the new year started with a shower of glitter for Primark as the discount fashion chain was named by *Vogue* as one of the unlikely hits of 2005 based on vital accessories such as boho skirts. But being named as one of last season's hottest items can be a backhanded compliment when it comes from fickle fashionistas, and the *Vogue* endorsement has proven a mixed blessing. Boho skirts have vanished from shop windows and the wardrobes of those in the know.

In fact, the chain has transformed the landscape of women's wear retailing in Britain, leading the charge of so-called fast-fashion by churning out imitations of catwalk clothing and must-have accessories in record time at unprecedented low prices. This formula has seen it grab market share from rivals at an impressive rate. In the second half of 2006, it posted a 12 per cent increase in like-for-like sales.

This sales growth came at the expense of discount rivals such as Matalan and larger chains such as Next, the mid-market clothing retailer, which had been suffering more than most. At the time in question, Next produced its worst trading figures since 2003. It warned the City that underlying sales would be down between 3 and 6 per cent in the financial year to January 2007. But when a sales slowdown was revealed by Primark it was seized on by rivals and analysts as a sign of a shift in the balance of power on the high street.

Maureen Hinton, senior analyst with Verdict Research, the retail consultancy, said: 'I think we were all surprised by the sales figures. It is quite surprising that they should have flat sales over the summer as value clothing tends to lend itself to this period, where for example vests and T-shirts sell well.' The analyst said that changing price architecture at large mid-market chains such as Marks & Spencer was challenging the value specialists. 'There is the resurgence of M&S that is selling high volumes at lower opening price points. People may be more likely to buy from M&S because of the inherent promise of quality and service. M&S is taking a lot of volume in the market so they have to be taking it from somewhere,' she says.

It did seem at the time that a rejuvenated M&S was enjoying an increase in market share as customers who had shunned it over the past few years were lured back in store with the promise of faster fashion – Limited Collection is M&S's version of on-trend lines – and cheaper items.

However, fashion editors who were quick to latch on to the rise of fast-fashion – advising readers to match a Chanel jacket with a Primark T-shirt – said the appeal of cheap chic has faded amid market saturation, and they continued to push this view.

Vanessa Gillingham, fashion director at Condé Nast's *Glamour* magazine said: 'I think it's like with anything great, after a while it flattens off a bit. Primark was the first to get on to the designer trend and put it into their stores and it seems that others such as George at Asda, Mark One, Tesco and Sainsbury's are all cashing in on it now and may have caught up.' Moira Beningson, retail specialist, said: 'People can't keep up. We're at the point where you have to change clothes every five minutes to wear everything you can buy at these stores.'

But John Bason, Primark's finance director, was relaxed about the slowdown in underlying sales. 'We always maintained that these very high like-for-like figures were unlikely to continue,' he said, pointing out that the chain would see a huge increase in sales due to the conversion of 41 stores acquired from Littlewoods, which it bought the previous year.

The retailer was already preparing for the possibility its UK growth would one day hit the buffers. It had just opened its first store in Madrid and, Mr Bason said, it was considering more aggressive expansion in Europe.

Primark's slowdown?

Then it got worse. Primark suffered its first really major slowdown in UK sales growth for five years, raising investor concerns about the stark deterioration in overall consumer spending since the start of 2011. Until this point the value chain had shown considerable resilience to economic malaise.

The discount clothing chain had seen viral-like expansion on the high street in recent years. But in 2011, Associated British Foods (owner of Primark) said it expected sales from its Primark stores in the UK and continental Europe open at least a year to rise just 3 per cent in the six months to 5 March – sharply down from the 8 per cent increase last year. ABF cited a 'noticeable slowing down of UK consumer demand' in contrast to continental Europe, which had seen 'very encouraging' sales.

Analysts at Shore Capital estimated Primark's UK like-for-like sales growth even entered negative territory in the seven weeks from 8 January 2011, expressing concern that value chains were not immune from the malaise elsewhere on the high street. Don't forget, the last time Primark had seen its sales growth stall was in September 2006, and it had managed impressive increases in like-for-like sales throughout the period since then. Shares in ABF fell nearly 6 per cent to 966½p on this trading statement.

'Primark is a best-in-class retailer and for it to be experiencing negative UK like-for-likes and volumes must send a shiver down the backbone of the trade,' said Clive Black, analyst at Shore Capital. Primark's fortunes highlight the challenging conditions on the British high street as consumers grappled with higher fuel and food prices, a rise in value added tax and concerns about unemployment ahead of expected public sector job cuts.

John Bason, finance director at ABF, said there had been a 'tipping point' for consumers since the start of year, noting that footfall on high streets had fallen since January. 'The UK consumer is feeling a little bit of a squeeze now,' he said. Mr Bason's comments follow those of Asda, the UK's second biggest grocer by market share, which said there had been a 'mindset shift' among consumers since the beginning of the year, and five weeks of lacklustre sales from John Lewis, the high street bellwether that has also been a winner during tougher times.

Primark's performance led to fears that that younger shoppers, who had kept spending during the downturn, were starting to feel the pinch. 'For the first time for quite a number of years, we are beginning to see some impact on the younger [shopper], who has been very resilient through the recession,' said Freddie George, analyst at Seymour Pierce. Primark cautioned that its operating profit margin would be lower than the year previously, as it absorbed the rising cost of cotton.

By late 2011, the budget retailer, was set to report annual sales growth half the rate of a year previously, showing that even value chains were not immune from tough conditions on the high street. Primark's like-for-like sales growth had slipped to 3 per cent in the year to 17 September, down from 6 per cent a year earlier. Although Primark's total sales were expected to be 13 per cent up on a year before, helped by a series of European store openings, analysts calculated that like-for-like sales growth in the UK and Ireland had been as low as 1 per cent. The retailer's strategy of not passing on high cotton prices to consumers to remain the cheapest on the high street meant margins fell in the second half of the year.

Darren Shirley, retail analyst at Shore Capital, said he anticipated a 200 basis point reduction when full-year figures were announced in November. 'If you're selling T-shirts for £1, it's obviously difficult to reprice that,' he said. 'However, there's been enough downward movement in the cotton price to give us confidence in the margin [in future].'

John Bason reiterated that sales growth at Primark's UK and Irish stores remained in positive territory for the year, although the market had got tougher. 'Other than the two bank holidays in April, it's been a tough year, and our planning assumptions are that it will continue to be tough next year,' he said. Pointing out that Primark's current fashion ranges were purchased in March, when the cotton price was at its peak, Mr Bason said he expected commodity pricing pressure to ease in 2012, which would help margins.

Noting strong growth in the group's growing European operations, he reported 'high single-digit' like-for-like sales growth in Spain and said he expected a further boost from the 350,000 sq ft of retail space in Germany that will open in the coming year.

Or maybe not so bad?

Critics of Primark had perhaps been a little too quick in their judgements. In fact, by 2012 it seemed that shoppers' desire for cheap clothes had kept the tills ringing at Primark, even as other, rival high street retailers were left reeling by consumers' thriftiness. Primark saw a 16 per cent increase in sales in the 16 weeks to 7 January. Stripping out new stores – and the group is increasing its footprint by some 10 per cent a year – like-for-like sales grew 2–3 per cent, on analysts' estimates. 'We had a slow autumn because it was warm,' said John Bason, finance director. 'But we had a really strong Christmas trading period, particularly in the UK.'

Some have attributed Primark's gain to others' pain, such as that of Barratt and Peacocks, which have collapsed into administration. But other analysts, noting that the latter's issues were more to do with debt, rather point to the retailer's value for money offerings which chime with cash-strapped consumers. The company took the hit when cotton prices soared the previous year, so margins could benefit now that prices have fallen sharply from the peaks. Because of this, the company was moving towards a stronger second half.

Alicia Forry, analyst at Collins Stewart, noted that operating margins were likely to be lower in the first half as a result of cotton prices and ramped-up promotions. 'We have to wait and see if they have outpaced on the top line, but when it comes to results and profits delivered [whether] they deliver less profit than their peers,' she said. The company, like its peers, could instead opt to pass the cheaper prices directly onto consumers in order to support sales growth.

However, Ms Forry saw sales growth as sustainable given the popularity of new stores in Germany and Spain – stores outside the UK now contribute one-third of Primark's turnover – and an offering that is popular with today's thriftier consumers. At Primark, Mr Bason said that, despite the 'torrid' economic climate, Spanish shoppers were flocking to the value clothing market. The Spanish market 'is probably where the UK was 10–15 years ago', he said.

And Primark now . . .

The Primark brand continued to hit the spot with savvy and choosy consumers as the UK came out of recession. There had been a blip in sales growth in 2011, when it looked like younger shoppers who had been very resilient through the recession were beginning to feel the pinch. However, Primark recovered faster than its rivals. Actually, Primark prospered as shoppers tightened their designer belts. A GfK research agency blind survey in 2012 asking consumers to rate a selection of fashion clothing items for quality, design and value for money, put Primark as top of the list – along with F&F (Tesco), and Tu (Sainsburys), the budget brand was way ahead of brands like Next, Marks & Spencer and Boden. Primark seemed to have the balance just right between quality and price for its consumers.

Primark continues to be under pressure from the media on conditions in its supply chains, including accusations that it was buying from a Manchester sweatshop using illegal immigrant labour. In 2013, Primark faced a crisis because it was one of the UK retailers sourcing products from the Bangladesh Rana Plaza factory, which collapsed killing 1,129 workers. Worldwide outrage over the disaster threatened to tarnish the names of firms like Primark. Nonetheless, Primark shoppers continued to buy in spite of the disaster. But Primark led the way in paying compensation to Bangladesh victims' families, and hired Paul Wright from Asda as sourcing director – Wright has a reputation for ethical sourcing and even installed web-cams in supplier factories to monitor working conditions when he was at Asda. Primark has also dropped some suppliers in action to prevent the use of child labour. But the director of 'War on Want' commented, 'Primark has a long way to go before it can be called an ethical retailer.'

Also in 2013, Primark took its first steps in online retailing through a relationship with Asos. After an initial trial with strong results, in 2013 Asos expanded the number of Primark products it carries from 70 to about 140. The Asos connection reinforces Primark's international ambitions.

By 2014, with 278 stores open, Primark had overtaken Zara in sales volume and was looking at a 17 per cent increase in sales over the previous year. Operating profits of £600 million on sales of £5 billion set Primark on course to outperform Marks & Spencer as well. M&S sales were nose-diving as shoppers turned from their frumpy collections to shop at Primark. Primark was apparently unaffected by the warm winter weather that blighted its competitors – Next and Supergroup issued profit warnings while Primark continued to grow. Other retailers claimed shoppers were waiting for colder weather to buy their warm winter clothes, while Primark shoppers appeared willing to buy whatever the temperature. Primark saw strong demand for its £25 Boucle Crombie coat, printed T-shirts featuring Disney's Frozen and Harry Potter characters, jog legs (a form of styled jogging trousers) and above the knee boots.

The company is in the midst of an international expansion drive with plans to grow on the east coast of America and to enter the Boston market in 2016, aiming to quickly have ten stores open and expand from that base. The selling pitch for the US is that buying at Primark is not trading down for the US consumer, but just normal low-price shopping, and they expect to make a big impact in the teen fashion space. One retail analyst says, 'What Primark offers is fashion at crazy low prices. Their gross margin is much lower, yet their merchandise and store designs are as good as you can get. It's been a winning combination in the UK and Europe, and could be in America in due course.' Meanwhile Primark stores in Spain and Germany were outperforming even the UK achievements – markets where people said Primark could never succeed, but it has.

Paul Marchant, Primark's chief executive, is only the second person to head the retailer in its 45-year history. In five years as chief executive, he has succeeded in accelerating Primark's expansion in Europe, while defying the recession in the UK – with the rapid growth in sales that has made Primark such a major force on the high street. Primark's 44 per cent increase in operating profit in 2013 earned him the UK fashion industry's most influential person award from industry journal *Drapers*. He is the one who now faces the challenge of breaking into the US – a challenge that has defeated many other European retailers.

Questions for discussion

1. What microenvironmental factors have influenced Primark's performance over the past few years?
2. What macroenvironmental factors have influenced Primark's performance during that period?

3. By focusing on low prices, has Primark pursued the best strategy? Why or why not?
4. What alternative strategy might Primark have followed in harsh economic conditions?
5. Given Primark's current position, what recommendations would you make to the chief executive for the company's future?
6. Does Primark have a robust marketing strategy or was it just lucky enough to be in the right place at the right time? List the arguments both ways and decide which are the most convincing.

Sources: Eoin Callan, Lucy Killgren and Elizabeth Rigby, 'Customers feel the quality not the width', *Financial Times*, 12 September 2006, p. 25; Claer Barrett and Andrea Felsted, 'Primark slowdown bodes ill', *Financial Times*, 1 March 2011, p. 19; Claer Barrett, 'Squeezed buyers halve Primark sales growth', *Financial Times*, 12 September 2011; Louise Lucas, 'Strong Primark sales boost ABF', *Financial Times*, 19 January 2012; Louise Eccles, 'How budget brands beat Boden and M&S', *Daily Mail*, 2 July 2012, p. 33; Andrea Felsted and Louise Lucas, 'Primark proves to be good fit at Asos', *Financial Times*, 13 June 2013, p. 21; Neil Craven, 'Primark soars after factory disaster fails to deter shoppers', *Daily Mail*, 20 April 2014, p. 89; Claer Barrett and Barney Jopson, 'Primark unveils US expansion plan', *Financial Times*, 9 September 2014, p. 24; Rupert Steiner, 'Primark leaves rival retailers in its wake', *Daily Mail*, 5 November 2014, p. 61.

CHAPTER FOUR

Managing marketing information to gain customer insights

Chapter preview

In this chapter, we continue our exploration of how marketers gain insights into consumers and the marketplace. We look at how companies develop and manage information about important marketplace elements: customers, competitors, products and marketing programmes. To succeed in today's marketplace, companies must know how to turn mountains of marketing information into fresh customer insights that will help them deliver greater value to customers.

Let's start by look at Tiger. Tiger has grown from a market stall to a huge company because it looks at what its customer's needs and wants. Sounds simple? It isn't. But it all starts with the head of the company.

Objectives outline

➤ **Objective 1** Explain the importance of information in gaining insights about the marketplace and customers.
Marketing information and customer insights
(pp. 104–106)

➤ **Objective 2** Define the marketing information system and discuss its parts.
Assessing marketing information needs (p. 106)
Developing marketing information (pp. 107–109)

➤ **Objective 3** Outline the steps in the marketing research process.
Marketing research (pp. 109–122)

➤ **Objective 4** Explain how companies analyse and use marketing information.
Analysing and using marketing information
(pp. 122–124)

➤ **Objective 5** Discuss the special issues some marketing researchers face, including public policy and ethics issues.
Other marketing information considerations
(pp. 124–127)

Tigers, Tigers everywhere!
By Eleri Rosier (Cardiff Business School)

Tiger is a variety store like no other. Originating in Scandinavia where it has caused a mini retail revolution selling stylish and innovative products at low prices, from homeware, kitchenware and stationery to toy and hobby items and offering a unique shopping experience.

Founded in 1995 by Lennart Lajboschitz, who started out running a market stall in Copenhagen's Israel Square, Tiger was conceived in Copenhagen as a pound shop. Its name is a play on 'tier', which is Danish slang for 10 kroner (£1.10). With the ethos to sell 'stylish own-branded products in a fun environment at astonishing low prices', it has quickly developed from a modest outlet to a recognised chain with over 400 stores across 25 European countries and Japan.

Speaking after analysing extensive competitor intelligence Lajboschitz suggested: 'When we started in 2005 I thought the average discount store was rubbish. There was just so much rubbish around then but customers now demand better quality from the discounters.' Tiger's success comes at a time when other high street stores are struggling, but cut-price discounter outlets such as TK Maxx, Poundland, Aldi and Lidl are thriving.

So what makes Tiger different? It's explicitly targeted at the savvy middle classes who are no longer embarrassed to shop in discount stores – but still like a nice shopping experience while they go in search of a bargain.

'Five or ten years ago you were either an M&S or an Asda shopper, but we are now sophisticated shoppers,' says Tiger UK managing director Philip Bier. 'We are not so worried about what people think. There used to be real stigma to middle-class customers going to a pound shop; that stigma has now more or less gone. Everybody is keen to be seen in Tiger despite its low prices because it's the smart place to spend your hard-earned cash.' The Tiger concept involves offering a constantly changing range – 300 new products hit the shelves each month – of unique items at very competitive prices that are sold in smart outlets.

The business ethos has been to take products away from being functional to more emotional so a plain mug will have a quirky design imprinted on it and it might be sold alongside other complementary items. Products are given the Tiger touch, adding smart Scandinavian design to make the ordinary extraordinary but with an enticing price tag, with 80 per cent of their products being sold at 5 euros or less. Whereas the business was predominantly about adding designs to base products bought in from China, the volume of goods now being sold have enabled it to increasingly create the base products themselves thereby adding to the unique nature of the goods and making the company as relevant and unique as possible. Sales data also showed that the products they designed and manufactured themselves sold 15 per cent faster. This shift has seen Tiger morph from discount to design stores with 70 per cent of goods produced in-house by a team of ten full-time designers, who come up with 300 new products a month.

Tiger targets savvy middle class shoppers who are no longer embarrassed to shop in discount stores in search of a bargain.

Source: Tiger Retail Ltd

Market research at Tiger is dynamic, gaining customer and marketplace insights through in-store observational research. Lajboschitz himself walks a Tiger store every day assessing in-store dynamics and watching how customers evaluate products in the store, so that they can quickly adapt to any subtle changes in customer desires, needs and wants. Tiger senior managers and designers are encouraged to travel widely, engage with young people, to listen, watch and learn from customers so that they can constantly innovate, adapt and change their products accordingly. This dynamic approach to gathering market information certainly seems to be working as a new store opens every three days in Europe and others are springing up in Japan where units double the European average of 250 sq m achieve four times the sales levels.

'Just because it is affordable, it doesn't need to be nasty and low quality,' explains Tiger UK Managing Director Philip Bier. Tiger's consumer research proved that all things Scandinavian really appealed to Britain, with UK shoppers having been quick to embrace Swedish and Danish brands, with the likes of H&M, Cos and Clas Ohlson. Bier believes Tiger can capitalise on this consumer trend to become as influential as IKEA, which changed the way British homes looked when it arrived with its trendy pine furniture and traditional folk print cushions in the late 1980s. However, Scandinavian design, particularly in interiors, was always considered to be desirable but expensive. Tiger's market research and competitor analysis showed that brands like IKEA and H&M had already done a lot to address the perception of high price. With more than 43,000 shops lying empty in the UK, high streets are crying out for new retailers and with many Britons yet to feel the economic recovery in their pocket, value retailers such as Poundland, Wilkinsons, Aldi and Lidl are having their moment in the sun. 'Our timing is really good in that there is a need for real shops on the high street,' says Bier. 'We are somewhere people can enjoy going to spend a few quid and leave without having to think too much about it.'

Bucking the online trend, Tiger is also flourishing without the Internet. With many British retailers looking to the web as their saviour, Tiger's website only allows customers to browse products and find out where the shops are located but not to purchase as the brand sees the high street as its biggest opportunity. With a transaction value of below £10 and items that can be quite bulky and fragile, delivery becomes complicated and expensive, and does not particularly lend itself to Internet shopping. Both Bier and Lajboschitz agree that their customer intelligence shows that much of their business is impulse shopping and their strategy is fuelled by opening new stores in urban affluent and fashionable high streets and shopping centres.[1]

Author comment

Marketing information by itself has little value. The value is in the *customer insights* gained from the information and how marketers use these insights to make better decisions.

Pinterest's unique insight into the Internet generation allowed them to fulfil the needs of consumers wanting to present themselves and their interest via organised online displays of images.

Source: Anatolii Babii/Getty Images

Excellent products and marketing programmes begin with good customer information. Companies also need an abundance of information on competitors, resellers and other actors and marketplace forces. But more than just gathering information, marketers must *use* the information to gain powerful *customer and market insights*.

MARKETING INFORMATION AND CUSTOMER INSIGHTS

To create value for customers and build meaningful relationships with them, marketers must first gain fresh, deep insights into what customers need and want. Such *customer insights* come from good marketing information. Companies use these customer insights to develop a competitive advantage.

For example, when it began a few years ago, social media site Pinterest needed to differentiate itself from the dozens, even hundreds, of existing social networking options.[2]

Pinterest's research uncovered a key customer insight. Many people want more than just Twitter or Facebook-like places to swap messages and pictures. They want a way to collect, organise and share things on the Internet related to their interests and passions. So Pinterest created a social scrapbooking site, where people can create and share digital pinboards – theme-based image collections on things that inspire them. 'Pinterest is your own little Internet of only the things you love,' says the company. Pinterest's mission is to provide a platform of 'inspiration and idea sharing' that connects people around the world through the 'things they find interesting'. Pinterest users can upload their own images grouped by topics, pin existing online images, and discover and re-pin images from others' pinboards.

Thanks to this unique customer insight, Pinterest has been wildly popular. Today, more than 70 million Pinterest users, including some 20 per cent of all Internet-using women, collectively pin more than 5 million articles a day and view more than 2.5 billion Pinterest pages a month. In turn, more than half a million businesses use Pinterest to engage and inspire their customer communities. Sephora, for example, has found that its nearly 226,000 Pinterest followers spend 15 times more than its Facebook fans.

Although customer and market insights are important for building customer value and engagement, these insights can be very difficult to obtain. Customer needs and buying motives are often anything but obvious – consumers themselves usually can't tell you exactly what they need and why they buy. To gain good customer insights, marketers must effectively manage marketing information from a wide range of sources.

Marketing information and today's 'big data'

With the recent explosion of information technologies, companies can now generate and find marketing information in great quantities. The marketing world is filled to the brim with information from innumerable sources. Consumers themselves are now generating tons of marketing information. Through e-mail, text messaging, blogging and social media, consumers now volunteer a tidal wave of bottom-up information to companies and to each other.

Far from lacking information, most marketing managers are overloaded with data and often overwhelmed by it. This problem is summed up in the concept of **big data**. The term *big data* refers to the huge and complex data sets generated by today's sophisticated information generation, collection, storage and analysis technologies. Every day, the people and systems of the world generate an amazing quintillion bytes of new data – about a trillion gigabytes of information each year. Put in perspective, that's enough data to fill 2.47 trillion good old CD-ROMs, a stack tall enough to go to the moon and back four times. If every word uttered by every human being who ever lived was written down and digitised, it would equal only two days' worth of the data being generated at today's rate.[3]

Big data presents marketers with both big opportunities and challenges. Companies that effectively tap this glut of big data can gain rich, timely customer insights. However, accessing and sifting through so much data is a daunting task. For example, when a company such as Pepsi monitors online discussions about its brands by searching key words in tweets, blogs, posts and other sources, its servers take in a stunning 6 million public conversations a day, more than 2 billion a year. That's far more information than any manager can digest.[4] Thus, marketers don't need *more* information; they need *better* information. And they need to make better use of the information they already have.

Managing marketing information

The real value of marketing information lies in how it is used – in the **customer insights** that it provides. Based on such thinking, companies ranging from Coca-Cola to Google and GEICO are restructuring their marketing information and research functions. They are creating *customer insights teams*, headed by a senior marketing executive with representatives from all of the firm's functional areas. For example, Coca-Cola's vice president of marketing strategy and insights heads up a team of 25 strategists who develop strategy based on marketing research insights. Similarly, GEICO's Customer Insights team analyses data from dozens of sources to gain insights into the GEICO customer experience, and then works with functional leaders across the organisation to find ways to improve that experience.[5]

Customer insights groups collect customer and market information from a wide variety of sources, ranging from traditional marketing research studies to mingling with and observing consumers to monitoring social media conversations about the company and its products. They mine big data from sources far and wide. Then they *use* this information to develop important customer insights from which the company can create more value for its customers.

Big data—The huge and complex data sets generated by today's sophisticated information generation, collection, storage and analysis technologies.

Customer insights—Fresh marketing information-based understandings of customers and the marketplace that become the basis for creating customer value, engagement and relationships.

Figure 4.1 The marketing information system

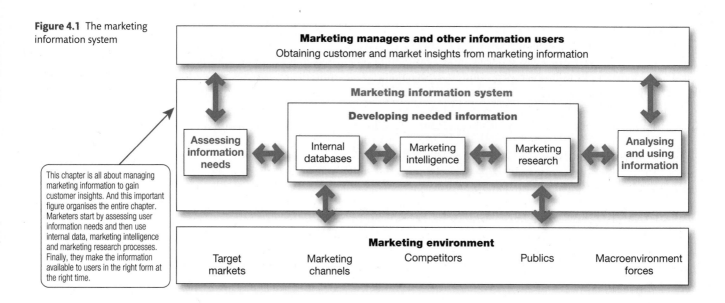

This chapter is all about managing marketing information to gain customer insights. And this important figure organises the entire chapter. Marketers start by assessing user information needs and then use internal data, marketing intelligence and marketing research processes. Finally, they make the information available to users in the right form at the right time.

Marketing information system (MIS)—People and procedures dedicated to assessing information needs, developing the needed information, and helping decision makers to use the information to generate and validate actionable customer and market insights.

Thus, companies must design effective marketing information systems that give managers the right information, in the right form, at the right time and help them to use this information to create customer value and stronger customer relationships. A **marketing information system** (**MIS**) consists of people and procedures dedicated to assessing information needs, developing the needed information, and helping decision makers use the information to generate and validate actionable customer and market insights.

Figure 4.1 shows that the MIS begins and ends with information users – marketing managers, internal and external partners, and others who need marketing information. First, it interacts with these information users to assess information needs. Next, it interacts with the marketing environment to develop needed information through internal company databases, marketing intelligence activities and marketing research. Finally, the MIS helps users to analyse and use the information to develop customer insights, make marketing decisions and manage customer relationships.

ASSESSING MARKETING INFORMATION NEEDS

The marketing information system primarily serves the company's marketing and other managers. However, it may also provide information to external partners, such as suppliers, resellers or marketing services agencies. For example, Walmart's Retail Link system gives key suppliers access to information on everything from customers' buying patterns and store inventory levels to how many items they've sold in which stores in the past 24 hours.[6]

A good MIS balances the information users would *like* to have against what they really *need* and what is *feasible* to offer. Some managers will ask for whatever information they can get without thinking carefully about what they really need. Too much information can be as harmful as too little. Other managers may omit things they ought to know, or they may not know to ask for some types of information they should have. For example, managers might need to know about surges in favourable or unfavourable consumer discussions about their brands on blogs or social media. But because they do not know about these discussions, they do not think to ask about them. The MIS must monitor the marketing environment to provide decision makers with information they should have to make key marketing decisions.

Finally, the costs of obtaining, analysing, storing and delivering information can mount quickly. The company must decide whether the value of insights gained from additional information is worth the costs of providing it, and both value and cost are often hard to assess.

DEVELOPING MARKETING INFORMATION

Marketers can obtain the needed information from *internal data*, *marketing intelligence* and *marketing research*.

Internal data

Many companies build extensive **internal databases**, collections of consumer and market information obtained from data sources within the company's network. Information in an internal database can come from many sources. The marketing department furnishes information on customer characteristics, in-store and online sales transactions, and web and social media site visits. The customer service department keeps records of customer satisfaction or service problems. The accounting department provides detailed records of sales, costs and cash flows. Operations reports on production, shipments and inventories. The sales force reports on reseller reactions and competitor activities, and marketing channel partners provide data on sales transactions. Harnessing such information can provide powerful customer insights and competitive advantage.

> A group of online advertising companies and publishers has launched a new code of conduct to help the industry cope with new European regulations around adverts based on tracking browsing habits. The European Advertising Standards Alliance guidelines commit to providing consumers with transparency about targeted advertising, protection for children and easier ways for consumers to complain if they feel their data have been misused. The new standards for online advertising using tracking cookies include an icon, to be appended to banners and other internet ads, linking to further information about targeting and giving consumers the opportunity to opt out of such tracking at youronlinechoices.eu. Companies committing to the system include Google, Microsoft, AOL and Yahoo, the last of which is already using a similar icon system on some of its sites. Publishers including *The Guardian*, the *Telegraph*, Yell and the *Financial Times* have also agreed to it. The EASA hopes that in the area of targeted advertising, its self-regulatory system will avoid the need for regular pop-ups or other clunky mechanisms to grant that permission. National industry bodies already checking that advertising does not mislead or offend, such as the UK's Advertising Standards Authority, will be enlisted to enforce the new rules. 'EASA's Best Practice Recommendation will provide European consumers with clear information and innovative ways to manage their choices concerning online behavioural advertising, as well as making available the use of the tried and tested national self-regulatory organisations if consumers wish to further complain', said Angela Mills Wade, vice-chairman of the EASA.[7]

Internal databases usually can be accessed more quickly and cheaply than other information sources, but they also present some problems. Because internal information is often collected for other purposes, it may be incomplete or in the wrong form for making marketing decisions. Data also ages quickly; keeping the database current requires a major effort. Finally, managing the mountains of information that a large company produces requires highly sophisticated equipment and techniques.

Competitive marketing intelligence

Competitive marketing intelligence is the systematic monitoring, collection and analysis of publicly available information about consumers, competitors and developments in the marketplace. The goal of competitive marketing intelligence is to improve strategic decision making by understanding the consumer environment, assessing and tracking competitors' actions, and providing early warnings of opportunities and threats. Marketing intelligence techniques range from observing consumers first-hand to quizzing the company's own employees, benchmarking competitors' products, researching on the Internet, and monitoring social media buzz.

Author comment

The problem isn't *finding* information; the world is bursting with information from a glut of sources. The real challenge is to find the *right* information — from inside and outside sources — and turn it into customer insights.

Internal databases— Collections of consumer and market information obtained from data sources within the company network.

Competitive marketing intelligence—The systematic monitoring, collection and analysis of publicly available information about consumers, competitors and developments in the marketing environment.

Good marketing intelligence can help marketers gain insights into how consumers talk about and engage with their brands. Many companies send out teams of trained observers to mix and mingle personally with customers as they use and talk about the company's products. Other companies – such as Dell, Cisco, PepsiCo and MasterCard – have set up sophisticated digital command centres that routinely monitor brand-related online consumer and market-place activity.

For example, MasterCard's digital intelligence command centre – called the Conversation Suite – monitors, analyses and responds in real time to millions of online conversations around the world:[8]

> MasterCard's Conversation Suite monitors online brand-related conversations across 43 markets and 26 languages. It tracks social networks, blogs, online and mobile video and traditional media — any and every digital place that might contain relevant content or commentary on MasterCard. At MasterCard's Purchase, New York, headquarters, Conversation Suite staff huddle with managers from various MasterCard departments and business units in front of a giant 40-foot LED screen that displays summaries of on-going global brand conversations, refreshed every four minutes. A rotating group of marketing and customer service people spends two or three hours a day in the command centre. 'It's a real-time focus group', says a MasterCard marketing executive. 'We track all mentions of MasterCard and any of our products, plus the competition.'
>
> MasterCard uses what it sees, hears, and learns in the Conversation Suite to improve its products and marketing, track brand performance, and spark meaningful customer conversations and engagement. MasterCard is even training 'social ambassadors' and 'social concierges', who can join online conversations and engage customers and brand influencers directly. 'Today, almost everything we do [across the company] is rooted in insights we're gathering from the Conversation Suite,' says another manager. '[It's] transforming the way we do business.'

Companies also need to actively monitor competitors' activities. They can monitor competitors' web and social media sites. For example, Amazon's Competitive Intelligence arm routinely purchases merchandise from competing sites to analyse and compare their assortment, speed and service quality. Companies can use the Internet to search specific competitor names, events or trends and see what turns up. And tracking consumer conversations about competing brands is often as revealing as tracking conversations about the company's own brands.

Much competitor intelligence can be collected from people inside the company – executives, engineers and scientists, purchasing agents and the sales force. The company can also obtain important intelligence information from suppliers, resellers and key customers. Intelligence seekers can also pore through many thousands of online databases. Some are free. For example, the European Patent Office provides free access to 70 million patent documents and Europages is a free directory of 2.3 million European suppliers.[9] For a fee, companies can also subscribe to any of the more than 3,000 online databases and information search services, such as Kompass, Hoover's and LexisNexis. Today's marketers have an almost overwhelming amount of competitor information only a few keystrokes away.

The intelligence game goes both ways. Facing determined competitive marketing intelligence efforts by competitors, most companies take steps to protect their own information. For example, Apple is obsessed with secrecy, and it passes that obsession along to its employees. 'At Apple everything is a secret,' says an insider. 'Apple

MasterCard and most progressive companies carefully monitor what people are saying about them and their products in a range of online forums.
Source: 123RF.com

wants new products to remain in stealth mode until their release dates.' Information leaks about new products before they are introduced gives the competition time to respond, raises customer expectations, and can steal thunder and sales from current products. So Apple employees are taught a 'loose-lips-sink-ships' mentality: A T-shirt for sale in the company store reads, 'I visited the Apple campus, but that's all I'm allowed to say.'[10]

One self-admitted corporate spy advises that companies should try conducting marketing intelligence investigations of themselves, looking for potentially damaging information leaks. They should start by 'vacuuming up' everything they can find in the public record, including job postings, court records, company advertisements and blogs, web pages, press releases, online business reports, social media postings by customers and employees, and other information available to inquisitive competitors.[11]

The growing use of marketing intelligence also raises ethical issues. Some intelligence-gathering techniques may involve questionable ethics. Clearly, companies should take advantage of publicly available information. However, they should not stoop to snoop. With all the legitimate intelligence sources now available, a company does not need to break the law or accepted codes of ethics to get good intelligence.

MARKETING RESEARCH

Author comment

Whereas marketing intelligence involves actively scanning the general marketing environment, marketing research involves more focused studies to gain customer insights relating to specific marketing decisions.

In addition to marketing intelligence information about general consumer, competitor and marketplace happenings, marketers often need formal studies that provide customer and market insights for specific marketing situations and decisions. For example, Heineken NV and the UniCredit Group want to know what appeals will be most effective in their UEFA Champions League Football advertising. Google wants to know how web searchers will react to a proposed redesign of its site. And Aéroport de Paris wants to know how many and what kinds of people want to use airports near Paris and when they wish to do so. In such situations, marketing intelligence will not provide the detailed information needed. In such situations, managers will need marketing research.

Marketing research is the systematic design, collection, analysis and reporting of data relevant to a specific marketing situation facing an organisation. Companies use marketing research in a wide variety of situations. For example, marketing research gives marketers insights into customer motivations, purchase behaviour and satisfaction. It can help them to assess market potential and market share or measure the effectiveness of pricing, product, distribution and promotion activities.

Marketing research—The systematic design, collection, analysis and reporting of data relevant to a specific marketing situation facing an organisation.

Some large companies have their own research departments that work with marketing managers on marketing research projects. In addition, these companies – like their smaller counterparts – frequently hire outside research specialists to consult with management on specific marketing problems and to conduct marketing research studies. Sometimes firms simply purchase data collected by outside firms to aid in their decision making.

The marketing research process has four steps (see Figure 4.2): defining the problem and research objectives, developing the research plan, implementing the research plan, and interpreting and reporting the findings.

Figure 4.2 The marketing research process

This first step in the marketing research process is probably the most difficult but also the most important. It guides the entire research process. It's frustrating to reach the end of an expensive research project only to learn that you've addressed the wrong problem!

Defining the problem and research objectives → Developing the research plan for collecting information → Implementing the research plan – collecting and analysing the data → Interpreting and reporting the findings

Defining the problem and research objectives

Marketing managers and researchers must work together closely to define the problem and agree on research objectives. The manager best understands the decision for which information is needed, whereas the researcher best understands marketing research and how to obtain the information. Defining the problem and research objectives is often the hardest step in the research process. The manager may know that something is wrong, without knowing the specific causes.

After the problem has been defined carefully, the manager and the researcher must set the research objectives. A marketing research project might have one of three types of objectives. The objective of **exploratory research** is to gather preliminary information that will help define the problem and suggest hypotheses. The objective of **descriptive research** is to describe things, such as the market potential for a product or the demographics and attitudes of consumers who buy the product. The objective of **causal research** is to test hypotheses about cause-and-effect relationships. For example, would a 10 per cent decrease in tuition at a private college result in an enrolment increase sufficient to offset the reduced tuition? Managers often start with exploratory research and later follow with descriptive or causal research.

The statement of the problem and research objectives guides the entire research process. The manager and the researcher should put the statement in writing to be certain that they agree on the purpose and expected results of the research.

Developing the research plan

Once researchers have defined the research problem and objectives, they must determine the exact information needed, develop a plan for gathering it efficiently, and present the plan to management. The research plan outlines sources of existing data and spells out the specific research approaches, contact methods, sampling plans and instruments that researchers will use to gather new data.

Research objectives must be translated into specific information needs. For example, suppose that Red Bull wants to know how consumers would react to a proposed new vitamin-enhanced water drink that would be available in several flavours and sold under the Red Bull name. Red Bull currently dominates the worldwide energy drink market with more than 43 per cent of the market share worldwide – it sold more than €2.7 billion worth of energy drinks last year. And the brand recently introduced Red Bull Editions flavoured energy drinks and Red Bull Total Zero, an energy drink for calorie-averse consumers.[12] A new line of enhanced, fizzless waters – akin to Glacéau's vitaminwater – might help Red Bull leverage its strong brand position even further. The proposed research might call for the following specific information:

- The demographic, economic and lifestyle characteristics of current Red Bull customers. (Do current customers also consume enhanced-water products? Are such products consistent with their lifestyles? Or would Red Bull need to target a new segment of consumers?)
- The characteristics and usage patterns of the broader population of enhanced-water users: What do they need and expect from such products, where do they buy them, when and how do they use them, and what existing brands and price points are most popular? (The new Red Bull product would need strong, relevant positioning in the crowded enhanced-water market.)
- Retailer reactions to the proposed new product line: Would they stock and support it? Where would they display it? (Failure to get retailer support would hurt sales of the new drink.)
- Forecasts of sales and profits of both the new and current Red Bull products. (Will the new enhanced waters create new sales or simply take sales away from current Red Bull products? Will the new product increase Red Bull's overall profits?)

Red Bull's marketers will need these and many other types of information to decide whether or not to introduce the new product and, if so, the best way to do it.

The research plan should be presented in a *written proposal*. A written proposal is especially important when the research project is large and complex or when an outside firm carries it out. The proposal should cover the management problems addressed, the research objectives, the information to be obtained, and how the results will help management's decision making. The proposal also should include estimated research costs.

To meet the manager's information needs, the research plan can call for gathering secondary data, primary data, or both. **Secondary data** consist of information that already exists somewhere, having been collected for another purpose. **Primary data** consist of information collected for the specific purpose at hand.

Gathering secondary data

Researchers usually start by gathering secondary data. The company's internal database provides a good starting point. However, the company can also tap into a wide assortment of external information sources.

Companies can buy secondary data reports from outside suppliers. For example, Nielsen sells shopper insight data from a consumer panel of more than 260,000 households in 27 countries worldwide, with measures of trial and repeat purchasing, brand loyalty and buyer demographics. Experian Consumer Research (Simmons) sells information consumer panel data on more than 8,000 brands in 450 product categories, including detailed consumer profiles that assess everything from the products consumers buy and the brands they prefer to their lifestyles, attitudes and media preferences. The MONITOR service by Yankelovich sells information on important social and lifestyle trends. These and other firms supply high-quality data to suit a wide variety of marketing information needs.[13]

Using *commercial online databases*, marketing researchers can conduct their own searches of secondary data sources. General database services such as Dialog, ProQuest and LexisNexis put an incredible wealth of information at the fingertips of marketing decision makers. Beyond commercial websites offering information for a fee, almost every industry association, government agency, business publication and news medium offers free information to those tenacious enough to find their websites or apps.

Internet search engines can also be a big help in locating relevant secondary information sources. However, they can also be very frustrating and inefficient. For example, a Red Bull marketer Googling 'enhancedwater products' would come up with more than 50,000 hits. Still, well-structured, well-designed online searches can be a good starting point to any marketing research project.

Secondary data can usually be obtained more quickly and at a lower cost than primary data. Also, secondary sources can sometimes provide data an individual company cannot collect on its own – information that either is not directly available or would be too expensive to collect. For example, it would be too expensive for Red Bull's marketers to conduct a continuing retail store audit to find out about the market shares, prices and displays of competitors' brands. But those marketers can buy the InfoScan service from SymphonyIRI Group, which provides this information based on scanner and other data from 34,000 retail stores.[14]

Secondary data can also present problems. Researchers can rarely obtain all the data they need from secondary sources. For example, Red Bull will not find existing information regarding consumer reactions about a new enhanced-water line that it has not yet placed on the market. Even when data can be found, the information might not be very usable. The researcher must evaluate secondary information carefully to make certain it is *relevant* (fits the research project's needs), *accurate* (reliably collected and reported), *current* (up-to-date enough for current decisions) and *impartial* (objectively collected and reported).

Red Bull Energy Drink is a unique combination of Taurine, Glucuronolactone, B-vitamins and other important nutrients. It improves performance, increases endurance and concentration, improves reaction speed and stimulates the metabolism. In short, Red Bull vitalizes both body and mind.

RED BULL GIVES YOU WIIINGS.

A decision by Red Bull to add a line of enhanced waters to its already successful mix of energy and cola drinks would call for marketing research that provides lots of specific information.

Source: Courtesy of © Red Bull Media House

Secondary data—Information that already exists somewhere, having been collected for another purpose.

Primary data—Information collected for the specific purpose at hand.

Table 4.1 Planning primary data collection

Research approaches	Contact methods	Sampling plan	Research instruments
Observation	Mail	Sampling unit	Questionnaire
Survey	Telephone	Sample size	Mechanical instruments
Experiment	Personal	Sampling procedure	
	Online		

Primary data collection

Secondary data provide a good starting point for research and often help to define research problems and objectives. In most cases, however, the company must also collect primary data. Table 4.1 shows that designing a plan for primary data collection calls for a number of decisions on *research approaches*, *contact methods*, the *sampling plan* and *research instruments*.

Research approaches

Research approaches for gathering primary data include observation, surveys and experiments. We discuss each one in turn.

Observational research

Observational research—Gathering primary data by observing relevant people, actions and situations.

Observational research involves gathering primary data by observing relevant people, actions and situations. For example, food retailer Carrefour might evaluate possible new store locations by checking traffic patterns, neighbourhood conditions, and the locations of competing Lidl, Aldi, Tesco and other retail chains.

Researchers often observe consumer behaviour to glean customer insights they cannot obtain by simply asking customers questions. For instance, Ricability is a UK charity providing consumer research and advice for older and disabled people. They use observational studies as their target customers – the elderly, infirm or disabled – often fail to notice or are unable to communicate potential health and safety hazards. Consequently, Ricability explores product experiences by observing end users' operation of products in their own homes rather than via direct questioning. In contrast, Fisher-Price has established an observation lab in which it can observe the reactions of little children to new toys. The Fisher-Price Play Lab is a sunny, toy-strewn space where lucky children get to test Fisher-Price prototypes, under the watchful eyes of designers who hope to learn what will get them worked up into a new-toy frenzy.

Marketers not only observe what consumers do but also observe what consumers are saying. As discussed earlier, marketers now routinely listen in on consumer conversations on blogs, social networks and websites. Observing such naturally occurring feedback can provide inputs that simply can't be gained through more structured and formal research approaches.

Ethnographic research—A form of observational research that involves sending trained observers to watch and interact with consumers in their 'natural environments'.

A wide range of companies now use **ethnographic research**. Ethnographic research involves sending observers to watch and interact with consumers in their 'natural environments'. The observers might be trained anthropologists and psychologists or company researchers and managers. Consider this example:[15]

Rank Group, the company behind Grosvenor casinos and Mecca bingo, has become the latest UK group to employ immersive market research to better understand its customers. Rank sends senior staff into the homes of customers to probe daily habits that would sometimes seem to have little to do with its products and services. In addition to long interviews, researchers photograph the subjects at home, travel with them on their journeys to bingo clubs or casinos and observe them throughout their visits. Unlike other companies, however, Rank wants its top executives to take part. Ian Burke, chief executive, has already spent a day following a couple from their home to one of the company's casinos and observing them there. 'At Mecca, there are already back-to-floor initiatives [in which head office staff work at the clubs]', said Jon McPherson, Rank's group head of insight and analytics. 'But immersion with a customer is very different from seeing things through the eyes of the employee.' The push follows a year in which Rank stemmed a decline in Mecca revenues by getting customers to spend more per visit — in part through new offerings, such as food and drink table service and 'After Dark' bingo, a looser form of the game. Luring more people in is the next task — and one Mr Burke has said cannot be accomplished without a better insight into customers. Hence, Jon McPherson hopes even to involve Rank Interactive, the group's online division. 'We have good technology for measuring how people move around a [web] page, but we don't know if people come home, put the children in bed, make a cup of tea and then sit down at the computer.'

P&G uses extensive ethnographic research to gain insights into serving the world's poor. Three years ago, P&G launched the '$2-a-day project', named for the average income of the people it targets worldwide. The project sends ethnographic researchers trekking through the jungles of Brazil, the slums of India, and farming villages in rural China seeking insights into the needs of very-low-income consumers. As an example, P&G researchers recently spent time with poor Chinese potato farmer Wei Xiao Yan, observing in detail as she washed her long black hair using only three cups of water. Her family's water supply is a precious commodity – it comes from storing rainwater. P&G must find affordable and practical solutions that work in Wei's harsh environment while also supporting her need to feel attractive.[16]

Insights from P&G's '$2-a-day project' have already produced some successful new products for emerging markets – such as a skin-sensitive detergent for women who wash clothing by hand. In the works is a body cleanser formulated to clean without much water – it generates foam, which can be easily wiped away, instead of lather. Another product is a leave-in hair conditioner that requires no water at all. For underserved customers like Wei Xiao Yan, P&G has learned, it must develop products that are not just effective and affordable but are also aspirational.

Beyond conducting ethnographic research in physical consumer environments, many companies now routinely conduct *Netnography* research – observing consumers in a natural context on the Internet and mobile space. Observing people as they interact and move about in the online world can provide useful insights into both online and offline buying motives and behaviour. And observing people's shopping patterns by tracking their mobile movement, both within and between stores, can provide retailers with valuable marketing information.[17]

Observational and ethnographic research often yield the kinds of details that just don't emerge from traditional research questionnaires or focus groups. Whereas traditional quantitative research approaches seek to test known hypotheses and obtain answers to well-defined product or strategy questions, observational research can generate fresh customer and market insights that people are unwilling or unable to provide. It provides a window into customers' unconscious actions and unexpressed needs and feelings.

In contrast, however, some things simply cannot be observed, such as attitudes, motives or private behaviour. Long-term or infrequent behaviour is also difficult to observe. Finally, observations can be very difficult to interpret. Because of these limitations, researchers often use observation along with other data collection methods.

Survey research

Survey research, the most widely used method for primary data collection, is the approach best suited for gathering descriptive information. A company that wants to know about people's knowledge, attitudes, preferences or buying behaviour can often find out by asking them directly.

The major advantage of survey research is its flexibility; it can be used to obtain many different kinds of information in many different situations. Surveys addressing almost any marketing question or decision can be conducted by phone or mail, in person or online.

However, survey research also presents some problems. Sometimes people are unable to answer survey questions because they cannot remember or have never thought about what they do and

Survey research—Gathering primary data by asking people questions about their knowledge, attitudes, preferences and buying behaviour.

why they do it. People may be unwilling to respond to unknown interviewers or about things they consider private. Respondents may answer survey questions even when they do not know the answer just to appear smarter or more informed. Or they may try to help the interviewer by giving pleasing answers. Finally, busy people may not take the time, or they might resent the intrusion into their privacy.

Experimental research

Whereas observation is best suited for exploratory research and surveys for descriptive research, **experimental research** is best suited for gathering causal information. Experiments involve selecting matched groups of subjects, giving them different treatments, controlling unrelated factors and checking for differences in group responses. Thus, experimental research tries to explain cause-and-effect relationships.

For example, before adding a new sandwich to its menu, Hard Rock Café might use experiments to test the effects on sales of two different prices it might charge. It could introduce the new sandwich at one price in one city and at another price in another city. If the cities are similar, and if all other marketing efforts for the sandwich are the same, then differences in sales in the two cities could be related to the price charged.

Contact methods

Information can be collected by mail, telephone, personal interview or online but there are strengths and weaknesses for each contact method.

Mail, telephone and personal interviewing

Mail questionnaires can be used to collect large amounts of information at a low cost per respondent. Respondents may give more honest answers to more personal questions on a mail questionnaire than to an unknown interviewer in person or over the phone. Also, no interviewer is involved to bias respondents' answers.

However, mail questionnaires are not very flexible; all respondents answer the same questions in a fixed order. Mail surveys usually take longer to complete, and the response rate – the number of people returning completed questionnaires – is often very low. Finally, the researcher often has little control over the mail questionnaire sample. Even with a good mailing list, it is hard to control *who* at a particular address fills out the questionnaire. As a result of the shortcomings, more and more marketers are now shifting to faster, more flexible and lower-cost e-mail, online and mobile phone surveys.

Telephone interviewing is one of the best methods for gathering information quickly, and it provides greater flexibility than mail questionnaires. Interviewers can explain difficult questions and, depending on the answers they receive, skip some questions or probe on others. Response rates tend to be higher than with mail questionnaires, and interviewers can ask to speak to respondents with the desired characteristics or even by name.

However, with telephone interviewing, the cost per respondent is higher than with mail, online or mobile questionnaires. Also, people may not want to discuss personal questions with an interviewer. The method introduces interviewer bias – the way interviewers talk, how they ask questions, and other differences that may affect respondents' answers. Finally, in this age of do-not-call lists and promotion-harassed consumers, potential survey respondents are increasingly hanging up on telephone interviewers rather than talking with them.

Personal interviewing takes two forms: individual interviewing and group interviewing. *Individual interviewing* involves talking with people in their homes or offices, on the street, or in shopping malls. Such interviewing is flexible. Trained interviewers can guide interviews, explain difficult questions, and explore issues as the situation requires. They can show subjects actual products, packages, advertisements or videos and observe reactions and behaviour. However, individual personal interviews may cost three to four times as much as telephone interviews.

Experimental research— Gathering primary data by selecting matched groups of subjects, giving them different treatments, controlling related factors, and checking for differences in group responses.

Group interviewing consists of inviting 6 to 10 people to meet with a trained moderator to talk about a good, service or organisation. Participants normally are paid a small sum for attending. A moderator encourages free and easy discussion, hoping that group interactions will bring out actual feelings and thoughts. At the same time, the moderator 'focuses' the discussion – hence the name **focus group interviewing**.

In traditional focus groups, researchers and marketers watch the focus group discussions from behind a one-way mirror and record comments in writing or on video for later study. Focus group researchers often use videoconferencing and Internet technology to connect marketers in distant locations with live focus group action. Using cameras and two-way sound systems, marketing executives in a far-off boardroom can look in and listen, using remote controls to zoom in on faces and pan the focus group at will.

Along with observational research, focus group interviewing has become one of the major qualitative marketing research tools for gaining fresh insights into consumer thoughts and feelings. In focus group settings, researchers not only hear consumer ideas and opinions, they can also observe facial expressions, body movements, group interplay and conversational flows. However, focus group studies present some challenges. They usually employ small samples to keep time and costs down, and it may be hard to generalise from the results. Moreover, consumers in focus groups are not always open and honest about their real feelings, behaviour and intentions in front of other people.

To overcome these problems, many researchers are tinkering with the focus group design. Some companies use *immersion groups* – small groups of consumers who interact directly and informally with product designers without a focus group moderator present. Other researchers are changing the environments in which they conduct focus groups to help consumers relax and elicit more authentic responses. For example, Lexus hosted a series of 'An evening with Lexus' dinners with groups of customers in customers' homes:[18]

According to Lexus group vice president and general manager Mark Templin, the best way to find out why luxury car buyers did or didn't become Lexus owners is to dine with them — up close and personal in their homes. At the first dinner, 16 owners of Lexus, Mercedes, BMW, Audi, Land Rover and other high-end cars traded their perceptions of the Lexus brand over a sumptuous meal prepared by a famous chef at a home. Templin gained many actionable insights. For example, some owners viewed Lexus vehicles as unexciting. 'Everyone had driven a Lexus at some point and had a great experience,' he says. 'But the Lexus they [had] wasn't as fun to drive as the car they have now. It's our challenge to show that Lexus is more fun to drive today than it was 15 years ago.' Templin was also surprised to learn the extent to which the grown children of luxury car buyers influence what car they purchase. Now, Templin says, future Lexus marketing will also target young adults who may not buy luxury cars but who influence their parents' decisions.

Individual and focus group interviews can add a personal touch as opposed to more numbers-oriented research. 'We get lots of research, and it tells us what we need to run our business, but I get more out of talking one-on-one,' confirms Lexus's Templin. 'It really comes to life when I hear people say it.'

Online marketing research

The growth of the Internet has had a dramatic impact on how marketing research is conducted. Increasingly, researchers are collecting primary data through **online marketing research**: Internet and mobile surveys, online panels, experiments, and online focus groups and brand communities.

Online research can take many forms. A company can use the Internet or mobile technology as a survey medium: It can include a questionnaire on its web or social media sites or use e-mail or mobile devices to invite people to answer questions. It can create online panels that provide regular feedback or conduct live discussions or online focus groups. Researchers

Focus group interviewing— Personal interviewing that involves inviting 6 to 10 people to gather for a few hours with a trained interviewer to talk about a product, service or organisation. The interviewer 'focuses' the group discussion on important issues.

Online marketing research— Collecting primary data online through Internet surveys, online focus groups, web-based experiments, or tracking of consumers' online behaviour.

can also conduct online experiments. They can experiment with different prices, headlines or product features on different web or mobile sites or at different times to learn the relative effectiveness of their offers. They can set up virtual shopping environments and use them to test new products and marketing programs. Or a company can learn about the behaviour of online customers by following their click streams as they visit the online site and move to other sites.

The Internet is especially well suited to *quantitative* research – for example, conducting marketing surveys and collecting data. Most Europeans now use the Internet, making it a fertile channel for reaching a broad cross-section of consumers.[19] As response rates for traditional survey approaches decline and costs increase, the Internet is quickly replacing mail and the telephone as the dominant data collection methodology.

Internet-based survey research offers many advantages over traditional phone, mail and personal interviewing approaches. The most obvious advantages are speed and low costs. By going online, researchers can quickly and easily distribute surveys to thousands of respondents simultaneously via e-mail or by posting them on selected online and mobile sites. Responses can be almost instantaneous, and because respondents themselves enter the information, researchers can tabulate, review and share research data as the information arrives.

Online research also usually costs much less than research conducted through mail, phone or personal interviews. Using the Internet eliminates most of the postage, phone, interviewer and data-handling costs associated with the other approaches. Moreover, sample size has little impact on costs. Once the questionnaire is set up, there's little difference in cost between 10 respondents and 10,000 respondents on the Internet.

Its low cost puts online research well within the reach of almost any business, large or small. In fact, with the Internet, what was once the domain of research experts is now available to almost any would-be researcher. Even smaller, less sophisticated researchers can use online survey services such as Snap Surveys (www.snapsurveys.com) and SurveyMonkey (www.surveymonkey .com) to create, publish and distribute their own custom online or mobile surveys in minutes.

Internet-based surveys also tend to be more interactive and engaging, easier to complete, and less intrusive than traditional phone or mail surveys. As a result, they usually garner higher response rates. The Internet is an excellent medium for reaching the hard to-reach consumer – for example, the often-elusive teen, single, affluent and well-educated audiences. It's also good for reaching people who lead busy lives, from working mothers to on-the-go executives. Such people are well represented online, and they can respond in their own space and at their own convenience.

Just as marketing researchers have rushed to use the Internet for quantitative surveys and data collection, they are now also adopting *qualitative* Internet-based research approaches, such as online focus groups, blogs and social networks. The Internet can provide a fast, low-cost way to gain qualitative customer insights.

Online focus groups— Gathering a small group of people online with a trained moderator to chat about a product, service or organisation and gain qualitative insights about consumer attitudes and behaviour.

A primary qualitative Internet-based research approach is **online focus groups**. For example, online research firm FocusVision offers its InterVu service, which harnesses the power of web conferencing to conduct focus groups with participants at remote locations, anywhere in the world, at any time. Using their own webcams, InterVu participants can log on to focus sessions from their homes or offices and see, hear and react to each other in real-time, face-to-face discussions.[20]

Such focus groups can be conducted in any language and viewed with simultaneous translation. They work well for bringing together people from different parts of the country or world at low cost. Researchers can view the sessions in real time from just about anywhere, eliminating travel, lodging and facility costs. Finally, although online focus groups require some advance scheduling, results are almost immediate.

Although growing rapidly, both quantitative and qualitative Internet-based research have some drawbacks. One major problem is controlling who's in the online sample. Without seeing respondents, it's difficult to know who they really are. To overcome such sample and context problems, many online research firms use opt-in communities and respondent panels. Alternatively, many companies are now developing their own custom social networks and using them to gain customer inputs and insights. For example, in addition to picking customers' brains in face-to-face events such as 'An evening with Lexus' dinners in customers' homes, Lexus has built an extensive online research community called the Lexus Advisory Board, which consists of 20,000 invitation-only Lexus owners representing a wide range of demographics, psychographics and model ownership. Lexus regularly surveys the group to obtain input on everything from perceptions of the brand to customer relationships with dealers.[21] Zoomerang offers an online consumer and business panel profiled on more than 500 attributes.[22] Alternatively, many companies are now developing their own custom social networks and using them to gain customer inputs and insights. Consider Adidas:[23]

When Adidas developed a Facebook fan page, it quickly attracted 2 million users. Ditto for its pages on Twitter and YouTube. But monitoring and analysing postings by 2 million members in public online communities is not realistic, so the sporting goods giant created its own private online community called Adidas Insiders, inviting only the most active users on its public pages to join. Through online conversations with and among Adidas Insiders, company marketers can quickly gather real-time consumer feedback about brand perceptions, product ideas and marketing campaigns. Adidas Insiders are surprisingly willing — and even anxious — to be involved. 'It's a great help to [us] spending time with consumers that love the brand as much as we do,' says Adidas' director of digital media.

Testing strategies and concepts with the Insiders group provides fast and actionable customer insights for Adidas' product marketing teams. 'We're able to play with colours and materials and get instant feedback from these fans, which allows us to be more efficient in development and go-to-market planning,' says the Adidas marketing executive. 'We've even asked about things like voiceovers for videos and received surprising feedback that's caused us to alter creative.'

Online customer social networks – such as Adidas Insiders – can help companies gain customer inputs and insights. Adidas Insiders are surprisingly willing – and even anxious – to be involved.

Source: Adidas

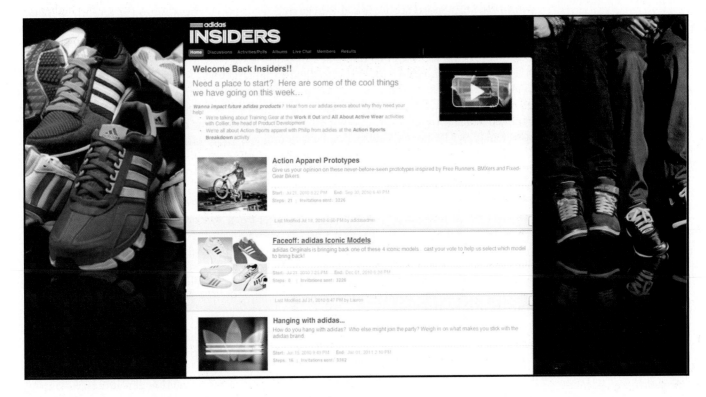

Online behavioural and social tracking and targeting

Thus, in recent years, the Internet has become an important tool for conducting research and developing customer insights. But today's marketing researchers are going even further – well beyond online surveys, focus groups and Internet communities. Increasingly, they are listening to and watching consumers by actively mining the rich veins of unsolicited, unstructured, 'bottom-up' customer information already coursing around the Internet. Whereas traditional marketing research provides more logical consumer responses to structured and intrusive research questions, online listening provides the passion and spontaneity of unsolicited consumer opinions.

Tracking consumers online might be as simple as scanning customer reviews and comments on the company's brand site or on shopping sites such as Amazon or BestBuy. Or it might mean using sophisticated online-analysis tools to deeply analyse the mountains of consumer brand-related comments and messages found in blogs or on social media sites, such as Facebook, Yelp, YouTube or Twitter. Listening to and engaging customers online can provide valuable insights into what consumers are saying or feeling about a brand. It can also provide opportunities for building positive brand experiences and relationships.

Information about what consumers do while surfing the vast expanse of the Internet – what searches they make, the sites they visit, how they shop and what they buy – is pure gold to marketers. And today's marketers are busy mining that gold. Then, in a practice called **behavioural targeting**, marketers use the online data to target ads and offers to specific consumers. For example, if you place a mobile phone in your Amazon shopping cart but don't buy it, you might expect to see some ads for that very type of phone the next time you visit your favourite ESPN site to catch up on the latest sports scores.

The newest wave of web analytics and targeting takes online eavesdropping even further – from *behavioural* targeting to *social* targeting. Whereas behavioural targeting tracks consumer movements across online sites, social targeting also mines individual online social connections and conversations from social networking sites. Research shows that consumers shop a lot like their friends and are much more likely to respond to ads from brands friends use. So, instead of just having a SportDirect.com ad for running shoes pop up because you've recently searched online for running shoes (behavioural targeting), an ad for a specific pair of running shoes pops up because a friend that you're connected to via Twitter just bought those shoes from Sport-Direct.com last week (social targeting).

Online listening, behavioural targeting and social targeting can help marketers to harness the massive amounts of consumer information swirling around the Internet. However, as marketers get more adept at trolling blogs, social networks and other Internet domains, many critics worry about consumer privacy. At what point does sophisticated online research cross the line into consumer stalking? Proponents claim that behavioural and social targeting benefit more than abuse consumers by feeding back ads and products that are more relevant to their interests. But to many consumers and public advocates, following consumers online and stalking them with ads feels more than just a little creepy.

Regulators and others are stepping in. Neelie Kroes, Vice-President of the European Commission has recommended the creation of a 'Do not track' system (the Internet equivalent to the 'Do not call' registry) – which would let people opt out of having their actions monitored online. Meanwhile, many major Internet browsers and social media have heeded the concerns by adding 'Do not track' features to their services.[24]

Sampling plan

Marketing researchers usually draw conclusions about large groups of consumers by studying a small sample of the total consumer population. A **sample** is a segment of the population selected for marketing research to represent the population as a whole. Ideally, the sample should be representative so that the researcher can make accurate estimates of the thoughts and behaviours of the larger population.

Behavioural targeting—Using online consumer tracking data to target advertisements and marketing offers to specific consumers.

Sample—A segment of the population selected for marketing research to represent the population as a whole.

Designing the sample requires three decisions. First, *who* is to be studied (what *sampling unit*)? The answer to this question is not always obvious. For example, to learn about the decision-making process for a family automobile purchase, should the subject be the husband, the wife, other family members, dealership salespeople, or all of these? Second, *how many* people should be included (what *sample size*)? Large samples give more reliable results than small samples. However, larger samples usually cost more, and it is not necessary to sample the entire target market or even a large portion to get reliable results.

Finally, *how* should the people in the sample be *chosen* (what *sampling procedure*)? Table 4.2 describes different kinds of samples. Using *probability samples*, each population member has a known chance of being included in the sample, and researchers can calculate confidence limits for sampling error. But when probability sampling costs too much or takes too much time, marketing researchers often take *non-probability samples*, even though their sampling error cannot be measured. These varied ways of drawing samples have different costs and time limitations as well as different accuracy and statistical properties. Which method is best depends on the needs of the research project.

Research instruments

In collecting primary data, marketing researchers have a choice of two main research instruments: *questionnaires* and *mechanical devices*.

Questionnaires

The questionnaire is by far the most common instrument, whether administered in person, by phone, by e-mail or online. Questionnaires are very flexible – there are many ways to ask questions. Closed-ended questions include all the possible answers, and subjects make choices among them. Examples include multiple-choice questions and scale questions. Open-ended questions allow respondents to answer in their own words. In a survey of airline users, Air France might simply ask, 'What is your opinion of Air France?' Or it might ask people to complete a sentence: 'When I choose an airline, the most important consideration is. . . .' These and other kinds of open-ended questions often reveal more than closed-ended questions because they do not limit respondents' answers.

Table 4.2 Types of samples

Probability sample	
Simple random sample	Every member of the population has a known and equal chance of selection.
Stratified random sample	The population is divided into mutually exclusive groups (such as age groups), and random samples are drawn from each group.
Cluster (area) sample	The population is divided into mutually exclusive groups (such as blocks), and the researcher draws a sample of the groups to interview.
Non-probability sample	
Convenience sample	The researcher selects the easiest population members from which to obtain information.
Judgement sample	The researcher uses his or her judgement to select population members who are good prospects for accurate information.
Quota sample	The researcher finds and interviews a prescribed number of people in each of several categories.

Open-ended questions are especially useful in exploratory research, when the researcher is trying to find out *what* people think but is not measuring *how many* people think in a certain way. Closed-ended questions, on the other hand, provide answers that are easier to interpret and tabulate.

Researchers should also use care in the *wording* and *ordering* of questions. They should use simple, direct and unbiased wording. Questions should be arranged in a logical order. The first question should create interest if possible, and difficult or personal questions should be asked last so that respondents do not become defensive.

Mechanical instruments

Although questionnaires are the most common research instrument, researchers also use mechanical instruments to monitor consumer behaviour. Nielsen Media Research attaches meters to television sets, cable boxes and satellite systems in selected homes to record who watches which programmes. Retailers use checkout scanners to record shoppers' purchases. Some companies are even building supermarket 'smart shelves'. The shelves use sensors to analyse facial structures and other characteristics that identify a shopper's age and sex and determine if and when the shopper selects a product off the shelf. Along with supplying a wealth of insights into consumer shopping behaviour, based on who's buying what, the smart shelves allow marketers to deliver real-time, personalised promotions via video screens on the shelves.[25]

Other mechanical devices measure subjects' physical responses to marketing offerings. Consider these example:[26]

Time Warner's new MediaLab at its New York headquarters looks more like a chic consumer electronics store than a research lab. But the lab employs a nifty collection of high-tech observation techniques to capture the changing ways that today's viewers are using and reacting to television and Web content. The MediaLab uses biometric measures to analyse every show subjects watch, every site they visit, and every commercial they skip. Meanwhile, mechanical devices assess viewer engagement via physiological measures of skin temperature, heart rate, sweat level, leaning in, and facial and eye movements. Observers behind two-way mirrors or using cameras that peer over each subject's shoulder make real-time assessments of web browsing behaviour. In all, the deep consumer insights gained from MediaLab observations are helping Time Warner prepare for marketing in today's rapidly changing digital media landscape.

And:[27]

Ipsos Mori, the market research firm, and its technology partner Eyetracker use equipment that measures every movement of a shopper's eyes. Encircling the head of participants is a plastic band supporting two miniature cameras wired up to a digital video recorder. One camera films everything in their field of vision. The other tracks tiny movements of their right eye to generate a visual record of every item of packaging, sign and shelf-label they look at. This cyborg-style headgear was initially developed to give combat pilots a split-second advantage in dogfights. Nowadays, it is high-street brands that are experimenting with its possibilities as they battle for the attention of time-pressed consumers. Richard Davies, senior vice-president of consumer and market insight at Unilever, the fast-moving consumer goods group, which has an in-house eye-tracking capability, says studying how people's eyes flit about has helped the company design packs that make its shampoos and detergents more noticeable on the supermarket shelf. When participants are asked what they have just looked at during a shopping trip, most people forget details or mix them up; but their eyes tell the true story of what they looked at and what they missed, where they went into the wrong aisle and the point they gave up hunting.

Still other researchers are applying *neuromarketing*, measuring brain activity to learn how consumers feel and respond. Marketing scientists using MRI scans and EEG devices have learned that tracking brain electrical activity and blood flow can provide companies with insights into what turns consumers on and off regarding their brands and marketing.

Companies ranging from Daimler AG , BMW and Honda UK to Unilever now hire neuromarketing research companies such as NeuroFocus and EmSense to help figure out what people are really thinking.[28]

Thirty men and women are studying a sporty silver test model of a next-generation Hyundai. The 15 men and 15 women are asked to stare at specific parts of the vehicle, including the bumper, the windshield and the tires. Electrode-studded caps on their heads capture the electrical activity in their brains as they view the car for an hour. That brain-wave information is recorded in a hard drive each person wears on a belt. Hyundai believes that their brain activity will show preferences that could lead to purchasing decisions. 'We want to know what consumers think about a car before we start manufacturing thousands of them,' says Hyundai's manager of brand strategy. He expects the carmaker will tweak the exterior based on the EEG reports, which track activity in all parts of the brain.

Similarly, eBay's PayPal began pitching its online payment service as 'fast' after brain-wave research showed that speed turns consumers on more than security and safety, earlier themes used in eBay advertising campaigns. Recently, *New Scientist* approached the world's leading neurological testing company, NeuroFocus, to evaluate three different cover designs for the August issue. 'We worked with NeuroFocus to select an appealing cover design for *New Scientist* using their neuromarketing technology,' said Graham Lawton, deputy editor. 'This issue of the magazine achieved strong UK newsstand sales, making it the second highest selling issue of the year, which is very unusual for the normally quiet month of August. This represents a 12 per cent increase over the same issue in the previous year and is much higher than we would expect for a similar cover story at that time of year, so we would certainly say the experiment was a big success.'[29]

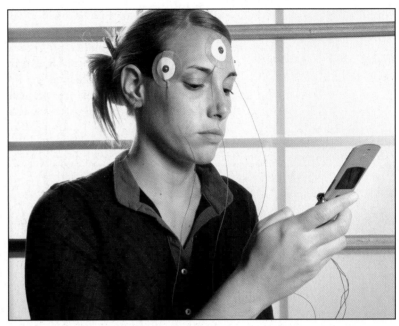

Brainwave information can generate fascinating and illuminating insight into what consumers are really thinking.
Source: Hannes Hepp/Fuse/Getty Images

Although neuromarketing techniques can measure consumer involvement and emotional responses second by second, such brain responses can be difficult to interpret. Thus, neuromarketing is usually used in combination with other research approaches to gain a more complete picture of what goes on inside consumers' heads.

Implementing the research plan

The researcher next puts the marketing research plan into action. This involves collecting, processing and analysing the information. Data collection can be carried out by the company's marketing research staff or outside firms. Researchers should watch closely to make sure that the plan is implemented correctly. They must guard against problems with data collection techniques and technologies, data quality and timeliness.

Researchers must also process and analyse the collected data to isolate important information and insight. They need to check data for accuracy and completeness and code it for analysis. The researchers then tabulate the results and compute statistical measures.

Interpreting and reporting the findings

The market researcher must now interpret the findings, draw conclusions and report them to management. The researcher should not try to overwhelm managers with numbers and fancy statistical techniques. Rather, the researcher should present important findings and insights that are useful in the major decisions faced by management.

However, interpretation should not be left only to researchers. Although they are often experts in research design and statistics, the marketing manager knows more about the problem and the decisions that must be made. The best research means little if the manager blindly accepts faulty interpretations from the researcher. Similarly, managers may be biased. They might tend to accept research results that show what they expected and reject those that they did not expect or hope for. In many cases, findings can be interpreted in different ways, and discussions between researchers and managers will help point to the best interpretations. Thus, managers and researchers must work together closely when interpreting research results, and both must share responsibility for the research process and resulting decisions.

ANALYSING AND USING MARKETING INFORMATION

Author comment

We've talked generally about managing customer relationships throughout the text. But here, 'customer relationship management' (CRM) has a much narrower data-management meaning. It refers to capturing and using customer data from all sources to manage customer interactions, engage customers and build customer relationships.

Information gathered in internal databases and through competitive marketing intelligence and marketing research usually requires additional analysis. Managers may need help applying the information to gain customer and market insights that will improve their marketing decisions. This help may include advanced statistical analysis to learn more about the relationships within a set of data. Information analysis might also involve the application of analytical models that will help marketers make better decisions.

Once the information has been processed and analysed, it must be made available to the right decision makers at the right time. In the following sections, we look deeper into analysing and using marketing information.

Customer relationship management and mining big data

The question of how best to analyse and use individual customer data presents special problems. In the current *big data* era, most companies are awash in information about their customers and the marketplace. Still, smart companies capture information at every possible customer *touch point*. These touch points include customer purchases, sales force contacts, service and support calls, web and social media site visits, satisfaction surveys, credit and payment interactions, market research studies – every contact between a customer and a company.

Customer relationship management (CRM)—
Managing detailed information about individual customers and carefully managing customer touch points to maximise customer loyalty.

Unfortunately, this information is usually scattered widely across the organisation or buried deep in big data databases. To overcome such problems, many companies are now turning to **customer relationship management** (**CRM**) to manage detailed information about individual customers and carefully manage customer touch points to maximise customer loyalty.

CRM first burst onto the scene in the early 2000s. Many companies rushed in, implementing overly ambitious CRM programmes that produced disappointing results and many failures. More recently, however, companies are moving ahead more cautiously and implementing CRM systems that really work. Last year, companies worldwide spent €4.7 billion on CRM systems from companies such as Oracle, Microsoft, Salesforce.com and SAS, up 9 per cent from the previous year, with cloud CRM approaches up by 24 per cent.[30]

CRM consists of sophisticated software and analytical tools from companies such as Salesforce.com, Oracle, Microsoft and SAS that integrate customer and marketplace information from all sources, analyse it in depth, and apply the results to build stronger customer relationships. CRM integrates everything that a company's sales, service and marketing teams know about individual customers, providing a 360-degree view of the customer relationship.

CRM analysts develop *big data warehouses* and use sophisticated *data mining* techniques to unearth the riches hidden in customer and marketplace data. A data warehouse is a company-wide database of finely detailed customer and market information that needs to be sifted through for gems. The purpose of a data warehouse is not only to gather information but also to pull it together into a central, accessible location. Then, once the data warehouse brings the data together, the company uses high-powered data mining and analytic techniques to sift through the mounds of big data and dig out interesting findings relevant to creating customer value.

These findings often lead to marketing opportunities. For example, in grocery retailing, product demand can vary by up to 300 per cent per day depending on the weather. In the UK Tesco have found that hotter days or days with longer sunshine hours boost sales of ready-washed salad by 19 per cent while sales of broccoli plummet.[31] Walmart's huge database provides deep insights for marketing decisions. A few years ago, as Hurricane Ivan roared toward the Florida coast, reports one observer, the giant retailer 'knew exactly what to rush onto the shelves of stores in the hurricane's path – strawberry Pop Tarts. By mining years of sales data from just prior to other hurricanes, [Walmart] figured out that shoppers would stock up on Pop Tarts – which don't require refrigeration or cooking.'[32]

> Data management might sound like a dry field, where statisticians and computer programmers haggle over terabytes and p-values. But as it becomes more sophisticated and yields ever richer portraits of customers and their behaviours, helped by social networking, it is increasingly becoming central to executive decision-making. The pioneers have reaped tremendous rewards. Sir Terry Leahy, former chief executive of Tesco, leaned so heavily on the customer portraits delivered by Dunnhumby that he ended up buying the company. Dunnhumby ploughed through the data yielded by Tesco's Clubcard programme to build ever more detailed customer profiles, to the point where it now has 12 million unique profiles of its 15 million customers. Its work is widely credited with helping Tesco open a wide lead over its UK supermarket rivals.[33]

By using CRM to understand customers better, companies can provide higher levels of customer service and develop deeper customer relationships. They can use CRM to pinpoint high-value customers, target them more effectively, cross-sell a company's products, and create offers tailored to specific customer requirements.

CRM and big data benefits don't come without costs or risk, either in collecting the original data or in maintaining and mining it. The most common CRM mistake is to view CRM as a technology and software process only. Yet technology alone cannot build profitable customer relationships. Companies can't improve customer relationships by simply installing some new software. Instead, marketers should start with the fundamentals of managing customer relationships and *then* employ high-tech data solutions. They should focus first on the R – it's the *relationship* that CRM is all about.

Distributing and using marketing information

Marketing information has no value until it is used to gain customer insights and make better marketing decisions. Thus, the marketing information system must make the information readily available to managers and others who need it, when they need it. In some cases, this means providing managers with regular performance reports, intelligence updates and reports on the results of research studies.

But marketing managers may also need access to non-routine information for special situations and on-the-spot decisions. For example, a sales manager having trouble with a large customer may want a summary of the account's sales and profitability over the past year. Or a brand manager may want to get a sense of the amount of the social media buzz surrounding the recent launch of a new product. These days, therefore, information distribution involves making information available in a timely, user-friendly way.

Many firms use a company *intranet* and internal CRM systems to facilitate this process. The internal information systems provide ready access to research information, customer contact information, reports, shared work documents, contact information for employees and other stakeholders, and more. For example, Cablecom, Switzerland's largest cable operator, discovered unhappy customers were most likely to quit after about nine months. So, it ran a feedback programme targeting people who had been customers for seven months. The data from the programme was analysed and more than 100 churn indicators identified – their exact nature is a closely guarded secret – but they have enabled the company to identify customers who may be about to leave. The 'customer retention team' is then activated before it's too late. In pilot studies, the technology has allowed Cablecom to reduce churn rates from 19 per cent to just 2 per cent.[34]

In addition, companies are increasingly allowing key customers and value-network members to access account, product and other data on demand through *extranets*. Suppliers, customers, resellers and select other network members may access a company's extranet to update their accounts, arrange purchases and check orders against inventories to improve customer service. For example, SkyHawke Tech Ltd produces one of the world's most popular portable golf GPS rangefinder called the SkyCaddie. Working with Mesacom Tech Ltd of the UK, SkyHawke established an extranet for the broad range of graphic designers, media organisations and publishers involved in different campaigns which produce a huge number of files and other materials. This extranet eases the administrative burden on the firm by allowing suppliers and designers to take responsibility for up-dating their content.[35]

Thanks to modern technology, today's marketing managers can gain direct access to a company's information system at any time and from virtually anywhere. They can tap into the system from a home office, customer location, airport or the local Starbucks – anywhere they can connect on a laptop, tablet or smartphone. Such systems allow managers to get the information they need directly and quickly and tailor it to their own needs.

Author comment

We finish this chapter by examining three special marketing information topics.

OTHER MARKETING INFORMATION CONSIDERATIONS

This section discusses marketing information in two special contexts: marketing research in small businesses and non-profit organisations and international marketing research. Then, we look at public policy and ethics issues in marketing research.

Marketing research in small businesses and non-profit organisations

Just like larger firms, small organisations need market information and the customer insights that it can provide. Managers of small businesses and non-profit organisations often think that marketing research can be done only by experts in large companies with big research budgets. True, large-scale research studies are beyond the budgets of most small organisations. However, many of the marketing research techniques discussed in this chapter also can be used by smaller organisations in a less formal manner and at little or no expense. Consider how one small-business owner conducted market research on a shoestring before even opening his doors:[36]

> After a string of bad experiences with his local dry cleaner, Robert Byerley decided to open his own dry-cleaning business. But before jumping in, he conducted plenty of market research. He needed a key customer insight: How would he make his business stand out from the others? To start, Byerley spent an entire week online, researching the dry-cleaning industry. To get input from potential customers, using a marketing firm, Byerley held focus groups on the store's name, look and brochure. He also took clothes to the 15 best competing cleaners in town and had focus group members critique their work. Based on his research, he made a list of features for his new business. First on his list: quality. His business would stand behind everything it did. Not on the list: cheap prices. Creating the perfect dry-cleaning establishment simply didn't fit with a discount operation.
>
> With his research complete, Byerley opened Bibbentuckers, a high-end dry cleaner positioned on high-quality service and convenience. It featured a bank-like drive-through area with curb-side delivery. A computerised barcode system read customer cleaning preferences and tracked clothes all the way through the cleaning process. Byerley added other differentiators, such as decorative awnings, TV screens and refreshments (even 'candy for the kids and a doggy treat for your best friend'). 'I wanted a place . . . that paired five-star service and quality with an establishment that didn't look like a dry cleaner,' he says. The market research yielded results. Today, Bibbentuckers is a thriving eight-store operation.

Thus, small businesses and non-profit organisations can obtain good marketing insights through observation or informal surveys using small convenience samples. Also, many associations, local media and government agencies provide special help to small organisations. For example, in the UK the Department of Business, Innovation and Skills offers dozens of free publications and a website (www.businesslink.gov.uk) that give advice on topics ranging from starting, financing and expanding a small business to ordering business cards. The European Commission supports the European Small Business portal that provides a wealth of helpful material and resources. Other excellent web resources for small businesses include the European Council for Small Business and Entrepreneurship (www.ecsb.org/) and Eurostat – the Statistical Office of the European Communities (http://ec.europa.eu/eurostat).

In summary, secondary data collection, observation, surveys and experiments can all be used effectively by small organisations with small budgets. However, although these informal research methods are less complex and less costly, they still must be conducted with care. Managers must think carefully about the objectives of the research, formulate questions in advance, recognise the biases introduced by smaller samples and less skilled researchers, and conduct the research systematically.[37]

International marketing research

International marketing research has grown tremendously over the past decade. International researchers follow the same steps as domestic researchers, from defining the research problem and developing a research plan to interpreting and reporting the results. However, these researchers often face more and different problems. Whereas domestic researchers deal with fairly homogeneous markets within a single country, international researchers deal with diverse markets in many different countries. These markets often vary greatly in their levels of economic development, cultures and customs, and buying patterns.

In many foreign markets, the international researcher may have a difficult time finding good secondary data. Whereas marketing researchers can obtain reliable secondary data from dozens of domestic research services, many countries have almost no research services at all. Some of the largest international research services operate in many countries. For example, The Nielsen Company (the world's largest marketing research company) has offices in more than 100 countries, from Wavre, Belgium to Oxford, UK, to Nicosia, Cyprus.[38] However, most research firms operate in only a relative handful of countries.[39] Thus, even when secondary information is available, it usually must be obtained from many different sources on a country-by-country basis, making the information difficult to combine or compare.

Because of the scarcity of good secondary data, international researchers often must collect their own primary data. However, obtaining primary data may be no easy task. For example, it can be difficult simply to develop good samples. Researchers can use current telephone directories, e-mail lists, census tract data, and any of several sources of socioeconomic data to construct samples. However, such information is largely lacking in many countries.

Once the sample is drawn, the researcher usually can reach most respondents easily by telephone, by mail, on the Internet or in person. Reaching respondents is often not so easy in other parts of the world. Researchers in some parts of the world cannot rely on telephone, Internet and mail data collection; most data collection is door to door and concentrated in three or four of the largest cities. In some countries, few people have phones or personal computers. In the UK, the World Bank lists over 83 per cent of the population as having access to the Internet. In Armenia the level is about 7 per cent.[40] In some countries, the postal system is notoriously unreliable. In Brazil, for instance, an estimated 30 per cent of the mail is never delivered. In many developing countries, poor roads and transportation systems make certain areas hard to reach, making personal interviews difficult and expensive.[41]

Cultural differences from country to country cause additional problems for international researchers. Language is the most obvious obstacle. For example, questionnaires must be prepared in one language and then translated into the languages of each country researched. Responses then must be translated back into the original language for analysis and interpretation. This adds to research costs and increases the risks of error. Even within a given country, language can be a problem. For example, in India, English is the language of business, but consumers may use any of 14 'first languages', with many additional dialects.

Translating a questionnaire from one language to another is anything but easy. Many idioms, phrases and statements mean different things in different cultures. For example, a Danish executive noted, 'Check this out by having a different translator put back into English what you've translated from English. You'll get the shock of your life. I remember [an example in which] "out of sight, out of mind" had become "invisible things are insane."'[42]

Consumers in different countries also vary in their attitudes toward marketing research. People in one country may be very willing to respond; in other countries, non-response can be a major problem. Customs in some countries may prohibit people from talking with strangers. In certain cultures, research questions often are considered too personal. For example, in many Muslim countries, mixed-gender focus groups are taboo, as is videotaping female-only focus groups. Even when respondents are *willing* to respond, they may not be *able* to because of high functional illiteracy rates.

Despite these problems, as global marketing grows, global companies have little choice but to conduct these types of international marketing research. Although the costs and problems associated with international research may be high, the costs of not doing it – in terms of missed opportunities and mistakes – might be even higher. Once recognised, many of the problems associated with international marketing research can be overcome or avoided.

Public policy and ethics in marketing research

Most marketing research benefits both the sponsoring company and its consumers. Through marketing research, companies gain insights into consumers' needs, resulting in more satisfying products and services and stronger customer relationships. However, the misuse of marketing research can also harm or annoy consumers. Two major public policy and ethics issues in marketing research are intrusions on consumer privacy and the misuse of research findings.

Intrusions on consumer privacy

Many consumers feel positive about marketing research and believe that it serves a useful purpose. Some actually enjoy being interviewed and giving their opinions. However, others strongly resent or even mistrust marketing research. They don't like being interrupted by researchers. They worry that marketers are building huge databases full of personal information about customers. Or they fear that researchers might use sophisticated techniques to probe our deepest feelings, track us as we browse and interact on the Internet, or peek over our shoulders as we shop and then use this knowledge to manipulate our buying.

When mining customer information, marketers must be careful not to cross over the privacy line. But there are no easy answers when it comes to marketing research and privacy. For example, is it a good or bad thing that marketers track and analyse consumers' online browsing or buying patterns to send them personalised promotions? Should we worry when marketers track consumer locations via their mobile phones to issue location-based ads and offers? Should we care that some retailers use mannequins with cameras hidden in one eye to record customer demographics and shopping behaviour? Similarly, should we applaud or resent companies that monitor consumer discussions on Facebook, Twitter, YouTube or other social media in an effort to be more responsive?[43]

Increasing consumer resentment has become a major problem for the marketing research industry, leading to lower survey response rates in recent years. Just as companies face the challenge of unearthing valuable but potentially sensitive consumer data while also maintaining consumer trust, consumers wrestle with the trade-offs between personalisation and privacy. Although many consumers willingly exchange personal information for free services, easy credit, discounts, upgrades and all sorts of rewards, they also worry about the growth in online identity theft.

A study by TRUSTe, an organisation that monitors the privacy practices of websites, found that more than 90 per cent of respondents view online privacy as a 'really' or 'somewhat' important issue. More than 75 per cent agreed with the statement, 'The Internet is not well regulated, and naïve users can easily be taken advantage of.' And 66 per cent of consumers do not want marketers to track their online behaviour and tailor advertisements to their interests. So it is no surprise that they are now less than willing to reveal personal information on websites.[44]

The marketing research industry is considering several options for responding to this problem. The European Federation of Associations of Market Research Organisations and ESOMAR recently jointly suggested a range of amendments to the European Commission's Directive 95/46/EC that deals with data protection. The industry also has considered adopting broad standards, perhaps based on the ESOMAR and International Chamber of Commerce world-wide code of ethical practice (the ICC/ESOMAR International Code on Market and Social Research). This code outlines researchers' responsibilities to respondents and the general public. For example, it says that researchers should make their names and addresses available to participants. It also bans companies from representing activities such as database compilation or sales and promotional pitches as research.

Most major companies – including Shell, Siemens, Deutsche Telekom, IBM and Microsoft – have now appointed a chief privacy officer (CPO), whose job is to safeguard the privacy of consumers who do business with the company. IBM's CPO claims that her job requires 'multidisciplinary thinking and attitude'. She needs to get all company departments, from technology, legal and accounting to marketing and communications working together to safeguard customer privacy.[45]

In the end, if researchers provide value in exchange for information, customers will gladly provide it. For example, Amazon's customers do not mind if the firm builds a database of products they buy as a way to provide future product recommendations. This saves time and provides value. Similarly, Bizrate users gladly complete surveys rating online seller sites because they can view the overall ratings of others when making purchase decisions. The best approach is for researchers to ask only for the information they need, use it responsibly to provide customer value, and avoid sharing information without a customer's permission.

Misuse of research findings

Research studies can be powerful persuasion tools; companies often use study results as claims in their advertising and promotion. Today, however, many research studies appear to be little more than vehicles for pitching the sponsor's products. In fact, in some cases, research surveys appear to have been designed just to produce the intended effect. For example, UK phone and broadband provider TalkTalk claimed that customers could save €160 per year. Their television advertisements exhorted customers to 'join our customers who are already saving an average of over £140 (€160) a year'. Competitors complained that such claims were misleading exaggerations as they were based on average savings of TalkTalk customers and not on the savings that could be achieved by new target customers. While TalkTalk argued that the on-screen text of their claims was surrounded by question marks (and thus was a question rather than a definitive statement), the UK Advertising Standards Authority heavily criticised TalkTalk's approach.

Recognising that surveys can be abused, several associations – including the European Society for Opinion and Market Research, European Marketing Association, the Academy of Marketing, the American Marketing Association, the Marketing Research Association and the Council of American Survey Research Organizations (CASRO) – have developed codes of research ethics and standards of conduct. For example, the CASRO Code of Standards and Ethics for Survey Research outlines researcher responsibilities to respondents, including confidentiality, privacy and avoidance of harassment. It also outlines major responsibilities in reporting results to clients and the public.[46]

In the end, however, unethical or inappropriate actions cannot simply be regulated away. Each company must accept responsibility for policing the conduct and reporting of its own marketing research to protect consumers' best interests and its own.

OBJECTIVES REVIEW AND KEY TERMS

To create value for customers and build meaningful relationships with them, marketers must first gain fresh, deep insights into what customers need and want. Such insights come from good marketing information. As a result of the recent explosion of 'big data' and marketing technology, companies can now obtain great quantities of information, sometimes even too much. The challenge is to transform today's vast volume of consumer information into actionable customer and market insights.

OBJECTIVE 1 Explain the importance of information in gaining insights about the marketplace and customers (pp. 104–106)

The marketing process starts with a complete understanding of the marketplace and consumer needs and wants. Thus, the company needs to turn sound consumer information into meaningful *customer insights* by which it can produce superior value for its customers. The company also requires information on competitors, resellers, and other actors and forces in the marketplace. Increasingly, marketers are viewing information not only as an input for making better decisions but also as an important strategic asset and marketing tool.

OBJECTIVE 2 Define the marketing information system and discuss its parts (pp. 106–109)

The *marketing information system (MIS)* consists of people and procedures for assessing information needs, developing the needed information, and helping decision makers use the information to generate and validate actionable customer and market insights. A well-designed information system begins and ends with users.

The MIS first *assesses information needs*. The MIS primarily serves the company's marketing and other managers, but it may also provide information to external partners. Then the MIS *develops information* from internal databases, marketing intelligence activities, and marketing research. *Internal databases* provide information on the company's own operations and departments. Such data can be obtained quickly and cheaply but often need to be adapted for marketing decisions. *Marketing intelligence* activities supply everyday information about developments in the external marketing environment, including listening and responding to the vast and complex digital environment. *Market research* consists of collecting information relevant to a specific marketing problem faced by the company. Last, the MIS helps users analyse and use the information to develop customer insights, make marketing decisions and manage customer relationships.

OBJECTIVE 3 Outline the steps in the marketing research process (pp. 109–122)

The first step in the marketing research process involves *defining the problem and setting the research objectives*, which may be exploratory, descriptive or causal research. The second step consists of *developing a research plan* for collecting data from primary and secondary sources. The third step calls for *implementing the marketing research plan* by gathering, processing and analysing the information. The fourth step consists of *interpreting and reporting the findings.* Additional information analysis helps marketing managers apply the information and provides them with sophisticated statistical procedures and models from which to develop more rigorous findings.

Both *internal* and *external* secondary data sources often provide information more quickly and at a lower cost than primary data sources, and they can sometimes yield information that a company cannot collect by itself. However, needed information might not exist in secondary sources. Researchers must also evaluate secondary information to ensure that it is *relevant, accurate, current* and *impartial.*

Primary research must also be evaluated for these features. Each primary data collection method — *observational, survey* and *experimental* — has its own advantages and disadvantages. Similarly, each of the various research contact methods — mail, telephone, personal interview and online — has its own advantages and drawbacks.

OBJECTIVE 4 Explain how companies analyse and use marketing information (pp. 122–124)

Information gathered in internal databases and through marketing intelligence and marketing research usually requires more analysis. To analyse individual customer data, many companies have now acquired or developed special software and analysis techniques — called *customer relationship management (CRM)* — that integrate, analyse and apply the mountains of individual customer and marketplace data contained in their databases.

Marketing information has no value until it is used to make better marketing decisions. Thus, the MIS must make the information available to managers and others who make marketing decisions or deal with customers. In some cases, this means providing regular reports and updates; in other cases, it means making non-routine information available for special situations and on-the-spot decisions. Many firms use company intranets and extranets to facilitate this process. Thanks to modern technology, today's marketing managers can gain direct access to marketing information at any time and from virtually any location.

OBJECTIVE 5 Discuss the special issues some marketing researchers face, including public policy and ethics issues (pp. 124–127)

Some marketers face special marketing research situations, such as those conducting research in small business, not-for-profit or international situations. Marketing research can be conducted effectively by small businesses and non-profit organisations with limited budgets. International marketing researchers follow the same steps as domestic researchers but often face more and different problems. All organisations need to act responsibly concerning major public policy and ethical issues surrounding marketing research, including issues of intrusions on consumer privacy and misuse of research findings.

NAVIGATING THE KEY TERMS

OBJECTIVE 1
Big data (p. 105)
Customer insights (p. 105)
Marketing information system (MIS) (p. 106)

OBJECTIVE 2
Internal databases (p. 107)
Competitive marketing intelligence (p. 107)

OBJECTIVE 3
Marketing research (p. 109)
Exploratory research (p. 110)
Descriptive research (p. 110)
Causal research (p. 110)
Secondary data (p. 111)
Primary data (p. 111)
Observational research (p. 112)
Ethnographic research (p. 112)
Survey research (p. 113)

Experimental research (p. 114)
Focus group interviewing (p. 115)
Online marketing research (p. 115)
Online focus groups (p. 116)
Behavioural targeting (p. 118)
Sample (p. 118)

OBJECTIVE 4
Customer relationship management (CRM) (p. 122)

DISCUSSION AND CRITICAL THINKING

Discussion questions

4-1 What is *big data* and what opportunities and challenges does it provide for marketers? (AACSB: Communication; Reflective thinking)

4-2 Explain how marketing intelligence differs from marketing research. (AACSB: Communication)

4-3 What is ethnographic research and how is it conducted online? (AACSB: Communication)

4-4 How are marketers using customer relationship management (CRM) to reveal customer insights from the vast amounts of data gathered? (AACSB: Communication)

4-5 What are the similarities and differences when conducting research in another country versus the domestic market? (AACSB: Communication)

Critical-thinking exercises

4-6 In a small group, identify a problem faced by a local business or charitable organisation and propose a research project addressing that problem. Develop a research proposal that implements each step of the marketing research process. Discuss how the research results will help the business or organisation. (AACSB: Communication; Reflective thinking)

4-7 Go to www.bized.co.uk/learn/business/marketing/research/index.htm and review the various resources available. Select one activity and present what you learned from that activity. (AACSB: Communication; Use of IT; Reflective thinking)

4-8 Research the marketing research industry and develop a presentation describing various types of marketing research jobs and compensation for those jobs. Create a graphical representation to communicate your findings. (AACSB: Communication; Use of IT; Reflective thinking)

Mini-cases and applications

Online, mobile and social media marketing: you are what you like

Marketers have always been interested in buyers' personality traits and how they influence behaviours, but it is difficult to measure personality. Until now, that is. Microsoft and researchers from the University of Cambridge analysed over 58,000 Facebook users' 'Likes' and developed an algorithm that matched them with demographic information and personality profiles. The resulting personality profiles determined with over 80 per cent accuracy factors such as users' gender, ethnicity, religion, sexual orientation, alcohol and drug use, and even whether their parents had separated before they turned

21 years old. Researchers even predicted IQ and found that users with higher IQs like curly fries and those with lower IQs like Harley-Davidson. All that and more can be predicted just from users' 'Like'-clicking behaviour on the Internet. This research gives marketers another research tool that will help them customise their offerings and communications with greater accuracy.

4-9 Visit www.youarewhatyoulike.com to see what your 'Likes' say about you. You will have to log on to Facebook to see the results. What characteristics are shown? Does the profile describe you accurately? (AACSB: Communication; Use of IT)

4-10 Critics claim that research activities such as this infringe on consumer privacy rights. Should marketers have access to such information? Discuss the advantages and disadvantages of such research for both marketers and consumers. (AACSB: Communication; Ethical reasoning)

Marketing ethics: research ethics

Marketing information helps develop insights into the needs of customers, and gathering competitive intelligence (CI) data supplies part of this information. CI has blossomed into a full-fledged industry, with most major companies establishing CI units. But not all CI gathering is ethical or legal – even at venerable P&G. In 1943, a P&G employee bribed a Lever Brothers (now Unilever) employee to obtain bars of Swan soap, which was then under development, to improve its Ivory brand. P&G settled the case by paying Unilever almost €4 million (about €43 million in today's money) for patent infringement – a small price to pay given the market success of Ivory. In 2001, P&G once again paid a €7.5 million settlement to Unilever for a case that involved a contractor rummaging through a trash dumpster outside Unilever's office, an infraction that was actually reported by P&G itself.

4-11 Find another example of corporate espionage and write a brief report on it. Did the guilty party pay restitution or serve prison time? Discuss what punishments, if any, should be levied in cases of corporate espionage. (AACSB: Communication; Ethical reasoning)

4-12 How can businesses protect themselves from corporate espionage? (AACSB: Communication; Reflective thinking)

Marketing by the numbers: sample size

Have you ever been disappointed because a television network cancelled one of your favourite television shows because of 'low ratings'? The network didn't ask your opinion, did it? It probably didn't task any of your friends, either. That's because in the UK estimates of television audience sizes are based on research done by the Broadcast Audience Research Board (BARB), which uses a sample of around 5,000 households out of the more than 62 million households in the UK to determine national ratings for television programmes. That doesn't seem like enough, does it? As it turns out, statistically, it's significantly more than enough.

4-13 Go to www.surveysystem.com/sscalc.htm to determine the appropriate sample size for a population of 115 million households (the number for the US). Assuming a confidence interval of 5, how large should the sample of households be if desiring a 95 per cent confidence level? How large for a 99 per cent confidence level? Briefly explain what is meant by *confidence interval* and *confidence level*. (AACSB: Communication; Use of IT; Analytical reasoning)

4-14 What sample sizes are necessary at population sizes of 1 billion, 10,000, and 100 with a confidence interval of 5 and a 95 per cent confidence level? Explain the effect population size has on sample size. (AACSB: Communication; Use of IT; Analytical reasoning)

REFERENCES

[1] Based on information found in H. Booth 'The Tiger who came to town', *The Guardian*, 19 Friday July 2013; CNN *What is the Tiger Touch?* cnn.com, 14 May 2014; G. Davis, 'Potential for hundreds of Tiger stores in UK', *Retail Insider*, 18 December 2013; A-M. Hourihane, 'We hate indifference: the rise of Tiger stores', *The Irish Times*, 9 December 2014; M. Power, 'Welcome to the posh Pound Shop: how the High Street's new arrival Tiger has become catnip to middle-class shoppers who love its VERY quirky bargains', *Daily Mail*, 22 May 2014; A. Wilson, 'Online? It's not really our top priority', *The Telegraph*, 12 January 2013; Z. Wood, 'Posh pound shop: Tiger sinks its claws into UK High Street', *The Guardian*, 13 March 2014; www.tigerstores.co.uk, accessed October 2015

[2] See Craig Smith, 'By the numbers: 31 amazing Pinterest stats', *Digital Marketing Ramblings*, 20 October 2013, http://expandedramblings.com/index.php/pinterest-stats/; 'Pinterest: what, why, how, and who?', *Just Creative*, 24 April 2012, http://justcreative.com/2012/04/24/pinterest-guide/; and Kevin

Roose, 'It's time to start taking Pinterest seriously', *New York Magazine*, 24 October 2013, http://nymag.com/daily/intelligencer/2013/10/time-to-start-taking-pinterest-seriously.html.

[3] See 'Big data', *Wikipedia*, http://en.wikipedia.org/wiki/Big_data, accessed October 2015; and Yuyu Chen, 'Marketers still struggle to harness power of big data', *ClickZ*, 12 November 2013, www.clickz.com/clickz/news/2303229/marketers-still-struggleto-harness-power-of-big-data-study.

[4] See Helen Leggatt, 'IBM: marketers suffering from data overload', *BizReport*, 12 October 2011, www.bizreport.com/2011/10/ibm-marketers-suffering-data-overload.html#; Carey Toane, 'Listening: the new metric', *Strategy*, September 2009, p. 45; and Margarita Tartakovsky, 'Overcoming information overload', *PsychCentral*, 21 January 2013, http://psychcentral.com/blog/archives/2013/01/21/overcoming-information-overload/.

[5] See Piet Levy, 'A day with Stan Sthanunathan', *Marketing News*, 28 February 2011, pp. 11ff.; and 'Customer insights analyst', http://jobs.geico.com/geico/customer-insights-analyst, accessed October 2015.

[6] See www.walmartstores.com/Suppliers/248.aspx, accessed October 2015.

[7] Example from Tim Bradshaw, 'Online advertisers issue tracking code', *Financial Times*, 15 April 2011, www.ft.com/cms/s/0/7e9e1368–66ce-11e0-8d88-00144feab49a.html#axzz1WOopxs9y, accessed October 2015

[8] Sheila Shayon, 'MasterCard harnesses the power of social with innovative Conversation Suite', *brandchannel*, 7 May 2013, www.brandchannel.com/home/post/2013/05/07/MasterCard-ConversationSuite-050713.aspx; Giselle Abramovich, 'Inside Mastercard's social command center', *Digiday*, 9 May 2013, http://digiday.com/brands/inside-mastercards-social-command-center/; and 'MasterCard Conversation Suite Video', http://newsroom.mastercard.com/videos/mastercard-conversation-suite-video/, accessed October 2015.

[9] See europages.com, accessed October 2015.

[10] See Adam Lashinsky, 'The secrets Apple keeps', *Fortune*, 6 February 2012, pp. 85–94; and Megan Rose Dickey, 'The most extreme examples of secrecy at Apple', *Business Insider*, 22 July 2013, www.businessinsider.com/the-most-extreme-examples-ofsecrecy-at-apple-2013-7.

[11] George Chidi, 'Confessions of a corporate spy', *Inc.*, February 2013, pp. 72-77.

[12] See http://biz.yahoo.com/ic/101/101316.html, accessed October 2015; 'The top 15 energy drink brands', *Energy Fiend*, www.energyfiend.com/the-15-top-energy-drink-brands, accessed October 2015; and http://energydrink-us.redbull.com/red-bull-energy-drink, accessed October 2015.

[13] For more on research firms that supply marketing information, see Jack Honomichl, 'Honomichl Top 50', special section, *Marketing News*, 30 June 2009. Other information from www.us.nielsen.com/products/cps.shtml; www.smrb.com/web/guest/core-solutions/national-consumer-study and www.yankelovich.com, accessed October 2015.

[14] See www.iriworldwide.com/SolutionsandServices/Detail.aspx?ProductID=181, accessed October 2015.

[15] Example from Rose Jacobs, 'Rank sets out to discover home truths', *Financial Times*, 7 February 2011, www.ft.com/cms/s/0/49bde8ca-32f9-11e0-9a61-00144feabdc0.html#axzz1UPifHx5H, accessed October 2015.

[16] See Jennifer Reingold, 'Can P&G make money in places where people earn $2 a day?' *Fortune*, 17 January 2011, pp. 86-91; C. K. Prahalad, 'Bottom of the pyramid as a source of breakthrough innovations', *Journal of Product Innovation Management*, January 2012, pp. 6-12; Jim Riley, 'How did P&G reach the top in China?' tutor2u, 22 September 2013, www.tutor2u.net/blog/index.php/business-studies/comments/how-did-pg-reach-the-topin-china; and 'P&G's push into rural china', www.youtube.com/watch?v=WvKmgP9A_5Y#t=47, accessed October 2015.

[17] For more discussion of online ethnography and mobile phone tracking, see Robert V. Kozinets, 'Netnography: the marketer's secret weapon', March 2010, http://info.netbase.com/rs/netbase/images/Netnography_WP; http://en.wikipedia.org/wiki/Online_ethnography, accessed October 2015; and Sam Grobart, 'Apple's secret retail weapon is already in your pocket', *Bloomberg Businessweek*, 16 October 2013, www.businessweek.com/articles/2013-10-16/apples-secret-retail-weapon-is-already-in-your-pocket.

[18] Example based on information found in 'My dinner with Lexus', *Automotive News*, 29 November 2010, www.autonews.com/article/20101129/RETAIL03/311299949/my-dinner-with-lexus; and 'An evening with Lexus', YouTube video, www.youtube.com/watch?v=LweS8EScADY, accessed October 2015.

[19] See 'Pew Internet: health', *Pew Internet*, 1 July 2013, http://pewinternet.org/Commentary/2011/November/Pew-Internet-Health.aspx; and 'Internet World Stats', www.internetworldstats.com/stats.htm, accessed October 2015.

[20] For more information, see www.focusvision.com and www.youtube.com/watch?v=PG8RZl2dvNY, accessed October 2015.

[21] Derek Kreindler, 'Lexus soliciting customer feedback with Lexus advisory board', 24 August 2010, *Automotive News*, www.autoguide.com/auto-news/2010/08/lexus-soliciting-customerfeedback-with-lexus-advisory-board.html; and www.lexusadvisory board.com, accessed October 2015.

[22] See 'Online Panel', http://www.zoomerang.com/online-panel/, accessed October 2015.

[23] Adapted from Jeremy Nedelka, 'Adidas relies on insiders for insight', *1to1 Media*, 9 November 2009, www.1to1media.com/view.aspx?DocID=31963&m=n.

[24] For more discussion of online behavioral and social tracking and targeting, see Amit Avner, 'How social targeting can lead to discovery', *Adotas*, 7 February 2012, www.adotas.com/2012/02/how-social-targeting-can-lead-to-discovery/; Thomas Claburn, 'Microsoft finds people want more privacy control', *Informationweek–Online*, 24 January 2013, www.informationweek.com/windows/security/microsoft-finds-people-want-more-privacy/240146932; Lisa M. Thomas, 'We know where you've been: emerging rules in online behavioral advertising', *Computer and Internet Lawyer*, February 2013, pp. 16-19; and Somini Sengupta, 'When privacy becomes a business imperative', *International New York Times*, 3 March 2013, www.nytimes.com/2013/03/04/technology/amiddo-not-track-effort-web-companies-race-to-look-privacy-friendly.html?_r=0; also see www.ec.europa.eu/commission_2010–2014/kroes/en/tags/do-not-track, accessed October 2015.

[25] See Clint Boulton, 'Snack maker modernizes the impulse buy', *Wall Street Journal*, 17 October 2013, p. B4; Aaron Taube, 'The maker of Oreos has invented a store shelf that spies on you while you're shopping', *Business Insider*, 18 October 2013, www.businessinsider.com/mondelez-smart-shelf-technology-2013–10.

[26] Based on information from 'Time Warner opens NYC NeuromarketingLab', *Neuromarketing*, 26 January 2012, www.neuroscience-marketing.com/blog/articles/new-labs.htm; Amy Chozick, 'These lab specimens watch 3-D television', *New York Times*, 25 January 2012, p. B3; and Sam Thielman, 'Time Warner's media lab knows what you like to watch', *Adweek*, 4 February 2013, www.adweek.com/news/technology/time-warner-s-media-lab-knowswhat-you-watch-147045; also see www.timewarnermedialab.com.

[27] Example from Alicia Clegg, 'Eyes in the aisles reveal shopping secrets', *Financial Times*, 17 February 2011, www.ft.com/cms/s/0/8f1665ac-3ac7-11e0-9c1a-00144feabdc0.html#axzz1UPifHx5H, accessed October 2015.

[28] This and the other neuromarketing examples are adapted from Laurie Burkitt, 'Neuromarketing: companies use neuroscience for consumer insights', *Forbes*, 16 November 2009, www.forbes.com/forbes/2009/1116/marketing-hyundai-neurofocus-brain-waves-battle-for-the-brain.html.

[29] Example from Anonymous, 'Sales success shows neuromarketing moves magazines: New Scientist reports 12% increase in newsstand sales for issue featuring NeuroFocus-tested cover design', *PR Newswire Europe*, 2 September 2010, www.prnewswire.com/news-releases/sales-success-shows-neuromarketing-moves-magazines-new-scientist-reports-12-increase-in-newsstand-sales-for-issue-featuring-neurofocus-tested-cover-design-102081328.htm, accessed October 2015.

[30] See Barney Beal, 'Gartner: CRM spending looking up', Search-CRM.com, 29 April 2008, http://searchcrm.techtarget.com/news/article/0,289142,sid11_gci1311658,00.htm; David White, 'CRM Magazine announces winners of 2009 CRM Service Awards', Business Wire, 1 April 2009; and 'Research and markets: global customer relationship management (CRM) sales automation software market 2008–2012', M2 Presswire, 14 January 2010; also see www.information-age.com/industry/software/123457830/crm-remains-top-it-priority-businesses-plan-spending-increase, accessed October 2015

[31] Example from Rod Addy, 'Tesco keeps a keen eye on its fair-weather customers', Foodmanufacture.co.uk, 26 March 2008, www.foodmanufacture.co.uk/Business-News/Tesco-keeps-a-keen-eye-on-its-fair-weather-customers, accessed October 2015.

[32] Mike Freeman, 'Data company helps Walmart, casinos, airlines analyze customers', San Diego Union Tribune. For another good CRM example, see 'SAS helps 1–800-Flowers.com grow deep roots with customers', www.sas.com/success/1800flowers.html, accessed October 2015.

[33] Example from Philip Delves Broughton, 'The added value of good information', Financial Times, 7 March 2011, www.ft.com/cms/s/0/cca74d5c-4907-11e0-af8c-00144feab49a.html#axzz1UPifHx5H, accessed October 2015.

[34] Example from Geoff Nairn, 'System gives a warning of unhappiness', Financial Times, 16 September 2009, www.ft.com/cms/s/0/cc18d792-a2ce-11de-ae7e-00144feabdc0.html#axzz1UPifHx5H, accessed October 2015.

[35] See www.mesacom.co.uk and specifically www.mesacom.co.uk/ProjectExtranetSoftware/Project_Extranet_CaseStudy_SkyCaddie.aspx for details of the SkyCaddie case.

[36] Based on information in Ann Zimmerman, 'Small business; do the research', Wall Street Journal, 9 May 2005, p. R3; with additional information and insights from John Tozzi, 'Market research on the cheap', BusinessWeek, 9 January 2008, www.businessweek.com/smallbiz/content/jan2008/sb2008019_352779.htm; 'Understanding the basics of small business market research', All Business, www.allbusiness.com/marketing/market-research/2587-1.html#axzz2K-8T92eOR, accessed October 2015; and www.bibbentuckers.com, accessed October 2015.

[37] For some good advice on conducting market research in a small business, search 'conducting market research', at www.sba.gov or see 'Researching your market', Entrepreneur, www.entrepreneur.com/article/43024-1, accessed October 2015.

[38] See http://en-us.nielsen.com/main/about/Profile, accessed October 2015.

[39] See 'Top 25 global market research organizations', Marketing News, August 2013, p. 24; and www.nielsen.com/us/en/about-us.html and www.nielsen.com/us/en.html?worldWideSelected=true, accessed October 2015.

[40] See http://data.worldbank.org/data-catalog/world-development-indicators?cid=GPD_WDI, accessed October 2015.

[41] Internet stats are from www.worldbank.org/, accessed October 2015; also see www.iwcp.hpg.ig.com.br/communications.html, accessed October 2015.

[42] Subhash C. Jain, International Marketing Management, 3rd ed. (Boston: PWS-Kent, 1990), p. 338. For more discussion on international marketing research issues and solutions, see Warren J. Keegan and Mark C. Green, Global Marketing, 7th ed. (Upper Saddle River, NJ: Prentice Hall, 2013), pp. 170–201.

[43] See Andrew Roberts, 'In some stores, all eyes are on you', Bloomberg Businessweek, 10 December 2012, pp. 32–33; and 'EyeSee Mannequin', www.almax-italy.com/en-US/ProgettiSpeciali/EyeSeeMannequin.aspx, accessed October 2015.

[44] See Stephanie Clifford, 'Many see privacy on the web as big issue, survey says', New York Times, 16 March 2009; and Mark Davis, 'Behavioral targeting of online ads is growing', McClatchy-Tribune Business News, 19 December 2009; also see 'Consumers encouraged to protect their privacy online', PR Newswire, 27 January 2010.

[45] See Jaikumar Vijayan, 'Disclosure laws driving data privacy efforts, says IBM exec', Computerworld, 8 May 2006, p. 26; 'Facebook Chief Privacy Officer – Interview', Analyst Wire, 18 February 2009; and Rita Zeidner, 'New face in the C-Cuite', HRMagazine, January 2010, pp. 39-41.

[46] Information at www.casro.org/codeofstandards.cfm#intro, accessed October 2015.

COMPANY CASE

Holland & Barrett by Dr Eleri Rosier, Cardiff Business School

Holland & Barrett has been on a health kick recently, increasing its presence on the high street and online while also working to boost its profits.

In the last year it has opened seven new stores and 42 new franchises as well as expanding overseas. It has fuelled this growth through cultivating its own-brand range and developing its position as a multi-channel retailer.

Holland & Barrett is one of Europe's leading retailers of vitamins, minerals and herbal supplements. The chain of health food shops has over 700 stores in the United Kingdom, Republic of Ireland, South Africa, China, Singapore, Spain, Malta and Gibraltar. The company also has stores in the Netherlands, where they trade as De Tuinen. Holland & Barrett was formed in 1870 by Alfred Slapps Barrett and Major William Holland, who bought a grocery store and developed their business into two shops; a grocery store and a clothing store. In the 1920s, Alfred Button & Sons bought the business and kept the name Holland & Barrett. Holland & Barrett has since changed hands a number of times. Notably, Lloyds Pharmacy purchased Holland & Barrett in 1992, after which NBTY, formerly known as Nature's Bounty Inc., an American manufacturer of vitamins and nutritional supplements, acquired Holland & Barrett in 1997. Private American equity firm the Carlyle Group subsequently bought NBTY in 2010.

Today, increasing competition from independent health stores, as well as national supermarket chains, chemists, drugstores and Internet traders, has led to the company to aim to differentiate itself from mass-market competitors by developing a specialist reputation. By shifting the focus of its marketing away from price promotions to the expertise of its staff, it aims to differentiate itself from supermarket chains. Phil Geary, group marketing director of Holland & Barrett parent company NBTY Europe, said the activity was intended to demonstrate that although supermarkets offer cheap vitamins, 'they can't compete with us on customer advice or product knowledge'. Offering high-quality products at low, value prices Holland & Barrett has been keen to promote itself as a specialist retailer in an increasingly fragmented market. Holland & Barrett prides itself on being amongst the first in the industry to introduce innovative products in response to new studies, research and consumer preferences. The company aims to maintain this position in order to appeal to the broad church of customers seeking healthy lifestyles. The company is also continuing to invest in new technologies to make it an omni-channel business. The rollout of new till and web platforms in 2014 has helped Holland & Barrett leverage this investment by improving upon its current level of performance.

The company has recently opened its 1,000th Holland & Barrett retail store in Manchester's Trafford Centre and plans to open a further 70 new outlets in Europe with a total investment of £40 million. The announcement coincides with annual financial figures showing increased profits of 8 per cent at Holland & Barrett on a turnover of more than £500 million. The chief executive of Holland & Barrett's parent company, Peter Aldis, said that the company was expanding in international markets as well as the United Kingdom, mentioning new territories as varied as Belgium, China, Iceland, Kuwait and Singapore.

One of the key factors behind the recent success of Holland & Barrett was consumers' increased understanding of the long-term health risks of food staples such as sugar, salt, red meat and processed meats. The drift towards an all-round healthier lifestyle for UK shoppers is leading to consumer demand for more and more 'free-from' foods and beauty product items said Mr Aldis. Holland & Barrett's own research charts significantly changing attitudes towards health over the past generation, with today's twenty-something's three times more likely to go to a gym than their parents' generation, and with five times as many people taking vitamins, mineral and supplements than in the 1980s. 'Through a combination of acquisition and franchising we are now operating 80 stores in eight territories and plan this financial year to open a further 70 new European stores. Although the UK high street has been challenging these past few years I believe the retail health sector benefits from the resilience of the 'health pound' against other demands on consumers' wallets,' predicted Mr Aldis.

In 2013 the health retailer recruited Neal Preece to the new role of e-commerce director who previously held a similar position at Next. His arrival coincided with a multimillion pound revamp of Holland and Barrett's IT systems and website. Customer insights revealed that convenience is key to store choice for ten million health food users. Steps to making stores more easily accessible, including online, can tap into the spending of this sizeable group. 2013 also saw the implementation of new EPOS software as the company sought to further improve its omni-channel offering, partnering with software provider Oracle in order to streamline its existing loyalty card scheme Rewards for Life and offering a card-based system to ensure a more personalised service. The aim here was to allow for a more strategic approach to customer insights and segmentation in order to improve their product offering.

The 1,000th store milestone came in the middle of a £40 million investment programme that will allow the business to better meet the demands of an increasingly younger client base and more complex shopping environment. Holland & Barrett's omni-channel strategy has seen the roll-out of a click and collect proposition to further boost Internet sales an a bid to tap into the 1.8 million visitors to its site each month. Also, new shop formats have been introduced and pilots for new store concepts such as protein shake bars and scent stations have proved very successful, underlining the continued importance shoppers attach to a real sensory retail experience.

Holland & Barrett is currently putting together a brief for a new concept store, dubbed a 'Store for the Future', where it will look to trial and test consumer reaction to new technologies including iBeacons. In so doing, Holland & Barrett has become the latest brand to eye the opportunities beacon technology offers — most recently House of Fraser, Hawes & Curtis and Bentalls eagerly threw themselves into trials across a number of stores, John Lewis invested £100k in a beacons start-up, and BA rolled out beacon tech at Heathrow Airport. It is a trend that has shown no sign of slowing.

As the retailer launches a two-year overhaul of its technology offering, chief marketing officer Lysa Hardy revealed that the new store, likely to be ready by the new year, will serve as a place to truly test out ideas on consumers, some of which will not make it country-wide. 'With the concept store, we will be putting things into it as a true concept store; some of which won't work and we won't roll out. The whole point of it is to see what customers react to and what they like and what we need to build on.' Hardy said that beacon technology is something the retailer will look to experiment with, and it is hoped

Holland & Barrett will eventually be able to target customers individually based on a profile they have set for themselves. Marketing spend has been increased as a result of the modernisation and a new multimillion pound ad campaign launched as a progression of Holland & Barrett's animated woodland creature format. Hardy said the idea behind updating the ad comes as other retailers, including John Lewis, have begun to use animation in their campaigns, and Holland & Barrett wanted to move the advert on. 'When we launched it last year people were saying it was very distinctive and very different and no one was doing that style of advertising,' said Hardy. 'But since then a few brands have picked up on that idea and even the John Lewis ad last year was an animated woodland creature. So we wanted to move it on and feel a little more dynamic, because

Source: D. Callcut/Alamy Images

we feel the brand is more dynamic and progressive now.' The ad campaign (endorsed by celebrity Louise Redknapp) famous for its 'weird and wonderful' snail gel product range, aimed to boost its popularity among a younger audience and help the brand feel more modern.

In late 2014 Holland & Barrett signed a deal with major supermarkets, including Tesco, Asda, Morrisons and Waitrose, as well as newsagent WH Smith to stock its health and well-being magazine, *Healthy*. The magazine had, until then, only been sold through Holland & Barrett's 720 stores.

From 2015 issues were available across the UK and Republic of Ireland at an increased price per issue. Holland & Barrett has also created what it is calling 'Good Life Insiders' to chalk up greater engagement across social media and offer consumers the chance of testing products ahead of their release. The idea behind the Good Life Insiders comes as the firm focuses on its website content marketing to provide a more cohesive and integrated approach for the offline *Healthy* magazine. Ellie Hughes, editorial director at Holland & Barrett's content agency, The River Group, explained: 'There is a lot of great content in Healthy, so we're trying to get more integrated with what we're doing in our campaigns and what's in Healthy and bring that together in a digital forum for people as well. Having our own customers generate some of that content is a great situation for us.' The aim of the magazine is to offer friendly, in-depth and trustworthy health advice to women of all ages on important health-related issues. This, combined with a food section investigating the latest trends, fitness and emotional health sections promoting the philosophy of a balanced life, is targeted at women wanting to lead a healthier, happier life. Current advertisers include Dr Organics, Pharmacare and Vitabiotics but Holland & Barrett hopes the new website together with the increased circulation from the newsstand will attract a greater breadth of advertisers.

Holland and Barrett's extensive research has shown that the UK vitamins market has continued to grow annually by 4 per cent, reaching £738 million in 2013. Cautious consumer spending, lower consumption and a lack of significant new product development has prevented the category from growing at a faster pace. The struggle to gain momentum in this sector bears witness to challenging trading conditions for companies in this industry. The data also shows that around 35 per cent of adults take vitamins, down from 41 per cent in 2008. Despite this, when it comes to health and wellness today's information-driven consumers seek advice from a number of quarters but it is recommendation that carries the highest weight, influencing purchase of vitamins amongst six in ten users. Holland & Barrett's data also shows that this trend has been linked to a growing desire among consumers to buy healthy food rather than vitamins, as well as studies questioning the efficacy of vitamin tablets compared with a decent diet. However, the uncertain economic climate has led some customers to view supplements as a luxury they don't actually need. Holland & Barrett continues to represent the leading company in the UK vitamins market with a 14 per cent value share. It would seem that the retailer's strategy of continuing the expansion of the number of stores, the introduction of new products, effective promotional activity and continued investment in its employees has paid off in terms of helping the company to maintain its leading position.

Questions for discussion

1. How has Holland & Barrett mined its big data to use market information more effectively?
2. With the streamlining of its loyalty card scheme what should Holland & Barrett do to enhance its customer relationship management?
3. How can Holland & Barrett use marketing information and customer insights to ensure that all the implemented changes have succeeded?

Sources: R. Baker, 'Holland & Barrett vies to change "old fashioned" perception', *Marketing Week*, 28 February 20113; M. Chapman, 'Holland & Barrett in health expert shift', *Marketing Magazine*, 11 October 2011; J. Faull, 'Holland & Barrett inks deal with supermarkets to sell *Healthy* magazine nationwide', *The Drum*, 12 December 2014; T. Holland, 'Holland & Barrett to launch click-and-collect and order in store within 12 months', *Retail Week*, 6 October 2014; Mintel, 'Vitamins and supplements – UK', September 2014; Mintel, 'Health food retailing UK consumer market research report', 2014; G. Montague-Jones, 'As Phil Geary quits Holland & Barrett, NBTY shakes up e-commerce and buying', *The Grocer*, 15 June 2013; N. Mortimer, 'Holland & Barrett preps "store for the future" to trial beacon technology', *The Drum*, 8 October 2014; N. Mortimer, N. 'Holland & Barrett aims to "modernise" its brand as it chases younger audience for £600k snailgGel campaign', *The Drum*, 26 November 2014.

CHAPTER FIVE

Consumer markets and buyer behaviour

Chapter preview

You've studied how marketers obtain, analyse and use information to develop customer insights and assess marketing programmes. In this chapter, we take a closer look at the most important element of the marketplace – customers. The aim of marketing is to engage consumers and affect how they think and act. To affect the *whats, whens* and *hows* of buyer behaviour, marketers must first understand the *whys*. In this chapter, we look at *final consumer* buying influences and processes. In the next chapter, we'll study the buyer behaviour of *business customers*. You'll see that understanding buyer behaviour is an essential but very difficult task.

To get a better sense of the importance of understanding consumer behaviour, we begin by first looking at Jack Wills, the UK-founded clothing brand. What makes Jack Wills buyers so loyal? Just what is it that makes the student-types flock to their stores, their events and parties? Partly, it's the way the clothes look and feel. But at the core, customers buy from Jack Wills because the brand itself is a part of their own self-expression and lifestyle. It's a part of what the loyal Jack Wills customer is.

Objective outline

➤ **Objective 1** Define the consumer market and construct a simple model of consumer buyer behaviour.
Model of consumer behaviour (p. 139)

➤ **Objective 2** Name the four major factors that influence consumer buyer behaviour.
Characteristics affecting consumer behaviour (pp. 140–153)

➤ **Objective 3** List and define the major types of buying decision behaviour and the stages in the buyer decision process.

➤ **Objective 4** Describe the adoption and diffusion process for new products.

Jack Wills: the university outfitters

t's a holiday weekend and the sun is out in Rock, the Cornish resort in the south of the UK. However, the teenagers in Rock are not heading for the sand and surf but towards a newly opened clothes shop, Jack Wills. Outside, there are bright flashes of colour – shopping bags in the Jack Wills signature colours of pink and navy blue stripes. The teenagers are all wearing branded Jack Wills clothing: denim mini-skirts worn over leggings, zip-up hoodies, vests, shirts and shorts. To the embarrassment of their parents and the admiration of their friends, some boys are wearing their trousers 'fashionably' low, the better to display 'Jack Wills' on the elastic of their underpants.

There is something cultish about its fans' devotion to the Jack Wills brand. Visit any upmarket university, boarding school or resort town, and the teens will be there, buying Jack Wills' expensive preppy sportswear (€79 for a hooded sweatshirt and up to €22 for a pair of socks.). Jack Wills ('university outfitters') isn't just on the high street. The firm annually hosts and sponsors three nights of events for thousands of students involved in the British Universities Council 'Main Event'. It sponsors university balls (such as the St. Andrews Kate Kennedy Charity May Ball, the Keble College, Oxford, May Ball) and puts on between-season 'tours' in university towns (giving away bespoke T-shirts for each town, plus mugs, underpants and other coveted trinkets).

The company is one of a number of brands, including the more established US label Abercrombie & Fitch, that target teenagers with money and sell them 'preppy' or 'surf-inspired' casual clothes. It prides itself on its stealth marketing and its very direct relationship with its consumers.

Jack Wills shuns advertising in favour of social media and organised events. About 700,000 Facebook, 125,000 Instagram followers, 125,000 Twitter followers tune in to watch videos of its sponsored events on its YouTube channel. Among its employees, there is a team monitoring followers' tweets and replying to questions. 'We get hundreds of mentions every day on Twitter and we reply to 90 per cent of them,' says marketing manager Freddie Wyatt. 'People ask a question and we'll tweet back an answer along with a video. It's one-to-one contact.' The firms generates buzz for its various collections by each year sending out four catalogues, or handbooks as they're known, to a huge UK readership to coincide with UK school terms (although many customers also use the Jack Wills App).

The first Jack Wills opened in Salcombe, Devon, in the south of the UK, in 1999. Having just graduated, Peter Williams, then 23, became lifestyle brand obsessed. He picked the sleepy resort of Salcombe because 'I'd been once in summer and it really just registered something. When I started thinking about a premium brand I dredged up this vision of what I remembered in Salcombe. I thought, "What if you could create a brand that could bottle what being at a British university was all about and all the cool amazing stuff that goes with that?" It's such a uniquely cherished part of your life. I thought if you could create a brand that epitomised that it would be very compelling.'

He joined forces with Robert Shaw, a university friend then working at a marketing firm, and they scraped together about €50,000 of their own capital from savings, credit cards and loans. They set up Jack Wills (named after Williams' grandfather, Jack Williams) as a summer shop on Fore Street (it's still there and has expanded into the two neighbouring sites). They sold vintage-inspired T-shirts and sweaters bearing the Jack Wills lettering while sleeping above the shop.

George Wallace, head of MHE Retail, a retail consultancy, says Jack Wills has 'created a very classy lifestyle brand with a very tribal following. They've got quite a narrow position – it's very public school – but they've got that group to buy in to it in a very big way. They've created something that persuades parents to pay premium prices for reasonable quality, and at very high margins. The worry is if this very fickle group falls out of love with them. It's such a volatile market. If they do, the fall could be spectacular, although I don't see that happening any time soon.'

Jack Wills also taps into the allure of 'privilege' as a selling point. Mat Bickley, founder of retail consultancy joynlondon.com, says: 'Posh is cool again, it's like the 1980s. If you look at all the celebrity endorsements, the bands, the actors and faces of Burberry even now, they're all "society" or public school educated.' There are now around 80 Jack Wills shops. Most stores are in the UK but there are two in in Ireland and the brand has opened a dozen stores in the US. It is also expanding into Asia and the Middle East, with the Jack Wills open in Dubai, Kuwait Beirut and Hong Kong. Recently, Jack Wills took a pop-up store

Source: Kumar Sriskandan/Alamy Images

in Terminal 5 complete with a branded Land Rover, while in 2013 they opened pop-up stores in the UK and the US to coincide with the Christmas and New Year sales.

Williams says, 'We're still very grassroots about things'. Grassroots are at the heart of everything Jack Wills is about, and its attention to its customers – its community – is what sets it apart from other shops selling to teenagers. Its tweeds, vintage hoodies and print prairie dresses are pleasant but they are not cutting-edge, individual or high fashion. Their sameness reinforces membership of an exclusive friendship group.

Events in the real world make the brand, which even sounds like a friend, into a companion for the good times. Jack Wills sponsors the varsity rugby union match between Oxford and Cambridge universities watched by many thousands of students, ex-students and teenagers. The Jack Wills' annual Varsity Polo is the biggest event in its calendar to date. In the summer of 2014, teams from Harvard, Yale, Oxford and Cambridge universities, and the UK public schools Eton and Harrow, played against each other with thousands of fans looking on. The company is the official sponsor. Max Reyner, insight editor at LSN Global, says: 'Events are key here and are taking over from social networking, which is still important for awareness but is seen as less cool to teens now, as parents join sites like Facebook. They used to be private spaces. With the events they have a sense of ownership. The fact that Jack Wills doesn't advertise also helps. Teens like the idea of discovery. The whole feel of Jack Wills is like you're in a club and you're shutting out the parents.'

One of Jack Wills' key innovations is its 'Seasonnaires' programme. The company recruits young good-looking people who seem cool and appear outgoing as summer-long interns. These 'influencers' attracted by the tagline 'Work hard, live louder', attend parties and circulate with guests, handing out free goods and merchandise. This summer a group of Seasonnaires, who are paid and given free clothing by the brand, will travel to targeted locations, hosting parties on the beach and in local clubs and pubs, giving out free Jack Wills gifts. When inviting people to apply Jack Wills say, 'Winners should expect to spend their summer hanging out on the beach, sailing and surfing during the day, and hosting parties in town at night.'

So far Jack Wills has been able to crystallise the essence of a particular group and sell it back to them to wear at the beach and in the nightclub. And those customers seem very, very happy about it. Says Isabelle, 15, standing outside the new Jack Wills in Rock, bedecked head-to-toe in Jack Wills merchandise. 'I like that Jack Wills feels British. I get the catalogue, everyone in my school does. I love their Facebook page too.'[1]

The Jack Wills story shows that factors at many levels affect consumer buying behaviour. Buying behaviour is never simple, yet understanding it is an essential task of marketing management. **Consumer buyer behaviour** refers to the buying behaviour of final consumers – individuals and households that buy goods and services for personal consumption. All of these final consumers combine to make up the **consumer market.** The EU consumer market consists of more than 507 million people who consume more than €13.70 trillion worth of goods and services each year, making it one of the most attractive consumer markets in the world.[2]

Consumers around the world vary tremendously in age, income, education level and tastes. They also buy an incredible variety of goods and services. How these diverse consumers relate with each other and with other elements of the world around them impacts their choices among various products, services and companies. Here we examine the fascinating array of factors that affect consumer behaviour.

Consumer buyer behaviour—The buying behaviour of final consumers – individuals and households that buy goods and services for personal consumption.

Consumer market—All the individuals and households that buy or acquire goods and services for personal consumption.

MODEL OF CONSUMER BEHAVIOUR

Consumers make many buying decisions every day, and the buying decision is the focal point of the marketer's effort. Most large companies research consumer buying decisions in great detail to answer questions about what consumers buy, where they buy, how and how much they buy, when they buy, and why they buy. Marketers can study actual consumer purchases to find out what they buy, where and how much. But learning about the *whys* behind consumer buying behaviour is not so easy – the answers are often locked deep within the consumer's mind. Often, consumers themselves don't know exactly what influences their purchases.

The central question for marketers is this: how do consumers respond to various marketing efforts the company might use? The starting point is the stimulus-response model of buyer behaviour shown in Figure 5.1. This figure shows that marketing and other stimuli enter the consumer's 'black box' and produce certain responses. Marketers must figure out what is in the buyer's black box.

Marketing stimuli consist of the four Ps: product, price, place and promotion. Other stimuli include major forces and events in the buyer's environment: economic, technological, social and cultural. All these inputs enter the buyer's black box, where they are turned into a set of buyer responses – the buyer's attitudes and preferences, brand engagements and relationships, and what he or she buys, when, where and how much.

Marketers want to understand how the stimuli are changed into responses inside the consumer's black box, which has two parts. First, the buyer's characteristics influence how he or she perceives and reacts to the stimuli. Second, the buyer's decision process itself affects his or her behaviour. We look first at buyer characteristics as they affect buyer behaviour and then discuss the buyer decision process.

Author comment

Despite the simple-looking model in Figure 5.1, understanding the *whys* of buying behaviour is very difficult. Says one expert, 'the mind is a whirling, swirling, jumbled mass of neurons bouncing around... .'

Figure 5.1 The model of buyer behaviour

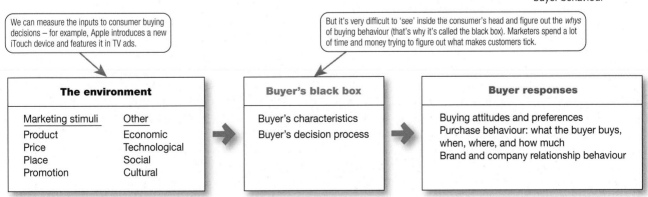

We can measure the inputs to consumer buying decisions – for example, Apple introduces a new iTouch device and features it in TV ads.

But it's very difficult to 'see' inside the consumer's head and figure out the *whys* of buying behaviour (that's why it's called the black box). Marketers spend a lot of time and money trying to figure out what makes customers tick.

The environment		Buyer's black box	Buyer responses
Marketing stimuli / Product / Price / Place / Promotion	**Other** / Economic / Technological / Social / Cultural	Buyer's characteristics / Buyer's decision process	Buying attitudes and preferences / Purchase behaviour: what the buyer buys, when, where, and how much / Brand and company relationship behaviour

CHARACTERISTICS AFFECTING CONSUMER BEHAVIOUR

Author comment

Many levels of factors affect our buying behaviour – from broad cultural and social influences to motivations, beliefs and attitudes lying deep within us. For example, why *did* you buy *that* specific phone you're carrying?

Consumer purchases are influenced strongly by cultural, social, personal and psychological characteristics, as shown in Figure 5.2. For the most part, marketers cannot control such factors, but they must take them into account.

Cultural factors

Cultural factors exert a broad and deep influence on consumer behaviour. Marketers need to understand the role played by the buyer's *culture, subculture* and *social class*.

Culture

Culture—The set of basic values, perceptions, wants and behaviours learned by a member of society from family and other important institutions.

Culture is the most basic cause of a person's wants and behaviour. Human behaviour is largely learned. Growing up in a society, a child learns basic values, perceptions, wants and behaviours from his or her family and other important institutions. A European child normally learns or is exposed to the following values: achievement and success, freedom, individualism, hard work, activity and involvement, efficiency and practicality, material comfort, youthfulness and fitness and health. Every group or society has a culture, and cultural influences on buying behaviour may vary greatly from both county to county and country to country.

Marketers are always trying to spot *cultural shifts* so as to discover new products that might be wanted. For example, the cultural shift toward greater concern about health and fitness has created a huge industry for health-and-fitness services, exercise equipment and clothing, organic foods and a variety of diets.

Subculture

Subculture—A group of people with shared value systems based on common life experiences and situations.

Each culture contains smaller **subcultures**, or groups of people with shared value systems based on common life experiences and situations. Subcultures include nationalities, religions, racial groups and geographic regions. Many subcultures make up important market segments and marketers often design products and marketing programmes tailored to their needs. Across Europe many thousands of subcultures exist, from cybergoths to bodybuilders to naturists to bikers to fundamental Christians. While subcultures are distinct, they are not mutually exclusive (which suggests that somewhere there is a subculture of cybergoth, bodybuilders who ride motorbikes to church in the nude). Two contrasting examples of subcultures are gamers and mature consumers.

Figure 5.2 Factors influencing consumer behaviour

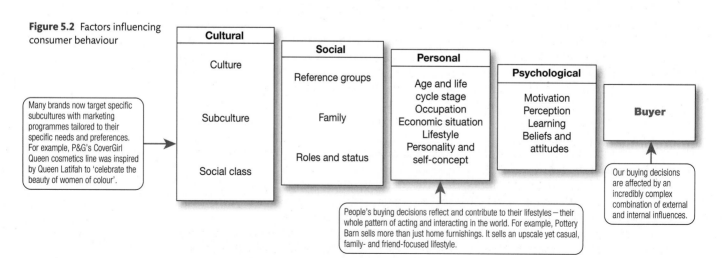

Many brands now target specific subcultures with marketing programmes tailored to their specific needs and preferences. For example, P&G's CoverGirl Queen cosmetics line was inspired by Queen Latifah to 'celebrate the beauty of women of colour'.

Cultural
Culture
Subculture
Social class

Social
Reference groups
Family
Roles and status

Personal
Age and life cycle stage
Occupation
Economic situation
Lifestyle
Personality and self-concept

Psychological
Motivation
Perception
Learning
Beliefs and attitudes

Buyer

People's buying decisions reflect and contribute to their lifestyles – their whole pattern of acting and interacting in the world. For example, Pottery Barn sells more than just home furnishings. It sells an upscale yet casual, family- and friend-focused lifestyle.

Our buying decisions are affected by an incredibly complex combination of external and internal influences.

Gamers

Originally the term 'gamer' referred to young people playing role-playing games and war-games (epitomised by players of the phenomenally successful Dungeons and Dragons dice-based, role-playing game). However, today the label of gamer is attributed to anybody who enjoys playing or learning about video games – both on and offline. According to a recent study,[3] around 25 per cent of Europe's population can be considered gamers (that is, playing computer games at least once a week) with the worldwide video game marketplace set to rise in value from €79 billion to €8 billion by the end of 2015.[4] While we might be unfairly tempted to stereotype gamers as adolescents with poor social skills and pale skin tones, recent research for the Interactive Software Federation of Europe by Game Vision Europe[5] defies such narrow-mindedness:

Over 25 percent of Europeans can be thought of as gamers.
Source: Cathy Yeulet/123RF.com

- Gamers are 55 per cent male and 45 per cent female (video gaming being far from the male-only preserve often portrayed in the press).
- 51 per cent of gamers are under 35 but 11 per cent are between 55 and 64 years old.
- Gaming is most popular among the young, however almost 49 of gamers are over 35 years old.
- 35 per cent of gamers have purchased a game in the past 12 months.
- In the Nordic countries many parents play video games with their children (56 per cent in Denmark, 55 per cent in Norway, 50 per cent in Finland and 47 per cent in Sweden).
- Across the EU 36 per cent of parents play video games with children to spend time with them with 34 per cent of parents arguing that video gaming is a fun activity for all the family.
- Around 46 per cent of parents argue that playing video games encourages their children to be more creative.
- Nevertheless, 279 per cent of European parent use Parental Control software to manage the gaming habits of their 6–9 year olds.

The growth in gaming is mirrored in the intensively competitive games consoles market that appears to be becoming increasingly competitive.[6]

Sony has topped Nintendo in annual sales of video game consoles for the first time in eight years – a bittersweet victory as both Japanese companies have failed to stop customers from abandoning specialised game equipment in favour of smartphones.

Both Sony and Nintendo suffered significant unit-sales declines in the financial year, but the drop at Sony was smaller – 20 per cent compared with Nintendo's 30 per cent – thanks in part to the launch of the new Sony PlayStation 4 game player in late 2013.

The difference put Sony ahead of its rival for the first time since Nintendo launched its hit Wii console in late 2006. Recent updates of the Wii and its handheld cousin, the Nintendo DS, have not sold as well as earlier versions, contributing to three straight years of net losses for Nintendo.

Sony sold 18.7 million home and portable players last financial year, against 16.3 million for Nintendo, according to company data.

Sales of specialised game consoles peaked at the end of 2009 and no recent machine has had the impact of the original Wii, whose innovative motion controller and simple, family-oriented games attracted millions of new fans from outside the ranks of hard-core gamers.

Many of those fans have drifted away again, however, attracted by the low cost and increasing sophistication of downloadable games for their smartphones or tablets. Nintendo has slashed sales targets for the Wii U, the latest incarnation of the Wii franchise, more than once since its launch in late 2012.

At Sony, the powerful PlayStation series of consoles has always been aimed at a more avid fan base than the Wii – a strategy that hurt the company during the Wii's ascendancy but has offered a measure of protection from the smartphone threat.

By way of comparison with Sony and Nintendo's sales figures, Apple has lately been shipping about 50 million iPhones and iPads each quarter, more than the latest full-year game console sales for the two Japanese groups combined.

Mature consumers

As the population ages, mature consumers are becoming a very attractive market. By 2015, when all the baby boomers will be 50-plus, people aged 50–75 will account for 40 per cent of adult consumers. By 2030, adults aged 65 and older will represent nearly 20 per cent of the population. Whereas in 1960 most European countries had three 0–14 year olds for each person over 65, by 2060 it is forecast that each 0–14 will be matched by two people over 65. And these mature consumer segments boast the most expendable cash. The 50-plus consumer segment now accounts for nearly 50 per cent of all consumer spending, more than any current or previous generation. They have 2.5 times the discretionary buying power of those aged 18 to 34. As one marketing executive puts it, they have 'assets, not allowances'. Despite some financial setbacks resulting from the recent economic crisis, mature consumers remain an attractive market for companies in all industries, from pharmaceuticals, furniture, groceries, beauty products and clothing to consumer electronics, travel and entertainment and financial services.[7]

For decades, many marketers stereotyped mature consumers as doddering, impoverished shut-ins who are less willing to change brands. One problem: brand managers and advertising copywriters tend to be younger. 'Ask them to do an ad targeting the 50-plus demographic,' bemoans one marketer, 'and they'll default to a grey-haired senior living on a beach trailed by an aging golden retriever'. For example, in a recent survey, advertising professionals regarded the term *over the hill* as meaning people over 57. In contrast, baby boomer respondents related the term to people over age 75.[8]

As a group, however, mature consumers are anything but 'stuck in their ways'. To the contrary, a recent AARP study showed that older consumers for products such as stereos, computers and mobile phones are more willing to shop around and switch brands than their younger counterparts. For example, notes one expert, 'some 25 per cent of Apple's iPhones – the epitome of cool, cutting-edge product – have been bought by people over 50'.[9]

And in reality, people whose ages would seem to place them squarely in the 'old' category usually don't act old or see themselves that way. Thanks to advances in longevity, people are redefining what the mature life stage means. 'They're having a second middle-age before becoming elderly,' says a generational marketing expert. Marketers need to appeal to these consumers in a vibrant but authentic way.[10]

Today's mature consumers create an attractive market for travel agents and holiday firms. Indeed, mature consumers are more likely than younger consumers to take longer (and more expensive) holidays. A good example of a firm catering to this market is Solitair, which specialises in holidays for single people. Recognising the volume of mature consumers who are single, Solitair has developed a range of holidays exclusively for single consumers with the aim 'to rejuvenate the energy level of our travellers above 50 years during their singles holidays'. The promotional material claims that 'we make sure that we not only cater you the best services but the adventure and fun which our over 50s travellers seek during their singles trips. With our Singles Holidays Over 50, you get to enjoy beaches, cruises and many adventurous activities like skiing holidays, scuba diving, sailing and even mountaineering.'[11]

The idea that all mature consumers spend their days knitting, feeding ducks and slowly walking around super-markets is, at best, dated.
Source: Steve Fitchett/Getty Images

Social class

Almost every society has some form of **social class** structure. Social classes are society's relatively permanent and ordered divisions whose members share similar values, interests and behaviours. Social scientists have identified seven social classes, as shown in Figure 5.3.

Social class is not determined by a single factor, such as income, but is measured as a combination of occupation, income, education, wealth and other variables. In some social systems, members of different classes are reared for certain roles and cannot change their social positions. In Europe, however, the lines between social classes are not fixed and rigid; people can move to a higher social class or drop into a lower one.

Marketers are interested in social class because people within a given social class tend to exhibit similar buying behaviour. Social classes show distinct product and brand preferences in areas such as clothing, home furnishings, travel and leisure activity, financial services and automobiles.

In the UK, the British Broadcasting Corporation (commonly known as the BBC) worked with some university professors to undertake the largest ever study of social class in order to develop a more contemporary view of social class. Rather than the traditional class groupings presented in Figure 5.3, the BBC study suggests seven, radically different distinct classes:[12]

Social class—Relatively permanent and ordered divisions in a society whose members share similar values, interests and behaviours.

Figure 5.3 The major social classes

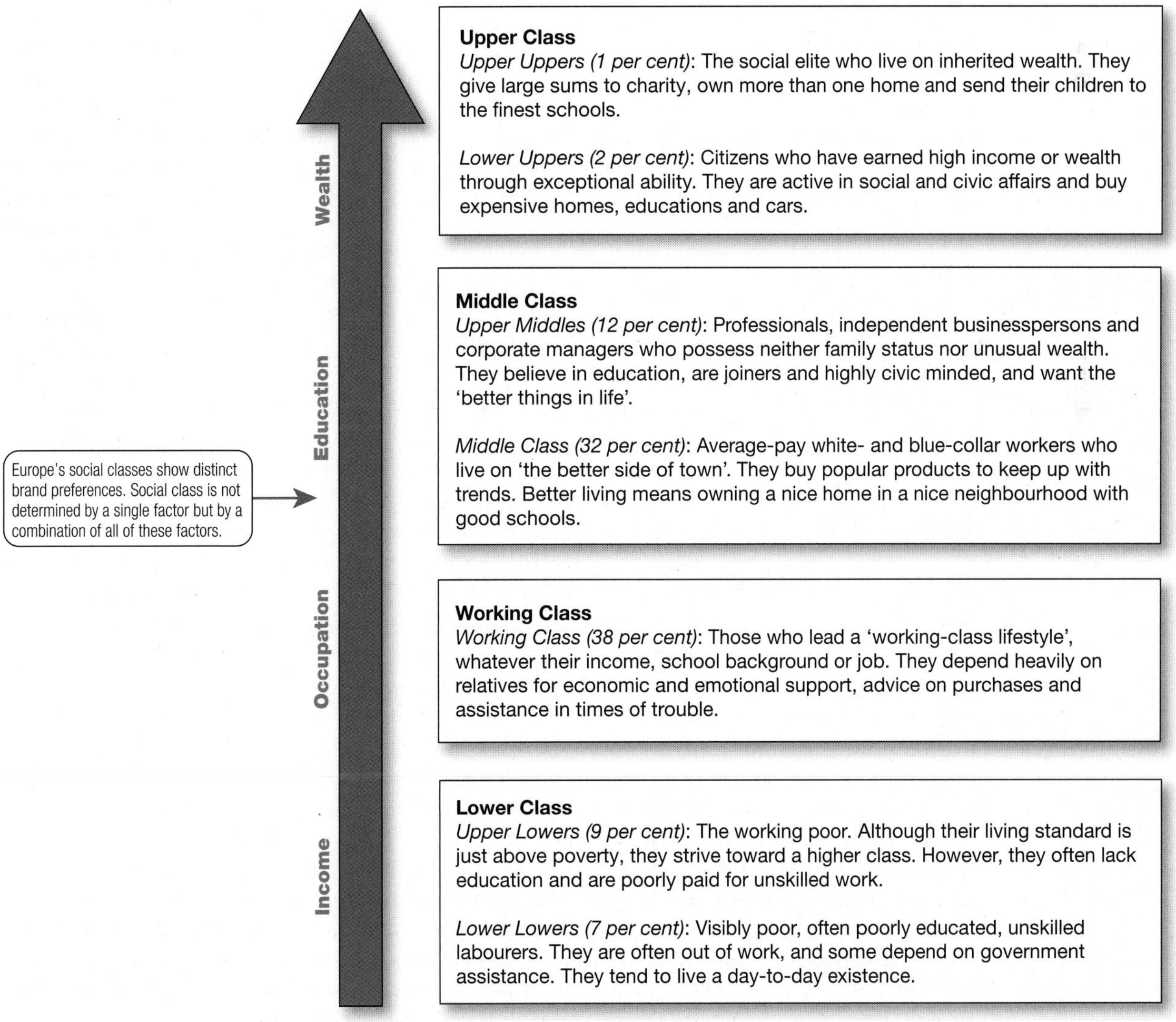

Wealth → Education → Occupation → Income

Upper Class
Upper Uppers (1 per cent): The social elite who live on inherited wealth. They give large sums to charity, own more than one home and send their children to the finest schools.

Lower Uppers (2 per cent): Citizens who have earned high income or wealth through exceptional ability. They are active in social and civic affairs and buy expensive homes, educations and cars.

Middle Class
Upper Middles (12 per cent): Professionals, independent businesspersons and corporate managers who possess neither family status nor unusual wealth. They believe in education, are joiners and highly civic minded, and want the 'better things in life'.

Middle Class (32 per cent): Average-pay white- and blue-collar workers who live on 'the better side of town'. They buy popular products to keep up with trends. Better living means owning a nice home in a nice neighbourhood with good schools.

Working Class
Working Class (38 per cent): Those who lead a 'working-class lifestyle', whatever their income, school background or job. They depend heavily on relatives for economic and emotional support, advice on purchases and assistance in times of trouble.

Lower Class
Upper Lowers (9 per cent): The working poor. Although their living standard is just above poverty, they strive toward a higher class. However, they often lack education and are poorly paid for unskilled work.

Lower Lowers (7 per cent): Visibly poor, often poorly educated, unskilled labourers. They are often out of work, and some depend on government assistance. They tend to live a day-to-day existence.

Europe's social classes show distinct brand preferences. Social class is not determined by a single factor but by a combination of all of these factors.

- **Elite:** This is the most privileged class in Great Britain who have high levels of all three capitals. Their high amount of economic capital sets them apart from everyone else.
- **Established middle class:** Members of this class have high levels of all three capitals although not as high as the Elite. They are a gregarious and culturally engaged class.
- **Technical middle class:** This is a new, small class with high economic capital but seem less culturally engaged. They have relatively few social contacts and so are less socially engaged.
- **New affluent workers:** This class has medium levels of economic capital and higher levels of cultural and social capital. They are a young and active group.
- **Emergent service workers:** This new class has low economic capital but has high levels of 'emerging' cultural capital and high social capital. This group are young and often found in urban areas.
- **Traditional working class:** This class scores low on all forms of the three capitals although they are not the poorest group. The average age of this class is older than the others.
- **Precariat:** This is the most deprived class of all with low levels of economic, cultural and social capital. The everyday lives of members of this class are precarious.

The key difference in these groupings is the dependence on social and cultural capital as pivotal reflectors of class and prospects (as well as the traditional measure of income).

Social factors

A consumer's behaviour also is influenced by social factors, such as the consumer's *small groups, social networks, family* and *social roles and status.*

Groups and social networks

Group—Two or more people who interact to accomplish individual or mutual goals.

Many small **groups** influence a person's behaviour. Groups that have a direct influence and to which a person belongs are called *membership groups*. In contrast, *reference groups* serve as direct (face-to-face interactions) or indirect points of comparison or reference in forming a person's attitudes or behaviour. People often are influenced by reference groups to which they do not belong. For example, an aspirational group is one to which the individual wishes to belong, as when a young football player hopes to someday emulate football star Gareth Bale and play in the La Liga.

Marketers try to identify the reference groups of their target markets. Reference groups expose a person to new behaviours and lifestyles, influence the person's attitudes and self-concept and create pressures to conform that may affect the person's product and brand choices. The importance of group influence varies across products and brands. It tends to be strongest when the product is visible to others whom the buyer respects.

Word-of-mouth influence and buzz marketing

Word-of-mouth influence—The impact of the personal words and recommendations of trusted friends, family, associates and other consumers on buying behaviour.

Word-of-mouth influence can have a powerful impact on consumer buying behaviour. The personal words and recommendations of trusted friends, family, associates and other consumers tend to be more credible than those coming from commercial sources, such as advertisements or salespeople. One recent study showed that 92 per cent of consumers trust recommendations from friends and family above any form of advertising.[13] Most word-of-mouth influence happens naturally: consumers start chatting about a brand they use or feel strongly about one way or the other. Often, however, rather than leaving it to chance, marketers can help to create positive conversations about their brands.

Opinion leader—A person within a reference group who, because of special skills, knowledge, personality, or other characteristics, exerts social influence on others.

Marketers of brands subjected to strong group influence must figure out how to reach **opinion leaders** – people within a reference group who, because of special skills, knowledge, personality, or other characteristics, exert social influence on others. Some experts call this group the *influentials or leading adopters*. When these influentials talk, consumers listen. Marketers try to identify opinion leaders for their products and direct marketing efforts toward them.

Buzz marketing involves enlisting or even creating opinion leaders to serve as 'brand ambassadors' who spread the word about a company's products. For example, Nike created a ton of buzz worldwide during the 2012 London Olympics when it shod 400 of its Nike-sponsored athletes in can't-miss incandescent green/yellow Volt Flyknit shoes. The shoes became the talk of the Olympics. And pop star Lady Gaga routinely enlists her most passionate fans – she calls them the Little Monsters – to spread the word about her new music. Gaga frequently leaks snippets of unreleased songs exclusively through Little Monster networks to create advance buzz. With more than 40 million fans on Twitter and 60 million fans on Facebook, engaging these diehard fans creates a big marketplace wallop.[14]

Philips' 'Wake-up Light' tapped into most people's desire to be woken naturally and gently each morning.
Source: Rachata Teyparsit/ Shutterstock.com

Many companies turn everyday customers into brand evangelists. For instance, Philips turned users into brand ambassadors for its novel Wake-up Light lighting system:[15]

A few years ago, Philips launched the first 'Wake-up Light' – a bedside lighting system that simulated a natural sunrise, helping people to wake up more naturally and happily. At first, however, Philips had difficulty explaining the complex benefits of the wake-up concept to sceptical consumers. The solution: create knowledgeable consumer advocates who could explain the product to others. Philips did this through an award-winning integrated media campaign called 'Wake up the town' in which it supplied the Wake-up Light to 200 residents in Longyearbyen, Norway – the northern-most town in the Arctic Circle. The town's 2,000 residents experience complete darkness 24 hours a day for 11 straight weeks each year. As you might imagine, waking up and starting the day in total darkness can be physically and mentally challenging. As the social experiment progressed, Philips asked consumers who used the Wake-up Light to honestly share their experiences on an interactive website, in blog posts and on Facebook. Philips also arranged media interviews and posted video mini-documentaries on the site. The three-month word-of-mouth campaign paid off handsomely as potential buyers followed the stories of those using the light. Of the 200 participants in 'Wake up the town', 87 per cent reported they were waking up feeling more refreshed, alert and ready for the day; 98 per cent reported that they would continue to use the Wake-up Light. During the campaign, purchase consideration in target markets in Sweden and the Netherlands grew by 17 per cent and 45 per cent, respectively. Unit demand grew by 29 per cent.

Online social networks

Over the past several years, a new type of social interaction has exploded onto the scene – online social networking. **Online social networks** are online communities where people socialise or exchange information and opinions. Social networking communities range from blogs (Consumerist, Gizmodo, Zenhabits) and message boards (Craigslist) to social media sites (Facebook, Twitter, YouTube, Pinterest and Foursquare) and virtual worlds (Second Life and Everquest). The new online forms of consumer-to-consumer and business-to-consumer dialogue have big implications for marketers.

Online social networks— Online social communities – blogs, social networking websites and other online communities – where people socialise or exchange information and opinions.

Marketers are working to harness the power of these new social networks and other 'word-of-web' opportunities to promote their products and build closer customer relationships. Instead of throwing more one-way commercial messages at consumers, they hope to use the Internet and mobile social networks to interact with consumers and become a part of their conversations and lives.

For example, brands ranging from Guinness and IKEA to Real Madrid CF are tweeting on Twitter. H&M connects with customers via the company's Facebook and YouTube pages, has a specific H&M iPad/iPhone App and a host of enthusiast groups. Benetton sponsors 'the United Blogs of Benetton' with blogs from the Netherlands, to Portugal to Italy to Mexico and even China.[16] And during the 2010 winter Olympics, VISA launched a 'Go World' microsite featuring athlete videos, photos and widgets that tied into nets like Facebook. VISA customised the campaign for global markets, featuring a different set of athletes for different countries.[17]

Most brands have built a comprehensive social media presence. Eco-conscious outdoor shoe and gear maker Timberland, for instance, has created an online community (http://community.timberland .com) that connects like-minded 'Earthkeepers' with each other and the brand through a network that includes several websites, a Facebook page, a YouTube channel, Pinterest pinboards, a Boot-makers Blog, an e-mail newsletter and several Twitter feeds. We will dig deeper into online social networks as a marketing tool in Chapter 17.

However, although much of the current talk about tapping social influence focuses on the Internet and social media, some 90 per cent of brand conversations still take place the old-fashioned way – face to face.[18] So most effective word-of-mouth marketing programmes begin with generating person-to-person brand conversations and integrating both offline and online social influence strategies. The goal is to create opportunities for customers to get involved with brands and then help them share their brand passions and experiences with others in both their real world and virtual social networks.

Traditional outdated roles are changing rapidly. Today, most men regularly act as the family grocery shopper, while half of women influence the family's technology purchases.

Source: Tyler Olson/Shutterstock. com

Family

Family members can strongly influence buyer behaviour. The family is the most important consumer buying organisation in society, and it has been researched extensively. Marketers are interested in the roles and influence of the husband, wife and children on the purchase of different products and services.

Husband–wife involvement varies widely by product category and by stage in the buying process. Buying roles change with evolving consumer lifestyles. For example, in Europe, the wife traditionally has been considered the main purchasing agent for the family in the areas of food, household products and clothing. But with more women working outside the home and the willingness of husbands to do more of the family's purchasing, all this is changing. A recent study found that 65 per cent of men grocery shop regularly and prepare at least one meal a week for others in the household. At the same time, women now influence 65 per cent of all new car purchases, 91 per cent of new home purchases, and 92 per cent of vacation purchases. In all, women make almost 85 per cent of all family purchases and control some 73 per cent of all household spending. Says one analyst, 'today's woman is … the designated chief operating officer of the home'.[19]

Such changes suggest that marketers in industries that have sold their products to only men or only women are now courting the opposite sex. For example, today women account for 50 per cent of all technology purchases. So consumer electronics companies are increasingly designing products that are easier to use and more appealing to female buyers:[20]

Consumer electronics engineers and designers are bringing a more feminine sensibility to products historically shaped by masculine tastes, habits and requirements. Designs are more 'feminine and softer', rather than masculine and angular. But many of the new touches are more subtle, like the wider spacing of the keys on a Sony netbook computer. It accommodates the longer fingernails that women tend to have. Some of the latest cell phones made by LG Electronics have the cameras' automatic focus calibrated to arm's length. The company observed that young women are fond of taking pictures of themselves with a friend. This isn't the case with men. Nikon and Olympus recently introduced lines of lighter, more compact and easy-to-use digital, single-lens reflex cameras that were designed with women in mind because they tend to be a family's primary keeper of memories.

A recent ad for Samsung's Galaxy smartphone features a new dad at home swaddling a baby while mom is out running errands – with the help of his Samsung phone, of course. While holding the baby with one hand, the dad uses the Air Gesture feature to activate the phone, then requests 'Hey Galaxy, search YouTube for swaddling tips'. As he follows the resulting video, Smart Pause pauses the video automatically as he works through the steps. Crisis averted. When mom calls to see if there are any problems, the relieved dad reports, 'No, we're having a dudes' day home. We're fiiiine.'[21]

Children may also have a strong influence on family buying decisions. For example, in the UK the Office for National Statistics predict that children under 16 years of age will increase to over 12 million by 2016. Between the ages of 7 and 15 these children will spend around €6,800 in pocket money and contribute €5.65 billion to the UK economy. Meanwhile each child will cost parents around €227,000 to clothe, feed and educate them to the age of 21.[22] In the US, 36 million children aged 8 to 12 wield an estimated €45 billion in disposable income. They also influence an additional €180 billion that their families spend on them in areas such as food, clothing, entertainment and personal care items. One study found that kids significantly influence family decisions about everything from where they take vacations to what cars and cell phones they buy.[23]

For example, to encourage families to take their children out to eat again following the recession, casual restaurants reached out to children with everything from sophisticated children's menus and special deals to a wealth of kid-focused activities. In the UK, at Pizza Hut children eat free all day and every day over the summer with the purchase of an adult entrée. To encourage parents to take holidays with their children, Forte Village in Sardinia even offer a dedicated Children's Restaurant, Children's Pool, complimentary kids clubs for children of all ages, a Chelsea Football Club Academy, rugby coaching, numerous water sports and even a special pool lagoon designed just for children.[24]

Roles and status

A person belongs to many groups – family, clubs, organisations, online communities. The person's position in each group can be defined in terms of both role and status. A role consists of the activities people are expected to perform according to the people around them. Each role carries a status reflecting the general esteem given to it by society.

People usually choose products appropriate to their roles and status. Consider the various roles a working mother plays. In her company, she may play the role of a brand manager; in her family, she plays the role of wife and mother; at her favourite sporting events, she plays the role of avid fan. As a brand manager, she will buy the kind of clothing that reflects her role and status in her company. At the game, she may wear clothing supporting her favourite team.

Personal factors

A buyer's decisions also are influenced by personal characteristics such as the buyer's age and life-cycle stage, occupation, economic situation, lifestyle and personality and self-concept.

Age and life-cycle stage

People change the goods and services they buy over their lifetimes. Tastes in food, clothes, furniture and recreation are often age related. Buying is also shaped by the stage of the family life cycle – the stages through which families might pass as they mature over time. Life stage changes usually result from demographics and life-changing events – marriage, having children, purchasing a home, divorce, children going to college, changes in personal income, moving out of the house and retirement. Marketers often define their target markets in terms of life-cycle stage and develop appropriate products and marketing plans for each stage.

Consumer information giant Acxiom's PersonicX life-stage segmentation system places households into distinct consumer segments and life-stage groups, based on specific consumer behaviour and demographic characteristics. PersonicX includes life-stage groups with names such as *Beginnings*, *Taking Hold*, *Cash & Careers*, *Jumbo Families*, *Transition Blues*, *Our Turn*, *Golden Years* and *Active Elders*. For example, the *Taking Hold* group consists of young, energetic, well-funded couples and young families who are busy with their careers, social lives and interests, especially fitness and active recreation. *Transition Blues* are blue-collar, less-educated, mid-income consumers who are transitioning to stable lives and talking about marriage and children.

'Consumers experience many life-stage changes during their lifetimes,' says Acxiom. 'As their life stages change, so do their behaviours and purchasing preferences. Marketers who are armed with the data to understand the timing and makeup of life-stage changes among their customers will have a distinct advantage over their competitors.'[25]

In line with today's tougher economic times, Acxiom has also developed a set of economic life-stage segments, including groups such as *Squeaking By*, *Eye on Essentials*, *Tight with a Purpose*, *It's My Life*, *Full Speed Ahead* and *Potential Rebounders*. The *Potential Rebounders* are those more likely to loosen up on spending sooner. This group appears more likely than other segments to use online research before purchasing electronics, appliances, home decor and jewellery. Thus, home improvement retailers appealing to this segment should have a strong online presence, providing pricing, features and benefits and product availability.

Different life-stage groups exhibit different buying behaviours. Life-stage segmentation provides a powerful marketing tool for marketers in all industries to better find, understand and engage consumers. Armed with data about the makeup of consumer life stages, marketers can create actionable, personalised campaigns based on how people consume and interact with brands and the world around them.

Occupation

A person's occupation affects the goods and services bought. Blue-collar workers tend to buy more rugged work clothes, whereas executives buy more business suits. Marketers try to identify the occupational groups that have an above-average interest in their products and services. A company can even specialise in making products needed by a given occupational group.

For example, Ede and Ravenscroft is a London bespoke tailor established in 1689. For over 300 years they have produced ceremonial gowns in the UK including the gowns for 12 royal coronations. Indeed, they are currently appointed as robe makers to Her Majesty Queen Elizabeth II, His Royal Highness The Duke of Edinburgh and His Royal Highness The Prince of Wales. However, Ede and Ravenscroft are probably best known as the dressers of the legal profession of barristers (not only in the UK but also across the world). The original Ede created the bespoke legal robes that barristers are required to wear during court appearances while Ravenscroft made the individually tailored legal wigs that barristers must wear when appearing in court.[26]

Economic situation

A person's economic situation will affect his or her store and product choices. Marketers watch trends in spending, personal income, savings and interest rates. In today's more frugal times, most companies have taken steps to create more customer value by redesigning, repositioning and re-pricing their products and services. For example:

Across Europe, retailers are facing a new reality: cash-strapped shoppers and rising costs. But it is mainly retailers that have traditionally relied on selling a high number of cheap items, from €1 T-shirts to €5 jeans, that are taking the biggest hit. 'What we are seeing is the end of the volume-driven market,' says Richard Hyman, strategic retail adviser to Deloitte. Stubbornly high inflation has been a feature of the economic downturn, exacerbated recently by rising fuel and food prices. Those with the lowest incomes are being hit hardest, as they spend a higher proportion of their money on essential items. At the same time, the costs that retailers themselves face are rising, from increases in cotton and wool prices, to rising wages in south-east Asia, although there has been some relief on cotton recently. There are also signs that younger customers, who have driven demand at companies such as the UK's ASOS, are now starting to feel the pinch. All retailers are faced with the unpalatable choice of passing higher costs on to customers, or taking a hit to their profits. Primark, owned by Associated British Foods, has decided not to pass inflation fully on to its customers in order to protect its long-term reputation for value. At the value end of the market, Sweden's Hennes & Mauritz has also refused to pass on higher input costs to consumers. In contrast, retailers that serve older, or more affluent customers, such as Marks and Spencer, or offer more cutting edge fashion, such as Spain's Inditex, are faring better. There is no value sector to speak of in Italy, given Italians' desire for top-end luxury. But some mid-market players, such as Gap, Banana Republic and Inditex's Zara have recently opened in the Italian market, with what are often higher prices than in their domestic markets, and are doing well. Inditex, the world's biggest clothing retailer by sales, can ship garments from its headquarters in northern Spain to stores within two weeks, allowing it to quickly interpret emerging trends. It can react within the fashion season – responding for example to a demand for bold colours – rather than creating a collection, and placing orders, months in advance. Being on trend provides real pricing power, although Inditex has said that it is keeping its prices stable. The strategy, and Inditex's international reach, has given the group a performance that soars above the rest of the troubled Spanish clothing market.[27]

Similarly, in line with worldwide economic trends, smartphone makers that once offered only premium-priced phones are now offering lower-priced models for consumers both at home and in the world's emerging economies. Google's Motorola division recently unveiled an ultra-cheap Moto G phone, with most of the features offered on more expensive phones. And Apple introduced a lower-end, lower-priced version of its iPhone, the iPhone SE. As their more affluent Western markets have become saturated and more competitive, the phone makers hope that their lower-priced phones will help them to compete effectively and grow in less-affluent emerging Eastern markets such as China and Southeast Asia.[28]

Lifestyle

People coming from the same subculture, social class and occupation may have quite different lifestyles. **Lifestyle** is a person's pattern of living as expressed in his or her psychographics. It involves measuring consumers' major AIO dimensions – activities (work, hobbies, shopping, sports, social events), interests (food, fashion, family, recreation) and opinions (about themselves, social issues, business, products). Lifestyle captures something more than the person's social class or personality. It profiles a person's whole pattern of acting and interacting in the world.

Lifestyle—A person's pattern of living as expressed in his or her activities, interests and opinions.

When used carefully, the lifestyle concept can help marketers understand changing consumer values and how they affect buying behaviour. Consumers don't just buy products; they buy the values and lifestyles those products represent. For example, Triumph doesn't just sell motorcycles, it sells an independent, 'Go your own way' lifestyle, Smirnoff vodka says consumers should 'Be there' and Adidas encourages consumers to 'Own the game'. Says one marketer, 'People's product choices are becoming more and more like value choices. It's not, "I like this water, the way it tastes." It's "I feel like this car, or this show, is more reflective of who I am."'[29]

For example, take the case with which we opened the chapter – retailer Jack Wills. They target young, educated middle and upper class consumers with a preppy, buzzing atmosphere, selling a cool and casual lifestyle to which its customers aspire:

There is something cultish about the Jack Wills brand and its fans' devotion to the brand. Visit any upmarket university, boarding school or resort town, across the UK, and the affluent teens will be there, buying Jack Wills' expensive preppy sportswear (€90 for a hooded sweatshirt and up to €25 for a pair of socks.) Even though Jack Wills is a rapidly expanding global business, you could be forgiven for never having come across it before. The company is one of a number of brands, including the more-established US label Abercrombie & Fitch, that target teens with money and sell them preppy or surf-inspired casual clothes. It prides itself on its stealth marketing and its very direct relationship with its consumers. George Wallace, head of MHE Retail, a retail consultancy. says Jack Wills has 'created a very classy lifestyle brand with a very tribal following.

They've got quite a narrow position – it's very public school – but they've got that group to buy into it in a very big way. They've created something that persuades parents to pay premium prices for reasonable quality, and at very high margins. The worry is if this very fickle group falls out of love with them. It's such a volatile market. If they do, the fall could be spectacular, although I don't see that happening any time soon.'[30]

Personality and self-concept

Each person's distinct personality influences his or her buying behaviour. **Personality** refers to the unique psychological characteristics that distinguish a person or group. Personality is usually described in terms of traits such as self-confidence, dominance, sociability, autonomy, defensiveness, adaptability and aggressiveness. Personality can be useful in analysing consumer behaviour for certain product or brand choices.

The idea is that brands also have personalities, and consumers are likely to choose brands with personalities that match their own. A *brand personality* is the specific mix of human traits that may be attributed to a particular brand. One researcher identified five brand personality traits: *sincerity* (down-to-earth, honest, wholesome and cheerful), *excitement* (daring, spirited, imaginative and up-to-date), *competence* (reliable, intelligent and successful), *sophistication* (glamorous, upper class, charming) and *ruggedness* (outdoorsy and tough). 'Your personality determines what you consume, what TV shows you watch, what products you buy, and [most] other decisions you make,' says one consumer behaviour expert.[31]

Most well-known brands are strongly associated with one particular trait: Land Rover with 'ruggedness', Apple with 'excitement', the BBC with 'fairness' and Dove with 'sincerity'. Hence, these brands will attract persons who are high on the same personality traits.

Many marketers use a concept related to personality – a person's *self-concept* (also called *self-image*). The idea is that people's possessions contribute to and reflect their identities – that is, 'we are what we have'. Thus, to understand consumer behaviour, marketers must first understand the relationship between consumer self-concept and possessions.

Apple applies these concepts in its long-running 'Get a Mac' commercials that characterise two people as computers: one guy plays the part of an Apple Mac, and the other plays a personal computer (PC). The two have very different personalities and self-concepts. 'Hello, I'm a Mac,' says the guy on the right, who's younger and dressed in jeans. 'And I'm a PC,' says the one on the left, who's wearing dweeby glasses and a jacket and tie. The two men discuss the relative advantages of Macs versus PCs, with the Mac coming out on top. The commercials present the Mac brand personality as young, laid back and cool. The PC is portrayed as buttoned down, corporate and a bit dorky. The message? If you see yourself as young and with it, you need a Mac.[32]

Psychological factors

A person's buying choices are further influenced by four major psychological factors: *motivation*, *perception*, *learning* and *beliefs and attitudes*.

Motivation

A person has many needs at any given time. Some are biological, arising from states of tension such as hunger, thirst or discomfort. Others are psychological, arising from the need for recognition, esteem or belonging. A need becomes a motive when it is aroused to a sufficient level of intensity. A **motive (or drive)** is a need that is sufficiently pressing to direct the person to seek satisfaction. Psychologists have developed theories of human motivation. Two of the most popular – the theories of Sigmund Freud and Abraham Maslow – carry quite different meanings for consumer analysis and marketing.

Sigmund Freud assumed that people are largely unconscious about the real psychological forces shaping their behaviour. His theory suggests that a person's buying decisions are affected by subconscious motives that even the buyer may not fully understand. Thus, an ageing baby boomer who buys a sporty BMW convertible might explain that he simply likes the feel of the wind in his thinning hair. At a deeper level, he may be trying to impress others with his success. At a still deeper level, he may be buying the car to feel young and independent again.

The term *motivation research* refers to qualitative research designed to probe consumers' hidden, subconscious motivations. Consumers often don't know or can't describe why they act as they do. Thus, motivation researchers use a variety of probing techniques to uncover underlying emotions and attitudes toward brands and buying situations.

Many companies employ teams of psychologists, anthropologists and other social scientists to carry out motivation research. One ad agency routinely conducts one-on-one, therapy-like interviews to delve into the inner workings of consumers. Another company asks consumers to describe their favourite brands as animals or cars (say, a Mercedes versus a Jaguar) to assess the prestige associated with various brands. Still others rely on hypnosis, dream therapy or soft lights and mood music to plumb the murky depths of consumer psyches.

Such projective techniques seem pretty goofy, and some marketers dismiss such motivation research as mumbo jumbo. But many marketers use such touchy-feely approaches, now sometimes called *interpretive consumer research*, to dig deeper into consumer psyches and develop better marketing strategies.

Abraham Maslow sought to explain why people are driven by particular needs at particular times. Why does one person spend a lot of time and energy on personal safety and another on gaining the esteem of others? Maslow's answer is that human needs are arranged in a hierarchy, as shown in Figure 5.4, from the most pressing at the bottom to the least pressing at the top. They include *physiological* needs, *safety* needs, *social* needs, *esteem* needs and *self-actualisation* needs.[33]

Motivation: an ageing baby boomer who buys a sporty convertible might explain that he simply likes the feel of the wind in his thinning hair. At a deeper level, he may be buying the car to feel young and independent again.

Source: Ysbrand Cosijn/ Shutterstock.com

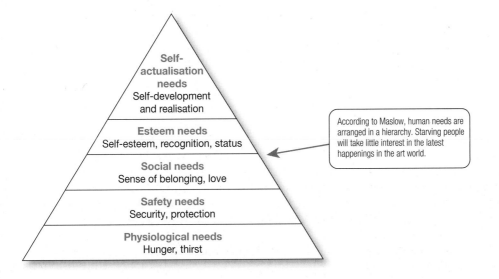

Figure 5.4 Maslow's hierarchy of needs

According to Maslow, human needs are arranged in a hierarchy. Starving people will take little interest in the latest happenings in the art world.

This view of motivation works on the basis that a person tries to satisfy the most important need first. When that need is satisfied, it will stop being a motivator, and the person will then try to satisfy the next most important need. For example, starving people (physiological need) will not take an interest in the latest happenings in the art world (self-actualisation needs) nor in how they are seen or esteemed by others (social or esteem needs) nor even in whether they are breathing clean air (safety needs). But as each important need is satisfied, the next most important need will come into play.

Perception

Perception—The process by which people select, organise and interpret information to form a meaningful picture of the world.

A motivated person is ready to act. How the person acts is influenced by his or her own perception of the situation. All of us learn by the flow of information through our five main senses: sight, hearing, smell, touch and taste. However, each of us receives, organises and interprets this sensory information in an individual way. **Perception** is the process by which people select, organise and interpret information to form a meaningful picture of the world.

People can form different perceptions of the same stimulus because of three perceptual processes: selective attention, selective distortion and selective retention. People are exposed to a great amount of stimuli every day. For example, individuals are exposed to an estimated 3,000 to 5,000 ad messages each day. The cluttered digital environment adds 5.3 trillion online display ads shown each year, 400 million tweets sent daily, 144,000 hours of video uploaded daily, and 4.75 billion pieces of content shared on Facebook every day.[34] It is impossible for people to pay attention to all the competing stimuli surrounding them. *Selective attention* – the tendency for people to screen out most of the information to which they are exposed – means that marketers must work especially hard to attract the consumer's attention.

Even noticed stimuli do not always come across in the intended way. Each person fits incoming information into an existing mind-set. *Selective distortion* describes the tendency of people to interpret information in a way that will support what they already believe. People also will forget much of what they learn. They tend to retain information that supports their attitudes and beliefs. *Selective retention* means that consumers are likely to remember good points made about a brand they favour and forget good points made about competing brands. Because of selective attention, distortion and retention, marketers must work hard to get their messages through.

Interestingly, although most marketers worry about whether their offers will be perceived at all, some consumers worry that they will be affected by marketing messages without even knowing it – through *subliminal advertising*. More than 50 years ago, a researcher announced that he had flashed the phrases 'Eat popcorn' and 'Drink Coca-Cola' on a screen in a New Jersey movie theatre every five seconds for 1/300th of a second. He reported that although viewers did not consciously recognise these messages, they absorbed them subconsciously and bought 58 per cent more popcorn and 18 per cent more Coke. Suddenly advertisers and consumer-protection groups became intensely interested in subliminal perception. Although the researcher later admitted to making up the data, the issue has not died. Some consumers still fear that they are being manipulated by subliminal messages.

Numerous studies by psychologists and consumer researchers have found little or no link between subliminal messages and consumer behaviour. Recent brain-wave studies have found that in certain circumstances, our brains may register subliminal messages. However, it appears that subliminal advertising simply doesn't have the power attributed to it by its critics. One classic ad from the pokes fun at subliminal advertising. 'So-called "subliminal advertising" simply doesn't exist,' says the ad. 'Overactive imaginations, however, most certainly do.'[35]

Learning

Learning—Changes in an individual's behaviour arising from experience.

When people act, they learn. **Learning** describes changes in an individual's behaviour arising from experience. Learning theorists say that most human behaviour is learned. Learning occurs through the interplay of drives, stimuli, cues, responses and reinforcement.

A *drive* is a strong internal stimulus that calls for action. A drive becomes a motive when it is directed toward a particular *stimulus object*. For example, a person's drive for self-actualisation might motivate him or her to look into buying a camera. The consumer's response to the idea of buying a camera is conditioned by the surrounding cues. *Cues* are minor stimuli that determine when, where and how the person responds. For example, the person might spot several camera brands in a shop window, hear of a special sale price, or discuss cameras with a friend. These are all cues that might influence a consumer's *response* to his or her interest in buying the product.

Suppose the consumer buys a Nikon camera. If the experience is rewarding, the consumer will probably use the camera more and more, and his or her response will be *reinforced*. Then the next time he or she shops for a camera, or for binoculars or some similar product, the probability is greater that he or she will buy a Nikon product. The practical significance of learning theory for marketers is that they can build up demand for a product by associating it with strong drives, using motivating cues, and providing positive reinforcement.

Beliefs and attitudes

Through doing and learning, people acquire beliefs and attitudes. These, in turn, influence their buying behaviour. A **belief** is a descriptive thought that a person holds about something. Beliefs may be based on real knowledge, opinion or faith and may or may not carry an emotional charge. Marketers are interested in the beliefs that people formulate about specific products and services because these beliefs make up product and brand images that affect buying behaviour. If some of the beliefs are wrong and prevent purchase, the marketer will want to launch a campaign to correct them.

People have attitudes regarding religion, politics, clothes, music, food and almost everything else. **Attitude** describes a person's relatively consistent evaluations, feelings and tendencies toward an object or idea. Attitudes put people into a frame of mind of liking or disliking things, of moving toward or away from them. Our camera buyer may hold attitudes such as 'Buy the best', 'The Japanese make the best camera products in the world', and 'Creativity and self-expression are among the most important things in life'. If so, the Nikon camera would fit well into the consumer's existing attitudes.

Attitudes are difficult to change. A person's attitudes fit into a pattern; changing one attitude may require difficult adjustments in many others. Thus, a company should usually try to fit its products into existing attitude patterns rather than attempt to change attitudes. For example, Firefly Tonics sells a small but growing range of distinctive drinks as it rides the wave of consumer interest in natural products. Consumers can choose from six formulations – de-tox, chill-out, sharpen up, health kick, wake-up and a special-edition love potion for St Valentine's Day. The drinks contain no added sugar or preservatives.[36] By matching today's attitudes about life and healthful living, the Firefly Tonic brand has become a well-known player in the New Age beverage category.

We can now appreciate the many forces acting on consumer behaviour. The consumer's choice results from the complex interplay of cultural, social, personal and psychological factors.

Belief—A descriptive thought that a person holds about something.

Attitude—A person's consistently favourable or unfavourable evaluations, feelings and tendencies toward an object or idea.

Complex buying behaviour—Consumer buying behaviour in situations characterised by high consumer involvement in a purchase and significant perceived differences among brands.

TYPES OF BUYING DECISION BEHAVIOUR

Buying behaviour differs greatly for a tube of toothpaste, a smartphone, financial services and a new car. More complex decisions usually involve more buying participants and more buyer deliberation. Figure 5.5 shows the types of consumer buying behaviour based on the degree of buyer involvement and the degree of differences among brands.

Complex buying behaviour

Consumers undertake **complex buying behaviour** when they are highly involved in a purchase and perceive significant differences among brands. Consumers may be highly involved when the product is expensive, risky, purchased infrequently and highly self-expressive. Typically, the

Author comment

Some purchases are simple and routine, even habitual. Others are far more complex — involving extensive information gathering and evaluation — and are subject to sometimes subtle influences. For example, think of all that goes into a new car buying decision.

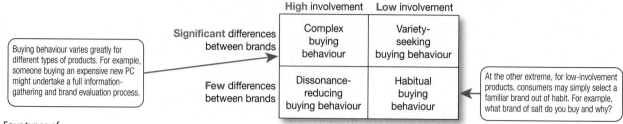

Figure 5.5 Four types of buying behaviour

Source: Adapted from Henry Assael, *Consumer Behaviour and Marketing Action* (Boston: Kent Publishing Company, 1987), p. 87. Used with permission of the author.

consumer has much to learn about the product category. For example, someone buying a new car might know what models, attributes and accessories to consider or what prices to expect.

This buyer will pass through a learning process, first developing beliefs about the product, then attitudes, and then make a thoughtful purchase choice. Marketers of high-involvement products must understand the information-gathering and evaluation behaviour of high-involvement consumers. They need to help buyers learn about product-class attributes and their relative importance. They need to differentiate their brand's features, perhaps by describing and illustrating the brand's benefits through printed promotional materials or in-depth online information and videos. They must motivate store salespeople and the buyer's acquaintances to influence the final brand choice.

Dissonance-reducing buying behaviour

Dissonance-reducing buying behaviour — Consumer buying behaviour in situations characterised by high involvement but few perceived differences among brands.

Dissonance-reducing buying behaviour occurs when consumers are highly involved with an expensive, infrequent or risky purchase but see little difference among brands. For example, consumers buying carpeting may face a high-involvement decision because carpeting is expensive and self-expressive. Yet buyers may consider most carpet brands in a given price range to be the same. In this case, because perceived brand differences are not large, buyers may shop around to learn what is available but buy relatively quickly. They may respond primarily to a good price or purchase convenience.

After the purchase, consumers might experience *post-purchase dissonance* (after-sale discomfort) when they notice certain disadvantages of the purchased carpet brand or hear favourable things about brands not purchased. To counter such dissonance, the marketer's after-sale communications should provide evidence and support to help consumers feel good about their brand choices.

Habitual buying behaviour

Habitual buying behaviour — Consumer buying behaviour in situations characterised by low consumer involvement and few significant perceived brand differences.

Habitual buying behaviour occurs under conditions of low consumer involvement and little significant brand difference. For example, take table salt. Consumers have little involvement in this product category – they simply go to the store and reach for a brand. If they keep reaching for the same brand, it is out of habit rather than strong brand loyalty. Consumers appear to have low involvement with most low-cost, frequently purchased products.

In such cases, consumer behaviour does not pass through the usual belief–attitude–behaviour sequence. Consumers do not search extensively for information about the brands, evaluate brand characteristics, and make weighty decisions about which brands to buy. Because they are not highly involved with the product, consumers may not evaluate the choice, even after purchase. Thus, the buying process involves brand beliefs formed by passive learning, followed by purchase behaviour, which may or may not be followed by evaluation.

Because buyers are not highly committed to any brands, marketers of low-involvement products with few brand differences often use price and sales promotions to promote buying. Alternatively, they can add product features or enhancements to differentiate their brands from the rest of the pack and raise involvement. For example, to set its brand apart, Charmin toilet tissue offers

Ultrastrong, Ultrasoft and Freshmate (wet) versions that are so absorbent that you can 'soften your bottom line' by using four times less than value brands. Charmin also raises brand involvement by offering a 'Sit or squat' website and cell phone app that helps travellers who 'Gotta go on the go!' find and rate clean public restrooms.

Variety-seeking buying behaviour

Consumers undertake **variety-seeking buying behaviour** in situations characterised by low consumer involvement but significant perceived brand differences. In such cases, consumers often do a lot of brand switching. For example, when buying cookies, a consumer may hold some beliefs, choose a cookie brand without much evaluation, and then evaluate that brand during consumption. But the next time, the consumer might pick another brand out of boredom or simply to try something different. Brand switching occurs for the sake of variety rather than because of dissatisfaction.

In such product categories, the marketing strategy may differ for the market leader and minor brands. The market leader will try to encourage habitual buying behaviour by dominating shelf space, keeping shelves fully stocked, and running frequent reminder advertising. Challenger firms will encourage variety seeking by offering lower prices, special deals, coupons, free samples and advertising that presents reasons for trying something new.

> **Variety-seeking buying behaviour**—Consumer buying behaviour in situations characterised by low consumer involvement but significant perceived brand differences.

THE BUYER DECISION PROCESS

Now that we have looked at the influences that affect buyers, we are ready to look at how consumers make buying decisions. Figure 5.6 shows that the buyer decision process consists of five stages: *need recognition*, *information search*, *evaluation of alternatives*, the *purchase decision* and *post-purchase behaviour*. Clearly, the buying process starts long before the actual purchase and continues long after. Marketers need to focus on the entire buying process rather than on the purchase decision only.

Figure 5.6 suggests that consumers pass through all five stages with every purchase in a considered way. But buyers may pass quickly or slowly through the buying decision process. And in more routine purchases, consumers often skip or reverse some of the stages. Much depends on the nature of the buyer, the product and the buying situation. A woman buying her regular brand of toothpaste would recognise the need and go right to the purchase decision, skipping information search and evaluation. However, we use the model in Figure 5.6 because it shows all the considerations that arise when a consumer faces a new and complex purchase situation.

> **Author comment**
>
> The actual purchase decision is part of a much larger buying process — starting with recognising a need through how you feel after making the purchase. Marketers want to be involved throughout the entire buyer decision process.

Need recognition

The buying process starts with **need recognition** — the buyer recognises a problem or need. The need can be triggered by *internal stimuli* when one of the person's normal needs — for example, hunger or thirst — rises to a level high enough to become a drive. A need can also be triggered by

> **Need recognition**—The first stage of the buyer decision process, in which the consumer recognises a problem or need.
>
> **Figure 5.6** Buyer decision process

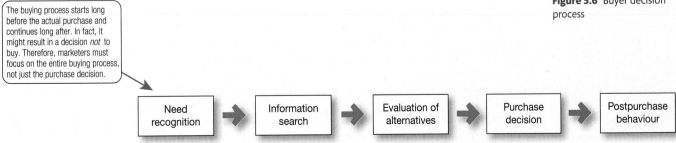

The buying process starts long before the actual purchase and continues long after. In fact, it might result in a decision *not* to buy. Therefore, marketers must focus on the entire buying process, not just the purchase decision.

| Need recognition | → | Information search | → | Evaluation of alternatives | → | Purchase decision | → | Postpurchase behaviour |

external stimuli. For example, an advertisement or a discussion with a friend might get you thinking about buying a new car. At this stage, the marketer should research consumers to find out what kinds of needs or problems arise, what brought them about, and how they led the consumer to this particular product.

Information search

Information search—The stage of the buyer decision process in which the consumer is motivated to search for more information.

An interested consumer may or may not search for more information. If the consumer's drive is strong and a satisfying product is near at hand, he or she is likely to buy it then. If not, the consumer may store the need in memory or undertake an **information search** related to the need. For example, once you've decided you need a new car, at the least, you will probably pay more attention to car ads, cars owned by friends and car conversations. Or you may actively search online, talk with friends, and gather information in other ways.

Consumers can obtain information from any of several sources. These include *personal sources* (family, friends, neighbours, acquaintances), *commercial sources* (advertising, sales people, dealer and manufacturer, web and mobile sites, packaging, displays), *public sources* (mass media, consumer rating organisations, social media, online searches and peer reviews) and *experiential sources* (examining and using the product). The relative influence of these information sources varies with the product and the buyer.

Traditionally, consumers have received the most information about a product from commercial sources – those controlled by the marketer. The most effective sources, however, tend to be personal. Commercial sources normally *inform* the buyer, but personal sources *legitimise* or *evaluate* products for the buyer. Few advertising campaigns can be as effective as a next-door neighbour leaning over the fence and raving about a wonderful experience with a product you are considering.

Increasingly, that 'neighbour's fence' is a digital one. Today, consumers share product opinions, images and experiences freely across social media. And buyers can find an abundance of user-generated reviews alongside the products they are considering at a range of sites including MumsNet, Trivago, TripAdvisor, Yelp and 'Which?'. Although individual user reviews vary widely in quality, an entire body of reviews often provides a reliable product assessment – straight from the fingertips of people like you who've actually purchased and experienced the product.

As more information is obtained, the consumer's awareness and knowledge of the available brands and features increase. In your car information search, you may learn about several brands that are available. The information might also help you to drop certain brands from consideration. A company must design its marketing mix to make prospects aware of and knowledgeable about its brand. It should carefully identify consumers' sources of information and the importance of each source.

Evaluation of alternatives

Alternative evaluation—The stage of the buyer decision process in which the consumer uses information to evaluate alternative brands in the choice set.

We have seen how consumers use information to arrive at a set of final brand choices. Next, marketers need to know about **alternative evaluation**, that is, how consumers process information to choose among alternative brands. Unfortunately, consumers do not use a simple and single evaluation process in all buying situations. Instead, several evaluation processes are at work.

How consumers go about evaluating purchase alternatives depends on the individual consumer and the specific buying situation. In some cases, consumers use careful calculations and logical thinking. At other times, the same consumers do little or no evaluating. Instead, they buy on impulse and rely on intuition. Sometimes consumers make buying decisions on their own; sometimes they turn to friends, online reviews or salespeople for buying advice.

Suppose you've narrowed your car choices to three brands. And suppose that you are primarily interested in four attributes – price, style, operating economy and performance. By this time, you've probably formed beliefs about how each brand rates on each attribute. Clearly, if one car rated best on all the attributes, the marketer could predict that you would choose it. However, the brands will no doubt vary in appeal. You might base your buying decision mostly on one attribute, and your choice would be easy to predict. If you wanted style above everything else, you would buy the car that you think has the most style. But most buyers consider several attributes, each with different importance. By knowing the importance that you assigned to each attribute, the marketer could predict and affect your car choice more reliably.

Marketers should study buyers to find out how they actually evaluate brand alternatives. If marketers know what evaluative processes go on, they can take steps to influence the buyer's decision.

Purchase decision

In the evaluation stage, the consumer ranks brands and forms purchase intentions. Generally, the consumer's **purchase decision** will be to buy the most preferred brand, but two factors can come between the purchase *intention* and the purchase *decision*. The first factor is the *attitudes of others*. If someone important to you thinks that you should buy the lowest-priced car, then the chances of you buying a more expensive car are reduced.

The second factor is *unexpected situational factors*. The consumer may form a purchase intention based on factors such as expected income, expected price and expected product benefits. However, unexpected events may change the purchase intention. For example, the economy might take a turn for the worse, a close competitor might drop its price, or a friend might report being disappointed in your preferred car. Thus, preferences and even purchase intentions do not always result in an actual purchase choice.

Buying things can be stressful and marketers need to understand how consumers evaluate different alternatives.
Source: Wavebreak Media Ltd/123RF.com

Purchase decision—The buyer's decision about which brand to purchase.

Post-purchase behaviour

The marketer's job does not end when the product is bought. After purchasing the product, the consumer will either be satisfied or dissatisfied and will engage in **post-purchase behaviour** of interest to the marketer. What determines whether the buyer is satisfied or dissatisfied with a purchase? The answer lies in the relationship between the *consumer's expectations* and the product's *perceived performance*. If the product falls short of expectations, the consumer is disappointed; if it meets expectations, the consumer is satisfied; if it exceeds expectations, the consumer is delighted. The larger the gap between expectations and performance, the greater the consumer's dissatisfaction. This suggests that sellers should promise only what their brands can deliver so that buyers are satisfied.

Almost all major purchases, however, result in **cognitive dissonance**, or discomfort caused by post-purchase conflict. After the purchase, consumers are satisfied with the benefits of the chosen brand and are glad to avoid the drawbacks of the brands not bought. However, every purchase involves compromise. So consumers feel uneasy about acquiring the drawbacks of the chosen brand and about losing the benefits of the brands not purchased. Thus, consumers feel at least some post-purchase dissonance for every purchase.[37]

Why is it so important to satisfy the customer? Customer satisfaction is a key to building profitable relationships with consumers – to keeping and growing consumers and reaping their customer lifetime value. Satisfied customers buy a product again, talk favourably to others about the product, pay less attention to competing brands and advertising, and buy other products from the company. Many marketers go beyond merely meeting the expectations of customers – they aim to *delight* customers.

A dissatisfied consumer responds differently. Bad word of mouth often travels farther and faster than good word of mouth. It can quickly damage consumer attitudes about a company and its products. But companies cannot simply wait for dissatisfied customers to volunteer their complaints. Most unhappy customers never tell the company about their problems. Therefore, a company

Post-purchase behaviour— The stage of the buyer decision process in which consumers take further action after purchase, based on their satisfaction or dissatisfaction.

Cognitive dissonance—Buyer discomfort caused by post-purchase conflict.

should measure customer satisfaction regularly. It should set up systems that *encourage* customers to complain. In this way, the company can learn how well it is doing and how it can improve.

By studying the overall buyer decision process, marketers may be able to find ways to help consumers move through it. For example, if consumers are not buying a new product because they do not perceive a need for it, marketing might launch advertising messages that trigger the need and show how the product solves customers' problems. If customers know about the product but are not buying because they hold unfavourable attitudes toward it, marketers must find ways to change either the product or consumer perceptions.

Author comment

Here we look at some special considerations in *new product* buying decisions.

THE BUYER DECISION PROCESS FOR NEW PRODUCTS

New product—A good, service, or idea that is perceived by some potential customers as new.

Adoption process—The mental process through which an individual passes from first hearing about an innovation to final adoption.

We now look at how buyers approach the purchase of new products. A **new product** is a good, service, or idea that is perceived by some potential customers as new. It may have been around for a while, but our interest is in how consumers learn about products for the first time and make decisions on whether to adopt them. We define the **adoption process** as the mental process through which an individual passes from first learning about an innovation to final adoption. *Adoption* is the decision by an individual to become a regular user of the product.[38]

Stages in the adoption process

Consumers go through five stages in the process of adopting a new product:

1. *Awareness*. The consumer becomes aware of the new product but lacks information about it.
2. *Interest*. The consumer seeks information about the new product.
3. *Evaluation*. The consumer considers whether trying the new product makes sense.
4. *Trial*. The consumer tries the new product on a small scale to improve his or her estimate of its value.
5. *Adoption*. The consumer decides to make full and regular use of the new product.

This model suggests that marketers should think about how to help consumers move through these stages. For example, if SodaStream finds that many consumers are evaluating its home soda makers favourably but are still tentative about buying one, it might offer sales at retail, rebates or other price incentives that help get consumers over the decision hump.

> Hyundai discovered many potential customers were interested in buying new cars but couldn't get past the evaluation stage of the buying process. Consumers worried that they might buy a car and then lose their jobs and subsequently their new cars and their good credit ratings. To help buyers over this hurdle, the carmaker offered the Hyundai Assurance Programme, which promised to let buyers who financed or leased a new Hyundai vehicle return their vehicles at no cost and with no harm to their credit rating if they lost their jobs or incomes within a year. The Assurance Programme, combined with a ten-year warranty and a five-year, 24-hour roadside assistance programme, all at no extra charge, made the buying decision much easier for customers concerned about the future economy. Sales of the Hyundai Sonata surged 85 per cent in the month following the start of the Assurance campaign, and the brand's market share grew at an industry-leading pace during the following year. Hyundai continued the programme on its 2010 models, and other carmakers soon followed with their own assurance plans.[39]

Individual differences in innovativeness

People differ greatly in their readiness to try new products. In each product area, there are 'consumption pioneers' and early adopters. Other individuals adopt new products much later. People can be classified into the adopter categories shown in Figure 5.7.[40]

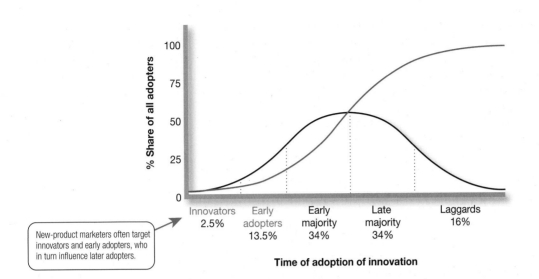

New-product marketers often target innovators and early adopters, who in turn influence later adopters.

As shown by the curve, after a slow start, an increasing number of people adopt the new product. As successive groups of consumers adopt the innovation, it eventually reaches its cumulative saturation level. Innovators are defined as the first 2.5 per cent of buyers to adopt a new idea (those beyond two standard deviations from mean adoption time); the early adopters are the next 13.5 per cent (between one and two standard deviations); and then come early mainstream, late mainstream and lagging adopters.

The five adopter groups have differing values. *Innovators* are venturesome – they try new ideas at some risk. *Early adopters* are guided by respect – they are opinion leaders in their communities and adopt new ideas early but carefully. *Early mainstream* adopters are deliberate – although they rarely are leaders, they adopt new ideas before the average person. *Late mainstream* adopters are sceptical – they adopt an innovation only after a majority of people have tried it. Finally, *lagging adopters* are tradition bound – they are suspicious of changes and adopt the innovation only when it has become something of a tradition itself.

This adopter classification suggests that an innovating firm should research the characteristics of innovators and early adopters in their product categories and direct initial marketing efforts toward them.

Influence of product characteristics on rate of adoption

The characteristics of the new product affect its rate of adoption. Some products catch on almost overnight. For example, Apple's iPod, iPhone and iPad flew off retailers' shelves at an astounding rate from the day they were first introduced. Others take a longer time to gain acceptance. For example, it is estimated that 55 per cent of Europeans are likely to buy a HDTV in the next five years.[41]

Five characteristics are especially important in influencing an innovation's rate of adoption. For example, consider the characteristics of HDTV in relation to the rate of adoption:

- *Relative advantage.* The degree to which the innovation appears superior to existing products. HDTV offers substantially improved picture quality. This accelerated its rate of adoption.
- *Compatibility.* The degree to which the innovation fits the values and experiences of potential consumers. HDTV, for example, is highly compatible with the lifestyles of the TV-watching public. However, in the early years, HDTV was not yet compatible with programming and broadcasting systems, which slowed adoption. As high-definition programmes and channels became the norm, the rate of HDTV adoption increased rapidly.
- *Complexity.* The degree to which the innovation is difficult to understand or use. HDTVs are not very complex. Therefore, as more programming became available and prices fell, the rate of HDTV adoption increased faster than that of more complex innovations.

- *Divisibility.* The degree to which the innovation may be tried on a limited basis. Early HDTVs and HD cable and satellite systems were very expensive, which slowed the rate of adoption. As prices fell, adoption rates increased.
- *Communicability.* The degree to which the results of using the innovation can be observed or described to others. Because HDTV lends itself to demonstration and description, its use spread faster among consumers.

Other characteristics influence the rate of adoption, such as initial and on-going costs, risk and uncertainty and social approval. The new product marketer must research all these factors when developing the new product and its marketing programme.

OBJECTIVES REVIEW AND KEY TERMS

The EU consumer market consists of more than 507 million people who consume more than €13.70 trillion worth of goods and services each year, making it one of the most attractive consumer markets in the world. Consumers vary greatly in terms of cultural, social, personal and psychological makeup. Understanding how these differences affect *consumer buying behaviour* is one of the biggest challenges marketers face.

OBJECTIVE 1 Define the consumer market and construct a simple model of consumer buyer behaviour (p. 139)

The *consumer market* consists of all the individuals and households that buy or acquire goods and services for personal consumption. The simplest model of consumer buyer behaviour is the stimulus–response model. According to this model, marketing stimuli (the four Ps) and other major forces (economic, technological, political, cultural) enter the consumer's 'black box' and produce certain responses. Once in the black box, these inputs produce observable buyer responses, such as brand choice, purchase location and timing and brand engagement and relationship behaviour.

OBJECTIVE 2 Name the four major factors that influence consumer buyer behaviour (pp. 140–153)

Consumer buyer behaviour is influenced by four key sets of buyer characteristics: cultural, social, personal and psychological. Although many of these factors cannot be influenced by the marketer, they can be useful in identifying interested buyers and shaping products and appeals to serve consumer needs better. *Culture* is the most basic determinant of a person's wants and behaviour. *Subcultures* are 'cultures within cultures' that have distinct values and lifestyles and can be based on anything from age to ethnicity. Many companies focus their marketing programmes on the special needs of certain cultural and subcultural segments, such as gamers or mature consumers.

Social factors also influence a buyer's behaviour. A person's *reference groups* — family, friends, social networks, professional associations — strongly affect product and brand choices. The buyer's age, life-cycle stage, occupation, economic circumstances, personality and other *personal characteristics* influence his or her buying decisions. Consumer *lifestyles* — the whole pattern of acting and interacting in the world — are also an important influence on purchase decisions. Finally, consumer buying behaviour is influenced by four major *psychological factors*: motivation, perception, learning, and beliefs and attitudes. Each of these factors provides a different perspective for understanding the workings of the buyer's black box.

OBJECTIVE 3 List and define the major types of buying decision behaviour and the stages in the buyer decision process (pp. 153–158)

Buying behaviour may vary greatly across different types of products and buying decisions. Consumers undertake *complex buying behaviour* when they are highly involved in a purchase and perceive significant differences among brands. *Dissonance reducing behaviour* occurs when consumers are highly involved but see little difference among brands. *Habitual buying behaviour* occurs under conditions of low involvement and little significant brand difference. In situations characterised by low involvement but significant perceived brand differences, consumers engage in *variety-seeking buying behaviour*.

When making a purchase, the buyer goes through a decision process consisting of *need recognition, information search, evaluation of alternatives, purchase decision* and *behaviour*. The marketer's job is to understand the buyer's behaviour at each stage and the influences that are operating. During *need recognition*, the consumer recognises a problem or need that could be satisfied by a product or service in the market. Once the need is recognised, the consumer is aroused to seek more information and moves into the *information search stage*. With information in hand, the consumer proceeds to *alternative evaluation*, during which the information is used to evaluate brands in the choice set. From there, the consumer makes a *purchase decision* and actually buys the product. In the final stage of the buyer decision process, *post purchase behaviour*, the consumer takes action based on satisfaction or dissatisfaction.

OBJECTIVE 4 Describe the adoption and diffusion process for new products (pp. 158–160)

The product *adoption process* is made up of five stages: awareness, interest, evaluation, trial and adoption. New-product marketers must think about how to help consumers move through these stages. With regard to the *diffusion process* for new products, consumers respond at different rates, depending on consumer and product characteristics. Consumers may be innovators, early adopters, early mainstream, late mainstream or lagging adopters. Each group may require different marketing approaches. Marketers often try to bring their new products to the attention of potential early adopters, especially those who are opinion leaders. Finally, several characteristics influence the rate of adoption: relative advantage, compatibility, complexity, divisibility and communicability.

NAVIGATING THE KEY TERMS

OBJECTIVE 1
Consumer buyer behaviour (p. 139)
Consumer market (p. 139)

OBJECTIVE 2
Culture (p. 140)
Subculture (p. 140)
Social class (p. 143)
Group (p. 144)
Word-of-mouth influence (p. 144)
Opinion leader (p. 144)
Online social networks (p. 145)
Lifestyle (p. 149)

Personality (p. 150)
Motive (drive) (p. 150)
Perception (p. 152)
Learning (p. 152)
Belief (p. 153)
Attitude (p. 153

OBJECTIVE 3
Complex buying behaviour (p.153)
Dissonance-reducing buying behaviour
   (p. 154)
Habitual buying behaviour (p. 154)

Variety-seeking buying
   behaviour (p. 155)
Need recognition (p. 155)
Information search (p. 156)
Alternative evaluation (p. 156)
Purchase decision (p. 157)
Post-purchase behaviour (p. 157)
Cognitive dissonance (p. 157)

OBJECTIVE 4
New product (p. 158)
Adoption process (p 158)

DISCUSSION AND CRITICAL THINKING

Discussing the concepts

5-1 What is subculture? Describe at least two subcultures to which you belong and identify any reference groups that might influence your consumption behaviour. (AACSB: Communication; Diversity; Reflective thinking)

5-2 Why are marketers interested in consumer lifestyles and what dimensions do they use to measure lifestyle? Describe your lifestyle along those dimensions and identify consumption-related activities based on your lifestyle. (AACSB: Communication; Reflective thinking)

5-3 What is a 'new product' and how do consumers go about deciding whether to adopt a new product? (AACSB: Communication)

5-4 What characteristics of a new product affect its rate of adoption? How will each factor influence the rate of adoption of electric automobiles? (AACSB: Communication; Reflective thinking)

Critical-thinking exercises

5-5 Researchers study the role of personality on consumer purchase behaviour. One research project – 'Beyond the purchase' – offers a range of surveys consumers can take to learn more about their own personality, in general, and their consumer personality, in particular. Register at www.beyondthepurchase.org/ and take the 'Spending habits' surveys, along with any of the other surveys that interest you. What do these surveys tell you about your general and consumer personality? Do you agree with the findings? Why or why not? (AACSB: Communication; Use of IT; Diversity; Reflective thinking)

5-6 Malcolm Gladwell published a book entitled *The Tipping Point*. He describes the Law of the Few, Stickiness, and the Law of Context. Research these concepts and describe how understanding them helps marketers better understand and target consumers. (AACSB: Communication; Reflective thinking)

5-7 In a small group, imagine that you work in an upscale international hotel that caters to guests from around the world. Discuss what you would serve at a breakfast, lunch or dinner buffet. Research what consumers eat in at least one country from every continent. The goal is to have a wide enough variety to satisfy all of the guests' tastes based on their cultures. Create a presentation with pictures of food that you would include in your buffet. (AACSB: Communication; Use of IT; Diversity; Reflective thinking)

Mini-cases and applications

Online, mobile and social media marketing: digital influencers

Jen Hsieh is a college student with a love for fashion who shares outfits and fashion sense on Jennifhsieh, her fashion blog. Her social influence earned an invite to Kate Spade's New York fashion week presentation, after which she blogged, 'I had to keep myself from drooling' when describing the collection. Digital influencers like Jen are often paid to write product reviews on their blogs and to post pictures of themselves on sites such as Pinterest and Instagram wearing clothes given to them by the sponsor. Some are given all-expenses paid trips to events. For example, Olivia Lopez, a personal-style blogger with a site called Lust for Life, was invited by Samsung to the South by Southwest and Lollapalloza music festivals and provided a phone with which to post pictures for her 90,000 Instagram followers. The hashtag, '#thenextbigthing', which is used in Samsung's product promotions, was included in her posts. Otherwise, Olivia included no indication that Samsung provided sponsorship.

5-8 Find an example of a blog on a topic that interests you. Are there advertisements on the blog? Does the blogger appear to be sponsored by any companies? Is there information regarding sponsorship? Write a brief report of your observations. (AACSB: Use of IT; Communication; Reflective thinking)

5-9 Summarise the FTC's disclosure rules on using social media to promote products and services. Does the blogger you reviewed in the previous question follow these rules? Explain. (AACSB: Communication; Reflective thinking)

Marketing ethics: liquid gold

Vitaminwater sounds healthy, right? Although Vitaminwater has vitamins, it also has 33 grammes — that's two heaping tablespoons – of sugar, making it not much better than a soda. Vitaminwater, owned by Coca-Cola, has been under fire from the Centre for Science in the Public Interest (CSPI), a consumer-advocacy group that fights for safer, more nutritious foods. The CSPI filed a class-action lawsuit against Coca-Cola, claiming names for Vitaminwater flavours such as 'endurance peach mango' and 'focus kiwi strawberry' are misleading for two reasons: (1) the drinks contain zero to one per cent juice, and (2) words like *endurance, focus, defence, rescue* and *energy* imply health benefits. Coca-Cola's defence was that reasonable consumers would not be misled into believing that Vitaminwater is healthy for them.

5-10 Debate whether or not Coca-Cola is deliberately trying to deceive consumers into believing that Vitaminwater is a healthy alternative to soda. Which psychological factor is most affected by the product name and ad claims and might influence consumers to purchase this product? (AACSB: Communication; Ethical reasoning)

5-11 Find two other examples of brands that use names, words, colours, package shapes or other elements to convey potentially deceptive meanings to consumers. (AACSB: Communication; Reflective Thinking)

5-12 What buying factors are most likely affecting consumers who purchase luxury bottled water? (AACSB: Communication; Reflective thinking)

5-13 Is it ethical to sell water, which is basically all the same, in a way that commands such high prices? Explain why or why not. (AACSB: Communication; Ethical reasoning)

Marketing by the numbers: evaluating alternatives

One way consumers can evaluate alternatives is to identify important attributes and assess how purchase alternatives perform on those attributes. Consider the purchase of a tablet. Each attribute, such as screen size, is given a weight to reflect its level of importance to that consumer. Then the consumer evaluates each alternative on each attribute. For example, in the following table, price (weighted at 0.5) is the most important attribute for this consumer. The consumer believes that Brand C performs best on price, rating it 7 (higher ratings indicate higher performance). Brand B is perceived as performing the worst on this attribute (rating of 3). Screen size and available apps are the consumer's next most important attributes. Operating system is least important.

A score can be calculated for each brand by multiplying the importance weight for each attribute by the brand's score on that attribute. These weighted scores are then summed to determine the score for that brand. For example, Score Brand A = $(0.2 \times 4) + (0.5 \times 6) + (0.1 \times 5) + (0.2 \times 4) = 0.8 + 3.0 + 0.5 + 0.8 = 5.1$. This consumer will select the brand with the highest score.

Attributes	Importance	Alternative brands		
	Weight (e)	A	B	C
Screen size	0.2	4	6	2
Price	0.5	6	3	7
Operating system	0.1	5	5	4
Apps available	0.2	4	6	7

1. Calculate the scores for brands B and C. Which brand would this consumer likely choose? (AACSB: Communication; Analytic reasoning)

2. Which brand is this consumer least likely to purchase? Discuss two ways the marketer of this brand can enhance consumer attitudes toward purchasing its brand. (AACSB: Communication; Reflective thinking; Analytic reasoning)

REFERENCES

1 This case study draws heavily on the excellent case studies and analyses of: Lucie Green, 'Pretty, posh and profitable', *Financial Times*, 13 May 2011, www.ft.com/cms/s/2/fcca7ebc-7ce4-11e0-a7c7-00144feabdc0.html#axzz1ZKhQf2fh, accessed October 2015; , Claer Barrett, 'High-spending tourists boost airport sales', *Financial Times*, 12 September 2011, www.ft.com/cms/s/0/3ecc0056-dd57-11e0-9dac-00144feabdc0.html#axzz1ZKhQf2fh, accessed October 2015; 'The best summer job in America', www.jackwills.com/media/1521037/job_spec-online-us.pdf, accessed October 2015.

2 Consumer expenditure figures from www.cia.gov/library/publications/the-world-factbook/geos/ee.html; population figures from http://ec.europa.eu/eurostat/tgm/table.do?tab=table&plugin=1&language=en&pcode=tps00001, accessed October 2015.

3 Example and data from www.isfe.eu/industry-facts, accessed October 2015.

4 www.gartner.com/newsroom/id/2614915, accessed October 2015.

5 The below bullet points are selected from the fuller report available at www.isfe.eu/industry-facts, accessed October 2015.

6 Example from Jonathan Soble, 'Sony outplays Nintendo in game console sales', *Financial Times*, 10 June 2014, www.ft.com/cms/s/0/1114c0c0-efb1-11e3-bee7-00144feabdc0.html#axzz3PRw3FUie, accessed October 2015.

7 See Gene Epstein, 'Boomer consumer', *Barron's*, 5 October 2009, http://online.barrons.com/article/SB125452437207860627.html; Stuart Elliott, 'The older audiences looking better than ever', *New York Times*, 20 April 2009; Ellen Byron, 'Seeing store shelves through senior eyes', *Wall Street Journal*, 14 September 2009, p. B1; and Brent Bouchez, 'Super Bowl ads need to age gracefully', *BusinessWeek*, February 2010, www.businessweek.com.

8 Stuart Elliott, 'The older audiences looking better than ever', *The New York Times*, 19 April 2009, www.nytimes.com/2009/04/20/business/20adcol.html?_r=0, accessed January 2016.

9 'Boom time of America's new retirees feel entitled to relax – and intend to spend', *Financial Times*, 6 December 2007, p. 9.

10 Mark Dolliver, 'Marketing to today's 65-Plus consumers', *Adweek*, 27 July 2009, www.adweek.com.

11 See www.holidaysforsinglepeople.co.uk/singles-holidays-over-50.php, accessed October 2015.

12 Definitions of classifications taken from the excellent report at: www.bbc.co.uk/science/0/21970879, accessed October 2015.

13 Adam Bluestein, 'Make money in 2013 (and beyond)', *Inc.*, December 2012/January 2013, pp. 58–65, here p. 64.

14 See 'How Lady Gaga co-marketed new album *ARTPOP* with diehard fans', *Forbes*, 10 November 2013, www.forbes.com/sites/jackiehuba/2013/11/10/how-lady-gaga-co-markets-new-albumartpop-with-diehard-fans/.

15 Based on information from Julie Liesse, 'The Big Idea', *Advertising Age*, 28 November 2011, pp. C4–C6; and 'Philips's "Wake up the Town"', www.ketchum.com/de/philips's-"wake-town", accessed October 2015.

16 See http://blog.benetton.com/, accessed October 2015.

17 See Brian Morrissey, 'Social rings', *Brandweek*, 18 January 2010, p. 20.

18 Digital Strategy Consulting, 'Word of mouth trends: how advertising influences real-world conversations', 2 November 2013, www.digital-strategyconsulting.com/intelligence/2013/02/word_of_mouth_trends_how_advertising_influences_realworld_conversations_infographic.php.

19 See Eleftheria Parpis, 'She's in charge', *Adweek*, 6–13 October 2008, p. 38; Abigail Posner, 'Why package-goods companies should market to men', *Advertising Age*, 9 February 2009, http://adage.com/print?article_id=134473; and Marissa Miley and Ann Mark, 'The new female consumer: the rise of the real mom', *Advertising Age*, 16 November 2009, pp. A1–A27.

20 Adapted from Michel Marriott, 'Gadget designers take aim at women', *New York Times*, 7 June 2007, p. C7. Also see Dean Takahashi, 'Philips focuses on TVs women buyers', *McClatchy-Tribune Business News*, 6 January 2008.

21 See Melissa Hoffman, 'Ad of the day: Samsung dad may be the swaddle master but kid has him beat in this Galaxy S4 spot', *Adweek*, 5 June 2013, www.adweek.com/news/advertisingbranding/ad-day-samsung-150028; and www.youtube.com/watch?v=NApR0dDSuPM[, accessed October 2015.

22 Example from Rebecca Smithers, 'How much does it cost to raise a child?', *The Guardian*, 23 February 2010, www.guardian.co.uk/news/datablog/2010/feb/23/cost-raising-child?INTCMP=SRCH, accessed October 2015; and Ryan Kisiel, 'Children have never had it so good', *Daily Mail*, 21 January 2010, www.dailymail.co.uk/news/article-1241841/Children-good-Average-weekly-pocket-money-rises-6-840.html, accessed October 2015.

23 R. K. Miller and Kelli Washington, *Consumer Behavior 2009* (Atlanta, GA: Richard K. Miller & Associates, 2009), Chapter 27. Also see Michael R. Sullivan, *Consumer Behavior: Buying, Having, and Being* (Upper Saddle River, New Jersey: Prentice Hall, 2011), pp. 439–445.

24 See www.justsardinia.co.uk/forte-village/, accessed October 2011.

25 For this quote and other information on Acxiom's PersonicX segmentation system, see 'Acxiom study reveals insight on evolving consumer shopping behaviors in trying economic times', *Reuters*, 13 January 2009, www.reuters.com/ article/pressRelease/idUS180299+13-Jan-2009+BW20090113; 'Acxiom study offers insight into leisure travelers who still spend freely despite a down economy',

Business Wire, 18 November 2009; and 'Acxiom PersonicX' and 'Intelligent solutions for the travel industry: life-stage marketing', www.acxiom.com, accessed October 2015.

26 See www.edeandravenscroft.co.uk/, accessed October 2015.

27 Example from Andrea Felsted, 'Europe's cheap chic brands feel the pinch', *Financial Times*, 22 June 2011, www.ft.com/cms/s/0/ed23fef6-9cf2-11e0-8678-00144feabdc0.html#ixzz1TNHvNhkG, accessed October 2015.

28 See 'Apple expected to increase marketing presence abroad with low-cost iPhone', *Advertising Age*, 10 September 2013, www.adage.com/print/244072; and Alistair Barr and Edward C. Baig, 'Google targets low-end smartphone market with Moto G', *USA Today*, 13 November 2013, www.usatoday.com/story/tech/2013/11/13/google-motorola-moto-g/3516039/.

29 Beth J. Harpaz, 'New book connects political and lifestyle choices', 4 November 2006, www.seattlepi.com/lifestyle/291052_lifestylevote04.html; for more on lifestyle and consumer behaviour, see Michael R. Solomon, *Consumer Behavior: Buying, Having, and Being* (Upper Saddle River, NJ: Prentice Hall, 2011), pp. 226–233.

30 From Lucie Greene, 'Pretty, posh and profitable', *Financial Times*, 13 May 2011, www.ft.com/cms/s/2/fcca7ebc-7ce4-11e0-a7c7-00144feabdc0.html#ixzz1TNV353IY, accessed October 2015.

31 See Jennifer Aaker, 'Dimensions of measuring brand personality', *Journal of Marketing Research*, August 1997, pp. 347–356; and Kevin Lane Keller, *Strategic Brand Management*, 4th ed. (Upper Saddle River, New Jersey: Pearson Publishing, 2012), Chapter 2.

32 See www.apple.com/getamac/ads/, accessed October 2015.

33 See Abraham H. Maslow, 'A theory of human motivation', *Psychological Review*, 50 (1943), pp. 370–396. Also see Maslow, *Motivation and Personality*, 3rd ed. (New York: HarperCollins Publishers, 1987); and Michael R. Solomon, *Consumer Behavior*, 11th ed. (Upper Saddle River, NJ: Prentice Hall, 2014), pp. 132–134.

34 See Ellen Moore, 'Letter to my colleague: we can do better', *Adweek*, 22 December 2010, www.adweek.com/news/advertisingbranding/letter-my-colleagues-we-can-do-better-104084; and Kelsey Libert and Kristin

Tynski, 'Research: the emotions that make marketing campaigns go viral', *Harvard Business Review*, 24 October 2013, http://blogs.hbr.org/2013/10/research-the-emotions-that-make-marketing-campaigns-go-viral/.

35 For more reading, see Lawrence R. Samuel, *Freud on Madison Avenue: Motivation Research and Subliminal Advertising in America* (Philadelphia: University of Pennsylvania Press, 2010); Charles R. Acland, *Swift Viewing: The Popular Life of Subliminal Influence* (Durham, NC: Duke University Press, 2011); Christopher Shea, 'The history of subliminal ads', *Wall Street Journal*, 15 February 2012, http://blogs.wsj.com/ideas-market/2012/02/15/the-history-of-subliminal-ads/; and Dominic Green, '15 corporate logos that contain subliminal messaging', *Business Insider*, 11 May 2013, www.businessinsider.com/subliminal-messages-in-12-popular-logos-2013-5#.

36 Example from Salamander Davoudi and Edward Blakeney, 'A business with natural energy', *Financial Times*, 7 November 2007, www.ft.com/cms/s/0/b31c690a-8cd4-11dc-b887-0000779fd2ac.html#axzz1UPifHx5H and www.fireflytonics.com/our-company/, accessed October 2015.

37 See Leon Festinger, *A Theory of Cognitive Dissonance* (Stanford, CA: Stanford University Press, 1957); Cynthia Crossen, '"Cognitive dissonance" became a milestone in the 1950s psychology', *Wall Street Journal*, 12 December 2006, p. B1; and Anupam Bawa and Purva Kansal, 'Cognitive dissonance and the marketing of services: some issues', *Journal of Services Research*, October 2008–March 2009, p. 31.

38 The following discussion draws from the work of Everett M. Rogers. See his *Diffusion of Innovations*, 5th ed. (New York: Free Press, 2003).

39 Nick Bunkley, 'Hyundai, using a safety net, wins market share', *New York Times*, 5 February 2009; Chris Woodyard and Bruce Horvitz, 'GM, Ford are latest offering help to those hit by job loss', *USA Today*, 1 April 2009; and 'Hyundai assurance enhanced for 2010', *PR Newswire*, 29 December 2009.

40 Based on Everett Rogers, *Diffusion of Innovation*, 5th edition, New York: Free Press, 2003, p. 281. For more discussion, see http://en.wikipedia.org/wiki/Everett_Rogers, accessed January 2016.

41 www.strategyanalytics.com/default.aspx?mod=pressreleaseviewer&a0=5485 accessed October 2015

COMPANY CASE

Porsche: guarding the old while bringing in the new

Porsche (pronounced Porsh-uh) is a unique company. It has always been a niche brand that makes cars for a small and distinctive segment of automobile buyers. Last year, Porsche sold around 155,000 vehicles globally and around 50,000 units within Europe. In contrast, Honda is aiming to sell 6 million units per year by 2017. In this sense, Porsche owners are as rare as

their vehicles. For that reason, top managers at Porsche spend a great deal of time thinking about customers. They want to know who their customers are, what they think and how they feel. They want to know why they buy a Porsche rather than a Jaguar, or a Ferrari, or a big Mercedes coupe. These are challenging questions — even Porsche owners themselves don't know exactly what motivates their buying. But given Porsche's low volume and the increasingly fragmented auto market, it is imperative that management understand its customers and what gets their motors running.

Profile of a Porsche owner

Porsche was founded in 1931 by Ferdinand Porsche, the man credited with designing the original Volkswagen Beetle, Adolf Hitler's 'people's car' and one of the most successful car designs of all time. For most of the first two decades, the company built Volkswagen Beetles for German citizens and tanks and Beetles for the military. As Porsche AG began to sell cars under its own nameplate in the 1950s and 1960s, a few constants developed. The company sold very few models, creating an image of exclusivity. Those early models had a rounded, bubble shape that had its roots in the original Beetle, but design evolved into something more Porsche-like with the world famous 356 and 911 models. Finally, Porsche's automobiles featured air-cooled four- and six-cylinder 'boxer' motors (cylinders in an opposed configuration) in the rear of the car. This gave the cars a unique and often dangerous characteristic — a tendency for the rear-end to swing out when cornering hard. That's one of the reasons that Porsche owners were drawn to them. They were challenging to drive and that kept most people away, making the car even more exclusive.

Since its early days, Porsche has appealed to a very narrow segment of financially successful people. These are achievers who see themselves as entrepreneurial, even if they work for a corporation. They set very high goals for themselves and then work doggedly to meet them. And they expect no less from the clothes they wear, the restaurants they go to, or the cars they drive. These individuals see themselves not as a part of the regular world, but as exceptions to it. They buy Porsches because the car mirrors their self-image — it stands for the things owners like to see in themselves and in their lives.

Most of us buy what Porsche executives call utility vehicles. That is, we buy cars to go to work, to deliver the kids and to run errands. Because we have to use our cars to accomplish these daily tasks, we base buying decisions on features such as price, size, fuel economy and other practical considerations. But a Porsche is more than a utility car. Its owners see it as a car to be enjoyed, not just used. Most Porsche buyers are not moved by information, but by feelings. A Porsche is like a piece of clothing, something the owner 'wears' and is seen in. They develop a personal relationship with their cars, one that has more to do with the way the car sounds, vibrates and feels than with how many cup holders it has or how much cargo it can tote. They admire their Porsches as machines that perform without being flashy or phoney.

People buy Porsches because they enjoy driving. If all they needed was something to get them from point A to point B, they could find something much less expensive. And whereas many Porsche owners are car enthusiasts, some of them are not. One successful businesswoman and owner of a high-end Porsche said, 'When I drive this car to the high school to pick up my daughter, I end up with five youngsters in the car. If I drive any other car, I can't even find her; she doesn't want to come home.'

From niche to numerous

For the first few decades, Porsche AG lived by the philosophy of Ferry Porsche, Ferdinand's son. Ferry created the Porsche 356 because no one else made a car like the one he wanted. 'We did not do market research, we had no sales forecasts, no return-on-investment calculations. None of that. I very simply built my dream car and figured that there would be other people who share that dream.' So really, Porsche AG from the beginning was very much like its customers: an achiever that set out to make the very best.

But as the years rolled on, Porsche management became concerned with a significant issue: were there enough Porsche buyers to keep the company afloat? Granted, the company never had illusions of churning out the numbers of Peugeot or BMW. But to fund innovation, even a niche manufacturer has to grow a little. And Porsche began to worry that the quirky nature of the people who buy Porsches might just run out on them.

This led Porsche to extend its brand outside the box. In the early 1970s, Porsche introduced the 914, a square-ish, mid-engine two-seater that was much cheaper than the 911. This meant that a different class of people could afford a Porsche. It was no surprise that the 914 became Porsche's top-selling model. By the late 1970s, Porsche replaced the 914 with a hatchback coupe that had something no other regular Porsche model had ever had: an engine in the front. At less than €16,000, more than €8,000 less than the 911, the 924 and later 944 models were once again Porsche's pitch to affordability. At one point, Porsche increased its sales goal by nearly 50 per cent to 60,000 cars a year.

Although these cars were in many respects sales successes, the Porsche faithful cried foul. They considered these entry-level models to be cheap and underperforming. Most loyalists never really accepted these models as 'real' Porsches. In fact, they were not at all happy that they had to share their brand with a customer who didn't fit the Porsche-owner profile. They were turned off by what they saw as a corporate strategy that had focused on *mass* over *class* marketing. This tarnished image was compounded by the fact that Nissan, Toyota, BMW and other carmakers had ramped up high-end sports car offerings, creating some fierce competition. In fact, both the Datsun 280-ZX and the Toyota Supra were not only cheaper than Porsche's 944, they were faster. A struggling economy threw more sand in Porsche's tank. By 1990, Porsche sales had plummeted and the company flirted with bankruptcy.

Return to its roots?

But Porsche wasn't going down without a fight. It quickly recognised the error of its ways and halted production of the entry-level models. It rebuilt its damaged image by revamping its higher-end model lines with more race-bred technology. In an effort to regain rapport with customers, Porsche once again targeted the high end of the market in both price and performance. It set modest sales goals and decided that moderate growth with higher margins would be more profitable in the long term. The company set out to make one less Porsche than the public demanded. According to one executive, 'We're not looking for volume, we're searching for exclusivity.'

Porsche's efforts had the desired effect. By the late 1990s, the brand was once again favoured by the same types of achievers who had so deeply loved the car for decades. The cars were once again exclusive. And the company was once again profitable. But by the early 2000s, Porsche management was asking itself a familiar question: to have a sustainable future, could Porsche rely on only the Porsche faithful? According to then CEO Wendelin Wiedeking, 'For Porsche to remain independent, it can't be dependent on the most fickle segment in the market. We don't want to become just a marketing department of some giant. We have to make sure we're profitable enough to pay for future development ourselves.'

So in 2002, Porsche did the unthinkable. It became one of the last car companies to jump into the insatiable SUV market. At roughly 5,000 pounds, the Porsche Cayenne was heavier than anything that Porsche had ever made with the exception of some prototype military tanks it made during WWII. Once again, the new model featured an engine up-front. And it was the first Porsche to ever be equipped with seat belts for five. As news spread about the car's development, howls of distress could be heard from Porsche's customer base.

But this time, Porsche did not seem too concerned that the loyalists would be put off. Could it be that the company had already forgotten what happened the last time it deviated from the mould? Apparently not. After driving one of the first Cayennes off the assembly line, one journalist stated, 'A day at the wheel of the 444 horsepower Cayenne Turbo leaves two overwhelming impressions. First, the Cayenne doesn't behave or feel like an SUV, and second, it drives like a Porsche.' This was no entry-level car. Porsche had created a two-and-a-half ton beast that could accelerate to 60 miles per hour in just over five seconds, corner like it was on rails, and hit 165 miles per hour, all while coddling five adults in sumptuous leather seats with almost no wind noise from the outside world. On top of that, it could keep up with a Land Rover when the pavement ended. Indeed,

Porsche had created the Porsche of SUVs

Recently, Porsche upped the ante one more time. It unveiled another large vehicle. But this time, it was a low-slung, five-door luxury sedan. The Porsche faithful and the automotive press again gasped in disbelief. But by the time the Panamera hit the pavement, Porsche had proven once again that Porsche customers could have their cake and eat it too. The Panamera is almost as big as the Cayenne but can move four adults down the road at speeds of up to 190 miles per hour, accelerate from a standstill to 60 miles per hour in 3.6 seconds, and still wring 23 miles out of a gallon of petrol.

Although some Porsche traditionalists would never be caught dead driving a front-engine Porsche that has more than two doors, Porsche insists that two trends will sustain these new models. First, a category of Porsche buyers has moved into life stages that have them facing inescapable needs – they need to haul more people and stuff. This not only applies to certain regular Porsche buyers, but Porsche is again seeing buyers enter its dealerships who otherwise wouldn't have. Only this time, the price points of the new vehicles are drawing only the well- heeled, allowing Porsche to maintain its exclusivity. These buyers also seem to fit the achiever profile of regular Porsche buyers.

The second trend is the growth of emerging economies. While Europe is home, the United States has long been the world's biggest consumer of Porsches, the company expects China to become its biggest customer before long. Twenty years ago, the United States accounted for about 50 per cent of Porsche's worldwide sales. Now, it accounts for less than 25 per cent. In China, many people who can afford to buy a car as expensive as a Porsche also hire a chauffeur. The Cayenne and the Panamera are perfect for those who want to be driven around in style but who may also want to make a quick getaway if necessary.

The most recent economic downturn brought down the sales of just about every maker of premium automobiles. When times are tough, buying a car like a Porsche is the ultimate postponable purchase. But as this downturn turns back up, Porsche is better positioned than ever to meet the needs of its customer base. Porsche is also in better shape than ever to maintain its brand image with the Porsche faithful, and with others as well. Understanding Porsche buyers is still a difficult task. But one former chief executive of Porsche summed it up this way: 'If you really want to understand our customers, you have to understand the phrase, "If I were going to be a car, I'd be a Porsche."'

Questions for discussion

1. Analyse the buyer decision process of a traditional Porsche customer.
2. Contrast the traditional Porsche customer decision process to the decision process for a Cayenne or Panamera customer.
3. Which concepts from the chapter explain why Porsche sold so many lower-priced models in the 1970s and 1980s?
4. Explain how both positive and negative attitudes toward a brand like Porsche develop. How might Porsche change consumer attitudes toward the brand?
5. What role does the Porsche brand play in the self-concept of its buyers?

Sources: Andre Tutu, 'Porsche announces 2011 sales increase', *Au-toevolution*, 3 January 2012, www.autoevolution.com/news/porsche-announces-2011-us-sales-increase-41571.html; David Gumpert, 'Porsche on Nichemanship', *Harvard Business Review*, March/April 1986, pp. 98–106; Peter Robinson, 'Porsche Cayenne – driving impression', *Car and Driver*, January 2003, www.caranddriver.conVreviews/porsche-cayenne-first-drive-review; Jens Meiners, '2010 Porsche Panamera S/4S/Turbo – first drive review', *Car and Driver*, June 2009, www.caranddrivercom/reviews/2010-porsche-panamera-s-4s-turbo-first-drive-review; http://wardsauto.com/north-america/honda-targets-6-million-global-sales-2017-north-american-output-rise and information from www.porsche.com/usa/aboutporsche/pressreleases/, accessed October 2015.

CHAPTER SIX

Business markets and business buyer behaviour

Chapter preview

In the previous chapter, you studied *final consumer* buying behaviour and factors that influence it. In this chapter, we'll do the same for business customers — those that buy goods and services for use in producing their own goods and services or for resale to others. As when selling to final buyers, firms marketing to businesses must engage business customers and build profitable relationships with them by creating superior customer value.

To start, let's look at UPS. You probably know UPS as a neighbourhood small package delivery company. It turns out, however, that a majority of UPS's business comes not from residential consumers like you, but from large *business* customers. To succeed in its business-to-business markets, UPS must do more than just pick up and deliver packages. It must work closely and deeply with its business customers to become a strategic logistics partner.

Objective outline

➤ **Objective 1** Define the business market and explain how business markets differ from consumer markets.
Business markets (pp. 170–172)

➤ **Objective 2** Identify the major factors that influence business buyer behaviour.
Business buyer behaviour (pp. 172–176)

➤ **Objective 3** List and define the steps in the business buying decision process.

The business buying process (pp. 176–179)
E-procurement and online purchasing (pp. 179–180)

➤ **Objective 4** Compare the institutional and government markets and explain how institutional and government buyers make their buying decisions.
Institutional and government markets (pp. 180–182)

UPS: a strategic logistics partner to business customers

Mention UPS and most people envision one of those familiar brown trucks with a friendly driver, rumbling around their neighbourhood dropping off parcels. For most of us, seeing a brown UPS truck evokes fond memories of past package deliveries. That makes sense.

With its European Headquarters in Brussels, Belgium and its main European airport hub in Cologne/ Bonn, Germany, UPS is a key player in European and global logistics. In Europe alone their 44,000 employees serve around 11,500 access points with nearly half a million square metres of warehouse space. Globally, the company's brown-clad drivers deliver more than 4.3 billion packages annually with around 400 flights in and out of Europe *every day*.

However, most of UPS's revenues come not from the residential customers who receive the packages, but from the business customers who send them. And for its business customers, UPS does more than just get Grandma's holiday package there on time. For businesses, physical package delivery is just part of a much more complex logistics process that involves purchase orders, inventories, order status checks, invoices, payments, returned merchandise, fleets of delivery vehicles and even international cross-border dealings. Companies need timely information about their outbound and inbound packages — what's in them, where they're now located, to whom they are going, when they'll get there and how much is owed. UPS knows that, for many companies, such logistics can be a real nightmare.

That's where UPS can help. Logistics is exactly what UPS does best. Over the years, UPS has grown to become much more than a neighbourhood package delivery service. It is now a €44 billion corporate giant providing a broad range of global logistics solutions. Whereas many business customers hate dealing with the logistics process, UPS proclaims 'We ♥ logistics'. To UPS's thinking, 'the new logistics' is 'the most powerful force in business today'. It's much more than just efficiently getting things where they need to be on time. 'Logistics is about using the movement of goods as a competitive advantage,' says the company. 'It makes running your business easier. It lets you serve your customers better. And it can help you grow. It's a whole new way of thinking.'

If it has to do with the new logistics, anywhere in the world, UPS can probably do it better than any other company. UPS offers business customers efficient multimodal package, mail and freight distribution services. But it can also help customers streamline sourcing, maintain leaner inventories, manage and fulfil orders, warehouse goods, assemble or even customise products, and manage post-sales warranty repair and returns services.

In its business markets, UPS does much more than just deliver packages. It works hand in hand with business customers to become a logistics *partner*, helping them to shape and sharpen their entire logistics strategy and operations.

UPS has the resources to handle the logistics needs of just about any size business. It employs nearly 400,000 people, owns almost 100,000 delivery vehicles, runs the world's ninth-largest airline, and maintains 1,907 operating facilities in more than 220 countries. The distribution giant is also the world's largest international customs broker. With some 882 international flights per day to or from 323 international destinations, UPS can also help businesses to navigate the complexities of international shipping.

At one level, UPS can simply handle a company's package shipments. On a deeper level, however, UPS can advise businesses on how to improve their own overall logistics operations. It can help clients redesign their logistics systems to better synchronise the flow of goods, funds and information up and down the entire supply chain. At a still deeper level, companies can let UPS take over and manage part or all of their logistics operations.

Consumer electronics maker Toshiba lets UPS handle its entire laptop PC repair process — lock, stock and barrel. UPS's logistics prowess helped Toshiba solve one of its biggest challenges — turnaround time on laptop repairs. According to Mike Simons of Toshiba, 'When we started off with UPS, we thought of them [only] as a mover of packages from point A to point B — how to get a PC from the factory floor into the customer's hands. But by sitting down with them and looking at our complete supply chain, talking about our repair process and parts management, we evolved into so much more.' Now, customers ship laptops needing repair to a special UPS facility near the World port air hub. There, UPS employees receive the units, run diagnostics to assess the repairs needed, pick the necessary parts, quickly complete the service, and return the laptops to their owners. UPS can now fix and ship a laptop in a single day, shortening a door-to-door repair process that once took two to three weeks down to four or fewer days. Together, UPS and Toshiba greatly improved the customer repair experience.

So, what does 'Big Brown' do for its customers? As it turns out, the answer depends on who you are. For residential consumers, UPS uses those familiar brown trucks to provide simple and efficient package pickup and delivery services. But in its business-to-business markets, it develops deeper and more in-volved customer relationships. UPS employees roll up their sleeves and work hand in hand with business customers to provide a rich range of logistics services that help customers sharpen their logistics strat-egies, cut costs and serve customers better. More than just providing shipping services, UPS becomes a strategic logistics *partner*. 'One of the things we've learned with UPS is their willingness to be a part-ner,' says Toshiba's Simon. 'They really understand the overall experience we're trying to create for the customers.'[1]

Business buyer behaviour—
The buying behaviour of organisations that buy goods and services for use in the production of other products and services that are sold, rented or supplied to others.

Business buying process—
The decision process by which business buyers determine which products and services their organisations need to purchase and then find, evaluate, and choose among alternative suppliers and brands.

In one way or another, most large companies sell to other organisations. Companies such as Unilever, Nestlé, Olivetti, Boeing, IBM, Caterpillar, and countless other firms sell *most* of their products to other businesses. Even large consumer-products companies, which make products used by final consumers, must first sell their products to other businesses. For example, Unilever makes many familiar consumer brands – food products (such as, Lipton, Bovril, Pot Noodle and Cornetto), homecare products (for example, Comfort, Surf, Peril and Domestos), personal care products (for instance, Dove, Lux, Brut and Vaseline), and others. But to sell these products to consumers, General Mills must first sell them to its wholesaler and retailer customers, who in turn serve the consumer market.

Business buyer behaviour refers to the buying behaviour of organisations that buy goods and services for use in the production of other products and services that are sold, rented or supplied to others. It also includes the behaviour of retailing and wholesaling firms that acquire goods to resell or rent to others at a profit. In the **business buying process**, business buyers determine which products and services their organisations need to purchase and then find, evaluate and choose among alternative suppliers and brands. *Business-to-business (B-to-B) marketers* must do their best to understand business markets and business buyer behaviour. Then, like businesses that sell to final buyers, they must engage business customers and build profitable relationships with them by creating superior customer value.

BUSINESS MARKETS

Author comment

Business markets operate 'behind the scenes' to most consumers. Most of the things you buy involve many sets of business purchases before you ever see them.

The business market is *huge*. In fact, business markets involve far more euros and items than do consumer markets. For example, think about the large number of business transactions involved in the production and sale of a single set of Pirelli tyres. Various suppliers sell Pirelli the rubber, steel, equipment and other goods that it needs to produce tyres. Pirelli then sells the finished tyres to retailers, who in turn sell them to consumers. Thus, many sets of *business* purchases were made for only one set of *consumer* purchases. In addition, Pirelli sells tyres as original equipment to manufacturers that install them on new vehicles and as replacement tyres to companies that maintain their own fleets of company cars, trucks, buses or other vehicles.

In some ways, business markets are similar to consumer markets. Both involve people who assume buying roles and make purchase decisions to satisfy needs. However, business markets differ in many ways from consumer markets. The main differences are in *market structure and demand*, the *nature of the buying unit*, and the *types of decisions and the decision process* involved.

Market structure and demand

The business marketer normally deals with *far fewer but far larger buyers* than the consumer marketer does. Even in large business markets, a few buyers often account for most of the purchasing. For example, when Goodyear sells replacement tyres to final consumers, its potential market includes millions of car owners around the world. But its fate in business markets depends on getting orders from only a handful of large automakers.

Further, many business markets have *inelastic and more fluctuating demand*. The total demand for many business products is not much affected by price changes, especially in the short run. A drop in the price of leather will not cause shoe manufacturers to buy much more leather unless it results in lower shoe prices that, in turn, increase consumer demand for shoes. And the demand for many business goods and services tends to change more – and more quickly – than does the demand for consumer goods and services. A small percentage increase in consumer demand can cause large increases in business demand.

Finally, business demand is **derived demand** – it ultimately derives from the demand for consumer goods. Consumers buy Intel processors only when they buy PCs, tablets, smartphones and other devices with Intel processors inside them from producers such as HP, Dell, Lenovo, Samsung, Sony and Toshiba. And demand for Gore-Tex fabrics derives from consumer purchases of outdoor apparel brands made from Gore-Tex. If consumer demand for these products increases, so does the demand for the Intel processors or Gore-Tex fabrics they contain. Therefore, B-to-B marketers sometimes promote their products directly to final consumers to increase business demand. For example, Intel's long-running Intel Inside consumer marketing campaign consists of ads and promotions extolling the virtues of both Intel processors and the brands that contain them:[2]

> During the recent holiday season, Intel opened pop-up retail stores in major cities – called Intel Experience Stores – featuring the latest products from Dell, Asus, Lenovo, Acer, Sony, HP, Samsung, Toshiba and other Intel-based brands. Intel also partnered with retailers such as Best Buy to set up online sites featuring Intel-based products (*BestBuy.com/IntelExperience*). And it posted an online holiday buying guide promoting Intel Atom-powered laptop and tablet brands. Intel even collaborated recently with Toshiba to produce several award-winning social media film series, called 'Inside', 'The Beauty Inside' and 'The Power Inside'. For example, the 63-episode 'The Beauty Inside' series followed the story of Alex, a man who wakes up every day as the same person but in a different body, forcing him to explore his inner self. Each episode featured actual brand fans who gave Alex hundreds of different faces. The film engaged consumers deeply and got even strangers discussing their own central identities, all celebrating the essential fact that 'it's what's inside that counts' (which just happens to be Intel's core marketing message). The award-winning film captured 70 million views and 26 million interactions. It even won an Emmy for Outstanding New Approach to Daytime Programming at the 40th Annual Daytime Emmy Awards. Based on its success, Intel and Toshiba followed with 'The Power Inside', a comedy/Sci-Fi adventure in which the hero calls on the power inside his Toshiba laptop and the power inside himself to defend earth from a race of extra-terrestrial moustaches and unibrows which take over people's faces. In all, the series garnered over 200 million views and the Intel Inside campaign has boosted demand for both Intel processors and the products containing them, benefiting both Intel and its business partners.

Derived demand—Business demand that ultimately comes from (derives from) the demand for consumer goods.

Nature of the buying unit

Compared with consumer purchases, a business purchase usually involves *more decision participants* and a *more professional purchasing effort*. Often, business buying is done by trained purchasing agents who spend their working lives learning how to buy better. The more complex the purchase, the more likely it is that several people will participate in the decision-making process. Buying committees composed of technical experts and top management are common in the buying of major goods. Beyond this, B-to-B marketers now face a new breed of higher-level, better-trained supply managers. Therefore, companies must have well-trained marketers and salespeople to deal with these well-trained buyers.

Types of decisions and the decision process

Business buyers usually face *more complex* buying decisions than consumer buyers. Business purchases often involve large sums of money, complex technical and economic considerations, and interactions among people at many levels of the buyer's organisation. The business buying process also tends to be *longer* and *more formalised*. Large business purchases usually call for detailed product specifications, written purchase orders, careful supplier searches and formal approval.

Finally, in the business buying process, the buyer and seller are often much *more dependent* on each other. B-to-B marketers may roll up their sleeves and work closely with their customers during all stages of the buying process – from helping customers define problems, to finding solutions, to supporting after-sale operation. They often customise their offerings to individual customer needs. In the short run, sales go to suppliers who meet buyers' immediate product and service needs. In the long run, however, business-to-business marketers keep customers by meeting current needs *and* by partnering with them to help solve their problems. For example, consider IKEA:

> IKEA, the world's largest furniture retailer, is the quintessential global cult brand. Customers from Thessaloniki in Greece to Bucharest in Romania flock to the €29 billion Scandinavian retailer's more than 315 huge stores in 27 countries, drawn by IKEA's trendy but simple and practical furniture at affordable prices. But IKEA's biggest obstacle to growth isn't opening new stores and attracting customers. Rather, it's finding enough of the right kinds of *suppliers* to help design and produce the billions of euros of affordable goods that customers will carry out of its stores. IKEA currently relies on some 1,046 suppliers in 52 countries to stock its shelves. IKEA can't just rely on spot suppliers who might be available when needed. Instead, it has systematically developed a robust network of supplier-partners that reliably provide the more than 9,500 items it stocks. IKEA's designers start with a basic customer value proposition. Then they find and work closely with key suppliers to bring that proposition to market. Thus, IKEA does more than just buy from suppliers; it also involves them deeply in the process of designing and making stylish but affordable products to keep IKEA's customers coming back.[3]

Supplier development—Systematic development of networks of supplier-partners to ensure an appropriate and dependable supply of products and materials for use in making products or reselling them to others.

As in IKEA's case, in recent years relationships between most customers and suppliers have been changing from downright adversarial to close and chummy. In fact, many customer companies are now practising **supplier development**, systematically developing networks of supplier-partners to ensure a dependable supply of the products and materials that they use in making their own products or reselling to others. For example, IKEA doesn't have a 'Purchasing Department', it has a 'Supplier Development Department'. The giant retailer knows that it can't just rely on spot suppliers who might be available when needed. Instead, IKEA manages a huge network of supplier-partners that help provide the hundreds of billions of euros of goods that it sells to its customers each year.

BUSINESS BUYER BEHAVIOUR

Author comment

Business buying *decisions* can range from routine to incredibly complex, involving only a few or very many decision makers and buying influences.

At the most basic level, marketers want to know how business buyers will respond to various marketing stimuli. Figure 6.1 shows a model of business buyer behaviour. In this model, marketing and other stimuli affect the buying organisation and produce certain buyer responses. To design good marketing strategies, marketers must understand what happens within the organisation to turn stimuli into purchase responses.

Within the organisation, buying activity consists of two major parts: the *buying centre*, composed of all the people involved in the buying decision, and the *buying decision process*. The

Figure 6.1 A model of business buying behaviour

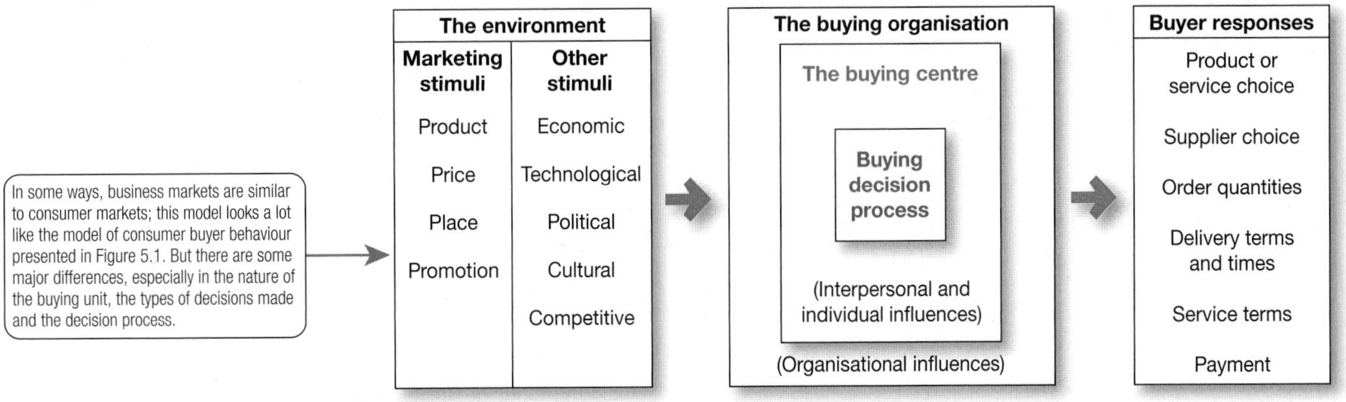

model shows that the buying centre and the buying decision process are influenced by internal organisational, interpersonal and individual factors as well as external environmental factors.

The model in Figure 6.1 suggests four questions about business buyer behaviour: What buying decisions do business buyers make? Who participates in the business buying process? What are the major influences on buyers? How do business buyers make their buying decisions?

Major types of buying situations

There are three major types of buying situations.[4] In a **straight rebuy**, the buyer reorders something without any modifications. It is usually handled on a routine basis by the purchasing department. To keep the business, 'in' suppliers try to maintain product and service quality. 'Out' suppliers try to find new ways to add value or exploit dissatisfaction so that the buyer will consider them.

In a **modified rebuy**, the buyer wants to modify product specifications, prices, terms or suppliers. The 'in' suppliers may become nervous and feel pressured to put their best foot forward to protect an account. 'Out' suppliers may see the modified rebuy situation as an opportunity to make a better offer and gain new business.

A company buying a product or service for the first time faces a **new task** situation. In such cases, the greater the cost or risk, the larger the number of decision participants and the greater the company's efforts to collect information. The new task situation is the marketer's greatest opportunity and challenge. The marketer not only tries to reach as many key buying influences as possible, but also provides help and information. The buyer makes the fewest decisions in the straight rebuy and the most in the new task decision.

Many business buyers prefer to buy a complete solution to a problem from a single seller rather than buying separate products and services from several suppliers and putting them together. The sale often goes to the firm that provides the most complete *system* for meeting the customer's needs and solving its problems. Such **systems selling (or solutions selling)** is often a key business marketing strategy for winning and holding accounts. Consider UPS and its customer Alcatel:[5]

Alcatel is one of Europe's (and indeed the world's) leading players in telecommunications and the Internet. Alcatel builds next generation networks while delivering integrated end-to-end data and voice networking solutions to consumers, enterprises and telecommunications carriers. Jean-Michel Fallet, Vice-President of Supply Chain and Support at Alcatel eND, says, 'We wished to develop a close relationship with a single partner whom we could work with to develop a solution tailored to Alcatel eND's needs. Above all, we wanted to boost the quality of service that our customers receive in terms of timeliness and flow traceability; reduce costs and inventory; and streamline our supply chain by eliminating the need for multiple suppliers across different geographic regions. We were

Straight rebuy—A business buying situation in which the buyer routinely reorders something without any modifications.

Modified rebuy—A business buying situation in which the buyer wants to modify product specifications, prices, terms or suppliers.

New task—A business buying situation in which the buyer purchases a product or service for the first time.

Systems selling (or solutions selling)—Buying a packaged solution to a problem from a single seller, thus avoiding all the separate decisions involved in a complex buying situation.

looking for a large-scale partner able to take over global management and be totally free to choose their own service providers simply by subcontracting on the basis of proven efficiency. UPS Supply Chain Solutions was uniquely able to meet these two criteria.'

UPS Supply Chain Solutions rose to this challenge and now acts as the sole point of contact between customers and suppliers by managing all supply chain activities through strategic, tactical and operational levels.

The single interface offered by UPS generates a much more effective solution than the multiple suppliers that previously operated in Alcatel's supply chain. However, the UPS Supply Chain Solutions offering extends far beyond the mere management of Alcatel's service delivery. UPS coordinates its own logistics organisation resources and wider information technology with those of other complementary service partners. Adopting innovative tracking of transactions and the wider monitoring of the supply chain, UPS optimises (at a European level) Alcatel's logistics. The outcome of this? Supply chain costs reduced from 5.8 per cent to 3.1 per cent and service levels up from 60 per cent to 90 per cent.

Participants in the business buying process

Who does the buying of the trillions of euros worth of goods and services needed by business organisations? The decision-making unit of a buying organisation is called its **buying centre**. It consists of all the individuals and units that play a role in the business purchase decision-making process. This group includes the actual users of the product or service, those who make the buying decision, those who influence the buying decision, those who do the actual buying and those who control buying information.

The buying centre includes all members of the organisation who play any of five roles in the purchase decision process.[6]

- **Users** are members of the organisation who will use the good or service. In many cases, users initiate the buying proposal and help define product specifications.
- **Influencers** often help define specifications and also provide information for evaluating alternatives. Technical personnel are particularly important influencers.
- **Buyers** have formal authority to select the supplier and arrange terms of purchase. Buyers may help shape product specifications, but their major role is in selecting vendors and negotiating. In more complex purchases, buyers might include high-level officers participating in the negotiations.
- **Deciders** have formal or informal power to select or approve the final suppliers. In routine buying, the buyers are often the deciders, or at least the approvers.
- **Gatekeepers** control the flow of information to others. For example, purchasing agents often have authority to prevent salespersons from seeing users or deciders. Other gatekeepers include technical personnel and even personal secretaries.

The buying centre is not a fixed and formally identified unit within the buying organisation. It is a set of buying roles assumed by different people for different purchases. Within the organisation, the size and makeup of the buying centre will vary for different products and for different buying situations. For some routine purchases, one person – say, a purchasing agent – may assume all the buying centre roles and serve as the only person involved in the buying decision. For more complex purchases, the buying centre may include 20 or 30 people from different levels and departments in the organisation.

The buying centre concept presents a major marketing challenge. The business marketer must learn who participates in the decision, each participant's relative influence, and what evaluation criteria each decision participant uses. This can be difficult.

The buying centre usually includes some obvious participants who are involved formally in the buying decision. For example, the decision to buy a corporate jet will probably involve the company's CEO, the chief pilot, a purchasing agent, some legal staff, a member of top management and others formally charged with the buying decision. It may also involve less obvious, informal

Buying centre—All the individuals and units that play a role in the purchase decision-making process.

Users—Members of the buying organisation who will actually use the purchased product or service.

Influencers—People in an organisation's buying centre who affect the buying decision; they often help define specifications and also provide information for evaluating alternatives.

Buyers—People in an organisation's buying centre who make an actual purchase.

Deciders—People in an organisation's buying centre who have formal or informal power to select or approve the final suppliers.

Gatekeepers—People in an organisation's buying centre who control the flow of information to others.

participants, some of whom may actually make or strongly affect the buying decision. Sometimes, even the people in the buying centre are not aware of all the buying participants. For example, the decision about which corporate jet to buy may actually be made by a corporate board member who has an interest in flying and who knows a lot about airplanes. This board member may work behind the scenes to sway the decision. Many business buying decisions result from the complex interactions of ever-changing buying centre participants.

Major influences on business buyers

Business buyers are subject to many influences when they make their buying decisions. Some marketers assume that the major influences are economic. They think buyers will favour the supplier who offers the lowest price or the best product or the most service. They concentrate on offering strong economic benefits to buyers. Such economic factors are very important to most buyers, especially in a tough economy. However, business buyers actually respond to both economic and personal factors. Far from being cold, calculating and impersonal, business buyers are human and social as well. They react to both reason and emotion.

Today, most B-to-B marketers recognise that emotion plays an important role in business buying decisions. Consider this example:[7]

> USG Corporation is a leading manufacturer of gypsum wallboard and other building materials for the construction and remodelling industries. Given its construction contractor, dealer and builder audience, you might expect USG's B-to-B ads to focus heavily on the performance features and benefits, such as strength, impact resistance, ease of installation and costs. USG does promote these benefits. However, a recent marketing campaign for USG's Sheetrock Ultralight wallboard panels also packed a decidedly more emotional wallop. Ultralight panels offer performance equal to or better than standard gypsum wallboard but are 30 per cent lighter. That makes them easier to lift, carry and install, reducing worker fatigue. Instead of just stating that Ultralight is lighter, USG's award-winning advertising campaign — called the 'Weight has been lifted' — visualised this benefit using dramatic, emotion-charged imagery showing that it's literally removing some weight from the backs and shoulders of its customers. Ads show contractors struggling to carry enormous objects such as a car, a giant anchor, a grand piano, or an elephant or dinosaur. The tagline: 'If you're not lifting Ultralight Panels, what are you lifting?'

Figure 6.2 lists various groups of influences on business buyers – environmental, organisational, interpersonal and individual. Business buyers are heavily influenced by factors in the current and expected *economic environment*, such as the level of primary demand, the economic outlook and the cost of money. Another environmental factor is the *supply* of key materials. Many companies now are more willing to buy and hold larger inventories of

Figure 6.2 Major influences on business buying behaviour

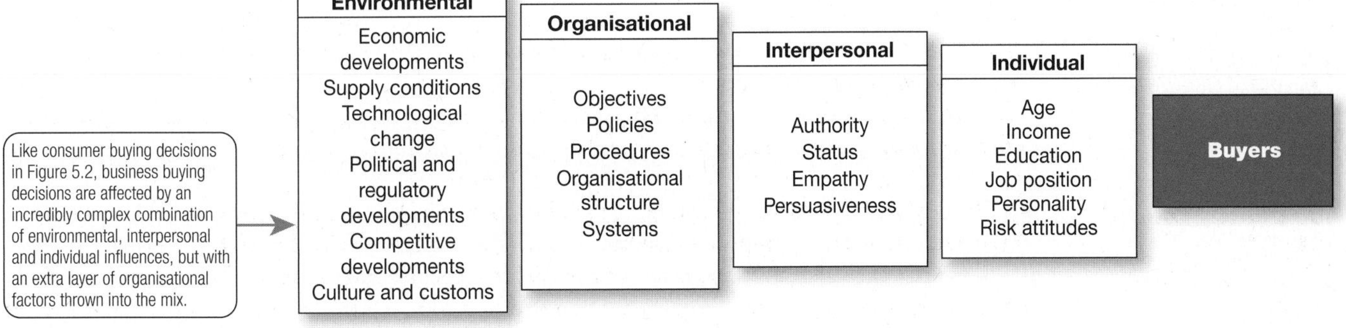

Like consumer buying decisions in Figure 5.2, business buying decisions are affected by an incredibly complex combination of environmental, interpersonal and individual influences, but with an extra layer of organisational factors thrown into the mix.

Environmental	Organisational	Interpersonal	Individual	
Economic developments				
Supply conditions	Objectives	Authority	Age	
Technological change	Policies	Status	Income	**Buyers**
Political and regulatory developments	Procedures	Empathy	Education	
	Organisational structure	Persuasiveness	Job position	
Competitive developments	Systems		Personality	
Culture and customs			Risk attitudes	

scarce materials to ensure adequate supply. Business buyers also are affected by *technological*, *political* and *competitive* developments in the environment. Finally, *culture and customs* can strongly influence business buyer reactions to the marketer's behaviour and strategies, especially in the international marketing environment. The business buyer must watch these factors, determine how they will affect the buyer, and try to turn these challenges into opportunities.

Organisational factors are also important. Each buying organisation has its own objectives, strategies, structure, systems and procedures, and the business marketer must understand these factors well. Questions such as these arise: How many people are involved in the buying decision? Who are they? What are their evaluative criteria? What are the company's policies and limits on its buyers?

The buying centre usually includes many participants who influence each other, so *interpersonal factors* also influence the business buying process. However, it is often difficult to assess such interpersonal factors and group dynamics. Buying centre participants do not wear tags that label them as 'key decision maker' or 'not influential'. Nor do buying centre participants with the highest rank always have the most influence. Participants may influence the buying decision because they control rewards and punishments, are well liked, have special expertise, or have a special relationship with other important participants. Interpersonal factors are often very subtle. Whenever possible, business marketers must try to understand these factors and design strategies that take them into account.

Each participant in the business buying decision process brings in personal motives, perceptions and preferences. These *individual factors* are affected by personal characteristics such as age, income, education, professional identification, personality and attitudes toward risk. Also, buyers have different buying styles. Some may be technical types who make in-depth analyses of competitive proposals before choosing a supplier. Other buyers may be intuitive negotiators who are adept at pitting the sellers against one another for the best deal.

The business buying process

Figure 6.3 lists the eight stages of the business buying process.[8] Buyers who face a new task buying situation usually go through all stages of the buying process. Buyers making modified or straight rebuys, in contrast, may skip some of the stages. We will examine these steps for the typical new task buying situation.

Problem recognition

Problem recognition—The first stage of the business buying process in which someone in the company recognises a problem or need that can be met by acquiring a good or a service.

The buying process begins when someone in the company recognises a problem or need that can be met by acquiring a specific product or service. **Problem recognition** can result from internal or external stimuli. Internally, the company may decide to launch a new product that requires new production equipment and materials. Or a machine may break down and need new parts. Perhaps a purchasing manager is unhappy with a current supplier's product quality, service, or prices. Externally, the buyer may get some new ideas at a trade show, see an ad, or receive a call from a salesperson who offers a better product or a lower price.

Figure 6.3 Stages of business buying behaviour

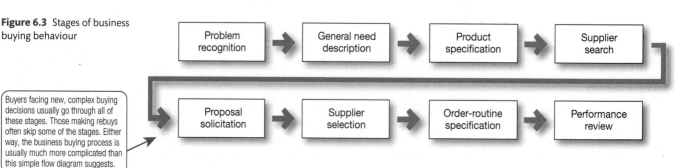

Buyers facing new, complex buying decisions usually go through all of these stages. Those making rebuys often skip some of the stages. Either way, the business buying process is usually much more complicated than this simple flow diagram suggests.

In fact, in their advertising, business marketers often alert customers to potential problems and then show how their products and services provide solutions. For example, consulting firm Accenture's award-winning 'High performance. delivered'. B-to-B ads do this. One Accenture ad points to the urgent need for a business to get up to speed with mobile technology. 'Are your customers drawn to you?' the ad asks, showing moths drawn to a brightly lit smartphone screen. Accenture's solution: 'We're helping clients leverage mobility not only to connect with customers – but also employees, businesses, and machines on web-enabled devices of every kind. That's high performance, delivered.'[9] Other ads in the series tell success stories of how Accenture has helped client companies recognise and solve a variety of other problems.

Source: Romantiche/Alamy Images

General need description

Having recognised a need, the buyer next prepares a **general need description** that describes the characteristics and quantity of the needed item. For standard items, this process presents few problems. For complex items, however, the buyer may need to work with others – engineers, users, consultants – to define the item. The team may want to rank the importance of reliability, durability, price and other attributes desired in the item. In this phase, the alert business marketer can help the buyers define their needs and provide information about the value of different product characteristics.

General need description– The stage in the business buying process in which a buyer describes the general characteristics and quantity of a needed item.

Product specification

The buying organisation next develops the item's technical **product specifications**, often with the help of a value analysis engineering team. *Product value analysis* is an approach to cost reduction in which components are studied carefully to determine if they can be redesigned, standardised or made by less costly methods of production. The team decides on the best product characteristics and specifies them accordingly. Sellers, too, can use value analysis as a tool to help secure a new account. By showing buyers a better way to make an object, outside sellers can turn straight rebuy situations into new task situations that give them a chance to obtain new business.

Product specification–The stage of the business buying process in which the buying organisation decides on and specifies the best technical product characteristics for a needed item.

Supplier search

The buyer now conducts a **supplier search** to find the best vendors. The buyer can compile a small list of qualified suppliers by reviewing trade directories, doing online searches or phoning other companies for recommendations. Today, more and more companies are turning to the Internet to find suppliers. For marketers, this has levelled the playing field – the Internet gives smaller suppliers many of the same advantages as larger competitors.

The newer the buying task, and the more complex and costly the item, the greater the amount of time the buyer will spend searching for suppliers. The supplier's task is to get listed in major directories and build a good reputation in the marketplace. Salespeople should watch for companies in the process of searching for suppliers and make certain that their firm is considered.

Supplier search–The stage of the business buying process in which the buyer tries to find the best vendors.

Proposal solicitation

In the **proposal solicitation** stage of the business buying process, the buyer invites qualified suppliers to submit proposals. In response, some suppliers will refer the buyer to its website or promotional materials or send a salesperson to call on the prospect. However, when the item is complex or expensive, the buyer will usually require detailed written proposals or formal presentations from each potential supplier.

Proposal solicitation–The stage of the business buying process in which the buyer invites qualified suppliers to submit proposals.

Business marketers must be skilled in researching, writing and presenting proposals in response to buyer proposal solicitations. Proposals should be marketing documents, not just technical documents. Presentations should inspire confidence and should make the marketer's company stand out from the competition.

Supplier selection

The members of the buying centre now review the proposals and select a supplier or suppliers. During **supplier selection**, the buying centre often will draw up a list of the desired supplier attributes and their relative importance. Such attributes include product and service quality, reputation, on-time delivery, ethical corporate behaviour, honest communication and competitive prices. The members of the buying centre will rate suppliers against these attributes and identify the best suppliers.

Buyers may attempt to negotiate with preferred suppliers for better prices and terms before making the final selections. In the end, they may select a single supplier or a few suppliers. Many buyers prefer multiple sources of supplies to avoid being totally dependent on one supplier and to allow comparisons of prices and performance of several suppliers over time. Today's supplier development managers want to develop a full network of supplier partners that can help the company bring more value to its customers.

Order-routine specification

The buyer now prepares an **order-routine specification**. It includes the final order with the chosen supplier or suppliers and lists items such as technical specifications, quantity needed, expected delivery time, return policies and warranties. In the case of maintenance, repair and operating items, buyers may use blanket contracts rather than periodic purchase orders. A blanket contract creates a long-term relationship in which the supplier promises to resupply the buyer as needed at agreed prices for a set time period.

Many large buyers now practise *vendor-managed inventory*, in which they turn over ordering and inventory responsibilities to their suppliers. Under such systems, buyers share sales and inventory information directly with key suppliers. The suppliers then monitor inventories and replenish stock automatically as needed. For example, most major suppliers to large retailers such as Carrefour, Tesco, Walmart and Sainsbury's assume vendor-managed inventory responsibilities.

Performance review

In this stage, the buyer reviews supplier performance. The buyer may contact users and ask them to rate their satisfaction. The **performance review** may lead the buyer to continue, modify or drop the arrangement. The seller's job is to monitor the same factors used by the buyer to make sure that the seller is giving the expected satisfaction.

In all, the eight-stage buying-process model shown in Figure 6.3 provides a simple view of the business buying as it might occur in a new task buying situation. However, the actual process is usually much more complex. In the modified rebuy or straight rebuy situation, some of these stages would be compressed or bypassed. Each organisation buys in its own way, and each buying situation has unique requirements.

Different buying centre participants may be involved at different stages of the process. Although certain buying-process steps usually do occur, buyers do not always follow them in the same order, and they may add other steps. Often, buyers will repeat certain stages of the process. Finally, a customer relationship might involve many different types of purchases on-going at a given time, all in different stages of the buying process. The seller must manage the total *customer relationship*, not just individual purchases.

E-procurement and online purchasing

Advances in information technology have changed the face of the B-to-B marketing process. Online purchasing, often called **e-procurement**, has grown rapidly in recent years. Virtually unknown a decade and a half ago, online purchasing is standard procedure for most companies today. E-procurement gives buyers access to new suppliers, lowers purchasing costs, and hastens order processing and delivery. In turn, business marketers can connect with customers online to share marketing information, sell products and services, provide customer support services and maintain on-going customer relationships.

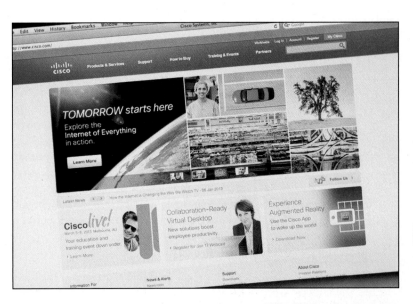

Companies can do e-procurement in any of several ways. They can conduct *reverse auctions*, in which they put their purchasing requests online and invite suppliers to bid for the business. Or they can engage in online *trading exchanges*, through which companies work collectively to facilitate the trading process. Companies also can conduct e-procurement by setting up their own *company buying sites*. For example, GE operates a company trading site on which it posts its buying needs and invites bids, negotiates terms and places orders. Or companies can create *extranet links* with key suppliers. For instance, they can create direct procurement accounts with suppliers such as Dell or Staples, through which company buyers can purchase equipment, materials and supplies directly. Staples operates a business-to-business procurement division called Staples Advantage, which serves the office supplies and services buying needs of businesses of any size, from 20 employees to the *Fortune* 1000.

B-to-B marketers can help customers who wish to purchase online by creating well-designed, easy-to-use web sites. For example, *BtoB* magazine rated the site of Cisco Systems – a global market leader in web networking hardware, software and services with offices in just about every European country – as one of its ten great B-to-B websites':[10]

Online buying: Cisco Systems website helps customers who want to purchase online by providing deep access to information about thousands of products. The site can also personalise the online experience for users and connect them with appropriate Cisco partner resellers.
Source: NetPhotos/Alamy Images

E-procurement—Purchasing through electronic connections between buyers and sellers — usually online.

To spur growth, Cisco Systems recently stepped up its focus on the small and midsize business (SMB) segment. Its award-winning new SMB-specific website is simple, action-oriented and engaging but gives SMB buyers deep access. At the most basic level, customers can find and download information about thousands of Cisco products and services. Digging deeper, the site is loaded with useful video content — everything from testimonials to 'how to' videos to informational and educational on-demand webcasts.

Cisco's SMB site gets customers interacting with both the company and its partner resellers. For example, its live click-to-chat feature puts users in immediate touch with Cisco product experts. Web-Ex web-conferencing software connects potential SMB customers with appropriate Cisco partner resellers, letting them share web pages, PowerPoint slides and other documents in a collaborative online space. Finally, the Cisco SMB site can actually personalise the online experience for users. For example, if it detects that someone from the legal industry is paying attention to wireless content, it might put together relevant pieces of content to create a page for that visitor. Such personalisation really pays off. Customers visiting personalised pages stay two times longer than other visitors and go much deeper into the site.

More generally, today's business-to-business marketers are using a wide range of digital and social marketing approaches – from websites, blogs and smartphone apps to mainstream social media such as Facebook, LinkedIn, YouTube and Twitter – to reach business customers and manage customer relationships anywhere, at any time. Digital and social media marketing has rapidly become *the* new space for engaging business customers.

Business-to-business e-procurement yields many benefits. First, it shaves transaction costs and results in more efficient purchasing for both buyers and suppliers. E-procurement reduces the time between order and delivery. And an online-powered purchasing programme eliminates the paperwork associated with traditional requisition and ordering procedures and helps an organisation keep better track of all purchases. Finally, beyond the cost and time savings, e-procurement frees purchasing people from a lot of drudgery and paperwork. In turn, it frees them to focus on more-strategic issues, such as finding better supply sources and working with suppliers to reduce costs and develop new products.

The rapidly expanding use of e-procurement, however, also presents some problems. For example, at the same time that the Internet makes it possible for suppliers and customers to share business data and even collaborate on product design, it can also erode decades-old customer–supplier relationships. Many buyers now use the power of the Internet to pit suppliers against one another and search out better deals, products and turnaround times on a purchase-by-purchase basis.

INSTITUTIONAL AND GOVERNMENT MARKETS

So far, our discussion of organisational buying has focused largely on the buying behaviour of business buyers. Much of this discussion also applies to the buying practices of institutional and government organisations. However, these two non-business markets have additional characteristics and needs. In this final section, we address the special features of institutional and government markets.

Institutional markets

Institutional market—Schools, hospitals, nursing homes, prisons and other institutions that provide goods and services to people in their care.

The **institutional market** consists of schools, hospitals, nursing homes, prisons and other institutions that provide goods and services to people in their care. Institutions differ from one another in their sponsors and their objectives. For example, in the UK Spire Healthcare runs 38 for-profit hospitals, generating €765 million in annual revenues. By contrast, the National Health Service in the UK is a huge non-profit organisation providing healthcare that is free at the point of delivery with over 2300 hospitals employing over 148,000 doctors and 331,000 nurses with an average net expenditure of €128 billion.

Institutional markets can be huge. Consider the massive and expanding European prisons economy. Across Europe prison populations vary considerably. Norway has 66 prisoners per 100,000 citizens while England and Wales has 148. Germany, Spain, the UK, Italy, Poland, Turkey, Ukraine and France each has prison populations over 50,000. Liechtenstein imprison a mere 7 offenders while 39 per cent of Switzerland's prisoners are unsentenced.[11] Although figures vary across Europe, the overall cost of the whole criminal justice system is around 2 per cent of Gross Domestic Product (GDP) with each prisoner costing around €47,000 each year.

Many institutional markets are characterised by low budgets and captive patrons. For example, hospital patients have little choice but to eat whatever food the hospital supplies. A hospital purchasing agent has to decide on the quality of food to buy for patients. Because the food is provided as a part of a total service package, the buying objective is not profit. Nor is strict cost minimisation the goal – patients receiving poor-quality

Institutional markets can be huge and are often neglected by marketers. Prisons, hospitals and other institutions form a sizeable part of most markets

Source: Paco Ayala/123RF.com

food will complain to others and damage the hospital's reputation. Thus, the hospital purchasing agent must search for institutional food vendors whose quality meets or exceeds a certain minimum standard and whose prices are low.

Many marketers set up separate divisions to meet the special characteristics and needs of institutional buyers. For example, Nestlé Professional helps institutional foodservice customers find creative meal solutions using Nestlé's broad assortment of food and beverage brands. Similarly, P&G's Procter & Gamble Professional Division markets professional cleaning and laundry formulations and systems to educational, healthcare and other institutional and commercial customers.[12]

Government markets

The **government market** offers large opportunities for many companies, both big and small. In most countries, government organisations are major buyers of goods and services. Government buying and business buying are similar in many ways. But there are also differences that must be understood by companies that wish to sell goods and services to governments. To succeed in the government market, sellers must locate key decision makers, identify the factors that affect buyer behaviour, and understand the buying decision process.

Government organisations typically require suppliers to submit bids, and normally they award the contract to the lowest bidder. In some cases, a governmental unit will make allowances for the supplier's superior quality or reputation for completing contracts on time. Governments will also buy on a negotiated contract basis, primarily in the case of complex projects involving major R&D costs and risks, and in cases where there is little competition.

Government organisations tend to favour domestic suppliers over foreign suppliers. A major complaint of multinationals operating in Europe is that each country shows favouritism toward its nationals in spite of superior offers that are made by foreign firms. The European Economic Commission is gradually removing this bias.

Like consumer and business buyers, government buyers are affected by environmental, organisational, interpersonal and individual factors. One unique thing about government buying is that it is carefully watched by outside publics, ranging from Congress to a variety of private groups interested in how the government spends taxpayers' money. Because their spending decisions are subject to public review, government organisations require considerable documentation from suppliers, who often complain about excessive paperwork, bureaucracy, regulations, decision-making delays and frequent shifts in procurement personnel.

Given all the red tape, why would any firm want to do business with governments? The reasons are quite simple: governments are huge buyers of products and services – in Europe, Switzerland is the only country with total government expenditure below 34 per cent of GDP while Slovenia tops the European chart with around 59 per cent.[13] For example, it is forecast that the five big economies of Western Europe will spend around €46 billions on hardware, software and IT services – around half of which will occur at governmental levels.[14]

Non-economic criteria also play a growing role in government buying. Government buyers are asked to favour depressed business firms and areas; small business firms; minority-owned firms; and business firms that avoid race, gender or age discrimination. Sellers need to keep these factors in mind when seeking government business.

Many companies that sell to the government have not been very marketing oriented for a number of reasons. Total government spending is determined by elected officials rather than by any marketing effort to develop this market. Government buying has emphasised price, making suppliers invest their effort in technology to bring costs down. When the product's characteristics are specified carefully, product differentiation is not a marketing factor. Nor do advertising or personal selling matter much in winning bids on an open-bid basis.

Several companies, however, have established separate government marketing departments, including GE, Boeing, Xerox and Goodyear. Other companies sell primarily to government buyers, such as Lockheed Martin, which makes 82 per cent of its sales from governments, either as a prime contractor or a subcontractor. These companies anticipate government needs and projects,

Government market— Governmental units — federal, state and local — that purchase or rent goods and services for carrying out the main functions of government.

participate in the product specification phase, gather competitive intelligence, prepare bids carefully, and produce stronger communications to describe and enhance their companies' reputations.

Other companies have established customised marketing programmes for government buyers. For example, Dell has specific business units tailored to meet the needs of federal as well as state and local government buyers. Dell offers its customers tailor-made Premier web pages that include special pricing, online purchasing, and service and support for each city, state and federal government entity.

During the past decade, a great deal of the government's buying has gone online. For example, in the UK the Efficiency and Reform Group (a part of the Cabinet Office) has an online procurement portal. Across Europe, the European Union has established PEPPOL, the Pan-European Public Procurement OnLine project to establish OpenPEPPOL in September 2012. OpenPEPPOL is a non-profit-making international association that consists of private and public sector members. The aim of OpenPEPPOL is to generate a range of benefits, including: 'providing economic operators, in particular SMEs, with new business opportunities and increased competitiveness, while lowering costs with automated tendering solutions; saving contracting authorities significant administrative and transaction costs through standardised, speedy and streamlined procedures; and boosting the development and the capabilities of the ICT industry with increased demand for new, user-friendly IT services.'[15]

OBJECTIVES REVIEW AND KEY TERMS

Business markets and consumer markets are alike in some key ways. For example, both include people in buying roles who make purchase decisions to satisfy needs. But business markets also differ in many ways from consumer markets. For one thing, the business market is *huge*, far larger than the consumer market. Within the United States alone, the business market includes organisations that annually purchase trillions of dollars' worth of goods and services.

OBJECTIVE 1 Define the business market and explain how business markets differ from consumer markets (pp. 170–172)

The *business market* comprises all organisations that buy goods and services for use in the production of other products and services or for the purpose of reselling or renting them to others at a profit. As compared to consumer markets, business markets usually have fewer but larger buyers. Business demand is derived demand, which tends to be more inelastic and fluctuating than consumer demand. The business buying decision usually involves more, and more professional, buyers. Business buyers usually face more complex buying decisions, and the buying process tends to be more formalised. Finally, business buyers and sellers are often more dependent on each other

OBJECTIVE 2 Identify the major factors that influence business buyer behaviour (pp. 172–176)

Business buyers make decisions that vary with the three types of *buying situations*: straight rebuys, modified rebuys and new tasks.

The decision-making unit of a buying organisation – the *buying centre* – can consist of many different persons playing many different roles. The business marketer needs to know the following: Who are the major buying centre participants? In what decisions do they exercise influence and to what degree? What evaluation criteria does each decision participant use? The business marketer also needs to understand the major environmental, organisational, interpersonal and individual influences on the buying process.

OBJECTIVE 3 List and define the steps in the business buying decision process (pp. 176–180)

The *business buying decision process* itself can be quite involved, with eight basic stages: problem recognition, general need description, product specification, supplier search, proposal solicitation, supplier selection, order-routine specification and performance review. Buyers who face a new task buying situation usually go through all stages of the buying process. Buyers making modified or straight rebuys may skip some of the stages. Companies must manage the overall customer relationship, which often includes many different buying decisions in various stages of the buying decision process.

Advances in information technology have given birth to 'e-procurement', by which business buyers are purchasing all kinds of products and services online. The Internet gives business buyers access to new suppliers, lowers purchasing costs, and hastens order processing and delivery. However, e-procurement can also erode customer–supplier relationships. Still, business marketers are increasingly connecting with customers online to share marketing information, sell products and services, provide customer support services and maintain on-going customer relationships.

OBJECTIVE 4 **Compare the institutional and government markets and explain how institutional and government buyers make their buying decisions (pp. 180–182)**

The *institutional market* consists of schools, hospitals, prisons and other institutions that provide goods and services to people in their care. These markets are characterised by low budgets and captive patrons. The *government market*, which is vast, consists of government units – federal, state and local – that purchase or rent goods and services for carrying out the main functions of government.

Government buyers purchase products and services for defence, education, public welfare and other public needs. Government buying practices are highly specialised and specified, with open bidding or negotiated contracts characterising most of the buying. Government buyers operate under the watchful eye of local, national and regional governments and many private watchdog groups. Hence, they tend to require more forms and signatures and respond more slowly and deliberately when placing orders.

NAVIGATING THE KEY TERMS

OBJECTIVE 1
Business buyer behaviour (p. 170)
Business buying process (p. 170)
Derived demand (p. 171)
Supplier development (p. 172)

OBJECTIVE 2
Straight rebuy (p. 173)
Modified rebuy (p. 173)
New task (p. 173)
Systems selling (solutions selling) (p. 173)

Buying centre (p. 174)
Users (p. 174)
Influencers (p. 174)
Buyers (p. 174)
Deciders (p. 174)
Gatekeepers (p. 174)

OBJECTIVE 3
Problem recognition (p. 176)
General need description (p. 177)
Product specification (p. 177)

Supplier search (p. 177)
Proposal solicitation (p. 177)
Supplier selection (p. 178)
Order-routine specification (p. 178)
Performance review (p. 178)
E-procurement (p. 179)

OBJECTIVE 4
Institutional market (p. 180)
Government market (p. 181)

DISCUSSION AND CRITICAL THINKING

Discussion questions

6-1 Explain how the market structure and demand differ for business markets compared to consumer markets. (AACSB: Communication; Reflective thinking)

6-2 Explain what is meant by systems selling and discuss why it is a preferred approach to buying for many organisations. (AACSB: Communication; Reflective thinking)

6-3 Discuss the major influences on business buyers. (AACSB: Communication)

6-4 List the steps for a typical new task buying process. What is product value analysis and in which step of the buying process does it occur? (AACSB: Communication; Reflective thinking)

6-5 Compare the institutional and government markets and explain how institutional and government buyers make their buying decisions. (AACSB: Communication)

Critical-thinking exercises

6-6 *Kaizen. Seiri. Seiton. Seiso. Seiketsu. Shitsako. Jishuken.* These Japanese words are related to continuous quality improvement and are applied in supplier development programmes, particularly Toyota's. Research Toyota's Production System (TPS) and describe how these concepts are applied in supplier development. (AACSB: Communication; Multicultural and diversity)

6-7 Interview a business person to learn how purchases are made in his or her organisation. Ask this person to describe a straight rebuy a modified rebuy and a new task buying situation that took place recently or of which he or she is aware (define them if necessary). Did the buying process differ based on the type of product or purchase situation? Ask the business person to explain the role he or she played in a recent purchase and to discuss the factors that influenced the decision. Write a brief report of your interview by applying the concepts you learned in this chapter regarding business buyer behaviour. (AACSB: Communication; Reflective thinking)

Mini-cases and applications

Online, mobile and social media marketing: e-procurement and mobile procurement

Many businesses outsource certain functions to save costs. For example, your university may contract with another company to run its bookstore or for its food service. One teaching hospital outsourced its coding and billing service for just one department and saved millions on billing services. The hospital might not have saved that much if it hadn't used MedPricer's e-sourcing platform to find the right supplier at the right cost for the job. E-sourcing, or e-procurement, is changing the way buyers and sellers do business. However, e-sourcing and reverse e-auctions are old news. The new kid on the block is mobile procurement, which offers a cloud-based platform that reduces the search, order and approval cycle and offers analytics-on-the go. Most large companies have adopted some form of e-sourcing, and a recent study found that 30 per cent plan to adopt mobile procurement and supply chain function mobile applications within the next year.

6-8 Discuss the advantages of e-procurement to both buyers and sellers. What are the disadvantages? (AACSB: Communication; Reflective thinking)

6-9 Research mobile procurement and discuss the roles in the buying centre that are impacted most by this technology. (AACSB: Communication; Reflective thinking)

Marketing ethics: commercial bribery

You are the senior buyer for a growing medical products company and an avid football fan. You have just opened an invitation to attend the Champions League Final. The invitation is from a supplier company that has been trying to sell you its new line of products for the past year. The supplier will pay for everything — travel, room, meals –and you'll even get an opportunity to meet some of the players. You have read the newly released employee manual and there is no reference or rule that specifically states that an employee cannot accept a fully paid trip from a vendor, although there are some vague restrictions on lunches and dinners paid for by suppliers.

6-10 Do you accept or decline the invitation?

6-11 Just because it is not specifically mentioned in the employee manual, would you be acting ethically if you accepted?

6-12 Do you think the supplier will expect 'special' treatment in the next buying situation?

6-13 How would other company employees interpret your acceptance of this invitation?

Marketing by the numbers: salespeople

B-to-B marketing relies heavily on sales reps. Salespeople do more than just sell products and services; they manage relationships with customers to deliver value to both the customer and their companies. Thus, for many companies, sales reps visit customers several times per year, often for hours at a time. Sales managers must ensure that their companies have enough salespeople to adequately deliver value to customers.

6-14 Refer to Appendix 2: Marketing by the numbers to determine the number of salespeople a company needs if it has 3,000 customers who need to be called on ten times per year. Each sales call lasts approximately 2.5 hours, and each sales rep has approximately 1,250 hours per year to devote to customers. (AACSB: Communication; Analytical reasoning)

6-15 If each sales rep earns a salary of €60,000 per year, what sales are necessary to break even on the sales force costs if the company has a contribution margin of 40 per cent? What effect will adding each additional sales representative have on the break-even sales? (AACSB: Communication; Analytical reasoning)

REFERENCES

[1] Based on information from http://thenewlogistics.ups.com/swf#/stories?page_1, accessed March 2014; www.thenewlogistics.com and www.pressroom.ups.com/Fact+Sheets/UPS+Fact+Sheet and www.pressroom.ups.com/Fact+Sheets/UPS+Europe+Region+Fact+Sheet, accessed October 2015.

[2] Based on information from Jessica Hansen, 'Intel opens pop-up retail stores featuring the latest Intel-based devices for the holidays', 22 November 2013, http://newsroom.intel.com/community/intel_newsroom/blog/2013/11/22/intel-opens-pop-up-retail-stores-featuring-the-latest-intel-based-devices-for-the-holidays; Beth Snyder Bulik, 'What's inside Intel/Toshiba's "Beauty Inside"', *Advertising Age*, 12 November 2013, http://adage.com/print/245136/; and www.youtube.com/watch?v=RMrcAQeDHbI, accessed October 2015.

[3] See Theresa Ooi, 'Amazing key to IKEA success', *Australian*, 22 September 2008; Kerry Capell, 'How the Swedish retailer became a global cult brand', *BusinessWeek*, 14 November 2005, p. 103; IKEA, *Hoover's Company Records*, 1 April 2010, p. 42925; and information from www.ikea.com, accessed October 2015.

[4] This classic categorisation was first introduced in Patrick J. Robinson, Charles W. Faris, and Yoram Wind, *Industrial Buying Behaviour and Creative Marketing* (Boston: Allyn & Bacon, 1967). Also see Philip Kotler and Kevin Lane Keller, *Marketing Management*, 14th ed. (Upper Saddle River, NJ: Prentice Hall, 2012), Chapter 7.

[5] Based on information from 'UPS supply chain solutions group provides fourth-party logistics support for Alcatel eND's supply chain', www.ups-scs.com/solutions/case_studies/cs_alcatel.pdf, accessed October 2015.

[6] See Frederick E. Webster Jr. and Yoram Wind, *Organizational Buying Behaviour* (Upper Saddle River, NJ: Prentice Hall, 1972), pp. 78–80. Also see Jorg Brinkman and Markus Voeth, 'An analysis of buying center decisions through the sales force', *Industrial Marketing Management*, October 2007, p. 998; and Philip Kotler and Kevin Lane Keller, *Marketing Management*, 14th ed. (Upper Saddle River, NJ: Prentice Hall, 2012), pp. 188–191.

[7] Based on information from 'USG print campaign', *Communications Arts*, 6 June 2012, www.commarts.com/exhibit/usg-corporation-print.html; 'BtoB's best-integrated campaign: USG Corp.', 8 October 2012, www.btobonline.com/article/20121008/ADVERTISING02/310089984/btobs-best-integrated-campaign-less-than-200–000-usg-corp; Kate Maddox, 'BtoB's best marketers', *BtoB*, 15 October 2013, www.

btobonline.com/article/20131015/PEOPLE0303/310149942/btobs-best-marketers-linda-mcgovern-usg-corp; and www.usg.com/company/about-usg.html and www.theweighthasbeenlifted.com, accessed October 2015.

[8] Patrick J. Robinson, Charles W. Faris, and Yoram Wind, *Industrial Buying Behaviour and Creative Marketing* (Boston: Allyn & Bacon, 1967) p. 14; Also see Philip Kotler and Kevin Lane Keller, *Marketing Management*, 14th ed. (Upper Saddle River, NJ: Prentice Hall, 2012) pp. 197–203.

[9] For more ads in this series, see www.accenture.com/us-en/company/overview/advertising/Pages/brand-print-advertising.aspx, accessed October 2015.

[10] For this and other examples, see '10 great web sites', *BtoB Online*, 15 September 2008; and '10 great websites', *BtoB Online*, 14 September 2009, both accessed at www.btobonline.com; other information from www.cisco.com/cisco/web/solutions/small_business/index.html, accessed October 2011.

[11] See www.prisonstudies.org, accessed October 2015.

[12] See www.nestleprofessional.com/united-states/en/Pages/home.aspx and www.pgpro.com, accessed October 2015.

[13] See www.epp.eurostat.ec..europe.eu, accessed October 2015.

[14] See 'U.K. continues to be the biggest public sector IT spender, according to IDC Government Insights Report', 15 September 2014, www.idc.com/getdoc.jsp?containerId=prUK25136214, accessed October 2015.

[15] See www.peppol.eu/, accessed October 2015.

COMPANY CASE

Industrial Internet at General Electric: why B-to-B doesn't stand for 'boring-to-boring' by Andrew Pressey, Birmingham Business School

For some time, B-to-B marketing has been stereotyped as staid, dull and lacking creativity, in comparison to B-to-C marketing for brands such as Apple, Coca-Cola and Zara. B-to-B marketing was thought to occupy the least imaginative point on the creative marketing spectrum. The new 'big data' concept – the Industrial Internet – promoted by General Electric, however, illustrates that this is far from reality, and stands to revolutionise both B-to-B markets and marketing.

Incorporated in 1892 in New York, The General Electric Company (GE) was the result of a merger between Edison General Electric and the Thomson-Houston Company, and has a large and diffuse product history, spanning jet engines, turbines,

locomotives, electricity transmission systems and distribution motors, and medical imaging equipment (www.ge.com). GE was an early proponent of industrial R&D laboratories, industrial parks, and was at the vanguard of management concepts such as decentralisation in the 1950s and strategic planning in the 1970s. Indeed, GE's influence 'extends well beyond its products. As one of the titans of American capitalism in the twentieth century, it has been respected by its peers and envied for its success, and has greatly influenced how governments and other corporations conduct their affairs'. It also played an influential role in the corporate advancement of the marketing concept. In their *Journal of Marketing* paper, Barksdale and Darden advance the argument that: 'the General Electric Company is usually acknowledged as the first firm to systematically structure its operations in accordance with the precepts of the marketing philosophy'.

In 2012 GE published the *Industrial Internet: Pushing the Boundaries of Minds and Machines*, which set out a bold agenda for the future of its business: 'The world is on the threshold of a new era of innovation and change with the rise of the Industrial Internet. It is taking place through the convergence of the global industrial system with the power of advanced computing, analytics, low-cost sensing and new levels of connectivity permitted by the Internet.'

The R&D division of GE coined the term 'Industrial Internet', where sensors are added to the multitude of networked machinery and equipment that GE produces in order to collect an abundance of data that will allow the manufacturer to improve the efficiency of GE's products by connecting its machinery to the digital world. The notion of adding sensors to equipment to communicate and collate data is not a new concept (it's often referred to as the 'Internet of Things'); however, the scale with which GE aims to operationalise the concept is far greater than previous attempts.

The Internet of Things, advanced in 1999 by Kevin Ashton, refers to the capability to capture identifiable physical objects as virtual symbols on digital platforms. Early applications included radio-frequency identification (RFID), which allowed for the tracking of objects in real-time. Adding sensors to people and objects allows for computers to capture huge amounts of data. GE is responding to the era of 'big data' by using data to increase the productivity of the machinery and equipment of its industrial clients.

'Things that spin' – the Industrial Internet and General Electric

GE created the fictional world of 'Datalandia' to help illustrate and promote the Industrial Internet and produced a series of short films, where 'sexy' vampires rub shoulders with 'menacing' aliens and werewolves. Digital marketers at GE created the series of films in Hamburg on the world's largest miniature trainset. In Datalandia – 'the small town saved by big data' – the films profile the potential benefits of the Industrial Internet where trains communicate with the Internet, jet engines transfer information to maintenance crews, ambulances communicate with personnel at hospitals, and wind turbines share data in real-time.

GE's has invested an estimated $1.5 billion on the project, and its potential big data revolution is centred on a new facility located in San Ramon, California, where the company is developing new software which has the potential to transform a number of industries. By adding a multitude of sensors to the machinery it produces, GE can measure equipment efficiency. For example, sensors added to GE's 20,000 jet engines currently operating can transmit real-time data to maintenance crews indicating which engines will need maintenance in advance of current checks, thus helping to avoid expensive delays. While data is currently collected on operational jet engines, this new approach would produce algorithms that would collate huge amounts of data and would potentially track readings in real-time from each flight

for study. GE estimates that it could record more data in a year than the company has collated previously in its entire aviation history; efficiency improvements by just one per cent in fuel efficiency could generate $2 billion in savings a year for the global airline industry. Such advances are not restricted to aviation, however; GE anticipates that the same techniques can be applied to its healthcare equipment by adding sensors to hospital beds in order to track which are in use and which are unoccupied, helping system efficiency and allowing medical facilities to treat more patients.

In essence, anything that 'spins' can produce data that can be used to improve equipment efficiency, starting 'with embedding sensors and other advanced instrumentation in an array of machines from the simple to the highly complex', that via machine-to-machine communication can yield data for real-time analysis and adjustment. It is estimated that in excess of 3 million major pieces of industrial equipment – or 'things that spin' – exist around the world which could be connected to digital platforms, allowing vast amounts of data capture. The Industrial Internet is underpinned by three key elements:

i. *Intelligent machines*. Finding new ways to connect the world's machines and equipment of all types to sensors that can record and analyse data such as performance results.
ii. *Advanced analytics*. Drawing on advances in predictive algorithms and other advanced analytical techniques to understand how very large systems and machines operate and perform.
iii. *Personnel*. Reporting real-time data updates to people wherever they are physically located in the world, enabling them to provide solutions to maintain and improve systems and operations, as well increasing service quality and safety.

By connecting these elements, the Industrial Internet data loop can help companies and organisations to seamlessly transfer data in real-time, in order to offer preventative solutions (such as providing the maintenance of equipment when needed rather than providing periodic maintenance that may be unnecessary), and reduce unplanned equipment downtime (e.g. power outages). For example, this could include oil rigs, jet engines and bridges that can alert their human operatives of impending failure or maintenance needs, or sensors on shipments of fruit and vegetables that can detect the freshness of the produce in transit and that can report any spoilage prior to delivery.

The power of one per cent

GE estimates that small improvements in efficiency could produce dramatic productivity gains. Collecting data that enables a one per cent improvement in efficiency could yield considerable savings to a variety of industries. For example, one per cent in fuel savings for gas-fired generators could produce $66 billion in savings over a 15-year period, a one per cent reduction in worldwide healthcare system inefficiencies could save $63 billion over a similar period, and a one per cent reduction in the cost of oil and gas exploration could result in savings of $90 billion by 2030. Similar savings could also be realised for a variety of industries such as rail freight and global energy production. By adding tagging devices (including QR codes and bar codes) networked computers can record vast amounts of data that stands to transform business, for example, by tracking inventories of goods for retailers that can be kept in real-time thus ensuring that stocks are not depleted.

One example of the potential benefits of Industrial Internet is in the aviation industry. Ten per cent of all flight cancellations and delays are due to unscheduled maintenance, which results in $8 billion in costs incurred every year. It is estimated that some 20,000 commercial aircraft are operational with 43,000 jet engines in operation; each jet engine has three key pieces of rotating equipment that can be connected to digital platforms for more accurate monitoring. 'Intelligent aircraft' can then transfer data to operators in real-time while in flight related to key operational issues such as fuel consumption and engine performance, which can then be factored into decisions around improved scheduling, allocation of aircraft crew, as well as fuel depletion and engine maintenance, all of which can help reduce unscheduled maintenance and costly delays. Comparative opportunities exist in almost all industries, spanning power plants, locomotives and industrial facilities.

Other companies are implementing similar 'data driven' applications. For example, the Google driverless car gathers real-time data from a roof-mounted machine to control the car's acceleration, braking and steering to avoid obstacles, while The Union Pacific Railroad uses sensors to scan passing trains and transmit information to its data centres where software can detect equipment in danger of failing.

What factors are driving these changes? Initially, the power of the Industrial Internet is being driven by a worldwide fall in prices for networked sensors (as well as their miniaturisation) and computing power, and advances in cloud-based computing and communications. The benefits of the Industrial Internet, however, can only be realised if certain driving forces are in place including the integration of sensors to the design of new industrial equipment, retrofitting existing industrial machinery with sensors, faster means of transmitting information (e.g. sufficient broadband spectrum), improved analytical capabilities to analyse large datasets and the development of talented personnel with appropriate technical, analytical and leadership skills.

The Industrial Internet and B-to-B marketing

The swiftness of networked computers has been dramatic; in 1981 there were fewer than 300 computers connected to the Internet, by the mid-1990s this had increased to almost 20 million, and numbers in the billions today. In some respects the Industrial Internet is analogous to the commercialisation of the Internet itself in the early 1990s by B-to-B firms. Many of the earliest corporate websites and e-marketplaces were B-to-B sites selling chemicals and metals, which were at the vanguard of web usage at a time when many consumer goods firms were attempting to understand how this new channel could be utilised. In the same way, B-to-B companies must learn how they might benefit from the Industrial Internet. By 2020, Forrester Research estimates that B-to-B e-commerce will reach $1.3 trillion in worldwide sales, considerably larger than e-commerce in B-to-C markets. Therefore, the usage of the Internet and e-commerce by B2B firms affords new opportunities via online platforms and networked computers. The Industrial Internet will also likely create new markets and business models that call for compelling new forms of marketing. Overall the potential impact of the Industrial Internet on B-to-B markets and marketing stands to be significant.

Business buyers base buying decisions on benefits rather than features. For the Industrial Internet this could include, for example, products that improve standards to the aviation industry which could also benefit consumers in B-to-C markets, such as fewer flight delays and maintaining low-cost air travel. In this way, B-to-B solutions can also help business customers create added value for their final customers. In addition, B-to-B marketers at GE need to communicate the benefits of the Industrial Internet to specific industries that may face challenges unique to that industry. Organisational buyers in the locomotive freight industry, for example, will differ in their specific needs to business buyers in aviation, power plants and automotive sectors.

GE's notion of the Industrial Internet also provides its customers with a packaged solution to a problem they may face (chiefly equipment and machinery efficiency). Such systems selling (or solutions selling), benefits companies by being able to purchase a total solution to a problem from a single provider, helping to avoid separate buying decisions that may create a complex buying situation. GE is able to provide a solution that helps its clients improve safety, quality, reliability, efficiency, and save costs, through increased data capture and analysis. The challenge to B-to-B marketers at GE is being able to communicate the benefits of the Industrial Internet to its stakeholders. Further, as B-to-B marketers have to appeal to a variety of individuals in the buying centres of its customers (such as influencers, gatekeepers and deciders), with a variety of concerns and needs unique to their roles, this task is made more complex. The potential gains for GE, however, are significant, and could change the way they do business during well into the next century of their existence.

Questions for discussion

1. What are the specific benefits of the Industrial Internet for each member of the buying centre? What is the key message that needs to be communicated to each member?

2. Business buyers focus on benefits (e.g. cost savings through equipment efficiency) rather than features (e.g. the colour of a piece of equipment). What are the potential benefits of the Industrial Internet for business buyers?

3. B-to-B marketers at GE used the creative concept of Datalandia to promote the potential benefits of the Industrial Internet. What approach to marketing the Industrial Internet would you take to a variety of B-to-B stakeholders such as customers, the business media and government accounts?

4. How can the Industrial Internet potentially benefit B-to-C markets and customers? What impact might it have and in what ways?

Sources: This case study draws extensively on Peter C. Evans and Marco Annunziata, 'Industrial Internet: pushing the boundaries of minds and machines', GE white paper, www.ge.com/docs/chapters/Industrial_Internet.pdf, accessed September 2015; Kevin Ashton, 'That 'Internet of Things' thing, in the real world things matter more than ideas', *RFID Journal*, 22 June 2009, www.rfidjournal.com/articles/view?4986, accessed September 2015; Hiram C. Barksdale and Bill Darden, 'Marketers' attitudes toward the marketing concept', *The Journal of Marketing*, 1971, 35, pp.29-36; Jessica Leber, 'General Electric pitches an Industrial Internet, *MIT Technology Review*, 28 November 2012, www.technologyreview.com/news/507831/general-electric-pitches-an-industrial-internet/, accessed September 2015; Steve Lohr 'The Internet gets physical', *The New York Times*, 17 December 2011; Chris Murphy, 'Union Pacific delivers Internet of Things reality check', 3 August 2012, informationweek.com, accessed September 2015; Bob Murphy, '4 ways to prep for the B-to-B e-commerce boom', *American Marketing Association B2B Marketing e-newsletter*, August 2015; Thomas F. O'Boyle, *At Any Cost: Jack Welch, General Electric, and the Pursuit of Profit*, Vintage: New York: 1999; Johnny Ryan, *A History of the Internet and the Digital Future*, Reaktion Books: London: 2010.

PART THREE

Designing a customer value-driven strategy and mix

CHAPTER SEVEN

Customer-driven marketing strategy: creating value for target customers

Chapter preview

So far, you have learned what marketing is and about and the importance of understanding consumers and the marketplace environment. With that as background, you're now ready to delve deeper into marketing strategy and tactics. This chapter looks further into key customer-driven marketing strategy decisions – dividing up markets into meaningful customer groups (*segmentation*), choosing which customer groups to serve (*targeting*), creating market offerings that best serve targeted customers (*differentiation*), and locating the offerings in the minds of consumers (*positioning*). The chapters that follow explore the tactical marketing tools – the four Ps – by which marketers bring these strategies to life.

To start our discussion of the ins and outs of segmentation, targeting, differentiation and positioning, Volkswagen, the leading European car maker, is an interesting illustration of the strength of actively marketing to clearly defined target markets and developing brands around those targets. Volkswagen became the world's leading car manufacturer by the strength and clever positioning of each of its portfolio of brands but now faces major challenges.

Objective outline

➤ **Objective 1** Define the major steps in designing a customer-driven marketing strategy: market segmentation, targeting, differentiation and positioning. Customer-driven marketing strategy (p. 194)

➤ **Objective 2** List and discuss the major bases for segmenting consumer and business markets. Market segmentation (pp. 194–203)

➤ **Objective 3** Explain how companies identify attractive market segments and choose a market-targeting strategy. Market targeting (pp. 203–208)

➤ **Objective 4** Discuss how companies differentiate and position their products for maximum competitive advantage. Differentiation and positioning (pp. 209–215)

Multi-branding at Volkswagen: becoming number one

For several years now, Volkswagen (VW) has been vying with Toyota for the title of the world's largest car maker by volume, both having left the traditional US motor industry giants General Motors and Ford behind some time ago. The answer to which of VW and Toyota is the larger comes down to how you count vehicles produced in joint ventures in China. If you include joint ventures in 2014 – then VW was the world leader and had been for several years. VW's car production reached 10.14 million vehicles in 2014 – up 5 per cent on the previous year – and it held around 14 per cent of the world passenger car market and 25 per cent of the European market. Sales in 2014 were valued at €212 billion.

Indeed, VW has three cars in the top ten list of best-selling cars of all time – the Volkswagen Golf, the Volkswagen Beetle and the Volkswagen Passat – with these three cars, VW has the most cars still being manufactured of any car maker on the list. VW operates 118 production plants in 20 European countries as well as a further eight countries in the Americas, Asia and Africa, and has almost 600,000 employees worldwide. VW sells vehicles in 153 countries.

Multi-branding strategy

The most distinctive aspect of the marketing strategy followed by VW has been its multi-branding. While competitors like BMW, Mercedes and Fiat have essentially one brand, to cover all their vehicles, VW has developed a stable of car brands, each aimed at a different part of the market, even though in some cases VW brands compete directly with each other for the same customers.

VW pioneered what has been called 'proactive cannibalisation' – becoming stronger by allowing different parts of your own portfolio to compete with each other. The logic is that by competing with your-self – you still win if you keep the customer within the group. Someone is going to compete with you for that customer – so why not do it yourself?

VW's multi-brand strategy started to cut the ice in the late 1990s when VW displaced Renault and Fiat to become the market leader in Western Europe. The four main mass-market brands – VW, Audi, Seat and Skoda – offered vehicles which in many cases shared the same engineering platform. VW had cut its platforms down to four at this time. So, for example, a single engineering design platform was shared by the VW Golf, the Audi A3, the Audi TT Roadster, the VW Jetta, the New VW Beetle, the Seat Toledo and the Skoda Octavia. The economy and design robustness of this move was massive, but the strategy relies on customers trading up and down and switching brands, but remaining within the VW Group. So, while the Skoda Octavia offers VW engineering and design at a lower price – customers trading down remain as VW Group customers.

The current brand portfolio consists of 12 brands from seven European countries covering mass-market brands, prestige brands and commercial brands. The goal is that each brand has a distinct and individual image and market positioning, each operates largely as an autonomous business, and each has its own marketing programmes – though VW does nothing to disguise its association with each brand.

VW mass market brands

- **VW – *Das Auto***. Three core brand attributes: innovative, enduring value, responsible. The largest selling of the mass market brands.
- **Audi – *Vorsprung durch Technik***. Aimed at the premium segment of the market with a brand

VW has three cars in the top ten list of best-selling cars of all time.

Source: Volkswagen Group

relying on its high-quality, sporty and progressive image. A brand strategy of innovative engineering solutions and emotional design language. A premium brand and a cash cow for the group – taking on BMW and Mercedes-Benz.

- **Seat – *Enjoyneering***. A Spanish brand with strong design appeal. The brand is focused on being dynamic, young and design-oriented. The brand claims 'Enjoyneering' to capture the character of the brand as a passionate perfectionist and emotional technology leader. Reputed to be loss-making and something of a problem-child.
- **Skoda – *Simply clever***. The brand proposition is dominated by a compelling value proposition (competitive prices) and attractive design which emphasises intelligent use of space and refined practical details for the family market. Skoda is the main focus for low-cost cars, responding for example to Renault's Dacia. In 2015, Skoda passed the million car sales point for the first time.

VW luxury brands

In the prestige or luxury car business, VW has Bentley, Bugati and Lamborghini. While varying in their degree of exclusivity and price level, these three brands are linked by elegance, exclusivity and power. Bentley is a UK marque and is expanding into 4×4s under the leadership of the man who produced the Porsche Cayenne. Bugati has tiny volumes (40–50 cars a year, at incredibly high prices) but provides an engineering test-bed for cutting edge technologies within VW. Lamborghini competes with Ferrari though it sells fewer cars than its Italian rival.

The Porsche sports car brand is now also part of VW's prestige brand portfolio. Porsche brand values are well-established across the world and focus on the one hand on exclusivity, tradition, performance and design, but balanced with acceptance, innovation, suitability for daily use and functionality, linked by the motto to achieve maximum output from minimum input. VW and Porsche have long cooperated in products like 4×4s.

Ducati motorcycles also fits in this part of the VW brand portfolio, providing premium motorcycles with Italian style and high levels of quality, craftsmanship and performance.

VW commercial vehicle brands

In additional to passenger vehicles, VW also has commercial vehicle brands emphasising reliability, economy and partnership. The main brands are Volkswagen Commercial Vehicles, Scania and MAN, all providing commercial vehicles of many kinds.

Clearly, there is competition between brands – particularly in the case of the mass market brands. Critics claim that Skoda offers VW technology at a lower price than VW and Audi, yet while Skoda is doing very well, so are VW and Audi, even if some customers trade down it seems others trade up. Others have sneered at some Porsche models as 'glorified VWs' because of the shared technology – yet this does not seem to have damaged the Porsche brand which remains extremely robust in the sports car market. It seems that for VW competing with yourself has worked.

Some problems for VW. . .

Established in Germany in 1937, it has not been all plain sailing for VW over the years. Indeed, in the 1970s, VW was in serious trouble with failing sales in Europe and the 1980s saw dramatic falls in sales to the US and Canada, when VW was faced with stiff competition from Japanese manufacturers equalling VW quality but at much lower prices. However, the 2000s saw an array of new VW models in response to tougher competition.

There has been some management turbulence with key managers leaving the business – most recently the resignation of Ferdinand Piech in 2015, the man who led the expansion of VW between 1993 and 2002, and then headed the supervisory board. He had close control over the group because the Piech and Porsche families, through ownership of the Porsche Group, also controlled a majority stake in VW. In 2015, Piech withdrew his support for current VW CEO Martin Winterkorn, his former protégé, over fundamental disagreements about the business: the relatively low profitability of the core VW brand, the failure to gain traction in the US market, and slow progress in launching a low-cost brand for developing markets. The problem of tension between controlling family interests and management remains a concern. VW has complicated relations with both unions and shareholders — for example, the German state of Lower Saxony holds 20 per cent of the stock.

In September 2015, Mr Winterkorn resigned as a result of the diesel emissions scandal (VW had fitted millions of diesel engines with software designed to cheat emissions tests). He was replaced by Matthias Müller, Head of Porsche. The spread of the global crisis looked likely to cost VW as much as £26 billion, as regulators claimed some 11 million VW vehicles were affected.

And there are other worries about the future for VW. The European car market remains difficult, the slowing growth in China, and the challenges of managing a large portfolio of brands are all challenges for the company. VW remains relatively weak in the giant US market — while it captures around 25 per cent of the Western Europe market, it has only around 3 per cent of the US market. Also, with a large part of its manufacturing in expensive European countries, VW succeeds only as long as customers are prepared to pay a premium for exceptionally well-built, mass-market cars. VW may be vulnerable to low-cost competition from outside Europe.

Currently VW remains estranged and in dispute with Suzuki — its chosen partner for India and in sharing technology on electric cars and diesel engine research.

Some worry too that the multi-brand strategy may be a weak position in the new global car business facing the impact of: electrification, car-sharing, a focus on connectivity, the digitisation of retail and customer relationships, and the prospect of non-traditional competitors like Tesla, Google and Apple. Plus VW is battling GM for supremacy in China. Maybe 12 brands is too many when the challenge is repositioning to meet the new competitive challenges? Certainly, managerial overstretch from too many brands caught out both GM and Toyota on their ascent to the top.

Overall, VW is under pressure in the US market where it has lost ground because it lacks a variety of 4×4 vehicles, while the slowdown in China, which accounts for more than a third of unit sales, is hitting growth. Efficiency is also an issue — VW and Toyota produce a similar amount of vehicles but the Japanese car maker employs about 40 per cent fewer people.

Consequently, margins are also an issue. In terms of operating profit as a percentage of sales, Toyota achieves 10.1 per cent. Within the VW Group, performance is mixed: Porsche (15.6 per cent), Audi (9.8 per cent), Scania (9.7 per cent), Skoda (8.1 per cent), Bentley (5.8 per cent), VW Commercial Vehicles (5.1 per cent), Man (2.8 per cent), VW (2.7 per cent) and Seat (1.2 per cent). Lifting return on sales is a priority.

VW strengths for the future

But there are also some important underlying advantages for VW.

With its mass market brands — VW, Audi, Skoda and Seat — although the brands operate separately, they share an engineering platform. The shared engineering base allows economy and the costs of innovation to be spread across the brands. VW is probably the motor industry's most skilled practitioner of platform sharing across its brands, which gives a major advantage over competitors in cost by virtue of its economies of scale. It will be interesting to see how the multi-brand strategy survives the 2015 diesel emissions scandal — will the effects be restricted to the VW brand or spread across the whole portfolio?

One major VW strength in Europe has been its lower borrowing costs, which allow it to offer consumers less expensive loans and build market share in this way. In a tough European car market which has shrunk in size, this competitive edge is important. While General Motor's Opel has been affected, Fiat and Peugeot Citroen have been particularly hard hit by VW's cheap loans, reflecting Germany's economic strength compared to its European neighbours. In 2012, it looked like this aggressive financing had been pivotal in increasing VW's market share in Western Europe from 20 per cent to 25 per cent. Financing customers at low rates reduces the need for price discounts and helps keep profit margins and resale values intact.

In the tough times of economic recession a couple of years ago, VW was able to weather the storm better than most of its European rivals through the development of modular assembly systems and escalating robot-based assembly in its plants.

But as always, the question for car makers is how well they can adapt to new types of competition and new customer needs and preferences.[1]

Figure 7.1 Designing a customer-driven marketing strategy

In concept, marketing boils down to two questions: (1) Which customers will we serve? and (2) How will we serve them? Of course, the tough part is coming up with good answers to these simple sounding yet difficult questions. The goal is to create more value for the customers we serve than competitors do.

Market segmentation— Dividing a market into smaller groups of buyers with distinct needs, characteristics or behaviours that might require separate marketing strategies or mixes.

Market targeting (targeting) – Evaluating each market segment's attractiveness and selecting one or more segments to enter.

Differentiation— Differentiating the market offering to create superior customer value.

Positioning—Arranging for a market offering to occupy a clear, distinctive and desirable place relative to competing products in the minds of consumers.

Companies today recognise that they cannot appeal to all buyers in the marketplace – or at least not to all buyers in the same way. Buyers are too numerous, widely scattered and varied in their needs and buying practices. Moreover, the companies themselves vary widely in their abilities to serve different segments of the market. Instead, like VW, a company must identify the parts of the market that it can serve best and most profitably. It must design customer-driven marketing strategies that build the right relationships with the right customers.

Thus, most companies have moved away from mass marketing and toward *target marketing*: identifying market segments, selecting one or more of them, and developing products and marketing programmes tailored to each. Instead of scattering their marketing efforts (the 'shotgun' approach), firms are focusing on the buyers who have greater interest in the values they create best (the 'rifle' approach).

Figure 7.1 shows the four major steps in designing a customer-driven marketing strategy. In the first two steps, the company selects the customers that it will serve. **Market segmentation** involves dividing a market into smaller groups of buyers with distinct needs, characteristics or behaviours that might require separate marketing strategies or mixes. The company identifies different ways to segment the market and develops profiles of the resulting market segments. **Market targeting** (or **targeting**) consists of evaluating each market segment's attractiveness and selecting one or more market segments to enter.

In the final two steps, the company decides on a value proposition – how it will create value for target customers. **Differentiation** involves establishing differences in a firm's market offering to create superior customer value. **Positioning** consists of arranging for a market offering to occupy a clear, distinctive and desirable place relative to competing products in the minds of target consumers. We discuss each of these steps in turn.

MARKET SEGMENTATION

Author comment

Market segmentation addresses the first simple-sounding marketing question: what customers will we serve? The answer will be different for each company. For example, the luxury hotels target the top spenders among of corporate and leisure travellers. Budget hotels target those who want to spend less because they travel for different reasons.

Buyers in any market differ in their wants, resources, locations, buying attitudes and buying practices. Through market segmentation, companies divide large, heterogeneous markets into smaller groups that can be reached more efficiently and effectively with products and services that match their unique needs. In this section, we discuss four important segmentation topics: segmenting consumer markets, segmenting business markets, segmenting international markets and the requirements for effective segmentation.

Segmenting consumer markets

There is no single way to segment a market. A marketer has to try different segmentation variables, alone and in combination, to find the best way to view market structure. Table 7.1 outlines the major variables that might be used in segmenting consumer markets. Here we look at the major *geographic*, *demographic*, *psychographic* and *behavioural* variables.

Table 7.1 Major segmentation variables for consumer markets

Segmentation Variable	Examples
Geographic	Countries, regions, cities, neighbourhoods, population density (urban, suburban, rural), climate
Demographic	Age, life-cycle stage, gender, income, occupation, education, religion, ethnicity, generation
Psychographic	Social class, lifestyle, personality
Behavioural	Occasions, benefits, user status, usage rate, loyalty status

Geographic segmentation

Geographic segmentation calls for dividing the market into different geographical units, such as countries, regions, cities or even specific neighbourhoods. A company may decide to operate in one or a few geographical areas or operate in all areas but pay attention to geographical differences in needs and wants.

Many companies today are localising their products, advertising, promotion and sales efforts to fit the needs of individual regions, cities and even neighbourhoods. For example, supermarket Tesco in the UK uses the information from its Clubcard loyalty programme to examine 40 different characteristics of every item in the shopper's basket, to develop an understanding of the customer's 'DNA' and to cluster customers into different types – 'upmarket', 'price sensitive', 'green' and so on. One gain from this wealth of data and insight is the ability to create stores which reflect local demographics and purchasing patterns with great precision. It is no coincidence that Tesco stores near big universities often have large displays featuring beer and frozen pizzas, while those in residential areas place more emphasis on cooking ingredients, fresh fruit and baby products. Tesco small format Metro stores focus on the needs of time-pressed commuters and similar groups, depending on location.

Similarly, one of Marriott International's lifestyle hotel brands, Renaissance Hotels, has rolled out its Navigator programme, which hyper-localises guest experiences at each of its 155 lifestyle hotels around the world:[2]

> Renaissance Hotels' Navigator programme puts a personal and local face on each location by 'micro-localising' recommendations for guests' food, shopping, entertainment and cultural experiences at each destination. The programme is anchored by on-site Renaissance Hotels 'Navigators' at each location. Whether it's James Elliott at the St. Pancras Renaissance London Hotel, a history buff and local pub expert, or Omar Bennett, a restaurant-loving Brooklynite at the Renaissance New York Times Square Hotel, Navigators are extensively trained locals who are deeply passionate about the destination and often have a personal connection to the locale. Based on their own personal experiences and ongoing research, they work with guests personally to help them experience 'the hidden gems throughout the neighbourhood of each hotel through the eyes of those who know it best'.
>
> Since introducing the hyper-localised Navigator programme as part of Renaissance Hotels' 'Live life to discover' campaign two years ago, the hotel's website traffic has grown more than 80 per cent, Facebook 'Likes' have exploded from 40,000 to more than 915,000, and Twitter followers have surged from 5,000 to 61,000.

Geographic segmentation— Dividing a market into different geographical units, such as countries, regions, cities or even specific neighbourhoods.

Geographic segmentation: Renaissance Hotels' 'Navigators' and 'Live Life to Discover' programmes help guests to experience the locality of each hotel, seen through the eyes of those who know it best.
Source: Roberto Machado Noa/ LightRocket via Getty Images

Demographic segmentation

Demographic segmentation divides the market into segments based on age group, gender, family size, family life cycle, income, occupation, education, religion, ethnicity, generation and nationality. Demographic factors are the most popular bases for segmenting customer groups. One reason is that consumer needs, wants and usage rates often vary closely with demographic variables. Another is that demographic variables are easier to measure than most other types of variables. Even when marketers first define segments using other bases, such as benefits sought from the product or customer behaviour, they must know a segment's demographic characteristics to assess the size of the target market and reach it efficiently.

Age and life-cycle stage

Consumer needs and wants change with age. Some companies use **age and life-cycle segmentation**, offering different products or using different marketing approaches for different age and life-cycle groups.

Some companies focus on the specific age of life-stage groups. Saga in the UK provides a wide range of products and services, including insurance, homecare, holidays and a magazine, exclusively for the over 50s. Other companies offer brands in their broader portfolios that target specific age or life-stage groups. For example, whereas most tablet makers have been busy marketing their devices to adults, Amazon has spotted a smaller tablet market. Feedback from parents suggested that they were handing their entertainment-packed Kindle Fire tablets over to their young children for entertainment, education and babysitting purposes. To tap this young-family market, Amazon introduced FreeTime Unlimited, a multimedia subscription service targeted toward three- to eight-year-olds. Complete with parental controls, the service provides access to a treasure trove of child-rated movies, games and books, including premium content from Nickelodeon, Disney, Sesame Street and DC Comics. Not only does FreeTime Unlimited generate revenues for Amazon, it helps sell more Kindle Fire tablets to young families.[3]

But marketers must be careful to guard against stereotypes when using age and life-cycle segmentation. Although some 80-year-olds fit the 'doddery', low-income stereotypes, others play tennis, ski and run marathons. Similarly, whereas some 40-year-old couples are sending their children off to university with a huge sigh of relief at getting their lives back, others are just beginning new families. Indeed, in the UK over-65s lead the rise in cohabitation outside marriage.[4]

For example, Saga has started offering motorbike insurance for the over-50s, who represent a third of all motorbike expenditure in the UK. It is also noteworthy that there is a trend for showing mature women in campaigns for jewellery and fashion – they are older, wiser and more affluent.[5]

Thus, age is often a poor predictor of a person's life cycle, health, work or family status, needs and buying power.

Gender

Gender segmentation has long been used in marketing clothing, cosmetics, toiletries and magazines. For example, in the United States, P&G was among the first with Secret deodorants and antiperspirants, a brand specially formulated for a woman's chemistry, packaged and advertised to reinforce the female image.

Nonetheless, more recently, the men's personal care industry has exploded and many cosmetics brands that previously catered mostly to women – from L'Oréal, Nivea and Sephora to Unilever's Dove brand – now successfully market men's lines. For example, L'Oréal's Men Expert line includes a host of products with decidedly unmanly names such as Men's Expert Vita Lift SPF 15 Anti-Wrinkle & Firming Moisturiser and Men's Expert Hydra-Energetic Ice Cold Eye Roller (for diminishing under-eye dark circles). Dove's Men+Care line crafts a more masculine position by offering practical solutions to men's personal care problems.[6]

Going in the other direction, GoldieBlox markets a collection of engineering and problem-solving toys for girls – now going international via Amazon. Designed by a female engineer from Stanford University, the brand's goal is 'to get girls building' and to inspire a future generation of female engineers. Aimed at girls five to nine years old, GoldieBlox consists of story books and construction sets that require young girls to solve a series of construction challenges. Initially funded by more than a quarter of a million dollars raised via crowdfunding platform Kickstarter, the innovative product has recently won two Toy Industry Foundation Toy of the Year awards – Educational and People's Choice.[7]

Income

The marketers of products and services such as motor cars, clothing, cosmetics, financial services and travel have long used **income segmentation**. Many companies target affluent consumers with luxury goods and convenience services. For example, luxury hotels often provide special packages to attract the most affluent travellers. Similarly, many retailers have adapted their strategies in pursuit of the 'platinum pound' – trying to attract a broader, younger, more international group of ultra-affluent shoppers to stores in locations like London and Birmingham. Personal shopping services raise the store appeal to the 'cash-rich, time-poor' shopper. And Russian and Chinese speaking personal shopping assistants raise the appeal to the wealthy visiting from those countries.

However, not all companies that use income segmentation target the affluent. For example, many budget retailers – such as the Poundland, Poundshop and Matalan retail chains and grocery stores Aldi and Lidl – successfully target low- and middle-income groups. The core market for such stores is represented by families with more modest incomes. With their low-income strategies, budget stores have shown impressive growth in the harsh economic conditions of recent years and are increasingly attracting more affluent customers as well.

Indeed, the recent troubled economy in Europe has provided challenges for marketers targeting all income groups. Consumers at all income levels – including affluent consumers – are cutting back on their spending and seeking greater value from their purchases. In many cases, luxury marketers targeting high-income consumers have been hardest hit. Even consumers who can still afford to buy luxuries appear to be pushing the pause button. 'It's conspicuous *non*consumption,' says one economist. 'The wealthy still have the wealth, [but] it's the image you project in a bad economy of driving a nice car when your friends or colleagues may be losing their businesses.'[8]

Psychographic segmentation

Psychographic segmentation divides buyers into different segments based on social class, lifestyle or personality characteristics. People in the same demographic group can have very different psychographic characteristics.

In Chapter 5, we discussed how the products people buy reflect their *lifestyles*. As a result, marketers often segment their markets by consumer lifestyles and base their marketing strategies on lifestyle appeals. This approach is frequently observed with lifestyle brands in the fashion industry, but is seen in other sectors too. For example, car-sharing innovator Zipcar (now owned by Avis) rents cars by the hour or the day, in US and European cities. But Zipcar doesn't see itself as a car-rental company. Instead it sees itself as enhancing its customers' urban lifestyles and targets accordingly. 'It's not about cars,' says Zipcar's CEO, 'It's about urban life.'[9]

Marketers also use *personality* variables to segment markets. For example, some holiday cruise lines target adventure seekers. Royal Caribbean appeals to high-energy couples and families by providing hundreds of activities, such as rock wall climbing and ice skating. Its commercials urge travellers to 'declare your independence and become a citizen of our nation – Royal Caribbean, The Nation of Why Not'. By contrast, the Regent Seven Seas Cruise Line targets more serene and cerebral adventurers, mature couples seeking a more elegant ambiance and exotic destinations, such as the Orient. Regent invites them to come along as 'luxury goes exploring'.[10]

Income segmentation – Dividing a market into different incomes segments.

Psychographic segmentation – Dividing a market into different segments based on social class, lifestyle or personality characteristics.

MAMILS: Middle-aged men in lycra, increasingly swapping the golf course for cycle road racing and spending huge sums on the latest kit.

Source: RDaniel/Shutterstock.com

Marketers sometimes refer to brand-focused psychographic segments as *brand 'tribes'* – communities of core customers with shared characteristics, brand experiences and strong affinities for a particular brand.[11] For example, the Apple tribe consists of stylish, tech-savvy nonconformists; the Nike tribe consists of high-performance athletes. Often, brands in the same product category target very different tribes. For example, although both MacDonald's and Starbucks are snack and coffee shops, their brand tribes are as different as day and night.

Halfords is the UK's largest retailer of bicycles, mainly because of its success in the family market – selling parents their children's first bikes, for example. But the challenge is attracting different types of cycling enthusiasts, and the MAMILs (middle-aged men in lycra) in particular:[12]

Cycling in Britain is soaring in popularity following Britain's triumphs at the 2012 Olympics, and in the Tour de France, as well as with those seeking more environmentally friendly urban transport. Setting aside families, conventional touring cyclists and club racers, the real prize for cycle and kit retailer Halfords is achieving success with one or more of the new 'cycling tribes':

- *MAMILs – middle-aged man in lyra*: increasingly swapping the golf course for cycle road racing and spending huge sums on the latest kit. Likely to have a top-end road bike from Evans Cycles for £10,000. Buys expensive kit from Wiggle (online shopping) and Rapha (clothes) – the Rapha Classic jersey sells for around £130. Goes to cycling events for the opportunity to forget being a 40-something executive with a paunch trying to look cool, and pretending to be an athlete.
- *Shoreditch hipsters*: the fixed-wheel bike (the 'fixie') is a fashion statement, just like the skinny jeans and loafers without socks. The bike will be heavily personalised with coloured wheels and pencil-thin handlebars, and will probably be handmade by an independent builder like Foffa Bikes, and the iPad will go in a cycle-courier shoulder bag probably made by Rapha.
- *Downhill mountain bikers*: ride fast, furious and with body armour, hoping not to 'bin' (their word for crash). Overwhelmingly male 20–30-year-olds, showing off their Intense, Orange and Trek bikes that cost between £2,000 and £6,500. Online they flock to pinkbike.com or buy from Chain Reaction, the expanding Northern Ireland retailer.

The problem for Halfords is that most tribe members would not be seen dead in a Halford's store. Developing a successful value offering to the new types of cycling enthusiast will be difficult and may not even be possible.

Behavioural segmentation

Behaviour segmentation— Dividing a market into segments based on consumer knowledge, attitudes, uses of a product or responses to a product.

Behavioural segmentation divides buyers into segments based on their knowledge, attitudes, uses or responses to a product. Many marketers believe that behavioural variables are the best starting point for building market segments.

Occasions

Occasion segmentation— Dividing the market into segments according to occasions when buyers get the idea to buy, actually make their purchase or use the purchased item.

Buyers can be grouped according to occasions when they get the idea to buy, actually make their purchase, or use the purchased item. **Occasion segmentation** can help firms build up product usage. Heinz and Campbell's advertise soups more heavily in the cold winter months, and B&Q runs special spring-time promotions for lawn and garden products. For more than a decade, Starbucks in the US has welcomed the autumn season with its Pumpkin Spice Latte (PSL). Sold only in the autumn, to date the coffee chain has sold more than 200 million cups of the eagerly anticipated concoction. 'I've never been happier about burning my tongue with a hot beverage,' tweeted a Starbucks customer recently. In 2013, PSL arrived at Starbucks in the UK.[13]

Other companies try to boost consumption by promoting usage during non-traditional occasions. For example, most consumers drink orange juice in the morning, but orange growers have promoted drinking orange juice as a cool, healthful refresher at other times of the day. Indeed, some holidays, such as Mother's Day and Father's Day, were originally promoted to increase the sale of chocolate, flowers, cards and other gifts. Many marketers prepare special offers and ads for these and other holiday occasions.

Source: Aleksandar Hubenov/ 123RF.com

Benefits sought

A powerful form of segmentation is grouping buyers according to the different *benefits* that they seek from a product. **Benefit segmentation** requires finding the major benefits people look for in a product class, the kinds of people who look for each benefit, and the major brands that deliver each benefit.

International sportswear company Champion is best known in Europe as producing kit for premier league football team Wigan United and the Wales national football team, as well as jerseys for the Greek national basketball team. Less well-known is that Champion invented the hoodie, the sports bra and reversible T-shirts. In sportswear Champion segments its markets according to benefits that different consumers seek from these clothes. For example, 'Fit and polish' consumers seek a balance between function and style – they exercise for results but want to look good doing it. 'Serious sports competitors' exercise heavily and live in and love their sports clothes – they seek performance and function. By contrast, 'Value-seeking' mothers have low sports interest and low sportswear involvement – they buy for the family and seek durability and value. Thus, each segment seeks a different mix of benefits. Champion aims to target the benefit segment or segments that it can serve best and most profitably, using appeals that match each segment's benefit preferences.

Benefit segmentation— Dividing the market into segments according to the different benefits that consumers seek from the product.

User status

Markets can be segmented into non-users, ex-users, potential users, first-time users and regular users of a product. Marketers want to reinforce and retain regular users, attract targeted non-users, and reinvigorate relationships with ex-users.

Included in the potential user group are consumers facing life-stage changes – such as newlyweds and new parents – who can be turned into heavy users. For example, IKEA supplies 10 per cent of the furniture purchased in the UK – indeed, the company claims that one-in-ten Europeans were conceived in an IKEA bed. IKEA actively targets the newly divorced. After the breakdown of a relationship, individuals face setting up new homes, often largely from scratch. IKEA's typically provocative advertising makes light of these traumatic problems and looks to turn the 'newly single' into major buyers of Ikea's low budget home furnishings.[14]

Usage rate

Markets can also be segmented into light, medium and heavy product users. Heavy users are often a small percentage of the market but account for a high percentage of total consumption. For example, global fast-food company Burger King targets what it calls 'Super Fans' in the US. They are young (ages 18 to 34), Whopper-wolfing males and females who make up 18 per cent of the chain's customers but account for almost half of all customer visits. They eat at Burger King an average of 13 times a month. Burger King targets these Super Fans openly with ads that exalt monster burgers suitable for the biggest appetites.[15]

Loyalty status

A market can also be segmented by consumer loyalty. Consumers can be loyal to brands (e.g., Heinz Beanz), stores (e.g., Waitrose) and companies (e.g., Apple). Buyers can be divided into groups according to their degree of loyalty. Some consumers are completely loyal – they buy one brand all the time and can't wait to tell others about it.

For example, whether they own a MacBook computer, an iPhone or an iPad, Apple devotees seem unmoveable in their devotion to the brand. At one end are the quietly satisfied Apple users – people who own one or several Apple devices and use them for browsing, texting, e-mail and social networking. At the other extreme, however, are the Apple zealots – the so-called MacHeads or Macolytes – who can't wait to tell anyone within earshot about their latest Apple gadget. Such loyal Apple devotees helped keep Apple afloat during the lean years a decade ago, and they are now at the forefront of Apple's huge iPod, iTunes and iPad empire.

Other consumers are somewhat loyal – they are loyal to two or three brands of a given product or favour one brand while sometimes buying others. Still other buyers show no loyalty to any brand – they either want something different each time they buy, or they buy whatever's on sale.

A company can learn a lot by analysing loyalty patterns in its market. It should start by studying its own loyal customers. For example, by studying Mac fanatics, Apple can better pinpoint its target market and develop marketing appeals. By studying its less-loyal buyers, the company can detect which brands are most competitive with its own. By looking at customers who are shifting away from its brand, the company can learn about its marketing weaknesses and take actions to correct them.

Using multiple segmentation bases

Marketers rarely limit their segmentation analysis to only one or a few variables. Rather, they often use multiple segmentation bases in an effort to identify smaller, better-defined target groups. Thus, a bank may not only identify a group of wealthy, retired adults but also, within that group, distinguish several segments based on their current income, assets, savings and risk preferences, housing and lifestyles.

Several business information services, such as A.C. Nielsen, TNS, GfK and Experian, provide multivariable segmentation systems that merge geographic, demographic, lifestyle and behavioural data to help companies segment their markets down to postal codes, neighbourhoods and even households. One of the leading segmentation systems is the ACORN product provided in the UK by CACI Ltd, the UK subsidiary of CACI International in the United States.[16]

ACORN is used to understand consumers' lifestyle, behaviour and attitudes, as well as the needs of local neighbourhoods or communities. ACORN (acronym for 'A Classification Of Residential Neighbourhoods') is a geodemographic segmentation of the UK's population around small neighbourhoods, postcodes or consumer households. ACORN classifies population into five categories (Wealthy Achievers, Urban Prosperity, Comfortably Off, Moderate Means and Hard-Pressed) and within these categories identifies 17 groups and 56 types. For example, Wealthy Achievers comprises around 25 per cent of the UK's population, and Affluent Greys is one group within this category, and those living in farming communities constitute one of the types within this category.

ACORN and other such systems can help marketers segment people and locations into marketable groups of like-minded consumers. Each category and group is likely to have its own pattern of likes, dislikes, lifestyles and purchase behaviours. For example, Affluent Greys living in Farming Communities have distinct demographic characteristics, but also differ from others regarding car ownership, shopping preferences, Internet activity and media usage.

Such segmentation approaches provide a powerful tool for marketers of all kinds (e.g., private and public sector). It can help companies identify and better understand key customer segments, target them more efficiently, and tailor market offerings and messages to their specific needs. It can assist public policy decision makers in identifying the needs of local communities of different kinds.

Segmenting business markets

Consumer and business marketers use many of the same variables to segment their markets. Business buyers can also be segmented geographically, demographically (e.g., by industry or company size), or by benefits sought, user status, usage rate and loyalty status. Yet, business marketers also use some additional variables, such as customer *operating characteristics*, *purchasing approaches*, *situational factors* and *personal characteristics*.

Almost every company serves at least some business markets. For example, Starbucks has developed distinct marketing programmes for each of its two business segments: the office coffee segment and the food service segment. In the office coffee and vending segment, Starbucks Office Coffee Solutions markets a variety of workplace coffee services to businesses of any size, helping them to make Starbucks coffee and related products available to their employees in their workplaces. Starbucks helps these business customers design the best office solutions involving its coffees, teas, syrups and branded paper products and methods of serving them – portion packs, single cups or vending machine packs. The Starbucks Foodservice division teams up with businesses and other organisations – ranging from airlines, restaurants, universities and hospitals to sports stadiums – to help them serve the well-known Starbucks brand to their own customers. Starbucks provides not only the coffee, tea and paper products to its food service partners, but also equipment, training and marketing and merchandising support.[17]

Many companies establish separate systems for dealing with larger or multiple-location customers. For example, Steelcase, the global leader in the office furniture industry, provides innovative office furniture products. The company first divides customers into seven segments, including biosciences, higher education, government buyers, local government, healthcare, professional services and retail banking. Next, company salespeople work with Steelcase dealers to handle smaller or local Steelcase customers in each segment. But many national, multiple-location customers, such as ExxonMobil or IBM, have special needs that may reach beyond the scope of individual dealers. So Steelcase uses national account managers to help its dealer networks handle national accounts.

Within a given target industry and customer size, the company can segment by purchase approaches and criteria. As in consumer segmentation, many marketers believe that *buying behaviour* and *benefits* provide the best basis for segmenting business markets.

Segmenting international markets

Few companies have either the resources or the will to operate in all, or even most, of the countries that dot the globe. Although some large companies, such as Unilever, Coca-Cola or Sony, sell products in more than 200 countries, most international firms focus on a smaller set. Operating in many countries presents new challenges. Different countries, even those that are close together, can vary greatly in their economic, cultural and political makeup. Thus, just as they do within their domestic markets, international firms need to group their world markets into segments with distinct buying needs and behaviours.

Companies can segment international markets using one or a combination of several variables. They can segment by *geographic location*, grouping countries by regions such as Western Europe, the Pacific Rim, the Middle East or Africa. Geographic segmentation assumes that nations close to one another will have many common traits and behaviours. Although this is often the case, there are many exceptions. For example, although the United Kingdom and France have much in common, both differ culturally and economically from neighbouring Spain. Even within a region, consumers can differ widely. For example, it may be tempting for international marketers to group all Central and South American countries together. However, the Dominican Republic is no more like Brazil than Italy is like Sweden. Many Central and South Americans don't even speak Spanish, including 200 million Portuguese-speaking Brazilians and the millions in other countries who speak a variety of Indian dialects.

World markets can also be segmented on the basis of *economic factors*. Countries might be grouped by population income levels or by their overall level of economic development. A country's economic structure shapes its population's product and service needs and, therefore, the marketing opportunities it offers. For example, many companies have been targeting the BRIC countries – Brazil, Russia, India and China – which were believed to be fast-growing developing economies with rapidly increasing buying power, although this growth has slowed recently.

Intermarket segmentation: Coca-Cola targets teens throughout the world with universal themes, such as music.

Source: Shirlaine Forrest/Getty Images for Coca-Cola

Intermarket (cross-market) segmentation—Forming segments of consumers who have similar needs and buying behaviours even though they are located in different countries.

Countries can also be segmented by *political and legal factors* such as the type and stability of government, receptivity to foreign firms, monetary regulations and amount of bureaucracy. *Cultural factors* can also be used, grouping markets according to common languages, religions, values and attitudes, customs and behavioural patterns.

Segmenting international markets based on geographic, economic, political, cultural and other factors presumes that segments consist of clusters of regions or countries. However, as new communications technologies, such as satellite television and the Internet, connect consumers around the world, marketers can define and reach segments of like-minded consumers no matter where in the world they are. Using **intermarket segmentation** (also called **cross-market segmentation**), they form segments of consumers who have similar needs and buying behaviours even though they are located in different countries.

For example, Lexus targets the world's well-to-do – the 'global elite' segment – regardless of their country. Retailer H&M targets fashion-conscious but frugal young shoppers in 43 countries with its low-priced, trendy fashion clothing and accessories. Swedish furniture giant IKEA targets the aspiring global middle class – it sells good-quality furniture that ordinary people worldwide can afford. And Coca-Cola creates special programmes to target teens, core consumers of its soft drinks the world over. By 2020, one-third of the world's population – some 2.5 billion people – will be under 18 years of age. Coca-Cola reaches this important market through the universal teen themes, such as music. For example, it recently joined forces with Spotify to provide a global music network that helps teens discover new music, connect with other music-loving teens, and share their experiences with friends worldwide both online and offline.[18]

Requirements for effective segmentation

Clearly, there are many ways to segment a market, but not all segmentation is effective. For example, buyers of table salt could be divided into blond and brunette customers. But hair colour obviously does not affect the purchase of salt. Furthermore, if all salt buyers bought the same amount of salt each month, believed that all salt is the same, and wanted to pay the same price, the company would not benefit from segmenting this market. (Segmentation only becomes interesting for salt when you look at the niche of gourmet cooks who will buy Mediterranean sea salt and pink rock salt to go with their range of balsamic vinegars.)

To be useful, market segments must be:

- *Measurable*: The size, purchasing power and profiles of the segments can be measured. Certain segmentation variables are difficult to measure. For example, around 10 per cent of the world's population of 7 billion people is left-handed. This group is larger than many countries. Yet few products are targeted toward this left-handed segment. The major problem may be that the segment is hard to identify and measure. There are no data on the demographics of left-handed people, and few governments keep track of left-handedness in their population surveys. Private data companies keep reams of statistics on other demographic segments but not on left-handers.
- *Accessible*: The market segments can be effectively reached and served. Suppose a fragrance company finds that heavy users of its brand are single men and women who stay out late and socialise a lot. Unless this group lives or shops at certain places and is exposed to certain media, its members will be difficult to reach.

- *Substantial*: The market segments are large or profitable enough to serve. A segment should be the largest possible homogeneous group worth pursuing with a tailored marketing programme. It would not pay, for example, for a motor manufacturer to develop cars especially for people whose height is greater than seven feet.
- *Differentiable*: The segments are conceptually distinguishable and respond differently to different marketing mix elements and programmes. If men and women respond similarly to marketing efforts for soft drinks, they do not constitute separate segments.
- *Actionable*: Effective programmes can be designed for attracting and serving the segments. For example, although one small airline identified seven market segments, its staff was too small to develop separate marketing programmes for each segment.

MARKET TARGETING

Market segmentation reveals a firm's market segment opportunities. A firm now has to evaluate the various segments and decide how many and which segments it can serve best. We now look at how companies evaluate and select target segments.

Evaluating market segments

In evaluating different market segments, a firm must look at three factors: segment size and growth, segment structural attractiveness and company objectives and resources.

First, a company wants to select segments that have the right size and growth characteristics. But 'right size and growth' is a relative characteristic. The largest, fastest-growing segments are not always the most attractive ones for every company. Smaller companies may lack the skills and resources needed to serve larger segments. Or they may find these segments too competitive. Such companies may target segments that are smaller and less attractive, in an absolute sense, because those segments are potentially more profitable for them.

Second, the company also needs to examine major structural factors that affect long-run segment attractiveness.[19] For example, a segment is less attractive if it already contains many strong and aggressive *competitors* or if it is too easy for *new entrants* to come into the segment. The existence of many actual or potential *substitute products* may limit prices and the profits that can be earned in a segment. The relative *power of buyers* also affects segment attractiveness. Buyers with strong bargaining power relative to sellers will try to force prices down, demand more services, and set competitors against one another – all at the expense of seller profitability. Finally, a segment may be less attractive if it contains *powerful suppliers* who can control prices or reduce the quality or quantity of ordered goods and services.

Third, even if a segment has the right size and growth and is structurally attractive, the company must consider its own objectives and resources. Some attractive segments can be dismissed quickly because they do not fit with the company's long-run objectives. Or the company may lack the skills and resources needed to succeed in an attractive segment. For example, given the current economic conditions, the economy segment of the motor car market is large and growing. But given its objectives and resources, it would make little sense for the luxury-performance carmaker Lexus to enter this segment. A company should only enter segments in which it can create superior customer value and gain advantages over its competitors.

Selecting target market segments

After evaluating different segments, the company must decide which and how many segments it will target. A **target market** consists of a set of buyers who share common needs or characteristics that the company decides to serve. Market targeting can be carried out at several different levels. Figure 7.2 shows that companies can target very broadly (*undifferentiated marketing*), very narrowly (*micromarketing*) or somewhere in between (*differentiated or concentrated* marketing).

Target market—A set of buyers sharing common needs or characteristics that the company decides to serve.

Figure 7.2 Marketing targeting strategies

This figure covers a broad range of targeting strategies, from mass marketing (virtually no targeting) to individual marketing (customising products and programmes to individual customers).

Undifferentiated (mass) marketing → Differentiated (segmented) marketing → Concentrated (niche) marketing → Micromarketing (local or individual marketing)

Targeting broadly

Targeting narrowly

Undifferentiated marketing

Undifferentiated (mass) marketing—A market coverage strategy in which a firm decides to ignore market segment differences and go after the whole market with one offer.

Using an **undifferentiated marketing** (or **mass marketing**) strategy, a firm might decide to ignore market segment differences and target the whole market with one offer. Such a strategy focuses on what is *common* in the needs of consumers rather than on what is *different*. The company designs a product and a marketing programme that will appeal to the largest number of buyers.

As noted earlier in the chapter, most modern marketers have strong doubts about this strategy. Difficulties arise in developing a product or brand that will satisfy all consumers. Moreover, mass marketers often have trouble competing with more-focused firms that do a better job of satisfying the needs of specific segments and niches.

Differentiated marketing

Differentiated (segmented) marketing—A market coverage strategy in which a firm decides to target several market segments and designs separate offers for each.

Using a **differentiated marketing** (or **segmented marketing**) strategy, a firm decides to target several market segments and designs separate offers for each. Toyota Corporation produces several different brands of cars – from the Prius to Toyota to Lexus – each targeting its own segments of car buyers. In most large country markets, P&G markets multiple laundry detergent brands, which compete with each other on supermarket shelves.

By offering product and marketing variations to segments, companies hope for higher sales and a stronger position within each market segment. Developing a stronger position within several segments creates more total sales than undifferentiated marketing across all segments. P&G's multiple detergent brands capture four times the market share of its nearest rival.

But differentiated marketing also increases the costs of doing business. A firm usually finds it more expensive to develop and produce, say, ten units of ten different products than 100 units of a single product. Developing separate marketing plans for the separate segments requires extra marketing research, forecasting, sales analysis, promotion planning and channel management. And trying to reach different market segments with different advertising campaigns increases promotion costs. Thus, the company must weigh increased sales against increased costs when deciding on a differentiated marketing strategy.

Concentrated marketing

Concentrated (niche) marketing—A market coverage strategy in which a firm goes after a large share of one or a few segments or niches.

Using a **concentrated marketing** (or **niche marketing**) strategy, instead of going after a small share of a large market, a firm goes after a large share of one or a few smaller segments or niches. For example, Whole Foods Market is a niche food retailer which has become the world's largest retailer of natural and organic foods, with stores throughout North America and several in the United Kingdom and China.[20] Whole Foods is small compared to giant rivals, such as Walmart in the US and Tesco in the UK. Yet, over recent years, the smaller, more upscale retailer has grown rapidly, though with some bumps on the way. Whole Foods Market thrives by catering to affluent customers who the mass retailers of the world can't serve well, offering them 'organic, natural and gourmet foods, all swaddled in Earth Day politics' – what others call 'foodie treats'. In fact, a typical Whole Foods Market customer is more likely to boycott the local mass market supermarket than to shop at it.

Through concentrated marketing, a firm achieves a strong market position because of its greater knowledge of consumer needs in the niches it serves and the special reputation it acquires.

It can market more *effectively* by fine-tuning its products, prices and programmes to the needs of carefully defined segments. It can also market more *efficiently*, targeting its products or services, channels and communications programmes toward consumers that it can serve best and most profitably.

Whereas segments are fairly large and normally attract several competitors, niches are smaller and may attract only one or a few competitors. Niching lets smaller companies focus their limited resources on serving niches that may be unimportant to, or overlooked by, larger competitors. Many companies start as nichers to get a foothold against larger, more resourceful competitors and then grow into broader competitors. For example, the original low-cost airline, Southwest Airlines, began by serving intra-state, no-frills commuters in Texas but is now one of the largest airlines in the US, and its example has been followed by European airlines like easyJet and Ryanair.

In contrast, as markets change, some mega-marketers develop niche products to create sales growth. For example, in recent years, as consumers have grown more health conscious, the demand for carbonated soft drinks has declined, and the market for energy drinks and juices has grown. With carbonated soft drink sales falling across the world, to meet this shifting demand, mainstream cola marketers PepsiCo and Coca-Cola have both developed or acquired their own niche products. PepsiCo developed Amp energy drink and purchased the SoBe and Izze brands of enhanced waters and juices. Similarly, Coca-Cola developed Vault and acquired the Vitaminwater and Odwalla brands.

Today, the low cost of setting up shop on the Internet makes it even more profitable to serve seemingly miniscule niches. Small businesses, in particular, are realising riches from serving small niches on the web. Consider Moonpig.com:

Moonpig.com sells personalised greeting cards online. The website was launched in July 2000, and in 2007 the company was responsible for 90 per cent of the online greeting card market in the United Kingdom. According to founder Nick Jenkins, 'Moonpig' was his nickname at school, hence the name of the brand. Customers visiting the website choose from a large selection of basic greeting card designs but then enter their own text to personalise them. As well as cards, the website offers customisable spoof magazine covers and invitations, where customers can upload their own photos for printing. The growth in broadband and use of digital cameras, together with news spreading by word-of-mouth, meant sales steadily increased, and the first profits were made in 2005. A television advertising campaign began in November 2006 to further build brand awareness, and in February 2008 Moonpig.com received a higher level of UK Internet traffic than any other company in the flower and gift industry. By summer 2009, the company had 2.57 million customers. The business expanded into the Australian market in 2004, and in late 2009, the business developed its offering to include a range of flowers and custom mug designs. In spring 2010, Moonpig launched in America. In July 2011, Moonpig agreed to be taken over by PhotoBox in a £120 million deal.[21]

Concentrated marketing can be highly profitable. At the same time, it involves higher-than-normal risks. Companies that rely on one or a few segments for all of their business will suffer greatly if the segment turns sour. Or larger competitors may decide to enter the same segment with greater resources. For these reasons, many companies prefer to diversify in several market segments. In fact, many large companies are developing or acquiring niche brands of their own – the goal is to allow them to compete effectively in smaller, specialised markets, and the hope is that some currently niche brands will grow into future powerhouse brands.[22]

Micromarketing

Differentiated and concentrated marketers tailor their offers and marketing programmes to meet the needs of various market segments and niches. At the same time, however, they do not customise their offers to each individual customer. **Micromarketing** is the practice of tailoring products and marketing programmes to suit the tastes of specific individuals and locations. Rather

Micromarketing—Tailoring products and marketing programmes to the needs and wants of specific individual and local customer segments — it includes *local marketing* and *individual marketing.*

than seeing a customer in every individual, micromarketers see the individual in every customer. Micromarketing includes local marketing and individual marketing.

Local marketing

Local marketing—Tailoring brands and marketing to the needs and wants of local customer segments — cities, neighbourhoods, and even specific stores.

Local marketing involves tailoring brands and promotions to the needs and wants of local customer groups – cities, neighbourhoods, and even specific stores. For example, Tesco customises its merchandise store by store to meet the needs of local shoppers. The retailer's store designers create each new store's format according to neighbourhood characteristics, based on the study of geodemographics – stores near offices, for instance, contain prominent islands featuring ready-made meals for busy workers. By using a wealth of customer data on daily sales in every store, Tesco tailors individual store merchandise with considerable precision. Different store formats – superstores, Extra, Metro, Express, One-Stop and Home-Plus – are closely matched to local market needs and opportunities.[23]

Advances in communications technology have given rise to a new high-tech version of location-based marketing. For example, retailers have long been intrigued by the promise of mobile phones, which live in people's pockets and send signals about shoppers' locations. The idea is to send people ads tailored to their location, like a coupon for cappuccino when passing a Starbucks. That idea is fast becoming a reality. For example, in the US, outdoor clothing retailer, the North Face, sends texts about promotions, like a free water bottle with a purchase or seasonal merchandise arrivals. In Europe, Starbucks and L'Oréal are among leading brands developing placecasting of this kind to position localised messages direct with consumers.[24]

Local marketing has some drawbacks, however. It can drive up manufacturing and marketing costs by reducing the economies of scale. It can also create logistics problems as companies try to meet the varied requirements of different regional and local markets. Further, a brand's overall image might be diluted if the product and message vary too much in different localities.

Still, as companies face increasingly fragmented markets, and as new supporting technologies develop, the advantages of local marketing often outweigh the drawbacks. Local marketing helps a company to market more effectively in the face of pronounced regional and local differences in demographics and lifestyles, both within individual countries and across national boundaries.

Individual marketing

Individual marketing—Tailoring products and marketing programmes to the needs and preferences of individual customers.

At the extreme, micromarketing becomes **individual marketing** – tailoring products and marketing programmes to the needs and preferences of individual customers. Individual marketing has also been labelled *one-to-one marketing*, *mass customisation* and *markets-of-one marketing*.

The widespread use of mass marketing has obscured the fact that for centuries consumers were served as individuals: the tailor custom-made a suit, the shoes were designed for an individual and the cabinetmaker made furniture to order. Today, however, new technologies are encouraging many companies to return to forms of customised marketing. More detailed databases, robot-based production, flexible manufacturing, 3-D printing to create unique products, and interactive communication media such as mobile phones and the Internet have combined to foster 'mass customisation'. *Mass customisation* is the process through which firms interact one-to-one with masses of customers to design products and services tailor-made to individual needs.

Unlike mass production, which eliminates the need for human interaction, individual marketing makes relationships with customers more important than ever. Just as mass production was the marketing principle of the twentieth century, interactive marketing is becoming a marketing principle for the twenty-first century. The world appears to be coming full circle – from the good old days when customers were treated as individuals to mass marketing when nobody knew your name, and then back again.

For example, Dell, HP and Apple create custom-configured computers. And at www.cricketbats.com, the enthusiast can buy a cricket bat made to specific design, size, weight, handle size and shape preferences. Visitors to Nike's Nike ID website can personalise their training shoes by choosing from hundreds of colours and putting an embroidered word or phrase on the tongue. Harley Davidson's H-D1 factory customisation programme lets customers go on-line, design their own Harley, and get it in as little as four weeks. It invites customers to explore some 8,000 ways to create their own masterpiece. 'You dream it. We build it,' says the company.

Marketers are also finding new ways to personalise promotional messages. For example, plasma screens placed in shopping centres around the country can now analyse shoppers' faces and place ads based on an individual shopper's gender, age or ethnicity. Facial recognition technology takes this a stage further by recognising the individual and tailoring messages and offers to their interests and past purchase behaviour.

Business-to-business marketers are also finding new ways to customise their offerings. For example, in the global market for agricultural machinery, John Deere manufactures farm seeding equipment that can be configured in more than 2 million versions to individual customer specifications. The seeders are produced one at a time, in any sequence, on a single production line. Mass customisation provides a way to stand out against competitors.

Choosing a targeting strategy

Companies need to consider many factors when choosing a market targeting strategy. Which strategy is best depends on the company's resources. When a firm's resources are limited, concentrated marketing makes the most sense. The best strategy also depends on the degree of product variability. Undifferentiated marketing is more suited for uniform products, such as fresh fruit or steel. Products that can vary in design, such as cameras and cars, are more suited to differentiation or concentration. A product's life-cycle stage also must be considered. When a firm introduces a new product, it may only be practical to launch one version, and undifferentiated marketing or concentrated marketing may make the most sense. In the mature stage of a product life-cycle, however, differentiated marketing often makes more sense.

Another factor is *market variability*. If most buyers have the same tastes, buy the same amounts, and react the same way to marketing efforts, undifferentiated marketing is appropriate. Finally, *competitors' marketing strategies* are important. When competitors use differentiated or concentrated marketing, undifferentiated marketing can be suicidal. Conversely, when competitors use undifferentiated marketing, a firm can gain an advantage by using differentiated or concentrated marketing, focusing on the needs of buyers in specific segments.

Socially responsible target marketing

Smart targeting helps companies become more efficient and effective by focusing on the segments that they can satisfy best and most profitably. Targeting also benefits consumers – companies serve specific groups of consumers with offers carefully tailored to their needs. However, target marketing sometimes generates controversy and concern. The biggest issues usually involve the targeting of vulnerable or disadvantaged consumers with controversial or potentially harmful products.

For example, over the years, marketers in a wide range of industries – from cereal, soft drinks and fast food to toys and fashion – have been heavily criticised for their marketing efforts directed toward children. Critics worry, for example, that premium offers and high-powered advertising appeals presented through the mouths of lovable animated characters will overwhelm children's defences.

Children are seen as an especially vulnerable audience. Problems also arise when the marketing of adult products spills over into the children's segment – intentionally or unintentionally. For example, US lingerie retailer Victoria's Secret targets its highly successful Pink line of young, hip and sexy clothing to young women from 18 to 30 years old. However, critics charge that Pink is now all the rage among girls as young as 11 years old. Responding to Victoria's Secret's designs and marketing messages, children are flocking into stores and buying Pink, with or without parental supervision. More broadly, critics worry that marketers of everything from lingerie and cosmetics to Barbie dolls are directly or indirectly targeting young girls with provocative products, promoting a premature focus on sex and appearance.[25] These concerns extend to the way in which some brands promote themselves to young people – as shown by the criticisms faced by trendy fashion brand Jack Wills in the UK:[26]

> Fashionable clothing from the Jack Wills brand has become the uniform of the wealthier set in British universities and public schools. The fashion brand describes itself as 'hedonistic' and designed for the young and wealthy consumer with its preppy, rowing-inspired fashion, and sponsorship of polo events for Harrow and Eton schools. Critics believe that the brand has gone too far in using explicitly sexual imagery in its advertising. The company defended partial nudity and suggestive images in its advertising as projecting a positive, fun and flirtatious image. While aimed at 18–20-year-olds, its catalogues have developed a reputation among teenagers as young as 13 for their racy imagery. Young fans even launched a Facebook page for the 'Jack Wills Nipple Appreciation Society'.

With food firms accused of texting confectionery adverts to children, critics accusing companies of damaging young girls by the sexualisation of toys, clothes and cartoons, and 'junk food' firms using the Internet and social media to bypass rules that prevent them from marketing their products to children, some critics feel that more control should be exercised, and some have even called for a complete ban on advertising to children.[27]

Indeed, there are fears that the digital era has made children even more vulnerable to targeted marketing messages. Traditional TV and print ads directed at children usually contain obvious pitches that are easily detected and controlled by parents. However, marketing in digital media may be subtly embedded within the content and viewed by children on personal, small-screen devices that are beyond even the most watchful parent's eye. Such marketing might take the form of immersive 'advergames' – video games specifically designed to engage children with products. Or they might consist of embedded ads, quizzes or product placements that let marketers cross-promote branded products, TV shows, popular characters or other marketable entities.

This said, not all attempts to target children or other special segments draw such criticism. In fact, most provide benefits to targeted consumers. For example, Samsung markets the Jitterbug, an easy-to-use phone, directly to older consumers who need a simpler mobile phone with bigger buttons, large screen text and a louder speaker. And Colgate makes a large selection of toothbrush shapes and toothpaste flavours for children – from Colgate Sponge-Bob SquarePants Mild Bubble Fruit toothpaste to Colgate Dora the Explorer character toothbrushes. Such products help make tooth brushing more fun and get children to brush longer and more often.

The growth of the Internet and other carefully targeted direct media has raised fresh concerns about potential targeting abuses. The Internet allows more precise targeting, letting the makers of questionable products or deceptive advertisers zero in on the most vulnerable audiences. Unscrupulous marketers can now send tailor-made, deceptive messages by e-mail directly to millions of unsuspecting consumers.

Today's marketers are using sophisticated analytical techniques to track consumers' digital movements and to build detailed customer profiles containing highly personal information. Such profiles can then be used to hyper-target individual consumers with personalised brand messages and offers. Hyper-targeting can benefit both marketers and consumers, getting the right brand information into the hands of the right customers. However, taken too far or used wrongly, hyper-targeting can harm consumers more than benefit them. Marketers must use these new targeting tools responsibly.

In target marketing, the issue is not really *who* is targeted but rather *how* and for *what*. Controversies arise when marketers attempt to profit inappropriately at the expense of targeted segments – when they unfairly target vulnerable segments or target them with questionable products or tactics. Socially responsible marketing calls for segmentation and targeting that serve not just the interests of a company but also the interests of those targeted.

Author comment

At the same time that the company is answering the first simple-sounding question (which customers will we serve?), the company must be asking the second question (how will we serve them?).

DIFFERENTIATION AND POSITIONING

Beyond deciding which segments of the market it will target, the company must decide on a *value proposition* – how it will create differentiated value for targeted segments and what positions it wants to occupy in those segments. A **product position** is the way a product is *defined by consumers* on important attributes – the place a product occupies in consumers' minds relative to competing products. Products are made in factories, but brands happen in the minds of consumers.

Daz is positioned as a powerful, all-purpose family detergent; Fairy is positioned as the gentle detergent for fine washables and baby clothes. At Tesco, 'Every little helps', while Sainsbury shoppers are urged to 'Try something new today', and Asda customers are promised 'Always low prices . . . Always'. In the car market, small Nissans and Hondas are positioned on economy, Mercedes and Lexus on luxury, and Porsche and BMW on performance. And Toyota positions its fuel-efficient, hybrid Prius as a high-tech solution to the energy shortage: 'Harmony between man, nature, and machine.' Ritz Carlton hotels serve the top 5 per cent of corporate and leisure travellers and its value proposition is 'The Ritz-Carlton Experience' – one that 'enlivens the senses, instills a sense of well-being, and fulfills even the unexpressed wishes and needs of our guests'. And IKEA does more than just sell affordable home furnishings – it's the 'life improvement store'.

Consumers are overloaded with information about products and services. They cannot re-evaluate products every time they make a buying decision. To simplify the buying process, consumers organise products, services and companies into categories and 'position' them in their minds. A product's position is the complex set of perceptions, impressions and feelings that consumers have for the product compared with competing products.

Consumers position products with or without the help of marketers. But marketers do not want to leave their products' positions to chance. They must *plan* positions that will give their products the greatest advantage in selected target markets, and they must design marketing mixes to create these planned positions.

> **Product position**–The way a product is defined by consumers on important attributes — the place the product occupies in consumers' minds relative to competing products.

Positioning maps

In planning their differentiation and positioning strategies, marketers often prepare *perceptual positioning maps* that show consumer perceptions of their brands versus competing products on important buying dimensions. Figure 7.3 shows a positioning map for the US large luxury sport utility vehicle (or four-wheel drive car – 4×4) market.[28] The position of each circle on the map indicates the brand's perceived positioning on two dimensions: price and orientation (luxury versus performance). The size of each circle indicates the brand's relative market share.

Thus, customers view the market-leading Cadillac Escalade as a moderately priced, large, luxury 4×4 with a balance of luxury and performance. The Escalade is positioned on urban luxury, and, in its case, 'performance' probably means power and safety performance. You'll find no mention of off-road adventuring in an Escalade ad.

By contrast, the Range Rover and the Land Cruiser are positioned on luxury with nuances of off-road performance. For example, the Toyota Land Cruiser began in 1951 as a four-wheel drive, Jeep-like vehicle designed to conquer the world's most gruelling terrains and climates. In recent years, the Land Cruiser has retained this adventure and performance positioning but with luxury added. Its website brags of 'legendary off-road capability', with off-road technologies such as an Acoustic Control Induction System to get the most out of the RPMs, 'so you make molehills out of mountains'. Despite its ruggedness, however, the company notes that 'it's available Bluetooth hands-free technology, DVD entertainment, and a sumptuous interior have softened its edges'.

Choosing a differentiation and positioning strategy

Some firms find it easy to choose a differentiation and positioning strategy. For example, a firm well known for quality in certain segments will go for this position in a new segment, if there are enough buyers seeking quality. But in many cases, two or more firms will go after the same position. Then

Figure 7.3 Positioning map: large luxury SUvs

Source: Based on data provided by WardsAuto.com and Edmunds.com, 2010.

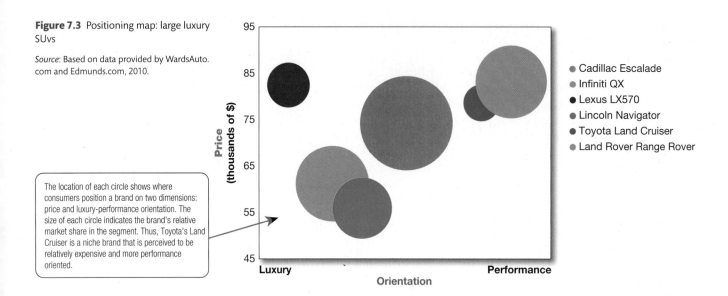

- Cadillac Escalade
- Infiniti QX
- Lexus LX570
- Lincoln Navigator
- Toyota Land Cruiser
- Land Rover Range Rover

The location of each circle shows where consumers position a brand on two dimensions: price and luxury-performance orientation. The size of each circle indicates the brand's relative market share in the segment. Thus, Toyota's Land Cruiser is a niche brand that is perceived to be relatively expensive and more performance oriented.

each will have to find other ways to set itself apart. Each firm must differentiate its offer by building a unique bundle of benefits that appeals to a substantial group within the segment.

Above all else, a brand's positioning must serve the needs and preferences of well-defined target markets. For example, although both McDonald's McCafe outlets and Starbucks are coffee and snack shops, they target very different customers, who want very different things from their favourite coffee seller. Starbucks targets more upscale professionals with more high-brow positioning. In contrast, McCafe targets the average person with a decidedly more low-brow, 'everyman' kind of positioning – no fancy pseudo-Italian names for coffees or cup sizes for example. Yet each brand succeeds because it creates the right value proposition for its unique mix of customers.

The differentiation and positioning task consists of three steps: identifying a set of differentiating competitive advantages on which to build a position, choosing the right competitive advantages, and selecting an overall positioning strategy. A company must then effectively communicate and deliver the chosen position to the market.

Identifying possible value differences and competitive advantages

To build profitable relationships with target customers, marketers must understand customer needs better than competitors do and deliver more customer value. To the extent that a company can differentiate and position itself as providing superior customer value, it gains **competitive advantage**.

Competitive advantage—An advantage over competitors gained by offering greater customer value, either by having lower prices or providing more benefits that justify higher prices.

But solid positions cannot be built on empty promises. If a company positions its product as *offering* the best quality and service, it must actually differentiate the product so that it *delivers* the promised quality and service. Companies must do much more than simply shout out their positions with slogans and taglines. They must first *live* the slogan. Avis' success in the car rental business is pinned on its 'we try harder' slogan, but this message is deeply embedded in the way the company is run as well as in its advertising. Online shoes and accessories seller Zappos' (now owned by Amazon) has a 'powered by service' positioning that would ring hollow if not backed by truly outstanding customer care. Zappos aligns its entire organisation and all of its people around providing the best possible customer service. The online seller's number-one core value: 'Deliver WOW through service.'[29]

To find points of differentiation, marketers must think through a customer's entire experience with the company's product or service. An alert company can find ways to differentiate itself at every customer contact point. In what specific ways can a company differentiate itself or its market offer? It can differentiate along the lines of *product*, *services*, *channels*, *people* or *image*.

Through *product differentiation*, brands can be differentiated on features, performance or style and design. Thus, Bose positions its speakers on their striking design and sound characteristics. Sandwich-maker Subway differentiates itself as the healthy fast-food choice. And Ecover – the biggest seller of 'eco' cleaning and laundry products in the UK – differentiates itself not so much by how its products perform as by the fact that its products are greener. Ecover products offer the eco-consumer the opportunity for 'feel good cleaning'.

Beyond differentiating its physical product, a firm can also differentiate the services that accompany the product. Some companies gain *services differentiation* through speedy, convenient or careful delivery. For example, innovative and unconventional new Metro Bank in the UK opens its stores seven days a week, including some evenings. Others differentiate their service based on high-quality customer care. In an age where customer satisfaction with airline service is in constant decline, Singapore Airlines sets itself apart through extraordinary customer care and the grace of its flight attendants. 'Everyone expects excellence from us,' says the international airline. '[So even] in the smallest details of flight, we rise to each occasion and deliver the Singapore Airlines experience.'[30]

Firms that practice *channel differentiation* gain competitive advantage through the way they design their channel's coverage, expertise and performance. Amazon.com sets itself apart with its smooth-functioning direct channel. Companies can also gain a strong competitive advantage through *people differentiation* – hiring and training better people than their competitors do. In all its global locations, Disney World people are known to be friendly and upbeat. People differentiation requires that a company select its customer-contact people carefully and train them well. For example, Disney trains its theme park people thoroughly to ensure that they are competent, courteous and friendly – from the hotel check-in staff, to the transport drivers, to the ride attendants, to the people who sweep the roads in the parks. Each employee is carefully trained to understand customers and to 'make people happy'.

Even when competing offers look the same, buyers may perceive a difference based on company or brand *image differentiation*. A company or brand image should convey a product's distinctive benefits and positioning. Developing a strong and distinctive image calls for creativity and hard work. A company cannot develop an image in the public's mind overnight by using only a few ads. If the Ritz-Carlton hotel means real quality, this image must be supported by everything the company says and does.

Symbols, such as the McDonald's golden arches, the colourful Google logo, the Twitter bird, the Nike swoosh or Apple's 'bite mark' logo, can provide strong company or brand recognition and image differentiation. The company might enhance a brand around a famous person, as H&M is doing with its David Beckham underwear range. Some companies even become associated with colours, such as Virgin (red), IBM (blue) or UPS (brown). The chosen symbols, characters and other image elements must be communicated through advertising that conveys the company's or brand's personality.

Product differentiation: premium speakers brand Bose promises better sound quality through research-based innovation and high quality kit.

Source: Robert Convery/Alamy Images

Choosing the right competitive advantages

Suppose a company is fortunate enough to discover several potential differentiations that provide competitive advantages. It now must choose the ones on which it will build its positioning strategy. It must decide how many differences to promote and which ones.

How many differences to promote

Many marketers think that companies should aggressively promote only one benefit to the target market. Rosser Reeves, an advertising executive, said a company should develop a *unique selling proposition* (USP) for each brand and stick to it. Each brand should pick an attribute and promote itself as 'number one' on that attribute. Buyers tend to remember number one better, especially in this over-communicated society. Thus, Tesco promotes its 'Every little helps' message, and across the world Burger King promotes personal choice – 'have it your way'.

Other marketers think that companies should position themselves on more than one differentiator. This may be necessary if two or more firms are claiming to be best on the same attribute.

Today, in a time when the mass market is fragmenting into many small segments, companies and brands are trying to broaden their positioning strategies to appeal to more segments. For example, whereas most laundry products marketers offer separate products for cleaning, softening and reducing static cling, Dial Corporation's Purex brand recently introduced a product that offers all three benefits in a single sheet: Purex Complete 3-in-1. 'It's like if bread came sliced, toasted, and pre-buttered,' says one ad. Clearly, many buyers want these multiple benefits. The challenge is to convince them that one brand can do it all. However, as companies increase the number of claims for their brands, they risk disbelief and a loss of clear positioning.

Which differences to promote

Not all brand differences are meaningful or worthwhile; not every difference makes a good differentiator. Each difference has the potential to create company costs as well as customer benefits. A difference is worth establishing to the extent that it satisfies the following criteria:

- *Important*: The difference delivers a highly valued benefit to target buyers.
- *Distinctive*: Competitors do not offer the difference, or one company can offer it in a more distinctive way.
- *Superior*: The difference is superior to other ways that customers might obtain the same benefit.
- *Communicable*: The difference is communicable and visible to buyers.
- *Pre-emptive*: Competitors cannot easily copy the difference.
- *Affordable*: Buyers can afford to pay for the difference.
- *Profitable*: A company can introduce the difference profitably.

Many companies have introduced differentiations that failed one or more of these tests. When the Westin Stamford Hotel in Singapore advertised that it was the world's tallest hotel, it was a distinction that was not important to most tourists – in fact, it turned many off. Similarly, Coca-Cola's now classic product failure – New Coke – failed the superiority and importance tests among core Coca-Cola drinkers. Extensive blind taste tests showed that 60 per cent of all soft drink consumers chose a new, sweeter Coca-Cola formulation over the original Coke, and 52 per cent chose it over Pepsi. So the brand dropped its original formula Coke and, with much fanfare, replaced it with New Coke, a sweeter, smoother version. However, in its research, Coca-Cola overlooked the many intangibles that have made Coca-Cola so popular for 125 years. To loyal Coke drinkers, the original beverage has traditional, iconic values. As it turns out, Coca-Cola differentiates its brand not just by taste, but by tradition. By dropping the original formula, Coca-Cola trampled on the sensitivities of the huge core of loyal Coke drinkers who loved Coke just the way it was. After only three months, the company brought the classic Coke back.

Thus, choosing competitive advantages on which to position a product or service can be difficult, yet such choices may be crucial to success. Choosing the right differentiators can help a brand stand out from the pack of competitors.

Selecting an overall positioning strategy

Value proposition—The full positioning of a brand – the full mix of benefits on which it is positioned.

The full positioning of a brand is called the brand's **value proposition** – the full mix of benefits on which a brand is differentiated and positioned. It is the answer to the customer's question 'why should I buy your brand?' For example, BMW's 'ultimate driving machine' value proposition

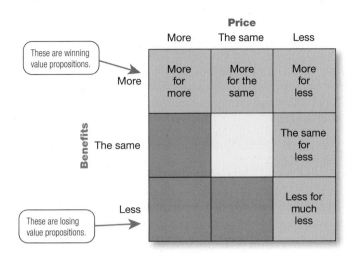

Figure 7.4 Possible value propositions

hinges on performance but also includes luxury and styling, all for a price that is higher than average but seems fair for this mix of benefits.

Figure 7.4 shows possible value propositions on which a company might position its products. In the figure, the five green cells represent winning value propositions – differentiation and positioning that gives the company competitive advantage. The red cells, however, represent losing value propositions. The centre yellow cell represents at best a marginal proposition. In the following sections, we discuss the five winning value propositions on which companies can position their products: more for more, more for the same, the same for less, less for much less and more for less.

More for more

More-for-more positioning involves providing the most upscale product or service and charging a higher price to cover the higher costs. A more-for-more market offering not only offers higher quality, it also gives prestige to the buyer. It symbolises status and a loftier lifestyle. Rolex watches, Mercedes cars and SubZero appliances – 'A SubZero is a refrigerator, just like a diamond is a stone' claims the advertising.[31] Each of these claims superior quality, craftsmanship, durability, performance or style and charges a high price to match. Often, the price difference exceeds the actual increment in quality.

Sellers offering 'only the best' can be found in every product and service category, from hotels, restaurants, food and fashion to cars and household appliances. Consumers are sometimes surprised, even delighted, when a new competitor enters a category with an unusually high-priced brand. Starbucks coffee entered as a very expensive brand in a commodity category. Dyson innovative carpet cleaners were priced way above conventional products in this category. When Apple premiered its iPhone, it offered higher-quality features than a traditional mobile phone, with a hefty price tag to match.

In general, companies should be on the lookout for opportunities to introduce a 'more-for-more' brand in any underdeveloped product or service category. Yet 'more-for-more' brands can be vulnerable. They often invite imitators that claim the same quality but at a lower price. For example, Starbucks now faces 'gourmet' coffee competitors ranging from Costa Coffee and Café Nero to McDonald's – McDonald's sells more coffee consumed away from the home in the UK than any competitor, including Starbucks. Also, luxury goods that sell well during good times may be at risk during economic downturns when buyers become more cautious in their spending. The recent gloomy economy hit premium brands, such as Starbucks, the hardest.

More for the same

Companies can attack a competitor's more-for-more positioning by introducing a brand offering comparable quality at a lower price. For example, Toyota introduced its Lexus line in the United States with a *more-for-the-same* (or even more-for-less) value proposition versus Mercedes and

BMW. Its first headline read: 'Perhaps the first time in history that trading a $72,000 car for a $36,000 car could be considered trading up.' It communicated the high quality of its new Lexus through rave reviews in car magazines and a widely distributed videotape showing side-by-side comparisons of Lexus and Mercedes models. It published surveys showing that Lexus dealers were providing customers with better sales and service experiences than were Mercedes dealerships. Many Mercedes owners switched to Lexus, and the Lexus repurchase rate has been 60 per cent, twice the industry average.

The same for less

Offering *the same for less* can be a powerful value proposition; everyone likes a good deal. Discount stores such as Poundshop and 'category killers' such as Toys R Us use this positioning. They don't claim to offer different or better products. Instead, they offer many of the same brands as department stores and speciality stores but at deep discounts based on superior purchasing power and lower-cost operations. Other companies develop imitative but lower-priced brands in an effort to lure customers away from the market leader. For example, AMD makes less-expensive versions of Intel's market-leading microprocessor chips, and Amazon.com offers the Kindle Fire tablet, which sells for less than 40 per cent of the price of the Apple iPad or Samsung Galaxy tablets.

Less for much less

A market almost always exists for products that offer less and therefore cost less. Few people need, want or can afford 'the very best' in everything they buy. In many cases, consumers will gladly settle for less than optimal performance or give up some of the bells and whistles in exchange for a lower price. For example, many travellers seeking overnight accommodation prefer not to pay for what they consider unnecessary extras, such as a swimming pool, an attached restaurant or mints on the pillow. Hotel chains such as Premier Inn, Formula 1, Travelodge and Days Inn forgo some of these amenities and accordingly charge less.

Less-for-much-less positioning involves meeting consumers' lower performance or quality requirements at a much lower price. For example, retailers Poundland and Poundshop offer more affordable goods at very low prices. Costco membership warehouses offer less merchandise selection and consistency and much lower levels of service – as a result, they charge rock-bottom prices. Successful budget airlines easyJet and Ryanair also practise less-for-much-less positioning, based on the Southwest Airlines model from the US.

More for less

Of course, the winning value proposition would be to offer *more for less*. Many companies claim to do this. And, in the short run, some companies can actually achieve such lofty positions. Yet in the long run, companies will find it very difficult to sustain such best-of-both positioning. Offering more usually costs more, making it difficult to deliver on the 'for-less' promise. Companies that try to deliver both may lose out to more focused competitors.

All said, each brand must adopt a positioning strategy designed to serve the needs and wants of its target markets. *More for more* will draw one target market, *less for much less* will draw another, and so on. Thus, in any market, there is usually room for many different companies, each successfully occupying different positions. The important thing is that each company must develop its own winning positioning strategy, one that makes it special to its target consumers.

Developing a positioning statement

Positioning statement—A statement that summarises company or brand positioning using this form: To (target segment and need) our (brand) is (concept) that (point of difference).

Company and brand positioning should be summed up in a **positioning statement**. The statement should follow the form: To (target segment and need) our (brand) is (concept) that (point of difference).[32] Here is an example using the popular digital information management application Evernote: 'To busy multi-taskers who need help remembering things, Evernote is a digital content management application that makes it easy to capture and remember moments and ideas from your everyday life using your computer, phone, tablet, and the web.' Another example is: 'To busy, mobile professionals who need to always be in the loop, the BlackBerry is a wireless connectivity solution that gives you an easier, more reliable way to stay connected to data, people, and resources while on the go.'

Note that the positioning statement first states the product's membership in a category (digital content management application, for Evernote) and then shows its point of difference from other members of the category (easily capture moments and ideas and remember them later). Evernote helps you 'remember everything' by letting you take notes, capture photos, create to-do lists and record voice reminders, and then makes them easy to find and access using just about any device, anywhere – at home, at work or on the go. The Blackberry offers (wireless connectivity solution) and then shows its point of difference from other members of the category (easier, more reliable connections to data, people and resources). Placing a brand in a specific category suggests similarities that it might share with other products in the category. But the case for the brand's superiority is made on its points of difference.

Source: maximimages.com/Alamy Images

Sometimes marketers put a brand in a surprisingly different category before indicating the points of difference. For example, when Nissan introduced its smallish, funky-looking city car – the Cube – it looked for a way to differentiate the brand in a market already crammed full of small-car models. So Nissan positioned the Cube not as a small *car* but as a personal *mobile device* – something that enhances young target customers' individual, mobile, connected lifestyles. Already hugely popular in Japan, the Nissan Cube was introduced in the United States as a device designed 'to bring young people together – like every mobile device they have'. It is 'a part of a fun, busy life that can be . . . personalised as easily as a cell phone ring or a web page'. Such out-of-category positioning helped make the Cube distinctive.[33]

Communicating and delivering the chosen position

Once it has chosen a position, the company must take effective steps to deliver and communicate the desired position to its target consumers. All the company's marketing mix efforts must support the positioning strategy.

Positioning the company calls for concrete action, not just talk. If the company decides to build a position on better quality and service, it must *deliver* that position. Designing the marketing mix – product, price, place and promotion – involves working out the tactical details of the positioning strategy. Thus, a firm that seizes on a more-for-more position knows that it must produce high-quality products, charge a high price, distribute through high-quality dealers, and advertise in high-quality media. It must hire and train more service people, find retailers who have a good reputation for service, and develop sales and advertising messages that broadcast its superior service. This is the only way to build a consistent and believable more-for-more position.

Companies often find it easier to come up with a good positioning strategy than to implement it. Establishing a position or changing one usually takes a long time. In contrast, positions that have taken years to build can quickly be lost. Once a company has built the desired position, it must take care to maintain the position through consistent performance and communication. It must closely monitor and adapt the position over time to match changes in consumer needs and competitors' strategies. However, the company should avoid abrupt changes that might confuse consumers. Instead, a product's position should evolve gradually as it adapts to the ever-changing marketing environment.

OBJECTIVES REVIEW AND KEY TERMS

In this chapter, you learned about the major elements of a customer-driven marketing strategy: segmentation, targeting, differentiation and positioning. Marketers know that they cannot appeal to all buyers in their markets or at least not to all buyers in the same way. Therefore, most companies today practise *target marketing* – identifying market segments, selecting one or more of them, and developing products and marketing mixes tailored to each.

OBJECTIVE 1 Define the major steps in designing a customer-driven marketing strategy: market segmentation, targeting, differentiation and positioning (p. 194)

A customer-driven marketing strategy begins with selecting which customers to serve and determining a value proposition that best serves the targeted customers. It consists of four steps. *Market segmentation* is the act of dividing a market into distinct groups of buyers with different needs, characteristics or behaviours who might require separate products or marketing mixes. Once the groups have been identified, *market targeting* evaluates each market segment's attractiveness and selects one or more segments to serve. *Differentiation* involves actually differentiating the market offering to create superior customer value. *Positioning* consists of positioning the market offering in the minds of target customers. A customer-driven marketing strategy seeks to build the *right relationships* with the *right customers*.

OBJECTIVE 2 List and discuss the major bases for segmenting consumer and business markets (pp. 194–203)

There is no single way to segment a market. Therefore, the marketer tries different variables to see which give the best segmentation opportunities. For consumer marketing, the major segmentation variables are geographic, demographic, psychographic and behavioural. In *geographic segmentation*, the market is divided into different geographical units, such as countries, regions, cities or even neighbourhoods. In *demographic segmentation*, the market is divided into groups based on demographic variables, including age, life-cycle stage, gender, income, occupation, education, religion, ethnicity and generation. In *psychographic segmentation*, the market is divided into different groups based on social class, lifestyle or personality characteristics. In *behavioural segmentation*, the market is divided into groups based on consumers' knowledge, attitudes, uses or responses to a product.

Business marketers use many of the same variables to segment their markets. But business markets also can be segmented by *business demographics* (industry, company size), *operating*

characteristics, *purchasing approaches*, *situational factors* and *personal characteristics*. The effectiveness of the segmentation analysis depends on finding segments that are *measurable*, *accessible*, *substantial*, *differentiable* and *actionable*.

OBJECTIVE 3 Explain how companies identify attractive market segments and choose a market-targeting strategy (pp. 203–208)

To target the best market segments, the company first evaluates each segment's size and growth characteristics, structural attractiveness and compatibility with company objectives and resources. It then chooses one of four market-targeting strategies – ranging from very broad to very narrow targeting. The seller can ignore segment differences and target broadly using *undifferentiated (or mass) marketing*. This involves mass producing, mass distributing and mass promoting the same product in the same way to all consumers. Or a seller can adopt *differentiated marketing* – developing different market offers for several segments. *Concentrated marketing* (or *niche marketing*) involves focusing on one or a few market segments only. Finally, *micromarketing* is the practice of tailoring products and marketing programmes to suit the tastes of specific individuals and locations. Micromarketing includes *local marketing* and *individual marketing*. Which targeting strategy is best depends on company resources, product variability, product life-cycle stage, market variability and competitive marketing strategies.

OBJECTIVE 4 Discuss how companies differentiate and position their products for maximum competitive advantage (pp. 209–215)

Once a company has decided which segments to enter, it must decide on its *differentiation and positioning strategy*. The differentiation and positioning task consists of three steps: identifying a set of possible differentiations that create competitive advantage, choosing advantages on which to build a position and selecting an overall positioning strategy.

A brand's full positioning is called its *value proposition* – the full mix of benefits on which a brand is positioned. In general, companies can choose from one of five winning value propositions on which to position their products: more for more, more for the same, the same for less, less for much less, or more for less. Company and brand positioning are summarised in positioning statements that state the target segment and need, the positioning concept and specific points of difference. The company must then effectively communicate and deliver the chosen position to the market.

NAVIGATING THE KEY TERMS

OBJECTIVE 1
Market segmentation (p. 194)
Market targeting (targeting) (p. 194)
Differentiation (p. 194)
Positioning (p. 194)

OBJECTIVE 2
Geographic segmentation (p. 195)
Demographic segmentation (p. 196)
Age and life-cycle segmentation (p. 196)
Gender segmentation (p. 196)
Income segmentation (p. 197)

Psychographic segmentation (p. 197)
Behavioural segmentation (p. 198)
Occasion segmentation (p. 198)
Benefit segmentation (p. 199)
Intermarket (cross-market) segmentation (p. 202)

OBJECTIVE 3
Target market (p. 203)
Undifferentiated (mass) marketing (p. 204)
Differentiated (segmented) marketing (p. 204)

Concentrated (niche) marketing (p. 204)
Micromarketing (p. 205)
Local marketing (p. 206)
Individual marketing (p. 206)

OBJECTIVE 4
Product position (p. 209)
Competitive advantage (p. 210)
Value proposition (p. 212)
Positioning statement (p. 214)

DISCUSSION AND CRITICAL THINKING

Discussion questions

7-1 Name and describe the four major steps in designing a customer-driven marketing strategy. (AACSB: Communication)

7-2 Compare and contrast consumer and business market segmentation. (AACSB: Communication)

7-3 Explain how companies segment international markets. (AACSB: Communication)

7-4 Explain how a company differentiates its products from competitors' products. (AACSB: Communication)

7-5 Discuss the criteria that should be evaluated in determining which differences a company should promote in its products. (AACSB: Communication)

Critical-thinking exercises

7-6 Advertisers use market segmentation when promoting products to consumers. For each major consumer segmention variable, find an example of a print ad that appears to be based on that variable. For each ad, identify the target market and explain why you think the advertiser is using the segmentation variable you identified for that ad. (AACSB: Communication; Reflective thinking)

7-7 Perceptual positioning maps are useful for showing consumer perceptions of brands in a product category. Search the Internet for guides on creating perceptual maps and create a map of your perceptions of brands in

a product category of your choice. How can the brand you perceived least favourably improve? (AACSB: Communication; Reflective thinking)

7-8 Form a small group and create an idea for a new reality television show. Using the approach provided in the chapter, develop a positioning statement for this television show. What competitive advantage does the show have over existing shows? How many and which differences would you promote? (AACSB: Communication; Reflective thinking)

Mini-cases and applications

Online, mobile and social media marketing: SoLoMo (Social + Local + Mobile)

Imagine walking into a retail store that has very little merchandise on display but still delights. In the United States, technology company Hointer is allowing retailers to do just that. For example, the company's store in Seattle only has one of every style of clothing hanging on display, seemingly floating in the air. With the store app, customers simply scan the tag to get information about each product, read reviews by others, access media clips and request that the product be added to their fitting room. Once in the fitting room, customers can request other sizes or styling advice via a tablet on the wall or through the mobile app on their phones. Customers return products they don't want through one chute and another size is delivered through another chute in about 30 seconds. With one click, customers can check out on a mobile device or at the sales counter, and they can share their purchases with others on Instagram, Facebook or Twitter. Sales associates still exist, but they are likely using the online tools to monitor customers' choices and suggest matching items of clothing and accessories. All this is possible with Hointer's suite of SoLoMo tools for retailers – eTag, Digital Connections, Omnicart, Associate Tools and Whoosh Fitting Room.

7-9 Search the Internet to find examples of retailers using SoLoMo and similar new technologies to target and engage potential customers, or describe your personal experience as a shopper in this type of retail technology environment. (AACSB: Communication; Use of IT; Reflective thinking)

7-10 Can manufacturers use SoLoMo? Find examples of or make suggestions as to how manufacturers can use this type of targeting. (AACSB: Communication; Reflective thinking)

Marketing ethics: unrealistic bodies

With a global population of overweight children and adolescents, you would think that Mattel's slender Barbie doll would be a good role model for little girls. Not so, according to some critics. If Barbie were a real woman, she would have less than 17 per cent body fat, a neck too thin to hold her head up, a waist too small to house a full liver and intestines, and ankles and feet too tiny to walk. One group of researchers estimated the likelihood of a woman having Barbie's body at one in 100,000. Yet some women strive for impossible bodies, with many suffering from eating disorders such as anorexia and bulimia. Other research has shown that 40 to 60 per cent of pre-adolescent girls are concerned about their weight, and almost 70 per cent of middle school-aged girls who read magazines say the pictures of thin models influence their perceptions of an ideal weight. Statistics like these cause consumer advocacy groups to call for action, especially when marketers target young girls.

7-11 Do you think it is wrong for Mattel and other doll manufacturers to market dolls with unrealistic body proportions to young girls? Explain why you think that way.

Discuss other examples of marketers targeting females with unrealistic body concepts. (AACSB: Communication; Ethical reasoning)

7-12 Give an example of a company that is countering this trend by offering more realistic dolls for young girls. (AACSB: Communication; Reflective thinking)

Marketing by the Numbers: USAA

USAA is an American insurance company that has won many awards for customer service. It is a financial services company formed in 1922 by 25 Army officers who came together to insure each other's motor cars, because they were deemed too high-risk by conventional insurers. USAA now has almost 25,000 employees and more than 9 million member customers. It consistently ranks in the top 10 car insurance companies in the USA and offers other types of insurance as well as banking, investment, retirement and financial planning services. USAA practises a niche marketing strategy – it targets only active and former military personnel and their immediate families. Members earn the right to be customers by serving in the forces and can pass that on to their spouses and children. The company was originally even more restrictive, targeting only military officers. However, in 1996, eligibility was extended to other personnel and is now extended to people who served and were honourably discharged from the forces and their immediate family members.

7-13 Discuss the factors used to evaluate the usefulness of the military personnel segment. (AACSB: Communication; Reflective thinking)

7-14 Using the chain ratio method described in Appendix 2: Marketing by the numbers, estimate the market potential in the military (active duty and veterans) market in the USA. Could this model be used in other countries – using the same approach, estimate the market potential in some of those countries? Be sure to state any assumptions you make. (AACSB: Communication; Use of IT; Analytical reasoning)

REFERENCES

[1] Vanessa Fuhrmans, 'VW bests rivals in Europe of haves and have-nots', *Wall Street Journal*, 15 November 2012, pp. 14–15; Peter Marsh, 'VW pins its growth hopes on concept of "modular assembly"', *Financial Times*, 15 March 2013, p. 20; www.autocar.co.uk/car-news/industry/volkswagen-topples-toyota-worlds-largest-car-maker, accessed August 2015; www.autoguide.com/auto-news/2012/02/top-10-best-selling-cars-of-all-time.html, accessed August 2015; www.automotiveit.com/analysis-vw-struggle-reflects-wider-auto-industry-dilemma/news/id-0010352, accessed August 2015; www.volkswagen.co.uk/, accessed August 2015; Chris Bryant, 'VW turns to Diess's 'Kostenkiller' instinct', *Financial Times*, 21 August 2015, p. 17; Laura Chesters, 'VW crisis set to cost £26bn', *Daily Mail*, 24 September 2015, p. 71.

[2] See Joan Voight, 'Marriott chain adds some local flavor', *Adweek*, 7 January 2013, p. 9; 'Renaissance Hotels launches new navigator program to help guests discover "hidden gems" of various cities around the world', 8 January 2013, www.adweek.com/print/146321; and http://renaissance-hotels.marriott.com/r-navigator, accessed September 2014.

[3] Sarah Perez, 'Amazon's Kindle FreeTime becomes an even better babysitter, with new educational feature that tells kids to "learn first", play later', *Tech Crunch*, 9 December 2013, http://techcrunch.com/2013/12/09/amazons-kindle-freetime-becomesan-even-better-babysitter-with-new-educational-feature-that-tellskids-to-learn-first-play-later/; Keenan Mayo, 'Amazon eyes the kids' tablet market', *Bloomberg Businessweek*, 12 December 2012, p. 34; and www.amazon.com/gp/feature.html?ie=UTF8&do cId=1000863021, accessed September 2014.

[4] Kate Allen and Valentina Romei, 'Over-65s lead rise in cohabitation outside marriage', *Financial Times*, 2 November 2012, p. 3.

[5] Salma Hayek, 'Older, wiser, more affluent', *Financial Times*, 5 March 2015, p. 8.

[6] See Matthew Boyle, 'Yes, real men drink beer and use skin moisturiser', *Bloomberg Businessweek*, 3 October 2013, www.businessweek.com/articles/2013-10-03/men-now-spend-more-on-toiletries-than-onshaving-products; and www.dovemencare.com/, accessed September 2014.

[7] See Oliver Wainwright, 'Meet GoldieBlox: the toy designed to get girls interested in engineering', *The Guardian*, 16 October 2012, www.theguardian.com/artanddesign/architecture-designblog/2012/oct/16/goldieblox-toy-girls-engineering-gender; Sarah Barness, 'GoldieBlox, world's coolest toys for girls, could win a super bowl TV spot', *Huffington Post*, 15 November 2013, www.huffingtonpost.com/2013/11/14/goldieblox-superbowl_n_4269101.html; and www.goldieblox.com/, accessed September 2014.

[8] John Waggoner, 'Even the wealthy feel tapped out', *USA Today*, 2 February 2009, p. B1; and Piet Levy, 'How to reach the new consumer', *Marketing News*, 28 February 2010, pp. 16–20.

[9] Elizabeth Olson, 'Car sharing reinvents the company wheels', *New York Times*, 7 May 2009, p. F2; www.zipcar.co.uk, accessed August 2015.

[10] Information from www.rssc.com, and www.creative.rccl.com/nation_of_why_not/, accessed August 2015.

[11] For more on brand tribes, see Tina Sharkey, 'What's your tribe?' *Forbes*, 25 January 2012, www.forbes.com/sites/tinasharkey/2012/01/25/whats-your-tribe-tap-into-your-core-consumers-aspirations-like-nikegatorade-babycenter-and-rei-do/; Seth Godin, *Tribes: We Need You to Lead Us* (Portfolio, 2008); 'Brand tribalism', *Wikipedia*, http://en.wikipedia.org/wiki/Brand_tribalism, accessed September 2014.

[12] Matthew Goodman, 'Halfords follows that Mamil', *The Sunday Times*, 26 May 2013, pp. 3–1, 3–9.

[13] Lisa Fleisher, 'Pumpkin spice latte, the drink that almost wasn't', *Wall Street Journal*, 30 August 2013, http://blogs.wsj.com/corporate-intelligence/2013/08/30/pumpkin-spice-latte-thedrink-that-almost-wasnt/; and www.starbucks.com/menu/drinks/espresso/pumpkin-spice-latte, accessed September 2014; www.telegraph.co.uk/finance/newsbysector/retailandconsumer/11198290/Why-the-UK-is-about-to-go-crazy-for-pumpkin-spice-lattes.html, accessed August 2015.

[14] Andrew Ward, 'Retailer still strong on the home front', *Financial Times*, 14 January 2011, p. 19; Sean Poulter, 'This flatpack nation', *Daily Mail*, 7 October 2010, p. 25.

[15] Blair Chancey, 'King, meet the world', *QSR Magazine*, February 2009, www.qsrmagazine.com/articles/interview/112/shaufelberger-3.phtml; and Julie Jargon, 'As sales drop, Burger King draws critics for courting "Super Fans"', *Wall Street Journal*, 1 February 2010, p. B1.

[16] See www.caci.co.uk/, accessed August 2015.

[17] See www.starbucksfs.com and http://starbucksocs.com/, accessed September 2014.

[18] See Jay Moy, 'Every song has a place: Coca-Cola, Spotify launch groundbreaking social music app', 11 June 2013, www.coca-colacompany.com/coca-cola-music/every-song-has-aplace-coca-cola-spotify-launch-groundbreaking-social-music-app; and www.coca-cola.com/music, accessed September 2014.

[19] See Michael Porter, *Competitive Advantage* (New York: Free Press,1985), pp. 4–8, 234–236; For a more recent discussion, see Philip Kotler and Kevin Lane Keller, *Marketing Management*, 14th ed. (Upper Saddle River, NJ: Prentice Hall, 2012), p. 232.

[20] Store information found at www.wholefoodsmarket.com, accessed August 2015.

[21] Tim Bradshaw, 'Moonpig bought by Photobox for £129m', *Financial Times*, 25 July 2011, www.moonpig.com, accessed August 2015.

[22] See Jack Neff, 'Making the case for the Titans', *Advertising Age*, 7 October 2013, p. 14.

[23] See Darell K. Rigby and Vijay Vishwanath, 'Localization: the revolution in consumer markets', *Harvard Business Review*, April 2006, pp. 82–92; also see Cecilie Rohwedder, 'Decoding needs and wants of shoppers', *Wall Street Journal*, 24–28 December 2007, p. 4.

[24] Jonathan Birchall, 'Codes open new front in retail wars', *Financial Times*, 18 May 2010, p. 23.

[25] Adapted from portions of Fae Goodman, 'Lingerie is luscious and lovely', *Chicago Sun-Times*, 19 February 2006, p. B2; and Stacy Weiner, 'Goodbye to girlhood', *Washington Post*, 20 February 2007, p. HE01; Also see Suzanne C. Ryan and Betsy Cummings, 'Tickled pink', *Brandweek*, 8 September 2008, pp. MO26–MO28; and India Knight, 'Relax: girls will be girls', *The Sunday Times* (London), 21 February 2010, p. 4.

[26] Sean Poulter, 'How one of Britain's trendiest brands is selling clothes to your children', *Daily Mail*, 5 April 2011, p. 13.

[27] Lois Rogers and Jonathan Carr-Brown, 'Food firms text sweet ads to children', *The Sunday Times*, 30 May 2004, S1, p. 5; Fiona MacRae and Neil Sears, 'Sexy marketing that corrupts young lives', *Daily Mail*, 21 February 2007, p. 22.

[28] SUV sales data furnished by www.WardsAuto.com, accessed March 2013; Price data from www.edmunds.com, accessed March 2013.

[29] See 'Zappos family core values', http://about.zappos.com/ourunique-culture/zappos-core-values; and http://about.zappos.com/, accessed September 2014.

[30] Quote from 'Singapore Airlines: company information', www.singaporeair.com, accessed August 2015.

[31] www.westye.co.uk, accessed August 2015.

[32] See Bobby J. Calder and Steven J. Reagan, 'Brand Design', in Dawn Iacobucci, ed., *Kellogg on Marketing* (New York: John Wiley & Sons, 2001), p. 61. For more discussion, see Philip Kotler and Kevin Lane Keller, *Marketing Management*, 14th ed. (Upper Saddle River, NJ: Prentice Hall, 2012), Chapter 10.

[33] See Stuart Elliott, 'With the car industry in trouble, Nissan rolls out the mobile device', *New York Times*, 6 April 2009, www.nytimes.com; Dan Neil, 'Nissan's cube is coolness in a box', *Los Angeles Times*, 6 March 2009, p. 1; and www.nissanusa.com/cube, accessed August 2015.

COMPANY CASE

Asos: fast fashion for fast consumers

From the outset, online fashion retailer Asos has confounded its critics by homing in on its target market and constantly adapting its business model. Asos segmented its market carefully and concentrated on serving its target customers better than its competitors. It homes in on its target market and has constantly refined its business model to deliver better value to customers. But things have not always been plain sailing for the company and there are major challenges for the future to be confronted.

The first attempt

When the original Internet clothing company As Seen On Screen (Asos) listed on London's Alternative Investment Market in 2001, it was known for its 'red carpet replicas' – selling copies of dresses worn by actresses. The concept was simple – when you saw clothes worn by an actress on TV or in a film, you could locate a low-cost version through the Asos website. The first concept for the business was identifying brands worn by stars in films and detailing how to get them. The business, founded by Nick Robertson with a £2 million loan from his brother, was originally conceived as a spin-off from Mr Robertson's TV product placement business. Right away fashionistas looked down on the start-up and many celebrities were uncomfortable with the idea. But ten years later, Asos had remodelled itself into a global fashion destination where celebrities are happy to shop themselves – for example, Asos numbers Michelle Obama among its customers – but with a different business model.

The second version

The original Asos model foundered and was replaced with selling products supplied by third parties, rather than just linking buyers to third party websites for commission (the brand owners did not want to pay the commission). The business took off quickly and by 2011 it was among the UK's biggest fashion retailers, generating 11 million unique users a month. 'On a daily basis, that's around 700,000 people,' says Nick Robertson. 'Imagine having a shop with that many people walking through the door every day.'

Critics have consistently tried – and failed – to turn the company's growth story into something resembling the tale of the emperor's new clothes. Online fashion would never take off, they said, underestimating the net-savvy generation who make up Asos' 16 to 34-year-old core customer base. More recently, the company has switched its focus to international sales. In 2007, non-UK sales made up 10 per cent of the company's annual retail sales. Today, it is more than half the business. Bounding around Asos's headquarters in Camden, north London, one gets a sense of the scale of the company's operation. Everything that appears on the website is done in-house, including photo shoots – the company photographs 2,000 items a week – and catwalk videos. Spread over four floors, the 700 staff based here call it 'the fashion factory' and the open-plan floors are stuffed with shoot rails of clothes and accessories ready to be modelled. 'It's like a teenager's bedroom times 100,' jokes Mr Robertson.

Keeping the fashion and technology arms of the company under one roof – the company employs its own design team, whose products for Asos' own label account for half of all sales, and 120 people in IT – enables both sides of the business to learn from each other. 'We are a fashion and technology business,' he says.

Unusually for an office, the only phone that rings is Mr Robertson's BlackBerry. All the other employees stare at their screens and are busy blogging, tweeting or on Facebook. While many companies would discourage the use of social media at the office, Mr Robertson says this is exactly what his staff should be doing. 'They're doing what they would be doing anyway – but they're doing it for Asos,' he says. This is no coincidence. Most of Asos' staff fit the demographic of the company's customer base: young, trendy and predominantly female. Understanding exactly who its customers are is perhaps Asos' greatest strength.

Since its launch, everything Asos does has been aimed at 'the imagined 22-year-old', the median age of its shoppers. This is divided into three target groups: *Fashion Forward* – those who set the trends; *Fashion Passengers* – those who follow them; and *Functional Fashion* – the less trend-conscious. Mr Robertson believes employing the same types of people that Asos sells to means the company knows how to reach them. 'Nobody has done this before. If I had a board of seasoned retailers, they might have made decisions that were right for the retail market ten years ago,' he says.

One result is a stealth marketing strategy built on social networking sites. Teenagers think they have 'discovered' Asos through blogs and tweets instead of feeling like they have swallowed a sales pitch. The company has also created its own sites that build on existing platforms, often before its competitors. In 2009, the company launched Asos Life, an 'online community' that is a blend of staff and shoppers who blog, chat and post on fashion forums.

In 2010, the company launched Asos Marketplace, which allows designers to set up boutique stores on its site selling their own creations and one-off vintage items. 'Like a concession in a department store, they are renting web space from us,' he says. Asos vets its traders and takes a 10–15 per cent cut of everything they sell.

In 2011, it started the Asos Facebook store, becoming one of the first retailers to launch a shop on the social networking site. Signing up automatically gives Asos the right to send you e-mails, post on your wall and view your friend lists, photographs and profile information. Much of Asos' success has, however, been built on a low-tech guarantee to customers: free returns. In the early days of internet shopping, allowing customers to send back anything they did not want was essential.

As the company shifted its focus to the global 22-year-old, it offered free shipping. Mr Robertson calls this 'the best marketing money can buy' and, in the US, France and Germany, returns are also free. Not everyone is convinced that this model is sustainable. 'Offering free delivery is an expensive way of getting new customers but it shows how high Asos's margins are that they can afford to do that,' notes Nick Bubb, retail analyst at Arden Partners.

Another tap on finances is the company's growing number of product lines, which have to be stored somewhere. 'They have to be a perfect 10, operationally, to achieve these ambitious growth targets,' notes a rival retailer. 'There is no margin for error. If we achieved 30 per cent sales growth, that would be fantastic from our point of view. But if Asos doesn't achieve 50 per cent, the City will lose faith in the growth story.'

At the same time, rivals are improving their own offerings. At the luxury end of the sector, this includes Net-a-Porter and My-wardrobe.com, while there is a plethora of mid-market competitors including NotOnTheHighStreet.com. Moreover, fashion brands themselves are improving their online sales outlets. Superdry, for example, makes more money through sales via its own website and has barred Asos from selling its goods in certain countries. 'It's the most profitable part of our whole business,' says Julian Dunkerton, chief executive of Supergroup, Superdry's parent company. 'If shoppers go on to Asos and find Superdry, I'm happy. But if they tap in Superdry to a search engine and it comes up with another website, that's wrong.'

Always prepared to confound his critics, Mr Robertson has launched Fashion Finder, a service that will publicise brands that Asos does not sell. A nod to US fashion aggregator sites Polyvore and ShopStyle, the idea is to turn Asos into a 'fashion destination' rather than just a store. 'If you work at a fashion magazine, your role in life is to guide the reader through the world of fashion and edit it for them,' he says. 'Why can't shops do that?'

Mr Robertson said he wanted Asos to achieve £1 billion in sales, spread across five markets in five years. The five target countries are the US, France, the UK, Germany and China. If Asos can crack Asia, the story will enter a new dimension. So far, Mr Robertson has been able to do exactly what everyone said he could not. That management style does not seem to be going out of fashion.

In 2011, a focus on fashion-conscious and Internet-savvy young men and women and a global expansion programme boosted fourth-quarter year-on-year revenues more than 60 per cent at Asos. The online clothes retailer said full-year pre-tax profit before exceptional items 'would be at the top end of expectations' of £24 million to £29.3 million, pushing its shares up 13 per cent.

In 2010 Asos launched websites in the US, France and Germany, and hoped to open at least five country-specific sites in the next financial year, including China. UK sales grew 24 per cent to £44.8 million, in spite of difficult economic conditions facing consumers. For the first time, turnover from the group's international businesses overtook UK sales, and now accounted for 52 per cent of revenues.

Mr Robertson said he expected international sales — which rose 161 per cent for the quarter year on year — to grow to more than 60 per cent of total sales 'before you can shake a stick'. Total revenues increased 63 per cent to £96.6 million in the final quarter year on year, and 53 per cent to £340 million for the full year. Asos provides free delivery and returns to many of its markets, but this initiative would knock 260 to 280 basis points from full-year gross margins, the group said.

The group's Facebook store, which it launched in February 2011, was 'performing above expectations', Mr Robertson said, while Asos' Fashion Finder service, which includes more than 50 brands that Asos does not sell, has driven web traffic. 'This is our journey from shop to destination,' Mr Robertson said. 'Customers can create outfits, build looks, tag things they like and comment on styles. It's a different way of engaging with them.'

In 2013, Asos was also partnering with Primark to bring their £22 studded parka online, in Primark's first online venture, though on a limited basis.

Asos had evolved hugely from the original three-person start-up. Importantly, where once Asos followed, now it leads. From emulating celebrity fashion, it has come so far that it is now actually setting celebrity fashion trends. Asos own-label creations are now worn by celebrities from Rihanna to Kate Hudson. Asos offers something for everyone — men and women of course, but also maternity-wear, beauty products and kidswear. Although it does sell premium items, the average price is reasonable and accessible, the site is easy to navigate, and it is painless to return items — which is more than can be said for some far more expensive online retailers. Then there is the generation it sells to, its key demographic — one that expects a snappy online experience as a matter of course. By this stage, Asos had become the most expensive retailer in the sector by some margin, trading on a whopping multiple of 70 times expected 2010–11 earnings. As the dominant online-only fashion player, it is natural that Asos should command a premium in share price.

The fall from grace – a perfect storm

Asos remained a hero of the fashion industry through 2013, driven by stunning sales growth – defying the economic downturn, it looked like Asos sales would indeed go through the £1 billion mark – and the value of shares had doubled in 12 months. Retail sales were rising at around 34 per cent a year, with 8.2 million active customers and 60 per cent of sales outside the UK. Asos had become a £5.2 billion retail giant.

But in 2014 Asos hit its perfect storm, and everything seemed to go wrong at the same time. Profits fell by a fifth in six months and analysts started talking about a new online bubble. The company issued a series of profit warnings and saw £1 billion wiped off its market value. It looked like the run of good form had come to an end. Asos was no longer the darling of the stock market.

With a 45 per cent rise in costs, associated with the expensive entry to China and heavy losses in that venture, it looked like expansion had been too rapid. The Chinese venture lost £8 million as the company struggled to get stock into the country.

The Barnsley warehouse was working beyond capacity forcing the company to open temporary centres in Bradford and Selby, pushing labour costs up 23 per cent. The company had no choice but to increase its investment in supply chain infrastructure and IT. Then the summer of 2014 saw a fire at the Barnsley warehouse, that is estimated to have cost Asos £30 million in lost sales.

Worse, the strong pound meant that customers in some markets faced price increases of up to 25 per cent. While 60 per cent of sales were international and higher margin than the UK, because all the products are sold from a single website the company was tied to a single price for each item and it was difficult to raise or lower prices for any specific market. General price discounting across the board reduced profitability further – around 10 per cent of all products were being discounted at any given time. The company has now introduced 'zonal pricing' in an attempt to be able to price differently in different markets.

A new era for Asos?

Asos' fall from grace was spectacular, but notwithstanding the problems of 2014, Asos continued to grow and to remain in profit. Results in 2015 still showed a 14 per cent growth in sales.

The quality of the Asos value proposition remains intact. All the relevant metrics remain positive – active customers, new customers, order frequency, units per basket. The company still has a major global growth opportunity. Certainly, Nick Robinson maintains the view that, 'We are totally focused on rolling out the Asos business model globally as the world's leading fashion destination for twenty-somethings'. He believes that the business has recovered from the shocks of 2014 and has increasing momentum, particularly in overseas markets.

In 2015 the company has been extending its delivery cut-off times in the UK, introducing next-day delivery across Europe, as well as upgrading its global warehousing and IT infrastructure. It has introduced country-specific smartphone apps and has invested in automating the Barnsley warehouse.

But the market may have changed in ways that demand a new strategy for Asos to deliver superior value to its customers. In the early days, Asos was able to dominate the online fashion business by selling primarily third-party brands to web-savvy shoppers. But rivals are realising the power of online fashion. While in the past they were happy to sell through Asos, now they want more control of their own brands and especially the relationship with consumers. Certainly, Asos' decision to discount prices in the run-up to Christmas 2014 severely irritated some brands.

Asos was once the only destination for cutting-edge fashion online, but now it faces competition from a plethora of online upstarts such as Boohoo and Missguided. Traditional retailers, such as Topshop and even M&S are upping their online game. Next, whose Directory business has long out-paced competitors, is expanding sales of third party brands, while Amazon has also set its sights on cracking the online fashion market.

The reality is that low prices and fast fulfilment are now becoming commonplace across Asos' core trading areas of UK and Europe, and no longer give a competitive edge.

Late 2014 saw rumours of a bid for Asos. Amazon and eBay were mentioned as possible purchasers, though more likely is Asos' largest shareholder, Bestseller from Denmark, which has already acquired Zalando, a German online shopping business.

Questions for discussion

1. Considering the full spectrum of segmentation variables, describe how Asos segmented the market and the segmentation strategy it adopted. Is this same approach likely to be effective for the future or does Asos have to reposition itself in the market?
2. What were the reasons for the crisis for Asos in 2014? How do these affect customer relationships? What happens if a company fails to deliver the promises it has made to customers?
3. Does Asos have a competitive advantage? If so, what is it? If not, how can it create one?

4. How do you suggest that Asos should respond to the ways in which customers and competitors are changing in the current marketplace?

5. Will Asos ever return to the revenue and profit growth that it once enjoyed? Why or why not?

Sources: Claer Barrett, 'Fast fashion for fast consumers', *Financial Times*, 22 February 2011, p. 14; Mark Wembridge and Claer Bennett, 'Asos boosted by international websites', *Financial Times*, 14 April 2011, p. 22; Andrea Felsted, 'Asos helps Primark make online debut with a £22 studded parka', *Financial Times*, 4 June 2013, p. 17; Andrea Felsted and Adam Jones, "Stunning" sales growth drives Asos', *Financial Times*, 20 September 2013. p. 23; Peter Campbell, 'Asos is hit by profit plunge', *Daily Mail*, 3 April 2014, p. 66; Duncan Robinson, 'Asos suffers growing pains as costs rise', *Financial Times*, 19 March 214, p. 21; Jana Weigand, 'Web retailer is hit hard', *Wall Street Journal*, 6–8 June 2014, p. 17; Peter Campbell, '£1bn wiped off Asos by second profit warning', *Daily Mail*, 6 June 2014, p. 73; Andrea Felsted, 'Asos must "take the pain in short term" to reinvigorate its business', *Financial Times*, 17 September 2014, p. 21; Kadhim Shubber, 'Asos regains footing despite profit tumble', *Financial Times*, 2 April 2015, p. 20.

CHAPTER EIGHT

Products, services and brands:
building customer value

Chapter preview

After examining customer value-driven marketing strategy, we now take a deeper look at the marketing mix: the tactical tools that marketers use to implement their strategies, engage customers, and deliver superior customer value. In this and the next chapter, we'll study how companies develop and manage products and brands. Then, in the chapters that follow, we'll look at pricing, distribution, and marketing communication tools. The product is usually the first and most basic marketing consideration. We start with a seemingly simple question: what *is* a product? As it turns out, the answer is not so simple.

Before starting the coverage in this chapter, we can looking at an interesting product story. Marketing is all about building products and brands that connect deeply with customers. So, when you think about top brands, which ones pop up first? Maybe it's traditional global mega-brands such as Coca-Cola, Nike or McDonald's that come to mind. Or maybe a trendy tech brand such as Google, Facebook or Amazon. But one of the most fascinating developments of recent years has been the Uber taxi service and its impact in cities throughout the world.

Objective outline

➤ **Objective 1** Define product and the major classifications of products and services.
What is a product? (pp. 226–231)

➤ **Objective 2** Describe the decisions companies make regarding their individual products and services, product lines, and product mixes.
Product and service decisions (pp. 231–237)

➤ **Objective 3** Identify the four characteristics that affect the marketing of services and the additional marketing considerations that services require.
Services marketing (pp. 237–242)

➤ **Objective 4** Discuss branding strategy – the decisions companies make in building and managing their brands.
Branding strategy: building strong brands (pp. 243–252)

Uber: a killer product from the new sharing economy

The world is seeing a battle for the future of personal transport and it is being waged right outside our homes and offices and it is happening right now. Uber and a growing group of well-funded start-ups (like rival ride-sharing service Lyft) are trying to make getting a taxi as easy as booking a dinner reservation online or checking a price on Amazon. They are making a taxi ride just another thing you get with your smartphone. But these companies have an even greater ambition — they want to make owning a personal car completely unnecessary in modern cities.

About five years ago, Uber was the company that introduced the idea of letting passengers book the nearest taxi ride by smartphone, then track the vehicle as it approaches the pick-up point. After the journey, the service automatically pays the driver from the customer's pre-loaded credit card — no awkward tipping involved. Uber provides a simple experience and a much more pleasant way to get a taxi than hailing one in the street.

To be part of the network, Uber drivers receive about an hour's orientation, a free iPhone with the Uber app, some equipment for the windshield of their car, and then they are in business. They are not employees but independent freelance drivers. Uber owns no cars, it connects passengers to pre-existing fleet vehicle owners through its smartphone app — that's the Uber product.

Uber was founded in San Francisco by Travis Kalanick and Garrett Camp — both with a history of online start-ups and app development — with the idea of giving consumers more convenience and the feeling of travelling in style (in the early days Uber cars were large and luxurious). At the time, like many other cities, San Francisco capped the number of licensed taxis, regardless of the rapid growth in the city's population, leaving many passengers with long waits for elusive cabs. Also, as a result of limited taxi availability, major taxi companies did not seem to care much about prompt customer service, because they made their money from leasing cabs to drivers.

To get started Uber raised $307 million from a group of backers including Google Ventures (Google's investment arm) and Jeff Bezos, founder of Amazon. By 2013, the company looked to be billing $1 billion for taxi rides in the 70 cities across the world that it then covered. By 2015, Uber was valued at $40 billion.

In the process of developing its business, Uber has managed to be at the same time one of the most loved and one of the most hated start-ups of the smartphone era. Customers love the reliability, speed and convenience of the service, but complain bitterly about the surge pricing — higher prices at times of peak demand. Uber uses pricing to balance supply and demand. Raising fares during peak times persuades more drivers to get on the road to meet demand. Out of a $10 Uber fare during non-peak times, the driver keeps about $8. During a surge when prices can quadruple — such as during holidays or bad weather — the total fare may be $40 and the driver gets $32. Uber does ask passengers to agree to the higher fare before they get in the car.

Uber has been blocked in several markets by regulators wanting to protect 'consumer interests' but more particularly the businesses of traditional taxi firms. In Paris, incensed taxi drivers blocked road exits to main airports and created a gridlock in the city to express their displeasure at this new form of competition. In London, in 2014, cabbies descended *en massse* on Trafalgar Square to bring traffic to a stand-still to protest about competition from Uber. Protests extended from Paris and London to Berlin and Madrid. There have been several attempts to ban Uber from European cities, in spite of the enthusiasm of consumers for the service. Uber seems to revel in the controversy and the additional publicity it creates for the service. Kalanick has, after all, been described as having the public relations savvy of Miley Cyrus and the pugnacity of Alec Baldwin.

Uber is trying to make getting a taxi as easy as making a dinner reservation or checking a price on Amazon.

Source: Russell Hart/Alamy Images

Outraged opponents of the company accuse Uber of risking passengers' lives by putting untested drivers into the taxi driving seat, offering questionable insurance when things go wrong, and lowering prices as part of a conspiracy to kill the competition.

Indeed, Uber has admitted to overly aggressive sales tactics in some cases. When taxi driver unions complain – as they often do – Uber rallies its customers to tweet or e-mail regulators to support its cause. The unfolding Uber story normally involves a fight: scuffling with German regulators over banning one of its services in that country; sneakily snatching drivers from up-and-coming rival ride-sharer Lyft; working around taxi regulators and government officials of all kinds to bring its personal transport revolution to the market. Uber is in a lot of dog-fights but generally is ready for confrontation.

By 2012, Uber was facing competition from new start-ups like Sidekick and Lyft. These companies also connect cars and passengers via smartphone apps, but go a step further and allow any driver with a spare seat to pick up passengers who have asked for a lift via their smartphones. Uber's response was to launch its own ride-sharing service – UberX – with drivers using their personal mid-range cars.

Uber is rapidly expanding globally, now covering major cities in India and China, as well as Europe. By 2014, the international expansion included 246 cities in 46 countries.

The term 'Uber-Nomics' has been coined to reflect the fact that Uber has been created as part of a new 'sharing economy' where there is an Uber-type model coming out for just about anything – laundry (Washio), massages (Zeel), alcohol (Minibar). But *Fortune* magazine believes that Uber-mania is a symbol of something much bigger. It is a new type of 'platform' product that synthesises the firm and the market – workers become entrepreneurs, supply chains become marketplaces, and users are empowered. The sharing economy is where you can rent out your spare room or holiday home on Airbnb or HomeAway, and call on Guesty or Urban Bellhop to welcome the guests and clean up after them. A flood of new products and services is on the way from new start-ups in the sharing economy that will change things radically in many traditional markets.[1]

As the Uber story shows, in their quest to create customer relationships, marketers must build and manage products, services and brands that connect with customers and deliver superior value, even if it means disrupting a traditional marketplace. This chapter begins with a deceptively simple question: what is a product? After addressing this question, we look at ways to classify products in consumer and business markets. Then we discuss the important decisions that marketers make regarding individual products, product lines and product mixes. Next, we examine the characteristics and marketing requirements of a special form of product – services. Finally, we look into the critically important issue of how marketers build and manage product and service brands.

Product—Anything that can be offered to a market for attention, acquisition, use or consumption that might satisfy a want or need.

Service—An activity, benefit or satisfaction offered for sale that is essentially intangible and does not result in the ownership of anything.

WHAT IS A PRODUCT?

We define a **product** as anything that can be offered to a market for attention, acquisition, use or consumption that might satisfy a want or need. Products include more than just tangible objects, such as cars, computers or mobile phones. Broadly defined, products also include services, events, persons, places, organisations, ideas, or a mixture of these. Throughout this text, we use the term *product* broadly to include any or all of these entities. Thus, an Apple iPhone, a Jaguar XF and a Caffè Mocha at Starbucks are all products. But so are a trip to Paris, E*Trade online investment services, your Facebook page and advice from your family doctor.

Because of their importance in the world economy, we give special attention to services. **Services** are a form of product that consists of activities, benefits or satisfactions offered for sale that are essentially intangible and do not result in the ownership of anything. Examples include banking, hotels, airline travel, retail, wireless communication and home-maintenance services. We will look at services more closely later in this chapter.

Products, services and experiences

Products are a key element in the overall *market offering*. Marketing mix planning begins with building an offering that brings value to target customers. This offering becomes the basis on which the company builds profitable customer relationships.

A company's market offering often includes both tangible goods and services. At one extreme, the market offer may consist of a *pure tangible good*, such as soap, toothpaste or salt – no services accompany the product. At the other extreme are *pure services*, for which the market offer consists primarily of a service. Examples include a doctor's examination or financial services like life insurance. Between these two extremes, however, many goods-and-services combinations are possible.

Today, as products and services become more commoditised, many companies are moving to a new level in creating value for their customers. To differentiate their offers, beyond simply making products and delivering services, they are creating and managing customer *experiences* with their brands or company.

Experiences have always been an important part of marketing for some companies. Disney has long manufactured dreams and memories through its cinema films and theme parks throughout the world. And Nike has long declared, 'It's not so much the shoes but where they take you'. Today, however, all kinds of firms are recasting their traditional goods and services to create experiences. For example, BMW knows that it is selling more than a motor car, it's selling a luxury car ownership experience. This is shown to perfection in BMW's car delivery centre in Munich, called BMW Welt (BMW World):[2]

Designed by the Viennese architectural firm Coop Himmelb(l)au at an estimated cost of $280 million, futuristic BMW Welt is intended to create excitement when a customer gets the keys to a new car. Instead of going to the dealer where the car was purchased, the customer can stroll through exhibits, view presentations on innovation, and see the car rotate on a turntable, while illuminated by a spotlight A recent BMW ad puts it this way: 'We realised a long time ago that what you make people feel is just as important as what you make.'

Companies that market experiences realise that customers are really buying much more than just products and services. They are buying what those offers will *do* for them. 'A brand, product, or service is more than just a physical thing. Humans that connect with the brand add meaning and value to it,' says one marketing executive. 'Successfully managing the customer experience is the ultimate goal,' adds another.[3]

Levels of product and services

Product planners need to think about products and services on three levels (see Figure 8.1). Each level adds more customer value. The first and most basic level is the *core customer value*, which addresses the question *what is the buyer really buying?* When designing products, marketers must first define the core, problem-solving benefits or services that consumers seek. Although a touch politically incorrect in modern times, it has often said that a woman buying lipstick buys more than lip colour – Charles Revson of Revlon saw this early: 'In the factory, we make cosmetics; in the store, we sell hope.' And people who buy an Apple iPad are buying much more than a tablet computer. they are buying entertainment, self-expression, productivity and on-the-go connectivity to people and resources – a mobile and personal window on the world.

Core, actual and augmented product: people who buy an iPad are buying much more than a tablet computer, they are buying entertainment, self-expression, productivity and connectivity - a mobile and personal window on the world.

Source: Betsie Van der Meer/ Getty Images

Figure 8.1 Three levels of product

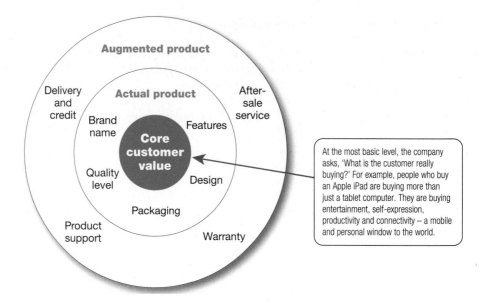

At the second level, product planners must turn the core benefit into an *actual product*. They need to develop product and service features, design, a quality level, a brand name and packaging. For example, the iPad is an actual product. Its name, parts, styling, features, packaging and other attributes have all been carefully combined to deliver the core customer value of staying connected.

Finally, product planners must build an *augmented product* around the core benefit and actual product by offering additional consumer services and benefits. The iPad is more than just a communications device. It provides consumers with a complete solution to mobile connectivity problems. Thus, when consumers buy an iPad, the company and its dealers also might give buyers a warranty on parts and workmanship, instructions on how to use the device, quick repair services when needed, and a customer service telephone number and website to use if they have problems or questions. Apple also provides access to a huge assortment of apps and accessories, along with an iCloud service that integrates buyers' photos, music, documents, apps, calendars, contacts and other content across all their devices from any location.

Consumers see products as complex bundles of benefits that satisfy their needs. When developing products, marketers first must identify the *core customer value* that consumers seek from a product. They must then design the *actual* product and find ways to *augment* it to create this customer value and the most satisfying customer experience.

Product and service classifications

Products and services fall into two broad classes based on the types of consumers that use them: *consumer products* and *industrial products*. Broadly defined, products also include other marketable entities such as experiences, organisations, persons, places and ideas.

Consumer products

Consumer product—A product bought by final consumers for personal consumption.

Consumer products are products and services bought by final consumers for personal consumption. Marketers usually classify these products and services further based on how consumers go about buying them. Consumer products include *convenience products*, *shopping products*, *specialty products* and *unsought products*. These products differ in the ways consumers buy them and, therefore, in how they are marketed (see Table 8.1).

Convenience product—A consumer product that customers usually buy frequently, immediately and with minimal comparison and buying effort.

Convenience products are consumer products and services that customers usually buy frequently, immediately and with minimal comparison and buying effort. Examples include washing powder, confectionery, magazines and fast food. Convenience products are usually low priced, and marketers place them in many locations to make them readily available when customers need or want them.

Table 8.1 Marketing considerations for consumer products

Marketing considerations	Type of consumer product			
	Convenience	**Shopping**	**Specialty**	**Unsought**
Customer buying behaviour	Frequent purchase; little planning, little comparison or shopping effort; low customer involvement	Less frequent purchase; much planning and shopping effort; comparison of brands on price, quality and style	Strong brand preference and loyalty; special purchase effort; little comparison of brands; low price sensitivity	Little product awareness or knowledge (or, if aware, little or even negative interest)
Price	Low price	Higher price	High price	Varies
Distribution	Widespread distribution, convenient locations	Selective distribution in fewer outlets	Exclusive distribution in only one or a few outlets per market area	Varies
Promotion	Mass promotion by the producer	Advertising and personal selling by both the producer and resellers	More carefully targeted promotion by both the producer and resellers	Aggressive advertising and personal selling by the producer and resellers
Examples	Toothpaste, magazines and laundry detergent	Major appliances, televisions, furniture and clothing	Luxury goods, such as Rolex watches or fine crystal	Life insurance and National Blood Service blood donations

Shopping products are less frequently purchased consumer products and services that customers compare carefully on suitability, quality, price and style. When buying shopping products and services, consumers spend much time and effort in gathering information and making comparisons. Examples include furniture, clothing, used cars, major appliances, and hotel and airline services. Shopping products marketers usually distribute their products through fewer outlets but provide deeper sales support to help customers in their comparison efforts.

Speciality products are consumer products and services with unique characteristics or brand identification for which a significant group of buyers is willing to make a special purchase effort. Examples include specific brands of cars, high-priced photographic equipment, designer clothes, gourmet foods and the services of medical or legal specialists. A Ferrari car, for example, is a specialty product because buyers are usually willing to travel great distances to buy one. Buyers normally do not compare speciality products. They invest only the time needed to reach dealers carrying the wanted products.

Unsought products are consumer products that a consumer either does not know about or knows about but does not normally consider buying. Most major new innovations are unsought until a consumer becomes aware of them through advertising. Classic examples of known but unsought products and services are life insurance, pre-planned funeral services and blood donations to the National Blood Service. By their very nature, unsought products require a lot of advertising, personal selling and other marketing efforts.

Industrial products

Industrial products are those purchased for further processing or for use in conducting a business. Thus, the distinction between a consumer product and an industrial product is based on the *purpose* for which a product is purchased. If a consumer buys a lawn mower for use at home, the lawn mower is a consumer product. If the same person buys the same lawn mower for use in a landscaping business, the lawn mower is an industrial product.

The three groups of industrial products and services are materials and parts, capital items, and supplies and services. *Materials and parts* include raw materials and manufactured materials and parts. Raw materials consist of farm products (e.g., wheat, cotton, livestock, fruits and vegetables) and natural products (e.g., fish, timber, crude petroleum and iron ore). Manufactured

Shopping products—A consumer product that the customer, in the process of selecting and purchasing, usually compares on such attributes as suitability, quality, price and style.

Speciality product—A consumer product with unique characteristics or brand identification for which a significant number of buyers is willing to make a special purchase effort.

Unsought product—A consumer product that the consumer either does not know about or knows about but does not normally consider buying.

Industrial product—A product bought by individuals and organisations for further processing or for use in conducting a business.

materials and parts consist of component materials (e.g., iron, yarn, cement and wires) and component parts (e.g., small motors, tyres and castings). Most manufactured materials and parts are sold directly to industrial users. Price and service are the major marketing factors – branding and advertising tend to be less important.

Capital items are industrial products that aid in a buyer's production or operations, including installations and accessory equipment. Installations consist of major purchases such as buildings (e.g., factories and offices) and fixed equipment (e.g., generators, drill presses, large computer systems and lifts). Accessory equipment includes portable factory equipment and tools (e.g., hand tools and lift trucks) and office equipment (e.g., computers, fax machines and desks). They have a shorter life than installations and simply aid in the production process.

The final group of industrial products is *supplies and services*. Supplies include operating supplies (e.g., lubricants, coal, paper and pencils) and repair and maintenance items (e.g., paint, nails and brooms). Supplies are the convenience products of the industrial field because they are usually purchased with a minimum of effort or comparison. Business services include maintenance and repair services (e.g., window cleaning and computer repair) and business advisory services (e.g., legal, management consulting and advertising). Such services are usually supplied under contract.

Organisations, persons, places and ideas

In addition to tangible products and services, marketers have broadened the concept of a product to include other market offerings: organisations, persons, places and ideas.

Organisations often carry out activities to 'sell' the organisation itself. *Organisation marketing* consists of activities undertaken to create, maintain or change the attitudes and behaviour of target consumers toward an organisation. Both profit and not-for-profit organisations practise organisation marketing. Business firms sponsor public relations or *corporate image advertising* campaigns to market themselves and polish their images.

For example, healthy-cereals producer Jordans promotes its Countryside Commitment to make its cereals more attractive to environmentally-minded consumers:[4]

Jordan's Countryside Commitment – We've all enjoyed our wonderful British countryside on a summer's day, however did you know that the number of herb-rich meadows has dramatically declined over the years, which, along with fewer hedgerows means there aren't enough places for wildlife to make their homes? And if they don't have homes and we lose pollinators like bees and butterflies it will heavily impact the food chain.

Hedgerow Homes – We are the only cereal company that insists the farmers who grow the grain that goes into our products, dedicate land specifically to create homes for wildlife. All the Conservation Grade farmers who grow grain for Jordan's use 10 per cent of their land just so that British wildlife, such as barn owls can have a home. Through Conservation Grade we've invested in the countryside for over 25 years and your support in buying Jordan's products has helped. But we can still do more . . .

People can also be thought of as products. *Person marketing* consists of activities undertaken to create, maintain or change attitudes or behaviour toward particular people. People ranging from politicians, entertainers and sports figures to professionals such as doctors, lawyers and architects use person marketing to build their reputations. And businesses, charities and other organisations use well-known personalities to help sell their products or causes. For example, Nike is represented by hundreds of well-known athletes around the globe in sports ranging from tennis and basketball to ice hockey and cricket.

The skilful use of marketing can turn a person's name into a powerhouse brand. Carefully managed and well-known names adorn everything from sports clothing, household products and magazines to book clubs and casinos. Such well-known names hold substantial branding power.

Place marketing involves activities undertaken to create, maintain or change attitudes or behaviour toward particular places. Cities, states, regions and even whole countries compete to attract tourists, new residents, conferences and conventions, and company offices and factories.

Slogans like 'Uniquely Singapore', 'Malaysia. Truly Asia', 'Incredible India' vie for attention. Tourism Ireland, the agency responsible for marketing Irish tourism to the rest of the world, invites travellers to 'Go where Ireland takes you'. The agency works with the travel trade, media and other partners in key world markets, such as the United States, Canada, Australia and a dozen European countries. At its Discover Ireland website, Tourism Ireland offers information about the country and its attractions, a travel planner, special vacation offers, lists of tour operators, and much more information that makes it easier to say 'yes' to visiting Ireland.[5]

Ideas can also be marketed. In one sense, all marketing is the marketing of an idea, whether it is the general idea of brushing your teeth or the specific idea that Colgate toothpastes and toothbrushes foster 'a world of oral care'. Here, however, we narrow our focus to the marketing of *social ideas*. This area has been called **social marketing**, described by the International Social Marketing Association (ISMA) as activity that seeks to develop and integrate marketing concepts with other approaches to influence behaviours that benefit individuals and communities for the greater social good.[6]

Social marketing programmes include public health campaigns to reduce smoking, drug abuse and obesity. Other social marketing efforts include campaigns to promote environmental protection, clean air and conservation. Still others address issues such as family planning, human rights and racial equality. But social marketing involves much more than just advertising; the SMI encourages the use of a broad range of marketing tools. It involves a broad range of marketing strategies and marketing mix tools designed to bring about beneficial social change.[7]

Social marketing—The use of commercial marketing concepts and tools in programmes designed to influence individuals' behaviour to improve their well-being and that of society.

PRODUCT AND SERVICE DECISIONS

Marketers make product and service decisions at three levels: individual product and service decisions, product line decisions, and product mix decisions. We discuss each in turn.

Individual product and service decisions

Figure 8.2 shows the important decisions in the development and marketing of individual products and services. We will focus on decisions about *product attributes*, *branding*, *packaging*, *labelling* and *product support services*.

Product and service attributes

Developing a product or service involves defining the benefits that it will offer. These benefits are communicated and delivered by product attributes such as *quality*, *features* and *style and design*.

Product quality

Product quality is one of the marketer's major positioning tools. Quality has a direct impact on product or service performance – thus, it is closely linked to customer value and satisfaction. In the narrowest sense, quality can be defined as 'no defects'. But most customer-centred companies go beyond this narrow definition. Instead, they define quality in terms of creating customer value and satisfaction. Quality is the characteristics of a product or service that bear on its ability to satisfy stated or implied customer needs. For example, German engineering company Siemens defines quality this way: 'Quality is when our customers come back and our products don't.'[8]

> **Author comment**
>
> Now that we've answered the 'what is a product?' question, we dig into the specific decisions that companies must make when designing and marketing products and services.

Product quality—The characteristics of a product or service that bear on its ability to satisfy stated or implied customer needs.

Figure 8.2 Individual product decisions

Don't forget Figure 8.1. The focus of all of these decisions is to create core customer value.

Product attributes → Branding → Packaging → Labelling → Product support services

Total quality management (TQM) is an approach in which all of the company's people are involved in constantly improving the quality of products, services and business processes. For most top companies, customer-driven quality has become a way of doing business. Today, companies are taking a *return on quality* approach, viewing quality as an investment and holding quality efforts accountable for bottom-line results.

Product quality has two dimensions: level and consistency. In developing a product, the marketer must first choose a *quality level* that will support a product's positioning. Here, product quality means *performance quality* – the ability of a product to perform its functions. For example, a Rolls-Royce car provides higher performance quality than a Škoda Fabia: it has a smoother ride, provides more luxury and 'creature comforts', and lasts longer. Companies rarely try to offer the highest possible performance quality level – few customers want or can afford the high levels of quality offered in products such as a Rolls-Royce motor car or a Rolex watch. Instead, companies choose a quality level that matches target market needs and the quality levels of competing products.

Beyond quality level, high quality also can mean high levels of quality consistency. Here, product quality means *conformance quality* – freedom from defects and *consistency* in delivering a targeted level of performance. All companies should strive for high levels of conformance quality. In this sense, a Škoda can have just as much quality as a Rolls-Royce.

Although a Škoda doesn't perform at the same level as a Rolls-Royce, it can deliver the quality that customers pay for and expect. Interestingly, Škoda does actually regularly win customer satisfaction awards for its cars.

Product features

A product can be offered with varying features. A stripped-down model, one without any extras, is the starting point. The company can create higher-level models by adding more features. Features are a competitive tool for differentiating the company's product from competitors' products. Being the first producer to introduce a valued new feature is one of the most effective ways to compete.

How can a company identify new features and decide which ones to add to its product? It should periodically survey buyers who have used the product and ask these questions: how do you like the product? which specific features of the product do you like most? which features could we add to improve the product? The answers to these questions should provide the company with a rich list of feature ideas. The company can then assess each feature's *value* to customers versus its *cost* to the company. Features that customers value highly in relation to costs should be added.

Product style and design

Another way to add customer value is through distinctive *product style and design*. Design is a larger concept than style. *Style* simply describes the appearance of a product. Styles can be eye-catching or yawn-producing. A sensational style may grab attention and produce pleasing aesthetics, but it does not necessarily make a product *perform* better. Unlike style, *design* is more than skin deep – it goes to the very heart of a product. Good design contributes to a product's usefulness as well as to its looks.

Good design doesn't start with brainstorming new ideas and making prototypes. Design begins with observing customers, understanding their needs and shaping their product use experience. Product designers should think less about product attributes and technical specifications and more about how customers will use and benefit from a product. Consider the impact of inventor James Dyson of the world of electrical appliances for the household and workplace:[9]

James Dyson is an inventor who started his electrical goods company in 1992, and in 2013 saw sales of products reach £1.3 billion. in spite of tough markets, Dyson is struggling to keep up with demand for products ranging from the bag-less cyclone carpet cleaner to the Airblade hand dryer and a bladeless cooling fan. The breakthrough was Dyson's cyclonic bag-less carpet cleaner, using centrifugal force to extract dirt from carpets. Dyson spent 14 years and produced more than 5,000 prototypes before he was satisfied he had come up with a better design. With innovative design and engineering, and a high price, Dyson's carpet cleaner has become the leading cleaner brand in the US, UK and Japan. The design aesthetics have made the Dyson cleaner a life style brand not simply a way of cleaning the carpet. Dyson's principle is to find things in everyday life that do not work very well and to make a better alternative. The Dyson Airblade commercial hand dryer works with a slim jet of air moving at 400 miles an hour. Although the Dyson approach is engineering-led, the industrial design principles are impressive too — Dyson products have been put on display in a host of museums, including the Metropolitan Museum of Art in New York. In 2010, Dyson's Air Multiplier (a 'fan without blades') hit the market with a futuristic appearance and innovative air cooling technology.

Branding

Perhaps the most distinctive skill of professional marketers is their ability to build and manage brands. A **brand** is a name, a term, a sign, a symbol or a design or a combination of these, that identifies the maker or seller of a product or a service. Consumers view a brand as an important part of a product, and branding can add value to a product. Customers attach meanings to brands and develop brand relationships.

Brands have meaning well beyond a product's physical attributes. For example, consider Coca-Cola and Pepsi as the most iconic soft drinks brands in the world:[10]

> In an interesting taste test of Coca-Cola versus Pepsi, 67 subjects were connected to brain-wave-monitoring machines while they consumed both products. When the soft drinks were unmarked, consumer preferences were split down the middle. But when the brands were identified, subjects chose Coke over Pepsi by a margin of 75 per cent to 25 per cent. When drinking the identified Coke brand, the brain areas that lit up most were those associated with cognitive control and memory — a place where culture concepts are stored. That didn't happen as much when drinking Pepsi. Why? According to one brand strategist, it's because of Coca-Cola's long-established brand imagery — the almost 100-year-old contour bottle and cursive font and its association with iconic images ranging from Polar Bears to Santa Claus. Pepsi's imagery isn't quite as deeply rooted. Although people might associate Pepsi with a hot celebrity or the 'Pepsi generation' appeal, they probably don't link it to the strong and emotional icons associated with Coke. The conclusion? Plain and simple: consumer preference isn't based on taste alone. Coke's iconic brand appears to make a difference.

Branding has become so strong that today hardly anything goes unbranded. Salt is packaged in branded containers, common nuts and bolts are packaged with a retailer's label, and car parts — for example, spark plugs, tyres and filters — bear brand names that differ from those of the car makers. Even fruits, vegetables, dairy products and poultry are branded, for example, Dole bananas, Florette's pre-packed salad range, Yeo Valley organic milk and Bernard Matthews turkey products.

Branding helps buyers in many ways. Brand names help consumers identify products that might benefit them. Brands also say something about product quality and consistency. Buyers who always buy the same brand know that they will get the same features, benefits and quality each time they buy. Branding also gives the seller several advantages. Brand name becomes the basis on which a whole story can be built about a product's special qualities. The seller's brand name and trademark provide legal protection for unique product features that otherwise might be copied by competitors. And branding helps the seller to segment markets. For example, Toyota Motor Corporation can offer the major Lexus and Toyota brands to European car buyers, each with numerous sub-brands — such as iQ, AYGO, Yaris, Verso, Auris, Avensis, RAV4, Land Cruiser and others — not just one general product for all consumers.

Building and managing brands are perhaps the marketer's most important tasks. We will discuss branding strategy in more detail later in the chapter.

Brand—A name, term, sign, symbol or design, or a combination of these, that identifies the products or services of one seller or group of sellers and differentiates them from those of competitors.

Packaging

Packaging—The activities of designing and producing the container or wrapper for a product.

Packaging involves designing and producing the container or wrapper for a product. Traditionally, the primary function of a package was to hold and protect a product. In recent times, however, numerous factors have made packaging an important marketing tool as well. Increased competition and clutter on retail store shelves means that packages must now perform many sales tasks – from attracting attention, to communicating brand positioning, to closing the sale. Not every customer will see a brand's advertising, social media pages or other promotions. However, all consumers who buy and use a product will interact regularly with its packaging. Thus, the humble package represents prime marketing space.

Companies are realising the power of good packaging to create immediate consumer recognition of a brand. For example, in the US an average supermarket stocks 43,000 items; the average Walmart supercentre carries 142,000 items. The typical shopper makes three out of four purchase decisions in-store and passes by some 300 items per minute. In this highly competitive environment, the package may be the seller's best and last chance to influence buyers. So the package itself has become an important promotional medium.[11]

Innovative packaging can give a company an advantage over competitors and boost sales. Sometimes even seemingly small packaging improvements can make a big difference. For example, Heinz revolutionised the 170-year-old condiments industry by inverting the ketchup bottle, letting customers quickly squeeze out even the last bit of ketchup. At the same time, it adopted a 'fridge-door-fit' shape that not only slots into shelves more easily but also has a cap that is simpler for children to open. In the four months following the introduction of the new package in the US, sales jumped 12 per cent. Even more, the new package does double duty as a promotional tool. Says a packaging analyst, 'When consumers see the Heinz logo on the fridge door every time they open it, it's taking marketing inside homes.'[12]

In recent years, product safety has also become a major packaging concern. We have all learned to deal with hard-to-open 'childproof' packaging, which it appears only children can open. After the rash of product tampering scares in the 1980s, most medicine producers and food makers now put their products in tamper-resistant packages. In making packaging decisions, the company also must heed growing environmental concerns. Fortunately, many companies have gone 'green' by reducing their packaging and using environmentally responsible packaging materials.

Labelling

Labels range from simple tags attached to products to complex graphics that are part of the packaging. They perform several functions. At the very least, the label *identifies* a product or a brand, such as the Dole label on bananas. The label might also *describe* several things about a product – who made it, where it was made, when it was made, its contents, how it is to be used and how to use it safely. Finally, the label might help to *promote* a brand, support its positioning and connect with customers. For many companies, labels have become an important element in broader marketing campaigns.

Labels and brand logos can support the brand's positioning and add personality to the brand. In fact, brand labels and logos can become a crucial element in the brand–customer connection. Customers often become strongly attached to logos as symbols of the brands they represent. Consider the feelings evoked by the logos of companies such as Coca-Cola, Google, Twitter, Apple and Nike. Logos must be redesigned from time to time. For example, brands ranging from Yahoo! and eBay to Tesco have successfully adapted their logos to keep them contemporary and to meet the needs of new interactive media such as the web and mobile apps and browsers. However, companies must take care when changing such important brand symbols. For example, when Gap introduced a more contemporary redesign of its familiar old logo – the well-known white text on a blue square – customers went ballistic and imposed intense online pressure. Gap reinstated the old logo after only one week.

Along with the positives, labelling also raises concerns. There has been a long history of legal concerns about packaging and labels. False, misleading or deceptive labels or packages constitute unfair competition. Labels can mislead customers, fail to describe important ingredients or fail to include needed safety warnings, and most countries have legal regulation applying to labelling standards.

Labelling has been affected in recent times by *unit pricing* (stating the price per unit of standard measure), *open dating* (stating the expected shelf life of a product) and *nutritional labelling* (stating the nutritional values in a product). As a minimum, sellers must ensure that their labels contain all information required by law, which may vary by country even within Europe.

Product support services

Customer service is another element of product strategy. A company's offer usually includes some support services, which can be a minor part or a major part of the total offering. Later in this chapter, we will discuss services as products in themselves. Here, we discuss services that augment actual products. Support services are an important part of a customer's overall brand experience.

The first step in designing support services is to survey customers periodically to assess the value of current services and obtain ideas for new ones. Once the company has assessed the quality of various support services to customers, it can take steps to fix problems and add new services that will both please customers and yield profits to the company.

Many companies are now using a sophisticated mix of phone, e-mail, fax, online and interactive voice and data technologies to provide support services that were not possible before. For example, in the computer business Hewlett-Packard (HP) offers a complete set of sales and after-sale services. It promises 'HP Total Care – expert help for every stage of your computer's life. From choosing it, to configuring it, to protecting it, to tuning it up – all the way to recycling it.' Customers can click on the HP Total Care service portal that offers online resources for HP products and 24/7 tech support, which can be accessed via e-mail, instant online chat and telephone.[13]

Added services may also be key innovations to enhance customer relationships. In the US, Starbucks has addressed the problem of the incoherent, caffeine-deprived customer who is daunted by the queue of people standing between them and the desperately needed coffee. The company is trialling a pre-order smartphone app, so the coffee is made and ready when the addict arrives at the store. Fast food chains are also testing and developing pre-order apps of this kind. It seems pre-order apps provide a new support service that enhances both restaurant efficiency and sales.[14]

Product line decisions

Beyond decisions about individual products and services, product strategy also calls for building a product line. A **product line** is a group of products that are closely related because they function in a similar manner, are sold to the same customer groups, are marketed through the same types of outlets or fall within given price ranges. For example, Nike produces several lines of sports shoes and clothing, and Marriott offers several lines of hotels.

The major product line decision involves *product line length* – the number of items in a product line. The line is too short if a manager can increase profits by adding items; the line is too long if a manager can increase profits by dropping items. Managers need to analyse their product lines periodically to assess each item's sales and profits and understand how each item contributes to the line's overall performance.

The product line length is influenced by company objectives and resources. For example, one objective might be to allow for up-selling. Thus BMW wants to move customers up from its 1-series models to 3-, 5-, 6- and 7-series models. Another objective might be to allow cross-selling: HP sells printers as well as computers. Still another objective might be to protect against economic swings – Marriott's different hotel chains cover different price points.

A company can expand its product line in two ways: by *line filling* or *line stretching*. *Product line filling* involves adding more items within the present range of the line. There are several reasons for product line filling: reaching for extra profits, satisfying dealers, using excess capacity, being the leading full-line company and plugging holes to keep out competitors. However, line filling is overdone if it results in cannibalisation of sales and customer confusion. The company

Product line—A group of products that are closely related because they function in a similar manner, are sold to the same customer groups, are marketed through the same type of outlets, or fall within given price ranges.

Product line stretching and filling: Samsung's large mobile devices line now offers a device size for any need or preference – even a wristwatch-like wearable smartphone.

Source: Oleksiy Maksymenko Photography/Alamy Images

should ensure that new items are noticeably different from existing ones.

Product line stretching occurs when a company lengthens its product line beyond its current range. The company can stretch its line downward, upward or both ways. Companies located at the upper end of the market can stretch their lines *downward*. A company may stretch downward to plug a market hole that otherwise would attract a new competitor or respond to a competitor's attack on the upper end. Or it may add low-end products because it finds faster growth taking place in the low-end segments. Honda stretched downward for all these reasons by adding its thrifty little Honda Jazz to its line. The Jazz, economical to drive and priced around £11,000, was designed to meet increasing consumer demands for more frugal cars and to pre-empt competitors in the new-generation mini-car segment.

Companies can also stretch their product lines *upward*. Sometimes, companies stretch upward to add prestige to their current products. Or they may be attracted by a faster growth rate or higher margins at the higher end. For example, some years ago, each of the leading Japanese auto companies introduced an up-market automobile: Honda launched Acura in its major global markets; Toyota launched Lexus; and Nissan launched Infiniti. They used entirely new names rather than their own existing brands.

Over the past few years Samsung has both stretched and filled its Galaxy line of premium smartphone and tablet mobile devices. Samsung started the Galaxy line with a 4" smartphone, then quickly added a 10.1" tablet. It now offers a bulging Galaxy line that includes a size for any need or preference. The basic Galaxy smartphones come with 5" screens. The popular Galaxy Note 'phablet' comes with a 5.7" screen in what Samsung calls 'the best of both' between a phone and tablet. Galaxy Tab buyers can now choose among any of three sizes – 7", 8" and 10.1". To top things off, Samsung offers the Galaxy Gear, a wristwatch-like wearable Galaxy smartphone. The Galaxy line still caters heavily to the top end of its markets. But to address the fastest-growing smartphone segment – phones that sell for less than $300 contract-free – Samsung is rumoured to have lower-priced Galaxy models in the works. As a result, through artful stretching and filling, Samsung's successful Galaxy line has broadened its appeal, improved its competitive position and boosted growth.

Product mix decisions

Product mix (or product portfolio)—The set of all product lines and items that a particular seller offers for sale.

An organisation with several product lines has a product mix. A **product mix** (or **product portfolio**) consists of all the product lines and items that a particular seller offers for sale. Colgate's European product mix consists of three major product lines: oral care, personal care and pet nutrition. Each product line consists of several sub-lines.[15] Each line and sub-line has many individual items. Altogether, Colgate's product mix includes dozens of items.

A company's product mix has four important dimensions: width, length, depth and consistency. Product mix *width* refers to the number of different product lines the company carries. For example, the 'Colgate World of Care' includes a fairly contained product mix, consisting of personal care products that you can 'trust to care for yourself, your home, and the ones you love'. By contrast, GE manufactures as many as 250,000 items across a broad range of categories, from light bulbs to jet engines and diesel locomotives.

The product mix *length* refers to the total number of items a company carries within its product lines. Colgate typically carries different brands within each line.

The product mix *depth* refers to the number of versions offered for each product in the line. Colgate toothpastes come in several varieties, including Colgate Total Advanced, Colgate Total Sensitive, Colgate Max and Colgate Smiles children's toothpaste. Each variety comes with special forms and formulations. For example, you can buy Colgate Total in whitening, freshening and clean versions.

Finally, the *consistency* of a product mix refers to how closely related the various product lines are in end use, production requirements, distribution channels or some other way. Colgate product lines are consistent insofar as they are consumer products and go through the same distribution channels. The lines are less consistent insofar as they perform different functions for buyers.

These product mix dimensions provide the handles for defining the company's product strategy. The company can increase its business in four ways. (1) It can add new product lines, widening its product mix. In this way, its new lines build on the company's reputation in its other lines. (2) The company can lengthen its existing product lines to become a more full-line company. (3) It can add more versions of each product and thus deepen its product mix. (4) The company can pursue more product line consistency – or less – depending on whether it wants to have a strong reputation in a single field or in several fields.

From time to time, a company may also have to streamline its product mix to pare out marginally performing lines and to regain its focus. For example, P&G pursues a mega-brand strategy built around 25 billion-dollar brands in the household care and beauty and grooming categories. During the past decade, the consumer products giant has sold off dozens of major brands that no longer fit either its evolving focus or the billion-dollar threshold, ranging from Jif peanut butter, Crisco shortening, Folgers coffee, Pringles snack chips and Sunny Delight drinks to Noxema skin care products, Right Guard deodorant and Aleve pain reliever. Such pruning is essential for maintaining a focused, healthy product mix.

SERVICES MARKETING

Services have grown dramatically in recent years. In the developed countries, the rapidly expanding services sector is contributing more to economic growth and job creation worldwide than any other sector. The services sector accounts for some three-quarters of the gross domestic product (GDP) of the European Union countries. In addition, over three-quarters of European Union jobs are now in the services sector.[16] Services are growing quickly in the world economy, making up almost 64 per cent of gross world product.[17]

Service industries vary greatly. *Governments* offer services through courts, employment services, hospitals, military services, police and fire services and schools. *Private not-for-profit organisations* offer services through museums, charities, churches, colleges, foundations and hospitals. A large number of *business organisations* offer services – airlines, banks, hotels, insurance companies, consulting firms, medical and legal practices, entertainment and telecommunications companies, property firms, retailers, and others.

The nature and characteristics of a service

A company must consider four special service characteristics when designing marketing programmes: intangibility, inseparability, variability and perishability (see Fig 8.3).

Service intangibility means that services cannot be seen, tasted, felt, heard or smelled before they are bought. For example, people undergoing cosmetic surgery cannot see the result before the purchase. Airline passengers have nothing but a ticket and a promise that they and their luggage will arrive safely at the intended destination, hopefully at the same time. To reduce uncertainty, buyers look for *signals* of service quality. They draw conclusions about quality from the place, people, price, equipment and communications that they can see.

Therefore, a service provider's task is to make the service tangible in one or more ways and send the right signals about quality. One analyst calls this *evidence management*, in which the service organisation presents its customers with organised, honest evidence of its capabilities.[18]

Author comment

As noted at the start of this chapter, services are 'products' too – intangible ones. So all the product topics we've discussed so far apply to services as well as to physical products. However, in this section, we'll focus on the special characteristics and marketing needs that set services apart.

Service intangibility—
Services cannot be seen, tasted, felt, heard or smelled before they are bought.

Figure 8.3 Four service characteristics

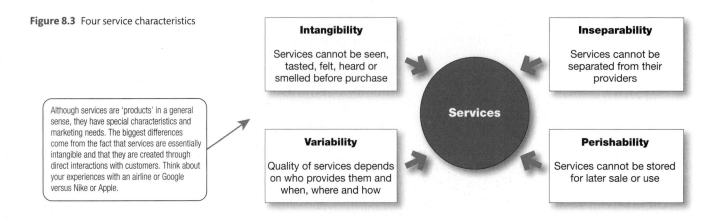

Although services are 'products' in a general sense, they have special characteristics and marketing needs. The biggest differences come from the fact that services are essentially intangible and that they are created through direct interactions with customers. Think about your experiences with an airline or Google versus Nike or Apple.

Service inseparability— Services are produced and consumed at the same time and cannot be separated from their providers.

Service variability—The quality of services may vary greatly depending on who provides them and when, where and how they are provided.

Service perishability— Services cannot be stored for later sale or use.

Physical goods are produced, then stored, later sold, and still later consumed. In contrast, services are first sold and then produced and consumed at the same time. In services marketing, a service provider is the product. **Service inseparability** means that services cannot be separated from their providers, whether the providers are people or machines. If a service employee provides a service, then the employee becomes a part of the service. And customers don't just buy and use a service, they play an active role in its delivery. Customer co-production makes *provider–customer interaction* a special feature of services marketing. Both the provider and the customer affect the service outcome.

Service variability means that the quality of services depends on who provides them as well as when, where and how they are provided. For example, some hotels – say, Marriott – have reputations for providing better service than others. Still, within a given Marriott hotel, one check-in counter employee may be cheerful and efficient, whereas another standing just a few feet away may be unpleasant and slow. Even the quality of a single Marriott employee's service varies according to his or her energy and frame of mind at the time of each customer encounter.

Service perishability means that services cannot be stored for later sale or use. Some private doctors and dentists charge patients for missed appointments because the service value existed only at that point and disappeared when the patient did not show up. The perishability of services is not a problem when demand is steady. However, when demand fluctuates, service firms often have difficult problems. For example, because of rush-hour demand, public transport companies have to own much more equipment than they would if demand were even throughout the day. Thus, service firms often design strategies for producing a better match between demand and supply. Hotels and holiday destinations charge lower prices in the off-season to attract more guests. And restaurants hire part-time employees to serve during peak periods.

Marketing strategies for service firms

Just like manufacturing businesses, good service firms use marketing to position themselves strongly in chosen target markets. British Airways is there 'To fly. To serve'; Tesco promises to support consumers through its 'Every little helps' message. Budget hotel Premier Inns offers 'Everything's premier but the price'. These and other service firms establish their positions through traditional marketing mix activities. However, because services differ from tangible products, they often require additional marketing approaches.

The service profit chain

In a service business, the customer and the front-line service employee *interact* to create the service. Effective interaction, in turn, depends on the skills of front-line service employees and on the support processes backing these employees. Thus, successful service companies focus their attention on both their customers and their employees. They understand the **service profit chain,** which links service firm profits with employee and customer satisfaction. This chain consists of five links:[19]

Service profit chain—The chain that links service firm profits with employee and customer satisfaction.

- *Internal service quality*: superior employee selection and training, a quality work environment and strong support for those dealing with customers, which results in . . .
- *Satisfied and productive service employees*: more satisfied, loyal and hardworking employees, which results in . . .
- *Greater service value*: more effective and efficient customer value creation and service delivery, which results in . . .
- *Satisfied and loyal customers*: satisfied customers who remain loyal, make repeat purchases and refer other customers, which results in . . .
- *Healthy service profits and growth*: superior service firm performance.

Therefore, reaching service profits and growth goals begins with taking care of those who take care of customers. Customer-service star Zappos, the online shoe, clothing and accessories retailer now owned by Amazon, knows that happy customers begin with happy, dedicated and energetic employees:[20]

> Most of Zappos' business is driven by word-of-mouth and customer interactions with company employees. So keeping *customers* happy really does require keeping *employees* happy. Zappos starts by recruiting the right people and training them thoroughly in customer-service basics. Then the Zappos culture takes over, a culture that emphasises 'a satisfying and fulfilling job . . . and a career you can be proud of. Work hard. Play hard. All the time!' The online retailer creates a relaxed, fun-loving, and close-knit family atmosphere, complete with free meals, full benefits, profit sharing, a nap room, and even a full-time life coach. Every year, the company publishes a 'culture book', filled with unedited, often gushy testimonials from Zapponians about what it's like to work there. And about what are Zapponians most passionate? The company's No. 1 core value: 'Creating WOW through service.'

Service marketing requires more than just traditional external marketing using the four Ps. Figure 8.4 shows that service marketing also requires *internal marketing* and *interactive marketing*.

Internal marketing means that a service firm must orient and motivate its customer-contact employees and supporting service people to work as a team to provide customer satisfaction. Marketers must get everyone in the organisation to be customer centred. In fact, internal marketing must *precede* external marketing. Service leaders start by hiring the right people and carefully orienting and inspiring them to give unparalleled customer service. The idea is to make certain that employees themselves believe in the brand, so they can authentically deliver the brand's promise to customers.

Internal marketing— Orienting and motivating customer contact employees and supporting service employees to work as a team to provide customer satisfaction.

For example, in retailing, even something as simple as a smile and polite greeting by staff can make a difference. Generally, shoppers who are cheered up by a nice welcome spend more

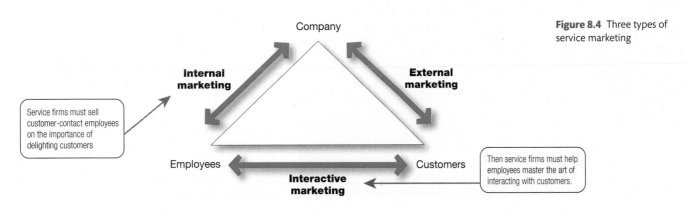

Figure 8.4 Three types of service marketing

money. Research in Mothercare stores in the UK suggests that shoppers who responded with a smile when greeted nicely by staff spent on average 67 per cent more than other customers. For retailers in this kind of business, improving the way staff interact with customers has a positive link to sales.[21] The exception appears to be luxury goods and designer labels where the snooty attitudes of shop assistants in high-end shops may actually boost sales. Research in Canada suggests that customers who felt 'rejected' by assistants in designer stores liked the brand more and were willing to pay more for it, than customers who were treated well.[22] Service marketers have to consider carefully the different ways in which employees may 'live' the brand message.

Interactive marketing– Training service employees in the fine art of interacting with customers to satisfy their needs.

Interactive marketing means that service quality depends heavily on the quality of the buyer–seller interaction during the service encounter. In product marketing, product quality often depends little on how a product is obtained. But in services marketing, service quality depends on both the service deliverer and the quality of delivery. Service marketers, therefore, have to master interactive marketing skills. Thus, the luxury hotels group Four Seasons selects only people with an innate 'passion to serve' and instructs them carefully in the fine art of interacting with customers to satisfy their every need. All new recruits complete three months of training, including improvisation exercises to help them improve their customer-interaction skills:[23]

> At Four Seasons Hotels & Resorts, every guest is a somebody. Other exclusive resorts pamper their guests, but Four Seasons has perfected the art of high-touch, carefully crafted service. Whether it's at the elegantly 're-imagined' Four Seasons London, the regally attentive Four Seasons Hotel Riyadh in Saudi Arabia, the tropical island paradise at the Four Seasons Resort Mauritius or the luxurious Sub-Saharan 'camp' at the Four Seasons Safari Lodge Serengeti, guests paying $1,000 or more a night expect to have their minds read. For these guests, Four Seasons doesn't disappoint. Its mission is to perfect the travel experience through the highest standards of hospitality. As a result, Four Seasons has a cult-like customer clientele, making it one of the most-decorated hotel chains in the world.
>
> But what makes Four Seasons so special? It's really no secret. Just ask anyone who works there. From the CEO to the doorman, they'll tell you — it's the quality of the Four Seasons staff. Its people are 'the heart and soul of what makes this company succeed', says Four Seasons founder Isadore Sharp. 'When we say people are our most important asset — it's not just talk.' Just as it does for customers, Four Seasons respects and pampers its employees. It knows that happy, satisfied employees make for happy, satisfied customers. The Four Seasons customer service legacy is deeply rooted in the company's culture, which in turn is grounded in the Golden Rule. In all of its dealings with both guests and staff, the luxury resort chain seeks to treat others as it wishes to be treated. 'How you treat your employees is a reflection of how you expect them to treat customers,' says Sharp.

Four Seasons' happy, dedicated and energetic employees – from the pool manager to the concierge to the financial manager - create an unparalleled customer experience.
Source: Dick Loek/Toronto Star via Getty Images

In today's marketplace, companies must know how to deliver interactions that are not only 'high touch' but also 'high tech'. For example, retail bank customers now expect to be able to log onto their bank's website and access account information, make transactions, receive investment information and get quotations for the bank's products. This is in addition to being able to contact service representatives by phone or visit a local branch. Thus, the challenge to banks has become to master interactive marketing at all three levels – calls, clicks *and* personal visits.

Today, as competition and costs increase, and as productivity and quality decrease, more service marketing sophistication is needed. Service companies face three major marketing tasks: They want to increase their *service differentiation*, *service quality* and *service productivity*.

Managing service differentiation

In these days of intense price competition, service marketers often complain about the difficulty of differentiating their services from those of competitors. To the extent that customers view the services of different providers as similar, they care less about the provider than the price. The solution to price competition is to develop a differentiated offer, delivery and image.

The *offer* can include innovative features that set one company's offer apart from competitors' offers. Some hotels offer no-wait computerised self-registration, car-rental, banking and business-centre services in their lobbies and free high-speed Internet connections in their rooms. Some retailers differentiate themselves by offerings that take you well beyond the products they stock. For example, Pets at Home isn't your average pet shop. The stores offer pet-food, toys, bedding, medication, insurance and accessories, with the choice of ordering online for home delivery or store collection. But many locations also offer Groom Room salons for sprucing up the scruffy pet (and microchipping them as well) and links to Companion Care, veterinary surgeries. The goal is to make Pets at Home your one-stop shop for all your pet's needs.

Innovative services closely tailored to customer needs provide unique offers. British start-up Luggage Mule takes away the stress of poor airline baggage handling (the deal when you go to Paris, France and your luggage goes to Paris, Texas). Luggage Mule collects your bags from the home or office a couple of days before you fly and couriers them to your destination address. You just show up at the airport with hand baggage knowing your bags are already safely at the destination – and the service is cheaper than excess baggage charges. The service now extends to bulky items like bicycles and to sea cruises.[24]

Service companies can also differentiate their service *delivery* by having more able and reliable customer-contact people, developing a superior physical environment in which the service product is delivered, or designing a superior delivery process. For example, most major grocery chains now offer online shopping and home delivery as a better way to shop than having to drive, park, wait in line and carry groceries home. And most banks allow you to access your account information from almost anywhere – from the ATM to your mobile phone or tablet device to get information and make transactions.

Finally, service companies also can work on differentiating their *images* through symbols and branding. For example, online insurance price comparison website Gocompare.com uses a flamboyant and incredibly annoying opera singer – Gio Compario – in TV and outdoor advertising. Singing his 'Gocompare' theme song and being extremely annoying, he has been the brand's mascot since 2009. Since 2013 he has been banned from singing but has been equally annoying in many other amusing situations – in 2015 Gio began singing again. Gio Compario has helped make the previously unknown insurance company memorable and approachable.

Managing service quality

A service firm can differentiate itself by delivering consistently higher quality than its competitors provide. Like manufacturers before them, most service industries have now joined the customer-driven quality movement. And like product marketers, service providers need to identify what target customers expect in regard to service quality.

Unfortunately, service quality is harder to define and judge than product quality. For instance, it is harder to agree on the quality of a haircut than on the quality of a hair dryer. Customer retention is perhaps the best measure of quality – a service firm's ability to hang onto its customers depends on how consistently it delivers value to them.

Top service companies set high service-quality standards. They watch service performance closely, both their own and that of competitors. They do not settle for merely good service; they strive for 100 per cent defect-free service. Unlike product manufacturers that can adjust their machinery and inputs until everything is perfect, service quality will always vary, depending on the interactions between employees and customers. As hard as they may try, even the best companies will have an occasional late delivery, a burned steak or a grumpy employee. However, good *service recovery* can turn angry customers into loyal ones. In fact, good recovery can win more customer purchasing and loyalty than if things had gone well in the first place.

For example, Southwest Airlines is the model for no-frills flyers throughout the world, including easyJet and Ryanair in Europe. Southwest stands out from its imitators through a proactive customer communications team whose job is to find the situations in which something went wrong – a mechanical delay, bad weather, a medical emergency or a berserk passenger – then remedy the bad experience quickly, within 24 hours, if possible.[25] The team's communications to passengers, usually e-mails these days, have three basic components: a sincere apology, a brief explanation of what happened and a gift to make it up, usually a voucher that can be used on their next Southwest flight. Surveys show that when Southwest handles a delay situation well, customers score it 14 to 16 points higher than on regular on-time flights.

These days, social media such as Facebook and Twitter can help companies root out and remedy customer dissatisfaction with service. Consider Marriott Hotels:[26]

> John Wolf, Marriott Hotel's director of public relations, heads a team of Marriott people who work full-time monitoring the company's Twitter feed and other social media. The team seeks out people who are complaining about problems they've had at Marriott. 'We'd rather know that there's an issue than not know it, and we'd rather be given the opportunity to solve the problem,' Wolf says. This strategy helps Marriott to solve customer problems as they arise and to recover previously dissatisfied customers. For example, when the team discovered an unhappy Marriott regular tweeting and blogging about an experience at a Marriott hotel that resulted in a ruined pair of shoes and big dry cleaning bill, they contacted him directly via Twitter, asking for his contact information. The next day, the disgruntled customer received a personal call from Marriott offering an explanation, a sincere apology and a generous amount of reward points added to his account to be applied to future stays at Marriott. The result: a once-again happy and loyal customer who now blogged and tweeted to others about his positive experience.

Managing service productivity

With their costs rising rapidly, service firms are under great pressure to increase service productivity. They can do so in several ways. They can train current employees better or recruit new ones who will work harder or more skilfully. Or they can increase the quantity of their service by giving up some quality. The provider can 'industrialise the service' by adding equipment and standardising production, as in McDonald's assembly-line approach to fast-food retailing. Finally, a service provider can harness the power of technology. Although we often think of technology's power to save time and costs in manufacturing companies, it also has great – and often untapped – potential to make service workers more productive.

However, companies must avoid pushing productivity so hard that doing so reduces quality. Attempts to industrialise a service or cut costs can make a service company more efficient in the short run. But that can also reduce its longer-run ability to innovate, maintain service quality, or respond to consumer needs and desires. For example, some airlines have learned this lesson the hard way as they attempt to economise in the face of rising costs. They stopped offering even the little things for free – such as in-flight snacks – and began charging extra for everything from luggage check-in to aisle seats. The result is a plane full of resentful customers who avoid the airline whenever they can. In their attempts to improve productivity, many airlines have mangled customer service.

Thus, in attempting to improve service productivity, companies must be mindful of how they create and deliver customer value. In short, they should be careful not to take the 'service' out of service. In fact, a company may purposely lower service productivity in order to improve service quality, in turn allowing it to maintain higher prices and profit margins.[27]

BRANDING STRATEGY: BUILDING STRONG BRANDS

Author comment

A brand represents everything that a product or service *means* to consumers. As such, brands are valuable assets to a company. For example, when you hear someone say 'Coca-Cola', what do you think, feel or remember? What about 'Nike'? Or 'Google'?

Some analysts see brands as *the* major enduring asset of a company, outlasting its specific products and facilities. A former CEO of McDonald's declared, 'If every asset we own, every building, and every piece of equipment were destroyed in a terrible natural disaster, we would be able to borrow all the money to replace it very quickly because of the value of our brand . . . The brand is more valuable than the totality of all these assets.'[28]

Thus, brands are powerful assets that must be carefully developed and managed. In this section, we examine the key strategies for building and managing product and service brands.

Brand equity

Brands are more than just names and symbols. They are a key element in the company's relationships with consumers. Brands represent consumers' perceptions and feelings about a product and its performance – everything that a product or a service *means* to consumers. In the final analysis, brands exist in the heads of consumers. As one well-respected marketer once said, 'Products are created in the factory, but brands are created in the mind.' Adds Jason Kilar, CEO of the online video service Hulu, 'A brand is what people say about you when you're not in the room.'[29]

A powerful brand has high *brand equity*. **Brand equity** is the differential effect that knowing the brand name has on customer response to a product and its marketing. It's a measure of the brand's ability to capture consumer preference and loyalty. A brand has positive brand equity when consumers react more favourably to it than to a generic or unbranded version of the same product. It has negative brand equity if consumers react less favourably than to an unbranded version.

Brands vary in the amount of power and value they hold in the marketplace. Some brands – such as Coca-Cola, Nike, Disney, GE, McDonald's, Harley-Davidson and others – become larger-than-life icons that maintain their power in the market for years, even generations. Other brands create fresh consumer excitement and loyalty, brands such as Google, Apple, YouTube, Twitter and Wikipedia. These brands win in the marketplace not simply because they deliver unique benefits or reliable service. Rather, they succeed because they forge deep connections with customers. For example, to devoted Vespa fans around the world, the Italian brand stands for much more than just a scooter. It stands for 'La Vespa Vida', a carefree, stylish lifestyle. Colourful, cute, sleek, nimble, efficient – the Vespa brand represents the freedom to roam wherever you wish and 'live life with passion'.[30]

Advertising agency Young & Rubicam's BrandAsset Valuator measures brand strength along four consumer perception dimensions: *differentiation* (what makes the brand stand out), *relevance* (how consumers feel it meets their needs), *knowledge* (how much consumers know about a brand), and *esteem* (how highly consumers regard and respect a brand). Brands with strong brand equity rate high on all four dimensions. A brand must be distinct, or consumers will have no reason to choose it over other brands. But the fact that a brand is highly differentiated doesn't necessarily mean that consumers will buy it. A brand must stand out in ways that are relevant to consumers' needs. But even a differentiated, relevant brand is far from an automatic winner. Before consumers will respond to a brand, they must first know about and understand it. And that familiarity must lead to a strong, positive consumer-brand connection.[31]

Thus, positive brand equity derives from consumer feelings about and connections with a brand. Consumers sometimes bond *very* closely with specific brands. As perhaps the ultimate expression of brand devotion, a surprising number of people – and not just Harley-Davidson fans – have their favourite brand tattooed on their bodies. Whether it's new brands such as Facebook or Amazon or old classics like Harley or Converse (Nike), strong brands are built around an ideal of engaging consumers in some relevant way.

A brand with high brand equity is a very valuable asset. **Brand value** is the total financial value of a brand. Measuring such value is difficult. However, according to one estimate, the brand value of Google in 2015 is a whopping $128 billion, with Samsung at $82 billion, Google at $77 billion,

Brand equity—The differential effect the brand name has on customer response to the product or its marketing.

Brand value—The total financial value of a brand.

Microsoft at $67 billion, and Verizon at $60 billion. Other brands rating among the world's most valuable include AT&T, Amazon, GE, China Mobile and Walmart.[32] Currently many of the fastest growth brands in value are from emerging markets like China.

The top global brands list is still dominated by familiar names like Google, Apple and IBM, but looking at the top 30 reveals brands like Tencent (China), China Mobile (China), ICBC (China/Thailand), Baidu (China), Toyota (Japan), Deutsche Telekom (Germany), Samsung (Korea) and Loius Vuitton (France). Branding is increasingly globalised and this trend looks set to continue, providing new challenges for Western brands. National identity may prove a weak defence. One study suggests that young consumers have little grasp of brand geography. US teenagers identified Nokia (from Finland) as Japanese; Lego (from Denmark) as American; Samsung (from Korea) as Japanese; Ericsson (from Sweden) as American; and Adidas (from Germany) as American. Young consumers may have less resistance to emerging market brands as a consequence.[33]

Of particular interest are new brands growing local strength and going international from emerging markets. In Latin America, for example, strong local brands include Peru's Inca Kola, which with a market share of 30 per cent easily beats Coca-Cola in that market. But more interesting is the new 'multi-latinas' going international, such as Chilean retailer Falabella expanding across the continent and banks like Brazil's Itau and Colombia's Bancolumbia.[34] It is already the case that some brands from China have dominant positions in their industries, for example Haier (appliances), Lenovo (computers), and other brands have been acquired (Weetabix is owned by Bright Food of China). Tata is the first Indian multinational and owns brands like Jaguar Land Rover. New brands from these markets are likely to escalate in importance.[35]

Partly as a consequence of new competition, brand values can and do change, and sometimes dramatically. In 2015, the biggest brand winners (by $million increase in brand value) were: Apple (+$23,623), China Mobile (+$16,071), Facebook (+$14,361), AT&T (+$13,409) and Amazon (+$10,977). Others on the top ten brand winners list are: Baidu, Google, China Construction Bank, Disney and Verizon. But correspondingly, in the same year, top brand losers were: Tesco (−$6,607), IBM (−$6.086), Hitachi (−$5,630), BNP Paribus (−$5,268) and Toshiba (−$4,645). Others on the top ten brand losers list were: GE, Sony, McDonald's, Vivendi and Mitsubishi. Marketers must watch carefully for signs of brand decline. For example, Croc's shoes were red hot six years ago, but today the share price is down 60 per cent from its peak. Nintendo seems to have similar problems. Brands may have to be redefined and relaunched.[36]

High brand equity provides a company with many competitive advantages. A powerful brand enjoys a high level of consumer brand awareness and loyalty. Because consumers expect stores to carry a particular brand, the company has more leverage in bargaining with resellers. Because a brand name carries high credibility, the company can more easily launch line and brand extensions. A powerful brand offers the company some defence against fierce price competition.

Above all, however, a powerful brand forms the basis for building strong and profitable customer relationships. The fundamental asset underlying brand equity is *customer equity* – the value of customer relationships that a brand creates. A powerful brand is important, but what it really represents is a profitable set of loyal customers. The proper focus of marketing is building customer equity, with brand management serving as a major marketing tool. Companies need to think of themselves not as portfolios of products but as portfolios of customers.

Building strong brands

Branding poses challenging decisions to the marketer. Figure 8.5 shows that the major brand strategy decisions involve *brand positioning*, *brand name selection*, *brand sponsorship* and *brand development*.

Brand positioning

Marketers need to position their brands clearly in target customers' minds. They can position brands at any of three levels.[37] At the lowest level, they can position a brand on *product attributes*. For example, P&G invented the disposable nappy category with its Pampers brand. Early

Figure 8.5 Major brand strategy decisions

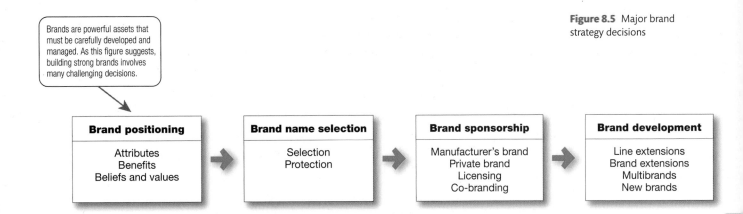

Brands are powerful assets that must be carefully developed and managed. As this figure suggests, building strong brands involves many challenging decisions.

Brand positioning

Attributes
Benefits
Beliefs and values

Brand name selection

Selection
Protection

Brand sponsorship

Manufacturer's brand
Private brand
Licensing
Co-branding

Brand development

Line extensions
Brand extensions
Multibrands
New brands

Pampers' marketing focused on attributes such as fluid absorption, fit and disposability. In general, however, attributes are the least desirable level for brand positioning. Competitors can easily copy attributes. More importantly, customers are not interested in attributes as such; they are interested in what the attributes will do for them.

A brand can be better positioned by associating its name with a desirable *benefit*. Thus, Pampers can go beyond technical product attributes and talk about the resulting containment and skin-health benefits from dryness. Some successful brands positioned on benefits are FedEx (guaranteed on-time delivery), Nike (performance), Tesco (save money) and Facebook (connections and sharing).

The strongest brands go beyond attribute or benefit positioning. They are positioned on strong *beliefs and values*, engaging customers on a deep, emotional level. For example, to parents, Pampers mean much more than just containment and dryness. The Pampers website (**www.pampers.com**) positions Pampers as a 'love, sleep and play' brand that's concerned about happy babies, parent–child relationships and total baby care. Says a former P&G executive, 'Our baby care business didn't start growing aggressively until we changed Pampers from being about dryness to helping mom with her baby's development.'[38]

Successful brands engage customers on a deep, emotional level. Advertising agency Saatchi & Saatchi suggests that brands should strive to become *lovemark*s – products or services that 'inspire loyalty beyond reason'. Lovemark brands pack an emotional wallop. Customers don't just like these brands, they have strong emotional connections with them and love them unconditionally.[39] Brands such as BMW's Mini, Aston Martin, Alexander McQueen, Jack Wills and Agent Provocateur rely less on a product's tangible attributes and more on creating surprise, passion and excitement surrounding a brand – they have earned the accolade of 'cool brands'.[40]

Some brands, for example, focus on the consumer's 'inner child' – the affection that adults felt for brands as children. Brands that play on nostalgia engage in a balancing act between the claims of three groups: loyalists to the brand, customers that have lapsed, and those that are yet to be. The appeal is strong when times are difficult, and in certain life stages, such as parenthood which causes people to think back to their own childhoods. Brands that have used this approach to beliefs and values include: Heinz Tomato Soup (the universal prescription for ill children at home in bed), Heinz Beanz (the classic tea-time comfort food for baby boomer children) and retro confectionery like sherbet flying saucers.[41]

One interesting example of brand positioning is the Ferrari brand owned by Fiat as one of its two luxury brands (Maserati is the other). Ferrari makes the $1.3 million LaFerrari hybrid supercar, among other models. Ferrari is pursuing a strategy of greater exclusivity for the brand because they believe that is a key value or benefit – in 2014 it cut production by 400 cars a year to 6,900 vehicles in total, and increased prices.[42]

When positioning a brand, the marketer should establish a mission for a brand and a vision of what a brand must be and do. A brand is the company's promise to deliver a specific set of features, benefits, services and experiences consistently to buyers. The brand promise must be simple and honest. Accor's French budget hotel Formula 1, for example, offers clean rooms, low prices and good service but does not promise expensive furnishings or large bathrooms. In contrast, the Ritz-Carlton offers luxurious rooms and a truly memorable experience but does not promise low prices.

Brand name selection

A good name can add greatly to a product's success. However, finding the best brand name is a difficult task. It begins with a careful review of a product and its benefits, the target market and proposed marketing strategies. After that, naming a brand becomes part science, part art, and a measure of instinct.

Desirable qualities for a brand name include the following: (1) It should suggest something about a product's benefits and qualities; some examples include Breathe Right (nose strips) and Food Saver (sealable packaging). (2) It should be easy to pronounce, recognise and remember; examples include Daz, iPod, and easyJet. (3) The brand name should be distinctive, such as Rolex and Uggs. (4) It should be extendable – Amazon.com began as an online bookseller but chose a name that would allow expansion into other categories. The move by Google to brand its operation as Alphabet provides an overall link while allowing the existing and new brands to develop their own identities – the new name also puts the company alphabetically ahead of arch-rivals Amazon and Apple, though this is said to be a coincidence! (5) The name should translate easily into foreign languages. Before changing its name to Exxon, Standard Oil of New Jersey rejected the name Enco, which it learned meant a stalled engine when pronounced in Japanese. (6) It should be capable of registration and legal protection. A brand name cannot be registered if it infringes existing brand names.

Choosing a new brand name is hard work. After a decade of choosing quirky names (e.g., Yahoo! and Google) or trademark-proof made-up names (e.g., Novartis, Aventis and Accenture), today's style is to build brands around names that have real meaning. For example, names like Blackboard (school software) are simple and make intuitive sense. Larry Page explains of the new Alphabet brand for what was Google: 'We liked the name Alphabet because it means a collection of letters that represent language, one of humanity's most important innovations, and is the core of how we index with Google search!'[43]

But with trademark applications soaring, *available* new names can be hard to find. Try it yourself. Pick a product and see if you can come up with a better name for it. How about Moonshot? Tickle? Vanilla? Treehugger? Simplicity? If you search for them on Google, you'll find that they're already taken.

Changing brand names is often controversial. When Kraft split its business into Kraft Foods (in the US) and Modelez (for the international marketplace) it was seen as a humiliating U-turn which broke away from the previous strategy of operating as a massive conglomerate, and people did not like or understand the Modelez brand (it is intended to be a portmanteau word that evokes the idea 'delicious world', and was one of 2000 ideas from employees around the world), and investors were unhappy. Other rebrandings have attracted controversy for other reasons: Philip Morris the cigarette producer became Altria, to distance itself from the tobacco industry; Andersen Consulting became Accenture to be more than an accounting firm; and the private military and security company Blackwater became Xe to avoid the association with allegations of misbehaviour by its employees in war zones. There are big questions to consider in making such moves and they should not be undertaken without adequate research into likely impact and effectiveness.[44]

Once chosen, a brand name must be protected. Many firms try to build a brand name that will eventually become identified with a product category. Brand names such as Kleenex, Levi's, Hoover, Formica and Velcro have succeeded in this way. However, their very success may threaten the company's rights to the name. Many originally protected brand names – such as cellophane, aspirin, nylon, linoleum, yo-yo, trampoline, escalator, thermos and shredded wheat – are now generic names that any seller can use. To protect their brands, marketers present them carefully using the word *brand* and the registered trademark symbol, as in 'BAND-AID® Brand Adhesive Bandages'.

Brand sponsorship

A manufacturer has four sponsorship options. A product may be launched as a *national brand* (or a *manufacturer's brand*), as when Samsung and Kellogg sell their output under their own brand names (Samsung Galaxy phone or Kellogg's Frosties). Or the manufacturer may sell to resellers who give a product a *private brand* (also called a *store brand* or a *distributor brand* or an *own-label*). Although most manufacturers create their own brand names, others market *licensed brands*. Finally, two companies can join forces and *co-brand* a product. We discuss each of these options in turn.

Manufacturers' brands versus retailer brands

Manufacturers' brands long dominated the retail scene. In recent times, however, an increasing number of retailers and wholesalers have created their own **store brands** (or **private brands or retailer brands or own-labels**). Although retailer brands have been gaining strength for more than a decade, recent tougher economic times have created a retailer-brand boom. Studies show that consumers are buying more private brands, and most don't plan to return to name brands anytime soon. Studies show that consumers are now buying even more private brands, which on average yield a 30 per cent savings.[45] More frugal times give retailer brands a boost as consumers become more price-conscious and less brand-conscious.

> **Store brand (or private brand or retailer brand or own-label)**—A brand created and owned by a reseller of a product or service.

Many large retailers skilfully market a deep assortment of store-brand merchandise. European retailers have generally been more successful than those in the US in positioning their own-brands as successful alternatives to manufacturers' brands. For example, in the UK, at leading supermarket Tesco own-brands account for around half of all sales, and Tesco *Finest* (premium) and *Value* (low price) brands are both worth more than £1 billion in annual sales. At the other end of the grocery spectrum, upscale Whole Foods Market offers an array of store brand products under its own label.

Once known as 'generic' or 'no-name' brands, today's retailer brands are shedding their image as cheap knock-offs of manufacturer brands. Retailer brands now offer much greater selection, and they are rapidly achieving manufacturer-brand quality. In fact, some retailers are out-innovating their manufacturer-brand competitors. As a result, consumers are becoming loyal to store brands for reasons besides price. Recent research showed that 80 per cent of all shoppers in the US believe retailer brand quality is equal to or better than that of manufacturer brands. 'Sometimes I think they don't actually know what is a store brand,' says one retail analyst.[46] In some cases, consumers are even willing to pay more for store brands that have been positioned as gourmet or premium items.

In the so-called *battle of the brands* between manufacturer and private brands, retailers have many advantages. They control what products they stock, where they go on the shelf, what prices they charge, and which ones they will feature in local promotions. Retailers often price their store brands lower than comparable manufacturer brands, and feature the side-by-side comparisons on store shelves. Although store brands can be hard to establish and costly to stock and promote, they also yield higher profit margins for the reseller. And they give resellers exclusive products that cannot be bought from competitors, resulting in greater store traffic and loyalty.

To compete with store brands, manufacturer brands must sharpen their value propositions, especially when appealing to today's more frugal consumers. Many manufacturer brands are fighting back by rolling out more discounts and sales promotions to defend their market share. In the long run, however, leading brand marketers must compete by investing in new brands, new features and quality improvements that set them apart. They must design strong advertising programmes to maintain high awareness and preference. And they must find ways to partner with major distributors to find distribution economies and improve joint performance.

For example, in response to the recent surge in private-label sales, consumer product giant Procter & Gamble has redoubled its efforts to develop and promote new and better products, particularly at lower price points. 'We invest $2 billion a year in research and development, $400 million on consumer knowledge, and about 10 per cent of sales on advertising,' says P&G's CEO. 'Store brands don't have that capacity.' As a result, P&G brands still dominate in their categories.

For example, P&G's premium laundry detergent brands capture a combined 50 per cent share of the $8.6 billion North American detergent market.[47]

Nonetheless, Nielsen research in 2013 suggests that cash-strapped shoppers across the world are continuing to opt for retailer own-labels. They found that two-thirds of shoppers across the globe are choosing retailer brands over manufacturer brands when it comes to new products. Consumers seem to be defecting even with 'innovation products' which firms like P&G, Unilever and Nestlé have sought to make their own. According to Nielsen, French consumers are the biggest fans of supermarkets' own-labels and 'value' products, with 80 per cent of them going for these when available, compared with 59 per cent of UK shoppers and 64 per cent of US shoppers. These trends are not restricted to Europe, but are hitting the Asia-Pacific and Latin American regions as well.[48]

Licensing

Most manufacturers take years and spend millions to create their unique brand names. However, some companies license names or symbols previously created by other manufacturers, names of well-known celebrities, or characters from popular movies and books. For a fee, any of these can provide an instant and proven brand name.

Clothing and accessories sellers pay large royalties to adorn their products – from blouses to ties and linens to luggage – with the names or initials of well-known fashion innovators such as Calvin Klein, Tommy Hilfiger, Gucci or Armani. Sellers of children's products attach an almost endless list of character names to clothing, toys, school supplies, linens, dolls, lunch boxes, cereals and other items. Licensed character names range from classics such as Sesame Street, Disney, Star Wars, the Muppets, Scooby Doo, Hello Kitty and Dr Seuss characters to the more recent Angry Birds and Hannah Montana. And currently a number of top-selling retail toys are products based on television shows and cinema films.

In a global retail market estimated by Deloittes as worth $4.3 trillion, retail sales of licensed merchandise account for about 6 per cent of all sales. There are more than 60 'billion dollar licensors', each selling more than a billion dollars a year of licensed merchandise at retail value – the top ten licensors account for around 50 per cent of the world's licensed merchandise business. Disney Consumer Products is by far the largest licensor in the world with $41 billion in licensed sales, including Marvel, LucasFilm, ABC Television and ESPN. Disney's portfolio includes hugely popular characters, from the Disney Princesses and Disney Fairies to heroes from *Toy Story* and *Cars*, to classic characters such as Mickey and Minnie Mouse.[49] But licensing extends beyond toys and superheroes. For example, Coca-Cola has a longstanding venture with Nestlé – Beverage Partners Worldwide (formerly Coca-Cola and Nestlé Refreshments), established in 2001 – to take its tea and coffee brands into global markets alongside Nestlé products. Recently, this venture was refocused on the ready-to-drink tea market – Nestlé tea brands are licensed to Coca-Cola outside the US, but Nestlé and Coca-Cola compete in coffee and non-tea beverages worldwide and in the ready-to-drink tea market in the US.

Co-branding

Co-branding—The practice of using the established brand names of two different companies on the same product.

Co-branding occurs when two established brand names of different companies are used on the same product. Co-branding offers many advantages. Because each brand dominates in a different category, the combined brands create broader consumer appeal and greater brand equity. For example, high-end shaving products brand The Art of Shaving partnered with mainstream marketer Gillette to create the Fusion Chrome Collection, featuring a power razor priced at more than £100 and billed as 'the world's most technologically advanced razor'. Through the partnership, The Art of Shaving gains access to Gillette's broader market; Gillette, in turn, adds high-end lustre to its shaving products line.

Co-branding can take advantage of the complementary strengths of two brands. For example, Nestlé has a very successful venture with its Nespresso operation – its Nespresso machines brew high-quality espresso coffee from expensive Nespresso coffee capsules. Nespresso capsules are sold exclusively by Nespresso But the coffee machines carry the brand names of well known kitchen equipment manufacturers such as Krups, Magimix, Siemens and DeLonghi. Indeed, Krups and Magimix store display models of Nespresso machines are also labelled as 'Made in Switzerland' (noted on the bottom of the machine). Nestlé's main business is selling the coffee capsules, but this business is supported by high-quality Nespresso coffee machines co-branded with up-market kitchen appliance specialists.

Seemingly unlikely partners KitKat (owned by Nestlé in Europe and Hershey in the US) and Google co-branded the latest Android KitKat operating system. Google has traditionally named versions of its Android operating system after sweet treats (because Android devices 'make our lives so sweet'), with names such as Cupcake, Honeycomb and Jelly Bean. This time, it named the new version 'after one of our favourite chocolate treats, KitKat'. In turn, KitKat launched specially branded KitKat chocolate bars featuring the Android robot. The co-branding effort added a touch of fun, familiarity and exposure to both brands.

Co-branding can take advantage of the complementary strengths of two brands. It also allows a company to expand its existing brand into a category it might otherwise have difficulty entering alone. For example, Nike and Apple co-branded the Nike+iPod Sport Kit, which lets runners link their Nike shoes with their iPods to track and enhance running performance in real time. 'Your iPod Nano [or iPod Touch] becomes your coach. Your personal trainer. Your favourite workout companion.' The Nike+iPod arrangement gives Apple a presence in the sports and fitness market. At the same time, it helps Nike bring new value to its customers.[50]

Co-branding can also have limitations. Such relationships usually involve complex legal contracts and licenses. Co-branding partners must carefully coordinate their advertising, sales promotion, and other marketing efforts. Finally, when co-branding, each partner must trust that the other will take good care of its brand. If something damages the reputation of the co-brand, it can tarnish the main brands as well.

Brand development

A company has four choices when it comes to developing brands (see Figure 8.6). It can introduce *line extensions*, *brand extensions*, *multibrands* or *new brands*.

Line extensions

Line extensions occur when a company extends existing brand names to new forms, colours, sizes, ingredients or flavours of an existing product category. Thus, the Nestlé Cheerios line of breakfast cereals includes the original Whole Grain, but also Honey Cheerios, Chocolatey Cheerios and Low Sugar Oat Cheerios.

A company can introduce line extensions as a low-cost, low-risk way to introduce new products. Or it might want to meet consumer desires for variety, use excess capacity, or simply command more shelf space from resellers. However, line extensions involve some risks. An over-extended brand name might cause consumer confusion and lose some of its specific meaning.

Line extension—Extending an existing brand name to new forms, colours, sizes, ingredients or flavours of an existing product category.

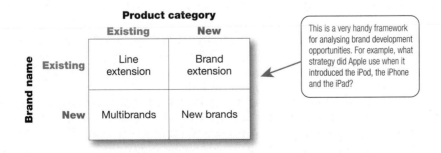

Figure 8.6 Brand development strategies

For example, in its efforts to offer something for everyone – from basic burger enthusiasts to practical parents to health-minded fast-food seekers – McDonald's has created a menu bulging with options. Some customers find the crowded menu a bit overwhelming, and offering so many choices has complicated the chain's food assembly process and slowed service at counters and drive-throughs. The extended menu may also be confusing the chain's positioning. According to one analyst, McDonald's 'doesn't have a clear marketing message right now'.[51]

Another risk is that sales of an extension may come at the expense of other items in the line. For example, how much would yet another Diet Coke extension steal from Coca-Cola's own lines versus Pepsi's? At some point, additional extensions might add little value to a line. A line extension works best when it takes sales away from competing brands, not when it 'cannibalises' a company's other items.

Brand extensions

Brand extension—Extending an existing brand name to new product categories.

A **brand extension** extends a current brand name to new or modified products in a new category. For example, Kellogg's has extended its Special K healthy breakfast cereal brand into a full line of cereals plus a line of biscuits, and snack and nutrition bars. Victorinox extended its venerable Swiss Army brand from multi-tool knives to products ranging from cutlery and ballpoint pens to watches, luggage and apparel. Starbucks has extended its retail coffee shops by adding packaged supermarket coffees, a coffee liqueur alcoholic drink, a chain of teahouses (Teavana Fine Teas + Tea Bar), and even a single-serve home coffee, espresso and latte machine – the Verismo.

For example, as it cuts production of its luxury sports cars to emphasise their exclusivity, Ferrari is looking to revenues from extending its brand to the Ferrari World indoor theme park in Abu Dhabi, and clothing lines like Prima (expensive leather jackets and other clothes for driving). Ferrari aims to be not just a car maker but a compilation of services and brand extension opportunities.[52]

A brand extension gives a new product instant recognition and faster acceptance. It also saves the high advertising costs usually required to build a new brand name. At the same time, a brand extension strategy involves some risk. The extension may confuse the image of the main brand. Brand extensions such as Heinz pet food met early deaths. And if a brand extension fails, it may harm consumer attitudes toward other products carrying the same brand name. Furthermore, a brand name may not be appropriate to a particular new product, even if it is well made and satisfying – would you consider flying on Hooters Air or wearing an Evian water-filled padded bra (both failed).

Each year, a survey by brand consultancy TippingSprung rates the year's best and worst brand extensions. Among the worst extensions – those that least fit a brand's core values – were Burger King men's clothing, Playboy energy drink, Kellogg's hip-hop streetwear, and a cake decorating kit from Harley-Davidson. 'Marketers have come to learn that the potential harm inflicted on the brand can more than offset short-term revenue opportunities,' says TippingSprung cofounder Robert Sprung. 'But that doesn't seem to stop many from launching extensions that in retrospect seem questionable or even ludicrous.' Thus, companies that are tempted to transfer a brand name must research how well the brand's associations fit the new product.[53]

In reality, a large majority of new products – tens of thousands of them every year – are extensions of already-successful brands. Compared with building new brands, extensions can create immediate new-product familiarity and acceptance. For example, it's not just any new wireless charging mat for your mobile devices, it's a Duracell Powermat. And it's not just a new, no-name over-the-counter sleep-aid, it's Vicks ZzzQuil. Extensions such as the Duracell Powermat and Vicks ZzzQuil make good sense – they connect well with the core brand's values and build on its strengths. But what separates brand extension hits from misses? According to brand extension consultancy Parham Santana, the success of a brand extension rests on three pillars: the extension should have a logical fit with the parent brand; the parent brand should give the extension a competitive advantage in a new category; and the extension should offer significant sales and profit potential.

Good fit goes both ways. Just as an extension should fit the parent brand, the parent brand should give the extension competitive advantage in its new category. The result is sales and profit success. For example, consumers have long associated the Vicks NyQuil brand with relieving cold symptoms so that they could get a better night's sleep. So the Vicks ZzzQuil name gave the extension a substantial boost in the sleep-aids segment. Similarly, when FedEx created FedEx TechConnect, a service that handles technology configuring, repairing and refurbishing for businesses, the FedEx brand's established reputation for speed, reliability and accessibility gave the new service immediate credibility over competitors.[54]

Before transferring a brand name to a new product, marketers must research how well the extension fits the parent brand's associations, as well as how much the parent brand will boost the extension's market success

Multi-brands

Companies often market many different brands in a given product category. For example, in the United States, P&G sells six brands of laundry detergent, five brands of shampoo and four brands of dishwashing detergent. Similarly in the US, PepsiCo markets at least eight brands of soft drinks, three brands of sports and energy drinks, four brands of bottled teas and coffees, three brands of bottled waters and nine brands of fruit drinks. Each brand includes a long list of sub-brands.

Multibranding offers a way to establish different features that appeal to different customer segments, lock up more reseller shelf space, and capture a larger market share. For example, P&G's six laundry detergent brands combined capture a whopping 62 per cent of the US laundry detergent market. And although PepsiCo's many brands of drinks compete with one another on supermarket shelves, the combined brands reap a much greater overall market share than any single brand ever could. Similarly, by positioning multiple brands in multiple segments, Pepsi's eight soft drink brands combine to capture much more market share than any single brand could capture by itself.

A major drawback of multi-branding is that each brand might obtain only a small market share, and none may be very profitable. The company may end up spreading its resources over many brands instead of building a few brands to a highly profitable level. These companies should reduce the number of brands they sell in a given category and set up tighter screening procedures for new brands. In the early 2000s, Unilever trimmed its brand portfolio from 1,600 brand names to 400, with the goal that the money saved by the cost cutting was then spent promoting Unilever's core, high-yield brands. The company has since focused on its core food brands (e.g., Ben & Jerry's, Lipton Teas), personal care (e.g., Dove, Lynx) and home care (e.g., Persil, Comfort).

New brands

A company might believe that the power of its existing brand name is waning, so a new brand name is needed. Or it may create a new brand name when it enters a new product category for which none of its current brand names are appropriate. For example, Toyota created the separate Lexus brand, targeted toward luxury car consumers, and the Scion brand, targeted toward Millennial consumers.

As with multi-branding, offering too many new brands can result in a company spreading its resources too thin. And in some industries, such as consumer packaged goods, consumers and retailers have become concerned that there are already too many brands, with too few differences between them. Thus, P&G, Kraft, Unilever and other large consumer-product marketers are now pursuing mega-brand strategies – weeding out weaker or slower-growing brands and focusing their marketing efforts on brands that can achieve the number-one or number-two market share positions with good growth prospects in their categories.

Managing brands

Companies must manage their brands carefully. First, a brand's positioning must be continuously communicated to consumers. Major brand marketers often spend huge amounts on advertising to create brand awareness and build preference and loyalty. For example, worldwide, Coca-Cola spends almost $3 billion annually to advertise its many brands, GM spends $3.2 billion, Unilever spends $7.4 billion and P&G spends an astounding $10.6 billion.[55]

Managing brands requires managing 'touch points'. Says a former Disney executive: 'A brand is a living entity, and it is enriched or undermined cumulatively over time, the product of a thousand small gestures'.

Source: tim gartside/Alamy Images

Such advertising campaigns can help create name recognition, brand knowledge, and perhaps even some brand preference. However, the fact is that brands are not maintained by advertising but by customers' *engagement* with brands and customers' *brand experiences*. Today, customers come to know a brand through a wide range of contacts and touch points. These include advertising but also personal experience with a brand, word of mouth and social media, company web pages and mobile apps, and many others. The company must put as much care into managing these touch points as it does into producing its ads. A one former Disney top executive agrees: 'A brand is a living entity, and it is enriched or undermined cumulatively over time, the product of a thousand small gestures.'[56]

A brand's positioning will not take hold fully unless everyone in the company lives the brand. Therefore the company needs to train its people to be customer-centred. Even better, the company should carry on internal brand building to help employees understand and be enthusiastic about the brand promise. Many companies go even further by training and encouraging their distributors and dealers to serve their customers well.

Finally, companies need to periodically audit their brands' strengths and weaknesses. They should ask: does our brand excel at delivering benefits that consumers truly value? is the brand properly positioned? do all of our consumer touch points support the brand's positioning? do the brand's managers understand what the brand means to consumers? does the brand receive proper, sustained support? The brand audit may turn up brands that need more support, brands that need to be dropped, or brands that must be re-branded or repositioned because of changing customer preferences or new competitors.

OBJECTIVES REVIEW AND KEY TERMS

A product is more than a simple set of tangible features. Each product or service offered to customers can be viewed on three levels. The *core customer value* consists of the core problem-solving benefits that consumers seek when they buy a product. The *actual product* exists around the core and includes the quality level, features, design, brand name and packaging. The *augmented product* is the actual product plus the various services and benefits offered with it, such as a warranty, free delivery, installation and maintenance.

OBJECTIVE 1 Define product and the major classifications of products and services (pp. 226–231)

Broadly defined, a *product* is anything that can be offered to a market for attention, acquisition, use or consumption that might satisfy a want or a need. Products include physical objects but also services, events, persons, places, organisations or ideas, or mixtures of these entities. *Services* are products that consist of activities, benefits or

satisfactions offered for sale that are essentially intangible, such as banking, hotel, tax preparation and home-repair services.

Products and services fall into two broad classes based on the types of consumers that use them. *Consumer products* – those bought by final consumers – are usually classified according to consumer shopping habits (convenience products, shopping products, speciality products and unsought products). *Industrial products* – purchased for further processing or for use in conducting a business – include materials and parts, capital items, and supplies and services. Other marketable entities – such as organisations, persons, places and ideas – can also be thought of as products.

OBJECTIVE 2 Describe the decisions companies make regarding their individual products and services, product lines and product mixes (pp. 231–237)

Individual product decisions involve product attributes, branding, packaging, labelling and product support services. *Product attribute* decisions involve product quality, features and style and design. *Branding* decisions include selecting a brand name and developing a brand strategy. *Packaging* provides many key benefits, such as protection, economy, convenience and promotion. Package decisions often include designing *labels*, which identify, describe and possibly promote a product. Companies also develop *product support services* that enhance customer service and satisfaction and safeguard against competitors.

Most companies produce a product line rather than a single product. A *product line* is a group of products that is related in function, customer-purchase needs or distribution channels. All product lines and items offered to customers by a particular seller make up the *product mix*. The mix can be described by four dimensions: width, length, depth and consistency. These dimensions are the tools for developing the company's product strategy.

OBJECTIVE 3 Identify the four characteristics that affect the marketing of services and the additional marketing considerations that services require (pp. 237–242)

Services are characterised by four key characteristics: they are *intangible*, *inseparable*, *variable* and *perishable*. Each characteristic poses problems and marketing requirements. Marketers work to find ways to make the service more tangible, increase the productivity of providers who are inseparable from their products, standardise quality in the face of variability, and improve demand movements and supply capacities in the face of service perishability.

Good service companies focus attention on *both* customers and employees. They understand the *service profit chain*, which links service firm profits with employee and customer satisfaction. Services marketing strategy calls not only for external marketing but also for *internal marketing* to motivate employees and *interactive marketing* to create service delivery skills among service providers. To succeed, service marketers must create

competitive differentiation, offer high *service quality* and find ways to increase *service productivity*.

OBJECTIVE 4 Discuss branding strategy – the decisions companies make in building and managing their brands (pp. 243–252)

Some analysts see brands as *the* major enduring asset of a company. Brands are more than just names and symbols – they embody everything that a product or a service *means* to consumers. *Brand equity* is the positive differential effect that knowing brand name has on customer response to a product or a service. A brand with strong brand equity is a very valuable asset.

In building brands, companies need to make decisions about brand positioning, brand name selection, brand sponsorship and brand development. The most powerful *brand positioning* builds around strong consumer beliefs and values. *Brand name selection* involves finding the best brand name based on a careful review of product benefits, the target market and proposed marketing strategies. A manufacturer has four *brand sponsorship* options: it can launch a *national brand* (or a manufacturer's brand), sell to resellers who use a *private brand*, market *licensed brands*, or join forces with another company to *co-brand* a product. A company also has four choices when it comes to developing brands. It can introduce *line extensions*, *brand extensions*, *multi-brands* or *new brands*.

Companies must build and manage their brands carefully. A brand's positioning must be continuously communicated to consumers. Advertising can help. However, brands are not maintained by advertising but by customers' *brand experiences*. Customers come to know a brand through a wide range of contacts and interactions. The company must put as much care into managing these touch points as it does into producing its ads. Companies must periodically audit their brands' strengths and weaknesses.

NAVIGATING THE KEY TERMS

OBJECTIVE 1
Product (p. 226)
Service (p. 226)
Consumer product (p. 228)
Convenience product (p. 228)
Shopping product (p. 229)
Specialty product (p. 229)
Unsought product (p. 229)
Industrial product (p. 229)
Social marketing (p. 231)

OBJECTIVE 2
Product quality (p. 231)
Brand (p. 233)

Packaging (p. 234)
Product line (p. 235)
Product mix (product portfolio)
   (p. 236)

OBJECTIVE 3
Service intangibility (p. 237)
Service inseparability (p. 238)
Service variability (p. 238)
Service perishability (p. 238)
Service profit chain (p. 239)
Internal marketing (p. 239)
Interactive marketing (p. 240)

OBJECTIVE 4
Brand equity (p. 243)
Brand value (p. 243)
Store brand (private brand)
   (p. 247)
Co-branding (p. 248)
Line extension (p. 249)
Brand extension (p. 250)

DISCUSSION AND CRITICAL THINKING

Discussion questions

8-1 What is a product? How do consumer products differ from industrial products? (AACSB: Communication; Reflective thinking)

8-2 Name and briefly describe the important decisions in developing and marketing individual products and services. (AACSB: Communication)

8-3 Explain the importance of product quality and discuss how marketers use quality to create customer value. (AACSB: Communication)

8-4 What is a brand? Describe the brand sponsorship options available to marketers and provide an example of each. (AACSB: Communication)

8-5 Discuss how service providers differentiate their services from those of competitors and provide an example of each. (AACSB: Communication)

Critical-thinking exercises

8-6 In many countries, regulators are requiring improvements to the standard nutrition labels on food items. In a small group, research the nutrition labelling requirements and likely changes in a country of your choice and create a report explaining them. Include history on nutrition labels in that country in your presentation. (AACSB: Communication; Use of IT; Reflective thinking)

8-7 A product's package must satisfy many criteria, such as sustainability, convenience, safety, efficiency, functionality and marketing. Research 'packaging awards' and develop a presentation analysing an award-winning product packaging effort. Describe the organisation hosting the award competition, the criteria for selecting winners, and one of the award-winning packages. (AACSB: Communication; Use of IT)

8-8 Find five examples of service-provider attempts to reduce service intangibility. Describe them. (AACSB: Communication; Reflective thinking)

Mini-cases and applications

Online, mobile and social media marketing: keeping tabs on Fido's health

Want to monitor your dog's health and fitness? Now, in the US you can do this with devices like Whistle and Voyce, wearable bands placed around a dog's neck like a regular collar. Only this is no regular collar. It monitors your dog's vital signs, such as heart and respiratory rates and calories burned. You can also learn if your dog is active or sleeps most of the day. Unlike humans, dogs do not exhibit symptoms and it is often too late when you notice something is wrong. Voyce gives dogs a 'voice' by letting owners 'connect the dots' to reveal anything that's amiss. Although the monitoring will not set off alarm bells, owners can track vital stats through a monthly subscription service synced with a computer, tablet or smartphone and share that data with a vet. Over time, the device gets to know a dog and sends owners customised articles, tips and advice. Using a mobile device, owners can remotely access their pet's data anytime through www.MyDogsVoyce.com. Voyce also makes it easy to share your pup's milestones with friends and family through social media. Such devices are not cheap, however, ranging from €130 for Whistle to €300 for Voyce, in addition to a monthly service fee. The makers of Voyce also hope to introduce a device to fit even the smallest dogs, cats and horses. These devices gained popularity in 2014 and 2015 and are likely to reach the dog-lovers of Europe very soon.

8-9 Describe the core, actual and augmented levels of product associated with this product. What level does the monitoring service represent? Explain. (AACSB: Communication; Reflective thinking)

8-10 Discuss two examples of similar types of wearable technology for humans. (AACSB: Communication; Reflective thinking)

Marketing ethics: $450 Starbucks gift card

For the second year running in the US, right around the holidays Starbucks offered the Limited Edition Medal Starbucks Card for $450, entitling the holder to $400 of Starbucks drinks, goodies and gold-level Starbucks membership status. The other $50 was to cover the cost to make the handcrafted, rose-coloured, laser-etched steel card. Sounds crazy, doesn't it? Well, 1,000 of the super-premium cards, which could only be purchased at the luxury goods website Gilt.com, sold out within minutes. Then they popped up on eBay selling at $500 to $1,000! The premium cards are refillable, allowing owners elite exclusivity. Some criticised Starbucks, claiming it is a card 'for the 1 per cent' and saying it is 'all about status' and that holders of the premium card have something others don't. Starbucks also rolled out a pricey brew for the other 99 per cent, charging $7 a cup.

8-11 What is it about Starbucks that allows the company to sell a gift card for $50 more than the $400 in merchandise the card can purchase? Should a brand be allowed to do that? (AACSB: Communication; Reflective thinking; Ethical reasoning)

8-12 How has Starbucks positioned its brand? Could this premium gift card offer or $7 cup of coffee harm Starbucks' brand image? (AACSB: Communication; Reflective thinking)

Marketing by the numbers: Pop-Tarts gone nutty!

Kellogg's, maker of Pop-Tarts, recently introduced Pop-Tarts Gone Nutty! The new product includes flavours such as peanut butter and chocolate peanut butter. Although the new Gone Nutty! product will reap a higher wholesale price for the company (€1.20 per eight-pack of the new product versus €1.00 per pack for the original product), it also comes with higher variable costs (€0.55 per eight-pack for the new product versus €0.30 per eight-pack for the original product).

8-13 What brand development strategy is Kellogg's undertaking? (AACSB: Communication; Reflective thinking)

8-14 Assume the company expects to sell 5 million packages of Pop-Tarts Gone Nutty! in the first year after introduction globally, but expects that 80 per cent of those sales will come from buyers who would normally purchase existing Pop-Tart flavours (that is, they will be cannibalised sales). Assuming the sales of regular Pop-Tarts are normally 300 million packs per year and that the company will incur an increase in fixed costs of €500,000 during the first year to launch Gone Nutty!, will the new product be profitable for the company? Refer to the discussion of cannibalisation in Appendix 2: Marketing by the Numbers for an explanation regarding how to conduct the analysis (AACSB: Communication; Analytical reasoning).

REFERENCES

[1] Brad Stone, 'Invasion of the taxi snatchers', *Bloomberg BusinessWeek*, 20 February 2014, pp. 38–42; Lisa Fleisher, 'Cabbies plan big protests against Uber in Europe', *Wall Street Journal*, 11 June 2014, p. 1; Adam Lashinsky, 'Uber banks on world domination', *Fortune*, 6 October 2014, pp. 35–37; Mark Milian and Serena Saitto, 'Uber alles', *Bloomberg BusinessWeek*, 24–30 November 2014, pp. 35–36; Alan Murray, 'Uber-Nomics', *Fortune*, 1 January 2015, p. 2; Sarah Mishkin, 'The back office start-ups that serve the sharing economy', *Financial Times*, 20 February 2015, p. 12.

[2] Alex Taylor, 'BMW ramps up', *Fortune*, 12 November 2007, pp. 14–15; www.bmw-welt.com/en/, accessed August 2015.

[3] R. K. Krishna Kumar, 'Effective marketing must begin with customer engagement', *Marketing News*, 15 April 2009, p. 15.

[4] See www.jordanscereals.co.uk/our-story/countryside-commitment/, accessed August 2015.

[5] Information from www.discoverireland.com/us, accessed August 2015; also see www.iloveny.com and www.visitcalifornia.com/, accessed August 2015.

[6] www.isocialmarketing.org/index.php?option=com_content& view=article&id=84:social-marketing-definition&catid= 28:front-page#.VcduIPlVikp, accessed August 2015.

[7] For more on social marketing, see Alan R. Andreasen, *Social Marketing in the 21st Century* (Thousand Oaks, CA: Sage Publications, 2006); Philip Kotler and Nancy Lee, *Social Marketing: Influencing Behaviors for Good*, 4th ed. (Thousand Oaks, CA: Sage Publications, 2011); and www.adcouncil.org and www.i-socialmarketing.org, accessed September 2014.

[8] Quotes and definitions from Philip Kotler, *Marketing Insights from A to Z* (Hoboken, NJ: Wiley, 2003), p. 148.

[9] Steve Hamm, 'The vacuum man takes on wet hands', *BusinessWeek*, 2 July 2007, pp. 84–86; Lucy Ballinger, 'That's cool, Mr Dyson', *Daily Mail*, 17 May 2010, p. 31; 'Dyson wants recruits', *Daily Mail*, 13 February 2012, p. 63.

[10] Andy Goldsmith, 'Coke vs. Pepsi: the taste they don't want you to know about', *The 60-Second Marketer*, www.60secondmarketer.com/60SecondArticles/Branding/cokevs.pepsitast.html.

[11] See '3 in 4 grocery purchase decisions being made in-store', *MarketingCharts*, 15 May 2012, www.marketingcharts.com/direct/3-in-4-grocery-purchase-decisions-being-made-in-store-22094; 'FMI – supermarket facts', www.fmi.org/research-resources/supermarket-facts, accessed April 2014; and 'Our retail divisions', http://news.walmart.com/news-archive/2005/01/07/our-retaildivisions, accessed April 2014.

[12] Sonja Reyes, 'Ad blitz, bottle design fuel debate over Heinz's sales', *Brandweek*, 12 February 2007, www.brandweek.com/bw/news/recent_display.jsp?vnu_content_id=1003544497.

[13] See the HP Total Care site at www8.hp.com/uk/en/support-drivers/total-care/total-care.html, accessed August 2015.

[14] Olga Kharif, 'The end of the coffee line', *Bloomberg BusinessWeek*, 26 November 2014, pp. 33–34.

[15] Information on Colgate's product mix from www.colgate.com/app/Colgate/US/HomePage.cvsp, accessed August 2015.

[16] See http://ec.europa.eu/trade/creating-opportunities/economic-sectors/services/, accessed August 2015.

[17] See CIA, *The World Factbook*, www.cia.gov/library/publications/the-world-factbook/geos/xx.html and www.cia.gov/library/publications/the-world-factbook/fields/2012.html, accessed August 2015; and information from the Bureau of Labor Statistics, www.bls.gov, accessed August 2015.

[18] See: Leonard Berry and Neeli Bendapudi, 'Clueing in customers', *Harvard Business Review*, February 2003, pp. 100–106.

[19] See James L. Heskett, W. Earl Sasser Jr., and Leonard A. Schlesinger, *The Service Profit Chain: How Leading Companies Link Profit and Growth to Loyalty, Satisfaction, and Value* (New York: Free Press, 1997); Heskett, Sasser, and Schlesinger, *The Value Profit Chain: Treat Employees Like Customers and Customers Like Employees* (New York: Free Press, 2003); Christian Homburg, Jan Wieseke, and Wayne D. Hoyer, 'Social identity and the service-profit chain', *Journal of Marketing*, March 2009, pp. 38–54; and Rachael W. Y. Yee and others, 'The service-profit chain: a review and extension', *Total Quality Management & Business Excellence*, 2009, pp. 617–632.

[20] Based on quotes and information from Pete Blackshaw, 'Zappos shows how employees can be brand-builders', *Advertising Age*, 2 September 2008, http://adage.com/print?article_id=130646; Jeremy Twitchell, 'Fun counts with web retailer', *Fort Wayne Journal-Gazette*, 16 February 2009, p. C5; Jeffrey M. O'Brien, 'Zappos knows how to kick it', *Fortune*, 2 February 2009, pp. 55–60; and http://about.zappos.com/jobs, accessed August 2015.

[21] Sean Poulter, 'We spend more if shop staff greet us with a smile', *Daily Mail*, 27 May 2013, p. 21.

[22] Fiona Macrae, 'So Mrs Slocombe was right all along – being snooty DOES help shop assistants sell more in fancy stores', *Daily Mail*, 29 April 2014, www.dailymail.co.uk/sciencetech/article-2616199/So-Mrs-Slocombe-right-snooty-DOES-help-shop-assistants-sell-fancy-stores.html, accessed online August 2015.

[23] Based on information from 'TripAdvisor names Four Seasons Resort Hualalai #1 Hotel in the World', 18 January 2013, http://press.fourseasons.com/hualalai/hotel-news/2013/01/tripadvisor_names_four_seasons_resort_hualalai_1_h/; Jeffrey M. O'Brien, 'A perfect season', *Fortune*, 22 January 2008, pp. 62–66; 'The 100 best companies to work for', *Fortune*, 4 February 2013, p. 85; Micah Solomon, 'Four Seasons Hotels: building a hospitality and customer service culture', *Forbes*, 1 September 2013, www.forbes.com/sites/micahsolomon/2013/09/01/four-seasons-hotels-building-a-hospitality-service-culture-without-starting-from-scratch/; and http://jobs.fourseasons.com/Pages/Home.aspx and www.fourseasons.com/about_us/, accessed September 2014.

[24] Sarah Bridge, 'Bag service lets travellers wave goodbye to stress', *Mail on Sunday*, 25 May 2014, p. 84; www.luggagemule.co.uk, accessed August 2015.

[25] See Terry Maxon, 'Horrible flight? Airlines' apology experts will make it up to you', *McClatchy-Tribune News Service*, 24 August 2010; Katie Morell, 'Lessons from Southwest Airlines' stellar customer service', *ehotelier.com*, 29 August 2012, http://ehotelier.com/hospitality-news/item.php?id=23931_0_11_0M_C; and Micah Solomon, 'Customer service: what Southwest knows and you don't (Hint: being nice isn't enough)', *Forbes*, 22 September 2013, www.forbes.com/sites/micahsolomon/2013/09/22/not-hiring-jerksisnt-enough-your-systems-have-to-love-your-customers-too/.

[26] Based on information from Sarah Kessler, 'The future of the hotel industry and social media', *Mashable!*, 19 October 2010, http://mashable.com/2010/10/18/hotel-industry-social-media/; and Jeff Williams, 'Marriott's SM team gets it', *HD Leader*, 14 September 2010, http://hdleader.com/2010/09/14/marriotts-sm-team-gets-it/. Also see https://twitter.com/MarriottIntl, accessed September 2014.

[27] For more discussion on the trade-offs between service productivity and service quality, see Roland T. Rust and Ming-Hui Huang, 'Optimizing service productivity', *Journal of Marketing*, March 2012, pp. 47–66.

[28] See 'McAtlas shrugged', *Foreign Policy*, May–June 2001, pp. 26–37; and Philip Kotler and Kevin Lane Keller, *Marketing Management*, 13th ed. (Upper Saddle River, NJ: Prentice Hall, 2009), p. 254.

[29] Quotes from Jack Trout, '"Branding" simplified', *Forbes*, 19 April 2007, www.forbes.com; and a presentation by Jason Kilar at the Kenan-Flagler Business School, University of North Carolina at Chapel Hill, Fall 2009.

[30] Pete Pachal, 'Love your Vespa? Now you can do it officially on social media', *Mashable*, 21 August 2012, http://mashable.com/2012/08/21/la-vespa-vita/; and www.lavespavita.com/, accessed September 2014.

[31] For more on Young & Rubicam's BrandAsset Valuator, see W. Ronald Lane, Karen Whitehill King, and Tom Reichert, *Kleppner's Advertising Procedure*, 18th ed. (Upper Saddle River, NJ: Pearson Prentice Hall, 2011), pp. 83–84; 'Brand Asset Valuator', *Value-BasedManagement.net*, www.valuebasedmanagement.net/methods_brand_asset_valuator.html, accessed June 2014; and http://bavconsulting.com, accessed June 2014.

[32] 'Yesterday's brand', *The Marketer*, March/April 2015, pp. 34–37.

[33.] See *FT Special Report: Global Brands*, 21 May 2014; Elizabeth Woyke 'Flunking brand geography', *Bloomberg BusinessWeek*, 18 June 2007, p. 14.

[34] See *FT Special Report: Latin American Brands*, 24 September 2014.

[35] Nirmalya Kumar and Jan-Benedict Steenkamp, *Brand Breakout: How Emerging Market Brands Will Go Global*, London: Palgrave MacMillan, 2015.

[36] 'Yesterday's brand', *The Marketer*, March/April 2015, pp. 34–37.

[37] See Scott Davis, *Brand Asset Management*, 2nd ed. (San Francisco: Jossey-Bass, 2002). For more on brand positioning, see Philip Kotler and Kevin Lane Keller, *Marketing Management*, 14th ed. (Upper Saddle River, NJ: Prentice Hall, 2012), Chapter 10.

[38] See 'For P&G, success lies in more than merely a dryer diaper', *Advertising Age*, 15 October 2007, p. 20; Jack Neff, 'Just how well-defined is your brand's ideal?' *Advertising Age*, 16 January 2012, p. 4; and www.pampers.com, accessed September 2014.

[39] See Aaron Ahuvia Rajeev and Richard P. Bagozzi, 'Brand love', *Journal of Marketing*, March 2012, pp. 1–16; and www.saatchi.com/the_lovemarks_company and www.lovemarks.com, accessed September 2014.

[40] *Cool Brands*, *Sunday Times* Supplement, 24 September 2006; Burt Helm, 'For your eyes only', *BusinessWeek*, 31 July 2006, p. 66.

[41] Alicia Clegg, 'The consumer's inner child', *Financial Times*, 30 October 2012, p. 12; Louise Lucas, 'Nostalgia prompts sweet taste of success', *Financial Times*, 12/13 November 2011, p. 17.

[42] Rachel Sanderson, 'Ferrari aims to pull away from the pack', *Financial Times*, 12 June 2013, p. 19.

[43] Larry Page's blog quoted in Peter Campbell, 'Google soups up its network with alphabet', *Daily Mail*, 12 August 2015, p. 68.

[44] Sarah Gordon, 'Investors chew over Kraft chief's change of heart', *Financial Times*, 6/7 August 2011, p. 14. Caitlin Kenting, 'Famous re-brandings', *Fortune*, 30 April 2012, p. 12.

[45] 'Store brands prices stay hot during the coldest months, saving shoppers 30% on average', *PRNewswire*, 12 February 2013, www.prnewswire.com/news-releases/store-brands-prices-stayhot-during-the-coldest-months-saving-shoppers-30-on-average-190846991.html.

[46] Scott Davis, 'How Target, Walgreens, and Home Depot have forever changed the private label game', *Forbes*, www.forbes.com/sites/scottdavis/2013/05/23/how-target-walgreens-and-homedepot-have-forever-changed-the-private-label-game/; and Stephanie Strom, 'Groceries are cleaning up in store-brand aisles', *New York Times*, 2 October 2013, p. B1.

[47] 'P&G targets thrifty customers with cheaper tide', *Trefis*, 11 September 2013, www.trefis.com/stock/pg/articles/205189/pg-targets-thrifty-customers-with-cheaper-tide-detergent/2013-09-11.

[48] Louise Lucas, 'Cash-strapped shoppers opt for own-labels', *Financial Times*, 21 January 2013, p. 23.

[49] See www.licensemag.com/license-global/top-150-global-licensors, accessed August 2015.

[50] Quote from www.apple.com/ipod/nike/, accessed April 2014.

[51] Julie Jargon, 'At McDonald's, salads don't sell', *Wall Street Journal*, 13 October 2013, http://online.wsj.com/news/articles/SB10001424052702304384104579139871559464960.

[52] Tomasso Ebhardt, 'Ferrari bets that less is more', *Bloomberg BusinessWeek*, 30 May 2013, pp. 25–26.

[53] The quote and the best/worst examples are from 'TippingSprung publishes results from fifth annual brand-extensions survey', 6 January 2009, www.tippingsprung.com/index.php?/knowledge/knowledge_article/tippingsprung_publishes_results_from_fifth_annual_brandextension_survey/; www.brandchannel.com/papers_review.asp?sp_id=1222, accessed February 8 2012.

[54] See: Robert Klara, 'The best (and worst) brand extensions', *Adweek*, 4 February 2013, pp. 26–27; Brad Tuttle, 'Why some brand extensions are brilliant and others are just awkward', *Time*, 7 February 2013, http://business.time.com/2013/02/07/why-some-brand-extensions-are-brilliant-and-others-are-just-awkward/; Gary Belsky, 'These companies stretched their brands to make even bigger bucks,' Time, 13 March 2012, http://business.time.com/2012/03/14/the-10-best-brand-extensions-ever-according-to-me/; Denise Lee Yohn, 'Great brands aim for customers' hearts, not their wallets', *Forbes*, January 2014, www.

forbes.com/sites/onmarketing/2014/01/08/great-brands-aim-for-customers-hearts-not-their-wallets/; www.clorox.com/products; www.duracellpowermat.com and www.zzzquil.com, accessed September 2014.

[55] 'Global marketers 2013', *Advertising Age*, 9 December 2013, p. 17.

[56] Quotes from Stephen Cole, 'Value of the brand', *CA Magazine*, May 2005, pp. 39–40; and Lawrence A. Crosby and Sheree L. Johnson, 'Experience required', *Marketing Management*, July/August 2007, pp. 21–27.

COMPANY CASE

John Lewis: Middle England's retailer of choice

In the past, John Lewis was often seen as a sleepy, conservative high street department store chain with a staid, middle class customer base and no more than that. But there is much more to the company than this suggests.

The John Lewis Partnership, which started life as a small drapers shop on Oxford Street in 1864, emerged as the clear winner over Christmas 2014 with sales up 8 per cent for the holiday period, and online sales increasing by 20 per cent, producing total sales of £4.42 billion for the year. John Lewis looked all set to take over from Marks & Spencer as Britain's favourite department store.

In fact, John Lewis has become a retail powerhouse after doubling in size in the last decade, by adding new stores, developing a market-leading Internet business, and from rapid growth in its Waitrose supermarket chain. In 2013, John Lewis led the list of Britain's most trusted brands, way ahead of Amazon, Virgin, M&S and Ocado. Indeed, to round off its spectacular successes, in 2014 John Lewis retained its title as Britain's favourite retailer in the survey of consumer satisfaction by Verdict, the retail research group. But why? 'It's the moral face of retailing', says one experienced retail analyst.

The John Lewis brand is renowned for the excellent quality of customer service and the value for money it provides to customers, as well as its partnership-based ownership. Its reputation has remained intact, even while other retailers have failed and closed during the tough years of the 2000s and early 2010s.

Part of John Lewis' winning formula is down to its unusual ownership structure. The John Lewis Partnership's 69,000 staff own John Lewis, Waitrose and the financial services arm Greenbee. Employees have a high degree of participation in running the organisation. Staff receive an annual bonus based on the profits of the business, and are called 'partners'. The more effort they put in, the more they get back. The company believes that this structure – put in place by John Spedan Lewis in 1929 – fosters better customer service, lower staff turnover and higher trust among customers. But sharing in profits via bonuses cuts both ways – if you share in the business risk of the company, then sometimes you lose out. In 2015, John Lewis employees found the staff bonus cut for the second year running. Lower profits at Waitrose were blamed as the impact of the new discounters Aldi and Lidl stimulated an intense grocery price war. Nonetheless, the bonus was still equivalent to about 11 per cent of pay, though down from 17 per cent a couple of years earlier.

Nonetheless, outsiders agree the structure has played a key part in John Lewis' success, although some rivals believe the set-up, which also gives staff a say in the running of the business, can be frustrating for managers. 'Is it the utopian business? Of course it's not. They have their flaws,' says the retail analyst. But it enables John Lewis to 'pay slightly more than the competition does, and they leverage that, to get more solid, wholesome people, who take more of a pride in what they do.'

The unusual ownership structure helps the chain to deliver incredibly strong customer service, while customers are also attracted by its long-held promise to be 'never knowingly undersold' by rivals (though in fact that promise is now restricted to stores within 8 miles and bricks-and-mortar retailers only). Mr Street says these factors came into their own in the downturn. At the time he said: 'What is really special about John Lewis [this year] is somehow we managed to hold customers' trust as we went through the recession,' he says. 'We had a very difficult first half of the year, but customers knew we were not compromising on quality of product, on price, or on service. As a consequence, when things got a little better for customers, they wanted to shop with us.' The company was able to continue its investment plan throughout the recession of the late 2000s to improve stores, product mix and the website operation.

Mr Street adds that the structure also enabled John Lewis to take a long-term view when economic times were difficult a few years ago: 'because we were not beholden to the City, I was not forced to do things that would damage the business, even if they promoted profit in the short term'.

But it is not just the ownership structure that has worked in the chain's favour. John Lewis carries a wide product range and in recent years has been sharpening its offer and refreshing its stores. 'Over the last ten years or so, a group of younger, more ambitious, more dynamic managers have come through the ranks and I think they have upped the pace, both in the department stores, and in Waitrose,' says the retail analyst. Managing director Andy Street says the key is to be contemporary, without being 'bleeding-edge trendy'. In the early 2010s, the John Lewis stores introduced high-fashion products from such names as Aspinal of London, Orla Kiely, DKNY, Guess, Gucci and Tag Heuer.

John Lewis' direct Internet operation has radically changed. The catalyst was a mocking advertisement from Dixons, then the leading discount electrical chain, which in 2009 urged shoppers to: 'Step into Middle England's best-loved department store, stroll through haberdashery to the audiovisual department where an awfully well brought-up man will bend over backwards to find the right television for you – and then go to dixons.co.uk and buy it.'

In fact, positioned at the other end of the market to Dixons, John Lewis built an enviable reputation for giving the best advice to shoppers. In the run-up to Christmas 2011, its consumer electronics floors were so overrun that customer ticketing machines were put into action to manage waiting shoppers. In 1950s-style queues shoppers waited patiently for their number to come up so they could to speak to an assistant. John Lewis beat the downward trend in sales in the tough environment of that time.

The John Lewis strategy – probably invisible to customers – has been based on innovation. But the company has grown organically through a consistent long-term strategy relying on innovation that matches customer expectations, and using feedback from highly motivated employee/partners. The company calls its approach 'logical incremental', in which change is implemented in small steps, with each phase informing the next. The partners play a key role in providing feedback and insights into changing consumer needs. The logical incremental strategy has been applied to:

- *Responding to customer requirements*: the frequent renewal of a wide range of products with a broad range of prices. In 2012, Waitrose carried 4,600 new products and John Lewis about 30 major new brands. The supermarket's new labels include 'Heston from Waitrose' in a tie-up with celebrity chef Heston Blumenthal.

- *New store formats*: John Lewis' new 'At Home' is a smaller version of its classic format, being typically a third of the size, carrying two-thirds of the stock, and for one-quarter of the cost. The flexible format allows all the stock to be showcased in half the usual space and customers can use in-store technology to make purchases. Waitrose has opened small convenience stores – Little Waitrose – with longer opening hours.

- *International expansion*: John Lewis has achieved international growth, trialling a shop within a store with South Korean department store Shinsegae and plans to repeat this elsewhere. Waitrose has ventured overseas through a licensing agreement with Spinneys of Dubai.

- *Online:* From the start, John Lewis aimed to extend its outstanding service ethos to online retailing. This meant ease of use, and reliable and speedy collection and return of items. The online platform is updated often – costing £40 million in 2012 alone. Collection of online orders has been made progressively easier – as well as courier delivery, pick-up points were extended to Waitrose and the company has now teamed up with a service that allows collection in the UK from 5,000 convenience stores. It was also the first department store to introduce a charge for 'click and collect' service. John Lewis online operations now cover 33 countries, with rapidly increasing sales.

Meantime, in the UK over recent years, John Lewis has opened a new department store in Cardiff, and also a smaller format home furnishings outlet in Poole. Based on the success of Poole, the group plans to open up to 50 home and electrical stores. They will be key to expansion after the company was forced to scale down its ambitions to open at least half a dozen full-scale department stores, as property developers shelved regional shopping centres. Waitrose has also been pushing ahead, most notably with the launch of its first-ever value range – essentials – which has contributed to its sales surge.

John Lewis may also have been in a sweet spot as far as customers are concerned. While unemployment has eaten into spending, those in jobs have benefited from low interest rates and energy costs. As the UK recovered from the recession, John Lewis continued to reap the benefits of a more affluent customer base than its rivals.

Nonetheless, life is going to get tougher for some of the people who had more money to spend in the late 2000s, and given the challenging outlook, the chain is already thinking ahead. While it will continue to focus on the middle to premium market, it has already introduced a value range of homewares such as cutlery and electrical appliances. But it is not just economic headwinds that may be against John Lewis this year. According to Mr Street: 'If we have a very good season . . . everyone will be trying to work out what we have done and will be gunning for us.'

But John Lewis is poised for expansion into Europe, bolstering its website to attract international orders and enabling the group to gather data on which European cities could support its department stores. The company is planning its first forays into the US and Australia, and is recruiting its first partners outside the UK for a buying office in India. In the UK, John Lewis is planning new 'space-age' shops packed with the latest shopping technology.

Interestingly, John Lewis is also in the headlines for other reasons. Early in 2012, then-Deputy Prime Minister Nick Clegg called for the UK to become 'more of a John Lewis economy'. The department store has become an emblem of a new capitalism for politicians, and more mutually owned businesses has been an oft-mooted ambition of all three main UK political parties.

The Partnership is even advising the British government on how its model could be applied to the public sector, for example in running hospitals. In 2011, John Lewis staff were giving long-overdue lessons to British police officers in how to be more professional and considerate when dealing with victims and witnesses of crime – i.e., polite to the people who pay their wages. Indeed, John Lewis has become something of a politicians' talisman – UK politicians are drawn to John Lewis, because it is owned by its staff and run on democratic principles, as a model for economic and organisational reform. This is part of the search for successful businesses to help reinvent, rebalance and revise capitalism in a post-recession world.

Indeed, Sir Charlie Mayfield, John Lewis' chairman, is championing employee owned businesses (EOBs) in a new venture. Some believe that EOBs are more resilient and prosperous and employees who own their own businesses are more robust when times are tough and more cooperative when redundancies and pay-cuts are in the offing. When employees run the business, managers are able to make long-term decisions, without the pressure to make risky deals and acquisitions that endanger livelihoods. There is very little hard evidence to back these claims but they are attracting a wider audience.

Questions for discussion

1. What do you think that the John Lewis brand means to consumers? Is this brand a strength or a weakness as the company moves forward?

2. What is John Lewis actually selling? What are loyal John Lewis customers buying? Discuss these questions in terms of the core benefit, actual product and augmented product levels.

3. What recommendations would you make to the managing director for the future of the John Lewis Partnership?

4. Can the elements of a successful service model like John Lewis really be transferred to public services? Can a hospital be like a John Lewis shop? What are the barriers likely to be?

Sources: Andrea Felsted, 'Consumer trust sees John Lewis set retail pace', *Financial Times*, 16/17 January 2010, p. 13; Jaya Narain, 'Long arm of the store', *Daily Mail*, 5 January 2011, p. 3; Andrea Felsted, 'Partners hold key to John Lewis success', *Financial Times*, 22/23 January 2011, p. 13; Claer Barrett, 'John Lewis to expand into Europe', *Financial Times*, 14 February 2011, p. 20; Kate Walsh, 'Middle England's store bites back', *The Sunday Times*, 13 March 2011, S3, pp. 1, 8; Phillip Blond, '"John Lewis Economy" talk is never knowingly undersold', *Financial Times*, 17 January 2012; Andrew Hill, 'A rather civil partnership', *Financial Times*, 21/22 January 2012, p. 9; Neil Craven, 'John Lewis set to grab retail throne from M&S', *Mail on Sunday*, 8 September 2013, p. 79; Abby Ghobadian, 'John Lewis Partnership', *Financial Times*, 23 July 2013, p. 12; Kate Burgess, 'Employee-owned businesses go for that John Lewis glow', 8 February 2015, FT.com, accessed August 2015; Kadhim Shudhar, 'John Lewis cuts staff bonus as price war bites', 12 March 2015, FT.com, accessed August 2015.

CHAPTER NINE

New product development and product life-cycle strategies

Chapter preview

In the previous chapter, you learned how marketers manage and develop products and brands. In this chapter, we examine two additional product topics: developing new products and managing products through their life cycles. New products are the lifeblood of an organisation. However, new product development is risky, and many new products fail. So, the first part of this chapter lays out a process for finding and growing successful new products. Once introduced, marketers want their products to enjoy long and happy lives. In the second part of this chapter, you'll see that every product passes through several stages, and each stage poses new challenges requiring different marketing strategies and tactics. Finally, we wrap up our product discussion by looking at two additional considerations: social responsibility in product decisions and international product and services marketing.

To open, consider Google – one of the world's most innovative companies. Google seems to come up with an almost unending flow of stunning new technologies and services. If it has to do with finding, refining or using information, there is probably an innovative Google solution for it. At Google, innovation is not just a process – it is in the very spirit of the place.

Objective outline

➤ **Objective 1** Explain how companies find and develop new product ideas.
New product development strategy (p. 263)

➤ **Objective 2** List and define the steps in the new product development process and the major considerations in managing this process.
New product development process (pp. 263–271)
Managing new product development (pp. 271–274)

➤ **Objective 3** Describe the stages of the product life cycle and how marketing strategies change during a product's life cycle.
Product life-cycle strategies (pp. 274–279)

➤ **Objective 4** Discuss two additional product issues: socially responsible product decisions and international product and services marketing.
Additional product and service considerations (pp. 279–282)

Google: the new product 'moonshot' factory

Google is wildly innovative. Over the past decade, it has become a top-five fixture in every list of most-innovative companies. Google simply refuses to get comfortable with the way things are. Instead, it innovates constantly, plunging into new markets and taking on new competitors.

As a result, Google is also spectacularly successful. Despite formidable competition from giants such as Microsoft and Yahoo!, Google's share in its core business — online search — stands at a decisive 86 per cent globally, more than five times the market shares of all other competitors combined. The company also dominates in paid online and mobile search-advertising revenue. Searches accounted for a majority of Google's $60 billion in revenues last year, 20 per cent of which filtered down into profits. And Google is growing at an incredible rate — its revenues have more than doubled in just the past three years.

But Google is rapidly becoming much more than just an online search and advertising company. Google's mission is 'to organise the world's information and make it universally accessible and useful'. In Google's view, information is a kind of natural resource — one to be mined, refined and universally distributed. That idea unifies what would otherwise appear to be a widely diverse set of Google projects, such as mapping the world, creating wearable computer technology, amassing the world's largest video library, or even providing for the early detection of flu epidemics. If it has to do with harnessing and using information, Google's got it covered in some innovative way.

Google knows how to innovate. At many companies, new product development is a cautious, step-by-step affair that might take years to unfold. In contrast, Google's freewheeling new product development process moves at the speed of light. The nimble innovator implements major new products and services in less time than it takes competitors to refine and approve an initial idea. As one Google executive explains, 'The hardest part about indoctrinating people into our culture is when engineers show me a prototype and I'm like, "Great, let's go!" They'll say, "Oh, no, it's not ready." I tell them, "The Googly thing is to launch it early [as a beta product] and then to iterate, learning what the market wants — and making it great."'

When it comes to new product development at Google, there are no two-year plans. The company's new product planning looks ahead only four to five months. Google would rather see projects fail quickly than see a carefully planned, drawn-out project fail. Whereas even highly innovative companies such as Apple prefer the safety of a 'perfect-it-before-you-sell it' approach, at Google, it's all about 'launching and iterating'. When Google developers face two paths and aren't sure which one to take, they invariably take the quickest one.

Google's famously chaotic innovation process has unleashed a seemingly unending stream of diverse products, most of which are market leaders in their categories. These include an e-mail service (Gmail), a digital media store (Google Play), an online payment service (Google Wallet), a photo sharing service (Google Picasa), a mobile operating system (Google Android), an ultra-high-speed residential broad-band network (Google Fiber), a cloud-friendly Internet browser (Chrome), projects for mapping and exploring the world (Google Maps and Google Earth), and even an early warning system for flu outbreaks in your area (Google Flu Trends).

Google's most recent innovations are taking it well beyond simply organising and searching for information. The company is now leading the way in harnessing the potential of the Internet to connect virtually everything in people's lives. For example, Google recently paid a massive $3.2 billion — twice what it paid for YouTube — to acquire Nest Labs, a maker of smart thermostats and smoke alarms. Nest has re-imagined these lowly home appliances into connected, digital devices worthy of the smartphone age, making them fun, easy and efficient to use. Although it may seem like Google paid a lot for a little with Nest, with Google's substantial resources and innovation prowess, Nest may soon be helping you run your entire home, a huge potential market. As one analyst explains, 'This is about whose service — Google, Amazon, Apple, Microsoft, and others — is going to coordinate your smart home for you.'

Nest may soon be helping you run your entire home, a huge potential market. As one analyst explains, 'This is about whose service – Google, Amazon, Apple, Microsoft and others – is going to coordinate your smart home for you.'
Source: David Paul Morris/ Bloomberg via Getty Images

If the concept of Internet-connected smart homes seems a bit far-fetched for Google, that's pretty tame next to some of the company's other grand ideas. Google's innovation machine is renowned for 'moonshots' – futuristic longshots that, if successful, will profoundly change how people live. According to one Google engineer, Google co-founders Larry Page and Sergey Brin 'have this idea that incremental improvements are not good enough. The standard for success is whether we can get these [moonshots] into the world and do audacious things.'

To foster moonshots, Google created Google X – a secretive research lab and kind of nerd heaven charged with developing things that seem audacious even for Google. 'Anything which is a huge problem for society we'll sign up for,' says the innovation unit's director. Google X's most notable innovation so far is Google Glass – the wearable smart-devices that have everyone buzzing, although subsequently withdrawn from the market for further iteration and development. But behind the secret curtain are numerous other futuristic projects, such as Google's driverless car – a project once thought to be pure science fiction but now a reality. Imagine buying something online, then having an automated Google Car pull up to your home and a Google Humanoid jump out to deliver the package to your door. Seem far-fetched? Maybe not. Google is now a leading robotics developer.

Google is open to new product ideas from just about any source. But the company also places responsibility for innovation on every employee. Google is famous for its Innovation Time-Off programme, which encourages engineers and developers to spend 20 per cent of their time – one day a week – developing their own 'cool and wacky' new product ideas. In the end, at Google, innovation is more than a process – it's part of the company's DNA. 'Where does innovation happen at Google? It happens everywhere,' says a Google research scientist.

Talk to Googlers at various levels and departments, one powerful theme emerges: these people feel that their work can change the world. The marvel of Google is its ability to continue to instil a sense of creative fearlessness and ambition in its employees. Prospective recruits are often asked, 'If you could change the world using Google's resources, what would you build?' But here, this isn't a goofy or even theoretical question: Google wants to know because thinking – and building – on that scale is what Google does. When it comes to innovation, Google is different. But the difference isn't tangible. It's in the air – in the spirit of the place.

In 2015, to expand even further its creative base, Google established Alphabet as the holding company for two divisions: 'Old Google', with the search engine and advertising, YouTube, Gmail, Android and Chrome; and 'New Google' including Google X (wild projects), Calico (biotechnology), Nest (home controls), Fiber (high-speed internet), Google Ventures (investments) and Google Capital (investment arm). The Old Google division is the current revenue-generators. But New Google houses the ambitious, and plain weird ventures in which Google is involved. Moonshots include contact lenses that detect a diabetic's blood sugar levels, but also floating hover boards (like in *Back to the Future*), lifts that could travel outside the Earth's atmosphere, and an entire unit dedicated to trying to develop eternal life. This part of Alphabet will be run by Google founders Larry Page and Sergey Brin. Google is very, very serious about innovation.[1]

As the Google, now Alphabet, story suggests, companies that excel at developing and managing new products reap big rewards. But every product seems to go through a life cycle: it is born, goes through several phases, and eventually dies as newer products come along that create new or greater value for customers.

The product life cycle presents two major challenges. First, because all products eventually decline, a firm must be good at developing new products to replace ageing ones (the challenge of *new product development*). Second, a firm must be good at adapting its marketing strategies in the face of changing tastes, technologies and competition as products pass through stages (the challenge of *product life-cycle strategies*). We first look at the problem of finding and developing new products and then at the challenges in managing them successfully over their life cycles.

NEW PRODUCT DEVELOPMENT STRATEGY

A firm can obtain new products in two ways. One is through *acquisition* – by buying a whole company, a patent or a licence to produce someone else's product. The other is through a firm's own **new product development** efforts. By *new products* we mean original products, product improvements, product modifications and new brands that a firm develops through its own R&D efforts. In this chapter, we concentrate on new product development.

New products are important – to both customers and the marketers who serve them. For customers, they bring new solutions and variety to their lives. For companies, new products are a key source of growth. In today's fast-changing environment, many companies rely on new products for the majority of their growth. For example, new products have almost completely transformed Apple in recent years. The iPhone and iPad – neither of which was available just eight years ago – are now the company's two biggest-selling products with the iPhone, bringing in more than half of Apple's total revenues.[2]

Yet innovation can be very expensive and very risky. New products face tough odds. By one estimate, 66 per cent of all new products introduced by established companies fail within two years. By another, 96 per cent of all innovations fail to return their development costs.[3] It is estimated that around 90 per cent of new consumer products launched in Europe fail.[4]

For example, Windows software is vitally important to Microsoft – it accounts for around 17 per cent of revenues and a quarter of profits at the company. Microsoft's Vista was perhaps the least-loved piece of software in the company's history, and by the time it was replaced Windows was used on only 19 per cent of the world's PCs. Windows 8 was an even bigger flop and just 16 per cent of PCs now use Windows. This compares to 2000, when Windows ran on 97 per cent of consumer devices. The 2015 launch of Windows 10 is a critical moment for Microsoft on which its ambitions for the future rest – particularly those for building and attracting developers to produce universal apps that run on Windows on any device. Microsoft promises that Windows 10 will reach one billion users in three years, but the jury is out on that one.[5]

But why do so many new products fail? There are several reasons. Although an idea may be good, the company may overestimate market size. The actual product may be poorly designed. Or it might be incorrectly positioned, launched at the wrong time, priced too high, or poorly advertised. A high-level executive might push a favourite idea despite poor marketing research findings. Sometimes the costs of product development are higher than expected, and sometimes competitors fight back harder than expected.

So, companies face a problem. They must develop new products, but the odds weigh heavily against success. To create successful new products, a company must understand its consumers, markets and competitors, and develop products that deliver superior value to customers.

NEW PRODUCT DEVELOPMENT PROCESS

Rather than leaving new products to chance, a company must carry out effective new product planning and set up a systematic, customer-driven *new product development process* for finding and growing new products. Figure 9.1 shows the eight major steps in this process.

Idea generation

New product development starts with **idea generation** – the systematic search for new product ideas. A company typically generates hundreds of ideas – even thousands – to find a few good ones. Major sources of new product ideas include internal sources and external sources such as customers, competitors, distributors and suppliers, and others.

Author comment

New products are the lifeblood of a company. As old products mature and fade away, companies must develop new ones to take their place. For example, only eight years after it unveiled its first iPod, 51 per cent of Apple's revenues came from iPods, iPhones and iTunes.

New product development– The development of original products, product improvements, product modifications and new brands through the firm's own new product development efforts.

Author comment

Companies cannot just hope that they will stumble across good new products. Instead, they must have a systematic new product development process.

Idea generation–The systematic search for new product ideas.

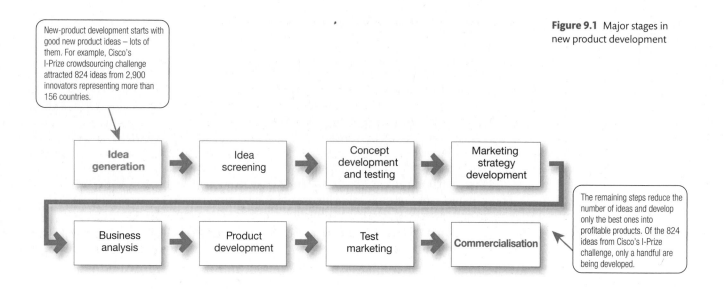

Figure 9.1 Major stages in new product development

New-product development starts with good new product ideas – lots of them. For example, Cisco's I-Prize crowdsourcing challenge attracted 824 ideas from 2,900 innovators representing more than 156 countries.

The remaining steps reduce the number of ideas and develop only the best ones into profitable products. Of the 824 ideas from Cisco's I-Prize challenge, only a handful are being developed.

Internal idea sources

Using *internal sources*, the company can find new ideas through formal R&D. However, according to one study, only 33 per cent of companies surveyed rated traditional R&D as a leading source of innovation ideas. In contrast, 41 per cent of companies identified customers as a key source, followed by heads of company business units (35 per cent), employees (33 per cent), and the sales force (17 per cent).[6]

Thus, beyond its internal R&D process, companies can pick the brains of its employees – from executives to scientists, engineers and manufacturing staff to salespeople. Many companies have developed successful internal social networks and 'intrapreneurial' programmes that encourage employees to develop new product ideas. For example, Google's Innovation Time-Off programme has resulted in blockbuster product ideas ranging from Gmail and Ad Sense to Google News. A similar programme at 3M, called Dream Days, has long encouraged employees to spend 15 per cent of their working time on their own projects, resulting in Post-it Notes and many other successful products.[7]

These days, online companies such as Facebook and Twitter sponsor periodic 'hackathons', in which employees take a day or a week away from their day-to-day work to develop new ideas. LinkedIn, the 250-million-member professional social media network, holds 'hackdays', a Friday each month when it encourages employees to work on whatever they want that will benefit the company. LinkedIn takes the process a step further with its InCubator programme, under which employees can form teams each quarter that pitch innovative new ideas to LinkedIn executives. If approved, the team gets up to 90 days away from its regular work to develop the idea into reality. So far, the programme has produced proposals for new products and business lines, internal tools and human resources programmes developed by employees from all over the company.[8]

External idea sources

Companies can also obtain good new product ideas from any of a number of external sources. For example, *distributors and suppliers* can contribute ideas. Distributors are close to the market and can pass along information about consumer problems and new product possibilities. Suppliers can tell the company about new concepts, techniques and materials that can be used to develop new products. For example, some major retailers invite thousands of would-be suppliers to submit product ideas and supporting videos, and make presentation to the company, to seek out possible new product ideas.

Competitors are another important source. Companies watch competitors' ads to get clues about their new products. They buy competing new products, take them apart to see how they work, analyse their sales, and decide whether they should bring out a new product of their own. Other idea sources include trade magazines, shows and seminars, websites, government agencies, advertising agencies, marketing research firms, university and commercial laboratories, and inventors.

Perhaps the most important source of new product ideas is *customers* themselves. The company can analyse customer questions and complaints to find new products that better solve consumer problems. Or it can invite customers to share suggestions and ideas. For example, the Danish-based LEGO Group, maker of the classic LEGO plastic bricks that have been fixtures in homes around the world for more than 60 years, systematically taps users for new product ideas and input:[9]

> In 2008, LEGO teamed with Japanese design co-creation platform firm CUUSOO SYSTEM to launch the LEGO CUUSOO website. At the site, LEGO invites users to submit ideas for 'the LEGO set of their dreams' and to vote for other users' ideas. Ideas supported by 10,000 votes are reviewed internally with a chance of being put into production. Consumers who have their ideas chosen earn 1 per cent of the total net sales of the product. So far, the efforts of LEGO CUUSOO fans have resulted in dozens of major product ideas and six new products. One recent release is the LEGO Back to the Future DeLorean Time Machine, which lets users build the classic time-travelling car in LEGO bricks. The idea pulled in the required 10,000 votes in nine months. During that time, the idea was viewed more than 400,000 times and attracted over 2,000 comments. A previous LEGO CUUSOO idea, the highly successful LEGO Minecraft Micro World, racked up its 10,000 votes in less than 48 hours.

New product ideas from customers: Lego's CUUSOO website invited users to submit and vote on product ideas. Lego Minecraft Micro World got the required 10,000 votes in less than 48 hours (Since 1 May 2014 LEGO CUUSOO is no longer in operation).

Source: © CUUSOO SYSTEM 2014

The LEGO CUUSOO website ceased operation on 1 May 2014.

Following the same logic, Starbucks sponsors My Starbucks Idea, a website that invites customers to share, discuss and vote on new product and service ideas. 'You know better than anyone else what you want from Starbucks,' says the site. 'So tell us. What's your Starbucks idea? Revolutionary or simple – we want to hear it.'[10] Similarly, to harness customer new product input, 3M has opened nearly two dozen customer innovation centres throughout the world, including sites in the United States, Brazil, Germany, India, China and Russia. The innovation centres not only generate plenty of customer-driven new product ideas but also help 3M establish productive, long-term customer relationships.[11]

Crowdsourcing

On an even broader front, many companies are now developing *crowdsourcing* or *open-innovation* new product idea programmes. Through **crowdsourcing** a company can invite broad communities of people – customers, employees, independent scientists and researchers, and even the public at large – into the new product innovation process. The idea, says one analyst, is that when it comes to helping to improve 'your products, services, website, or marketing efforts . . . two heads – or 2,000 or 20,000 – are better than one.'[12]

Companies ranging from giants like P&G and Samsung to innovative manufacturing start-ups are throwing the innovation doors wide open. Consider the P&G approach:

Crowdsourcing—Inviting broad communities of people – customers, employees, independent scientists and researchers, and even the public at large – into the new product innovation process.

> P&G has long set the gold standard for breakthrough innovation and new product development in its industry. P&G's Tide detergent was the first synthetic laundry detergent for automatic washing machines, its Pampers brand was the first successful disposable nappy, and P&G's Febreze was the first air freshener that eliminated odours rather than just covering them up. Such breakthrough innovations have been pivotal in P&G's success. Until recently, most of P&G's innovations came from within its own R&D labs. P&G employs more than 8,000 R&D researchers in 26 facilities around the globe, some of the best research talent in the world. But P&G's research labs alone simply can't provide the quantity of innovation required to meet the growth needs of the $84 billion company.

So about 12 years ago, P&G began inviting outside partners to help develop new products and technologies. It launched P&G Connect + Develop, a major crowdsourcing programme that invites entrepreneurs, scientists, engineers and other researchers – even consumers themselves – to submit ideas for new technologies, product designs, packaging, marketing models, research methods, engineering or promotion – anything that has the potential to create better products that will help P&G meet its goal of 'improving more consumers' lives'.

P&G isn't looking to replace its 8,000 researchers; it wants to leverage them better. Through careful crowdsourcing, it can extend its inside people with millions of brilliant minds outside. Through Connect + Develop, says the company, 'Together, we can do more than either of us could do alone.'

Today, thanks to Connect + Develop, P&G has a truly global open-innovation network. More than 50 per cent of its innovations involve some kind of external partner. So far, the programme has resulted in more than 2,000 successful agreements. P&G Connect + Develop is 'at the heart of how P&G innovates'.

Companies large and small, across all industries, are using crowdsourcing rather than relying only on their own R&D labs to produce all of the needed new product innovations. For example, Samsung recently launched an Open Innovation Program, by which it connects broadly with outside collaborators and entrepreneurs to develop new products and technologies. The programme's mission is to break down the walls surrounding its own innovation process and open the doors to fresh new ideas from outside the company. Through the programme, Samsung creates alliances with top industry and university researchers around the world, participates actively in industry-wide forums, works with suppliers on innovation, and seeks out and invests in promising start-up companies. 'In the 21st century, no company can do all the research alone,' says a Samsung executive, 'and we see it as critically important to partner with [others] across the world to build and strengthen a vibrant research community'.[13]

In practice, rather than creating and managing their own crowdsourcing platforms, companies can use third-party crowdsourcing networks, such as InnoCentive, TopCoder, CloudSpokes and jovoto. For example, organisations ranging from Audi, Microsoft and Nestlé to Swiss Army Knife maker Victorinox have tapped into jovoto's network of 50,000 creative professionals for ideas and solutions, offering prizes of $100 to $100,000. For the past three years, Victorinox has used jovoto to capture new designs for a limited fashion edition of its Swiss Army Knife. The aim of fashion designs is to attract younger buyers to the product. The first year, more than 1,000 artists submitted designs via jovoto. The limited edition, consisting of ten designs selected after review by jovoto community members and voting on Facebook by Victorinox brand fans, had 20 per cent better sales success than any previous internally created limited edition models.[14]

> Victorinox used third-party crowdsourcing network jovoto to capture creative designs for limited editions of its Swiss Army Knife. The crowdsourced designed models had 20 per cent better sales success than any previous internally-created limited editions.
>
> *Source:* Victorinox owns the rights.

Crowdsourcing can produce a flood of innovative ideas. In fact, opening the floodgates to anyone and everyone can overwhelm the company with ideas – some good and some bad. Of course, truly innovative companies don't rely only on one source or another for new product ideas. Instead, they develop extensive innovation networks that capture ideas and inspiration from every possible source, from employees and customers to outside innovators and multiple points beyond.

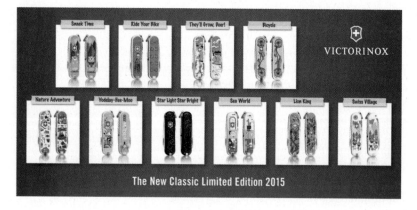

The New Classic Limited Edition 2015

Idea screening

> **Idea screening**—Screening new product ideas to spot good ones and drop poor ones as soon as possible.

The purpose of idea generation is to create a large number of ideas. The purpose of the succeeding stages is to *reduce* that number. The first idea-reducing stage is **idea screening**, which helps spot good ideas and drop poor ones as soon as possible. Product development costs rise greatly in later stages, so the company wants to go ahead only with those product ideas that will turn into profitable products.

Many companies require their executives to write up new product ideas in a standard format that can be reviewed by a new product committee. The write-up describes a product or a service, the proposed customer value proposition, the target market and the competition. It makes some rough estimates of market size, product price, development time and costs, manufacturing costs, and rate of return. The committee then evaluates the idea against a set of general criteria.

One marketing expert proposes an R-W-W ('real, win, worth doing') product screening framework that asks three questions. First, *Is it real?* Is there a real need and desire for a particular product and will customers buy it? Is there a clear product concept and will such a product satisfy the market? Second, *Can we win?* Does a particular product offer a sustainable competitive advantage? Does the company have the resources to make such a product a success? Finally, *Is it worth doing?* Does a particular product fit the company's overall growth strategy? Does it offer sufficient profit potential? The company should be able to answer yes to all three R-W-W questions before developing a new product idea further.[15]

Concept development and resting

An attractive idea must be developed into a **product concept**. It is important to distinguish between a product idea, a product concept and a product image. A *product idea* is an idea for a possible product that the company can see itself offering to the market. A *product concept* is a detailed version of the idea stated in meaningful consumer terms. A *product image* is the way consumers perceive an actual or potential product.

Product concept—A detailed version of the new product idea stated in meaningful consumer terms.

Concept development

Suppose a car manufacturer has developed a practical, battery-powered, all-electric car. Its initial prototype is a sleek, sporty roadster convertible that sells for more than £70,000.[16]

However, in the near future, it plans to introduce more affordable, mass-market versions that will compete with recently introduced hybrid-electric and all-electric cars, such as the Nissan Leaf and Ford Focus Electric. This 100 per cent electric car will accelerate from zero to 60 miles per hour in 4 seconds, travel more than 300 miles on a single charge, recharge in 45 minutes from a normal electrical outlet, and cost about one penny per mile to operate.

Looking ahead, the marketer's task is to develop this new product into alternative product concepts, find out how attractive each concept is to customers, and choose the best one. It might create the following product concepts for this electric car:

- *Concept 1*: An affordably priced mid-size car designed as a second family car to be used around town for running errands and visiting friends.
- *Concept 2*: A mid-priced, sporty, small family car appealing to young singles and couples.
- *Concept 3*: A 'green' car appealing to environmentally conscious people who want practical, low-polluting transportation.
- *Concept 4*: A high-end midsize 4×4 vehicle appealing to those who love the space 4×4s provide but lament the poor fuel consumption.

Concept testing

Concept testing calls for testing new product concepts with groups of target consumers. The concepts may be presented to consumers symbolically or physically. Here, in more detail, is concept 3:

Concept testing—Testing new product concepts with a group of target consumers to find out if the concepts have strong consumer appeal.

> An efficient, fun-to-drive, battery-powered small family car that seats four. This 100 per cent electric wonder provides practical and reliable transport with no pollution. It goes more than 300 miles on a single charge and costs pennies per mile to operate. It is a sensible, responsible alternative to today's pollution-producing gas-guzzlers. Its fully equipped price is £20,000.

Many firms routinely test new product concepts with consumers before attempting to turn them into actual new products. For some concept tests, a word or picture description might be sufficient. However, a more concrete and physical presentation of the concept will increase the

Table 9.1 Questions for the all-electric car concept test

1. Do you understand the concept of a battery-powered electric car?
2. Do you believe the claims about the car's performance?
3. What are the major benefits of an all-electric car compared with a conventional car?
4. What are its advantages compared with a petrol-electric hybrid car?
5. What improvements in the car's features would you suggest?
6. For what uses would you prefer an all-electric car to a conventional car?
7. What would be a reasonable price to charge for the car?
8. Who would be involved in your decision to buy such a car? Who would drive it?
9. Would you buy such a car (definitely, probably, probably not, definitely not)?

reliability of the concept test. After being exposed to the concept, consumers then may be asked to react to it by answering questions similar to those in Table 9.1.

The answers to such questions will help the company decide which concept has the strongest appeal. For example, the last question asks about a consumer's intention to buy. Suppose 2 per cent of consumers say they 'definitely' would buy, and another 5 per cent say 'probably'. The company could project these figures to the full population in this target group to estimate sales volume. Even then, the estimate is uncertain because people do not always carry out their stated intentions.

Marketing strategy development

Marketing strategy development—Designing an initial marketing strategy for a new product based on the product concept.

Suppose the carmaker finds that concept 3 for the electric car tests best. The next step is **marketing strategy development**, designing an initial marketing strategy for introducing this car to the market.

The *marketing strategy statement* consists of three parts. The first part describes the target market; the planned value proposition; and the sales, market share and profit goals for the first few years. Thus:

> The target market is younger, well-educated, moderate- to high-income individuals, couples, or small families seeking practical, environmentally responsible transportation. The car will be positioned as more fun to drive and less polluting than today's internal combustion engine or hybrid cars. The company will aim to sell 50,000 cars in the first year, at a loss of not more than £10 million. In the second year, the company will aim for sales of 90,000 cars and a profit of £20 million.

The second part of the marketing strategy statement outlines the product's planned price, distribution and marketing budget for the first year:

> The battery-powered electric car will be offered in three colours — red, white and blue — and will have a full set of accessories as standard features. It will sell at a retail price of £20.000, with 15 per cent off the list price to dealers. Dealers who sell more than 10 cars per month will get an additional discount of 5 per cent on each car sold that month. A marketing budget of £35 million will be split fifty-fifty between a national media campaign and local event marketing. Advertising, the website and mobile sites, and various social media content will emphasise the car's fun spirit and low emissions. During the first year, £75,000 will be spent on marketing research to find out who is buying the car and what their satisfaction levels are.

The third part of the marketing strategy statement describes the planned long-run sales, profit goals and marketing mix strategy:

> We intend to capture a 3 per cent long-run share of the total car market and realise an after-tax return on investment of 15 per cent. To achieve this, product quality will start high and be improved over time. Price will be raised in the second and third years if competition and the economy permit. The total marketing budget will be raised each year by about 10 per cent. Marketing research will be reduced to £40,000 per year after the first year.

Business analysis

Once management has decided on its product concept and marketing strategy, it can evaluate the business attractiveness of the proposal. **Business analysis** involves a review of the sales, costs and profit projections for a new product to find out whether they satisfy the company's objectives. If they do, a product can move to the product development stage.

To estimate sales, the company might look at the sales history of similar products and conduct market surveys. It can then estimate minimum and maximum sales to assess the range of risk. After preparing a sales forecast, management can estimate the expected costs and profits for a product, including marketing, R&D, operations, accounting and finance costs. The company then uses the sales and costs figures to analyse a new product's financial attractiveness.

Business analysis—A review of the sales, costs and profit projections for a new product to find out whether these factors satisfy the company's objectives.

Product development

For many new product concepts, a product may exist only as a word description, a drawing, or perhaps a crude mock-up. If a product concept passes the business test, it moves into **product development**. Here, R&D or engineering develops the product concept into a physical product. The product development step, however, now calls for a huge jump in investment. It will show whether a product idea can be turned into a workable product.

The R&D department will develop and test one or more physical versions of the product concept. R&D hopes to design a prototype that will satisfy and excite consumers and that can be produced quickly and at budgeted costs. Developing a successful prototype can take days, weeks, months, or even years depending on the product and prototype methods.

However, the speed of producing prototypes has been dramatically increased by new technologies like 3D printing, and digital simulations are replacing traditional mock-up prototypes in industries like carmaking:[17]

Product development—Developing the product concept into a physical product to ensure that the product idea can be turned into a workable market offering.

> Carmakers spend a fortune on prototypes of new models which can cost as much as $1 million each. Now manufacturers are shifting towards digital simulation methods instead. The Jaguar XE saloon which started shipping in the UK in 2015, was produced without using any prototypes – a first for a mainstream model. Jaguar Land Rover aims to eliminate all physical prototypes by 2020. They are committed to ordering expensive factory tooling on the back of computer modelling alone. The car industry spends $10 billion a year on building prototypes, but computer simulations are replacing conventional approaches because they are cheaper, quicker and more accurate.

One way or another, products undergo rigorous tests to make sure that they perform safely and effectively, or that consumers will find value in them. Companies can do their own product testing or outsource it to other firms that specialise in testing.

Marketers often involve actual customers in product testing. For example, HP signs up consumers to evaluate prototype imaging and printing products in their homes and offices. Participants work with pre-release products for periods ranging from a few days to eight weeks and share their experiences about how the products perform in an actual use environment. The product-testing programme gives HP a chance to interact with customers and gain insights about their entire 'out-of-box experience', from product set-up and operation to system compatibility. HP personnel might even visit participants' homes to directly observe installation and first use of the product.

A new product must have the required functional features and also convey the intended psychological characteristics. A all-electric car, for example, should strike consumers as being well built, comfortable and safe. Management must learn what makes consumers decide that a car is well built. To some consumers, this means that the car has 'solid-sounding' doors. To others, it means that the car is able to withstand heavy impact in crash tests. Consumer tests are conducted in which consumers test-drive the car and rate its attributes.

For example, in developing Windows 10, Microsoft employed 5 million volunteer bug testers, known as Windows Insiders, not only to make the product better but to try to build loyalty. In the Windows Insider programme, a group of consumers and business users agreed to download a series of early versions and try them out. Members of the programme sent feedback – shaping Windows 10 to a degree that would have been unthinkable at Microsoft only a few years ago.[18]

Test marketing

Test marketing—The stage of new product development in which the product and its proposed marketing programme are tested in realistic market settings.

If a product passes both the concept test and the product test, the next step is **test marketing**, the stage at which a product and its proposed marketing programme are introduced into realistic market settings. Test marketing gives the marketer experience with marketing a product before going to the great expense of full introduction. It lets the company test a product and its entire marketing programme – targeting and positioning strategy, advertising, distribution, pricing, branding and packaging and budget levels.

The amount of test marketing needed varies with each new product. Test marketing costs can be high, and it takes time that may allow competitors to gain advantages. When introducing a new product requires a big investment, when the risks are high, or when management is not sure of the product or its marketing programme, a company may do a lot of test marketing. Starbucks spent 20 years developing the Starbucks VIA instant coffee – one of its most risky product roll-outs ever – and several months testing the product in Starbucks shops before fully releasing it. The testing paid off. The Starbucks VIA line is now a best-selling instant coffee for Starbucks' global business.[19]

When the costs of developing and introducing a product are low, or when management is already confident about a new product, the company may do little or no test marketing. In fact, test marketing by consumer goods firms has been declining in recent years. Companies often do not test market simple line extensions or copies of successful competitor products.

As an alternative to extensive and costly standard test markets, companies can use controlled test markets or simulated test markets. In *controlled test markets*, new products and tactics are tested among controlled groups of customers and stores. In each market, a marketing research agency can be used to measure purchases by a panel of shoppers who report all of their purchases in participating stores. Within test stores, the agency can control such factors as shelf placement, price and in-store promotions for the products being tested. The research agency can also measure television viewing in each panel household and in some situations send special commercials to panel members' television sets to test the effect on shopping decisions.

By combining information on each consumer's purchases with consumer demographic and television viewing information, a skilled marketing research agency can provide store-by-store, week-by-week reports on the sales of tested products and the impact of in-store and in-home marketing efforts. Such controlled test markets usually cost much less than standard test markets and can provide accurate forecasts in as little as 12 to 24 weeks. Naturally, the choice of research agency will be important and should reflect the strength of different agencies in local markets.

Companies can also test new products using *simulated test markets*, in which researchers measure consumer responses to new products and marketing tactics in laboratory stores or simulated shopping environments. Many marketers are now using new online simulated marketing technologies to reduce the costs of test marketing and speed up the process.

Commercialisation

Commercialisation—Introducing a new product into the market.

Test marketing gives management the information needed to make a final decision about whether to launch the new product. If the company goes ahead with **commercialisation** – introducing a new product into the market – it will face high costs. The company may need to build or rent a manufacturing facility. And, in the case of a major new consumer product, it may spend large amounts for advertising, sales promotion and other marketing efforts in the first year. For instance, to introduce the Surface tablet, Microsoft spent close to $400 million on an advertising blitz that spanned TV, print, outdoor, the Internet, events, public relations and sampling.

The company launching a new product must first decide on introduction *timing*. If a carmaker's new battery-powered electric car will eat into the sales of its other cars, the introduction may be delayed. If the car can be improved further, or if the economy is down, the company may wait until the following year to launch it. However, if competitors are ready to introduce their own battery-powered models, the company may push to introduce its car sooner.

Next, the company must decide *where* to launch the new product – in a single location, a region, the national market or the international market. Few companies have the confidence, capital and capacity to launch new products into full country-wide national or international distribution from the start. Instead, they develop a planned *market rollout* over time. (Though in smaller European countries global launch may be essential early on, to achieve adequate volume.) Some companies, however, may quickly introduce new models into their full country-market while companies with international distribution systems may introduce new products through swift global rollouts. For example, Microsoft launched its Windows 8 operating system with a massive $1 billion global marketing campaign spanning 42 countries. The initial launch featured a series of events that began with preview parties in Shanghai and New York City and the opening of 31 pop-up stores worldwide.[20]

MANAGING NEW PRODUCT DEVELOPMENT

The new product development process shown in Figure 9.1 highlights the important activities needed to find, develop and introduce new products. However, new product development involves more than just going through a set of steps. Companies must take a holistic approach to managing this process. Successful new product development requires a customer-centred, team-based and systematic effort.

Customer-centred new product development

Above all else, new product development must be customer-centred. When looking for and developing new products, companies often rely too heavily on technical research in their R&D laboratories. But like everything else in marketing, successful new product development begins with a thorough understanding of what consumers need and value. **Customer-centred new product development** focuses on finding new ways to solve customer problems and create more customer-satisfying experiences.

One study found that the most successful new products are ones that are differentiated, solve major customer problems, and offer a compelling customer value proposition. Another study showed that companies that directly engage their customers in the new product innovation process had twice the return on assets and triple the growth in operating income of firms that did not. Thus, customer involvement has a positive effect on the new product development process and product success.[21]

For example, Intuit – maker of world-leading financial software such as TurboTax, QuickBooks and Quicken – is a strong proponent of customer-driven new product development:[22]

Intuit follows a 'Design for Delight (D4D)' development philosophy that products should delight customers by providing experiences that go beyond their expectations. Design for Delight starts with customer empathy – knowing customers better than they know themselves. To that end, each year, Intuit conducts 10,000 hours of what it calls 'follow-me-homes', in which design employees observe first-hand how customers use its products at home and at work. They look to understand problems and needs

Author comment

Above all else, new product development must focus on creating customer value. A senior Samsung executive says, 'We get our ideas from the market. The market is the driver.'

Customer-centred new product development—New product development that focuses on finding new ways to solve customer problems and create more customer-satisfying experiences.

Customer centred new product development: financial software maker Intuit follows a 'Design for Delight' philosophy that products should delight customers by providing experiences that go beyond their expectations.
Source: Intuit

HOW WE INNOVATE

DEEP CUSTOMER EMPATHY

DELIGHT

GO BROAD TO GO NARROW

RAPID EXPERIMENTS WITH CUSTOMERS

Intuit. simplify the business of life   QuickBooks   TurboTax   Mint that even customers themselves might not recognise. Based on customer observations, the next D4D step is to 'go broad, go narrow' – developing many customer-driven product ideas, then narrowing them down to one or a few great ideas for products that will solve customer problems. The final D4D step involves turning the great ideas into actual products and services that create customer delight, collecting customer feedback steadily throughout the development process. Intuit works relentlessly to embed Design for Delight concepts deeply into its culture. 'D4D comes to life through every employee – it's part of all of our jobs,' says Eileen Fagan, the company's vice president of innovation and transformational change programmes. 'It requires us to come to work everyday with a learning mentality, adaptability and vulnerability to truly deliver 'delight' to our customers.' Thanks to customer-centred new product development, Intuit's revenues have grown to $4.2 billion annually, a 27 per cent increase in just the past four years.

For products ranging from consumer packaged goods to financial services, today's innovative companies get out of the research laboratory and mingle with customers in the search for new customer value. For instance, when Danish toy-maker LEGO faced sagging sales, and losses of $300 million a year, the underlying problem was that the classic toy company had fallen out of touch with its customers. In the age of the Internet, videogames, iPods and high-tech playthings, traditional toys such as LEGO bricks had been pushed to the back of the cupboard:[23]

> The LEGO product makeover, however, didn't start with engineers working in design laboratories. First, LEGO had to reconnect with customers. So it started by listening to customers, understanding them, and including them in the new product development process. To get to know its customers better, for instance, LEGO conducted up-close-and-personal ethnographic studies – hanging out with and observing children aged seven to nine on their home turf. 'We thought we understood our consumers, the children of the world,' says a LEGO marketer, but it turns out that 'we didn't know them as well as we thought'.
>
> For example, LEGO had long held fast to a 'keep it simple' mantra. From the beginning, it offered only basic play sets – bricks, building bases, beams, doors, windows, wheels and slanting roof tiles – with few or no instructions. The philosophy was that giving children unstructured building sets would stimulate their imaginations and foster creativity. But that concept just wasn't cutting it in the modern world. Today's children get bored easily, and in today's fast-moving environment, they are exposed to many more characters and themes. In response, LEGO shifted toward more-specialised, more-structured products.
>
> Thanks to customer-centred new product development, LEGO is now thriving. In the past five years, even as the overall toy market has declined in a weakened economy and as competitors such as Mattel and Hasbro have struggled, LEGO's sales have soared 66 per cent, and its profits have jumped tenfold. 'Kids [including the adult variety] are ruthless,' says a senior LEGO executive. 'If they don't like the product, then at the end of the day . . . all the rest of it won't make any difference. What counts, all that counts, is that you're at the top of kids' wish lists.' Thanks to all that listening and customer involvement, that's where LEGO is again.

Thus, customer-centred new product development begins and ends with understanding customers and involving them in the process. Successful innovation boils down to finding fresh ways to meet customer needs.

Team-based new product development

Good new product development also requires a total-company, cross-functional effort. Some companies organise their new product development process into the orderly sequence of steps shown in Figure 9.1, starting with idea generation and ending with commercialisation. Under this *sequential product development* approach, one company department works individually to complete its stage of the process before passing the new product along to the next department and stage. This orderly, step-by-step process can help bring control to complex and risky projects. But it can also be dangerously slow. In fast-changing, highly competitive markets, such slow-but-sure product development can result in product failures, lost sales and profits, and crumbling market positions.

To get their new products to market more quickly, many companies use a **team-based new product development** approach. Under this approach, company departments work closely together in cross-functional teams, overlapping the steps in the product development process to save time and increase effectiveness. Instead of passing a new product from department to department, the company assembles a team of people from various departments that stays with the new product from start to finish. Such teams usually include people from the marketing, finance, design, manufacturing and legal departments and even supplier and customer companies. In the sequential process, a bottleneck at one phase can seriously slow an entire project. In the team-based approach, if one area hits snags, that area can work to resolve the snag while the remainder of the team moves on.

The team-based approach does have some limitations, however. For example, it sometimes creates more organisational tension and confusion than the more orderly sequential approach. However, in rapidly changing industries facing increasingly shorter product life cycles, the rewards of fast and flexible product development far exceed the risks. Companies that combine a customer-centred approach with team-based new product development gain a big competitive edge by getting the right new products to market faster.

For example, in Sweden, Electrolux, the world's number two appliance maker, has redesigned its new product development around teams to speed product development and achieve customer-focused innovation:[24]

> Electrolux researchers spent hours in homes in Australia, France and Russia asking people questions as they vacuumed their carpets to catalogue the 'pain points' — the annoying things that irritate users, such as the dust flying around when the cleaner is emptied. The result of the research was the UltraCapic bagless vacuum cleaner that compresses the dirt into a spongy pellet to prevent fly-away dust particles when the machine is emptied. For much of its 94-year history, Electrolux had product development run by its engineers. But Electrolux has now brought in what it calls an 'innovation triangle', bringing together design, research and development and marketing departments to jointly make decisions on new products. For the UltraCapic, the fly-away dust pain point found in the market research led to a brief for designers. They proposed a built-in compactor to compress the dirt into a disk that could be removed without creating a dust-storm. The idea was tested in another round of focus groups. R&D then weighed in with different approaches to compacting — manual versus electric for example. Before settling on a final design, additional focus groups were convened to review the alternatives and to compare with competitors' products from Dyson and Hoover. At all stages everything had to get a 70 per cent approval rating to proceed. Electrolux is changing the way it tackles design and product development to know more, know it faster and be ready to react.

Systematic new product development

Finally, the new product development process should be holistic and systematic rather than compartmentalised and haphazard. Otherwise, few new ideas will surface, and many good ideas will fizzle-out and die. To avoid these problems, a company can install an *innovation management system* to collect, review, evaluate and manage new product ideas.

The company can appoint a respected senior person to be the company's innovation manager. It can create web-based idea management software and encourage all company stakeholders – employees, suppliers, distributors and dealers – to become involved in finding and developing new products. It can assign a cross-functional innovation management committee to evaluate proposed new product ideas and help bring good ideas to market. It can create recognition programmes to reward those who contribute the best ideas.

The innovation management system approach yields two favourable outcomes. First, it helps create an innovation-oriented company culture. It shows that top management supports, encourages and rewards innovation. Second, it will yield a larger number of new product ideas, among which will be found some especially good ones. The good new ideas will be more systematically developed, producing more new product successes. No longer will good ideas wither for the lack of a sounding board or a senior product advocate.

Thus, new product success requires more than simply thinking up a few good ideas, turning them into products, and finding customers for them. It requires a holistic approach for finding

Team-based new product development—New product development in which various company departments work closely together, overlapping the steps in the product development process to save time and increase effectiveness.

new ways to create valued customer experiences, from generating and screening new product ideas to creating and rolling out want-satisfying products to customers.

More than this, successful new product development requires a whole-company commitment. At companies known for their new product prowess, such as Google, Apple, Reckitt Benckiser, IDEO, 3M and P&G, the entire culture encourages, supports and rewards innovation.

New product development in turbulent times

When tough economic times hit, or when a company faces financial difficulties, management may be tempted to reduce spending on new product development. However, such thinking is usually shortsighted. By cutting back on new products, the company may make itself less competitive during or after the downturn. In fact, tough times might call for even greater new product development, as the company struggles to better align its market offerings with changing consumer needs and tastes. In difficult times, innovation more often helps than hurts in making the company more competitive and positioning it better for the future.

Companies such as Apple, Google, Samsung and Amazon keep the innovations flowing during tough economic times. For example, Apple created its blockbuster iPod, iPhone and iTunes innovations in the midst of some very difficult times it faced more than a decade ago. Those innovations not only saved the company, they propelled it into the innovative powerhouse it is today. P&G launched two of its most successful (and highest-priced) new products, Swiffer (innovative household cleaning products) and Crest Whitestrips (tooth whitening products), during recessions. Thus, rain or shine, good times or bad, a company must continue to innovate and develop new products if it wants to grow and prosper.

Product life cycle—The course of a product's sales and profits over its lifetime.

PRODUCT LIFE-CYCLE STRATEGIES

After launching a new product, management wants that product to enjoy a long and happy life. Although it does not expect that product to sell forever, the company wants to earn a decent profit to cover all the effort and risk that went into launching it. Management is aware that each product will have a life cycle, although its exact shape and length is not known in advance.

Figure 9.2 shows a typical **product life cycle** (PLC) – the course that a product's sales and profits take over its lifetime. The PLC has five distinct stages:

1. *Product development* begins when the company finds and develops a new product idea. During product development, sales are zero and the company's investment costs mount.

2. *Introduction* is a period of slow sales growth as a product is introduced in the market. Profits are non-existent in this stage because of the heavy expenses of product introduction.

3. *Growth* is a period of rapid market acceptance and increasing profits.

4. *Maturity* is a period of slowdown in sales growth because a product has achieved acceptance by most potential buyers. Profits level off or decline because of increased marketing outlays to defend a product against competition.

5. *Decline* is the period when sales fall off and profits drop.

Not all products follow all five stages of the PLC. Some products are introduced and die quickly; others stay in the mature stage for a long, long time. Some enter the decline stage and are then cycled back into the growth stage through strong promotion or repositioning. It seems that a well-managed brand could live forever. Venerable brands like Coca-Cola, Gillette, Budweiser, Guinness, American Express and Wells Fargo, for instance, are still going strong after more than 100 years. Guinness beer from Ireland recently celebrated its 250th anniversary.

The product life-cycle concept can describe a *product class* (petrol-powered motor cars), a *product form* (four-wheel drives or 4×4s) or a *brand* (the amazing BMW X5). The product

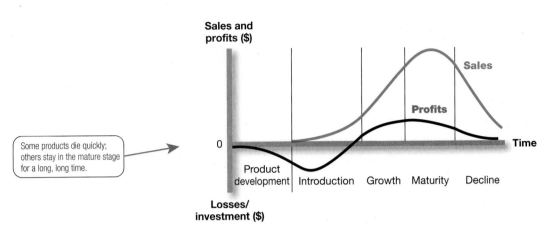

Figure 9.2 Sales and profits over the product's life from inception to decline

Some products die quickly; others stay in the mature stage for a long, long time.

Style—A basic and distinctive mode of expression.

Brompton folding bicycles have attracted a cult following among commuters as a solution to an urban living problem and a life-style choice.

Source: Juice Images/Alamy Images

life-cycle concept applies differently in each case. Product classes have the longest life cycles; the sales of many product classes stay in the mature stage for a long time. Product forms, in contrast, tend to have the standard PLC shape. Product forms such as 'dial telephones' and 'VHS tapes' passed through a regular history of introduction, rapid growth, maturity and decline.

A specific brand's life cycle can change quickly because of changing competitive attacks and responses. For example, although laundry soaps (product class) and powdered detergents (product form) have enjoyed fairly long life cycles, the life cycles of specific brands have tended to be much shorter. In the United States, today's leading brands of powdered laundry soap are Tide and Gain – the leading brands 100 years ago were the long-defunct and forgotten Fels-Naptha, Octagon and Kirkman.

The product life-cycle concept also can be applied to what are known as styles, fashions and fads. Their special life cycles are shown in Figure 9.3. A **style** is a basic and distinctive mode of expression. For example, styles appear in homes (e.g., country cottage, townhouse, functional, art deco), clothing (e.g., formal and casual) and art (e.g., realist, surrealist and abstract). Once a style is created, it may last for generations, passing in and out of vogue. A style has a cycle showing several periods of renewed interest.

For example, based in London, Brompton folding bicycles have attracted a cult following among commuters in UK cities and those in Germany, Hong Kong, Singapore, Japan and the US, who buy around 45,000 bikes a year. The distinctively styled bicycle can be folded in a few easy movements. It is not aimed at cycling enthusiasts but at city commuters who are linked by their weariness with public transport and inner city traffic – it is a solution to an urban living problem and a life-style choice. It has also achieved fanatical loyalty and a strong group identity among users.[25]

Figure 9.3 Styles, fashions, and fads

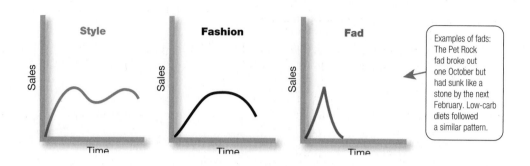

Examples of fads: The Pet Rock fad broke out one October but had sunk like a stone by the next February. Low-carb diets followed a similar pattern.

Fashion—A currently accepted or popular style in a given field.

A **fashion** is a currently accepted or popular style in a given field. For example, the more formal 'business attire' look of corporate dress of the 1980s and 1990s gave way to the 'business casual' look of the 2000s and 2010s. Fashions tend to grow slowly, remain popular for a while, and then decline slowly.

Fad—A temporary period of unusually high sales, driven by consumer enthusiasm and immediate product or brand popularity.

Fads are temporary periods of unusually high sales driven by consumer enthusiasm and immediate product or brand popularity. A fad may be part of an otherwise normal life cycle, as in the case of recent surges in the sales of poker chips and accessories. Or a fad may comprise a brand's or product's entire life cycle. Pet Rocks are a classic example. Upon hearing his friends complain about how expensive it was to care for their dogs, advertising copywriter Gary Dahl joked about his pet rock. He soon wrote a spoof of a dog-training manual for it, titled *The Care and Training of Your Pet Rock*. Soon Dahl was selling some 1.5 million ordinary beach pebbles at $4 each. Yet the fad, which started one October, had sunk just like a stone by the next February. Dahl's advice to those who want to succeed with a fad: 'Enjoy it while it lasts.' Other examples of fads include Silly Bandz, Furbies, Crocs and Pogs.[26]

In Britain, chocolate and nut spread Nutella has been described as the fad that the 'health police' hate:[27]

> Nutella was invented in at Italian bakery half a century ago. In Britain the product now sells around 11 million jars a year with revenue around £30 million, growing 22 per cent last year alone. Nuttella's Facebook page has a global audience of 26 million people. Nutella is a thick brown gloop containing hazelnuts that is spread on toast, used as a pancake filling, and provides the 'secret' ingredient for delicious chocolate cakes. In an age of anti-obesity campaigns it is an anachronism, but one which inspires incredible loyalty amongst its fans. Nutella has been embraced by the British middle class, even though it is unhealthy. For owner Ferrero SpA, Nutella has become big business. The Nutella fad shows no sign of slowing – Ferrero has opened Nutella cafés in Chicago and New York, selling Nutella pastries and treats, and the product's 50th birthday was celebrated with a special stamp issued by the Italian postal service, street parties throughout Europe, and a pop concert in Naples. And this for a product where a single tablespoon has 100 calories, which is sickly sweet, and bad for the teeth and the waistline.

Marketers can apply the product life-cycle concept as a useful framework for describing how products and markets work. And when used carefully, the concept can help in developing good marketing strategies for different life-cycle stages. But using the product life-cycle concept for forecasting product performance or developing marketing strategies presents some practical problems. For example, in practice, it is difficult to forecast the sales level at each life-cycle stage, the length of each stage, and the shape of the life-cycle curve. Using the product life-cycle concept to develop marketing strategy also can be difficult because strategy is both a cause and a result of the life-cycle. A product's current product life-cycle position suggests the best marketing strategies, and the resulting marketing strategies affect product performance in later stages.

Moreover, marketers should not blindly push products through the traditional product life-cycle stages. Instead, marketers often defy the 'rules' of the life cycle and position or reposition their products in unexpected ways. By doing this, they can rescue mature or declining products and return them to the growth phase of the life cycle. Or they can leapfrog obstacles to slow consumer acceptance and propel new products forward into the growth phase.

The moral of the product life cycle is that companies must continually innovate or else they risk extinction. No matter how successful its current product line-up, a company must skilfully manage the life cycles of existing products for future success. And to grow, it must develop a steady stream of new products that bring new value to customers.

We looked at the product development stage of the product life cycle in the first part of this chapter. We now look at strategies for each of the other life-cycle stages.

In Britain, chocolate and nut spread Nuttella has been described as the fad that the 'health police' hate.
Source: MASP Food Photography/ Alamy Images

Introduction stage

The **introduction stage** starts when a new product is first launched. Introduction takes time, and sales growth is apt to be slow. Well-known products such as frozen foods and HDTVs lingered for many years before they entered a stage of more rapid growth.

In this stage, as compared to other stages, profits are negative or low because of the low sales and high distribution and promotion expenses. Much money is needed to attract distributors and build their inventories. Promotion spending is relatively high to inform consumers of a new product and get them to try it. Because the market is not generally ready for product refinements at this stage, the company and its few competitors produce basic versions of a product. These firms focus their selling on those buyers who are the most ready to buy.

A company, especially a *market pioneer*, must choose a launch strategy that is consistent with the intended product positioning. It should realise that the initial strategy is just the first step in a grander marketing plan for a product's entire life cycle. If the pioneer chooses its launch strategy to make a 'killing', it may be sacrificing long-run revenue for the sake of short-run gain. As the pioneer moves through later stages of the life cycle, it must continuously formulate new pricing, promotion, and other marketing strategies. It has the best chance of building and retaining market leadership if it plays its cards correctly from the start.

Introduction stage—The product life-cycle stage in which a new product is first distributed and made available for purchase.

Growth stage

If a new product satisfies the market, it will enter a **growth stage**, in which sales will start climbing quickly. The early adopters will continue to buy, and later buyers will start following their lead, especially if they hear favourable word-of-mouth. Attracted by the opportunities for profit, new competitors will enter the market. They will introduce new product features, and the market will expand. The increase in competitors leads to an increase in the number of distribution outlets, and sales jump just to build reseller stocks. Prices remain where they are or decrease only slightly. Companies keep their promotion spending the same or at a slightly higher level. Educating the market remains a goal, but now the company must also meet the competition.

Profits increase during the growth stage as promotion costs are spread over a larger volume and as unit manufacturing costs decrease. A firm uses several strategies to sustain rapid market growth as long as possible. It improves product quality and adds new product features and models. It enters new market segments and new distribution channels. It shifts some advertising from building product awareness to building product conviction and purchase, and it lowers prices at the right time to attract more buyers.

In the growth stage, a firm faces a trade-off between high market share and high current profit. By spending a lot of money on product improvement, promotion and distribution, the company can capture a dominant position. In doing so, however, it gives up maximum current profit, which it hopes to make up in the next stage.

Growth stage—The product life-cycle stage in which a product's sales start climbing quickly.

Maturity stage

Maturity stage—The product life-cycle stage in which a product's sales growth slows or levels off.

At some point, a product's sales growth will slow down, and it will enter the **maturity stage**. This maturity stage normally lasts longer than the previous stages, and it poses strong challenges to marketing management. Most products are in the maturity stage of the life cycle, and therefore most of marketing management deals with a mature product.

The slowdown in sales growth results in many producers with many products to sell. In turn, this over-capacity leads to greater competition. Competitors begin marking down prices, increasing their advertising and sales promotions, and upping their product development budgets to find better versions of the product. These steps lead to a drop in profit. Some of the weaker competitors start dropping out, and the industry eventually contains only well-established competitors.

Although many products in the mature stage appear to remain unchanged for long periods, most successful ones are actually evolving to meet changing consumer needs. Product managers should do more than simply ride along with or defend their mature products; a good offence is the best defence. They should consider modifying the market, product and marketing mix.

In *modifying the market*, the company tries to increase consumption by finding new users and new market segments for its brands. For example, brands such as Harley-Davidson and Axe fragrances, which have typically targeted male buyers, are introducing products and marketing programmes aimed at women. Conversely, Weight Watchers has typically targeted women, but has now created products and programmes aimed at men.

The company may also look for ways to increase usage among present customers. For example, 3M recently ran a marketing campaign to inspire more usage of its Post-It products:[28]

> The Post-It brand's 'Go ahead' campaign hopes to convince customers that the sticky pieces of paper are good for much more than just scribbling temporary notes and reminders. Instead, it positions Post-It Notes as a means of self-expression by showing creative, non-traditional ways that consumers around the world use them. In the past, 3M promoted mostly functional uses of Post-It products, but research showed that consumers have a surprisingly strong emotional relationship with the brand. 'They're using it to communicate, using it to collaborate, using it to organise themselves,' says a 3M marketing executive. The 'Go ahead' campaign was motivated by customers' 'quirky and inspired uses of our product'. An initial ad shows people on a college campus blanketing a wall outside a building with Post-It Notes answering the question, 'What inspires you?' 'Share on a real wall,' the announcer explains. Other scenes show a young man filling a wall with mosaic artwork created from multiple colours of Post-It Notes, teachers using Post-It Notes to enliven their classrooms, and a man posting a 'Morning, beautiful' note on the bathroom mirror as his wife is brushing her teeth. 'Go ahead,' says the announcer, 'keep the honeymoon going'. The ad ends with a hand peeling Post-It Notes off a pad one by one to reveal new, unexpected uses: 'Go ahead, connect, 'Go ahead, inspire', and 'Go ahead, explore'.

Inspiring more usage: 3M's 'Go ahead, Post-It' campaign portrays Post-It Notes as good for much more than just scribbling temporary notes and reminders. Instead they are a means of self-expression.
Source: 3M Company

The company might also try *modifying a product* – changing characteristics such as quality, features, style or packaging, or technology platforms to inspire more usage among current customers and attract new users. Thus, to freshen up their products for today's technology-obsessed children, many classic toy and game makers are creating new digital versions or add-ons for old favourites. More than 75 per cent of children eight years old and younger now use mobile devices such as tablets and smartphones. So toy makers are souping-up their products to meet the tastes of the new generation. For example, the electronic banking edition of Monopoly uses bank cards instead of paper money, Hot Wheels cars can zoom across an iPad using the Hot Wheels Apptivity app, and the Barbie Photo Fashion doll has a digital camera built in.[29]

In another example of product modification, Heinz Tomato Ketchup has been around since 1876, and has long been a staple in the British diet. To keep the brand young, Heinz now markets

the product as: Tomato Ketchup, Tomato Ketchup Jalapeno Chilli, Tomato Ketchup Organic, Tomato Ketchup 50% Less Sugar, and Tomato Ketchup Sweet Chilli.

Finally, the company can try *modifying the marketing mix* – improving sales by changing one or more marketing mix elements. The company can offer new or improved services to buyers. It can cut prices to attract new users and competitors' customers. It can launch a better advertising campaign or use aggressive sales promotions – trade deals, money-off, premiums and contests. In addition to pricing and promotion, the company can also move into new marketing channels to help serve new users.

Decline stage

The sales of most product forms and brands eventually dip. The decline may be slow, as in the cases of postage stamps and porridge for breakfast, or rapid, as in the cases of cassette and VHS tapes. Sales may plunge to zero, or they may drop to a low level where they continue for many years. This is the **decline stage** (see Table 9.2).

Sales decline for many reasons, including technological advances, shifts in consumer tastes and increased competition. As sales and profits decline, some firms withdraw from the market. Those remaining may prune their product offerings. They may drop smaller market segments and marginal trade channels, or they may cut the promotion budget and reduce their prices further.

Carrying a weak product can be very costly to a firm, and not just in profit terms. There are many hidden costs. A weak product may take up too much of management's time. It often requires frequent price and stock-level adjustments. It requires advertising and sales-force attention that might be better used to make 'healthy' products more profitable. A product's failing reputation can cause customer concerns about the company and its other products. The biggest cost may well lie in the future. Keeping weak products delays the search for replacements, creates a lopsided product mix, hurts current profits and weakens the company's foothold on the future.

Decline stage—The product life-cycle stage in which a product's sales fade away.

Table 9.2 Summary of product life-cycle characteristics, objectives and strategies

	Introduction	Growth	Maturity	Decline
Characteristics				
Sales	Low sales	Rapidly rising sales	Peak sales	Declining sales
Costs	High cost per customer	Average cost per customer	Low cost per customer	Low cost per customer
Profits	Negative	Rising profits	High profits	Declining profits
Customers	Innovators	Early adopters	Mainstream adopters	Lagging adopters
Competitors	Few	Growing number	Stable number beginning to decline	Declining number
Marketing objectives				
	Create product engagement and trial	Maximise market share	Maximise profit while defending market share	Reduce expenditure and milk the brand
Strategies				
Product	Offer a basic product	Offer product extensions, service, and warranty	Diversify brand and models	Phase out weak items
Price	Use cost-plus	Price to penetrate market	Price to match or beat competitors	Cut price
Distribution	Build selective distribution	Build intensive distribution	Build more intensive distribution	Go selective: phase out unprofitable outlets
Advertising	Build product awareness among early adopters and dealers	Build engagement and interest in the mass market	Stress brand differences and benefits	Reduce to level needed to retain hard-core loyals
Sales promotion	Use heavy sales promotion to entice trial	Reduce to take advantage of heavy consumer demand	Increase to encourage brand switching	Reduce to minimal level

Source: from *Marketing Management*, 13th ed., Prentice Hall (Kotler P., Keller K.L. 2009) p. 288, Pearson Education Inc. (NJ), Reproduced by permission of Pearson Education Inc., Upper Saddle River, New Jersey.

For these reasons, companies must identify products in the decline stage and then decide whether to maintain, harvest or drop each of these declining products. Management may decide to *maintain* its brand, repositioning or reinvigorating it in hopes of moving it back into the growth stage of the product life cycle. P&G has done this with several brands, including Mr Clean in the US and Canada, and Old Spice internationally.

Management may decide to *harvest* a product, which means reducing various costs (plant and equipment, maintenance, R&D, advertising, sales force), hoping that sales hold up. If successful, harvesting will increase the company's profits in the short run. Finally, management may decide to *drop* a product from its line. It can sell it to another firm or simply liquidate it at salvage value. In recent years, P&G has sold off several lesser or declining brands, such as Folgers coffee, Crisco oil, Comet cleanser, Sure deodorant, Duncan Hines cake mixes, Jif peanut butter, and most recently its last food business in the form of Pringles snacks. If the company plans to find a buyer, it will not want to run down a product through harvesting.

Table 9.2 above summarises the key characteristics of each stage of the PLC. The table also lists the marketing objectives and strategies for each stage.[30]

ADDITIONAL PRODUCT AND SERVICE CONSIDERATIONS

Author comment

Let's look at a few more product topics, including regulatory and social responsibility issues and the special challenges of marketing products internationally.

We wrap up our discussion of products and services with two additional considerations: public policy issues and social responsibility in product decisions, and issues of international product and services marketing.

Product decisions and social responsibility

Marketers should carefully consider public policy issues and regulations regarding acquiring or dropping products, patent protection, product quality and safety and product warranties.

Regarding new products, the national and international regulators (e.g., the European Union) may prevent companies from adding products through acquisitions if the effect threatens to lessen competition. Companies dropping products must be aware that they have legal obligations, written or implied, to their suppliers, dealers and customers who have a stake in the dropped product. Companies must also obey the patent and trademark laws of different countries when developing new products. A company cannot make its product illegally similar to another company's established product.

Manufacturers must comply with specific laws regarding product quality and safety, which vary considerably across different countries. Generally, if consumers are injured by a product with a defective design, they can sue manufacturers or dealers. A recent survey of manufacturing companies found that product liability was the second-largest litigation concern, behind only labour and employment matters. Although manufacturers are found at fault in a small minority of all product liability cases, when they are found guilty, the damages awarded are often very substantial. For example, after it recalled 11 million vehicles for accelerator-pedal-related issues, Toyota faced more than 100 class-actions and individual lawsuits and ended up paying a $1.6 billion settlement to compensate owners for financial losses associated with the defect.[31]

This issue has resulted in huge increases in product liability insurance premiums, causing big problems in some industries. Some companies pass these higher rates along to consumers by raising prices. Others are forced to discontinue high-risk product lines. Some companies are now appointing 'product stewards', whose job is to protect consumers from harm and the company from liability by proactively ferreting out potential product problems.

International product and services marketing

Innovation and new product development is a global phenomenon. For example, money is flowing into Europe's creative hubs faster than ever, in spite of a tough regulatory environment. So, while exciting US-based start-ups include Uber (taxi hailing app), Airbnb (room and home rental service), Palantir (cyber security and big data) and Snapchat (messaging), parallel European start-ups include Spotify (music streaming service from Sweden), Delivery Hero (take-away service in Germany), Supercell (games maker from Finland behind *Clash of Titans*) and Blippar (augmented reality app from London). Companies need to maintain an international perspective on innovation and change in their industries.[32]

Moreover, it is important for marketers to be aware that, increasingly, emerging markets may be the key driver of new product innovation in the rest of the world. For example, studies of product innovation in India point to the strength of 'frugal innovation' – based on the observation of the innovative brilliance of Indian entrepreneurs with limited means at their disposal, and a focus on simplicity, rather than endless new product features:[33]

When the then-CEO of Renault visited Russia in 1997, he was uncomfortable to find that the $6,000 locally produced Lada was outselling Renault's more expensive and showy cars by a big margin. Five years later, Renault unveiled its $6,000 no-frills Logan. The Logan was designed for emerging markets, but sold so well in prosperous western Europe that Renault launched a line of low-cost vehicles that today constitutes nearly half its global sales. The authors of *Frugal Innovation* see Renault as a pioneer of working in a way which will increasingly characterise the way Western companies innovate and create new products. Developing the Logan involved a shift for Renault's engineers away from plentiful resources and a rich market to constrained resources and value-hungry customers. This change is on the way for all businesses, they warn.

The term 'reverse innovation' is also used to describe the creation of low-cost products in emerging markets which then take on the developed markets. For example, Mahindra & Mahindra is India's biggest tractor maker. Their machines are affordable and suit the tastes and pockets of emerging market customers in India and China. But those products are now starting to do well in the United States – well enough to motivate John Deere to launch its own low-cost tractor in India. It looks like increasingly Western businesses must learn new tricks and develop new products for emerging markets at much lower cost, and then bring these products back into their domestic markets.[34]

Reverse innovation – also known as 'trickle-up innovation' – is already well-established at companies like GE and Unilever. It means turning products created for emerging markets into low-cost goods for developed world customers. GE is committed to major new product development expenditure in health care to substantially lower costs, increase access and improve quality, by developing products in emerging markets that can then succeed in developed markets. This reverses the traditional approach of modifying Western products and selling them in emerging markets. When GE developed a low-cost portable ultrasound scanner for doctors – in and for China – it achieved sales growth rates of 50–60 per cent a year when it was launched globally.[35]

In addition, international product and services marketers have always faced special challenges of other kinds as well. First they must figure out what products and services to introduce and in which countries. Then they must decide how much to standardise or adapt their products and services for world markets.

On the one hand, companies would like to standardise their offerings. Standardisation helps a company develop a consistent worldwide image. It also lowers the product design, manufacturing and marketing costs of offering a large variety of products. On the other hand, markets and consumers around the world differ widely. Companies must usually respond to these differences by adapting their product offerings. For example, Swiss company Nestlé sells a variety of very popular Kit Kat flavours in Japan that might make the average Western chocolate-lover's stomach turn, such as green tea, red bean and red wine.

Packaging also presents many practical challenges for international marketers. Packaging issues can be subtle. For example, names, labels and colours may not translate easily from one country to another. A firm using yellow flowers in its logo might fare well in the United States but meet with disaster in Mexico, where a yellow flower symbolises death or disrespect. Similarly, although Nature's Gift might be an appealing name for gourmet mushrooms in Britain, it would be deadly in Germany, where *gift* means poison. Packaging may also need to be tailored to meet the physical characteristics of consumers in various parts of the world. For instance, soft drinks are sold in smaller cans in Japan to better fit the smaller Japanese hand. Thus, although product and package standardisation can produce benefits, companies must usually adapt their offerings to the unique needs of specific international markets.

On the other hand, one of the strengths of digital businesses is that they offer globally services which are near-identical to those they offer in their home markets. What the British customer receives from Google, Facebook, YouTube, Amazon or Netflix is almost the same as what the US customer receives, because these online businesses are less constrained by individual market size and characteristics. Changes tend to be only those mandated by local regulators, for example the EU privacy pressures on Google, and the China government restrictions on Internet access.

Service marketers also face special challenges when going global. Some service industries have a long history of international operations. For example, the commercial banking industry was one of the first to grow internationally. Banks had to provide global services to meet the foreign exchange and credit needs of their home country clients wanting to sell overseas. In recent years, many banks have become truly global. Germany's Deutsche Bank, for example, serves more than 19 million customers through 2,984 branches in more than 70 countries. For its clients around the world that wish to grow globally, Deutsche Bank can raise money not only in Frankfurt but also in Zurich, London, Paris, Tokyo and Moscow.[36]

Professional and business services industries, such as accounting, management consulting and advertising, have also undertaken globalisation. The international growth of these firms followed the globalisation of the client companies they serve. For example, as more clients employ worldwide marketing and advertising strategies, advertising agencies have responded by globalising their own operations. For example, London-based WPP is the world's largest communications services group,. (WPP stands for Wire and Plastic Products, the name of the UK manufacturer of wire baskets which was the foundation company for what is now the WPP group.) WPP employs 165,000 people working in 3,000 offices in 110 countries. WPP companies work with 350 of the Fortune Global 500, all 30 of the Dow Jones 30, 63 of the NASDAQ 100, and 31 of the Fortune e-50. Some 760 clients are served worldwide. There are 30 WPP team leaders assigned to focus on clients such as Bayer, Colgate-Palmolive, Danone, Dell, Ford, HSBC, Johnson & Johnson, Kimberly-Clark, Mazda, Procter & Gamble, Shell and Vodafone. Over 25 WPP team leaders are assigned to focus on clients such as Bayer, Colgate, Danone, Dell, Ford, HSBC, Johnson & Johnson, Kimberly-Clark, Mazda, Procter & Gamble, Shell and Vodafone.[37]

Retailers are among the latest service businesses to go global. As their home markets become saturated, retailers in mature, developed markets are expanding into faster-growing markets abroad. For example, since 1991, US mega-retailer Walmart has entered 27 countries outside the United States – its international division's sales account for 29 per cent of total sales. Carrefour, the world's second-largest retailer, now operates more than 10,000 stores in more than 33 countries. It is the leading retailer in Europe, Brazil and Argentina and the largest foreign retailer in China. Asian shoppers can now buy American and European goods in French-owned Carrefour stores in China. Britain's leading supermarket retailer, Tesco, now has a range of successful businesses outside the UK, with more than 500,000 employees worldwide and 7,817 stores (including franchises). Tesco has particular strengths in the former eastern European countries (Czech Republic, Hungary, Slovakia, Poland), and has expanded rapidly into Asia (Thailand, Malaysia, India, China) as well as markets like the Republic of Ireland and Turkey.[38]

The trend towards growth of global service companies will continue, especially in banking, airlines, telecommunications and professional services. Today, service firms are no longer simply following their manufacturing customers. Instead, they are taking the lead in international expansion.

OBJECTIVES REVIEW AND KEY TERMS

A company's current products face limited life spans and must be replaced by newer products. But new products can fail – the risks of innovation are as great as the rewards. The key to successful innovation lies in a customer-focused, holistic, total-company effort, strong planning and a systematic *new product development process*.

OBJECTIVE 1 Explain how companies find and develop new product ideas (p. 263)

Companies find and develop new product ideas from a variety of sources. Many new product ideas stem from *internal sources*. Companies conduct formal R&D, or they pick the brains of their employees, urging them to think up and develop new product ideas. Other ideas come from *external sources*. Companies track *competitors'* offerings and obtain ideas from *distributors and suppliers*, who are close to the market and can pass along information about consumer problems and new product possibilities.

Perhaps the most important source of new product ideas is customers themselves. Companies observe customers, invite them to submit their ideas and suggestions, or even involve customers in the new product development process. Many companies are now developing *crowdsourcing* or *open-innovation* new product idea programmes, which invite broad communities of people – customers, employees, independent scientists and researchers, and even the general public – into the new product innovation process. Truly innovative companies do not rely only on one source for new product ideas.

OBJECTIVE 2 List and define the steps in the new product development process and the major considerations in managing this process (pp. 263–274)

The new product development process consists of eight sequential stages. The process starts with *idea generation*. Next comes *idea screening*, which reduces the number of ideas based on the company's own criteria. Ideas that pass the screening stage continue through *product concept development*, in which a detailed version of a new product idea is stated in meaningful consumer terms. In the next stage, *concept testing*, new product concepts are tested with a group of target consumers to determine whether the concepts have strong consumer appeal. Strong concepts proceed to *marketing strategy development*, in which an initial marketing strategy for a new

product is developed from a product concept. In the *business-analysis* stage, a review of the sales, costs and profit projections for a new product is conducted to determine whether the new product is likely to satisfy the company's objectives. With positive results here, the ideas become more concrete through *product development* and *test marketing* and finally are launched during *commercialisation*.

New product development involves more than just going through a set of steps. Companies must take a systematic, holistic approach to managing this process. Successful new product development requires a customer-centred, team-based, systematic effort.

OBJECTIVE 3 Describe the stages of the product life cycle (PLC) and how marketing strategies change during a product's life cycle (pp. 274–279)

Each product has a *life-cycle* marked by a changing set of problems and opportunities. The sales of the typical product follow an S-shaped curve composed of five stages. The cycle begins with the *product development stage* in which the company finds and develops a new product idea. The *introduction stage* is marked by slow growth and low profits as a product is distributed to the market. If successful, a product enters a *growth stage*, which offers rapid sales growth and increasing profits. Next comes a *maturity stage* in which a product's sales growth slows down and profits stabilise. Finally, a product enters a *decline stage* in which sales and profits dwindle. The company's task during this stage is to recognise the decline and decide whether it should maintain, harvest or drop a product. The different stages of the product life cycle require different marketing strategies and tactics.

OBJECTIVE 4 Discuss two additional product issues: socially responsible product decisions and international product and services marketing (pp. 279–282)

Marketers must consider two additional product issues. The first is *social responsibility*. This includes public policy issues and regulations involving acquiring or dropping products, patent protection, product quality and safety and product warranties. The second involves the special challenges facing international product and services marketers. International marketers must decide how much to standardise or adapt their offerings for world markets.

NAVIGATING THE KEY TERMS

OBJECTIVE 1
New product development (p. 263)

OBJECTIVE 2
Idea generation (p. 263)
Crowdsourcing (p. 265)
Idea screening (p. 266)
Product concept (p. 267)
Concept testing (p. 267)

Marketing strategy development (p. 268)
Business analysis (p. 269)
Product development (p. 269)
Test marketing (p. 270)
Commercialisation (p. 270)
Customer-centred new product
development) (p. 271)
Team-based new product development
(p. 273)

OBJECTIVE 3
Product life cycle (PLC) (p. 274)
Style (p. 275)
Fashion (p. 276)
Fad (p. 276)
Introduction stage (p. 277)
Growth stage (p. 277)
Maturity stage (p. 278)
Decline stage (p. 279)

DISCUSSION AND CRITICAL THINKING

Discussion questions

9-1 What activities are performed in the marketing strategy development step of the new product development process? What is required in a good marketing strategy statement? (AACSB: Communication; Reflective thinking)

9-2 What decisions must be made once a company decides to go ahead with commercialisation for a new product? (AACSB: Communication)

9-3 What are the benefits of an *innovation management system* and how can a company install such a system? (AACSB: Communication)

9-4 Name and define the stages of the product life cycle. Do all products follow this pattern? Explain. (AACSB: Communication; Reflective thinking)

Critical-thinking exercises

9-5 It appears that the sky is the limit regarding ideas for smartphone/tablet apps. In a small group, create an idea for new apps related to (1) business, (2) health, (3) education, (4) sports and (5) shopping. (AACSB: Communication; Use of IT; Reflective thinking)

9-6 Find an example of a company that launched a new consumer product within the last five years. Develop a presentation showing how the company implemented the 4 Ps in launching the product and report on the product's success since the launch. (AACSB: Communication; Reflective thinking)

9-7 The 'Internet of Things' — a term that refers to everyday objects being connected to the Internet — is growing. Thermostats, ovens, cars, toothbrushes, and even baby clothes are connecting to the Internet. Research this phenomenon and suggest five innovative product ideas connected to the 'Internet of Things'. (AACSB: Communication; Use of IT; Reflective thinking)

Mini-cases and applications

Online, mobile and social media marketing: Reading Rainbow app

Many Americans have grown up watching LeVar Burton on PBS's *Reading Rainbow* show. He hosted the children's educational show for 26 years and now has taken it mobile. Burton purchased the rights to the show and launched a *Reading Rainbow* mobile app, making it the App Store's top-grossing app in less than a year. The app is free to try, but a €10 per month or €30 per six-month subscription allows kids unlimited access to the library and adventures on themed islands, such as the Animal Kingdom and others from the iconic television show, as well as new adventure field trips. Kids have gobbled up more than 10 million books. Audio and video storytelling brings books to life for children, and interactive elements encourage curiosity and learning. Adventures incorporate segments from the TV show and brand new video. Up to five children in a household can customise their own reading adventures, and reading lists are suggested based on their abilities and interests. The parent dashboard lets parents monitor their child's reading progress. LeVar Burton personally starts each day with a 'Good morning, y'all' tweet followed by 15 to 20 more tweets each day to his followers. The service is always expanding, offering new adventures that are often based on user feedback through social media.

9-8 In what stage of the product life cycle is the *Reading Rainbow* television programme? Has the mobile app changed that? Explain. (AACSB: Communication; Reflective thinking)

9-9 Discuss other existing products that have created new life for the product by embracing Internet, mobile or social media platforms. Suggest an app for another tangible product or service that does not currently use online, mobile or social media, along with ways to encourage customer engagement and social sharing for the brand. (AACSB: Communication; Use of IT; Reflective thinking)

Marketing ethics: orphan drugs

For years, rare diseases were unattractive markets for pharmaceutical companies. This changed with the 'orphan drug' designation. For example, in the US, the Food and Drug Administration now offers incentives for producers of orphan drugs, such as: faster approval, tax incentives and longer patent protections, and patient groups raise large sums of money to aid in their development. Now, in the US, more than 200 orphan drugs a year enter development, and about a third of them gain FDA approval. But these drugs are expensive to users. For example, Isis Pharmaceutical's cholesterol drug for a rare condition costs $235,000 to $295,000 per year. NPS Pharmaceuticals has a drug for a rare bowel condition, Gattex, that costs patients $295,000 per year. In Europe, Sanofi's enzyme-replacement therapy drug, Myozyme, costs €700,000 per year. These high prices fetched more than $1 billion in annual sales for a third of orphan drug makers, and the category has more than $50 billion in worldwide sales that grow more than 20 per cent a year. This has become an attractive market segment for pharmaceutical companies, which have seen many of their blockbuster drugs go off-patent and are looking for new revenue streams. But who pays for these expensive orphan drugs? Right now, private health plans and governments foot the bill.

9-10 Discuss the ethical issues surrounding orphan drugs. Should pharmaceutical companies be allowed to charge such high prices for these drugs? (AACSB: Communication; Ethical reasoning)

9-11 Discuss the impact of austerity measures in Europe and the implementation of health care reform in the United States on the future of orphan drugs. (AACSB: Communication; Reflective thinking)

Marketing by the numbers: dental house calls

With the population of the US, Europe and China ageing, and patients who dread sitting in a sterile dental office, some dentists are finding an opportunity in dental house-calls. In the US, the Blende Dental Group has taken its service on the road in San Francisco and New York City, performing everything from routine exams and cleaning to root canal surgery. Some patients are wealthy and prefer the personal service, whereas others are elderly, home-bound people who cannot get out to the dentist's office. Recreating a dental office in a home requires additional equipment, such as a portable X-ray machine that looks like a ray gun, sterile water tanks, a dental drill, lights and a laptop. A portable X-ray machine alone costs €8,000. Refer to Appendix 2: Marketing by the numbers to answer the following questions.

9-12 What types of fixed costs are associated with this service? Estimate the total fixed costs for this additional service, and, assuming a contribution margin of 40 per cent, determine the amount of sales necessary to break even on this increase in fixed costs to offer this additional service. (AACSB: Communication; Analytical thinking)

9-13 What other factors must a dentist consider before offering this service in addition to their in-office service? (AACSB: Communication; Reflective thinking)

REFERENCES

[1] Based on information found in Brad Stone, 'Inside the moonshot factory', *Bloomberg Businessweek*, 22 May 2013, pp. 56–61; Chuck Salter, 'Google: the faces and voices of the world's most innovative company', *Fast Company*, March 2008, pp. 74–88; John Markoff, 'Google puts money on robots, using the man behind Android', *New York Times*, 4 December 2013, p. 1; Larry Popelka, 'Google is winning the innovation war against Apple', *Bloomberg Businessweek*, 20 May 2013, www.businessweek.com/articles/2013-05-20/google-is-winning-the-innovation-waragainst-apple; Ben Paynter, 'Google: for adding fiber to our Internet diet', *Fast Company*, 11 February 2013, www.fastcompany.com/most-innovative-companies/2013/google; Rolfe Winkler and Daisuke Wakabayashi, 'Google to buy nest labs for $3.2 Billion', *Wall Street Journal*, 13 January 2014; and www.google.com and http://investor.google.com/financial/tables.html, accessed September 2014; Peter Campbell, 'Google soups up its network with Alphabet', *Daily Mail*, 12 August 2015, p. 68.

[2] Austino Fontevecchia, 'Apple's strong iPhone sales mask falling revenue per unit as gross margins contract', *Forbes*, 22 July 2013, www.forbes.com/sites/afontevecchia/2013/07/23/applesstrong-iphone-sales-mask-falling-revenue-per-unit-as-gross-margins-contract/.

[3] Marsha Lindsey, '8 ways to ensure your new-product launch succeeds', *Fast Company*, 3 April 2012, www.fastcompany.com/1829483/8-ways-ensure-your-new-product-launch-succeeds; and Vijaya Kumar, 'Improving the success rate of new product introduction through digital social media', *PDMA*, 27 August 2013, www.pdma.org/p/bl/et/blogid=2&blogaid=115.

[4] See www.scribd.com/doc/20269401/Product-Failures-and-Their-Strategies, accessed July 2015.

[5] Richard Waters, 'Microsoft pins hopes on Windows 10 as it challenges rivals for leading role in app world', *Financial Times*, 29 July 2015, p. 19; Dina Bass and Ashlee Vance, 'The new old Windows', *Bloomberg Businessweek*, 3–9 August 2015, pp. 32–33.

[6] See Paul Sloane, 'Source of innovative ideas', *Yahoo! Voices*, 16 June 2010, http://voices.yahoo.com/sources-innovativeideas-6185898.html; and 'R&D spending returns to pre-recession levels, finds Booz & Company Global Innovation 1000 Study', 10 October 2012, www.booz.com/global/home/press/display/51296501.

[7] For these and other examples, see Dan Schawbel, 'Why companies want you to become an intrapreneur', *Forbes*, 9 September 2013, www.forbes.com/sites/danschawbel/2013/09/09/why-companieswant-you-to-become-an-intrapreneur/; and 'Time to think', http://solutions.3m.com/innovation/en_US/stories/time-to-think, accessed September 2014.

[8] Kevin Scott, 'The LinkedIn [in]cubator', 7 December 2012, http://blog.linkedin.com/2012/12/07/linkedin-incubator/; and www.linkedin.com/static?key=what_is_linkedin, accessed September 2014.

[9] Based on information from Matthew Kronsberg, 'How LEGO's great adventure in geek-sourcing snapped into place and boosted the brand', *Fast Company*, 2 February 2012, www.fastcompany.com/1812959/LEGO-cuusoo-minecraft-lord-of-rings-hayabusa; Yun Mi Antorini and Albert M. Muniz, Jr., 'The benefits and challenges of collaborating with user communities', *Research Technology Management*, May/June 2013, pp. 21–28; Kurt Wagner, '5 brands that got fans to lend a hand', *Fortune*, 24 June 2013, http://money.cnn.com/gallery/leadership/2013/06/24/crowdsourcing-brands.fortune/; and http://LEGO.cuusoo.com/, accessed September 2014.

[10] See http://mystarbucksidea.force.com/ideaHome, accessed July 2015.

[11] Mary Tripsas, 'Seeing customers as partners in invention', *New York Times*, 27 December 2009, www.nytimes.com.

[12] See Brian Morrissey, 'The social sell?' *Brandweek*, 14 February 2010, www.brandweek.com; and www.ideastorm.com, accessed July 2015.

[13] 'Samsung is fueling its future with open innovation', *Inno Centive*, 23 October 2013, www.innocentive.com/blog/2013/10/23/samsung-is-fueling-its-future-with-open-innovation/.

[14] See 'Victorinox Success!' September 2012, www.jovoto.com/blog/2012/09/success-story-victorinox/; Bastian Unterberg et al., *Crowdstorm: The Future of Ideas, Innovation, and Problem Solving Is Collaboration* (Somerset, NJ: Wiley, 2013), pp. 175–177; and http://victorinox.jovoto.com and www.jovoto.com/clients, accessed September 2014.

[15] See George S. Day, 'Is it real? Can we win? Is it worth doing?' *Harvard Business Review*, December 2007, pp. 110–120.

[16] This example is based on Tesla Motors and information obtained from www.teslamotors.com, accessed April 2014; also see Ryan Bradley, 'Full charge ahead', *Fortune*, 4 February 2013, pp. 10–13; Leah Hunter, 'How Tesla protects the romance of driving while disrupting the industry', *Co. Design*, 7 November 2013, www.fastcodesign.com/3021312; and 'Electric car', *Wikipedia*, http://en.wikipedia.org/wiki/Electric_car, accessed September 2014.

[17] Andy Sharman, 'Car prototyping moves from workshop to digital simulation', *Financial Times*, 24 July 2015, p. 12.

[18] Dina Bass and Ashlee Vance, 'The new old Windows', *Bloomberg BusinessWeek*, 3–9 August 2015, pp. 32–33.

[19] See Maureen Morrison, 'Marketer of the Year: Taco Bell', *Advertising Age*, 2 September 2013, pp. 15–16; Susan Berfield, 'Baristas, patrons steaming over Starbucks VIA', *Bloomberg BusinessWeek*, 13 November 2009; and Tamara Walsh, 'Starbucks makes a big bet on new product mix in 2014', *The Motley Fool*, 8 January 2014, www.fool.com/investing/general/2014/01/08/starbucks-makesa-big-bet-on-new-product-mix-in-20.aspx.

[20] Beth Snyder Bulik, 'Microsoft spends $1B on operating system launch, but are ads Windows-washing?' *Advertising Age*, 29 October 2012, p. 10; and Mary Jo Foley, 'Microsoft to open its holiday pop-up retail stores on October 26', *ZDNet*, 2 October 2012, www.zdnet.com/microsoft-to-open-its-holiday-pop-up-retailstores-on-october-26-7000005113/.

[21] See Robert G. Cooper, 'Formula for success', *Marketing Management*, March–April 2006, pp. 19–23; Barry Jaruzelski and Kevin Dehoff, 'The Global Innovation of 1000', *Strategy + Business*, Issue 49, fourth quarter, 2007, pp. 68–83; Shu-Hua Chien and Jyh-jye Chen, 'Supplier involvement in customer involvement effect on new product development success in the financial service industry', *The Service Industries Journal*, February 2010, p. 185.

[22] See Chris O'Brien, 'How Intuit became a pioneer of "Delight"', *Los Angeles Times*, 10 May 2013; Bob Thompson, "Delight, by Design. Innovation sets Intuit apart as a customer-centric leader', *Customer Think*, 6 June 2013, http://customerthink.com/delight_by_design_innovation_sets_intuit_apart_as_customer_centric_leader/; Intuit: Immersive Customer Experience, Michele Marut and Duncan Wannamaker, *Design for Experience Awards*, http://awards.designforexperience.com/gallery/2013/promoting-empathy-forusers/intuit, accessed June 2014; and http://investors.intuit.com/financial-information/annual-reports/default.aspx and intuitlabs.com/innovation.html, accessed September 2014.

[23] Adapted from: 'LEGO grows by listening to customers', *Advertising Age*, 9 November 2009, p. 15; Nelson D. Schwartz, 'Beyond the blocks', *The New York Times*, 6 September 2009, p. BU1; Jon Henley, 'Toy Story', *The Guardian*, 26 March 2009, p. F4; Kevin O'Donnell, 'Where do the best ideas come from? The unlikeliest sources', *Advertising Age*, 14 July 2008, p. 15; Lewis Borg Cardona, 'LEGO learns a lesson', *Change Agent*, June 2008, www.synovate.com/changeagent; and www.LEGO.com/eng/info/ and http://mindstorms.LEGO.com/en-us/community/default.aspx, accessed April 2010.

[24] Carol Matlack, 'Electrolux's Holy Trinity', *Bloomberg BusinessWeek*, 31 October 2013, pp. 55–56.

[25] Brendan Greeley, 'Into the fold', *Bloomberg BusinessWeek*, 3 April 2014, pp. 83–85.

[26] See Katya Kazakina and Robert Johnson, 'A fad's father seeks a sequel', *New York Times*, 30 May 2004, www.nytimes.com; John Schwartz, 'The joy of silly', *New York Times*, 20 January 2008, p. 5; Drew Guarini, '11 surprising product fads', *Huffington Post*, 8 August 2012, www.huffingtonpost.com/2012/08/22/productfads_n_1819710.html#slide=1410262; and www.crazyfads.com, accessed September 2014.

[27] David Derbyshire, 'How Britain went nuts for a spread the heath police hate', *Daily Mail*, 26 May 2014, p. 22.

[28] Based on information from Stuart Elliott, '3M says, "Go ahead, make something of it"', *New York Times*, 28 January 2013, www.nytimes.com/2013/01/28/business/mutfund/3m-says-goahead-make-something-of-it.html?pagewanted=2&tntemail0=y&_r=3&emc=tnt; and 'Post-It brand. Go ahead', www.youtube.com/watch?v=F1zOJTonK5s, accessed September 2014.

[29] Stephanie Clifford, 'Go digitally, directly to jail? Classic toys learn new clicks', *New York Times*, 25 February 2012; Anya Kamenetz, 'Study: 75% of kids under age 8 use mobile devices', *Fast Company*, 28 October 2013, www.fastcompany.com/3020755/fast-feed/study-75-of-kids-under-age-8-use-mobile-devices; and http://mattelapptivity.com/app-toys-games/hot-wheels/, accessed September 2014.

[30] For a more comprehensive discussion of marketing strategies over the course of the PLC, see Philip Kotler and Kevin Lane Keller, *Marketing Management*, 15th ed. (Upper Saddle River, NJ: Prentice Hall, 2015).

[31] Jaclyn Trop, 'Toyota will pay $1.6 billion over faulty accelerator suit', *New York Times*, 20 July 2013, p. 3B.

[32] Murad Ahmed, 'In Silicon Valley's shadow', *Financial Times*, 22 July 2015, p. 11.

[33] See Navi Radjou and Jaideep Prabhu, *Frugal Innovation: How to Do More With Less*, London: Profile Books, 2015. Mian Ridge, 'A revolution

in business by doing more with less', *Financial Times*, 12 February 2015, p. 12; Kevin Roberts, Navi Radjou, Jaideep Prabhu and Simone Ahuja, *Jugaad Innovation: Think Frugal, Be Flexible, Generate Breakthrough Growth*, London: Wiley, 2012

34 See: Vijay Govinda Rajan and Chris Trimble, *Reverse Innovation: Create Far From Home, Win Everywhere*, Boston MA: Harvard Business Review Press, 2012; James Crabtree, 'The new markets for low-cost and profitable ideas', *Financial Times*, 12 April 2012, p. 14.

35 Jeffrey R Immelt, Vijay Govindarajan and Chris Trimble, 'How GE is disrupting itself', *Harvard Business Review*, October 2009, pp. 56–65.

36 Information from www.db.com, accessed September 2014.

37 See www.wpp.com, accessed July 2015.

38 See 'Global powers of retailing 2014', www2.deloitte.com/content/ dam/ Deloitte/global/Documents/Consumer-Business/dttl_CB_Global-Powers-of-Retailing-2014.pdf; 'Walmart Corporate International', http:// corporate.walmart.com/our-story/locations, accessed September 2014; information from www.carrefour.com, accessed September 2014; www. tescoplc.com/index.asp?pageid=71, accessed July 2015.

COMPANY CASE

Reckitt Benckiser: building a brand powerhouse

Reckitt Benckiser is far from being a household name, but it has become a cleaning products superstar, at times outshining Procter & Gamble and Unilever with its new products and marketing prowess. Reckitt's strong suit is finding niche markets with high growth potential, So instead of trying to compete in the saturated laundry detergent market, for example, Reckitt focuses on the growing segment for automatic dishwasher products, where it achieved a massive worldwide market share. By pioneering new brands, often in market niches, Reckitt has emerged as one of Europe's top performers.

Reckitt Benckiser (RB) was formed in 1999 by the merger of Dutch group Benckiser with the UK's Reckitt & Colman. In 2005, RB acquired Boots Healthcare International for £1.9 billion, expanding its presence in the over-the-counter healthcare market. In 2007 the company acquired Adams Respiratory Therapeutics, allowing it to enter the US over-the-counter pharmaceuticals market. In 2010, RB made a £2.5 billion offer for SSL International, maker of Durex and Scholl products, pursuing further geographic diversification and new product areas.

RB has become a global leader in household, healthcare and personal products. The group's 19 'Powerbrands' are sold in more than 200 countries. The Powerbrands include well-known names like: Air Wick (air fresheners), Cillit Bang (household cleaners), Dettol (antiseptics), Durex (contraceptives), Gaviscon (indigestion remedies), Harpic (bleaches), Nurofen (painkillers), Strepsils (sore throat remedies), Veet (body hair removal products). Heavy investment in the Powerbrands, focused on areas where high growth was possible, meant that at one point 16 of the Powerbrands could claim to be number 1 or 2 in their categories in the global marketplace. In fact, RB markets hundreds of products, many of which are local leaders in the global marketplace.

RB's brand strategy is captured as follows:

Innovation drives the strategy, which drives innovation

RB reinforces its brands with an exceptional rate of innovation. Innovations must be Great Performers, Fast to Market and Cost-effective. The innovation pipeline is built around brand strategy. So innovative cost savings improve margins and fuel growth. And it's a full time job — RB changes a formula about every eight hours.

Consumers are at the centre of RB innovation

Innovation starts and ends with consumers — the small ways RB can make life better. So RB builds consumers into product development, validating every idea with them. It doesn't focus on ideas, but ideas that sell because they meet consumer needs. This creates powerful global brands that can adapt to local preferences.

Where do those ideas come from?

Above all, from consumer insights. RB spends time with consumers in the lab and in their homes. But RB has its own technology insights too. The RB-Idealink website sources ideas the world over. RB also keeps a close eye on technological and societal trends. And puts all these ideas to the test.

Product innovation is at the core of RB strategy, relying on 'value-added' products to keep customers buying even during the recession. Then-CEO Bart Becht said: 'It is even more important [during difficult times] to sort our brands apart from the cheap stuff.' The focus is on regular improvements to the Powerbrands. In 2010, in spite of tough economic conditions, RB released Finish Quantumatic, a detergent that can be clipped to the racks of dishwashers; Airwick Aqua Mist, a 'natural' air freshener that comes in a bottle with no chemical propellants; and Vanish Oxi Action Extra Hygiene, a stain remover that claims to remove bacteria from clothes washed at low temperatures. It also brought out the Lysol No-Touch Hand Soap System, a dispenser that 'senses' the presence of hands and pumps out soap without requiring physical contact.

Becht's Legacy at Benckeiser

In April 2011, Bart Becht stood down as CEO at Benckiser. Even then, listening to Bart Becht enthusing about the latest Reckitt Benckiser twist on air fresheners or dishwasher tablets, it was easy to imagine him checking friends' bathroom cabinets and kitchen cupboards for his group's products. His evident passion – extending even to the unpromising categories of cockroach killers and toilet cleaners – makes it hard to understand why he was quitting the group he had led since it was formed in 1999 from the merger of Dutch group Benckiser with the UK's Reckitt and Colman.

Mr Becht said at this time that it was a good time to announce his exit plans. 'The executive team is very strong and SSL [the maker of Durex condoms and Scholl footwear, bought last year for £2.5 billion ($4 billion)] is bedding down very well. Sixteen years is a long time. The fact that you have passion doesn't mean you can't retire at some time.'

Mr Becht's time at the helm has transformed the merged group into a powerhouse that delivered years of great returns for shareholders. This earned him City plaudits and a great deal of money: including vested share options, his pay in 2009 totalled £92 million. During his tenure, RB shares have outperformed the FTSE by three and a half times, as well as beating the peer group: Reckitt's shares have outperformed Procter & Gamble's by 225 per cent and L'Oréal's by 256 per cent.

Julian Hardwick, an analyst at RBS who has covered Mr Becht's career since Benckiser's initial public offering in 1997, said: 'He is outstanding for his understanding of the business, the intensity he brings to his work and the way he has created the culture of Reckitt Benckiser'. Reckitt's success is based on zealous cost-cutting, frenetic innovation and hefty marketing spend to promote its main brands. In 2010, about 35 per cent of revenues came from products launched in the previous three years, and the group's 19 'Powerbrands' accounted for 69 per cent of sales.

The years immediately after the original merger were marked by a lack of large acquisitions, driven by a fear of overpaying. But latterly the business was better prepared to do significant deals – notably SSL, Boots Healthcare International and Adams Respiratory Therapeutics.

Nevertheless, Mr Becht left the group facing strategic challenges. One relates to the drug Suboxone, which treats opiate dependency and has come off-patent in the US. This drug had built to constitute 8 per cent of RB's total sales. The likelihood is the rapid emergence of generic methadone-substitute products.

The core household cleaners business is under siege from Procter & Gamble which has launched detergents and stain removers to compete directly with Reckitt's Finish and Vanish brands.

'The shares have underperformed the European Consumer Staples space over the past two years for two reasons,' Mr Hardwick said. 'The first is the huge uncertainty over what sort of generic challenge Suboxone will face. The second is that base business growth has slowed down as the company has faced weaker developed market growth and increased competition in some categories, especially from Procter & Gamble.'

Mr Deboo agreed about the competitive threat to niche products from the US consumer goods group. 'Reckitt's success was built on going into 'shoulder' categories such as washing additives that were too small for the majors to touch. But P&G's need for growth is such that it is pushing into these categories now too.'

Nonetheless, Becht was handing over a company which had become a £25 billion behemoth selling in 180 countries, but facing growing competition and recession-hit consumers trading down from premium products to cheaper alternatives like retailer brands.

Incoming CEO Rakesh Kapoor in 2011, formerly Reckitt's marketing chief, faced the challenge of returning Reckitt to its stellar growth record after the economic downturn, after sales growth fell in 2009 and 2010. Kapoor faced the tough challenge of stepping into the shoes of a chief executive who hardly put a foot wrong during his reign.

The next phase for RB

Kapoor's vision for the business from the outset was captured in his mantra 'health, hygiene and home' and the goal of unifying the hotch-potch of brands and businesses, but he remains focused on the power brands which provide around half of revenues. But he also faced the challenge that times have changed, and the days of 'swimming between the big giants' were over – for example, P&G had marched straight into the one-time gaps RB traditionally monopolised, such as premium dishwasher tablets, air fresheners and laundry stain removers.

In 2014, RB demerged its pharmaceuticals business (best known for the heroin substitute Suboxone) to focus on healthcare (including Scholl footcare products and Durex condoms), and bought the KY personal lubricant brand from Johnson & Johnson. RB tried to buy Merck's consumer health unit, but was outbid by Bayer. Kapoor believes he has an advantage over the science-based pharmaceuticals companies who have dominated healthcare products in the past because, he says: 'Innovation in consumer health means considering mums not molecules. At RB the consumer is at the core of the business.

By 2015, RB was looking at increasing profits and restoring growth targets based on a strong pipeline of new products. The company was in the midst of a £150 million cost-cutting campaign – including 'Supercharge,' a project aimed at reducing duplication of functions between the businesses. Healthcare, which Kapoor aims to make the main focus of the business, accounts for one-third of sales and was driving performance. Kapoor is rumoured to be looking for further acquisitions in the healthcare area. But RB remains strong mainly in developed markets rather than emerging markets – two-thirds of sales are in Europe and North America. The company has recently improved its developed country position by reorganising into divisions based on customer type rather than geography – European and North American customers have similar buying habits and form one division, while Russians, Arabs and Africans are grouped into a separate division.

Questions for discussion

1. How has Reckitt been able to achieve leadership positions in so many different areas?
2. Is Reckitt's product development customer-centred? Systematic? Justify and explain your answer.
3. Based on the product life cycle, what challenges does Reckitt face in managing its brand portfolio? Are the challenges for Mr Kapoor different to those faced earlier by Mr Brecht? In what ways?
4. Will Reckitt be able to maintain its market position in so many areas when strong competitors enter with their own niche products? Why or why not?
5. Can Reckitt extend its position in emerging markets. If so, how can this be achieved?

Sources: Laura Cohn, 'Why it pays to reinvent the mop', *BusinessWeek*, 24 January 2005, p. 23; Alison Smith, 'Succession challenge for incoming Reckitt chief', *Financial Times*, 15 April 2011, p. 18; Sarah Shannon, 'The British upstart challenging P&G', *Bloomberg BusinessWeek*, 2–19 August 2010, pp. 26–27; Jenny Wiggins and Adam Jones, 'Reckitt deals with burgeoning cash pile', *Financial Times*, 11 February 2010, p. 19; Elizabeth Rigby, Adam Jones and Kate Burgess, 'Teckitt Benckiser chief's pay-out reached £92 million after decade of success', *Financial Times*, 8 April 2010, p. 1; Paul Sonne, 'Reckitt Benckiser's CEO to step down', *Wall Street Journal*, 15–22 April 2011, p. 7; Scheherezade Daneshku, 'RB looks to future in "health, hygiene and home"', *Financial Times*, 5 December 2014, p. 25; Scheherazade Daneshku, 'Reckitt restores growth forecasts as profit soar', *Financial Times*, 29 July 2015, p. 22.

CHAPTER TEN

Pricing: understanding and capturing customer value

Chapter preview

In this chapter, we look at the second major marketing mix tool – pricing. If effective product development, promotion and distribution sow the seeds of business success, effective pricing is the harvest. Firms successful at creating customer value with the other marketing mix activities must still capture some of this value in the prices they earn. In this chapter, we discuss the importance of pricing, dig into three major pricing strategies, and look at internal and external considerations that affect pricing decisions. In the next chapter, we examine some additional pricing considerations and approaches.

To start, let's examine pricing at Ryanair. Over the past two decades, Ryanair has changed the airline-pricing world – and annoyed, frustrated and irritated in equal measures the 'old-fashioned' airlines while growing and growing its market share. For Ryanair – 'no-frills' is not just the way forward, it is an obsession.

Objective outline

➤ **Objective 1** Answer the question 'What is a price?' and discuss the importance of pricing in today's fast-changing environment.
What is a price? (pp. 292–293)

➤ **Objective 2** Identify the three major pricing strategies and discuss the importance of understanding customer-value perceptions, company costs and competitor strategies when setting prices.
Major pricing strategies (pp. 293–300)

➤ **Objective 3** Identify and define the other important external and internal factors affecting a firm's pricing decisions.
Other internal and external considerations affecting price decisions (pp. 301–305)

Ryanair: really good-value pricing – flying for free!

The major airlines are struggling with difficult pricing strategy decisions in these tough air-travel times. Pricing strategies vary widely. One airline, however, appears to have found a radical new pricing solution, one that customers are sure to love: Make flying *free!* That's right. Michael O'Leary, CEO of Dublin-based Ryanair, has a dream that someday all Ryanair passengers will fly for free. And with a current average price of €83.45 per ticket (compared to €89.97 for closest UK competitor easyJet and a whopping €206.76 for FlyThomasCook Southwest), Ryanair is getting closer. While this is somewhat behind the sector leaders, Pegasus at €63.19 (see Chapter 1), Ryanair leads the Western European 'no-frills' flight market.

They proudly proclaim that 'We are Europe's only ultra low cost carrier, and that means we bring you the lowest fares on flights to all of our destinations – and that's guaranteed. From the moment Ryanair embraced a no-frills, low-cost, get-you-from-A-to-B model, we've pretty much revolutionised the air travel industry. We get you from A to B, and we get you there cheaper, and more reliably, than any other airline.'

Even without completely free flights, Ryanair has become Europe's most popular carrier. Last year Ryanair flew over 80 million passengers to more than 179 European destinations in 29 countries. The budget airline is also Europe's most profitable one. Over the past decade, even as the global airline industry collectively lost nearly €40 billion, Ryanair has turned healthy net profits in nine out of ten years. Given the prospects of rising fuel costs, collapsing European economies, and other troubled times ahead for the airline industry, Ryanair seems well positioned to weather the turbulence.

What's the secret? Ryanair's frugal cost structure makes even cost-conscious Southwest look like a reckless spender. In addition, the Irish airline makes money on everything *but* the ticket, from charging for baggage check-in to revenues from seat-back advertising space. Ryanair's low-cost strategy is modelled after Southwest's. Twenty years ago, when Ryanair was just another struggling European carrier, Ryanair's O'Leary went to Dallas to meet with Southwest executives and see what he could learn. The result was a wholesale revamping of the Irish carrier's business model. Following Southwest's lead, to economise, Ryanair began employing only a single type of aircraft – the good-old Boeing 737. Also like Southwest, it began focusing on smaller, secondary airports and offering unassigned passenger seating.

But Ryanair has since taken Southwest's low-cost pricing model even further. When it comes to keeping costs down, O'Leary – who wears jeans, trainers and off-the-peg short-sleeved shirts – is an absolute fanatic. He wants Ryanair to be known as the Walmart of flying. Like the giant retailer, Ryanair is constantly on the lookout for new ways to cut costs – for example, hard plastic seats with no seat-back pockets reduce both weight and cleaning expense. Ryanair flight crews even buy their own uniforms and headquarters staff supply their own pens.

O'Leary equates every cost reduction with the benefit to customers in terms of lower ticket prices. Removing all but one toilet from each plane would cut 5 per cent off the average ticket price. Replacing the last ten rows with a standing cabin – another 20 to 25 per cent off. O'Leary's sometimes nutty proposals for cost-cutting – deliberately provocative so that they're sure to gain free publicity – have even included flying planes with only one pilot ('Let's take out the second pilot. Let the bloody computer fly it.') and having customers place their own bags in the belly of Ryanair planes ('You take your own bag with you. You bring it down. You put it on'). It all sounds crazy, but think again about those zero-euro ticket prices.

O'Leary's dream of customers flying free rests on the eventuality that, someday, all of Ryanair's revenues will come from 'ancillary' fees. The penny-pinching

O'Leary's vision is that one day tickets will be free for customers with the airline generating revenue from ancillary fees.

Source: Stefan Kiefer/imageBROKER/REX/Shutterstock

airline currently takes in only 20 per cent of its revenue from such non-ticket charges. But Ryanair is the industry leader in charging passengers for virtually every optional amenity they consume. The brash airline brags about being the first to charge for checked bags and in-flight refreshments. Such tactics, once shunned by the industry, are now standard procedure and bring in billions in airline revenues. But Ryanair takes it much further. It now charges customers for printing boarding passes, paying with a debit or credit card, or using wheelchairs. It has even proposed charging for overweight customers, or charging a fee for using that one remaining toilet.

In addition to charging customers for every aspect of the flight, Ryanair also envisions big revenues from selling products for other companies. The interiors of Ryanair planes are almost as littered with advertising as Times Square. Once in the air, flight attendants hawk everything from scratch-card games to digital cameras to their captive audience. They peddle croissants and cappuccino; digital gadgets and perfumes; raffle tickets for the airline's sponsored charity; and even smokeless cigarettes for €6 a pack.

Upon arrival at a usually out-of-the-way airport, Ryanair will sell passengers bus or train tickets into town. The company also gets commissions from rental cars, hotel rooms, ski packages and travel insurance. Every chance it gets, Ryanair tries to squeeze just a little more out of its passengers.

Ryanair makes no excuses for both the additional charges and the absence of creature comforts. In fact, it sees its 'less-for-less' value-pricing approach as long overdue in the airline industry. 'In many ways, travel is pleasant and enriching,' O'Leary states. But 'the physical process of getting from point A to point B shouldn't be pleasant, nor enriching. It should be quick, efficient, affordable and safe'. As Ryanair's success suggests, customers seem to agree. Passengers are getting exactly what they want – outrageously low prices. And the additional purchases are discretionary.

Despite the lack of amenities, most passengers seem to appreciate rather than resent Ryanair's open and straight forward approach to pricing. Compared with the so-called 'sophisticated' approaches of other airlines, proclaims one passenger, 'I prefer [Ryanair's] crude ways, with its often dirt-cheap tickets and shameless [but plain-speaking] efforts to get its hand in my purse.'

And commenting on what some analysts have referred to as Ryanair's 'cattle-car' approach to passengers, another good-humoured flier observes, 'Only O'Leary will call you a cow, lick his chops, and explain how he plans to carve you up for dinner.' O'Leary's philosophy that commercial air passengers don't need to be coddled to make them loyal appears to fly in the face of modern marketing's focus on providing an exceptional customer experience. But Ryanair is proving that companies can provide customer value in more ways than one. When you look at Ryanair's falling prices and rising profits, O'Leary's dream of flying for free doesn't seem so far-fetched after all. With Ryanair's knack for good-value pricing, not even the sky's the limit.[1]

Companies today face a fierce and fast-changing pricing environment. Value-seeking customers have put increased pricing pressure on many companies. Thanks to tight economic times in recent years, the pricing power of the Internet, and value-driven retailers, such as Primark, today's more frugal consumers are pursuing spend-less strategies. In response, it seems that almost every company has been looking for ways to cut prices.

Yet cutting prices is often not the best answer. Reducing prices unnecessarily can lead to lost profits and damaging price wars. It can cheapen a brand by signalling to customers that price is more important than the customer value a brand delivers. Instead, in both good economic times and bad, companies should sell value, not price. In some cases, that means selling lesser products at rock-bottom prices. But in most cases, it means persuading customers that paying a higher price for the company's brand is justified by the greater value they gain.

WHAT IS A PRICE?

Price—The amount of money charged for a product or service, or the sum of the values that customers exchange for the benefits of having or using the product or service.

In the narrowest sense, **price** is the amount of money charged for a product or a service. More broadly, price is the sum of all the values that customers give up to gain the benefits of having or using a product or service. Historically, price has been the major factor affecting buyer choice. In recent decades, however, non-price factors have gained increasing importance. Even so, price remains one of the most important elements that determine a firm's market share and profitability.

Price is the only element in the marketing mix that produces revenue; all other elements represent costs. Price is also one of the most flexible marketing mix elements. Unlike product features and channel commitments, prices can be changed quickly. At the same time, pricing is the number-one problem facing many marketing executives, and many companies do not handle pricing well. Some managers view pricing as a big headache, preferring instead to focus on other marketing mix elements.

However, smart managers treat pricing as a key strategic tool for creating and capturing customer value. Prices have a direct impact on a firm's bottom line. A small percentage improvement in price can generate a large percentage increase in profitability. More important, as part of a company's overall value proposition, price plays a key role in creating customer value and building customer relationships. So, instead of shying away from pricing, smart marketers are embracing it as an important competitive asset.[2]

MAJOR PRICING STRATEGIES

The price the company charges will fall somewhere between one that is too low to produce a profit and one that is too high to produce any demand. Figure 10.1 summarises the major considerations in setting prices. Customer perceptions of the product's value set the ceiling for its price. If customers perceive that the product's price is greater than its value, they will not buy the product. Likewise, product costs set the floor for a product's price. If the company prices the product below its costs, the company's profits will suffer. In setting its price between these two extremes, the company must consider several external and internal factors, including competitors' strategies and prices, the overall marketing strategy and mix, and the nature of the market and demand.

Figure 10.1 suggests three major pricing strategies: customer value-based pricing, cost based pricing and competition-based pricing.

Customer value-based pricing

In the end, the customer will decide whether a product's price is right. Pricing decisions, like other marketing mix decisions, must start with customer value. When customers buy a product, they exchange something of value (the price) to get something of value (the benefits of having or using the product). Effective customer-oriented pricing involves understanding how much value consumers place on the benefits they receive from the product and setting a price that captures that value.

Customer value-based pricing uses buyers' perceptions of value as the key to pricing. Value-based pricing means that the marketer cannot design a product and marketing programme and then set the price. Price is considered along with all other marketing mix variables before the marketing programme is set.

Author comment

Setting the right price is one of the marketer's most difficult tasks. A host of factors come into play. But finding and implementing the right pricing strategy is critical to success.

Author comment

Like everything else in marketing, good pricing starts with *customers* and their perceptions of value.

Customer value-based pricing—Setting price based on buyers' perceptions of value rather than on the seller's cost.

Figure 10.1 Considerations in setting price

If customers perceive that a product's price is greater than its value, they won't buy it. If a company prices a product below its costs, profits will suffer. Between the two extremes, the 'right' pricing strategy is one that delivers both value to the customer and profits to the company.

Customer perceptions of value		Other internal and external considerations		Product costs
Customer perceptions of value **Price ceiling** No demand above this price	⬌	**Other internal and external considerations** Competitors' strategies and prices Marketing strategy, objectives and mix Nature of the market and demand	⬌	**Product costs** **Price floor** No profits below this price

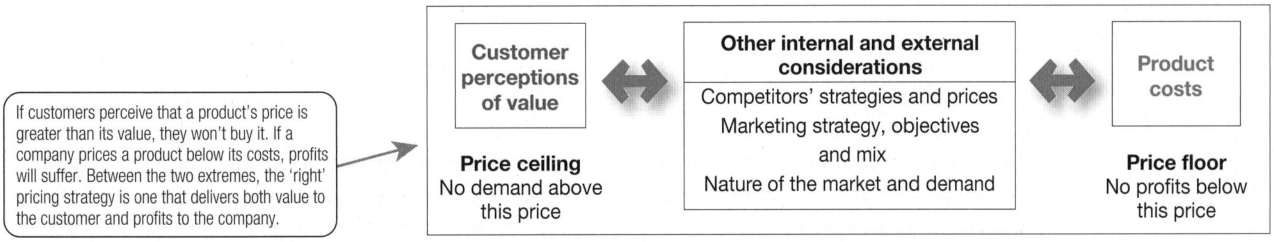

Figure 10.2 Value-based pricing versus cost-based pricing

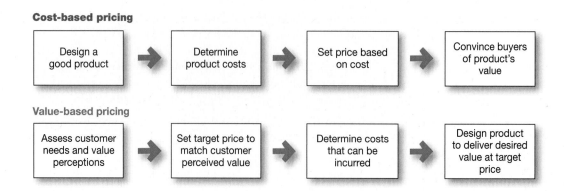

Figure 10.2 compares value-based pricing with cost-based pricing. Although costs are an important consideration in setting prices, cost-based pricing is often product driven. The company designs what it considers to be a good product, adds up the costs of making the product, and sets a price that covers costs plus a target profit. Marketing must then convince buyers that the product's value at that price justifies its purchase. If the price turns out to be too high, the company must settle for lower mark-ups or lower sales, both resulting in disappointing profits.

Value-based pricing reverses this process. The company first assesses customer needs and value perceptions. It then sets its target price based on customer perceptions of value. The targeted value and price drive decisions about what costs can be incurred and the resulting product design. As a result, pricing begins with analysing consumer needs and value perceptions, and the price is set to match perceived value.

It's important to remember that 'good value' is not the same as 'low price'. For example, some owners consider a luxurious Patek Philippe watch a real bargain, even at eye-popping prices ranging from €15,000 to €400,000:[3]

Listen up here, because I'm about to tell you why a certain watch costing €15,000, or even €400,000, isn't actually expensive, but is in fact a tremendous value. Every Patek Philippe watch is handmade by Swiss watchmakers from the finest materials and can take more than a year to make. Still not convinced? Beyond keeping precise time, Patek Philippe watches are also good investments. They carry high prices but retain or even increase their value over time. Many models achieve a kind of cult status that makes them the most coveted timepieces on the planet. But more important than just a means of telling time or a good investment is the sentimental and emotional value of possessing a Patek Philippe. These watches are unique possessions steeped in precious memories, making them treasured family assets. According to the company, 'The purchase of a Patek Philippe is often related to a personal event – a professional success, a marriage, or the birth of a child – and offering it as a gift is the most eloquent expression of love or affection.' A Patek Philippe watch is made not to last just one lifetime, but many. Says one ad: 'You never actually own a Patek Philippe, you merely look after it for the next generation.' That makes it a real bargain, even at twice the price.

A company will often find it hard to measure the value customers attach to its product. For example, calculating the cost of ingredients in a meal at a fancy restaurant is relatively easy. But assigning value to other measures of satisfaction such as taste, environment, relaxation, conversation and status is very hard. Such value is subjective; it varies both for different consumers and different situations.

Still, consumers will use these perceived values to evaluate a product's price, so the company must work to measure them. Sometimes, companies ask consumers how much they would pay for a basic product and for each benefit added to the offer. Or a company might conduct experiments to test the perceived value of different product offers. According to an old Russian proverb, there are two fools in every market – one who asks too much and one who asks too little. If the seller charges more than the buyers' perceived value, the company's sales will suffer. If the seller charges less, its products sell very well, but they produce less revenue than they would if they were priced at the level of perceived value.

We now examine two types of value-based pricing: *good-value pricing* and *value-added pricing*.

Good-value pricing

The recent recession caused a fundamental and lasting shift in consumer attitudes toward price and quality. In response, many companies have changed their pricing approaches to bring them in line with changing economic conditions and consumer price perceptions. More and more, marketers have adopted the strategy of **good-value pricing** – offering the right combination of quality and good service at a fair price.

In many cases, this has involved introducing less-expensive versions of established, brand-name products. To meet tougher economic times and more frugal consumer spending habits, fast-food restaurants such as Quick and McDonald's offer value meals and €1 menu items. Armani offers the less-expensive, more-casual Armani Exchange fashion line. Alberto-Culver's TRESemmé hair care line promises, 'A salon look and feel at a fraction of the price.' And every car company now offers small, inexpensive models better suited to the cash-strapped consumer's budget.

In other cases, good-value pricing has involved redesigning existing brands to offer more quality for a given price or the same quality for less. Some companies even succeed by offering less value but at very low prices. For example, the Aldi supermarket chain has established an impressive good-value pricing position by which it gives customers 'more "mmm" for the euro'.

Aldi practises an important type of good-value pricing at the retail level called *everyday low pricing (EDLP)*. EDLP involves charging a constant, everyday low price with few or no temporary price discounts. Other retailers such as Asda (owned by Walmart) and Carrefour practice EDLP. However, the king of EDLP is Walmart, which practically defined the concept. Except for a few sale items every month, Walmart promises everyday low prices on everything it sells. In contrast, *high–low pricing* involves charging higher prices on an everyday basis but running frequent promotions to lower prices temporarily on selected items. Department stores such as Debenhams and Marks & Spencers practise high–low pricing by having frequent sale days, early-bird savings and bonus earnings for store credit-card holders.

Good-value pricing—Offering just the right combination of quality and good service at a fair price.

Value-added pricing

Value-added pricing doesn't mean simply charging what customers want to pay or setting low prices to meet competition. Instead, many companies adopt value-added pricing strategies. Rather than cutting prices to match competitors, they attach value-added features and services to differentiate their offers and thus support their higher prices. For example, even as frugal consumer spending habits linger, some movie theatre chains are *adding* amenities and charging *more* rather than cutting services to maintain lower admission prices:[4]

Value-added pricing—Attaching value-added features and services to differentiate a company's offers and charging higher prices.

Some theatre chains are turning their multiplexes into smaller, roomier luxury outposts. The new premium theatres offer value-added features such as online reserved seating, high-backed leather executive or rocking chairs with armrests and footrests, the latest in digital sound and super-wide screens, dine-in restaurants serving fine food and drinks, and even valet parking. For example, AMC Theatres (the second-largest American theatre chain) operates more than 50 theatres with some kind of enhanced food and beverage amenities, including Fork & Screen (upgraded leather seating, seat-side service, extensive menu including dinner offerings, beer, wine and cocktails) and Cinema Suites (additional upscale food offerings in addition to premium cocktails and an extensive wine list, seat-side service, red leather reclining chairs, and eight to nine feet of spacing between rows).

So at the Cinema Suites at the AMC Easton 30 with IMAX in Columbus, Ohio, bring on the mango margaritas! For €8–€14 a ticket (depending on the time and day), moviegoers are treated to reserved seating, a strict 21-and-over-only policy, reclining leather seats, and the opportunity to pay even more to have dinner and drinks brought to their seats. Such theatres are so successful that AMC plans to add more. 'Once people experience it,' says a company spokesperson. 'More often than not they don't want to go anywhere else.'

A Steinway piano may cost a lot of money but Steinway argue that it reflects value. 'A Steinway takes you places you've never been'.

Source: Action Press/REX/Shutterstock

Author comment

Costs set the floor for price, but the goal isn't always to *minimise* costs. In fact, many firms invest in higher costs so that they can claim higher prices and margins (think back about Patek Philippe watches). The key is to manage the *spread* between costs and prices — how much the company makes for the customer value it delivers.

Cost-based pricing—Setting prices based on the costs of producing, distributing and selling the product plus a fair rate of return for effort and risk.

Fixed costs (overhead)— Costs that do not vary with production or sales level.

Variable costs—Costs that vary directly with the level of production.

Total costs—The sum of the fixed and variable costs for any given level of production.

Cost-based pricing

Whereas customer value perceptions set the price ceiling, costs set the floor for the price that the company can charge. **Cost-based pricing** involves setting prices based on the costs of producing, distributing and selling the product plus a fair rate of return for the company's effort and risk. A company's costs may be an important element in its pricing strategy.

Some companies, such as Lidl and Ryanair, work to become the *low-cost producers* in their industries. Companies with lower costs can set lower prices that result in smaller margins but higher sales and profits. However, other companies – such as Apple, BMW and Steinway – intentionally pay higher costs so that they can add value and claim higher prices and margins. For example, it costs more to make a 'handcrafted' Steinway piano than a Yamaha production model. But the higher costs result in higher quality, justifying an average €50,000 price. The key is to manage the spread between costs and prices – how much the company makes for the customer value it delivers.

Types of costs

A company's costs take two forms: fixed and variable. **Fixed costs** (also known as **overhead**) are costs that do not vary with production or sales level. For example, a company must pay each month's bills for rent, heat, interest and executive salaries regardless of the company's level of output. **Variable costs** vary directly with the level of production. Each PC produced by HP involves a cost of computer chips, wires, plastic, packaging and other inputs. Although these costs tend to be the same for each unit produced, they are called variable costs because the total varies with the number of units produced. **Total costs** are the sum of the fixed and variable costs for any given level of production. Management wants to charge a price that will at least cover the total production costs at a given level of production.

The company must watch its costs carefully. If it costs the company more than its competitors to produce and sell a similar product, the company will need to charge a higher price or make less profit, putting it at a competitive disadvantage.

Costs at different levels of production

To price wisely, management needs to know how its costs vary with different levels of production. For example, suppose Nokia built a plant to produce 1,000 mobile phones per day. Figure 10.3a shows the typical short-run average cost curve (SRAC). It shows that the cost per mobile phone is high if Nokia's factory produces only a few per day. But as production moves up to 1,000 mobile phones per day, the average cost per unit decreases. This is because fixed costs are spread over more units, with each one bearing a smaller share of the fixed cost. It can try to produce more than 1,000 mobile phones per day, but average costs will increase because the plant becomes inefficient. Workers have to wait for machines, the machines break down more often, and workers get in each other's way.

If Nokia believed it could sell 2,000 mobile phones a day, it should consider building a larger plant. The plant would use more efficient machinery and work arrangements. Also, the unit cost of producing 2,000 cell phones per day would be lower than the unit cost of producing 1,000 units per day, as shown in the long-run average cost (LRAC) curve (Figure 10.3b). In fact, a

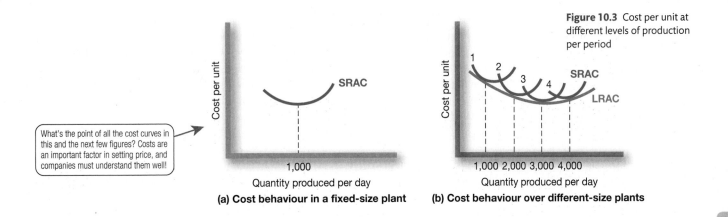

Figure 10.3 Cost per unit at different levels of production per period

What's the point of all the cost curves in this and the next few figures? Costs are an important factor in setting price, and companies must understand them well!

3,000-capacity plant would be even more efficient, according to Figure 10.3b. But a 4,000-daily production plant would be less efficient because of increasing diseconomies of scale – too many workers to manage, paperwork slowing things down, and so on. Figure 10.3b shows that a 3,000-daily production plant is the best size to build if demand is strong enough to support this level of production.

Costs as a function of production experience

Suppose Nokia operates a plant that produces 3,000 mobile phones per day. As Nokia gains experience in producing mobile phones, it learns how to do it better. Workers learn shortcuts and become more familiar with their equipment. With practice, the work becomes better organised, and Nokia finds better equipment and production processes. With higher volume, Nokia becomes more efficient and gains economies of scale. As a result, the average cost tends to decrease with accumulated production experience. This is shown in Figure 10.4.[5] Thus, the average cost of producing the first 100,000 mobile phones is €10 per phone. When the company has produced the first 200,000 phones, the average cost has fallen to €8.50. After its accumulated production experience doubles again to 400,000, the average cost is €7. This drop in the average cost with accumulated production experience is called the **experience curve** (or the **learning curve**).

If a downward-sloping experience curve exists, this is highly significant for the company. Not only will the company's unit production cost decrease, but it will decrease faster if the company makes and sells more during a given time period. But the market has to stand ready to buy the higher output. And to take advantage of the experience curve, Nokia must get a large market share early in the product's life cycle. This suggests the following pricing strategy: Nokia should price its mobile phones low; its sales will then increase, and its costs will decrease through gaining more experience, and then it can lower its prices further.

Experience curve (learning curve)—The drop in the average per unit production cost that comes with accumulated production experience.

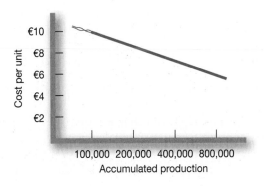

Figure 10.4 Cost per unit as a function of accumulated production: the experience curve

Some companies have built successful strategies around the experience curve. However, a single-minded focus on reducing costs and exploiting the experience curve will not always work. Experience-curve pricing carries some major risks. The aggressive pricing might give the product a cheap image. The strategy also assumes that competitors are weak and not willing to fight it out by meeting the company's price cuts. Finally, while the company is building volume under one technology, a competitor may find a lower-cost technology that lets it start at prices lower than those of the market leader, which still operates on the old experience curve.

Cost-plus pricing

Cost-plus pricing (mark-up pricing)—Adding a standard mark-up to the cost of the product.

The simplest pricing method is **cost-plus pricing** (or **mark-up pricing**) – adding a standard mark-up to the cost of the product. Construction companies, for example, submit job bids by estimating the total project cost and adding a standard mark-up for profit. Lawyers, accountants and other professionals typically price by adding a standard mark-up to their costs. Some sellers tell their customers they will charge cost plus a specified mark-up; for example, aerospace companies often price this way to the government.

To illustrate mark-up pricing, suppose a toaster manufacturer had the following costs and expected sales:

Variable cost	€10
Fixed costs	€300,000
Expected unit sales	50,000

Then the manufacturer's cost per toaster is given by the following:

$$\text{unit cost} = \text{variable cost} + \frac{\text{fixed costs}}{\text{unit sales}} = €10 + \frac{€300,000}{50,000} = €16$$

Now suppose the manufacturer wants to earn a 20 per cent mark-up on sales. The manufacturer's mark-up price is given by the following:[6]

$$\text{markup price} = \frac{\text{unit cost}}{(1 - \text{desired return on sales})} = \frac{€16}{1 - 0.2} = €20$$

The manufacturer would charge dealers €20 per toaster and make a profit of €4 per unit. The dealers, in turn, will mark up the toaster. If dealers want to earn 50 per cent on the sales price, they will mark up the toaster to €40 (€20 + 50% of €40). This number is equivalent to a *mark-up on cost* of 100 per cent (€20/€20).

Does using standard mark-ups to set prices make sense? Generally, no. Any pricing method that ignores demand and competitor prices is not likely to lead to the best price. Still, mark-up pricing remains popular for many reasons. First, sellers are more certain about costs than about demand. By tying the price to cost, sellers simplify pricing; they do not need to make frequent adjustments as demand changes. Second, when all firms in the industry use this pricing method, prices tend to be similar, so price competition is minimised. Third, many people feel that cost-plus pricing is fairer to both buyers and sellers. Sellers earn a fair return on their investment but do not take advantage of buyers when demand becomes great.

Break-even pricing (target return pricing)—Setting price to break even on the costs of marketing and marketing a product or setting price to make a target return.

Break-even analysis and target profit pricing

Another cost-oriented pricing approach is **break-even pricing** (or a variation called **target return pricing**). The firm tries to determine the price at which it will break even or make the target return it is seeking.

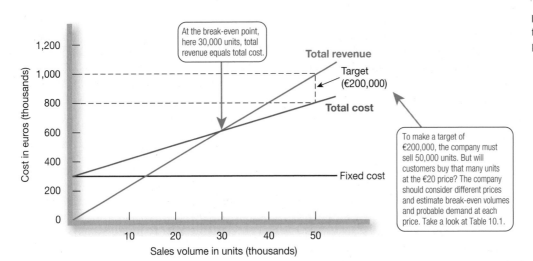

Figure 10.5 Break-even chart for determining target return price and break-even volume

Target return pricing uses the concept of a *break-even chart*, which shows the total cost and total revenue expected at different sales volume levels. Figure 10.5 shows a break-even chart for the toaster manufacturer discussed here. Fixed costs are €300,000 regardless of sales volume. Variable costs are added to fixed costs to form total costs, which rise with volume. The total revenue curve starts at zero and rises with each unit sold. The slope of the total revenue curve reflects the price of €20 per unit.

The total revenue and total cost curves cross at 30,000 units. This is the *break-even volume*. At €20, the company must sell at least 30,000 units to break even, that is, for total revenue to cover total cost. Break-even volume can be calculated using the following formula:

$$\text{break} - \text{even volume} = \frac{\text{fixed cost}}{\text{price} - \text{variable cost}} = \frac{\text{€300,000}}{\text{€20} - \text{\$10}} = 30,000$$

If the company wants to make a profit, it must sell more than 30,000 units at €20 each. Suppose the toaster manufacturer has invested €1,000,000 in the business and wants to set a price to earn a 20 per cent return, or €200,000. In that case, it must sell at least 50,000 units at €20 each. If the company charges a higher price, it will not need to sell as many toasters to achieve its target return. But the market may not buy even this lower volume at the higher price. Much depends on price elasticity and competitors' prices.

The manufacturer should consider different prices and estimate break-even volumes, probable demand and profits for each. This is done in Table 10.1. The table shows that as price increases, the break-even volume drops (column 2). But as price increases, the demand for toasters also decreases (column 3). At the €14 price, because the manufacturer clears only €4 per toaster (€14 less €10 in variable costs), it must sell a very high volume to break even. Even though the low price attracts many buyers, demand still falls below the high break-even point, and the manufacturer loses money. At the other extreme, with a €22 price, the manufacturer clears €12 per toaster and must sell only 25,000 units to break even. But at this high price, consumers buy too few toasters, and profits are negative. The table shows that a price of €18 yields the highest profits. Note that none of the prices produce the manufacturer's target return of €200,000. To achieve this return, the manufacturer will have to search for ways to lower the fixed or variable costs, thus lowering the break-even volume.

Competition-based pricing

Competition-based pricing involves setting prices based on competitors' strategies, costs, prices and market offerings. Consumers will base their judgements of a product's value on the prices that competitors charge for similar products.

Competition-based pricing—Setting prices based on competitors' strategies, prices, costs and market offerings.

Table 10.1 Break-even volume and profits at different prices

(1)	(2)	(3)	(4)	(5)	(6)
Price	Unit demand needed to break even	Expected unit demand at given price	Total revenue (1) × (3)	Total costs*	Profit (4) – (5)
€14	75,000	71,000	€994,000	€1,010,000	−€16,000
16	50,000	67,000	$1,072,000	$970,000	$102,000
18	37,500	60,000	$1,080,000	$900,000	$180,000
20	30,000	42,000	$840,000	$720,000	$120,000
22	25,000	23,000	$506,000	$530,000	−€24,000

*Assumes fixed costs of €300,000 and constant unit variable costs of €10.

In assessing competitors' pricing strategies, the company should ask several questions. First, how does the company's market offering compare with competitors' offerings in terms of customer value? If consumers perceive that the company's product or service provides greater value, the company can charge a higher price. If consumers perceive less value relative to competing products, the company must either charge a lower price or change customer perceptions to justify a higher price.

Next, how strong are current competitors, and what are their current pricing strategies? If the company faces a host of smaller competitors charging high prices relative to the value they deliver, it might charge lower prices to drive weaker competitors from the market. If the market is dominated by larger, low-price competitors, the company may decide to target un-served market niches with value-added products at higher prices.

For example, Daunt Books, an independent bookseller in London, UK, isn't likely to win a price war against Amazon or Barnes & Noble; it doesn't even try. Instead, the shop relies on its personal approach, cosy atmosphere and friendly and knowledgeable staff to turn local book lovers into loyal patrons, even if they have to pay a little more.

James Daunt, 46, is the founder of Daunt Books, the independent bookshop based in London's Marylebone High Street, with branches in Belsize Park, Hampstead, Holland Park and Chelsea. The shops are known for their old-fashioned interiors and organisation of books by country instead of subject. The shops are original Edwardian bookshops with beautiful, long oak galleries and graceful skylights. The interiors whisper old-fashioned charm, tradition and conservative geniality. No loud music blares, no crass assistants atone 'Have a nice day'; instead the aged floors and relaxed atmosphere generates a feeling of tranquillity and calm.[7]

Daunt books shops are renowned for their beautiful, long oak galleries and graceful skylights.

Source: Lonely Planet/Getty Images

What principle should guide decisions about what price to charge relative to those of competitors? The answer is simple in concept but often difficult in practice: no matter what price you charge – high, low or in between – be certain to give customers superior value for that price.

OTHER INTERNAL AND EXTERNAL CONSIDERATIONS AFFECTING PRICE DECISIONS

Author comment

Now that we've looked at the three general pricing strategies – value-, cost- and competitor-based pricing – let's dig into some of the many other factors that affect pricing decisions.

Beyond customer value perceptions, costs and competitor strategies, the company must consider several additional internal and external factors. Internal factors affecting pricing include the company's overall marketing strategy, objectives and marketing mix, as well as other organisational considerations. External factors include the nature of the market and demand and other environmental factors.

Overall marketing strategy, objectives and mix

Price is only one element of the company's broader marketing strategy. So, before setting price, the company must decide on its overall marketing strategy for the product or service. Sometimes, a company's overall strategy is built around its price and value story. For example, when Honda developed its Acura brand to compete with European luxury-performance cars in the higher-income segment, this required charging a high price. In contrast, when it introduced the Honda Fit model – billed as 'a pint-sized fuel miser with feisty giddy up' – this positioning required charging a low price. Thus, pricing strategy is largely determined by decisions on market positioning.

If a company has selected its target market and positioning carefully, then its marketing mix strategy, including price, will be fairly straightforward. For example, Amazon positions its Kindle Fire tablet as offering the same (or even more) for less, and prices it at 40 per cent less than Apple's iPad and Samsung's Galaxy tablets. It recently began targeting families with young children, positioning the Kindle Fire as the 'perfect family tablet', with models priced as low as €40, bundled with Kindle FreeTime, an all-in-one subscription service starting at €10 per month that brings together books, games, educational apps, films and TV shows for kids aged three to eight. Thus, the Kindle pricing strategy is largely determined by decisions on market positioning.

Pricing may play an important role in helping to accomplish company objectives at many levels. A firm can set prices to attract new customers or profitably retain existing ones. It can set prices low to prevent competition from entering the market or set prices at competitors' levels to stabilise the market. It can price to keep the loyalty and support of resellers or avoid government intervention. Prices can be reduced temporarily to create excitement for a brand. Or one product may be priced to help the sales of other products in the company's line.

Price decisions must be coordinated with product design, distribution and promotion decisions to form a consistent and effective integrated marketing mix programme. Decisions made for other marketing mix variables may affect pricing decisions. For example, a decision to position the product on high-performance quality will mean that the seller must charge a higher price to cover higher costs. And producers whose resellers are expected to support and promote their products may have to build larger reseller margins into their prices.

Companies often position their products on price and then tailor other marketing mix decisions to the prices they want to charge. Here, price is a crucial product-positioning factor that defines the product's market, competition and design. Many firms support such price-positioning strategies with a technique called **target costing**. Target costing reverses the usual process of first designing a new product, determining its cost, and then asking, 'Can we sell it for that?' Instead, it starts with an ideal selling price based on customer value considerations and then targets costs that will ensure that the price is met. For example, when Honda initially designed the Honda Fit, it began with a €10,000 starting price point and highway mileage of 33 miles per gallon firmly in mind. It then designed a stylish, peppy little car with costs that allowed it to give target customers those values.

Target costing—Pricing that starts with an ideal selling price, then targets costs that will ensure that the price is met.

Other companies de-emphasise price and use other marketing mix tools to create *non-price* positions. Often, the best strategy is not to charge the lowest price but rather to differentiate the marketing offer to make it worth a higher price. For example, luxury smartphone maker Vertu puts very high value into its products and charges premium prices to match that

Vertu phones are handcrafted and targeted at the luxury market.

Source: Vertu Corporation

value. Vertu phones are made from high-end materials such as titanium and sapphire crystal, and each phone is hand assembled by a single craftsman in England. Phones come with additional services such as Vertu Concierge, which helps create personal, curated user experiences and recommendations. Vertu phones sell for an average price of €4,750, with top models going for more than €8,000. But target customers recognise Vertu's very high quality and are willing to pay more to get it.[8]

Some marketers even position their products on *high* prices, featuring high prices as part of their product's allure. For example, Grand Marnier offers a €160 bottle of Cuvée du Cent Cinquantenaire that's marketed with the tagline 'Hard to find, impossible to pronounce, and prohibitively expensive'. And Stella Artois' famous advertising campaign which proudly informed consumers that the premium lager was 'Reassuringly expensive' and the height of sophisticated European modernity.

Thus, marketers must consider the total marketing strategy and mix when setting prices. But again, even when featuring price, marketers need to remember that customers rarely buy on price alone. Instead, they seek products that give them the best value in terms of benefits received for the prices paid.

Organisational considerations

Management must decide who within the organisation should set prices. Companies handle pricing in a variety of ways. In small companies, prices are often set by top management rather than by the marketing or sales departments. In large companies, pricing is typically handled by divisional or product managers. In industrial markets, salespeople may be allowed to negotiate with customers within certain price ranges. Even so, top management sets the pricing objectives and policies, and it often approves the prices proposed by lower level management or salespeople.

In industries in which pricing is a key factor (airlines, aerospace, steel, railroads, oil companies), companies often have pricing departments to set the best prices or help others set them. These departments report to the marketing department or top management. Others who have an influence on pricing include sales managers, production managers, finance managers and accountants.

The market and demand

As noted earlier, good pricing starts with an understanding of how customers' perceptions of value affect the prices they are willing to pay. Both consumer and industrial buyers balance the price of a product or service against the benefits of owning it. Thus, before setting prices, the marketer must understand the relationship between price and demand for the company's product. In this section, we take a deeper look at the price–demand relationship and how it varies for different types of markets. We then discuss methods for analysing the price–demand relationship.

Pricing in different types of markets

The seller's pricing freedom varies with different types of markets. Economists recognise four types of markets, each presenting a different pricing challenge.

Under *pure competition*, the market consists of many buyers and sellers trading in a uniform commodity, such as wheat, copper or financial securities. No single buyer or seller has much effect on the going market price. In a purely competitive market, marketing research, product development, pricing, advertising and sales promotion play little or no role. Thus, sellers in these markets do not spend much time on marketing strategy.

Under *monopolistic competition*, the market consists of many buyers and sellers trading over a range of prices rather than a single market price. A range of prices occurs because sellers can differentiate their offers to buyers. Because there are many competitors, each firm is less affected by competitors' pricing strategies than in oligopolistic markets. Sellers try to develop differentiated offers for different customer segments and, in addition to price, freely use branding, advertising and personal selling to set their offers apart. Thus, Toyota sets its Prius brand apart through strong branding and advertising, reducing the impact of price. It advertises that the third generation Prius takes you from 'zero to sixty in 70 per cent fewer emissions'. Because there are many competitors in such markets, each firm is less affected by competitors' pricing strategies than in oligopolistic markets.

The Toyota Prius is positioned as a car of good quality that is environmentally friendlier – setting the offer apart from the mainstream market.

Source: Courtesy of Toyota (GB) Ltd

Under *oligopolistic competition*, the market consists of a few sellers who are highly sensitive to each other's pricing and marketing strategies. Because there are few sellers, each seller is alert and responsive to competitors' pricing strategies and moves.

In a *pure monopoly*, the market consists of one seller. The seller may be a government monopoly (e.g., in Sweden, Finland, Iceland and Norway governments hold monopolies for selling alcoholic beverages), a private regulated monopoly (e.g., a power company), or a private non-regulated monopoly (e.g., DuPont when it introduced nylon). Pricing is handled differently in each case.

Analysing the price–demand relationship

Each price the company might charge will lead to a different level of demand. The relationship between the price charged and the resulting demand level is shown in the **demand curve** in Figure 10.6. The demand curve shows the number of units the market will buy in a given time period at different prices that might be charged. In the normal case, demand and price are inversely related – that is, the higher the price, the lower the demand. Thus, the company would sell less if it raised its price from P1 to P2. In short, consumers with limited budgets probably will buy less of something if its price is too high.

The French food conglomerate Danone's overall strategy is reliant on a clear understanding of consumers' willingness to pay. To Danone, volume is more important than sales growth and careful pricing is needed to maintain volume.[9]

Demand curve—A curve that shows the number of units the market will buy in a given time period, at different prices that might be charged.

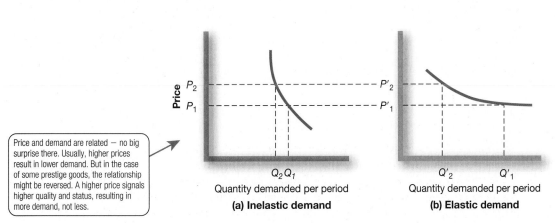

Price and demand are related — no big surprise there. Usually, higher prices result in lower demand. But in the case of some prestige goods, the relationship might be reversed. A higher price signals higher quality and status, resulting in more demand, not less.

Figure 10.6 Demand curves

(a) Inelastic demand

(b) Elastic demand

Franck Riboud is the executive chairman of Danone. He has shifted Danone's strategy to volume growth rather than sales growth. His view appears to be that setting a high sales target in the current economic environment would put undue pressure on managers, risking mistakes and short-cuts to achieve the growth. Much better to cut prices and increase volumes than to shut factories, he has said. The company sells its products – including Activia yoghurt and Actimel yoghurt drink, as well as Evian, Badoit and baby food, including Milupa, to 700 million people worldwide. It aims to achieve its mission to 'bring health through food to the largest number of people' by selling to 1 billion people by the end of 2011. Although its international sales are expanding, it still relies on Western Europe for 48 per cent of its sales. For Danone, the shift towards volume rather than sales growth means targeting and expanding sales in emerging markets. But because people in these countries are less wealthy than in more prosperous countries, the company cannot expect to generate the same profit margins. Its cheapest yoghurt is sold in Bangladesh at 6 euro cents for an 80g cup. In France, plain Activia yoghurt sells for 26 euro cents for 125g.

Most companies try to measure their demand curves by estimating demand at different prices. The type of market makes a difference. In a monopoly, the demand curve shows the total market demand resulting from different prices. If the company faces competition, its demand at different prices will depend on whether competitors' prices stay constant or change with the company's own prices.

Price elasticity of demand

Price elasticity—A measure of the sensitivity of demand to changes in price.

Marketers also need to know **price elasticity** – how responsive demand will be to a change in price. If demand hardly changes with a small change in price, we say demand is *inelastic*. If demand changes greatly, we say the demand is *elastic*.

If demand is elastic rather than inelastic, sellers will consider lowering their prices. A lower price will produce more total revenue. This practice makes sense as long as the extra costs of producing and selling more do not exceed the extra revenue. At the same time, most firms want to avoid pricing that turns their products into commodities. In recent years, forces such as deregulation and the instant price comparisons afforded by the Internet and other technologies have increased consumer price sensitivity, turning products ranging from telephones and computers to new automobiles into commodities in some consumers' eyes.

The economy

Economic conditions can have a strong impact on the firm's pricing strategies. Economic factors such as a boom or recession, inflation and interest rates affect pricing decisions because they affect consumer spending, consumer perceptions of the product's price and value, and the company's costs of producing and selling a product.

In the aftermath of the recent recession, many consumers rethought the price–value equation. They tightened their belts and become more value conscious. Consumers have continued their thriftier ways well beyond the economic recovery. As a result, many marketers have increased their emphasis on value-for-the-money pricing strategies.

The most obvious response to the new economic realities is to cut prices and offer discounts. Thousands of companies have done just that. Lower prices make products more affordable and help spur short-term sales. However, such price cuts can have undesirable long-term consequences. Lower prices mean lower margins. Deep discounts may cheapen a brand in consumers' eyes. And once a company cuts prices, it's difficult to raise them again when the economy recovers.

Rather than cutting prices, many companies have instead shifted their marketing focus or added more affordable lines to their product mixes. For example, in line with tighter consumer budgets and thriftier spending habits, P&G has added lower-price versions of its premium brands to make them more affordable. It has introduced 'Basic' versions of its Bounty and Charmin brands that sell for less. It brought back its Vidal Sassoon Pro Series hair products line as an affordable alternative to the company's higher-priced Pantene brand. And P&G recently launched Iams So Good dog food, a line designed as a 'more accessible' addition to its premium Iams brand. Making Iams 'more accessible' is 'a big move for us', says a P&G marketing executive. In these thriftier times, 'we realise a lot of our brands need to "tier down" to appeal to more consumers'. Iams So Good is positioned as a '100 per cent wholesome' product without added sugar, dyes and artificial ingredients. The brand's lower prices are conveyed mostly through store displays and packaging.[10] Other companies are holding prices but redefining the 'value' in their value propositions. For instance, Unilever has repositioned its higher-end Bertolli frozen meals as an eat-at-home brand that's more affordable than eating out. And Kraft's Velveeta cheese ads tell shoppers to 'forget the cheddar, Velveeta is better', claiming that a package of Velveeta is 'twice the size of cheddar, for the same price'.[11]

Remember, even in tough economic times, consumers do not buy based on prices alone. They balance the price they pay against the value they receive. For example, according to a recent survey, despite selling its shoes for as much as €335 a pair (the Nike Mercurial Superfly SG), Nike commands the highest consumer loyalty of any brand in the footwear segment.[12] Customers perceive the value of Nike's products and the Nike ownership experience to be well worth the price. Thus, no matter what price they charge – low or high – companies need to offer great *value for the money*.

Nike commands widespread band loyalty: for Nike consumers the Nike experience is worth the price.

Source: YanLev/Shutterstock.com

Other external factors

Beyond the market and the economy, the company must consider several other factors in its external environment when setting prices. It must know what impact its prices will have on other parties in its environment. How will resellers react to various prices? The company should set prices that give resellers a fair profit, encourage their support and help them to sell the product effectively. The *government* is another important external influence on pricing decisions. Finally, *social concerns* may need to be taken into account. In setting prices, a company's short-term sales, market share and profit goals may need to be tempered by broader societal considerations. We will examine public policy issues in pricing in Chapter 11.

OBJECTIVES REVIEW AND KEY TERMS

Companies today face a fierce and fast-changing pricing environment. Firms successful at creating customer value with the other marketing mix activities must still capture some of this value in the prices they earn. This chapter examines the importance of pricing, general pricing strategies, and the internal and external considerations that affect pricing decisions.

OBJECTIVE 1 Answer the question 'What is a price?' and discuss the importance of pricing in today's fast changing environment (pp. 292–293)

Price can be defined narrowly as the amount of money charged for a product or service. Or it can be defined more broadly as the sum of the values that consumers exchange for the benefits of having and using the product or service. The pricing challenge is to find the price that will let the company make a fair profit by getting paid for the customer value it creates.

Despite the increased role of non-price factors in the modern marketing process, price remains an important element in the marketing mix. It is the only marketing mix element that produces revenue; all other elements represent costs. More important, as a part of a company's overall value proposition, price plays a key role in creating customer value and building customer relationships. Smart managers treat pricing as a key strategic tool for creating and capturing customer value.

OBJECTIVE 2 Identify the three major pricing strategies and discuss the importance of understanding customer value perceptions, company costs and competitor strategies when setting prices (pp. 293–300)

Companies can choose from three major pricing strategies: customer value-based pricing, cost-based pricing and competition-based pricing. *Customer value-based pricing* uses buyers' perceptions of value as the basis for setting price. Good pricing begins with a complete understanding of the value that a product or service creates for customers and setting a price that captures that value. Customer perceptions of the product's value set the ceiling for prices. If customers perceive that a product's price is greater than its value, they will not buy the product.

Companies can pursue either of two types of value-based pricing. *Good-value pricing* involves offering just the right combination of quality and good service at a fair price. EDLP is an example of this strategy. Value-added pricing involves attaching value-added features and services to differentiate the company's offers and support charging higher prices.

Cost-based pricing involves setting prices based on the costs for producing, distributing and selling products plus a fair rate of return for effort and risk. Company and product costs are an important consideration in setting prices. Whereas customer value perceptions set the price ceiling, costs set the floor for pricing. However, cost-based pricing is product driven rather than customer driven. The company designs what it considers to be a good product and sets a price that covers costs plus a target profit. If the price turns out to be too high, the company must settle for lower mark-ups or lower sales, both resulting in disappointing profits. If the company prices the product below its costs, its profits will also suffer. Cost-based pricing approaches include *cost-plus pricing* and *break-even pricing* (or target profit pricing).

Competition-based pricing involves setting prices based on competitors' strategies, costs, prices and market offerings. Consumers base their judgements of a product's value on the prices that competitors charge for similar products. If consumers perceive that the company's product or service provides greater value, the company can charge a higher price. If consumers perceive less value relative to competing products, the company must either charge a lower price or change customer perceptions to justify a higher price.

OBJECTIVE 3 Identify and define the other important external and internal factors affecting a firm's pricing decisions (pp. 301–305)

Other *internal* factors that influence pricing decisions include the company's overall marketing strategy, objectives and marketing mix, as well as organisational considerations. Price is only one element of the company's broader marketing strategy. If the company has selected its target market and positioning carefully, then its marketing mix strategy, including price, will be fairly straight forward. Common pricing objectives might include customer retention and building profitable customer relationships, preventing competition, supporting resellers and gaining their support, or avoiding government intervention. Price decisions must be coordinated with product design, distribution and promotion decisions to form a consistent and effective marketing programme. Finally, in order to coordinate pricing goals and decisions, management must decide who within the organisation is responsible for setting price.

Other *external* pricing considerations include the nature of the market and demand and environmental factors such as the economy, reseller needs and government actions. Ultimately, the customer decides whether the company has set the right price. The customer weighs the price against the perceived values of using the product – if the price exceeds the sum of the values, consumers will not buy. So the company must understand such concepts as demand curves (the price–demand relationship) and price elasticity (consumer sensitivity to prices).

Economic conditions can have a major impact on pricing decisions. The Great Recession caused consumers to rethink the price–value equation, and consumers have continued their thriftier ways well beyond the economic recovery. Marketers have responded by increasing their emphasis on value-for-money pricing strategies. No matter what the economic times, however, consumers do not buy based on prices alone. Thus, no matter what price they charge – low or high – companies need to offer superior value for the money.

NAVIGATING THE KEY TERMS

OBJECTIVE 1
Price (p. 292)

OBJECTIVE 2
Customer value-based pricing (p. 293)
Good-value pricing (p. 295)
Value-added pricing (p. 295)
Cost-based pricing (p. 296)

Fixed costs (overhead) (p. 296)
Variable costs (p. 296)
Total costs (p. 296)
Experience curve (learning curve) (p. 297)
Cost-plus pricing (mark-up pricing) (p. 298)
Break-even pricing (target return pricing) (p. 298)
Competition-based pricing (p. 299)

OBJECTIVE 3
Target costing (p. 301)
Demand curve (p. 303)
Price elasticity (p. 304)

DISCUSSION AND CRITICAL THINKING

Discussion questions

10-1 How does value-based pricing differ from cost-based pricing? (AACSB: Communication)

10-2 Name and describe the types of costs marketers must consider when setting prices. Describe the types of cost-based pricing and the methods of implementing each. (AACSB: Communication)

10-3 What is target costing and how is it different from the usual process of setting prices? (AACSB: Communication)

10-4 Name and describe the four types of markets recognised by economists and discuss the pricing challenges posed by each. (AACSB: Communication)

10-5 What other issues beyond the market and the economy must marketers consider when setting prices? (AACSB: Communication)

Critical-thinking exercises

10-6 If you've ever travelled to another country, such as Germany, you may have noticed that the price on a product is the total amount you actually pay when you check out. That is, no sales tax is added to the purchase price at the checkout as it is in the United States. That is because many countries impose a value added tax (VAT). In a small group, research value added taxes and debate whether or not such taxes benefit consumers. Do marketers support or dislike these types of taxes? (AACSB: Communication; Reflective thinking)

10-7 In a small group, discuss your perceptions of value and how much you are willing to pay for the following products: automobiles, frozen dinners, jeans and athletic shoes. Are there differences among members of your group? Explain why those differences exist. Discuss some examples of brands of these products that are positioned to deliver different value to consumers. (AACSB: Communication; Reflective thinking)

10-8 What is the Consumer Price Index (CPI)? Select one of the reports available at www.bls.gov/cpi/home.htm and create a presentation on price changes over the past two years. Discuss reasons for that change. (AACSB: Communication; Use of IT; Reflective thinking)

Mini-cases and applications

Online, mobile and social media marketing: online price tracking

Got your eye on a new 32-inch Samsung television? Well, you'd better not purchase it in December – that's when the price was highest on Amazon (€500 versus €400 in November or February). Most consumers know that prices fluctuate throughout the year, but did you know they even fluctuate hourly? You probably can't keep up with that, but there's an app that can. Camelcamelcamel.com hosts a tool that tracks Amazon's prices for consumers and sends alerts when a price hits the sweet spot. This app allows users to import entire Amazon wish-lists and to set desired price levels at which e-mails or tweets are sent to inform them of the prices. All of this is free. Camel makes its money from an unlikely partner – Amazon – which funnels price data directly to Camel. Camel is a member of Amazon's Affiliate programme, kicking back 8.5 per cent of sales for each customer Camel refers. It would seem that Amazon would want customers to buy when prices are higher, not lower. But the online behemoth sees this as a way to keep the bargain hunters happy while realising more profitability from less price-sensitive customers. This is an improvement over Amazon's earlier pricing tactics, which charged different customers different prices based on their buying behaviour.

10-9 Go to http://us.camelcamelcamel.com/ and set up a free account. Track ten products that interest you. Did any of the products reach your desired price? Write a report on the usefulness of this type of app for consumers. (AACSB: Communication; Use of IT)

10-10 Camel is not the only Amazon tracking or online price tracking application. Find and describe an example of another online price tracking tool for consumers. (AACSB: Communication; Use of IT)

Marketing ethics: psychology of mobile payments

Consumers love to play games on their mobile devices, and Japanese consumers seem to be the most passionate. Mobile game publishers in Japan have mastered the art of getting as much revenue as possible from players – some earning more than €4 million per day. The makers of *Puzzle & Dragons* have seemingly cracked the revenue code by using the psychology of mobile payments to squeeze more revenue from players by encouraging them to play longer. One *Puzzle & Dragons* secret was to issue its own virtual currency, called magic stones, so consumers don't feel like they are spending real money for chances to enhance play. Then, the game offers a little reward at the end with a reminder of what is lost if the player doesn't take the offer. Limited-time sales offer monsters to use in battle for just a few magic stones, and if players run out of space, the game reminds them that they will lose their monsters if they don't purchase more space. All the while, mathematicians and statisticians work behind the scenes to track game play and make it easier or more challenging to keep players engaged and spending. One expert called *Puzzle & Dragons* 'truly diabolical' in convincing players to pay and play more. These and other game producers' tactics have propelled Japan's game revenue alone to exceed revenue from all apps in the United States.

10-11 Is it ethical for game producers to use game playing data to encourage consumers to spend more? Explain why or why not. (AACSB: Communication; Ethical reasoning)

10-12 Is this similar to the 'freemium' model used by many US game producers? Explain this model and discuss examples of games that use this model. (AACSB: Communication; Reflective thinking; Ethical reasoning)

Marketing by the numbers: reseller margins

One external factor that manufacturers must consider when setting prices is reseller margins. Manufacturers do not have the final say concerning the price to consumers; retailers do. So manufacturers must start with their suggested retail prices and work back, subtracting out the mark-ups required by resellers that sell the product to consumers. Once that is considered, manufacturers know at what price to sell their products to resellers, and they can determine what volume they must sell to break *even* at that price and cost combination. To answer the following questions, refer to Appendix 2.

10-13 A consumer purchases a computer for €800 from a retailer. If the retailer's mark-up is 30 per cent and the wholesaler's mark-up is 10 per cent, both based on their respective selling prices, at what price does the manufacturer sell the product to the wholesaler? (AACSB: Communication; Analytical reasoning)

10-14 If the unit variable cost for each computer is €350 and the manufacturer has fixed costs totalling €2 million, how many computers must this manufacturer sell to break *even*? How many must it sell to realise a profit of €50 million? (AACSB: Communication; Analytical reasoning)

REFERENCES

[1] Quotes and other information from Cecilia Rodriguez, 'Airlines look to raise revenue the Ryanair way', *Forbes*, 5 March 2012, www.forbes.com/sites/ceciliarodriguez/2012/03/05/105/; Jane Leung, 'Ryanair's five "cheapest" money-saving schemes', *CNNTravel*, 17 October 2011, www.cnn.com/2011/10/17/traveV ryanair-money-saving-schemes/index.htm; Felix Gillette, 'Ryanair's O'Leary: The Duke of Discomfort', *Business-week*, 2 September 2010, www.businessweek.com/magazine/content/10_37/b4194058006755.htm; and Steve Rothwell, 'Ryanair lifts profit goal as winter capacity cuts buoy fares', *Bloomberg Businessweek*, 30 January 2012, www.bloomberg.com/news/2012-01-30/ryanair-lifts-proftt-goal-on-wintercapacity.html, all accessed October 2015. Emi Boscamp, 'The world's busiest airlines' *Huffington Post*, www.huffingtonpost.com/2013/06/18/busiest-airlines-world_n_3460451.html, accessed January 2016 Isabel Choat, 'Which is the cheapest budget airline?', *The Guardian*, www.theguardian.com/travel/2013/nov/19/cheapest-flights-in-europe-pegasus-easyjet, accessed October 2015;

'Welcome to Ryanair', www.ryanair.com/en/about/, accessed October 2015.

[2] For more on the importance of sound pricing strategy, see Thomas T. Nagle, John Hogan, and Joseph Zale, *The Strategy and Tactics of Pricing: A Guide to Growing More Profitably*, 5th ed. (Upper Saddle River, NJ: Prentice Hall, 2011), Chapter 1.

[3] See Megan Willett, 'How Swiss watchmaker Patek Philippe hand-crafts its famous $500,000 watches', *Business Insider*, 12 July 2013, www.businessinsider.com/how-a-patek-philippe-watch-is-made-2013-7; and www.patek.com/contents/default/en/values.html, accessed October 2015.

[4] See Maria Puente, 'Theaters turn up the luxury', *USA Today*, 12 March 2010, p. 1A; 'iPic Entertainment and Alberta Development Partners announce visionary luxury movie theater escape planned for Dallas', *PR*

Newswire, 23 January 2013; and information from http://dinein.amctheatres.com, accessed October 2015.

[5] Accumulated production is drawn on a semilog scale so that equal distances represent the same percentage increase in output.

[6] The arithmetic of mark-ups and margins is discussed in Appendix 2: Marketing by the numbers.

[7] Example from Natalie Graham, 'My first million: James Daunt', *Financial Times*, 19 February 2010, www.ft.com/cms/s/2/798781da-1d81-11df-a893-00144feab49a.html#axzz1UPifHx5H and www.dauntbooks.co.uk/shops.asp?TAG=&CID=, accessed October 2011.

[8] See Stan Schroeder, 'Vertu's luxury Android smartphone costs $10,000', *Mashable*, 12 February 2013, http://mashable. com/2013/02/12/vertu-ti/; Matt Vella, 'The ulter-luxe phone', *Fortune*, 29 April 2013, pp. 10–12; Lara O'Reilly, 'Vertu seeks to broaden appeal with marketing', *Marketing Week*, 13 October 2013, www.marketingweek.co.uk/news/vertu-seeks-to-broaden-appeal-with-marketing/4008105.article; and www.vertu.com, accessed October 2015.

[9] Example from Scheherazade Daneshkhu and Jenny Wiggins, 'Food group shifts strategy to volume growth', *Financial Times*, 10 January 2010, www.ft.com/cms/s/0/3181527e-fe11-11de-9340-00144feab49a. html#axzz3xaj3cVqp, accessed October 2015.

[10] See Stuart Elliott, 'Courting thrifty shoppers with quality and value', *New York Times*, 3 June 2013, p. B4; and www.iams.com/dog-food/about-so-good-dog-food, accessed October 2015.

[11] Petrecca, 'Marketers try to promote value without cheapening image', *USA Today*, 17 November 2008, p. B1; Anne D'Innocenzio, 'Butter, Kool-Aid in limelight in advertising shift', 21 April 2009, www.azcentral.com/business/articles/2009/04/21/20090421biz-NewFrugality0421.html; and Judann Pollack, 'Now's the time to reset marketing for post-recession', *Advertising Age*, 1 February 2010, p. 1.

[12] Kenneth Hein 'Study: value trumps price among shoppers', *Brandweek*, 2 March 2009, p. 6.

COMPANY CASE

Cath Kidston: nostalgic fantasy that creates value for consumers

This case study examines the pricing strategy of Cath Kidston, one UK-based company that sells furnishings, home and personal accessories as well as clothes, operating mainly in the UK, Europe and Asia regions.

How much are you willing to pay for a key ring? The market price charges just a bit more than €1. But would you pay €3 for a comparable product? How about €12? A low-price strategy is often used by companies if their products are not well differentiated. Although a low-price strategy might seem attractive, especially in an economic downturn, some companies are focusing on creating value for customers and adopting customer-value-added pricing strategy. Cath Kidston Ltd is one UK-based company that understands that sometimes it pays to charge more. Cath Kidston's key rings sells for roughly €6 to €12, whereas the market price charges less than a third of that. To understand how Cath Kidston has succeeded with this pricing strategy, let's look at what makes the brand so special.

The cheery colours and fun patterns Cath Kidston created allows it not to focus on price-sensitive market segments but instead lure customers with a value-added pricing strategy. It is important for a brand to create something that people respond to with their hearts, which is a sure-fire way to breed success for a brand. Cath Kidston is one of the brands that is confident in its design style and fun in its character.

From humble beginnings

Cath Kidston Ltd was founded in 1993 when designer Cath Kidston opened a tiny shop in London's Holland Park with a €19,000 (£15,000) investment in her business, selling towels, vintage fabrics and wallpaper and brightly painted 'junk' furniture she remembered fondly from her childhood. While her first print design 'Rose Bouquet' was inspired by a Welsh wallpaper, Cath Kidston's designs epitomised 1950s English heritage. Cath Kidston's clever re-working of traditional English country style made her tiny shop soon become a cult success. Today, the brand carries a wide product range, everything from furnishings, crockery, cutlery, cloths, toys, china, bed linen and bags, to women's and children's wear and accessories, charging price premiums that fans are gladly paying.

Today Cath Kidston has around 66 shops and concessions in the UK (not counting a dozen or so 'pop-up' outlets): 1 in Jersey, 3 in Ireland, 6 in Spain, 4 in France, 27 in Japan, 18 in South Korea, 16 in Thailand, 6 in China, 6 in Hong Kong, 5 in Indonesia and 9 in Taiwan. The business is also driven by successful web, mail-order and wholesale divisions, with UK, Euro and US transactional websites. Cath Kidston has become a powerhouse of British design and retail, up there with the likes of Burberry and Pringle.

Design is core part of Cath Kidston's brand. However, it is more than the vintage-inspired patterns and the stunning shop interiors. Walk into any Cath Kidston shop and you are able to 'experience' the brand that other retail shops do not offer. And this 'experience' permeates Cath Kidston's websites and all of its printed communications. If you are a fan, you can feel the essence of the brand in every aspect. In colour psychology terms, Cath Kidston is pure spring – fun, creative, warm, inspiring and young, adding a splash of colour and vintage charm to a routine day.

Cath Kidston not only offers a wide product range but is actually a lifestyle store. You can buy almost everything for your home, children or yourself. The broad product range maximises the brand's appeal and means that it works for both gift and personal purchases. Cath Kidston allows its brand personality (fun and brightness) to shine through its brand identity (colours and typography), hence becoming a brand consumers can fall in love with.

Vague versus price

In certain respects, cross-comparing personal products such as key rings can be problematic, because there is so much variation in both features and price. But consider some popular Cath Kidston products. Its scarves sell for roughly €58, whereas comparable products from apparel retailers such as Marks & Spencer or Monsoon range from roughly €20 to €30. Cath Kidston's plastic-coated fabric bags sell from roughly €35 to €150, whereas other apparel retailers only charge similar prices for their leather bags. The fantasy of the English country childhood that Cath Kidston creates for customers enables the brand to charge price premiums as compared to competitors, such as John Lewis, Marks & Spencer and Monsoon. For the fans of Cath Kidston, her products excite them in a way that IKEA and other competitors cannot hope to grasp.

In terms of competition, in the product category of home accessories, Cath Kidston competes directly with UK retailers like John Lewis and Marks & Spencer. In the clothing category, apparel retailers such as Monsoon and Marks & Spencer are the key competitors of Cath Kidston, while it competes with retailers like IKEA in the furniture category. Compared to the above main competitors, the weakness of Cath Kidston is its product offerings are still relatively limited and narrow. However, Cath Kidston's unique strength is the product design offers its customers strong personal statement and identify that other competitors found hard to achieve. The biggest challenge of Cath Kidston brand is to continue its success with the traditional English country style and fun brand character, while satisfying its loyal customers with innovative product design and product line extension.

Retro brands in hard times

Given the harsh economic climate, you might expect to see the cheerful floral prints that made Cath Kidston a household name withering a little. However, Cath Kidston has survived the recession very well, selling the retro-styling and a rose-tinted antidote to an uncertain world in the uncertain economic climate. The brand is now a seemingly recession-proof 'global lifestyle brand'. In 2009, while other brands were chalking up serious losses due to the economic downturn, Cath Kidston saw profits leap by

60 per cent while, post-recession, last year sales grew by a year-on-year increases of 10 per cent with non-UK sales up by 37 per cent. The reason for this phenomenon is that in these uncertain times, consumers, although cash-conscious, have an appetite for nostalgia. The products of Cath Kidston fulfil consumer needs for value and meaning, because they are inspired by a comforting and familiar 1950s aesthetic. For Cath Kidston, its premium pricing strategy coincided with a trend of consumer preference toward nostalgia, which seemed to provide comfort in the time of recession. Thus, the value derived from Cath Kidston products was enough to justify the high prices for many of its products. In an economic downturn, consumers want a bit of security and comfort, and this trend shows in the recession of the 1990s and today. UK retailers such as Asda reported a surge in sales of nostalgic brands, as people seem to look back to their childhood in an attempt to cheer themselves up. Consumers want the comfort and security that retro brands can give them, reminding them of their childhoods and even their parents' childhoods.

In times of economic downturn, people are worried about the credit crunch and losing jobs, and thus brands that act as an antidote to anxiety will do well. A lot of people didn't see the most recent economic crisis coming, and that makes them nervous about looking forward. The reflex is to seek comfort in things that reference the past. Also, as people stay at home more in a recession time to reduce consumption, stylish home comforts become more important, which also helps explain why Cath Kidston has done well in hard times.

Cath Kidston is conquering the world with her floral and polka dot designs, and it is not surprising to see how such a powerful brand can divide people. Consumers either love it or hate it. For those who hate it, the products of Cath Kidston look like the junk from a late granny's attic. However, as the key target audiences of Cath Kidston are 30- to 40-year-old middle-class working women, their strong purchasing power sustains the growth of the brand. Today the company claims that around 50 per cent of 18–65 women are aware of the brand, while the numerous men that are viewed slouching outside stores suggest that an equal number of men are aware of the brand (albeit, arguably less fondly!). Amongst teenage girls, brand awareness is huge (quite possibly 'frenzied') – most likely in part driven by approving parental gifts and nostalgic grandparents.

Pressing on with price premiums

The core idea of Cath Kidston brand is a product-centric strategy. The control and expansion of the brand to a wider product range is still the focus after the shifting of company ownership. The product-centric concept of a brand is a business model that embodies perhaps the most essential brand ingredient for business success: simplicity. Cath Kidston Ltd is far from resting and is looking for further business expansion, with plans to open more shops in Europe, Japan and the Far East, including China, Hong Kong and South Korea. The brand is pressing on with its nostalgic designs that create value for its customers, justifying the premium price of its products.

Questions for discussion

1. Does Cath Kidston's pricing strategy truly differentiate it from the competition?
2. Has Cath Kidston executed value-based pricing, cost-based pricing or competition-based pricing? Explain.
3. Could Cath Kidston have been successful as a design-focused product marketer had it employed a low-price strategy? Explain.
4. Is Cath Kidston's pricing strategy sustainable? Explain.

Sources: This case study relies on extensive and drearily long periods of 'market research' by Amelia C. Harris and Tabitha C. Harris for which we are 'grateful' – albeit considerably poorer. Additional sources include: Beth Hale, 'Cath Kidston to pocket £50m from sale of brand 20 years after shop assistant created famous nostalgic designs', *Daily Mail*, 23 February 2010, www.dailymail.co.uk/femail/article-1252954/ Cath-Kidston-pocket-30m-sale-brand-20-years-shop-assistant-created-famous-nostalgic-designs.html; Kathryn Hopkins, 'Designer Cath Kidston in deal to sell off her retail empire', *The Guardian*, 7 March 2010, www.guardian.co.uk/business/2010/mar/07/cath-kidston-private-equity-buyout; Rachel Porter, 'The REAL domestic goddess: how Cath Kidston is conquering the world with her floral and polka dot designs', *Daily Mail*, 11 August 2009, www.dailymail.co.uk/femail/article-1205665/ The-REAL-domestic-goddess-How-Cath-Kidston-conquering-world-floral-polka-dot-designs.html; and other information from www.cathkidston.com/, accessed October 2015.

CHAPTER ELEVEN

Pricing strategies: additional considerations

Chapter preview

In the previous chapter, you learned that price is an important marketing mix tool for both creating and capturing customer value. You explored the three main pricing strategies – customer value-based, cost-based and competition-based pricing – and the many internal and external factors that affect a firm's pricing decisions. In this chapter, we'll look at some additional pricing considerations: new product pricing, product mix pricing, price adjustments, and initiating and reacting to price changes. We close the chapter with a discussion of public policy and pricing.

To start, let's examine the importance of pricing strategy in sport. Our case looks at the pricing approach of Borussia Dortmund, a Bundesliga team with huge local support. But Dortmund's pricing strategy isn't just about local fans – their pricing strategy recognises that real fans will travel long distances for the elusive goal of high-quality football combined with a fanatic atmosphere!

Objective outline

➤ **Objective 1** Describe the major strategies for pricing new products.
New product pricing strategies (pp. 314–315)

➤ **Objective 2** Explain how companies find a set of prices that maximises the profits from the total product mix.
Product mix pricing strategies (pp. 315–317)

➤ **Objective 3** Discuss how companies adjust their prices to take into account different types of customers and situations.
Price adjustment strategies (pp. 318–324)

➤ **Objective 4** Discuss the key issues related to initiating and responding to price changes.
Price changes (pp. 325–328)

➤ **Objective 5** Overview the social and legal issues that affect pricing decisions.
Public policy and pricing (pp. 328–330)

Borussia Dortmund: supporting a fair price
by Leif Brandes, Warwick Business School

Football made in Germany is becoming increasingly popular – and not only among German supporters who might still be in a dream-like trance after Germany's victory in the 2014 FIFA World Cup final. In addition, German football has also managed to attract some of its fiercest critics from the past: English football fans. According to a recent BBC article, more than 1,000 supporters are leaving their country each weekend to attend Bundesliga matches in Germany. The destination? Dortmund. The motivation? Attending high-quality football matches for a reasonable price.

Located in the Ruhr area, Ballsportverein Borussia 09 e.V. Dortmund (BVB) was founded in 1909, and is now one of the most successful clubs in the German Bundesliga. In 2010 and 2011, the club won the national championships twice, and the national cup once. In the following two years, the team finished the league second behind Bayern Munich, and reached the UEFA Champions League final in 2013 (where they lost to Bayern Munich in the first ever German final). This outstanding sporting performance also shows up in the team's stock price: from 2010 to 2014, BVB's stock market value increased by an impressive 280 per cent! However, Dortmund does not only attract spectators because of their sporting performance, but because of the unique culture of their fans, who create an incredible stadium atmosphere during the games.

Borussia Dortmund's slogan '*echte liebe*' means 'true love', and supporters stand by it. Need an example? How about this: when Dortmund reached the 2013 Champions League final, the club received 502,567 applications for 24,042 tickets. Not bad for a city with a total population of 580,956. The fans' true love also shows up in attendance figures for Bundesliga home matches: with a stadium capacity of 80,645, Dortmund has an average attendance of 80,291, which makes it currently the highest in the world. 25,000 of these spectators stand on the terrace during the games and form the '*Gelbe Wand*' ('yellow wall'). The atmosphere that these fans create is indeed legendary and even feared by other teams: when asked whether he was more scared of Dortmund's players or manager, Bayern Munich and Germany midfielder Bastian Schweinsteiger responded: 'It is the yellow wall that scares me the most.' Eager to become part of this atmosphere in every home game, 30,000 people are currently on the club's waiting list for one of the 55,000 season tickets.

With such a degree of excess demand, many football clubs around the world would be tempted to raise their prices — especially if current prices are as low as in Dortmund where season ticket holders pay, on average, just €11 to see a match. But Dortmund is different. Here, the club wants to ensure that fandom is affordable for their customers in the longer run. To this end, the club recently refused caterers' requests to increase the beer price for the first time in three years. Similarly, Dortmund said no when their shirt manufacturer, Puma, urged them to increase the price of the kit for the first time in three years.

The club understands that fans are co-producers in creating an unforgettable match experience for every visitor, and place this experience before revenues. For example, Dortmund do not sell drinks in their corporate boxes during the game to make sure that fans spend the match time supporting the team by clapping and singing. In a similar vein, Dortmund's stadium announcer demands fans return to their seats in time for the start of the second half. The club could allow fans to spend more money buying food and drink, but this would reduce product quality in the eyes of officials. 'We are a football club,' says marketing director Carsten Cramer. 'If the football doesn't run properly, the rest of the business would not work. The business is part of a train, but not the engine.'

Dortmund's business philosophy is what makes the experience so affordable for every member of society, not just the rich and old. Even the British fans are thrilled about the low cost: 'We make a weekend of it. With tickets, accommodation, transport, this trip will cost €82. When you think it cost me €64 to see the Arsenal game last season, you can see the benefits.'

The atmosphere at a Borussia Dortmund home game is considered one of the best in any football league.

Source: Alexandre Simoes/ Borussia Dortmund/Getty Images

The high prices in England have changed the composition of fans who can afford to attend the matches. Says a Dortmund fan: 'When I was young, we all watched English football, the Kop and said "yes, that is what football is all about". Now, when we go to English football, the stadiums are quiet and we say that it is actually quite boring. If you price people out, you change the atmosphere. If you price people out, it isn't the people's game anymore.' Another English fan agrees: 'Prices are too high in England. But here, everything is cheap. It's a better experience for the fan and the atmosphere is incredible.'

Dortmund's pricing approach, however, results in substantial forgone revenues that not every club around the world would be willing to bear. Take Arsenal, London, for example. Despite having 20,000 fewer seats, the amount of money the club generates on match days dwarfs that of the BVB. In times when clubs generate a significant part of revenues from success in international competitions like the Champions League, a team's spending power becomes an important competitive advantage. So why does Dortmund continue leaving money on the table every single home match?

The answer is simple: because the club is owned by the fans. This particular ownership structure reflects on the Bundesliga's '50+1' rule, which requires clubs to be owned by their members. Currently, all but three of the 18 clubs in the Bundesliga are owned or controlled by their members, with Wolfsburg, Leverkusen and Hoffenheim the exceptions. It is thus clear that low ticket prices are likely to prevail in Germany as long as the fan is king – and many kings there are: according to a recent Deloitte report, the Bundesliga is now the number one European football league in terms of weekly attendance figures and profitability.[1]

As the Borussia Dortmund story suggests, and as we learned in the previous chapter, pricing decisions are subject to a complex array of company, environmental and competitive forces. To make things even more complex, a company does not set a single price but rather a *pricing structure* that covers different items in its line. This pricing structure changes over time as products move through their life cycles. The company adjusts its prices to reflect changes in costs and demand and to account for variations in buyers and situations. As the competitive environment changes, the company considers when to initiate price changes and when to respond to them.

This chapter examines additional pricing approaches used in special pricing situations or to adjust prices to meet changing situations. We look in turn at *new product pricing* for products in the introductory stage of the product life cycle, *product mix pricing* for related products in the product mix, *price adjustment tactics* that account for customer differences and changing situations, and strategies for initiating and responding to *price changes*.

NEW PRODUCT PRICING STRATEGIES

Pricing strategies usually change as the product passes through its life cycle. The introductory stage is especially challenging. Companies bringing out a new product face the challenge of setting prices for the first time. They can choose between two broad strategies: *market-skimming pricing* and *market-penetration pricing*.

Market-skimming pricing

Many companies that invent new products set high initial prices to *skim* revenues layer by layer from the market. Apple frequently uses this strategy, called **market-skimming pricing (or price skimming)**. When Apple first introduced the iPhone, its initial price was as much as €417 per phone. The phones were purchased only by customers who really wanted the sleek new gadget and could afford to pay a high price for it. Six months later, Apple dropped the price to €278 for an 8GB model and €348 for the 16GB model to attract new buyers. Within a year, it dropped prices again to €138 and €208, respectively, and you can now buy an 8GB model for €69. In this way, Apple skimmed the maximum amount of revenue from the various segments of the market.

Market skimming makes sense only under certain conditions. First, the product's quality and image must support its higher price, and enough buyers must want the product at that price. Second, the costs of producing a smaller volume cannot be so high that they cancel the advantage of charging more. Finally, competitors should not be able to enter the market easily and undercut the high price.

Market-penetration pricing

Rather than setting a high initial price to skim off small but profitable market segments, some companies use **market-penetration pricing**. Companies set a low initial price to *penetrate* the market quickly and deeply – to attract a large number of buyers quickly and win a large market share. The high sales volume results in falling costs, allowing companies to cut their prices even further. For example, Samsung has used penetration pricing to quickly build demand for its mobile devices in fast-growing emerging markets.[2]

In Kenya, Nigeria and other African countries, Samsung recently unveiled an affordable yet full-function Samsung Galaxy Pocket model that sells for only about €95 with no contract. The Samsung Pocket is designed and priced to encourage millions of first-time African buyers to trade up to smartphones from their more basic handsets. Samsung also offers a line of Pocket models in India, selling for as little as €60. Through penetration pricing, the world's largest smartphone maker hopes to make quick and deep inroads into India's exploding mobile device market, which consists of mostly first-time users and accounts for nearly one-quarter of all smartphones sold globally each year. Samsung's penetration pricing has set off a price war in India with Apple, which has responded in emerging markets with heavy discounts and more affordable models of its own. Apple iPhones have typically sold for more than €250 in India, limiting Apple's market share to only about 2 per cent there.

Several conditions must be met for this low-price strategy to work. First, the market must be highly price sensitive so that a low price produces more market growth. Second, production and distribution costs must decrease as sales volume increases. Finally, the low price must help keep out the competition, and the penetration price must maintain its low-price position. Otherwise, the price advantage may be only temporary.

Market-penetration pricing— Setting a low price for a new product in order to attract a large number of buyers and a large market share.

Cheaper but full-function mobile smartphones are facilitated through a market penetration strategy by Samsung.

Source: Adrian Pope/Getty Images

PRODUCT MIX PRICING STRATEGIES

The strategy for setting a product's price often has to be changed when the product is part of a product mix. In this case, the firm looks for a set of prices that maximises its profits on the total product mix. Pricing is difficult because the various products have related demand and costs and face different degrees of competition. We now take a closer look at the five product mix pricing situations summarised in Table 11.1: *product line pricing, optional-product pricing, captive-product pricing, by-product pricing* and *product bundle pricing*.

Product line pricing

Companies usually develop product lines rather than single products. For example, Rossignol offers seven different collections of alpine skis of all designs and sizes, at prices that range from €133 for its junior skis, such as Fun Girl, to more than €985 for a pair from its Radical racing

Author comment

Most individual products are part of a broader product mix and must be priced accordingly. For example, Gillette prices its Fusion razors low. But once you buy the razor, you're a captive customer for its higher-margin replacement cartridges.

Table 11.1 Product mix pricing

Pricing situation	Description
Product line pricing	Setting prices across an entire product line
Optional-product pricing	Pricing optional or accessory products sold with the main product
Captive-product pricing	Pricing products that must be used with the main product
By-product pricing	Pricing low-value by-products to get rid of or make money on them
Product bundle pricing	Pricing bundles of products sold together

Product line pricing—Setting the price steps between various products in a product line based on cost differences between the products, customer evaluations of different features and competitors' prices.

collection. It also offers lines of Nordic and backcountry skis, snowboards and ski-related apparel. In **product line pricing**, management must determine the price steps to set between the various products in a line.

The price steps should take into account cost differences between products in the line. More important, they should account for differences in customer perceptions of the value of different features. For example, Sage offers an entire line of financial management software, including Sage One Accounts, Instant Accounts, Instant Accounts Plus, 50 Accounts and 50 Accounts Plus versions priced at around €14, €170, €275, €775 and €1,116, respectively. Although it costs Sage no more to produce the CD containing the 50 Accounts Plus version than the CD containing the Sage One version, many buyers happily pay more to obtain additional features. Sage's task is to establish perceived value differences that support the price differences.

Optional-product pricing

Optional-product pricing—The pricing of optional or accessory products along with a main product.

Many companies use **optional-product pricing** – offering to sell optional or accessory products along with the main product. For example, a car buyer may choose to order a navigation system and premium entertainment system. Refrigerators come with optional ice makers. And when you order a new computer, you can select from a bewildering array of processors, hard drives, docking systems, software options and service plans. Pricing these options is a sticky problem. Companies must decide which items to include in the base price and which to offer as options.

Captive-product pricing

Captive-product pricing—Setting a price for products that must be used along with a main product, such as blades for a razor and games for a video-game console.

Companies that make products that must be used along with a main product are using **captive-product pricing**. Examples of captive products are razor blade cartridges, video games, printer cartridges, single-serve coffee pods and e-books. Producers of the main products (razors, video-game consoles, printers, single-cup coffee brewing systems and tablet computers) often price them low and set high mark-ups on the supplies. For example, Amazon makes little or no profit on its Kindle readers and tablets. It hopes to more than make up for thin margins through sales of digital books, music, movies, subscription services and other content for the devices. 'We want to make money when people use our devices, not when they buy our devices,' declares Amazon CEO Jeff Bezos.[3]

When Sony first introduced its PlayStation3 (PS3) videogame console, priced at €347 and €417 for the regular and premium versions, respectively, it lost as much as €213 per unit sold. Sony hoped to recoup the losses through the sales of more lucrative PS3 games. However, companies that use captive product pricing must be careful. Finding the right balance between the main product and captive product prices can be tricky. For example, despite industry-leading PS3 videogame sales, Sony has yet to earn back its losses on the PS3 console. Even more, consumers trapped into buying expensive captive products may come to resent the brand that ensnared them.

Customers of single-cup coffee brewing systems such as Nescafé's Dolce Gusto or Nestlé's Nespresso may cringe at what they must pay for those handy little coffee portion packs. Although they might seem like a bargain when compared on a cost-per-cup basis versus Costa

Coffee, Starbucks, Tchibo or Segafredo, the pods' prices can seem like highway robbery when broken down by the pound. One investigator calculated the cost of pod coffee at a shocking €40 per pound.[4] At those prices, you'd be better off cost-wise brewing a big pot of premium coffee and pouring out the unused portion. For many buyers, the convenience and selection offered by single cup brewing systems outweigh the extra costs. However, such captive product costs might make others avoid buying the device in the first place or cause discomfort during use after purchase.

In the case of services, captive-product pricing is called *two-part pricing*. The price of the service is broken into a *fixed fee* plus a *variable usage rate*. Thus, at Aqualand in the South of France and other amusement parks, you pay a daily ticket or season pass charge plus additional fees for food and other in-park features.

By-product pricing

Producing products and services often generates by-products. If the by-products have no value and if getting rid of them is costly, this will affect the pricing of the main product. Using **by-product pricing**, the company seeks a market for these by-products to help offset the costs of disposing of them and help make the price of the main product more competitive.

> **By-product pricing**—Setting a price for by-products in order to make the main product's price more competitive.

The by-products themselves can even turn out to be profitable – turning trash into cash. For example, whisky can fuel you in more than one way:[5]

> Viobuttanol is a biofuel made from whisky by-products, it can be used in ordinary cars, and is predicted to be the generation of biofuel which they estimate gives 30 per cent more output power than ethanol. Scientists were provided with samples of whisky distilling by-products from Diageo's Glenkinchie Distillery in East Lothian, which makes The Edinburgh Malt. It uses the two main by-products of whisky production — pot ale, the liquid from the copper stills, and draff, the spent grains, as the basis for producing the butanol that can then be used as fuel. The scientists at the university's biofuel research centre have filed for a patent and intend to create a spin-out company to take the new fuel to market. With 1.6 million litres of pot ale and 187,000 tonnes of draff produced by the malt whisky industry annually, the scientists believe there is real potential for biofuel to be available at local garage forecourts alongside traditional fuels. Unlike ethanol, the nature of the innovative biofuel means that ordinary cars could use the more powerful fuel, instead of traditional petrol, without modification. The product can also be used to make other green renewable biochemicals, such as acetone.

> **Product bundle pricing**— Combining several products and offering the bundle at a reduced price.

Product bundle pricing

Using **product bundle pricing**, sellers often combine several products and offer the bundle at a reduced price. For example, fast-food restaurants bundle a burger, fries and a soft drink at a 'combo' price. Body Shop (owned by L'Oréal) with 2,500 stores in 61 countries is offering 'three-for' deals on its soaps and lotions (such as buy three lotions and save €5, buy three save €10). And Sky, France Telecom, Virgin, Deutsche Telecom and British Telecom, and other telecommunications companies bundle TV service, phone service and high-speed Internet connections at a low combined price. Price bundling can promote the sales of products consumers might not otherwise buy, but the combined price must be low enough to get them to buy the bundle.

> **By-product pricing: you can make biofuel from whisky byproducts.**
>
> *Source:* Tim Graham/Alamy Images

Author comment

Setting the base price for a product is only the start. The company must then adjust the price to account for customer and situational differences. When was the last time you paid the full suggested retail price for something?

PRICE ADJUSTMENT STRATEGIES

Companies usually adjust their basic prices to account for various customer differences and changing situations. Here we examine the seven price adjustment strategies summarised in Table 11.2: *discount and allowance pricing, segmented pricing, psychological pricing, promotional pricing, geographical pricing, dynamic pricing and international pricing*.

Discount and allowance pricing

Most companies adjust their basic price to reward customers for certain responses, such as paying bills early, volume purchases and off-season buying. These price adjustments – called *discounts* and *allowances* – can take many forms.

Discount—A straight reduction in price on purchases during a stated period of time or of larger quantities.

One form of **discount** is a *cash discount*, a price reduction to buyers who pay their bills promptly. A typical example is '2/10, net 30', which means that although payment is due within 30 days, the buyer can deduct 2 per cent if the bill is paid within 10 days. *A quantity discount* is a price reduction to buyers who buy large volumes. A seller offers a *functional discount* (also called a *trade discount*) to trade-channel members who perform certain functions, such as selling, storing and record keeping. A *seasonal discount* is a price reduction to buyers who buy merchandise or services out of season.

Allowance—Promotional money paid by manufacturers to retailers in return for an agreement to feature the manufacturer's products in some way.

Allowances are another type of reduction from the list price. For example, *trade-in allowances* are price reductions given for turning in an old item when buying a new one. Trade-in allowances are most common in the automobile industry, but they are also given for other durable goods. *Promotional allowances* are payments or price reductions that reward dealers for participating in advertising and sales-support programmes.

Segmented pricing

Companies will often adjust their basic prices to allow for differences in customers, products and locations. In **segmented pricing**, the company sells a good or service at two or more prices, even though the difference in prices is not based on differences in costs.

Segmented pricing—Selling a product or service at two or more prices, where the difference in prices is not based on differences in costs.

Segmented pricing takes several forms. Under *customer-segment pricing*, different customers pay different prices for the same product or service. Museums and movie theatres, for example,

Table 11.2 Price adjustments

Strategy	Description
Discount and allowance pricing	Reducing prices to reward customer responses such as volume purchases, paying early, or promoting the product
Segmented pricing	Adjusting prices to allow for differences in customers, products or locations
Psychological pricing	Adjusting prices for psychological effect
Promotional pricing	Temporarily reducing prices to spur short-run sales
Geographical pricing	Adjusting prices to account for the geographic location of customers
Dynamic pricing	Adjusting prices continually to meet the characteristics and needs of individual customers and situations
International pricing	Adjusting prices for international markets

may charge a lower admission for students and senior citizens. Under *product form pricing*, different versions of the product are priced differently but not according to differences in their costs. For instance, a one-litre bottle (about 34 ounces) of Evian mineral water may cost €1 at your local supermarket. But a five-ounce aerosol can of Evian Brumisateur Mineral Water Spray sells for a suggested retail price of €8 at beauty boutiques and spas. The water is all from the same source in the French Alps, and the aerosol packaging costs little more than the plastic bottles. Yet you pay about €0.03 an ounce for one form and €1.60 an ounce for the other.

Using *location-based pricing*, a company charges different prices for different locations, even though the cost of offering each location is the same. For instance, state universities charge higher tuition for out-of-state students, and theatres vary their seat prices because of audience preferences for certain locations. Tickets for a Monday night performance of *Les Misérables* in London's West End cost €17 for a seat in the upper circle, whereas seats in the stalls go for €88. Finally, using *time-based pricing*, a firm varies its price by the season, the month, the day, and even the hour. For example, cinemas charge matinee pricing during the daytime, and resorts give weekend and seasonal discounts.

For segmented pricing to be an effective strategy, certain conditions must exist. The market must be segmentable, and segments must show different degrees of demand. The costs of segmenting and reaching the market cannot exceed the extra revenue obtained from the price difference. Of course, the segmented pricing must also be legal.

Most important, segmented prices should reflect real differences in customers' perceived value. Consumers in higher price tiers must feel that they're get-

Product-form pricing: Evian water in a one-litre bottle might cost you €0.03 an ounce at your local supermarket, whereas the same water might run to €1.60 an ounce when sold in five ounce aerosol cans as Evian Brumisateur Mineral Water Spray moisturiser.

Source: Photo by Jim Whitmer

ting their extra money's worth for the higher prices paid. By the same token, companies must be careful not to treat customers in lower price tiers as second-class citizens. Otherwise, in the long run, the practice will lead to customer resentment and ill will. For example, in recent years, the airlines have incurred the wrath of frustrated customers at both ends of the airplane. Passengers paying full fare for business or first-class seats often feel that they are being gouged. At the same time, passengers in lower-priced coach seats feel that they're being ignored or treated poorly.

Psychological pricing

Price says something about the product. For example, many consumers use price to judge quality. A €100 bottle of perfume may contain only $3 worth of scent, but some people are willing to pay the €100 because this price indicates something special.

In using **psychological pricing**, sellers consider the psychology of prices, not simply the economics. For example, consumers usually perceive higher-priced products as having higher quality. When they can judge the quality of a product by examining it or by calling on past experience with it, they use price less to judge quality. But when they cannot judge quality because they lack

Psychological pricing— Pricing that considers the psychology of prices and not simply the economics; the price is used to say something about the product.

the information or skill, price becomes an important quality signal. For instance, who's the better barrister or advocate, one who charges €50 per hour or one who charges €500 per hour? You'd have to do a lot of digging into the respective lawyers' credentials to answer this question objectively; even then, you might not be able to judge accurately. Most of us would simply assume that the higher-priced lawyer is better.

Reference prices—Prices that buyers carry in their minds and refer to when they look at a given product.

Another aspect of psychological pricing is **reference prices** – prices that buyers carry in their minds and refer to when looking at a given product. The reference price might be formed by noting current prices, remembering past prices or assessing the buying situation. Sellers can influence or use these consumers' reference prices when setting price. For example, a grocery retailer might place its store brand of bran flakes and raisins cereal priced at €2.49 next to Kellogg's Raisin Bran priced at €3.79. Or a company might offer more expensive models that don't sell very well to make its less expensive but still-high-priced models look more affordable by comparison. For example, Ralph Lauren was selling a 'Ricky' alligator bag for €10,000, making its Tiffin Bag a steal at just €1,800. Williams-Sonoma once offered a fancy bread maker at the steep price of €220. However, it then added a €340 model. The expensive model flopped but sales of the cheaper model doubled.[6]

For most purchases, consumers don't have all the skill or information they need to figure out whether they are paying a good price. They don't have the time, ability or inclination to research different brands or stores, compare prices and get the best deals. Instead, they may rely on certain cues that signal whether a price is high or low. Interestingly, such pricing cues are often provided by sellers, in the form of sales signs, price-matching guarantees, loss-leader pricing, and other helpful hints.

Even small differences in price can signal product differences. A 9 or 0.99 at the end of a price often signals a bargain. You see such prices everywhere. For example, browse the online sites of top discounters such as Lidl or Netto, where almost every price ends in 9. In contrast, high-end retailers might favour prices ending in a whole number (for example, €6, €25 or €200). Others use 00-cent endings on regularly priced items and 99-cent endings on discount merchandise.

Even small differences in price can signal product differences. For example, in a recent American study, people were asked how likely they were to choose among LASIK eye surgery providers based only on the prices they charged: $299 or $300 (around €211). The actual price difference was only $1 (€0.81), but the study found that the psychological difference was much greater. Preference ratings for the providers charging $300 were much higher. Subjects perceived the $299 price as significantly less, but it also raised stronger concerns about quality and risk.[7] Some psychologists even argue that each digit has symbolic and visual qualities that should be considered in pricing. Thus, eight (8) is round and even and creates a soothing effect, whereas seven (7) is angular and creates a jarring effect.[8]

Promotional pricing

Promotional pricing—Temporarily pricing products below the list price, and sometimes even below cost, to increase short-run sales.

With **promotional pricing**, companies will temporarily price their products below list price – and sometimes even below cost – to create buying excitement and urgency. Promotional pricing takes several forms. A seller may simply offer *discounts* from normal prices to increase sales and reduce inventories. Sellers also use *special-event pricing* in certain seasons to draw more customers. Thus, TVs and other consumer electronics are promotionally priced in November and December to attract holiday shoppers into the stores. *Limited-time offers*, such as online *flash sales*, can create buying urgency and make buyers feel lucky to have gotten in on the deal.

Manufacturers sometimes offer *cash rebates* to consumers who buy the product from dealers within a specified time; the manufacturer sends the rebate directly to the customer. Rebates have been popular with automakers and producers of mobile phones and small appliances, but they are also used with consumer packaged goods. Some manufacturers offer *low-interest financing, longer warranties* or *free maintenance* to reduce the consumer's 'price'. This practice has become another favourite of the auto industry.

Promotional pricing, however, can have adverse effects. Used too frequently and copied by competitors, price promotions can create 'deal-prone' customers who wait until brands go on sale before buying them. Or, constantly reduced prices can erode a brand's value in the eyes of customers. Marketers sometimes become addicted to promotional pricing, especially in difficult economic times. They use price promotions as a quick fix instead of sweating through the difficult process of developing effective longer-term strategies for building their brands. But companies must be careful to balance short-term sales incentives against long-term brand building. One analyst advises:[9]

> When times are tough, there's a tendency to panic. One of the first and most prevalent tactics that many companies try is an aggressive price cut. Price trumps all. At least, that's how it feels these days: 20% off. 30% off. 50% off. Buy one, get one free. Whatever it is you're selling, you're offering it at a discount just to get customers in the door. But aggressive pricing strategies can be risky business. Companies should be very wary of risking their brands' perceived quality by resorting to deep and frequent price cuts. Some discounting is unavoidable in a tough economy, and consumers have come to expect it. But marketers have to find ways to shore up their brand identity and brand equity during times of discount mayhem.

Promotional pricing, however, can have adverse effects. During most holiday seasons, for example, it's an all-out bargain war. Marketers carpet-bomb consumers with deals, causing buyer wear-out and pricing confusion. Used too frequently, price promotions can create 'deal-prone' customers who wait until brands go on sale before buying them. In addition, constantly reduced prices can erode a brand's value in the eyes of customers.

Marketers sometimes become addicted to promotional pricing, especially in tight economic times. They use price promotions as a quick fix instead of sweating through the difficult process of developing effective longer-term strategies for building their brands. Companies must be careful to balance short-term sales incentives against long-term brand building.

Geographical pricing

A company also must decide how to price its products for customers located in different parts of Europe or the world. Should the company risk losing the business of more distant customers by charging them higher prices to cover the higher shipping costs? Or should the company charge all customers the same prices regardless of location? We will look at five **geographical pricing** strategies for the following hypothetical situation:

> The Peerless Paper Company is located in Madrid, Spain, and sells paper products to customers all over Europe. The cost of freight is high and affects the companies from which customers buy their paper. Peerless wants to establish a geographical pricing policy. It is trying to determine how to price a €10,000 order to three specific customers: Customer A (Lisbon, Portugal), Customer B (Florence, Italy), and Customer C (Riga, Latvia).

One option is for Peerless to ask each customer to pay the shipping cost from the Madrid factory to the customer's location. All three customers would pay the same factory price of €10,000, with Customer A paying, say, €100 for shipping; Customer B, €150; and Customer C, €250. Called **FOB-origin pricing**, this practice means that the goods are placed *free on board* (hence, *FOB*) a carrier. At that point the title and responsibility pass to the customer, who pays the freight from the factory to the destination. Because each customer picks up its own cost, supporters of FOB pricing feel that this is the fairest way to assess freight charges. The disadvantage, however, is that Peerless will be a high-cost firm to distant customers.

Uniform-delivered pricing is the opposite of FOB pricing. Here, the company charges the same price plus freight to all customers, regardless of their location. The freight charge is set at the average freight cost. Suppose this is €150. Uniform-delivered pricing therefore results in a higher charge to the Lisbon customer (who pays €150 freight instead of €100) and a lower charge to the Riga customer (who pays €150 instead of €250). Although the Lisbon customer would prefer to buy paper from another local paper company that uses FOB-origin pricing, Peerless has a better chance of winning over the Latvian customer in Riga.

Geographical pricing— Setting prices for customers located in different parts of the country or world.

FOB-origin pricing—A geographical pricing strategy in which goods are placed free on board a carrier; the customer pays the freight from the factory to the destination.

Uniform-delivered pricing—A geographical pricing strategy in which the company charges the same price plus freight to all customers, regardless of their location.

Zone pricing—A geographical pricing strategy in which the company sets up two or more zones. All customers within a zone pay the same total price; the more distant the zone, the higher the price.

Base-point pricing—A geographical pricing strategy in which the seller designates some city as a basing point and charges all customers the freight cost from that city to the customer.

Freight-absorption pricing—A geographical pricing strategy in which the seller absorbs all or part of the freight charges in order to get the desired business.

Zone pricing falls between FOB-origin pricing and uniform-delivered pricing. The company sets up two or more zones. All customers within a given zone pay a single total price; the more distant the zone, the higher the price. For example, Peerless might set up a West-Europe Zone and charge €100 freight to all customers in this zone, a Mid-Europe Zone in which it charges €150, and an East-Europe Zone in which it charges €250. In this way, the customers within a given price zone receive no price advantage from the company. For example, customers in Lisbon and Madrid pay the same total price to Peerless. The complaint, however, is that the Lisbon customer is paying part of the Madrid customer's freight cost.

Using **base-point pricing**, the seller selects a given city as a 'base point' and charges all customers the freight cost from that city to the customer location, regardless of the city from which the goods are actually shipped. For example, Peerless might set Paris as the base point and charge all customers €10,000 plus the freight from Paris to their respective locations. This means that a Madrid customer pays the freight cost from Paris to Madrid, even though the goods may be shipped from Madrid. If all sellers used the same base-point city, delivered prices would be the same for all customers, and price competition would be eliminated.

Finally, the seller that is anxious to do business with a certain customer or geographical area might use **freight-absorption pricing**. Using this strategy, the seller absorbs all or part of the actual freight charges to get the desired business. The seller might reason that if it can get more business, its average costs will decrease and more than compensate for its extra freight cost. Freight-absorption pricing is used for market penetration and to hold on to increasingly competitive markets.

Dynamic and Internet pricing

Throughout most of history, prices were set by negotiation between buyers and sellers. *Fixed-price* policies – setting one price for all buyers – is a relatively modern idea that arose with the development of large-scale retailing at the end of the nineteenth century. Today, most prices are set this way. However, some companies are now reversing the fixed-pricing trend. They are using **dynamic pricing** – adjusting prices continually to meet the characteristics and needs of individual customers and situations.

Dynamic pricing—Adjusting prices continually to meet the characteristics and needs of individual customers and situations.

For example, think about how the Internet has affected pricing. From the mostly fixed pricing practices of the past century, the Internet seems to be taking us back into a new age of fluid pricing. The flexibility of the Internet allows web sellers to instantly and constantly adjust prices on a wide range of goods based on demand dynamics (sometimes called *real-time pricing*). In other cases, customers control pricing by bidding on auction sites such as eBay or negotiating on sites such as Priceline.

> CarTrawler uses innovative technology to link airlines, hotel chains and other travel industry customers with 500 multinational and independent car rental companies. Annual turnover is around €100m. CarTrawler is based in Dublin but it has 85 employees and offices in the US and Alicante in Spain, the main European market for car hire. The CarTrawler platform is installed in a number of international airlines, such as Malaysia Airlines and Virgin Blue, and the booking service is available to about 200 million airline passengers worldwide. The platform, which can be installed directly into a hotel or airline's own booking software, acts like a car rental exchange, pricing the product in real time to match the market and maximise the returns. An airline might no longer have an exclusive deal with one rental car supplier but can use the CarTrawler system to get the best deal from all available operators.[10]

Dynamic pricing is especially prevalent online, where the Internet seems to be taking us back to a new age of fluid pricing. Such pricing offers many advantages for marketers. For example, Internet sellers such as Amazon or Dell can mine their databases to gauge a specific shopper's desires, measure his or her means, instantaneously tailor offers to fit that shopper's behaviour and price products accordingly.

Services ranging from retailers, airlines and hotels to sports teams change prices on the fly according to changes in demand, costs or competitor pricing, adjusting what they charge for specific items on a daily, hourly, or even continuous basis. Done well, dynamic pricing can help sellers to optimise sales and serve customers better. However, done poorly, it can trigger margin-eroding price wars and damage customer relationships and trust. Companies must be careful not to cross the fine line between smart dynamic pricing strategies and damaging ones.

In the extreme, some companies customise their offers and prices based on the specific characteristics and behaviours of individual customers, mined from online browsing and purchasing histories. These days, online offers and prices might well be based on what specific customers search for and buy, how much they pay for other purchases, and whether they might be willing and able to spend more. For example, a consumer who recently went online to purchase a first-class ticket to London or customise a new Mercedes coupe might later get a higher quote on a new Bose Wave Radio. By comparison, a friend with a more modest online search and purchase history might receive an offer of 5 per cent off and free shipping on the same radio.[11]

Although such dynamic pricing practices seem legally questionable, they're not. Dynamic pricing is legal as long as companies do not discriminate based on age, gender, location or other similar characteristics. Dynamic pricing makes sense in many contexts – it adjusts prices according to market forces and consumer preferences. But marketers need to be careful not to use dynamic pricing to take advantage of certain customer groups, thereby damaging important customer relationships.

The practice of online pricing, however, goes both ways, and consumers often benefit from online and dynamic pricing. Thanks to the Internet, the centuries-old art of haggling is suddenly back in vogue. For example, consumers can negotiate prices at online auction sites and exchanges. Want to sell that antique pickle jar that's been collecting dust for generations? Post it on eBay or Gumtree. Want to name your own price for a hotel room or rental car? Visit Bidroom or another reverse auction site. Want to bid on a ticket to a hot show or sporting event? Check out Ticketmaster, which offers an online auction service for event tickets.

Also thanks to the Internet, consumers can get instant product and price comparisons from thousands of vendors at price comparison sites such as Trivago, Skyscanner or Moneysupermarket.com, or using mobile apps such as TheFind, eBay's Red-Laser, Google Shopper or Amazon's Price Check. For example, a growing number of different mobile apps let customers scan barcodes or QR codes (or search by voice or image) while shopping in stores. It then searches online and at nearby stores to provide thousands of reviews and comparison prices, and even offers buying links for immediate online purchasing. Armed with this information, consumers can often negotiate better in-store prices.

In fact, many retailers are finding that ready online access to comparison prices is giving consumers too much of an edge. Store retailers are now devising strategies to combat the consumer practice of *showrooming*. Consumers armed with smartphones now routinely come to stores to see an item, compare prices online while in the store, and then buy the item online at a lower price. Such behaviour is called showrooming because consumers use retailers' stores as de facto 'showrooms' for online resellers such as Amazon.

Dynamic pricing: CarTrawler uses innovative technology to link airlines, hotel chains and other travel industry customers with 500 multinational and independent car retail companies. (source: Car Trawler.com).

Source: Shutterstock.com

International pricing

Companies that market their products internationally must decide what prices to charge in different countries. In some cases, a company can set a uniform worldwide price. For example, Boeing sells its jetliners at about the same price everywhere, whether the buyer is in the United States, Europe or a third-world country. However, most companies adjust their prices to reflect local market conditions and cost considerations.

The price that a company should charge in a specific country depends on many factors, including economic conditions, competitive situations, laws and regulations, and the nature of the wholesaling and retailing system. Consumer perceptions and preferences also may vary from country to country, calling for different prices. Or the company may have different marketing objectives in various world markets, which require changes in pricing strategy. For example, Apple introduces sophisticated, feature-rich, premium smartphones in carefully segmented mature markets in highly developed countries using a market-skimming pricing strategy. By contrast, it's now under pressure to discount older models and develop a more basic phone for sizable but less affluent markets in developing countries, supported by penetration pricing.

Costs play an important role in setting international prices. Travellers abroad are often surprised to find that goods that are relatively inexpensive at home may carry outrageously higher price tags in other countries. A pair of Levi's selling for €30 in the United States might go for €63 in Tokyo and €88 in Paris. A McDonald's Big Mac selling for a modest €3.57 in the United States might cost €5.29 in Norway, and an Oral-B toothbrush selling for €2.49 at home may cost €10 in China. Conversely, a Gucci handbag going for only €140 in Milan, Italy, might fetch €240 in the United States. In some cases, such *price escalation* may result from differences in selling strategies or market conditions. In most instances, however, it is simply a result of the higher costs of selling in another country – the additional costs of operations, product modifications, shipping and insurance, import tariffs and taxes, exchange-rate fluctuations and physical distribution.

Price has become a key element in the international marketing strategies of companies attempting to enter less affluent emerging markets. Typically, entering such markets has meant targeting the exploding middle classes in developing countries such as China, India, Russia and Brazil, whose economies have been growing rapidly. More recently, however, as the weakened global economy has slowed growth in both domestic and emerging markets, many companies are shifting their sights to include a new target – the so-called 'bottom of the pyramid', the vast untapped market consisting of the world's poorest consumers.

Not long ago, the preferred way for many brands to market their products in developing markets – whether consumer products or cars, computers and smartphones – was to paste new labels on existing models and sell them at higher prices to the privileged few who could afford them. However, such a pricing approach put many products out of the reach of the tens of millions of poor consumers in emerging markets. As a result, many companies developed smaller, more basic and affordable product versions for these markets. For example, Unilever – the maker of such brands as Dove, Sunsilk, Lipton and Vaseline – shrunk its packaging and set low prices that even the world's poorest consumers could afford. It developed single-use packages of its shampoo, laundry detergent, face cream and other products that it could sell profitably for just pennies a pack. As a result, today, more than half of Unilever's revenues come from emerging economies.[12]

Although this strategy has been successful for Unilever, most companies are learning that selling profitably to the bottom of the pyramid requires more than just repackaging or stripping down existing products and selling them at low prices. Just like more well-to-do consumers, low-income buyers want products that are both functional and aspirational. Thus, companies today are innovating to create products that not only sell at very low prices but also give bottom-of-the-pyramid consumers more for their money, not less.

International pricing presents many special problems and complexities. We discuss international pricing issues in more detail in Chapter 19.

PRICE CHANGES

After developing their pricing structures and strategies, companies often face situations in which they must initiate price changes or respond to price changes by competitors.

Initiating price changes

In some cases, the company may find it desirable to initiate either a price cut or a price increase. In both cases, it must anticipate possible buyer and competitor reactions.

Initiating price cuts

Several situations may lead a firm to consider cutting its price. One such circumstance is excess capacity. Another is falling demand in the face of strong price competition or a weakened economy. In such cases, the firm may aggressively cut prices to boost sales and market share. But as the airline, fast-food, automobile, retailing and other industries have learned in recent years, cutting prices in an industry loaded with excess capacity may lead to price wars as competitors try to hold on to market share.

A company may also cut prices in a drive to dominate the market through lower costs. Either the company starts with lower costs than its competitors, or it cuts prices in the hope of gaining market share that will further cut costs through larger volume. For example, computer and electronics maker Lenovo uses an aggressive low-cost, low-price strategy to increase its share of the PC market in developing countries.

Initiating price increases

A successful price increase can greatly improve profits. For example, if the company's profit margin is 3 per cent of sales, a 1 per cent price increase will boost profits by 33 per cent if sales volume is unaffected. A major factor in price increases is cost inflation. Rising costs squeeze profit margins and lead companies to pass cost increases along to customers. Another factor leading to price increases is over-demand: when a company cannot supply all that its customers need, it may raise its prices, ration products to customers, or both – consider today's worldwide oil and gas industry.

When raising prices, the company must avoid being perceived as a *price gouger*. For example, when gasoline prices rise rapidly, angry customers often accuse the major oil companies of enriching themselves at the expense of consumers. Customers have long memories, and they will eventually turn away from companies or even whole industries that they perceive as charging excessive prices. In the extreme, claims of price gouging may even bring about increased government regulation.

There are some techniques for avoiding these problems. One is to maintain a sense of fairness surrounding any price increase. Price increases should be supported by company communications telling customers why prices are being raised.

Wherever possible, the company should consider ways to meet higher costs or demand without raising prices. For example, it might consider more cost-effective ways to produce or distribute its products. It can 'unbundle' its market offering,

Author comment

When and how should a company change its price? What if costs rise, putting the squeeze on profits? What if the economy sags and customers become more price sensitive? Or what if a major competitor raises or drops its prices? As Figure 11.1 suggests, companies face many price-changing options.

Sometimes raising prices can be viewed as unfair and generate negative press and social media responses. Marketers should take such issues into account before any price rises.
Source: Paul Taggart/Bloomberg via Getty Images

removing features, packaging or services and separately pricing elements that were formerly part of the offer. Or it can shrink the product or substitute less-expensive ingredients instead of raising the price. P&G recently did this with Tide by holding price while shrinking 100-ounce containers to 92 ounces and 50-ounce containers to 46 ounces, creating a more than 8 per cent price increase per ounce without changing package prices. Imperial Leather soap recently reduced the size of its bars from 125g to 100g while Cadbury's Dairy Milk bars shrank from 140g to 120g (that's two whole chunks!) while the price remained unchanged.[13] Similarly, Kimberly-Clark raised Kleenex prices by 'desheeting' – reducing the number of sheets of toilet paper or facial tissues in each package. And a regular Snickers bar now weighs 1.86 ounces, down from 2.07 ounces in the past, effectively increasing prices by 11 per cent.[14]

Buyer reactions to price changes

Customers do not always interpret price changes in a straightforward way. A price *increase*, which would normally lower sales, may have some positive meanings for buyers. For example, what would you think if Rolex raised the price of its latest watch model? On the one hand, you might think that the watch is even more exclusive or better made. On the other hand, you might think that Rolex is simply being greedy by charging what the traffic will bear.

Similarly, consumers may view a price cut in several ways. For example, what would you think if Rolex were to suddenly cut its prices? You might think that you are getting a better deal on an exclusive product. More likely, however, you'd think that quality had been reduced, and the brand's luxury image might be tarnished. A brand's price and image are often closely linked. A price change, especially a drop in price, can adversely affect how consumers view the brand. Tiffany found this out when it attempted to broaden its appeal by offering a line of more affordable jewellery:[15]

> Tiffany is all about luxury and the cachet of its blue boxes. However, in the late 1990s, the high-end jeweller responded to the 'affordable luxuries' craze with a new 'Return to Tiffany' line of less expensive silver jewellery. The 'Return to Tiffany' silver charm bracelet quickly became a must-have item, as teens jammed Tiffany's hushed stores clamouring for the €78 silver bauble. Sales skyrocketed. But despite this early success, the bracelet fad appeared to alienate the firm's older, wealthier and more conservative clientele, damaging Tiffany's reputation for luxury. So, over ten years ago, the firm began re-emphasising its pricier jewellery collections. Although high-end jewellery has once again replaced silver as Tiffany's fastest growing business, the company has yet to fully regain its exclusivity. Says one well-heeled customer: 'You used to aspire to be able to buy something at Tiffany, but now it's not that special anymore.'

Competitor reactions to price changes

A firm considering a price change must worry about the reactions of its competitors as well as those of its customers. Competitors are most likely to react when the number of firms involved is small, when the product is uniform, and when the buyers are well informed about products and prices.

How can the firm anticipate the likely reactions of its competitors? The problem is complex because, like the customer, the competitor can interpret a company price cut in many ways. It might think the company is trying to grab a larger market share or that it's doing poorly and trying to boost its sales. Or it might think that the company wants the whole industry to cut prices to increase total demand.

The company must guess each competitor's likely reaction. If all competitors behave alike, this amounts to analysing only a typical competitor. In contrast, if the competitors do not behave alike – perhaps because of differences in size, market shares or policies – then separate analyses are necessary. However, if some competitors will match the price change, there is good reason to expect that the rest will also match it.

Responding to price changes

Here we reverse the question and ask how a firm should respond to a price change by a competitor. The firm needs to consider several issues: Why did the competitor change the price? Is the price change temporary or permanent? What will happen to the company's market share and profits if it does not respond? Are other competitors going to respond? Besides these issues, the company must also consider its own situation and strategy and possible customer reactions to price changes.

Figure 11.1 shows the ways a company might assess and respond to a competitor's price cut. Suppose the company learns that a competitor has cut its price and decides that this price cut is likely to harm its sales and profits. It might simply decide to hold its current price and profit margin. The company might believe that it will not lose too much market share, or that it would lose too much profit if it reduced its own price. Or it might decide that it should wait and respond when it has more information on the effects of the competitor's price change. However, waiting too long to act might let the competitor get stronger and more confident as its sales increase.

If the company decides that effective action can and should be taken, it might make any of four responses. First, it could *reduce its price* to match the competitor's price. It may decide that the market is price sensitive and that it would lose too much market share to the lower-priced competitor. However, cutting the price will reduce the company's profits in the short run. Some companies might also reduce their product quality, services and marketing communications to retain profit margins, but this will ultimately hurt long-run market share. The company should try to maintain its quality as it cuts prices.

Alternatively, the company might maintain its price but *raise the perceived value* of its offer. It could improve its communications, stressing the relative value of its product over that of the lower-price competitor. The firm may find it cheaper to maintain price and spend money to improve its perceived value than to cut price and operate at a lower margin. Or, the company might *improve quality* and *increase price*, moving its brand into a higher price–value position. The higher quality creates greater customer value, which justifies the higher price. In turn, the higher price preserves the company's higher margins.

Price competition is a core element of our free-market economy. In setting prices, companies usually are not free to charge whatever prices they wish. Many federal, state and even local laws govern the rules of fair play in pricing. In addition, companies must consider broader societal pricing concerns. In setting their prices, for example, pharmaceutical firms must balance their development costs and profit objectives against the sometimes life-and-death needs of drug consumers.

Figure 11.1 Responding to competitor price changes

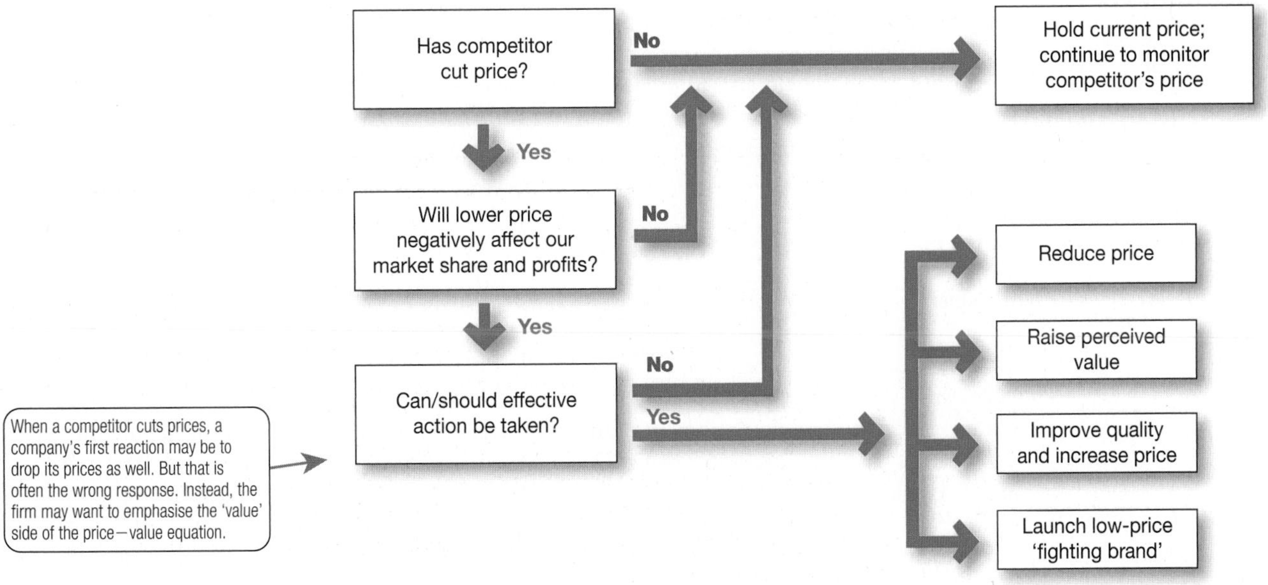

When a competitor cuts prices, a company's first reaction may be to drop its prices as well. But that is often the wrong response. Instead, the firm may want to emphasise the 'value' side of the price—value equation.

Finally, the company might *launch a low-price 'fighter brand'* – adding a lower-price item to the line or creating a separate lower-price brand. This is necessary if the particular market segment being lost is price sensitive and will not respond to arguments of higher quality. For example, France Telecom, Vivendi's SFR and Bouygues Telecom have all reacted to the imminent entry of a new rival Iliad into France's €40 billion-a-year telecoms market. Of that €40 billion market, €7 billion comes from broadband, €2 billion from fixed lines, €6 billion from business-to-business services and €25 billion from mobile services. In order to protect its share of the mobile market and to protect its Orange brand, France Telecom launched 'Sosh', a new low-cost brand to compete with Iliad's 'Free'.[16] Another example is Bosch's fighter brand 'Viva'. While Bosch white goods competed well at the higher end of the market, their white goods were at a major disadvantage when competing in the low-price category. Consequently, Bosch launched the Viva brand to compete with white good price-discounters in the low-price market while protecting its brand reputation, image and premium position for Bosch branded white goods in the premium market.

To counter store brands and other low-price entrants in a tighter economy, P&G turned a number of its brands into fighter brands. Luvs disposable nappies give parents 'premium leakage protection for less than pricier brands'. And P&G offers popular budget-priced basic versions of several of its major brands. For example, Charmin Basic 'holds up at a great everyday price', and Puffs Basic gives you: 'Everyday softness. Everyday value.' And Tide Simply Clean & Fresh is about 35 per cent cheaper than regular Tide detergent. However, companies must use caution when introducing fighter brands, as such brands can tarnish the image of the main brand. In addition, although they may attract budget buyers away from lower-priced rivals, they can also take business away from the firm's higher-margin brands.

PUBLIC POLICY AND PRICING

Price competition is a core element of our free-market economy. In setting prices, companies usually are not free to charge whatever prices they wish. Many federal, state, and even local laws govern the rules of fair play in pricing. In addition, companies must consider broader societal pricing concerns. In setting their prices, for example, pharmaceutical firms must balance their development costs and profit objectives against the sometimes life-and-death needs of drug consumers.

Across Europe there are many different statutory provisions governing pricing and competition. For example, in the European Union Article 82 (c) of the European Commission Treaty deals with abuses of dominant positions. In addition member states of the European Union seek to protect consumers and firms through national-level laws and organisations such as the UK's Office of Fair Trading.

Figure 11.2 shows the major public policy issues in pricing. These include potentially damaging pricing practices within a given level of the channel (price-fixing and predatory pricing) and across levels of the channel (retail price maintenance, discriminatory pricing and deceptive pricing).[17]

Pricing within channel levels

EU legislation on *price-fixing* states that sellers must set prices without talking to competitors. Otherwise, price collusion is suspected. Price-fixing is illegal per se – that is, the government does not accept any excuses for price-fixing. As such, companies found guilty of these practices can receive heavy fines. Recently, governments at the state and national levels have been aggressively enforcing price-fixing regulations in industries ranging from gasoline, insurance and concrete to credit cards, CDs and computer chips. Price-fixing is also prohibited in many international markets. For example, Apple was recently fined €529,000 on price-fixing charges for its iPhones in Taiwan.[18]

Sellers are also prohibited from using *predatory pricing* – selling below cost with the intention of punishing a competitor or gaining higher long-run profits by putting competitors out of

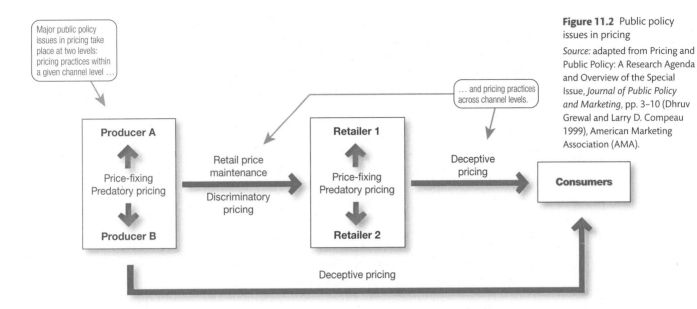

Major public policy issues in pricing take place at two levels: pricing practices within a given channel level …

… and pricing practices across channel levels.

Figure 11.2 Public policy issues in pricing

Source: adapted from Pricing and Public Policy: A Research Agenda and Overview of the Special Issue, *Journal of Public Policy and Marketing*, pp. 3–10 (Dhruv Grewal and Larry D. Compeau 1999), American Marketing Association (AMA).

business. This protects small sellers from larger ones that might sell items below cost temporarily or in a specific locale to drive them out of business. The biggest problem is determining just what constitutes predatory pricing behaviour. Selling below cost to unload excess inventory is not considered predatory; selling below cost to drive out competitors is. Thus, a given action may or may not be predatory depending on intent, and intent can be very difficult to determine or prove.

In recent years, several large and powerful companies have been accused of predatory pricing. However, turning an accusation into a lawsuit can be difficult. For example, many publishers and booksellers have expressed concerns about Amazon's predatory practices, especially its book pricing:[19]

> Many booksellers and publishers complain that Amazon's book pricing policies are destroying their industry. During past holiday seasons, Amazon has sold top-10 bestselling hardback books as loss leaders at cut-rate prices of less than €10 each. And Amazon now sells e-books at fire-sale prices in order to win customers for its Kindle e-reader. Such very low book prices have caused considerable damage to competing booksellers, many of whom view Amazon's pricing actions as predatory. Says one observer, 'The word "predator" is pretty strong, and I don't use it loosely, but . . . I could have sworn we had laws against predatory pricing. I just don't understand why [Amazon's pricing] is not an issue.' Still, no predatory pricing charges have ever been filed against Amazon. It would be extremely difficult to prove that such loss-leader pricing is purposefully predatory as opposed to just plain good competitive marketing. Earlier, Amazon challenged French law by refusing to eliminate its free shipping on books offer. The action, brought by the French Booksellers' Union (*Syndicat de la librairie française*) argued that Amazon offered illegal discounts. Amazon said it would pay the €1,000 per day fine rather than abide with a French High Court ruling.[20]

Pricing across channel levels

As in the US, the European Union also seeks to prevent unfair *price discrimination* by ensuring that sellers offer the same price terms to customers at a given level of trade. For example, every retailer is entitled to the same price terms from a given manufacturer, whether the retailer is Halfords or your local bicycle shop. However, price discrimination is allowed if the seller can prove that its costs are different when selling to different retailers – for example, that it costs less per unit to sell a large volume of bicycles to Halfords than to sell a few bicycles to the local dealer.

The seller can also discriminate in its pricing if the seller manufactures different qualities of the same product for different retailers. The seller has to prove that these differences are proportional.

Price differentials may also be used to match competition in good faith, provided the price discrimination is temporary, localised and defensive rather than offensive.

Laws also prohibit *retail (or resale) price maintenance*; a manufacturer cannot require dealers to charge a specified retail price for its product. Although the seller can propose a manufacturer's *suggested* retail price to dealers, it cannot refuse to sell to a dealer that takes independent pricing action nor can it punish the dealer by shipping late or denying advertising allowances.

Deceptive pricing occurs when a seller states prices or price savings that mislead consumers or are not actually available to consumers. This might involve bogus reference or comparison prices, as when a retailer sets artificially high 'regular' prices and then announces 'sale' prices close to its previous everyday prices. For example, in the US Overstock.com recently came under scrutiny for inaccurately listing manufacturer's suggested retail prices, often quoting them higher than the actual price. Such comparison pricing is widespread.

Other deceptive pricing issues include *scanner fraud* and price confusion. The widespread use of scanner-based computer checkouts has led to increasing complaints of retailers overcharging their customers. Most of these overcharges result from poor management – from a failure to enter current or sale prices into the system. Other cases, however, involve intentional overcharges.

Many federal and state statutes regulate against deceptive pricing practices. For example, the European Union has recently addressed the issue of extra credit card charges for online purchases:[21]

> Hefty credit card charges when paying online for goods or services – such as airline tickets – could soon be a thing of the past after European Union lawmakers passed rules on consumer rights in Europe. Buried in the myriad of new rules is a provision which states: 'Member states shall prohibit traders from charging consumers, in respect of a given means of payment, fees that exceed the cost borne by the trader for the use of such means.' 'This law will put an end to growing unfair business practices – like, when buying flights, consumers will not be charged unjustified fees just to use their credit card,' said Monique Goyens, director-general of Beuc, the European consumers' organisation. Consumer advocates say a common source of complaint in this area relates to budget airlines, which are apt to charge travellers significant additional sums depending merely on what type of card they use for the purchase. For example, a €32.15 Aberdeen–London ticket with easyJet could cost €47.02 if purchased with a credit card, €41.33 with a debit card and incur no premium if purchased with Visa Electron. easyJet says its fees 'stand comparison with any other airline – which is why people choose to fly with us'. The aim of the legislation is to provide consumers across the EU with harmonised minimum rights, and although that intention has been watered down to some extent during long and difficult negotiations, consumers will now have a 14-day, EU-wide 'cooling off' period when shopping online, during which they can change their minds about purchases.

However, reputable sellers go beyond what is required by law. Treating customers fairly and making certain that they fully understand prices and pricing terms is an important part of building strong and lasting customer relationships.

OBJECTIVES REVIEW AND KEY TERMS

In this chapter, we examined some additional pricing considerations – new product pricing, product mix pricing, price adjustments, initiating and reacting to prices changes, and pricing and public policy. A company sets not a single price but rather a *pricing structure* that covers its entire mix of products. This pricing structure changes over time as products move through their life cycles. The company adjusts product prices to reflect changes in costs and demand and account for variations in buyers and situations. As the competitive environment changes, the company considers when to initiate price changes and when to respond to them.

OBJECTIVE 1 Describe the major strategies for pricing new products (pp. 314–315)

Pricing is a dynamic process, and pricing strategies usually change as the product passes through its life cycle. The introductory stage – setting prices for the first time – is especially challenging. The company can decide on one of several strategies for pricing innovative new products. It can use *market-skimming pricing* by initially setting high prices to 'skim' the maximum amount of revenue from various segments of the market. Or it can use *market-penetrating pricing* by setting a low initial price to penetrate the market deeply and win a large market share. Several conditions must be set for either new product pricing strategy to work.

OBJECTIVE 2 Explain how companies find a set of prices that maximises the profits from the total product mix (pp. 315–317)

When the product is part of a product mix, the firm searches for a set of prices that will maximise the profits from the total mix. In *product line pricing*, the company determines the price steps for the entire product line it offers. In addition, the company must set prices for *optional products* (optional or accessory products included with the main product), *captive products* (products that are required for using the main product), *by-products* (waste or residual products produced when making the main product) and *product bundles* (combinations of products at a reduced price).

OBJECTIVE 3 Discuss how companies adjust their prices to take into account different types of customers and situations (pp. 318–324)

Companies apply a variety of *price adjustment strategies* to account for differences in consumer segments and situations. One is *discount and allowance pricing*, whereby the company establishes cash, quantity, functional or seasonal discounts, or varying types of allowances. A second strategy is *segmented pricing*, where the company sells a product at two or more prices to accommodate different customers, product forms, locations or times. Sometimes companies consider more than economics in their pricing decisions, using *psychological pricing* to better communicate a product's intended position. In *promotional pricing*, a company offers discounts or temporarily sells a product below list price as a special event, sometimes even selling

below cost as a loss leader. Another approach is *geographical pricing*, whereby the company decides how to price to distant customers, choosing from such alternatives as FOB origin pricing, uniform-delivered pricing, zone pricing, basing point pricing and freight-absorption pricing. Using *dynamic pricing*, a company can adjust prices continually to meet the characteristics and needs of individual customers and situations. Finally, *international pricing* means that the company adjusts its price to meet different conditions and expectations in different world markets.

OBJECTIVE 4 Discuss the key issues related to initiating and responding to price changes (pp. 325–328)

When a firm considers initiating a *price change*, it must consider customers' and competitors' reactions. There are different implications to *initiating price cuts* and *initiating price increases*. Buyer reactions to price changes are influenced by the meaning customers see in the price change. Competitors' reactions flow from a set reaction policy or a fresh analysis of each situation. There are also many factors to consider in responding to a competitor's price changes. The company that faces a price change initiated by a competitor must try to understand the competitor's intent as well as the likely duration and impact of the change. If a swift reaction is desirable, the firm should pre-plan its reactions to different possible price actions by competitors. When facing a competitor's price change, the company might sit tight, reduce its own price, raise perceived quality, improve quality and raise price, or launch a fighter brand.

OBJECTIVE 5 Overview the social and legal issues that affect pricing decisions (pp. 328–330)

Many federal, state, and even local laws govern the rules of fair pricing. Also, companies must consider broader societal pricing concerns. The major public policy issues in pricing include potentially damaging pricing practices *within* a given level of the channel, such as price-fixing and predatory pricing. They also include pricing practices across channel levels, such as retail price maintenance, discriminatory pricing and deceptive pricing. Although many federal and state statutes regulate pricing practices, reputable sellers go beyond what is required by law. Treating customers fairly is an important part of building strong and lasting customer relationships.

NAVIGATING THE KEY TERMS

OBJECTIVE 1
Market-skimming pricing (price skimming) (p. 314)
Market-penetration pricing (p. 315)

OBJECTIVE 2
Product line pricing (p. 316)
Optional-product pricing (p. 316)
Captive-product pricing (p. 316)

By-product pricing (p. 317)
Product bundle pricing (p. 317)

OBJECTIVE 3
Discount (p. 318)
Allowance (p. 318)
Segmented pricing (p. 318)
Psychological pricing (p. 319)
Reference prices (p. 320)

Promotional pricing (p. 320)
Geographical pricing (p. 321)
FOB-origin pricing (p. 321)
Uniform-delivered pricing (p. 321)
Zone pricing (p. 322)
Basing-point pricing (p. 322)
Freight-absorption pricing (p. 322)
Dynamic pricing (p. 322)

DISCUSSION AND CRITICAL THINKING

Discussion questions

11-1 Compare and contrast market-skimming and market penetration pricing strategies and discuss the conditions under which each is appropriate. For each strategy, give an example of a recently introduced product that used that pricing strategy. (AACSB: Communication; Reflective thinking)

11-2 Define captive-product pricing and give examples. What must marketers be concerned about when implementing this type of pricing? (AACSB: Communication)

11-3 What is dynamic pricing? Why is it especially prevalent online? Is it legal? (AACSB: Communication)

11-4 Should a company always respond to a competitor's price cut, and what options are available if it does decide to respond? (AACSB: Communication)

11-5 Briefly discuss the major policy issues across levels of the channel of distribution. (AACSB: Communication)

Critical-thinking exercises

11-6 You are an owner of a small independent chain of coffee houses competing head-to-head with Costa Coffee. The retail price your customers pay for coffee is exactly the same as at Costa Coffee. The wholesale price you pay for roasted coffee beans has increased by 25 per cent. You know that you cannot absorb this increase and that you must pass it on to your customers. However, you are concerned about the consequences of an open price increase. Discuss three alternative price-increase strategies that address these concerns. (AACSB: Communication; Reflective thinking)

11-7 Identify three online price-comparison shopping sites or apps and shop for a product you are interested in

purchasing. Compare the price ranges given at the three sites. Based on your search, determine a 'fair' price for the product. (AACSB: Communication; Use of IT; Reflective thinking)

11-8 One psychological pricing tactic is 'just-below' pricing. It is also called '9-ending' pricing because prices usually end in the number 9 (or 99). In a small group, have each member select five different products and visit a store to learn the price of those items. Is there a variation among the items and stores with regard to 9-ending pricing? Why do marketers use this pricing tactic? (AACSB: Communication; Reflective thinking)

Mini-cases and applications

Online, mobile and social media marketing: online price glitches

The Internet is great for selling products and services. But don't make a pricing mistake online! Intercontinental Hotels mistakenly priced rooms at one of its four-star hotels near Venice, Italy, for 1 euro per night instead of the actual price of 150 euros per night. Internet users booked 1,400 nights before the mistake was realised. Intercontinental Hotels honoured the reservations at a cost of 90,000 euros to the company. In Taiwan, an eight-hour online pricing snafu on Dell's website created tremendous problems for the company, such as 40,000 orders for a laptop computer priced at about one-quarter the intended price. Unlike Intercontinental Hotels, however, Dell refused to honour the erroneous price and offered a discount instead. The Taiwanese government disagreed, ordered Dell to honour orders for erroneously priced products, and fined the company.

11-9 Find two other examples of online pricing mistakes. How did the companies handle the problems resulting from the pricing errors? (AACSB: Communication; Reflective thinking)

11-10 Research ways in which marketers protect against the consequences of online pricing errors and write a brief report summarising what you learn. (AACSB: Communication; Reflective thinking)

Marketing ethics: airfare pricing

You'd think that the farther you fly, the more expensive your airfare would be. According to easily accessible data, however, that's not the case. For example, one study compared five US and EU city-pairs (Los Angeles–San Francisco, New York–Boston, Chicago–Detroit, Denver–Las Vegas, Miami–Orlando versus London–Edinburgh, Paris–Nice, Milan–Rome, Dusseldorf–Berlin, Barcelona–Madrid). The total distance of all five US-based flights is a total (return) distance of 3,172 miles while for the five European flights the total distance travelled would be slightly more at 3,338 miles. Yet the European flights are about half of the cost of those in the US at around €276 versus €527! That's the average cost; fliers sitting next to each other most likely paid different prices. Many factors influence the pricing of airfares; distance has minor impact, even though two major expenses–fuel and labour–increase the longer the flight. Airlines claim they are just charging what the market will bear.

11-11 Should airlines be required to charge standard prices based on distance and equal airfares for passengers seated in the same class (such as coach or business class) on the same flight? What will be likely to happen to prices if the government requires airlines to base fares only on distance and passenger class? (AACSB: Communication; Ethical reasoning; Reflective thinking)

11-12 What factors account for the variation in airfares? Should airlines be permitted to get as much as they can for a seat? (AACSB: Communication; Reflective thinking)

Marketing by the numbers: Louis Vuitton price increase

One way to maintain exclusivity for a brand is to raise its price. That's what luxury fashion and leather goods maker Louis Vuitton did. The company did not want the brand to become overexposed and too common, so it raised prices 10 per cent and is slowing its expansion in China. The Louis Vuitton brand is the largest contributor to the company's €11.8 billion revenue from its fashion and leather division, accounting for over €7 billion of those sales. It might seem counterintuitive to want to encourage fewer customers to purchase a company's products, but when price increases, so does the product's contribution margin, making each sale more profitable. Thus, sales can drop and the company can still maintain the same profitability as before the price hike.

11-13 If the company's original contribution margin was 40 per cent, calculate the new contribution margin if price is increased 10 per cent. Refer to Appendix 2: Marketing by the numbers, paying attention to endnote 6 on the price change explanation in which the analysis is done by setting price equal to €1.00. (AACSB: Communications; Analytic reasoning)

11-14 Determine by how much sales can drop and let the company still maintain the total contribution it had when the contribution margin was 40 per cent. (AACSB: Communication; Analytic reasoning)

REFERENCES

[1] Based on information from BBC 'Price of football 2014: why fans flock to Borussia Dortmund', www.bbc.co.uk/sport/0/football/29624410; Deloitte, *Annual Report of Football Finance – Highlights*, Deloitte, Sports Business Group, 2013; Stock price information for Borussia Dortmund has been obtained from www.maxblue.de/de/maerkte-aktie.html?symbol=BVB.ETR; Historical sporting performance information for Borussia Dortmund has been obtained from www.kicker.de, accessed October 2015.

[2] 'Lower cost Samsung GALAXY unveiled in Kenya', *BiztechAfrica*, 23 May 2014, www.biztechafrica.com/article/lower-cost-samsungsamsung-galaxy-unveiled-kenya/2967/#.Uvo4bfldV8F; Ed Sutherland, 'Apple vs Samsung price war in India', *iDownloadBlog*, 17 April 2013, www.idownloadblog.com/2013/04/17/apple-samsung-indiaprice-war/; Panjaj Mishra, 'Apple turns to old iPhone models, and lower prices, to woo users in India', *TechCrunch*, 17 January 2014, http://techcrunch.com/2014/01/17/apple-turns-to-old-iphone-modelsand-lower-prices-to-woo-users-in-india/; and 'Samsung Galaxy Pocket Neo', www.mysmartprice.com/mobile/samsung-galaxy-pocketneo-msp2810, accessed October 2015.

[3] Karis Hustad, 'Kindle Fire HDX keeps Amazon's low price, adds extra features', *Christian Science Monitor*, 26 September 2013, www.csmonitor.com/Innovation/2013/0926/Kindle-Fire-HDXkeeps-Amazon-s-low-price-adds-extra-features.

[4] See Oliver Strand, 'With coffee, the price of individualism can be high', *New York Times*, 8 February 2012, p. D6; and '$51 per pound: the deceptive cost of single-serve coffee', *New York Times*, www.thekitchn.com/51-per-pound-the-deceptive-cost-of-singleserve-coffee-the-new-york-times-165712, accessed October 2015.

[5] Example from Andrew Bolger, 'Scottish scientists develop whisky biofuel', *Financial Times*, 17 August 2010, www.ft.com/cms/s/0/62e0f67a-aa0b-11df-8eb1-00144feabdc0.html#ixzz1UWPinXkk, accessed October 2015.

[6] Peter Coy, 'Why the price is rarely right', *Bloomberg BusinessWeek*, 1 and 8 February 2010, pp. 77–78.

[7] Anthony Allred, E. K. Valentin, and Goutam Chakraborty, 'Pricing risky services: preference and quality considerations', *The Journal of Product*

and Brand Management, vol. 19, no. 1, 2010, p. 54; Also see Kenneth C. Manning and David E. Sprott, 'Price endings, left-digit effects, and choice', *Journal of Consumer Research*, August 2009, pp. 328–336.

[8] See Anthony Allred, E. K. Valentin, and Goutam Chakraborty, 'Pricing risky services: preference and quality considerations', *Journal of Product and Brand Management*, Vol. 19, No. 1, 2010, p. 54; Kenneth C. Manning and David E. Sprott, 'Price endings, left-digit effects, and choice', *Journal of Consumer Research*, August 2009, pp. 328–336; Martin Lindstrom, 'The psychology behind the sweet spots of pricing', *Fast Company*, 27 March 2012, www.fastcompany.com/1826172/psychology-behind-sweetspots-pricing; and Travis Nichols, 'A penny saved: psychological pricing', *Gumroad*, 18 October 2013, http://blog.gumroad.com/post/64417917582/a-penny-saved-psychological-pricing.

[9] Adapted from information found in Elizabeth A. Sullivan, 'Stay on course', *Marketing News*, 15 February 2009, pp. 11–13; also see Stuart Elliott, 'Never mind what it costs. Can I get it 70 percent off?' *New York Times*, 27 April 2009, www.nytimes.com/2009/04/28/business/media/28adco.html?_r=1&scp=1&sq=Never%20Mind%20What%20It%20Costs&st=cse; and 'Consumer "new frugality" may be an enduring feature of post-recession economy, finds Booz & Company survey', *Business Wire*, 24 February 2010.

[10] See www.cartrawler.com

[11] See Justin D. Martin, 'Dynamic pricing: Internet retailers are treating us like foreign tourists in Egypt', *Christian Science Monitor*, 7 January 2011; Patrick Rishe, 'Dynamic pricing: the future of ticket pricing in sports', *Forbes*, 6 January 2012, www.forbes.com/sites/prishe/2012/01/06/dynamic-pricing-the-future-of-ticketpricing-in-sports/; and Mike Southon, 'Time to ensure the price is right', *Financial Times*, 21 January 2012, p. 30.

[12] Matthew Boyle, 'Unilever: taking on the world, one stall at a time', *Bloomberg Businessweek*, 7 January 2013, pp. 18–20; and Martinne Geller, 'Unilever sticks with emerging markets as sales rebound', *Reuters*, 21 January 2014, http://uk.reuters.com/article/2014/01/21/uk-unilever-results-idUKBREA0K09A20140121.

[13] See www.bbc.co.uk/news/magazine-13725050, accessed October 2015.

[14] See Serena Ng, 'Toilet-tissue "desheeting" shrinks rolls, plumps margins', *Wall Street Journal*, 24 July 2013, http://online.wsj.com/news/articles/SB10001424127887323971204578626223494483866; and Serena Ng, 'At P&G, new Tide comes in, old price goes up', *Wall Street Journal*, 10 February 2014, http://online.wsj.com/news/articles/SB10001424052702304450904579368852980301572.

[15] Example adapted from information found in Ellen Byron, 'Fashion victim: to refurbish its image, Tiffany risks profits', *Wall Street Journal*, 10 January 2007, p. A1; and Aliza Rosenbaum and John Christy, 'Financial insight: Tiffany's boutique risk; by breaking mall fast, high-end exclusivity may gain touch of common', *Wall Street Journal*, 20 October 2007, p. B14. Also see Brian Burnsed, 'Where discounting can be dangerous', *BusinessWeek*, 3 August 2009, p. 49.

[16] Example from James Boxell, 'France Telecom earmarks disposals', *Financial Times*, 28 July 2011, www.ft.com/cms/s/0/263d5932-b8ee-11e0-bd87-00144feabdc0.html#axzz1UPifHx5H, accessed October 2015; and from Ross Tieman, 'France's Free is wired for telecoms success', *Financial Times*, 17 March 2011, www.ft.com/cms/s/0/9e2bfb0e-440b-11e0-8f20-00144feab49a.html#axzz1TD6Um28m, accessed October 2015.

[17] For discussions of these issues, see Dhruv Grewel and Larry D. Compeau, 'Pricing and public policy: a research agenda and overview of the special issue', *Journal of Public Policy and Marketing*, Spring 1999, pp. 3–10; Walter L. Baker, Michael V. Marn, and Craig C. Zawada, *The Price Advantage* (Hoboken, New Jersey: John Wiley & Sons, 2010), Appendix 2; and Thomas T. Nagle, John E. Hogan, and Joseph Zale, *The Strategy and Tactics of Pricing*, 5th ed. (Upper Saddle River, NJ: Prentice Hall, 2011).

[18] See Tim Worstall, 'Apple fined $670,000 in Taiwan for price fixing', *Forbes*, 25 December 2013, www.forbes.com/sites/timworstall/2013/12/25/apple-fined-670000-in-taiwan-for-price-fixing.

[19] Based on information found in Lynn Leary, 'Publishers and booksellers see a 'predatory' Amazon', *NPR Books*, 23 January 2012, www.npr.org/2012/01/23/145468105; Allison Frankel, 'Bookstores accuse Amazon (not Apple!)' and Andrew Albanese, 'Court denies bid to examine Amazon's e-book pricing', *Publishers Weekly*, 14 November 2013, www.publishersweekly.com/pw/by-topic/digital/content-and-e-books/article/60002-court-denies-bid-to-examine-amazon-s-e-book-pricing.html.

[20] Example from Victoria Shannon, 'Amazon.com is challenging French competition law', *New York Times*, 14 January 2008, www.nytimes.com/2008/01/14/technology/14iht-amazon.4.9204272.html, accessed October 2015.

[21] Example from Nikki Tait, 'Brussels targets online credit card fees', *Financial Times*, 23 June 2011, www.ft.com/cms/s/0/3ed2e7e4-9dd4-11e0-b30c-00144feabdc0.html#ixzz1UWarBS2y, accessed October 2015.

COMPANY CASE

Coach: riding the wave of premium pricing

Victor Luis stood looking out the window of his office on 34th Street in Manhattan's Hell's Kitchen neighbourhood. It had been just over a year since he had taken over as CEO of Coach, Inc., a position that had previously been held by Lewis Frankfort for 28 years. Under Frankfort's leadership, it seemed Coach could do no wrong. Indeed, over the previous decade, the 73-year-old company had seen its revenues skyrocket from about €0.92 billion to over €4.6 billion as its handbags became one of the most coveted luxury items for women in the United States and beyond. On top of that, the company's €0.92 billion bottom line – a 20 per cent net margin – was typical. Coach's revenues made it the leading handbags seller in the nation. The brand's premium price and profit margins made the company a financier's darling.

Right around the time Luis took over, however, Coach's fortunes began to shift. Although the company had experienced promising results with expansion into men's lines and international markets, it had just recorded the fourth straight quarter of declining revenues in the United States, a market that accounted for 70 per cent of its business. North American comparable sales were down by a whopping 21 per cent over the previous year. Once the trendsetter, for two years in a row Coach lost market share to younger and more nimble competitors. Investors were jittery, causing Coach's stock price to drop by nearly 50 per cent in just two years. After years of success, it now seemed that Coach could do little right.

Artisanal origins

In a Manhattan loft in 1941, six artisans formed a partnership called Gail Leather Products and ran it as a family-owned business. Employing skills handed down from generation to generation, the group handcrafted a collection of leather goods, primarily wallets and billfolds. Five years later, the company hired Miles and Lillian Cahn – owners of a leather handbag manufacturing firm – and by 1950, Miles was running things.

As the business grew, Cahn took particular interest in the distinctive properties of the leather in baseball gloves. The gloves were stiff and tough when new, but with use they became soft and supple. Cahn developed a method that mimicked the wear-and-tear process, making a leather that was stronger, softer, and more flexible. As an added benefit, the worn leather also absorbed dye to a greater degree, producing deep, rich tones. When Lillian Cahn suggested adding women's handbags to the company's low-margin line of wallets, the Coach brand was born.

Over the next 20 years, Coach's uniquely soft and feminine cowhide bags developed a reputation for their durability. Coach bags also became known for innovative features and bright colours, rather than the usual browns and tans. As the Coach brand expanded into shoes and accessories, it also became known for attractive integrated hardware pieces – particularly the silver toggle that remains an identifying feature of the Coach brand today. In 1985, the Cahns sold Coach to the Sara Lee Corporation, which housed the brand within its Hanes Group. Lewis Frankfort became Coach's director and took the brand into a new era of growth and development.

Under Frankfort's leadership, Coach grew from a relatively small company to a widely recognised global brand. This growth not only included new designs for handbags and new product lines, but a major expansion of outlets as well. When Frankfort assumed the top position, Coach had only six boutiques located within department stores and a flagship Coach store on Madison Avenue. By the time Frankfort stepped down, there were more than 900 Coach stores in North America, Asia and Europe, with hundreds of Coach boutiques in department stores throughout those same markets as well as in Latin America, the Middle East and Australia. In addition to the bricks-and-mortar outlets, Coach had developed a healthy stream of online sales through its websites.

High price equals high sales

With the expansion in Coach's product lines and distribution outlets, women everywhere were drawn to the brand's quality and style. But perhaps more than anything, they were attracted to the brand as a symbol of luxury, taste and success. Over the years, Coach had taken great care to find an optimal price point, well above that of ordinary department store brands. Whereas stores that carried Coach products also sold mid-tier handbag brands for moderate prices, Coach bags were priced as much as five times higher.

It might seem that such a high price would scare buyers off. To the contrary. As Coach's reputation grew, women aspired to own its products. And although the price of a Coach bag is an extravagance for most buyers, it is still within reach for even middle-class women who want to splurge once in a while. And with comparable bags from Gucci, Fendi or Prada priced five to ten times higher, a Coach bag is a relative bargain.

With its image as an accessible status symbol, Coach was one of the few luxury brands that maintained steady growth and profits throughout the Great Recession. And it did so without discounting its prices. Fearing that price cuts would damage the brand's image, Coach instead introduced its 'Poppy' line at prices about 30 per cent lower than regular Coach bags. Coach concentrated on its factory stores in outlet malls. And it maintained an emphasis on quality to drive perceptions of value. As a result, Coach's devoted customer base remained loyal throughout the tough times.

At about the same time, Coach also invested in new customers. It opened its first men's-only store, stocked with small leather goods, travel accessories, footwear, jewellery and swimsuits. Coach also expanded men's collections in other stores. As a result, its revenue from men's products doubled in one year. The company saw similar success with international customers, pressing hard into Europe, China and other Asian markets.

But just as it seemed that Coach was untouchable, the brand showed signs of frailty. Coach's US handbag business started slowing down. During Luis' first year on the job, Coach's share of the US handbag market fell from 19 per cent to 17.5 per cent — the second straight year for such a loss. During that same period, Michael Kors, Coach's biggest competitive threat, saw its market share increase from 4.5 per cent to 7 per cent. Up-and-comers Kate Spade and Tory Burch also saw increases. Because the US market accounted for such a large portion of the company's business, overall revenue took a dip despite the brand's growth in new markets.

What's the problem?

Many factors could be blamed. During the most recent holiday season, Coach had to contend with the same problem many other retailers faced — less traffic in shopping malls. But Kate Spade and Michael Kors, which operate their own stores and sell through department stores in malls just as Coach does, experienced double-digit gains during the same period. Coach's performance also ran counter to the dynamics of the handbag and accessory market as a whole, which grew by nearly 10 per cent over the previous year.

The difference in sales trends between Coach and its competitors have led some analysts to speculate that the long-time leader has lost its eye for fashion. 'These guys are definitely losing share,' said analyst Brian Yarbrough. 'Fashionwise, they're missing the beat.' Yarbrough isn't alone. Many others assert that, under the same creative direction for 17 years, Coach's designs have grown stale.

Then there is the issue of Coach's price structure — in short, Coach may have taken the premium price point too far. 'Coach tried to eliminate coupon promotions tied directly to its discount outlets, which are the company's biggest source of revenue, and which attract customers looking to stretch their dollars,' said one luxury retail expert. 'The number of people willing and able to pay a premium for luxury brands, like Coach, is getting small as this weak economy continues.' However, price alone would not explain why Coach's business slid at the same time that sales by comparably priced competitors rose. Additionally, while Coach's North American revenues were down last year, sales of its high-end handbags (priced above $400) actually increased.

Some analysts have also questioned the effect of Coach's popularity on its image of exclusivity. A luxury brand's image and customer aspirations often rest on the fact that not everyone can afford it. But Coach has become so accessible, anyone that wants a Coach product can usually find a way to buy one. This availability has been fostered by Coach's outlet stores — company-owned stores that carry prior season merchandise, seconds and lower-quality lines at much lower prices. With the number of customers drawn in by low prices, Coach's outlet stores now account for a sizable 60 per cent of revenues and an even higher percentage of unit sales. Combine that with a healthy secondary market through eBay and other websites, and Coach products are no longer as exclusive as they once were.

Although new as CEO, Luis has been with Coach for the past eight years and oversaw Coach's international expansion. And although Frankfort has stepped down, he is still involved as chairman of the board. Led by these seasoned fashion executives, Coach has a turnaround plan. For starters, the company has hired a new creative director who, according to Luis, is 'providing a fashion relevance for the brand like we have never had'. Both the fashion and investment worlds anxiously await the first designs from the new regime.

In addition to the creative and design changes, Coach is rebalancing its product portfolio. To win back shoppers, Coach will be positioned as a lifestyle brand with greater expansion into footwear, clothing and accessories. Additionally, the company will increase the number of handbag offerings priced at €400 or more, a move that could raise the average price point of Coach's handbags. With all that the brand has at stake, those in charge will not give up easily. The question is, will the new strategy restore Coach to its former glory days?

Questions for discussion

1. What challenges does Coach face relative to pricing its vast product line?
2. Based on principles from the chapter, explain how price affects customer perceptions of the Coach brand.
3. How has increased competition at Coach's price points affected the brand's performance?
4. Will the plan proposed by current Coach leadership be successful in reversing the brand's slide in market share? Why or why not?
5. What recommendations would you make to Coach?

Sources: Andrew Marder, 'Coach, Inc. can't get it together', *Motley Fool*, 30 April 2014, www.fool.com/investing/general/2014/04/30/coach-inc-cant-get-it-together.aspx; Phil Wahba, 'Coach sales in North America plummet as market share erodes', Reuters, 22 January 2014, http://in.reuters.com/article/2014/01/22/coach-results-idINL3N0KW3V920140122; Ashley Lutz, 'Coach is slipping fast, and it can all be traced to one major mistake', *Business Insider*, 22 October 2012, www.businessinsider.com/coach-is-losing-its-value-2012-10; and additional information taken from www.coach.com/online/handbags/genWCM-10551-10051-en-/Coach_US/CompanyInformation/Investor-Relations/CompanyProfile, accessed January 2016.

CHAPTER TWELVE

Marketing channels: delivering customer value

Chapter preview

We now arrive at the third marketing mix tool – distribution. Companies rarely work alone in creating value for customers and building profitable customer relationships. Instead, most are only a single link in a larger supply chain and marketing channel. An individual firm's success depends not only on how well *it* performs but also on how well its *entire marketing channel* competes with competitors' channels. The first part of this chapter explores the nature of marketing channels and the marketer's channel design and management decisions. We then examine physical distribution – or logistics – an area that is growing dramatically in importance and sophistication. In the next chapter, we'll look more closely at two major channel intermediaries: retailers and wholesalers.

We start by looking at Netflix. Through innovative distribution, Netflix has become the world's largest video subscription service. But to stay on top in the turbulent video distribution industry, Netflix must continue to innovate at a breakneck pace or risk being pushed aside by others.

Objective outline

> **Objective 1** Explain why companies use marketing channels and discuss the functions these channels perform.
> Supply chains and the value delivery network
> (pp. 340–341)
> The nature and importance of marketing channels
> (pp. 341–345)

> **Objective 2** Discuss how channel members interact and how they organise to perform the work of the channel.
> Channel behaviour and organisation (pp. 345–351)

> **Objective 3** Identify the major channel alternatives open to a company.
> Channel design decisions (pp. 351–356)

> **Objective 4** Explain how companies select, motivate and evaluate channel members.
> Channel management decisions (pp. 356–357)
> Public policy and distribution decisions (pp. 357–358)

> **Objective 5** Discuss the nature and importance of marketing logistics and integrated supply chain management.
> Marketing logistics and supply chain management
> (pp. 358–365)

Netflix's channel innovation: finding the future by abandoning the past

Time and again, Netflix has innovated its way to the top in the distribution of video entertainment. In the early 2000s, Netflix's revolutionary DVD-by-mail service put all but the most powerful video-rental stores out of business. In 2007, Netflix's then-groundbreaking move into digital streaming once again revolutionised how people accessed cinema and other video content. Now, with Netflix leading the pack, video distribution has become a boiling pot of emerging technologies and high-tech competitors, one that offers both frightening risks and mind-bending opportunities.

Just ask Blockbuster. Only a few years ago, the giant bricks-and-mortar video-rental chain just about owned the industry. Then along came Netflix, the fledgling DVD-by-mail service. First thousands, then millions, of subscribers were drawn to Netflix's innovative distribution model – no more trips to the video rental store, no more late fees, and a selection of more than 100,000 titles that dwarfed anything Blockbuster could offer in a conventional retail shop. Even better, Netflix's $5-a-month subscription rate in the US cost little more than renting a single video from Blockbuster. In 2010, as Netflix surged, once-mighty Blockbuster fell into bankruptcy.

The Blockbuster riches-to-rags story underscores the turmoil that typifies today's video distribution business. In only the past few years, a glut of video access options has materialised. At the same time that Netflix ascended and Blockbuster plunged, Coinstar's Redbox came out of nowhere to build a novel network of $1-a-day DVD-rental kiosks in the US. Then high-tech start-ups such as Hulu – with its high-quality, ad-supported free access to films and current TV shows – began pushing digital streaming via the Internet.

All along the way, Netflix has acted boldly to stay ahead of the competition. For example, in 2007, rather than sitting on the success of its still-hot DVD-by-mail business, Netflix and its CEO, Reed Hastings, set their sights on a then-revolutionary new video distribution model: to deliver the Netflix service to every Internet-connected screen, from laptops to Internet-ready TVs to mobile phones and other Wi-Fi-enabled devices. Netflix began by launching its Watch Instantly service, which let Netflix members stream movies instantly to their computers as part of their monthly membership fee, even if it came at the expense of Netflix's still-booming DVD business.

Although Netflix didn't pioneer digital streaming, it poured resources into improving the technology and building the largest streaming library. It built a huge subscriber base and sales and profits soared. With its massive physical DVD library and a streaming library of more than 20,000 high-definition movies accessible via 200 different Internet-ready devices, it seemed that nothing could stop Netflix.

Netflix has innovated its way to the top in the distribution of video material.

Source: Andrew Harrer/Bloomberg via Getty Images

But Netflix's stunning success drew a slew of resourceful competitors. In 2010, video giants such as Google's YouTube and Apple's iTunes began renting movie downloads, and Hulu introduced its subscription-based Hulu Plus. To stay ahead, even to survive, Netflix needed to keep the innovation pedal to the metal. So in the summer of 2011, in an ambitious but risky move, CEO Hastings made an all-out bet on digital streaming. He split off Netflix's still-thriving DVD-by-mail service into a separate business named Qwikster and required separate subscriptions for DVD rentals and streaming (at a startling 60 per cent price increase for customers using both). The Netflix name would now stand for nothing but digital streaming, which would be the primary focus of the company's future growth.

Although perhaps visionary, Netflix's abrupt changes didn't sit well with customers. Some 800,000 subscribers dropped the service, and Netflix's stock price plummeted by almost two-thirds. To repair the damage, within only weeks, Netflix admitted its blunder and reversed its decision to set up a separate Qwikster operation. However, despite the setback,

Netflix retained its separate, higher pricing for DVDs by mail. Netflix rebounded quickly, replacing all of its lost subscribers and then some. What's more, with a 60 per cent higher price, revenues and profits rose as well. Netflix's stock price was once again skyrocketing.

Now more than ever, Hastings seems bent on speeding up the company's leap from success in DVDs to success in streaming. Although customers can still access Netflix's world's-biggest DVD library, the company's promotions and online site barely mention that option. The focus is now squarely on streaming video. Netflix's current 48 million paid subscribers watch an astounding 1.4 billion hours of movies and TV programmes every month.

Despite its continuing success, Netflix knows that it can't rest its innovation machine. Competition continues to move at a blurring rate. For example, Amazon's Prime Instant Video offers instant streaming of thousands of films and TV shows to Amazon Prime members at no extra cost. Google has moved beyond its YouTube rental service with Google Play, an all-media entertainment portal for movies, music, e-books and apps. Comcast offers Xfinity Streampix, which lets subscribers stream older movies and television programmes via their TVs, laptops, tablets or smartphones. Coinstar and Verizon have now joined forces to form Redbox Instant by Verizon, which offers subscription-based streaming of older movies and newer pay-per-view content. And Apple and Samsung are creating smoother integration with streaming content via smart TVs.

Moving ahead, as the industry settles into streaming as the main delivery model, content – not just delivery – will be a key to distancing Netflix from the rest of the pack. Given its head start, Netflix remains well ahead in the content race. However, Amazon, Hulu Plus and other competitors are working feverishly to sign contracts with big film and TV content providers. But so is Netflix. It recently scored a big win with a Disney exclusive – soon, Netflix will be the only place viewers can stream Disney's deep catalogue and new releases from Walt Disney Animation, Marvel, Pixar and Lucasfilm.

But as content-licensing deals with film and television studios become harder to get, in yet another innovative video distribution twist, Netflix and its competitors are now developing their own original content at a feverish pace. Once again, Netflix appears to have the upper hand. For example, it led the way with the smash hit *House of Cards*, a US version of a hit British political drama series produced by Hollywood bigwigs David Fincher and Kevin Spacey. Based on its huge success with *House of Cards*, Netflix developed a number of other original series, including *Hemlock Grove, Lillyhammer* and *Orange is the New Black*, its most successful release to date. Such efforts have left the rest of the video industry scrambling to keep up. And Netflix is just getting started. It plans to invest $300 million a year in developing new original content, adding at least five original titles annually.

Thus, from DVDs by mail, to Watch Instantly, to video streaming on almost any device, to developing original content, Netflix has stayed ahead of the howling pack by doing what it does best – innovate and revolutionise distribution. What's next? No one really knows. But one thing seems certain: whatever's coming, if Netflix doesn't lead the change, it risks being left behind – and quickly. In this fast-changing business, new tricks grow old in a hurry. To stay ahead, as one headline suggests, Netflix must 'find its future by abandoning its past'.[1]

As the Netflix story shows, good and innovative distribution strategies can contribute strongly to enhancing customer value and create competitive advantage for a firm. But firms cannot bring value to customers by themselves. Instead, they must work closely with other firms in a larger value delivery network.

Author comment

A company can't go it alone in creating customer value. It must work within an entire network of partners to accomplish this task. Individual companies and brands don't compete, their entire value delivery networks do.

SUPPLY CHAINS AND THE VALUE DELIVERY NETWORK

Producing a product or a service and making it available to buyers requires building relationships not only with customers but also with key suppliers and resellers in the company's *supply chain*. This supply chain consists of upstream and downstream partners. Upstream from the company is the set of firms that supply the raw materials, components, parts, information, finances and expertise needed to create a product or a service. Marketers, however, have traditionally focused on the downstream side of the supply chain – on the *marketing channels* (or *distribution channels*) that look toward the customer. Downstream marketing channel partners, such as wholesalers and retailers, form a vital connection between the firm and its customers.

In fact, the term *supply chain* may be too limited; it takes a *make-and-sell* view of the business. It suggests that raw materials, productive inputs and factory capacity should serve as the starting point for market planning. A better term would be *demand chain* because it suggests a *sense-and-respond* view of the market. Under this view, planning starts by identifying the needs of the target customers, to which the company responds by organising a chain of resources and activities with the goal of creating customer value.

Yet even a demand chain view of a business may be too limited because it takes a step-by-step, linear view of purchase, production and consumption activities. Instead, most large companies today are engaged in building and managing a complex, continuously evolving *value delivery network*.

As defined in Chapter 2, a **value delivery network** is composed of the company, suppliers, distributors and, ultimately, customers who 'partner' with each other to improve the performance of the entire system. For example, Adidas makes great sports shoes and clothing. But to make and market just one of its many lines – say, its new Adidas originals line of retro shoes and vintage street wear – Adidas manages a huge network of people within the company. It also coordinates the efforts of thousands of suppliers, retailers ranging from JD Sports to online seller Amazon, and advertising agencies and other marketing service firms that must work together to create customer value and establish the line's 'unite all originals' positioning.

This chapter focuses on marketing channels – on the downstream side of the value delivery network. We examine four major questions concerning marketing channels: What is the nature of marketing channels and why are they important? How do channel firms interact and organise to do the work of the channel? What problems do companies face in designing and managing their channels? What role do physical distribution and supply chain management play in attracting and satisfying customers? In Chapter 13, we will look at marketing channel issues from the viewpoint of retailers and wholesalers.

Value delivery network— A network composed of the company, suppliers, distributors and, ultimately, customers who 'partner' with each other to improve the perfomance of the entire system in delivering customer value.

THE NATURE AND IMPORTANCE OF MARKETING CHANNELS

Few producers sell their goods directly to final users. Instead, most use intermediaries to bring their products to market. They try to forge a **marketing channel (or distribution channel)** – a set of interdependent organisations that help make a product or a service available for use or consumption by the consumer or business user.

A company's channel decisions are directly linked to every other marketing decision. Pricing depends on whether the company works with discount chains, uses high-quality specialty stores, or sells directly to consumers online. The firm's sales force and communications decisions depend on how much persuasion, training, motivation and support its channel partners need. Whether a company develops or acquires certain new products may depend on how well those products fit the capabilities of its channel members.

Companies often pay too little attention to their distribution channels – sometimes with damaging results. In contrast, many companies have used imaginative distribution systems to gain a competitive advantage. Enterprise revolutionised the car-rental business by establishing rental offices away from airports. Apple turned the retail music business on its head by selling music for the iPod via the Internet on iTunes. And FedEx's creative and imposing distribution system made it a leader in express delivery.

Author comment

In this section, we look at the downstream side of the value delivery network - the marketing channel organisations that connect the company and its customers. To understand their value, imagine life without retailers - say, without grocery stores or department stores.

Marketing channel (distribution channel)—A set of interdependent organisations that help make a product or service available for use or consumption by the consumer or business user.

Brandy Melville is the hottest teen retailer you have never heard of - unless you are a tween- or teen-age girl (or one of their parents.

Source: Kevin George/Alamy Images

The impact of the Internet may be substantial. For example, Brandy Melville in the US has been described as Instagram's first retail success, as social media change the shape of distribution channels, and it is one of many developments in the fashion business that blur the distinction between online and conventional retail channels:[2]

Brandy Melville is the hottest teen retailer you have never heard of — unless you are a tween- or teen-age girl (or one of their parents). The company was founded in Italy in the 1990s and now has 45 stores in the US, Canada and Europe. And it is growing fast — sales estimated at $125 million and expanding at 20–25 per cent a year. Storefronts are discreet, the company does little advertising, and the stores' popularity is driven almost exclusively through social media — it has 2.2 million followers on its main Instagram site, 65,000 followers on Twitter and 218,000 Likes on Facebook. Brandy Melville sets trends — it offers clothing that allows the teen consumer to define their own look — basic styling with a unique approach to layering. Teens who are into the brand seem to like the idea that Brandy Melville clothes are not for everyone, and there is a degree of exclusivity. Most of the clothes come in one size only on the basis that 'one size fits most'.

Increasingly, new types of competition based on innovative channel designs can disrupt markets anywhere. Chinese e-commerce phenomenon Alibaba became the world's largest stock market flotation in 2014 with a $22 billion valuation on the New York stock exchange, which some see as heralding the end of US dominance in e-commerce:[3]

Founded by Jack Ma in 1999, Alibaba dominates the Chinese e-commerce sector and this dominant market position has made it hugely profitable. Alibaba started as a listings page for Chinese firms looking for overseas buyers but has ballooned since those days. Alibaba is the world's largest online marketplace for trade between companies and has built an unrivalled online retail platform in China. It ships around £90 billion worth of goods a year, and handles more packages annually than Amazon and eBay combined. Its Taobao website has been the engine of growth by linking consumers together on a peer-to-peer model. More recent emphasis is on the Tmall website that hosts large retailers selling to consumers. Alibaba has taken the fragmented market of the most heterogeneous market in the world — China — and united it on the Internet. For example, Alibaba is famous for 'singles' day' — the biggest annual e-commerce discounting day in China, in the course of which last year Alibaba processed 254 million orders billing $5.8 billion on the day, dwarfing the equivalent Cyber Monday in the US.

   In 2014, Alibaba alone accounted for 8 per cent of all retail sales in China. The company has 280 million customers who are habitual digital shoppers. Alibaba operates on a net margin of 50 per cent because its model is to connect buyers and sellers and leave others with the costly business of moving goods around. Helping merchants to market their goods in China accounts for half Alibaba's sales; sellers' commissions account for a quarter; and most of the rest comes from the wholesale business and international commerce. Cost of sales is incredibly low. The wall around Alibaba's business is the network effect – the company has the most buyers and sellers giving current users an excellent reason to stay and new users reasons to come. This volume translates into revenues and profit so Alibaba can invest in other businesses. Businesses in China using Alibaba account for the majority of the 27 million packages shipped in China each day. Alibaba is already helping small businesses throughout the United States. For example, 2015 saw Alibaba team up with peer-to-peer lender Lending Club to provide small

Alibaba is the world's largest online marketplace for trade between companies and has built an unrivalled online retail platform in China. It ships around £90 billion worth of goods a year, and handles more packages than Amazon and eBay combined.

Source: ERIC FEFERBERG/AFP/ Getty Images

business loans to US customers. However, Mr Ma is more interested in developing markets in Asia and Africa than going head-to-head with rivals Amazon and eBay in the developed world. Central to the Alibaba channel is brokering sales into and out of China in a new age of border-hopping commerce that bypasses traditional intermediaries. While Amazon and eBay have single online hubs with regional versions across the world, Alibaba has created multiple sites – each tailored for a different style of transaction, and each with the potential for massive global reach. Alibaba is a global channel in a way that Amazon is not, because it facilitates so much business into and out of China. Since the flotation, rivals have been braced for Alibaba's inevitable push overseas.

Distribution channel decisions often involve long-term commitments to other firms. For example, companies such as Ford, McDonald's or Nike can easily change their advertising, pricing or promotion programmes. They can scrap old products and introduce new ones as market tastes demand. But when they set up distribution channels through contracts with franchisees, independent dealers or large retailers, they cannot readily replace these channels with company-owned stores or Internet sites if the conditions change. Therefore, management must design its channels carefully, with an eye on both today's likely selling environment and tomorrow's as well.

How channel members add value

Why do producers give some of the selling job to channel partners? After all, doing so means giving up some control over how and to whom they sell their products. Producers use intermediaries because they create greater efficiency in making goods available to target markets. Through their contacts, experience, specialisation and scale of operation, intermediaries usually offer the firm more than it can achieve on its own.

Figure 12.1 shows how using intermediaries can provide economies. Figure 12.1A shows three manufacturers, each using direct marketing to reach three customers. This system requires nine different contacts. Figure 12.1B shows the three manufacturers working through one distributor, which contacts the three customers. This system requires only six contacts. In this way, intermediaries reduce the amount of work that must be done by both producers and consumers.

From the economic system's point of view, the role of marketing intermediaries is to transform the assortments of products made by producers into the assortments wanted by consumers. Producers make narrow ranges of products in large quantities, but consumers want broad ranges of products in small quantities. Marketing channel members buy large quantities from many producers and break them down into the smaller quantities and broader ranges desired by consumers.

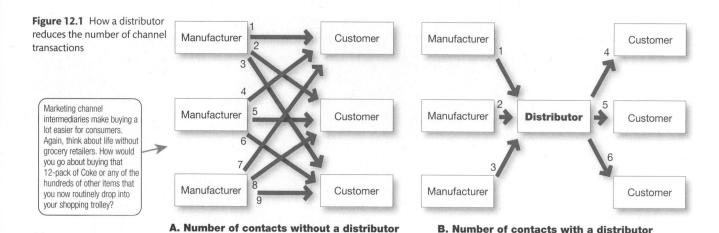

Figure 12.1 How a distributor reduces the number of channel transactions

Marketing channel intermediaries make buying a lot easier for consumers. Again, think about life without grocery retailers. How would you go about buying that 12-pack of Coke or any of the hundreds of other items that you now routinely drop into your shopping trolley?

A. Number of contacts without a distributor

B. Number of contacts with a distributor

For example, Unilever makes millions of bars of hand soap each week, but you want to buy only a few bars at a time. So big food, pharmaceuticals and discount retailers, such as Tesco, Boots and Superdrug, buy Unilever's soaps by the lorry-load to stock their stores' shelves. In turn, you can buy a single bar of soap, along with a shopping basket full of small quantities of toothpaste, shampoo and other related products as you need them. Thus, intermediaries play an important role in matching supply and demand.

In making products and services available to consumers, channel members add value by bridging the major time, place and possession gaps that separate goods and services from those who use them. Members of the marketing channel perform many key functions:

- *Information*: Gathering and distributing marketing research and intelligence information about actors and forces in the marketing environment needed for planning and aiding exchange.
- *Promotion*: Developing and spreading persuasive communications about an offer.
- *Contact*: Finding and engaging prospective buyers.
- *Matching*: Shaping offers to the buyer's needs, including activities such as manufacturing, grading, assembling and packaging.
- *Negotiation*: Reaching an agreement on price and other terms so that ownership or possession can be transferred.

Others help to fulfil the completed transactions:

- *Physical distribution*: Transporting and storing goods.
- *Financing*: Acquiring and using funds to cover the costs of the channel work.
- *Risk taking*: Assuming the risks of carrying out the channel work.

The question is not *whether* these functions need to be performed – they must be – but rather *who* will perform them. To the extent that the manufacturer performs these functions, its costs go up, and, therefore, its prices must be higher. When some of these functions are shifted to intermediaries, the producer's costs and prices may be lower, but the intermediaries must charge more to cover the costs of their work. In dividing the work of the channel, the various functions should be assigned to the channel members who can add the most value for the cost.

Number of channel levels

Companies can design their distribution channels to make products and services available to customers in different ways. Each layer of marketing intermediaries that performs some work in bringing the product and its ownership closer to the final buyer is a **channel level**. Because both the producer and the final consumer perform some work, they are part of every channel.

The *number of intermediary levels* indicates the *length* of a channel. Figure 12.2 shows both consumer and business channels of different lengths. Figure 12.2A shows several common

Channel level—A layer of intermediaries that performs some work in bringing the product and its ownership closer to the final buyer.

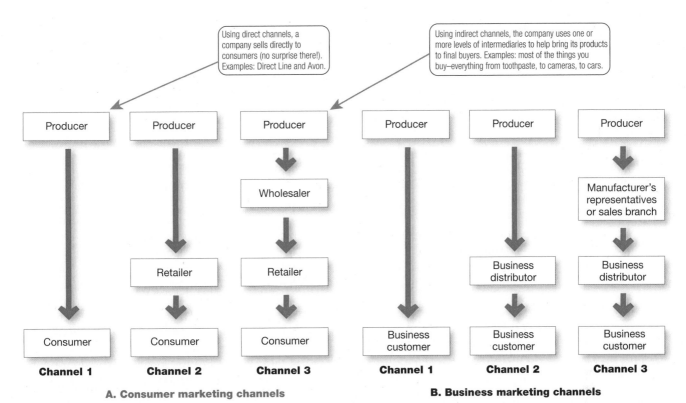

Figure 12.2 Consumer and business marketing channels

consumer distribution channels. Channel 1, called a **direct marketing channel**, has no intermediary levels – the company sells directly to consumers. For example, companies like Avon Cosmetics sell their products direct to consumers – door-to-door, through home and office sales parties, and on the Internet. Another example is Amway, with a sales force of more than 3 million people, Amway markets and sells health, beauty, durables and homecare and personal care products to consumers in more than 90 countries and territories worldwide. In the UK, Direct Line sells insurance direct via the telephone and the Internet. The remaining channels in Figure 12.2A are **indirect marketing channels**, containing one or more intermediaries.

Figure 12.2B shows some common business distribution channels. The business marketer can use its own sales force to sell directly to business customers. Or it can sell to various types of intermediaries, who in turn sell to these customers. Although consumer and business marketing channels with even more levels can sometimes be found, these are less common. From the producer's point of view, a greater number of levels means less control and greater channel complexity. Moreover, all the institutions in the channel are connected by several types of *flows*. These include the *physical flow* of products, the *flow of ownership*, the *payment flow*, the *information flow* and the *promotion flow*. These flows can make channels with only one or a few levels very complex.

CHANNEL BEHAVIOUR AND ORGANISATION

Distribution channels are more than simple collections of firms tied together by various flows. They are complex behavioural systems in which people and companies interact to accomplish individual, company and channel goals. Some channel systems consist of only informal interactions among loosely organised firms. Others consist of formal interactions guided by strong organisational structures. Moreover, channel systems do not stand still – new types of intermediaries emerge, and whole new channel systems evolve. Here we look at channel behaviour and how members organise to do the work of the channel.

Direct marketing channel—A marketing channel that has no intermediary levels.

Indirect marketing channel—A marketing channel containing one of more intermediary levels.

Author comment

Channels are composed of more than just boxes and arrows on paper. They are behavioural systems composed of real companies and people who interact to accomplish their individual and collective goals. Like groups of people, sometimes they work well together and sometimes they don't work well together.

Channel behaviour

A marketing channel consists of firms that have partnered for their common good. Each channel member depends on the others. For example, a Jaguar car dealer depends on Jaguar to design cars that meet customer needs. In turn, Jaguar depends on the dealer to attract customers, persuade them to buy Jaguar cars, and service the cars after the sale. Each Jaguar dealer also depends on other dealers to provide good sales and service that will uphold the brand's reputation. In fact, the success of individual Jaguar dealers depends on how well the entire Jaguar marketing channel competes with the channels of other car manufacturers.

Each channel member plays a specialised role in the channel. For example, the role of consumer electronics maker Samsung is to produce electronics products that consumers will like and create demand through advertising in each country. The retailer's role is to display the Samsung products in convenient locations or online, answer buyers' questions and complete sales. The channel will be most effective when each member assumes the tasks it can do best.

Ideally, because the success of individual channel members depends on overall channel success, all channel firms should work together smoothly. They should understand and accept their roles, coordinate their activities, and cooperate to attain overall channel goals. However, individual channel members rarely take such a broad view. Cooperating to achieve overall channel goals sometimes means giving up individual company goals. Although channel members depend on one another, they often act alone in their own short-run best interests. They often disagree on who should do what and for what rewards. Such disagreements over goals, roles and rewards generate **channel conflict**.

Horizontal conflict occurs among firms at the same level of the channel. For instance, some Ford dealers in a particular location might complain that other dealers in the same location steal sales from them by pricing too low or advertising outside their assigned territories. Or Holiday Inn franchisees might complain about other Holiday Inn operators overcharging guests or giving poor service, hurting the overall Holiday Inn image.

Vertical conflict, conflicts between different levels of the same channel, is even more common. For example, McDonald's has recently faced growing conflict with its corps of independent franchisees:[4]

Channel conflict—
Disagreements among marketing channel members on goals, roles and rewards – who should do what and for what rewards?

> In a recent company webcast, based on rising customer complaints that service isn't fast or friendly enough, McDonald's told its franchisees that their cashiers need to smile more. At the same time, it seems, the franchisees weren't very happy with McDonald's, either. A recent survey of franchise owners reflected growing franchisee discontent with the corporation. Much of the conflict stems from a recent slowdown in system-wide sales that has both sides on edge. The most basic conflicts are financial. McDonald's makes its money from franchisee royalties based on total system sales. In contrast, franchisees make money on margins — what's left over after their costs.
>
> To reverse the sales slump, McDonald's has increased emphasis on low-price menu items, a strategy that increases corporate sales but squeezes franchisee margins. Franchisees are also grumbling about adding popular but more complex menu items, such as Snack Wraps, that increase the top line for McDonald's but add preparation and staffing costs for franchisees while slowing down service. McDonald's is also asking franchisees to make costly restaurant upgrades and overhauls. As one survey respondent summarised, there's 'too much reliance on price-pointing and discounting to drive top-line sales, which is where the corporate cow feeds'. In all, the survey rates McDonald's current franchisee relations at a decade-low 1.93 out of a possible 5, in the 'fair' to 'poor' range. That fact might explain both the lack of smiles and the increasing customer complaints. According to one restaurant consultant, 'there's a huge connection' between franchisee satisfaction and customer service.

Some conflict in the channel takes the form of healthy competition. Such competition can be good for the channel – without it, the channel could become passive and non-innovative. For example, McDonald's conflict with its franchisees might represent normal give-and-take over the respective rights of the channel partners. However, severe or prolonged conflict can disrupt channel effectiveness and cause lasting harm to channel relationships. McDonald's must manage the channel conflict carefully to keep it from getting out of hand.

Vertical marketing systems

For the channel as a whole to perform well, each channel member's role must be specified, and channel conflict must be managed. The channel will perform better if it includes a firm, agency or mechanism that provides leadership and has the power to assign roles and manage conflict.

Historically, *conventional distribution channels* have lacked such leadership and power, often resulting in damaging conflict and poor performance. One of the biggest channel developments over the years, particularly in the huge US market, has been the emergence of *vertical marketing systems* that provide channel leadership. Figure 12.3 contrasts the two types of channel arrangements.

A **conventional distribution channel** consists of one or more independent producers, wholesalers and retailers. Each is a separate business seeking to maximise its own profits, perhaps even at the expense of the system as a whole. No channel member has much control over the other members, and no formal means exist for assigning roles and resolving channel conflict.

In contrast, a **vertical marketing system** (**VMS**) consists of producers, wholesalers and retailers acting as a unified system. One channel member owns the others, has contracts with them, or wields so much power that they must all cooperate. The VMS can be dominated by the producer, the wholesaler or the retailer.

There are three major types of VMSs: *corporate, contractual* and *administered*. Each uses a different means for setting up leadership and power in the channel.

Corporate VMS

A **corporate VMS** integrates successive stages of production and distribution under single ownership. Coordination and conflict management are attained through regular organisational channels. For example, little-known Italian eyewear maker Luxottica is the world's largest eye wear business. The company produces many famous eyewear brands – including its own Ray-Ban and Oakley brands and licensed brands such as Burberry, Chanel, Polo Ralph Lauren, Dolce & Gabbana, Donna Karan, Prada, Versace and Bulgari. It then sells these brands through some of the world's largest optical chains – LensCrafters, Pearle Vision and Sunglass Hut – that it also owns.[5]

Integrating the entire distribution chain – from its own design and manufacturing operations to distribution through its own managed stores – has turned Spanish clothing chain Zara into the world's fastest-growing fast-fashion retailer:[6]

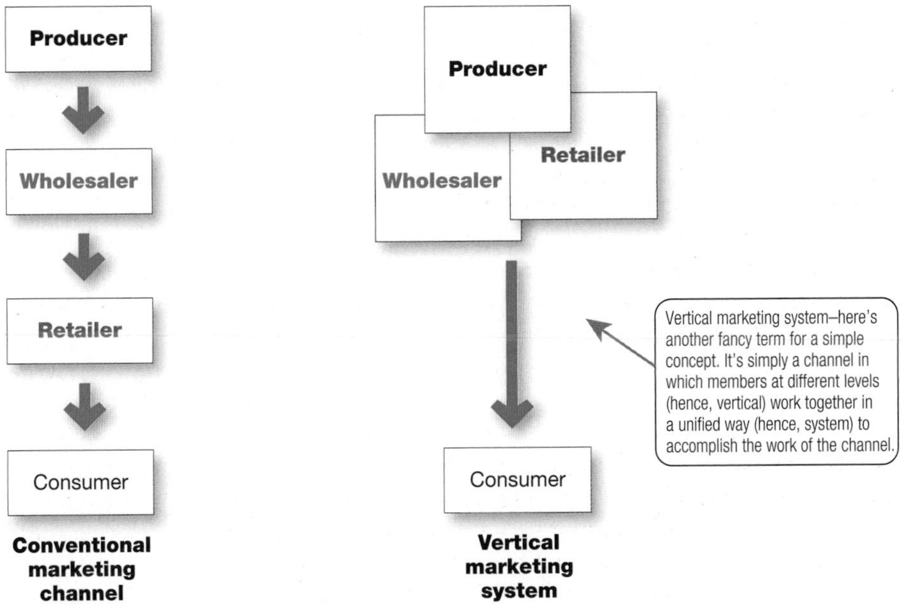

Conventional distribution channel—A channel consisting of one or more independent producers, wholesalers, and retailers. Each a separate business seeking to maximise its own profits, perhaps even at the expense of profits for the system as a whole.

Vertical marketing system (VMS)—A channel structure in which producers, wholesalers and retailers act as a unified system, One channel member owns the others, has contracts with them, or has so much power that they all cooperate.

Corporate VMS—A vertical marketing system that combines successive stages of production and distribution under single ownership – channel leadership is established through common ownership.

Figure 12.3 Comparison of conventional distribution channel with vertical marketing system

Vertical marketing system—here's another fancy term for a simple concept. It's simply a channel in which members at different levels (hence, vertical) work together in a unified way (hence, system) to accomplish the work of the channel.

Conventional marketing channel

Vertical marketing system

In recent years, fashion retailer Zara has attracted a near cult-like clientele of shoppers swarming to buy its 'cheap chic' — stylish designs that resemble those of big-name fashion houses but at moderate prices. However, Zara's amazing success comes not just from *what* it sells, but from *how fast* its cutting-edge distribution system *delivers* what it sells. Zara delivers fast fashion — really fast fashion. Thanks to vertical integration, Zara can take a new fashion concept through design, manufacturing and store-shelf placement in as little as three weeks, whereas competitors such as Gap, Benetton or H&M often take six months or more. And the resulting low costs let Zara offer the very latest mid-market chic at down-market prices.

Speedy design and distribution allows Zara to introduce a copious supply of new fashions — at three times the rate of competitor introductions. Then, Zara's distribution system supplies its stores with small shipments of new merchandise twice a week, compared with competing chains' outlets, which get large shipments seasonally, usually just four to six times per year. The combination of a large number of timely new fashions delivered in frequent small batches gives Zara stores a continually updated merchandise mix that brings customers back more often. Fast turnover also results in less outdated and discounted merchandise. 'Instead of betting on tomorrow's hot look,' says one analyst, 'Zara can wait to see what customers are actually buying — and make that.'

Contractual VMS

Contractual VMS—A vertical marketing system in which independent firms at different levels of production and distribution join together through contracts.

A **contractual VMS** consists of independent firms at different levels of production and distribution who join together through contracts to obtain more economies or sales impact than each could achieve alone. Channel members coordinate their activities and manage conflict through contractual agreements.

Franchise organisation—A contractual vertical marketing system in which a channel member called a franchisor, links several stages in the production–distribution process.

The **franchise organisation** is the most common type of contractual relationship. A channel member called a *franchisor* links several stages in the production-distribution process. In Europe, even though American brands are still hugely popular, many franchises originating in European countries have also become big names across the continent and beyond. Some of the most successful European franchises include: Tecnocasa, an Italian estate agency franchise founded in 1986, that has 2,654 units in ten countries; Jean Louis David, a French hairdressing company which has a worldwide network of more than a thousand units; and, Foto-Quelle, a German franchise that has become the world's largest dealer in photographic equipment. Almost every kind of business has been franchised – from hotels and fast-food restaurants to dental centres and dating services, from wedding consultants and cleaning services to fitness centres and funeral homes.

There are three types of franchises. The first type is the *manufacturer-sponsored retailer franchise system*. Ford Motor Company and its network of independent franchised dealers is an example of a manufacturer-sponsored system. The second type is the *manufacturer-sponsored wholesaler franchise system*. For example, Coca-Cola licenses bottlers (wholesalers) in various world markets, who buy Coca-Cola syrup concentrate and then bottle and sell the finished product to retailers in their local markets. The third type is the *service-firm-sponsored retailer franchise system* – for example, Burger King and its nearly 12,100 franchisee-operated restaurants around the world. Other examples can be found in everything from car rentals (e.g., Hertz and Avis), clothing retailers (e.g., The Athlete's Foot, Laura Ashley), and hotels (e.g., Holiday Inn and Ramada Inn) to estate agencies (e.g., Century 21) and personal services (e.g., Mr. Handyman, and Molly Maid).

The fact that most consumers cannot tell the difference between contractual and corporate VMSs shows how successfully the contractual organisations compete with corporate chains. Chapter 13 presents a fuller discussion of the various contractual VMSs.

Administered VMS

Administered VMS—A vertical marketing system that coordinates successive stages of production and distribution through the size and power of one of the parties.

In an **administered VMS**, leadership is assumed not through common ownership or contractual ties but through the size and power of one or a few dominant channel members. Manufacturers of a top brand can obtain strong trade cooperation and support from resellers. For example,

P&G, and Apple can command an unusually high level of cooperation from resellers regarding displays, shelf space, promotions and price policies. In turn, large retailers such as Walmart, Carrefour, Metro and Tesco can exert a very strong influence on the many manufacturers that supply the products they sell.

In the normal push and pull between mega-retailers like Walmart in the US or Tesco in the UK, and consumer goods suppliers, the retailer usually gets its own way. For example, for a branded cleaning product manufacturer in the UK, sales to Tesco might be 30 per cent of its total sales, whereas the product is only a fraction of a per cent of the retailer's total sales. For the many such brands, maintaining a strong relationship with the giant retailer is crucial.[7]

Horizontal marketing systems

Another channel development is the **horizontal marketing system**, in which two or more companies at one level join together to follow a new marketing opportunity. By working together, companies can combine their financial, production or marketing resources to accomplish more than any one company could alone.

Companies might join forces with competitors or non-competitors. They might work with each other on a temporary or permanent basis, or they may create a separate company. For example, competing big media companies Fox Broadcasting, Disney-ABC and NBCUniversal (Comcast) jointly own and market Hulu, the successful online subscription service that provides on-demand streaming of TV shows, films and other video content. Together, they compete more effectively against digital streaming competitors such as Netflix. Walmart partners with non-competitor McDonald's to place 'express' versions of McDonald's restaurants in Walmart stores. McDonald's benefits from Walmart's heavy store traffic, and Walmart keeps hungry shoppers from needing to go elsewhere to eat. In the UK, Tesco has a similar arrangement with Krispy Kreme doughnuts.

Such channel arrangements also work well globally. For example, competitors General Mills and Nestlé operate a joint venture – Cereal Partners Worldwide – to market General Mills BigG cereal brands in 130 countries outside North America. General Mills supplies a kitchen cabinet full of quality cereal brands, whereas Nestlé contributes its extensive international distribution channels and local market knowledge. The 30-year-old alliance produces $1.1 billion in revenues for General Mills.[8]

Currently, excess capacity in UK supermarkets is driving retailers to collaborate by placing concession stores within major supermarkets. With rapid expansion now a thing of the past, supermarkets are looking to high street retailers and leisure operators to take up their unproductive floor space. The first two Argos stores opened in Sainsbury's in 2015 with more to follow. Sainsbury's has also signed agreements with Jessops, the photographic retailer, and Western Union, to being global money transfer services to its stores. Asda has partnered with French sports retailer Decathlon, while it is expected that Tesco will bring Sports Direct into its stores. Deals between supermarkets and dentists, opticians and hairdressers are expected to follow. These horizontal collaborations have not always been successful in the past: an earlier collaboration between Sainsbury's and Boots ended in acrimony; Tesco's addition of Giraffe restaurants and Harris + Hoole coffee shops to stores did not attract consumers. Nonetheless, it looks like these horizontal collaborations will expand, driven by the excess selling space in large supermarkets, who face tough competition from discounters and convenience stores.[9]

Multi-channel distribution systems

In the past, many companies used a single channel to sell to a single market or market segment. Today, with the proliferation of customer segments and channel possibilities, more and more companies have adopted **multi-channel distribution systems**. Such multi-channel marketing occurs when a single firm sets up two or more marketing channels to reach one or more customer segments.

Horizontal marketing system—A channel arrangement in which two or more companies at one level join together to follow a new marketing opportunity.

Multi-channel distribution system—A distribution system in which a single firm sets up two or more marketing channels to reach one or more customer segments.

Figure 12.4 Multichannel distribution system

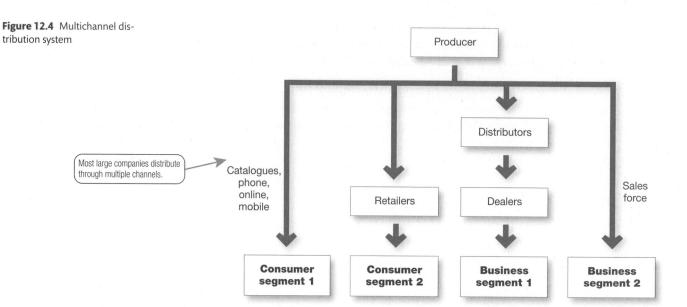

Figure 12.4 shows a multi-channel marketing system. In the figure, the producer sells directly to consumer segment 1 using catalogues, telemarketing, online and mobile channels, and reaches consumer segment 2 through retailers. It sells indirectly to business segment 1 through distributors and dealers and to business segment 2 through its own sales force.

These days, almost every large company, and many small ones, distribute through multiple channels. Multi-channel distribution systems offer many advantages to companies facing large and complex markets. With each new channel, the company expands its sales and market coverage and gains opportunities to tailor its products and services to the specific needs of diverse customer segments. But such multi-channel systems are harder to control, and they generate conflict as more channels compete for customers and sales. For example, in moving from a direct model to a multi-channel distribution approach, Dell faced the challenge of managing the competing demands of third-party computer re-sellers, independent retailers, its own retail operations, and balancing those demands with its direct selling and online operation. Complex channels bring additional risks of conflict.

Changing channel organisation

Changes in technology and the explosive growth of direct and online marketing are having a profound impact on the nature and design of marketing channels. One major trend is toward **disintermediation**. Disintermediation occurs when product or service producers cut out intermediaries and go directly to final buyers or when radically new types of channel intermediaries displace traditional ones.

For example, in the UK, Direct Line changed an industry. It pioneered direct online selling of insurance, cutting out the insurance brokers and their fees. Direct Line prospered through disintermediation. But then, in turn, Direct Line was squeezed out by the next stage of disintermediation in the form of price comparison websites like Gocompare.com and Comparethemarket.com and has had to redesign its brand offer accordingly.[10]

Thus, in many industries, traditional intermediaries are dropping by the wayside. For example, online music download services such as iTunes and Amazon MP3 have pretty much put traditional music retailers out of business. In fact, many once-dominant music retailers such as Tower Records have declared bankruptcy and closed their doors for good. In turn, streaming music services such as Spotify and Vevo are now disintermediating digital download services – digital downloads peaked last year while music streaming increased 32 per cent. Similarly, Amazon.com has devastated traditional booksellers across the world. And the burgeoning online-only merchant has forced highly successful big-box store-based retailers to dramatically rethink their entire operating

Disintermediation—The cutting out of marketing channel intermediaries by product or service producers or the displacement of traditional resellers by radical new types of intermediary.

models. In fact, many retailing experts question whether traditional stores can compete in the long run against online rivals in fields like electronics and computing products and services, as online marketers continue to take business away from traditional bricks-and-mortar retailers.[11]

Similarly, no-frills airlines like Ryanair in Europe and Southwest Airlines in the US, sell their tickets direct to final buyers, cutting travel agents from their marketing channels altogether. There are a growing number of cases where new forms of resellers are displacing traditional intermediaries. Consumers can buy hotel rooms and airline tickets from Expedia.com and Travelocity.com; electronics from eBuyer.com; clothes and accessories from Asos.com; home appliances from AO.com; and books, videos, toys, jewellery, sports, consumer electronics, home and garden items, and almost anything else from Amazon.com – all without ever stepping into a traditional retail store.

Disintermediation presents both opportunities and problems for producers and resellers. Channel innovators who find new ways to add value in the channel can sweep aside traditional resellers and reap the rewards. In turn, traditional intermediaries must continue to innovate to avoid being swept aside.

Innovation in channel designs is not restricted to consumer products but takes place in business-to-business channels as well. For several years, Amazon has been developing a new approach to business-to-business wholesaling:[12]

In 2012, Amazon quietly launched Amazon Supply – a venture into the lucrative world of business-to-business wholesaling. The goal was to grab a share of the $160 billion market for industrial supplies in the US, by using Amazon's power to destroy traditional sales patterns and undercut competitors. By 2014, Amazon Supply was offering 2.2 million products for sale in 17 categories ranging from tools and home improvement to stainless steel. Industry insiders were concerned about the potential impact on America's 35,000 distribution companies, almost all of which are regional and family-run. In 2015, Amazon replaced Amazon Supply with Amazon Business – a new platform to do for business customers what Amazon.com has done for consumers. Companies that register for an Amazon Business account will have access to business-only products ranging from IT and laboratory equipment to food service supplies, with bulk discounts and free two-day shipping on orders over $50. The new launch was Amazon's response to feedback from customers saying they wanted the same Amazon shopping experience when they were buying for work as they received when buying for themselves. Industry experts see Amazon Business as a boon not just for business buyers but also for sellers, who will benefit from Amazon's infrastructure and e-commerce expertise and services.

Like resellers, to remain competitive, many product and service producers must develop new channel opportunities, such as the Internet and other direct channels. However, developing these new channels often brings them into direct competition with their established channels, resulting in conflict.

To ease this problem, companies often look for ways to make going direct a plus for the entire channel. For example, guitar and amp maker Fender knows that many customers would prefer to buy its guitars, amps and accessories online. But selling directly through its website would create conflicts with retail partners, from large chains stocking the instruments to small shops scattered throughout the world, such as Hollywood Music in Milton Keynes in the UK or Freddy for Music in Amman, Jordan. So Fender's website provides detailed information about the company's products, but you can't buy a new Fender Stratocaster or Acoustasonic guitar there. Instead, the Fender website refers you to resellers' websites and stores. Thus, Fender's direct marketing helps both the company and its channel partners.

CHANNEL DESIGN DECISIONS

Author comment

Like everything else in marketing, good channel design begins with analysing customer needs. Remember, marketing channels are really *customer-value delivery networks*.

We now look at several channel decisions manufacturers face. In designing marketing channels, manufacturers struggle between what is ideal and what is practical. A new firm with limited capital usually starts by selling in a limited market area. Deciding on the best channels might not be a problem – the problem might simply be how to convince one or a few good intermediaries to handle the line.

If successful, the new firm can branch out to new markets through existing intermediaries. In smaller markets, the firm might sell directly to retailers; in larger markets, it might sell through distributors. In one part of the country or region, it might grant exclusive franchises while in another, it might sell through all available outlets. Then it might add an Internet store that sells directly to hard-to-reach customers. In this way, channel systems often evolve to meet market opportunities and conditions.

For maximum effectiveness, however, channel analysis and decision making should be more purposeful. **Marketing channel design** calls for analysing consumer needs, setting channel objectives, identifying major channel alternatives and evaluating those alternatives.

Analysing consumer needs

As noted previously, marketing channels are part of the overall *customer-value delivery network*. Each channel member and level adds value for the customer. Thus, designing the marketing channel starts with finding out what target consumers want from the channel. Do consumers want to buy from nearby locations or are they willing to travel to more distant and centralised locations? Would customers rather buy in person, by phone or online? Do they value breadth of assortment of products or do they prefer specialisation? Do consumers want many add-on services (e.g., delivery, installation and repairs) or will they obtain these services elsewhere? The faster the delivery, the greater the assortment provided, and the more add-on services supplied, the greater the channel's service level.

Providing the fastest delivery, the greatest assortment, and the most services may not be possible, practical or desirable. The company and its channel members may not have the resources or skills needed to provide all the desired services. Also, providing higher levels of service results in higher costs for the channel and higher prices for consumers. For example, your local high street hardware store probably provides more personalised service, a more convenient location, and less shopping hassle than the nearest huge B&Q store. But it may also charge higher prices. The company must balance consumer needs not only against the feasibility and costs of meeting these needs but also against customer price preferences. The success of discount retailing shows that consumers will often accept lower service levels in exchange for lower prices. Thus, companies must balance consumer needs not only against the feasibility and costs of meeting these needs but also against customer price preferences.

For example, it has been predicted that the car dealership of the future will be located inside a shopping centre, display only three vehicles, employ no salesmen and be staffed mainly by females. Hyundai, the Korean car manufacturer, has chosen a small retail unit wedged between Body Shop and the Disney Store at Kent's Bluewater shopping centre, as it seeks to capture the eyes of potential customers. This development is a sign of the need for car makers to chase their customers to where they shop, rather than try to lure them to traditional isolated out-of-town car distributorships. The age of the car dealership that relied on family trips to vast forecourts is rapidly passing, giving way to more shopping centre outlets, pop-up shops and online showrooms.[13]

Setting channel objectives

Companies should state their marketing channel objectives in terms of targeted levels of customer service. Usually, a company can identify several segments wanting different levels of service. The company should decide which segments to serve and the best channels to use in each case. In each segment, the company wants to minimise the total channel cost of meeting customer-service requirements.

The company's channel objectives are also influenced by the nature of the company, its products, its marketing intermediaries, its competitors and the environment. For example, the company's size and financial situation determine which marketing functions it can handle itself and which it must give to intermediaries. Companies selling perishable products, like fresh foods, may require more direct marketing to avoid delays and too much handling.

Marketing channel design— Designing effective marketing channels by analysing customer needs, setting channel objectives, identifying major channel alternatives and evaluating those alternatives.

In some cases, a company may want to compete in or near the same outlets that carry competitors' products. For example, top-of-the market Maytag and Amana want their designer kitchen appliances displayed alongside competing brands to facilitate comparison shopping in Costco or Kitchen Zone, or online at Amazon or AO.com. In other cases, companies may avoid the channels used by competitors. Avon Cosmetics, for example, sells directly to consumers through its corps of more than six and a half million representatives worldwide, and has generally avoided going head-to-head with other cosmetics makers for scarce positions in retail stores. Direct Line primarily markets car and homeowner's insurance directly to consumers via the telephone and the Internet rather than through insurance agents or price comparison websites.

Finally, environmental factors such as economic conditions and legal constraints may affect channel objectives and design. For example, in a depressed economy, producers want to distribute their goods in the most economical way, using shorter channels and dropping unneeded services that add to the final price of the goods.

Identifying major alternatives

When the company has defined its channel objectives, it should next identify its major channel alternatives in terms of the *types* of intermediaries, the *number* of intermediaries and the *responsibilities* of each channel member.

Types of intermediaries

A firm should identify the types of channel members available to carry out its channel work. Most companies face many channel member choices. For example, until recently, Dell sold directly to final consumers and business buyers only through its sophisticated phone and Internet marketing channel. It also sold directly to large corporate, institutional and government buyers using its direct sales force. However, to reach more consumers and match competitors such as Samsung and Apple, Dell now sells indirectly through retailers, value-added resellers and independent distributors and dealers who develop computer systems and applications tailored to the special needs of small- and medium-sized business customers – Dell has a multi-channel strategy.

Using many types of resellers in a channel provides both benefits and drawbacks. For example, by selling through retailers and value-added resellers in addition to its own direct channels, Dell can reach more and different kinds of buyers. However, the new channels will be more difficult to manage and control. And the direct and indirect channels will compete with each other for many of the same customers, causing potential conflict. In fact, Dell often finds itself 'stuck in the middle', with its direct sales reps complaining about competition from retail stores, while its value-added resellers complain that the direct sales reps are undercutting their business.

Number of marketing intermediaries

Companies must also determine the number of channel members to use at each level. Three strategies are available: intensive distribution, exclusive distribution and selective distribution. Producers of convenience products and common raw materials typically seek **intensive distribution** – a strategy in which they stock their products in as many outlets as possible. These products must be available where and when consumers want them. For example, toothpaste, confectionery and other similar items are sold in millions of outlets to provide maximum brand exposure and consumer convenience. Many fast-moving consumer goods companies like Kraft, Coca-Cola, Kimberly-Clark and Unilever distribute their products in this way.

By contrast, some producers purposely limit the number of intermediaries handling their products. The extreme form of this practice is **exclusive distribution**, in which the producer gives only a limited number of dealers the exclusive right to distribute its products in their territories. Exclusive distribution is often found in the distribution of luxury brands. For example, exclusive Bentley cars are typically sold by only a handful of authorised dealers in any given market. By granting exclusive distribution, Bentley gains stronger dealer selling support and more control

Intensive distribution—
Stocking the product in as many outlets as possible.

Exclusive distribution—
Giving a limited number of dealers the exclusive right to distribute the company's products in their territories.

over dealer prices, promotion and services. Exclusive distribution also enhances the brand's image and allows for higher mark-ups.

Between intensive and exclusive distribution lies **selective distribution** – the use of more than one but fewer than all the intermediaries who are willing to carry a company's products. Most television, furniture and home appliance brands are distributed in this manner. For example, Hotpoint and Dyson sell their major appliances through dealer networks and selected large retailers. By using selective distribution, they can develop good working relationships with selected channel members and expect a better-than-average selling effort. Selective distribution gives producers good market coverage with more control and less cost than does intensive distribution.

Responsibilities of channel members

The producer and the intermediaries need to agree on the terms and responsibilities of each channel member. They should agree on price policies, conditions of sale, territory rights and the specific services to be performed by each party. The producer should establish a list price and a fair set of discounts for the intermediaries. It must define each channel member's territory, and it should be careful about where it places new resellers.

Mutual services and duties need to be spelled out carefully, especially in franchise and exclusive distribution channels. For example, McDonald's provides franchisees with promotional support, a record-keeping system, training at Hamburger University, and general management assistance. In turn, franchisees must meet company standards for physical facilities and food quality, cooperate with new promotion programmes, provide requested information, and buy specified food products.

Evaluating the major alternatives

Suppose a company has identified several channel alternatives and wants to select the one that will best satisfy its long-run objectives. Each alternative should be evaluated against economic, control and adaptability criteria.

Using *economic criteria*, a company compares the likely sales, costs and profitability of different channel alternatives. What will be the investment required by each channel alternative, and what returns will result? The company must also consider *control issues*. Using intermediaries usually means giving them some control over the marketing of the product, and some intermediaries take more control than others. Other things being equal, the company prefers to keep as much control as possible. Finally, the company must apply *adaptability criteria*. Channels often involve long-term commitments, yet the company wants to keep the channel flexible so that it can adapt to environmental changes. Thus, to be considered, a channel involving long-term commitments should be greatly superior on economic and control grounds.

Designing international distribution channels

International marketers face many additional complexities in designing their channels. Each country or region has its own unique distribution system that has evolved over time and changes very slowly. These channel systems can vary widely from country to country. Thus, global marketers must usually adapt their channel strategies to the existing structures within each country.

In some markets, the distribution system is complex and hard to penetrate, consisting of many layers and large numbers of intermediaries. For example, many Western companies find Japan's distribution system difficult to navigate – it is steeped in tradition and very complex, with many distributors touching a product before it makes it to the store shelf.

At the other extreme, distribution systems in developing countries may be scattered, inefficient, or altogether lacking. For example, China and India are huge markets – each with a population well over one billion people. However, because of inadequate distribution systems, most companies can profitably access only a small portion of the population located in each country's most affluent cities. 'China is a very decentralised market', notes a China trade expert. '[It is] made up of two dozen distinct markets sprawling across 2,000 cities. Each has its own culture.... It's like operating in an asteroid belt.' China's distribution system is so fragmented that logistics costs to wrap, bundle, load, unload, sort, reload and transport goods amount to more than 18 per cent of the country's GDP, far higher than in most other countries. (In the US logistics costs account for about 8.5 per cent of GDP.) After years of effort, global retailers continue to struggle with the challenge of assembling efficient supply chains in China.[14]

Sometimes local conditions can greatly influence how a company distributes products in global markets. For example, in low-income neighbourhoods in Brazil where consumers have limited access to supermarkets, Nestlé supplements its distribution with thousands of self-employed salespeople who sell Nestlé products from refrigerated carts door to door. And in crowded cities in Asia and Africa, fast-food restaurants such as McDonald's and KFC offer home delivery:[15]

The McDonald's delivery guy: in cities like Beijing, Seoul and Cairo armies of motorbike delivery drivers, wearing colourful uniforms and bearing food in specially designed boxes strapped to their backs, make their way through bustling traffic to deliver Big Macs.

Source: Brent Lewin/Bloomberg via Getty Images

> Whereas Americans who want a quick meal delivered to their homes are likely to order in a Chinese meal, people in China and elsewhere around the world are now ordering in from McDonald's or KFC. In big cities such as Beijing, Cairo and Tokyo, where crowded streets and high property costs make drive-throughs impractical, delivery is becoming an important part of fast-food strategy. In these markets, McDonald's and KFC now dispatch legions of motorbike delivery drivers in colourful uniforms to dispense Big Macs and buckets of chicken to customers who call in. In McDonald's Asia/Pacific, Middle East and Africa division, more than 1,500 of its 8,800 restaurants now offer 'McDelivery'. 'We've used the slogan, "If you can't come to us, we'll come to you"', says the division's president. More than 30 per cent of McDonald's total sales in Egypt and 12 per cent of its Singapore sales come from delivery. Similarly, for KFC, delivery accounts for nearly half of all sales in Kuwait and a third of sales in Egypt.

On occasion, international market customs or government regulation can greatly restrict how a company distributes products in global markets. For example, an inefficient distribution structure wasn't the cause of problems for Avon in China – the cause was restrictive government regulation. Fearing the growth of multilevel marketing schemes, the Chinese government banned door-to-door selling altogether in 1998, forcing Avon to abandon its traditional direct marketing approach and sell through retail shops. In 2006, the Chinese government gave Avon and other direct sellers permission to sell door-to-door again, but that permission is tangled in a web of restrictions. Fortunately for Avon, its earlier focus on store sales is helping it weather the restrictions better than most other direct sellers. In fact, through a combination of direct and retail sales, Avon's sales in China are now booming.[16]

Indeed, complications from government policies and local customs affecting marketing and distribution also occur in Europe. For example, in France, the government still regulates the setting of retail prices and sets minimum prices that retailers must pay suppliers. In Germany it took years of debate to eliminate laws that prohibited haggling and put limits on bonus schemes like store-loyalty cards – designed to protect small shopkeepers from large stores. For decades, European retailers could cut prices only during certain periods set by the government and winter sales were in the new year, not at Christmas. In many European countries, the hours stores are open is also regulated by local and central government – even in Britain, one of the most deregulated European states, stores can only open six hours on Sundays. Some retailers in Europe like

Galeries Lafayette in Paris and Harrods in London still stick to a full-priced Christmas, on the grounds it makes little sense to discount when people are desperate to buy.[17]

International marketers face a wide range of channel alternatives. Designing efficient and effective channel systems between and within various country markets poses a difficult challenge. We discuss international distribution decisions further in Chapter 19.

CHANNEL MANAGEMENT DECISIONS

Once the company has reviewed its channel alternatives and determined the best channel design, it must implement and manage the chosen channel. **Marketing channel management** calls for selecting, managing and motivating individual channel members and evaluating their performance over time.

Selecting channel members

Producers vary in their ability to attract qualified marketing intermediaries. Some producers have no trouble signing up channel members. For example, when Toyota first introduced its luxury Lexus line into the United States, it had no trouble attracting new dealers. In fact, it had to turn down many would-be resellers.

At the other extreme are producers that have to work hard to line up enough qualified intermediaries. For example, Swedish firm NEVS, which purchased the Saab motor car brand out of bankruptcy in 2011, is now attempting to sell its cars via the Internet because the Saab dealer network no longer exists. As another example, when Timex first tried to sell its inexpensive watches through regular jewellery stores, most jewellery stores refused to carry them. The company then managed to get its watches into mass-merchandise outlets. This turned out to be a wise decision because of the rapid growth of mass merchandising.

Even established brands may have difficulty gaining and keeping desired distribution, especially when dealing with powerful resellers. Major retailers like Walmart, Tesco, Aldi, CostCo, Metro and Carrefour are renowned for their tough policies in regularly streamlining product assortments and favouring their own-brands over manufacturer brands. For example, many major store groups have opted not to sell cigarettes, in spite of attractive margins, in the face of health lobby pressures. As more major retail chains such as follow suit, tobacco companies will have to seek new channels for selling their brands.[18]

When selecting intermediaries, the company should determine what characteristics distinguish the better ones. It will want to evaluate each channel member's years in business, other lines carried, growth and profit record, cooperativeness and reputation. If the intermediaries are sales agents, the company will want to evaluate the number and character of other lines carried and the size and quality of the sales force. If the intermediary is a retail store that wants exclusive or selective distribution, the company will want to evaluate the store's customers, location and future growth potential.

Managing and motivating channel members

Once selected, channel members must be continuously managed and motivated to do their best. The company must sell not only *through* the intermediaries but also *to* and *with* them. Most companies see their intermediaries as first-line customers and partners. They practise strong *partner relationship management* (PRM) to forge long-term partnerships with channel members. This creates a value delivery system that meets the needs of both the company *and* its marketing partners.

In managing its channels, a company must convince distributors that they can succeed better by working together as a part of a cohesive value delivery system. Thus, P&G works closely with its major retailer customers across the world to create superior value for final consumers,

Author comment

Now it's time to implement the chosen channel design and work with selected channel members to manage and motivate them.

Marketing channel management—Selecting, managing and monitoring individual channel members and evaluating their performance over time.

jointly planning merchandising goals and strategies, stock levels, and advertising and promotion programmes. Similarly, heavy-equipment manufacturer Caterpillar and its worldwide network of independent dealers work in close harmony to find better ways to bring value to customers.[19]

Many companies are now installing integrated high-tech partnership relationship management (PRM) systems to coordinate their whole-channel marketing efforts. Just as they use customer relationship management (CRM) software systems to help manage relationships with important customers, companies can now use PRM and supply chain management (SCM) software to help recruit, train, organise, manage, motivate and evaluate relationships with channel partners.

Evaluating channel members

The company must regularly check channel member performance against standards such as sales quotas, average stock levels, customer delivery time, treatment of damaged and lost goods, cooperation in company promotion and training programmes, and services to the customer. The company should recognise and reward intermediaries who are performing well and adding good value for consumers. Those who are performing poorly should be assisted or, as a last resort, replaced.

Finally, companies need to be sensitive to their channel partners. Those who treat their partners poorly risk not only losing their support but also causing some legal problems. The next section describes various rights and duties pertaining to companies and other channel members.

PUBLIC POLICY AND DISTRIBUTION DECISIONS

For the most part, and in most countries, companies are legally free to develop whatever channel arrangements suit them. In fact, the commonest laws affecting channel choices seek to prevent the exclusionary tactics of some companies that might keep another company from using a desired channel. Most legal requirements influencing distribution channels deal with the mutual rights and duties of channel members once they have formed a relationship. Marketers need to be aware that legal frameworks vary greatly across different countries, and in some cases are subject to government (or EU) policies to protect local companies.

One problem area may be because many producers and wholesalers like to develop exclusive channels for their products. When the seller allows only certain outlets to carry its products, this strategy is called *exclusive distribution*. When the seller requires that these dealers not handle competitors' products, its strategy is called *exclusive dealing*. Both parties can benefit from exclusive arrangements: the seller obtains more loyal and dependable outlets, and the dealers obtain a steady source of supply and stronger seller support. But exclusive arrangements also exclude other producers from selling to these dealers, in a way which may be regarded as anti-competitive. In most countries, exclusive arrangements are legal as long as they do not substantially lessen competition or tend to create a monopoly and as long as both parties enter into the agreement voluntarily.

Exclusive dealing often includes *exclusive territorial agreements*. The producer may agree not to sell to other dealers in a given area, or the buyer may agree to sell only in its own territory. The first practice is normal under franchise systems as a way to increase dealer enthusiasm and commitment. Usually, this is also perfectly legal – a seller has no legal obligation to sell through more outlets than it wishes. The second practice, whereby the producer tries to keep a dealer from selling outside its territory, may be more likely to conflict with local laws. Where the boundaries are borders between countries with different legal jurisdictions, the issue may become considerably more complex.

Producers of a strong brand sometimes sell it to dealers only if the dealers will take some or all the rest of the line. This is called *full-line forcing*. Such tying agreements are not necessarily illegal, but may be questionable under some countries' legal frameworks if they tend to lessen competition substantially. In particular, local regulators may consider that the practice may prevent consumers from freely choosing among competing suppliers of these other brands.

Finally, producers are free to select their dealers, but their right to terminate dealers is somewhat restricted in some countries. In general, sellers can drop dealers for a justifiable reason. However, they usually cannot drop dealers if, for example, the dealers refuse to cooperate in a doubtful legal arrangement, such as exclusive dealing or tying agreements. In some countries terminating contracts with local distributors may be expensive and a very drawn-out process.

The legal and government policy differences facing marketers in markets like India and China are especially large. Specialist advice is usually essential before committing to channel strategy in such markets.

MARKETING LOGISTICS AND SUPPLY CHAIN MANAGEMENT

Author comment

Marketers used to call this plain old 'physical distribution'. But the topic has grown in importance, complexity and sophistication.

In today's global marketplace, selling a product is sometimes easier than getting it to customers. Companies must decide on the best way to store, handle and move their products and services so that they are available to customers in the right assortments, at the right time, and in the right place. Logistics effectiveness has a major impact on both customer satisfaction and company costs. Here we consider the nature and importance of logistics management in the supply chain, the goals of the logistics system, major logistics functions, and the need for integrated supply chain management.

Nature and importance of marketing logistics

Marketing logistics (physical distribution)—Planning, implementing and controlling the physical flow of materials, final goods and related information from points of origin to points of consumption to meet customer requirements at a profit.

To some managers, marketing logistics means only lorries and warehouses. But modern logistics is much more than this. **Marketing logistics** – also called **physical distribution** – involves planning, implementing and controlling the physical flow of goods, services and related information from points of origin to points of consumption to meet customer requirements at a profit. In short, it involves getting the right product to the right customer in the right place at the right time. At its simplest – it takes around 10,000 bricks to build the average British home, and if bricks are in short supply, as they were in 2014, builders cannot construct new homes.[20]

In the past, physical distribution planners typically started with products at the plant and then tried to find low-cost solutions to get them to customers. However, today's *customer-centred* logistics starts with the marketplace and works backward to the factory or even to sources of supply. Marketing logistics involves not only *outbound distribution* (moving products from the factory to resellers and ultimately to customers) but also *inbound distribution* (moving products and materials from suppliers to the factory) and *reverse logistics* (moving broken, unwanted or excess products returned by consumers or resellers). That is, it involves entire **supply chain management** – managing upstream and downstream value-added flows of materials, final goods, and related information among suppliers, the company, resellers and final consumers, as shown in Figure 12.5.

Supply chain management— Managing upstream and downstream value-added flows of materials, final goods and related information among suppliers, the company, resellers and final consumers.

The logistics manager's task is to coordinate the activities of suppliers, purchasing managers, marketers, channel members and customers. These activities include forecasting, information systems, purchasing, production planning, order processing, stocks, warehousing and transport planning.

Companies today are placing greater emphasis on logistics for several reasons. First, companies can gain a powerful competitive advantage by using improved logistics to give customers better service or lower prices. Second, improved logistics can yield tremendous cost savings to both a company and its customers. As much as 20 per cent of an average product's price is accounted for by shipping and transport alone. This far exceeds the cost of advertising and many other marketing costs. Even more, when fuel and other costs rise, so do logistics costs. For example, American companies spend $1.33 trillion each year – about 8.5 per cent of GDP – to wrap, bundle, load, unload, sort, reload and transport goods. That's more than the total national GDPs of all but 13 countries worldwide.[21] Additional costs come from international markets with limited infrastructure and distribution systems – India is a compelling example of the problems faced in international marketing logistics caused by weak infrastructure like roads.

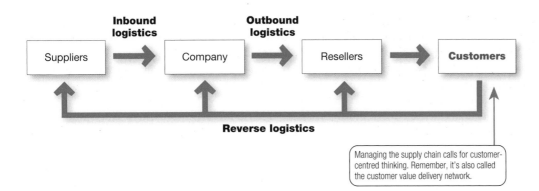

Figure 12.5 Supply chain management

Shaving off even a small fraction of logistics costs can mean substantial savings. For example, both in the United States and its global operations, Walmart is currently implementing a programme of logistics improvements through more efficient international sourcing, better stock management, and greater supply chain productivity, that will reduce supply chain costs by 5 to 15 per cent over five years – that's a whopping $4 billion to $12 billion.[22] Many of the world's top retailers are looking for similar supply chain efficiency improvement.

Third, the explosion in product variety has created a need for improved logistics management. For example, in 1911 the typical local grocery store carried only about 270 items. The store manager could keep track of this inventory on about ten pages of notebook paper stuffed in a shirt pocket. Today, the average local store carries a bewildering stock of more than 25,000 items. At the extreme, superstores run by companies like Tesco, Carrefour, CostCo and Walmart can carry more than 100,000 products.[23] Ordering, shipping, stocking and controlling such a variety of products presents a sizable logistics challenge.

Improvements in information technology have created opportunities for major gains in distribution efficiency. Today's companies are using sophisticated supply chain management (SCM) software, Internet-based logistics systems, point-of-sale scanners, RFID tags, satellite tracking and electronic transfer of order and payment data. Such technology lets them quickly and efficiently manage the flow of goods, information and finances through the supply chain.

Nonetheless, UK research suggests that many companies are wide open to supply chain risks because they have little visibility of their supply chains. Businesses in many sectors seem to have little knowledge of where their suppliers are sourcing goods:[24]

The 2013 fire in a Bangladesh clothing factory, which killed more than 600 people, heaped scrutiny on retailers like Primark and Benetton, which had clothes made at the site. The same year, the British horsemeat scandal, when supermarket food products were found to contain the meat, was another example of companies being hurt be weaknesses in their complex, cross-border supply chains. Companies are at risk if they do not even know who their suppliers' suppliers are. This is why Jaguar Land Rover and Aston Martin have teamed up with Toyota to create a joint supply chain map showing where they are all exposed to natural disasters (like the 2011 Japanese earthquake and tsunami, which left factories closed for weeks), and hence to financial and reputational risks.

Finally, more than almost any other marketing function, logistics affects the environment and a firm's environmental sustainability efforts. Transport, warehousing, packaging and other logistics functions are typically the biggest contributors to the company's environmental footprint. At the same time, they also provide one of the most fertile areas for cost savings.

Goals of the logistics system

Some companies state their logistics objective as providing maximum customer service at the least cost. Unfortunately, as nice as this sounds, no logistics system can *both* maximise customer service *and* minimise distribution costs. Maximum customer service implies rapid delivery, large stocks, flexible product assortments, liberal returns policies and other services – all of which raise distribution costs. In contrast, minimum distribution costs imply slower delivery, smaller stocks in reserve and larger shipping lots – which represent a lower level of overall customer service.

The goal of marketing logistics should be to provide a *targeted* level of customer service at the least cost. A company must first research the importance of various distribution services to customers and then set desired service levels for each segment. The objective is to maximise *profits*, not sales. Therefore, the company must weigh the benefits of providing higher levels of service against the costs. Some companies offer less service than their competitors and charge a lower price. Other companies offer more service and charge higher prices to cover higher costs.

Major logistics functions

Given a set of logistics objectives, the company designs a logistics system that will minimise the cost of attaining these objectives. The major logistics functions include *warehousing*, *stock management*, *transport* and *logistics information management*.

Warehousing

Production and consumption cycles rarely match, so most companies must store their goods while they wait to be sold. For example, manufacturers producing products like lawn mowers with seasonal demand are likely to want to run their factories all year long and so need to store products for the heavy spring and summer buying seasons. The storage function overcomes differences in needed quantities and timing, ensuring that products are available when customers are ready to buy them.

Distribution centre—A large, highly automated warehouse designed to receive goods from various plants and suppliers, take orders, fill them efficiently, and deliver goods to customers as quickly as possible.

A company must decide on *how many* and *what types* of warehouses it needs and *where* they will be located. The company might use either *storage warehouses* or *distribution centres*. Storage warehouses store goods for moderate to long periods. **Distribution centres** are designed to move goods rather than just store them. They are large and highly automated warehouses designed to receive goods from various plants and suppliers, take orders, fill them efficiently, and deliver goods to customers as quickly as possible.

For example, even though Amazon.com is the world's most successful Internet business platform, obviously it still faces the physical challenge of getting products to customers. For this reason, Amazon's business is supported by a group of huge, highly automated fulfilment centres operating in the US, Europe and Asia, supported by a network of smaller distribution centres. For example, at Marston Gate, Milton Keynes in the UK, Amazon's fulfilment centre is half a mile long and stocks everything from cuddly toys to saucepans. At peak times like holiday seasons, thousands of casual workers pick and pack customer orders. Amazon places considerable emphasis on environmental impact – recycling packaging, avoiding packaging waste, reducing transport and energy saving – in its distribution network. Indeed, to improve efficiency in its massive distribution centres, Amazon recently purchased robot maker Kiva Systems:[25]

> When you buy from Amazon, the chances are still good that your order will be plucked from warehouse shelves by human hands. However, the humans in Amazon's distribution centres are increasingly being assisted by an army of squat, ottoman-size, day-glo orange robots. The robots bring racks of merchandise to workers, who in turn fill boxes. Dubbed the 'magic shelf', racks of items simply materialise in front of workers, with red lasers pointing to items to be picked. The robots then drive off and new shelves appear. The super-efficient robots work tirelessly 16 hours a day, seven days a week. They never complain about the workload or ask for pay raises, and they are pretty much maintenance free. 'When they run low on power, they head to battery-charging terminals,' notes one observer, 'or, as warehouse personnel say, "They get themselves a drink of water."'

Stock management

The management of stock also affects customer satisfaction. Here, managers must maintain the delicate balance between carrying too little stock and carrying too much. With too little stock, the firm risks not having products when customers want to buy. To remedy this, the firm may need costly emergency shipments or production. Carrying too much stock results in higher-than-necessary stock-carrying costs and stock obsolescence. Thus, in managing stock levels, firms must balance the costs of carrying larger stocks against resulting sales and profits.

Many companies have greatly reduced their stock levels and related costs through *just-in-time* logistics systems. With such systems, producers and retailers carry only small stocks of parts or merchandise, often enough for only a few days of operations. New stock arrives exactly when needed, rather than being stored until being used. Just-in-time systems require accurate forecasting along with fast, frequent and flexible delivery so

High-tech distribution centres: Amazon enjoys a team of super-retrievers - in day-glo orange - to keep its warehouse running.
Source: Justin Sullivan/Getty Images

that new supplies will be available when needed. However, these systems result in substantial savings in stock-carrying and handling costs.

Marketers are always looking for new ways to make stock management more efficient. In the not-too-distant future, handling stock might even become fully automated. For example, in Chapter 3 we discussed RFID or 'smart tag' technology, by which small transmitter chips are embedded in or placed on products and packaging on everything from flowers and razors to tyres. 'Smart' products could make the entire supply chain – which often accounts for as much as 75 per cent of a product's cost – intelligent and automated.

Companies using RFID would know, at any time, exactly where a product is located physically within the supply chain. 'Smart shelves' would not only tell them when it's time to reorder but also place the order automatically with their suppliers. Such exciting new information technology applications are revolutionising distribution as we know it. Many large and resourceful marketing companies, such as Tesco, P&G, Kraft, IBM, HP and major retail groups, are investing heavily to make the full use of RFID technology a reality.[26]

Transport

The choice of transport carriers affects the pricing of products, delivery performance and the condition of goods when they arrive – all of which will affect customer satisfaction. In shipping goods to its warehouses, dealers and customers, depending on the country in question, the company can choose among five main transportation modes: truck, rail, water, pipeline and air, along with an alternative mode for digital products – the Internet.

Across the European Union countries, road transport dominates the inland freight market, accounting for 75 per cent of all freight. Rail transport comprises around 18 per cent of freighting, while 5–6 per cent is constituted by inland waterways. Freighting in Europe in 2012 amounted to 2100 billion tonne-kilometres.[27]

Road transport has generally increased its share of transportation steadily, in spite of the controversial environmental impact associated with this mode of freighting. Lorries are highly flexible in their routing and time schedules, and they can usually offer faster service than railways. They are efficient for short hauls of high-value merchandise. Trucking firms have evolved in recent years to become full-service providers of global transportation services. For example, large trucking firms now offer everything from satellite tracking, Internet-based shipment management and logistics planning software to cross-border shipping operations.

Railways are one of the most cost-effective modes for shipping large amounts of bulk products – coal, sand, minerals and farm and forest products – over long distances. In recent years, railways have increased their customer services by designing new equipment to handle special categories of goods, providing flatcars for carrying lorry trailers by rail (piggyback), and providing in-transit services such as the diversion of shipped goods to other destinations en route and the processing of goods en route.

Inland waterways can transport large amounts of goods by ships and barges. Although the cost of water transportation is very low for shipping bulky, low-value, non-perishable products such as sand, coal, grain, oil and metallic ores, water transportation is the slowest mode and may be affected by the weather. *Pipelines* are a specialised means of shipping petroleum, natural gas, and chemicals from sources to markets. Most pipelines are used by their owners to ship their own products.

Although *air* carriers transport a small proportion of all goods, they are an important transportation mode. Airfreight rates are much higher than railway or road rates, but airfreight is ideal when speed is needed or distant markets have to be reached. Among the most frequently airfreighted products are perishables (e.g., fresh fish and cut flowers) and high-value, low-bulk items (e.g., technical instruments and jewellery). Companies find that airfreight also reduces stock levels, packaging costs and the number of warehouses needed.

The *Internet* carries digital products from producer to customer via satellite, cable or phone wire. Software firms, the media, music and video companies and education all make use of the Internet to transport digital products. Although these firms primarily use traditional transportation to distribute DVDs, newspapers, and more, the Internet holds the potential for lower product distribution costs. Whereas planes, trucks and trains move freight and packages, digital technology moves information bits.

Successful firms do not stand still – they innovate constantly, even in mundane areas like transport and delivery. Amazon is even testing a car boot delivery service in Germany:[28]

> Amazon customers will be able to order parcels delivered direct to the boot of their car in a pilot scheme launched by Amazon with car maker Audi. When ordering, Amazon Prime customers will indicate the rough location of the vehicle and desired delivery time. A DHL delivery agent will later be notified of the exact location of the car via a smartphone app. The agent is granted one-time keyless access to the boot, which locks automatically when it is shut again. The customer agrees that the vehicle can be tracked for a time and is notified via e-mail of successful delivery. (The vehicle has to be adapted to allow third-party boot access.) A product return service is planned using the same route. Parcel-to-car delivery aims to reduce the number of failed delivery attempts at homes, or the log-jam of parcels in offices when employees have Amazon deliver to their workplace.

Multimodal transport—
Combining two or more modes of transport.

Some shippers also use **multimodal transport** – combining two or more modes of transport. *Piggyback* describes the use of rail and lorries; *fishyback*, water and lorries; *trainship*, water and rail; and *airtruck*, air and trucks. Combining modes provides advantages that no single mode can deliver. Each combination offers advantages to the shipper. For example, not only is piggyback cheaper than trucking alone, but it also provides flexibility and convenience.

In choosing a transportation mode for a product, shippers must balance many considerations: speed, dependability, availability, cost, and others. Thus, if a shipper needs speed, air and road are the prime choices. If the goal is low cost, then water or rail might be best. The environmental impact of transportation mode chosen is a growing concern because of the impact on customer perceptions of companies and their products.

Logistics information management

Companies manage their supply chains through information. Channel partners often link up to share information and make better joint logistics decisions. From a logistics perspective, flows of information, such as customer transactions, billing, shipment and stock levels, and even customer data, are closely linked to channel performance. Companies need simple, accessible, fast and accurate processes for capturing, processing and sharing channel information.

Information can be shared and managed in many ways, but most sharing takes place through traditional or Internet-based *electronic data interchange* (EDI), the computerised exchange of data between organisations, which primarily is transmitted via the Internet. Major retailers like Tesco and Carrefour in Europe and Walmart in the US, for example, require EDI links with their suppliers. If new suppliers don't have EDI capability, the retailers will work with the supplier to find and implement the needed software. 'EDI has proven to be the most efficient way of conducting business with our product suppliers,' says Walmart. 'This system of exchanging information . . . allows us to improve customer service, lower expenses, and increase productivity.'[29]

In some cases, suppliers might actually be asked to generate orders and arrange deliveries for their customers. Many large retailers – such as Tesco, Carrefour and B&Q – work closely with major suppliers such as P&G or Black & Decker to set up *vendor-managed inventory* (VMI) systems or *continuous inventory replenishment* systems. Using VMI, the customer shares real-time data on sales and current stock levels with the supplier. The supplier then takes full responsibility for managing stocks and deliveries. Some retailers even go so far as to shift stocking and delivery costs to the supplier. Such systems require close cooperation between the buyer and seller.

Integrated logistics management

Today, more and more companies are adopting the concept of **integrated logistics management**. This concept recognises that providing better customer service and trimming distribution costs require *teamwork*, both inside the company and among all the marketing channel organisations. Inside, the company's various departments must work closely together to maximise its own logistics performance. Outside, the company must integrate its logistics system with those of its suppliers and customers to maximise the performance of the entire distribution network.

> **Integrated logistics management**—The logistics concept that emphasises teamwork – both inside the company and among all the marketing channel organisations – to maximise the performance of the entire distribution system.

Cross-functional teamwork inside the company

Most companies assign responsibility for various logistics activities to many different departments – marketing, sales, finance, operations and purchasing. Too often, each function tries to optimise its own logistics performance without regard for the activities of the other functions. However, transport, stock-holding, warehousing and information management activities interact, often with an inverse relationship – for example, lower stock levels reduce stock-carrying costs, but they may also reduce customer service and increase costs from stock-outs, back-orders, special production runs and costly fast-freight shipments. Because distribution activities involve such major trade-offs, decisions by different functions must be coordinated to achieve better overall logistics performance.

The goal of integrated supply chain management is to harmonise all of the company's logistics decisions. Close working relationships among departments can be achieved in several ways. Some companies have created permanent logistics committees composed of managers responsible for different physical distribution activities. Companies can also create supply chain manager positions that link the logistics activities of functional areas. For example, P&G has created product supply managers who manage all the supply chain activities for each product category. Many companies have a director of logistics with cross-functional authority.

Finally, companies can employ sophisticated, system-wide supply chain management software, now available from a wide range of software enterprises large and small, from SAP and Oracle to Infor and Logility. The worldwide market for SCM software topped $9.9 billion in 2014, with

> Integrated logistics management: Logility's Voyager Solutions software offers tools for managing every aspect of the supply chain, from value chain collaboration to stock holding optimization to transportation and logistics management.
> *Source:* Stockbroker/Alamy Images

SAP and Oracle the market leaders.[30] The important thing is that the company must coordinate its logistics and marketing activities to create high market satisfaction at a reasonable cost.

Building logistics partnerships

Companies must do more than improve their own logistics. They must also work with other channel partners to improve whole-channel distribution. The members of a marketing channel are linked closely in creating customer value and building customer relationships. One company's distribution system is another company's supply system. The success of each channel member depends on the performance of the entire supply chain. For example, IKEA can create its stylish but affordable furniture and deliver the 'IKEA lifestyle' only if its entire supply chain – consisting of thousands of merchandise designers and suppliers, transport companies, warehouses and service providers – operates at maximum efficiency and customer-focused effectiveness.

Smart companies coordinate their logistics strategies and forge strong partnerships with suppliers and customers to improve customer service and reduce channel costs. Many companies have created *cross-functional, cross-company teams*. For example, in the US, Swiss company Nestlé has a Purina pet food unit which has a team of dozens of people working in Bentonville, Arkansas, the home base of Walmart. The Purina team members work jointly with their counterparts at Walmart to find ways to squeeze costs out of their distribution system. Working together benefits not only Purina and Walmart but also their shared, final consumers. This cross-company working to reduce logistics costs is becoming more usual at major retail groups across the world – Disney has recently established a team at Tesco's head office, for example.

Other companies partner through *shared projects*. For example, many large retailers conduct joint in-store programmes with suppliers, in some cases allowing key suppliers to use their stores as a testing ground for new merchandising programmes. The suppliers can spend time in stores watching how their product sells and how customers relate to it. They then create programmes specially tailored to the retailer and its customers. Clearly, both the supplier and the customer can benefit from such partnerships. The point is that all supply chain members must work together in the cause of bringing value to final consumers.

Third-party logistics

Third-party logistics (3PL) provider—An independent logistics provider that performs any or all of the functions required to get a client's product to market.

Although most big companies love to make and sell their products, many loathe the associated logistics 'grunt work'. They detest the bundling, loading, unloading, sorting, storing, reloading, transporting, customs clearing and tracking required to supply their factories and get products to their customers. They hate it so much that a growing number of firms now outsource some or all of their logistics to **third-party logistics (3PL) providers**, such as FedEx Logistics or DHL Logistics.

A group of around 25 third-party logistics providers (3PLs) increasingly dominate logistics outsourcing around the world, as they have taken on an increasingly important role for multinational manufacturers and retailers. Manufacturers need absolutely reliable sources of supply. Retailers need flexible links to suppliers with low-cost production. But these suppliers are often in remote regions. At the same time, retailers need rapid delivery channels for an ever-expanding distribution network of consumers. These global 3PLs provide transportation, consolidation, forwarding and customs brokerage, warehousing, fulfilment, distribution and virtually any logistics and trade-related services that their international customers need. In a global 3PL market worth $270 billion a year, the top three companies turn over around $42 billion a year. The global market leaders are Excel (UK), Kuene & Nagel (Switzerland) and Schenkler (Germany). Unsurprisingly, the top 7 global 3PL providers are European, since 3PL use is more widespread in Europe than America.[31]

Companies use 3PL providers for several reasons. First, because getting the product to market is their main focus, these providers can often do it more efficiently and at lower cost. Outsourcing typically results in 15–30 per cent in cost savings. Second, outsourcing logistics frees a company to focus more intensely on its core business. Finally, integrated logistics companies understand increasingly complex logistics environments. According to one report, 86 per cent of *Fortune 500* companies use 3PL (also called *outsourced logistics* or *contract logistics*) services. General Motors, P&G and Walmart each use 50 or more 3PLs.[32]

3PL partners can be especially helpful to companies attempting to expand their global market coverage. For example, companies distributing their products across Europe face a bewildering array of environmental restrictions that affect logistics, including packaging standards, lorry size and weight limits, and noise and emissions pollution controls. By outsourcing its logistics, a company can gain a complete pan-European distribution system without incurring the costs, delays and risks associated with setting up its own system.

OBJECTIVES REVIEW AND KEY TERMS

Some companies pay too little attention to their distribution channels, but others have used imaginative distribution systems to gain competitive advantage. A company's channel decisions directly affect every other marketing decision. Management must make channel decisions carefully, incorporating today's needs with tomorrow's likely selling environment.

OBJECTIVE 1 Explain why companies use marketing channels and discuss the functions these channels perform (pp. 340–345)

In creating customer value, a company can't go it alone. It must work within an entire network of partners – a value delivery network – to accomplish this task. Individual companies and brands don't compete, their entire value delivery networks compete.

Most producers use intermediaries to bring their products to market. They forge a *marketing channel* (or *distribution channel*) – a set of interdependent organisations involved in the process of making a product or service available for use or consumption by the consumer or business user. Through their contacts, experience, specialisation and scale of operation, intermediaries usually offer the firm more than it can achieve on its own.

Marketing channels perform many key functions. Some help *complete transactions* by gathering and distributing *information* needed for planning and aiding exchange, developing and spreading persuasive *communications* about an offer, performing *contact* work (finding and communicating with prospective buyers), *matching* (shaping and fitting the offer to the buyer's needs) and entering into *negotiation* to reach an agreement on price and other terms of the offer so that ownership can be transferred. Other functions help to *fulfil* the completed transactions by offering *physical distribution* (transporting and storing goods), *financing* (acquiring and using funds to cover the costs of the channel work) and *risk taking* (assuming the risks of carrying out the channel work.

OBJECTIVE 2 Discuss how channel members interact and how they organise to perform the work of the channel (pp. 345–351)

The channel will be most effective when each member assumes the tasks it can do best. Ideally, because the success of individual channel members depends on overall channel success, all channel firms should work together smoothly. They should understand and accept their roles, coordinate their goals and activities, and cooperate to attain overall channel goals. By cooperating, they can more effectively sense, serve and satisfy the target market.

In a large company, the formal organisation structure assigns roles and provides needed leadership. But in a distribution channel composed of independent firms, leadership and power are not formally set. Traditionally, distribution channels have lacked the leadership needed to assign roles and manage conflict. In recent years, however, new types of channel organisations have appeared that provide stronger leadership and improved performance.

OBJECTIVE 3 Identify the major channel alternatives open to a company (pp. 351–356)

Channel alternatives vary from direct selling to using one, two, three or more intermediary *channel levels*. Marketing channels face continuous and sometimes dramatic change. Three of the most important trends are the growth of *vertical*, *horizontal* and *multichannel marketing systems*. These trends affect channel cooperation, conflict and competition.

Channel design begins with assessing customer channel service needs and company channel objectives and constraints. The company then identifies the major channel alternatives in terms of the *types* of intermediaries, the *number* of intermediaries and the *channel responsibilities* of each. Each channel alternative must be evaluated according to economic, control and adaptive criteria. *Channel management* calls for selecting qualified intermediaries and motivating them. Individual channel members must be evaluated regularly.

OBJECTIVE 4 Explain how companies select, motivate and evaluate channel members (pp. 356–358)

Producers vary in their ability to attract qualified marketing intermediaries. Some producers have no trouble signing up channel members. Others have to work hard to line up enough qualified intermediaries. When selecting intermediaries, the company should evaluate each channel member's qualifications and select those that best fit its channel objectives.

Once selected, channel members must be continuously motivated to do their best. The company must sell not only *through* the intermediaries but also *with* them. It should forge strong partnerships with channel members to create a marketing system that meets the needs of both the manufacturer *and* the partners.

OBJECTIVE 5 Discuss the nature and importance of marketing logistics and integrated supply chain management (pp. 358–365)

Marketing logistics (or *physical distribution*) is an area of potentially high cost savings and improved customer satisfaction. Marketing logistics addresses not only *outbound logistics* but also *inbound logistics* and *reverse logistics*. That is, it involves the entire *supply chain management* — managing value-added flows between suppliers, the company, resellers and final users. No logistics system can both maximise customer service and minimise distribution costs. Instead, the goal of logistics management is to provide a *targeted* level of service at the least cost. The major logistics functions include *warehousing, stock management, transportation* and *logistics information management*.

The *integrated supply chain management concept* recognises that improved logistics requires teamwork in the form of close working relationships across functional areas inside the company and across various organisations in the supply chain. Companies can achieve logistics harmony among functions by creating cross-functional logistics teams, integrative supply manager positions and senior-level logistics executives with cross-functional authority. Channel partnerships can take the form of cross-company teams, shared projects and information-sharing systems. Today, some companies are outsourcing their logistics functions to 3PL providers to save costs, increase efficiency and gain faster and more effective access to global markets.

NAVIGATING THE KEY TERMS

OBJECTIVE 1
Value delivery network (p. 341)
Marketing channel (distribution channel)
   (p. 341)
Channel level (p. 344)
Direct marketing channel (p. 345)
Indirect marketing channel (p. 345)

OBJECTIVE 2
Channel conflict (p. 346)
Conventional distribution channel
   (p. 347)
Vertical marketing system (VMS) (p. 347)

Corporate VMS (p. 347)
Contractual VMS (p. 348)
Franchise organisation (p. 348)
Administered VMS (p. 348)
Horizontal marketing system (p. 349)
Multichannel distribution system (p. 349)
Disintermediation (p. 350)

OBJECTIVE 3
Marketing channel design (p. 352)
Intensive distribution (p. 353)
Exclusive distribution (p. 353)
Selective distribution (p. 354)

OBJECTIVE 4
Marketing channel management (p. 356)

OBJECTIVE 5
Marketing logistics (physical distribution)
   (p. 358)
Supply chain management (p. 358)
Distribution centre (p. 360)
Multimodal transportation (p. 362)
Integrated logistics management (p. 363)
Third-party logistics (3PL) provider
   (p. 364)

DISCUSSION AND CRITICAL THINKING

Discussion questions

12-1 Describe how marketing channel members add value in the channel of distribution between manufacturers and consumers. (AACSB: Communication)

12-2 Explain how a vertical marketing system differs from a conventional distribution channel. (AACSB: Communication)

12-3 What types of exclusive arrangements do manufacturers develop with resellers? Are these arrangements legal? (AACSB: Communication; Reflective thinking)

12-4 Describe inter-modal transportation and list the different combinations used to distribute products and the benefits of using this mode of transportation. (AACSB: Communication)

12-5 What are third-party logistics providers and why do companies use them? (AACSB: Communication)

Critical-thinking exercises

12-6 Distribution channel concerns for pharmaceutical drugs – especially the problem of counterfeit drugs – can be a matter of life and death. There have been moves in some parts of the world to require the keeping of a record of the chain of custody ('pedigree') from manufacturer through resellers to the point of dispensing, and some regulators are requiring an electronic pedigree using serialisation and track-and-trace systems. Write a report on this development and the current status of track-and-trace systems in the global pharmaceutical drug distribution channel, as well as other initiatives to fight counterfeit drugs in different parts of the world. (AACSB: Communication; Reflective thinking)

12-7 The most common type of contractual vertical marketing system is the franchise organisation. Visit the International Franchise Association at www.franchise.org/ and find a franchise that interests you. Write a report describing the franchise. Identify what type of franchise it represents and research the market opportunities for that product or service. (AACSB: Communication; Use of IT; Reflective thinking)

12-8 The term *last mile* is often used in the telecommunications industry. Research what is going on in this industry and how the *last mile* has evolved in recent years, then predict where it is heading in the future. What companies are major players in the last mile and how does the concept of net neutrality fit in? (AACSB: Communication; Reflective thinking)

Mini-cases and applications

Online, mobile and social media marketing: self-publishing

Do you think that you have what it takes to write a bestselling novel? In the past, authors had to go through traditional publishing houses to print and distribute their work, but technology has turned the publishing industry on its head. Although aspiring authors could always self-publish a book, selling it through the traditional channels – book shops – was only a pipedream for most. But that has all changed thanks to the Internet and social media. Amazon's Kindle Direct Publishing is a popular platform for self-publishers, but other online services offer similar opportunities with hundreds of thousands of authors and titles. For example, Amanda Hocking's self-published e-book sales caught the attention of a publisher, and now the former social worker is a millionaire. Self-published books have grown nearly 300 per cent in less than ten years, with the majority being e-books. A large proportion of readers worldwide now own e-readers, such as Kindles and iPads. That creates opportunities for anyone wanting to distribute their works to these avid readers. For example, after being turned away by traditional publishers, author Christine Bronstein created her own online social network to promote her book, *Nothing But the Truth, So Help Me God: 51 Women Reveal the Power of Positive Female Connection*, which launched on Amazon and Barnes & Noble sites. She's even expanded access to her readers. For just €20 (no copy-edit) or €95 (copy-edited), you can publish your own *Nothing But the Truth, So Help Me God: My Story* at http://nothingbutthetruth.com/submit.

12-9 Visit a self-publishing site such as Amazon's Kindle Direct (https://kdp.amazon.com/) and create a presentation to give to aspiring authors about distributing their works this way. (AACSB: Communication; Use of IT; Reflective thinking)

12-10 What other industries' channels of distribution have been impacted dramatically by online, mobile and social media? (AACSB: Communication; Reflective thinking)

Marketing ethics: supplier safety

Fast-fashion retailers, such as Zara, H&M and others, demand short lead times and quick changes from suppliers, to feed consumers' demand for changing fashions. Retailers used to place orders almost a year in advance and suppliers produced high volumes cheaply. But fast-fashion retailers now offer new stock in their stores almost weekly to get customers coming back. Additionally, many retailers are placing small initial orders, and if styles take off with consumers, they quickly re-order – a tactic known as 'chasing'. Appropriate stock levels in the clothing industry have always been difficult to predict, but it appears that retailers are pushing this worry back onto suppliers. Bangladesh is the second largest clothing producer for US and European brands and retailers. However, recent fires and building collapses due to lax safety concerns are killing thousands of workers and even some of the factory executives. Unlike more developed countries, the industry in Bangladesh is loosely regulated. That, coupled with the demands to feed the fast-fashion industry, is alleged to be the cause of these tragedies. As a result, US and European brands and retailers are coming under greater scrutiny concerning supplier issues. IndustriALL, a Geneva-based international union, organised a proposal to enhance supplier safety in Bangladesh that many, but not all, Western retailers/brands accepted.

12-11 Write a brief report on the Bangladesh Accord on Fire and Building Safety proposed by IndustriALL. Which retailers signed the agreement and why have some retailers refused to sign the pact? (AACSB: Communication; Reflective thinking)

12-12 Should retailers be responsible for safety conditions in garment factories in other countries? (AACSB: Communication; Reflective thinking; Ethical reasoning)

Marketing by the numbers: Tyson expanding distribution

Tyson Foods is the largest US beef and chicken supplier, processing more than 100,000 head of cattle and 40-plus million chickens weekly. Their primary distribution channels are supermarket meat departments. However, the company is now expanding distribution into convenience stores. There are almost 150,000 gas stations and convenience stores, where the company would like to sell hot Buffalo chicken bites near the checkout. This is a promising channel, as sales are growing considerably at these retail outlets and profit margins on prepared foods are higher than selling raw meat to grocery stores. Tyson will have to hire ten more sales representatives at a salary of $45,000 each to expand into this distribution channel because many of these types of stores are independently owned. Each convenience store is expected to generate an average of $50,000 in revenue for Tyson. Refer to Appendix 2: Marketing by the numbers to answer the following questions.

12-13 If Tyson's contribution margin is 30 per cent on this product, what increase in sales will it need to break even on the increase in fixed costs to hire the new sales reps? (AACSB: Communication; Analytical reasoning)

12-14 How many new retail accounts must the company acquire to break even on this tactic? What average number of accounts must each new rep acquire? (AACSB: Communication; Analytical reasoning)

REFERENCES

[1] Based on information from Rip Empson, 'Netflix tops HBO in paid US subscribers as members stream 5 billion hours of content in Q3', *Tech Crunch*, 21 October 2013, http://techcrunch.com/2013/10/21/netflix-tops-hbo-in-paid-u-s-subscribers-asmembers-stream-5-billion-hours-of-content-in-q3/; Ronald Grover and Cliff Edwards, 'Can Netflix find its future by abandoning its past?' *Bloomberg Businessweek*, 26 September–2 October 2011, pp. 29–30; Stu Woo and Ian Sherr, 'Netflix recovers subscribers', *Wall Street Journal*, 26 January 2012, p. B1; David Carr, 'Giving viewers what they want', *New York Times*, 25 February 2013, p. B1; Brian Stelter, 'Netflix grabs a slice of Star Wars', *CNNMoney*, 13 February 2014, http://money.cnn.com/2014/02/13/technology/netflix-star-wars/; Mike Snider, 'Netflix, adding customers and profits, will raise prices', *USA Today*, 22 April 2014, www.usatoday.com/story/tech/2014/04/21/netflix-results/7965613/; and www.netflix.com, accessed September 2014.

[2] Lisa Marsh, 'Instagram's first retail success', *Bloomberg BusinessWeek*, 15–21 December 2014, pp. 18–19.

[3] See: Kathrin Hille, 'Rivals braced for Alibaba push overseas', *Financial Times*, 13 May 2013, p. 17; Brad Stone, 'Alibaba's IPO may herald the end of US e-commerce dominance', *Bloomberg BusinessWeek*, 7 August 2014, pp. 8–10; John Noble and Nicole Bullock, 'Alibaba notches up biggest IPO', *Financial Times*, 23 September 2014, p. 21; Lucy Colback and Robert Armstrong, 'Alibaba', *Financial Times*, 10 September 1014, p. 11; Peter Campbell, 'Alibaba's treasure trove', *Daily Mail*, 9 September 2014, p. 69.

[4] Based on information from Joe Cahill, 'Mind your franchisees, Mayor McCheese', *Crain's Chicago Business*, 26 April 2013, www.chicagobusiness.com/article/20130426/BLOGS10/130429841; and 'McDonald's customer service push irritates some franchisees', *Chicago Business Journal*, 17 April 2014, www.bizjournals.com/chicago/news/2013/04/17/mcdonalds-riding-fine-line-franchisees.html.

[5] Information accessed at www.luxottica.com/en/company/quick_view, accessed July 2015.

[6] See 'Fashion forward; Inditex', *The Economist*, 24 March 2012, pp. 63–64; Susan Berfield, 'Zara's fast-fashion edge', *Bloomberg Businessweek*, 14 November 2013, www.businessweek.com/articles/2013-11-14/2014-outlook-zaras-fashion-supply-chainedge; and information from the Inditex Press Dossier, www.inditex.com/en/press/information/press_kit, accessed September 2014.

[7] See Eric Platt, '22 companies that are addicted to Walmart', 13 June 2012, *Business Insider*, www.businessinsider.com/22-companies-who-are-completely-addicted-to-walmart-2012-6#; and Stacy Mitchell, 'Will Walmart replace the supermarket?' *Salon*, 28 March 2013, www.salon.com/2013/03/28/will_wal_mart_replace_the_supermarket_partner/.

[8] See 'General Mills: joint ventures', www.generalmills.com/en/Company/Businesses/International/Joint_ventures.aspx, accessed September 2014.

[9] Kadhim Shubber, 'Supermarkets battle to mop up excess space, *FT.com*, 29 May 2015, www.ft.com/cms/s/0/a94436d2-05fe-11e5-b676-00144feabdc0.html#axzz3xQ4cib90, accessed August 2015.

[10] 'Yesterday's brand?', *The Marketer*, March/April 2015, pp. 34–37.

[11] For more discussion, see Eleazar David Melendez, 'Best buy is still alive, but how?' *Huffington Post*, 20 August 2014, www.huffingtonpost.com/2013/08/20/best-buy-turnaround_n_3786695.html; Matthew Yglesias, 'Best buy 'still basically sucks despite successful turnaround', *Huffington Post*, 9 September 2013, www.huffingtonpost.com/2013/09/20/best-buy-turnaround_n_3962408.html; and Steve Knopper, 'Beats enters streaming wars', *Rolling Stone*, 13 February 2014, p. 15.

[12] See: Hal Weitzman, 'Supply chain resists pull of Amazon', *Financial Times*, 21 May 2012, p. 18; Clare O'Connor, 'Amazon launches Amazon Business Marketplace. Will close Amazon supply', *Forbes*, 28 April 2015.

[13] Andy Sharman, 'Carmakers chase consumers in drive to boost sales', *Financial Times*, 27 October 2014, p. 4.

[14] See 'Ministry of Commerce tackles China's high logistics costs'', *WantChinaTimes.com*, 30 November 2013, www.wantchinatimes.com /news-subclass-cnt.aspx?id=20131130000004&cid=1102; and Benjamin Robertson, 'Walmart keeps on expansion path in China', *South China Morning Post*, 19 December 2013, www.scmp.com/business/companies /article/1385419/walmartkeeps-expansion-path-china.

[15] Based on information from Julie Jargon, 'Asia delivers for McDonald's', *Wall Street Journal*, 13 December 2011, http://online.wsj.com/article /SB10001424052970204397704577074982151549316.html; 'Feel like a burger? Dial M for McDonald's Japan', *Asia Pulse*, 23 January 2012; and McDonald's annual reports, www.aboutmcdonalds.com/mcd/investors /annual_reports.html, accessed September 2014.

[16] Nanette Byrnes, 'Avon calls. China opens the door', *BusinessWeek Online*, 28 February 2006, p. 19; Mei Fong, 'Avon's calling, but China opens door only a crack', *Wall Street Journal*, 26 February 2007, p. B1; 'Cosmetic changes in China market', 11 October 2007, www.chinadaily.com.cn; and David Barboza, 'Direct selling flourishes in China', *New York Times*, 26 December 2009, p. B1;

[17] Cecilie Rohwedder, 'European shoppers enjoy novelty: Christmas sales', *Wall Street Journal*, 24–26 December 2007, pp. 1–2.

[18] See Stephanie Strom, 'CVS vows to quit selling tobacco products', *New York Times*, 5 February 2014, p. B1; and http://info.cvscaremark.com/ cvs-insights/cvs-quits, accessed September 2014.

[19] Quotes and other information from Alex Taylor III, 'Caterpillar', *Fortune*, 20 August 2007, pp. 48–54; Donald V. Fites, 'Make our dealers your partners," *Harvard Business Review*, March–April 1996, pp. 84–95; and information at www.cat.com, accessed July 2015.

[20] James Salmon, 'Brick shortage hurts builders', *Daily Mail*, 3 September 2014, p. 57.

[21] See Rosalyn Wilson, '24th Annual State of Logistics Report: is this the new normal?', www.fmsib.wa.gov/reports/powerPoints/RosalynWilson-StateofLogisticsReport2013.pdf, 21 August 2013.

[22] William B. Cassidy, 'Walmart squeezes costs from supply chain', *Journal of Commerce*, 5 January 2010; and 'Walmart to save $150 million thanks to sustainability programs', *Triple Pundit*, 16 October 2012, www.triplepundit.com/2012/10/walmart-save-150-million-sustainability-programs/.

[23] Shlomo Maital, 'The last frontier of cost reduction', *Across the Board*, February 1994, pp. 51–52; and information http://walmartstores.com// default.aspx, accessed June 2010.

[24] See: Claire Jones, 'Companies seen as "wide open" to supply chain risks', *Financial Times*, 7 May 2013, p. 5

[25] See Scott Kirsner, 'Amazon acquisition puts Amazon rivals in awkward spot', *Boston Globe*, 1 December 2013, www.bostonglobe.com/ business/2013/12/01/will-amazon-owned-robot-makersell-tailer-rivals/FON7bVNKvfzS2sHnBHzfLM/story.html; and www.kivasystems .com, accessed September 2014.

[26] See Maida Napolitano, 'RFID surges ahead', *Logistics Management*, April 2012, pp. 47–49; 'Research and markets: global RFID market forecast to 2014', *Business Wire*, April 2012; and Bob Trebilcock, 'RFID: The Macy's Way', *Modern Materials Handling*, 1 June 2013, www.mmh.com /article/rfid_the_macys_way.

[27] See http://ec.europa.eu/eurostat/statistics-explained/index.php /Freight_transport_statistics_-_modal_split, accessed July 2015.

[28] Chris Bryant, 'Amazon and Audi test car boot delivery service', *Financial Times*, 23 April 2015, p. 16.

[29] See Walmart's supplier requirements at http://corporate.walmart .com/suppliers, accessed September 2014.

[30] See www.supplymanagement.com/news/2015/supply-chain-management-software-market-worth-99-billion, accessed July 2015.

[31] See www.supplychainbrain.com/content/nc/sponsored-channels/ kenco-logistic-services-third-party-logistics/single-article-page/article/ top-25-third-party-logistics-providers-extend-their-global-reach/, accessed July 2015.

[32] '3PL Customers Report identifies service trends, 3PL market segment sizes and growth rates', Armstrong & Associates, Inc., 11 July 2013, www.3plogistics.com/PR_3PL_Customers-2013.htm.

COMPANY CASE

Amazon and P&G: taking channel partnering to a new level

Until recently, if you were in the United States and you ordered Bounty paper towels, Pampers nappies, Charmin toilet paper, or any of the dozens of other P&G consumer products from Amazon.com, they probably came to your doorstep by a circuitous distribution route. The paper towels, for example, might well have been produced in one of P&G's regional factories and shipped by the lorry load to one of its warehouses, where the paper goods were unloaded and repacked with other P&G goods and shipped to Amazon's regional fulfilment centre. At the fulfilment centre, they were unloaded and shelved, and then finally picked and packed by Amazon employees for shipment to you via UPS, FedEx or mail.

But today, in a move that could turn consumer package goods distribution upside down, Amazon and P&G are quietly blazing a new, simpler, lower-cost distribution trail for such goods. Now, for example, at the P&G warehouse, rather than reloading lorry-loads of P&G products and shipping them to Amazon fulfilment centres, P&G employees simply cart the goods to a fenced-off area inside their own warehouse. The fenced-in area is run by Amazon. From there, Amazon employees pack, label and ship items directly to customers who have ordered them online. Amazon calls this venture Vendor Flex — and it's revolutionising how people buy low-priced, low-margin everyday household products.

Amazon's Vendor Flex programme offers big potential for both Amazon and supplier-partners like P&G. In the US, consumers currently buy only about 2 per cent of their non-food consumer packaged goods online. Boosting online sales of these staples to 6 per cent — the percentage that the Internet now captures of overall retail sales — would give Amazon an additional $10 billion a year in revenues, up from the current $2 billion in the US alone.

But there's a reason why household staples have lagged behind other kinds of products in online sales. Such goods have long been deemed too bulky or too cheap to justify the high shipping costs involved with Internet selling. To sell household staples profitably online, companies like Amazon and P&G must work together to streamline the distribution process and reduce costs. That's where Vendor Flex comes in.

Vendor Flex takes channel partnering to an entirely new level. Co-locating 'in the same tent' creates advantages for both partners. For Amazon, Vendor Flex reduces the costs of storing bulky items, such as nappies and toilet paper, in its own distribution centres, and it frees up space in Amazon's centres for more higher-margin goods. The sharing arrangement lets Amazon extend its consumer package goods selection without building more distribution centre space. For example, the P&G warehouse also stocks other popular P&G household brands, from Gillette razors to Pantene shampoo to Iams pet food. Finally, locating at the source guarantees Amazon immediate availability and facilitates quick delivery of P&G products to customers.

P&G also benefits from the Vendor Flex partnership. It saves money by cutting out the costs of transporting goods to Amazon's fulfilment centres, which in turn lets it charge more competitive prices to the e-commerce giant. And although P&G is a superb in-store brand marketer, it is still a relative newcomer to online selling, one of the company's top priorities. By partnering more closely with Amazon, P&G gets Amazon's expert help in moving its brands online.

Amazon considers household staples to be one of its next big frontiers for Internet sales. Its presence inside the P&G warehouse is just the tip of the iceberg for Vendor Flex. Amazon and P&G quietly began sharing warehouse space three years ago, and the online merchant has set up shop inside at least seven other P&G distribution centres worldwide, including facilities in Japan and Germany. Amazon is also inside or talking with other major consumer goods suppliers — such as Kimberly Clark — about co-locating distribution facilities. Moreover, Amazon has invested heavily to build an infrastructure for profitably selling all kinds of everyday household items to consumers online. For example, in late 2010, Amazon in the US acquired Quidsi, the owner of Diapers.com and Soap.com, online retailers of baby products and household essentials. Since the Amazon acquisition, Quidsi has added a half-dozen new sites selling, among other things, toys (YoYo.com), pet supplies (Wag.com), premium beauty products (BeautyBar.com) and home products (Casa.com).

Vendor Flex looks like a win–win for everyone involved — Amazon, P&G and final consumers. However, the close Amazon–P&G partnership has caused some grumbling among other important channel participants. For example, what about US mega-retailer Walmart, P&G's largest customer by far? The giant store retailer is locked in a fierce online battle with Amazon, yet one of its largest suppliers appears to be giving Amazon preferential treatment. At the same time, Amazon's courtship of P&G may upset other important suppliers that compete with P&G on Amazon's site. Both P&G and Amazon must be careful that their close Vendor Flex relationship doesn't damage other important channel partnerships.

More broadly, some analysts assert that even with Vendor Flex, Amazon won't be able to sell products such as paper towels, detergent or shaving cream profitably online. They reason that the margins on such items are simply too low to cover shipping costs. Amazon is already losing an estimated $1 billion to $2 billion annually on its Amazon Prime shipping programme. And, they suggest, if there is money to be made by shipping a heavy jug of Tide or a bulky three-pack of Bounty paper towels from P&G's warehouse to your front door, P&G would have been doing that long ago.

However, such doom-and-gloom predictions seem to overlook recent rapid changes in the distribution landscape, especially in online retailing. Mega-shippers like UPS and FedEx are continuing to drive down small-package delivery times and costs. And Amazon is moving aggressively toward same-day delivery in major market areas, including grocery and related items. The Vendor Flex programme seems to align well with such distribution trends.

As for the Amazon–P&G Vendor Flex partnership, it looks like an ideal match for both companies. If P&G wants to be more effective in selling its brands online, what better partner could it have than Amazon, the undisputed master of online retailing? If Amazon wants to be more effective in selling household staples, what better partner could it have than P&G, the acknowledged master of consumer package goods marketing? Together, under Amazon's Vendor Flex, these respective industry leaders can flex their distribution muscles to their own benefit, and to the benefit of the consumers they jointly serve.

Questions for discussion

1. What are the advantages of a channel partnership like that between P&G and Amazon from the points of view of the partners and the consumer?

2. What potentials are there for disagreements between the partners which could undermine the partnership system? For example, as P&G expands its own online operation, are there potential conflicts with Amazon on the way?

3. Are there any potential risks and disadvantages to a close cooperative partnership of this kind — from the points of view of the partners and the consumer? List them and discuss how serious they are.

4. How can competitors respond effectively to the P&G/Amazon partnership with new channels of their own?

5. Consider what other types of channel partnering may revolutionise conventional channels in other markets.

Sources: Serena Ng, 'Soap opera: Amazon moves in with P&G', *Wall Street Journal*, 15 October 2013, p. A1; Andre Mouton, 'Amazon considers "co-creation" with Procter & Gamble', *USA Today*, 21 October 2013, www.usatoday.com/story/tech/2013/10/21/amazon-proctor-gamble-products/3143773/; and David Streitfeld, 'Amazon to raise fees as revenue disappoints', *New York Times*, 31 January 2014, p. B1.

CHAPTER THIRTEEN

Retailing and wholesaling

Chapter preview

We now look more deeply into the two major intermediary channel functions: retailing and wholesaling. You already know something about retailing – retailers of all shapes and sizes serve you every day, both in stores and online. However, you probably know much less about the hoard of wholesalers that work behind the scenes. In this chapter, we examine the characteristics of different kinds of retailers and wholesalers, the marketing decisions they make, and trends for the future.

Retailing is a highly changeable business. Although we always think first of the mega-companies like Walmart, Carrefour, CostCo, Metro and Tesco, there are other 'movers and shakers' as well, with a big impact on the global retail scene. Consider how relatively unknown discount supermarket Aldi is achieving high impact not simply in its German home market, but also globally. What Aldi shares with other successful retailers is an unrelenting focus on bringing value to its customers.

Objective outline

➤ **Objective 1** Explain the role of retailers in the distribution channel and describe the major types of retailers.
Retailing (pp. 375–381)

➤ **Objective 2** Describe the major retailer marketing decisions.
Retailer marketing decisions (pp. 381–386)

➤ **Objective 3** Discuss the major trends and developments in retailing.
Retailing trends and developments (pp. 386–392)

➤ **Objective 4** Explain the major types of wholesalers and their marketing decisions.
Wholesaling (pp. 393–397)

Aldi: putting a beach towel over the UK and the US?

Aldi has never been a 'household name' in the way that Tesco, Sainsburys, Asda/Walmart and Carrefour can claim, but its performance in recent years has been quite remarkable. The essence of the business is low prices through store-brand goods, sold in no-frills stores. The original Aldi shops had bare neon lights, the goods were stacked on pallets, there was no refrigerated produce, and there were few staff. Now, the Aldi group operates more than 9,000 stores in 18 countries worldwide, including Trader Joe's in the US. Key to the business model is limited product ranges – Aldi stores stock maybe 1,000 to 3,000 items, compared to more than 50,000 at a conventional hypermarket. Efficiency drives prices down to unprecedented levels.

Aldi has been able to grow quickly under the radar because it is private – it is one the world's largest private companies. The group does not report results, but global sales are estimated at €67 billion, and Aldi is one of the fastest-growing retailers in the world. Aldi has pioneered a distinct brand of pile-it-high, sell-it-cheap shopping that has transformed retailing in Germany and much of Europe. Aldi buys in bulk from suppliers and commissions them to make its store-brand groceries cheaper than those of its rivals. The thing is that although the stores are no-frills to the extreme, Aldi is so cheap that even the mighty Walmart closed its stores in Germany, selling them to Metro and losing a billion dollars in the process, partly because shoppers found the US giant too expensive in comparison with Aldi.

Originally, Aldi, short for 'Albrecht Discount', was a discount supermarket chain based in Germany. The chain is still made up of two separate groups, Aldi Nord, headquartered in Essen, and Aldi Süd, headquartered in Mülheim an der Ruhr, which operate independently from each other within specific market boundaries. The individual groups were originally owned and managed by brothers Karl Albrecht and Theo Albrecht; Karl has since retired and is Germany's richest man. Theo was Germany's second richest man until his death in July 2010. The brothers were always secretive and reclusive, and many senior Aldi executives spent their whole careers at the company without ever seeing one of the brothers.

Aldi's German operations currently consist of Aldi Nord's 35 individual regional companies with about 2,500 stores in western, northern and eastern Germany, and Aldi Süd's 31 regional companies with 1,600 stores in western and southern Germany. According to a survey by the German market research institute Forsa, 95 per cent of blue-collar workers, 88 per cent of white-collar workers, 84 per cent of public servants and 80 per cent of self-employed Germans shop at Aldi. Aldi and the other deep discounters account for 40 per cent of all grocery sales in Germany. Internationally, Aldi Nord operates in Denmark, France, the Benelux countries, the Iberian peninsula and Poland, while Aldi Süd operates in countries including Ireland, the United Kingdom, Hungary, Greece, Switzerland, Austria, Slovenia (operating as Hofer in Austria and Slovenia) and Australia. In the United States, Aldi Nord is the parent company of the Trader Joe's niche food stores, while Aldi Süd operates the regular Aldi stores in the country.

In 2009, having struggled to make inroads after first arriving in the UK in the early 1990s, Aldi became one of the few retail winners in the economic downturn, with sales rising 25 per cent in a single year. The momentum of the brand was fuelled by a customer base increasingly made up of the wealthier sections of society – half the customer base is now made up of more affluent ABC1 consumers. But with only 3 per cent of the UK groceries market, Aldi believed it had plenty of scope for further growth. Some estimates suggest that discount supermarkets' share of UK groceries could rise from less than 5 per cent to more than 20 per cent.

Certainly, in 2010, when consumer group Which? surveyed consumers regarding store quality, staff attitude and range of products and prices, discounters Aldi (and its smaller German rival Lidl) both came out ahead of the 'big four' (Tesco, Sainsbury's, Asda and Morrisons) in consumer satisfaction. In addition to its very low-price standard assortment, Aldi has weekly special offers on more expensive products like electronics, tools and computers – the computer offers like the £80 tablet regularly sell out within hours.

Aldi is one the fastest-growing retailers in the world. Aldi has pioneered a distinct brand of pile-it-high, sell-it-cheap shopping that has transformed shopping in Germany and much of Europe.

Source: Susan Norwood/Alamy Images

Tesco is so worried it has built a mock-up of an Aldi store at its headquarters, where its executives, marketers and product buyers can study the tactics being used by the enemy. Tesco has already had to respond to the discounters by introducing its own discount brand range. But the established competitors in the British grocery market made the mistake of underestimating Aldi until it was too late.

In the harsh economic conditions of the late 2000s, the no-frills discount supermarkets (mainly Aldi but also Lidl) were attracting droves of new shoppers as unemployment figures rocketed and the credit crunch forced households to slash spending. Offering high-quality products on a limited number of lines at low prices, the discounters were luring shoppers away from Tesco, Sainsbury, Asda and Morrisons, as the British middle classes tightened their belts in the face of soaring energy and food bills. Aldi has doubled in size in the UK in the three years up to 2015. By 2015, the proportion of Aldi customers in the wealthiest AB demographic had increased to 31 per cent, up from just 12 per cent in 2013.

Aldi prices were running around one-third cheaper than its competitors. Product choice is restricted, but that keeps costs lower than rivals – while Aldi stocks one variety of tomato ketchup, Tesco stocks about 24 varieties. Lower costs meant that Aldi could sell a £7.99 bottle of Chateau-Neuf-du-Pape to go with a £4.99 Canadian lobster from Lidl. Paul Foley, Aldi's UK chief says: 'If you offer the consumer the lowest prices and the highest quality, then you shouldn't be surprised that we take market share.' Indeed, Aldi regularly comes top in taste tests for its products – in 2013 its hams, tea and cakes beat M&S and Harrods in the Grocer's taste test of own-label products.

Aldi's advertising campaign likes to use quirky, slightly bizarre consumers making direct comparisons between expensive branded products and the much cheaper Aldi own-label, emphasising the equivalence of the competing offers in quality, linked by the slogan suggesting that Aldi is 'Like brands. Only cheaper'.

In 2015, a landmark was that Aldi had overtaken Waitrose in share of the UK grocery market – half a million new Aldi shoppers have gained it a 5.3 per cent market share compared to Waitorose's 5.1 per cent. Aldi is now the sixth largest grocery chain in the UK. Aldi and the other discounters have led the deflation of grocery prices and played havoc with the big four grocers which are struggling to achieve sales growth amid an intensifying price war. More than half of families in the UK now shop at discount stores rather than traditional grocery chains.

Aldi has consistently maintained a price advantage of up to 30 per cent compared to the 'big five' supermarkets. The pressure was stepped up yet further when Aldi opted to accept credit cards for the first time. In 2015, Aldi was in the midst of a two-year investment of £600 million to open new stores and upgrade existing ones – planning 65 new stores in 2015, and aims to reach 1,000 stores by 2022. In four years, Aldi has taken its sales density from £10 per square foot per week to £25.

The US arm of Aldi is expanding on Walmart's home turf in America, looking to seize on the economic downturn to lure consumers to its spartan stores and cheap groceries and then keep their loyalty in economic recovery. The company exploited the downturn to break through a traditional barrier – that US grocery shoppers tend to be loyal to big-name brands. According to Nielsen Co. store-brand goods generally make up about 22 per cent of US sales (it is closer to 30 per cent in Europe), but at Aldi 95 per cent of the goods on sale are the retailer's own-brands. In the US Midwest, Aldi prices are between 15 per cent and 20 per cent less than Walmart and 30 per cent to 40 per cent cheaper than regional chains. In fact, Aldi has been in the US since 1976, and has more than 1,000 stores. Seen as something of a 'sleeping giant' of US groceries, Aldi is braced for the arrival in the US of rival discounter Lidl, which should shake things up.

At the same time, Aldi has upgraded its German retailing by improving food ranges and offering more upscale non-food promotions to bring in middle-class shoppers with more disposable income. At one time in the US and UK, Aldi located unattractive stores in low-income areas and sold very few products and little fresh food. Store designs have been improved and grocery ranges enhanced. In the US, Aldi is locating new stores near Walmart Supercentres to draw customers. The test is whether Aldi can repeat its UK success by moving up the market in the huge US market.[1]

The Aldi story sets the stage for examining the fast-changing world of today's resellers. This chapter looks at *retailing* and *wholesaling*. In the first section, we look at the nature and importance of retailing, the major types of store and non-store retailers, the decisions retailers make and the future of retailing. In the second section, we discuss these same topics as they apply to wholesalers.

RETAILING

Author comment

You already know a lot about retailers. You deal with them every day – store retailers, service retailers, online and mobile retailers, and others.

What is retailing? We all know that Aldi, B&Q, Alliance Boots, PCWorld and Dixons Carphone are retailers, but so are Avon representatives, Amazon, the local Holiday Inn and a doctor seeing patients. **Retailing** includes all the activities involved in selling products or services directly to final consumers for their personal, non-business use. Many institutions – manufacturers, wholesalers and retailers – do retailing. But most retailing is done by **retailers**, businesses whose sales come *primarily* from retailing.

Retailing plays a very important role in most marketing channels. They connect brands to consumers in what OgilvyAction, a marketing agency, calls 'the last mile' – the final stop in the consumer's path to purchase. It's the 'distance a consumer travels between an attitude and an action', explains OgilvyAction's CEO. Some 40 per cent of all consumer decisions are made in or near the store. Thus, retailers 'reach consumers at key moments of truth, ultimately [influencing] their actions at the point of purchase'.[2]

In fact, many marketers are now embracing the concept of **shopper marketing** – focusing the entire marketing process – from product and brand development to logistics, promotion and merchandising – toward turning shoppers into buyers as they approach the point of sale.

Shopper marketing emphasises using in-store promotions and advertising to extend brand equity to 'the last mile' and encourage favourable in-store purchase decisions, and recognises that the retail store itself is an important marketing medium. What differentiates the concept of shopper marketing is the suggestion that these efforts should be coordinated around the shopping process itself. For example, P&G follows a 'store back' concept, in which all marketing ideas need to be effective at the store-shelf level and work back from there. The strategy builds around what P&G calls the 'First Moment of Truth' – the critical three to seven seconds that a shopper considers a product on a store shelf.[3]

The dramatic growth of online and mobile shopping has added new dimensions to shopper marketing. The retailing 'moment of truth' no longer takes place only in stores. Instead, Google defines a 'zero moment of truth', when consumers begin the buying process by searching for and learning about products online. Today's consumers are increasingly *omni-channel buyers,* who make little distinction between in-store and online shopping, and for whom the path to a retail purchase runs across multiple channels. For these buyers, a particular purchase might consist of researching a product online and buying it from an online retailer, without ever setting foot in a retail store. Alternatively, they might use a smartphone to research a purchase on the move, or even in retail store aisles. For example, it's common to see a consumer examining an item on a shelf in John Lewis while at the same time using a mobile app to check product reviews and prices at Amazon.com. Thus, shopper marketing isn't just about in-store buying these days. Influencing consumers' buying decisions as they shop involves efforts aimed at online search and in-store, online and mobile shopping.[4]

Although most retailing is still done in retail stores, in recent years direct and online retailing have been growing much faster than store retailing. We discuss direct and online retailing in detail later in this chapter and in Chapter 17. For now, we will focus on store retailing.

Retailing—All the activities involved in selling goods and services to final consumers for their personal, non-business use.

Retailer—A business whose sales come primarily from retailing.

Shopper marketing—Using in-store promotions and advertising to extend brand equity to 'the last mile' and encourage favourable hi-store purchase decisions.

Shopper marketing: the dramatic growth in online and mobile shopping has added new dimensions to 'point of purchase'. Influencing consumers buying decisions as they shop now involves efforts aimed at online search and in-store, online and mobile shopping.
Source: Lev Dolgachov/Alamy Images

Types of retailers

Retail stores come in all shapes and sizes – from your local hairdressing salon or family-owned restaurant to national speciality chain retailers, such as J D Sports or Lakeland, to mega-retailers such as Costco, Tesco or Carrefour. The most important types of retail stores are described in Table 13.1 and discussed in the following sections. They can be classified in terms of several characteristics, including the *amount of service* they offer, the breadth and depth of their *product lines*, the *relative prices* they charge and how they are *organised*.

Table 13.1 Major store retailer types

Type	Description	Examples
Speciality store	A store that carries a narrow product line with a deep assortment, such as clothing stores, sporting-goods stores, furniture stores, florists and bookstores.	Charles Tyrwhitt (men's clothes), J D Sports (sporting goods), Lakeland (specialised kitchenware)
Department store	A store that carries several product lines – typically clothing, home furnishings and household goods – with each line operated as a separate department managed by specialist buyers or merchandisers.	Macy's (US), House of Fraser (UK), Le Bon Marché (France), Karstadt (Germany)
Supermarket	A relatively large, low-cost, low-margin, high-volume, self-service operation designed to serve the consumer's total needs for grocery and household products.	Tesco, Sainsbury's (UK), Auchan, Carrefour (France), Aldi, Metro, Lidl (Germany)
Convenience store	A relatively small store located near residential areas, open long hours seven days a week, and carrying a limited line of high-turnover convenience products at slightly higher prices.	Tesco Express (UK), Spar (throughout Europe), Albert Heijn To Go (Netherlands)
Discount store	A store that carries standard merchandise sold at lower prices with lower margins and higher volumes.	Poundworld, B&M (UK), Dia (Carrefour's hard discount stores across Europe)
Off-price retailer	A store that sells merchandise bought at less-than-regular wholesale prices and sold at less than retail. These include *factory outlets* owned and operated by manufacturers; *independent off-price retailers* owned and run by entrepreneurs or by divisions of larger retail corporations; and *warehouse (or wholesale) clubs* selling a limited selection of brand-name groceries, appliances, clothing and other goods at deep discounts to consumers who pay membership fees.	Mikasa (factory outlet); Superdrug (UK and Ireland), Costco, Sam's Club, BJ's Wholesale Club (warehouse clubs in US and UK), TK Maxx (UK and Europe), Gap Outlet (UK and Europe)
Superstores	A very large store traditionally aimed at meeting consumers' total needs for routinely purchased food and non-food items. This category includes *supercentres*, combined supermarket and discount stores and *category killers*, which carry a deep assortment in a particular category.	Tesco Superstores (UK), Auchan and Carrefour hypermarkets (Europe), Walmart Supercenter, SuperTarget, Meijer (discount stores); PetSmart, Staples (UK and Europe), ToysRUs (category killer)

Amount of service

Different types of customers and products require different amounts of service. To meet these varying service needs, retailers may offer one of three service levels: self-service, limited service and full service.

Self-service retailers serve customers who are willing to perform their own 'locate-compare-select' process to save time or money, and increasingly also operate self-service checkouts. Self-service is the basis of all discount operations and is typically used by retailers selling convenience goods (such as supermarkets) and nationally branded, fast-moving shopping goods (such as Tesco or Auchan). *Limited-service retailers*, such as PCWorld or Halfords (electrical goods, motoring and cycling products), provide more sales assistance because they carry more goods about which customers need information. Their increased operating costs may result in higher prices.

In *full-service retailers*, such as high-end speciality stores (for example, up-market jewellery stores or specialists in products like expensive kitchenware) and first-class department stores (such as Harrods and John Lewis in the UK), salespeople assist customers in every phase of the shopping process. Full-service stores usually carry more speciality goods for which customers need or want assistance or advice. They provide more services, resulting in much higher operating costs, which are normally passed along to customers as higher prices.

Product line

Retailers can also be classified by the length and breadth of their product assortments. Some retailers, such as **speciality stores**, carry narrow product lines with deep assortments within those lines. In many cases, speciality stores are flourishing; for example, The Pen Shop carries high-quality writing instruments for a specialised market. The increasing use of market segmentation, market targeting and product specialisation has resulted in a greater need for stores that focus on specific products and segments.

By contrast, **department stores** carry a wide variety of product lines. In recent years, department stores have been squeezed between more focused and flexible speciality stores on the one hand and more efficient, lower-priced discounters on the other. In response, many have added promotional pricing to meet the discount threat. Others have stepped up the use of store brands and single-brand 'designer shops' to compete with speciality stores. Still others are trying catalogue, telephone and web selling. Service remains the key differentiating factor. High-end department stores do well by emphasising exclusive merchandise and high-quality service.

Supermarkets are the most frequently shopped type of retail store. However, even in the grocery business they face an increase in competition from discount supercentres (Tesco, Carrefour) and speciality food stores (e.g., Whole Foods Market and local delicatessens). In the harsh economic conditions of the late 2000s, supermarkets regained ground in some countries through heavy price discounting to attract consumers, but have been hard hit by discounters like Aldi and Lidl in the UK, as well as growth in out-of-home eating by consumers.

In the battle for 'share of stomachs', some supermarkets have moved upscale, providing improved store environments and higher-quality food offerings, such as fresh bakeries, gourmet deli counters, natural foods and fresh seafood departments. Others, however, are attempting to compete head-on with food discounters such as Tesco, Auchen, Aldi and Carrefour by cutting costs, establishing more-efficient operations and lowering prices. For example, in the UK, Waitrose (a division of the John Lewis Partnership) has successfully rebuilt its market position in tough economic conditions:

> While its major competitors have their own segments – research agency Experian says Sainsbury appeals to younger, well-educated shoppers with cosmopolitan tastes, compared to the broader appeal of Tesco to the price-conscious, while Asda aims at more down-to-earth types – Waitrose is frequented by career professionals and the well-educated. Some call it the posh people's supermarket, which is famed for its emphasis on quality. In spite of the economic downturn, 2010 saw new customers flocking to Waitrose stores, and the company was expanding faster than its bigger competitors, and was for a time the UK's fastest growing grocery retailer. The company benefited from expanding its 'Essential Waitrose' range of value items (to counter perceptions that Waitrose was more expensive than rivals on everyday items), as well as by expanding the high-end Duchy Originals ranges (natural, organic food and other high-quality products made to traditional methods, associated with the Prince of Wales' estates and his well-known environmental proselytising). Advertising campaigns featured designer chef Heston Blumenthal and British icon chef Delia Smith to promote upmarket recipes and products. Waitrose has been successfully persuading customers to do more of their everyday shopping at the store, rather than regarding Waitrose as a shop only for the special occasion. They have been attracting customers from both the mainstream rivals like Tesco and Sainsbury but also at times from the hard discounters like Aldi and Lidl – though in 2015 Waitrose was overtaken in market share by Aldi. Waitrose is looking for growth through a renewed online operation, franchised stores overseas and small units in petrol service stations.[5]

Speciality store—A retail store that carries a narrow product line with a deep assortment within that line.

Department store—A retail store that carries a wide range of product lines, each operated as a separate department managed by specialist buyers or merchandisers.

Supermarket—A large, low-cost, low-margin, high-volume, self-service store that carries a wide variety of grocery and household products.

Convenience store—A small store, located near a residential area, that is open long hours seven days a week and carries a limited line of high-turnover convenience goods.

Superstore—A store much larger than a regular supermarket that offers a large assortment of routinely purchased food products, non-food items and services.

Category killer—A giant speciality store that carries a very deep assortment of a particular line.

Service retailer—A retailer whose product line is actually a service, including hotels, airlines, banks, colleges and many others

Convenience stores are small stores that carry a limited line of high-turnover convenience goods. For example, Tesco Express and Sainsbury Local are chains of convenience stores operated by the major supermarket companies, with the aim of allowing consumers to do local 'top-up' shopping as well as the main shop at a supermarket or superstore. The big companies have purchased small chains of local convenience outlets and re-branded them, as well as opening new sites and locating at petrol stations. Other convenience stores are operated as independent ventures or as small regional chains.

Superstores are much larger than regular supermarkets and offer a large assortment of routinely purchased food products, non-food items and services. These discount retailers offer *supercentres*, very large combination food and discount stores. Recent years have also seen the explosive growth of superstores that are actually giant speciality stores, the so-called **category killers** (e.g., B&Q, ToysRUs). They feature huge stores that carry a very deep assortment of a particular line with a knowledgeable staff. Category killers are prevalent in a wide range of categories, including electronics, home-improvement products, books, baby products, toys and sporting goods. They are particularly significant channels of distribution in the United States.

Finally, for many retailers, the product line is actually a service. **Service retailers** include hotels, banks, airlines, colleges, hospitals, cinemas, sports and fitness clubs, restaurants, repair services, hairdressers and dry cleaners. In many countries, service retailers are growing faster than product retailers.

Relative prices

Retailers can also be classified according to the prices they charge (see Table 13.1). Most retailers charge regular prices and offer normal-quality goods and customer service. Others offer higher-quality goods and service at higher prices. Retailers that feature low prices are discount stores and 'off-price' retailers.

Discount stores

Discount store—A retail operation that sells standard merchandise at lower prices by accepting lower margins and selling at higher volume.

A **discount store** sells standard merchandise at lower prices by accepting lower margins and selling higher volume. Aldi and Lidl are discount stores in UK grocery retailing. The early discount stores cut expenses by offering few services and operating in warehouse-like facilities in low-rent, high-traffic areas. Today's discounters have impoved their store environments and increased their services, while at the same time keeping prices low through lean, efficient operations.

Leading 'big-box' discounters, such as Walmart, Costco and Target, dominate the retail scene in the US, although that dominance by this type of retailer is much less pronounced in Europe. However, even 'small-box' discounters are thriving in the current economic environment. For example, Poundland is Europe's biggest single-price discount store (all items sell for £1), and has done well during the recession. Poundland has moved from its low-income consumer base into mainstream shopping centres and attracts a broader market. Poundland is expanding its non-UK business as D€ALZ, although not using the single price policy. The Poundland slogan is 'Amazing value every day'.

Off-price retailers

Off-price retailer—A retailer that buys at less-than-regular wholesale prices and sells at less than retail.

As the major discount stores have tended to trade up, a new wave of **off-price retailers** moved in to fill the ultralow-price, high-volume gap. Ordinary discounters buy at regular wholesale prices and accept lower margins to keep prices down. In contrast, off-price retailers buy at less-than-regular wholesale prices and charge consumers less than retail. Off-price retailers can be found in all areas, from food, clothing and electronics to no-frills banking and discount brokerages.

Independent off-price retailer—An off-price retailer that is independently owned and operated or a division of a larger retail corporation.

The three main types of off-price retailers are *independents*, *factory outlets* and *warehouse clubs*. **Independent off-price retailers** either are independently owned and run, or are divisions of larger retail corporations. Although many off-price operations are run by smaller independents, most large off-price retailer operations are owned by bigger retail chains. Examples include

Discount stores: Poundland is Europe's largest single-price discount store (all items sell for £1) and has done well during the recession.
Source: Iconic Cornwall/Alamy Images

stores like TK Maxx and online sellers such as Overstock.com. TK Maxx promises brand name and designer fashions for 20 to 60 per cent off department store prices. How does it fulfil this promise? Its buyer are constantly on the lookout for deals. 'So when a designer overproduces and department stores overbuy,' says the company, 'We swoop in, negotiate the lowest possible price, and pass the savings on.'[6]

Factory outlets

Manufacturer-owned and operated stores by firms such as Gap, Levi Strauss and others sometimes group together in *factory outlet malls* and *value-retail centres*, where dozens of outlet stores offer prices as much as 50 per cent below retail on a wide range of mostly surplus, discounted or irregular goods. Whereas outlet malls consist primarily of manufacturers' outlets, value-retail centres combine manufacturers' outlets with off-price retail stores and department store clearance outlets. Factory outlet malls have become one of the hottest growth areas in retailing in the United States, and are growing in popularity in several European countries.

These malls in general are now moving upscale – and even dropping 'factory' from their descriptions. A growing number of outlet malls now feature luxury brands such as Coach, Polo Ralph Lauren, Brooks Brothers, Dolce&Gabbana, Giorgio Armani, Burberry and Versace. As consumers become more value-minded, even upper-end retailers are accelerating their factory outlet strategies, placing more emphasis on these outlets. Many companies now regard outlets not simply as a way of disposing of problem merchandise but as an additional way of gaining business for fresh merchandise. The combination of highbrow brands and lowbrow prices found at outlets provides powerful shopper appeal, especially in a tighter economy.[7]

Warehouse clubs (or *wholesale clubs* or *membership warehouses*), such as Costco in the US and UK, and Makro in Europe and Asia, operate in huge, draughty, warehouse-like facilities and offer few frills. However, they offer ultralow prices and surprise deals on selected branded merchandise. Warehouse clubs have grown rapidly in recent years. These retailers appeal not only to low-income consumers seeking bargains on bare-bones products but also all kinds of customers shopping for a wide range of goods, from necessities to extravagances.

Consider Costco, now the third-largest retailer in the United States, behind only Walmart and Kroger, and with stores in the UK, the Asia-Pacific region and Latin America. Low price is an important part of Costco's equation, but what really sets Costco apart is the products it carries and the sense of urgency that it builds into the Costco shopper's store experience.[8]

Factory outlet—An off-price retailing operation that is owned and operated by a manufacturer and normally carries the manufacturer's surplus, discontinued or irregular goods.

Warehouse club—An off-price retailer that sells a limited selection of brand name grocery items, appliances, clothing, and other goods at deep discounts to members who pay annual membership fees.

Table 13.2 Major types of retail organisations

Type	Description	Examples
Corporate chain	Two or more outlets that are commonly owned and controlled. Corporate chains appear in all types of retailing, but they are strongest in department stores, discount stores, food stores, drug stores and restaurants.	John Lewis (UK department stores), Tesco (UK discount stores), Sainsbury (UK grocery stores), Alliance Boots (UK pharmacies)
Voluntary chain	Wholesaler-sponsored group of independent retailers engaged in group buying and merchandising.	Spar (European voluntary chain)
Retailer cooperative	Group of independent retailers who jointly establish a central buying organisation and conduct joint promotion efforts.	The Cooperative Group (UK consumer cooperative)
Franchise organisation	Contractual association between a franchisor (a manufacturer, wholesaler or service organisation) and franchisees (independent businesspeople who buy the right to own and operate one or more units in the franchise system).	McDonald's, Subway, Pizza Hut

Corporate chains (or multiples)—Two or more outlets that are commonly owned and controlled.

Franchise—A contractual association between a manufacturer, wholesaler or service organisation (a franchisor) and independent businesspeople (franchisees) who buy the right to own and operate one or more units in the franchise system.

Retailer cooperatives: founded in the Netherlands in 1932, Spar is the world's largest independent voluntary retail trading chain, trading from approximately 12,500 stores in 35 countries worldwide.

Source: Jeffrey Blackler/Alamy Images

Organisational approach

Although many retail stores are independently owned, others band together under some form of corporate or contractual organisation. Table 13.2 describes four major types of retail organisations – *corporate chains*, *voluntary chains*, *retailer cooperatives* and *franchise organisations*.

Corporate chains (or multiples) are two or more outlets that are commonly owned and controlled. They have many advantages over independents. Their size allows them to buy in large quantities at lower prices and gain promotional economies. They can hire specialists to deal with areas such as pricing, promotion, merchandising, inventory control and sales forecasting.

The great success of corporate chains caused many independent retailers to band together in one of two forms of contractual associations. One is the *voluntary chain* – a wholesaler-sponsored group of independent retailers that engages in group buying and common merchandising. The other type of contractual association is the *retailer cooperative* – a group of independent retailers that bands together to set up a jointly owned, central wholesale operation and conduct joint merchandising and promotion efforts. Founded in the Netherlands in 1932, Spar is the world's largest independent voluntary retail trading chain, trading from approximately 12,500 stores in 35 countries worldwide. These organisations give independents the buying and promotion economies they need to meet the prices of corporate chains.

Another form of contractual retail organisation is a **franchise**. The main difference between franchise organisations and other contractual systems (voluntary chains and retail cooperatives) is that franchise systems are normally based on some unique product or service; a method of doing business; or the trade name, goodwill or patent that the franchisor has developed. Franchising has been prominent in fast-food restaurants, hotels, health and fitness centres, motor car sales and service, and estate agency.

But franchising covers a lot more than just burger joints and fitness centres. Franchises have sprung up to meet just about any need. For example, Mad Science Group franchisees put on science programmes for schools, children's clubs and birthday parties. And Mr Handyman provides repair services for homeowners, while Merry Maids tidies up their houses.

Once considered upstarts among independent businesses, the International Franchise Association estimates that franchised brands account for 56 per cent of quick service restaurants, 18 per cent of lodging establishments, 14 per cent of retail food businesses, and 13 per cent of table/full service restaurants. In this study franchises were found to employ almost 10 million people, with direct output close to $625 billion and a payroll of $230 billion.[9] Certainly, franchises now command 40 per cent of all retail sales in the United States. These days, it's nearly impossible to stroll down a high street without seeing a McDonald's, Subway or Holiday Inn. One of the best-known and most successful franchisers, McDonald's, now has more than 34,000 stores in 118 countries, including almost 14,000 in the United States. It serves 69 million customers a day and racks up more than $97 billion in annual system-wide sales. More than 80 per cent of McDonald's restaurants worldwide are owned and operated by franchisees. Now a larger business than McDonalds, Subway is one of the fastest-growing franchises, with more than 41,000 shops in 105 countries, including more than 25,500 in the United States.[10]

Retailer marketing decisions

Retailers are always searching for new marketing strategies to attract and hold customers. In the past, retailers attracted customers with unique product assortments and more or better services. Today, retail assortments and services are looking more and more alike. Many manufacturers, in their drive for volume, have placed their brands almost everywhere. You can find most consumer brands not only in department stores but also in mass-merchandise discount stores, off-price discount stores and all over the Internet. Thus, it's now more difficult for any one retailer to offer exclusive merchandise.

Service differentiation among retailers has also eroded. Many department stores have trimmed their services, whereas discounters have increased theirs. Customers have become smarter and more price sensitive. They see no reason to pay more for identical brands, especially when service differences are shrinking. For all these reasons, many retailers today are rethinking their marketing strategies.

As shown in Figure 13.1, retailers face major marketing decisions about *segmentation and targeting*, *store differentiation and positioning*, and the *retail marketing mix*.

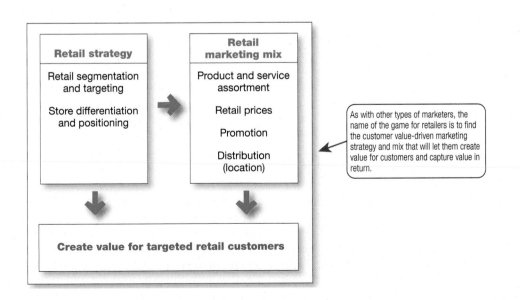

Figure 13.1 Retailer marketing strategies

Segmentation, targeting, differentiation and positioning decisions

Retailers must first segment and define their target markets and then decide how they will differentiate and position themselves in these markets. Should they focus on upscale, midscale or downscale shoppers? Do target shoppers want variety, depth of assortment, convenience or low prices? Until they define and profile their markets, retailers cannot make consistent decisions about product assortment, services, pricing, advertising, store décor, or any of the other decisions that must support their positions. Too many retailers, even big ones, fail to clearly define their target markets and positions. In contrast, successful retailers define their target markets well and position themselves strongly.

For example, Tesco positions itself strongly on low prices and what those always low prices mean to its customers. It consistently promises customers that 'Every little helps'. But if giant Tesco, with roughly a third of the UK grocery market, dominates the low-price position, how can other retailers hope to compete? Again, the answer is good targeting and positioning. For example, Waitrose has fewer than 250 stores in the UK and slightly more than 5 per cent of the market versus Tesco's global network of stores in multiple trading formats and 30 per cent of the UK market. How does this small grocery chain compete with Tesco? Waitrose succeeds by carefully positioning itself *away* from Tesco. It targets a select group of upscale customers and offers them high-quality products with outstanding provenance. In fact, not only is Waitrose growing much faster than Tesco, some devoted Waitrose customers are more likely to boycott the local Tesco than to shop at it.

Waitrose can't match Tesco's massive economies of scale, incredible volume purchasing power, ultra-efficient logistics, wide selection and hard-to-beat prices. But then again, it doesn't generally try. By positioning itself strongly away from Tesco and other discounters, Waitrose has grown solidly, even in tighter economic times.

With robust targeting and positioning, a retailer can compete effectively against even the largest and strongest competitors.

Product assortment and services decision

Retailers must decide on three major product variables: product assortment, services mix and store atmosphere.

The retailer's product assortment should differentiate the retailer while matching target shoppers' expectations. One strategy is to offer merchandise that no other competitor carries, such as store brands, or manufacturer brands on which it holds exclusives. For example, a department store like John Lewis may get exclusive rights to carry a well-known designer's labels, and also offer its own private-label lines.

Another strategy is to feature blockbuster merchandising events. In the US, department store Bloomingdale's is known for running spectacular shows featuring goods from a certain country, such as India or China. Or the retailer can offer surprise merchandise, as when Aldi and Lidl or Poundland offer surprise assortments of seconds, overstocks and closeouts (products no longer manufactured). Finally, the retailer can differentiate itself by offering a highly targeted product assortment: High & Mighty carries extra large clothing sizes; Gadget Shop offers an unusual assortment of gadgets and gifts; and Accessorize offers about every imaginable kind of hair decoration and cheap jewellery.

The *services mix* can also help set one retailer apart from another. For example, some retailers invite customers to ask questions or consult service representatives in person or via phone or keyboard. The John Lewis Partnership promises 'The Partnership aims to deal honestly with its customers and secure their loyalty and trust by providing outstanding choice, value and service'; do-it-yourself home improvement giant B&Q Home Depot offers a diverse mix of services for do-it-yourselfers, from 'how-to' guides to advice to inspire.

The *store's atmosphere* is another important element in the reseller's product arsenal. Retailers desire to create a unique store experience, one that suits the target market and moves customers to buy. Many retailers practise *experiential retailing*. For example, at several REI stores

(Recreational Equipment Inc.) in the US, consumers can get hands-on experience with merchandise, before buying it, via the store's mountain bike test trail, gear-testing stations, a huge rock climbing wall, or an in-store simulated rain shower.

Today's digital technologies present many new challenges and opportunities for shaping retail experiences. The surge in online and mobile shopping has changed retail customer behaviours and expectations. As a result, a wide range of store retailers – from high-tech sellers such as Apple to high-touch sellers like Audi and Build-A-Bear – are digitising the in-store experience. They are merging the physical and digital worlds to create new-age experiential retailing environments:[11]

> Digitising in-store retail is not just for technology retailers like Apple. Companies in a wide range of other industries are also pioneering the concept. Take German automaker Audi, for instance. In the lead-up to the 2012 Summer Olympics in London, Audi threw open the doors to its first Audi City, a stunningly innovative digitised showroom in London's busy Piccadilly Circus area.
>
> Rather than displaying a sea of shiny new vehicles, the Audi City showroom contains very few actual cars and future Audi showrooms may have none at all. Instead, Audi City is all-digital. Prospective customers use touchscreens and cameras to design and manipulate virtual, life-size cars of their dreams displayed on massive screens surrounding the showroom space. When they've finished, a video shows the car they've designed in action, complete with the exact sound of the chosen engine in full stereo fidelity. The car is then loaded onto a memory stick that the customer can take for later remembering and sharing.
>
> The idea of buying a car without actually seeing it flies in the face of car retailing tradition. But these car-buying times are anything but traditional. Audi sees digitisation as a way to fit showrooms into smaller urban settings and to overcome the limitations of physical dealerships. With 12 different models, each with up to six different trim levels, all with numerous options, no physical dealership can have every possible model on hand. Virtual showrooms, however, can present every model in Audi's extensive portfolio in every possible permutation. Moreover, customers can call them up instantly and make changes on the fly.
>
> So far, the Audi City virtual experience is producing very real-world results. Audi City showrooms in London, Beijing and Dubai are outselling their traditional counterparts by 70 per cent, with an average increase in margin per vehicle of 30 per cent. And the digitised auto lounges are bringing more new customers through the doors. Ninety per cent of Audi City visitors are new to the brand.

Today's successful retailers carefully orchestrate virtually every aspect of the consumer store experience. The next time you step into a retail store – whether it sells consumer electronics, hardware or high fashion – stop and carefully consider your surroundings. Think about the store's layout and displays. Listen to the background sounds. Smell the smells. Check the colours and lighting. Chances are good that everything in the store, from the layout and lighting to the music and even the smells, has been carefully orchestrated to help shape the customer's shopping experience – and open their wallets. At a Sony Style store, for instance, the environment is designed to encourage touch, from the silk wallpaper to the smooth maple wood cabinets, to the etched-glass countertops. Products are displayed like museum pieces and are set up to be touched and tried.

For example, retailers choose the colours in their logos and interiors carefully: black suggests sophistication, orange is associated with fairness and affordability, white signifies simplicity and

Audi City is a stunningly innovative digitised showroom that contains very few cars. Prospective customers use touchscreens and cameras to design and manipulate life-size cars of their dreams displayed on massive screens surrounding the showroom.
Source: Clemens Bilan/Getty Images

383

purity (think Apple stores) and blue connotes trust and dependability (financial institutions use it a lot).[12]

> Luxury shirtmaker Thomas Pink pipes the smell of clean, pressed shirts into its stores – its signature 'line-dried linen' scent. Bloomingdale's uses different essences in different departments: the soft scent of baby powder in the baby store, coconut in the swimsuit area, lilacs in intimate apparel, and sugar cookies and evergreen scent during the holiday season. At a Sony Style store, the subtle fragrance of vanilla and mandarin orange – designed exclusively for Sony – wafts down on shoppers, relaxing them and helping them believe that this is a very nice place to be. Such scents can increase customer 'dwell times' and, in turn, buying. Says the founder of ScentAir, a company that produces such scents, 'Developing a signature fragrance is much like [developing] a message in print or radio: What do you want to communicate to consumers and how often?'

Such 'experiential retailing' confirms that retail stores are much more than simply assortments of goods. They are environments to be experienced by the people who shop in them. Store atmospheres offer a powerful tool by which retailers can differentiate their stores from those of competitors.

In fact, retail establishments sometimes become small communities in themselves – places where people get together. These places include coffee shops and cafés, bookstores, children's play spaces, superstores and urban greenmarkets. For example, today's bookstores have become part bookstore, part library, part living room and part coffee-house. On an early evening at your local Waterstones, for example, you'll most likely find school students with backpacks doing their homework with friends in the coffee bar. Nearby, retirees sit in cushy chairs thumbing through travel or gardening books, while parents read aloud to their small children. Waterstones tries to sell more than just books; it sells comfort, relaxation and community.

Price decision

A retailer's price policy must fit its target market and positioning, product and service assortment, the competition and economic factors. All retailers would like to charge high mark-ups and achieve high volume, but the two seldom go together. Most retailers seek *either* high mark-ups on lower volume (most speciality stores) *or* low mark-ups on higher volume (mass merchandisers and discount stores).

Thus, Harvey Nichols, founded in 1813, caters to the upper crust by selling clothing, shoes and jewellery created by designers such as Chanel, Prada and Hermes. The up-market retailer pampers its customers with services such as a personal shopper and in-store showings of the upcoming season's trends with cocktails and hors d'oeuvres. By contrast, TK Maxx sells brand-name clothing at discount prices aimed at the budget-conscious. Stocking new products each week, the discounter provides a treasure hunt for bargain shoppers. 'No sales. No gimmicks,' says the retailer. 'Just brand name and designer fashions for you . . . for up to 60 per cent off department store prices.'

Retailers must also decide on the extent to which they will use sales and other price promotions. Some retailers use no price promotions at all, competing instead on product and service quality rather than on price. For example, it's difficult to imagine Harvey Nichols holding a two-for-the-price-of-one sale on Chanel handbags, even in a tough economy. Other retailers – such as Asda, Costco and Poundland – practise *everyday low pricing*, charging constant, everyday low prices with few sales or discounts.

Still other retailers practice *high–low pricing* – charging higher prices on an everyday basis, coupled with frequent sales and other price promotions to increase store traffic, create a low-price image, or attract customers who will buy other goods at full prices. The recent economic downturn caused a rash of high–low pricing, as retailers poured on price cuts and promotions to coax bargain-hunting customers into their stores. Which pricing strategy is best depends on the retailer's overall marketing strategy, the pricing approaches of its competitors and the economic environment.

Promotion decision

Retailers use any or all of the five promotion tools – advertising, personal selling, sales promotion, public relations (PR), and direct and social media marketing – to reach consumers. They advertise in newspapers and magazines and on the radio, television and the Internet. Advertising may be supported by newspaper inserts and catalogues. Store salespeople greet customers, meet their needs, and build relationships. Sales promotions may include in-store demonstrations, displays, sales and loyalty programmes. PR activities, such as new-store openings, special events, newsletters and blogs, store magazines and public service activities, are also available to retailers.

Most retailers also interact digitally with consumers using websites and digital catalogues, online ads and video, social media, mobile ads and apps, blogs and e-mail. Almost every retailer, large or small, maintains a full social media presence. Digital communications offer customers information and other features and sell merchandise directly.

Digital promotions let retailers reach individual customers with carefully targeted messages. For example, office products retailer Staples supports its stores with print catalogues and online catalogue links e-mailed to regular customers. The online links provide a reminder that it is time to reorder some office supplies, and highlight special offers and awards for additional purchases, which may be made online, over the telephone or in the store.

Place decision

Retailers often point to three critical factors in retailing success: *location, location* and *location*! It's very important that retailers select locations that are accessible to the target market in areas that are consistent with the retailer's positioning. For example, Apple locates its stores in high-end shopping centres and trendy shopping districts. Small retailers may have to settle for whatever locations they can find or afford. Large retailers, however, usually employ specialists who use advanced methods to select store locations.

Most stores today cluster together to increase their customer pulling power and give consumers the convenience of one-stop shopping. In the US and most European countries, *city centres* were the main form of retail cluster until the 1950s. Every large city and town had a central area with department stores, speciality stores, banks and cinemas. When people began to move to the suburbs, however, city centres, with their traffic, parking and crime problems, began to lose business. In recent years, many cities have joined with retailers to try to revive city centre shopping areas, generally with only mixed success.

A **shopping centre** is a group of retail businesses built on a site that is planned, developed, owned and managed as a unit. The most complex differentiation between different levels and types of shopping centres is shown in American retailing, reflecting the size of that country, and the model is scaled down in smaller countries, so these distinctions may be less clear-cut in Europe. In the US, a *regional shopping centre*, or *regional shopping mall*, the largest and most dramatic shopping centre, can have from 50 to more than 100 stores, including two or more full-line department stores. It is like a covered mini-downtown and attracts customers from a wide area. A *community shopping centre* contains between 15 and 50 retail stores. It normally contains a branch of a department store or variety store, a supermarket, speciality stores, professional offices and sometimes a bank. Most shopping centres are *neighbourhood shopping centres* or *strip malls* that generally contain between 5 and 15 stores. They are close and convenient for consumers. They usually contain a small supermarket, perhaps a discount store, and several service stores – dry cleaner, pharmacist, video-rental store, hardware store, local restaurant or other stores.[13]

In Europe, while there has been considerable development of more attractive central shopping malls, like the giant Bluewater out-of-town shopping centre in Kent, and new Westfield shopping centres throughout the UK, market size limits the potential more than is the case in the United States.

A newer form of shopping centre is the so-called power centre. *Power centres* are huge unenclosed shopping centres consisting of a long strip of retail stores, including large stores acting as free-standing anchors. Each store has its own entrance with parking directly in front for shoppers who wish to visit

Shopping centre—A group of retail businesses built on a site that is planned, developed, owned and managed as a unit.

only one store. In contrast, *lifestyle centres* are smaller, open-air malls with upscale stores, convenient locations and non-retail activities, such as a playground, skating rink, hotel, dining establishments and a cinema complex. In fact, the original power centre and lifestyle centre concepts are now morphing into hybrid lifestyle-power centres that combine the convenience and community feel of a neighbourhood centre with the brute force of a power centre. Meanwhile, traditional regional shopping malls are adding lifestyle elements – such as fitness centres, common areas and multiplex cinemas – to make themselves more social and welcoming. In all, today's centres are more like places to hang out rather than just places to shop. 'The line between shopping, entertainment, and community building has blurred,' says one analyst. 'Shopping centres aren't just places to buy things. They're social centres, places for entertainment, and employment hubs.'[14]

Some similar developments are occurring in the UK, where giant retail centres are attracting visitors with a mix of leisure and entertainment facilities as well as shops. The Trafford Centre in Manchester has a miniature Legoland; Bluewater in Kent has a pirate theme park for children and a live music venue; and Westfield London has Gymbox, a trendy fitness centre with classes such as Thug Box, as well as a huge cinema complex and 50 bars and restaurants. However, the rise of the 'supermall' is at the expense of smaller, secondary centres.[15]

Bear in mind that the 'mall' is an American icon, as in 'hanging out at the mall' as a prime leisure activity. However, in the UK and Europe, the intensity of large shopping centres is generally less, although the situation varies across the different countries involved. While the American shopping centre types are of interest, the European picture is complicated by the smaller geographical area of most individual countries, a longer history of urbanisation, longer established city centres, and cultural differences which are reflected in consumer shopping preferences and attitudes towards shopping. You should not expect to find a direct replication of the American model in any European country, although there will be examples of each of the shopping centre types in each country, varying from local shopping areas to major regional centres and malls. It is not feasible to generalise about shopping centre types and developments Europe-wide, and marketers need to look closely at differences between countries of interest regarding retail developments. Marketers must recognise that retail structures vary considerably across the countries in Europe.

Retailing trends and developments

Retailers operate in a harsh and fast-changing environment, which offers threats as well as opportunities. For example, in some countries, the retail industry suffers from chronic overcapacity (too many shops), resulting in fierce competition for customer expenditure, especially in tough economic times. Customer demographics, lifestyles and spending patterns are changing rapidly, as are retailing technologies. To be successful, retailers need to choose target segments carefully and position themselves strongly. They need to take the following retailing developments into account as they plan and execute their competitive strategies.

Tighter consumer spending

Following many years of good economic times for retailers, economic downturn and recession turned many retailers' fortunes from boom to bust. Even as the world economy has recovered, retailers will feel the effects of changed consumer spending patterns well into the future. To a greater or lesser extent, these comments hold true for most of the developed economies in Europe.

Nonetheless, some retailers actually benefit from economic downturn. For example, as consumers cut back and look for ways to spend less on what they buy, big discounters scoop up new business from bargain-hungry shoppers. Think of retailers like Aldi and Poundland in the UK. Similarly, lower-priced fast-food chains, such as McDonald's, have taken business from their pricier eating-out competitors.

For most retailers, however, tighter consumer spending means tough times. Some large and familiar retailers have declared bankruptcy and closed their doors completely over recent years – for example, in the UK this includes household names such as Woolworths, Past Times, La Senza,

Focus DIY, Oddbins and Borders, to name a few, and others remain at risk. Other retailers have laid off employees, cut their costs, and offered deep price discounts and promotions aimed at luring cash-strapped customers back. Beyond cost-cutting and price promotions, many retailers have also added new value pitches to their positioning.

When reacting to economic difficulties, retailers must be careful that their short-run actions don't damage their long-run images and positions. Drastic price discounting is 'a sign of panic', says a retail strategist. 'Anyone can sell product by dropping their prices, but it does not breed loyalty.'[16] Instead of relying on cost-cutting and price reductions, retailers should focus on building greater customer value within their long-term store positioning strategies. For example, in the long run, a retailer like Waitrose cannot afford to abandon the quality, innovation and service that differentiate it from Tesco and other discounters.

New retail forms, shortening retail life cycles and retail convergence

New retail forms continue to emerge to meet new situations and consumer needs, but the life cycle of new retail forms is getting shorter. Department stores took about 100 years to reach the mature stage of the life cycle; more recent forms, such as warehouse stores, reached maturity in about ten years. In such an environment, seemingly solid retail positions can crumble quickly. For example, in the US, of the top 10 discount retailers in 1962 (the year that Walmart and Kmart began), not one exists today. Even the most successful retailers can't sit back with a winning formula. To remain successful, they must keep adapting.

New retail forms are always emerging. The most recent blockbuster retailing trend is the advent of online retailing, by both online-only and bricks-and-mortar retailers, via websites, mobile apps and social media.

Other lesser innovations occur regularly as well. For example, many retailers are now using limited-time *pop-up stores* that let them promote their brands to seasonal shoppers and create buzz in busy areas. In the UK, pop-up shops were once reserved for edgy fashion and low-quality electrical goods but now extend to restaurants, galleries and even nightclubs. eBay runs a pop-up shop in London for a week and McDonald's had a temporary outlet in the Olympic Park for six weeks. John Lewis, Chanel and US boutiques have all run temporary premises in central London. Using empty shops – or in the case of Dum Dums Donutterie selling gourmet doughnuts from a converted shipping container – pop-up shops allow entrepreneurs, merchants, designers and artists to try out an idea before committing to permanent premises. Dum Dums now sell in Harrods. In 2013 the Crown Estate opened Piccadilly to pop-ups for niche newcomers as part of moves to reinvent Britain's high street. Even hotels have pop-ups:[17]

New retail forms: many retailers are now using limited-time pop-up stores that let them promote their brands to seasonal shoppers and create a buzz in busy areas.

Source: M-dash/Alamy Images

Snoozebox was born when veteran hotelier Robert Breare was sheltering from the rain at the Le Mans 24-hour motor race. The idea was to build comfortable, portable cabins and transport them – by air, land or sea – to sporting and musical events. By 2013, Snoozebox was shipping stackable containers to house guests at events including Le Mans, the Edinburgh Festivals of plays and concerts, and the G8 Summit. Snoozebox can go most places where events are being held but there is not enough accommodation for the people visiting. Snoozebox negotiates with event promoters to drop its serviced, air-conditioned rooms closest to the event action. That does not come cheap – three nights in a Snoozebox for two adults and a child at the Formula 1 Santander British grand Prix costs around £800 but you are right next to the race track. Snoozebox is a pop-up hotel.

New retail forms: Snooze-box was born when veteran hotelier Robert Breare was sheltering from the rain at the Le Mans 24-hour race. The idea was to build comfortable, portable cabins and transport them to sporting and musical events. Snoozebox is a pop-up hotel.

Source: Matthew Horwood/ Alamy Images

The online and mobile equivalent is *flash sales* sites, such as Marks & Spencer time-limited sales events on fashion and household goods offered to customers by e-mail. Similarly, Groupon offers flash deals on travel through Groupon Getaways.[18]

In addition, new retail forms are always emerging. Increasingly, different types of retailers now sell the same products at the same prices to the same consumers. For example, you can buy brand-name home appliances at department stores, discount stores, home improvement stores, off-price retailers, electronics specialists, supermarkets and many websites that all compete for the same customers. So if you can't find the microwave oven you want at John Lewis, step across the street and find one for a better price at Tesco or Aldi – or just order one online from Amazon or a more specialised home appliance website. This merging of consumers, products, prices and retailers is called *retail convergence*. Such convergence means greater competition for retailers and greater difficulty in differentiating the product assortments of different types of retailers.

The rise of mega-retailers

The rise of huge mass merchandisers and speciality superstores, the formation of vertical marketing systems, and a rash of retail mergers and acquisitions have created a core of superpower mega-retailers, usually operating globally. Through their superior information systems and buying power, these giant retailers can offer better merchandise selections, good service and strong price savings to consumers. As a result, they grow even larger by squeezing out their smaller, weaker competitors.

The mega-retailers have shifted the balance of power between retailers and producers. A small handful of retailers now control access to enormous numbers of consumers, giving them the upper hand in their dealings with manufacturers. For example, you may never have heard of speciality coatings and sealants manufacturer RPM International, but you've probably used one or more of its many familiar do-it-yourself brands – such as Rust-Oleum paints, Plastic Wood and Dap fillers, and Testors hobby cements and paints – all of which you can buy at your local hardware or hobby store. However, a dominant hardware retailer like Home Depot in the US is a very important customer to RPM, accounting for a significant share of its consumer sales. Home Depot's sales of $66 billion are close to 20 times RPM's sales of $3.4 billion. As a result, the giant retailer can, and often does, use this power to wring concessions from RPM and thousands of other smaller suppliers.[19]

Growth of non-store retailing

Many consumers still make most of their purchases the old-fashioned way: They go to a store, find what they want, wait patiently in line to put down their cash or credit card, and bring home the goods. However, consumers now have a broad array of non-store alternatives, including direct and digital shopping via websites, mobile apps and social media, as well as mail order and catalogues. Consumers everywhere are increasingly avoiding the hassles and crowds at shops by doing more of their buying by phone or computer. As we'll discuss in Chapter 17, direct and digital marketing are currently the fastest-growing forms of marketing.

Today, thanks to advanced technologies, easier-to-use and enticing online sites and mobile apps, improved online services, and the increasing sophistication of search technologies, online retailing is thriving. In the United States, online retailing still accounts for only around 5.8 per cent of total US retail sales, but is growing at a much faster rate than retail buying as a whole. Last year's US online retail sales reached an estimated $263 billion, up 16.9 per cent over the previous year versus a 4.2 per cent increase in overall retail sales. Online retail will reach an estimated $370 billion by 2017.[20]

The Centre for Retail Research estimates that across Europe online retail sales increased by 7.2 per cent in 2015, while growth in the UK was 15.2 per cent and in Germany 11.6 per cent – way above the overall growth rate for all retail sales in those countries. Europe-wide online spending rose from £132 billion in 2014 to just under £160 billion in 2015.[21] In the UK, online sales account for around 12 per cent of all retail in 2015.[22]

Retailer online sites, mobile apps and social media also influence a large amount of in-store buying. For example, consider the situation in the US: an estimated 46 per cent of total US retail sales were either transacted directly or influenced by online research; an estimated 15 per cent of all online sales now take place on mobile devices, a number that will grow to 25 per cent by 2017; and, according to a recent survey, nearly 20 per cent of online holiday shoppers made at least some purchases based on personal connections or promotions on Facebook. Increasingly, retailers of all kinds rely on social media to engage their buyer communities. For example, Victoria's Secret is second only to iTunes among retailers in YouTube subscribers.[23]

The digital age has spawned a whole new breed of shopper – people who just can't buy anything unless they first look it up online and find out what's what.

Source: Zurijeta/Shutterstock.com

The spurt in online, mobile and social media retailing is both a blessing and a curse to store retailers. Although it gives them new channels for engaging and selling to customers, it also creates more competition from online-only retailers. To the dismay of some store retailers, many shoppers now check out products at physical-store showrooms but then buy them online using a computer or mobile device, sometimes while in the store – a process called **showrooming**. These days, as many as half of all shoppers who buy products online first check them out at a traditional store. Store retailers in fields as diverse as homewares, home electronics and toys are being hit hard by showrooming. Today, however, many store retailers are developing strategies to counter showrooming. Others are even embracing it as an opportunity to highlight the advantages of shopping in stores versus online-only retailers.[24]

Showrooming—The shopping practice of coming into retail store showrooms to check out merchandise and prices but instead buying from an online-only rival, sometimes while in the store.

Thus, it's no longer a matter of customers deciding whether to shop in a store *or* shop online. Increasingly, customers are merging store, websites, social media and mobile outlets into a single shopping process. The Internet and digital devices have spawned a whole new breed of shopper and way of shopping. Whether shopping for electronics, consumer products, cars, homes or medical care, many people just can't buy anything unless they first look it up online and get the lowdown. And they've become used to buying anywhere, anytime – whether it's in the store, online, on the go, or even online while in the store.

All types of retailers now employ direct and online channels. The web and mobile online sales of large bricks-and-mortar retailers, such as Tesco, John Lewis, Staples and Dixons Carphone, are increasing rapidly. Many large online-only retailers – Amazon, Netflix, online travel companies such as Travelocity.com and Expedia.com, and others – are now making it big on the Internet. At the other extreme, hordes of niche marketers are using the Internet to reach new markets and expand their sales.

Still, much of the anticipated growth in online sales will go to multi-channel retailers – the clicks-and-bricks marketers that can successfully merge the virtual and physical worlds. In a recent ranking of the top 25 online retail sites, 15 were owned by store-based retail chains. Another study showed that, among the top 500 online retailers, online sales by store chains were growing 8 per cent faster than those of online-only retailers and 40 per cent faster than overall e-commerce.[25] For example, John Lewis' enhanced website complements its stores around the UK. Although many John Lewis customers make purchases online, the site offers a range of features designed to build loyalty to the Partnership and pull customers into stores. Like many retailers, John Lewis has discovered that its best customers shop both online and offline. Similarly, in the US at the famous department store chain Macy's: 'When our customers shop [both] online and in stores they spend 20 per cent more in stores than the average in-store shopper and 60 per cent more online than the average online shopper at Macys.com,' says the chairperson. But the website aims to do more than just sell products online. 'We see Macys.com as far more than a selling site. We see it as the online hub of the Macy's brand.'[26] What is more, through its international website and electronic commerce partner Borderfree Ecommerce, Macy's entire offering is also available online to European countries.

Growing importance of retail technology

Retail technologies have become critically important as competitive tools. Progressive retailers are using advanced information technology (IT) and software systems to produce better forecasts, control inventory costs, interact electronically with suppliers, send information between stores, and even sell to customers within stores. They have adopted sophisticated systems for checkout scanning, RFID stock tracking, merchandise handling, information sharing and interacting with customers.

Perhaps the most startling advances in retail technology concern the ways in which retailers are connecting with consumers. Today's customers have gotten used to the speed and convenience of buying online and to the control that the Internet gives them over the buying process. The web lets consumers shop when they like and where they like, with instant access to huge storehouses of information about competing products and prices. At the same time, websites, blogs, social media and mobile apps give retailers a whole new avenue for establishing brand connections and community with customers. No real-world store can do all that.

Increasingly, retailers are bringing online and digital technologies into their physical stores. Many retailers now routinely use technologies ranging from touchscreen kiosks and handheld shopping assistants to interactive dressing-room mirrors and virtual sales associates. For example, in the US stores can use Shopkick's shopBeacon indoor positioning system to engage customers digitally as they shop around the stores. When opted-in customers enter the store, a Bluetooth signal wakes up the shopBeacon app on their smartphone or tablet, which welcomes them and alerts them to location-specific rewards, deals, discounts and product recommendations within the store. The technology can also link in-store and at-home browsing; if the customer 'likes' a specific product online, shopBeacon can remind them where to find it in the store and maybe pass along a for-you-only deal. The goal of shopBeacon is to engage tech-savvy and social customers as a trusted companion and to personalise their in-store shopping experience.[27]

But the future of technology in retailing lies in merging online and offline shopping into a seamless shopping experience. It's not a matter of online retailing growing while physical retailing declines. Instead, both will be important, and the two must be integrated. One view of the potential transformation of the retail experience is provided by analysts Deloitte from their research into global retailing.[28] They ask us to picture retailing a decade into the future if technologies come together:

- You go into your favourite clothing store, and the store's electronic monitoring recognises you by the devices you carry and wear, as well as the RFID tags on your clothes, and triggers your personal digital shopping assistant.
- The digital assistant suggests the look for your new outfit by accessing your wardrobe from past purchases and needs from recent online searches.
- The retailer's 3D printer begins production of your new clothes by using MRI scanned custom fit data.
- You donate or recycle part of your current wardrobe to offset the cost of the new outfit.
- Finally, you pay with a secure biometric authorisation – no cards or devices required.

Deloitte make the telling point that actually the technology is there to make this a reality today – it is a matter of assembling and integrating these technical capabilities into the next generation of retail experience.

Green retailing

Today's retailers are increasingly adopting environmentally sustainable practices. They are 'greening' their stores and operations, promoting more environmentally responsible products, launching programmes to help customers be more responsible, and working with channel partners to reduce their environmental impact.

At the most basic level, most large retailers – such as Tesco and Sainsbury's in the UK – are making their stores more environmentally friendly through sustainable building design, construction and operations. For example, new retail stores commonly employ extensive recycling and compost programmes, wind energy and solar panels for power, and locally sourced sustainable building materials. Similarly, even McDonald's' Golden Arches are now going green. Its new eco-friendly restaurants are designed from the bottom up with a whole new eco-attitude.[29]

New 'green' McDonald's restaurants are built and furnished mostly with reclaimed building materials. The car parks are made with permeable surfaces, which absorb and clean storm water and filter it back into the water table. Exterior and interior lighting uses energy-efficient LEDs, which consume as much as 78 per cent less energy and last 10 to 20 times longer than traditional lighting. The restaurants are landscaped with hearty, drought-resistant native plants, which require less water. Then, what little water they do need comes from rainwater channelled from the roof and condensation from the super-high efficiency HVAC system. Inside the restaurant, solar-tube skylights bring in natural light and reduce energy use. A sophisticated lighting system adjusts indoor illumination based on light entering through the skylights. The dining room is filled with materials made from recycled content (recycled floor tiles, for example, and counters made from recycled glass and concrete), and paints and cleaning chemicals are chosen for their low environmental impact. Other green features include high-efficiency kitchen equipment and water-saving, low-flow water taps and toilets. Some new restaurants even offer electric vehicle charging stations for customers.

Retailers are also greening up their product assortments and in some cases different approaches to niche retailing have developed. For example, Green Baby was set up by Canadian mother Jill Barker in the UK. Green Baby provides organic products, washable nappies, wooden toys, toiletries and maternity wear from four London stores and a mail order business. Their knitwear is produced by a Women's Fair Trade cooperative in Uruguay. They use luxurious natural fibres sourced via MANOS, which economises on water use and other resources and avoids using harmful chemicals during the kettle dyeing process. And clothing retailer H&M has launched an eco-friendly 'Conscious Collection', clothing made from materials such as organic cotton and recycled fibres. Such products can both boost sales and lift the retailer's image as a responsible company.[30]

Many large retailers have also launched programmes that help consumers make more environmentally responsible decisions. For example, global office products retailer Staples' EcoEasy programme helps customers identify green products sold in its stores and makes it easy to recycle printer cartridges, mobile phones, computers and other office technology products. As one of the world's leading ink sellers, Staples was one of the first international retailers to offer an in-store technology recycling programme. As a result, Staples recycles more than 30 million printer cartridges and 4.5 million kilos of technology each year. Staples has recycled more than 100,000 mobile phones and PDAs since 2005 through its partnership with Collective Good, which recycles and refurbishes small electronics.[31]

Finally, many large retailers are joining forces with suppliers and distributors to create more sustainable products, packaging and distribution systems. For example, Amazon works closely with the producers of many of the products it sells to reduce and simplify their packaging. And beyond their own substantial sustainability initiatives, mega-retailers like Tesco and Carrefour in the UK and Europe wield their huge buying power to urge their armies of suppliers to improve their environmental impact and practices.

Green retailing yields both top and bottom line benefits. Sustainable practices lift a retailer's top line by attracting consumers looking to support environmentally friendly sellers and products. They also help the bottom line by reducing costs. For example, Amazon's reduced-packaging efforts increase customer convenience and eliminate 'wrap rage' while at the same time save packaging costs. And an earth-friendly McDonald's restaurant not only appeals to customers and helps save the planet but costs less to operate. 'Green retailing has recently become another legitimate differentiator in the [retail] brand equation, and it creates significant quick-hit ROI opportunities, as well,' concludes a retail analyst.[32]

Global expansion of major retailers

Retailers with unique formats and strong brand positioning are increasingly developing international expansion strategies. Many are expanding globally to escape mature and saturated home markets. Revenues for the world's top ten global retailers are around $1.3 trillion. Over the years, some giant retail operations, such as McDonald's and KFC, have become globally prominent as a result of their marketing prowess. The world's largest retailer, Walmart, is rapidly establishing a global presence. Walmart, which now operates more than 6,300 stores in 26 non-US markets, sees exciting global potential. Its international division alone last year racked up sales of more than $135 billion, almost 88 per cent more than rival Target's *total* sales of $72 billion.[33]

However, in fact most US retailers are still significantly behind Europe and Asia when it comes to global expansion. Only eight of the world's top 20 retailers are US companies; and only four of these retailers have established stores outside North America (Walmart, Home Depot, Sears and Costco). Among the top 250 global retailers in the world, around 37 per cent are US-based, 33 per cent are European, and 24 per cent are Asia-Pacific-based. Of the 12 non-US retailers in the world's top 20, most have stores in at least ten countries. Among non-US retailers that have gone global are France's Carrefour, Groupe Casino and Auchan chains, Germany's Metro, Lidl and Aldi chains, Britain's Tesco, and Japan's Seven & I. Generally, global expansion by European and Asian retailers has been more successful than that of US retailers.[34]

For example, French discount retailer Carrefour, the world's second-largest retailer, has embarked on an aggressive mission to extend its role as a leading international retailer:

> The Carrefour Group has an interest in more than 15,400 stores in over 30 countries in Europe, Asia and the Americas, including over 1,000 hypermarkets (supercentres). It leads Europe in supermarkets and the world in hypermarkets. Carrefour has outpaced Walmart in several emerging markets, including South America, China and the Pacific Rim. It's the leading retailer in Brazil and Argentina, where it operates more than 1,000 stores, compared to Walmart with half that number of units in those two countries. Carrefour is the largest foreign retailer in China, where it operates more than 443 stores versus Walmart's 279. In short, although Walmart has more than three times Carrefour's overall sales, Carrefour is forging ahead of Walmart in many markets outside North America. The big question: can the French retailer hold its lead? Although no one retailer can safely claim to be in the same league with Walmart as an overall retail presence, Carrefour stands a better chance than most to hold its own in global retailing.[35]

Nonetheless, international retailing operations carry risks. Carrefour has had disappointing results in some areas, and the UK's Tesco has withdrawn totally from its Fresh & Easy chain in the United States, losing an estimate £1 billion. International retailing presents challenges as well as opportunities. Retailers can face dramatically different retail environments when crossing countries, continents and cultures. Simply adapting the operations that work well in the home country is usually not enough to create success abroad. Instead, when going global, retailers must understand and meet the needs of local markets.

Perhaps the biggest challenge for international retailers in their globalisation is how to succeed in emerging markets like India and China, where local trading conditions and regulatory environments are very different to those in the West. It is also worth bearing in mind that globalisation means exactly that – for example, leading Asian retailers such as Aeon, Dairy Farm and Seiyu are extending their operations across the Asia-Pacific possibly with ambitions beyond those confines including the European and American marketplaces. Don't forget – companies which have developed ways of doing business that are effective in some of the world's toughest markets (the emerging markets) may see considerable prospects for their ways of doing business in the austerity-dominated European and American markets.

WHOLESALING

Wholesaling includes all the activities involved in selling goods and services to those buying for resale or business use. Firms engaged *primarily* in wholesaling activities are called **wholesalers**.

Wholesalers buy mostly from producers and sell mostly to retailers, industrial consumers and other wholesalers. As a result, many of the largest and most important wholesalers are largely unknown to final consumers. For example, in Britain, the Institute of Grocery Distribution estimates that sales through the grocery and foodservice wholesaling sector in 2014 reached £29.8 billion, and are likely to reach £32.3 billion by 2019, in a grocery market worth around £150 billion at the retail level.[36] Convenience and traditional grocery retailers get their supplies mainly from wholesalers. Outside grocery, while Boots the Chemist is familiar to British consumers as a high street retailer, consumers are generally less aware of the Alliance Boots International wholesale business or the importance of wholesalers in supplying small pharmacies throughout the country:

> Pharmaceutical distributors provide 90 per cent of Britain's medicines, covering all of the UK's population. Full line wholesalers act as a one stop shop for almost all pharmaceutical products and services, playing a key role in the cost effective and safe distribution of a diverse and comprehensive range of healthcare products, all to exact orders on a same day basis. The National Health Service relies on the efficient and effective service they provide, delivering to pharmacists, doctors, hospitals, sometimes even to individual patients across the whole country.
>
> Boots the Chemist is one of Britain's best-known high street retailers. But Boots UK is a member of Alliance Boots, an international pharmacy-led health and beauty group. Alliance Boots is a pharmaceutical wholesale business, which together with associates and joint ventures, supplies medicines, other healthcare products and related services to over 160,000 pharmacies, doctors, health centres and hospitals from over 370 distribution centres in 21 countries. The business provides high service levels to pharmacists in terms of frequency of delivery, product availability, delivery accuracy, timeliness and reliability at competitive prices. Retail customers are offered innovative added-value services which help pharmacists develop their own businesses. In addition to wholesaling of medicines and other healthcare products, Alliance Boots provides services to pharmaceutical manufacturers that are increasingly seeking to gain greater control over their product distribution. These services include pre-wholesale and contract logistics, direct deliveries to pharmacies, and specialised medicine delivery including related home healthcare. Alliance Boots is the largest pharmaceutical wholesaler/distributor in Europe and has recently merged with WalGreens in the US.[37]

Why are wholesalers important to sellers? For example, why would a producer use wholesalers rather than selling directly to retailers or consumers? Simply put, wholesalers add value by performing one or more of the following channel functions:

- *Selling and promoting*: Wholesalers' sales forces help manufacturers reach many small customers at a low cost. The wholesaler has more contacts and is often more trusted by the buyer than the distant manufacturer.
- *Buying and assortment building*: Wholesalers can select items and build assortments needed by their customers, thereby saving much work.
- *Bulk breaking*: Wholesalers save their customers money by buying in large lots and breaking bulk (breaking large lots into small quantities).
- *Warehousing*: Wholesalers hold stocks, thereby reducing the stocking costs and risks of suppliers and customers.

Author comment

Whereas retailers primarily sell goods and services directly to final consumers for personal use, wholesalers sell primarily to those buying for resale or business use. Because wholesalers operate behind the scenes, they are largely unknown to final consumers. But they are very important to their business customers.

Wholesaling—All the activities involved in selling goods and services to those buying for resale or business use.

Wholesaler—A firm engaged primarily in wholesaling activities.

Wholesaling: while Boots the Chemists is familiar to British shoppers as a high street retailer, consumers are generally less aware of the Alliance Boots International wholesale business or the importance of wholesalers in supplying small pharmacies throughout the country.
Source: Oli Scarff/Getty Images

- *Transportation*: Wholesalers can provide quicker delivery to buyers because they are closer to buyers than are producers.
- *Financing*: Wholesalers finance their customers by giving credit, and they finance their suppliers by ordering early and paying bills on time.
- *Risk bearing*: Wholesalers absorb risk by taking title and bearing the cost of theft, damage, spoilage and obsolescence.
- *Market information*: Wholesalers give information to suppliers and customers about competitors, new products and price developments.
- *Management services and advice*: Wholesalers often help retailers train their sales staff, improve store layouts and displays and set up accounting and stock control systems.

Types of wholesalers

Merchant wholesaler—An independently owned wholesale business that takes title to the merchandise it handles.

Wholesalers fall into three major groups (see Table 13.3): *merchant wholesalers*, *agents and brokers*, and *manufacturers' and retailers' branches and offices*. **Merchant wholesalers** are generally the largest single group of wholesalers in a trade. Merchant wholesalers include two broad types: full-service wholesalers and limited-service wholesalers. *Full-service wholesalers* provide a full set of services, whereas the various *limited-service wholesalers* offer fewer services to their suppliers and customers. The different types of limited-service wholesalers perform varied specialised functions in the distribution channel.

Table 13.3 Major types of wholesalers

Type	Description
Merchant wholesalers	Independently owned businesses that take title to all merchandise handled. They include full-service wholesalers and limited-service wholesalers.
Full-service wholesalers	Provide a full line of services: carrying stock, maintaining a sales force, offering credit, making deliveries and providing management assistance. Full-service wholesalers include wholesale merchants and industrial distributors.
Wholesale merchants	Sell primarily to retailers and provide a full range of services. General merchandise wholesalers carry several merchandise lines, whereas general line wholesalers carry one or two lines in great depth. Speciality wholesalers specialise in carrying only part of a line.
Industrial distributors	Sell to manufacturers rather than to retailers. Provide several services, such as carrying stock, offering credit and providing delivery. May carry a broad range of merchandise, a general line, or a speciality line.
Limited-service wholesalers	Offer fewer services than full-service wholesalers. There are many types of limited-service wholesalers, including cash-and-carry wholesalers, truck wholesalers, drop shippers, rack jobbers, producers' cooperatives and mail-order or web wholesalers.
Cash-and-carry wholesalers	Carry a limited line of fast-moving goods and sell to small retailers for cash. Normally do not deliver.
Truck wholesalers (or truck jobbers)	Perform primarily a selling and delivery function. Carry a limited a line of semi-perishable merchandise (such as milk, bread, snack foods), which they sell for cash as they make their rounds, deliveries are made to supermarkets, small grocery stores, hospitals, restaurants, factory cafeterias and hotels.
Drop shippers	Do not carry stock or handle the product. On receiving an order, drop shippers select a manufacturer, which then ships the merchandise directly to the customer. Drop shippers operate in bulk industries, such as coal, timber and heavy equipment.
Rack jobbers	Serve grocery and pharmaceutical retailers, mostly in non-food items. Rack jobbers send delivery trucks to stores, where the delivery people set up toys, paperbacks, hardware items, health and beauty aids, or other items. Rack jobbers price the goods, keep them fresh, set up point-of-purchase displays and keep stock records.
Producers' cooperatives	Farmer-owned members that assemble farm produce to for sell sale in local markets. Producers' cooperatives often attempt to improve product quality and promote a co-op brand name, such as Sun-Maid raisins, Sunkist oranges or Diamond walnuts.

Table 13.3 Major types of wholesalers (*continued*)

Type	Description
Mail-order or web wholesalers	Send catalogues to or maintain websites for retail, industrial and institutional customers featuring jewellery, cosmetics, speciality foods and other small items. Main customers are small businesses often in small outlying areas.
Brokers and agents	Do not take title to goods. Main function is to facilitate buying and selling, for which they earn a commission on the selling price. Generally specialise by product line or customer type.
Brokers	Bring buyers and sellers together and assist in negotiation. Brokers are paid by the party who hired them and do not carry stock, get involved in financing or assume risk. Examples: include food brokers, property brokers, insurance brokers and security brokers.
Agents	Represent either buyers or sellers on a more permanent basis than brokers do. There are four types of agents: manufacturers' agents, selling agents, purchasing agents and commission merchants.
Manufacturers' agents	Represent two or more manufacturers of complementary lines. Often used in such lines as clothing, furniture and electrical goods. A manufacturer's agent is hired by small manufacturers who cannot afford their own field sales forces and by large manufacturers who use agents to open new territories or to cover territories that cannot support full-time salespeople.
Selling agents	Have contractual authority to sell a manufacturer's entire output. The selling agent serves as a sales department and has significant influence over prices, terms and conditions of sale. Found in product areas such as textiles, industrial machinery and equipment, coal and coke, chemicals and metals.
Purchasing agents	Generally have a long-term relationship with buyers and make purchases for them, often receiving, inspecting, warehousing and shipping the merchandise to the buyers. Purchasing agents help clients obtain the best goods and prices available.
Commission merchants	Take physical possession of products and negotiate sales. Used most often in agricultural marketing by farmers who do not want to sell their own output. Takes a truckload of commodities to a central market, sells it for the best price, deducts a commission and expenses and remits the balance to the producers.
Manufacturers' and retailers' branches and offices	Wholesaling operations conducted by sellers or buyers themselves rather than through independent wholesalers. Separate branches and offices can be dedicated to either sales or purchasing.
Sales branches and offices	Set up by manufacturers to improve stock control, selling and promotion. Sales branches carry stock and are found in industries such as timber and automotive equipment and parts. Sales offices do not carry stock and are most prominent in industries like clothing, accessories and dry goods.
Purchasing officers	Perform a role similar to that of brokers or agents but are part of the buyer's organisation. Many retailers establish purchasing offices in major market centres, such as London, New York, Paris and Frankfurt.

Brokers and *agents* differ from merchant wholesalers in two ways: they do not take title to goods, and they perform only a few functions. Like merchant wholesalers, they generally specialise by product line or customer type. A **broker** brings buyers and sellers together and assists in negotiation. **Agents** represent buyers or sellers on a more permanent basis. *Manufacturers' agents* (also called *manufacturers' representatives*) are the most common type of agent wholesaler. The third major type of wholesaling is that done in **manufacturers' sales branches and offices** by sellers themselves rather than through independent wholesalers.

Wholesaler marketing decisions

Wholesalers now face growing competitive pressures, more demanding customers, new technologies, and more direct-buying programmes on the part of large industrial, institutional and retail buyers. As a result, they have taken a fresh look at their marketing strategies. As with retailers,

Broker—A wholesaler who does not take title to goods and whose function is to bring buyers and sellers together and assist in negotiation.

Agent—A wholesaler who represents buyers or sellers on a relatively permanent basis, performs only a few functions, and does not take title to goods.

Manufacturers' and retailers' branches and offices—Wholesaling by sellers and buyers themselves rather than through independent wholesalers.

Figure 13.2 Wholesaler
marketing strategies

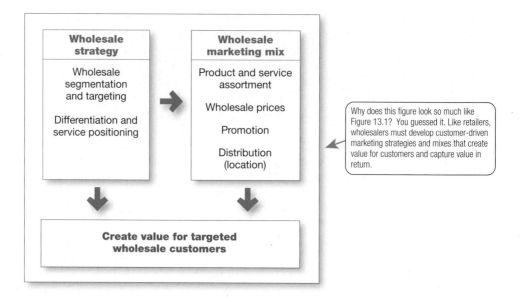

their marketing decisions include choices of segmentation and targeting, differentiation and positioning, and the marketing mix – product and service assortments, price, promotion and distribution (see Figure 13.2).

Segmentation, targeting, differentiation and positioning decisions

Like retailers, wholesalers must segment and define their target markets and differentiate and position themselves effectively – they cannot serve everyone. They can choose a target group by size of customer (large retailers only), type of customer (convenience stores only), the need for service (customers who need credit), or other factors. Within the target group, they can identify the more profitable customers, design stronger offers, and build better relationships with them. They can propose automatic reordering systems, establish management-training and advisory systems, or even sponsor a voluntary chain. They can discourage less-profitable customers by requiring larger orders or adding service charges to smaller ones.

Marketing mix decisions

Like retailers, wholesalers must decide on product and service assortments, prices, promotion and place. Wholesalers add customer value though the *products and services* they offer. They are often under great pressure to carry a full line and stock enough for immediate delivery. But this practice can damage profits. Wholesalers today are cutting down on the number of lines they carry, choosing to carry only the more profitable ones. They are also rethinking which services count most in building strong customer relationships and which should be dropped or paid for by the customer. The key is to find the mix of services most valued by their target customers.

Price is also an important wholesaler decision. Wholesalers usually mark up the cost of goods by a standard percentage – say 20 per cent. Expenses may run to 17 per cent of the gross margin, leaving a profit margin of 3 per cent. In grocery wholesaling, the average profit margin is often less than 2 per cent. Wholesalers are trying new pricing approaches. The recent economic downturn put heavy pressure on wholesalers to cut their costs and prices. As their retail and industrial customers face sales and margin declines, these customers turn to wholesalers looking for lower prices. Wholesalers may cut their margins on some lines to keep important customers. They may ask suppliers for special price breaks, when they can turn them into an increase in the supplier's sales.

Although *promotion* can be critical to wholesaler success, most wholesalers are not promotion minded. They often use largely scattered and unplanned trade advertising, sales promotion, personal selling and public relations. Many are behind the times in personal selling; they still see selling as a single salesperson talking to a single customer instead of as a team effort to sell, build and service major accounts. Wholesalers also need to adopt some of the non-personal promotion techniques used by retailers. They need to develop an overall promotion strategy and make greater use of supplier promotion materials and programmes. Digital and social media are playing an increasingly important role. Some successful wholesalers maintain an active presence on Facebook, YouTube, Twitter, LinkedIn and Google+, and provide feature-rich mobile apps and videos on topics ranging such as the company and its products and services, and keeping down inventory costs.

Finally, *distribution* (location) is important. Wholesalers must choose their physical locations, facilities and web locations carefully. There was a time when wholesalers could locate in low-cost areas and invest little money in their buildings, equipment and systems. Today, however, as technology zooms forward, such behaviour results in outdated systems for material handling, order processing and delivery.

Instead, today's large and progressive wholesalers have reacted to rising costs by investing in automated warehouses and IT systems. Orders are fed from the retailer's information system directly into the wholesaler's, and the items are picked up by mechanical devices and automatically taken to a shipping platform where they are assembled. Most large wholesalers use technology to carry out accounting, billing, stock control and forecasting. Modern wholesalers are adapting their services to the needs of target customers and finding cost-reducing methods of doing business. They are also transacting more business online.

Trends in wholesaling

Today's wholesalers face considerable challenges. The industry remains vulnerable to one of its most enduring trends – the need for ever-greater efficiency. Recent economic conditions have led to demands for even lower prices and the winnowing out of suppliers who are not adding value based on cost and quality. Progressive wholesalers constantly watch for better ways to meet the changing needs of their suppliers and target customers. They recognise that their only reason for existence comes from adding value by increasing the efficiency and effectiveness of the entire marketing channel. As with other types of marketers, the goal is to build value-adding customer relationships.

The distinction between large retailers and large wholesalers continues to blur. Many retailers now operate formats such as wholesale clubs and supercentres that perform many wholesale functions. One of the greatest strengths of the large retailer is to integrate wholesale and retail operations under direct control. Companies like Tesco, Carrefour and Walmart make relatively little use of independent wholesalers, usually dealing direct with manufacturers and managing their own logistics operations for greater efficiency. Retailers like these maintain buying functions actively seeking products direct from manufacturers across the world.

Although it is relatively unusual to date, there is also the potential for wholesale businesses to enter the retail market. For example, in the United States until recently, SuperValu was classified as a food wholesaler, with a majority of its business derived from supplying grocery products to independent grocery retailers. However, over the past decade, SuperValu has started or acquired several retail food chains of its own – including Shop 'n Save – to become one of America's food retailers. Thus, even though it remains the largest food wholesaler in the US, SuperValu is now classified as a retailer because 75 per cent of its sales come from retailing.[38] Nonetheless, such moves are unusual in a European context.

Independent wholesalers are likely to continue to increase the services they provide to retailers – retail pricing, cooperative advertising, marketing and management information reports, accounting services, online transactions, and others. The weak economy, the growing power of large retailers that deal direct with manufacturers, and the demand for increased services from smaller customers are putting the squeeze on wholesaler profits. Wholesalers that do not find efficient ways to deliver value to their customers will soon drop by the wayside. However, the increased use of computerised, automated and web-based systems will help wholesalers contain the costs of ordering, shipping and stock holding, thus boosting their productivity in some markets.

OBJECTIVES REVIEW AND KEY TERMS

Retailing and wholesaling consist of many organisations bringing goods and services from the point of production to the point of use. In this chapter, we examined the nature and importance of retailing, the major types of retailers, the decisions retailers make, and the future of retailing. We then examined these same topics for wholesalers.

OBJECTIVE 1 Explain the role of retailers in the distribution channel and describe the major types of retailers (pp. 375–381)

Retailing includes all the activities involved in selling goods or services directly to final consumers for their personal, non-business use. Retailers play an important role in connecting brands to consumers in the final phases of the buying process. *Shopper marketing* involves focusing the entire marketing process on turning shoppers into buyers as they approach the point of sale, whether during in-store, online or mobile shopping.

Retail stores come in all shapes and sizes, and new retail types keep emerging. Store retailers can be classified by the *amount of service* they provide (self-service, limited service or full service), *product line sold* (speciality stores, department stores, supermarkets, convenience stores, superstores and service businesses) and *relative prices* (discount stores and off-price retailers). Today, many retailers are banding together in corporate and contractual *retail organisations* (corporate chains, voluntary chains, retailer cooperatives and franchise organisations).

OBJECTIVE 2 Describe the major retailer marketing decisions (pp. 381–386)

Retailers are always searching for new marketing strategies to attract and hold customers. They face major marketing decisions about segmentation and targeting, store differentiation and positioning, and the retail marketing mix.

Retailers must first segment and define their target markets and then decide how they will differentiate and position themselves in these markets. Those that try to offer 'something for everyone' end up satisfying no market well. In contrast, successful retailers define their target markets well and position themselves strongly.

Guided by strong targeting and positioning, retailers must decide on a retail marketing mix – product and services assortment, price, promotion and place. Retail stores are much more than simply an assortment of goods. Beyond the products and services they offer, today's successful retailers carefully orchestrate virtually every aspect of the consumer store experience. A retailer's price policy must fit its target market and positioning,

products and services assortment and competition. Retailers use any or all of the five promotion tools – advertising, personal selling, sales promotion, public relations and direct marketing – to reach consumers. Finally, it's very important that retailers select locations that are accessible to the target market in areas that are consistent with a retailer's positioning.

OBJECTIVE 3 Discuss the major trends and developments in retailing (pp. 386–392)

Retailers operate in a harsh and fast-changing environment, which offers threats as well as opportunities. Following years of good economic times for retailers, they have now adjusted to the new economic realities and more thrift-minded consumers. New retail forms continue to emerge. At the same time, however, different types of retailers are increasingly serving similar customers with the same products and prices (retail convergence), making differentiation more difficult. Other trends in retailing include the rise of mega-retailers, the rapid growth of direct, online and social media marketing, the growing importance of retail technology, a surge in green retailing and the global expansion of major retailers.

OBJECTIVE 4 Explain the major types of wholesalers and their marketing decisions (pp. 393–397)

Wholesaling includes all the activities involved in selling goods or services to those who are buying for the purpose of resale or business use. Wholesalers fall into three groups. First, *merchant wholesalers* take possession of the goods. They include *full-service wholesalers* (wholesale merchants and industrial distributors) and *limited-service wholesalers* (cash-and-carry wholesalers, truck wholesalers, drop shippers, rack jobbers, producers' cooperatives and mail-order wholesalers). Second, *brokers and agents* do not take possession of the goods but are paid a commission for aiding buying and selling. Finally, *manufacturers' sales branches and offices* are wholesaling operations conducted by non-wholesalers to bypass the wholesalers.

Like retailers, wholesalers must target carefully and position themselves strongly. And, like retailers, wholesalers must decide on product and service assortments, prices, promotion and place. Progressive wholesalers constantly watch for better ways to meet the changing needs of their suppliers and target customers. They recognise that, in the long run, their only reason for existence comes from adding value by increasing the efficiency and effectiveness of the entire marketing channel. As with other types of marketers, the goal is to build value-adding customer relationships.

NAVIGATING THE KEY TERMS

OBJECTIVE 1
Retailing (p. 375)
Retailer (p. 375)
Shopper marketing (p. 375)
Speciality store (p. 377)
Department store (p. 377)
Supermarket (p. 377)
Convenience store (p. 378)
Superstore (p. 378)
Category killer (p. 378)
Service retailer (p. 378)

Discount store (p. 378)
Off-price retailer (p. 378)
Independent off-price retailer (p. 378)
Factory outlet (p. 379)
Warehouse club (p. 379)
Corporate chains (p. 380)
Franchise (p. 380)

OBJECTIVE 2
Shopping centre (p. 385)

OBJECTIVE 3
Showrooming (p. 389)

OBJECTIVE 4
Wholesaling (p. 393)
Wholesaler (p. 393)
Merchant wholesaler (p. 394)
Broker (p. 395)
Agent (p. 395)
Manufacturers' sales branches and
    offices (p. 395)

DISCUSSION AND CRITICAL THINKING

Applying the concepts

13-1 Explain how retailers can be classified based on the amount of service offered and give an example of each retailer type. (AACSB: Communication; Reflective thinking)

13-2 Define the concept of shopper marketing and explain why it has grown in prominence. (AACSB: Communication)

13-3 Name and describe the types of corporate or contractual organisation of retail stores and the advantages of each. (AACSB: Communication)

13-4 Explain how wholesalers add value in the channel of distribution. (AACSB: Communication)

13-5 Compare and contrast brokers and agents with merchant wholesalers. (AACSB: Communication; Reflective thinking)

Critical-thinking exercises

13-6 Visit a local shopping centre where you are and evaluate five stores. What type of retailer is each of these stores? What is the target market for each? How is each store positioned? Do the retail atmospherics of each store enhance this positioning effectively to attract and satisfy the target market? (AACSB: Communication; Reflective thinking)

13-7 Deciding on a target market and positioning for a retail store are very important marketing decisions. In a small group, develop the concept for a new retail store. What is the target market for your store? How is your store positioned? What retail atmospherics will enhance this positioning effectively to attract and satisfy your target market? (AACSB: Communication; Reflective thinking)

13-8 The majority of shoppers agree that online reviews can be very helpful. However, some online reviews are fake. Research this issue and write a report on how to spot fake online reviews and the steps retailers take to minimise fake reviews. (AACSB: Communication; Use of IT; Reflective thinking)

Mini-cases and applications

Online, mobile and social media marketing: local retailers

It seems you can't get away from the buzz of online, mobile and social media marketing from the likes of Amazon, ao.com, johnlewis.com, and other large retailers. But what about the small independent retailers? Are they also getting on the online, mobile and social media bandwagon? Some independent retailers are using these tools. Consider some examples from the United States. A convenience store owner in Miami tweets a picture to 7,000 followers of a new beer he just stocked that morning, and by late afternoon customers come streaming in to check it out. Emerson Salon in Seattle, a hairdresser, sources 75 per cent of its business from Facebook, Twitter and its blog. Butter Lane cupcake bakery in New York City has found success using social media as well. Although these retailers have embraced online, mobile and social media marketing, to most small retailers, using Facebook, Twitter, Pinterest, Tumblr, Groupon, Instagram, Yelp, Foursquare, and other digital media can seem downright intimidating. Nonetheless, the US examples underline the potential for small retailers using online promotion in markets as diverse as Europe, Africa and Asia.

13-9 Find an example of a local retailer in your country or locality that uses online, mobile and social media marketing. Interview the owner of the store or restaurant and ask about the challenges and successes they've experienced when implementing this strategy. (AACSB: Communication; Use of IT; Reflective thinking)

13-10 Create a presentation to give to local retailers in your locality explaining how they can effectively use online, mobile and social media marketing to engage customers and enhance their business. (AACSB: Communication; Reflective thinking)

Marketing ethics: marketplace fairness

The desire of many governments to regulate online marketing, particularly where taxes, security or censorship are involved, is a global issue. For example, in the US, the Marketplace Fairness Act of 2013 allows US States to require online retailers to collect sales taxes, in the same way that conventional retailers do. Most consumers purchase online knowing that they may not have to pay sales tax, which essentially lowers prices for consumers. This anomaly in the US results from a 1992 Supreme Court ruling stipulating that catalogue and online sellers need only collect sales taxes for states in which they have a physical presence. Consumers are supposed to remit taxes to their state if an online retailer does not collect them, but consumers often do not pay the taxes, causing States to miss out on millions in tax revenues. Online giant Amazon saw this as a competitive advantage and was very careful regarding how its employees behaved when conducting business in certain states to avoid the 'physical presence' requirement. Amazon opposed any initiatives to require online resellers to collect sales taxes. Bricks-and-mortar retailers cried foul, claiming online sellers have an unfair competitive price advantage. The Marketplace Fairness Act aims to eliminate that advantage. But will it? With more than 9,000 different tax jurisdictions, can a small retailer that also has an online presence compete with the Amazons and other online giants? While Amazon was initially against such legislation, the online reseller changed direction and supported the Act. The Act is now law in the US, subject to the States simplifying their sales tax arrangements.

13-11 Why did Amazon change its position regarding online sales taxes and why does it now support the Marketplace Fairness Act? (AACSB: Communication; Reflective thinking)

13-12 Discuss the impact the Marketplace Fairness Act will have on small retailers in the US. Is it fair that small retailers should have to collect sales taxes on online sales to customers outside of their state? (AACSB: Communication; Ethical reasoning; Reflective thinking)

Marketing by the numbers: stockturn rate

Retailers need merchandise to make sales. In fact, a retailer's stock is its biggest asset. Not stocking enough merchandise can result in lost sales, but carrying too much stock increases costs and lowers margins. Both circumstances reduce profits. One measure of a reseller's stock management effectiveness is its stockturn rate. The key to success in retailing is realising a large volume of sales on as little stock as possible, while maintaining enough stock to meet customer demands.

13-13 Refer to Appendix 2: Marketing by the numbers, and determine the stockturn rate of a retailer carrying an average inventory at cost of €350,000, with a cost of goods sold of €800,000. (AACSB: Communication; Analytical reasoning)

13-14 If this company's stockturn rate was 3.5 last year, is the stockturn rate calculated above better or worse? Explain. (AACSB: Communication; Reflective thinking)

REFERENCES

[1] *Sources*: Cecilie Rohwedder and Davod Kesmodel, 'German discounter Aldi invades Wal-Mart's turf', *Wall Street Journal*, 14 January 2009, p. 5; Elizabeth Rigby, 'Aldi sales rise 25% as it lures wealthy', *Financial Times*, 13 January 2009, p. 19; Neil Craven, 'Belt-tightening shoppers are defecting to discounter Aldi', *Mail on Sunday*, 8 June 2008, p. 53; Neil Craven, 'Germans' cut-price lobster puts the squeeze on Tesco in the battle over middle Britain', *Mail on Sunday*, 17 February 2008, p. 57; Sean Poulter, 'Cut-price stores cash in as families feel the squeeze', *Daily Mail*, 24 January 2008, p. 34; Sean Poulter, 'Aldi tops the taste test', *Daily Mail*, 4 June 2013, p. 20; Andrea Felsted, 'Aldi and Lidl rattle the UK's big grocers', *Financial Times*, 10 July 2014, p. 17; Kadhim Subber, 'Aldi overtakes Waitrose in battle for sales', *Financial Times*, 9 April 2015, p. 20; Sean Poulter, 'Aldi's still the cheapest. . . even after price war', *Daily Mail*, 17 March 2015, p. 24; Neil Craven, 'Aldi snaps at heels of top five supermarkets', *Mail on Sunday*, 6 June 2015.

[2] Quotes and other information on OgilvyAction from Katy Bachman, 'Suit your shelf', *AdweekMedia*, 19 January 2009, pp. 10–12; 'Ogilvy action takes regional marketers to the last mile', 23 January 2008, www.entrepreneur.com/tradejournals/article/173710015.html; Jack Neff, 'Trouble in store for shopper marketing', *Advertising Age*, 2 March 2009, pp. 3–4; Retail sales statistics from 'Monthly and Annual Retail Trade', US Census Bureau, www.census.gov/retail/, accessed February 2010.

[3] Jack Neff, 'P&G pushes design in brand-building strategy', 12 April 2010, http://adage.com/print?article_id=143211; Gil Press, 'What do CMOs want? On big data, better focus, and moments of truth', *Forbes*, 25 November 2013, www.forbes.com/sites/gilpress/2013/11/25 /what-do-cmos-want-on-big-data-betterfocus-and-moments-of-truths/.

[4] For more on digital aspects of shopper marketing, see Christopher Heine, 'Marketing to the omnichannel shopper', *Adweek*, 3 June 2013, pp. S1–S2; John Balla, 'Customer I love – it's all about the connection', *loyalty360*, 14 February 2014, http://loyalty360.org/loyalty-today/ article/customer-love-its-all-about-the-connection; www.shoppermar- ketingmag.com/home/, accessed June 2014; and 'ZMOT', *Google Digital Services*, www.zeromomentoftruth.com/, accessed September 2014.

[5] Illustration based on: David Wilkes, 'Supermarket snobs', *Daily Mail*, 10 October 2007, p. 25; Rupert Steiner, 'Waitrose prospers despite friction with John Lewis', *Daily Mail*, 13 November 2010, p. 101; Andrea Felsted, 'Waitrose upsurge signals revival', *Financial Times*, 19 August 2009, p. 16; Andrea Felsted, 'Value range boosts Waitrose', *Financial Times*, 22 June 2009, p. 1; Andrea Felsted, 'Big supermarkets rewrite their grocery lists', *Financial Times*, 12 September 2014, p. 23.

[6] 'How we do it', http://tjmaxx.tjx.com/store/jump/topic/how- wedo-it/2400087, accessed September 2014.

[7] Extract adapted from information found in Sandra M. Jones, 'Outlets proved promising for high-end retailers: luxury goods for less attract shoppers', *McClatchy-Tribune Business News*, 11 April 2009; also see Karen Talley, 'Bloomingdale's to open outlet stores', *Wall Street Journal*, 21 January 2010; and David Moin, 'VCs considering outlets', *WWD*, 22 January 2010, p. 2.

[8] Based on information from '2013 Top 250 global retailers', *Stores*, January 2014; Matthew Boyle, 'Why Costco is so addictive', *Fortune*, 25 October 2006, pp. 126–132; Rick Aristotle Munarriz, 'For Costco, $1.50 hot dog combos and $4.99 chickens aren't enough', *Daily Finance*, 10 October 2013, www.dailyfinance.com/2013/10/10/costco-earn- ings-disappointment-analysis-hotdogs-chicken/; and www.costco.com and www.costco.com/insider-guide-amazing-facts.html, accessed Sep- tember 2014.

[9] See www.franchiseeurope.com/top500/article/europeanfranchising- trendsanddevelopments/1/, accessed 21 February 2012.

[10] Company and franchising information from '2013 Franchise Times Top 200 franchise systems', *Franchise Times*, October 2013, www.franchisetimes .com/pdf/Top-200-2013.pdf; www.score.org/resources/should-i-buy- franchise; www.aboutmcdonalds.com/mcd and www.subway.com/ subwayroot/About_Us/default.aspx, accessed September 2014.

[11] Rajesh Setty, 'Re-imagining the retail experience: the Audi City Store', *Huffington Post*, 29 December 2013, www.huffingtonpost.com/rajesh /setty/re-imagining-the-retail-eb4514046.html; and www.youtube.com /watch?v=GDdPN6mVLPM, accessed September 2014.

[12] See Yelena Moroz Alpert, 'How color affects your spending', *Real Sim- ple*, March 2013, p. 148; James Archer, 'Let them sniff, customers will buy more', *Inc.*, 23 January 2013, www.inc.com/james-archer/let-them-sniff- customers-will-buy-more.html; Justine Sharrock, 'How manufactured smells are making people shop longer and kill better', *BuzzFeed*, 15 March 2013, www.buzzfeed.com/justinesharrock/how-manufactured- smells-are-making-peopleshop-longer-and-ki; Alexandra Sifferlin, 'My nose made me buy it', *Time*, 16 December 2013, http://healthland.time. com/2013/12/16/my-nose-made-me-buy-it-how-retailers-use-smell- and-other-tricksto-get-you-to-spend-spend-spend/; and www.scentair .com/whyscentair-scent-studies/, accessed September 2014.

[13] For definitions of these and other types of shopping centres, see 'Dic- tionary', *American Marketing Association*, www.marketingpower.com/_ layouts/Dictionary.aspx, accessed September 2014.

[14] See 'Brick by brick: the state of the shopping center', Nielsen, 17 May 2013, http://nielsen.com/us/en/reports/2013/brick-by-brick- thestate-of-the-shopping-center.html; 'It's the end of the mall as we know it', *Real Estate Weekly*, 22 February 2013, www.rew-online. com/2013/02/22/its-the-end-of-the-mall-as-we-know-it/; and Judy Keen, 'As enclosed malls decline, "lifestyle centers" proliferate', MIN- NPOST, 30 August 2013, www.minnpost.com/cityscape/2013/08 /enclosed-malls-decline-lifestyle-centers-proliferate.

[15] Kate Walsh, 'Supermalls, the pleasure domes of the 21st century', *The Sunday Times*, 6 March 2011, S3, p. 9.

[16] Kenneth Hein, 'Target tries first price point driven TV ads', *Brandweek*, 14 January 2009, www.brandweek.com, p. 1.

[17] Patricia Laya, 'First, pop-up stores, now, pop-up hotels', *Bloomberg BusinessWeek*, 21 June 2013, pp. 26–27.

[18] See 'A summer's worth of pop-up shops in NYC', *Guest of a Guest*, http://guestofaguest.com/new-york/nyc/a-summers-worthof-pop-up- shops-in-nyc&slide=5, accessed March 2014; Lauren Sherman, 'Pop-up shops prove to be more than just a passing trend', *Fashionista*, 7 Novem- ber 2013, http://fashionista.com/2013/11/pop-up-shops-prove-to-be- more-than-just-a-passing-trend/; Peter Evans, 'Pop-up shops arrive', *Wall Street Journal*, 4 September 2012, p. 19; Duncan Robinson, 'Pop-up stores rise to challenge of reviving retail', *Financial Times*, 16 May 2014, p. 4; Andrew Bounds, 'Crown Estate opens Piccadilly pop-ups to niche newcomers', *Financial Times*, 31 July 2013, p. 12.

[19] See www.rpminc.com/leading-brands/consumer-brands, accessed September 2014.

[20] '60% of U.S. retail sales will involve the web by 2017', *Internet Retailer*, 30 October 2013, www.internetretailer.com/2013/10/30/60-us-retail- sales-will-involve-web-2017; and US Census Bureau News, 'Quarterly retail e-commerce sales, 4rd quarter 2013', 18 February 2014, www .census.gov/retail/mrts/www/data/pdf/ec_current.pdf.

[21] See www.retailresearch.org/onlineretailing.php, accessed July 2015.

[22] See www.ons.gov.uk/ons/rel/rsi/retail-sales/january-2015/stb-rsi- january-2015.html, accessed July 2015.

[23] See Lucia Moses, 'Data points: mobile shopping', *Adweek*, 20 May 2013, pp. 20–21; and 'Retail social media top 10', *Retail Customer Expe- rience.com*, 10 January 2013, www.retailcustomerexperience.com /blog/9655/Retail-Social-Media-Top-10-Infographic.

[24] See Ann Zimmerman, 'Can retailers halt "showrooming"?' *Wall Street Journal*, 11 April 2012, p. B1; 'Data points: spending it', *Adweek*, 16 April 2012, pp. 24–25; and 'Consumers visit retailers, then go online for cheaper sources', *Adweek*, 14 March 2013, www.adweek. com/print/147777; and '60% of US retail sales will involve the web by 2017', *Internet Retailer*, 30 October 2013, www.internetretailer. com/2013/10/30/60-us-retail-sales-will-involve-web-2017.

[25] 'Top 500 Guide', *Internet Retailer*, www.top500guide.com/top-500/ the-top-500-list/, accessed June 2014; and 'Store-based retailers take the early lead among Top 500 retailers in online sales growth', *Inter- net Retailer*, 18 February 2014, www.internetretailer.com/2014/02/18 /store-based-retailers-take-earlylead-among-top-500.

[26] See Don Davis, 'M is for multi-channel', *Internet Retailer*, June 2007, www.internetretailer.com/2007/06/01/m-is-for-multi-channel; Macy's, Inc., 'Online selling sites enhance integration with bricks-and-mortar stores', *Business Wire*, 8 December 2008; and information from www. macys.com, accessed June 2010.

[27] For another example, see 'American Eagle Outfitters and Shop- kick announce 100-store trial of new shopBeacon technology', *PRNewswire*, 16 January 2014, www.prnewswire.com/news-releases

/american-eagle-outfitters-and-shopkick-announce-100-store-tria-lof-new-shopbeacon-technology-240487111.html; and Ingrid Lunden, 'Shopkick starts 100-store iBeacon trial for American Eagle, biggest apparel rollout yet', *TechCrunch*, 16 January 2014, http://techcrunch.com/2014/01/16/shopkick-starts-100-store-ibeacontrial-for-american-eagle-outfitters-the-biggest-apparel-rollout-yet/.

[28] http://www2.deloitte.com/content/dam/Deloitte/global/Documents/Consumer-Business/dttl-CB-GPR14STORES.pdf, accessed July 2015.

[29] See Jordan Cooke, 'McDonald's eco-friendly seal', *McClatchy-Tribune Business News*, 13 January 2010; 'The Golden Arches go green: McDonald's first LEED certified restaurant', 11 December 2008, accessed at www.greenbe-anchicago.com/leed-certified-permeable-pavers-led-lighting-recycling-golden-arches-green-mcdonalds-leed-certified-restaurant/; 'McDonald's green prototype uses 25 per cent less energy', *Environmental Leader*, 8 April 2009, accessed at www.environmentalleader.com/2009/04/08/mcdonalds-green-restaurant-uses-25-percent-less-energy/; and D. Gail Fleenor, 'Green light', *Stores*, October 2009, p. 52.

[30] Quotes and other information from Peter Berlinski, 'Green keeps growing', *Private Label Magazine*, www.privatelabelmag.com/feature.cfm, accessed 31 March 2010, p. 1; www.www.jcpenney.com/jcp/

default.aspx, accessed April 2010; www.greenbaby.co.uk, accessed February 22. 2012.

[31] See www.staples.com/sbd/cre/marketing/easy-on-the-planet/recycling-and-eco-services.html, accessed September 2014.

[32] Peter Berlinski, 'Green keeps growing', *op cit.*; Also see Kee-hung Lai, T.C.E. Cheng, and Ailie K.Y. Tang, 'Green retailing: factors for success', *California Management Review*, Winter 2010, pp. 6+.

[33] See http://news.walmart.com/walmart-facts/corporate-financial-fact-sheet, accessed September 2014.

[34] See www2.deloitte.com/content/dam/Deloitte/global/Documents/Consumer-Business/dttl-CB-GPR14STORES.pdf, accessed July 2015.

[35] Information from www.carrefour.com, accessed July 2015.

[36] See www.igd.com/Research/Retail/Wholesaling-and-foodservice/25729/2014-a-year-of-mixed-fortunes-for-wholesale-/, accessed July 2015.

[37] See www.bapw.net/, accessed February 2012; and http://www.boots-uk.com/, accessed July 2015.

[38] Facts from www.supervalu.com/sv-webapp/, accessed July 2015.

COMPANY CASE

Auchen: maybe Walmart is not unbeatable after all?

Auchen is sometimes called the French Walmart. It is a mega-retailer with a powerful patriarch, and a goal of expansion, headquartered in Croix, France. Auchan is France's second-largest supermarket group after Carrefour. It is one of the world's principal distribution groups. In fact, Gérard Mulliez is the plain-speaking, small-town entrepreneur who has built a sprawling retail empire from a single store. Mulliez leads a secretive family that controls one of the world's biggest retail operations.

The Mulliez family has more than two dozen companies including Auchan (a big-box retailer similar to Walmart), Decathlon (the world's biggest sporting goods retailer – not part of the Auchen group), and the European and Latin American operations of the US Midas car exhaust replacement chain. Auchan is gaining ground against competitors, especially in emerging markets. The major Auchan businesses are shown above.

In fact, Auchen Groupe has diverse interests, spanning: hypermarkets, sports stores, car repairs, DIY shopes, electronic devices shops, fabric stores, banking, clothes shops, cultural products and girls' clothes – mostly organised as separate divisions and brands.

The Mulliez family has an estimated $22 billion fortune, making them one of France's wealthiest families, but also one that goes to extreme lengths to avoid publicity. Even most French people do not realise the extent of the family's holdings.

Brand	Business	Outlets
Auchan	Hypermarkets	1,245 in 13 countries
Leroy Merlin	Home improvement	452 in 9 countries
Decathlon	Sporting goods	424 in 14 countries
3 Suisses*	Catalogue/online	Websites for 24 countries
Midas**	Car repairs	1,100 in 11 countries

*44% owned by Mulliez family **Only in Europe and Latin America

Source: The Major Auchen Businesses, *Business Week* (Matlack, C.), Bloomberg L.P.

Despite being thoroughly international, Auchan has preserved a decentralised way of working. Each chain, in each country, is independent, although it operates in synergy with the others and moves forward by sharing experiences and pooling its resources. The company says that this way of working allows for considerable closeness to customers, who are placed at the centre of every policy. The company's view is also that Auchan was created in an enterprise culture which, more than 50 years on, is still very much part of the company's mindset and ethos. Through laboratories and business incubators, the company invests the necessary time and money in innovation, improving existing activities and helping new concepts and solutions to emerge. The group conducts numerous experiments, supporting them, fine-tuning them and – once the right formula has been discovered – transforming them into strategy. This process recognises the right to fail: innovation, after all, depends on trial and error. Furthermore, the autonomy that every Groupe Auchan company enjoys encourages it to innovate in order to achieve sustainable and lasting growth.

Auchen's 2011 sales revenue was reported as €44.4 billion, with 269,000 employees worldwide. As of this year Auchen had 639 hypermarkets and 2,412 supermarkets located around the world. Auchen's slogan is '*la vie Auchen, elle change la vie*' (Auchen's lifestyle changes life itself).

Auchan is the only Mulliez business to publish an annual report. Economist Benoît Boussemart's investigation of the Auchan empire suggests it is very strong, with most of the companies nearly debt-free. The network that binds the Mulliez businesses together is strong, but invisible. While legally separate, the Mulliez businesses are controlled by an extended family of about 550 people. Although Gérard Mulliez retired in 2006, his son, cousins, nephews and nieces hold top positions in nearly all the businesses. All the companies are privately held. A family agreement allows the family to trade shares to each other, but not to outsiders.

While Auchan's sales level means it is smaller than global leaders Walmart and Carrefour, it is on a par with Tesco and Germany's Metro. Auchan has been a particularly fast mover in emerging markets like China and Russia, where it has performed better than global peers Walmart, Tesco and Carrefour.

Indeed, Auchan's China operations have outperformed rivals from the start. While close competitor Carrefour designed its China stores to mimic raucous street markets, Auchan's stores are designed to appeal to upwardly mobile and more refined shoppers. Consultancy Planet Retail estimates that Auchan's 145 China stores average $45 million in annual sales, compared to around $26 million for Walmart's mainland outlets.

In fact, Walmart's emphasis in China on very low prices seems to have backfired. It seems that Chinese consumers often assume that cheaper goods are counterfeit or dangerous. The affluent, modern Chinese consumer has very little taste for fakes and low-quality products, or even perhaps for undiluted Western-style retailing.

For example, RT-Mart, the best-performing foreign big-box retailer in China, is also one of the most local of the foreign-owned retailers. It is owned by Sun Art, a joint venture of Taiwan's Ruentex Group and Auchan, and it listed in Hong Kong last year. RT-Mart's per-store sales are nearly double those of its main foreign competitors, according to Kantar Retail. On a weekday evening at its flagship store in Beijing, RT-Mart's blend of Western-style efficiency and Chinese touches is on display. The vegetable section resembles that of any modern supermarket but for the burly female employee who stands in the aisle barking out bargains. The feel is more akin to the street markets the locals know so well, than to the sterility of big-box stores.

The Mulliez operations are growing rapidly in Russia as well, and 'Russia is poised to become the largest consumer market in Europe,' says Per Hong, Moscow-based partner at management consultancy AT Kearney. After the economic downturn of the late 2000s, Russia now has a new middle class that likes to shop. Seven years after opening its first Moscow outlet, Auchen has become Russia's top foreign hypermarket business, with 34 stores and around $6 billion in sales. By contrast, Walmart and Tesco are not in Russia and Carrefour has pulled out. Decathlon and the family Leroy Merlin home improvement chain are piling into Russia. Support comes from property group Immochan, yet another Mulliez business, which acquires properties for the other family companies.

In 2012, Auchan, seen by local commentators as the most aggressive rival to Walmart globally, held talks with the Landmark Group for a possible India entry, reported by *The Times of India*. The discussions centred around a potential joint venture, but the final agreement will depend on whether India moves ahead with plans for foreign direct investment (FDI) in multi-brand retailing, which is politically sensitive in India. The stores which will be opened in India, if the agreement is signed between the two groups, may operate with the Auchan brand name, although the finer details are still to be worked out.

Nonetheless, in spite of its global success, Auchan has not prospered in the US or the UK. Auchan and Decathlon tried stores in America in the 1980s and 1990s but pulled out. The family bought Britain's Allied Carpets in 1999, but then sold it on after sales slumped.

Questions for discussion

1. Describe Auchan according to the different types of retailers discussed in this chapter.
2. As a retail brand, assess the Auchan retail strategy with respect to segmentation, targeting, differentiation and positioning.
3. What are Auchan's long-term prospects and what threats does the company face in its dependence on emerging markets?
4. What recommendations would you make to Auchan's management for the future of their global business?

Sources: Carol Matlack, 'A French Wal-Mart's global blitz', *Bloomberg BusinessWeek*, 21 December 2009, pp. 64-65; Laurie Burkitt, 'Chinese shoppers lose taste for fakes', *Wall Street Journal*, 14 February 2012, p. 17; Simon Rabinovitch, 'China growth paradox baffles Walmart', *Financial Times*, 14 February 2012. Paul Gould, 'Consumers: a new middle class that likes to shop', *Financial Times*, 3 October 2011; Samidha Sharma and Boby Kurian 'French company Auchan eyes landmark joint venture', *The Times of India*, 13 February 2012; www.groupe-auchan.com/en/who-is-auchan/innovations/, accessed July 2015.

CHAPTER FOURTEEN

Engaging customers and communicating customer value: integrated marketing communications strategy

Chapter preview

In this and the next three chapters, we'll examine the last of the marketing mix tools – promotion. Companies must do more than just create customer value. They must also clearly and persuasively communicate that value. Promotion is not a single tool but rather a mix of several tools. Ideally, under the concept of *integrated marketing communications*, a company will carefully coordinate these promotion elements to engage customers and build a clear, consistent and compelling message about the organisation and its brands.

We begin by introducing the various promotion mix tools. Next, we'll examine the rapidly changing communications environment – especially the addition of new digital and social media and the need for integrated marketing communications. Finally, we discuss the steps in developing marketing communications and the promotion budgeting process. In the next three chapters, we'll present the specific marketing communications tools: advertising and public relations (Chapter 15); personal selling and sales promotion (Chapter 16); and direct, online, mobile and social media marketing (Chapter 17).

Let's start by looking at a good integrated marketing communications approach. Tesco's strapline, 'Every little helps, has consistently been a key focus in its marketing communications campaigns and has endured for over 20 years. It has successfully worked within its marketing communication mix to communicate the brand's unique proposition and made it the leading supermarket in the UK.

Objective outline

➤ **Objective 1** Define the five promotion mix tools for communicating customer value.
The promotion mix (pp. 408–409)

➤ **Objective 2** Discuss the changing communications landscape and the need for integrated marketing communications.
Integrated marketing communications (pp. 409–412)

➤ **Objective 3** Outline the communication process and the steps in developing effective marketing communications.

A view of the communication process (pp. 412–414)
Steps in developing effective marketing communication pp. 414–420)

➤ **OBJECTIVE 4** Explain the methods for setting the promotion budget and factors that affect the design of the promotion mix.
Setting the total promotion budget and mix (pp. 420–424)
Socially responsible marketing communication (pp. 424–425)

Tesco: 'Every little helps', a beautifully integrated marketing communications campaign

Apart from being the UK's number one supermarket, Tesco is also recognised for its wide-ranging marketing activities that encompass several product lines in the mix as communicated through various media. Many wonder how it consistently tops the list among competitors, including Asda/Walmart, Morrison and Sainsbury with Aldi and Lidl following on behind. The answer is not farfetched: a brilliantly packaged marketing communications strategy. Although the success of the organisation could be linked to its entire package of marketing strategy, including an effective blend of all its marketing mix elements, the contribution of its marketing communications strategy in this regard is considerable.

There are a number of reasons why Tesco's marketing communications strategy works so well. One of these is that the organisation embraces integrated marketing communications (IMC) by carefully integrating and co-ordinating its communication channels to deliver a clear, consistent, comprehensive and compelling message about the organisation and its various offerings. This is clearly evident in Tesco's use of advertising, sales promotion, personal selling, public relations, direct marketing and other marketing communications tools.

Meanwhile, a key factor in its marketing communications that cannot be ignored is its strapline, 'Every little helps', which was introduced in 1992 to communicate the firm's brand and the associated unique proposition. The introduction of this strapline became necessary as Tesco acknowledged that consumers are bombarded with many marketing communications messages from different sources, and a clear-cut message on how the firm is positioned to help customers solve their problems is fundamentally needed. The organisation has taken this slogan as a philosophy that drives everything it has done over the past 25 years, as well as into the future. For example, as detailed in the company's website, the slogan communicates that customers can get what they want, it informs them that the prices are competitive, it indicates improved customer service because the time the customer has to wait has been reduced, and it signals that the employees are helpful and courteous. It is therefore not surprising that it has been named the top UK retailer by Climate Change. Clearly, this strapline is a key part of the firm's heritage and has remained so over the years.

The consistency with which this message spreads across all of the marketing communications media that Tesco uses is noteworthy. Evidence shows that the company uses the traditional marketing communications tools effectively, and it has been spending more than the sector average on every one of the media it uses since 2005. For instance, its direct mail cost, which was €18.25 million in 2005, was more than four times the sector average. In 2010, press advertising was almost double the sector average at around €76 million. Today Tesco spends around €150 million on advertising in the UK alone (compared to Asda/Walmart's €124m and Morrison's €103m) – €10 million alone on TV advertising over the festive season.

It is crystal clear that the elements of the marketing environment keep changing, and so do customers' modes of communication. This is emphasised by the fact that we are now in the digital age; hence it is logical that the relevant tools associated with these developments be integrated with the traditional media toward making a compelling case about the brand of the organisation. This is exactly what Tesco does. It has a presence in various social media, including Facebook, Twitter and YouTube, which is managed by a dedicated team of experts through which it offers personalised local service to the biggest fan base in the UK. A significant step taken by Tesco in this direction was the appointment of Coca-Cola's interactive manager, Jude Brooks, to head its social media unit. Meanwhile, despite the increase in the number of means of communications available to Tesco, its focus on the key emphasis in the messages still remains 'Every

While recent times have not been great for Tesco, their integrated marketing communications strategy has been a bulwark against a period of tough trading and strategy changes.
Source: Greg Balfour Evans/ Alamy Images

little helps'. It basically ensures that its mass-media advertisements effectively deliver the same message as shown in the in-store promotion stimuli, which is consistent with what is shown on its website and also corroborates what is communicated through the company's various social media links. Simply put, the marketing information about Tesco and its offerings as shown on YouTube, Facebook, Twitter and other social media are coherently integrated with other traditional media to echo the same message.

As expected in an effective marketing communications process, Tesco often begins by identifying its target audience. This helps the organisation to decide on the content of its message, as well as how it will be delivered, when it will be delivered, who will deliver it, and where it will be delivered. It also determines the communication objectives early enough in the process for successful outcomes. Although some would argue that the key objective of marketing communication campaigns is to get consumers to buy the offerings, Tesco's view extends this understanding. Essentially, it emphasises that customers pass through the buyer-readiness stages – awareness, knowledge, liking, preference, conviction and purchase. Accordingly, it sets its marketing communications objectives to be consistent with this model as circumstances demand. It carefully designs the message in such a way that ensures consistency between all the marketing communication tools used, selects the message source, collects feedback, and selects the marketing communication budget in relation to the appropriate mix of the marketing communication tools.

As an example, in a move to strengthen its IMC system, recently Tesco launched an advertising campaign to communicate the improved quality of its Everyday own label range to replace Tesco's value range. The new range is reportedly healthier and features more stylish packaging. The press advertising designed for this purpose, which was handled by the RED Brick Road Agency, features images of this range of products, focusing on products for breakfast and dinner. According to the marketing director, this strategic move was adopted because feedback from customers indicated that they wanted products with a good level of taste, and health and visual appeal – but they wanted this at low prices. But something that is strikingly important here and noteworthy is that its marketing communications for this new range of products still emphasise the 'Every little helps' strapline.

It is clear that as the economic environment becomes increasingly challenging, firms are also challenged to review their marketing strategies to see whether they can succeed in the complex environment. Against this backdrop, Tesco has also begun a critical look into its marketing activities, with marketing communications being one of the key areas of focus. It put its advertising account up for grabs, which propelled many agencies to pitch for the firm's investment in marketing communications. After the process, Wieden and Kennedy London emerged as the favourite to handle the firm's $174.3 million advertising account. It has been reported that it is also reviewing its brand communications, including the 'Every little helps' slogan. However, the reactions of most commentators have been very positive on the impacts of the slogan in the firm's IMC package. In fact, it has been stated that although the new agency is poised to exhibit its creativity in creating clear and compelling messages, it will still maintain the use of 'Every little helps', which has been running for over 20 years. Overall, the choice of this slogan is a small step that has worked hugely well for Tesco and epitomises the concept of integrated marketing communications.[1]

Building good customer relationships calls for more than just developing a good product, pricing it attractively, and making it available to target customers. Companies must also communicate their value propositions to customers, and what they communicate should not be left to chance. All communications must be planned and blended into carefully integrated programmes. Just as good communication is important in building and maintaining any other kind of relationship, it is a crucial element in a company's efforts to engage customers and build profitable customer relationships.

THE PROMOTION MIX

A company's total **promotion mix** – also called its **marketing communications mix** – consists of the specific blend of advertising, public relations, personal selling, sales promotion and direct marketing tools that the company uses to engage consumers, persuasively communicate customer value, and build customer relationships. The five major promotion tools are defined as follows:[2]

- **Advertising.** Any paid form of non-personal presentation and promotion of ideas, goods or services by an identified sponsor.
- **Sales promotion.** Short-term incentives to encourage the purchase or sale of a good or service.
- **Personal selling.** Personal customer interactions by the firm's sales force for the purpose of engaging customers, making sales and building customer relationships.
- **Public relations.** Building good relations with the company's various publics by obtaining favourable publicity, building up a good corporate image, and handling or heading off unfavourable rumours, stories and events.
- **Direct and digital marketing.** Engaging directly with carefully targeted individual consumers and customer communities to both obtain an immediate response and build lasting customer relationships.

Each category involves specific promotional tools that are used to communicate with customers. For example, *advertising* includes broadcast, print, online, mobile, outdoor and other forms. *Sales promotion* includes discounts, coupons, displays and demonstrations. *Personal selling* includes sales presentations, trade shows and incentive programmes. *Public relations (PR)* includes press releases, sponsorships, events and web pages. And *direct and digital marketing* includes direct mail, catalogues, online and social media, mobile marketing, and more.

At the same time, marketing communication goes beyond these specific promotion tools. The product's design, its price, the shape and colour of its packaging, and the stores that sell it – *all* communicate something to buyers. Thus, although the promotion mix is the company's primary engagement and communications activity, the entire marketing mix – promotion, *as well as* product, price and place – must be coordinated for greatest impact.

INTEGRATED MARKETING COMMUNICATIONS

In past decades, marketers perfected the art of mass marketing: selling highly standardised products to masses of customers. In the process, they developed effective mass-media communication techniques to support these strategies. Large companies now routinely invest millions or even billions of dollars in television, magazine or other mass-media advertising, reaching tens of millions of customers with a single ad. Today, however, marketing managers face some new marketing communications realities. Perhaps no other area of marketing is changing so profoundly as marketing communications, creating both exciting and challenging times for marketing communicators.

The new marketing communications model

Several major factors are changing the face of today's marketing communications. First, *consumers* are changing. In this digital, wireless age, consumers are better informed and more communications empowered. Rather than relying on marketer-supplied information, they can use the Internet, social media and other technologies to find information on their own. They can connect easily with other consumers to exchange brand-related information or even create their own brand messages and experiences.

Second, *marketing strategies* are changing. As mass markets have fragmented, marketers are shifting away from mass marketing. More and more, they are developing focused marketing programmes designed to build closer relationships with customers in more narrowly defined micro-markets.

Finally, sweeping advances in *digital technology* are causing remarkable changes in the ways companies and customers communicate with each other. The digital age has spawned a host

Promotion mix (marketing communications mix)—The specific blend of promotion tools that the company uses to persuasively communicate customer value and build customer relationships.

Advertising—Any paid form of non-personal presentation and promotion of ideas, goods or services by an identified sponsor.

Sales promotion—Short-term incentives to encourage the purchase or sale of a product or a service.

Personal selling—Personal presentation by the firm's sales force for the purpose of engaging customers, making sales and building customer relationships.

Public relations (PR)—Building good relations with the company's various publics by obtaining favourable publicity, building up a good corporate image, and handling or heading off unfavourable rumours, stories and events.

Direct and digital marketing—Engaging directly with carefully targeted individual consumers and customer communities to both obtain an immediate response and build lasting customer relationships.

Author comment

IMC is a really hot marketing topic these days. No other area of marketing is changing so quickly and profoundly. A big part of the reason is the huge surge in customer engagement through digital media – online, mobile and social media marketing.

of new information and communication tools – from smartphones and tablets to satellite and cable television systems to the many faces of the Internet (brand websites, e-mail, blogs, social media and online communities, the mobile web, and so much more). These explosive developments have had a dramatic impact on marketing communications. Just as mass marketing once gave rise to a new generation of mass-media communications, the new digital and social media have given birth to a more targeted, social and engaging marketing communications model.

Although network television, magazines, newspapers and other traditional mass media remain very important, their dominance is declining. In their place, advertisers are now adding a broad selection of more specialised and highly targeted media to engage smaller customer segments with more personalised, interactive content. The new media range from speciality cable television channels and made-for-the-web videos to online display ads, Internet catalogues, e-mail and texting, blogs, mobile coupons and other content, and social media such as Twitter, Facebook, Google+ and Pinterest. Such new media have taken marketing by storm.

Some advertising industry experts even predict that the old mass-media communications model will eventually become obsolete. Mass-media costs are rising, audiences are shrinking, ad clutter is increasing, and viewers are gaining control of message exposure through technologies such as video streaming or DVRs that let them skip disruptive television commercials. As a result, the sceptics suggest, marketers are shifting ever-larger portions of their marketing budgets away from old-media mainstays and moving them to online, social, mobile and other new-age media.

In recent years, although TV still dominates as an advertising medium with around 38 per cent share of ad spending, its growth has stagnated. Spending in magazines, newspapers and radio has lost ground. Meanwhile, digital media have come from nowhere during the past few years with digital advertising spending in Europe increasing by 11.9 per cent last year surpassing €27 billon.[3]

Walkers use of social media has proved an excellent way to engage customers with the brand.

Source: Dave J Hogan/Getty Images for Walkers Do Us A Flavour

In Europe, the UK leads the way in digital marketing with mobile advertising beginning to dominate – of the €8.4 billion spend in the UK on Internet advertising, €1.4 billion is mobile telephone oriented.[4] By far the fastest-growing ad-spending category, digital's share is expected to grow to 31 per cent by 2017. P&G, the world's biggest advertiser, now spends a full third of its marketing budget on digital media.[5]

In some cases, marketers are skipping traditional media altogether. For example, when Rovio introduced the Angry Birds Space version of its popular game, it used only online video. It began by posting a 20-second video teaser containing only the game title and launch date – that video landed 2.2 million online views. Next, in an inspired move, Rovio teamed with NASA and astronaut Don Petit to do a video in outer space on the International Space Station, which demonstrated the actual physics of a stuffed Angry Bird in space – that video went viral. Six millions views and a few days later, Rovio released a video trailer briefly introducing the game's characters, which grabbed another cool 1 million views in only two days. Finally, at launch time, Rovio posted a two-minute video fully introducing the new game. In total, the award-winning online video campaign reaped an astonishing 134 million views and 168,570 social shares.[6]

In an interesting link-up between digital and physical promotions, Walkers in the UK recently transformed bus shelters into tweet activated vending machines. As part of their search for new flavours (the 'Do us a flavour' campaign) the campaign featured a well-known UK ex-footballer and TV personality Gary Lineker. Commuters were required to tweet @Walkers_busstop with an additional code to be given a free packet of new-flavour crisps by a virtual image of the ex-England footballer. Consumers were then encouraged to vote for their favourite new recipe flavour online and via a Facebook page.

In the new marketing communications world, rather than using old approaches that interrupt customers and force-feed them mass messages, new media formats let marketers reach smaller communities of consumers in more interactive, engaging ways. For example, think about television viewing these days. Consumers can now watch their favourite programmes on just about anything with a screen – on televisions but also laptops, mobile phones or tablets. And they can choose to watch programmes whenever and wherever they wish, often without commercials. Increasingly, some programmes, ads and videos are being produced only for Internet viewing.

Despite the shift toward new digital media, however, traditional mass media still capture a large share of the promotion budgets of most major marketing firms, a fact that probably won't change quickly. Thus, rather than the old-media model collapsing completely, most industry insiders foresee a shifting mix of both traditional mass media and a wide array of online, mobile and social media that engage more targeted consumer communities in a more personalised, interactive way. Many advertisers and ad agencies are still grappling with this transition. In the end, however, regardless of the communications channel, the key is to integrate all of these media in a way that best engages customers, communicates the brand message and enhances the customer's brand experiences.

As the marketing communications environment shifts, so will the role of marketing communicators. Rather than just creating and placing 'TV ads' or 'print ads' or 'Facebook display ads', many marketers now view themselves more broadly as **content marketing** managers. As such, they create, inspire and share brand messages and conversations with and among customers across a fluid mix of *paid, owned, earned* and *shared* communication channels. These channels include media that are both traditional and new, controlled and not controlled.

Content marketing— Creating, inspiring and sharing brand messages and conversations with and among consumers across a fluid mix of paid, owned, earned and shared channels.

The need for integrated marketing communications

The shift toward a richer mix of media and brand content approaches poses a problem for marketers. Consumers today are bombarded by brand content from a broad range of sources. But consumers don't distinguish between content sources the way marketers do. In the consumer's mind, brand content from different sources – whether it's a Champions League football ad, in-store display, mobile app or a friend's social media post – all become part of a single message about the brand or company. Conflicting content from these different sources can result in confused company images, brand positions and customer relationships.

All too often, companies fail to integrate their various communication channels. The result is a hotchpotch of brand content to consumers. Mass-media ads say one thing, whereas an in-store promotion sends a different signal, and the company's Internet site, e-mails, social media pages or videos posted on YouTube say something altogether different. The problem is that these communications often come from different parts of the company. Advertising messages are planned and implemented by the advertising department or an ad agency. Other company departments or agencies are responsible for public relations (PR), sales promotion events, and online or social media content. However, whereas companies may have separated their communications tools, customers don't. Mixed content from these sources results in blurred brand perceptions by consumers.

The new world of online, mobile, social media marketing presents tremendous opportunities but also big challenges. It can 'give companies increased access to their customers, fresh insights into their preferences, and a broader creative palette to work with', says one marketing executive. But 'the biggest issue is complexity and fragmentation . . . the amount of choice out there', says another. The challenge is to 'make it come together in an organised way'.[7]

To that end, more companies today are adopting the concept of **integrated marketing communications (IMC)**. Under this concept, as illustrated in Figure 14.1, the company carefully integrates its many communication channels to deliver a clear, consistent and compelling message about the organisation and its brands.

Integrated marketing communications calls for recognising all touch points where the customer may encounter content about the company and its brands. Each contact with the brand will deliver a message – whether good, bad or indifferent. The company's goal should be to deliver a consistent and positive message at each contact. Integrated marketing communications ties together all of the company's messages and images. Its television and print ads have the same brand message as its e-mail and personal selling communications. And its PR materials are consistent with website, online, social media and mobile marketing content.

Integrated marketing communications (IMC)— Carefully integrating and coordinating the company's many communications channels to deliver a clear, consistent and compelling message about the organisation and its products.

Figure 14.1 Integrated marketing communications

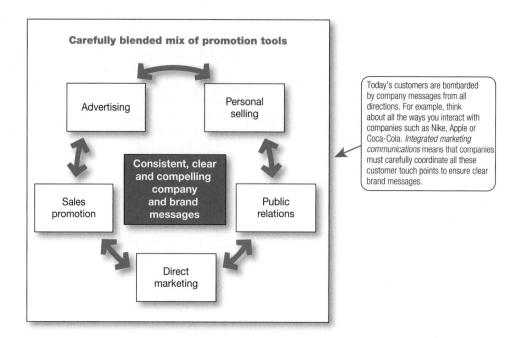

Often, different media play unique roles in engaging, informing and persuading consumers. For example, a recent study showed that more than two-thirds of advertisers and their agencies are planning video ad campaigns that stretch across multiple viewing platforms, such as traditional TV and digital, mobile and social media. Such *digital video ad convergence*, as it's called, combines TV's core strength – vast reach – with digital's better targeting, interaction and engagement.[8] These varied media and roles must be carefully coordinated under the overall marketing communications plan.

A great example of a well-integrated marketing communications effort is that of the ALS Foundation in the Netherlands:[9]

> The ALS Foundation's 'I have already died' campaign is the deserved winner of a raft of prestigious awards and is widely acknowledged as an excellent integrated campaign that genuinely changed the world. The 'I have already died' campaign sought to increase awareness of 'ALS', commonly known as Lou Gehrig's disease, while encouraging pharmaceutical companies to devote more research into a search for a cure. As ALS sufferers usually pass on within three years of diagnosis, limited research has been conducted. In response, the agency Publicis Amsterdam adopted a confrontational strategy – recording appeals from patients and airing them after they had died. The campaign received very heavy play on a wide range of media from TV to print with truly breath taking results. Donations rose by 500 per cent, awareness increased from 60 per cent to 81 per cent and willingness to give rose from 27 per cent to 40 per cent.

In the past, no one person or department was responsible for thinking through the communication roles of the various promotion tools and coordinating the promotion mix. To help implement integrated marketing communications, some companies have appointed a marketing communications director who has overall responsibility for the company's communications efforts. This helps to produce better communications consistency and greater sales impact. It places the responsibility in someone's hands – where none existed before – to unify the company's image as it is shaped by thousands of company activities.

Author comment

To develop effective marketing communications, you must first understand the general communication process.

A VIEW OF THE COMMUNICATION PROCESS

Integrated marketing communications involves identifying the target audience and shaping a well-coordinated promotional programme to obtain the desired audience response. Too often, marketing communications focus on immediate awareness, image or preference goals in the target

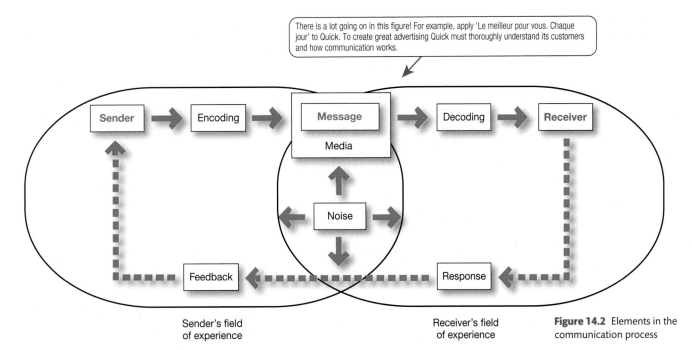

> There is a lot going on in this figure! For example, apply 'Le meilleur pour vous. Chaque jour' to Quick. To create great advertising Quick must thoroughly understand its customers and how communication works.

Figure 14.2 Elements in the communication process

market. But this approach to communication is too short-sighted. Today, marketers are moving toward viewing communications *as* managing on-going customer engagement and relationships with the company and its brands.

Because customers differ, communications programmes need to be developed for specific segments, niches and even individuals. And, given today's interactive communications technologies, companies must ask not only 'How can we engage our customers?' but also 'How can we let our customers engage us?'

Thus, the communications process should start with an audit of all the potential touch points that target customers may have with the company and its brands. For example, someone purchasing a new phone plan may talk to others, see television or magazine ads, visit various online sites for prices and reviews, and check out plans at a high-street phone shop, their local supermarket or a provider's kiosk or store. The marketer needs to assess what influence each communication experience will have at different stages of the buying process. This understanding helps marketers allocate their communication dollars more efficiently and effectively.

To communicate effectively, marketers need to understand how communication works. Communication involves the nine elements shown in Figure 14.2. Two of these elements are the major parties in a communication – the *sender* and the *receiver*. Another two are the major communication tools – the *message* and the *media*. Four more are major communication functions – *encoding*, *decoding*, *response* and *feedback*. The last element is *noise* in the system.

Definitions of these elements follow and are applied to a Quick (the pan-Europe burger chain) '*Le meilleur pour vous. Chaque jour*' ('The best for you. Every day) television commercial.

- *Sender*: The *party sending the message* to another party – here, Quick.
- *Encoding*: The process of *putting thought into symbolic form* – for example, Quick's ad agency assembles words, sounds and illustrations into an ad that will convey the intended message.
- *Message*: The *set of symbols* that the sender transmits – the actual Quick ad.
- *Media*: The *communication channels* through which the message moves from the sender to the receiver – in this case, television and the specific television programmes that Quick selects.
- *Decoding*: The process by which the receiver *assigns meaning to the symbols* encoded by the sender – a consumer watches the Quick commercial and interprets the words and images it contains.
- *Receiver*: The *party receiving the message* sent by another party – the customer who watches the Quick ad.

- *Response*: The *reactions of the receiver* after being exposed to the message – any of hundreds of possible responses, such as the consumer likes Quick better, is more likely to eat at Quick next time, hums the 'Best for You' jingle, or does nothing.
- *Feedback*: The part of the *receiver's response communicated back to the sender* – Quick's research shows that consumers are either struck by and remember the ad or they write or call Quick, praising or criticising the ad or its products.
- *Noise*: The *unplanned static or distortion* during the communication process, which results in the receiver getting a different message than the one sent – the consumer is distracted while watching the commercial and misses its key points.

For a message to be effective, the sender's encoding process must mesh with the receiver's decoding process. The best messages consist of words and other symbols that are familiar to the receiver. The more the sender's field of experience overlaps with that of the receiver, the more effective the message is likely to be. Marketing communicators may not always *share* the customer's field of experience. For example, an advertising copywriter from one socioeconomic level might create ads for customers from another level – say, wealthy business owners. However, to communicate effectively, the marketing communicator must *understand* the customer's field of experience.

This model points out several key factors in good communication. Senders need to know what audiences they wish to reach and what responses they want. They must be good at encoding messages that take into account how the target audience decodes them. They must send messages through media that reach target audiences, and they must develop feedback channels so that they can assess an audience's response to the message. Also, in today's interactive media environment, companies must be prepared to 'flip' the communications process – to become good receivers of and responders to messages sent by consumers.

STEPS IN DEVELOPING EFFECTIVE MARKETING COMMUNICATION

We now examine the steps in developing an effective integrated communications and promotion programme. Marketers must do the following: identify the target audience, determine the communication objectives, design a message, choose the media through which to send the message, select the message source collect feedback.

Identifying the target audience

A marketing communicator starts with a clear target audience in mind. The audience may be current users or potential buyers, those who make the buying decision or those who influence it. The audience may be individuals, groups, special publics or the general public. The target audience will heavily affect the communicator's decisions on *what* will be said, *how* it will be said, *when* it will be said, *where* it will be said and *who* will say it.

Determining the communication objectives

Buyer-readiness stages—The stages consumers normally pass through on their way to a purchase: awareness, knowledge, liking, preference, conviction and, finally, the actual purchase.

Once the target audience has been defined, marketers must determine the desired response. Of course, in many cases, they will seek a *purchase* response. But purchase may result only after a lengthy consumer decision-making process. The marketing communicator needs to know where the target audience now stands and to what stage it needs to be moved. The target audience may be in any of six **buyer-readiness stages**, the stages consumers normally pass through on their way to making a purchase. These stages are *awareness, knowledge, liking, preference, conviction* and *purchase* (see Figure 14.3).

The marketing communicator's target market may be totally unaware of the product, know only its name, or know only a few things about it. Thus, the marketer must first build *awareness* and *knowledge*. For example, to introduce consumers to its innovative new Microsoft Surface tablet, Microsoft spent millions of euros on marketing. The current campaign introduces the

Figure 14.3 Buyer-readiness stages

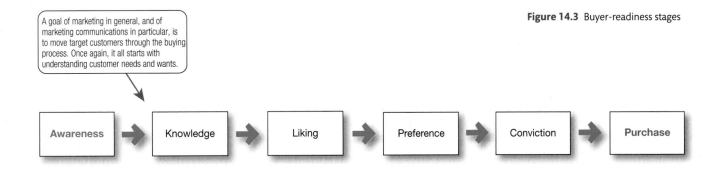

> A goal of marketing in general, and of marketing communications in particular, is to move target customers through the buying process. Once again, it all starts with understanding customer needs and wants.

Awareness → Knowledge → Liking → Preference → Conviction → Purchase

Surface Pro 3 tablet as the 'One device for everything in your life' – it's lighter and thinner than a laptop but with a click-in keyboard and fuller features than competing tablets. The extensive introductory campaign used a broad range of traditional, digital, mobile, social and in-store media to quickly create awareness and knowledge across the entire market.

Assuming that target consumers *know* about a product, how do they *feel* about it? Once potential buyers know about Microsoft's Surface tablet, marketers want to move them through successively stronger stages of feelings toward the model. These stages include *liking* (feeling favourable about the Surface), *preference* (preferring the Surface to competing tablets) and *conviction* (believing that the Surface is the best tablet for them).

Microsoft Surface marketers use a combination of promotion mix tools to create positive feelings and conviction. Initial TV commercials help build anticipation and an emotional brand connection. Images and videos on the Microsoft Surface's YouTube, Facebook and Pinterest pages engage potential buyers and demonstrate the product's use and features. Press releases and other PR activities help keep the buzz going about the product. A packed microsite provides additional information and buying opportunities.

Finally, some members of the target market might be convinced about the product but not quite get around to making the *purchase*. The communicator must lead these consumers to take the final step. To help reluctant consumers over such hurdles, Microsoft might offer buyers special promotional prices and upgrades, and support the product with comments and reviews from customers at its web and social media sites and elsewhere.

Of course, marketing communications alone cannot create positive feelings and purchases for the Surface. The product itself must provide superior value for the customer. In fact, outstanding marketing communications can actually speed the demise of a poor product. The more quickly potential buyers learn about a poor product, the more quickly they become aware of its faults. Thus, good marketing communications call for 'good deeds followed by good words'.

Microsoft have spent millions of euros to influence potential customers' buyer-readiness stages regarding their innovative Surface computer.

Source: imageBROKER/REX/Shutterstock

Designing a message

Having defined the desired audience response, the communicator then turns to developing an effective message. Ideally, the message should get *attention*, hold *interest*, arouse *desire* and obtain *action* (a framework known as the *AIDA model*). In practice, few messages take the consumer all the way from awareness to purchase, but the AIDA framework suggests the desirable qualities of a good message.

When putting a message together, the marketing communicator must decide what to say (*message content*) and how to say it (*message structure* and *format*).

Message content

The marketer has to figure out an appeal or theme that will produce the desired response. There are three types of appeals: rational, emotional and moral. *Rational appeals* relate to the audience's self-interest. They show that the product will produce the desired benefits. Examples are messages showing a product's quality, economy, value or performance. Thus, in one ad, Virgin Atlantic simply states, 'Fly Virgin Atlantic Upper Class and get your own suite'. 'Quaker Instant Oatmeal. A warm, yummy way to help lower your cholesterol'. And a Weight Watchers ad states this simple fact: 'The diet secret to end all diet secrets is that there is no diet secret.'

Emotional appeals attempt to stir up either negative or positive emotions that can motivate purchase. Communicators may use emotional appeals ranging from love, joy and humour to fear and guilt. Advocates of emotional messages claim that they attract more attention and create more belief in the sponsor and the brand. The idea is that consumers often feel before they think, and persuasion is emotional in nature. Thus, Michelin sells tyres using mild fear appeals, showing families riding in cars and telling parents: 'Michelin: because so much is riding on your tyres.' And De Beers' iconic emotional ads showing silhouettes of men surprising the women they love with diamond jewellery. One recent ad concludes, 'Celebrate your loving marriage. A diamond is forever.'[10]

Moral appeals are directed to an audience's sense of what is 'right' and 'proper'. They are often used to urge people to support social causes, such as a cleaner environment or aid to the disadvantaged. For example, the Red Cross urges people to donate money to help people in emergencies and to save and rebuild lives. In the recent West Africa Ebola Outbreak Appeal the Red Cross argued that 'there is no quick fix to stopping Ebola in West Africa' and that 'this is not a normal disaster where everybody is running to help, because of the fear around Ebola'.[11] They presented the morally appealing story of Daniel a volunteer, who says: 'I keep going and working . . . because it is the right thing to do. People are dying and if nobody is managing the dead bodies, the disease is going to spread.'[12]

These days, it seems as if every company is using humour in its advertising. Properly used, humour can capture attention, make people feel good, and give a brand personality. However, advertisers must be careful when using humour. Used poorly, it can detract from comprehension, wear out its welcome fast, overshadow the product, and even irritate consumers.

Many brands manage to be sporadically funny but those that successfully build themselves around humour are far more unusual. The UK soft drink brand Tango did it from the mid-1990s with a series of advertisements. The most popular featured an orange blobby man who slapped drinkers with the catchphrase 'You've been Tangoed', a slogan that passed into common usage. A more recent example is Comparethemarket.com, the insurance comparison site whose brand identity centres on a Russian meerkat called Aleksandr Orlov and the fact that comparethemarket.com is easily confused with comparethemeerkat.com. 'In 2008, we'd been going for a year and research suggested we had a big issue with name recognition,' says Kal Atwal, the website's managing director. All the comparison sites 'had "compare" in their names'. The campaign had a tangible impact: monthly site visits have gone up from 50,000 to 2 million. The meerkat has proved so popular that a number of spin-off products were launched, including an 'autobiography' of Orlov that was published in time for Christmas. 'Even the Russians seem to like him,' says Ms Atwal. 'Russian TV covered the book launch.' Humour can also reinvigorate older brands. Old Spice has found a new audience with its 'Smell like a man, man' ads. Iain Tait of Wieden & Kennedy, the agency behind the campaign, says because a lot of men's toiletries are bought for them by women, 'we needed to create a character who was adored by ladies but who men don't find threatening'. The answer was a character who combines extreme handsomeness with being funny. 'It's a very knowing kind of humour that comes from the character playing it straight,' says Mr Tait. Why don't more brands take the plunge? Mr Prior says companies worry that being amusing makes people question their credibility. But, he argues, 'consumers are more sophisticated than that. If you take an airline, passengers know that airlines take safety very seriously'. '[The Old Spice ads don't] send up the product and he doesn't make fun of himself,' explains Mr Tait. 'You need to treat the audience with a bit of respect and credit them with intelligence. When you try and spoon-feed them the gag, that's when it becomes embarrassing.'[13]

Message structure

Marketers must also decide how to handle three message structure issues. The first is whether to draw a conclusion or leave it to the audience. Research suggests that, in many cases, rather than drawing a conclusion, the advertiser is better off asking questions and letting buyers come to their own conclusions.

The second message structure issue is whether to present the strongest arguments first or last. Presenting them first gets strong attention but may lead to an anticlimactic ending.

The third message structure issue is whether to present a one-sided argument (mentioning only the product's strengths) or a two-sided argument (touting the product's strengths while also admitting its shortcomings). Usually, a one-sided argument is more effective in sales presentations – except when audiences are highly educated or likely to hear opposing claims or when the communicator has a negative association to overcome. In this spirit, Marmite (the yeast extract spread) ran the 'You either love it or hate it' campaign with the follow-up of 'Show your love'. Heinz ran the message 'Heinz Ketchup is slow good', and Listerine ran the message 'Listerine tastes bad twice a day'. In such cases, two-sided messages can enhance an advertiser's credibility and make buyers more resistant to competitor attacks.

IMC: colour increases brand recognition by up to 80 per cent.

Source: Ashley Cooper/Alamy Images

Message format

The marketing communicator also needs a strong *format* for the message. In a print ad, the communicator has to decide on the headline, copy, illustration and colours. To attract attention, advertisers can use novelty and contrast; eye-catching pictures and headlines; distinctive formats; message size and position; and colour, shape and movement.

If a message is to be carried on television or in person, then all these elements plus body language must be planned. Presenters plan every detail – facial expressions, gestures, dress, posture and hairstyles. If a message is carried on a product or its package, the communicator must watch texture, scent, colour, size and shape. For example, colour alone can enhance message recognition for a brand. One study suggests that colour increases brand recognition by up to 80 per cent – for example, Veuve Cliquot's (trademark orange), KitKat's (red and white), Ecover's (blue and green), Quick Burger Restaurant's (red and white), Dove's (predominately white with blue text); or UPS (brown). Thus, in designing effective marketing communications, marketers must consider colour and other seemingly unimportant details carefully.[14]

Choosing communication channels and media

The communicator must now select the *channels of communication*. There are two broad types of communication channels: *personal* and *non-personal*.

Personal communication channels

In **personal communication channels**, two or more people communicate directly with each other. They might communicate face to face, on the phone, via mail or e-mail, or even through texting or an Internet chat. Personal communication channels are effective because they allow for personal addressing and feedback.

Personal communication channels—Channels through which two or more people communicate directly with each other, including face to face, on the phone, via mail or e-mail, or even through an Internet 'chat'.

Some personal communication channels are controlled directly by the company. For example, company salespeople contact business buyers. But other personal communications about the product may reach buyers through channels not directly controlled by the company. These channels might include independent experts – consumer advocates, bloggers and others – making statements to buyers. Or they might be neighbours, friends, family members, associates, or other consumers talking to target buyers, in person or via social media or other interactive media. This last channel, **word-of-mouth influence**, has considerable effect in many product areas.

Personal influence carries great weight, especially for products that are expensive, risky or highly visible. One survey found that recommendations from friends and family are far and away the most powerful influence on consumers worldwide: More than 50 per cent of consumers said friends and family are the number one influence on their awareness and purchase. Another study found that 90 per cent of customers trust recommendations from people they know and 70 per cent trust consumer opinions posted online, whereas trust in ads runs from a high of about 62 per cent to less than 24 per cent, depending on the medium.[15] Is it any wonder, then, that few consumers buy a big-ticket item before checking out what existing users have to say about the product at a site such as Amazon? Who hasn't made an Amazon purchase based on another customer's review or the 'Customers who bought this also bought …' section; or decided against purchase because of negative customer reviews?

Companies can take steps to put personal communication channels to work for them. For example, as we discussed in Chapter 5, they can create *opinion leaders* for their brands – people whose opinions are sought by others – by supplying influencers with the product on attractive terms or by educating them so that they can inform others. **Buzz marketing** involves cultivating opinion leaders and getting them to spread information about a product or a service to others in their communities. For example, headquartered in Germany, trnd is a Europe-wide company that specialises (amongst other things) in the use of collaborative marketing formats to generate brand awareness and increase brand visibility of innovative products. Working with L'Oréal Paris, trnd assembled 2,500 fashion-oriented brand ambassadors to promote L'Oréal's Sublime Mousse. This involved equipping each ambassador (whose hair colour varied from dark brown to light blond) with an appropriate hair colour shaded mousse. Thereafter the brand ambassadors were encouraged to distribute samples to a wide range of friends and family. The resulting word-of-mouth was not only considerable but also highly targeted and therefore hugely efficient.[16]

Social marketing firm BzzAgent takes a different approach to creating buzz. It creates customers for a client brand, then turns them into influential brand advocates:[17]

> BzzAgent has assembled a volunteer army of natural-born buzzers, millions of actual shoppers around the world who are highly active in social media and who love to talk about and recommend products. Once a client signs on, BzzAgent searches its database and selects 'agents' that fit the profiles of the product's target customers. Selected volunteers receive product samples, creating a personal brand experience. BzzAgent then urges the agents to share their honest opinions of the product through face-to-face conversations and via tweets, Facebook posts, online photo and video sharing, blogs and other social sharing venues. If the product is good, the positive word-of-mouth spreads quickly. If the product is iffy – well, that's worth learning quickly as well. BzzAgent advocates have successfully buzzed the brands of hundreds of top marketing companies, from P&G, Nestle, Coca-Cola and Estee Lauder to Kroger and Disney. BzzAgent's appeal is its authenticity. The agents aren't scripted. Instead, the company tells its advocates, 'Here's the product; if you believe in it, say whatever you think. Bzz is no place for excessive, repetitive, or unauthentic posts.'

Non-personal communication channels

Non-personal communication channels are media that carry messages without personal contact or feedback. They include major media, atmospheres and events. Major *media* include print

---

Word-of-mouth influence—Personal communications about a product between target buyers and neighbours, friends, family members and associates.

Buzz marketing—Cultivating opinion leaders and getting them to spread information about a product or a service to others in their communities.

Non-personal communication channels—Media that carry messages without personal contact or feedback, including major media, atmospheres and events.

media (newspapers, magazines, direct mail), broadcast media (television, radio), display media (billboards, signs, posters) and online media (e-mail and company websites). *Atmospheres* are designed environments that create or reinforce the buyer's leanings toward buying a product. Thus, lawyers' offices and banks are designed to communicate confidence and other qualities that might be valued by clients. *Events* are staged occurrences that communicate messages to target audiences. For example, public relations departments arrange grand openings, shows and exhibits, public tours, and other events.

Non-personal communication affects buyers directly. In addition, using mass media often affects buyers indirectly by causing more personal communication. For example, communications might first flow from television, magazines and other mass media to opinion leaders and then from these opinion leaders to others. Thus, opinion leaders step between the mass media and their audiences and carry messages to people who are less exposed to media. Interestingly, marketers often use non-personal communication channels to replace or stimulate personal communications by embedding consumer endorsements or word-of-mouth testimonials in their ads and other promotions.

Selecting the message source

In either personal or non-personal communication, the message's impact also depends on how the target audience views the communicator. Messages delivered by highly credible sources are more persuasive. Thus, many food companies promote to doctors, dentists and other healthcare providers to motivate these professionals to recommend specific food products to their patients. And marketers hire celebrity endorsers – well-known athletes, actors, musicians and even cartoon characters – to deliver their messages. Premier League football star Wayne Rooney lends his image to brands such as Nike and E. A. Sports, Sarah Jessica Parker speaks for Garnier, Keith Richards endorses Louis Vuitton and the end of every Formula 1 race finds drivers scrabbling to put on their latest endorsed watches and hats.[18]

But companies must be careful when selecting celebrities to represent their brands. Picking the wrong spokesperson can result in embarrassment and a tarnished image. For example, a dozen or more big brands – including Nike, Anheuser-Busch, Radio Shack, Oakley, Trek bikes and Giro helmets – faced embarrassment when pro cyclist Lance Armstrong was stripped of his Tour de France titles and banned for life from competitive cycling for illegal use of performance-enhancing drugs. Previously considered a model brand spokesman, Armstrong once earned nearly €16 million in endorsement income in a single year. 'Arranged marriages between brands and celebrities are inherently risky,' notes one expert. 'Ninety-nine per cent of celebrities do a strong job for their brand partners,' says another, 'and 1 per cent goes off the rails.'[19] More than ever, it's important to pick the right celebrity for the brand.

Collecting feedback

After sending the message or other brand content, the communicator must research its effect on the target audience. This involves asking target audience members whether they remember the content, how many times they saw it, what points they recall, how they felt about the content, and their past and present attitudes toward the brand and company. The communicator would also like to measure behaviour resulting from the content – how many people bought the product, talked to others about it, or visited the store.

Feedback on marketing communications may suggest changes in the promotion programme or in the product offer itself. For example, Stockmann's uses television and newspaper advertising to inform area consumers about its stores, services and merchandising events. Suppose feedback research shows that 80 per cent of all shoppers in an area recall seeing the store's ads and are aware of its merchandise and sales. Sixty per cent of these aware shoppers have visited a Stockmann's store in the past month, but only 20 per cent of those who visited were satisfied with the shopping experience.

These results suggest that although promotion is creating *awareness*, Stockmann's stores aren't giving consumers the *satisfaction* they expect. Therefore, Stockmann's needs to improve the shopping experience while staying with the successful communications programme. In contrast, suppose research shows that only 40 per cent of area consumers are aware of the store's merchandise and events, only 30 per cent of those aware have shopped recently, but 80 per cent of those who have shopped return soon to shop again. In this case, Stockmann's needs to strengthen its promotion programme to take advantage of its power to create customer satisfaction in the store.

Author comment

In this section, we'll look at the promotion budget setting process and at how marketers blend the various marketing communication tools into a smooth-functioning integrated promotion mix.

SETTING THE TOTAL PROMOTION BUDGET AND MIX

We have looked at the steps in planning and sending communications to a target audience. But how does the company determine its total *promotion budget* and the division among the major promotional tools to create the *promotion mix*? By what process does it blend the tools to create integrated marketing communications? We now look at these questions.

Setting the total promotion budget

One of the hardest marketing decisions facing a company is how much to spend on promotion. John Wanamaker, the department store magnate, once said, 'I know that half of my advertising is wasted, but I don't know which half. I spent $2 million for advertising, and I don't know if that is half enough or twice too much.' Thus, it is not surprising that industries and companies vary widely in how much they spend on promotion. Promotion spending may be 10–12 per cent of sales for consumer packaged goods, 20 per cent for cosmetics, and only 1.9 per cent for household appliances. Within a given industry, both low and high spenders can be found.[20]

How does a company determine its promotion budget? Here, we look at four common methods used to set the total budget for advertising: the *affordable method*, the *percentage-of-sales method*, the *competitive parity method* and the *objective-and-task method*.

Affordable method

Affordable method—Setting the promotion budget at the level management thinks the company can afford.

Some companies use the **affordable method:** they set the promotion budget at the level they think the company can afford. Small businesses often use this method, reasoning that the company cannot spend more on advertising than it has. They start with total revenues, deduct operating expenses and capital outlays, and then devote some portion of the remaining funds to advertising.

Unfortunately, this method of setting budgets completely ignores the effects of promotion on sales. It tends to place promotion last among spending priorities, even in situations in which advertising is critical to the firm's success. It leads to an uncertain annual promotion budget, which makes long-range market planning difficult. Although the affordable method can result in overspending on advertising, it more often results in underspending.

Percentage-of-sales method

Percentage-of-sales method—Setting the promotion budget at a certain percentage of current or forecasted sales or as a percentage of the unit sales price.

Other companies use the **percentage-of-sales method**, setting their promotion budget at a certain percentage of current or forecasted sales. Or they budget a percentage of the unit sales price. The percentage-of-sales method is simple to use and helps management think about the relationships between promotion spending, selling price and profit per unit.

Despite these claimed advantages, however, the percentage-of-sales method has little to justify it. It wrongly views sales as the *cause* of promotion rather than as the *result*. Although studies have found a positive correlation between promotional spending and brand strength, this relationship often turns out to be effect and cause, not cause and effect. Stronger brands with higher sales can afford the biggest ad budgets.

Thus, the percentage-of-sales budget is based on the availability of funds rather than on opportunities. It may prevent the increased spending sometimes needed to turn around falling sales. Because the budget varies with year-to-year sales, long-range planning is difficult. Finally, the method does not provide any basis for choosing a *specific* percentage, except what has been done in the past or what competitors are doing.

Competitive-parity method

Still other companies use the **competitive-parity method**, setting their promotion budgets to match competitors' outlays. They monitor competitors' advertising or get industry promotion spending estimates from publications or trade associations and then set their budgets based on the industry average.

Competitive-parity method—Setting the promotion budget to match competitors' outlays.

Two arguments support this method. First, competitors' budgets represent the collective wisdom of the industry. Second, spending what competitors spend helps prevent promotion wars. Unfortunately, neither argument is valid. There are no grounds for believing that the competition has a better idea of what a company should be spending on promotion than does the company itself. Companies differ greatly, and each has its own special promotion needs. Finally, there is no evidence that budgets based on competitive parity prevent promotion wars.

Objective-and-task method

The most logical budget-setting method is the **objective-and-task method**, whereby the company sets its promotion budget based on what it wants to accomplish with promotion. This budgeting method entails (1) defining specific promotion objectives, (2) determining the tasks needed to achieve these objectives, and (3) estimating the costs of performing these tasks. The sum of these costs is the proposed promotion budget.

Objective-and-task method—Developing the promotion budget by (1) defining specific promotion objectives, (2) determining the tasks needed to achieve these objectives, and (3) estimating the costs of performing these tasks. The sum of these costs is the proposed promotion budget.

The advantage of the objective-and-task method is that it forces management to spell out its assumptions about the relationship between dollars spent and promotion results. But it is also the most difficult method to use. Often, it is hard to figure out which specific tasks will achieve the stated objectives. For example, suppose Samsung wants a 95 per cent awareness level for its latest smartphone model during the six-month introductory period. What specific advertising messages, marketing content and media schedules should Samsung use to attain this objective? How much would this content and media cost? Samsung management must consider such questions, even though they are hard to answer.

Shaping the overall promotion mix

The concept of integrated marketing communications suggests that the company must blend the promotion tools carefully into a coordinated *promotion mix*. But how does it determine what mix of promotion tools to use? Companies within the same industry differ greatly in the design of their promotion mixes. For example, cosmetics maker Avon in the UK spends most of its promotion funds on personal selling and direct marketing, whereas competitors Rimmel and Max Factor spends heavily on consumer advertising. We now look at factors that influence the marketer's choice of promotion tools.

The nature of each promotion tool

Each promotion tool has unique characteristics and costs. Marketers must understand these characteristics in shaping the promotion mix.

Author comment

In this section, we'll look at how marketers blend the various marketing communication tools into a smooth-functioning, integrated and engaging promotion mix.

Advertising

Advertising can reach masses of geographically dispersed buyers at a low cost per exposure, and it enables the seller to repeat a message many times. For example, television advertising can reach huge audiences. An estimated 380 million people worldwide watched the last Champions League Final (considerably more people than watched the US Super Bowl). A cricket World Cup match between India and Pakistan can be watched by over 1 billion viewers while the 2014 Fifa World Cup final between Germany and Argentina brought 35 million Germans to their TV sets – around 86.3 per cent of TV watchers! For companies that want to reach a mass audience, TV is the place to be. Beyond its reach, large-scale advertising says something positive about the seller's size, popularity and success. Because of advertising's public nature, consumers tend to view advertised products as more legitimate. Advertising is also very expressive; it allows the company to dramatise its products through the artful use of visuals, print, sound and colour. On the one hand, advertising can be used to build up a long-term image for a product (such as Coca-Cola ads). On the other hand, advertising can trigger quick sales (as when Burger King advertises weekend specials).

Advertising also has some shortcomings. Although it reaches many people quickly, advertising is impersonal and lacks the direct persuasiveness of company salespeople. For the most part, advertising can carry on only a one-way communication with an audience, and the audience does not feel that it has to pay attention or respond. In addition, advertising can be very costly. Although some advertising forms, such as newspaper and radio advertising, can be done on smaller budgets, other forms, such as network TV advertising, require very large budgets. For example, a recent one-minute Microsoft 'Empowering' Super Bowl ad cost €7 million for media time alone, not counting the costs of producing the ad.

Personal selling

Personal selling is the most effective tool at certain stages of the buying process, particularly in building up buyers' preferences, convictions and actions. It involves personal interaction between two or more people, so each person can observe the other's needs and characteristics and make quick adjustments. Personal selling also allows all kinds of customer relationships to spring up, ranging from matter-of-fact selling relationships to personal friendships. An effective salesperson keeps the customer's interests at heart to build a long-term relationship by solving a customer's problems. Finally, with personal selling, the buyer usually feels a greater need to listen and respond, even if the response is a polite 'No thank-you'.

These unique qualities come at a cost, however. A sales force requires a longer-term commitment than does advertising – although advertising can be turned up or down, the size of a sales force is harder to change. Personal selling is also the company's most expensive promotion tool, costing companies on average €475 or more per sales call, depending on the industry.[21] Firms spend up to three times as much on personal selling as they do on advertising.

Sales promotion

Sales promotion includes a wide assortment of tools – coupons, contests, discounts, premiums and others – all of which have many unique qualities. They attract consumer attention, engage consumers, offer strong incentives to purchase, and can be used to dramatise product offers and boost sagging sales. Sales promotions invite and reward quick response. Whereas advertising says, 'Buy our product,' sales promotion says, 'Buy it now'. Sales promotion effects can be short-lived, however, and often are not as effective as advertising or personal selling in building long-run brand preference and customer relationships.

Public relations

Public relations is very believable – news stories, features, sponsorships and events seem more real and believable to readers than ads do. PR can also reach many prospects who avoid salespeople and advertisements – the message gets to buyers as 'news and events' rather than as a sales-directed communication. And, as with advertising, public relations can dramatise a company or product. Marketers tend to underuse public relations or use it as an afterthought. Yet a well-thought-out public relations campaign used with other promotion mix elements can be very effective and economical.

Direct and digital marketing

The many forms of direct and digital marketing – from direct mail, catalogues and telephone marketing to online, mobile and social media – all share some distinctive characteristics. Direct marketing is more targeted: it's usually directed to a specific customer or customer community. Direct marketing is immediate and personalised: messages can be prepared quickly – even in real time – and tailored to appeal to specific consumers or brand groups. Finally, direct marketing is interactive: it allows a dialogue between the marketing team and the consumer, and messages can be altered depending on the consumer's response. Thus, direct and digital marketing are well suited to highly targeted marketing efforts, creating customer engagement and building one-to-one customer relationships.

Promotion mix strategies

Marketers can choose from two basic promotion mix strategies: *push* promotion or *pull* promotion. Figure 14.4 contrasts the two strategies. The relative emphasis given to the specific promotion tools differs for push and pull strategies. A **push strategy** involves 'pushing' the product through marketing channels to final consumers. The producer directs its marketing activities (primarily personal selling and trade promotion) toward channel members to induce them to carry the product and promote it to final consumers. For example, Husqvarna (the originally Swedish but now truly global firm) does very little promoting of its outdoor products to final consumers. Instead, Husqvarna's sales force works with national-level

Push strategy—A promotion strategy that calls for using the sales force and trade promotion to push the product through channels. The producer promotes the product to channel members who in turn promote it to final consumers.

Figure 14.4 Push versus pull promotion strategy

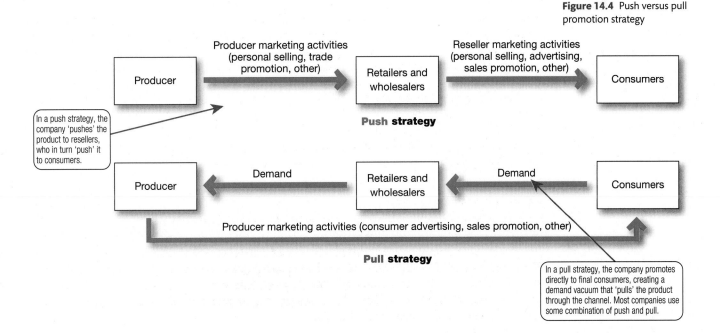

In a push strategy, the company 'pushes' the product to resellers, who in turn 'push' it to consumers.

In a pull strategy, the company promotes directly to final consumers, creating a demand vacuum that 'pulls' the product through the channel. Most companies use some combination of push and pull.

retailers, independent dealers and other channel members, who in turn push Husqvarna's products to final consumers.

Using a **pull strategy**, the producer directs its marketing activities (primarily advertising, consumer promotion, and direct and digital media) towards final consumers to induce them to buy the product. For example, Unilever promotes its Axe grooming products directly to its young male target market using TV and print ads, its web and social media brand sites, and other channels. If the pull strategy is effective, consumers will then demand the brand from retailers, such as Carrefour, Tesco or Walmart, which will in turn demand it from Unilever. Thus, under a pull strategy, consumer demand 'pulls' the product through the channels.

Some industrial-goods companies use only push strategies; likewise, some direct marketing companies use only pull strategies. However, most large companies use some combination of both. For example, Unilever spends more than €7.2 billion worldwide each year on consumer marketing and sales promotions to create brand preference and pull customers into stores that carry its products.[22] At the same time, it uses its own and distributors' sales forces and trade promotions to push its brands through the channels, so that they will be available on store shelves when consumers come calling.

Companies consider many factors when designing their promotion mix strategies, including the type of product and market. For example, the importance of different promotion tools varies between consumer and business markets. Business-to-consumer companies usually pull more, putting more of their funds into advertising, followed by sales promotion, personal selling, and then public relations. In contrast, business-to-business marketers tend to push more, putting more of their funds into personal selling, followed by sales promotion, advertising and public relations.

Integrating the promotion mix

Having set the promotion budget and mix, the company must now take steps to see that each promotion mix element is smoothly integrated. Guided by the company's overall communications strategy, the various promotion elements should work together to carry the firm's unique brand messages and selling points. Integrating the promotion mix starts with customers. Whether it's advertising, personal selling, sales promotion, public relations, or digital and direct marketing, communications at each customer touch point must deliver consistent marketing content and positioning. An integrated promotion mix ensures that communications efforts occur when, where and how *customers* need them.

To achieve an integrated promotion mix, all of the firm's functions must cooperate to jointly plan communications efforts. Many companies even include customers, suppliers and other stakeholders at various stages of communications planning. Scattered or disjointed promotional activities across the company can result in diluted marketing communications impact and confused positioning. By contrast, an integrated promotion mix maximises the combined effects of all a firm's promotional efforts.

SOCIALLY RESPONSIBLE MARKETING COMMUNICATION

In shaping its promotion mix, a company must be aware of the many legal and ethical issues surrounding marketing communications. Most marketers work hard to communicate openly and honestly with consumers and resellers. Still, abuses may occur, and public policy makers have developed a substantial body of laws and regulations to govern advertising, sales promotion, personal selling and direct marketing. In this section, we discuss issues regarding advertising, sales promotion and personal selling. We discuss digital and direct marketing issues in Chapter 17.

Pull strategy—A promotion strategy that calls for spending a lot on consumer advertising and promotion to induce final consumers to buy the product, creating a demand vacuum that 'pulls' the product through the channel.

Advertising and sales promotion

By law, companies must avoid false or deceptive advertising. Advertisers must not make false claims, such as suggesting that a product cures something when it does not. They must avoid ads that have the capacity to deceive, even though no one actually may be deceived. An automobile cannot be advertised as getting 32 miles per gallon unless it does so under typical conditions, and diet bread cannot be advertised as having fewer calories simply because its slices are thinner.

Sellers must avoid bait-and-switch advertising that attracts buyers under false pretences. For example, a large retailer advertised a sewing machine at €150. However, when consumers tried to buy the advertised machine, the seller downplayed its features, placed faulty machines on showroom floors, understated the machine's performance, and took other actions in an attempt to switch buyers to a more expensive machine. Such actions are both unethical and illegal.

A company's trade promotion activities also are closely regulated. For example, under the EU Unfair Commercial Practices Directives sellers cannot undertake misleading or aggressive practices that disadvantage customers.

Beyond simply avoiding legal pitfalls, such as deceptive or bait-and-switch advertising, companies can use advertising and other forms of promotion to encourage and promote socially responsible programmes and actions. For example, Ecover, the Belgium-based manufacturer and distributor of domestic cleaning products has the mission to 'offer efficient and sustainable solutions for the hygienic needs of people today and of future generates', with a vision 'to contribute to the process of creating economic, ecological and social change within our society to build as sustainable future for everyone'. The Ecover company slogan is 'Powered by nature'. A recent print ad for Ecover washing up liquid simply states 'protect our future. Begin with the Washing up!'[23]

The Ecover company slogan is 'Powered by nature'.

Source: Andy Lauwers/REX/Shutterstock

Personal selling

A company's salespeople must follow the rules of 'fair competition'. Most states have enacted deceptive sales acts that spell out what is not allowed. For example, salespeople may not lie to consumers or mislead them about the advantages of buying a particular product. To avoid bait-and-switch practices, salespeople's statements must match advertising claims.

Different rules apply to consumers who are called on at home or who buy at a location that is not the seller's permanent place of business versus those who go to a store in search of a product. Because people who are called on may be taken by surprise and may be especially vulnerable to high-pressure selling techniques, the EU Distance Selling Directive is most commonly interpreted as allowing a *seven-day cooling-off rule* to give special protection to customers who are not seeking products. Under this rule, customers who agree to sales via mail order, the Internet, digital TV or telephone have a week in which to cancel a contract or return merchandise and get their money back – no questions asked.

Much personal selling involves business-to-business trade. In selling to businesses, salespeople may not offer bribes to purchasing agents or others who can influence a sale. They may not obtain or use technical or trade secrets of competitors through bribery or industrial espionage. Finally, salespeople must not disparage competitors or competing products by suggesting things that are not true.

OBJECTIVES REVIEW AND KEY TERMS

In this chapter, you learned how companies use integrated marketing communications (IMC) to communicate customer value. Modern marketing calls for more than just creating customer value by developing a good product, pricing it attractively, and making it available to target customers. Companies also must clearly and persuasively engage current and prospective consumers and *communicate* that value to them. To do this, they must blend five promotion mix tools, guided by a well-designed and implemented IMC strategy.

OBJECTIVE 1 Define the five promotion mix tools for communicating customer value (pp. 408–409)

A company's total promotion mix – also called its marketing communications mix – consists of the specific blend of advertising, personal selling, sales promotion, public relations and direct and digital marketing tools that the company uses to engage consumers, persuasively communicate customer value and build customer relationships. Advertising includes any paid form of non-personal presentation and promotion of ideas, goods or services by an identified sponsor. In contrast, public relations focuses on building good relations with the company's various publics. Personal selling is personal presentation by the firm's sales force for the purpose of making sales and building customer relationships. Firms use sales promotion to provide short-term incentives to encourage the purchase or sale of a product or service. Finally, firms seeking immediate response from targeted individual customers use direct and digital marketing tools to engage directly with customers and cultivate relationships with them.

OBJECTIVE 2 Discuss the changing communications landscape and the need for integrated marketing communications (pp. 409–412)

The explosive developments in communications technology and changes in marketer and customer communication strategies have had a dramatic impact on marketing communications. Advertisers are now adding a broad selection of more specialised and highly targeted media and content – including online, mobile and social media – to reach smaller customer segments with more personalised, interactive messages. As they adopt richer but more fragmented media and promotion mixes to reach their diverse markets, they risk creating a communications hotchpotch for consumers. To prevent this, companies are adopting the concept of *integrated marketing communications (IMC)*. Guided by an overall IMC strategy, the company works

out the roles that the various promotional tools and marketing content will play and the extent to which each will be used. It carefully coordinates the promotional activities and the timing of when major campaigns take place.

OBJECTIVE 3 Outline the communication process and the steps in developing effective marketing communications (pp. 412–420)

The communication process involves nine elements: two major parties (sender, receiver), two communication tools (message, media), four communication functions (encoding, decoding, response and feedback) and noise. To communicate effectively, marketers must understand how these elements combine to communicate value to target customers.

In preparing marketing communications, the communicator's first task is to *identify the target audience* and its characteristics. Next, the communicator has to determine the *communication objectives* and define the response sought, whether it be *awareness, knowledge, liking, preference, conviction* or *purchase*. Then a *message* should be constructed with an effective content and structure. *Media* must be selected, both for personal and non-personal communication. The communicator must find highly credible sources to deliver messages. Finally, the communicator must collect *feedback* by watching how much of the market becomes aware, tries the product and is satisfied in the process.

OBJECTIVE 4 Explain the methods for setting the promotion budget and factors that affect the design of the promotion mix (pp. 420–425)

The company must determine how much to spend for promotion. The most popular approaches are to spend what the company can afford, use a percentage of sales, base promotion on competitors' spending, or base it on an analysis and costing of the communication objectives and tasks. The company has to divide the *promotion budget* among the major tools to create the *promotion mix*. Companies can pursue a *push* or a *pull* promotional strategy – or a combination of the two. The best specific blend of promotion tools depends on the type of product/market, the buyer's readiness stage, and the PLC stage. People at all levels of the organisation must be aware of the many legal and ethical issues surrounding marketing communications. Companies must work hard and proactively at communicating openly, honestly and agreeably with their customers and resellers.

NAVIGATING THE KEY TERMS

OBJECTIVE 1
Promotion mix (or marketing communications mix) (p. 409)
Advertising p. 409)
Sales promotion (p. 409)
Personal selling p.409)
Public relations (PR) (p. 409)
Direct and digital marketing (p. 409)

OBJECTIVE 2
Content marketing (p. 411)

Integrated marketing communications (IMC) (p. 411)

OBJECTIVE 3
Buyer-readiness stages (p. 414)
Personal communication channels (p. 417)
Word-of-mouth influence (p. 418)
Buzz marketing (p. 418)
Non-personal communication channels (p.418)

OBJECTIVE 4
Affordable method (p. 420)
Percentage-of-sales method (p. 420)
Competitive-parity method (p. 421)
Objective-and-task method (p. 421)
Push strategy (p. 423)
Pull strategy (p. 424)

DISCUSSION AND CRITICAL THINKING

Discussion questions

14-1 List and briefly describe the five major promotion mix tools. (AACSB: Communication)

14-2 Why is there a need for integrated marketing communications and how do marketers go about implementing it? (AACSB: Communication; Reflective thinking)

14-3 Name and briefly describe the nine elements of the communications process. Why do marketers need to understand these elements? (AACSB: Communication; Reflective thinking)

14-4 Name and describe the two basic promotion mix strategies. In which strategy is advertising more important? (AACSB: Communication; Reflective thinking)

Critical-thinking exercises

14-5 In a small group, select a company and research its marketing communications activities for the past several years. Has the company changed its advertising campaign in that time? Has the type of appeal remained the same or has it changed? Create a presentation of your findings. (AACSB: Communication; Use of IT; Reflective thinking)

14-6 Marketers use Q Scores to determine a celebrity's appeal to his or her target audience. Research Q Scores and write a report of a celebrity's Q Score for the past several years. If the score changed considerably, what could be the reason? What other types of Q Scores are there besides scores for celebrities? (AACSB: Communication; Reflective thinking)

14-7 Find three examples of advertisements that incorporate socially responsible marketing in the message. Some

companies are criticised for exploiting social issues or organisations by promoting them for their own gain. Do the examples you found do that? Explain. (AACSB: Communication; Ethical reasoning; Reflective thinking)

Mini-cases and applications

Online, mobile and social media: marketing native advertising

Marketers have always advertised in traditional media such as newspapers, television and magazines, but today they are increasingly creating content for the online platforms of these media through *native advertising*, also called sponsored content. This form of promotion is not new. It dates back to the late 1880s as 'reading notices' that placed information about brands and companies in news stories, usually without indicating the advertiser's sponsorship. However, the sponsorship of today's native advertising is often clearly labelled. Native advertising is growing quickly, generating billions annually for online content publishers. It is offered by 73 per cent of online publishers and more than 40 per cent of brands currently use it. For example, Facebook reaped more than €1 billion in mobile native advertising alone in just one quarter. The rapid growth of native advertising has caught the attention of regulators, leaving some to wonder if further regulations are forthcoming.

14-8 Find examples of native advertising on various publishers' websites. Create a presentation with screen shots showing the content and how it is identified. Has the content been shared with others via social media? (AACSB: Communication; Use of IT)

14-9 Debate whether or not current regulations and guidelines regarding online advertising are adequate for this type of promotion. Is it likely that the regulators will issue new guidelines or regulations? (AACSB: Communication; Reflective thinking)

Marketing ethics: racist promotion?

A Unilever brand in Thailand ran into some problems with one of its promotion campaigns, the 'Citra 3D brightening girls search'. Citra Pearly White UV Body Lotion is marketed as a skin-whitening product. Skin whitening is popular in many Asian countries because lighter skin colour is associated with higher economic status. However, this belief is not created by marketers. Anthropologists point out that Asian cultures, and Thailand in particular, have long histories of associating darker skin tones with outdoor peasants and field workers and lighter skin tones with higher socio-economic status. Citra's advertising was criticised because it showed two female students – one lighter-skinned than the other – and asked them what would make them 'outstanding in uniform'. The darker girl seemed confused and didn't answer, while the lighter girl answered with Citra's product slogan. After considerable social media outcry, Citra pulled the ad, but it did not stop a related scholarship competition. The competition offered a 100,000 baht (€3,750) prize for the college student best demonstrating 'product efficacy' – that is, the whitest skin. The company claims its products help people feel good about themselves and enhances their self-esteem.

14-10 Since lighter skin and skin whitening are popular in Thailand, is it wrong for marketers to offer and promote products that encourage this belief and behaviour? Explain why or why not. (AACSB: Communication; Reflective thinking; Ethical reasoning)

14-11 Find other examples of marketers creating controversy by promoting culture-based products that could be viewed as inappropriate by others outside of that culture. (AACSB: Communication; Reflective thinking)

Marketing by the numbers: advertising-to-sales ratios

Using the percentage-of-sales method, an advertiser sets its budget at a certain percentage of current or forecasted sales. However, determining what percentage to use is not always clear. Many marketers look at industry averages and competitor spending for comparisons. Websites and trade publications publish data regarding industry averages to guide marketers in setting the percentage to use.

14-12 Find industry advertising-to-sales ratio data. Why do some industries have higher advertising-to-sales ratios than others? (AACSB: Communication; Use of IT; Reflective thinking)

14-13 Determine the advertising-to-sales ratios for two competing companies and compare them to the industry advertising-to-sales ratio found above. Why do you think there is a difference between competitors and the industry average? (AACSB: Communication; Use of IT; Analytical reasoning; Reflective thinking)

REFERENCES

[1] 'Tesco spends a whopping £132.1m in 2010, its highest ever spend and £57.4m above the average', the UK Top 100 Advertisers 2011, *Brad Insight*, www.bradtop100.co.uk/01-retail/01-tesco-stores-ltd, accessed 14 November 2012; S. Kimberly, 'Tesco appoints W & K to £110m ad account', *Campaign*, 20 July 2012, www.campaignlive.co.uk/news/1142068/; Z. Wood, 'Tesco advertising up for grabs', *The Guardian*, 11 April 2012, www.guardian.co.uk/business/2012/apr/11/tesco-advertising-up-for-grabs; R. Baker, 'Tesco rolls out ads for everyday value', *Marketing Week*, 20 April 2012, www.marketingweek.co.uk/news/tesco-rolls-out-ads-for-everydayvalue/4001402.article; 'Wieden & Kennedy to use Tesco's 'Every little helps' strapline', *Campaign*, 26 July 2012, www.campaignlive.co.uk/news/1142982/; L Gibbons, 'Tesco appoints Coca-Cola boss as social media manager', 13 November 2012, www.foodmanufacture.co.uk/PeopleITesco-appoints-Coca-Cola-boss-as-social-media-manager; and 'Tesco named top UK retailer on climate change', Tesco PLC News Release, 12 October 2012, www.tescoplc.com/index.asp?pageid=17&newsid=690,; Ben Bold, 'Top 100 UK advertisers: BSkyB increases lead as P&G, BT and Unilever reduce adspend', available at, www.marketingmagazine.co.uk/article/1289560/top-100-uk-advertisers-bskyb-increases-lead-p-g-bt-unilever-reduce-adspend, accessed October 2015.

[2] For other definitions, see www.marketingpower.com/_layouts/Dictionary.aspx, accessed October 2015.

[3] Ronan Shields, 'IAB Europe: digital ad revenues record double digit growth', available at www.exchangewire.com/blog/2014/05/20/iab-europe-digital-ad-revenues-record-double-digit-growth/, accessed October 2015.

[4] Juliette Garside, 'Britain's ad spend to hit £20bn a year', available at www.theguardian.com/media/2014/apr/28/britain-advertising-spend-20bn-2015 accessed October 2015.

[5] 'US total media ad spend inches up, pushed by digital', *eMarketer*, 22 August 2013, www.emarketer.com/Article/US-Total-Media-Ad-Spend-Inches-Up-Pushed-by-Digital/1010154; Serena Ng and Suzanne Vranica, 'P&G shifts marketing dollars to online, mobile', *Wall Street Journal*, 1 August 2013, http://online.wsj.com/news/articles/SB10001424127887323681904578641993173406444; 'Total media ad spend continues slow and steady trajectory', *eMarketer*, 26 December 2013, www.emarketer.com/Article/Total-Media-Ad-Spend-Continues-Slow-Steady-Trajectory/1010485; and Anthony Ha, 'IAB report: US Internet ad revenue grew to $42.8 billion in 2013, overtaking broadcast TV', *Tech Crunch*, 10 April 2014, http://techcrunch.com/2014/04/10/iab-2013-report/.

[6] Chris Anderson, 'The 'Angry Birds in Space' video marketing campaign', *The Video Marketer*, 22 March 2012, http://blog.wooshii.com/the-angry-birds-in-space-video-marketingcampaign/; and 'Samsung, Wieden & Kennedy rule *Ad Age*'s 2013 Viral Video Awards', *Advertising Age*, 16 April 2013, http://adage.com/print/240900/.

[7] See Jon Lafayette, '4A's conference: agencies urged to embrace new technologies', *Broadcasting & Cable*, 8 March 2011, www.broadcasting-cable.com/news/advertising-and-marketing/4asconference-agencies-urged-embrace-new-technologies/52550; and David Gelles, 'Advertisers rush to master fresh set of skills', *Financial Times*, 7 March 2012, www.ft.com/intl/cms/s/0/8383bbae-5e20-11e1-b1e9-00144feabdc0.html#axzz1xUrmM3KK.

[8] See 'Advertisers blend digital and TV for well-rounded campaigns', *eMarketer*, 12 March 2014, www.emarketer.com/Article/Advertisers-Blend-Digital-TV-Well-Rounded-Campaigns/1010670.

[9] See www.caples.org//i-have-already-died, accessed October 2015.

[10] De Beers Commercial (2009), see www.popisms.com/TelevisionCommercial/4544/De-Beers-Commercial-2009.aspx, accessed October 2015.

[11] See www.redcross.org.uk/About-us/News/2014/December/Ebola-crisis-is-long-term-fight, accessed October 2015.

[12] See www.redcross.org.uk/ebolavirus?gclid=CP3drKy5scMCFYLn-wgodgDYAHQ&utm_expid=7932746-25.kdFJhosJTBueu8-, accessed October 2015.

[13] Example from Rhymer Rigby, 'Brands that laugh all the way to the bank', *Financial Times*, 6 January 2011, www.ft.com/cms/s/0/cd02d8c4-19c4-11e0-b921-00144feab49a.html#ixzz1Trdnoyod, accessed October 2015.

[14] See 'Brand design: cracking the colour code', *Marketing Week*, 11 October 2007, p. 28; and Joe Tradii, 'Available for your brand: burnt umber! Any takers?' *Brandweek*, 17 November 2009, www.brandweek.com/bw/content_display/esearch/e3i45e1bcc0b65a294f442520efa2d3b051.

[15] Jonah Bloom, 'The truth is: consumers trust fellow buyers before marketers', *Advertising Age*, 13 February 2006, p. 25; and 'Jack Morton publishes new realities 2012 research', press release, 26 January 2012, www.jackmorton.com/news/article.aspx?itemID=106.

[16] See http://company.trnd.com/en, accessed October 2015.

[17] See www.bzzagent.com and http://about.bzzagent.com/, accessed October 2015.

[18] See Lacey Rose, 'The 10 most trusted celebrities', *Forbes*, 25 January 2010, www.forbes.com/2010/01/25/most-trusted-celebrities-business-entertainment-trust.html; Robert Klara, 'I'm with the celebrity, get me out of here!' *Brandweek*, 8 March 2010, p. 13; and 'Which athletes can lift brands?' *Mediaweek*, 19 April 2010, p. 23.

[19] T. L. Stanley, 'Dancing with the stars', *Brandweek*, 8 March 2010, pp. 10–12; and Chris Isidore, 'Lance Armstrong: how he'll make money now', *CNNMoney*, 18 January 2013, http://money.cnn.com/2013/01/16/news/companies/armstrong-endorsements/.

[20] For more on advertising spending by company and industry, see '100 leading national advertisers: U.S. ad spending by category', *Advertising Age*, 24 June 2013, pp. 14–22; and '2014 marketing fact pack', *Advertising Age*, 30 December 2014, pp. 8–12.

[21] See discussions at Mike Ishmael, 'The cost of a sales call', 22 October 2012, http://4dsales.com/the-cost-of-a-sales-call/; Jeff Green, 'The new Willy Loman survives by staying home', *Bloomberg Businessweek*, 14 January–20 January, 2013, pp. 16–17; and 'What is the real cost of a B2B sales call?' www.marketingplaybook.com/sales-marketing-strategy/what-is-the-real-cost-of-ab2b-sales-call, accessed October 2015.

[22] Jack Neff, 'Unilever plans to cut 800 marketers as it slashes agency fees, products', *Advertising Age*, 5 December 2013, http://adage.com/article/news/unilever-eliminate-800-marketersglobally-cut-launches/245542/.

[23] See www.evover.comcall, accessed October 2015.

COMPANY CASE

Red Bull: a different kind of integrated campaign

It's a calm day in the desert town of Roswell, New Mexico. Thirteen miles above the ground, a giant helium balloon ascends with a space capsule tethered beneath it. The capsule door slides open, revealing the Earth as a sphere – the curve of the horizon bending dramatically around the planet, the sky above almost black. A man in a full space suit steps out onto a small platform and secures his footing. Then, with a quick salute to the camera, he jumps.

A NASA test? No. It's the latest promotional effort from Red Bull – another extreme stunt designed to evoke reactions of shock and awe while driving home the now famous slogan, 'Red Bull gives you wiings'. Today, through a bevy of other such events, Red Bull's message is broadcast far and wide via an army of celebrity endorsers as well as sports, music and entertainment event sponsorships. Red Bull is not the most conventional marketer. It spreads its brand message across an eclectic mix of promotional efforts while largely shunning traditional media. But the manner in which Red Bull has integrated its diverse messages is a model of success that cuts straight to the heart of building deep emotional connections with customers.

An unlikely start

It all started about 30 years ago when Austrian toothpaste sales-man Dietrich Mateschitz travelled to Thailand. While there, he tried a 'tonic' called Krating Daeng – Thai for 'water buffalo'. It tasted terrible but instantly cured his jet lag. One thing led to another, and within a few years Mateschitz and a partner had acquired the rights to sell the formula throughout the rest of the world. They named it Red Bull.

From the beginning, nothing about Red Bull was conventional. The slim blue-and-silver can, emblazoned with two muscular red bulls about to smash heads in front of a yellow sun, was unlike anything on the market. At 8.3 ounces, so was its size. With mystical ingredients such as taurine and glucuronol-actone, and a sickeningly sweet taste often described as 'liquid sweet tarts' or 'cough medicine in a can', the drink didn't fit any established beverage category. And with a €1.65 price tag, Red Bull was by far the most expensive carbonated beverage on any shelf. But with that unlikely combination, Red Bull gave birth to the energy drink category.

Mateschitz launched Red Bull in his native Austria under the only slogan to ever accompany the brand, 'Red Bull gives you wings'. The moment he heard it, Mateschitz knew that this slogan would be the core of Red Bull's brand image. He didn't care about the product's taste. 'It's not just another fla-voured sugar water differentiated by colour or taste or fla-vour,' he says. 'It's an efficiency product. I'm talking about improving endurance, concentration, reaction time, speed, vigilance and emotional status. Taste is of no importance whatsoever.' Despite negative initial product reviews, Red Bull's young male target market agreed. Sales in Europe were positively bullish.

An unlikely promotional programme

As head of a young company without much of an advertising budget, Mateschitz continued in his unorthodox ways when launching Red Bull (in the United Kingdom in 1994, the United States in 1997 and the Middle East in 2000). He bucked the trend of aggressive and excessive promotional campaigns flaunted by other start-ups in the 1990s. Instead, his young, attractive army of marketers tossed out free cans of Red Bull from a fleet of shiny logo-bearing off-roaders with giant cans attached to the trunk. Word-of-mouth took care of the rest. In this manner, Mateschitz introduced Red Bull to the masses and built a brand image for next to nothing.

As a product that thrived on grassroots marketing, Red Bull depended on word-of-mouth. As word about Red Bull spread throughout Europe's all-night-party circuit, so did rumours. Tales circulated that taurine was a derivative of bull testicles or even bull semen. Even worse, there were rumours that young people had died while partying too hard and drinking too much Red Bull.

Although none of these rumours was ever substantiated, Mates-chitz is convinced that one of the most important promotional techniques the company ever employed was to let the rumours fly and say nothing. 'In the beginning, the high-school teachers who were against the product were at least as important as the students who were for it,' said Mateschitz. 'Newspapers asked, "Is it a drug? Is it harmless? Is it dangerous?" That ambivalence is so important. The most dangerous thing for a branded product is low interest.'

Bit by bit, Red Bull's portfolio of promotional weapons grew. At times, the company dabbled in TV and print adver-tising. But Red Bull's primary tactics have steered clear of such mainstream techniques. Instead, it was Mateschitz's plan to promote the brand in a way that would go way beyond reach and frequency of coverage. He wanted the brand to hit young people right in the face in a way that they experienced Red Bull to the fullest. He wanted to engage customers through activities so meaningful to them that deep relationships would form quickly.

With that philosophy, Red Bull's promotional mix evolved into what it is today. The following descriptions are just a sample of Red Bull's promotional techniques.

Athletes and teams

With the claim that Red Bull improves athletic performance at the centre of its promotional message, the brand took a page right out of the book used by Nike and Gatorade and began signing up athlete endorsers early on. Today, Red Bull sponsors more than 650 athletes in 97 sports, mostly 'extreme' sports. And sticking with its unconventional ways, Red Bull brings these ath-letes into the 'family' with nothing more than a verbal agree-ment to 'support' them in achieving their dreams. Today, Red Bull's family includes such top-tier athletes as German runner Sabrina Mockenhaupt and Irish triathlete Con Doherty, British racing driver Andrew Jordon, and French skier Alexis Pinturault as well as niche athletes such as Romanian paraglider Nicolau Alexandru and French wind surfer Alice Arutkin. Indeed, at the last Winter Olympics if Red Bull were a country it would have tied for fifth position in the overall medal chart (ahead of France and China!). Whenever these athletes make official public appearances, the Red Bull name or logo is visible somewhere on their person.

However, Red Bull's endorsement strategy goes beyond propping individual athletes. Red Bull owns five soccer teams: New York's Red Bulls, Red Bull Salzburg, Red Bull Brazil, Red Bull Ghana and RB Leipzig. The brand also owns a NASCAR team, two Formula 1 racing teams, ice hockey teams, hockey teams and other racing teams. Many have asserted that team owner-ship is merely a hobby for Mateschitz, noting that none of these teams makes money. But Mateschitz says that misses the point.

'In literal financial terms, our sports teams are not yet profitable, but in value terms, they are,' he says. 'The total editorial media value plus the media assets created around the teams are superior to pure advertising expenditures.'

Sports events

As Red Bull built relationships through athletes and teams, it wasn't long before it began sponsoring events. Today, Red Bull has its name on dozens of major annual events, including the Red Bull Romaniacs Hard Enduro Rallye (an extreme enduro off-road motorcycle race run annually in Romania), Red Bull Dolomitenmann (billed as the world's toughest team relay race), Red Bull X-Alps (a 1,000 km race from Austria to Monaco – via the Alps), Red Bull Wake Open (wake boarding), Red Bull Rampage (mountain biking) and Red Bull Sharpshooters (basketball). With such event sponsorships, Red Bull has more than once invented an entirely new sport.

Consider Red Bull Crashed Ice, a world tour winter extreme sport. It's similar to ski cross or snowboard cross – only with skates, on ice. In this sport, some of the toughest ice hockey players in the world jockey for position at speeds of up to 40 miles per hour. But the real catch is that the race takes place in a 500-metre ice canal filled with bumps, jumps, berms, and other obstacles. The cameras capture all the action as competitors race past screaming fans and Red Bull banners.

Music and entertainment

Recognising that its target customers weren't 'all sports all the time', Red Bull extended its strategy for endorsements and events to the world of music and entertainment. With its penchant for sniffing out the unique, Red Bull sponsors artists, teams and events in dance, music, film, video games and other creative media. Red Bull Flying Bach is a performance troupe that wraps breakdancing around the music of Bach. The Red Bull Canvas Cooler is a nationwide invitational competition for top artists to redesign the iconic Red Bull cooler. And Red Bull Common Thread is a new concept on the concert circuit – back-to-back performances by bands that shared members at different points in their evolution.

Programming

As the producer of such TV programmes as *No Limits* on ESPN and such films as *That's It*, *That's All*, Red Bull is not new to media production. But in perhaps its most ambitious undertaking yet, Red Bull has created Red Bull Media House – 'the centre of the global Red Bull media network' and 'your gateway into the World of Red Bull'. The network spans TV, print, mobile, digital and music. With this move, Red Bull has defined itself as a major multimedia content provider.

As just one example of how extensive this network is, consider the music arm of Red Bull Media House. Nothing short of a complete music division, it includes Red Bull Publishing (a hub for all music and audio generated in the Red Bull Media House), Red Bull Records (its own music label) and Red Bull Radio Services (an Internet-based radio network and original shows). Through this music media network, Red Bull puts its brand at the centre of a cooperative of companies, brands and artists, encouraging them to take part in Red Bull's resources.

Multiplying this across the other major media in the Red Bull Media House network, it's clear that Mateschitz sees Red Bull not as a beverage brand, but as a global lifestyle brand with boundaries that have not yet been reached. He calls the recent multimedia assault 'our most important line extension so far', with the goal to 'communicate and distribute the "World of Red Bull" in all major media segments'. As with all the other promotional ventures, Mateschitz hopes Red Bull Media House will turn a profit. But as with his sport teams, he's willing to be patient and bank on the promotional value of these activities.

Doing it all for customers

Felix Baumgartner's successful jump from 17 miles up was only a dry run. When he made the real jump later in the year, it was from the stratosphere, 23 miles above sea level. In the process, he broke four world records: the highest manned balloon flight, the highest skydive, the longest freefall, and the first parachutist to break the sound barrier. He also tested the next-generation space suit to be worn by astronauts. And the Red Bull brand was plastered all over the entire event. But more than promotional coverage, this feat served the same purpose that all other Red Bull promotions serve – to forge deep relationships with customers through emotional experiences.

From its unlikely origins, Red Bull has grown into a massive enterprise. Last year, the company sold around 5.5 billion cans of the drink with revenues of more than €5 billion. As Red Bull's growth continues, Mateschitz has no intention of slowing down. In fact, he confesses, he has always been attracted to the idea of creating an independent nation state – the country of Red Bull. 'The rules would be simple. Nobody tells you what you have to do – only what you don't have to do.'

Questions for discussion

1. List all the ways that Red Bull's promotional efforts are unique from those of the mainstream.
2. Which promotional mix elements does Red Bull use? What grade would you give Red Bull on integrating these elements into a core marketing communications campaign?

3. Will Red Bull eventually need to embrace more traditional media marketing techniques in order to keep growing? Why or why not?

4. Describe Red Bull's target audience. Are Red Bull's promotional techniques consistent with that audience?

5. At some point, will Red Bull have to branch out beyond its target market? Will it need to alter its promotional strategy in order to do so?

Sources: 'Felix Baumgartner prepares for daredevil freefall from 17 Miles', *Fox News*, 24 July 2012, www.foxnews.com/scitech/2012/07/24/final-test-jump-from-edge-space-set-for-tuesday/; 'Red Bull's adrenaline marketing mastermind pushes into media', *Business Week*, 19 May 2011, www.bloomberg.com/news/print/2011-05-19/red-bull-s-adrena-line-marketing-billionaire-mastermind.html; David Browne, 'The republic of Red Bull', www.mensjournal.com/travel/ski-snow/the-republic-of-red-bull-20140128; and other information found at www.redbullusa.com and www.redbullmedia-house.com, accessed October 2015.

CHAPTER FIFTEEN

Advertising and public relations

Chapter preview

Following our analysis of overall integrated marketing communications (IMC) planning, we now dig more deeply into the specific marketing communications tools. In this chapter, we explore advertising and public relations (PR). Advertising involves communicating the company's or brand's value proposition by using paid media to inform, persuade and remind consumers. PR involves building good relations with various company publics – from consumers and the general public to the media, investor, donor and government publics. As with all the promotion mix tools, advertising and PR must be blended into the overall IMC programme. In Chapters 16 and 17, we will discuss the remaining promotion mix tools: personal selling, sales promotion, and direct and digital marketing.

Let's start with a question: does advertising really make a difference? One of the most striking creative advertising and PR campaigns of recent years has been the one dominated by talking meerkats drawing consumers' attention to the comparethemarket.com price comparison website for financial services and other products. As you read the creative story, think about the impact of advertising on the fortunes of what was not long ago a little-known brand.

Objectives outline

The mighty meerkats – simples!

Aleksandr Orlov is a talking meerkat, with heavily accented and barely passable English, who stars in television ads for comparethemarket.com, the insurance, credit card and utilities price comparison website. Usually appearing in a threadbare smoking jacket or velvet dressing gown that has seen better days, Aleksandr's urged people to compare meerkats on his website – comparethemeerkats.com. The bane of his life appeared to be consumers who confuse the two websites, visiting the meerkat site when in fact looking for cheap car insurance. Aleksandr's TV campaign was so effective that the actual comparethemeerkat.com site receives more than 2 million hits a month.

In fact, there are those who would say that Sergei, Aleksandr's stooge and quieter companion meerkat, is the real star of the ads. Sergei's involvement is that the core storyline is based on the supposed confusion among consumers between the comparethemarket.com and the fictional comparethemeerkat.com, and the meerkats' pleas to consumers to go to the right website to avoid overloading the meerkat's own page and causing Sergei excessive work and suffering. The story expanded to include the great historical meerkat battles of the past with their mongoose enemies, their excursion as émigrés from Russia, and the danger that Sergei may have worms and moult excessively.

The fascination of the public with Aleksandr's and Sergei saw the establishment of the actual compare-the-meerkat website, www.comparethemeerkat.com, offering fans the opportunity to delve further into the complexity of meerkat 'history' and Meerkova, the meerkat village, as well as download ads and other treats.

Christmas 2010 saw the autobiography of the furry Aleksandr's outselling the life stories of stars such as Michael McIntyre and Keith Richards, and sitting at the top of *The Sunday Times* non-fiction bestseller list. The royalties were not destined for a good cause because Aleksandr's, the little furry author, said 'I am hope to remarble roof on Orlov family mansion. Please enjoyment'. Rival author, comedian Paul O'Grady fumed: 'Now we have the life and times of a meerkat – a piece of stuffed vermin who flogs insurance. What next? Churchill, the life of a dog?'

Aleksandr's ornate family life detailed in *A Simples Life* includes ancestors struggling through the Kalahari, the meerkat-mongoose war of 1728, and the ancient village of Meerkova. The website has downloads such as wallpapers, ringtones, text alerts, voicemail messages and videos. The iPhone app has background information, a database of English phrases in 'meerkat' pronunciation, a mongoose 'detector', and some videos.

A master of social media, Aleksandr's has 770,000 friends on Facebook, 700,000 subscribers to his iPhone app (iSimples) and more than 44,000 followers on Twitter. A limited edition replica meerkat toy in Aleksandr's image sold through Harrods and became an immediate collectible. Undoubtedly, Aleksandr's Orlov is heading towards advertising immortality as the star of one of the UK's most acclaimed ad campaigns. For some months in 2009, traffic to the fictional meerkat site exceeded that to comparethemarket.com itself.

But this was all created by advertising agency VCCP in 2009 to help a flagging insurance site sell more quotes. The campaign has transformed the fortunes of the client. The first year of the meerkat campaign saw very strong growth of comparethemarket.com of 189 per cent. In 2010, BGL Group which own comparethemarket.com saw a 6 per cent rise in revenue in a tough trading environment, and a jump in pre-tax profit to £62.3 million. The first two meerkat years drove a £33 million dividend payment for comparethemarket.com's owners.

In a category with no functional differentiation between the competitors and a once-a-year relationship with customers, the campaign has pulled off the neat trick of creating a marketing conversation that has

nothing to do with the product, but links the name with something people like. Moreover, the creatives have seen off the risk of overkill by continuing to keep it fresh.

Early in 2009, comparethemarket.com had been languishing in fourth place in its sector, and trading conditions were difficult. The advertising challenge was to make an essentially boring product something which was fun and to put some life into the comparethemarket.com brand. In fact, within days of the first ad hitting TV screens, it achieved the most modern of accolades: it was a YouTube sensation. In the first nine weeks of the campaign, quotes on the insurance site increased by 80 per cent and awareness of the brand tripled.

In 2012, comparethemarket.com became the sponsor of the long-running soap opera *Coronation Street* for three years, necessitating the appearance of Aleksandr's and Sergei before and after the advertising slot, indulging in typically annoying meerkat behaviour.

Other comparison websites like Confused.com and GoCompare have slipped down the rankings since the arrival of the meerkats on the scene. When the meerkats first appeared, comparethemarket.com controlled between 5 per cent and 7 per cent of the price comparison market. Within weeks of the meerkat campaign this had become 18 per cent, and by 2015 comparethemarket.com accounted for 40 per cent of the market. Although 2015 saw the meerkat campaign reach its sixth year, comparethemarket.com sees no need to stop — the CEO says the meerkats are now the company's 'key differentiator' and the 'catalyst' of its success.

Indeed, 2015 saw the launch of another part of the meerkat empire. Comparethemarket.com signed a deal to take over Britain's two-for-one cinema ticket service. The company sees this as a membership model that rewards customers for loyalty — buyers get membership and two-for-one cinema tickets for a year when they buy a product. They aim to build from 5 million to 7 million customers over three years. The meerkat involvement is shown in ads where Aleksandr and Sergei visit Hollywood to disrupt the studios and film sets, bully Arnold Schwarzenegger, and beat down studio bosses to get the cinema ticket deal. It was apparently Aleksandr's idea all along and is called Meerkat Movies.

Aleksandr's is one of the more prominent examples of the trend for animated characters or puppets to act as brand ambassadors. US consumers have long been charmed by the frogs that feature in Budweiser's advertising or the cockney gecko that stars in Geico's campaigns. Meanwhile, Domo, the saw-toothed mascot for Japanese broadcaster NHK, has gone on to appear in video games and comics, and spread virally online.

But the proliferation and popularity of these creations and the merchandising they have spawned raises questions for both brand owners and advertising agencies hoping to capitalise on the value of the intellectual property.

For brand owners, the appeal of creating characters is that they are cheaper and more reliable than the celebrities often enlisted to star in campaigns. 'Quite often celebrities do things outside of your advertising campaign which can reflect badly back on your brand,' says Charlie Herbert, director of e-commerce and marketing at Travelodge, the budget UK hotel chain that has just launched a campaign featuring Mr Sleep and the Zzz Squad, a group of gangster teddy bears with a vendetta against night-time noise. 'With puppets, you can control your iconography.'

The Zzz Squad was developed by London-based agency Mother, which insists on sharing profits from future merchandising with the client. 'In these last few years, the consideration of how we retain IP on our characters has been at the forefront when we create them,' says Stuart Outhwaite, a creative director at the agency. Mother's stance follows its experience with Monkey, a cuddly character it created in 2001 for the UK broadcaster ITV Digital. When ITV Digital went into administration, a row erupted over who controlled the intellectual property rights to Monkey. After a legal battle, the rights to the character were donated to the charity Comic Relief. In 2007, Monkey was revived for Unilever's PG Tips brand of tea under licence from the charity, working with Mother as part of the deal.

In spite of not holding the rights, Mr Outhwaite says the agency remains Monkey's legal 'carers' and 'creative guardians'. 'Monkey and Mother are intrinsically linked,' he says. 'As a creative property, he has been fantastic. Beyond any significant financial gain, he has won us two or three awards and brought in enough business. He's earned his fair share over the years.' Nonetheless, proceeds from Monkey merchandise — from toys to babywear — go to Comic Relief.

By contrast, VCCP, the agency behind Aleksandr's and Sergei, does not receive any direct proceeds from meerkat merchandise. Kal Atwal, managing director of comparethemarket.com, argues that the absence of revenue-sharing arrangements is fair because, as the client, her company has taken the bigger risk by investing in it. 'There were a number of pitches and the brief was quite specific,' she says. 'You work in partnership.'

Chris Satterthwaite, chief executive of Chime Communications, VCCP's parent company, points out that a successful campaign creates more work for that client and attracts new ones. 'Lots of agencies have talked about creating their own IP and I really haven't seen any who have succeeded in doing it,' he says. They are in the services business. You produce it to a brief and [the IP] belongs to the client.'

But, with the advertising industry's traditional business model under pressure from moves towards time-based remuneration, sharing in the upside of creative work through IP ownership could unlock a new form of revenue for agencies. Moreover, the guarantee of a ten-year royalty stream would be very welcome for agencies as long-term retainers become scarcer.

Some agencies have set up dedicated brand licensing units in response to the new challenges. M&C Saatchi established one such division earlier this year. 'Traditional advertising is becoming less important, new ways of communicating are growing, yet no one was really doing licensing,' says Matthew Conrad, a former IP lawyer who leads the unit. 'The way we look at licensing, it's a response to a specific marketing challenge. By doing that you'll mitigate the huge risk of brand [dilution].' He also hopes to incorporate licensing into more agency contracts for traditional marketing work to avoid missing out on meerkat-like opportunities.

Another unit has been set up by BBH, the agency behind Flat Eric, the orange puppet who shot to fame ten years ago in adverts for Levi's Sta-Prest jeans. As well as T-shirts, toys and other merchandising, Flat Eric even topped the charts with the techno anthem *Flat Beat*. But BBH shared in little of the upside, prompting it to create Zag, its own brand invention business.

'It's a challenging model that requires a long-term commitment but if you get it right it will be game-changing for you as a business,' says Neil Munn, who runs the unit.

But for all the valuable merchandising opportunities they generate, the main purpose of all these cute and cuddly characters remains to promote the brand. 'I almost don't see it as brand extension,' says comparethemarket.com's Ms Atwal. 'It's more about how we've broadened the communications platform that we have.'

In spite of all the spin-off merchandising, the managing director of comparethemarket.com, denies that the meerkat franchise is becoming overextended. 'If we wanted to, we could do a lot more on merchandising,' she says. 'But we have this asset that we need to protect and we don't want to have overexposure', insisting that any tie-ins are meant to promote the car insurance site, not generate revenue themselves. 'We have been strict at focusing on elements that are important to the campaign,' she says. 'It would be too short term from our perspective to do it as a revenue driver.'[1]

As we discussed in the previous chapter, companies must do more than simply create customer value. They must also engage target customers and persuasively communicate that value to them. In this chapter, we take a closer look at two marketing communications tools: *advertising* and *public relations (PR)*.

ADVERTISING

Author comment

You already know a lot about advertising; you are exposed to it every day. But here we'll look behind the scenes at how companies make advertising decisions.

Advertising can be traced back to the very beginnings of recorded history. Archaeologists working in countries around the Mediterranean have dug up signs announcing various events and offers. The Romans painted walls to announce gladiator fights, and the Phoenicians painted pictures on large rocks to promote their wares along parade routes. During the golden age in Greece, town criers announced the sale of cattle, crafted items, and even cosmetics. An early 'singing commercial' went as follows: 'For eyes that are shining, for cheeks like the dawn / For beauty that lasts after girlhood is gone / For prices in reason, the woman who knows / Will buy her cosmetics from Aesclyptos.'

Modern advertising, however, is a far cry from these early efforts. Global advertising expenditure in 2015 is estimated at around $545 billion. US advertisers alone now run up an estimated annual bill of more than $176 billion on measured advertising media, with the next largest advertising markets being: China ($45 billion), Japan ($45 billion), Germany ($25 billion), UK ($23 billion), Brazil ($17 billion), France ($13 billion), Australia ($12 billion), South Korea ($12 billion) and Canada ($11 billion). Of these major advertising areas, China, Brazil and South Korea are expected to grow between 20 and 36 per cent by 2017, while the developed countries are expected to grow far less.[2]

Advertising—Any paid form of non-personal presentation and promotion of ideas, goods or services by an identified sponsor.

Figure 15.1 Major advertising decisions

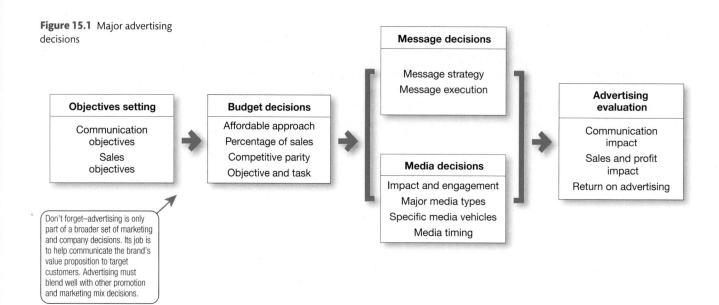

Don't forget–advertising is only part of a broader set of marketing and company decisions. Its job is to help communicate the brand's value proposition to target customers. Advertising must blend well with other promotion and marketing mix decisions.

Although advertising is employed mostly by business firms, a wide range of not-for-profit organisations, professionals and social agencies also employ advertising to promote their causes to various target publics. In fact, in most countries one of the largest advertising spenders is a not-for-profit organisation – the government. In the US federal agency spending on advertising was $892 million in 2013.[3] In the UK, government advertising spending in 2015 grew by 22 per cent on 2014 to nearly £300 million. Key campaigns were those explaining deficit reduction, the Scottish independence referendum, and 'improving public confidence' in Britain's role in Afghanistan – their advertising has three themes: economic confidence, fairness and attribution and Britain in the world.[4] And in 2015, it was revealed that the advertising spending by the European Commission had reached £2.4 billion a year – more than the £2.13 billion Coca-Cola spent worldwide in advertising its brands.[5] Advertising is a good way to inform and persuade, whether the purpose is to sell soft drinks worldwide or educate people in developing nations on how to live healthier lives.

Marketing management must make four important decisions when developing an advertising programme (see Figure 15.1): *setting advertising objectives*, *setting the advertising budget*, *developing advertising strategy* (*message decisions* and *media decisions*) and *evaluating advertising campaigns*.

Setting advertising objectives

The first step is to set *advertising objectives*. These objectives should be based on past decisions about the target market, positioning and the marketing mix, which define the job that advertising must do in the total marketing programme. The overall advertising objective is to help engage customers and build customer relationships by communicating customer value. Here, we discuss specific advertising objectives.

Advertising objective–A specific communication *task* to be accomplished with a specific *target audience* during a specific *period of time*.

An **advertising objective** is a specific communication *task* to be accomplished with a specific *target* audience during a specific period of *time*. Advertising objectives can be classified by their primary purpose – to *inform*, *persuade* or *remind*. Table 15.1 lists examples of each of these specific objectives.

Informative advertising is used heavily when introducing a new product category. In this case, the objective is to build primary demand. So, early producers of HDTVs first had to inform consumers about the image quality and size benefits of the new product. *Persuasive advertising* becomes more important as competition increases. Here, the company's objective is to build selective demand. For example, once HDTV's became established, Samsung began trying to persuade consumers that *its* brand offered the best quality for their money. Such advertising wants to engage customers and create brand community.

Some persuasive advertising has become *comparative advertising* (or *attack advertising*), in which a company directly or indirectly compares its brand with one or more other brands. You

Table 15.1 Possible advertising objectives

Informative advertising	
Communicating customer value	Suggesting new uses for a product
Building a brand and company image	Informing the market of a price change
Telling the market about a new product	Describing available services and support
Explaining how a product works	Correcting false impressions
Persuasive advertising	
Building brand preference	Persuading customers to purchase now
Encouraging switching to a brand	Creating customer engagement
Changing customer perceptions of product value	Building brand community
Reminder advertising	
Maintaining customer relationships	Reminding consumers where to buy the product
Reminding consumers that the product may be needed in the near future	Keeping the brand in a customer's mind during off-seasons

see examples of comparative advertising in many product categories, ranging from sports drinks, coffee and soup, to computers, car rentals, credit cards, wireless phone services, and even retail pricing. For example, Unilever ran into trouble in 2011 with the UK's Advertising Standards Authority for adverts promoting its Knorr gravy granules, which contained headlines that said 'unbeatable taste vs Bisto'. The ads contained further text that said Knorr's gravy had recorded 'unbeatable scores for taste, appearance, consistency and aroma' in testing. One of the adverts claimed Knorr gravy recorded 'unbeatable scores' over 'main competitors'. Premier Goods Group who owned Bisto took some exception to this advertising and the ASA agreed.[6] Meanwhile in the US, Dunkin' Donuts ran a TV and web campaign comparing the chain's coffee to Starbuck's brews. 'In a recent national blind taste test,' proclaimed the ads, 'more Americans preferred the taste of Dunkin' Donuts coffee over Starbucks. It's just more proof it's all about the coffee (not the couches or music)', which is intentionally somewhat provocative.

Indeed, Microsoft has recently run an extensive campaign directly comparing its Bing search engine and Windows computers to Google's leading search engine and other products:

> It all began with Microsoft's 'Bing it on' campaign, which directly challenged consumers to make side-by-side comparisons of its Bing search engine results to Google search results without knowing which results were from which search engine. According to Microsoft, to the surprise of many people, those making the comparison choose Bing over Google by a two-to-one margin. Microsoft next launched an aggressive 'Scroogled' campaign, which attacked Google's search engine for 'Scroogling' users by exploiting their personal data with everything from invasive ads in Gmail to sharing data with app developers to maximise advertising profits. 'For an honest search engine,' said the Scroogled ads, 'try Bing'. More recent Scroogled attack ads have disparaged Google Chromebook laptops – inexpensive, stripped-down, web-only machines that Google and partners like Acer, Samsung and HP market as an alternative to fully fledged laptops. The hard-hitting Scroogled ads point out that Chromebooks won't run Microsoft Windows and other popular programs like Office, iTunes and Photoshop and suggest that a Chromebook is 'pretty much a brick' when not connected to the Internet. Although controversial, the Scroogled campaign has been effective in getting many consumers to look at Bing and other Microsoft products in a new light versus competitor Google.[7]

Comparison advertising: Microsoft's hard-hitting 'Scroogled' campaign directly challenges competitor Google. 'For an honest search engine try Bing'.

Source: Microsoft

But advertisers should use comparative advertising with caution. All too often, such ads invite competitor responses, resulting in an advertising war that neither competitor can win. Upset competitors might decide to take more drastic action, such as filing complaints with the regulatory authorities (e.g., the Advertising Standards Authority in the UK and the National Advertising Division of the Council of Better Business Bureaus in the US) or even filing false-advertising lawsuits. Note that Unilever's Knorr advertising mentioned above was, for example, banned by the ASA.[8]

Reminder advertising is important for mature products; it helps to maintain customer relationships and keep consumers thinking about the product. Expensive Coca-Cola television ads primarily build and maintain the Coca-Cola brand relationship rather than inform or persuade customers to buy it in the short run.

Advertising's goal is to help move consumers through the buying process. Some advertising is designed to move people to immediate action. For example, a direct-response television ad by Weight Watchers urges consumers to pick up the phone and sign up right away, and a PCWorld newspaper insert for a weekend sale encourages immediate store visits. However, many ads focus on building or strengthening long-term customer relationships. For example, a Nike television ad in which well-known athletes work through extreme challenges in their Nike gear never directly asks for a sale. Instead, the goal is to somehow change the way the customers think or feel about the brand.

Setting the advertising budget

Advertising budget—The financial allocation and other resources allocated to a product or company advertising programme.

After determining its advertising objectives, a company next sets its **advertising budget** for each product. Four commonly used methods for setting promotion budgets were discussed in Chapter 14. Here we discuss some specific factors that should be considered when setting the advertising budget.

A brand's advertising budget often depends on its *stage in the product life cycle*. For example, new products typically need relatively large advertising budgets to build awareness and gain consumer trial. In contrast, mature brands usually require lower budgets as a ratio to sales. *Market share* also impacts on the amount of advertising needed: because building market share or taking market share from competitors requires larger advertising spending than does simply maintaining current share, low-share brands usually need more advertising spending as a percentage of sales.

Also, brands in a market with many competitors and high advertising clutter must be advertised more heavily to be noticed above the noise in the marketplace. Undifferentiated brands – those that closely resemble other brands in their product class (e.g., soft drinks and laundry detergents) – may require heavy advertising to set them apart. When one product differs greatly from competing products, advertising can be used to point out the differences to consumers.

No matter what method is used, setting the advertising budget is no easy task. How does a company know if it is spending the right amount? Some critics charge that large consumer packaged-goods firms tend to spend too much on advertising and that B-to-B marketers generally under spend on advertising. They claim that, on the one hand, large consumer companies use lots of image advertising without really knowing its effects. They overspend as a form of 'insurance' against not spending enough. On the other hand, business advertisers tend to rely too heavily on their sales forces to bring in orders. They underestimate the power of company image and product image in pre-selling to industrial customers. Thus, they do not spend enough on advertising to build customer awareness and knowledge.

Companies such as Coca-Cola, Unilever and Kraft have built sophisticated statistical models to determine the relationship between promotional spending and brand sales, which helps determine the 'optimal investment' across various media. Still, because so many factors affect advertising effectiveness, some controllable and others not, measuring the results of advertising spending remains an inexact science. In most cases, managers must rely on large doses of judgement along with more quantitative analysis when setting advertising budgets.[9]

As a result, advertising is one of the easiest budget items to cut when economic times get tough. Cuts in brand-building advertising appear to do little short-term harm to sales. For example, in the wake of the economic downturn and recession, US advertising expenditures plummeted 12 per cent from the previous year. In the early 2010s economic turmoil in the Eurozone and the rest of Western Europe encouraged companies to reduce advertising expenditures. In the long run, however, slashing ad spending risks long-term damage to a brand's image and market share. In fact, companies that can maintain or even increase their advertising spending while competitors are decreasing theirs can gain competitive advantage.

For example, during the recent recession, while competitors were cutting back, car maker Audi actually increased its marketing and advertising spending. Audi 'kept its foot on the pedal while everyone else [was] pulling back,' said an Audi ad executive. 'Why would we go backwards now when the industry is generally locking the brakes and cutting spending?' As a result, Audi's brand awareness and buyer consideration reached record levels during the recession, outstripping those of BMW, Mercedes and Lexus, and positioning Audi strongly for the post-recession era. Audi is now one of the hottest auto brands on the market, neck and neck with BMW and Mercedes in global luxury car sales.[10]

Developing advertising strategy

Advertising strategy consists of two major elements: creating advertising *messages* and selecting advertising *media*. In the past, companies often viewed media planning as secondary to the message-creation process. The creative department first created good ads; then the media department selected and purchased the best media for carrying those ads to desired target audiences. This often caused friction between creatives (copy-writers, artists, graphic designers) and media planners.

Today, however, soaring media costs, more-focused target marketing strategies, and the blizzard of new digital and interactive media have promoted the importance of the media-planning function. The decision about which media to use for an ad campaign – television, newspapers, magazines, video, a website or an online social media, mobile devices or e-mail – is now sometimes more critical than the creative elements of the campaign. As a result, more and more advertisers are orchestrating a closer harmony between their messages and the media that deliver them. In fact, in a really good ad campaign, you often have to ask 'Is that a media idea or a creative idea?'

Advertising strategy—The strategy by which the company accomplishes its advertising objectives. It consists of two major elements: creating advertising messages and selecting advertising media.

Creating the advertising message and brand content

No matter how big the budget, advertising can succeed only if it gains attention, engages consumers and communicates well. Good ad messages are especially important in today's costly and cluttered advertising environment.

In 1950, the average US household received only three network television channels and a handful of major national magazines. Today, the average American household receives more than 180 channels, and consumers have more than 20,000 magazines from which to choose.[11] Add in the countless radio stations and a continuous barrage of catalogues, direct mail, e-mail and online ads, and out-of-home media, mobile and social media exposure, and consumers are being bombarded with ads at home, work and all points in between. For example, Americans are exposed to a cumulative 5.3 trillion online ad impressions each year and a daily diet of 400 million tweets, 144,000 hours of uploaded YouTube video, and 4.75 billion pieces of shared content on Facebook.[12] Though the change is less extreme in European countries, the same dramatic media expansion is occurring here and throughout the world.

Breaking through the clutter

If all this clutter bothers some consumers, it also causes huge headaches for marketers. Take the situation facing television advertisers in the US. They pay an average of $354,000 to produce a single 30-second commercial. Then, each time they show it, they pay an average of $122,000 for 30 seconds of advertising time during a popular primetime programme. They pay even more if it's

Advertising clutter: today's consumers, armed with an arsenal of weapons, can choose what they watch and don't watch. Increasingly they are choosing not to watch TV ads.

Source: Gallo Images/Alamy Images

Madison & Vine—A term that has come to represent the merging of advertising and entertainment in an effort to break through the clutter and create new avenues for reaching customers with more engaging messages.

an especially popular programme, such as *American Idol* ($355,000) or *The Big Bang Theory* ($317,000), or a mega-event such as the Super Bowl (averaging $4 million per 30 seconds!). Then their ads are sandwiched in with a clutter of other commercials, announcements and network promotions, totalling as much as 20 minutes of non-programme material per primetime hour, with long commercial breaks coming every six minutes on average. Such clutter in television and other ad media has created an increasingly hostile advertising environment.[13]

According to one recent study, more than 70 per cent of Americans think there are too many ads on TV, and 62 per cent of national advertisers believe that TV ads have become less effective, citing clutter as the main culprit.[14]

Media costs are lower outside the US, but European advertisers are experiencing exactly the same pressures as those in America to stand out from the crowd in busy and increasingly fragmented advertising media.

Until recently, television viewers were essentially a captive audience for advertisers. But today's digital wizardry has given consumers a rich new set of information and entertainment choices. With the growth in cable and satellite TV, the Internet, video on demand (VOD), video streaming, tablets and smartphones, today's viewers have many more options.

Digital technology has also armed consumers with an arsenal of weapons for choosing what they watch or don't watch. Increasingly, thanks to the growth of digital video recorder (DVR) systems, consumers are choosing *not* to watch ads. Half of American TV households now have DVRs, and two-thirds of DVR owners use the device to skip commercials. One ad agency executive calls these DVR systems 'electronic weedwhackers' when it comes to commercials. At the same time, video downloads and streaming are expanding rapidly, letting viewers watch entertainment on their own time – with or without commercials.[15] In addition, the globalisation of the world technology market underlines the rapid spread of this technology across the world.

Thus, advertisers can no longer force-feed the same old conventional ad messages to captive consumers through traditional media. Just to gain and hold attention, today's advertising messages must be better planned, more imaginative, more entertaining and more emotionally engaging. Simply interrupting or disrupting consumers no longer works. Instead, unless ads provide information that is interesting, useful or entertaining, many consumers will simply skip by them.

Merging advertising and entertainment

To break through the clutter, many marketers are now subscribing to a new merging of advertising and entertainment, dubbed '**Madison & Vine**' in the US. You've probably heard of Madison Avenue. It's the New York City street that houses the headquarters of many of America's largest advertising agencies. You may also have heard of Hollywood & Vine, the intersection of Hollywood Avenue and Vine Street in Hollywood, California, long the symbolic heart of the US entertainment industry. Now, Madison Avenue and Hollywood & Vine are coming together to form a new intersection – Madison & Vine – that represents the merging of advertising and entertainment in an effort to create new avenues for reaching customers with more engaging messages.

This merging of advertising and entertainment takes one of two forms: advertisement or branded entertainment. The aim of *advertainment* is to make ads themselves so entertaining, or so useful, that people *want* to watch them. There's no chance that you'd watch ads on purpose, you say? Think again. Reconsider the impact of comparethemarket.com's meerkat advertising described in the case at the beginning of of this chapter, and the loyal fans of the meerkats on the website, Facebook and Twitter.

These days, it's not unusual to see an entertaining ad or other brand content on YouTube before you see it on TV. And you might well seek it out at a friend's suggestion rather than having it forced on you by the advertiser. Moreover, beyond making their regular ads more engaging, advertisers are also creating new content forms that look less like ads and more like short films or shows. A range of new brand messaging platforms – from webisodes and blogs to online videos and apps – now blur the line between ads and entertainment.

For example, as part of its long-running and highly successful Campaign for Real Beauty, Unilever's Dove brand created a thought-provoking three-minute video, called 'Dove real beauty sketches', about how women view themselves. The video compares images of women drawn by a sketch artist based on their self-descriptions versus strangers' descriptions. Side-by-side comparisons show that the stranger-described images are invariably more accurate and more flattering, creating strong reactions from the women. The tagline concludes, 'You're more beautiful than you think'. Although the award-winning video was never shown on TV, it drew more than 163 million global YouTube views within just two months, making it the most watched video ever.[16]

Branded entertainment (or *brand integration*) involves making the brand an inseparable part of some other form of entertainment. The most common form of branded entertainment is product placements – embedding brands as props within other programming. This technique is so highly developed in the US, it is almost compulsory for programme makers. It might be a brief glimpse of the latest LG phone on *Grey's Anatomy*. It could be worked into the show's overall storyline, as it is on *The Big Bang Theory*, whose character Penny works at the Cheesecake Factory restaurant. The product placement might even be scripted into an episode. For example, one entire episode of US comedy programme *Modern Family* centres around finding geeky father character Phil Dunphy the recently released, hard-to-find Apple iPad he covets as his special birthday present.[17]

Originally created with TV in mind, branded entertainment has spread quickly into other sectors of the entertainment industry. It's widely used in films (remember all those GM vehicles in the *Transformers* series; the prominence of Purina Puppy Chow in *Marley & Me*; and the appearance of brands ranging from Audi and Oracle to LG in *Iron Man 2*?). In fact, 2013's top 39 films contained 325 identifiable brand placements.[18] If you look carefully, you'll also see product placements in video games, comic books, Broadway musicals and even pop music. For example, there's a sandwich-making scene featuring Wonder Bread and Miracle Whip in the middle of Lady Gaga's ten-minute 'Telephone' video (which captured more than 50 million YouTube views in less than a month).

The highly acclaimed film, *The LEGO Movie*, was pretty much a 100-minute product placement for iconic LEGO construction bricks. According to one writer, 'The audience happily sits through a cinematic sales pitch … that shows off the immense versatility of the product while placing it in a deeply personal context. The majority of the film is a breathtaking display of what LEGO bricks are capable of as creative tools, but the personal element is what really elevates this film to product-placement perfection.'[19]

Many companies are even producing their own branded entertainment. For example, Ford created 'Random Acts of Fusion', a web-only show that followed TV celebrities Joel McHale and Ryan Seacrest as they hosted video contests and free food festivals across America, letting people interact with the latest-model Ford Fusion as they went (www.youtube.com/user/fordfusion). The show increased traffic to the Ford Fusion website by 20 per cent.

Similarly, IKEA has produced several web-only series. One of the latest is the 'IKEA Home Tour', which follows five IKEA employees on a year-long road trip to provide families with home makeovers using merchandise from local IKEA stores. In keeping with the retailer's long-time practice of showing diversity in its ads and marketing, the employees visit many non-traditional families, such as a male couple in the Bronx planning to be married. 'Consumers no longer want just a 30-second commercial,' says an IKEA marketer. 'They want to know who a company is, what it believes, and what its personality is.'

While at its most developed and sophisticated the US media, product placement and related communication activities are rapidly spreading to

Branded entertainment: the highly acclaimed film, *The LEGO Movie*, was pretty much a 100-minute product placement for iconic LEGO construction bricks, what one writer calls 'product-placement perfection'.

Source: Richard McDowell/Alamy Images

Europe. In France, Spain and Germany, companies have embraced product placement since the relaxation of strict European Union laws in 2007. The new EU rules bring Europe broadly into line with the US on product placement regulation. In 2011, the new rules allowed product placement for the first time in the UK. Nonetheless, in the UK an onscreen 'P' logo must be displayed at the start and end of programmes and between ad breaks to warn viewers when shows contain product placement, and Ofcom, the UK regulator, enforces more stringent rules and restrictions than most countries (children's and religious programming are exempt and some products like gambling and alcohol are excluded).[20]

So, there is a new meeting place for the advertising and entertainment industries. The goal is for brand messages to become a part of the entertainment rather than interrupting it. As JWT, an ad agency, puts it, 'We believe advertising needs to stop interrupting what people are interested in and be what people are interested in.' However, advertisers must be careful that the new intersection itself doesn't become too congested. With all the new ad formats and product placements, Madison & Vine threatens to create even more of the very clutter that it was designed to break through. At that point, consumers might decide to take yet a different route.

Message strategy

The first step in creating effective advertising messages is to plan a *message strategy* – the general message that will be communicated to consumers. The purpose of advertising is to get consumers to think about or react to the product or company in a certain way. People will react only if they believe they will benefit from doing so. Thus, developing an effective message strategy begins with identifying customer *benefits* that can be used as advertising appeals. Ideally, the message strategy will follow directly from the company's broader positioning and customer value-creation strategies.

Message strategy statements tend to be plain, straightforward outlines of benefits and positioning points that an advertiser wants to stress. The advertiser must next develop a compelling **creative concept** – or 'big idea' – that will bring the message strategy to life in a distinctive and memorable way. At this stage, simple message ideas become great ad campaigns. Usually, a copy writer and an art director will team up to generate many creative concepts, hoping that one of these concepts will turn out to be the big idea. The creative concept may emerge as a visualisation, a phrase or a combination of the two.

The creative concept will guide the choice of specific appeals to be used in an advertising campaign. *Advertising appeals* should have three characteristics. First, they should be *meaningful*, pointing out benefits that make the product more desirable or interesting to consumers. Second, appeals must be *believable*. Consumers must believe that the product or service will deliver the promised benefits.

However, the most meaningful and believable benefits may not be the best ones to feature. Appeals should also be *distinctive*. They should tell how one product is better than its competing brands. For example, the most meaningful benefit of using a body wash or fragrance is that it makes you feel cleaner or smell better. But Axe's Anarchy brand for men and women sets itself apart by the extreme nature of the 'Axe effect' it promises to create – Axe Anarchy For Him + For Her will 'Unleash the chaos'. Similarly, the most meaningful benefit of owning a wristwatch is that it keeps accurate time, yet few watch ads feature this benefit. Instead, based on the distinctive benefits they offer, watch advertisers might select any of a number of advertising themes. For years, Timex has been the affordable watch. In contrast, Rolex ads talk about the brand's 'obsession with perfection' and the fact that 'Rolex has been the preeminent symbol of performance and prestige for more than a century'.

For example, consider the massive impact of Cadbury's gorilla advertising in 2007 (you can see the ad at www.youtube.com/watch?v=TnzFRV1LwIo):

Publicis creative agency Fallow Worldwide designed an advertising campaign for Cadbury's Dairy Milk chocolate which started with an ad showing a man in a gorilla suit smiling while playing the drums to Phil Collins' 'In the Air Tonight', and showing the bar of chocolate only in the fade-out shot at the end with the slogan 'A glass and a half full of joy'. Fallow is renowned for persuading large advertisers to make unconventional ads. The ad was first shown during the final of the programme

---

Creative concept—The compelling 'big idea' that will bring an advertising message strategy to life in a distinctive and memorable way.

Big Brother, then a major hit. Importantly, after the 90-second ad appeared on British television it quickly became an Internet hit and was downloaded 7 million times on YouTube as well as generating dozens of imitative spoofs and its own Wikipedia page.

Almost as soon as the ad aired the questions began. Did it feature a real or fake gorilla playing the drums? Was it Phil Collins, the rock drummer who wrote the original song, in a costume? How could this help a staid confectionery brand regain its traditional hold on Britain's chocoholic youth? The secret to its success was the benefit of free 'viral' distribution of the advert as consumers e-mailed, blogged, created and posted spoof versions. This, in turn, provided free editorial coverage in mainstream media, including an uninterrupted full showing of the ad on Australian TV news where the ad itself is not even on the air.

CEO, Todd Stitzer, went on record as saying that the campaign worked because it communicated the joy of eating a chocolate bar 'without being obvious about it'. Cadbury Dairy Milk chocolate sales rose 9 per cent in the two months after the ad was aired, stealing market share from rival Mars. Internal company e-mails refer to 'the gorilla phenomenon'. Cadbury has since been bought by Kraft Foods.[21]

Nonetheless, sometimes creatives may go too far and shock audiences. In a light-hearted attempt to sell garden furniture, one IKEA campaign featured people destroying garden gnomes in increasingly violent ways – one scene showing a heart-broken gnome standing over a fallen friend, with a tear running down his cheek. The tagline was 'Make more of your garden. Say no to gnomes'. However, the humour backfired badly and the company found some viewers affronted at the violence and complaining that the images were distressing. The company reassured viewers that 'We can confirm that no gnomes were harmed in the making of the advert, thanks to some brave stunt doubles', but had to change the ads.[22]

Message execution

The advertiser now must turn the big idea into an actual ad execution that will capture the target market's attention and interest. The creative team must find the best approach, style, tone, words and format for executing a message. A message can be presented in various **execution styles**, such as the following:

- *Slice of life*: This style shows one or more 'typical' people using a particular product in a normal setting. Dairylea cheese triangles are shown being consumed by children in various settings to underline the taste and healthy dimensions of the product.
- *Lifestyle*: This style shows how a product fits in with a particular lifestyle. For example, an ad for Gap's Athleta womens' active wear shows a woman in a complex yoga pose and states: 'If your body is your temple, build it one piece at a time.'
- *Fantasy*: This style creates a fantasy around the product or its use. For example, Dreamies luxury cat biscuits shows a cat repeatedly diving through a wall, and leaving an endearing cat-size hole, in response to the rattle of the biscuits. And giant M&Ms talk to people and play out unreal situations varying from a petrol station hostage drama to a nightclub pick-up scene.
- *Mood or image*: This style builds a mood or image around the product or service, such as beauty, love, intrigue or serenity. Few claims are made about the product or service except through suggestion. For example, staple British bread brand Hovis advertising showcases over 100 years of British history through a boy's eyes to celebrate the 122 years since Hovis was established.
- *Musical*: This style shows people or cartoon characters singing about the product. For example, many advertisers have recently chosen to use iconic rock songs as the background to their ads.
- *Personality symbol*: This style creates a character that represents the product. The character might be animated (e.g., Alexsandr Orlov the meerkat, Michelin Man, Mr. Clean, or Tony the Tiger) or real (e.g., Ronald McDonald, the Fox from Foxy Bingo).

Execution style—The approach, style, tone, words and format used for executing an advertising message.

Message execution: staple British bakery brand Hovis showcases historical scenes and moods.

Source: Hovis Ltd/History of Advertising Trust

- *Technical expertise*: This style shows the company's expertise in making the product. Thus, Kenco Coffee shows the care with which coffee beans are selected for its brands.
- *Scientific evidence*: This style presents survey or scientific evidence that the brand is better or better liked than one or more other brands. For years, P&G's Crest toothpaste (Blend-A-Med in some European markets) has used scientific evidence to convince buyers that the brand is better than others at fighting tooth decay.
- *Testimonial evidence or endorsement*: This style features a highly believable or likable source endorsing the product. It could be ordinary people saying how much they like a given product.

The advertiser also must choose a *tone* for the ad. For example, P&G always uses a positive tone: its ads say something very positive about its products. Other advertisers now use edgy humour to break through the commercial clutter.

The advertiser must use memorable and attention-getting *words* in the ad. The skill of the copy writer is in achieving clarity of message, distinctiveness and impact.

Finally, *format* elements make a difference in an ad's impact as well as in its cost. A small change in an ad design can make a big difference in its effect. In a print ad, the *illustration* is the first thing the reader notices; it must be strong enough to draw attention. Next, the *headline* must effectively entice the right people to read the copy. Finally, the *copy* – the main block of text in the ad – must be simple but strong and convincing. Moreover, these three elements must effectively work *together* to engage customers and persuasively present customer value. However, novel formats can help an ad stand out from the clutter. For example, in one striking print ad from Volkswagen, the illustration does most of the work in catching relevant attention for the car maker's precision parking assist feature. It shows a porcupine 'parked' in a tight space between goldfish in water-filled plastic bags. The small-print headline says only 'Precision parking. Park assist by Volkswagen'. Enough said!

Consumer-generated content

Taking advantage of today's interactive technologies, many companies are now tapping consumers for message content, message ideas, or even actual ads and videos. They are searching existing video sites, setting up their own sites, and sponsoring ad-creation contests and other promotions. Sometimes the results are outstanding; sometimes they are forgettable. If done well, however, user-generated content can incorporate the voice of the customer into brand messages and generate greater consumer brand involvement. The dramatic growth of social networking sites like Facebook and Twitter is encouraging advertisers to step up their experiments with user-generated Internet content. Many brands develop brand websites or hold contests that invite consumers to submit ad message ideas and videos.

For example, for the past several years, in the US PepsiCo's Doritos brand has held its annual 'Crash the Super Bowl Challenge' contest that invites consumers to create their own video ads about the tasty triangular corn chips. The consumer-generated Doritos ads have been a success – winners receive large cash awards and have their ads run during the Super Bowl.

At the other end of the spectrum, international online crafts marketplace/community Etsy.com – 'Your best place to buy and sell all things handmade' – ran a contest inviting consumers to tell the Etsy.com story in 30-second videos. The results were what one well-known former advertising critic called 'positively remarkable'.[23]

The ten semi-finalists are, as a group, better thought-out and realised than any ten random commercials running on TV anywhere in the world. The best user-created Etsy ad features a simple, sad, animated robot, consigned to a life of soul-crushing assembly-line production. 'See, there's a lot of robots out there,' says the voice of the unseen Etsy craftswomen who crafted him. 'A lot of these robots are sad, because they're stuck making these boring, mass-produced things. Me, I really can believe all that great stuff about how it helps the environment and microeconomics and feeling special about getting something handmade by someone else. But the real reason I make handmade goods is because every time somebody buys something handmade, a robot gets its wings.' The user-made ad 'is simply magnificent', concludes the ad critic, 'in a way that the agency business had better take note of'.

But brands across a wide range of industries – from carmakers and fast-food chains to clothing brands and pet food marketers – are inviting customers to participate in generating marketing content. For example, Chevrolet held an Oscars Program Video Contest that produced 72 imaginative ad videos for its Chevy Cruze model in the US. The winner – a delightfully quirky one-minute video called 'Speed Chaser' – was shot in an open field for only $4,000. Similarly, Purina conducted a video contest on its YouTube page, inviting owners of everyday dogs to submit videos showing 'How is your dog great?' Using a compilation of clips from more than 500 submitted videos, Purina created a 60-second 'How I'm great' commercial and aired it during the broadcast of the Westminster Kennel Club Dog Show. And to help boost digital and social media engagement, Taco Bell invited YouTube stars and influencers to create video content for its new Fiery Doritos Locos Tacos. Taco Bell ended up choosing 65 video ads to distribute online through Twitter feeds and social networks, and used one clever video – featuring a '3D Doritos Taco printer' – in subsequent paid online advertising.[24]

Consumer-generated content can make customers an everyday part of the brand conversation. Yogawear company Lululemon recently launched its #TheSweatLife campaign, in which it invited customers to tweet or Instagram photos of themselves 'getting their sweat on' in Lululemon gear. 'Your perspiration is our inspiration,' said the brand on its website. Within only a few months, the brand had received more than 7,000 photos, which it featured in a #TheSweatLife online gallery, quickly drawing more than 40,000 unique visitors. The user-generated content campaign created substantial customer engagement for Lululemon. 'We created the programme as a way to connect with our guests and showcase how they're authentically sweating in our product offline,' says a Lululemon brand manager. 'We see it as a unique way to bring their offline experiences into our online community.'[25]

Not all consumer-generated advertising efforts, however, are so successful. As many big companies have learned, ads made by amateurs can be … well, pretty amateurish. If done well, however, consumer-generated advertising efforts can produce new creative ideas and fresh perspectives on the brand from consumers who actually experience it. Such campaigns can boost consumer involvement and get consumers talking and thinking about a brand and its value to them.[26]

Selecting advertising media

The major steps in **advertising media** selection are (1) defining *reach*, *frequency*, *impact* and *engagement*; (2) choosing among major *media types*; (3) selecting specific *media vehicles*; and (4) choosing *media timing*.

Advertising media—The vehicles through which advertising messages are delivered to their intended audiences.

Determining reach, frequency, impact and engagement

To select media, an advertiser must determine the reach and frequency needed to achieve the advertising objectives. *Reach* is a measure of the *percentage* of people in the target market who are exposed to an ad campaign during a given period of time. For example, an advertiser might try to reach 70 per cent of the target market during the first three months of the campaign. *Frequency* is a measure of how many *times* the average person in the target market is exposed to a message. For example, an advertiser might want an average exposure frequency of three.

But advertisers want to do more than just reach a given number of consumers a specific number of times. The advertiser also must determine the desired *media impact* – the *qualitative value* of message exposure through a given medium. For example, the same message in one magazine (say, *The Economist*) may be more believable than in another (say, *Hello!*). For products that need to be demonstrated, messages on television may have more impact than messages on radio because television uses sight, motion *and* sound. Products for which consumers provide input on design or features might be better promoted at an interactive website or social media page than in a direct mailing.

More generally, the advertiser wants to choose media that will *engage* consumers rather than simply reach them. For example, a DIY superstore might decide that although it lacks the broad reach of TV or print ads, combining mobile and online media can engage customers more deeply and personally – a web banner ad could link to the retailer's mobile website, which highlights products matching the season and the local weather forecast (e.g., when it's snowing offer special deals on snow shovels and snow blowers).

Although research agency Nielsen is beginning to measure the levels of *media engagement*, for some television, radio and social media, such measures are still hard to come by for most media. Current media measures are things such as ratings, readership, listenership and click-through rates for websites. However, engagement happens inside the consumer. Notes one expert, 'Just measuring the number of eyeballs in front of a television set is hard enough without trying to measure the intensity of those eyeballs doing the viewing.'[27] Still, marketers need to know how customers connect with an ad and brand idea as a part of the broader brand relationship.

Engaged consumers are more likely to act upon brand messages and even share them with others. Thus, rather than simply tracking *consumer impressions* for a media placement – how many people see, hear or read an ad – Coca-Cola now also tracks the *consumer expressions* that result, such as a comment, a 'Like', uploading a photo or video, or sharing brand content on social networks. Today's empowered consumers often generate more messages about a brand than a company can.

For example, Coca-Cola estimates that on YouTube there are about 146 million views of content related to Coca-Cola. However, only about 26 million of those are of content that Coca-Cola created. The other 120 million are of content created by engaged consumers. 'We can't match the volume of our consumers' output,' says Coca-Cola's chief marketing officer, 'but we can spark it with the right type [and placement] of content'. To that end, many Coca-Cola marketing campaigns are aimed at generating expressions rather than just impressions. For example, the brand's recent 'Ahh effect' campaign called on pre-teens to share the 'ahh moments' they experience while drinking Coke at a www.AHH.com website and via social media using the hashtag #ThisisAHH. It then featured the user-generated personal expressions in 'This is AHH' commercials on youth-oriented TV channels.[28]

Choosing among major media types

Media planners have to know the reach, frequency and impact of each major media type. As summarised in Table 15.2, the major media types are television, digital and social media, newspapers, direct mail, magazines, radio and outdoor. Each medium has its advantages and its limitations. Media planners want to choose media that will effectively and efficiently present the advertising message to target customers. Thus, they must consider each medium's impact, message effectiveness and cost. As discussed in the previous chapter, it's typically not a question of which one medium to use. Rather, the advertiser selects a mix of media and blends them into a fully integrated marketing communications campaign.

The mix of media must be re-examined regularly. For a long time, television and magazines dominated the media mixes of major consumer goods advertisers, with other media often neglected. However, as discussed previously, the media mix appears to be shifting dramatically. As mass-media costs rise, audiences shrink, and exciting new digital and interactive media emerge, many advertisers are finding new ways to reach consumers. They are supplementing the traditional mass media with more specialised and highly targeted media that cost less, target more effectively, and engage customers more fully. Today's marketers want to assemble a full mix of *paid, owned, earned* and *shared media* that create and deliver engaging brand content to target consumers.

In addition to the explosion of online, mobile and social media, cable and satellite television systems are thriving, such as Sky in the UK, as well as Freeview. Such systems allow narrow programming formats, such as all sports, all news, nutrition, arts, home improvement and gardening, cooking, travel, history, finance and others that target select groups. Some operators are even testing systems that will let them target specific types of ads to TVs in specific neighbourhoods or

Table 15.2 Profiles of major media types

Medium	Advantages	Limitations
Television	Good mass-marketing coverage; low cost per exposure; combines sight, sound, and motion; appealing to the senses	High absolute costs; high clutter; fleeting exposure; less audience selectivity
Digital and social media	High selectivity; low cost; immediacy; engagement capabilities	Potentially low impact; high audience control of content and exposure
Newspapers	Flexibility; timeliness; good local market coverage; broad acceptability; high believability	Short life; poor reproduction quality; small pass-along audience
Direct mail	High audience selectivity; flexibility; no ad competition within the same medium; allows personalisation	Relatively high cost per exposure; 'junk mail' image
Magazines	High geographic and demographic selectivity; credibility and prestige; high-quality reproduction; long life and good pass-along readership	Long ad purchase lead time; high cost; no guarantee of position
Radio	Good local acceptance; high geographic and demographic selectivity; low cost	Audio only; fleeting exposure; low attention ('the half-heard' medium); fragmented audiences
Outdoor	Flexibility; high repeat exposure; low cost; low message competition; good positional selectivity	Little audience selectivity; creative limitations

individually to specific types of customers. For example, ads for a Polish-language channel would run in only Polish-speaking neighbourhoods, or only pet owners would see ads from pet food companies. Advertisers can take advantage of such narrowcasting to 'rifle in' on special market segments rather than use the 'shotgun' approach offered by network broadcasting.

Finally, in their efforts to find less costly and more highly targeted ways to reach consumers, advertisers have discovered a dazzling collection of *alternative media*. These days, no matter where you go or what you do, you will probably run into some new form of advertising. This search for new media opportunities is at its most extreme in the United States but is spreading rapidly to Europe and other parts of the world:

Tiny billboards attached to shopping carts urge you to buy Pampers while ads roll by on the store's checkout conveyor publicising your local car dealer. Step outside and there goes a local authority rubbish truck sporting an ad for rubbish bags or a local bus for schools displaying a Domino's pizza ad. A nearby bus shelter is emblazoned with advertising for KFC's 'fiery' chicken wings. You escape to the football ground, only to find giant video screens running beer ads while a hot air balloon with an electronic message board circles lazily overhead. In mid-winter, you wait in a bus shelter that looks like an oven – with heat coming from the coils – shouting out the local coffee shop's line-up of hot breakfasts.

These days, you're likely to find ads – well – anywhere. Taxi cabs sport electronic messaging signs tied to GPS location sensors that can pitch local stores and restaurants wherever they roam. Ad space is being sold on car park tickets, airline boarding passes, Underground turnstiles, golf scorecards, ATMs, litter bins, and even police cars, doctors' examining tables and church bulletins. One company even sells space on toilet paper furnished free to restaurants, football grounds and shopping centres – the paper carries advertiser logos, coupons and codes you can scan with your smartphone to download digital coupons or link to advertisers' social media pages. Now that's a captive audience.

Alternative media: Cambridge graduates launched a business selling their faces as advertising hoardings.

Source: BuyMyFace.com

Such alternative media seem a bit far-fetched, and they sometimes irritate consumers who resent it all as 'ad nauseam'. But for many marketers, these media can save money and provide a new way to hit selected consumers where they live, shop, work and play. For example, Cambridge graduates launched a business selling advertisers their faces (and those of thousands of like-minded volunteers) as advertising hoardings, sold through their website Buymyface.com. While seemingly bizarre, advertisers have already included Airfix model kits, Paddy Power the bookmakers, and Ernst & Young the accountants.[29]

Another important trend affecting media selection is the rapid growth in the number of *media multi-taskers*, people who absorb more than one medium at a time. For example, it's not uncommon to find someone watching TV with a smartphone in hand, tweeting, snapchatting with friends, and chasing down product information on Google. One recent survey found that as many as 88 per cent of tablet owners and 86 per cent of smartphone owners use the devices while watching TV. Although some of this multitasking is related to TV viewing – such as looking up related product and programme information – most multitasking involves tasks unrelated to the shows being watched. Marketers need to take such media interactions into account when selecting the types of media they will use.[30]

Selecting specific media vehicles

Media planners must also choose the best *media vehicles* – specific media within each general media type. For example, particular television programmes, specific special interest magazines, or online and mobile vehicles like Twitter, Facebook, Pinterest and YouTube.

Media planners must compute the cost per 1,000 persons reached by a vehicle. For example, if a full-page, four-colour advertisement in the US national edition of *Forbes* costs $148,220 and *Forbe's* readership is 900,000 people, the cost of reaching each group of 1,000 persons is about $164. The same advertisement in *Bloomberg BusinessWeek* regional edition may cost only $48,100 but reach only 155,000 people – at a cost per 1,000 of about $310.[31] The media planner ranks each magazine by cost per 1,000 and favours those magazines with the lower cost per 1,000 for reaching target customers. However, in the previous case, if a marketer is targeting regional business managers, *BusinessWeek* might be the more cost-effective buy, even at a higher cost per thousand. Media planners must also consider the costs of producing ads for different media. Whereas newspaper ads may cost very little to produce, flashy television ads can be very costly. Many online ads cost little to produce, but costs can climb when producing made-for-the-web videos and ad series.

In selecting specific media vehicles, media planners must balance media costs against several media effectiveness factors. First, the planner should evaluate the media vehicle's *audience quality*. For a Huggies disposable nappies advertisement, for example, *Mother & Baby* magazine would have a high exposure value; *GQ* magazine would have a low exposure value. Second, the media planner should consider *audience engagement*. Readers of *Vogue*, for example, typically pay more attention to ads than do *Economist* readers. Third, the planner should assess the vehicle's *editorial quality*. The *Economist* and the *Financial Times* are more believable and prestigious than the *Sun* or the *National Enquirer*.

Deciding on media timing

An advertiser must also decide how to schedule the advertising over the course of a year. Suppose sales of a product peak in December and drop in March (for winter sports gear, for instance). The firm can vary its advertising to follow the seasonal pattern, oppose the seasonal pattern, or be the same all year. Most firms do some seasonal advertising. For example, confectionery manufacturers run special ads for their sweets for almost every holiday and 'season', from Christmas, to Easter to Halloween. Moonpig.com, the online customised greetings card producer, is likely to advertise more heavily before major holidays or special days, such as Christmas, Easter, Mothers'

Day, Fathers' Day and Valentine's Day. Some marketers do *only* seasonal advertising: For instance, P&G advertises its cold remedies only during the annual cold and flu season.

Finally, the advertiser must choose the pattern of the ads. *Continuity* means scheduling ads evenly within a given period. *Pulsing* means scheduling ads unevenly over a given time period. Thus, 52 ads could either be scheduled at one per week during the year or pulsed in several bursts. The idea behind pulsing is to advertise heavily for a short period to build awareness that carries over to the next advertising period. Those who favour pulsing feel that it can be used to achieve the same impact as a steady schedule but at a much lower cost. However, some media planners believe that although pulsing achieves minimal awareness, it sacrifices depth of advertising communications.

Today's online and social media let advertisers create ads that respond to events in real time. For example, luxury car brand Lexus recently introduced a new model through live streaming from the North American International Auto Show via Facebook's News Feed. Some 100,000 people watched the introduction live in only the first ten minutes; another 600,000 viewed it online within the next few days. Biscuit brand Oreos reacted in a timely way to a power failure during the US Super Bowl XLVII with the darkness-related 'You can still dunk in the dark' tweet ad. The fast-reaction ad was retweeted and favourited thousands of times in only 15 minutes.[32]

Evaluating advertising effectiveness and the return on advertising investment

Measuring advertising effectiveness and the **return on advertising investment** has become a hot issue for most companies, especially in the tight economic environment. Even in a recovering economy with marketing budgets again on the rise, like consumers, advertisers are still pinching their pennies and spending conservatively. A less friendly economy 'has obligated us all to pinch pennies all the more tightly and squeeze blood from a rock', says one advertising executive.[33] That leaves top management at many companies asking their marketing managers, 'How do we know that we're spending the right amount on advertising?' and 'What return are we getting on our advertising investment?'

Advertisers should regularly evaluate two types of advertising results: the communication effects, and the sales and profit effects. Measuring the *communication effects* of an ad or ad campaign tells whether the media are communicating the ad message well. Individual ads can be tested before or after they are run. Before an ad is placed, an advertiser can show it to consumers, ask how they like it, and measure message recall or attitude changes resulting from it. After an ad is run, an advertiser can measure how the ad affected consumer recall or product awareness, knowledge and preference. Pre- and post-evaluations of communication effects can be made for entire ad campaigns as well.

Advertisers have gotten pretty good at measuring the communication effects of their ads and ad campaigns. However, *sales and profit* effects of advertising are often much harder to measure. For example, what sales and profits are produced by an ad campaign that increases brand awareness by 20 per cent and brand preference by 10 per cent? Sales and profits are affected by many factors other than advertising – such as product features, price and availability.

One way to measure the sales and profit effects of advertising is to compare past sales and profits with past advertising expenditures. Another way is through experiments. For example, to test the effects of different advertising spending levels, Coca-Cola could vary the amount it spends on advertising in different market areas and measure the differences in the resulting sales and profit levels. More complex experiments could be designed to include other variables, such as differences in the ads or media used.

However, because so many factors affect advertising effectiveness, some controllable and others not, measuring the results of advertising spending remains an inexact science. For example, dozens of advertisers spend lavishly on high-profile ads around major sporting events each year. Although they sense that the returns are worth the sizable investment, few can actually measure or prove it. One study by the Association of National Advertisers in the US asked advertising managers if they would be able to 'forecast the impact on sales' of a 10 per cent cut in advertising

Return on advertising investment—The net return on advertising investment divided by the costs of the advertising investment.

spending. Sixty-three per cent said no. Another recent survey found that more than one-third of the surveyed firms have made no effort at all to measure marketing ROI, and another one-third have been working on it for less than two years.[34]

'Marketers are tracking all kinds of data and they still can't answer basic questions' about advertising accountability, says a marketing analyst, 'because they don't have real models and metrics by which to make sense of it'. Advertisers are measuring 'everything they can, and that ranges from how many people respond to an ad to how many sales are closed and then trying to hook up those two end pieces,' says another analyst. 'The tough part is, my goodness, we've got so much data. How do we sift through it?'[35] Thus, although the situation is improving as marketers seek more answers, managers often must rely on large doses of judgement along with quantitative analysis when assessing advertising performance.

Other advertising considerations

In developing advertising strategies and programmes, the company must address two additional questions. First, how will the company organise its advertising function – who will perform which advertising tasks? Second, how will the company adapt its advertising strategies and programmes to the complexities of international markets?

Organising for advertising

Different companies organise in different ways to handle advertising. In small companies, advertising might be handled by someone in the sales department. Large companies have advertising departments whose job it is to set the advertising budget, work with the ad agency, and handle other advertising not done by the agency. Most large companies use outside advertising agencies because they offer several advantages.

Advertising agency—A marketing services firm that assists companies in planning, preparing, implementing and evaluating all or portions of their advertising programmes.

How does an **advertising agency** work? Advertising agencies were originated in the mid-to-late 1800s by salespeople and brokers who worked for the media and received a commission for selling advertising space to companies. As time passed, the salespeople began to help customers prepare their ads. Eventually, they formed agencies and grew closer to the advertisers than to the media.

Today's agencies employ specialists who can often perform advertising tasks better than the company's own staff can. Agencies also bring an outside point of view to solving the company's problems, along with lots of experience from working with different clients and situations. So, today, even companies with strong advertising departments of their own use advertising agencies.

Some ad agencies are huge. In recent years, many agencies have grown by gobbling up other agencies, thus creating huge agency holding companies. The largest of these 'mega-groups' in the world is London-based WPP, employing around 165,000 people in 3,000 offices across 110 countries. WPP includes several large advertising, PR and promotion agencies – among them Millward Brown, Grey, Burson-Marsteller, Hill & Knowlton, JWT, Ogilvy & Mather, TNS, Young & Rubicam and Cohn & White – with combined worldwide revenues of £10.4 billion and billings of £44.4 billion. WPP is closely followed by the Paris-based Publicis Groupe, which had global revenues of €7.3 billion in 2014 from: its global network including Saatchi & Saatchi and Leo Burnett Worldwide, its creative agencies including Fallon Worldwide and Bartle Bogie Hegarty, and its digital and media businesses including Sapient Corporation, Rosetta and ZenithOptiMedia. Around half Publicis revenues come from digital activities and high-growth emerging countries.

Most large advertising agencies have the staff and resources to handle all phases of an ad campaign for their clients, from creating a marketing plan to developing ad campaigns and preparing, placing and evaluating ads and other brand content. Smaller advertising agencies tend to specialise in particular countries or types of communications, such as online. Large brands commonly employ several agencies that handle everything from mass-media advertising campaigns to shopper marketing and social media content.

International advertising decisions

International advertisers face many complexities not encountered by domestic advertisers. The most basic issue concerns the degree to which global advertising should be adapted to the unique characteristics of various country markets.

Some large advertisers have attempted to support their global brands with highly standardised worldwide advertising, with campaigns that work as well in Bangkok as they do in Bolton. For example, McDonald's unifies its creative elements and brand presentation under the familiar 'I'm lovin' it' theme in all its 100-plus markets worldwide. Coca-Cola pulls advertising together for its flagship brand under the theme, 'Open happiness'. And Visa coordinates worldwide advertising for its debit and credit cards under the 'more people go with Visa' creative platform, which works as well in Korea as it does in the United States or Europe.

In recent years, the increased popularity of online social networks and video sharing has boosted the need for advertising standardisation for global brands. Most big marketing and ad campaigns include a large online presence. Connected consumers can now zip easily across borders via the Internet and social media, making it difficult for advertisers to roll out adapted campaigns in a controlled, orderly fashion. As a result, at the very least, most global consumer brands coordinate their websites internationally. For example, visit the McDonald's websites from Germany to Jordan to China. You'll find the golden arches logo, the 'I'm lovin it' logo and jingle, a Big Mac equivalent, and maybe even Ronald McDonald himself.

Standardisation produces many benefits – lower advertising costs, greater global advertising coordination and a more consistent worldwide image. But it also has drawbacks. Most importantly, it ignores the fact that country markets differ greatly in their cultures, demographics and economic conditions. Thus, most international advertisers 'think globally but act locally'. They develop global advertising *strategies* that make their worldwide efforts more efficient and consistent. Then they adapt their *programmes* to make them more responsive to consumer needs and expectations within local markets. For example, although VISA employs its 'Everywhere you want to be' theme globally, ads in specific locales employ local language and inspiring local imagery that make the theme relevant to the local markets in which they appear.

And Snickers runs similar versions of its 'You're not you when you're hungry' ads in 80 different countries, from the United States and the United Kingdom to Mexico, Australia and even Russia. No matter what the country, the ads strike a common human emotion that everyone can relate to – people get out of sorts and do uncharacteristic things when they are hungry. A Snickers bar can help them get back to being their real selves. Snickers lets local markets make adjustments for local languages and personalities. Otherwise, the ads are similar worldwide.[36]

Global advertisers face several special problems. For instance, advertising media costs and availability differ vastly from country to country. Countries also differ in the extent to which they regulate ad practices. Many countries have extensive systems of laws restricting how much a company can spend on advertising, the media used, the nature of advertising claims, and other aspects of the programme. Such restrictions often require advertisers to adapt their campaigns from country to country.

For example, alcohol products cannot be advertised in India or in Muslim countries. In many countries, such as Sweden and Canada, junk food ads are banned from children's television programming. To play it safe, McDonald's advertises itself as a family restaurant in Sweden. Comparative ads, although acceptable and even common in the United States and Canada, are less commonly used in the United Kingdom and are actually illegal in India and Brazil. China bans sending e-mail for advertising purposes to people without their permission, and all advertising e-mail that is sent must be titled 'advertisement'.

China also has restrictive censorship rules for TV and radio advertising; for example, the words *the best* are banned, as are ads that 'violate social customs' or present women in 'improper ways'. McDonald's once avoided government sanctions in China by publicly apologising for an ad that crossed cultural norms by showing a customer begging for a discount. Similarly, Coca-Cola's Indian subsidiary was forced to end a promotion that offered prizes, such as a trip to Hollywood, because it violated India's established trade practices by encouraging customers to 'gamble'.

Thus, although advertisers may develop global strategies to guide their overall advertising efforts, specific programmes must usually be adapted to meet local cultures and customs, media characteristics and regulations.

PUBLIC RELATIONS

Author comment

Not long ago, PR was considered a marketing stepchild because of its limited marketing use. That situation is changing fast, however, as more marketers recognise PR's brand-building power.

Another major mass-promotion tool is **public relations** (PR) – engaging and building good relationships with the company's various publics by obtaining favourable publicity; building up a good corporate image; and handling or heading off unfavourable rumours, stories and events. PR specialists may perform any or all of the following functions:[37]

- *Press relations or press agency*. Creating and placing newsworthy information in the news media to attract attention to a person, product or service.
- *Product publicity*. Publicising specific products.
- *Public affairs*. Building and maintaining national or local community relationships.
- *Lobbying*. Building and maintaining relationships with law-makers and government departments to influence legislation and regulation.
- *Investor relations*. Maintaining relationships with shareholders and others in the financial community.
- *Development*. Working with donors or members of non-profit organisations to gain financial or volunteer support.

Public relations (PR)—
Building a good reputation with the company's various publics by obtaining favourable publicity; building up a good corporate image; and handling or heading off unfavourable rumours, stories and events.

PR is used to promote products, people, places, ideas, activities, organisations and even nations. Companies use PR to build good relationships with consumers, investors, the media and their communities. Industry associations have used PR to rebuild interest in declining commodities, such as eggs, apples, potatoes and milk. Even government organisations use PR to build awareness – for example, of heart disease, poor diet, alcohol consumption, smoking issues.

The role and impact of PR

PR can have a strong impact on public awareness at a much lower cost than advertising can. When using public relations, the company does not pay for the space or time in the media. Rather, it pays for the staff to develop and circulate information and manage events. If the company develops an interesting story or event, it could be picked up by several different media, having the same effect as advertising that would cost much more. And it would have more credibility than advertising – PR has the power to engage consumers and make them a part of the brand story.

PR results can sometimes be spectacular. Consider the launch of Apple's iPad:[38]

Apple's iPad was one of the most successful new-product launches in history. The funny thing: whereas most big product launches are accompanied by huge pre-launch advertising campaigns, Apple pulled this one off with no advertising. None at all. Instead, it simply fed the PR fire. It built buzz months in advance by distributing iPads for early reviews, feeding the offline and online press with tempting tidbits, and offering fans an early online peek at thousands of new iPad apps that would be available. At launch time, it fanned the flames with a cameo on the US TV sitcom *Modern Family*, a flurry of launch-day appearances on TV talk shows, and other launch-day events. In the process, through PR alone, the iPad launch generated unbounded consumer excitement, a media frenzy, and long lines outside retail stores on launch day. Apple sold more than 300,000 of the sleek gadgets on the first day alone and more than 2 million in the first two months – even as demand outstripped supply. Apple repeated the feat a year later with the equally successful launch of iPad 2, which sold close to 1 million devices the weekend of its launch.

Despite its potential strengths, PR is sometimes described as a marketing stepchild because of its often limited and scattered use. If there is a PR department, it is often located at corporate headquarters or PR may be handled by a third-party agency. Its staff is so busy dealing with various publics – shareholders, employees, politicians and the press – that PR programmes to support product marketing objectives may be ignored. Moreover, marketing managers and PR practitioners do not always speak the same language. Whereas many PR practitioners see their jobs as simply communicating, marketing managers tend to be much more interested in how advertising and PR affect brand building, sales and profits, and customer engagement and relationships.

This situation is changing, however. Although public relations still captures only a small portion of the overall marketing budgets of many firms, PR can be a powerful brand-building tool. Especially in this digital age, the lines between advertising and PR are becoming more and more blurred. For example, are brand websites, blogs, brand videos and social media activities advertising or PR efforts? All are both. And as the use of shared digital content grows rapidly, PR may play a bigger role in brand content management. More than any other department, PR has always been responsible for creating relevant marketing content that draws consumers to a brand rather than pushing messages out. 'Knowing where influence and conversations are to be found is PR's stock in trade,' says one expert. 'PR pros are an organisation's master storytellers. In a word, they *do* content.'[39] The point is that PR should work hand in hand with advertising within an integrated marketing communications programme to help build customer engagement and relationships.

The role and impact of PR: through PR alone Apple's iPad launch generated unbounded consumer excitement throughout the world.
Source: DAMIEN MEYER/AFP/ Getty Images

Major public relations tools

PR encompasses several tools. One of the major tools is *news*. PR professionals find or create favourable news stories about the company and its products or people. Sometimes news stories occur naturally; sometimes the PR person can suggest events or activities that would create news. *Speeches* can also create product and company publicity. Increasingly, company executives must field questions from the media or give talks at trade associations or sales meetings, and these events can either build or hurt the company's image. Another common PR tool is *special events*, ranging from news conferences, press tours, grand openings and fireworks displays to laser light shows, multimedia presentations or educational programmes designed to reach and interest target publics.

PR people also prepare *written materials* to reach and influence their target markets. These materials include annual reports, brochures, articles and company newsletters and magazines. *Audiovisual materials*, such as slide-and-sound programmes, DVDs and online videos are being used increasingly as communication tools. *Corporate identity materials* can also help create a corporate identity that the public immediately recognises. Logos, stationery, brochures, signs, business forms, business cards, buildings, uniforms and company cars and trucks all become marketing tools when they are attractive, distinctive and memorable. Finally, companies can improve public goodwill by contributing money and time to *public service activities*.

As discussed previously, the web and social media are also an increasingly important PR channels. websites, blogs and social media such as YouTube, Facebook, Pinterest and Twitter are providing interesting new ways to reach and engage more people. 'The core strengths of public relations – the ability to tell a story and spark conversation – play well into the nature of such social media,' says a PR expert.

By itself, a company's website is an important PR vehicle. Consumers and other publics often visit websites for information or entertainment. Websites can also be ideal for handling crisis situations, such as computer network malfunctions at banks, product recalls of electrical appliances, or product safety alerts for cars.

As with the other promotion tools, in considering when and how to use product PR, management should set PR objectives, choose the PR messages and vehicles, implement the PR plan, and evaluate the results. The firm's PR should be blended smoothly with other promotion activities within the company's overall integrated marketing communications effort. The company case at the end of the chapter looks at Coca-Cola's PR and customer engagement strategy.

OBJECTIVES REVIEW AND KEY TERMS

Companies must do more than make good products; they have to inform consumers about product benefits and carefully position products in consumers' minds. To do this, they must master *advertising* and *public relations*.

OBJECTIVE 1 Define the role of advertising in the promotion mix (pp. 437–438)

Advertising – the use of paid media by a seller to inform, persuade and remind buyers about its products or its organisation – is an important promotion tool for communicating the value that marketers create for their customers. Advertising takes many forms and has many uses. Although advertising is employed mostly by business firms, a wide range of not-for-profit organisations, professionals and public agencies also employ advertising to promote their causes to various target publics. *PR* – gaining favourable publicity and creating a favourable company image – is the least used of the major promotion tools, although it has great potential for building consumer awareness and preference.

OBJECTIVE 2 Describe the major decisions involved in developing an advertising programme (pp. 438–454)

Advertising decision making involves making decisions about the advertising objectives, budget, message and media, and evaluation of the results. Advertisers should set clear target, task and timing *objectives*, whether the aim is to inform, engage, persuade or remind buyers. Advertising's goal is to move consumers through the buyer-readiness stages discussed in Chapter 14. Some advertising is designed to move people to immediate action. However, many of the ads you see today focus on building or strengthening long-term customer engagement and relationships. The advertising *budget* depends on many factors. No matter what method is used, setting the advertising budget is no easy task.

Advertising strategy consists of two major elements: creating advertising *messages* and selecting advertising *media*. The *message decision* calls for planning a message strategy and executing it effectively. Good messages are especially important in today's costly and cluttered advertising environment. Just to gain and hold attention, today's messages must be better planned, more imaginative, more entertaining and more rewarding to consumers. In fact, many marketers are now subscribing to a new merging of advertising and entertainment, dubbed *Madison & Vine*. The *media decision* involves defining reach, frequency and impact goals; choosing major media types; selecting media vehicles; and choosing media timing. Message and media decisions must be closely coordinated for maximum campaign effectiveness.

Finally, *evaluation* calls for evaluating the communication and sales effects of advertising before, during and after ads are placed. Advertising accountability has become a hot issue for most companies. Increasingly, top management is asking: 'What return are we getting on our advertising investment?' and 'How do we know that we're spending the right amount?' Other important advertising issues involve *organising* for advertising and dealing with the complexities of *international advertising*.

OBJECTIVE 3 Define the role of PR in the promotion mix (pp. 454–455)

Public relations or PR – gaining favourable publicity and creating a favourable company image – is the least used of the major promotion tools, although it has great potential for building consumer awareness and preference.

PR is used to promote products, people, places, ideas, activities, organisations and even nations. Companies use PR to build good relationships with consumers, investors, the media and their communities. PR can have a strong impact on public awareness at a much lower cost than advertising can, and PR results can sometimes be spectacular. Although PR still captures only a small portion of the overall marketing budgets of most firms, PR is playing an increasingly important brand-building role. In the digital age, the lines between advertising and PR are becoming more and more blurred.

OBJECTIVE 4 Explain how companies use PR to communicate with their publics (pp. 455–456)

Companies use PR to communicate with their publics by setting PR objectives, choosing PR messages and vehicles, implementing the PR plan and evaluating PR results. To accomplish these goals, PR professionals use several tools, such as *news*, *speeches* and *special events*. They also prepare *written*, *audiovisual* and *corporate identity materials* and contribute money and time to *public service activities*. The Internet has also become an increasingly important PR channel, as websites, blogs and social media are providing interesting new ways to reach more people.

NAVIGATING THE KEY TERMS

OBJECTIVE 1
Advertising (p. 437)

OBJECTIVE 2
Advertising objective (p. 438)
Advertising budget (p. 440)

Advertising strategy (p. 441)
Madison & Vine (p. 442)
Creative concept (p. 444)
Execution style (p. 445)
Advertising media (p. 447)

Return on advertising investment (p. 451)
Advertising agency (p. 452)

OBJECTIVE 3
Public relations (p. 454)

DISCUSSION AND CRITICAL THINKING

Discussion questions

15-1 Describe the major elements of a firm's advertising strategy. (AACSB: Communication)

15-2 Compare and contrast advertainment and branded entertainment. (AACSB: Communication)

15-3 Why has measuring advertising effectiveness become so important? What types of advertising results do marketers measure and what are the issues related to this assessment? (AACSB: Communication)

15-4 What are the role and functions of public relations within an organisation? (AACSB: Communication)

15-5 Discuss the tools used by public relations professionals. Is public relations free promotion for a company? (AACSB: Communication)

Critical-thinking exercises

15-6 Any message can be presented using different execution styles. Select a brand and target audience and design two advertisements, each using a different execution style to deliver the same message to the target audience, but in a different way. Identify the types of execution styles you are using and present your advertisements. (AACSB: Communication; Reflective thinking)

15-7 According to a recently released study, mascots create more social media buzz than do celebrity endorsers. In a small group, find an example of a company using a mascot to create social media buzz and suggest ways the company can create even more buzz. How is social media buzz measured? (AACSB: Communication; Use of IT; Reflective thinking)

15-8 The Public Relations Society of America (PRSA) in the USA, and the Chartered Institute of Public Relations in the UK, make awards for the best public relations campaigns in their countries. Visit www.prsa.org/Awards/Search, or www.cipr.co.uk/content/awards-events/excellence-awards, and review several case reports of previous winners. What does the field of public relations seem to encompass? Write a report on one of the award winners, focusing on marketing-related activities. (AACSB: Communication; Use of IT; Reflective thinking)

Mini-cases and applications

Online, mobile and social media marketing: Facebook audience network

Facebook has more than a billion monthly users, and a large majority of users typically visit the site daily on a mobile device. One day in August 2015, Facebook had a billion visits on a single day – equivalent to one person in seven on the planet visiting the site. What started as an online social network, allowing people to connect with each other, has transformed into a massive media mogul that promises to be a game-changer in mobile advertising. Facebook has announced its new mobile ad platform called Audience Network to deliver targeted mobile ads for advertisers. While there are other mobile ad platforms (Google is the dominant player), Facebook has a treasure trove of data that is useful for advertisers. Google is strong in search data, but Facebook is part of our lives. Facebook has been placing ads on its site for advertisers, but now it will be pushing those ads to third-party apps. This is a win–win–win situation for advertisers, app developers and Facebook, because advertisers get their mobile ads to people based on very personal information, app developers get ad revenue, and Facebook gets a cut of the ad revenue for placing the ad. And it's no small cut – in just the last quarter of 2013, Facebook earned $1.3 billion in mobile ad revenue. That's 60 per cent of Facebook's overall ad revenue.

15-9 Compare and contrast Facebook's, Google's and Twitter's ad networks. Which is most effective for advertisers? (AACSB: Communication; Reflective thinking)

15-10 Mobile advertising is one of the fastest growing sectors of digital advertising, but how is mobile advertising effectiveness measured? Research this issue and create a report of your findings. (AACSB: Communication; Reflective thinking)

Marketing ethics: Amazon's dronerama

On the eve of the biggest e-commerce shopping day of the year in the US, Amazon's normally secretive founder and CEO, Jeff Bezos, scored a public relations victory by going on CBS's *60 Minutes* programme to unveil the company's Prime Air unmanned aircraft project to deliver packages to consumers' doorsteps. Forget that it couldn't be implemented because many countries' regulators do not allow such use of drones in their air-space, and that it will most likely be 2026 before drone delivery might even be possible. The interview set off the 'Dronerama', as some have called it. The next morning – Cyber Monday – the media were abuzz about drone delivery, with news organisations and Internet sites throughout the world replaying the video of Amazon's cool drone delivering a package. The normally hard-hitting *60 Minutes* interview has been criticised because the interviewer seemed to gush all over Bezos and ignore other controversial issues, such as working conditions at Amazon. The same interviewer further eulogised Amazon during the *60 Minutes* overtime digital supplement to the show. Critics believe the normally unattainable Bezos called the shots in return for appearing on the show. The 'Dronerama' not only got Amazon on every cyber shoppers' lips across the world, and on that all-important

US online shopping day, it seemed to take some of the wind out of the sails of a recently released critical book about Bezos at a time when Amazon needed customers the most.

15-11 Watch the *60 Minutes* interview at www.cbsnews.com/news/amazons-jeff-bezos-looks-to-the-future/. Is it ethical for companies to use the media this way to gain favourable exposure? Did Jeff Bezos acknowledge the fact that drones are not feasible any time soon? (AACSB: Communication; Ethical reasoning; Reflective thinking)

15-12 Create a presentation of the worldwide publicity Amazon received as a result of the *60 Minutes* interview. Would you judge this campaign a success or failure? (AACSB: Communication; Use of IT; Reflective thinking)

Marketing by the numbers: C3, CPM and CPP

Nielsen ratings are very important to both advertisers and television programmers because the cost of television advertising time is based on these ratings. A show's rating is the number of households in Nielsen's sample that are tuned to that show, divided by the number of television-owning households – for example, 115.6 million in the United States. One rating point represents 1 per cent of the households (HHS) in the TV market. Nielsen's TV ratings are referred to as C3 and measure viewers who watch commercials live or watch recorded commercials up to three days later. A common measure of advertising efficiency is cost per thousand (CPM), which is the ad cost per thousand potential audience contacts. Advertisers also assess the cost per rating point by dividing the ad cost by the rating (CPP). These numbers are used to assess the efficiency of a media buy. Use the following average price and rating information for programmes that are shown at the 8.00 pm hour on television to answer the questions:

Programme	Cost per: 30 Spot	C3 Rating
Sunday Night Football	$594,000	7.9
The Big Bang Theory	$317,000	5.1
The Voice	$264,575	3.9
How I Met Your Mother	$168,435	3.2
Agents of S.H.I.E.L.D.	$169,730	3.1

15-13 How many households are expected to watch each programme? (AACSB: Communication; Analytical reasoning)

15-14 Calculate the cost per thousand (CPM) and cost per point (CPP) for each programme. How should advertisers use these measures when planning a television media buy? (AACSB: Communication; Analytical reasoning; Reflective thinking)

REFERENCES

[1] 'Meerkat makes millions', *Sunday Times*, 17 October 2010, S3, p. 1; Giles Hattersley, 'How to hit the Jackpot: Simples!', *Sunday Times*, 5 December 2010, S1, p. 24; Richard Gold, 'The public image: comparethemarket. com', *Financial Times*, 11 January 2010, www.ft.com, accessed February 2012; Tim Bradshaw, 'Cute, cuddly and commercial', *Financial Times*, 22 June 2010, www.ft.com, accessed February 2012; Graham Ruddick, 'Meerkat Movies will be explosive', *Daily Telegraph*, 21 March 2015.

[2] Figures extracted from www.zenithoptimedia.com/wp-content/uploads/2014/12/Adspend-forecasts-December-2014-executive-summary.pdf, accessed July 2015.

[3] See Congressional Research Services, Report for Congress: www.fas.org/sgp/crs/misc/R41681.pdf, accessed July 2015.

[4] See www.theguardian.com/media/2014/may/14/governemnet-ad-spend-deficit-scottish-referendum-afghanistan, accessed July 2015.

[5] See, for example, www.dailymail.co.uk/news/article-2438112/EUs-2-4bn-ad-budget-higher-Coca-Colas-Huge-revealed-new-fiscal-fact-book-details-44-diplomats-Barbados.html, accessed July 2015.

[6] See http://www.out-law.com/page-11979, accessed February 2012.

[7] 'Take the Bing it on challenge', 6 September 2012, www.bing.com/blogs/site_blogs/b/search/archive/2012/09/06/challengeannounce. aspx; www.bingiton.com, accessed June 2014; Alex Kantrowitz, 'Microsoft's Google bashing is having an impact', *Advertising Age*, 14 October 2013, p. 24; and www.scroggled.com/Home, accessed September 2014.

[8] For these and other examples of comparative advertising, see Emily Bryson York and Natalie Zmuda, 'So sue me: why big brands are taking claims to court', *Advertising Age*, 4 January 2010, pp. 1, 23; 'AT&T ends Verizon ad lawsuit', *Techweb*, 2 December 2009; 'Pepsi suing Coca-Cola over Powerade ads', *New York Times*, 13 April 2009, accessed at www.nyt.com; Emily Bryson York, 'Book of tens: nasty comparative campaigns of 2009', *Advertising Age*, 14 December 2009, accessed at http://adage.com/print?article_id=141025; and Isabella Soscia, Simona Girolamo and Bruno Busacca, 'The effect of comparison advertising on consumer perceptions: similarity or differentiation?' *Journal of Business and Psychology*, March 2010, pp. 109–118.

[9] For more on advertising budgets, see Ronald Lane, Karen King and Thomas Russell, *Kleppner's Advertising Procedure*, 18th ed. (Upper Saddle River, NJ: Prentice Hall, 2011), Chapter 6.

[10] See Jean Halliday, 'Thinking big takes Audi from obscure to awesome', *Advertising Age*, 2 February 2009, http://adage.com/print/134234; Chad Thomas and Andreas Cremer, 'Audi feels a need for speed in the US', *Bloomberg Businessweek*, 22 November 2010, p. 1; and Kyle Stock, 'Audi swipes BMW's luxury crown. Keeping it will be harder', *Bloomberg BusinessWeek*, 11 March 2014, www.businessweek.com/articles/2014–03–11/where-audi-will-win-or-lose-the-luxury-car-race.

[11] Justin Bachman, 'The ugly numbers behind unbundled cable', *Bloomberg Businessweek*, 6 December 2013, www.business week.com/articles/2013–12–06/the-ugly-numbers-behindunbundled-cable-tv; and Thad McIlroy, 'The future of magazines', *The Future of Publishing*, 10 July 2013, http://thefutureofpublishing.com/industries/the-future-of-magazines/.

[12] Kelsey Libert and Kristen Tynski, 'Research: the emotions that make marketing campaigns go viral', HBR Blog Network, 24 October 2013, http://blogs.hbr.org/2013/10/research-the-emotions-that-make-marketing-campaigns-go-viral/.

[13] 'Results of 4A's 2011 television production cost survey', 22 January 2013, www.aaaa.org/news/bulletins/pages/tvprod_01222013.aspx; Sam Thielman, 'The new hour is 43 minutes long', *Adweek*, 24 June 2013, p. 12; Jeanine Poggi, 'TV ad prices', *Advertising Age*, 20 October 2013, http://adage.com/print/244832; and 'Who bought what in Super Bowl XLVIII', *Advertising Age*, 3 February 2014, http://adage.com/print/244024.

[14] 'Advertising in the U.S.: Synovate Global Survey shows Internet, innovation and online privacy a must', 3 December 2009, accessed at www.synovate.com/news/article/2009/12/advertising-in-the-us-synovate-global-survey-shows-internet-innovation-and-online-privacy-a-must.html; and Katy Bachman, 'Survey: clutter causing TV ads to lack effectiveness', *MediaWeek*, 8 February 2010.

[15] Caleb Garling, 'How television advertising deals with DVRs destroying their business', *SFGate*, 27 December 2013, http://blog.sfgate.com/techchron/2013/12/27/dvr-advertisements/; and 'No hardware, no problem: VOD lets users time-shift with ease', 9 September 2013, www.nielsen.com/us/en/newswire/2013/no-hardware-no-problem-vod-lets-users-time-shift-with-ease.html.

[16] 'Real beauty shines through: Dove wins Titanium Grand Prix, 163 million views on YouTube', *Google: Think Insights*, June2013, www.thinkwithgoogle.com/case-studies/dove-real-beauty-sketches.html; Nina Bahadur, 'Dove 'Real Beauty' campaign turns 10: How a brand tried to change the conversation about female beauty', *Huffington Post*, 6 February 2014, www.huffingtonpost.com/2014/01/21/dove-real-beauty-campaign-turns-10_n_4575940.tml; and www.youtube.com/watch?v=XpaOjMXyJGk, accessed June 2014.

[17] See Alessandra Stanley, 'Commercials you can't zap', *New York Times*, 7 June 2009, p. MT1; Sam Schechner and Suzanne Vranica, 'IPad gets star turn in television comedy', *Wall Street Journal*, 2 April 2010, p. B8; and Rupal Parekh, 'Why long-form ads are the wave of the future', *Advertising Age*, 3 May 2010, accessed at http://adage.com/madisonandvine/article?article_id=143603.

[18] Abe Sauer, 'The envelope, please: The 2014 Brandcameo Product Placement Awards', BrandChannel, 27 February 2014, www.brandchannel.com/home/post/2014/02/27/140227–2014-Brandcameo-Product-Placement-Awards.aspx#continue.

[19] 'Why *The Lego Movie* is the perfect piece of product placement', *A.V. Club*, 11 February 2014, www.avclub.com/article/whythe-lego-movie-is-the-perfect-piece-of-product-201102.

[20] David Gelles and Tim Bradshaw, 'When props pay for production', *Financial Times*, 1 March 2011, p. 16.

[21] Aaron O. Patrick, 'Fallon in London hones an unconventional edge', *Wall Street Journal*, 11 December 2007, p. 6; Jenny Wiggins and Maggie Urry, 'Cadbury benefits from gorilla tactics', *Financial Times*, 12 December 2007, p. 23; Carlos Grande, 'Aping of ad helps to drum up chocolate brand interest', *Financial Times*, 12 December 2007, p. 23.

[22] Jaya Narain, 'IKEA declares war on our garden gnomes. . . Call in Elf and Safety!', *Daily Mail*, 29 May 2013, p. 21.

[23] Adapted from information found in Bob Garfield, 'How etsy made us rethink consumer-generated ads', *Advertising Age*, 21 September 2009, p. 4.

[24] For these and other examples, see David Gianatasio, 'Ad of the day: cute, quirky Chevy commercial on the Oscars was made for $4,000', *Adweek*, 3 March 2014, www.adweek.com/print/156071; 'Purina Pro Plan debuts new consumer-generated ad during Westminster Kennel Club Dog Show', *PRNewswire*, 11 February 2013; and 'Taco Bell commissions

user-generated YouTube ads to promote new fiery Doritos Locos Taco', *Viral Gains*, www.viralgains.com/2013/08/taco-bell-commissions-user-generated-youtube-adspromote-fiery-doritos-locos-taco/, accessed September 2014.

25 Quotes and other information from Lauren Drell, 'User generated content: lessons from 4 killer ad campaigns', *American Express Open Forum*, 28 January 2013, www.openforum.com/articles/lessons-from-4-killer-ugc-campaigns/; and http://thesweatlife.lululemon.com/, accessed June 2014.

26 For more on consumer-generated advertising, see Emma Hall, 'Most winning creative work involves consumer participation', *Advertising Age*, 6 January 2010, accessed at http://adage.com/print?article_id=141329; Stuart Elliott, 'Do-it-yourself Super Ads', *New York Times*, 8 February 2010; Michael Learmonth, 'Brands team up for user-generated-ad contests', *Advertising Age*, 23 March 2009, p. 8; and Rich Thomaselli, 'If consumer is your agency, it's time for review', *Advertising Age*, 17 May 2010, p. 2.

27 Brian Steinberg, 'Viewer-engagement rankings signal change for TV industry', *Advertising Age*, 10 May 2010, p. 12.

28 Joe Tripoti, 'Coca-Cola marketing shifts from impressions to expressions', 27 April 2011, http://blogs.hbr.org/cs/2011/04/coca-colas_marketing_shift_fro.html; Devon Glenn, 'Coca-Cola on social content: "expressions are more valuable than impressions"', *Social Times*, 11 September 2012, http://socialtimes.com/coca-cola-on-social-content-expressions-are-more-valuable-thanimpressions_b104547; and Anna Rudenko, 'Coca-Cola USA prompting youngsters to contribute their "Ahh moments"', *POPSOP*, 24 March 2014, http://popsop.com/2014/03/coca-cola-usaprompting-youngsters-to-contribute-their-ahh-coke-moments/.

29 Jack Grimston, 'We're no mugs, we've sold our faces', *Sunday Times*, 4 March 2012, S1, p. 11.

30 For these and other multi-tasking stats, See 'Nielsen: most tablet/smartphone users watch TV at same time', *Electronista*, 5 April 2012, www.electronista.com/articles/12/04/05/simultaneous.use.prevalent.in.us.market/; Lucia Moses, 'Second-screen effect', *Adweek*, 1 April 2013, pp. 16–17; and 'TiVo social media and multitasking survey', *Yahoo! Finance*, 23 January 2013, http://finance.yahoo.com/news/tivo-social-media-multitasking-survey-120600364.html.

31 *Forbes* and *Bloomberg Businessweek* cost and circulation data found online at www.bloombergmedia.com/magazine/businessweek/rates/ and www.forbesmedia.com/forbes-magazine-rates/, accessed September 2014.

32 For these and other examples, see Christopher Heine, 'Lexus nabs 100K video views on Facebook – in 10 minutes', *Adweek*, 23 January 2013, www.adweek.com/news/technology/print/146726; Matt McGee, 'Oreo, Audi, and Walgreens Newsjack Super Bowl "Blackout Bowl"', *Marketing Land*, 3 February 2013, http://marketingland.com/oreo-audi-walgreens-market-quickly-duringsuper-bowl-blackout-32407; and 'Arby's slayed the Grammys with this tweet about Pharrell Williams' hat', *Adweek*, 27 January 2014, www.adweek.com/print/155237.

33 Kate Maddox, 'Optimism, accountability, social media top trends', *BtoB*, 18 January 2010, p. 1.

34 See Lawrence A. Crosby, 'Getting serious about marketing ROI', *Marketing Management*, May/June 2009, pp. 10–17.

35 Elliott, 'How effective is this ad, in real numbers? Beats me', p. C8; and 'Taking measure of which metrics matter', *BtoB*, 5 May 2008.

36 See E. J. Schultz, 'Behind the Snickers campaign that launched a global comeback', *Advertising Age*, 4 October 2013, http://adage.com/print/244593; and http://adsoftheworld.com/media/outdoor/snickers_running and http://cargocollective.com/mirceaandronescu/SNICKERS-OOH, accessed September 2014.

37 Based on Glen Broom and Bey-Ling Sha, *Cutlip & Center's Effective Public Relations*, 11th ed. (Upper Saddle River, NJ: Prentice Hall, 2013), Chapter 1.

38 See Geoffrey Fowler and Ben Worthen, 'Buzz powers iPad launch', *Wall Street Journal*, 2 April 2010; 'Apple iPad sales top 2 million since launch', *Tribune-Review* (Pittsburgh), 2 June 2010; 'PR pros must be Apple's iPad as a true game-changer', *PRweek*, May 2010, p. 23; and 'Apple launches new iPad', 7 March 2012, www.apple.com/pr/library/2012/03/07Apple-Launches-New-iPad.html.

39 Sarah Skerik, 'An emerging PR trend: Content PR strategy and tactics', *PR Newswire*, 15 January 2013, http://blog.prnewswire.com/2013/01/15/an-emerging-pr-trend-content-pr-strategy-tactics/.

COMPANY CASE

Public relations and customer engagement at Coca-Cola: from impressions to expressions to transactions

Coca-Cola aims to do much more with public relations than just create passive 'impressions'. It's looking to create customer engagement and inspire customer 'expressions'. According to Coca-Cola's chief marketing officer, Joe Tripodi, the PR goal is to develop 'strongly sharable pieces of communication information that generate huge numbers of impressions online – and then, crucially, lead to expressions from consumers, who join the story and extend it, and then finally to transactions'. That is, Coca-Cola uses PR to engage consumers and start customer conversations that will inspire consumers themselves to extend the brand's theme of open happiness and optimism.

Consider Coca-Cola's recent 'Hug me' campaign, in which the company installed a 'happiness' vending machine overnight at a university in Singapore. The machine had a solid red front and trademark wavy white stripe, but it contained no Coca-Cola logo, no coin slot and no soda selection buttons. Only the words 'Hug me' were visible in large white letters printed in Coca-Cola's famous script. With hidden cameras rolling, Coca-Cola captured the quizzical reactions of passers-by as they first scratched their heads, then slowly approached the machine and, finally, with smiles on their faces, gave it a big hug. Responding to that simple act of happiness, the machine magically dispensed a cold can of Coca-Cola, free of charge.

Coca-Cola's 'Hug me' video shows one person after another hugging the machine, receiving a Coke, and sharing their delight with others. Coca-Cola placed the video online, then stepped back and let the media and consumers carry the story forward. Within only one week's time, the video generated 112 million impressions. Given the low costs of the free Cokes and producing the video, the 'Hug me' campaign resulted in an amazingly low cost per impression. But even more valuable were the extensive customer expressions that followed, such as 'Liking' the video and forwarding it to others. 'The Coca-Cola Hug Machine is a simple idea to spread some happiness,' says a Coca-Cola marketer. 'Our strategy is to deliver doses of happiness in an unexpected, innovative way ... and happiness is contagious.'

The 'Hug me' campaign was only the most recent in a long line of similar conversation-starting PR tactics by Coca-Cola.

One Valentine's Day, the company placed a modified vending machine in the middle of a busy shopping centre that dispensed free Cokes to people who confirmed their 'couple' status with a hug or a kiss. A few years ago, another Coca-Cola Happiness machine placed at a university dispensed everything from free Cokes to popcorn, pizza, flowers, handshakes and Polaroid photos. Making periodic 'jackpot' sounds, the machine dispensed dozens of Cokes and a long plank layered with colourful cupcakes. These unexpected actions not only prompted smiles and cheers, but recipients could hardly wait to share their bounty and the story with anyone and everyone, extending Coke's happiness positioning.

Coca-Cola has fielded many other PR campaigns that employ its 'impressions-expressions-transactions' model to inspire brand conversations. In its 'Project connect' campaign, the company printed 150 common first names on Coke bottles, an exploit that had consumers by the hundreds of thousands rifling through Coca-Cola displays in retail stores looking for their names.

Coca-Cola's long-running Arctic Home campaign employs the power of publicity and shared media to create engagement by connecting the company's brands to a culturally relevant cause. In that campaign, Coca-Cola has partnered with the World Wildlife Fund (WWF) to protect the habitat of polar bears – a cause that fits perfectly with Coke's longstanding use of digitally produced polar bears as 'spokes-critters' in its ads. The Arctic Home campaign goes well beyond clever seasonal ads by integrating PR efforts with virtually every aspect of promotion and marketing. The campaign includes a dedicated website, a smartphone app, a pledge of $3 million to the WWF, advertisements and online videos featuring footage from the IMAX film To the Arctic 3D, and attention-grabbing white Coke cans highlighting the plight of polar bears. In its first year, Arctic Home produced an astounding 1.3 billion impressions, which in turn inspired untold customer engagement and expressions.

Coca-Cola's 'BHAG', or 'big hairy audacious goal', is not just to hold its market share in the soft drink category, where sales have been flat for years, but to double its business by the end of the decade. Public relations and the social media will play a central role in achieving this goal by making customers a part of the brand story and turning them into an army of brand advocates who will carry the Coca-Cola Open Happiness message forward. 'It's not just about pushing stuff out as we've historically done,' says CMO Tripodi. 'We have to create experiences that perhaps are had only by a few but are compelling enough to fuel conversations with many.'

Questions for discussion

1. How would you summarise Coca-Cola's PR strategy in this case and how does it relate to an integrated marketing communications approach?

2. What measures would you take to evaluate the short-term and longer-term effectiveness of the Coca-Cola strategy?

3. What do you see as the disadvantages of a PR-based communications strategy as opposed to a conventional media advertising approach?

4. Has the Coca-Cola communications strategy been effective? Support your answer.

5. To what extent can an engaged brand community protect Coca-Cola from changes in market tastes that favour other kinds of soft drinks and refreshments?

Sources: Tim Nudd, 'Coca-Cola joins the revolution in a world where the mob rules', *Adweek*, 19 June 2012, www.adweek.com/print/141217; 'WWF and the Coca-Cola Company team up to protect polar bears', http://worldwildlife.org/projects/wwf-and-the-coca-cola-company-team-up-to-protect-polar-bears, accessed June 2014; Natalie Zmuda, 'Coca-Cola gets real with polar bears', *Advertising Age*, 25 October 2011, http://adage.com/ print/230632/; Anthony Wing Kosner, 'Hug me: Coca-Cola introduces gesture based marketing in Singapore', *Forbes*, 11 April 2012, www.forbes.com/sites/anthonykosner/2012/04/11/hug-me-coca-cola-introduces-gesture-based-marketing-in-singapore/; 'Cannes Lions 2012: five-points to a great marketing strategy', afaqs.com, 20 June 2012, www.afaqs.com/news/story/34444; and www.youtube.com/watch?feature=endscreen&N-R=1&v=-A-7H4aOhq0 and www.youtube.com/watch?v=D3j_pB3STsQ, accessed September 2014.

CHAPTER SIXTEEN

Personal selling and sales promotion

Chapter preview

In the previous two chapters, you learned about communicating customer value through integrated marketing communications (IMC) and two elements of the promotion mix: advertising and PR. In this chapter, we examine two more IMC elements: personal selling and sales promotion. Personal selling is the interpersonal arm of marketing communications, in which the sales force interacts with customers and prospects to build relationships and make sales. Sales promotion consists of short-term incentives to encourage the purchase or sale of a product or a service. As you read, remember that although this chapter presents personal selling and sales promotion as separate tools, each must be carefully integrated with the other elements of the promotion mix.

First, we can look at a real-life sales force. What is your first reaction when you think of a salesperson or a sales force? Perhaps you think of pushy retail sales assistants, 'yell and sell' television advertising, or the stereotypical smarmy 'used-car salesman'. But such stereotypes simply don't fit the reality of most of today's salespeople – sales professionals who succeed not by taking advantage of customers but by listening to their needs and helping to create solutions. For most companies, personal selling plays an important role in building profitable customer relationships. Consider Procter & Gamble (P&G), whose customer-focused sales force has long been considered one of the most effective in the world.

Objective outline

➤ **Objective 1** Discuss the role of a company's salespeople in creating value for customers and building customer relationships.
Personal selling (pp. 466–469)

➤ **Objective 2** Identify and explain the six major sales force management steps.
Managing the sales force (pp. 470–482)

➤ **Objective 3** Discuss the personal selling process, distinguishing between transaction-oriented marketing and relationship marketing.
The personal selling process (pp. 482–486)

➤ **Objective 4** Explain how sales promotion campaigns are developed and implemented.
Sales promotion (pp. 486–492)

Procter & Gamble

For decades, P&G has been at the top of almost every expert's A-list of outstanding marketing companies. The experts point to P&G's stable of top-selling consumer brands, or that, year in and year out, P&G is the world's largest advertiser. Consumers seem to agree. You will find least one of P&G's blockbuster brands in 99 per cent of all American households; in many homes, there will be a dozen or more familiar P&G products. But P&G is also highly respected for something else – its top-notch, customer-focused sales force.

P&G's sales force has long been an icon for selling at its very best. When it comes to selecting, training and managing salespeople, P&G sets the gold standard. The company employs a massive sales force of more than 5,000 salespeople worldwide. At P&G, however, the company rarely calls it 'sales'. Instead, it's 'Customer Business Development' (CBD). And P&G sales reps aren't 'salespeople'; they are 'CBD managers' or 'CBD account executives'. All this might seem like 'corp-speak', but at P&G the distinction goes to the very core of how selling works.

P&G understands that if its customers don't do well, neither will the company. To grow its own business, therefore, P&G must first grow the business of the retailers that sell its brands to final consumers. And at P&G, the primary responsibility for helping customers grow falls to the sales force. Rather than just selling *to* its retail and wholesale customers, CBD managers partner strategically *with* customers to help develop their business in P&G's product categories. 'We depend on them as much as they depend on us,' says one CBD manager. By partnering with each other, P&G and its customers create 'win–win' relationships that help both to prosper.

Most P&G customers are huge and complex businesses – such as Walmart, Dollar General, Tesco, Metro or Carrefour – with thousands of stores and billions in revenues. Working with and selling to such customers can be a very complex undertaking, more than any single salesperson or sales team could accomplish. Instead, P&G assigns a full CBD team to every large customer account. Each CBD team contains not only salespeople but also a full complement of specialists in every aspect of selling P&G's consumer brands at the retail level.

CBD teams vary in size depending on the customer. For example, P&G's largest single customer, Walmart, which accounts for an amazing 20 per cent of the company's sales, commands a 350-person CBD team. By contrast, the P&G Dollar General team consists of about 30 people. Regardless of size, every CBD team constitutes a complete, multifunctional customer-service unit. Each team includes a CBD manager and several CBD account executives (each responsible for a specific P&G product category), supported by specialists in marketing strategy, product development, operations, information systems, logistics, finance and human resources.

To deal effectively with large accounts, P&G salespeople must be smart, well trained and strategically grounded. They deal daily with high-level retail category buyers who may purchase hundreds of millions of dollars worth of P&G and competing brands annually. It takes a lot more than a friendly smile and a firm handshake to interact with such buyers. Yet individual P&G salespeople can't know everything, and thanks to the CBD sales structure, they don't have to. Instead, as members of a full CBD team, P&G salespeople have at hand all the resources they need to resolve even the most challenging customer problems. 'I have everything I need right here,' says a household care account executive. 'If my customer needs help from us with in-store promotions, I can go right down the hall and talk with someone on my team in marketing about doing some kind of promotional deal. It's that simple.'

Trade fairs and retail demonstrations are ways for P&G to keep in touch with its markets.
Source: Everett Collection/REX/ Shutterstock

CBD involves partnering with customers to jointly identify strategies that create shopper value and satisfaction and drive profitable sales at the store level. When it comes to profitably moving Tide, Pampers, Gillette or other P&G brands off store shelves and into consumers' shopping trolleys, P&G reps and their teams often know more than the retail buyers they advise. In fact, P&G's retail partners often rely on CBD teams to help them manage not only the P&G brands on their shelves but also entire product categories, including competing brands.

Wait a minute. Does it make sense to let P&G advise on the stocking and placement of competitors' brands as well as its own? Would a P&G CBD rep ever tell a retail buyer to stock fewer P&G products and more of a competing brand? Believe it or not, it happens all the time. The CBD team's primary goal is to help the customer win in each product category. Sometimes, analysis shows that the best solution for the customer is 'more of the other guy's product'. For P&G, that's okay. It knows that creating the best situation for the retailer ultimately pulls in more customer traffic, which in turn will most likely lead to increased sales for other P&G products in the same category. Because most of P&G's brands are market share leaders, it stands to benefit more from the increased traffic than competitors do. Again, what's good for the customer is good for P&G; it's a win–win situation.

Honest and open dealings also help to build long-term customer relationships. P&G salespeople become trusted advisors to their retailer-partners, a status they work hard to maintain. 'It took me four years to build the trust I now have with my buyer,' says a veteran CBD account executive. 'If I talk her into buying P&G products that she can't sell or out of stocking competing brands that she should be selling, I could lose that trust in a heartbeat.'

Finally, collaboration is usually a two-way street: P&G gives and customers give back in return. 'We'll help customers run a set of commercials or do some merchandising events, but there's usually a return-on-investment,' explains another CBD manager. 'Maybe it's helping us with distribution of a new product or increasing space for fabric care. We're very willing if the effort creates value for us as well as for the customer and the final consumer.'

According to P&G, 'Customer Business Development is selling and a whole lot more. It's a P&G-specific approach [that lets us] grow business by working as a "strategic partner" with our accounts, focusing on mutually beneficial business building opportunities. All customers want to improve their business; it's [our] role to help them identify the biggest opportunities.'

Thus, P&G salespeople aren't the stereotypical road warriors that some people have come to expect when they think of selling. In fact, they aren't even called 'salespeople'. They are CBD managers – talented, well-educated, well-trained sales professionals who do all they can to help customers succeed. They know that good selling involves working with customers to solve their problems for mutual gain. They know that if customers succeed, they succeed.[1]

In this chapter, we examine two more promotion mix tools: *personal selling* and *sales promotion*. Personal selling consists of interpersonal interactions with customers and prospects to make sales and maintain customer relationships. Sales promotion involves using short-term incentives to encourage customer purchasing, reseller support and sales force efforts.

PERSONAL SELLING

Robert Louis Stevenson once noted, 'Everyone lives by selling something'. Companies around the world use sales forces to sell products and services to business customers and final consumers. But sales forces are also found in many other kinds of organisations. For example, universities use recruiters to attract new students, and faith organisations use membership committees to attract new members. Museums and fine arts organisations use fundraisers to contact donors and raise money. Even public sector organisations use sales forces to sell commercial services, for example, to corporate customers. In the first part of this chapter, we examine personal selling's role in the organisation, sales force management decisions, and the personal selling process.

The nature of personal selling

Personal selling is one of the oldest professions in the world. The people who do the selling go by many names, including salespeople, sales representatives, agents, district managers, account executives, sales consultants and sales engineers.

People have many stereotypes of salespeople – including some very unfavourable ones. 'Salesman' may bring to mind the image of Arthur Miller's pitiable Willy Loman in *Death of a Salesman* or Chris Finch, the brashly confident, openly sexist, rasping-voiced, bullying Wernham Hogg paper salesman from the TV comedy programme *The Office*. And then there are the real-life 'yell-and-sell' 'pitchmen', who hawk everything from 'buy one, get one free' Safestyle replacement windows to Cillit Bang cleaning products in TV commercials, and the irritating cold-callers on the telephone trying to sell financial services or house maintenance products. However, the majority of salespeople are a far cry from these stereotypes. Even so, cold-callers and 'yell-and-sell' selling is mainly annoying when they reach the wrong target at the wrong time. When they reach the right target at the right time, they sell products.

Nonetheless, as the opening P&G story shows, most salespeople are well-educated and well-trained professionals who add value for customers and maintain long-term customer relationships. They listen to their customers, assess customer needs and organise the company's efforts to solve customer problems. Or, consider Boeing and Airbus, the aerospace giants competing head-to-head in the rough-and-tumble worldwide commercial aircraft market. It takes more than fast talk and a warm smile to sell expensive aircraft. Selling high-tech aircraft at $150 million or more a copy is complex and challenging. A single big sale to an airline, airfreight carrier, government or military customer can easily run into billions of dollars. In this type of selling, salespeople head up an extensive team of company specialists – sales and service technicians, financial analysts, planners, engineers – all dedicated to finding ways to satisfy a large customer's needs.

Some assumptions about what makes someone a good salesperson are dead wrong. There's this idea that the classic sales personality is overbearing, pushy and outgoing – the kind of people who walk in and suck all the air out of the room. But the best salespeople are good at one-on-one contact. They create loyalty and customers because people trust them and want to work with them. It's a matter of putting the client's interests first, which is the antithesis of how most people view salespeople. The most successful salespeople are successful for one simple reason: they know how to build relationships. You can go in with a big personality and convince people to do what you want them to do, but that really isn't selling; it's manipulation, and it only works in the short term. A good salesperson can read customer emotions without exploiting them because the bottom line is that he or she wants what's best for the customer.

Consider GE's diesel locomotive business. A batch of high-tech locomotives may have a price tag of $2 million or more per locomotive. A single big sale can easily run into the hundreds of millions of dollars. GE salespeople head up an extensive team of company specialists. The selling process can take years from the first sales presentation to the day the sale is announced. The real challenge is to win a buyer's business by building partnerships with them – day-in, day-out, year-in, year-out – based on superior products and close collaboration.

Clearly, the term **salesperson** covers a wide range of positions. At one extreme, a salesperson might be largely an *order taker*, such as the retail store salesperson standing behind the counter. At the other extreme are *order getters*, whose

Personal selling—Personal presentations by the firm's sales force for the purpose of engaging customers, making sales and building customer relationships.

Salesperson—An individual who represents a company to customers by performing one or more of the following activities: prospecting, communicating, selling, servicing, information gathering and relationship building.

Professional selling: it takes more than fast talk and a warm smile to sell expensive airplanes. Boeing's real challenge is to win business by building partnerships - day-in, day-out, year-in, year-out - with its airline customers.
Source: Stephen Brashear/Getty Images

positions demand *creative selling* and *relationship building* for products and services ranging from appliances, industrial equipment and locomotives to insurance and IT services.[2] Here, we focus on the more creative types of selling and the process of building and managing an effective sales force.

The role of the sales force

Personal selling is the interpersonal arm of the promotion mix. Advertising consists largely of non-personal communication with large groups of consumers. By contrast, personal selling involves interpersonal interactions between salespeople and individual customers – whether face-to-face, by telephone, via e-mail or social media, through video or online conferences, or by other means. Personal selling can be more effective than advertising in more complex selling situations. Salespeople can probe customers to learn more about their problems and then adjust the marketing offer and presentation to fit the special needs of each customer.

The role of personal selling varies from company to company. Some firms have no salespeople at all – for example, companies that sell only online or through catalogues, or companies that sell through manufacturer's reps, sales agents or brokers. In most firms, however, the sales force plays a major role. In companies that sell business products and services, such as IBM, BP or Airbus, salespeople work directly with customers. In consumer product companies such as P&G and Nestlé, the sales force plays an important behind-the-scenes role. It works with wholesalers and retailers to gain their support and help them be more effective in selling the company's products to end-users.

Linking the company with its customers

The sales force serves as a critical link between a company and its customers. In many cases, salespeople serve two masters: the seller and the buyer. First, they *represent the company to customers*. They find and develop new customers and communicate information about the company's products and services. They sell products by approaching customers, presenting their offerings, answering objections, negotiating prices and terms, closing sales, servicing accounts and maintaining account relationships. In addition, salespeople carry out market research and intelligence work.

At the same time, salespeople *represent customers to the company*, acting inside the firm as 'champions' of customers' interests and managing the buyer–seller relationship. Salespeople relay customer concerns about company products and actions back inside to those who can handle them. They learn about customer needs and work with other marketing and non-marketing people in the company to develop greater customer value.

Salespeople link the company with its customers. To many customers, the salesperson is the company.

Source: Monkey Business Images/Shutterstock.com

In fact, to many customers, the salesperson *is* the company – the only tangible manifestation of the company that they see. Hence, customers may become loyal to salespeople as well as to the companies and products they represent. This concept of 'salesperson-owned loyalty' lends even more importance to the salesperson's customer relationship building abilities. Strong relationships with the salesperson will result in strong relationships with the company and its products. Conversely, poor relationships will probably result in poor company and product relationships.

Research by Harvard Business Review Analytical Services underlines the importance of meeting customers and business contacts in person, particularly when economic times are tough, and in building relationships in international markets with customers and distributors, particularly where cultural traditions favour face-to-face communications in buying and selling.[3]

Given its role in linking the company with its customers, the sales force must be strongly customer-solutions focused. In fact, such a customer-solutions focus is a must not only for the sales force but also for the entire organisation. Says Anne Mulcahy, successful former CEO and chairperson of Xerox, who started her career in sales, a strong customer-service focus 'has to be the centre of your universe, the heartland of how you run your company':

Today, for most companies, personal selling plays an important role in building profitable customer relationships. In turn, those relationships contribute greatly to overall company success. Just ask Anne Mulcahy, recently retired CEO and current chairperson of the board at Xerox. She took the reins of the then-nearly-bankrupt copier company in early 2001 and transformed it into a successful, modern-day, digital technology and services enterprise. She began her career in 1976 as a Xerox sales rep in Boston. From there, she worked her way up the sales ladder to become Xerox's vice president of global sales in the late 1990s. Then, 25 years after first knocking on customer doors, she was appointed CEO of Xerox. As CEO, Mulcahy brought with her a sales and marketing mentality that now permeates the entire Xerox organisation, with a new focus on solving customer problems. Looking back, Mulcahy recalls, Xerox had lost touch with its markets. 'Sales helps you understand what drives the business and that customers are a critical part of the business,' Mulcahy says. 'This will be important in any business function, but you learn it [best] in sales management where it is critical, the jewel in the crown.' Implementing this customer-first sales philosophy, one of Mulcahy's first actions as CEO was to put on her old sales hat and hit the road to visit customers. Mulcahy knows that putting customers first isn't just a sales force responsibility; it's an emphasis for everyone in the company. To stress that point at all levels, she quickly set up a rotating 'customer officer of the day' programme at Xerox, which requires a top executive to answer customer calls that come to corporate headquarters. As the customer officer of the day, the executive has three responsibilities: listen to the customer, resolve the problem, and take responsibility for fixing the underlying cause. That sounds a lot like sales. So if you're still thinking of salespeople as fast-talking, ever-smiling peddlers who foist their wares on reluctant customers, you're probably working with an out-of-date stereotype. Good salespeople succeed not by taking customers in but by helping them out – by assessing customer needs and solving customer problems. In fact, that isn't just good sales thinking; it applies to the entire organisation.[4]

Coordinating marketing and sales

Ideally, the sales force and other marketing functions (marketing planners, brand managers, marketing content managers and researchers) should work together closely to jointly create value for customers. Unfortunately, however, some companies still treat sales and marketing as separate functions. When this happens, the separate sales and marketing groups may not get along well. When things go wrong, marketers blame the sales force for its poor execution of what they see as an otherwise splendid strategy. In turn, the sales team blames the marketers for being out of touch with what's really going on with customers. Neither group fully values the other's contributions. If not repaired, such disconnects between marketing and sales can damage customer relationships and company performance.

A company can take several actions to help bring its marketing and sales functions closer together. At the most basic level, it can increase communications between the two groups by arranging joint meetings and spelling out communications channels. It can create opportunities for salespeople and marketers to work together. Brand managers and researchers can occasionally go along on sales calls or sit in on sales planning sessions. In turn, salespeople can play a role in marketing planning sessions and share their first-hand customer knowledge.

A company can also create joint objectives and reward systems for sales and marketing teams or appoint marketing-sales liaisons – people from marketing who 'live with the sales force' and help coordinate marketing and sales force programmes and efforts. Finally, it can appoint a high-level marketing executive to oversee both marketing and sales. Such a person can help infuse marketing and sales with the common goal of creating value for customers to capture value in return.[5]

MANAGING THE SALES FORCE

Author comment

Here's another definition of sales force management: 'Planning, organising, leading and controlling personal contact programmes designed to achieve profitable customer relationships.' Once again, the goal of every marketing activity is to create customer value and build customer relationships.

We define **sales force management** as analysing, planning, implementing, and controlling sales force activities. It includes designing the sales force strategy and structure and recruiting, selecting, training, compensating, supervising and evaluating the firm's salespeople. These major sales force management decisions are shown in Figure 16.1 and are discussed in the following sections.

Designing sales force strategy and structure

Marketing managers face a number of important sales force strategy and design questions. How should salespeople and their tasks be structured? How big should the sales force be? Should salespeople sell alone or work in teams with other people in the company? Should they sell in the field, by telephone, or using online and social media? We address these issues next.

Sales force management—
Analysing, planning, implementing and controlling sales force activities

Sales force structure ,

A company can divide sales responsibilities along any of several lines. The structure decision is simple if the company sells only one product line to one industry with customers in many locations. In that case the company would use a *territorial sales force structure*. This remains the commonest sales force structure in Europe. However, if the company sells many products to many types of customers, it might need a *product sales force structure*, a *customer sales force structure*, or a combination of the two.

Territorial sales force structure—A sales force organisation that assigns each salesperson to an exclusive geographic territory in which that salesperson sells the company's full line.

In the **territorial sales force structure**, each salesperson is assigned to an exclusive geographic area and sells the company's full line of products or services to all customers in that territory. This organisation clearly defines each salesperson's job and fixes accountability. It also increases the salesperson's desire to build local customer relationships that, in turn, improve selling effectiveness. Finally, because each salesperson travels within a limited geographic area, travel expenses are relatively small. A territorial sales organisation is often supported by several levels of sales management positions. While in global sales organisations multiple levels are common, in smaller European and other specialised markets fewer sales force management levels are more usual.

Product sales force structure—A sales force organisation in which salespeople specialise in selling only a portion of the company's products or lines.

If a company has many and complex products, it can adopt a **product sales force structure**, in which the sales force specialises in product lines. For example, global giant GE employs different sales forces within different product and service divisions of its major businesses. Within GE Infrastructure, for instance, the company has separate sales forces for aviation, energy, transportation, and water processing products and technologies. No single salesperson can become expert in all these product categories, so product specialisation is required. Similarly, GE Healthcare employs different sales forces for diagnostic imaging, life sciences, and integrated IT products and services. In all, a company as large and complex as GE might have dozens of separate sales forces serving its diverse product and service portfolio across its global markets.

However, the product structure may have limits, if a single large customer buys many different company products. For example, several different GE salespeople might end up calling on the same large healthcare customer in a given period. This means that they travel over the same routes

Figure 16.1 Major steps in sales force management

> The goal of this process? You guessed it! The company wants to build a skilled and motivated sales team that will help to create customer value, engage customers and build strong customer relationships.

and wait to see the same customer's purchasing managers. These extra costs must be compared with the benefits of better salesperson product knowledge and attention to individual products.

More and more companies are now using a **customer (or market) sales force structure**, in which they organise the sales force along customer or industry lines. Separate sales forces may be set up for different industries, serving current customers versus finding new ones, and serving major accounts versus regular accounts. Many companies even have special sales forces to handle the needs of individual large customers. For example, Stanley Black & Decker has a sales organisation specifically focused on individual mass-retailer customers. Many companies have developed sales and account structures around the needs of their most important customers.[6]

Organising the sales force around customers can help a company build closer relationships with important customers. Consider Hill-Rom, a global supplier of medical equipment, including hospital beds, stretchers and nurse communication systems, which restructured its product-based US sales force into a customer-based one:[7]

> Hill-Rom divided its sales force into two customer-based teams. One sales force focuses on 'key' customers – large accounts that purchase high-end equipment and demand high levels of sales force collaboration. The second sales force focuses on 'prime' customers – smaller accounts that are generally more concerned about getting the features and functions they need for the best possible price. Assigning the separate sales forces helps Hill-Rom better understand what the different types of customers need. It also lets the company track how much attention the sales force devotes to each customer group.
>
> Prior to restructuring its sales force, Hill-Rom had been treating both key and prime customers the same way. As a result, it was trying to sell to smaller prime customers with a level of service and innovation that they did not value or could not afford. So the cost of sales for prime customers was four to five times higher than for key customers. Now, a single account manager and team focus intensely on all the areas of each key customer's business, working together to find product and service solutions. Such intensive collaboration would have been difficult under the old product-based sales structure, in which multiple Hill-Rom sales reps serviced the different speciality areas within a single key account. In the two years following the sales force redesign, Hill-Rom's sales growth doubled.

When a company sells a wide variety of products to many types of customers over a broad geographic area, it often employs a *complex sales force structure*, which combines several types of organisation. Salespeople can be specialised by customer and territory; product and territory; product and customer; or territory, product and customer. For example, Stanley Black & Decker specialises its sales force by customer (with different sales forces calling on mass-merchandisers like B&Q and Bauhaus, and smaller independent retailers) *and* by territory for each key customer group (territory representatives, territory managers, and so on). No single structure is best for all companies and situations. Each company should select a sales force structure that best serves the needs of its customers and fits its overall marketing strategy.

A good sales structure can mean the difference between success and failure. Over time, sales force structures can grow complex, inefficient and unresponsive to customers' needs, and become a barrier to salespeople achieving their real potential performance. For this reason, companies should periodically review their sales force organisations to be certain that they serve the needs of the company and its customers.

Sales force size

Once the company has established its structure, it is ready to consider sales force size. Sales forces may range in size from only a few salespeople to tens of thousands. Some sales forces in global companies are huge: for example, PepsiCo employs 36,000 salespeople; American Express, 23,400; GE, 16,400; and Cisco Systems, 14,000.[8] Salespeople constitute one of the company's most productive – and most expensive – assets. Therefore, increasing their numbers will increase sales but also costs. Tough economic times in Europe have seen sales force downsizing in some companies and across some sectors like financial services.

Customer (or market) sales force structure—A sales force organisation in which salespeople specialise in selling only to certain customers or industries.

Many companies use some form of *workload approach* to establish sales force size. Using this approach, a company first groups accounts into different classes according to size, account status, or other factors related to the amount of effort required to maintain the account. It then determines the number of salespeople needed to call on each class of accounts the desired number of times.

The company might reason as follows: suppose we have 1,000 A-level accounts and 2,000 B-level accounts. A-level accounts require 36 calls per year, and B-level accounts require 12 calls per year. In this case, the sales force's *workload* – the number of calls it must make per year – is 60,000 calls [(1,000 × 36) + (2,000 × 12) = 36,000 + 24,000 = 60,000]. Suppose the average salesperson can make 1,000 calls a year, then we need 60 salespeople (60,000 ÷ 1,000).[9]

Other sales force strategy and structure issues

Sales management must also determine who will be involved in the selling effort and how various sales and sales support people will work together.

Outside and inside sales forces

The company may have an **outside sales force (or field sales force)**, an **inside sales force**, or both. Outside salespeople travel to call on customers in the field. By contrast, inside salespeople conduct business from their offices via telephone, online and social media interactions, or visits from buyers. The use of inside sales has grown in recent years because of increased outside selling costs and the surge in online, mobile phone and social media technologies. One estimate is that for every one person hired today for an outside sales job, ten are being recruited for inside sales posts. This shift reflects market changes, but also costs: industry estimates are that each contact with an internal salesperson might cost a company $25–$30, while each contact with a field salesperson might cost $300–$500.[10]

Some inside salespeople provide support for the outside sales force, freeing them to spend more time selling to major accounts and finding new prospects. For example, *technical sales support people* provide technical information and answers to customers' questions. *Sales assistants* provide administrative backup for outside salespeople. They track down sales leads, call ahead and confirm appointments, follow up on deliveries, and answer customers' questions when outside salespeople cannot be reached. Using such combinations of inside and outside salespeople can help serve important customers better. The inside rep provides daily access and support; the outside rep provides face-to-face collaboration and relationship building.

Other inside salespeople do more than just provide support. *Telemarketers* and *online sellers* use the phone, Internet and social media to find new leads, learn about customers and their business, or sell and service accounts directly. Telemarketing and online selling can be very effective, less costly ways to sell to smaller, harder-to-reach customers. Depending on the complexity of the product, a telemarketer can make from 20 to 33 decision-maker contacts a day, compared to the average of four that an outside salesperson can make. And whereas an average B-to-B field sales call can cost £250 or more, a routine industrial telemarketing call costs only about £3–5 and a complex call about £15.[11]

Although the government regulators in many countries have developed 'opt-out' schemes, which have put a dent in telephone sales to consumers, telemarketing remains a vital tool for many B-to-B marketers. For some smaller companies, telephone and online selling may be the primary sales approaches. However, larger companies also use these tactics, either to sell directly to small and mid-size customers or to assist the sales force in selling to larger ones. Especially in the leaner times following the recession, many companies have reduced their in-person customer visits in favour of more telephone, e-mail and online selling.

In addition to cost savings, in today's digital, mobile and social media environments, many buyers are more receptive to – or even

Outside sales force (or field sales force)—Salespeople who travel to call on customers in the field.
Inside sales force—Salespeople who conduct business from their offices via telephone, online and social media interactions, or visits from prospective buyers.

Inside salespeople conduct business from their offices, via telephone, the Internet, or visits from buyers.
Source: Climax Portable Machine Tools

prefer – phone and online contact versus the high level of face-to-face contact once required with field salespeople. Many customers are more inclined to gather information online – one study showed that a typical buyer reports contacting a sales rep only after independently completing about 60 per cent of the buying process. Then, they routinely use the phone, online meetings and social media interactions to engage sellers and close deals. 'With virtual meeting software such as GoToMeeting.com and WebEx, communications tools such as Skype, and social media sites such as Twitter, Facebook and LinkedIn, it's become easier to sell with few if any face-to-face meetings,' says an inside sales consultant.[12]

As a result of these trends, telephone and online selling are growing much faster than in-person selling. One study also notes the emergence of the 'hybrid sales rep', a modern cross between a field sales rep and an inside rep, who often works from a remote location. Some 41 per cent of outside sales activity is now done over the phone or a mobile device, from either a home office, a company office, or on the go.[13]

For many types of products and selling situations, phone or online selling can be as effective as a personal sales call. Climax Portable Machine Tools is an American company with a base in the north of England, as well as a worldwide distributor network.

Climax Portable Machine Tools, which manufactures portable maintenance tools for the metal cutting industry, has proven in its US business that telemarketing can save money and still lavish attention on buyers. Under the old system, Climax sales engineers spent one-third of their time on the road, training distributor salespeople and accompanying them on calls. They could make about four contacts a day. Now, each of five sales engineers on Climax's inside sales team calls about 30 prospects a day, following up on leads generated by ads and e-mails. Because it takes about five calls to close a sale, the sales engineers update a prospect's profile after each contact, noting the degree of commitment, requirements, next call date and personal comments. 'If anyone mentions he's going on a fishing trip, our sales engineer enters that in the sales information system and uses it to personalise the next phone call,' says Climax's president, noting that this is one way to build good relations.

Another is that the first direct contact with a prospect includes the sales engineer's business card with his or her picture on it. Climax's customer information system also gives inside reps instant access to customer information entered by the outside sales force and service people. Armed with all the information, inside reps can build surprisingly strong and personal customer relationships. Of course, it takes more than friendliness to sell $15,000 machine tools over the phone (special orders may run to $200,000), but the telemarketing approach works well. When Climax customers were asked, 'Do you see the sales engineer often enough?' the response was overwhelmingly positive. Obviously, many people didn't realise that the only contact they had with Climax had been on the phone.[14]

Team selling—Using teams of people from sales, marketing, engineering, finance, technical support and even upper management to service large, complex accounts.

For many types of selling situations, phone or web selling can be as effective as a personal sales call. At Climax Portable Machine Tools, telephone reps build surprisingly strong and personal customer relationships.

Source: Tetra Images/Alamy Images

Team selling

As products become more complex, and as customers grow larger and more demanding, a single salesperson simply can't handle all of a large customer's needs. Instead, most companies now use **team selling** to service large, complex accounts. Sales teams can unearth problems, solutions and sales opportunities that no individual salesperson could do. Such teams might include experts from any area or level of the selling firm – sales, marketing, technical and support services, R&D, engineering, operations, finance and others.

In many cases, the move to team selling mirrors similar changes in customers' buying organisations. 'Buyers implementing team-based purchasing decisions have necessitated the equal and opposite creation of team-based selling – a completely new way of doing business for many independent, self-motivated salespeople,' says a sales force analyst. 'Today, we're calling on teams of buying people, and that requires more firepower on our side,' agrees one sales vice president. 'One salesperson just can't do it all – can't be an expert in everything we're bringing to the customer. We have strategic account teams, led by customer business managers, who basically are our quarterbacks.'[15] Many large buyers are emphasising supplier relationship management approaches in a similar way to the adoption of account management teams by sellers.

Some companies, such as IBM Xerox and P&G, have used teams for a long time, as we saw in the chapter-opening story. P&G sales reps are organised into Customer Business Development (CBD) teams. Each CBD team is assigned to a major P&G retailer customer. The CBD organisation places the focus on serving the complete needs of each major customer. It lets P&G 'grow business by working as a "strategic partner" with our accounts,' not just as a supplier.[16] Indeed, major retailer Walmart in the United States has some 450 suppliers locating account teams at its headquarters, and the same process is happening with Tesco in the UK.

Team selling does have some pitfalls. For example, salespeople are by nature competitive and have often been trained and rewarded for outstanding individual performance. Salespeople who are used to having customers all to themselves may have trouble learning to work with and trust others on a team. In addition, selling teams can confuse or overwhelm customers who are used to working with only one salesperson. Finally, difficulties in evaluating individual contributions to the team selling effort can create some difficult compensation issues.

Recruiting and selecting salespeople

At the heart of any successful sales force operation is the recruitment and selection of good salespeople. The performance difference between an average salesperson and a top salesperson can be substantial. In a typical sales force, the top 30 per cent of the salespeople might bring in 60 per cent of the sales. Thus, careful salesperson selection can greatly increase overall sales force performance. Beyond the differences in sales performance, poor selection results in costly turnover. When a salesperson leaves, the costs of finding and training a new salesperson – plus the costs of lost sales – can be very high. One sales consulting firm calculates the total costs of a bad sales hire at a massive $616,000.[17] Also, a sales force with many new people is less productive, and turnover disrupts important customer relationships.

Great salespeople: the best salespeople possess intrinsic motivation, a disciplined work style, the ability to close a sale and, perhaps most important, the ability to build relationships with customers.

Source: Mint Images – Tim Robbins/Getty Images

What sets great salespeople apart from all the rest? In an effort to profile top sales performers, Gallup Consulting, a division of the well-known Gallup polling organisation in the US, interviewed hundreds of thousands of salespeople. Its research suggests that the best salespeople possess four key talents: intrinsic motivation, a disciplined work style, the ability to close a sale, and, perhaps most important, the ability to build relationships with customers.[18]

High performing salespeople are motivated from within; they have an unrelenting drive to excel. Some salespeople are driven by money, a desire for recognition, or the satisfaction of competing and winning. Others are driven by the desire to provide service and build relationships. The best salespeople possess some of each of these motivations. However, another analysis has found that the best salespeople are driven by a strong sense of purpose: 'The salespeople who sold with noble purpose, who truly want to make a difference to customers, consistently outsold the salespeople focused on sales goals and money.' Selling with such a sense of customer-related purpose is not only more successful, it's also more profitable and more satisfying to salespeople.[19]

Excellent salespeople also have a disciplined work style. They lay out detailed, organised plans and then follow through in a timely way. But motivation and discipline mean little unless they result in closing more sales and building better customer relationships. Top salespeople build the skills and knowledge they need to get the job done. Perhaps most important, high performing salespeople are excellent customer problem solvers and relationship builders. They understand their customers' needs. Talk to sales executives and they'll describe top performers in these terms: good listeners, empathetic, patient, caring and responsive. Top performers can put themselves on the buyer's side of the desk and see the world through their customers' eyes. They don't want just to be liked; they want to add value for their customers. Some of the techniques used by the world's top sellers are universal, regardless of product type.[20]

That said, there is no one right way to sell. Each successful salesperson uses a different approach, one that best applies his or her unique strengths and talents. For example, some salespeople enjoy the thrill of a harder sell in confronting challenges and winning people over. Others might apply 'softer' talents to reach the same goal. 'The key is for sales reps to understand and nurture their innate talents so they can develop their own personal approach and win business their way,' says a selling expert.[21]

When recruiting, a company should analyse the sales job itself and the characteristics of its most successful salespeople to identify the traits needed by a successful salesperson in their industry. Then it must recruit the right salespeople. The human resources department looks for applicants by getting names from current salespeople, using employment agencies, searching the Internet, placing classified ads, and working through school and university placement services. Another source is to attract top salespeople from other companies. Proven salespeople need less training and can be productive immediately.

Recruiting will attract many applicants from which a company must select the best. The selection procedure can vary from a single informal interview to lengthy testing and interviewing. Many companies give formal tests to sales applicants. Tests typically measure sales aptitude, analytical and organisational skills, personality traits, and other characteristics. But test scores provide only one piece of the information pie that includes personal characteristics, references, past employment history, social media traces and interviewer reactions.

Training salespeople

New salespeople may spend anywhere from a few weeks or months to a year or more in training. After initial training ends, most companies provide continuing sales training via seminars, sales meetings and Internet e-learning throughout the salesperson's career. Across the world, companies spend huge sums annually on training salespeople, and sales training typical captures the largest share of the training budget. According to one source, US companies spend nearly $20 billion a year. Although training can be expensive, it can also yield dramatic returns. For instance, one recent study showed that sales training conducted by ADP, an administrative services firm operating internationally, resulted in an ROI of nearly 340 per cent in only 90 days.[22]

Training programmes have several goals. First, salespeople need to know about customers and how to build relationships with them. So the training programme must teach them about different types of customers and their needs, buying motives and buying habits. It must also teach them how to sell effectively and train them in the basics of the selling process. Salespeople also need to know and identify with the company – its products and its competitors. Thus, an effective training programme teaches them about the company's objectives, organisation, products and the strategies of major competitors.

Today, many companies are adding e-learning to their sales training programmes. Online training may range from simple text and video-based product training and Internet-based sales exercises that build sales skills, to sophisticated simulations that re-create the dynamics of real-life sales calls. One of the most basic forms is virtual instructor-led training (VILT). Using this method, a small group of salespeople at remote locations logs on to an online conferencing site, where a sales instructor leads training sessions using online video, audio and interactive learning tools.

E-training can make sales training more efficient - and more fun. Bayer Healthcare Pharmaceuticals' role-playing video game - Rep Race - helped improve salesperson effectiveness by 20 per cent.

Source: MBI/Alamy Images

Training online instead of on-site can cut travel and other training costs, and it takes up less of a salesperson's selling time. It also makes on-demand training available to salespeople, letting them train as little or as much as needed, whenever and wherever needed, and overcomes language barriers in global markets. Although most e-learning is web-based, many companies now offer on-demand training from anywhere via smartphones and mobile tablet devices.

Many companies are now using imaginative and sophisticated e-learning techniques to make sales training more efficient – and sometimes even more fun. For example, Bayer HealthCare Pharmaceuticals (an international business with divisions based in the US and Germany) worked with Concentric RX, a healthcare marketing agency in America, to create a role-playing simulation video game to train its sales force on a new drug marketing programme:[23]

> Most people don't usually associate fast-paced rock music and flashy graphics with online sales training tools. But Concentric Rx's innovative role-playing video game – 'Rep Race: The Battle for Office Supremacy' – has all that and a lot more. Rep Race gives Bayer sales reps far more entertainment than the staid old multiple-choice skills tests it replaces. The game was created to help breathe new life into a mature Bayer product – Betaseron, a 17-year-old multiple sclerosis therapy treatment. The aim was to find a fresh, more active way to help Bayer sales reps apply the in-depth information they learned about Betaseron to actual selling and objections-handling situations. Bayer also wanted to increase rep engagement through interactive learning and feedback through real-time results. Bayer reps liked Rep Race from the start. According to Bayer, when the game was first launched, reps played it as many as 30 times. In addition to its educational and motivational value, Rep Race allowed Bayer to measure sales reps' individual and collective performance. In the end, Bayer calculated that the Rep Race simulation helped improve the Betaseron sales team's effectiveness by 20 per cent.

Compensating salespeople

To attract good salespeople, a company must have an appealing compensation plan. Compensation consists of four elements: a fixed amount, a variable amount, expenses and fringe benefits. The fixed amount, usually a salary, gives the salesperson some stable income. The variable amount, which might be commission or bonuses based on sales performance, rewards the salesperson for greater effort and success.

Management must determine what *mix* of these compensation elements makes the most sense for each sales job. Different combinations of fixed and variable compensation give rise to four basic types of compensation plans: straight salary, straight commission, salary plus bonus and salary plus commission. According to one study of sales force compensation, 18 per cent of companies pay straight salary, 19 per cent pay straight commission and 63 per cent pay a combination of salary plus incentives. A study showed that the average salesperson's pay consists of about 67 per cent salary and 33 per cent incentive pay.[24]

A sales force compensation plan can both motivate salespeople and direct their activities. Compensation should direct salespeople toward activities that are consistent with overall sales force and marketing objectives. For example, if the strategy is to acquire new business, grow rapidly, and gain market share, the compensation plan might include a larger commission component, coupled with a new-account bonus to encourage high sales performance and new account development. In contrast, if the goal is to maximise current account profitability, the compensation plan might contain a larger base-salary component with additional incentives for current account sales or customer satisfaction.

In fact, more and more companies are moving away from high commission plans that may drive salespeople to make short-term grabs for business. They worry that a salesperson who is pushing too hard to close a deal may ruin the customer relationship. Instead, companies are designing compensation plans that reward salespeople for building customer relationships and growing the long-run value of each customer. Nonetheless, there is considerable international variation in company policies on salesperson compensation, reflecting historical and cultural differences.

When the times are tough economically, some companies are tempted to cut costs by reducing sales compensation. However, although some cost-cutting measures make sense when business is difficult, cutting sales force compensation across the board is usually a last resort. Top salespeople are always in demand, and paying them less might mean losing them at a time when they are most needed. Thus, short-changing key sales people can result in short-changing important customer relationships. One sales compensation expert says: 'Keep in mind that if you burn the salesperson, you might burn the customer relationship.' If a company must reduce its compensation expenses, says the expert, a better strategy than across-the-board cuts is to 'keep the pay up for top performers and turn the [low performers] loose'.[25]

Supervising and motivating salespeople

New salespeople need more than a territory, compensation and training; they need supervision and motivation. The goal of *supervision* is to help salespeople 'work smart' by doing the right things in the right ways. The goal of *motivation* is to encourage salespeople to 'work hard' and energetically toward sales force goals. If salespeople work smart and work hard, they will realise their full potential – to their own and the company's benefit.

Supervising salespeople

Companies vary in how closely they supervise their salespeople. Many help salespeople identify target customers and set call objectives. Some may also specify how much time the sales force should spend prospecting for new accounts and set other time management priorities. One tool is the weekly, monthly or annual *call plan* that shows which customers and prospects to call on and which activities to carry out. Another tool is *time-and-duty analysis*. In addition to time spent selling, the salesperson spends time travelling, waiting, taking breaks and doing administrative chores.

Figure 16.2 shows how salespeople spend their time. On average, active selling time accounts for only 37 per cent of total working time.[26] Companies are always looking for ways to save time – simplifying administrative duties, developing better sales-call and routing plans, supplying more and better customer information, and using phone, e-mail, online or mobile conferencing instead of travelling. Consider the changes GE made to increase its sales force's face-to-face selling time.[27]

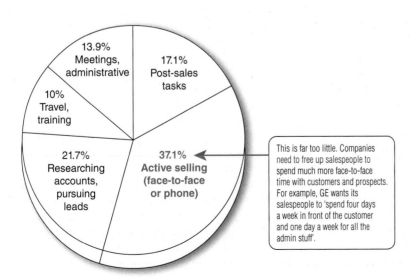

Figure 16.2 How salespeople spend their time

When Jeff Immelt became GE's new chairman, he was dismayed to find that members of the sales team were spending far more time on deskbound administrative chores than in face-to-face meetings with customers and prospects. 'He said we needed to turn that around,' recalls Venki Rao, an IT leader in global sales and marketing at GE Power Systems, a division focused on energy systems and products. '[We need] to spend four days a week in front of the customer and one day for all the admin stuff.' GE Power's salespeople spent much of their time at their desks because they had to go to many sources for the information needed to sell multimillion-dollar turbines, turbine parts and services to energy companies worldwide. To fix the problem, GE created a new sales portal, a kind of 'one-stop shop' that connects the vast array of GE databases, providing salespeople with everything from sales tracking and customer data to parts pricing and information on planned outages. GE also added external data, such as news feeds. 'Before, you were randomly searching for things,' says Bill Snook, a GE sales manager. Now, he says, 'I have the sales portal as my home page, and I use it as the gateway to all the applications that I have.' The sales portal has freed Snook and 2,500 other users around the globe from once time-consuming administrative tasks, greatly increasing their face time with customers.

Many firms have adopted *sales force automation systems*: computerised, digitised sales force operations that let salespeople work more effectively anytime, anywhere. Companies now routinely equip their salespeople with technologies such as laptops, smartphones, wireless connections, webcams for videoconferencing and customer-contact and relationship management software. Armed with these technologies, salespeople can more effectively and efficiently profile customers and prospects, analyse and forecast sales, schedule sales calls, make presentations, prepare sales and expense reports, and manage account relationships. The result is better time management, improved customer service, lower sales costs and higher sales performance. In all, technology has substantially reshaped the ways in which salespeople carry out their duties and engage customers.

Motivating salespeople

Beyond directing salespeople, sales managers must also motivate them. Some salespeople will do their best without any special urging from management. To them, selling may be the most fascinating job in the world. But selling can also be frustrating. Salespeople often work alone, and they must sometimes travel away from home. They may face aggressive competing salespeople and difficult customers. Therefore, salespeople often need special encouragement to do their best.

Management can boost sales force morale and performance through its organisational climate, sales quotas and positive incentives. *Organisational climate* describes the feeling that salespeople have about their opportunities, value and rewards for a good performance. Some companies treat salespeople as if they are not very important, so performance suffers accordingly. Other companies treat their salespeople as valued contributors and allow virtually unlimited opportunity for income and promotion. Not surprisingly, these companies enjoy higher sales force performance and less personnel turnover.

Many companies motivate their salespeople by setting **sales quotas**: standards stating the amount they should sell and how sales should be divided among the company's products. Compensation is often related to how well salespeople meet their quotas. Companies also use various *positive incentives* to increase the sales force effort. *Sales meetings* provide social occasions, breaks from the routine, opportunities to meet and talk with 'company brass', and opportunities to air feelings and identify with a larger group. Companies also sponsor *sales contests* to spur the sales force to make a selling effort above and beyond what is normally expected. Other incentives include honours, merchandise and cash awards, trips and profit-sharing plans.

Sales quota—A standard that states the amount a salesperson should sell and how sales should be divided among the company's products.

Evaluating salespeople and sales force performance

We have thus far described how management communicates what salespeople should be doing and how it motivates them to do it. This process requires good feedback. And good feedback means getting regular information about salespeople to evaluate their performance.

Management gets information about its salespeople in several ways. The most important source is *sales reports*, including weekly or monthly work plans and longer-term territory marketing plans. Salespeople also write up their completed activities on *call reports* and turn in *expense reports* for which they are partly or wholly reimbursed. The company can also monitor the sales and profit performance data in the salesperson's territory. Additional information comes from personal observation, customer surveys and discussions with other salespeople.

Using various sales force reports and other information, sales management evaluates the members of the sales force. It evaluates salespeople on their ability to 'plan their work and work their plan'. Formal evaluation forces management to develop and communicate clear standards for judging performance. It also provides salespeople with constructive feedback and motivates them to perform well.

On a broader level, management should evaluate the performance of the sales force as a whole. Is the sales force accomplishing its customer relationship, sales and profit objectives? Is it working well with other areas of the marketing and company organisation? Are sales force costs in line with outcomes? As with other marketing activities, the company wants to measure its *return on sales investment*.

SOCIAL SELLING: ONLINE, MOBILE AND SOCIAL MEDIA TOOLS

Author comment

Like just about everything else these days, digital technologies have impacted on selling big time. Today's sales forces are mastering the use of online, mobile and social media tools to engage business customers, build relationships and make sales.

The fastest-growing sales trend is the explosion in **social selling** – the use of online, mobile and social media to engage customers, build stronger customer relationships and augment sales performance. New digital sales force technologies are creating exciting new avenues for connecting with and engaging customers in the digital and social media age. Some analysts even predict that the Internet will mean the death of person-to-person selling, as salespeople are ultimately replaced by websites, online social media, mobile apps, video and conferencing technologies, and other tools that allow direct customer contact. 'Don't believe it,' says one sales expert – used properly, online and social media technologies won't make salespeople obsolete; they will make salespeople more productive and effective.[28]

Social selling—Using online, mobile and social media to engage customers, build stronger customer relationships and augment sales performance.

New digital technologies are providing salespeople with powerful tools for identifying and learning about prospects, engaging customers, creating customer value, closing sales and nurturing customer relationships. Social selling technologies can produce big organisational benefits for sales forces. They help conserve salespeople's valuable time, save travel expenses, and give salespeople new vehicles for selling and servicing accounts.

But social selling hasn't really changed the fundamentals of selling. Sales forces have always taken the primary responsibility for reaching out to, and engaging, customers and managing customer relationships. It's just that now more of that is being done digitally. Online and social media are dramatically changing the customer buying process, so as a result, they are also changing the selling process. In today's digital world, many customers no longer rely as much as they once did on information and assistance provided by salespeople. Instead, they carry out more of the buying process on their own – especially the early stages. Increasingly, they use online and social media resources to analyse their own problems, research solutions, get advice from colleagues and rank buying options before ever speaking to a salesperson. A recent study of business buyers found that 92 per cent of buyers start their searches online and that, on average, buyers completed nearly 60 per cent of the buying process before contacting a supplier.[29]

Thus, today's customers have much more control over the sales process than they had in the days when brochures, pricing and product advice were only available from a sales rep. Customers can now browse corporate websites, blogs and YouTube videos to identify and qualify sellers. They can mix with other buyers on social media such as LinkedIn, Google+, Twitter or Facebook to share experiences, identify solutions and evaluate products they are considering. As a result, if and when salespeople do enter the buying process, customers often know almost as much about a company's products as the salespeople do. 'It's not just that buyers start the sales process without you,' says an analyst, 'they typically complete most of the purchase journey before having any contact with sales. And by that point they are far more informed about your business than you are about theirs.'[30]

The role of salespeople in a digital and social media age

It may be hard to imagine a world without salespeople, but according to some analysts, there will be a lot fewer of them a decade from now. With the explosion of technologies that link customers directly with companies, they reason, who needs face-to-face selling anymore? According to the doubters, salespeople are rapidly being replaced by websites, e-mail, blogs, mobile apps, video sharing, virtual trade shows, social media such as LinkedIn and Facebook, and a host of other digital-age interaction tools. For example, research firm Gartner predicts that by 2020, 85 per cent of all interactions between businesses will be executed without human intervention, requiring fewer salespeople. 'The world no longer needs salespeople,' one doomsayer boldly proclaims. 'Sales is a dying profession and soon will be as outmoded as oil lamps and the rotary phone.' Says another, 'If we don't find and fill a need faster than a computer, we won't be needed.'

So, is business-to-business selling really dying out? Will the Internet, mobile technologies and social media replace the age-old art of selling face to face? To answer these questions, *Selling Power* magazine called together a panel of sales experts and asked them to consider the future of B-to-B sales. The panel members agreed that technology is radically transforming the selling profession. Today's revolutionary changes in how people communicate are affecting every aspect of business, and selling is no exception. But, says the *Selling Power* panel: technology, the Internet and social media will not soon be replacing person-to-person buying and selling. Selling has changed, agrees the panel, and the technology can greatly enhance the selling process. But it can't replace many of the functions that salespeople perform. 'The Internet can take orders and disseminate content, but what it can't do is discover customer needs,' says one panellist. 'It can't build relationships, and it can't prospect on its own.' Adds another panellist, 'Someone must define the company's value proposition and unique message and communicate it to the market, and that person is the sales rep.' What is dying, however, is what one panellist calls the account-maintenance role – the simple, routine order taker. Such salespeople are not creating value and can easily be replaced by automation. However, salespeople who excel at new customer acquisition, relationship management and account growth with existing customers will always be in high demand. For example, many companies are moving rapidly into online-community-based selling:

Several years ago, enterprise-software company SAP set up EcoHub, its own online, community-powered social media and mobile marketplace consisting of customers, SAP software experts, partners, and almost anyone else who wanted to join. The EcoHub community grew quickly to more than 2 million users in 200 countries, extending across a broad online spectrum – a dedicated website, mobile apps, Twitter channels, LinkedIn groups, Facebook and Google+ pages, YouTube channels, and more. EcoHub grew to more than 600 'solution storefronts', where visitors could 'discover, evaluate and buy' software solutions and services from SAP and its partners. EcoHub also let users rate and share the solutions and advice they got from other community members.

SAP was surprised to learn that what it had originally seen as a place for customers to discuss issues, problems and solutions turned into a significant point of sale. The information, give-and-take discussions, and conversations at the site drew in customers, even for big-ticket sales of $20–$30 million or more. In fact, EcoHub has now evolved into SAP Store, a gigantic SAP marketplace where customers can engage with SAP, its partners and each other to share information, post comments and reviews, discover problems, and evaluate and buy SAP solutions.

However, although the SAP Store draws in new potential customers and takes them through many of the initial stages of product discovery and evaluation, it doesn't replace SAP's or its partners' salespeople. Instead, it extends their reach and effectiveness. Its real value is the flood of sales leads it creates for the SAP and partner sales forces. Once prospective customers have discovered, discussed and evaluated SAP solutions online, SAP invites them to initiate contact, request a proposal, or start the negotiation process. That's where the person-to-person selling begins.

All this suggests that B-to-B selling isn't dying, just changing. The tools and techniques may be different as sales forces leverage technology and adapt to selling in the digital and social media age, but B-to-B marketers will never be able to do without strong sales teams. Sales people who can discover customer needs, solve customer problems and build relationships will be needed and successful, regardless of what else changes. Especially for those big-ticket B-to-B sales, 'all the new technology may make it easier to sell by building strong ties to customers even before the first sit-down, but when the signature hits the dotted line, there will be a sales rep there'.[31]

Indeed, sales remains the single biggest function in business, with millions more employed in sales jobs than in manufacturing or marketing – in the US, it is expected that 1.9 million sales and related jobs will be added by 2020, including at the retail level.[32] The art and science of selling is undergoing its greatest revolution, so even where the classic salesperson is disappearing a new form is being born.[33]

Online selling tools, such as SAP's EcoHub and SAP Store online community-based marketplaces, can help build customer engagement and generate buying interest and sales. But rather than replacing salespeople, such efforts extend their reach and effectiveness.

Source: Akos Stiller/Bloomberg via Getty Images

The new digital selling environment

In response to a new digital buying environment, sellers are reorienting their selling processes around the new customer buying process. They are 'going where customers are' – social media, web forums, online communities, blogs – in order to engage customers earlier. They are engaging customers not just where and when they are buying, but also where and when they are learning about and evaluating what they will buy.

Salespeople now routinely use digital tools that monitor customer social media exchanges to spot trends, identify prospects and learn what customers would like to buy, how they feel about a vendor, and what it would take to make a sale. They generate lists of prospective customers from online databases and social networking sites, such as InsideView, Hoovers and LinkedIn. They create dialogues when prospective customers visit their web and social media sites through live chats with the sales team. They use Internet conferencing tools such as WebEx, Zoom, GoToMeeting or TelePresence to talk live with customers about products and services. They provide videos and other information on their YouTube channels and Facebook pages.

Today's sales forces are also escalating their own use of social media to engage customers throughout the buying process. A recent survey of business-to-business marketers found that, although they have recently cut back on traditional media and event spending, 68 per cent are investing more in social media, ranging from proprietary online customer communities to Webinars and social media and mobile applications. Consider industrial and consumer products giant GE:[34]

GE complements its sales force efforts through a wide variety of digital and social media that inform and engage business customers, connect them with GE salespeople, and promote customer purchasing and relationships. For example, GE's various divisions – from GE Aviation to GE Healthcare and GE Energy – offer dozens of industry-specific websites, containing thousands of individual site areas and tens of thousands of pages that provide B-to-B customers with purchasing solutions, product overviews, detailed technical information, online videos and webinars, live chats and real-time customer support. GE also builds brand awareness and helps its sales force engage business customers deeply through a comprehensive presence in major social media, such as Facebook, Twitter, LinkedIn, Google+, Salesforce.com, and even Instagram, Pinterest and Vine. 'We have a core belief that business is social', says GE's chief marketing officer. 'If you're in business you need social because it's going to get you closer to your customers. We want to get our sales team 100 per cent digitised'.

Ultimately, social selling technologies are helping to make sales forces more efficient, cost-effective and productive. The technologies help salespeople do what good salespeople have always done – build customer relationships by solving customer problems – but do it better, faster and cheaper. However, social selling also has some drawbacks. For starters, it's not cheap. In addition, such systems can intimidate low-tech salespeople or clients. Even more, there are some things you just can't present or teach via the Internet – things that require personal interactions. For these reasons, some high-tech experts recommend that sales executives use online and social media technologies to spot opportunities, provide information, maintain customer contact and make preliminary client sales presentations but resort to old-fashioned, face-to-face meetings when the time draws near to close a big deal.

THE PERSONAL SELLING PROCESS

<div class="sidebar">

Author comment

So far, we've examined how sales management develops and implements overall sales force strategies and programmes. In this section, we'll look at how individual salespeople and sales teams sell to customers and build relationships with them.

</div>

We now turn from designing and managing a sales force, and considering the impact of the new digital environment for selling, to the personal selling process. The **selling process** consists of several steps that salespeople must master. These steps focus on the goal of getting new customers and obtaining orders from them. However, most salespeople spend much of their time maintaining existing accounts and building long-term customer relationships. We discuss the relationship aspect of the personal selling process in a later section.

Steps in the selling process

As shown in Figure 16.3, the selling process consists of seven steps: prospecting and qualifying, pre-approaching, approaching, presenting and demonstrating, handling objections, closing and following up.

Prospecting and qualifying

<div class="sidebar">

Selling process—The steps that salespeople follow when selling, which include prospecting and qualifying, pre-approach, approach, presentation and demonstration, handling objections, closing and follow-up.

Prospecting—The sales step in which a salesperson or company identifies qualified potential customers.

</div>

The first step in the selling process is **prospecting** – identifying qualified potential customers. Approaching the right potential customers is crucial to the selling success. Salespeople don't want to call on just any potential customers. They want to call on those who are most likely to appreciate and respond to the company's value proposition – those the company can serve well and profitably. As one sales expert puts it, 'If the sales force starts chasing anyone who is breathing and seems to have a budget, you risk accumulating a roster of expensive-to-serve, hard-to-satisfy customers who never respond to whatever value proposition you have.' He continues, 'The solution to this isn't

Figure 16.3 Steps in the selling process

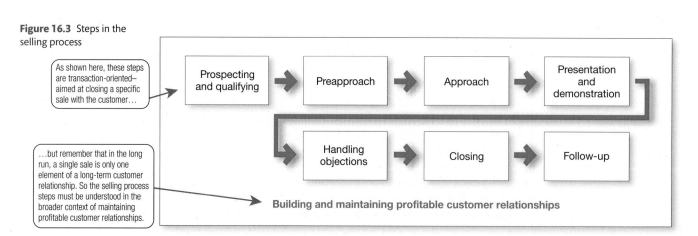

482

rocket science. [You must] train salespeople to actively scout the right prospects.' Another expert concludes, 'Increasing your prospecting effectiveness is the fastest single way to boost your sales.'[35]

A salesperson must often approach many prospects to get only a few sales. Although the company supplies some leads, salespeople need skill in finding their own. The best source is referrals. Salespeople can ask current customers for referrals and cultivate other referral sources, such as suppliers, dealers, non-competing salespeople and online or social media contacts. They can also search for prospects in directories or on the Internet and track down leads using telephone, e-mail and social media. Or they can drop in unannounced on various offices (a practice known as *cold calling*).

Salespeople also need to know how to *qualify* leads – that is, how to identify the good ones and screen out the poor ones. Prospects can be qualified by looking at their financial ability, volume of business, special needs, location and possibilities for growth.

Preapproach

Before calling on a prospect, the salesperson should learn as much as possible about an organisation (what it needs, who is involved in the buying) and its buyers (their characteristics and buying styles). This step is known as **preapproach**. 'Revving up your sales starts with your preparation,' says one sales consultant. 'A successful sale begins long before you set foot in the prospect's office.' Preapproaching begins with good research. The salesperson can consult standard industry and online sources, acquaintances and others to learn about the company. He or she can scour the prospect's web and social media sites for information about its products, buyers and buying processes. Then that salesperson must apply the research to develop a customer strategy. 'Being able to recite the prospect's product line in your sleep isn't enough,' says the consultant. 'You need to translate the data into something useful for your client.'[36]

The salesperson should set *call objectives*, which may be to qualify the prospect, gather information or make an immediate sale. Another task is to determine the best approach, which might be a personal visit, a phone call, a letter, an e-mail, or text or tweet. The best timing should be considered carefully because many prospects are busiest at certain times of the day or week. Finally, the salesperson should give thought to an overall sales strategy for the account.

Preapproach—The sales step in which a salesperson learns as much as possible about a prospective customer before making a sales call.

Approach

During the **approach** step, the salesperson should know how to meet and greet the buyer and get the relationship off to a good start. The approach might take place offline or online, in-person or via digital conferencing or social media. This step involves the salesperson's appearance, opening lines and follow-up remarks. The opening lines should be positive to build goodwill from the outset. This opening might be followed by some key questions to learn more about the customer's needs or by showing a display or sample to attract the buyer's attention and curiosity. As in all stages of the selling process, listening to the customer is crucial.

Approach—The sales step in which a salesperson meets the customer for the first time.

Presentation and demonstration

During the **presentation** step of the selling process, the salesperson tells the 'value story' to the buyer, showing how the company's offer would solve the customer's problems. The *customer-solution approach* fits better with today's relationship marketing focus than does a hard sell or glad-handing approach. 'Stop selling and start helping,' advises one sales consultant. 'Your goal should be to sell your customers exactly what will benefit them most,' says another.[37] Buyers today want answers, not smiles; results, not razzle-dazzle. Moreover, they don't want just products. More than ever in today's economic climate, buyers want to know how a particular product will add value to their businesses. They want salespeople who will listen to their concerns, understand their needs, and respond with the right products and services.

But before salespeople can *present* customer solutions, they must *develop* solutions to present. The solutions approach calls for good listening and problem-solving skills. The qualities that

Presentation—The sales step in which a salesperson tells the 'value story' to the buyer, showing how the company's offer solves the customer's problems.

buyers *dislike most* in salespeople include being pushy, late, deceitful, unprepared, disorganised or overly talkative. The qualities they *value most* include good listening, empathy, honesty, dependability, thoroughness and follow-through. Great salespeople know how to sell, but more importantly they know how to listen and build strong customer relationships. Says one professional, 'You have two ears and one mouth. Use them proportionally.' Says another, 'Everything starts with listening. I think the magic of these days is we've got so many more ways to listen.'[38] A classic ad from office products maker Boise Cascade makes the listening point. It shows a Boise salesperson with huge ears drawn on. 'With Boise, you'll notice a difference right away, especially with our sales force,' says the ad. 'At Boise . . . our account representatives have the unique ability to listen to your needs.'

Finally, salespeople must also plan their presentation methods. Good interpersonal communication skills count when it comes to making effective sales presentations. However, today's media-rich and cluttered communications environment presents many new challenges for sales presenters. Information-overloaded customers demand richer presentation experiences. And presenters now face multiple distractions during presentations from mobile phones, text messages and other digital competition. Salespeople must deliver their messages in more engaging and compelling ways.

Thus, today's salespeople are employing advanced presentation technologies that allow for full multimedia presentations to only one or a few people. The venerable old flip chart has been replaced with sophisticated tablet computers, presentation software, online presentation technologies, interactive whiteboards and digital projectors.

Handling objections

Handling objections—The sales step in which a salesperson seeks out, clarifies and overcomes any customer objections to buying.

Customers almost always have objections during the presentation or when asked to place an order. The problem can be either logical or psychological, and objections are often unspoken. In **handling objections**, the salesperson should use a positive approach, seek out hidden objections, ask the buyer to clarify any objections, take objections as opportunities to provide more information, and turn the objections into reasons for buying. Every salesperson needs training in the skill of handling objections.

Closing

Closing—The sales step in which a salesperson asks the customer for an order.

After handling the prospect's objections, the salesperson next tries to close the sale. Some salespeople do not get around to **closing** or handle it well. They may lack confidence, feel guilty about asking for the order, or fail to recognise the right moment to close the sale. Salespeople should know how to recognise closing signals from the buyer, including physical actions, comments and questions. For example, the customer might sit forward and nod approvingly or ask about prices and credit terms.

Salespeople can use one of several closing techniques. They can ask for an order, review points of agreement, offer to help write up an order, ask whether the buyer wants this model or that one, or note that the buyer will lose out if an order is not placed now. The salesperson may offer the buyer special reasons to close, such as a lower price, an extra quantity at no charge, or additional services.

Follow-up

Follow-up—The sales step in which a salesperson follows up after the sale to ensure customer satisfaction and repeat business.

The last step in the selling process – **follow-up** – is necessary if the salesperson wants to ensure customer satisfaction and repeat business. Right after closing, the salesperson should complete any details on delivery time, purchase terms and other matters. The salesperson then should schedule a follow-up call immediately after the buyer receives the initial order to make sure proper installation, instruction and servicing occur. This visit would reveal any problems, assure the buyer of the salesperson's interest, and reduce any buyer concerns that might have arisen since the sale.

Personal selling and managing customer relationships

The steps in the selling process as just described are *transaction oriented*; their aim is to help salespeople close a specific sale with a customer. But in most cases, the company is not simply seeking a sale. Rather, it wants to serve the customer over the long term in a mutually profitable *relationship*. The sales force usually plays an important role in customer relationship building. Thus, as shown in Figure 16.3, the selling process must be understood in the context of building and maintaining profitable customer relationships. Moreover, as discussed in a previous section, today's buyers are increasingly moving through the early stages of the buying process themselves, before even engaging with sellers. Salespeople must adapt their selling process to match the new buying process. That means discovering and engaging customers on a relationship basis rather than a transaction basis.

Value selling: sales management's challenge is to transform salespeople from customer advocates for price cuts into company advocates for value.

Source: 123RF.com

Successful sales organisations recognise that winning and keeping accounts requires more than making good products and directing the sales force to close lots of sales. If the company wishes only to close sales and capture short-term business, it can do this by simply slashing its prices to meet or beat those of competitors. Instead, most companies want their salespeople to practise *value selling* – demonstrating and delivering superior customer value and capturing a return on that value that is fair for both the customer and the company. For example, as we discovered in the chapter-opening story, companies like P&G understand that they aren't just selling products to and through their retailer customers. They are partnering with these retail accounts to create more value for final consumers to their mutual benefit. P&G knows that it can succeed only if its retail partners succeed.

Unfortunately, in the heat of closing sales – especially in a tough economy – salespeople too often take the easy way out by cutting prices rather than selling value. Thus, the challenge of sales management is to transform salespeople from customer advocates for price cuts into company advocates for value. Here's how Rockwell Automation – a global provider of industrial automation, power, control and information solutions and regularly named One of World's Most Ethical Companies – sells value and relationships rather than price:[39]

Facing pressure . . . to lower its prices, a condiment producer hastily summoned several competing supplier representatives – including Rockwell Automation sales rep Jeff Policicchio – who were given full access to the plant for one day and asked to find ways to dramatically reduce the customer's operating costs. Policicchio quickly learned that a major problem stemmed from lost production and down time due to poorly performing pumps on 32 huge condiment tanks. Policicchio gathered relevant cost and usage data and then used a Rockwell Automation laptop value-assessment tool to construct the best pump solution for the customer.

The next day, Policicchio and the competing reps presented their solutions to plant management. Policicchio's value proposition was as follows: 'With this Rockwell Automation pump solution, through less downtime, reduced administrative costs in procurement, and lower spending on repair parts, your company will save at least $16,268 per pump – on up to 32 pumps – relative to our best competitor's solution.' It turns out the Policicchio was the only rep to demonstrate tangible cost savings for his proposed solution. Everyone else made fuzzy promises about possible benefits or offered to save the customer money by simply shaving their prices.

The plant managers were so impressed with Policicchio's value proposition that – despite its higher initial price – they immediately purchased one Rockwell Automation pump solution for a trial. When the actual savings were even better than predicted, they placed orders for the remaining pumps. Thus, Policicchio's value-selling approach rather than price-cutting approach not only landed the initial sale but also provided the basis for a profitable long-term relationship with the customer.

Value selling requires listening to customers, understanding their needs, and carefully coordinating the whole company's efforts to create lasting relationships based on customer value.[40]

SALES PROMOTION

Sales promotion—Short-term incentives to encourage the purchase or sale of a product or a service.

Personal selling and advertising often work closely with another promotion tool, sales promotion. **Sales promotion** consists of short-term incentives to encourage the purchase or sales of a product or service. Whereas advertising offers reasons to buy a product or service, sales promotion offers reasons to buy *now*.

Examples of sales promotions are found everywhere. A freestanding insert in the local newspaper or posted through the letterbox contains a coupon offering 50p off new Dreamies treats for your cat. A Marks & Spencer ad in your favourite magazine offers 20 per cent off your next purchase of clothing. The health food store offers 'buy one, get one free' on vitamins and remedies. The end-of-the-aisle display in the local supermarket tempts impulse buyers with a wall of Coca Zero – four eight-packs for £10. An executive buys a new HP laptop and gets a free memory upgrade. A hardware store receives a 10 per cent discount on selected Stihl power lawn and garden tools if it agrees to advertise them in local newspapers. Sales promotion includes a wide variety of promotion tools designed to stimulate earlier or stronger market response.

The rapid growth of sales promotion

Sales promotion tools are used by most organisations, including manufacturers, distributors, retailers and not-for-profit institutions. They are targeted toward final buyers (*consumer promotions*), retailers and wholesalers (*trade promotions*), business customers (*business promotions*) and members of the sales force (*sales force promotions*). Today, in the average American consumer packaged-goods company, sales promotion accounts for 60 per cent of all marketing expenditures.[41] In Europe, overall companies probably spend at least as much on sales promotion as they do on higher-profile media advertising.

Several factors have contributed to the rapid growth of sales promotion, particularly in consumer markets. First, inside the company, product managers face greater pressures to increase current sales, and they view promotion as an effective short-run sales tool. Second, externally, the company faces more competition, and competing brands are less differentiated. Increasingly, competitors are using sales promotion to help differentiate their offers. Third, advertising efficiency has declined because of rising costs, media clutter and legal restraints. Finally, consumers have become more value oriented, particularly as a result of economic downturn and recession across the developed world. In the current economy, consumers are demanding lower prices and better deals.[42] Sales promotions can help attract today's more thrift-oriented consumers.

However, the growing use of sales promotion has resulted in *promotion clutter*, similar to advertising clutter. With so many products being sold on special offers, a given promotion runs the risk of being lost in a sea of other promotions, weakening its ability to trigger an immediate purchase. Manufacturers are now searching for ways to rise above the clutter, such as offering larger value deals, creating more dramatic point-of-purchase displays, or delivering promotions through new digital media – such as the Internet or mobile phones. According to one study, 88 per cent of retailers now see digital promotions – such as mobile coupons, shopper e-mails and online deals – as an important part of their shopper marketing efforts.[43]

In developing a sales promotion programme, a company must first set sales promotion objectives and then select the best tools for accomplishing these objectives.

Sales promotion objectives

Sales promotion objectives vary widely. Sellers may use *consumer promotions* to urge short-term customer buying or enhance customer brand involvement. Objectives for *trade promotions* include getting retailers to carry new items and stock more product, buy ahead, or promote the company's products and give them more shelf space. *Business promotions* are used to generate business leads, stimulate purchases, reward customers and motivate salespeople. For the *sales force*, objectives include getting more sales force support for current or new products or getting salespeople to sign up new accounts.

Sales promotions are usually used together with advertising, personal selling, direct marketing or other promotion mix tools. Consumer promotions must usually be advertised and can add excitement and pulling power to ads. Trade and sales force promotions support the firm's personal selling process.

When the economy is in trouble and sales slow down, it is tempting to offer deep promotional discounts to spur consumer spending. In general, however, rather than creating short-term sales or temporary brand switching, sales promotions should help to reinforce the product's position and build long-term customer relationships. If properly designed, every sales promotion tool has the potential to build both short-term excitement and long-term consumer engagement and relationships. Marketers should avoid 'quick fix', price-only promotions in favour of promotions that are designed to build brand equity. Examples include the various *loyalty programmes* and cards that have mushroomed in recent years. Most hotels, supermarkets and airlines offer frequent-guest/buyer/flyer programmes that give rewards to regular customers to keep them coming back. All kinds of companies now offer rewards programmes. Such promotional programmes can build loyalty through added value rather than discounted prices.

For example, Starbucks suffered sales setbacks resulting from the economic downturn, coupled with the introduction of cheaper gourmet coffees by a host of competitors. Starbucks could have lowered its prices or offered promotional discounts. But deep discounts might have damaged the chain's long-term premium positioning. So instead, Starbucks dropped its prices only slightly and ran ads telling customers why its coffee was worth a higher price. With headlines such as 'Beware of a cheaper cup of coffee. It comes with a price,' the ads laid out what separates Starbucks from the competition, such as its practices of buying fair-trade beans and providing healthcare for employees who work more than 20 hours a week. At the same time, to build loyalty, Starbucks promoted its Starbucks Card Rewards programme.[44]

Major sales promotion tools

Many tools can be used to accomplish sales promotion objectives. Descriptions of the main consumer, trade and business promotion tools follow.

Consumer promotions

Consumer promotions include a wide range of tools – from samples, coupons, refunds, premiums and point-of-purchase displays to contests, sweepstakes and event sponsorships.

Samples are offers of a trial amount of a product. Sampling is the most effective – but most expensive – way to introduce a new product or create new excitement for an existing one. Some samples are free; for others, the company charges a small amount to offset its cost. The sample might be sent by mail, handed out in a store or at a kiosk, attached to another product, or featured in an advert, an e-mail or a mobile offer. Sometimes, samples are combined into sample packs, which can then be used to promote other products and services. Sampling can be a powerful promotional tool. For example, in the United States Pizza Hut handed out more than 10,000 free slices of its hand-tossed pizza at Super Bowl XLVIII-related events (the premier American football event) in New York and New Jersey. 'It's a massive opportunity to sample our new product,' said a Pizza Hut marketer.

As with social selling examined earlier, companies are increasingly combining new technology with the conventional tool of free samples:

> The Christmas grocery shop was a little more bearable for some this year thanks to – almost literally – all-singing, all-dancing machines that cascaded free slices of Christmas cake to shoppers at the press of a button, alongside bursts of festive aroma and carol singing. The cake dispensers were dreamt up by Premier Foods to woo consumers on the street.

Consumer promotions–
Sales promotion tools used to boost short-term customer buying and engagement or enhance long-term customer relationships.

Kelloggs, the US-based cereals manufacturer, launched its move into savoury snacks by offering free samples to anyone who dropped in to a pop-up, temporary shop and sent a tweet about it. Visitors to the tweet shop got to share their opinions of the new product. The pop-up shop quickly generated 3,000 tweets of which 96 per cent were positive, generating a positive buzz around the new product.

Nestlé points to social media to show the success of its GPS-tracked cash giveaway. Chocolate bar KitKat gained 150,000 Facebook fans over the period of the campaign. Nestlé's 'We will find you' campaign involved hiding GPS chips in six chocolate bars including KitKat, Aero and Yorkie. When opened, the wrapper sent a signal of the location to Nestle, who then sent a representative to hand over £10,000 in cash. Offers to claim smaller prizes not involving GPS were included in further wrappers.[45]

Coupons are certificates that save buyers money when they purchase specified products. Many consumers love coupons, although it is a tradition better established in the US than Europe. In Europe, couponing is more frequently associated with the rewards paid out by retailer loyalty cards like Tesco Clubcard and Marks & Spencer's credit card. For example, Nielsen research reports that while 38 per cent of European consumers they surveyed indicate they use coupons to save, there is wide variation within the Continent. At least half of consumers reported coupon use in several western and southern European countries, such as Belgium and Portugal (63 per cent each), Greece (55 per cent), France (53 per cent) and Spain (50 per cent), yet in other markets, particularly in northern and eastern Europe, reported coupon use is much less prevalent. In countries such as Germany and the Netherlands, coupon use is very marginal. Reported coupon use is also less common as a saving strategy in Latin America (25 per cent) and the Middle East/Africa (18 per cent).

Nonetheless, US consumer packaged goods companies distributed 315 billion coupons with an average face value of $1.62 in 2013. Consumers redeemed more than 2.8 billion of them for a total savings of about $3.5 billion.[46] While European retailers are frequently reluctant to use coupons, coupons can promote early trial of a new brand or stimulate sales of a mature brand. However, in the US as a result of coupon clutter, redemption rates have been declining in recent years. Thus, most major consumer-goods companies are issuing fewer coupons and targeting them more carefully.

Marketers are also cultivating new outlets for distributing coupons, such as supermarket shelf dispensers, electronic point-of-sale coupon printers, and online and mobile phone coupon programmes. According to a recent study, digital coupons now outpace printed newspaper coupons by 10 to 1. Digital coupons accounted for nearly 9 per cent of all coupons redeemed last year in the United States; about 7 per cent were printed from a computer at home, and about 3 per cent were redeemed via smartphone or other mobile devices. In one study, more than half of all US adults redeemed a digital coupon last year, and nearly 20 per cent of adults used a mobile phone coupon, up more than 40 per cent from the prior year.[47] This trend is also apparent in Europe:

The total number of people using coupon sites in Europe in a month grew 162 per cent to 34.9 million visitors in December 2010 when compared to the prior year. The sizeable growth can largely be attributed to the emergence of Groupon, which was not a significant player in Europe prior to this time in 2009. Groupon, buoyed by its acquisition of its leading competitor in Europe, was able to establish a presence in more than 100 European cities in the past year and now reaches more than 12 million visitors a month, approximately one-third of the total coupon market.[48]

Cash refunds (or *rebates* or *cashback*) are like coupons except that the price reduction occurs after the purchase rather than at the retail outlet. The customer sends a 'proof of purchase' to the manufacturer, which then refunds part of the purchase price by mail. For example, global company Lowrance is world leader in the design, manufacture and marketing of high-quality sport fishing sonar and global positioning system mapping instruments. In this specialised market, the company's carefully timed Spring Rebate scheme in Europe offers customers cash back per product purchased, which then qualifies the customer for additional extra cashback on further purchases. The timing is aimed to attract users before the new season starts.

Price packs (also called *money-off deals*) offer consumers savings off the regular price of a product. The producer marks the reduced prices directly on the label or package. Price packs can be single packages sold at a reduced price (such as two for the price of one) or two related products banded together (such as a toothbrush and toothpaste). Price packs are very effective – even more so than coupons – in stimulating short-term sales. One of the commonest forms of this promotion in Europe is 'BOGOF' offers (buy one, get one free).

Premiums are goods offered either free or at low cost as an incentive to buy a product, ranging from toys included with children's products to phone cards and DVDs. A premium may come inside the package (in-pack), outside the package (on-pack) or through the mail. For example, over the years, McDonalds has offered a variety of premiums in its Happy Meals – from Madagascar characters to Beanie Babies and LEGO hologram drink cups. Customers can visit www.happymeal.com to play games and watch commercials associated with the current Happy Meal sponsor.[49] The giveaway is backed by a major TV campaign, with McDonalds' claiming the initiative is about increasing literacy and creativity among children.

Advertising specialities, also called *promotional products*, are useful articles imprinted with an advertiser's name, logo or message that are given as gifts to consumers. Typical items include T-shirts and other clothing, pens, coffee mugs, calendars, key rings, mouse pads, matches, holdalls, memory sticks, golf balls and baseball caps. US marketers spent more than $18.5 billion on advertising specialities last year and UK expenditure is estimated at around £800 million.[50] Such items can be very effective. The 'best of them stick around for months, subtly burning a brand name into a user's brain', notes a promotional products expert.[51]

Point-of-purchase (POP) promotions include displays and demonstrations that take place at the point of sale. Think of your last visit to your local supermarket. Chances are good that you were tripping over aisle displays, promotional signs, 'shelf talkers' or demonstrators offering free tastes of featured food or drink products. Unfortunately, many retailers do not like to handle the hundreds of displays, signs and posters they receive from manufacturers each year, and in Europe some refuse to have these materials in their stores at all, because they believe it undermines the image of the store. Manufacturers have responded by offering better POP materials; offering to set them up, and tying them in with television, print or online messages. Some upmarket retailers remain uncooperative.

Indeed, in the UK, when upmarket supermarket Waitrose chose to fight online and discounter competition by giving free coffee and newspapers to its customers, it managed both to upset Labour Party politicians who accused Waitrose of stealing business from small high street shops, and to annoy some of its loyal consumers who thought the free drinks were attracting the 'wrong type' of customers to its upmarket stores. The unrepentant Managing Director of Waitrose described this as a 'storm in a coffee cup'.[52]

Contests, sweepstakes and *games* give consumers the chance to win something, such as cash, trips or goods, by luck or through extra effort. A *contest* calls for consumers to submit an entry – a jingle, guess or suggestion, for example – to be judged by a panel that will select the best entries. A *sweepstake* calls for consumers to submit their names for a draw. A *game* presents consumers with something – for example, bingo numbers or missing letters – every time they buy, which may or may not help them win a prize. Such promotions can create considerable brand attention and consumer involvement. Nonetheless, most European countries have strict laws regarding running lotteries (contests where no skill is required of participants) and illegal gaming, so some care is needed in designing consumer contests which remain within the law.

All kinds of companies use sweepstakes and contests to create brand attention and boost consumer involvement. For example, Google's 'Doodle 4 Google' contest invited children to design a Google logo, based on the theme 'If I could invent one thing to make the world a better place . . .', with prizes ranging from T-shirts and tablet computers to a college scholarship. The 'OXO I do sweepstakes' invites soon-to-be-married couples to 'Like' OXO's Facebook page and earn a chance to win $500 toward their Amazon wedding registry.

Nonetheless, events like competitions require very careful planning and management. Consider the following example of how things can go wrong:

> In 2011 the UK's largest fresh soup brand – New Covent Garden Soup Co. – ran a competition offering the winner £500,000 to buy a small farm of their own. More than 260,000 people took part in the competition. But whoever had the pack with the winning number apparently discarded it without checking, so no one won the prize, and the competition was closed. As a result, Facebook and consumer websites were inundated with complaints from disgruntled competition participants, and the company got adverse media attention nationally. The company promised to review how future promotions should be run, but there was no escape from the negative impact on loyal consumers.[53]

Event marketing (or event sponsorships)—Creating a brand-marketing event or serving as a sole or participating sponsor of events created by others.

Finally, marketers can promote their brands through **event marketing (or event sponsorships)**. They can create their own brand-marketing events or serve as sole or participating sponsors of events created by others. The events might include anything from mobile brand tours to festivals, reunions, marathons, concerts or other sponsored gatherings. Event marketing is huge, and it may be the fastest-growing area of promotion, especially in tough economic times. One variation is the use of paid-for 'flash mobs' to add excitement. Effective event marketing links events and sponsorships to a brand's value proposition. And with the social sharing power of today's digital media, even local events can have far-reaching impact.

Event marketing can provide a less costly alternative to expensive TV commercials. When it comes to event marketing, sports are in a league of their own. Marketers spend large sums to associate their brands with sporting events and clubs. For example, Manchester United football club attracts multiple corporate sponsorships, including: AON (insurance and outsourcing) as official sponsor; DHL as official logistics partner; Betfair as official betting partner; Casillero del Diablo as official wine partner; Hublot as official time-keeper; Smirnoff as official responsible drinking partner; Mister Potato as official snack partner; Nike as official kit manufacturer; Audi as official car supplier; Singha as official beer; Thomas Cook as official travel partner; Turkish Airlines as official airline partner; Epson as official office products supplier; STC as official integrated telecommunications partner; plus some 14 more companies partnering in some form.[54] All these companies hope that sponsorship will connect their brands with major audiences throughout the world through the matches the club plays and the strength of its sporting brand – Manchester United has an estimated worldwide following of 333 million people with 92 million in Asia, and a uniquely strong brand in football. Manchester United sponsorship agreements are worth in excess of £130 million, including a recent ground-breaking £40m deal with logistics firm DHL to sponsor the club's training kit.

But according to one business reporter, energy drink maker Red Bull is the 'mother of event marketers':[55]

> Event pioneer Red Bull holds hundreds of events each year in dozens of sports around the world. Each event features off-the-grid experiences designed to bring the high-octane world of Red Bull to its community of enthusiasts. The brand even hosts a 'Holy S**t' tab on its website, featuring videos of everything from 27-metre ocean cliff dives at its Cliff Diving Series event in Grimstad, Norway, to dare-devil free-skiing feats at its Red Bull Cold Rush event in the Colorado mountain peaks, to absolutely breathtaking wing suit flights at Red Bull events staged in exotic locations from Monterrey, Mexico, to Hunan Province, China. The Red Bull Final Descent series is a mountain biking challenge that pushes riders to the brink and back, over some of the most technically challenging terrain in North America. Red Bull events draw large crowds and plenty of media coverage. But it's about more than just the events – it's about customer engagement. It's about creating face-to-face experiences in which customers can actually feel the excitement and live the brand. 'It's about deepening and enhancing relationships,' says one analyst.

Trade promotions

Trade promotions—Sales promotion tools used to persuade resellers to carry a brand, give it shelf space and promote it in advertising

Manufacturers direct more sales promotion dollars, in the United States, toward retailers and wholesalers (79 per cent of all promotions dollars) than to final consumers (21 per cent).[56] **Trade promotions** can persuade resellers to carry a brand, give it shelf space, promote it in advertising and push it to consumers. Shelf space is so scarce these days that manufacturers often have to offer price-offs, allowances, buy-back guarantees or free goods to retailers and wholesalers to get products on the shelf and, once there, to keep them there.

Manufacturers use several trade promotion tools. Many of the tools used for consumer promotions – such as contests, premiums and displays – can also be used as trade promotions. Or the manufacturer may offer a straight *discount* off the list price on each case purchased during a stated period of time (also called a *price-off*, *off-invoice* or *off-list*). Manufacturers also may offer an *allowance* (usually so much off per case) in return for the retailer's agreement to feature the manufacturer's products in some way. An advertising allowance compensates retailers for advertising the product. A display allowance compensates them for using special displays. Powerful retailers in Europe like Tesco and Carrefour sometimes require suppliers to make large cash payments for access to their stores, the cost of advertising, or to have special displays in-store.

'Event marketing: Red Bull hosts hundreds of events each year in dozens of sports around the world, designed to bring the high-octane world of Red Bull to its community of enthusiasts.

Source: Christopher Lee/Getty Images for Red Bull

Manufacturers may offer *free goods*, which are extra cases of merchandise, to resellers who buy a certain quantity or who feature a certain flavour or size. They may offer *push money* – cash or gifts to dealers or their sales forces to 'push' the manufacturer's goods. Manufacturers may give retailers free *speciality advertising items* that carry the company's name, such as pens, pencils, calendars, paperweights, matchbooks, memo pads and other attractive free gifts. However, in the UK and Europe suppliers have to be very careful not to breach strict anti-bribery laws in European countries – both local and EU-wide. Under new laws in the UK, even minor gifts or payments to individuals are liable to be seen as bribes, with severe penalties for the donors.

Business promotions

Companies spend huge amounts each year on promotion to industrial customers. **Business promotions** are used to generate business leads, stimulate purchases, reward customers and motivate salespeople. Business promotions include many of the same tools used for consumer or trade promotions. Here, we focus on two additional major business promotion tools: conferences and trade shows, and sales contests.

Business promotions—Sales promotion tools used to generate business leads, stimulate purchases, reward customers and motivate salespeople.

Some trade shows are huge. At the Bauma mining and construction equipment trade show in Munich, Germany, more than 3,400 exhibitors from 57 countries presented their latest product innovations to over 530,000 attendees from more than 200 countries.

Source: Photograph: Messe München

Many companies and trade associations organise *conferences, exhibitions* and *trade shows* to promote their products. Firms selling to a particular industry show their products at an industrial trade show. Sellers receive many benefits, such as opportunities to find new sales leads, contact customers, introduce new products, meet new customers, sell more to present customers, and educate customers with publications and audiovisual materials. Trade shows also help companies reach many prospects not reached through their sales forces.

Some trade shows are huge. For example, at the 2012 International Consumer Electronics Show, 3,000 exhibitors attracted 125,850 professional visitors. Even more impressive, at the 2013 BAUMA mining and construction equipment trade show in Munich, Germany, 3,421 exhibitors from 57 countries presented their latest product innovations to 535,065 attendees from more than 200 countries. Total exhibition space equalled about 575,000 m².[57]

A *sales contest* is a contest for salespeople or dealers to motivate them to increase their sales performance over a given period. Sales contests motivate and recognise good company performers, who may receive travel, cash prizes or other gifts. Some companies award points for performance, which a receiver can cash in for any of a variety of prizes. Sales contests work best when they are tied to measurable and achievable sales objectives (such as finding new accounts, reviving old accounts or increasing account profitability).

Developing the sales promotion programme

Beyond selecting the types of promotions to use, marketers must make several other decisions in designing the full sales promotion programme. First, they must determine the *size of the incentive*. A certain minimum incentive is necessary if the promotion is to succeed; a larger incentive will produce more sales response. The marketer also must establish *conditions for participation*. Incentives might be offered to everyone or only to select groups.

Marketers must determine how to *promote and distribute the promotion* programme itself. A £1-off coupon could be given out in a package, at the store, via the Internet, or in an mobile download. Each distribution method involves a different level of reach and cost. Increasingly, marketers are blending several media into a total campaign concept. The *length of the promotion* is also important. If the sales promotion period is too short, many prospects (who may not be buying during that time) will miss it. If the promotion runs too long, the deal will lose some of its 'act now' force.

Evaluation is also very important. Many companies fail to evaluate their sales promotion investments, and others evaluate them only superficially. Marketers should work to measure the returns on their sales promotion investments, just as they should seek to assess the returns on other marketing activities. The most common evaluation method is to compare sales before, during and after a promotion. Marketers should ask: Did the promotion attract new customers or more purchasing from current customers? Can we hold onto these new customers and purchases? Will the long-run customer relationship and sales gains from the promotion justify its costs?

Clearly, sales promotion plays an important role in the total promotion mix. To use it well, the marketer must define the sales promotion objectives, select the best tools, design the sales promotion programme, implement the programme and evaluate the results. Moreover, sales promotion must be coordinated carefully with other promotion mix elements within the overall IMC programme.

OBJECTIVES REVIEW AND KEY TERMS

This chapter is the third of four chapters covering the final marketing mix element – promotion. The previous two chapters dealt with overall integrated marketing communications and with advertising and public relations. This chapter investigated personal selling and sales promotion. Personal selling is the interpersonal arm of the communications mix. Sales promotion consists of short-term incentives to encourage the purchase or sale of a product or service.

OBJECTIVE 1 Discuss the role of a company's salespeople in creating value for customers and building customer relationships (pp. 466–469)

Most companies use salespeople, and many companies assign them an important role in the marketing mix. For companies selling business products, the firm's sales force works directly with customers. Often, the sales force is the customer's only direct contact with the company and therefore may be viewed by customers as representing the company itself. In contrast, for consumer-product companies that sell through intermediaries, consumers usually do not meet salespeople or even know about them. The sales force works behind the scenes, dealing with wholesalers and retailers to obtain their support and helping them become more effective in selling the firm's products.

As an element of the promotion mix, the sales force is very effective in achieving certain marketing objectives and carrying out such activities as prospecting, communicating, selling and servicing, and information gathering. But with companies becoming more market oriented, a customer-focused sales force also works to produce both customer satisfaction and company profit. The sales force plays a key role in developing and managing profitable customer relationships.

OBJECTIVE 2 Identify and explain the six major sales force management steps (pp. 470–482)

High sales force costs necessitate an effective sales management process consisting of six steps: designing sales force strategy and structure, recruiting and selecting, training, compensating, supervising and evaluating salespeople and sales force performance.

In designing a sales force strategy, sales management must address various issues, including what type of sales force structure will work best (territorial, product, customer or complex structure), sales force size, who will be involved in selling, and how its various salespeople and sales-support people will work together (inside or outside sales forces and team selling).

Salespeople must be recruited and selected carefully. In recruiting salespeople, a company may look to the job duties and the characteristics of its most successful salespeople to suggest the traits it wants in its salespeople. It must then look for applicants through recommendations of current salespeople, advertising, and the Internet and social media, as well as university recruitment/placement centres. After the selection process is complete, training programmes familiarise new salespeople not only with the art of selling but also with the company's history, its products and policies, and the characteristics of its market and competitors.

The sales force compensation system helps to reward, motivate and direct salespeople. In addition to compensation, all salespeople need supervision, and many need continuous encouragement because they must make many decisions and face many frustrations. Periodically, the company must evaluate their performance to help them do a better job. In evaluating salespeople, the company relies on getting regular information gathered through sales reports, personal observations, customers' letters and complaints, customer surveys and conversations with other salespeople.

The fastest-growing sales trend is the explosion in social selling – using online, mobile and social media in selling. The new digital technologies are providing salespeople with powerful tools for identifying and learning about prospects, engaging customers, creating customer value, closing sales and nurturing customer relationships. Many of today's customers no longer rely as much on assistance provided by salespeople. Instead, increasingly, they use online and social media resources to analyse their own problems, research solutions, get advice from colleagues, and rank buying options before ever speaking to a salesperson. In response, sellers are reorienting their selling processes around the new customer buying process. They are using social media, web forums, online communities, blogs and other digital tools to engage customers earlier and more fully. Ultimately, online and social media technologies are helping to make sales forces more efficient, cost effective and productive.

OBJECTIVE 3 Discuss the personal selling process, distinguishing between transaction-oriented marketing and relationship marketing (pp. 482–486).

Selling involves a seven-step process: prospecting and qualifying, pre-approach, approach, presentation and demonstration, handling objections, closing and follow-up. These steps help marketers close a specific sale and, as such, are transaction-oriented. However, a seller's dealings with customers should be guided by the larger concept of relationship marketing. The company's sales force should help to orchestrate a whole-company effort to develop profitable long-term relationships with key customers based on superior customer value and satisfaction.

OBJECTIVE 4 Explain how sales promotion campaigns are developed and implemented (pp. 486–492)

Sales promotion campaigns call for setting sales promotions objectives (in general, sales promotions should be *consumer relationship building*); selecting tools; and developing and implementing the sales promotion programme by using *consumer promotion tools* (from coupons, refunds, premiums and point-of-purchase promotions to contests, sweepstakes and events), *trade promotion tools* (from discounts and allowances to free goods and push money) and *business promotion tools* (conferences, exhibitions, trade shows and sales contests), as well as determining such things as the size of the incentive, the conditions for participation, how to promote and distribute the promotion package, and the length of the promotion. After this process is completed, the company must evaluate its sales promotion results.

NAVIGATING THE KEY TERMS

OBJECTIVE 1
Personal selling (p. 467)
Salesperson (p. 467)

OBJECTIVE 2
Sales force management (p. 470)
Territorial sales force structure (p. 470)
Product sales force structure (p. 470)
Customer (or market) sales force
    structure (p. 471)
Outside sales force (or field sales force)
    (p. 472)

Inside sales force (p. 472)
Team selling (p. 473)
Sales quota (p. 478)
Social selling (p. 479)

OBJECTIVE 3
Selling process (p. 482)
Prospecting (p. 482)
Pre-approach (p. 483)
Approach (p. 483)
Presentation (p. 483)
Handling objections (p. 484)

Closing (p. 484)
Follow-up (p. 484)

OBJECTIVE 4
Sales promotion (p. 486)
Consumer promotions (p. 487)
Event marketing (or event sponsorship)
    (p. 490)
Trade promotions (p. 490)
Business promotions (p. 491)

DISCUSSION AND CRITICAL THINKING

Discussion questions

16-1 Compare the three sales force structures outlined in the chapter. Which structure is most effective? (AACSB: Communication; Reflective thinking)

16-2 Compare an inside sales force and an outside sales force. Why might a company have both? (AACSB: Communication; Reflective thinking)

16-3 Discuss how online, mobile and social media tools are changing the selling function. (AACSB: Communication; Reflective thinking)

16-4 Define sales promotion and discuss its objectives. (AACSB: Communication)

16-5 Discuss the different types of trade sales promotions and distinguish these types of promotions from business promotions. (AACSB: Communication)

Critical-thinking exercises

16-6 Hiring the right people for sales jobs is an important sales management function. Aptitude tests are used often to assist in assessing a candidate's abilities and traits. Search the Internet for information on sales assessment tests and present the characteristics and traits most often assessed. (AACSB: Communication; Use of IT; Reflective thinking)

16-7 Select a product or service and role-play a sales call – from the approach to the close – with another student. Have one member of the team act as the salesperson with the other member acting as the customer, raising at least three objections. Select another product or service and perform this exercise again with your roles reversed. (AACSB: Communication; Reflective thinking)

16-8 Find an example of each type of consumer sales promotion tool. Explain how you obtained the promotion (that is, how did the marketer distribute it to consumers?) and what you think the marketer was trying to achieve with the sales promotion tool. (AACSB: Communications; Reflective thinking)

Mini cases and applications

Online, mobile and social media marketing: sales promotions

Sales promotion has always been an effective tool for influencing behaviour and providing a means for measuring effectiveness. Marketers can measure how many buyers redeem a coupon, enter a contest, receive a premium or buy bonus packs. But now,

new technologies are taking sales promotion to a new level – generating consumer engagement. For example, consider some examples from the US. When AMC Theaters wanted to encourage movie goers to watch a movie on Sunday, typically a slow day for AMC, it offered a coupon for popcorn and fountain drinks on Facebook for the week prior to a specific Sunday, and encouraged respondents to invite their friends to claim a coupon as well. The result? More than 200,000 takers in six days and almost 50,000 of them driving their friends to AMC's fan page as well. Similarly, when Edible Arrangements wanted to acquire fans for its Facebook page and increase awareness for the company, it offered free boxes of chocolate-covered fruit to consumers who entered and 'Liked' the page. When the company quickly ran out of free samples, it changed the offer to a coupon and experienced double-digit growth as tens of thousands of customers flooded the stores to redeem the coupon – all in less than a week. When Nintendo Wii wanted to raise awareness and generate excitement for its NBA Jam game, it used an essay contest of 'jamisms', with voting done in a bracket style like the NBA playoffs. In addition to the 3,000 entries, the contest generated buzz and thousands of impressions and new Facebook fans. The link between online and sales promotion is rapidly becoming important in every country.

16-9 Throughout the world, businesses large and small are using online, social media and mobile marketing to influence buyer behaviour and generate customer engagement. Research the tips available for offering an online promotion. What should marketers consider when designing and launching online sales promotions? (AACSB: Communication; Use of IT; Reflective thinking)

16-10 Design a sales promotion campaign using online, social media and mobile marketing for a small business or organisation in your locality. Develop a presentation to pitch your campaign to the business or organisation and incorporate what you've learned about the selling process. (AACSB: Communication; Reflective thinking)

Marketing ethics: drug dealing

The pharmaceutical industry is innovating at a dizzying pace, but it is getting more difficult for pharmaceutical sales reps to reach doctors to inform them of new or improved products. One option is to host educational seminars. However, many educational seminars are held at lavish restaurants or exotic destinations underwritten by pharmaceutical companies and doctors providing the education are paid generous consulting and speaking fees. In some cases, speakers are given scripts developed by the pharmaceutical company, leading to the criticism that this is company-scripted marketing and the distinguished speaker is merely a 'paid parrot' selling drugs for the company. Critics also claim that such promotion results in needlessly increased prescriptions for expensive drugs that are no better than generic alternatives. Many drug makers are reducing expenditures for such product promotions because they are increasingly seen as unacceptable sales practices.

16-11 Do you believe it is wrong for pharmaceutical companies to explain the benefits of their products to physicians in this way? Suggest other alternatives for reaching doctors to inform them of the benefits of a company's products. (AACSB: Communication; Ethical reasoning; Reflective thinking)

16-12 Research published stories of the incentives offered to doctors by pharmaceutical companies to persuade them to prescribe particular drugs, and the sanctions being applied by governments in the US, Europe and China to curb such practices. Write a report on what you find, and how pharmaceuticals selling is changing. (AACSB: Communication; Use of IT; Reflective thinking)

Marketing by the numbers: sales force analysis

Wheels, Inc. is a manufacturer of bicycles sold through retail bicycle shops in the south-eastern United States. The company has two salespeople who do more than just sell the products – they manage relationships with the bicycle shops to enable them to better meet consumers' needs. The company's sales reps visit the shops several times per year, often for hours at a time. The owner of Wheels is considering expanding to the rest of the US and would like to have distribution through 1,000 bicycle shops. To do so, however, the company would have to hire more salespeople. Each salesperson earns $40,000 plus 2 per cent commission on all sales. Another alternative is to use the services of sales agents instead of its own salesforce. Sales agents would be paid 5 per cent of sales.

16-13 Refer to Appendix 2: Marketing by the numbers, to answer this question. Determine the number of salespeople Wheels needs if it has 1,000 bicycle shop accounts that need to be called on four times per year. Each sales call lasts approximately 2.5 hours, and each sales rep has approximately 1,250 hours per year to devote to customers. (AACSB: Communication; Analytical reasoning)

16-14 At what level of sales would it be more cost-efficient for Wheels to use sales agents compared to its own sales force? To determine this, consider the fixed and variable costs for each alternative. What are the pros and cons of using a company's own sales force over independent sales agents? (AACSB: Communication; Analytical reasoning; Reflective thinking)

REFERENCES

[1] Based on information from numerous P&G managers; with information from '500 largest sales forces in America', *Selling Power*, September 2013, pp. 34, 40; Cassandra Jowett, 'Schulich Grand finds her calling in Customer Business Development at P&G', *TalentEgg*, 8 January 2013, http://talentegg.ca/incubator/2013/01/08/schul-ch-grad-finds-calling-customer-business-development-pg/; 'Then and now: going to great lengths to get P&G products into the hands of consumers', *P&G Corporate Newsroom*, 13 February 2013, http://news.pg.com/blog/company-strategy/then-and-now-going-great-lengths-get-pg-products-hands-consumers; and http://we.experiencepg.com/home/customer_business_development_cbd_sales.html, accessed September 2014.

[2] See, for example: Nigel F. Piercy and Nikala Lane, *Strategic Customer Management: Strategizing the Sales Organization*, Oxford: Oxford university Press, 2009.

[3] Andrew Palliser 'Business is better face-to-face', *Daily Telegraph*, 3 November 2009, p. B4.

[4] Henry Canaday, 'Sales rep to CEO: Anne Mulcahy and the Xerox revolution', *Selling Power*, November/December 2008, pp. 53–57; '2008 Chief Executive of the Year', *Chief Executive*, September/October 2008, p. 68; Andrea Deckert, 'Mulcahy describes the keys to Xerox turnaround', 2 November 2007, p. 3; 'Women CEOs, Xerox', *Financial Times*, 31 December 2008, p. 10; and 'Anne Mulcahy to retire as Xerox CEO', *Wireless News*, 27 May 2009.

[5] See Philip Kotler, Neil Rackham and Suj Krishnaswamy, 'Ending the war between sales and marketing', *Harvard Business Review*, July–August 2006, pp. 68–78; Christian Homburg, Ove Jensen and Harley Krohmer, 'Configurations of marketing and sales: a taxonomy', *Journal of Marketing*, March 2008, pp. 133–154; and Paul Greenberg, 'The shotgun marriage of sales and marketing', *Customer Relationship Management*, February 2010, pp. 30–36.

[6] Nigel F. Piercy and Nikala Lane, *Strategic Customer Management: Strategizing the Sales Organization*, Oxford: Oxford university Press, 2009.

[7] Example based on Ernest Waaser and others, 'How you slice it: smarter segmentation for your sales force', *Harvard Business Review*, March 2004, pp. 105–111.

[8] 'Selling Power 500: the largest sales force in America', *Selling Power*, July/August/September 2013, p. 32.

[9] For more on this and other methods for determining sales force size, see Mark W. Johnston and Greg W. Marshall, *Sales Force Management*, 11th ed. (London: Routledge, 2013).

[10] Jeff Green 'The new Willy Loman survives by staying home', *Bloomberg BusinessWeek*, 14–20 January 2013, p. 16–18.

[11] See discussions in Mike Ishmael, 'The cost of a sales call', 22 October 2012, http://4dsales.com/the-cost-of-a-sales-call/; Jeff Green, 'The new Willy Loman survives by staying home', *Bloomberg Businessweek*, 14–20 January 2013, pp. 16–17; and 'What is the real cost of a B2B sales call?' www.marketing-playbook.com/sales-marketing-strategy/what-is-the-real-cost-of-a-b2b-sales-call, accessed September 2014.

[12] Jeff Green, 'The new Willy Loman survives by staying home', *Bloomberg Businessweek*, 14–20 January 2013, pp. 16–17; and Dave Stein, 'The evolution of social selling', *Sales & Marketing Management*, May/June 2013, p. 14.

[13] Quote and facts from Jim Domanski, 'Special Report: The 2012 B@B Tele-Sales Trend Report', www.salesopedia.com/down-loads/2012%20B2B%20Tele-Sales%20Trend%20Special%20 Reportl.pdf, accessed July 2013.

[14] See 'Case study: climax portable-machine tools', www.selltis.com/products.aspx?menuid=13, accessed August 2010.

[15] Jennifer J. Salopek, 'Bye, bye, used car guy', *T+D*, April 2007, pp. 22–25; William F. Kendy, 'No more Lone Rangers', *Selling Power*, April 2004, pp. 70–74; Michelle Nichols, 'Pull together - or fall apart', *BusinessWeek*, 2 December 2005, accessed at www.businessweek.com/smallbiz/content/may2005/sb20050513_6167.htm; and John Boe, 'Cross-selling takes teamwork', *American Salesman*, March 2009, pp. 14–16.

[16] 'Customer Business Development', http://we.experiencepg.com/home/customer_business_development_cbd_sales.html, accessed September 2014.

[17] Scott Fuhr, 'Good hiring makes good cents', *Selling Power*, July/August/September 2012, pp. 20–21.

[18] For this and more information and discussion, see www.gallupaustralia.com.au/consulting/118729/sales-force-effectiveness.aspx, accessed July 2012; Lynette Ryals and Iain Davies, 'Do you really know who your best salespeople are?' *Harvard Business Review*, December 2010, pp. 34–35; 'The 10 skills of super salespeople', www.businesspartnerships.ca/articles/the_10_skills_of_super_salespeople.phtml, accessed July 2012; 'Profile of a super seller', *Selling Power*, October/November/December 2012, pp. 12–13; and Gerhard Gschwandtner, 'Love and aggression', *Selling Power*, April/May/June 2013, pp. 37–39.

[19] See Steve Denning, 'The one thing the greatest salespeople all have', *Forbes*, 29 November 2013, www.forbes.com/sites/stevedenning/2012/11/29/the-one-thing-the-greatest-salespeople-all-have/.

[20] See, for example, the discussion in: Philip Delves Broughton, 'Portrait of a perfect salesman', *Financial Times*, 3 May 2012, p. 14.

[21] Barbara Hendricks, 'Strengths-based selling', 8 February 2011, www.gallup.com/press/146246/Strengths-Based-Selling.aspx.

[22] Corporate Visions, Inc., 'ADP Case Study', http://corporatevisions.com/v5/documents/secure_downloads/CVI_caseStudy_ADP.pdf, accessed June 2014; and Henry Canaday, 'The transformation of enterprise sales training', *Selling Power*, https://wwwimages2.adobe.com/content/dam/Adobe/en/products/adobeconnect/pdfs/elearning/transformation-of-enterprise-sales-training.pdf, accessed September 2014.

[23] Based on information found in Sara Donnelly, 'Staying in the game', *Pharmaceutical Executive*, May 2008, pp. 158–159; 'Improving sales force effectiveness: Bayer's experiment with new technology', Bayer Healthcare Pharmaceuticals, Inc., 2008, www.icmrindia.org/casestudies/catalogue/Marketing/MKTG200.htm; and Tanya Lewis, 'Concentric', *Medical Marketing and Media*, July 2008, p. 59. For more on e-learning, see 'Logging on for sale school', *CustomRetailer*, November 2009, p. 30; and Sarah Boehle, 'Global sales training's balancing act', *Training*, January 2010, p. 29.

[24] For this and more discussion, see Joseph Kornak, '07 compensation survey: what's it all worth?', *Sales & Marketing Management*, May 2007, pp. 28–39; Ken Sundheim, 'How sales professionals are paid', *SellingProf*, www.sellingprof.com/leadership/how-sales-professionals-are-paid, accessed June 2014; and Alexander Group, '2014 sales compensation trends survey results', January 2014, www.alexandergroup.com/resources/survey-findings.

[25] Susan Greco, 'How to reduce your cost of sales', *Inc*, 5 March 2010, www.inc.com/guide/reducing-cost-of-sales.html, accessed October 2015.

[26] See Louis Columbus, 'Top-five focus areas for improving sales effectiveness initiatives', *Accenture*, 2013, www.accenture.com/SiteCollectionDocuments/PDF/Accenture-Top-Five-Improvements-Sales-Effectiveness.pdf; and '2014 sales performance optimization study', CSO Insights, www.csoinsights.com/Publications/.

[27] See Gary H. Anthes, 'Portal powers GE sales', *Computerworld*, 2 June 2003, pp. 31–32; also see Henry Canaday, 'How to boost sales productivity and save valuable time', *Agency Sales*, November 2007, p. 20; and 'According to IDC, one-third of potential selling time is wasted due to poor sales enhancement', *Business Wire*, 13 November 2008.

[28] Lain Chroust Ehmann, 'Sales up!' *Selling Power*, January/February 2011, p. 40; also see Scott Gillum, 'The disappearing sales process', *Forbes*, 7 January 2013, www.forbes.com/sites/gyro/2013/01/07/the-disappearing-sales-process/; and Matt Dixon and Steve Richard, 'Solution selling is dead: why 2013 is the year of B2B insight selling', *Openview*, http://labs.openviewpartners.com/solution-selling-is-dead-2013-year-of-b2b-insight-selling/.

[29] See 'The digital evolution in B2B marketing', Marketing Leaderships Council, 2 December 2012, p. 3; Scott Gillum, 'The disappearing sales process', *Forbes*, 7 January 2013, www.forbes.com/sites/gyro/2013/01/07/the-disappearing-sales-process/; and Alice Myerhoff, 'How selling has gone social in the last 15 years', *Salesforce Blog*, 13 March 2014, http://blogs.salesforce.com/company/2014/03/social-selling-15-years-gp.html.

[30] See Barbara Giamanco and Kent Gregoire, 'Tweet me, friend me, make me buy', *Harvard Business Review*, July–August 2012, pp. 88–94; and John Bottom, 'Research: are B2B buyers using social media?' *Slideshare*, 10 September 2013, www.slideshare.net/basebot/b2b-buyer-behaviour.

[31] This section is based on information from Lain Chroust Ehmann, 'Sales up!' *SellingPower*, January/February 2011, p. 40; Gerhared Gschwandtner, 'How many salespeople will be left by 2020?' *SellingPower*, May/June 2011, p. 7; Neil Baron, 'Death of sales people?', *Fast Company*, 17 August 2013, www.fastcompany.com/3020103/death-of-the-sales-people; 'Getting started with SAP EcoHub', http://ecohub.sap.com/getting-started, accessed November 2013; 'SAP EcoHub to the SAP Store: the evolution of the online channel at SAP', www.youtube.com/watch?v=WADFf6k34V8, accessed June 2014; and https://store.sap.com/ and https://scn.sap.com, accessed September 2014.

[32] Jeff Green, 'The new Willy Loman survives by staying home', *Bloomberg BusinessWeek*, 14–20 January 2013, p. 16–18.

[33] Philip Delves Broughton, 'Selling deserves a corner office', *Financial Times*, 1 May 212, p. 14; also Walter Friedman, *The Birth of a Salesman: The Transformation of Selling in America*, Boston MA, Harvard University Press, 2005.

[34] See 'GE's social story', www.salesforcemarketingcloud.com/resources/videos/ges-social-story/, accessed June 2014; David Moth, 'How General Electric uses Facebook, Twitter, Pinterest and Google+', *Velocify*, May 2013, https://econsultancy.com/blog/62684-how- general-electric-uses-facebook-twitter-pinterest-and-google; and 'GE social media', www.ge.com/news/social, accessed September 2014.

[35] Quotes from Bob Donath, 'Delivering value starts with proper prospecting', *Marketing News*, 10 November 1997, p. 5; and Bill Brooks, 'Power-packed prospecting pointers', *Agency Sales*, March 2004, p. 37; also see Maureen Hrehocik, 'Why prospecting gets no respect', *Sales & Marketing Management*, October 2007, p. 7; and 'Referrals', *Partner's Report*, January 2009, p. 8.

[36] Quotes in this paragraph from Lain Ehmann, 'Prepare to win', *Selling Power*, April 2008, pp. 27–29.

[37] John Graham, 'Salespeople under siege: the profession redefined', *Agency Sales*, January 2010, pp. 20–25; and Rick Phillips, 'Don't pressure, persuade', *Selling Power*, January/February 2010, p. 22.

[38] 'For B-to-B, engagement, retention are key', *Marketing News*, 15 April 2009, p. 9; and Nancy Peretsman, 'Stop talking and start listening', *Fortune*, 9 November 2009, p. 24.

[39] Example based on information from James C. Anderson, Nirmalya Kumar and James A. Narus, 'Be a value merchant', *Sales & Marketing Management*, 6 May 2008; and 'Business market value merchants', *Marketing Management*, March/April 2008, pp. 31; Also see John A. Quelch and Katherine E. Jocz, 'How to market in a downturn', *Harvard Business Review*, April 2009, pp. 52–62.

[40] See, for example: Nigel F. Piercy and Nikala Lane, *Strategic Customer Management: Strategizing the Sales Organization*, Oxford: Oxford University Press, 2009.

[41] Kantar Retail, *Making Connections: Trade Promotion Integration across the Marketing Landscape*, Wilton, CT: Kantar Retail, July 2012, p. 5.

[42] Nigel F. Piercy, David W. Cravens and Nikala Lane, 'Marketing out of the recession: recovery is coming, but things will never be the same again', *The Marketing Review*, vol. 10, no. 1, 2010, pp3–23.

[43] Kantar Retail, *Making Connections: Trade Promotion Integration across the Marketing Landscape*, p. 6.

[44] Based on information and quotes from Richard H. Levey, 'A slip between cup and lip', *Direct*, 1 May 2008, http://directmag.com /roi/0508-starbucks-loyalty-program/index.html; Emily Bryson York, 'Starbucks: don't be seduced by lower prices', *Advertising Age*, 30 April 2009, accessed at http://adage.com/print?article_id=136389; and Emily Bryson York, 'Starbucks gets its business brewing again with social media', *Advertising Age*, 22 February 2010, p. 34.

[45] Lucas, Louise, 'The pull of treats on the streets', *Financial Times*, 29 January 2013, p. 12.

[46] NCH Marketing Services, 'NCH annual topline US CPG coupon facts report for year-end 2013', February 2014, www2.nchmarketing .com/ResourceCenter/assets/0/22/28/76/226/457/0bddc7b288724-aac83e8215e9a16f854.pdf.

[47] See NCH Marketing Services, 'NCH annual topline U.S. CPG coupon facts report for year-end 2013', February 2014, www2.nchmarketing .com/ResourceCenter/assets/0/22/28/76/226/457/ 0bddc7b288724aac83e8215e9a16f854.pdf; 'Majority of US Internet users will redeem digital coupons in 2013', *eMarketer*, 21 October 2013, www.emarketer.com/Article/Majority-of-US-Internet-Users-Will-Redeem-Digital-Coupons-2013/1010313; and 'Mobile spurs digital coupon user growth', *eMarketer*, 31 January 2014, www.emarketer.com /Article/Mobile-Spurs-Digital-Coupon-User-Growth/1009639.

[48] See www.comscoredatamine.com/2011/02/groupon-contributes-to-significant-growth-for-coupon-sites-in-europe/

[49] See www.happymeal.com/en_US/, accessed June 2014.

[50] See www.bpma-sourcing.co.uk/ accessed 26 February 2012.

[51] See 'PPAI reports positive results, U.S. promotional products industry's annual sales volume increases to $18.5 billion', *PPAI News*, 8 July 2013, www.ppai.org/press/documents/ppai%20reports%20positive%20 results%20u.s.%20promotional%20products%20industrys%20annual%20 sales%20volume%20increases%20to%20 18.5%20bil.pdf.

[52] Andrea Felsted and Andy Sharman, 'Waitrose defends its free coffee scheme', *Financial Times*, 7 March 2014, p. 25.

[53] Sean Poulter, 'Win-a-farm competition where everyone is a loser', *Daily Mail*, 22 February 2012, p. 7.

[54] See www.manutd.com/en/Club/Sponsors.aspx

[55] Based on information found in Patrick Hanlon, 'Face slams: event marketing takes off', *Forbes*, 9 May 2012, www.forbes.com/sites /patrickhanlon/2012/05/09/face-slams-event-marketing-takes-off/; and www.redbull.com/us/en/events and www.redbull.com/cs/Satellite /en_INT/RedBull/HolyShit/011242745950125, accessed June 2014. The referenced wing suit flying video can be found at http://player.vimeo. com/video/31481531?autoplay=1.

[56] Kantar Retail, *Making Connections: Trade Promotion Integration across the Marketing Landscape*, p. 10.

[57] See Erica Ogg, 'CES attendance bounces back', *Circuit Breaker-CNET News*, 11 January 2010, accessed at http://news.cnet.com/8301– 31021_3-10432369-260.html; and the Bauma website, www.bauma.de, accessed October 2010.

COMPANY CASE

HP: overhauling a vast corporate sales force

Imagine this scenario: You need a new digital camera. You're not sure which one to buy or even what features you need. So you visit your nearest electronics superstore to talk with a salesperson. You walk through the camera section but can't find anyone to help you. When you finally find a salesperson, he yawns and tells you that he's responsible for selling all the products in the store, so he doesn't really know all that much about cameras. Then he reads some information from the box of one of the models that you ask about, as if he is telling something that you can't figure out for yourself. He then suggests that you should talk to someone else. You finally find a camera-savvy salesperson. However, after answering a few questions, she disappears to handle some other task, handing you off to someone new. And the new salesperson seems to contradict what the first salesperson said, even quoting different prices on a couple of models you like.

That imaginary situation may actually have happened to you. If so, then you can understand what many business buyers face when attempting to buy from a large corporate supplier. This was the case with business customers of technology giant Hewlett-Packard before Mark Hurd took over as HP's CEO a few years ago. Prior to Hurd assuming command, HP's revenues and profits had flattened, and its stock price had plummeted. To find out why, Hurd first talked directly with 400 corporate customers. Mostly what he heard were gripes about HP's corporate sales force.

Customers complained that they had to deal with too many salespeople, and HP's confusing management layers made it hard to figure out whom to call. They had trouble tracking down HP sales representatives. And once found, the reps often came across as apathetic, leaving the customer to take the initative. HP reps were responsible for a broad range of complex products, so they sometimes lacked the needed depth of knowledge on any subset of them. Customers grumbled that they received varying price quotes from different sales reps, and it often took weeks for reps to respond to seemingly simple requests. In all, HP's corporate customers were frustrated, not a happy circumstance for a company that gets more than 70 per cent of its revenues from businesses.

But customers weren't the only ones frustrated by HP's unwiedly and unresponsive sales force structure. HP was organised into three main product divisions: the Personal Systems Group (PSG), the Technology Solutions Group (TSG), and the Image and Printing Group (IPG). However, HP's corporate sales force was housed in a fourth division, the Customer Sales Group (CSG). All salespeople reported directly to the CSG and were responsible for selling products from all three product divisions. To make matters worse, the CSG was bloated and underperforming. According to one reporter, 'of the 17,000 people working in HP's corporate sales, only around 10,000 sold directly to customers. The rest were support staff or in management.' HP division executives were frustrated by the CSG structure. They complained that they had little or no direct control over the salespeople who sold their products. And multiple layers of management slowed sales force decision making and customer responsiveness.

Finally, salespeople themselves were frustrated by the structure. They weren't being given the time and support they needed to serve their customers well. Burdened with administrative tasks and bureaucratic red tape, they were spending less than one-third of their time with customers. And they had to work through multiple layers of bureaucracy to get price quotes and sample products for customers. 'The customers focus was lacking,' says an HP sales vice president. 'Trying to navigate HP was difficult. It was unacceptable.'

As Hurd peeled back the layers, it became apparent that HP's organisational problems went deeper than the sales force. The entire company had become so centralised, with so many layers of management, that it was unresponsive and out of touch with customers. Hurd had come to HP with a reputation for cost-cutting and ruthless efficiency. Prior to his new position, he spent 25 years at NCR, where he ultimately headed the company. Although it was a considerably smaller company than HP, Hurd had it running like a well-oiled machine. Nothing bothered him more than the discoveries he made about HP's inefficient structure.

Thus began what one observer called 'one of Hurd's biggest management challenges: overhauling HP's vast corporate sales force.' For starters, Hurd eliminated the CSG division, instead assigning salespeople directly to the three product divisions. He also did away with three layers of management and cut hundreds of unproductive sales workers. This move gave divisional marketing and sales executives direct control over a leaner, more efficient sale process, resulting in speedier sales decisions and quicker market response.

Hurd also took steps to reduce salesperson and customer frustrations. Eliminating the CSG meant that each salesperson was responsible for selling a smaller number of products and was able to devlop expertise in a specific product area. Hurd urged sales managers to cut back on salesperson administrative requirements and improve sales support so that salespeople could spend more quality time with customers. As a result, salespeople now spend more than 40 per cent of their time with customers, up from just 30 per cent before. And HP salespeople are noticing big changes in the sales support they receive:

Salesman Richard Ditucci began noticing some of the changes late last year. At the time, Ditucci was trying to sell computer servers to Staples. As part of the process, Staples had asked him to provide a sample server for the company to evaluate. In the past, such requests typically took two three weeks to fulfil because of HP's bureaucracy. This time, Ditucci got the server he needed within three days. The quick turnaround helped him win the contract, valued at several million dollars.

To ensure that important customers are carefully tended, HP assigned each salesperson three or fewer accounts. The top 2,000 accounts were assigned just one salesperson – 'so they'll always know whom to contact.' Customers are noticing differences in the attention that they get from HP salespeople:

James Farris, a senior technology executive at Staples, says HP has freed up his salesman to drop by Staples at least twice a month instead of about once a month before. The extra face time enabled the HP salesman to create more valuable interactions, such as arranging a workshop recently for Staples to explain HP's technology to the retailer's executives. As a result, Farris says he is planning to send more business HP's way. Similarly, Keith Morrow, chief information officer of convenience-store chain 7-Eleven, says his HP sales representative is now 'here all the time' and has been more knowledgeable in pitching products tailored to his business. As a result, last October, 7-Eleven began deploying in its US stores 10,000 HP pen pads — a mobile device that helps 7-Eleven workers on the sales floor.

A salesman at heart

Once the new sales force started to take shape, Hurd began to focus on the role of the client in the sales process. The fact that HP refers to its business buyers as 'partners' says a lot about its philosophy. 'We heavily rely on [our partners]. We look at them as an extension of the HP sales force, 'Hurd said. To strengthen the relationship between HP and its partners, HP and its partners, HP has partners participating in account planning and strategy development, an activity that teams the partners with HP sales reps and its top executive team.

Because Hurd wants the sales force to have strong relationships with its partners, he practises what he preaches. He spends up to 60 per cent of the year on the road with various channel partners and *their* customers. Part of his time is funnelled through HP's Executive Connections programme, roundtable meetings that take place worldwide. But many of Hurd's interactions with HP partners take place outside that programme as well. This demonstration of customer commitment at the highest level has created some fierce customer loyalty toward HP.

'I've probably met Mark Hurd more times in the last three or four years than all the CEOs of our other vendors combined,' said Simon Palmer, president of California-based STA, one of HP's fastest growing solution provider partners. 'There's no other CEO of any company that size that's even close. He's such a down-to-earth guy. He presents the HP story in very simple-to-understand terms.' 'Mark Sarazin, executive vice president of AdvizeX Technologies, an HP partner for 25 years, sings similar praises. 'He spent two-and-a-half hours with our customers. He talked in terms they could relate with, about his own relationship with HP IT. He knocked the ball out of the park with our 25-plus CIOs who were in the room. One said it was the best event he'd been to in his career.'

In the four years since Hurd took over as CEO, HP's revenues, profits and stock price have increased by 44 per cent, 123 per cent, and 50 per cent, respectively. Still, with HP's markets as volatile as they've been, Hurd has taken HP into new equipment markets as well as gaining a substantial presence in service solutions. Each time the company enters a new market and faces new competitors, the HP sales force is at the centre of the activity. In an effort to capture market share from Dell, Cisco and Lexmark in the server market, HP opened a new sales operation in New Mexico called the SMB Exchange. It combines a call centre, inside sales and channel sales teams. Observers have noted that whereas HP's sales force was known for being more passive in the past, it is now much more aggressive – like Cisco's.

Hurd knows that because of HP's enormous size, it walks a fine line. In fact, he refers to the company' size, as a 'strange friend'. On the one hand, it allows the company to offer a tremendous portfolio of products and services with support from a massive sales force. On the other hand, multiple organisational layers can make it more difficult to create solutions for partners and customers. Hurd is doing everything he can to make HP leaner and meaner so that it can operate with the nimbleness and energy of a much smaller company.

The changes that have taken place at HP have made most everyone more satisfied. And happier salespeople are more productive, resulting in happier customers. That should mean a bright future for HP. Hurd knows that there's still much more work to be done. But with a continued focus on the sales force and the sales process, HP is creating a structure that creates better value for its business customers. Now, if your local electronics superstore could only do the same for you . . . .

Questions for discussion

1. Which of the sales force structures described in the text best describes HP's structure?
2. What are the positive and negative aspects of HP's new sales force structure?
3. Describe some of the differences in the selling process that an HP sales rep might face in selling to a long-term established customer versus a prospective customer.
4. Given that Hurd has an effective sales force, does he really need to meet with HP partners as much as he does?
5. Is it possible for HP to function like a smaller company? Why or why not?

Sources: Quotes and adapted examples from Pui-Wing Tam, 'System Reboot: Hurd's Big Challenge at HP: Overhauling Corporate Sales,' *Wall Street Journal*, 3 April 2006, A1; Christopher Hosford, 'Rebooting Hewlett-Packard,' *Sales & Marketing Management*, july – August 2006, pp. 32–35; Steven Burke, 'HP vs Ciscoe: It's Personal,' *Computer Reseller News*, 1 November, 2009, p. 8; Damon Poeter, 'Never Enough,' *Computer Reseller News*, 1 April 2010, p. 24.

CHAPTER SEVENTEEN

Direct, online, social media and mobile marketing

Chapter preview

In the previous three chapters, you learned about engaging consumers and communicating customer value through integrated marketing communications (IMC), and about four elements of the marketing communications mix: advertising, publicity, personal selling and sales promotion. In this chapter, we examine direct marketing and its fastest growing form, digital marketing (online, social media and mobile marketing). Spurred by the surge in Internet usage and buying, as well as rapid advances in digital technologies – from smartphones, tablets and other digital devices to the spate of online mobile and social media – direct marketing has undergone a dramatic transformation – a blend of communication and distribution channels all rolled into one. As you read this chapter, remember that although direct and digital marketing are presented as separate tools, they must be carefully integrated with each other and with the other elements of the promotion and marketing mixes.

Let's start by looking at Facebook, a company that markets only directly and digitally. The giant online social media network promises to become one of the world's most powerful and profitable digital marketers. Yet, as a money-making marketing company, Facebook is just getting started.

Objective outline

> **Objective 1** Define direct and digital marketing and discuss their rapid growth and benefits to customers and companies.
> Direct and digital marketing (pp. 502–505)

> **Objective 2** Identify and discuss the major forms of direct and digital marketing.
> Forms of direct and digital marketing (pp. 505–506)
> Digital and social media marketing (p. 506)

> **Objective 3** Explain how companies have responded to the Internet and the digital age with new online marketing strategies.
> Marketing, the Internet and the digital age (pp. 506–507)
> Online marketing (pp. 507–511)

> **Objective 4** Discuss how companies use social media and mobile marketing to engage consumers and create brand community.
> Social media marketing (pp. 511–514)
> Mobile marketing (pp. 514–516)

> **Objective 5** Identify and discuss the traditional direct marketing forms and overview public policy and ethical issues presented by direct marketing.
> Traditional direct marketing forms (pp. 516–520)
> Public policy issues in direct and digital marketing (pp. 520–523)

Facebook: going online, social and mobile: and making money doing it

The world has rapidly gone online, social and mobile. And no company is more online, social and mobile than Facebook. The world's largest social network has a deep and daily impact on the lives of more than a billion members around the world. But despite Facebook's massive size and growth, it continues to grapple with a crucial question: How can it profitably tap the marketing potential of its massive online community to make money without driving off its legions of loyal users?

Facebook is huge. In little more than a decade, it has acquired some 1.3 billion active monthly users – one-seventh of the world's population. More than a billion members now access Facebook on mobile devices, and some 757 million visit the site daily. Collectively, the Facebook community uploads 350 million photos, 'Likes' 4.5 billion items, and shares 4.75 billion pieces of content daily.

With that many eyeballs glued to one virtual space for that much time, Facebook has tremendous impact and influence. Facebook's power comes not just from its size and omnipresence; rather, it lies in the deep social connections with and among users. Facebook's mission is 'to give people the power to share and make the world more open and connected'. It's a place where friends and family meet, share their stories, display their photos and chronicle their lives. Hordes of people have made Facebook their digital home 24/7.

By wielding all that influence, Facebook has the potential to become one of the world's most powerful and profitable online marketers. Yet the burgeoning social network is only now beginning to tap its financial potential. Initially, CEO Mark Zuckerberg and the network's other idealistic young co-founders focused on building a user base and gave little thought to making money. In fact, without any help from Facebook, companies themselves were first to discover the social medium's commercial value. Most brands – small and large – built their own Facebook pages, gaining free access to the gigantic community's socialsharing potential.

However, as it has matured, Facebook has come to realise that it must make its own marketing moves. It is now developing a growing portfolio of products that will let it connect everyone in the world and make money doing it. The social network's first and best bet for converting the value of its massive user base into real dollars is online advertising. In fact, during the past three years, as Facebook's revenues nearly quadrupled from $2 billion to $7.9 billion, advertising accounted for nearly 90 per cent of those revenues.

Many online marketers make money through advertising. But Facebook has two unique advantages – unprecedented user data and deep user engagement. Facebook maintains one of the richest collections of user profile data in the world. So ads on Facebook can be carefully targeted, based on user location, gender, age, likes and interests, relationship status, workplace and education. But Facebook ads do far more than simply capture the right eyeballs. They are 'engagement ads' that take advantage of the network's social sharing power to move people to action. Facebook ads blend in with regular user activities, and users can interact with ads by leaving comments, making recommendations, clicking the 'Like' button, or following a link to a brand-sponsored Facebook page.

Facebook's appeal to both users and advertisers hinges on its ability to target specific kinds of content to well-defined user segments. However, Facebook's former 'all things to all people' approach left many users, especially younger ones, visiting Facebook less and shifting time to more specialised competitive social networks. To meet that growing threat, Facebook is now pursuing a multi-app strategy of providing 'something for any and every individual'. According to Zuckerberg, 'Our vision for Facebook is to create a set of products that help you share any kind of content you want with any audience you want.'

Facebook's first move under this new multi-app strategy was to pay a stunning $1 billion to acquire Instagram, the rapidly growing photo-sharing app. Although Facebook already had its own photo-sharing

In August 2015, Facebook had a billion visits on a single day – equivalent to one-seventh of the world's total population visiting the site.

Source: epa european pressphoto agency b.v./Alamy Images

features, the Instagram acquisition brought a younger, 27-million-strong user base into the Facebook fold. And rather than incorporating Instagram as just another Facebook feature, Facebook has maintained Instagram as an independent brand, with its own personality and user base. Instagram and Facebook customers can choose their desired level of integration, including Instagram membership without a Facebook account. 'The fact that Instagram is connected to other services beyond Facebook is an important part of the experience,' says Zuckerberg.

Not long after the Instagram acquisition, in its quest to add unique new products and user segments, Facebook announced the creation of Creative Labs, a Facebook division charged with developing single-purpose mobile apps. It also unveiled the new division's first product – Paper, a mobile app that provides easy and personalised access to Facebook's News Feed. Although the core Facebook mobile app already provides access to this content, Paper lets users organise the feed by themes, interests and sources, serving it all up in a full-screen, distraction-free layout.

On the heels of the Paper launch came another stunning Facebook mega-acquisition. Much bigger than its Instagram deal, Facebook paid a shocking $19 billion for stand-alone messaging app WhatsApp. Facebook's own Messenger had already grown quickly to 200 million users. But similar to Instagram, WhatsApp immediately gave Facebook something it could not easily build on its own – an independent brand with more than 450 million registered international users, many of whom were not on Facebook. Most recently, Facebook acquired fitness and activity tracking app Moves, which will also continue to operate as a standalone brand.

By developing and acquiring such new products and apps, Facebook is doing what it does best – growing its membership and giving its diverse users more ways and reasons to connect and engage. Facebook's fuller portfolio lets users meet their individual needs within the broadening framework of the Facebook family. In turn, more and more-targetable users who spend increased time on the network create more opportunities for Facebook to attract advertising revenues.

Will increased advertising and commercialisation alienate loyal Facebook users? Not if it's done right. Recent studies show that online users readily accept – even welcome – well-targeted online advertising and marketing. Tasteful and appropriately targeted offers can enhance rather than detract from the Facebook user experience. Moreover, although Facebook's founders initially opposed running ads or other marketing, worried that marketing might damage Facebook's free (and commercial-free) sharing culture, they've now come to realise that if Facebook doesn't make money, it can't continue to serve its members.

Whatever its future, Facebook seems to have barely scratched the surface. Its new multi-app, multi-segment strategy, combined with its massive, closely knit social structure, gives Facebook staggering potential. Carolyn Everson, Facebook's vice president of global sales, sums up Facebook's growth potential this way: 'I'm not sure the marketing community understands our story yet. We evolve so quickly. We have a saying here: "We are one per cent done with our mission."'[1]

Direct and digital marketing—Engaging directly with carefully targeted individual consumers and customer communities to both obtain an immediate response and build lasting customer relationships.

Many of the marketing and promotion tools that you have read about in previous chapters were developed in the context of mass marketing: targeting broad markets with standardised messages and offers distributed through intermediaries like retailers and distributors. However, with the trend toward narrower targeting and the growth in digital and social media technologies, many companies are adopting direct marketing, either as a primary marketing approach or as a supplement to other approaches. In this section, we explore the exploding world of direct marketing and its fastest-growing form – digital marketing using online, social media and mobile marketing channels.

DIRECT AND DIGITAL MARKETING

Direct and digital marketing involve engaging directly with carefully targeted individual consumers and customer communities to both obtain an immediate response and build lasting customer relationships. Companies use direct marketing to tailor and customise their offers and content to the needs and interests of narrowly defined segments or even individual buyers. In this way, they build customer engagement, brand community and sales.

For example, Amazon.com interacts directly with customers via its website or mobile app to help them discover and buy almost anything and everything online. Similarly, many financial services companies interact directly with customers – by telephone, through websites or phone apps, or on Facebook, Twitter and YouTube pages – to build individual brand relationships, give insurance quotes, sell policies or service customer accounts.

The new direct marketing model

Early direct marketers – catalogue companies, direct mailers and telemarketers – gathered customer names and sold goods mainly by mail and telephone. Today, however, direct marketing has undergone a dramatic transformation, spurred by the growth in Internet usage and buying, and by rapid advances in digital technologies – from smartphones, tablets and other digital devices to the spate of online social and mobile media.

In the previous chapters, we discussed direct marketing as direct distribution – marketing channels that contain no intermediaries like retailers. We also included direct and digital marketing elements of the promotion mix – as an approach for engaging consumers directly and creating brand community. In reality, direct marketing is both of these things but much more.

Most companies still use direct marketing as a supplementary channel or medium. So, most department stores, such as John Lewis or Debenhams, sell the majority of their products from their store shelves and displays, but they also sell through direct mail, online catalogues and social media pages. For example, Pepsi's Mountain Dew soft drink brand makes heavy use of mass-media advertising and retailer promotion, but it also supplements these channels with direct marketing. It uses its several brand websites and a long list of social media to engage its customer community in everything from designing their own Mountain Dew lifestyle pages to co-creating advertising campaigns and deciding which limited-edition flavours should be launched or retired. Through such direct interactions, Mountain Dew has created one of the most passionately loyal fan bases of any soft drink brand. By one estimate, simply letting fans pick flavours has generated $200 million in incremental revenues per year for Mountain Dew.[2]

However, for many companies, direct and digital marketing are more than just supplementary channels or advertising media – they constitute a complete model for doing business. Firms employing this direct model use it as the only approach. Companies such as Facebook, Amazon, Google, eBay and Netflix have successfully built their entire approach to the marketplace around direct and digital marketing. For example, Priceline.com, the online travel company, sells its services exclusively through online, mobile and social media channels. Priceline.com and other online travel agency competitors such as Expedia and Lastminute.com, have pretty much driven traditional offline travel agencies to extinction.[3]

Rapid growth of direct and digital marketing

Direct and digital marketing have become the fastest-growing form of marketing. According to the Direct Marketing Association (DMA) in America, US companies spent almost $133 billion on direct and digital marketing last year. As a result, direct-marketing-driven sales now amount to more than $2 trillion, accounting for 13 per cent of the US economy. The DMA estimates that direct marketing sales will grow 4.9 per cent annually through 2016, compared with a projected 4.1 per cent annual growth for total US sales.[4] Meanwhile in the UK, Direct Marketing Association research suggests direct marketing spend had reached £15.2 billion by 2012, with annual growth topping 7 per cent, and their report reveals that UK companies on average attribute 23 per cent of their total sales to direct marketing, with this rising to 32 per cent for the travel and leisure sector, 30 per cent for the retail and wholesale sectors and 28 per cent for the financial services sector.[5]

Similar patterns exist in most European markets, though with some national differences and the continuing negative impact of economic downturn on advertising expenditure generally to be taken into account. But this is a dynamic and fast-changing area of marketing just about everywhere. For example, in emerging markets, shops are few and transport is rudimentary, making direct selling an attractive option for companies. So, in Mexico direct sales account for a quarter of sales of cosmetics, fragrances and toiletries, while the same figure for Brazil is around one-third of sales.[6]

Direct marketing continues to become more Internet-based, and digital direct marketing is claiming a surging share of marketing spending and sales, with highest growth in e-mail marketing and social media campaigns. For example, in the US marketers spent an estimated $43 billion on digital advertising alone last year, an amount expected to increase more than 14 per cent this year, generating more than $260 billion in online consumer spending. Total digital advertising spending – including online display and search advertising, video, social media, mobile and e-mail – now accounts for the second-largest share of media spending, behind only television. Over the next four years, digital marketing expenditures and digitally driven sales are expected to grow at a blistering 9 per cent a year in the United States.[7]

In fact, total global media advertising expenditure is estimated as $546 billion in 2014 by research agency eMarketer, and of this around 27 per cent is digital advertising and 8 per cent mobile internet advertising spend.[8] Among the world's top advertiser countries (US, China, Japan, Germany and the UK), the proportion of advertising spend which is online varies from 28 per cent in Germany to 50 per cent in China and 62 per cent of the total spend in the UK. The share of advertising media expenditure going online is expected to increase still further as Asia-Pacific, Eastern Europe and Latin America markets have a growing impact.

Consequently, consumers in Britain spend more money online per head than any other developed country – averaging £2000 per head in 2013, which is 50 per cent more than the next-highest valued market of Australia. This appears boosted by the widespread access of consumers to broadband and a long history of home shopping in various forms by British consumers (catalogues, door-to-door selling, Tupperware parties). With nearly eight in ten UK homes accessing fast broadband, the UK is ahead of France, Germany, Italy and Spain.[9]

Benefits of direct and digital marketing to buyers and sellers

For buyers, direct and digital marketing are convenient, easy and private. They give buyers anywhere, anytime access to an almost unlimited assortment of goods and a wealth of product and buying information. For example, on its website and mobile app, Amazon.com offers more information than most of us can digest, ranging from top 10 product lists, extensive product descriptions, and expert and user product reviews to recommendations based on customers' previous searches and purchases. Through direct marketing, buyers can interact with sellers by phone or on the seller's website or app to create exactly the configuration of information, products or services they want and then order them on the spot. Finally, for consumers who want it, digital marketing through online, mobile and social media provides a sense of brand engagement and community – a place to share brand information and experiences with other brand fans.

For sellers, direct marketing often provides a low-cost, efficient, speedy alternative for reaching their markets. Today's direct marketers can target small groups or individual customers. Because of the one-to-one nature of direct marketing, companies can interact with customers by phone or online, learn more about their needs, and personalise products and services to specific customer tastes. In turn, customers can ask questions and volunteer feedback.

Direct and digital marketing also offer sellers greater flexibility. They let marketers make ongoing adjustments to prices and programmes, or create immediate, timely and personal engagement and offers. For example, General Electric celebrated last year's National Inventors' Day by asking its Twitter followers for offbeat invention ideas, then created illustrations of the best ones, such as a 'handholding robot'.

Particularly in today's digital environment, direct marketing provides opportunities for *real-time marketing* that links brands to important moments and trending events in customers' lives. It is a powerful tool for moving customers through the buying process and for building customer engagement, community and personalised relationships. For example consider Starbucks.

Starbucks is a social media powerhouse with nearly 37 million Facebook fans and 6 million Twitter followers, and has long and systematically used real-time marketing to link the brand and what it stands for to current events important to its customers. For example, after a bad winter storm in the north-eastern United States, with heavy snowfall and hurricane-force winds in early 2013, Starbucks Twitter and Facebook promotions offered free coffee to customers in affected areas. 'We wanted to make a grand [and timely] gesture,' said a Starbucks digital marketer.

On an even grander stage, in autumn 2013, shortly after bipartisan bickering in Washington resulted in a partial shutdown of the US federal government – sending home hundreds of thousands of government employees, closing national parks, reducing many public health services, and much more – Starbucks launched a #ComeTogether campaign. It began with tweets and Facebook postings by CEO Howard Schultz asking 'How can we #cometogether to take care of each other?' and announcing that Starbucks would give a free tall brewed coffee to anyone kind enough to #payitforward and buy the next person in line their favourite beverage. That effort had customers flocking to Starbucks, and tweeting messages like this one: 'Bought coffee for the stranger in front of me @Starbucks. Got mine for free. Feels good to #payitforward.'[10]

Whether connected to a social cause, a trending topic or event, a consumer's personal situation, or something else, the essential concept behind successful real-time marketing is pretty simple. Find or create ongoing connections between the brand and what's happening and important in consumers' lives, then engage consumers genuinely in the moment. One marketing executive suggests that real-time marketers should equate the practice to 'meeting somebody in a social gathering – you don't accost them, instead you try to find a commonality of interest'.

FORMS OF DIRECT AND DIGITAL MARKETING

Author comment

Direct marketing is rich in tools, from traditional favourites such as direct mail and catalogues to dazzling new digital tools – online, mobile and social media.

The major forms of direct and digital marketing are shown in Figure 17.1. Traditional direct marketing tools include face-to-face selling, direct-mail marketing, catalogue marketing, telemarketing, direct-response television marketing and kiosk marketing. In recent years, however, a dazzling new set of digital direct marketing tools has burst onto the marketing scene, including online marketing (websites, online ads and promotions, e-mail, online videos and blogs), social media marketing and mobile marketing. We'll begin by examining the new direct digital and social media marketing tools that have received so much attention lately. Then, we'll look at the still heavily used and very important traditional direct marketing tools. As always, however, it's important to

Figure 17.1 Forms of direct and digital marketing

remember that all of these tools – both the new digital and the more traditional forms – must be blended into a fully integrated marketing communications programme.

DIGITAL AND SOCIAL MEDIA MARKETING

As noted earlier, **digital and social media marketing** is the fastest-growing form of direct marketing. It uses digital marketing tools such as websites, online video, e-mail, blogs, social media, mobile ads and apps, and other digital platforms to directly engage consumers anywhere, anytime via their computers, smartphones, tablets, Internet-ready TVs and other digital devices. The widespread use of the Internet and digital technologies is having a dramatic impact on both buyers and the marketers who serve them.

Marketing, the Internet and the digital age

Digital and social media marketing—Using digital marketing tools such as websites, social media, mobile apps and ads, online video, e-mail and blogs that engage consumers anywhere, anytime via their digital devices.

Much of the world's business today is carried out over digital networks that connect people and companies. These days, people connect digitally with information, brands and each other at almost any time and from almost anywhere. The digital age has fundamentally changed customers' notions of convenience, speed, price, product information, service and brand interactions. As a result, it has given marketers a whole new way to create customer value, engage customers and build customer relationships.

Digital usage and impact continues to grow steadily across the world. In the United States, more than 85 per cent of all adults use the Internet, and the average US Internet user spends more than five hours a day using digital media. Moreover, more than 60 per cent of smartphone owners access the Internet via their devices. Worldwide, more than 40 per cent of the population has Internet access, and 22 per cent have access to the mobile Internet – a number that's expected to double over the next five years as mobile becomes an ever-more-popular way to get online.[11]

This means that internationally, around 3.1 billion people have Internet access, i.e., 42 per cent of the world's population. The areas where the highest proportions of the population have internet access are: North America (86.9 per cent), Oceania/Australia (72.1 per cent) and Europe (70.4 per cent), but by far the fastest growth in Internet penetration is in Africa, Asia, the Middle East and Latin America.[12]

As a result, consumer shopping online has grown rapidly across the world with more and more purchasing being shifted from physical to digital stores. Online sources provide information to assist consumers in making purchase decisions and a growing number of consumers armed with smartphones and tablets use them as they shop in stores to find better deals and score price-matching offers. In emerging markets like Africa, this has been accompanied by the development of payment and banking systems to overcome an infrastructure that would otherwise impede buying and selling.

To reach this burgeoning market, most companies now market online. Some companies operate *only* online. They include a wide array of firms, from *e-tailers* such as Amazon.com and Expedia.com that sell products and services directly to final buyers via the Internet, to *search engines and portals* (such as Google, Yahoo! and Bing), *transaction sites* (eBay), *content sites* (the *Financial Times* on the web, BBC News and *Encyclopædia Britannica*), and *online social media* (Facebook, YouTube, Pinterest, LinkedIn, Twitter and Flickr).

Multichannel marketing—Marketing both through stores and other traditional offline channels and through digital, online, social media and mobile channels.

Today, it's hard to find a company that doesn't have a substantial online presence. Even companies that have traditionally operated offline have now created their own online sales, marketing and brand community channels. In fact, **multichannel marketing** companies are having more online success than their online-only competitors. A recent ranking of the world's ten largest online retail sites contained only three online-only retailers (Amazon.com, which was ranked number one, Netflix and CDW). All the others were multichannel retailers.[13]

For example, number two on the list of online retail sites is Staples, the global office supply retailer. Staples operates more than 2,000 superstores worldwide. But you might be surprised to learn that almost half of Staples' sales are generated online, from its website and mobile app; its presence on social media such as Facebook, Google+, Twitter, YouTube and LinkedIn; and its own Staples.com community.[14]

Selling online lets Staples build deeper, more personalised relationships with customers large and small. A large customer, such as GE or P&G, can create lists of approved office products at discount prices and then let company departments or even individuals do their own online and mobile purchasing. This reduces ordering costs, cuts through the red tape, and speeds up the ordering process for customers. At the same time, it encourages companies to use Staples as a sole source for office supplies. Even the smallest companies and individual consumers find 24/7 online ordering via the web, Staples mobile app or social media sites easier and more efficient.

In addition, Staples' online, mobile and social media efforts complement store sales by engaging customers, enlarging product assortments, offering hot deals, and helping customers find a local store and check stock and prices.

Direct digital and social media marketing takes any of the several forms shown in Figure 17.1. These forms include online marketing, social media marketing and mobile marketing. We discuss each in turn, starting with online marketing.

Online marketing

Online marketing refers to marketing via the Internet using company websites, online advertising and promotions, e-mail marketing, online video and blogs. In the UK, two-fifths of advertising spending is now online – more than other European countries or the US.[15] Social media and mobile marketing also take place online and must be closely coordinated with other forms of digital marketing. However, because of their special characteristics, we discuss the fast-growing social media and mobile marketing approaches in separate sections.

Online marketing—Marketing via the Internet using company websites, online ads and promotions, e-mail, online video and blogs.

Websites and branded web communities

For most companies, the first step in conducting online marketing is to create a website. websites vary greatly in purpose and content. Some websites are primarily **marketing websites**, designed to engage customers and move them closer to a direct purchase or other marketing outcome.

In contrast, **branded community websites** don't try to sell anything at all. Instead, their primary purpose is to present brand content that engages consumers and creates customer-brand community. Such sites typically offer a rich variety of brand information, videos, blogs, activities, and other features that build closer customer relationships and generate engagement with and between the brand and its customers.

For example, consider Harley-Davidson's website – the Harley Owners Group (HOG). You can't buy a motor bike, but instead, the site creates a vast branded community that stretches across the world.[16]

Marketing website—A website that engages consumers to move them closer to a direct purchase or other marketing outcome.

Branded community website—A website that presents brand content that engages consumers and creates customer community around a brand.

Harley Owners Group (HOG) is a special community provided by Harley-Davidson where enthusiasts for the company's motor bikes share more than their loyalty to a brand. For them, it represents a way of life, a culture, and it is one that can be found all over the world. Since the 1980s, Harley-Davidson have been diligently building up a brand community based around shared lifestyle, taste and ethos. HOG was born as a way for the brand's highly passionate consumers to connect and engage online. With more than 1 million active members, the strength of the community lies in the openness and enthusiasm of members it tries to foster and serve. This creates an incredibly strong community, that extends beyond online communities. HOG acts as a connector for enthusiasts around the world.

Of course, creating a website is one thing, while getting people to visit the site is another. To attract visitors, companies aggressively promote their websites in offline print and broadcast advertising and through ads and links on other sites. But today's web users are quick to abandon any website that doesn't measure up. The key is to create enough engaging and valued content to get consumers to come to the site, stick around, and come back again.

At the very least, a website should be easy to use and visually appealing. Ultimately, however, websites must also be *useful*. When it comes to online browsing and shopping, most people prefer substance over style and function over flash. Effective websites contain deep and useful information, interactive tools that help find and evaluate content of interest, links to other related sites, changing promotional offers, and entertaining features that lend relevant excitement.

Online advertising

Online advertising— Advertising that appears while consumers are browsing online, including display ads, search-related ads, online classifieds and other forms.

As consumers spend more and more time online, companies are shifting more of their marketing dollars to **online advertising** to build brand sales or attract visitors to their Internet, mobile and social media sites. Online advertising has become a major promotional medium. The main forms of online advertising are display ads and search-related ads. Together, display and search-related ads account for the largest portion of firms' digital marketing budgets, capturing 30 per cent of all digital marketing spending.[17]

Online display ads might appear anywhere on an Internet user's screen and are often related to the information being viewed. For instance, while browsing vacation packages on Travelocity.com, you might encounter a display ad offering a free upgrade on car hire from Enterprise Rent-A-Car. Online display ads have come a long way in recent years in terms of attracting and holding consumer attention. Today's *rich media* ads incorporate animation, video, sound and interactivity. The action-packed 'takeover' ad takes only a few seconds but delivers major impact.[18]

The largest form of online advertising is *search-related ads* (or *contextual advertising*), which accounted for nearly half of all online advertising spending last year. In search advertising, text- and image-based ads and links appear atop or alongside search engine results on sites such as Google, Yahoo! and Bing. For example, search Google for 'LCD TVs'. At the top and side of the resulting search list, you'll see inconspicuous ads for ten or more advertisers, ranging from Samsung, LG and Panasonic to Tesco.com and Amazon.com, as well as discount suppliers. Ninety-six per cent of Google's $50 billion in revenues last year came from ad sales. Search is an always-on kind of medium, and the results are easily measured.[19]

A search advertiser buys search terms from the search site and pays only if consumers click through to its site. For instance, type 'Coke' or 'Coca-Cola' or even just 'soft drinks' or 'rewards' into your search engine and almost without fail 'My Coke Rewards' comes up as one of the top options, perhaps along with a display ad and link to Coca-Cola's official Google+ page. This is no coincidence. Coca-Cola supports its popular online loyalty programme largely through search buys. The soft drink giant started first with traditional TV and print advertising but quickly learned that search was the most effective way to bring consumers to its www.mycokerewards.com website to register. Now, any of dozens of purchased search terms will return mycokerewards.com at or near the top of the search list.

E-mail marketing

E-mail marketing—Sending highly targeted, highly personalised, relationship-building marketing messages via e-mail.

E-mail marketing is an important and growing digital marketing tool. 'Social media is the hot new thing,' says one observer, 'but e-mail is still the king'.[20] For example, by one estimate, 91 per cent of all consumers in the United States use e-mail every day. What's more, e-mail is no longer limited to PCs and workstations; 65 per cent of all e-mails are now opened on mobile devices. Not surprisingly, then, a recent study found that e-mail is 40 times more effective at capturing customers than Facebook and Twitter combined. Marketers sent an estimated more than 838 *billion* e-mails last year. Despite all the e-mail clutter, thanks to its low costs, e-mail marketing still brings one of the highest marketing returns on investment. According to the US Direct

Marketing Association, marketers in America get a return of $44.25 on every $1 they spend on e-mail. US companies spent $2 billion on e-mail marketing last year, up from only $243 million 11 years earlier.[21]

When used properly, e-mail can be the ultimate direct marketing medium. Most blue-chip marketers use it regularly and with great success. E-mail lets these marketers send highly targeted, tightly personalised, relationship-building messages. And today's e-mails are anything but the staid, text-only messages of the past. Instead, they are colourful, inviting, personalised and interactive.

But there's a dark side to the growing use of e-mail marketing. The explosion of **spam** – unsolicited, unwanted commercial e-mail messages that clog up our e-mail boxes – has produced consumer irritation and frustration. According to one research company, spam now accounts for 70 per cent of all e-mail sent worldwide.[22] E-mail marketers walk a fine line between adding value for consumers and being intrusive and annoying.

To address these concerns, most legitimate marketers now practise permission-based e-mail marketing, sending e-mail pitches only to customers who 'opt in'. Many companies use configurable e-mail systems that let customers choose what they want to get. Amazon.com targets opt-in customers with a limited number of helpful 'we thought you'd like to know' messages based on their expressed preferences and previous purchases. Few customers object, and many actually welcome such promotional messages. Amazon.com benefits through higher return rates and by avoiding alienating customers with e-mails they don't want.

Inbox (8)
Spam (99)
Trash (3)

E-mail marketing: the explosion of spam has produced consumer irritation and frustration.
Source: ScottMurph/ Shutterstock.com

Spam—Unsolicited, unwanted commercial e-mail messages.

Online videos

Another form of online marketing is posting digital video content on brand websites or social media sites such as YouTube, Facebook and others. Some videos are made for the web and social media. Such videos range from 'how-to' instructional videos and public relations (PR) pieces to brand promotions and brand-related entertainment. Other videos are ads that a company makes primarily for TV and other media but posts online before or after an advertising campaign to extend their reach and impact.

Good online videos can engage consumers by the millions. The online video audience is soaring – for example, over 60 per cent of the US population now stream video.[23] Marketers hope that some of their videos will go viral. **Viral marketing**, the digital version of word-of-mouth marketing, involves creating videos, ads and other marketing content that is so infectious that customers will seek them out or pass them along to their friends. Because customers find and pass along the message or promotion, viral marketing can be very inexpensive. And when video or other information comes from a friend, the recipient is much more likely to view or read it.

All kinds of videos can go viral, producing engagement and positive exposure for a brand. For example, in one simple but honest McDonald's video, the director of marketing at McDonald's Canada answers an online viewer's question about why McDonald's products look better in ads than in real life by conducting a behind-the-scenes tour of how a McDonald's ad is made. The award-winning three-and-a-half-minute video pulled almost 15 million views and 15,000 shares, earning the company praise for its honesty and transparency. As another example, in association with the 2012 London Olympics and 2014 Sochi Winter Olympics, P&G produced heart-warming two-minute 'Proud sponsors of moms' videos thanking the mums who helped the athletes reach Olympic heights. Those videos garnered tens of millions of views and shares. They also formed the basis for TV ads shown during the events.[24]

Evian, called by one reporter 'the master of online video', has long reaped huge viral video rewards.[25]

Viral marketing—The digital version of word-of-mouth marketing: videos, ads and other marketing content that is so infectious that customers will seek it out or pass it along to friends.

Evian's first viral success, a 2009 'Roller-skating babies' ad video playing off the brand's, Live young' positioning, became the most-viewed ad of all time – but that was then. The sequel, titled 'Amazing baby & me', which showed adults break-dancing with baby-faced reflections of themselves in city store windows, did even better. It became the most-watched YouTube video of 2013, pulling down an amazing 39 million (and counting) views in more than 80 countries, and generating over 120,000 tweets, more than 1 million shares, and over 289,000 Facebook comments. Less than a year later, the babies were back in another Evian ad video, 'Amazing baby & me 2', in which Spiderman suddenly encounters a baby version of himself for a dance-off in the streets of New York City. By mid-year, that Evian ad video was well on its way to becoming the most-watched YouTube video of 2014. 'Our job is to tell a great brand story which creates desire,' says the digital director of Danone, Evian's parent company. 'Digital formats amplify that story by allowing enthusiasm and excitement to spread.'

However, marketers usually have little control over where their viral messages end up. They can seed content online, but that does little good unless the message itself strikes a chord with consumers. Says one creative director, 'You hope that the creative is at a high enough mark where the seeds grow into mighty oaks. If they don't like it, it ain't gonna move. If they like it, it'll move a little bit; and if they love it, it's gonna move like a fast-burning fire through the Hollywood hills.'[26]

Blogs and other online forums

Brands also conduct online marketing through various digital forums that appeal to specific special-interest groups. **Blogs** (or weblogs) are online journals where people and companies post their thoughts and other content, usually related to narrowly defined topics. Blogs can be about anything, from politics or baseball to haiku, car repair, brands, or the latest television series. According to one study, there are now more than 31 million blogs in the United States alone. Many bloggers use social networks such as Twitter, Facebook and Instagram to promote their blogs, giving them huge reach. Such numbers can give blogs – especially those with large and devoted followings – substantial influence.[27]

Blogs—Online journals where people and companies post their thoughts and other content, usually related to narrowly defined topics.

Most marketers are now tapping into the blogosphere with brand-related blogs that reach their customer communities. For example, on the Netflix blog, members of the Netflix team (themselves enthusiastic movie fans) tell about the latest Netflix features, share tricks for getting the most out of the Netflix experience, and collect feedback from subscribers. The Disney Parks blog is a place to learn about and discuss all things Disney, including a 'Behind the scenes' area with posts about dance rehearsals, sneak peeks at new construction sites, interviews with employees, and more. Whole Foods Market's 'Whole story' blog features videos, images and posts about healthy eating, recipes and what's happening inside the store.

Beyond their own brand blogs, many marketers use third-party blogs to help get their messages out. For example, McDonald's systematically reaches out to key 'mommy bloggers', those who influence the nation's homemakers, who in turn influence their families' eating-out choices:[28]

McDonald's recently hosted 15 bloggers on an all-expenses-paid tour of its headquarters in Oak Brook, Illinois. The bloggers toured the facilities (including the company's test kitchens), met McDonald's USA president, and had their pictures taken with Ronald at a nearby Ronald McDonald House. McDonald's knows that these mommy bloggers are very important. They have loyal followings and talk a lot about McDonald's in their blogs. So McDonald's is turning the bloggers into believers by giving them a behind-the-scenes view. McDonald's doesn't try to tell the bloggers what to say in their posts about the visit. It simply asks them to write one honest recap of their trip. However, the resulting posts (each acknowledging the blogger's connection with McDonald's) were mostly very positive. Thanks to this and many other such efforts, mommy bloggers around the country are now more informed about and connected with McDonald's. 'I know they have smoothies and they have yogurt and they have other things that my kids would want,' says one prominent blogger. 'I really couldn't tell you what Burger King's doing right now,' she adds. 'I have no idea.'

As a marketing tool, blogs offer some advantages. They can offer a fresh, original, personal and cheap way to enter into consumer online and social media conversations. However, the blogosphere is cluttered and difficult to control. And although companies can sometimes leverage blogs to engage customers in meaningful relationships, blogs remain largely a consumer-controlled medium. Whether or not they actively participate in the blogs, companies should monitor and listen to them. Marketers can use insights from consumer online conversations to improve their marketing programmes.

Social media marketing

As we've discussed throughout the text so far, the surge in Internet usage and digital technologies and devices has spawned a dazzling array of online **social media** and digital communities. Countless independent and commercial social networks have arisen that give consumers online places to congregate, socialise, and exchange views and information. These days, it seems, almost everyone is making friends on Facebook or Google+, checking in with Twitter, tuning into the day's hottest videos at YouTube, pinning images on social scrapbooking site Pinterest, or sharing photos with Instagram and Snapchat. And, of course, wherever consumers congregate, marketers will surely follow. Most marketers are now riding the huge social media wave. According to one survey, nearly 90 per cent of US companies now use social media networks as part of their marketing mix.[29] Nonetheless, in the UK the proportion of adults accessing social networks is falling. Social network use is also declining in the US, Japan and China. This most likely reflects the growth of other means of keeping in touch, such as online video sites, games platforms and instant messaging.[30]

Using social media

Marketers can engage in social media in two ways: They can use existing social media or they can set up their own. Using existing social media seems the easiest. Thus, most brands – large and small – have set up shop on a host of social media sites. Check the websites of brands ranging from Coca-Cola and Nike to Victoria's Secret or even Manchester United and you'll find links to each brand's Facebook, Google+, Twitter, YouTube, Flickr, Instagram, or other social media pages. Such social media can create substantial brand communities. Coca-Cola has an incredible 80 million fans.

Some of the major social networks are huge. More than 1.2 billion people access Facebook every month, nearly 20 times the whole population of the UK. Similarly, Twitter has more than 645 million registered users, and more than 1 billion unique users visit YouTube monthly, watching more than 6 billion hours of video. The list goes on: Google+ has 400 million active users, LinkedIn 240 million and Pinterest 70 million.[31]

Although these large social media networks grab most of the headlines, countless niche social media have also emerged. Niche online social networks cater to the needs of smaller communities of like-minded people, making them ideal vehicles for marketers who want to target special interest groups. There's at least one social media network for just about every interest, hobby or group. Kaboodle.com is for shopaholics, whereas mums share advice and commiseration at CafeMom.com. GoFISHn, a Facebook community of 4,000 anglers, features maps that pinpoint where fish are biting and a photo gallery where members can show off their catches. At Birdpost.com, avid bird watchers can keep an online list of birds they've seen and share bird sightings with other members using modern satellite maps. And myTransponder.com is a Facebook community where pilots find work, students locate flight instructors, and trade-specific advertisers home in on a hard-to-reach audience of people who love aviation.[32]

Beyond these independent social media, many companies have created their own online brand communities. For example, in Nike's Nike+ running community – consisting of more than 20 million runners who together have logged more than 1 billion running miles worldwide – members join together online to upload, track and compare their performances. Due to its success, Nike has expanded Nike+ to both basketball and general training, each with its own unique community site, app and corresponding products.[33]

Author comment

As in about every other area of our lives, social media and mobile technologies have taken the marketing world by storm. They offer some amazing marketing possibilities. But truth be told, many marketers are still struggling over how to use them most effectively.

Social media—Independent and commercial online communities where people congregate, socialise and exchange views and information.

Social media marketing advantages and challenges

Using social media presents both advantages and challenges. On the plus side, social media are *targeted* and *personal* – they allow marketers to create and share tailored brand content with individual consumers and customer communities. Social media are *interactive*, making them ideal for starting and participating in customer conversations and listening to customer feedback. For example, Volvo uses its #Swedespeak Tweetchat platform as a kind of digital focus group to engage customers and obtain immediate input on everything from product features to creating ads. The regular Twitter chats are 'creating good conversations', says Volvo's head marketer. 'People enjoy being part of [the process].'[34]

Social media are also *immediate* and *timely*. They can be used to reach customers anytime, anywhere with timely and relevant marketing content regarding brand happenings and activities. As discussed earlier in the chapter, the rapid growth in social media usage has caused a surge in *real-time marketing*, allowing marketers to create and join consumer conversations around situations and events as they occur. Marketers can now watch what's trending and create content to match.

Social media can be very *cost effective*. Although creating and administering social media content can be costly, many social media are free or inexpensive to use. Thus, returns on social media investments are often high compared with those of expensive traditional media such as television or print. The low cost of social media puts them within easy reach of even small businesses and brands that can't afford the high costs of big-budget marketing campaigns.

Perhaps the biggest advantage of social media is their *engagement and social sharing capabilities*. Social media are especially well suited to creating customer engagement and community – for getting customers involved with the brand and with each other. More than any other channels, social media can involve customers in shaping and sharing brand content and experiences. By tapping into the relationships social media influencers build with their followers, companies aim to get 'word-of-mouth at a far greater scale' – some social net influencers have more followers than the circulation of some magazines.[35] For example, one interesting target for advertisers is 'parent bloggers' – mainly women with children who provide a high-spending and sought-after group for advertising. The BritMums network in the UK has 6,000 bloggers, while in the US Mom Bloggers Club has 20,000 members and Bloggy Mums has 15,000. Parent blogging is spreading rapidly across Europe and Asia.[36]

Social media marketing provides an excellent way to create brand communities, places where brand loyalists can share experiences, information and ideas. For example, organic food retailer Whole Foods Market uses a host of social media to create a Whole Foods lifestyle community, where customers can research foods, access recipes, connect with other customers, discuss relevant food-related topics, and link to in-store events. In addition to its very active Facebook, Twitter, YouTube and Google+ pages, Whole Foods engages nearly 180,000 brand followers with 59 boards on social scrapbooking site Pinterest. Broad topics range from 'Food tips and tricks', 'Delicious art' and 'Edible celebrations' to Super HOT Kitchens, which is loaded with pictures of captivating kitchens. Whole Foods isn't in the kitchen remodelling business, but cooking and kitchens are a big part of the Whole Foods customer lifestyle.[37]

Social media marketing also presents challenges. First, many companies are still experimenting with how to use them effectively, and results are hard to measure. Second, such social networks are largely user controlled. The company's goal in using social media is to make the brand a part of consumers' conversations and

Social media marketing: Whole Foods Market uses a host of social media to create a Whole Foods lifestyle community.

Source: Julian Eales/Alamy Images

their lives. However, marketers can't simply force their way into consumers' digital interactions – they need to earn the right to be there. Rather than intruding, marketers must become a valued part of the online experience by developing a steady flow of engaging content. Nonetheless, there is a risk of being caught out by the speed and immediacy of social media:

Jimmy Choo is a luxury women's shoe brand, which found itself with a global best-seller. The shoe is a $625 model called the Abel, in a sparkly grey colour. The shoe unexpectedly sold out in Asia – only a few hundred pairs had been produced in the first place, and production had moved on to the next season's models. It took more than four months to produce more Abel shoes (several thousand pairs this time) and get them to customers who were waiting in Europe, the Middle East, the US and Asia (that's how long it takes to make hand-made shoes that require custom-made materials). The shoe had appeared in an episode of a popular new Korean television drama show. The social media lit up as followers of the shoes asked where they could get it. Stores in Asia sold out and started waiting lists, and demand spread to other parts of the world. Jimmy Choo had received no warning of the shoe's big TV moment, where it was pivotal to the Cinderella-like story line. A global best-seller had taken the brand by surprise because of the speed and power of social media in building demand.[38]

Because consumers have so much control over social media content, even the seemingly most harmless social media campaign can backfire. For example, Frito-Lay in the United States recently launched a 'Do us a flavour' contest, in which it asked people to come up with new potato crisp flavours, submit them to its web or Facebook site, and design package art for their creations. Many consumers took the contest (and the $1 million grand prize) seriously, submitting flavours that people would truly want to eat. However, others hijacked the contest by submitting sometimes amusing but completely bogus flavours, ranging from 'crunchy frog' and 'blue cheese', 'toothpaste' and 'orange juice', and '90 per cent air and like 4 chips'. Unfortunately, with each submission, no matter how bogus, the website responded cheerfully with a colourful rendition of the bag and flavour name, along with a message like the following: 'That does sound yummy as a chip! Keep those tasty ideas coming for your next chance to win $1 million.' With social media, 'You're going into the consumer's backyard. This is their place,' warns one social marketer. 'Social media is a pressure cooker,' says another. 'The hundreds of thousands, or millions, of people out there are going to take your idea, and they're going to try to shred it or tear it apart and find what's weak or stupid in it.'[39]

Integrated social media marketing

Using social media might be as simple as posting some messages and promotions on a brand's Facebook or Twitter pages or creating brand buzz with videos or images on YouTube or Pinterest. However, most large companies are now designing full-scale social media efforts that blend with and support other elements of a brand's marketing strategy and tactics. More than making scattered efforts and chasing 'Likes' and tweets, companies that use social media successfully are integrating a broad range of diverse media to create brand-related social sharing, engagement and customer community.

Managing a brand's social media efforts can be a major undertaking. For example, Starbucks, one of the most successful social media marketers, manages 51 Facebook pages (including 43 outside the United States); 31 Twitter handles (19 of them international); 22 Instagram names (14 international); plus Google+, Pinterest, YouTube and Foursquare accounts. Managing and integrating all that social media content is challenging, but the results are worth the investment. Customers can engage with Starbucks digitally without ever setting foot in a store – and engage they do. With more than 36 million fans on its main US page alone, Starbucks is the sixth-largest brand on Facebook. It ranks fifth on Twitter with 88.5 million followers.

But more than just creating online engagement and community, Starbucks' social media presence also drives customers into its stores. For example, in its first big social media promotion four years ago, Starbucks offered a free pastry with a morning drink purchase. A million people showed up. Its more recent 'tweet-a-coffee' promotion, which let customers give a $5 gift card to a friend by putting both #tweetacoffee and the friend's handle in a tweet, resulted in $180,000 in purchases within little more than one month. Social media 'are not just about engaging and telling a story and connecting,' says Starbucks' head of global digital marketing. 'They can have a material impact on the business.'[40]

Mobile marketing

Mobile marketing—
Marketing messages, promotions and other content delivered to on-the-go consumers through mobile phones, smartphones, tablets and other mobile devices.

Mobile marketing features marketing messages, promotions and other marketing content delivered to on-the-go consumers through their mobile devices. Marketers use mobile marketing to engage customers anywhere, anytime during the buying and relationship-building processes. The widespread adoption of mobile devices and the surge in mobile web traffic have made mobile marketing a must for most brands.

With the recent proliferation of mobile phones, smartphones and tablets, mobile device penetration is now greater than 100 per cent in the United States (many people possess more than one mobile device). Almost 40 per cent of US households are currently mobile-only households with no landline phone. More than 65 per cent of people in the United States own a smartphone, and over 60 per cent of smartphone users use it to access the mobile Internet. They not only browse the mobile Internet but are also avid mobile app users. The mobile apps market has exploded globally: there are more than 2 million apps available and the average smartphone has 25 apps installed on it.[41]

Most people love their phones and rely heavily on them. According to one study, nearly 90 per cent of consumers who own smartphones, tablets, computers and TVs would give up all of those other screens before giving up their phones. On average, people check their phones 150 times a day – once every six-and-one-half minutes – and spend 58 minutes a day on their smartphones talking, texting and visiting websites. Thus, although TV is still a big part of people's lives, mobile is rapidly becoming their 'first screen'. Away from home, it's their only screen.[42]

This incredibly rapid diffusion of smartphones (e.g., Samsung, Blackberry, iPhone) and pad devices (e.g., iPad) has also happened in the global marketplace and provides a growing method of gaining direct access to targeted individuals throughout the world. It is estimated that there are 6.6 billion mobile phone and device users in the world (around 94 per cent of the world's population), with growth led mainly by India and China, which together account for a third of all world mobile subscriptions. There are 1.3 billion mobile subscribers in China and 0.9 billion in India, dwarfing the number of subscribers in third place US (0.3 billion). Interestingly, Indonesia, Brazil and Russia are the leading countries for mobile broadband penetration, with the UK and US ranked much lower.[43] In the UK, 2014 saw advertising spend for mobile devices set to exceed traditional press advertising for the first time, while in the US mobile advertising spend rose 76 per cent last year, overtaking display advertising to become the second largest online ad format.[44]

Access to mobile users emphasises texting and instant messaging as well as e-mail. Mobile technology is quickly developing payment and banking systems, as well as several ticketing and couponing approaches. It is likely that expanding ownership of mobile devices will encourage further developments. For example, placecasting is a growing way of making direct contact with consumers through their mobile phones:

> Starbucks and L'Oréal are among leading brands developing placecasting to position their marketing and product messages direct with European consumers. Placecasting involves consumers receiving offers and discounts over their mobile phones by text message and uses a 'geofencing' system that directs text messages to consumers' mobile phones, when they are in the proximity of stores. Also, supermarkets have begun issuing 'digital coupons' on the Internet that can be downloaded to mobile phones, and scanned against purchases at the store checkout. Quick Response codes can be scanned by a smartphone camera to link the device to a retailer's mobile website. Youth-oriented cosmetics retailer, Sephora, uses this to link customers' phones to its Tarina Tarantino website and also has a mobile phone link for customer-generated product reviews, which can be uploaded to Facebook.[45]

Research agency eMarketer estimates that 2014 mobile Internet advertising spend reached $42.6 billion, with the largest spending countries being: US (44 per cent of the global spend), China (17 per cent of the total), UK (9 per cent), Japan (7 per cent) and Germany (3 per cent). Asia is expected to dominate global mobile advertising spending in the future.[46] In the US, Google is the main recipient of mobile advertising revenues.[47] Leading US retailers including Walmart, Sears and Gap, as well as companies like John Lewis in the UK, have launched mobile versions of their websites, together with shopping and browsing applications for iPhones and Blackberrys. Other retailers, such as JC Penney and Sephora, participate in Facebook's initiative to allow users to populate their Facebook pages with product, information, images and reviews, and access their through mobile devices, even when in the store.[48]

For consumers, a smartphone or tablet can be a handy shopping companion. It can provide on-the-go product information, price comparisons, advice and reviews from other consumers, access to instant deals and digital coupons, and even act as a payment device. Not surprisingly, then, mobile devices provide a rich platform for engaging consumers more deeply as they move through the buying process with tools ranging from mobile ads, coupons and texts to apps and mobile websites.

Almost every major marketer – from P&G and Tesco to your local bank or supermarket to non-profits such as charities – is now integrating mobile marketing into its direct marketing programmes. Such efforts can produce very positive outcomes. For example, 49 per cent of mobile users search for more information after seeing a mobile ad.[49]

Companies use mobile marketing to stimulate immediate buying, make shopping easier, enrich the brand experience, or all of these. It lets marketers provide consumers with information, incentives and choices at the moment they are expressing an interest or when they are in a position to make a buying choice. For example, McDonald's uses mobile marketing to promote new menu items, announce special promotions and drive immediate traffic at its restaurants. One recent interactive ad on a mobile app read: 'Taste buds. Any size soft drink or sweet tea for $1. Tap to visit site.' A tap on the mobile ad took customers to a mobile site promoting McDonald's ongoing summer promotion. Another McDonald's mobile campaign used a word scrabble game to entice customers to try the restaurant's dollar menu items. Such efforts create both customer engagement and store traffic. Using a game 'inside a mobile campaign is all about finding and maintaining engagement', says a McDonald's marketer.[50]

Today's rich-media mobile ads can create substantial engagement and impact. For example, American budget airline JetBlue recently created a voice-activated mobile ad that interacts with customers and talks back. It starts with a JetBlue mobile banner ad that says, 'Click here to learn how to speak pigeon.' A click expands the ad, which then instructs users by voice to repeat words on the screen, such as 'coo, coo, coo'. When they've completed two full sentences in pigeon, users receive a virtual medal and the option to play again. Hitting 'Learn more' takes users to the JetBlue Landing Perch, where they can explore and send messages to friends via digital carrier pigeons. The mobile ad is part of JetBlue's 'Air on the side of humanity' campaign, which features pigeons – the ultimate frequent fliers. Rather than making direct sales pitches, the voice ad aims simply to enrich the JetBlue experience. The airline hopes people will 'watch the ads, play with the pigeons, and remember us when they want to book tickets,' says JetBlue's advertising manager.[51]

Retailers can use mobile marketing to enrich the customer's shopping experience at the same time that they stimulate buying. Many marketers have created their own mobile online sites, optimised for specific phones and mobile service providers. Armed only with a smartphone or other mobile device, Zipcar's app lets you find and reserve a Zipcar, honk the horn (so you can find it in a crowd), and even lock and unlock the doors – all from your phone. Similarly, Starbucks' mobile app lets customers use their phones as a Starbucks card to make fast and easy purchases.

Naturally, as with other forms of direct marketing, companies must use mobile marketing responsibly or risk angering already ad-weary consumers. Most people don't want to be interrupted regularly by advertising, so marketers must be smart about how they engage people on mobiles. The key is to provide genuinely useful information and offers that will make consumers want to engage. And many marketers target mobile ads on an opt-in-only basis.

In all, digital direct marketing – online, social media and mobile marketing – offers both great promise and many challenges for the future. Its most ardent apostles still envision a time when the Internet and digital marketing will replace magazines, newspapers and even stores as sources for information, engagement and buying. Most marketers, however, hold a more realistic view. For most companies, digital and social media marketing will remain just one important approach to the marketplace that works alongside other approaches in a fully integrated marketing mix.

However, although the fast-growing digital marketing tools have grabbed most of the headlines lately, traditional direct marketing tools are very much alive and still heavily used. We now examine the traditional direct marketing approaches shown on the right side of Figure 17.1.

TRADITIONAL DIRECT MARKETING FORMS

Author comment

Again, although online, social media and mobile direct marketing seem to be getting much of the attention these days, traditional direct media still carry a lot of the direct marketing freight. Just think about your often overstuffed postbox.

The major traditional forms of direct marketing – as shown in Figure 17.1 – are face-to-face or personal selling, direct-mail marketing, catalogue marketing, telemarketing, direct-response television (DRTV) marketing and kiosk marketing. We examined personal selling in depth in Chapter 16. Here, we look into the other forms of traditional direct marketing.

Direct-mail marketing

Direct-mail marketing— Marketing that occurs by sending an offer, announcement, reminder, or other item directly to a person at a particular address.

Direct-mail marketing involves sending an offer, announcement, reminder, or other item to a person at a particular address. Using highly selective mailing lists, direct marketers send out millions of mail pieces each year – letters, catalogues, ads, brochures, samples, videos, and other 'salespeople with wings'. US marketers spent an estimated more than $45 billion on direct mail last year (including both catalogue and non-catalogue mail), which accounted for 30 per cent of all direct marketing spending and generated 31 per cent of all direct marketing sales. According to the DMA, every dollar spent on direct mail generates $12.57 in sales. UK expenditure on direct mail is around £1.7 billion a year – Germany, France and the UK are the largest direct mail markets in Europe.[52]

Direct mail is well suited to direct, one-to-one communication. It permits high target-market selectivity, can be personalised, is flexible and allows the easy measurement of results. Although direct mail costs more per thousand people reached than mass media such as television or magazines, the people it reaches are much better prospects. Direct mail has proved successful in promoting all kinds of products, from books, insurance, travel, gift items, gourmet foods, clothing and other consumer goods to industrial products of all kinds. Charities also use direct mail heavily to raise donations.

Some analysts predict a decline in the use of traditional forms of direct mail in the coming years, as marketers switch to newer digital forms, such as e-mail and online marketing, social media marketing and mobile marketing. The newer digital direct marketing approaches deliver messages at incredible speeds and lower costs compared to the post office's 'snail mail' pace.

However, even though new digital forms of direct marketing are bursting onto the scene, traditional direct mail is still heavily used by most marketers, although in some countries e-mail has already overtaken print as the main way of delivering marketing offers. Nonetheless, mail marketing offers some distinct advantages over digital forms. It provides something tangible for people to hold and keep and it can be used to send samples. 'Mail makes it real,' says one analyst. It 'creates an emotional connection with customers that digital cannot. They hold it, view it and engage with it in a manner entirely different from their [digital] experiences.' In contrast, e-mail and other digital forms are easily filtered or trashed. '[With] spam filters and spam folders to keep our messaging away from consumers' inboxes,' says a direct marketer, 'Sometimes you have to lick a few stamps.'[53]

Traditional direct mail can be an effective component of a broader integrated marketing campaign. For example, most large insurance companies rely heavily on TV advertising to establish broad customer awareness and positioning. However, the insurance companies also use lots of good old direct mail to break through the glut of insurance advertising on TV. Whereas TV advertising talks to broad audiences, direct mail communicates in a more direct and personal way. 'Mail is a channel that allows all of us to find the consumer with a very targeted, very specific message that you can't do in broadcast,' says John Ingersoll, vice president of marketing communications for Farmers Insurance in the US. And 'most people are still amenable to getting marketing communications in their mailbox, which is why I think direct mail will grow'.[54]

Direct mail may be resented as *junk mail* if sent to people who have no interest in it. For this reason, smart marketers are targeting their direct mail carefully so as not to waste their money and recipients' time. They are designing permission-based programmes that send direct mail only to those who want to receive it and have clearly indicated this.

Catalogue marketing

Advances in technology, along with the move toward personalised, one-to-one marketing, have resulted in exciting changes in **catalogue marketing.** In the US, traditional home of catalogue shopping, *Catalog Age* magazine used to define a *catalogue* as 'a printed, bound piece of at least eight pages, selling multiple products, and offering a direct ordering mechanism'. Today, this definition is sadly out of date – things are changing fast.

With the stampede to the Internet and digital marketing, more and more catalogues are going digital. A variety of online-only cataloguers have emerged, and most print cataloguers have added web-based catalogues and smartphone catalogue shopping apps to their marketing mixes. For example, in the days before the latest Lands' End clothing catalogue arrives in the mail, customers can access it digitally at landsend.com, at social media outlets such as Facebook, or via the Lands' End mobile app. 'With Lands' End Mobile,' says the company, 'You're carrying every item we carry'.[55]

Digital catalogues eliminate printing and mailing costs. And whereas space is limited in a print catalogue, online catalogues can offer an almost unlimited amount of merchandise. They also offer a broader assortment of presentation formats, including search and video. Finally, online catalogues allow real-time merchandising; products and features can be added or removed as needed, and prices can be adjusted instantly to match demand. Customers can carry digital catalogues anywhere they go, even when shopping at physical stores.

However, despite the advantages of digital catalogues, as your over-filled postbox may suggest, printed catalogues are still thriving in some areas. In the US, direct marketers mailed out some 12.5 billion catalogues last year – more than 100 per American household.[56] Why aren't companies ditching their old-fashioned paper catalogues in this new digital era? For one thing, paper catalogues create emotional connections with customers. Somehow, turning actual catalogue pages engages some consumers in a way that digital images simply can't.

In addition, printed catalogues are one of the best ways to drive online and mobile sales, making them more important than ever in the digital era. According to one study, about 58 per cent of online shoppers browse physical catalogues for ideas, and 31 per cent have a retailer's catalogue with them when they make a purchase online. Catalogue users look at more than double the number of online pages per visit to the company's site than the average visitor and spend twice the amount of time there.[57]

Similarly, in the UK, catalogues are continuing to boost online retail success by encouraging shoppers to buy online, according to research from Royal Mail's MarketReach initiative.[58] The study, which looks at the role of printed catalogues in the digital age, found the benefits of posting catalogues can be 'instant', with 60 per cent of people going online to make a purchase within a week of receiving one. It also found that more than half of catalogue users will spend over £40 on their first purchase, showing that companies that overlook catalogues could be missing out on sales. The MarketReach study found that for over 50 per cent of people, catalogues are a convenient way to review products. More than a third of people (36 per cent) said it allows them to compare products before a purchase. When they go online, consumers with catalogues were found to look at more than double the number of pages viewed by the average person per visit (121 per cent). They also spend 109 per cent more time on any given website than the average site visitor.

Catalogue marketing—Direct marketing through print, video or digital catalogues that are mailed to select customers, made available in stores, or presented online.

Telemarketing

Telemarketing involves using the telephone to sell directly to consumers and business customers. US marketers spent an estimated $42 billion on telemarketing last year, almost as much as on direct mail.[59] We're all familiar with telephone marketing directed toward consumers, but business-to-business (B-to-B) marketers also use telemarketing extensively. Marketers use *outbound* telephone marketing to sell directly to consumers and businesses. They also use *inbound* free phone numbers to receive orders from television and print ads, direct mail or catalogues.

Properly designed and targeted telemarketing provides many benefits, including purchasing convenience and increased product and service information. However, the explosion in unsolicited outbound telephone marketing over the years annoyed many consumers, who objected to the almost daily 'junk phone calls' or 'cold calls'. Mobile phone users can also become concerned about the impact of unwanted calls on their battery life while out and about. For these reasons, an increasing number of countries have laws and voluntary agreements allowing people to opt out of receiving commercial messages over the phone, if they do not want to receive them. Automated re-dial systems for calling back are generally not allowed either in most European states. The penalties for breaching these legal and voluntary restrictions vary by country.

Do-not-call rules have hurt parts of the consumer telemarketing industry. But two major forms of telemarketing – inbound consumer telemarketing and outbound B-to-B telemarketing – remain strong and growing. Telemarketing also remains a major fundraising tool for non-profit and political groups. Interestingly, do-not-call regulations appear to be helping some direct marketers more than it's hurting them. Rather than making unwanted calls, many of these marketers are developing 'opt-in' calling systems, in which they provide useful information and offers to customers who have invited the company to contact them by phone or e-mail. The opt-in model provides better returns for marketers than the formerly invasive one.

Direct-response television marketing

Direct-response television (DRTV) marketing takes one of two major forms: direct-response television advertising and interactive TV (iTV) advertising. Using *direct-response television advertising*, direct marketers air television spots, often 60 or 120 seconds in length, which persuasively describe a product and give customers a free phone number or an online site for ordering. It also includes full 30-minute or longer advertising programmes, called *infomercials*, for a single product. The widest use of infomercials is in the United States. In other countries, like the UK, there are stringent compliance procedures making it more difficult to use this approach and it has been relatively uncommon in the past. Nonetheless, High Street TV is pioneering the development of infomercials in the UK, for example for the Zumba dance fitness programme for which it has the UK rights, so things are changing.[60]

The US experience is that successful direct-response television advertising campaigns can ring up big sales. For example, little-known infomercial maker Guthy-Renker has helped propel its Proactiv Solution acne treatment and other 'transformational' products into power brands that pull in $1.8 billion in sales annually to 5 million active customers (compare that to only about $150 million in annual drugstore sales of acne products in the United States). Guthy-Renker now combines DRTV with social media campaigns using Facebook, Pinterest, Google+, Twitter and YouTube to create a powerful integrated direct marketing channel that builds consumer involvement and buying.[61]

DRTV ads are often associated with somewhat loud or questionable pitches for cleaners, stain removers, kitchen gadgets and nifty ways to stay in shape without working very hard at it. In recent years, however, a number of large companies – from P&G, Disney, Revlon and Apple to Toyota, Coca-Cola, Anheuser-Busch, and even the US Navy – have begun using infomercials to sell their wares, refer customers to retailers, recruit members, or attract buyers to their online, mobile and social media sites.

A more recent form of direct-response television marketing is *interactive TV (iTV)*, which lets viewers interact with television programming and advertising. Thanks to technologies such as interactive cable systems, Internet-ready smart TVs and smartphones and tablets, consumers can now use their TV remotes, phones or other devices to obtain more information or make purchases directly from TV ads. For example, fashion retailer H&M recently ran ads that let viewers with certain Samsung smart TVs use their remotes to interact directly with the commercials. A small pop-up menu, shown as the ads ran, offered product information, the ability to send that information to another device and the option to buy directly.[62]

Interestingly, British people use more Internet-connected televisions than the rest of Europe. Almost a quarter of UK consumers have a smart TV, and about four-fifths of those are connected to the Internet. Traditional TV viewing is declining in the UK as consumers use the Internet to watch TV programmes and films and on-demand programming, suggesting new opportunities are opening up.[63]

Increasingly, as the lines continue to blur between TV screens and other video screens, interactive ads and infomercials are appearing not just on TV, but also on mobile, online and social media platforms, adding even more TV-like interactive direct marketing venues. For example, US retailer Target recently placed dozens of products from its new home collection in an episode of a popular television comedy series, which was also simulcast online. When the products appeared on the television screen, viewers were encouraged to purchase them on their phones or other screens. Thus, when viewers watching the show saw, say, a lamp they liked, they could click on a red plus sign flashing on the product in the online version, which took them to Target.com where they could buy it. 'It's a combination of being a product integration that's really integrated into the story line of the script, being on a major network, and with a unique shopping experience,' concludes Target's marketing vice president.[64]

Kiosk marketing: in the UK a visit to Boots the Chemists provides kiosk access to photo printing technology.
Source: Courtesy of Boots UK

Kiosk marketing

As consumers become more and more comfortable with digital and touchscreen technologies, many companies are placing information and ordering machines – called *kiosks* (good old-fashioned vending machines but so much more) – in stores, airports, hotels, university campuses and other locations. Kiosks are everywhere these days, from self-service hotel and airline check-in devices, to unmanned product and information kiosks in malls, to in-store ordering devices that let you order merchandise not carried in the store. 'Vending machines, which not long ago had mechanical levers and coin trays, now possess brains,' says one analyst. Many modern 'smart kiosks' are now wireless-enabled. And some machines can even use facial recognition software that lets them guess gender and age and make product recommendations based on those data.[65] In-store Kodak, Fuji and HP kiosks let customers transfer pictures from memory cards, mobile phones and other digital storage devices, edit them, and make high-quality colour prints.

In the US, for example, to ensure the American consumer is never far away from a purchase opportunity, ZoomSystems creates small, free-standing kiosks called Zoom-Shops for retailers ranging from Apple, Sephora and The Body Shop to Macy's and Best Buy. For example, 100 Best Buy Express ZoomShop kiosks across the country – conveniently located in airports, busy shopping centres and resorts – automatically dispense an assortment of portable media players, digital cameras, gaming consoles, headphones, phone chargers, travel gadgets and other popular products. According to ZoomSystems, today's automated retailing 'offers [consumers] the convenience of online shopping with the immediate gratification of traditional retail'.[66]

PUBLIC POLICY ISSUES IN DIRECT AND DIGITAL MARKETING

Direct marketers and their customers usually enjoy mutually rewarding relationships. Occasionally, however, a darker side emerges. The aggressive and sometimes shady tactics of a few direct marketers can bother or harm consumers, giving the entire industry a black eye. Abuses range from simple excesses that irritate consumers to instances of unfair practices or even outright deception and fraud. The direct marketing industry has also faced growing privacy concerns, and online marketers must deal with Internet and mobile security issues.

Irritation, unfairness, deception and fraud

Direct marketing excesses sometimes annoy or offend consumers. For example, most of us dislike television commercials that are too loud, long, strident and insistent. Our postboxes fill up with unwanted junk mail, our e-mailboxes bulge with unwanted spam, and our computer, phone and tablet screens flash with unwanted online or mobile display ads, pop-ups or pop-unders.

Beyond irritating consumers, some direct marketers have been accused of taking unfair advantage of impulsive or less-sophisticated buyers. In the US in particular, television shopping channels and programme-long infomercials targeting television-addicted shoppers seem to be the worst culprits. They feature smooth-talking hosts, elaborately staged demonstrations, claims of drastic price reductions, 'while they last' time limitations, and unequalled ease of purchase to inflame buyers who have low sales resistance. Taking unfair advantage of vulnerable consumers is not restricted to the US:

> In the UK in 2015, after a newspaper investigation, charity organisations were accused of 'aggressive, ruthless and cynical' behaviour in cold telephone calling to raise donations, and using intensive, high-pressure 'boiler room' call centres. Callers were allegedly told by trainers, 'Be brutal . . . these people have no excuse for not giving'. They were accused of asking elderly dementia sufferers to commit to direct debits, taking money from those who admitted to confusion and memory problems, and repeatedly calling people aged in their 90s for donations even when they had opted out. When this story hit the news, major charities were forced to cease these fundraising activities and Government ministers threatened new laws to crack down on their 'grotesque' practices.[67]

Worse yet, so-called 'heat merchants' design mailers and write copy intended to mislead buyers. Fraudulent schemes, such as investment scams or phoney collections for charity, have also multiplied in recent years. *Internet fraud*, including identity theft and financial scams, has become a serious problem. In the United States alone, according to the Federal Bureau of Investigations' Internet Crime Complaint Center, since 2005, Internet scam complaints have more than tripled to almost 300,000 per year. The monetary loss of scam complaints exceeds $500 million per year.[68] Comparable figures are not available for Europe, although the new European Cybercrime Centre becomes fully operational in 2015.

One common form of Internet fraud is *phishing*, a type of identity theft that uses deceptive e-mails and fraudulent online sites to fool users into divulging their personal data. For example, consumers may receive an email, supposedly from their bank or credit card company, saying that their account's security has been compromised. The sender asks them to log on to a provided web address and confirm their account number, password, and perhaps even other personal details. If they follow the instructions, users are actually turning this sensitive information over to criminals. Although many consumers are now aware of such schemes, phishing can be extremely costly to those caught in the net. It also damages the brand identities of legitimate online marketers who have worked to build user confidence in web, e-mail and other digital transactions.

Many consumers also worry about *online and digital security*. They fear that unscrupulous snoopers will eavesdrop on their online transactions and social media postings, picking up personal information or intercepting credit and debit card numbers. Although online shopping has grown rapidly, one study showed that 75 per cent of participants were still concerned about identity theft.[69]

Another Internet marketing concern is that of *access by vulnerable or unauthorised groups*. For example, marketers of adult-oriented materials and sites have found it difficult to restrict access by minors. Although Facebook allows no children under age 13 to have a profile, an estimated 40 per cent of under-18 Facebook users are actually under 13. Facebook removes 200,000 underage accounts every day. And it's not just Facebook. Young users are logging onto social media such as Formspring, tweeting their locations to the web, and making friends with strangers on Disney and other game sites. Concerned governments are currently debating laws that would help better protect children online. Unfortunately, this requires the development of technology solutions, and as Facebook puts it, 'That's not so easy'.[70]

Consumer privacy

Invasion of privacy is perhaps the toughest public policy issue now confronting the direct marketing industry. Consumers often benefit from database marketing; they receive more offers that are closely matched to their interests. However, many critics worry that marketers may know *too* much about consumers' lives and that they may use this knowledge to take unfair advantage of consumers. At some point, they claim, the extensive use of databases intrudes on consumer privacy. Consumers, too, worry about their privacy. Although they are now much more willing to share personal information and preferences with marketers via digital and social media, they are still nervous about it. In one recent survey, some three-quarters of consumers agreed with the statement, 'No one should ever be allowed to have access to my personal data or web behaviour'. Another showed that 92 per cent of US Internet users worry about their privacy online.[71]

These days, it seems that almost every time consumers post something on social media or send a tweet, visit a website, enter a competition, apply for a credit card or order products by phone or online, their names are entered into some company's already bulging database. Using sophisticated computer technologies, direct marketers can mine these databases to 'micro-target' their selling efforts. Most marketers have become highly skilled at collecting and analysing detailed consumer information both online and offline.

Some consumers and policy makers worry that the ready availability of information may leave consumers open to abuse. For example, they ask, should online sellers be allowed to plant cookies in the browsers of consumers who visit their sites and use tracking information to target ads and other marketing efforts? Should credit card companies be allowed to make data on their millions of cardholders worldwide available to the retailers who accept their cards? Or is it right for government agencies to sell the names and addresses of driver's licence holders?

A need for action

To curb direct marketing excesses, various government agencies in different countries are investigating not only do-not-call lists but also do-not-mail lists, do-not-track online lists and 'Can spam' legislation. In response to online privacy and security concerns, many national government and European agencies are considering numerous legislative actions to regulate how online, social media and mobile operators obtain and use consumer information. New laws promise to give consumers more control over how web information is used, and to allow regulators to take a more active role in policing online privacy. European regulators have already several times taken action to curb what they regard as unwarranted invasion of consumer privacy. For example, in Europe in 2014 consumers gained 'the right to be forgotten' following a ruling of the European Union's top court, whereby individuals can ask that Google removes results that turn up in Internet searches for their own names, and Google is responding to thousands of requests from individuals who want data removed from searches.[72]

Consumer privacy: to support consumer privacy interests, with Internet-based advertising, by clicking on the little AdChoices advertising option icon in the upper right of the online ad, consumers can find out why they are seeing the ad and opt out if they wish. The Digital Advertising Alliance has expanded the use of its AdChoices icon into 35 countries and 26 languages as of 2016. This self-regulatory programme from the advertising industry is increasingly a global initiative with broad impact across Europe and North America.

Source: Digital Advertising Alliance

For example, in addition to the Privacy and Electronic Communications Regulations introduced in the EU in 2003, in 2012 the EU Privacy and Electronic Communications Directive came into force, apparently heralding a new era of regulation for digital business models. The new directive is designed to protect users' privacy if they do not wish their browsing habits to be tracked. The regulations have been driven by complaints from privacy campaigners concerned about cookies tracking details of web use to allow targeted advertising based on the web user's behaviour online. The directive introduces an 'opt-in' regime where users have to agree to cookies being used. However, it is clear that different European countries are taking different views on how to interpret and apply the new regulations, and the EU Information Commissioner faces a considerable challenge in enforcing them.[73]

In addition, regulators struggle to control the actions of powerful global organisations like Facebook and Google. Early 2012 saw Google rolling out a new privacy policy which makes it possible for Google to take what it has learnt about a consumer from one of its services, such as search or Gmail, and use it to tailor what the user sees on other services. The content of e-mails sent on Gmail could, for example, be used to influence what advertising is shown to that person on YouTube. Google made these changes in spite of repeated requests from regulators to delay, and warnings that the policy might not be lawful in the European Union.[74]

> Particular concern relating to privacy issues relates to Google and Facebook. The ability of Google to use its records of individuals' Internet searches to identify them as targets for advertising and marketing offers on the basis of their search interests is a major worry for privacy advocates. The capacity of Facebook to track online behaviour and connections of users of its social network provides a unique database relating to people's behaviour and preferences. The argument about whether these companies breach people's rights continues.

All of these concerns call for strong actions by marketers to monitor and prevent privacy abuses before legislators step in to do it for them. For example, to head off increased government regulation, six advertiser groups in the United States – the American Association of Advertising Agencies, the American Advertising Federation, the Association of National Advertisers, the Direct Marketing Association, the Interactive Advertising Bureau and the Network Advertising Initiative – recently issued a set of online advertising principles through the Digital Advertising Alliance. Among other measures, the self-regulatory principles call for online marketers to provide transparency and choice to consumers if web viewing data is collected or used for targeting interest-based advertising. The ad industry has agreed on an *advertising option icon* – a little 'i' inside a triangle – that it will add to behaviourally targeted online ads (including web sites, mobile web sites, and in-app environments) to tell consumers why they are seeing a particular ad and allowing them to opt out.[75]

Of special concern are the privacy rights of children. With the advent of online social networks, mobile phones and other devices, and high levels of use by young people in particular, the main concern is the amount of data mined by third parties from social networks, as well as the networks' own hazy privacy policies. In the United States, 2000 saw the Children's Online Privacy Protection Act (COPPA), which requires online operators targeting children to post privacy policies on their sites. They must also notify parents about any information they're gathering and obtain parental consent before collecting personal information from children under age 13. COPPA extended in 2013 to include 'identifiers such as cookies that track a child's activity online, as well as geolocation information, photos, videos and audio recordings'.[76] Privacy groups are pressing the US government to further extend COPPA to include both new technologies and teenagers. However, while there is a comparable European legal framework surrounding privacy issues, there are significant differences between EU data protection and that in the US. Critics on both sides of the Atlantic fear that legal protections for individuals are inadequate.

Many companies have responded positively to consumer privacy and security concerns with actions of their own. Still others are taking an industry-wide approach. For example, TRUSTe, a non-profit self-regulatory organisation, works with many large corporate sponsors, including

Microsoft, Yahoo!, AT&T, Facebook, Disney and Apple, to audit privacy and security measures and help consumers navigate the Internet safely. According to the company's website, 'TRUSTe believes that an environment of mutual trust and openness will help make and keep the Internet a free, comfortable, and richly diverse community for everyone.' To reassure consumers, the company lends its TRUSTe privacy seal to websites, mobile apps, e-mail marketing and other online and social media channels that meet its privacy and security standards. However, the TRUSTe seal does not indicate that a website complies with any specific set of privacy rules, such as the European Union's Data Protection Directive, but only that the site has self-certified as complying with the site's own privacy statement.[77]

The direct marketing industry as a whole is also addressing public policy issues. Professional bodies like the DMA in the US make substantial efforts to build consumer confidence in shopping direct through their explicit privacy promises. The comparable bodies in Europe make similar though less developed undertakings (e.g., the UK Direct Marketing Association).[78]

Direct marketers know that, if left untended, such direct marketing abuses will lead to increasingly negative consumer attitudes, lower response and engagement rates, and calls for more restrictive legal control by government. Most direct marketers want the same things that consumers want: honest and well-designed marketing offers targeted only toward consumers who will appreciate and respond to them. Direct marketing is just too expensive to waste on consumers who don't want it.

OBJECTIVES REVIEW AND KEY TERMS

This chapter is the last of four chapters covering the final marketing mix element – promotion. The previous chapters dealt with advertising, public relations, personal selling and sales promotion. This one investigates the burgeoning field of direct and digital marketing, including online, social media and mobile marketing.

OBJECTIVE 1 Define direct and digital marketing and discuss their rapid growth and benefits to customers and companies (pp. 502–505)

Direct and digital marketing involve engaging directly with carefully targeted individual consumers and customer communities to both obtain an immediate response and build lasting customer relationships. Companies use direct marketing to tailor their offers and content to the needs and interests of narrowly defined segments or individual buyers to build direct customer engagement, brand community and sales. Today, spurred by the surge in Internet usage and buying, and by rapid advances in digital technologies – from smartphones, tablets and other digital devices to the spate of online social and mobile media – direct marketing has undergone a dramatic transformation.

For buyers, direct and digital marketing are convenient, easy to use and private. They give buyers anywhere, anytime access to an almost unlimited assortment of products and buying information. Direct marketing is also immediate and interactive, allowing buyers to create exactly the configuration of information, products or

services they desire and then order them on the spot. Finally, for consumers who want it, digital marketing through online, mobile and social media provides a sense of brand engagement and community – a place to share brand information and experiences with other brand fans. For sellers, direct and digital marketing are powerful tools for building customer engagement and close, personalised, interactive customer relationships. They also offer greater flexibility, letting marketers make ongoing adjustments to prices and programmes, or make immediate, timely and personal announcements and offers.

OBJECTIVE 2 Identify and discuss the major forms of direct and digital marketing (pp. 505–506)

The main forms of direct and digital marketing include traditional direct marketing tools and the new direct digital marketing tools. Traditional direct approaches are face-to-face personal selling, direct-mail marketing, catalogue marketing, telemarketing, DRTV marketing and kiosk marketing. These traditional tools are still heavily used and very important in most firm's direct marketing efforts. In recent years, however, a dazzling new set of direct digital marketing tools has burst onto the marketing scene, including online marketing (websites, online ads and promotions, e-mail, online videos and blogs), social media marketing and mobile marketing. The chapter first discusses the fast-growing new digital direct marketing tools and then examines the traditional tools.

OBJECTIVE 3 **Explain how companies have responded to the Internet and the digital age with various online marketing strategies (pp. 506–511)**

The Internet and digital age have fundamentally changed customers' notions of convenience, speed, price, product information, service and brand interactions. As a result, they have given marketers a whole new way to create customer value, engage customers and build customer relationships. The Internet now influences a staggering 50 per cent of total sales – including sales transacted online plus those made in stores but encouraged by online research. To reach this burgeoning market, most companies now market online.

Online marketing takes several forms, including company websites, online advertising and promotions, e-mail marketing, online video and blogs. Social media and mobile marketing also take place online. But because of their special characteristics, we discuss these fast-growing digital marketing approaches in separate sections. For most companies, the first step in conducting online marketing is to create a website. The key to a successful website is to create enough value and engagement to get consumers to come to the site, stick around and come back again.

Online advertising has become a major promotional medium. The main forms of online advertising are display ads and search-related ads. E-mail marketing is also an important form of digital marketing. Used properly, e-mail lets marketers send highly targeted, tightly personalised, relationship-building messages. Another important form of online marketing is posting digital video content on brand websites or social media. Marketers hope that some of their videos will go viral, engaging consumers by the millions. Finally, companies can use blogs as effective means of reaching customer communities. They can create their own blogs and advertise on existing blogs or influence content there.

OBJECTIVE 4 **Discuss how companies use social media and mobile marketing to engage consumers and create brand community (pp. 511–516)**

In the digital age, countless independent and commercial social media have arisen that give consumers online places to congregate, socialise and exchange views and information. Most marketers are now riding this huge social media wave. Brands can use existing social media or they can set up their own. Using existing social media seems the easiest. Thus, most brands – large and small – have set up shop on a host of social media sites. Some of the major social networks are huge; other niche social media cater to the needs of smaller communities of like-minded people. Beyond these independent social media, many companies have created their own online brand communities. More than making just scattered efforts and chasing 'Likes' and tweets, most companies are integrating a broad range of diverse media to create brand-related social sharing, engagement and customer community.

Using social media presents both advantages and challenges. On the plus side, social media are targeted and personal, interactive, immediate and timely and cost effective. Perhaps the biggest advantage is their engagement and social sharing capabilities, making them ideal for creating customer community. On the down side, consumers' control over social media content make social media difficult to control.

Mobile marketing features marketing messages, promotions and other content delivered to on-the-go consumers through their mobile devices. Marketers use mobile marketing to engage customers anywhere, anytime during the buying and relationship-building processes. The widespread adoption of mobile devices and the surge in mobile web traffic have made mobile marketing a must for most brands, and almost every major marketer is now integrating mobile marketing into its direct marketing programmes. Many marketers have created their own mobile online sites. Others have created useful or entertaining mobile apps to engage customers with their brands and help them shop.

OBJECTIVE 5 **Identify and discuss the traditional direct marketing forms and overview the public policy and ethical issues presented by direct marketing (pp. 516–523)**

Although the fast-growing digital marketing tools have grabbed most of the headlines lately, traditional direct marketing tools are very much alive and still heavily used. The major forms are face-to-face or personal selling, direct-mail marketing, catalogue marketing, telemarketing, direct-response television (DRTV) marketing and kiosk marketing.

Direct-mail marketing consists of the company sending an offer, announcement, reminder or other item to a person at a specific address. Some marketers rely on catalogue marketing – selling through catalogues mailed to a select list of customers, made available in stores or accessed online. Telemarketing consists of using the telephone to sell directly to consumers. DRTV marketing has two forms: direct-response advertising (or infomercials) and interactive television (iTV) marketing. Kiosks are information and ordering machines that direct marketers place in stores, airports, hotels and other locations.

Direct marketers and their customers usually enjoy mutually rewarding relationships. Sometimes, however, direct marketing presents a darker side. The aggressive and sometimes shady tactics of a few direct marketers can bother or harm consumers, giving the entire industry a black eye. Abuses range from simple excesses that irritate consumers to instances of unfair practices or even outright deception and fraud. The direct marketing industry has also faced growing concerns about invasion-of-privacy and Internet security issues. Such concerns call for strong action by marketers and public policy makers to curb direct marketing abuses. In the end, most direct marketers want the same things that consumers want: honest and well-designed marketing offers targeted only toward consumers who will appreciate and respond to them.

NAVIGATING THE KEY TERMS

OBJECTIVE 1
Direct and digital marketing (p. 502)

OBJECTIVE 2
Digital and social media marketing
    (p. 506)

OBJECTIVE 3
Multichannel marketing (p. 506)
Online marketing (p. 507)
Marketing website (p. 507)

Branded community website (p. 507)
Online advertising (p. 508)
E-mail marketing (p. 508)
Spam (p. 509)
Viral marketing (p. 509)
Blogs (p. 510)

OBJECTIVE 4
Social media (p. 511)
Mobile marketing (p. 514)

OBJECTIVE 5
Direct-mail marketing (p. 516)
Catalogue marketing (p. 517)
Telemarketing (p. 518)
Direct-response television (DRTV)
    marketing (p. 518)

DISCUSSION AND CRITICAL THINKNG

Discussion questions

17-1 List and briefly describe the various forms of direct digital and social media marketing. (AACSB: Communication)

17-2 Compare and contrast a marketing website and a branded community website. (AACSB: Communication)

17-3 Name and describe the two main forms of online advertising. (AACSB: Communication)

17-4 Discuss the advantages and challenges of social media marketing. (AACSB: Communication)

17-5 List and briefly describe the major traditional forms of direct marketing. (AACSB: Communication)

Critical-thinking exercises

17-6 In a small group, design and deliver a direct-response television ad (DRTV) for a national brand not normally associated with this type of promotion, such as an athletic shoe, motor car or food product. (AACSB: Communication; Reflective thinking)

17-7 Will the pressure towards greater openness and disclosure requirements regarding ads and endorsers make Twitter less effective as an advertising medium? (AACSB: Communication; Use of IT; Reflective thinking)

17-8 Develop a presentation about phishing. In your presentation, define phishing, show three examples (search Google Images for phishing examples), and discuss how consumers and businesses used in scams can protect themselves. (AACSB: Communication; Use of IT; Reflective thinking)

Mini-cases and applications

Online, mobile and social media marketing: big business for small business

Mobile marketing is the place to be for small businesses. When rain pounded New Orleans right before its famous Jazz & Heritage Festival, the owner of a local shoe store saw an opportunity. She tweeted about rain boots available at her store, Feet First, and sold out in two hours. Feet First is no stranger to online marketing; it has a website, online shopping cart and a Facebook page. But mobile is where the action is. Employees update the store's Facebook, Twitter, Instagram, Pinterest, Tumblr and Snapette – a local fashion app – accounts frequently. Consumers are increasingly turning to mobile devices to find information and purchase products. The Polkadot Alley, an online store, found that 90 per cent of orders come from mobile phones. Even though Yelp's app traffic is a fraction of the overall website's traffic, 45 per cent of all Yelp searches come from its mobile app. Local retailers see the advantages of mobile marketing. As a result, Google changed its ad platform to accommodate the growth in mobile ad campaigns. Advertisers not only bid for search words, but also on the searcher's device used to search, their location and time of day. If it's Saturday before Mother's Day and you use your phone to search for a florist, Emily's Flower Shop half a mile away probably bid 30 per cent higher to get its ad at the top of your results list.

17-9 What local businesses in your community are using online, social media and/or mobile marketing? Interview the owner or manager of one of the businesses to learn how the business uses these marketing activities and discuss their satisfaction with them. (AACSB: Communication; Reflective thinking)

17-10 Mobile marketing can be confusing for a small business owner. Develop a presentation to present to small business owners that describes mobile marketing, its advantages and disadvantages, and examples of how small businesses in your locality are using mobile marketing. (AACSB: Communication; Reflective thinking)

Marketing ethics: tracking in 'meat space'

By now, you know about behavioural targeting – marketers tracking consumers' online behaviour in cyberspace to send them targeted advertising. Krux Digital reports that the average visit to a web page generated 56 instances of data collection, a fivefold increase in just one year. An investigation by the *Wall Street Journal* found that the 50 most popular US websites installed more than 3,000 tracking files on the computer used in the study. The total was even higher – 4,123 tracking files – for the top 50 sites that are popular with children and teens. Many sites installed more than 100 tracking tools each during the tests. Tracking tools include files placed on users' computers and on websites. Marketers use this information to target online advertisements. But now, wearable and mobile devices allow marketers to track consumer movements in the physical world. The term 'meat space' refers to the physical world in which our bodies move and do things, and marketers are using information obtained from wearable and mobile devices to personalise offers while consumers move around their space. For example, Disney's Magic Bands and mobile app allow users to unlock hotel room doors, enter parks, use FastPasses, and reserve, order and pay for food. But the real magic for Disney is the ability to track everything the user does as he or she moves around the 'meat space'. Since

users willingly give their names and birthdates when ordering Magic Bands, Goofy just might walk up to your child to say, 'Happy birthday, Billy!'

17-11 Debate whether or not it is ethical to track consumers' physical movements, especially children's. (AACSB: Communication; Ethical reasoning)

17-12 Discuss other ways marketers can track consumers in 'meat space'. (AACSB: Communication; Reflective thinking)

Marketing by the numbers: mobile advertising

Consumers spend a quarter of their media-viewing time on mobile, but advertisers devote 1 per cent of their media budgets to mobile devices. Although mobile advertising makes up a small percentage of online advertising, it is one of the fastest-growing advertising channels. One source reported more than 100 per cent growth in mobile advertising between 2012 and 2013. But one obstacle is measuring return on investment in mobile. A study of chief marketing officers by eMarketer found that 41 per cent of those investing in mobile advertising indicated that success of their mobile ad spending was 'inconsistent' or 'not sure'.

17-13 Research on the web how much is spent on mobile marketing and what is the growth rate of expenditures in this medium in different parts of the world? Compare those expenditures to spending on other advertising media. (AACSB: Communication; Analytical reasoning; Reflective thinking)

17-14 How are marketers measuring the return on investment in mobile advertising? Develop a presentation suggesting metrics that marketers should use to measure the effectiveness of mobile advertising. (AACSB: Communication; Use of IT; Reflective thinking)

REFERENCES

[1] Based on information from Sarah Kessler, 'With Paper, Facebook stops trying to be everything for everyone', *Fast Company*, 30 January 2014, www.fastcompany.com/3025762/with-paper-facebookstops-trying-to-be-everything-for-everyone; Josh Constine, 'Zuck says ads aren't the way to monetise messaging', *Techcrunch*, 19 February 2014, http://techcrunch.com/2014/02/19/whatsapp-will-monetize-later/; Shayndi Raice and Spencer E. Ante, 'Insta-rich: $1 billion for Instagram', *Wall Street Journal*, 10 April 2012, http://online.wsj.com/news/articles/SB10001424052702303815404577333840377381670; 'Facebook's sales chief: Madison Avenue doesn't understand us yet', *Advertising Age*, 29 April 2011, www.adage.com/print/227314/; Craig Smith, 'By the numbers: 105 amazing Facebook user statistics', *Digital Marketing Ramblings*, 13 March 2014, http://expandedramblings.com/index.php/by-thenumbers-17-amazing-facebook-stats/#.U2F1gtxH38u; and www.facebook.com, www.instagram.com and www.whatsapp.com, accessed September 2014.

[2] ComBlu, 'The state of online branded communities', http://comblu.com/downloads/ComBlu_StateOfOnlineCommunities_2012.pdf, accessed November 2012; 'The strangest Mountain Dew flavors ever made', *Huffington Post*, 2 April 2014, www.huffingtonpost.com/the-daily-meal/the-strangest-mountain-de_b_5076837.html; and www.mountaindew.com, accessed September 2014.

[3] See 'Priceline profit tops estimates as bookings rise', *Reuters*, 20 February 2014, www.reuters.com/article/2014/02/21/us-priceline-results-idUSBREA1J26X20140221; and http://ir.pricelinegroup.com/financials.cfm, accessed September 2014.

[4] For these and other direct marketing statistics in this section, see Direct Marketing Association, *The DMA Statistical Fact Book 2014*, 36th ed., April 2014; and a wealth of other information at www.thedma.org, accessed September 2014.

[5] See www.dma.org.uk/uploads/putting-price-direct-marketing_53fdbe53b4863.pdf, accesssed July 2015.

[6] Louise Lucas, 'Moving on from door-to-door', *Financial Times*, 21 February 2012, p. 14.

[7] Ginger Conlon, 'Outlook 2014: marketing spending to rise', *Direct Marketing News*, January 10, 2014, www.dmnews.com/outlook-2014-marketing-spending-to-rise/article/328925/; Thad Reuter, 'U.S. e-commerce to grow to 13% in 2013', *Internet Retailer*, 13 March 2013, www.internetretailer.com/2013/03/13/us-e-commerce-grow-13-2013; Sucharita Mulpuru, 'US online retail forecast, 2012 to 2017', 13 March 2013, www.forrester.com/US+Online+Retail+Forecast+2012+To+2017/fulltext/-/E-RES93281?objectid=RES93281; 'Marketing fact pack 2014', *Advertising Age*, December 30, 2013, p. 14; and 'Monthly and annual retail trade', US Census Bureau, www.census.gov/retail, accessed September 2014.

[8] For more detailed analysis see: www.emarketer.com/adspendtool, accessed July 11 2015.

[9] Daniel Thomas, 'UK turns into a nation of online shoppers', *Financial Times*, 11 December 2014, www.ft.com, accessed July 10 2015.

[10] More information about this an other real time marketing examples can be found in Georgia Wells, 'Real-time marketing in a real-time world', *Wall Street Journal*, 24 March 2014, p. R3; Rachel VanArsdale, 'Starbucks real-time marketing asks America to come together', 17 October 2013, http://themrsite.com/blog/2013/10/starbucks-real-time-marketing-asks-america-to-come-together/; Jeff Dachis, 'Stop whining about real-time marketing', *Advertising Age*, 10 October 2013, http://adage.com/print//244665; Christopher Heine, 'Ads in real time, all the time', *Adweek*, 18 February 2013, p. 9; Lucia Moses, 'Real-time marketing', *Adweek*, 14 October 2013, p. 17; Tim Nudd, 'Real-time rules: eight opportunities for marketing in the moment, and the brands that got it right', *Adweek*, 9 September 2013, pp. 22–25; and www.360i.com/work/oreo-daily-twist/, accessed September 2014.

[11] See Pew Research Center's Internet & American Life Project, 'Internet user demographics', www.pewinternet.org/data-trend/internet-use/latest-stats/, accessed June 2014; 'Digital set to surpass TV in time spent with US media', *eMarketer*, 1 August 2013, www.emarketer.com/Article/Digital-Set-Surpass-TV-Time-Spent-with-US-Media/1010096; 'ITU release latest tech figures & global rankings', 7 October 2013, www.itu.int/net/pressoffice/press_releases/2013/41.aspx#.Uumujvad6cC; John Heggestuen, 'One in every 5 people in the world own a smartphone, one in every 17 own a tablet', *Business Insider*, 15 December 2013, www.businessinsider.com/smartphone-and-tablet-penetration-2013-10; and James O'Tolle, 'Mobile apps overtake PC Internet usage in US', *CNN Money*, 28 February 2014, http://money.cnn.com/2014/02/28/technology/mobile/mobile-apps-internet//.

[12] See www.internetworldstats.com/stats.htm, accessed July 11 2015.

[13] See 'Internet Retailer: Top 500 Guide', www.top500guide.com/top-500/the-top-500-list, accessed September 2014.

[14] See Paul Davidson, 'Staples closing 225 stores, strengthens online focus', *USA Today*, 7 March 2014, www.usatoday.com/story/money/business/2014/03/06/staples-closings/6114525/; 'Staples aims to change image with new slogan', *Boston Globe*, 3 January 2014; and annual reports and other information found at www.staples.com, accessed September 2014.

[15] Daniel Thomas 'UK turns into a nation of online shoppers', *Financial Times*, 11 December 2014, www.ft.com, accessed July 10 2015.

[16] See www.momentology.com/4359–10-exceptional-examples-of-brand-communities/, accessed July 10 2015.

[17] Ginger Conlon, 'Outlook 2014: marketing spending to rise', *Direct Marketing News*, 10 January 2014, www.dmnews.com/outlook-2014-marketing-spending-to-rise/article/328925.

[18] See 'IAC Internet advertising competition: best rich media online ad', www.iacaward.org/iac/ winners_detail.asp?yr=all&award_level=best&medium=Rich%20media%20Online%20Ad'; and 'Gatorade – prime rich media takeover', www.iacaward.org/iac/winner.asp?eid=10379, both accessed July 2014.

[19] Ginger Conlon, 'Outlook 2014: marketing spending to rise'; and Google annual reports, http://investor.google.com/proxy.html, accessed September 2014.

[20] 'Social media is the hot new thing, but email is still the king', *Advertising Age*, 30 September 2013, p. 18.

[21] See Nora Aufreiter et al., 'Why marketers keep sending you emails', January 2014, www.mckinsey.com/Insights/Marketing_Sales/Why_marketers_should_keep_sending_you_emails; Niti Shah, '18 email marketing stats that'll make you better at your job', *HubSpot*, 5 December 2013, http://blog.hubspot.com/marketing/email-marketing-stats-list; and Amy Gesenhues, 'Report: marketing emails opened on mobile devices jumped 61% to 65% in Q4 2013', 23 January 2014, http://marketingland.com/report-65-of-marketing-emails-were-opened-on-mobile-device-sin-q4–2013-71387.

[22] Larry Bennett, 'Worldwide spam rate falls 2.5 percent but new tactics emerge', *ZDNet*, 23 January 2014, www.zdnet.com/worldwide-spam-rate-falls-2–5-percent-but-new-tacticsemerge-7000025517/.

[23] Linda Moses, 'Online video ads have higher impact than TV ads', *Adweek*, 1 May 2013, www.adweek.com/print/148982; and 'comScore releases December 2013 U.S. online video rankings', 10 January 2014, www.comscore.com/Insights/Press_Releases/2014/1/comScore_Releases_December_2013_US_Online_Video_Rankings.

[24] For these and other examples, see 'Samsung, Wieden & Kennedy rule Ad Age's 2013 viral video awards', *Advertising Age*, 16 April 2013, http://adage.com/article/240900/; and Alexander Coolidge, 'P&G aims for moms' heart with latest "thank you" ad', *USA Today*, 8 January 2014, www.usatoday.com/story/money/business/2014/01/08/pg-olympics-thank-you-ad/4380229/.

[25] 'Evian: masters of online video', *The Guardian*, www.theguardian.com/media-network/ebuzzing-partner-zone/evian-online-videoadvertising-baby-me, accessed June 2014; and Emma Bazilian, 'Ad of the day: Evian spins a familiar web with a dancing Baby Spider-Man', *Adweek*, 3 April 2014, www.adweek.com/news/advertising-branding/ad-day-evian-spins-familiar-web-dancingbaby-spider-man-156755.

[26] Troy Dreier, 'The force was strong with this one', *Streaming Media Magazine*, April/May 2011, pp. 66–68; also see Thales Teixeira, 'The new science of viral ads', *Harvard Business Review*, March 2012, pp. 25–28; and Hilary Masell Oswald, 'The biology of a marketplace sensation', *Marketing News*, September 2013, pp. 31–35.

[27] 'State of the blogging world in 2012', *New Media Expo Blog*, 25 July 2012, www.blogworld.com/2012/07/25/state-of-the-bloggingworld-in-2012/; and 'The blogconomy: blogging statistics', *Social Media Today*, 28 August 2013, http://socialmediatoday.com/mikevelocity/1698201/blogging-stats-2013-infographic.

[28] Based on information found in Keith O'Brien, 'How McDonald's came back bigger than ever', *New York Times*, 6 May 2012, p. MM44.

[29] Stuart Feil, 'How to win friends and influence people', *Adweek*, 10 September 2013, pp. S1–S2.

[30] Daniel Thomas, 'UK turns into a nation of online shoppers', *Financial Times*, 11 December 2014, www.ft.com, accessed July 10 2015.

[31] See http://newsroom.fb.com/company-info; www.youtube.com/yt/press/statistics.html; and www.statisticbrain.com/twitter-statistics/, accessed September 2014.

[32] For these and other examples, see www.kaboodle.com, www.farmersonly.com, www.birdpost.com, and www.cafemom.com, all accessed September 2014.

[33] See http://nikeinc.com/news/nike-coach-feature-motivates-runners-with-customized-training-plans and www.nikeplus.com, accessed June 2013.

[34] Karl Greenberg, 'Volvo uses Twitter chat for digital focus groups', Marketing Daily, 29 May 2013, www.mediapost.com/publications/article/201309/#axzz2UsMXTPXB.

[35] Hannah Kuchler and Shannon Bond, 'Online gurus shake up marketing by 'word of mouth at a far greater scale', Financial Times, 7 January 2015, p. 15.

[36] Maija Palmer 'The power of parent bloggers', Financial Times, 15 July 2014, p. 14.

[37] See http://pinterest.com/wholefoods/, accessed September 2014.

[38] Christina Binkley 'The making of a global best seller', Wall Street Journal, 24 May 2014, p. 25.

[39] Example and quotes from 'Meme watch: Lay's "Do us a flavor" crowdsourcing hilariously backfires', Uproxx, 5 February 2014, http://uproxx.com/gammasquad/2014/02/best-of-lays-do-us-aflavor-parodies/?showall=true; Michael Bourne, 'Sailing of 14 social Cs', Mullen Advertising, 13 February, 2012, www.mullen.com/sailing-the-14-social-cs/; and Jenna Mullins, 'The submissions for new Lay's chip flavors are getting out of control (but we love it)', EOnline, 6 February 2014, www.eonline.com/news/508137/thesubmissions-for-new-lays-chip-flavors-are-getting-out-of-controlbut-we-love-it.

[40] Melissa Allison, 'Re-creating the coffee klatch online', Raleigh News & Observer, 6 May 2013, p. 1D; Todd Wassermann, MAshable, 13 December 2013, http://mashable.com/2013/12/05/starbucksstweet-a-coffee-180000/; and www.facebook.com/Starbucks and https://twitter.com/Starbucks, accessed September 2014.

[41] Facts in this paragraph are from 'Wireless quick facts', www.ctia.org/your-wireless-life/how-wireless-works/wireless-quick-facts, accessed June 2014; Tara Siegel Bernard, 'Weighing the need for landline in a cellphone world', New York Times, 17 January 2014, www.nytimes.com/2014/01/18/your-money/weighing-theneed-for-a-landline-in-a-cellphone-world.html?_r=0; 'Smartphone penetration tops 65% of the US mobile market in Q4 2013', MarketingCharts, 5 February 2014, www.marketingcharts.com/wp/online/smartphone-penetration-tops-65-of-the-us-mobile-marketin-q4-2013-39595/; Pew Research Center's Internet & American Life Project, 'Cell phone activities', www.pewinternet.org/datatrend/mobile/cell-phone-activities/, accessed June 2014; and Zoe Fox, 'The average smartphone user downloads 25 Apps', Mashable, 5 September 2013, http://mashable.com/2013/09/05/most-apps-download-countries/.

[42] Jonathan Nelson, 'Voice: one screen to rule them all', Adweek, 13 February 2013, p. 15; Stephen Willard, 'Study: people check their cell phones every six minutes, 150 times a day', Elite Daily, 11 February 2013, http://elitedaily.com/news/world/study-people-check-cell-phones-minutes-150-times-day/; and John Fetto, 'Americans spend 58 minutes a day on their smartphones', Experian, 28 May 2013, www.experian.com/blogs/marketing-forward/2013/05/28/americans-spend-58-minutes-a-day-on-their-smartphones/.

[43] Statistics extracted from: http://mobiforge.com/research-analysis/global-mobile-statistics-2014-part-a-mobile-subscribers-handset-market-share-mobile-operators#topmobilemarkets, accessed July 10 2015.

[44] Robert Cookson, 'Mobile to pass UK press in ad spend for first time', Financial Times, 10 March 2014, p. 16; Shannon Bond, 'US spending on mobile advertising soars', Financial Times, 23 April 2015, p.17.

[45] Jonathan Birchall, 'Codes open new frontiers in retail wars', Financial Times, 18 May 2010, p. 23; Jonathan Birchall, 'Placecast signals change for shop offers', Financial Times, 15 October 2010, p. 23.

[46] Statistics extracted from: http://mobiforge.com/research-analysis/global-mobile-statistics-2014-part-a-mobile-subscribers-handset-market-share-mobile-operators#topmobilemarkets, accessed July 11 2015.

[47] MobiThinking, 'Global mobile statistics 2011', www.mobithinking.com/mobile-marketing-tools/latest-mobile-stats, accessed August 22, 2011.

[48] Jonathan Birchall, 'Codes open new front in retail wars', Financial Times, 18 May 2010, p. 23.

[49] 'IAB Internet Advertising Revenue Report', April 2013, www.iab.net/media/file/IAB_Internet_Advertising_Revenue_Report_FY_2012_rev.pdf; 'The mobile movement', accessed at www.thinkwithgoogle.com/insights/emea/library/studies/the-mobile-movement, May 2013; and 'Mobile advertising fast facts', Advertising Age, 4 April 2014, pp. 20+.

[50] See Lauren Johnson, 'McDonald's beefs up advertising strategy with mobile game', Mobile Marketer, 28 March 2013, www.mobilemarketer.com/cms/news/advertising/12447.html; and Rimma Kats, 'McDonald's beefs up mobile efforts via targeted campaign', Mobile Marketing, 16 August 2013, www.mobilemarketer.com/cms/news/advertising/13553.html.

[51] See Judith Acquino, 'JetBlue voice-activated ad teaches people to speak "Pigeon"', Ad Exchanger, 26 September 2013, www.adexchanger.com/online-advertising/jetblue-voice-activated-adsteach-people-to-speak-pigeon/; and Lauren Johnson, 'Top 10 mobile advertising campaigns of 2013', 24 December 2013, www.mobilemarketer.com/cms/news/advertising/16847.html.

[52] See 'Stats & facts: direct marketing', CMO Council, www.cmocouncil.org/facts-stats-categories.php?view=all&category=directmarketing, access September 2014 and http://stakeholders.ofcom.org.uk/market-data-research/market-data/communications-market-reports/cmr12/post/uk-6.11, accessed July 10 2015.

[53] Julie Liesse, 'When times are hard, mail works', Advertising Age, 30 March 2009, p. 14; Paul Vogel, 'Marketers are rediscovering the value of mail', Deliver Magazine, 11 January 2011, www.delivermagazine.com/2011/01/marketers-are-rediscovering-the-value-of-mail/; Laurie Beasley, 'Why direct mail still yields the lowest cost-per-lead and highest conversion rate', Online Marketing Insights, 13 June 2013, www.onlinemarketinginstitute.org/blog/2013/06/why-direct-mail-still-yields-the-lowestcost-per-lead-and-highest-conversion-rate/; and Lois Geller, 'If direct mail is dying, it's sure taking its time about it', Forbes, 4 December 2013, www.forbes.com/sites/loisgeller/2013/12/04/if-direct-mail-is-dying-its-sure-taking-its-time-about-it/.

[54] Bruce Britt, 'Marketing leaders discuss the resurgence of direct mail', Deliver Magazine, 18 January 2011, www.delivermagazine.com/2011/01/marketing-leaders-discuss-resurgence-of-directmail/; also see Alex Palmer, 'Insurance marketers leverage targeted marketing', Direct Marketing, 1 February 2012, www.dmnews.com/insurance-marketers-leverage-targeted-marketing/article/225127/.

[55] See www.landsend.com/mobile/index.html and http://catalogspree.com/, accessed September 2014.

[56] Allison Schiff, 'Catalogs are part of a balanced marketing diet', *Direct Marketing*, 11 March 2013, www.dmnews.com/catalogs-are-part-of-a-balanced-marketing-diet/article/283668/.

[57] Kurt Solomon, 'Is the catalog dead?' 5 November 2013, www.kurtsalmon.com/US/vertical-insight/Is-the-Catalog-Dead-?vertical=Retail&id=936&language=en-us#.UzTUVV5dCcC.

[58] See http://postandparcel.info/53976/news/it/royal-mail-says-printed-catalogues-drive-online-shopping/

[59] 'Data-driven marketing's growth accelerates', *Direct Marketing News*, http://media.dmnews.com/images/2014/01/10/direct_and_digital_529467.jpg, accessed June 2014.

[60] Andrew Bounds, 'TV retailer joining forces with shops on the high street', *Financial Times*, 11 July 2012, p. 14.

[61] See Rachel Brown, 'Perry, Fischer, Lavigne tapped for proactiv', *WWD*, 13 January 2010, p. 3; Rahul Parikh, 'Proactiv's celebrity shell game', Salon.com, 28 February 2011, www.salon.com/2011/02/28/proactiv_celebrity_sham; 'Guthy-Renker honored with nine Era Moxie awards for year's best direct marketing campaigns', *Marketing Weekly News*, 19 October 2013, p. 145; and www.proactiv.com, accessed September 2014.

[62] Jeanine Poggi, 'H&M Super Bowl ad lets you buy Beckham bodywear by remote control', *Advertising Age*, 6 January 2014, www.adage.com/print/290915.

[63] Daniel Thomas, 'UK turns into a nation of online shoppers', *Financial Times*, 11 December 2014, www.ft.com, accessed 10 July 2015.

[64] See 'Cougar Town episode doubles as a half-hour long target ad', *psfk*, March 2014, www.psfk.com/2014/03/cougar-town-target-ad.html#!Eo1Q8; and Andrew Adam Newman, 'Like that vase on TV? Click your phone to buy it', *New York Times*, 18 March 2014, p. B6.

[65] Stephanie Rosenbloom, 'The new touch-face of vending machines', *New York Times*, 25 May 2010, www.nytimes.com/2010/05/26/business/26vending.html; 'Automating retail success', www.businessweek.com/adsections/2011/pdf/111114_Verizon3.pdf, accessed July 2012; and 'The kiosk and self-service top five', *Kiosk Marketplace*, 17 April 2013, www.kioskmarketplace.com/article/211559/.

[66] 'Best buy: consumer electronics retailing on the go', www.zoomsystems.com/our-partners/partner-portfolio/; and www.zoomsystems.com/about-us/company-overview/, accessed September 2014.

[67] This example comes from: Katherine Faulkner, 'Inside the call centre sweatshop', *Daily Mail*, 7 July 2015, pp. 4–5; Katherine Faulkner, Jack Doyle and Lucy Osborne, 'Charities in crisis over cold call menace', *Daily Mail*, 10 July 2015, p. 1, p. 4.

[68] See Internet Crime Complaint Center, www.ic3.gov, accessed June 2014.

[69] See 'Many consumers fear identity theft yet still engage in risky behavior', *PRNewswire*, 21 October 2013, www.prnewswire.com/news-releases/many-consumers-fear-identity-theft-yet-stillengage-in-risky-behavior-228595151.html.

[70] See Susan Dominus, 'Underage on Facebook', *MSN Living*, 15 March 2012, http://living.msn.com/family-parenting/underageon-facebook-5; Josh Wolford, 'Facebook still has a big problem with underage users, and they know it', *WebProNews*, 24 January 2013, www.webpronews.com/facebook-still-has-a-big-problemwith-underage-users-and-they-know-it-2013–01.

[71] See Hadley Malcolm, 'Millennials don't worry about online privacy', *USA Today*, 21 April 2013; and '2014 TRUSTe US Consumer Confidence Index', *TRUSTe*, www.truste.com/us-consumerconfidence-index-2014/.

[72] Sam Schechner, 'Google acts on "forgotten" rule', *Wall Street Journal*, 27–29 June 2014, p. 1 & 5.

[73] Muireann Bolger, 'Cookie Monster', *The Marketer*, March/April 2012, pp. 34–37.

[74] Maija Palmer, Tim Bradshaw and Alex Barker, 'Google rolls out privacy policy in defiance of EU legality warnings', *Financial Times*, 2 March 2012, p. 1; Tim Bradshaw, 'Google's privacy policy given airing', *Financial Times*, 3 March, 2012, p. 17.

[75] See 'Facebook to make targeted ads more transparent for users', *Advertising Age*, 4 February 2013, http://adage.com/article/239564/; and www.aboutads.info/, accessed September 2014.

[76] See Richard Byrne Reilly, 'Feds to mobile marketers: stop targeting kids, or else', *Venture Beat*, 27 March 2014, http://venturebeat.com/2014/03/27/feds-to-mobile-marketers-stop-targeting-kidsor-else-exclusive/; and www.business.ftc.gov/privacy-and-security/childrens-privacy, accessed September 2014.

[77] Information on TRUSTe at www.truste.com, accessed September 2014.

[78] Information on the DMA Privacy Promise at www.the-dma.org/cgi/dispissue?article=129 and www.dmaconsumers.org/privacy.html, accessed September 2014.

[79] Statistics extracted from: http://mobithinking.com/mobile-marketing-tools/latest-mobile-stats, accessed February 2012.

COMPANY CASE

Ocado: taking on the Internet giants direct

The online grocery market is one of the fastest-growing, most competitive retail markets in the UK. While the online grocery market is still only 2 per cent of the total market, it is growing over six times as fast.

Ocado is the upmarket British-based online grocery retailer, mainly selling Waitrose products (Waitrose is the supermarket division of the John Lewis Partnership in the UK – the country's 'posh' department store group). Sales in 2015 are running at around £950 million a year, and Ocado has around 450,000 million users. The operation reaches about 60 per cent of British households and around a third of orders come through mobile devices – phones and tablets.

The founders of Ocado were Tim Steiner, an investment banker, Jonathan Faiman, a friend of Steiner's since nursery school and also previously an investment banker, and Jason Gissing. In 2000, the John Lewis Partnership struck a deal to take a 40 per cent stake in Ocado (the last of which holding it sold in 2011, after Ocado went public in 2010), and for its Waitrose business to act as Ocado's supplier (though Ocado has developed its own branded fresh food ranges as well). Intriguingly, in 2008 Procter & Gamble took a stake in Ocado despite its loss-making status at that time, in its first-ever retailer investment.

Sir Terry Leahy, then the respected Tesco boss, made no secret of his doubts about an upstart business set up by inexperienced youngsters in the early 2000s, when the dot-com boom was at its height, compared to his own market-leading Tesco Direct operation. The upstarts at Ocado retaliated with the claim that Tesco Direct model was not profitable, with its results an artefact of misleading internal cost allocations – an accusation that Tesco vehemently rejected at the time, though subsequent events suggest it may not have been far off the mark. Sir Terry's swipe at Ocado's business model, which he said was not viable, escalated the ferocity of competition in the online grocery business. Bitter rivalry emerged between Tesco and Ocado, as Ocado began to corner the online market within the M25. Price wars ensued with Ocado targeting price parity with Tesco on its top 100 lines. This is a battle between business models – warehouse-based distribution

(Ocado) and orders picked from stores (Tesco, Sainsbury, Asda). The warehouse-based system is faster, more accurate, offers better product availability, creates less waste and is more environmentally responsible. Ocado became the first retailer taking market share away from Tesco, as it quickly gained an 18 per cent share of the online grocery market

Ocado has pioneered its own approach to online grocery shopping and won awards for its customer service. Like the Boden 'posh' clothing catalogue, Pilates classes and honey-blonde highlights, the weekly Ocado delivery has become a 'must-have' for the affluent, urban tribe of yummy mummies. Ocado's fans are an emblem of middle-class aspirations. Its affluent customers, half of them inside the M25, love Ocado's emphasis on service. The company has cultivated an image of selling high-class food, while caring for the environment because customers don't need to drive to a store. Ocado service and environmental innovations include: green deliveries which enable customers to select vans already in their area, bio-diesel powered delivery vehicles, colour-coded grocery bags, SMS alerts on delivery day, driver boot mitts and delivery into the kitchen. Ocado has added two new websites to tap into its position with this part of the consumer market: Sizzle – selling posh kitchenware to enthusiasts; and Fetch – a pet store providing high-quality petfood. It is not unheard-of for Ocado fans to refuse to move house to areas not served by Ocado vans.

From the outset, Ocado's unique concept was to pick orders and despatch them direct to consumers from a huge, semi-automated, low-cost warehouse in Hertfordshire. The warehouse has the space of ten football pitches, with a 15km network of conveyor belts handling as many as 7,200 grocery crates an hour, ready for despatch to customers. This is a much faster and more accurate way of picking orders. Direct distribution means Ocado can boast that every fresh item it delivers will have at least six days' shelf life, and that its food waste is the lowest in the industry at 0.3 per cent of sales. By contrast, rivals such as Tesco began their Internet operations by picking goods from store shelves, meaning that some items would be out of stock and others towards the end of their shelf-life (and stores were disrupted for regular shoppers by the order pickers with their giant shopping trolleys). Tesco is now getting its act together with Ocado-style warehouses. Indeed, 2010 saw Tesco and Asda opening 'ghost stores' in London, closed to customers, from which to pick online orders, to try and challenge Ocado's strong position in this important market.

Nonetheless, the floatation of the company in July 2010 saw Ocado's shares fall within weeks from the offer price of 180p to 135p. Ocado lost a quarter of its market value in its first month as a public company. Investors were concerned about Ocado's capacity to deliver and expand. The situation was not helped when Amazon chose this moment to announce it would start selling groceries online in the UK. Since then the shares have seen a slow and erratic recovery, reaching a low point of 55p before the company announced its first annual profit in 2015.

Ocado's critics doubted whether the business would ever gain enough scale to make a profit. One worry was Waitrose's plans to ramp up its own Internet operation (basically selling the same products as Ocado in much the same areas). Waitrose occupies the dual role of supplier and competitor to Ocado, and in 2011 Waitrose invested $10 million in its own online grocery business and rolling out its new website. Indeed, when John Lewis held shares in Ocado, there was an ownership role as well. Nonetheless, in 2010, Ocado signed a further exclusive ten-year supply deal with Waitrose extending the relationship until 2020. There are also concerns that as the online grocery market matures, latecomers like Marks & Spencer will enter at the same time that Waitrose expands, all threatening Ocado's current strong position.

In 2011, Ocado announced a tie-up with Carrefour in France to sell a range of French products in the UK, alongside those from Waitrose. The relationship with Waitrose was further strained in 2013, when Ocado started talks with supermarket chain Morrisons to distribute its products. The Morrisons deal with Ocado was struck mid-2013, and Waitrose claimed it was a breach of its contract with Ocado, although this view was not supported. The Ocado/Morrisons deal is worth £200 million and is for 25 years. In fact, Morrisons products are sold from a Morrisons website and delivered in a Morrsions van with a Morrisons driver, using Ocado's technology and infrastructure. Ocado believes this licensing and distribution deal is completely different to its sourcing deal with Waitrose. The Morrisons deal gave a major boost to Ocado's share price.

In fact, some analysts, like Morgan Stanley, believe that the online grocery market is already mature and its relatively small share of the total grocery business is because over half of Britain's households have tried online and have gone back to shopping in-store, because they find it just as convenient as online.

This suggests the relatively low penetration of online grocery shopping is because the proposition simply is not attractive for most consumers.

However, early in 2011, Ocado defied its critics by posting its first quarterly profit, after a tough year in which its shares tanked following the controversial stock market debut. At this time Ocado's chief executive, Tim Steiner, said the business would step up its challenge to industry heavyweights like Tesco by selling more and cheaper groceries. Ocado expects more British shoppers to switch to shopping online using mobile phones.

At the same time, Ocado warned that customer demand had exceeded the capacity of its Hatfield depot. The company has rented warehouses in Bristol and Wimbledon, increasing its coverage by 1 million households to over 70 per cent of UK households, and allowing the firm to break into South Wales for the first time. A new warehouse opened in 2013. Work started on a further warehouse in 2014.

In 2013, Sir Stuart Rose became Ocado's chairman, sparking rumours that the company was being prepared for sale–possibly to Rose's former employer, Marks & Spencer, providing M&S with an online grocery business for the first time. In 2015, Ocado declared its first ever annual profit on the back of surging sales over the year and a higher number of customers. Sales had risen 20 per cent year-on-year to £950 million, and active customers rose to 453,000 from 385,000 the year before.

This year saw the start of the contract with Morrisons, to handle the supermarket chain's online delivery service. Significantly, Ocado announced at this time that it was in talks with multiple potential international partners to further expand the platform business – developing third-party service platforms like that for Morrisons. News is expected soon of the first customers signed up for Ocado's Smart Platform, thereby growing Ocado's online grocery fulfilment business beyond the existing deal with Morrisons. The question being raised is whether Ocado aims to become the Amazon of online grocery shopping.

Questions for discussion

1. How would you describe the competitive advantage in Ocado's business, compared to its larger rivals?
2. Can Ocado maintain its current strong position in this market?

3. Is online grocery shopping really likely to become a bigger part of Britain's food shopping, or has the market reached its maximum potential? What does your evaluation suggest for Ocado's future?

4. Is Ocado doing the right thing by sticking to its current strategy? What changes or new developments would you recommend to the company?

Sources: Neil Craven, 'Supermarket giants in online price war', *Mail on Sunday*, 24 February 2008, pp. 53-54; Elizabeth Rigby, 'P&G takes stake in loss-making Ocado in boost to online retailer, *Financial Times*, 27 November 2008, p. 19; Jenny Davey, 'For sale: loss-making delivery firm. Price: £1bn', *Sunday Times*, 2 February 2010, S3, p. 9; Jenny Davey, 'Waitrose looks to take on its rivals with online drive', *The Sunday Times*, 8 February 2009, S1, p. 33; Andrew Davidson, 'Ocado retailer stands on the brink of delivering', *The Sunday Times*, 27 June 2010, S3, p. 6; Andrea Felsted and Elizabeth Rigby, 'Ocado extends exclusive Waitrose deal to 2010', *Financial Times*, 27 May 2010, p. 19; Kate Walsh, 'Web pioneers fashion future of retailing', *The Sunday Times*, 22 August 2010, S3, p. 8; Ian Lyall, 'Can Ocado deliver on the city's demanding targets?', *Daily Mail*, 18 September 2010, p. 108; 'Ocado shares hit highs on maiden profit, *Daily Mail*, 2 February 2011, p. 64; Ruth Sutherland, 'How tycoons made a mint from Ocado', *Daily Mail*, 9 March 2011, p. 72; Rupert Steiner, 'Ocado set to deliver maiden annual profit despite gloom', *Daily Mail*, 5 March 2011, p. 93; Mark Wembridge, 'John Lewis Trust offloads Ocado', *Financial Times*, 12/13 February 2011, p. 14; Sam Unsted, 'Ocado posts first annual pretax profit as sales surge', http://morningstar.co.uk/uk/news, accessed 12 July 2015; Andrea Felsted and David Oakley, 'Sir Stuart's return cranks up Ocado rumours', *Financial Times*, 23 January 2013, p. 23.

PART FOUR

Extending marketing

CHAPTER EIGHTEEN

Creating competitive advantage

Chapter preview

In previous chapters, you explored the basics of marketing. You learned that the aim of marketing is to engage customers and to create value for them in order to capture value from them in return. Good marketing companies win, keep and grow customers by understanding customer needs, designing customer-driven marketing strategies, constructing value-delivering marketing programmes, engaging customers, and building customer and marketing partner relationships. In the final three chapters, we'll extend this concept to three special areas: creating competitive advantage, global marketing, and social and environmental marketing sustainability.

To start, let's dig into the competitive strategy of SodaStream, a relatively small brand competing among the giants of the carbonated-beverage industry. Rather than competing head-on with the likes of Coca-Cola and PepsiCo, SodaStream prospers by dominating its own special home-carbonation niche, positioning itself as a smarter alternative to bottled and canned beverages.

Objective outline

➤ **Objective 1** Discuss the need to understand competitors as well as customers through competitor analysis.
Competitor analysis (pp. 537–543)

➤ **Objective 2** Explain the fundamentals of competitive marketing strategies based on creating value for customers.
Competitive strategies (pp. 543–551)

➤ **Objective 3** Illustrate the need for balancing customer and competitor orientations in becoming a truly market-centred organisation.
Balancing customer and competitor orientations (pp. 551–552)

Sodastream: putting new fizz in the US?
Updated for this edition by Dr Navdeep Athwal, Sheffield Business School

The carbonated-beverage market is dominated by huge competitors. Together Coca-Cola and PepsiCo capture a whopping 67 per cent share of the €25 billion market. Number three Dr Pepper Snapple Group which owns brands such as Dr Pepper, 7-Up, Schweppes, Canada Dry and Crush captures another 21 per cent. These soft drink giants are investing vast sums in new product development and marketing to expand their positions even further, so there's precious little left over for smaller brands or new entrants.

However, one small start-up brand – SodaStream – is putting new fizz into carbonated beverages. How does this small brand survive among the giants? Through smart competitive strategy. SodaStream doesn't compete head-on against the likes of Coca-Cola and Pepsi. Instead, it has carved out its own special market niche. Unlike Coke and Pepsi, SodaStream doesn't actually sell carbonated beverages and waters. Instead, it sells a line of home soda makers that allows consumers to make their own.

SodaStream isn't just surviving, it's thriving. Although still comparatively tiny – about $534 million in annual sales versus Coca-Cola's €43 billion and PepsiCo's €58 billion – SodaStream is growing fast and profitably. Its sales have quadrupled in just the past four years, even as the bottled carbonated-beverage market has declined 1 to 2 per cent per year. In its niche, as the world leader in home-carbonation systems, SodaStream – not Coca-Cola or Pepsi – dominates.

Rather than taking on Coca-Cola and Pepsi directly, SodaStream positions itself as a sensible, responsible alternative to the bottled and canned beverages of its supersized competitors. Its tagline: 'SodaStream: Smart. Simple. Bubbles.' SodaStream's countertop drink makers are simple and convenient to use. Powered by a pressurised carbon dioxide canister, SodaStream transforms ordinary tap water into fresh carbonated beverages in only a few seconds, with no heavy bottles to lug around, store or recycle. Empty canisters can be returned to the store and swapped for full ones. Compared with bottled and canned soft drinks and sparkling water, the SodaStream system is also economical. SodaStream can produce the equivalent of an eight-pack of 12-ounce bottles at a 50 per cent lower cost than buying the product at the store.

Using a SodaStream is empowering, even fun. SodaStream invites customers to be creative and 'set the bubbles free'. The home carbonation system lets users customise their beverages in terms of flavour and amount of fizz. SodaStream offers more than 100 different SodaStream flavour syrups. The SodaStream appliances and bottles themselves offer a measure of self-expression. The devices come in eight different modern designs intended to spiff up countertops, even a penguin-shaped model and two models that carbonate water in glass carafes. Bottles come in a variety of designs, including bottles for holiday seasons and special occasions (expect customisable SodaStream bottles soon). Match that, Coke and Pepsi!

Sodastream is positioned as fun, empowering and creative.

Source: Mike Coppola/Getty Images for SodaStream

But wait, there's more. The carbonated beverages made at home with SodaStream are generally better for you. SodaStream flavour mixes contain no high-fructose corn syrup and about a third of the carbs and calories of shop-bought brands. And many SodaStream users mix in fruit juices, or even just a splash of lemon or lime, making concoctions that are healthier than off-the-shelf sodas. Finally, SodaStream is more eco-friendly than bottled or canned sodas. It largely eliminates the energy consumption and harmful emissions associated with making, filling, transporting and recycling plastic bottles and aluminium cans. The carbon footprint for beverages produced using the SodaStream system is 80 per cent lower than for store-bought bottled beverages. According to the company, one reusable SodaStream bottle ends up replacing more than 10,000 conventional ones.

All of these consumer benefits create big opportunities for SodaStream and the home-carbonation niche that it dominates. And the brand is moving aggressively to grow its niche through innovation, product development and marketing. For example, in line with recent beverage trends, SodaStream has developed Xstream Energy mixes (a line of flavours made to 'revitalise your mind and body'), SodaStream Isotonic (a sports drink mix designed to 'help replace lost fluids and boost your performance') and SodaStream Sparkling Natural (100 per cent free of artificial flavours, colourings, sweeteners and preservatives).

SodaStream has also partnered with Kraft, Campbell and Ocean Spray to develop new syrups for some of America's favourite drink flavours – from Country Time, Crystal Light and Kool-Aid to V8 juice and Ocean Spray Cranberry. Beyond just adding new flavours and appliance designs, SodaStream recently partnered with Samsung to make a new Samsung Sparkling Refrigerator, with a SodaStream-powered still or sparkling water dispenser in the door.

As another key aspect of its competitive strategy, SodaStream is rapidly bubbling into new markets and channels. For example, five years ago, SodaStream products were sold in only 300 US stores. Last year, that number increased to 15,000 stores (more than 60,000 worldwide), including US big hitters such as Walmart, Target, Macy's, Kohl's, Costco, Williams-Sonoma, Amazon and Bed Bath & Beyond. Because SodaStream sells an appliance rather than bottled beverages, it avoids the intense competition for shelf space on crowded beverage aisles. In fact, one of SodaStream's biggest challenges in new markets is just keeping shelves stocked. Its products fly off the shelves and sell-outs are common.

Whereas SodaStream avoids head-on competition with the beverage big shots in store aisles, it takes them on directly in edgy comparative ads. For example, in one ad designed for Super Bowl XLVII, Soda-Stream showed exploding Coke and Pepsi bottles, underscoring the environmental pitch that SodaStream could 'save 500 million bottles on game day alone if you let the bubbles set you free'. Under pressure from Coca-Cola and PepsiCo (two of the Super Bowl's biggest sponsors), CBS rejected the ad – SodaStream ran a revised version without the direct comparisons. However, the original comparative ad racked up 5 million online views. Again, in SodaStream's Super bowl XLVIII ad, Fox made the brand remove its ad-ending line, 'Sorry, Coke and Pepsi'. So for the end-of-the-year holiday season, SodaStream took its edgy comparative health and ecology messages to social media. For example, it took a swipe at Coke by posting renderings on Pinterest of a slimmer, healthier Santa dressed in green. Tweets with the hashtag #GreenSanta also chronicled the Jolly Old Elf's transformation using SodaStream while cutting back on bottled brands.

Despite benefiting from first-mover advantage in this niche market, SodaStream has not gone unnoticed by the key competitors. Recently acquiring a 10 per cent stake in Keurig Green Mountain's cold beverage system, Coca-Cola is threatening SodaStream's global dominance. With the American coffee brewer manufacturer Keurig providing the technology behind dispensing systems for carbonated drinks and Coca-Cola offering its products (such as Coca-Cola and Dr Pepper) as well as Keurig's own branded craft sodas and other cold drinks for use in the system, this could seriously undermine the future performance and success of SodaStream.

Dark and uncertain times lie ahead for this thriving and relatively young company; SodaStream must look to acquire new customers while retaining existing ones. Focusing on positioning itself as a supplier of naturally flavoured drinks and low-calorie drink mixes rather than a purely soda maker will enable SodaStream to enter less-mature markets such as the health drinks. Developing innovative digital and outdoor marketing strategies are all a part of SodaStream's future plans to raise awareness, reach and frequency amongst the company's key demographic target: over 25s who are mostly parents and married individuals. By continuing to adopt a smart competitive strategy, SodaStream can continue prosper in the shadows of the carbonated-beverage giants.[1]

Today's companies face their toughest competition ever. In previous chapters, we argued that to succeed in today's fiercely competitive marketplace, companies must move from a product-and-selling philosophy to a customer-and-marketing philosophy.

This chapter spells out in more detail how companies can go about outperforming competitors to win, keep and grow customers. To win in today's marketplace, companies must become adept not only in managing products but also in managing customer relationships in the face of determined competition and a difficult marketing environment. Understanding customers is crucial, but it's not enough. Building profitable customer relationships and gaining **competitive advantage**

Competitive advantage—An advantage over competitors gained by offering consumers greater value.

requires delivering more value and satisfaction to target customers than competitors do. Customers will see competitive advantages as customer advantages, giving the company an edge over its competitors.

In this chapter, we examine competitive marketing strategies – how companies analyse their competitors and develop successful, customer-value-based strategies for engaging customers and building profitable customer relationships. The first step is **competitor analysis**, the process of identifying, assessing and selecting key competitors. The second step is developing **competitive marketing strategies** that strongly position the company against competitors and give the company the strongest possible strategic advantage.

COMPETITOR ANALYSIS

To plan effective marketing strategies, a company needs to find out all it can about its competitors. It must constantly compare its marketing strategies, products, prices, channels and promotions with those of close competitors. In this way, the company can find areas of potential competitive advantage and disadvantage. As shown in Figure 18.1, competitor analysis involves first identifying and assessing competitors and then selecting which competitors to attack or avoid.

Identifying competitors

Normally, identifying competitors would seem to be a simple task. At the narrowest level, a company can define its competitors as other companies offering similar products and services to the same customers at similar prices. Thus, El Corte Inglés in Spain might see French discount operators such as Carrefour and Auchan as competitors, but Debenhams or Marks & Spencer would not be a competitor. The Ritz-Carlton might see the Four Seasons hotels as a major competitor, but Holiday Inn, Ibis, or any of the thousands of bed-and-breakfasts that dot the nation would not be competitors.

However, companies actually face a much wider range of competitors. The company might define its competitors as all firms with the same product or class of products. Thus, the Ritz-Carlton would see itself as competing against all other hotels. Even more broadly, competitors might include all companies making products that supply the same service. Here the Ritz-Carlton would see itself competing not only against other hotels but also against anyone who supplies rooms for busy travellers. Finally, and still more broadly, competitors might include all companies that compete for the same consumer euros. Here the Ritz-Carlton would see itself competing with travel and leisure products and services, from cruises and summer homes to vacations abroad.

Companies must avoid 'competitor myopia'. A company is more likely to be 'buried' by its latent competitors than its current ones. For example, it wasn't direct competitors that put an end to British Telecom's telegram business after 153 years; it was

Competitor analysis— Identifying key competitors; assessing their objectives, strategies, strengths and weaknesses and reaction patterns; and selecting which competitors to attack or avoid.

Competitive marketing strategies—Strategies that strongly position the company against competitors and give it the greatest possible competitive advantage.

Author comment

Creating competitive advantage begins with a thorough understanding of competitors' strategies. But before a company can analyse its competitors, it must first identify them – a task that's not as simple as it seems.

A cheap and cheerful Bed and Breakfast services an important niche but does not compete with high-end luxury hotels.
Source: Pabkov/Fotolia

| Identifying the company's competitors | → | Assessing competitors' objectives, strategies, strengths and weaknesses, and reaction patterns | → | Selecting which competitors to attack or avoid |

Figure 18.1 Steps in analysing competitors

cell phones and the Internet. Music superstores Our Price and Tower Records didn't go bankrupt at the hands of other traditional music stores; it fell victim to unexpected competitors such as supermarkets, online retailers and iTunes and other digital download services. Another classic example of competitor myopia is the Royal Mail of the UK:[2]

> The Royal Mail is currently losing money at a rapid rate – millions of euros per year. But it's not direct competitors such as FedEx or UPS that are the problem. Instead, it's a competitor that the Royal Mail could hardly have even imagined a decade and a half ago – the soaring use of personal and business e-mail and online transactions. Last year they experienced a 4 per cent fall in core mail volumes. In the future, the Royal Mail expects more declines of about 5 per cent a year as customers switch to e-mail and other forms of electronic communication. The response of the Royal Mail: increases in postage stamp prices and a reduction in delivery time, moves that will almost certainly reduce mail volume further. The solution? When I figure it out, I'll e-mail you.

Companies can identify their competitors from an *industry* point of view. They might see themselves as being in the oil industry, the pharmaceutical industry or the beverage industry. A company must understand the competitive patterns in its industry if it hopes to be an effective player in that industry. Companies can also identify competitors from a *market* point of view. Here they define competitors as companies that are trying to satisfy the same customer need or build relationships with the same customer group.

From an industry point of view, Pepsi might see its competition as Coca-Cola, Orangina, Fanta, 7UP and the makers of other soft drink brands. From a market point of view, however, the customer really wants 'thirst quenching' – a need that can be satisfied by bottled water, energy drinks, fruit juice, iced tea, and many other fluids. Similarly, Google once defined its competitors as other search engine providers, such as Yahoo! or Microsoft's Bing. Now Google takes a broader view of serving market needs for online and mobile access to the digital world. Under this market definition, Google squares off against once-unlikely competitors such as Apple, Samsung, Microsoft, and even Amazon and Facebook. The maker of Crayola crayons might define its competitors as other makers of crayons and children's drawing supplies. But from a market point of view, it would include all firms making recreational and educational products for children. In general, the market concept of competition opens the company's eyes to a broader set of actual and potential competitors.

Assessing competitors

Having identified the main competitors, marketing management now asks: What are the competitors' objectives? What does each seek in the marketplace? What is each competitor's strategy? What are various competitors' strengths and weaknesses, and how will each react to actions the company might take?

Determining competitors' objectives

Each competitor has a mix of objectives. The company wants to know the relative importance that a competitor places on current profitability, market share growth, cash flow, technological leadership, service leadership and other goals. Knowing a competitor's mix of objectives reveals whether the competitor is satisfied with its current situation and how it might react to different competitive actions. For example, a company that pursues low-cost leadership will react much more strongly to a competitor's cost-reducing manufacturing breakthrough than to the same competitor's increase in advertising.

A company also must monitor its competitors' objectives for various segments. If the company finds that a competitor has discovered a new segment, this might be an opportunity. If it finds that competitors plan new moves into segments now served by the company, it will be forewarned and, hopefully, forearmed.

Identifying competitors' strategies

The more that one firm's strategy resembles another firm's strategy, the more the two compete. In most industries, the competitors can be sorted into groups that pursue different strategies. A **strategic group** is a group of firms in an industry following the same or a similar strategy in a given target market. For example, in the major appliance industry, Bosch and Zanussi belong to the same strategic group. Each produces a full line of medium-price appliances supported by good service. In contrast, Smeg and Miele belong to a different strategic group. They produce a narrower line of higher-quality appliances, offer a higher level of service and charge a premium price. Bosch's focus is on high-end home appliances proudly offering 'a new generation of high-performance products'. Bosch claim that they are 'constantly developing new ways to reduce energy and water usage while maintaining product performance and efficiency'.[3]

Some important insights emerge from identifying strategic groups. For example, if a company enters a strategic group, the members of that group become its key competitors. Thus, if the company enters a group containing GE and Whirlpool, it can succeed only if it develops strategic advantages over these two companies.

Although competition is most intense within a strategic group, there is also rivalry among groups. First, some strategic groups may appeal to overlapping customer segments. For example, no matter what their strategy, all major appliance manufacturers will go after the apartment and homebuilders segment. Second, customers may not see much difference in the offers of different groups; they may see little difference in quality between Bosch and Zanussi. Finally, members of one strategic group might expand into new strategy segments. Thus, Bosch's Logixx Premium range of appliances compete in the premium-quality, premium-price line with Smeg and Miele

The company needs to look at all the dimensions that identify strategic groups within the industry. It must understand how each competitor delivers value to its customers. It needs to know each competitor's product quality, features and mix; customer services; pricing policy; distribution coverage; sales force strategy; and advertising, sales promotion and online and social media programmes. And it must study the details of each competitor's research and development (R&D), manufacturing, purchasing, financial and other strategies.

Strategic group—A group of firms in an industry following the same or a similar strategy.

Assessing competitors' strengths and weaknesses

Marketers need to carefully assess each competitor's strengths and weaknesses to answer a critical question: What can our competitors do? As a first step, companies can gather data on each competitor's goals, strategies and performance over the past few years. Admittedly, some of this information will be hard to obtain. For example, business-to-business (B-to-B) marketers find it hard to estimate competitors' market shares because they do not have the same syndicated data services that are available to consumer packaged-goods companies.

Companies normally learn about their competitors' strengths and weaknesses through secondary data, personal experience and word-of-mouth. They can also conduct primary marketing research with customers, suppliers and dealers. They can check competitors' online and social media sites. Or they can try **benchmarking** themselves against other firms, comparing the company's products and processes to those of competitors or leading firms in other industries to identify best practices and find ways to improve quality and performance. Benchmarking is a powerful tool for increasing a company's competitiveness.

Benchmarking—Comparing the company's products and processes to those of competitors or leading firms in other industries to identify best practices and find ways to improve quality and performance.

Estimating competitors' reactions

Next, the company wants to know: What will our competitors do? A competitor's objectives, strategies, and strengths and weaknesses go a long way toward explaining its likely actions. They also suggest its likely reactions to company moves, such as price cuts, promotion increases or new-product introductions. In addition, each competitor has a certain philosophy of doing business, a certain internal culture and guiding beliefs. Marketing managers need a deep understanding of a competitor's mentality if they want to anticipate how that competitor will act or react.

Each competitor reacts differently. Some do not react quickly or strongly to a competitor's move. They may feel their customers are loyal, they may be slow in noticing the move, or they may lack the funds to react. Some competitors react only to certain types of moves and not to others. Other competitors react swiftly and strongly to any action. Thus, P&G does not allow a competitor's new product to come easily into the market. Many firms avoid direct competition with P&G and look for easier prey, knowing that P&G will react fiercely if it is challenged. Knowing how major competitors react gives the company clues on how best to attack them or how best to defend its current positions.

In some industries, competitors live in relative harmony; in others, competitors are more openly combative. For example, competitors in the UK grocery market have been at each others' throats for years. Tesco, Sainsbury, Walmart/Asda and Morrisons have aggressively attacked each other in comparative ads. Tesco ads constantly compare its prices (favourably) to its rivals while extolling its automatic price promise. In contrast, Asda promises customers that it is the cheapest while guaranteeing customers the difference in price to competitors if it is *not* 10 per cent cheaper. Meanwhile, Sainsbury's has launched legal objections to Tesco's 'price promise'; while Morrison's recently announced €1.25 of discounts over the next three years on basic items.[4]

Selecting competitors to attack and avoid

A company has already largely selected its major competitors through prior decisions on customer targets, positioning and its marketing mix strategy. Management now must decide which competitors to compete against most vigorously.

Strong or weak competitors

A company can focus on one of several classes of competitors. Most companies prefer to compete against weak competitors. This requires fewer resources and less time. But in the process, the firm may gain little. You could argue that a firm also should compete with strong competitors to sharpen its abilities. And sometimes a company can't avoid its largest competitors, as in the case of Tesco, Sainsbury, Walmart/Asda and Morrisons. But even strong competitors have some weaknesses, and succeeding against them often provides greater returns.

Customer value analysis—An analysis conducted to determine what benefits target customers value and how they rate the relative value of various competitors' offers.

A useful tool for assessing competitor strengths and weaknesses is **customer value analysis**. The aim of customer value analysis is to determine the benefits that target customers value and how customers rate the relative value of various competitors' offers. In conducting a customer value analysis, the company first identifies the major attributes that customers value and the importance customers place on these attributes. Next, it assesses its performance against competitors on those valued attributes.

The key to gaining competitive advantage is to examine how a company's offer compares to that of its major competitors in each customer segment. The company wants to find the place in the market where it meets customers' needs in a way rivals can't. If the company's offer delivers greater value than the competitor's offer on important attributes, it can charge a higher price and earn higher profits, or it can charge the same price and gain more market share. But if the company is seen as performing at a lower level than its major competitors on some important attributes, it must invest in strengthening those attributes or finding other important attributes where it can build a lead.

Close or distant competitors

Most companies will compete with close competitors – those that resemble them most – rather than distant competitors. Thus, Nike competes more against Adidas than against Timberland or Keen. And Target competes against Walmart rather than Neiman Marcus or Nordstrom.

At the same time, the company may want to avoid trying to 'destroy' a close competitor. For example, in the late 1970s, then-market leader Bausch & Lomb moved aggressively against other soft contact lens manufacturers with great success. However, this forced weak competitors to sell out to larger firms such as Johnson & Johnson (J&J). As a result, Bausch & Lomb then faced much larger competitors – and it suffered the consequences. J&J acquired Vistakon, a small nicher with only €17.5 million in annual sales. Backed by J&J's deep pockets, the small but nimble Vistakon developed and introduced its innovative Acuvue disposable lenses. With Vistakon leading the way, J&J is now the dominant contact lens maker, with 42 per cent market share, while Bausch & Lomb lags in fourth place with about a 10 per cent market share. In this case, success in hurting a close rival brought in tougher competitors.[5]

Good or bad competitors

A company really needs and benefits from competitors. The existence of competitors results in several strategic benefits. Competitors may share the costs of market and product development and help legitimise new technologies. They may serve less-attractive segments or lead to more product differentiation. Finally, competitors may help increase total demand.

For example, you might think that Apple's introduction of its stylish and trendy iPad tablet would have spelled trouble for Amazon's smaller, dowdier Kindle e-reader, which had been on the market for three years prior to the iPad's debut. Many analysts thought that Apple had created the 'Kindle killer'. However, as it turns out, the competing iPad created a stunning surge in tablet demand that benefited both companies. Kindle e-reader sales increased sharply with the iPad introduction, and new tablet demand spurred Amazon to introduce its own full line of Kindle tablets. As an added bonus, the surge in iPad usage increased Amazon's sales of e-books and other digital content, which can be read on the iPad using a free Kindle for iPad app. Burgeoning tablet demand following the iPad introduction also opened the market to a host of new competitors, such as Samsung, Google and Microsoft.[6]

Further you might think that an independent coffeehouse surrounded by Starbucks stores might have trouble staying in business. But that's often not the case:[7]

> Coffee shop owners around the country have discovered that the corporate steamroller known as Starbucks is actually good for their business. It turns out that when a Starbucks comes to the neighbourhood, the result is new converts to the latte-drinking fold. When all those converts overrun the local Starbucks, the independents are there to catch the spill-over. In fact, some independent storeowners now actually try to open their stores near a Starbucks if they can. That's certainly not how the coffee behemoth planned it. 'Starbucks is actually *trying* to be ruthless,' says the owner of a small coffeehouse chain. But 'in its predatory store-placement strategy, Starbucks has been about as lethal a killer as a fluffy bunny rabbit'.

However, a company may not view all its competitors as beneficial. An industry often contains *good competitors* and *bad competitors*. Good competitors play by the rules of the industry. Bad competitors, in contrast, break the rules. They try to buy share rather than earn it, take large risks, and play by their own rules.

For example, the nation's traditional newspapers face a lot of bad competitors these days. Digital services that overlap with traditional newspaper content are bad competitors because they offer for free real-time content that subscription-based newspapers printed once a day can't match. An example is Craigslist, the online community that lets local users post largely free classified ads. Started as a hobby about 20 years ago by Craig Newmark, Craigslist has never cared all that much about profit margins, and that's about as bad as the competitor can get. Another example Gumtree.com which is owned by Kijiji, eBay's internal classifieds group. Gumtree.com is popular across the UK, Ireland and Poland and has Kijiji affiliates across the rest of Europe. Essentially similar to Craigslist, Gumtree.com offers consumers a network of online classified advertisements and local/community web-sites. Consumers can browse local classified ads or post free or paid ads (depending on what they are advertising).

Finding uncontested market spaces

Rather than competing head to head with established competitors, many companies seek out unoccupied positions in uncontested market spaces. They try to create products and services for which there are no direct competitors. Called a 'blue-ocean strategy', the goal is to make competition irrelevant:[8]

> Companies have long engaged in head-to-head competition in search of profitable growth. They have fought for competitive advantage, battled over market share, and struggled for differentiation. Yet in today's overcrowded industries, competing head-on results in nothing but a bloody 'red ocean' of rivals fighting over a shrinking profit pool. In their book *Blue Ocean Strategy*, two strategy professors contend that although most companies compete within such red oceans, the strategy isn't likely to create profitable growth in the future. Tomorrow's leading companies will succeed not by battling competitors but by creating 'blue oceans' of uncontested market space. Such strategic moves – termed value innovation – create powerful leaps in value for both the firm and its buyers, creating all new demand and rendering rivals obsolete. By creating and capturing blue oceans, companies can largely take rivals out of the picture.

Apple has long practised this strategy, introducing product firsts such as the iPod, iTunes, iPhone and iPad that created whole new categories. One example of a company exhibiting blue-ocean thinking is Cirque du Soleil, which reinvented the circus as a higher form of modern entertainment. At a time when the circus industry was declining, Cirque du Soleil innovated by eliminating high-cost and controversial elements such as animal acts and instead focused on the theatrical experience. Cirque du Soleil did not compete with then market leader Ringling Bros. and Barnum & Bailey; it was altogether different from anything that preceded it. Instead, it created an uncontested new market space that made existing competitors irrelevant. The results have been spectacular. Thanks to its blue-ocean strategy, in only its first 20 years, Cirque du Soleil achieved more revenues than Ringling Brothers and Barnum & Bailey achieved in its first 100 years.

Designing a competitive intelligence system

We have described the main types of information that companies need about their competitors. This information must be collected, interpreted, distributed and used. Gathering competitive intelligence can cost much money and time, so the company must design a cost-effective competitive intelligence system.

The competitive intelligence system first identifies the vital types of competitive information needed and the best sources of this information. Then, the system continuously collects information from the field (sales force, channels, suppliers, market research firms, Internet and social media sites, online monitoring and trade associations) and published data (government publications, speeches and online databases). Next the system checks the information for validity and reliability, interprets it and organises it in an appropriate way. Finally, it sends relevant information to decision makers and responds to inquiries from managers about competitors.

With this system, company managers receive timely intelligence about competitors in the form of reports and assessments, posted bulletins, newsletters, and e-mail and mobile alerts. Managers can also connect when they need to interpret a competitor's sudden move, know a competitor's weaknesses and strengths, or assess how a competitor will respond to a planned company move.

COMPETITIVE STRATEGIES

Having identified and evaluated its major competitors, a company now must design broad marketing strategies by which it can gain competitive advantage. But what broad competitive marketing strategies might the company use? Which ones are best for a particular company or for the company's different divisions and products?

Author comment

Now that we've identified competitors and know all about them, it's time to design a strategy for gaining competitive advantage.

Approaches to marketing strategy

No one strategy is best for all companies. Each company must determine what makes the most sense given its position in the industry and its objectives, opportunities and resources. Even within a company, different strategies may be required for different businesses or products.

Swiss-based pharmaceutical giant Novartis uses one marketing strategy for its leading brands in stable consumer markets, such as Nicotinell, and a different marketing strategy to medical professionals when marketing Glivec – a drug used to treat a range of cancers that generates revenue of €2.2 billion, potentially costing €70,000 per patient per year.

Companies also differ in how they approach the strategy-planning process. Many large firms develop formal competitive marketing strategies and implement them religiously. However, other companies develop strategy in a less formal and orderly fashion. Some companies, such as Harley-Davidson, Red Bull, Virgin Atlantic Airways and BMW's MINI unit, succeed by breaking many of the rules of marketing strategy. Such companies don't operate large marketing departments, conduct expensive marketing research, spell out elaborate competitive strategies, and spend huge sums on advertising. Instead, they sketch out strategies on the fly, stretch their limited resources, live close to their customers, and create more satisfying solutions to customer needs. They form buyer's clubs, use buzz marketing, and focus on winning customer loyalty. It seems that not all marketing must follow in the footsteps of marketing giants such as Nestlé and Unilever.

In fact, approaches to marketing strategy and practice often pass through three stages – entrepreneurial marketing, formulated marketing and intrepreneurial marketing:

- *Entrepreneurial marketing.* Most companies are started by individuals who live by their wits. They visualise an opportunity, construct flexible strategies on the backs of envelopes, and knock on every door to gain attention. For example, Jamie Murray-Wells, founder of online spectacles business Glasses Direct, launched Glasses Direct nine years ago. Mr Murray-Wells has a provocative style of marketing that shook up a sleepy industry. He also had a disruptive business model: selling cheap glasses online using prescriptions provided to customers by high street opticians as loss leaders for their own spectacle sales. In the start-up phase of the company, Glasses Direct took a characteristically direct approach to competition by targeting the optician chain Specsavers. Glasses Direct launched its Specspensive campaign that saw people wearing sheep outfits wandering around city centres handing out flyers that advised the public 'Don't get fleeced by Specsavers'. Accompanied by billboard ads, radio and other events the campaign proved newsworthy and great publicity for the fledgling firm.[9]
- *Formulated marketing.* As small companies achieve success, they inevitably move toward more formulated marketing. They develop formal marketing strategies and adhere to them closely. As brands grow, companies adopt a more formal approach to their marketing efforts. In the case of Glasses Direct, branding was improved, PR companies hired, sales promotion introduced, social media integrated and a number of other initiatives. Although Glasses Direct will no doubt remain less formal in its marketing than the Specsavers of the marketing world, as it grows, it will adopt more developed marketing tools.
- *Intrepreneurial marketing.* Many large and mature companies get stuck in formulated marketing. They pore over the latest Nielsen numbers, scan market research reports, and try to fine-tune their competitive strategies and programmes. These companies sometimes lose

the marketing creativity and passion they had at the start. They now need to re-establish within their companies the entrepreneurial spirit and actions that made them successful in the first place. They need to encourage more marketing initiative and 'intrepreneurship' at the local level.

Many companies build intrepreneurship into their core marketing operations. For example, IBM encourages employees at all levels to interact on their own with customers through blogs, social media and other platforms. Google's Innovation Time-Off programme encourages all of its engineers and developers to spend 20 per cent of their time developing 'cool and wacky' new-product ideas – blockbusters such as Google News, Gmail and AdSense are just a few of the resulting products. And Facebook sponsors regular 'hackathons', during which it encourages internal teams to come up with and present intrepreneurial ideas. One of the most important innovations in the company's history – the 'Like button' – resulted from such a hackathon.[10]

The bottom line is that there are many approaches to developing effective competitive marketing strategies. There will be a constant tension between the formulated side of marketing and the creative side. It is easier to learn the formulated side of marketing, which has occupied most of our attention in this book. But we have also seen how marketing creativity and passion in the strategies of many of the companies studied – whether small or large, new or mature – have helped to build and maintain success in the marketplace. With this in mind, we now look at the broad competitive marketing strategies companies can use.

Basic competitive strategies

Three decades ago, Michael Porter suggested four basic competitive positioning strategies that companies can follow – three winning strategies and one losing one.[11] The three winning strategies are as follows:

- *Overall cost leadership.* Here the company works hard to achieve the lowest production and distribution costs. Low costs let the company price lower than its competitors and win a large market share. Carrefour and Aldi are leading practitioners of this strategy.
- *Differentiation.* Here the company concentrates on creating a highly differentiated product line and marketing programme so that it comes across as the class leader in the industry. Most customers would prefer to own this brand if its price is not too high. Mercedes cars and Bang & Olufsen follow this strategy in the car and audio goods markets, respectively.
- *Focus.* Here the company focuses its effort on serving a few market segments well rather than going after the whole market. For example, Ritz-Carlton focuses on the top 5 per cent of corporate and leisure travellers. Tetra Food supplies 80 per cent of pet tropical fish food. Similarly, Hohner owns a stunning 85 per cent of the harmonica market.

Hohner has a breathtaking 85 per cent of the global harmonica market!

Source: music Alan King/Alamy Images

Companies that pursue a clear strategy – one of the above – will most likely perform well. The firm that carries out that strategy best will make the most profits. But firms that do not pursue a clear strategy – *middle-of-the-roaders* – do the worst. Recently, Tesco and Holiday Inn have encountered difficult times because they did not stand out as the lowest in cost, highest in perceived value, or best in serving some market segment. Middle-of-the-roaders try to be good on all strategic counts but end up being not very good at anything.

Two marketing consultants, Michael Treacy and Fred Wiersema, offer a more customer-centred classification of competitive marketing strategies.[12] They suggest that companies gain leadership positions by delivering superior value to their customers. Companies can pursue any of three strategies – called *value disciplines* – for delivering superior customer value:

- *Operational excellence.* The company provides superior value by leading its industry in price and convenience. It works to reduce costs and create a lean and efficient value delivery system. It serves customers who want reliable, good-quality products or services but want them cheaply and easily. Examples include IKEA, Zara and Southwest Airlines.

- *Customer intimacy*. The company provides superior value by precisely segmenting its markets and tailoring its products or services to exactly match the needs of targeted customers. It specialises in satisfying unique customer needs through a close relationship with and intimate knowledge of the customer. It empowers its people to respond quickly to customer needs. Customer-intimate companies serve customers who are willing to pay a premium to get precisely what they want. They will do almost anything to build long-term customer loyalty and to capture customer lifetime value. Examples include Lexus, British Airways, Visa and Ritz-Carlton.
- *Product leadership*. The company provides superior value by offering a continuous stream of leading-edge products or services. It aims to make its own and competing products obsolete. Product leaders are open to new ideas, relentlessly pursue new solutions, and work to get new products to market quickly. They serve customers who want state-of-the-art products and services, regardless of the costs in terms of price or inconvenience. Examples include Apple, Dyson and Rolls Royce Aero-engines.

From the very beginning, Apple has churned out one cutting-edge product after another. It all started with the Apple Macintosh, the first personal computer ever to feature a graphic user interface and mouse. The innovative Mac changed the computer industry forever, gained an enthusiastic throng of brand fans, and began a chain of events that would establish Apple as one of the world's premier product leaders. Apple's product leadership results from understanding what makes its customer tick, then creating ahead-of-the-curve products.

Many tech companies make products that just occupy space and do work. By contrast, Apple has a genius for sparking consumer imaginations and creating 'life-feels-good' products that customers want – usually before consumers themselves even know what they want. The result has been one Apple-led revolution after another. Groundbreaking Apple products such as the iPod, iTunes, iPhone and iPad have all created whole new categories where none previously existed. Such product leadership has produced a consumer love affair with Apple. Diehard fans and gadget geeks around the world have long anointed Apple 'the keeper of all things cool'. In turn, the consumer love affair with Apple has produced stunning sales and profit results over the years.[13]

Some companies successfully pursue more than one value discipline at the same time. For example, FedEx excels at both operational excellence and customer intimacy. However, such companies are rare; few firms can be the best at more than one of these disciplines. By trying to be *good at all* value disciplines, a company usually ends up being *best at none*.

Thus, most excellent companies focus on and excel at a single value discipline, while meeting industry standards on the other two. Such companies design their entire value delivery network to single-mindedly support the chosen discipline. For example, Carrefour knows that customer intimacy and product leadership are important. Compared with other discounters, it offers very good customer service and an excellent product assortment. Still, it purposely offers less customer service and less product depth than other supermarkets which pursue customer intimacy. Instead, Carrefour focuses obsessively on operational excellence – on reducing costs and streamlining its order-to-delivery process to make it convenient for customers to buy just the right products at the lowest prices. By the same token, Ritz-Carlton wants to be efficient and employ the latest technologies. But what really sets the luxury hotel chain apart is its customer intimacy. The Ritz-Carlton creates custom-designed experiences to coddle its customers – to fulfil even the unexpressed desires of its very demanding clientele.

Classifying competitive strategies as value disciplines is appealing. It defines marketing strategy in terms of the single-minded pursuit of delivering superior value to customers. Each value discipline defines a specific way to build lasting customer relationships.

Competitive positions

Firms competing in a given target market, at any point in time, differ in their objectives and resources. Some firms are large; others are small. Some have many resources; others are strapped for funds. Some are mature and established; others new and fresh. Some strive for rapid market share growth; others for long-term profits. And these firms occupy different competitive positions in the target market.

We now examine competitive strategies based on the roles firms play in the target market – leader, challenger, follower or nicher. Suppose that an industry contains the firms shown in Figure 18.2. As you can see, 40 per cent of the market is in the hands of the **market leader**, the firm with the largest market share. Another 30 per cent is in the hands of **market challengers**, runner-up firms that are fighting hard to increase their market share. Another 20 per cent is in the hands of **market followers**, other runner-up firms that want to hold their share without rocking the boat. The remaining 10 per cent is in the hands of **market nichers**, firms that serve small segments not being pursued by other firms.

Table 18.1 shows specific marketing strategies that are available to market leaders, challengers, followers and nichers.[14] Remember, however, that these classifications often do not apply to a whole company but only to its position in a specific industry. Large companies such as Unilever, Nestlé, GE, Microsoft or Disney might be leaders in some markets and nichers in others. For example, Unilever leads in many segments, such as hand soaps, but challenges P&G in other segments, such as laundry detergents and shampoo, and Kimberly-Clark in facial tissues. Such companies often use different strategies for different business units or products, depending on the competitive situations of each.

Market leader—The firm in an industry with the largest market share.

Market challenger—A runner-up firm that is fighting hard to increase its market share in an industry.

Market follower—A runner-up firm that wants to hold its share in an industry without rocking the boat.

Market nicher—A firm that serves small segments that the other firms in an industry overlook or ignore.

Market leader strategies

Most industries contain an acknowledged market leader. The leader has the largest market share and usually leads the other firms in price changes, new-product introductions, distribution coverage and promotion spending. The leader may or may not be admired or respected, but other firms concede its dominance. Competitors focus on the leader as a company to challenge, imitate or avoid. Some of the best-known market leaders are Facebook (social networking), L'Oréal (cosmetics) McDonald's (fast food), Amazon (online books), Coca-Cola (beverages), Microsoft (computer software), Caterpillar (earth-moving equipment) and Google (Internet search services).

Table 18.1 Strategies for market leaders, challengers, followers and nichers

Market leader strategies	Market challenger strategies	Market follower strategies	Market nicher strategies
Expand total market	Full frontal attack	Follow closely	By customer, market, quality, price, service
Protect market share	Indirect attack	Follow at a distance	
Expand market share			Multiple niching

Figure 18.2 Competitive market positions and roles

Each market position calls for a different competitive strategy. For example, the market leader wants to expand total demand and protect or expand its share. Market nichers seek market segments that are big enough to be profitable but small enough to be of little interest to major competitors.

Market leader 40% | Market challengers 30% | Market followers 20% | Market nichers 10%

A leader's life is not easy. It must maintain a constant watch. Other firms keep challenging its strengths or trying to take advantage of its weaknesses. The market leader can easily miss a turn in the market and plunge into second or third place. A product innovation may come along and hurt the leader (as when Netflix's direct marketing and video streaming unseated then-market leader Blockbuster or when Apple developed the iPod and iTunes and took the market lead from Sony's Walkman portable audio devices). The leader might grow arrogant or complacent and misjudge the competition (as when Sainsbury lost its lead of the UK grocery market to Tesco). Or the leader might look old-fashioned against new and peppier rivals (as when the Sony Walkman lost serious ground to the funky, stylish Apple iPods.)

To remain number one, leading firms can take any of three actions. First, they can find ways to expand total demand. Second, they can protect their current market share through good defensive and offensive actions. Third, they can try to expand their market share further, even if market size remains constant.

Expanding total demand

The leading firm normally gains the most when the total market expands. If Europeans eat more fast food, McDonald's stands to gain the most because it holds more than three times the fast-food market share of its nearest competitors, Subway and Burger King. If McDonald's can convince more Europeans that fast food is the best eating-out choice in these economic times, it will benefit more than its competitors.

Market leaders can expand the market by developing new users, new uses and more usage of its products. They usually can find new users or untapped market segments in many places. For example, traditionally boy-focused LEGO – Europe's biggest toymaker – now successfully targets girls:[15]

> Three years ago, 90 per cent of LEGO toys were purchased for boys. However, the brand's sales to girls tripled in recent years with the introduction of LEGO Friends, a girl-specific line featuring five cute little dolls with fetching names and background stories. Based on extensive research into differences between how boys and girls play, the LEGO Friends line features pastel colour bricks and construction sets that encourage girls to build everything from Olivia's House or Emma's Pet Salon to Andrea's City Park Café. LEGO Friends has become one of the most successful lines in LEGO history, helping to boost the company's sales by 25 per cent and profits by 35 per cent, even as other toy companies struggled.

Marketers can also expand markets by discovering and promoting *new uses* for the product. For example, since its founding, Velcro Industries has been finding all kinds of 'creative ways to connect this to that'. But its recent 'A million uses' ad, video and social media campaign aims to increase product usage by showcasing all the amazing ways that consumers can use Velcro hook-and-loop fasteners in their daily lives – around the home or office, in the garden or for craft and do-it-yourself projects. One ad shows how a gadget geek uses Velcro One-Wrap ties to organise all those wires behind his desk, while a gardener uses them to hold orchids upright and an outdoorsman uses them to bundle fishing rods. 'It's one wrap with a million uses,' the ad concludes. Velcro's Facebook, YouTube and Pinterest sites are also loaded with imaginative new uses, such as a guide on Pinterest for making Velcro jewellery.[16]

Finally, market leaders can encourage *more usage* by convincing people to use the product

LEGO have been hugely successful at targeting new female consumers.

Source: Rene van den Berg/Alamy Images

more often or use more per occasion. For example, Nestlé urges people to eat Carnation branded desserts and milk products more often by running ads containing new recipes. It also offers a tailored website (www.carnation.co.uk) that lets visitors search for or exchange recipes, view and sign up for a newsletter, and even watch podcasts (rather predictably listed as 'pud'casts) of famous chefs and celebrities making Carnation-based puddings and snacks.

Protecting market share

While trying to expand total market size, the leading firm also must protect its current business against competitors' attacks. BMW versus Lexus; Caterpillar against Komatsu; and BA against Virgin Atlantic.

What can the market leader do to protect its position? First, it must prevent or fix weaknesses that provide opportunities for competitors. It must always fulfil its value promise and work tirelessly to engage valued customers in strong relationships. Its prices must remain consistent with the value that customers see in the brand. The leader should 'plug holes' so that competitors do not jump in.

But the best defence is a good offence, and the best response is continuous innovation. The market leader refuses to be content with the way things are and leads the industry in new products, customer services, distribution effectiveness, promotion and cost cutting. It keeps increasing its competitive effectiveness and value to customers. And when attacked by challengers, the market leader reacts decisively. For example, in the laundry products category, Unilever faced huge problems breaking into the US market because of the decisive actions of the US market leader P&G.

In one of the most fabled marketing battles of the past century, P&G won the laundry war because it was bigger, better, more focused and more aggressive than challenger Unilever. Entering this millennium, even though its US laundry detergent market share was well over 50 per cent, P&G kept raining blows on Unilever and all other comers with stepped-up product launches. By 2007, P&G was outgunning Unilever on US media spending for laundry brands by €153 million to €17 million. New products such as Tide with Downey, Tide Coldwater, and the scent-focused Simple Pleasures line-up for Tide and Downey helped P&G steadily gain a share point or two per year, so that by 2008, it owned a 62.5 per cent share of the €2.6 billion laundry-detergent market to Unilever's 12.9 per cent (including Unilever's All, Wisk and Surf brands). It had an even bigger lead in fabric softeners – 66 per cent to Unilever's 8.4 per cent (Unilever's Snuggle brand). Globally, P&G went from being the number two laundry player in the early 1990s to a dominant market leader, with a global market share of 34 per cent to Unilever's 17 per cent. In the face of P&G's relentless assault, in mid-2008, Unilever finally threw in the towel and sold its North American detergents business.[17]

Expanding market share

Market leaders also can grow by increasing their market shares further. In many markets, small market share increases mean very large sales increases. For example, in the European beer market, a 1 per cent increase in market share is worth €2 billion; while in the spirits market it is €1 billion.

Studies have shown that, on average, profitability rises with increasing market share. Because of these findings, many companies have sought expanded market shares to improve profitability. GE, for example, declared that it wants to be at least number one or two in each of its markets or else get out. GE shed its computer, air-conditioning, small appliances and television businesses because it could not achieve top-dog position in those industries.

However, some studies have found that many industries contain one or a few highly profitable large firms, several profitable and more focused firms, and a large number of medium-sized firms with poorer profit performance. It appears that profitability increases as a business gains share relative to competitors in its served market. For example, Lexus holds only a small share of the total car market, but it earns a high profit because it is a leading brand in the luxury-performance car segment. And it has achieved this high share in its served market because it does other things right, such as producing high-quality products, creating outstanding service experiences, and building close customer relationships.

Companies must not think, however, that gaining increased market share will automatically improve profitability. Much depends on their strategy for gaining increased share. There are many high-share companies with low profitability and many low-share companies with high profitability. The cost of buying higher market share may far exceed the returns. Higher shares tend to produce higher profits only when unit costs fall with increased market share or when the company offers a superior-quality product and charges a premium price that more than covers the cost of offering higher quality.

Market challenger strategies

Firms that are second, third or lower in an industry are sometimes quite large, such as Royal Dutch Shell, Peugeot, Quick Restaurants, Samsung and Hertz. These runner-up firms can adopt one of two competitive strategies: They can challenge the market leader and other competitors in an aggressive bid for more market share (market challengers), or they can play along with competitors and not rock the boat (market followers).

A market challenger must first define which competitors to challenge and its strategic objective. The challenger can attack the market leader, a high-risk but potentially high-gain strategy. Its goal might be to take over market leadership. Or the challenger's objective may simply be to wrest more market share.

Although it might seem that the market leader has the most going for it, challengers often have what some strategists call a 'second-mover advantage'. The challenger observes what has made the market leader successful and improves on it. For example, BookStacks or books.com is attributed as the first online book store, founded by Charles Stack in 1991 and launched online in 1992. However, in 1994 Jeff Bezos founded Amazon and subsequently launched online in 1995. After rapidly expanding the product line (to for example DVDs and CDs), the second-mover advantage of Amazon is reflected in a turnover that is about three times that of Stacks Inc.

In fact, challengers often become market leaders by imitating and improving on the ideas of pioneering predecessors. For example, McDonald's first imitated and then mastered the fast-food system first pioneered by White Castle. And founder Sam Walton admitted that Walmart borrowed most of its practices from discount pioneer Sol Price's FedMart and Price Club chains and then perfected them.

Alternatively, the challenger can avoid the leader and instead challenge firms its own size or smaller local and regional firms. These smaller firms may be underfinanced and not serving their customers well. Several of the major beer companies grew to their present size not by challenging large competitors but by gobbling up small local or regional competitors. For example, SABMiller became the world's number two brewer by acquiring brands such as Miller, Molson, Coors and dozens of others. If the challenger goes after a small local company, its objective may be to put that company out of business. The important point remains: the challenger must choose its opponents carefully and have a clearly defined and attainable objective.

How can the market challenger best attack the chosen competitor and achieve its strategic objectives? It may launch a full *frontal attack*, matching the competitor's product, advertising, price and distribution efforts. It attacks the competitor's strengths rather than its weaknesses. The outcome depends on who has the greater strength and endurance. PepsiCo challenges Coca-Cola in this way, and Ford challenges Toyota frontally.

If the market challenger has fewer resources than the competitor, however, a frontal attack makes little sense. Thus, many new market entrants avoid frontal attacks, knowing that market leaders can head them off with ad blitzes, price wars and other retaliations. Rather than challenging head-on, the challenger can make an *indirect attack* on the competitor's weaknesses or on gaps in the competitor's market coverage. It can carve out toeholds using tactics that established leaders have trouble responding to or choose to ignore.

For example, consider how challenger Red Bull entered the US soft drink market in the late 1990s against market leaders Coca-Cola and PepsiCo.[18] Red Bull tackled the leaders indirectly by selling a high-priced niche product in non-traditional distribution points. It began by selling Red Bull via unconventional outlets that were under the radar of the market leaders, such as nightclubs and bars where young revellers gulped down their caffeine fix so they could go all night. Once it had built a core customer base, the brand expanded into more traditional outlets. 'Red Bull used the pull of high margins to elbow its way into the corner store, where it now sits in refrigerated bins within arm's length of Coke and Pepsi,' says an analyst. Finally, Red Bull used a collection of guerrilla marketing tactics rather than the high-cost traditional media used by the market leaders. The indirect approach worked for Red Bull. Despite rapidly intensifying competition in the United States, Red Bull captures a 43 per cent share of the energy drink market.

Market follower strategies

Not all runner-up companies want to challenge the market leader. The leader never takes challenges lightly. If the challenger's lure is lower prices, improved service or additional product features, the market leader can quickly match these to defuse the attack. The leader probably has more staying power in an all-out battle for customers. For example, a few years ago, when Walmart/Asda in the UK renewed its low-price 'Saving you money everyday' campaign, directly challenging Tesco, Tesco immediately responded with its own cut-price campaign. Thus, many firms (even if they are market dominant elsewhere – as Walmart is in the US) prefer to follow rather than challenge the market leader.

A follower can gain many advantages. The market leader often bears the huge expenses of developing new products and markets, expanding distribution and educating the market. By contrast, as with challengers, the market follower can learn from the market leader's experience. It can copy or improve on the leader's products and programmes, usually with much less investment. Although the follower will probably not overtake the leader, it often can be as profitable.

Following is not the same as being passive or a carbon copy of the market leader. A follower must know how to hold current customers and win a fair share of new ones. It must find the right balance between following closely enough to win customers from the market leader and following at enough of a distance to avoid retaliation. Each follower tries to bring distinctive advantages to its target market – location, services, financing. A follower is often a major target of attack by challengers. Therefore, the market follower must keep its manufacturing costs and prices low or its product quality and services high. It must also enter new markets as they open up.

Nichers: Logitech is only a fraction of the size of Apple or Microsoft. Yet, through skilful niching, it dominates the mouse market

Source: Business Wire via Getty Images

Market nicher strategies

Almost every industry includes firms that specialise in serving market niches. Instead of pursuing the whole market or even large segments, these firms target sub-segments. Nichers are often smaller firms with limited resources. But smaller divisions of larger firms also may pursue niching strategies. Firms with low shares of the total market can be highly successful and profitable through smart niching.

Why is niching profitable? The main reason is that the market nicher ends up knowing the target customer group so well that it meets their needs better than other firms that casually sell to that niche. As a result, the nicher can charge a substantial mark-up over costs because of the added value. Whereas the mass marketer achieves high volume, the nicher achieves high margins.

Nichers try to find one or more market niches that are safe and profitable. An ideal market niche is big enough to be profitable and has growth potential. It is one that the firm can serve effectively. Perhaps most important, the niche is of little interest to major competitors. And the firm can build the skills and customer goodwill to defend itself against a major competitor as the niche grows and becomes more attractive.

The key idea in niching is specialisation. Nichers thrive by meeting in depth the special needs of well-targeted customer groups. For example, when it comes to online dating sites, general sites such as eHarmony.com and Match.com get the most notice. But recently, there's been an explosion of niche dating sites that focus on the narrower preferences of small but well-defined audiences:[19]

Maturedatinguk.com pairs singles of all backgrounds while upforit.com, with their 'where hotties meet' focus on the young promiscuous singles market. Meninlove.com concentrates on the gay market. Alternatively, ethicalsingle.com has members that include 'green business practitioners, vegan vixens, organic farmers, human rights supporters, eco warriors, pacifist, wildlife protectors, charity workers and earth friendly consumers'. Those wishing to date rich partners seem especially well-provided for with datemillionaire.com or even sugerdaddyforme.com (it also links 'sugar mommies'). Finally, you could try meeting a partner who shares your favourite activity, be it dining out (foodlover.co.uk), keeping fit (sportssingle.com), horse riding (lovehorse.co.uk) or even rugby (rugbylover.co.uk).

Although some of these niche sites seem a bit extreme, they can be ideal for people who think they know precisely what kind of person they want. For example, FarmersOnly.com serves 100,000 country-folk members seeking like-minded mates with rural persuasions. Farmers Only founder Jerry Miller started the dating site after noticing that the isolated and demanding farming lifestyle makes it hard to find understanding partners. He cites an example in which a country girl and her city boyfriend discussed marriage. Their relationship went to seed when she said that she wanted to raise horses; he said they could keep the horses in the garage. At that point, says Miller, 'She knew they were not compatible.' Hence the dating service's popular tagline: FarmersOnly.com, because 'City folks just don't get it.'

A market nicher can specialise along any of several market, customer, product or marketing mix lines. For example, it can specialise in serving one type of *end user*, as when a law firm specialises in the criminal, civil or business law markets. The nicher can specialise in serving a given *customer-size* group. Many nichers specialise in serving small and midsize customers that are neglected by the majors.

Some nichers focus on one or a few *specific customers*, selling their entire output to a single company, such as Unilever or Nestlé. Still other nichers specialise by *geographic market*, selling only in a certain locality, region or area of the world. *Quality-price* nichers operate at the low or high end of the market. For example, HP specialises in the high-quality, high-price end of the hand-calculator market. Finally, *service nichers* offer services not available from other firms. For example, www.datingvegetarian.co.uk is a website dedicated to matching couples who are vegetarian or vegan - 'leaving the meat out of meeting' being a very good tag line!

Niching carries some major risks. For example, the market niche may dry up, or it might grow to the point that it attracts larger competitors. That is why many companies practise *multiple niching*. By developing two or more niches, a company increases its chances for survival. Even some large firms prefer a multiple niche strategy to serving the total market.

BALANCING CUSTOMER AND COMPETITOR ORIENTATIONS

Whether a company is the market leader, challenger, follower or nicher, it must watch its competitors closely and find the competitive marketing strategy that positions it most effectively. And it must continually adapt its strategies to the fast-changing competitive environment. This question

Figure 18.3 Evolving
company orientations

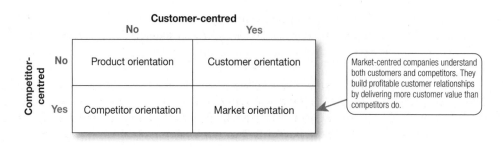

now arises: Can the company spend too much time and energy tracking competitors, damaging its customer orientation? The answer is yes. A company can become so competitor centred that it loses its even more important focus on maintaining profitable customer relationships.

A **competitor-centred company** is one that spends most of its time tracking competitors' moves and market shares and trying to find strategies to counter them. This approach has some pluses and minuses. On the positive side, the company develops a fighter orientation, watches for weaknesses in its own position, and searches out competitors' weaknesses. On the negative side, the company becomes too reactive. Rather than carrying out its own customer relationship strategy, it bases its own moves on competitors' moves. As a result, it may end up simply matching or extending industry practices rather than seeking innovative new ways to create more value for customers.

A **customer-centred company**, by contrast, focuses more on customer developments in designing its strategies. Clearly, the customer-centred company is in a better position to identify new opportunities and set long-run strategies that make sense. By watching customer needs evolve, it can decide what customer groups and what emerging needs are the most important to serve. Then it can concentrate its resources on delivering superior value to target customers.

In practice, today's companies must be **market-centred companies**, watching both their customers and their competitors. But they must not let competitor watching blind them to customer focusing.

Figure 18.3 shows that companies might have any of four orientations. First, they might be product oriented, paying little attention to either customers or competitors. Next, they might be customer oriented, paying attention to customers. In the third orientation, when a company starts to pay attention to competitors, it becomes competitor oriented. Today, however, companies need to be market oriented, paying balanced attention to both customers and competitors. Rather than simply watching competitors and trying to beat them on current ways of doing business, they need to watch customers and find innovative ways to build profitable customer relationships by delivering more customer value than competitors do.

Competitor-centred company—A company whose moves are mainly based on competitors' actions and reactions.

Customer-centred company—A company that focuses on customer developments in designing its marketing strategies and delivering superior value to its target customers.

Market-centred company—A company that pays balanced attention to both customers and competitors in designing its marketing strategies.

OBJECTIVES REVIEW AND KEY TERMS

Today's companies face their toughest competition ever. Understanding customers is an important first step in developing strong customer relationships, but it's not enough. To gain competitive advantage, companies must use this understanding to design market offers that deliver more value than the offers of competitors seeking to win over the same customers. This chapter examines how firms analyse their competitors and design effective competitive marketing strategies.

OBJECTIVE 1 **Discuss the need to understand competitors as well as customers through competitor analysis (pp. 537–543)**

To prepare an effective marketing strategy, a company must consider its competitors as well as its customers. Building profitable customer relationships requires satisfying target consumer needs *better than competitors do*. A company must continuously analyse competitors and develop *competitive marketing strategies* that position it effectively against competitors and give it the strongest possible *competitive advantage*.

Competitor analysis first involves identifying the company's major competitors, using both an industry-based and a market-based analysis. The company then gathers information on competitors' objectives, strategies, strengths and weaknesses, and reaction patterns. With this information in hand, it can select competitors to attack or avoid. Competitive intelligence must be collected, interpreted and distributed continuously. Company marketing managers should be able to obtain full and reliable information about any competitor affecting their decisions.

OBJECTIVE 2 Explain the fundamentals of competitive marketing strategies based on creating value for customers (pp. 543–551)

Which competitive marketing strategy makes the most sense depends on the company's industry and on whether it is the market leader, challenger, follower or nicher. The *market leader* has to mount strategies to expand the total market, protect market share, and expand market share. A *market challenger* is a firm that tries aggressively to expand its market share by attacking the leader, other runner-up companies, or smaller firms in the

industry. The challenger can select from a variety of direct or indirect attack strategies.

A *market follower* is a runner-up firm that chooses not to rock the boat, usually from fear that it stands to lose more than it might gain. But the follower is not without a strategy and seeks to use its particular skills to gain market growth. Some followers enjoy a higher rate of return than the leaders in their industry. A *market nicher* is a smaller firm that is unlikely to attract the attention of larger firms. Market nichers often become specialists in some end use, customer size category, specific customer group, geographic area, or service.

OBJECTIVE 3 Illustrate the need for balancing customer and competitor orientations in becoming a truly market-centred organisation (pp. 551–552)

A competitive orientation is important in today's markets, but companies should not overdo their focus on competitors. Companies are more likely to be hurt by emerging consumer needs and new competitors than by existing competitors. *Market-centred companies* that balance customer and competitor considerations are practising a true market orientation.

NAVIGATING THE KEY TERMS

OBJECTIVE 1
Competitive advantage (p. 536)
Competitor analysis (p. 537)
Competitive marketing strategies (p. 537)
Strategic group (p. 539)
Benchmarking (p. 539)

Customer value analysis (p. 540)

OBJECTIVE 2
Market leader (p. 546)
Market challenger (p. 546)
Market follower (p. 546)

Market nicher (p. 546)

OBJECTIVE 3
Competitor-centred company (p. 552)
Customer-centred company (p. 552)
Market-centred company (p.552)

DISCUSSION AND CRITICAL THINKING

Discussion questions

18-1 Briefly describe the activities involved when conducting a competitor analysis. (AACSB: Communication)

18-2 Name and describe the three stages that marketing strategy and practice often pass through. (AACSB: Communication)

18-3 Describe the three winning strategies suggested by Michael Porter. What is the losing strategy identified by Porter? (AACSB: Communication)

18-4 Describe the strategies market challengers can adopt and explain why challengers might have an advantage over market leaders. (AACSB: Communication)

18-5 Compare and contrast competitor-centred, customer-centred and market-centred companies. Which orientation is best? (AACSB: Communication; Reflective thinking)

Critical-thinking exercises

18-6 Companies pursuing a blue-ocean strategy attempt to find uncontested market spaces. Apple is described in the chapter as an example of a company pursuing and succeeding with such a strategy. Describe another example of a company that is successfully pursuing a blue ocean strategy. (AACSB: Communication; Reflective thinking)

18-7 Form a small group and conduct a customer value analysis for competing companies in an industry of your choice. Who are the strong and weak competitors? For the strong competitors, what are their vulnerabilities? (AACSB: Communication; Reflective thinking)

18-8 One source of competitive information is product teardowns. Information such as a bill of materials (BOM) – a listing of all the elements of a product and their costs – can be very useful. Find an example of a product tear down with cost information and discuss the value of that information for competitors. (AACSB: Communication; Reflective thinking)

Mini-cases and applications

Online, mobile and social media: marketing social logins

How many times have you left a website or app because of the hassle of setting up a login account, or you forgot your username or password for one you had set up? If you are like the 90 per cent of users bothered by having to log in, you probably just leave the site and never return. Social networks are helping with that problem by offering social logins on third-party sites and applications. With more than 1.3 billion users and 680 million mobile users, Facebook is the largest social network, and the company is using that power to become even more valuable to both users and businesses. Facebook Login allows website visitors and app users to use their Facebook login credentials to log in instead of establishing a separate login for each site and app. Google+, Twitter, LinkedIn and other social networks also offer social login capabilities, but Facebook is the leader, powering more than half of all social logins online and more than 60 per cent of mobile logins. This seems to be a winning arrangement for all parties – users conveniently log in to multiple sites with one username and password, third-party sites and apps gain access to Facebook users' demographic data, and Facebook gathers useful information on users' behaviour to better sell advertising.

18-9 How is Facebook Login expanding the total demand for social networks? (AACSB: Communication; Reflective thinking)

18-10 A major criticism of social logins is consumer privacy. How has Facebook addressed this issue, and do you think it will hurt the company's competitive advantage in this area? (AACSB: Communication; Reflective thinking)

Marketing ethics

Deconstruction experts eagerly anticipate the release of Apple's new iPad. Some like Luke Soules wanted to be the first to get his hands on the device so that he could take it apart and analyse it, called *teardowns* in the industry. He even spread video of his purchase and teardown on the Internet and bragged about feeding intimate information about the device's innards to folks before stores even opened. Although Soules' company, iFixit, makes teardown information public, most deconstruction firms provide data only to paying clients. Apple's gadgets are particularly tricky to crack; there are no screws. The tool of choice for prying open the iPhone was a dental pick. Apple is very secretive of the components that make up its gadgets; some components carry the Apple name rather than the manufacturer's name. However, experts armed with X-ray machines and scanning electron microscopes, with a little bit of sleuthing mixed in, are often able to determine the origins and cost of parts.

18-11 Using Google, search for 'iPad teardown' to find what information is available on the iPad. Is it ethical to 'tear down' a product and share that information publicly or sell it to other firms? (AACSB: Communication; Ethical reasoning; Reflective thinking)

18-12 iFixit used the iPad teardown as a publicity stunt to promote its repair business. Apple is a 'closed company' and doesn't want users repairing its products. In fact, users cannot replace a battery in an iPad; they have to return it to Apple and purchase a refurbished device for around €73 plus shipping. Replacing a battery is not as simple as popping in a new one because the batteries are soldered in. Is it right for Apple to be so restrictive regarding what customers can do with the product? (AACSB: Communication; Ethical reasoning; Reflective thinking)

Marketing by the numbers

The base Wi-Fi 16 GB iPad2 was introduced at around €570; like all electronic products, Apple will likely lower the price within a year or two of introduction. The 16 GB iPad's cost of goods sold is €250. Refer to Appendix 2: Marketing by the numbers to answer the following questions.

18-13 Calculate Apple's gross margin per unit and gross margin as a percentage of sales for the 16 GB iPad2. What is Apple's gross margin if the company sells 10 million iPads? (AACSB: Communication; Analytical reasoning)

18-14 What will happen to the gross margin generated by the iPad if Apple reduces the price by €100? (AACSB: Communication; Analytical reasoning)

REFERENCES

[1] Based on information from: 'Keurig's cold beverage maker set at chilly price', *Fortune*, http://fortune.com/2015/05/14/keurig-cold-beverage-machine/, accessed July 2015; 'Coca-Cola invests £767m to take on SodaStream', *Marketing Magazine*, www.marketingmagazine.co.uk/article/1230190/coca-cola-invests-767m-sodastream, accessed July 2015; Natalie Zmuda and Jeanine Poggi, 'SodaStream plots "edgy" return to Super Bowl', *Advertising Age*, 1 November 2013, http://adage.com/print/245079/; Rick Aristotle Munarriz, 'SodaStream takes a snarky swipe at Coke with Green Santa campaign', *Daily Finance*, 13 December 2013, www.dailyfinance.com/on/sodastream-snarky-green-santa-viral-adcampaign-coke/; Nadav Shemer, 'SodaStream: for making DIY carbonation sexy', *Fast Company*, 11 February 2013, www.fastcompany.com/most-innovative-companies/2013/sodastream; Jayson Derrick, 'SodaStream: tremendous growth prospects and potential buy-out target', Seekingalpha.com, 9 September 2013, seekingalpha.com/article/1681552; Bruce Horovitz, 'SodaStream's Super Bowl ad gets rejected – again', *USA Today*, 25 January 2014; 'SodaStream investor presentation', http://sodastream.investorroom.com/sodastreamoverview, accessed February 2014; and www.sodastream.com, accessed September 2014.

[2] Example adapted from information found in Frank James, 'Postal service quarterly losses surge; Internet gets blamed', 5 August 2009, www.NPR.org/blogs/thetwoway/2009/08/postal_service_quarterly_losse.html; Brian Groom, 'Royal Mail losses cast doubt on sell-off', *Financial Times*, 14 June 2011, www.ft.com/cms/s/0/a6489e86-9682-11e0-afc5-00144feab49a.html#ixzz1U4bQykWD, accessed January 2016

[3] See www.bosch.co.uk/en/uk/our_company_2/business_sectors_and_divisions_2/household_appliances_2/household-appliances.html, accessed October 2015.

[4] See www.telegraph.co.uk/finance/newsbysector/retailandconsumer/10717921/Sainsburys-wins-second-bite-at-Tesco-price-promise.html, accessed October 2015.

[5] See 'Contact lenses 2013', *Contact Lens Spectrum*, 1 January 2014, www.clspectrum.com/articleviewer.aspx?articleID=107853; and 'Bausch & Lomb', www.wikinvest.com/wiki/Bausch_&_Lomb, accessed October 2015;

[6] See Casey Johnston, 'Kindle Fire nabs 33% of Android tablet market, Nexus 7 just 8%', *ars technica*, 8 January 2013, http://arstechnica.com/gadgets/2013/01/kindle-fire-nabs-33-of-android-tabletmarket-nexus-7-just-8/; and Jim Edwards, 'Samsung is stealing Apple's iPad share', *Business Insider*, 21 October 2013, www.businessinsider.com/samsung-is-stealing-apples-ipad-market-share-2013-10.

[7] Adapted from Taylor Clark, 'Who's afraid of the big bad Starbucks?', *The Week*, 18 January 2008, p. 46.

[8] Adapted from information found in W. Chan Kim and Renée Mauborgne, 'Blue ocean strategy: how to create uncontested market space and make competition irrelevant', www.blueoceanstrategy.com/pre/downloads/BlueOceanStrategySummary.pdf, accessed October 2015; also see Kim and Mauborgne, *Blue Ocean Strategy: How to Create Uncontested Market Space and Make Competition Irrelevant* (Boston: Harvard Business Press, 2005). For other discussion, see 'Blue Ocean Strategy', www.blueoceanstrategy.com/, accessed October 2015.

[9] Example from Jonathan Guthrie, 'The young ones, older and wiser', *Financial Times*, 16 November 2010, www.ft.com/cms/s/0/1921f98c-f1b2-11df-bb5a-00144feab49a.html#ixzz1U5FW3brs, accessed October 2011; and see www.glassesdirect.co.uk/about/story/, accessed October 2015.

[10] For these and other examples, see Dan Schwabel, 'Why companies want you to become an intrapreneur', *Forbes*, 9 September 2013, www.forbes.com/sites/danschawbel/2013/09/09/why-companieswant-you-to-become-an-intrapreneur/.

[11] Michael E. Porter, *Competitive Strategy: Techniques for Analyzing Industries and Competitors* (New York: Free Press, 1980), Chapter 2; and Porter, 'What is strategy?' *Harvard Business Review*, November–December 1996, pp. 61–78; Also see Stefan Stern, 'May the force be with you and your plans for 2008', *Financial Times*, 8 January 2008, p. 14; and 'Porter's generic strategies', www.quickmba.com/strategy/generic.shtml, accessed October 2015.

[12] See Michael Treacy and Fred Wiersema, 'Customer intimacy and other value disciplines', *Harvard Business Review*, January–February 1993, pp. 84–93; also Treacy and Wiersema, *The Discipline of Market Leaders: Choose Your Customers, Narrow Your Focus, Dominate Your Market* (New York: Perseus Press, 1997); and Wiersema, *Double-Digit Growth: How Great Companies Achieve It – No Matter What* (New York: Portfolio, 2003). Also see Elaine Cascio, 'Fast, cheap, or good – pick two', *Inter@ction Solutions*, January/February 2012, p. 8; Jürgen Kai-Uwe Brock and Josephine Yu Zhou, 'Customer intimacy', *Journal of Business and Industrial Marketing*, 2012, pp. 370–383; and Joe Weinman, 'How customer intimacy is evolving to collective intimacy, thanks to big data', *Forbes*, 4 June 2013, www.forbes.com/sites/joeweinman/2013/06/04/howcustomer-intimacy-is-evolving-to-collective-intimacy-thanks-to-bigdata/.

[13] For a history of Apple see www.macworld.com/article/1050112/30moments.html, accessed January 2016.

[14] For more discussion, see Philip Kotler and Kevin Lane Keller, *Marketing Management*, 13th ed. (Upper Saddle River, NJ: Prentice Hall, 2009), Chapter 11.

[15] Robert Klara, 'New kid with the block', *Adweek*, 15 April 2013, pp. 30–31; Neda Ulaby, 'Girls' Legos are a hit, but why do girls need special Legos?' *NPR*, 29 June 2013, www.npr.org/blogs/monkeysee/2013/06/28/196605763; Christian Wienberf, 'Lego profit soars 35% as toy bricks for girls drive sales growth', *BloombergBusinessweek*, 21 February 2013, www.businessweek.com/news/2013-02-21/lego-profit-soars-35-percent-as-toy-bricksfor-girls-drive-sales-growth; and http://friends.lego.com/en-us/products, accessed October 2015.

[16] See 'Velcro Industries launches integrated marketing campaign to promote VELCRO brand One-Wrap ties', *BusinessWire*, 28 May 2013, www.businesswire.com/news/home/20130528005147/en/; Rupal Parekh, 'Can marketing push make Velcro stick?' *Advertising Age*, 3 June 2013, p. 8; and www.velcro.com and www.pinterest.com/velcrobrand/, accessed October 2015.

[17] Adapted from information found in Jack Neff, 'Why Unilever lost the laundry war', *Advertising Age*, 6 August 2007, pp. 1, 25; 'Bidders Eye Unilever's US detergent arm', *Financial Times*, 9 April 2008, p. 24; 'Unilever sells North American detergents unit', 28 July 2008, accessed at www.msnbc.msn.com/id/25884712.

[18] Example based on information from David J. Bryce and Jeffrey H. Dyer, 'Strategies to crack well-guarded markets', *Harvard Business Review*, May 2007, pp. 84–91; with information from Teressa Iezzi, 'For showing what it really means to transform yourself into a media brand', *Fast Company*, www.fastcompany.com/most-innovative-companies/2012/redbull-media-house, accessed October 2015; and 'The top 15 energy

drink brands', *caffeineinformer*, www.caffeineinformer.com/the-15-top-energydrink-brands, accessed October 2015.

[19] See Angela Chen, 'The rise of niche online dating sites', *Wall Street Journal*, 15 October 2013, http://online.wsj.com/news/articles/SB1000142405270230456100457913744126 9527948; Laura T. Coffey, 'From

farmers to salad toppings: 26 weirdly niche dating sites', *USA Today*, 5 August 2013, www.today.com/health/farmers-salad-toppings-26-weirdly-niche-dating-sites-6C10843053; and www.farmersonly.com, accessed October 2015.

COMPANY CASE

Amazon's Kindle Fire versus Apple's iPad: let battle commence!

When Steve Jobs, the inspirational co-founder and visionary passed away in October 2011 the battle lines had already been drawn, the troops mobilised and the opening shots fired – Amazon had declared at war on Apple. While Steve Jobs had spent the last few years of his life fighting to secure the long-term position of the company he led, the rapidly changing world of mobile telephones, tablet computers and linked technology provides no guarantees of stability. That said, Apple begins the post-Jobs era in a strong position, largely down to the drive and insight of Mr Jobs. The firm currently holds a truly massive war chest of €134bn in net cash and equivalents on its balance sheet of which €7 billion is in hard cash. Somewhat ironically, this is more than enough to buy the two top PC makers by revenue, Hewlett-Packard (HP) and Dell, outright.

These companies are among those scrambling to come up with a plausible rival to the iPad. A tough challenge given that the iPad tablet (in various versions) has sold over 70 million units in 2013, and while sales at the start of 2014 were sluggish, the launch of new versions in late 2014 were predicted to lead to significant sales increases throughout 2015. Such was the impact of the iPad that Léo Apotheker, the outgoing Chief Executive of HP, admitted the iPad was transforming the world of personal computing.

Not everything has been easy for Apple however. Apple and Samsung had undertaken a year-long global legal battle that in early 2014 saw the companies agree to limit their legal actions to the US, where in mid-2014 a US, jury ruled that Samsung should pay Apple around €100m in damages for patent infringement although Samsung is appealing against any such findings

However, notwithstanding these irritating distractions, Apple's real competitor in the tablet market seems to be Amazon's Kindle Fire. Priced at a wafer-thin margin, near cost of about €70, Amazon intends to demonstrate that a clever, persistent, well-planned and deep-pocketed competitor is able and willing to take on Apple in the entire chain of distribution: not merely in term of content – music, video and books – but also via the devices on which they are consumed. Central to Amazon's technology approach is a stripped-down (literally and metaphorically) piece of hardware that is designed to fit neatly into the new world of 'cloud computing'. This modern view of technology sets it apart from a raft of other tablets, most of which have tried – and (largely) failed – to match the explicitly high-end iPad in design, looks, innovativeness and capabilities while lacking the enormous economies of scale that Apple has benefited from as the first-mover in the new tablet market.

After numerous rumours, denials, general malarkey and much shenanigans, Jeff Bezos, Amazon's founder and Chief Executive, announced the launch of the Kindle Fire in autumn 2011 (the actual product launch being two months later in time for Christmas sales). Mr Bezos' presentation was beautiful to watch – even hardened Apple fans found his arguments persuasive. As he strolled confidently through his presentation unveiling the Kindle Fire tablet computer, the target whose name hung unspoken in the air was 'Apple'. At one point, a surprisingly deadpan Mr Bezos pulled up a huge image of a dangling and ostentatiously white USB cable (a cable that millions of consumers have used to send content between their laptops and Apple's iPods and iPads). The media present audibly chuckled because they guessed what backhanded dig was coming. 'Syncing should be done invisibly, in the background, wirelessly – and it should actually work,' Mr Bezos said.

Commentators noted that Mr Bezos couldn't resist a little smirk as he announced the low price of his new competitor to the costly Apple iPad – and to the entire ecosystem of films, music, magazines and books that can appear on Apple's device: 'This is unbelievable value. We are building premium products at non-premium prices. We are determined to do that, and we are doing it.' This seems to sum up Amazon's approach – their new business mantra and business model is simply *premium products at non-premium prices*. For Apple this seems to be a deliberate statement that Amazon intends to market devices that compete with Apple's and have similarly sophisticated technology but are much, much cheaper.

In many regards, Amazon has long been positioning itself as the online equivalent of Walmart, in that the firm has consistently attempted to operate at mass scale with wafer-thin margins which drive out smaller, higher-margin competitors. In some senses, Amazon's business model for their Kindle tablets can be viewed as a classic follower strategy. That strategy of driving down prices to exert market power was evident in the updated Kindle e-readers, which now sell for around €100 each (or less). Traditional book stores and book publishers will be feeling even more threatened by Amazon than before. The Nook e-reader originated by Barnes & Noble (B&N) is seen by many industry commentators as out-classed by the Kindle reader. Indeed, 17 years after Mr Bezos founded Amazon, taking on the then mighty US bookstore chain B&N, his company had long ago left its detractors behind (most of which predicted Amazon's demise and B&N's continued dominance). Amazon is now worth around €133 billion – over 100 times the value of B&N, Nook HD and HD+ e-readers seem hopelessly outgunned, out-dated and out-of-touch.

Industry observers claimed that while the first Fire tablets looked compelling, well-designed and innovative, later additions have just got better and better. At less than half the price of Apple's cheapest iPad, the latest Kindle Fire has a colour touchscreen, front and rear cameras, four case colours, two screen size choices and a new higher-speed browser optimised for accessing online content. Amazon's growing music and video libraries are easily accessible. With both six- and seven-inch screen versions, the Fire is intended to take on and beat the both sizes of iPad (and the larger iPhones) as an easier-to-hold and even better designed media consumption device. While some commentators claimed the first Kindle Fires were not 'full' tablet computers, as they were WiFi-only, lacked a camera, and some other features, Amazon quickly overcame such objections by adding these to later versions – a clear follower strategy. Indeed, Richard Doherty, an analyst at Envisioneering, a tech research firm, claims 'it's incredible value for its specifications'.

In announcing the launch of the Kindle Fire in 2011 and the more recent Fire Phone in 2014, Mr Bezos did more than announce a competitor for the iPad and iPhone suite, he finally unveiled a strategy for a full-scale assault on Apple. During his presentation there was just a touch of steel and fire in the geeky-zany Bezos – when he stood playing the video game 'Ninja Fruit' on the Fire, slashing his finger across a screen full of leaping fruit. 'I have to admit that I find this a little uncomfortably therapeutic,' he joked as his virtual Ninja's destroyed pieces of fruit in a none-too-subtle reference to his main fruit-named Apple target. Mr Bezos' subsequent (and none-too-subtle) letter to customers on the Amazon home page about the new

Kindles expresses his business philosophy even more bluntly: 'There are two types of companies: those that work hard to charge customers more, and those that work hard to charge customers less. Both approaches can work. We are firmly in the second camp.' This is not to suggest that the targeting of Apple is a spontaneous decision – Amazon has been plotting for years to rival and surpass the Apple 'ecosystem' of blended offerings. However, while Apple is set up to make their profits from the hardware, Amazon intend to make their money from the add-ons and extras, enabling them to sell the Kindle at truly cut-down prices.

Amazon have ostentatiously struck deals with media companies, including arrangements to stream video content from Fox, CBS and NBC. Their site proudly proclaims that their streaming service Amazon Instant Video 'offers two great ways to watch movies and TV shows instantly, anywhere. Rent or buy from a selection of more than 50,000 titles or subscribe to and get unlimited streaming of more than 15,000 movies and TV episodes'. Amazon also announced deeper cooperation with Hearst, the magazine and newspaper publisher. 'The good news for Amazon is that, unlike everyone else who has tried to compete, they have spent a lot of time building out the services before they launched the device,' said Michael Gartenberg, Gartner analyst.

These linkages are synergistic with Amazon's virtual store dedicated to distributing applications for the Android-based mobile phones and tablets. This provided a much-needed boost to the adoption of the operating system. Another competitor, Google's official Android Market, was viewed as chaotic because it allows any developer to place apps in it, while Apple's iPhone applications were too closely vetted and controlled by Apple. Some hardware makers and wireless carriers, including Verizon, had set out to make their own stores dedicated to Android devices, but none have the extensive customer base and expertise in online sales that Amazon has fought hard to develop. The Amazon store 'will definitely help with the fragmentation issue', said analyst Michael Gartenberg of Gartner. Innovatively, the Amazon Appstore has many of the company's usual features, including customer reviews and recommendations based on past purchases but also includes new functions that are not typically available via Apple's iTunes, such as the ability to test an application through a standard PC web browser.

Aaron Rubenson, category leader for the Amazon Appstore, said the company's extensive retail experience gave it the best marketing and promotional capabilities to direct people to the apps that they would be interested in. Soon it seems that Amazon will not merely recommend the consumer's next book or CD purchase but also slip in suggestions for useful apps. With each app tested by Amazon, security and reliability could prove major draws (something that some iPad users have found frustrating with some apps). Interestingly, Amazon's Appstore keep around 30 per cent of the revenue from paid apps. However, Amazon determine the price, raising or lowering of the cost to consumers in order to drive maximum sales.

With its own growing Appstore and a suite of media delivery applications, the Amazon tablet and phone suite are the first coherent effort to replicate Apple's comfortable and convenient 'ecosystem', in which users can purchase music, video and reading material from one source. The Fire Tablet and Phone offers music through Amazon's Cloud Player music service, video through Amazon's Instant Video service, and books and periodicals through its well-established Kindle platform. Through shifting computing effort on to Amazon's own infrastructure, this plays to its strengths as a 'cloud computing' company. As one of the biggest global digital infrastructure companies, Amazon currently hosts plenty of content on behalf of other companies and (as evidenced by their deals with other media companies) will be able to attract more media companies by offering to manage and distribute their content more efficiently.

Amazon's history in e-commerce will also give it an advantage as it seeks to increase its digital media sales. 'They have millions and millions of credit cards,' said Mr Gartenberg. 'It becomes really easy to charge for these services. One click and you can rent a movie.' 'Few companies are poised to enter the market with the resources they have,' said Mr Gartenberg. and, of course, the Kindle range is 'prominently placed on the Amazon homepage, which is another home court advantage that few other players have.'

After a period littered with failed attempts to match the iPad, from the HP TouchPad to the BlackBerry PlayBook, it might seem rash (or, at least, ill-timed) for yet another pretender to kick sand in the face of the mighty Apple. This time, though, things feel different. With a technology architecture and business strategy that differ markedly from the earlier flops, according to tech industry analysts, Amazon has positioned itself to act as the first true challenger to the iPad. Which company will win? Well time will tell. But it will be fun to watch . . . via a tablet, of course.

Questions for discussion

1. What advantages has Apple's iPad over the Kindle Fire?
2. Conversely, what advantages has Amazon's new entrant Kindle Fire over the more elderly Apple iPad?
3. Why have other products fared so badly when competing with the iPad?
4. Which strategy is Amazon pursuing in its attack on Apple? Will it work? Why?

Sources: John Gapper, 'Jeff Bezos of Amazon takes aim at Apple', *Financial Times*, 28 September 2011, http://blogs.ft.com/businessblog/2011/09/jeff-bezos-of-amazon-takes-aim-at-apple/#ixzz1aYEijlqM, accessed October 2015; John Gapper and Barney Jopson, 'An inventor with Fire in his belly and Jobs in his sights', 30 September 2011, www.ft.com/cms/s/0/4ada7e06-ea98-11e0-b0f5-00144feab49a.html#ixzz1aYVqzXB3, accessed October 2015; Joseph Menn, 'No guarantees in the era after Jobs', *Financial Times*, 6 October 2011, www.ft.com/cms/s/2/12349726-f033-11e0-977b-00144feab49a.html#ixzz1aYHttsyb, accessed October 2015; Richard Waters, Barney Jopson and David Gelles, 'Amazon tablet fires its ambitions', *Financial Times*, 29 September 2011, www.ft.com/cms/s/2/ce7860cc-ea14-11e0-b997-00144feab49a.html#ixzz1aYEAbU4C, accessed October 2015; also www.amazon.co.uk/Instant-Video/b/ref=topnav_storetab_atv?_encoding=UTF8&node=3010085031; Joan E. Solsman, 'Nook's last stand? B&N still must battle Amazon', www.cnet.com/news/nooks-last-stand-b-n-still-must-battle-amazon/, accessed October 2015; Sean Farrell, 'Apple's burden: a mountain of money it can't really use', www.theguardian.com/technology/2014/sep/07/apple-iphone-6-cash-pile-tax-avoidance-us, accessed October 2015; Amit Chowdhry, 'Apple and Samsung drop patent disputes against each other outside of the U.S.', www.forbes.com/sites/amitchowdhry/2014/08/06/apple-and-samsung-drop-patent-disputes-against-each-other-outside-of-the-u-s/, accessed October 2015.

CHAPTER NINETEEN

The global marketplace

Chapter preview

You've now learned the fundamentals of how companies develop competitive marketing strategies to engage customers, create customer value and build lasting customer relationships. In this chapter, we extend these fundamentals to global marketing. Although we discussed global topics in each previous chapter – it's difficult to find an area of marketing that doesn't contain at least some international elements – here we'll focus on special considerations that companies face when they market their brands globally. Advances in communication, transportation and digital technologies have made the world a much smaller place. Today, almost every firm, large or small, faces international marketing issues. In this chapter, we will examine six major decisions marketers make in going global.

To start our exploration of global marketing, let's look at Coca-Cola, a truly global operation. You'll find a Coca-Cola product within arm's length of almost anyone, anywhere in the world. With 3,500 products and 14 billion-euro brands, the company sells 'moments of happiness' more than 1.9 billion times a day in more than 200 countries. Like many companies, Coca-Cola's greatest growth opportunities lie in international markets. Here, we examine the company's odyssey into Africa.

Objective outline

Coca-Cola in Africa: 'Everything is right there to have it happen'

Coca-Cola is one of the world's truly iconic brands – a €38-billion global powerhouse. It puts Coke products within 'an arm's length' of 98 per cent of the world's population. Already the world's number-one soft drink maker, Coca-Cola is three-quarters of the way through a 12-year plan to double its global system revenues by 2020. But achieving such growth won't be easy. The major problem: soft drink sales growth has lost its fizz in North America and Europe, two of Coca-Cola's largest and most profitable markets. In fact, the US soft drink market has shrunk for five straight years. With sales stagnating in its mature markets, Coca-Cola must look elsewhere to meet its ambitious growth goals.

In recent years, Coca-Cola has sought growth primarily in developing global markets such as China and India, which boast large emerging middle classes but relatively low per capita consumption of Coke. However, both China and India are now crowded with competitors and notoriously difficult for outsiders to navigate. So while Coca-Cola will continue to compete heavily in those countries, it has set its sights on an even more promising long-term growth opportunity – Africa.

Many Western companies view Africa as an African untamed final frontier – a kind of no man's land plagued by poverty, political corruption and instability, unreliable transportation, and shortages of fresh water and other essential resources. But Coca-Cola sees plenty of opportunity to justify the risks. According to one source, six of the world's ten fastest-growing markets are in Africa. The continent has a growing population of more than 1 billion people and a just-emerging middle class. The number of African households earning at least €4,000 – the income level where families begin to spend at least half their income on non-food items – has tripled over the past 30 years to more than a third of the population. 'You've got an incredibly young population, a dynamic population,' says Coca-Cola CEO Muhtar Kent, '[and] huge disposable income. I mean €1.3 trillion of GDP, which is bigger than Russia, bigger than India.'

Coca-Cola is no stranger to Africa. It has operated there since 1929, and it's the only multinational that offers its products in every African country. The company has a dominant 29 per cent market share in Africa and the Middle East, as compared with Pepsi's 15 per cent share. Coca-Cola's sparkling beverage revenues in Africa and the Middle East grew by 6 per cent last year, compared with a 2 per cent decline in North America and 1 per cent decline in Europe.

But there's still plenty of room for Coca-Cola to grow in Africa. For example, annual per capita consumption of Coke in Kenya is just 40 servings, compared with more developed countries like Mexico, where consumption runs at an eye-popping 728 servings per year. So the stage is set for Coca-Cola on the African continent, not just for its flagship Coke brand but also for its large stable of other soft drinks, waters and juices. Whereas the beverage giant invested €4.8 billion in the African market over the past decade, it plans to invest twice that amount during the next ten years – an effort that includes bottling plants, distribution networks, retailer support and an Africa-wide promotional campaign called 'One billion reasons to believe in Africa'.

Marketing in Africa is a very different proposition from marketing in more developed regions. 'Africa … is not Atlanta,' observes one analyst, 'and Coke is, in a sense, sticking its hand into a bees' nest to get some honey'. To grow its sales in Africa, beyond just marketing through traditional channels in larger African cities, Coca-Cola is now invading smaller communities with more grassroots tactics. '[Just] being in a country is very easy; you can go and set up a depot in every capital city,' says CEO Kent. But in Africa, 'That's not what we're about. There's nowhere in Africa that we don't go. We go to every town, every village, every community, every township.' In Africa, every small shop in every back alley has become important, as Coca-Cola

Coca-Cola's strategy in Africa has been hugely successful.
Source: REDA &CO srl/Alamy Images

launches what another analyst describes as 'a street-by-street campaign to win drinkers … not yet used to guzzling Coke by the gallon'. For example, take the Mamakamau Shop in Uthiru, a poor community outside Nairobi, Kenya. Piles of trash burn outside the shop and sewage trickles by in an open trench. Besides Coca-Cola products, the shop – known as a duka – also carries everything from mattresses to plastic buckets, all in a room about the size of a small bedroom. Still, proprietor Mamakamau Kingori has earned Coca-Cola's 'Gold' vendor status, its highest level, for selling about 72 cola products a day, priced at 30 Kenyan shillings (€0.27) for a 500-millilitre bottle. Most customers drink the soda in the store while sitting on overturned red crates – they can't afford to pay the bottle deposit. Coca-Cola's Kenyan bottler will reuse the glass bottles up to 70 times.

To earn her 'Gold' status, Kingori follows carefully prescribed selling techniques. She uses a red, Coke-provided, refrigerated cooler by the front entrance, protected by a blue cage. Like other mom-and-pop stores in her area, she keeps the cooler fully stocked with Coke on top, Fanta in the middle, and large bottles at the bottom. Inside the store, she posts red menu signs provided by Coca-Cola that push combo meals, such as a 300-millilitre Coke and a ndazi, a type of local donut, for 25 Kenyan shillings.

In Kabira, another poor Nairobi neighbourhood, the crowded streets are lined with shops painted Coke red. The local bottler hires an artist to paint the shops with logos and Swahili phrases like 'Burudika na Coke Baridi', meaning 'Enjoy Coke cold'. In countless communities across Africa, whether it's the dukas in Nairobi or tuck shops in Johannesburg, South Africa, small stores play a big role in helping Coca-Cola grow.

Such shops are supplied by a rudimentary but effective network of Coca-Cola distributors. For example, in downtown Nairobi, men in red lab coats load hand-pulled trolleys with 22 to 40 crates of Coke and other soft drinks from Rosinje Distributors, one of 3,200 Micro Distribution Centres (MDCs) that Coca-Cola operates in Africa. These centres are the spine of Coca-Cola's African distribution network. For example, the Nairobi plant ships Coke, Fanta, Stoney Ginger Beer, and other Coca-Cola brands to almost 400 area MDCs. From there, crews hustle the products – sometimes a case at a time carried on their heads – to local shops and beverage kiosks. Because of the poor roads crowded with traffic, moving drinks by hand is often the best method. The MDCs help Coca-Cola to get its products into remote areas, making them available as people develop a taste for soft drinks and have the income to buy them.

Despite their elemental nature, Coca-Cola's marketing approaches in Africa are proving effective. The company's first rule is to get its products 'cold and close'. 'If they don't have roads to move products long distances on trucks, we will use boats, canoes, or trolleys,' says the president of Coca-Cola South Africa. For example, in Nigeria's Makako district – a maze of stilt houses on the Lagos lagoon – women criss-cross the waterways selling Coca-Cola directly from canoes to residents.

There's little doubt that Coca-Cola's increased commitment to Africa will be key to its achieving its global goals. As CEO Muhtar Kent concludes: 'Africa is the untold story and could be the big story of the next decade, like India and China were this past decade.… Everything is right there to have it happen.'[1]

In the past, European companies paid little attention to international trade. If they could pick up some extra sales via exports, that was fine. But the big market was at home, and it teemed with opportunities. The home market was also much safer. Managers did not need to learn other languages, deal with strange and changing currencies, face political and legal uncertainties, or adapt their products to different customer needs and expectations. Today, however, the situation is much different. Organisations of all kinds, from BASF, Google, Fiat and BMW to Michelin and even Champions League Football, have gone global.

Author comment

The rapidly changing global environment provides both opportunities and threats. It's difficult to find a marketer today that isn't affected in some way by global developments.

GLOBAL MARKETING TODAY

The world is shrinking rapidly with the advent of faster digital communication, transportation and financial flows. Products developed in one country – McDonald's hamburgers, Netflix video service, Samsung electronics, Zara fashions, Caterpillar construction equipment, German BMWs, Facebook social networking – have found enthusiastic acceptance in other countries. It would not be surprising to hear about a German businessman wearing an Italian suit meeting an English friend at a Japanese restaurant who later returns home to drink Russian vodka while watching American Idol on TV and checking Facebook posts from friends around the world.

International trade has boomed over the past three decades. Since 1990, the number of multinational corporations in the world has more than doubled to more than 63,000. Some of these multinationals are true giants. In fact, of the largest 150 economies in the world, only 77 are countries. The remaining 73 are multinational corporations. Walmart, the world's largest company (based on a weighted average of sales, profits, assets and market value), has annual revenues greater than the gross domestic product (GDP) of all but the world's 25 largest countries.[2] Despite a dip in world trade caused by the recent worldwide recession, the world trade of products and services last year was valued at more than €14.7 trillion, about 31.8 per cent of GDP worldwide.[3]

Many European companies have long been successful at international marketing: BMW, Nestlé, IKEA, Siemens and Rolls-Royce and dozens of other European firms have made the world their market. However, non-European firms have also become well-established with such names such as McDonald's, Coca-Cola, Starbucks, GE, IBM, Colgate, Caterpillar and Boeing. Other products and services that appear to be European are, in fact, produced or owned by foreign companies, such as Campbell Soups, Asda (now owned by US giant Walmart), Cadbury (the quintessential British chocolate maker), Mulberry (the British lifestyle brand is owned by Singaporean business tycoon Christina Ong), Laura Ashley, Lanvin, Crabtree and Evelyn (all owned by Asian companies), Michelin, the oh-so-French tyre manufacturer, now does 34 per cent of its business in North America. And America's own Caterpillar belongs more to the wider world, with 61 per cent of its sales coming from outside the United States.[4]

Many European companies have made the world their market.

Source: mauritius images GmbH/ Alamy Images

But as global trade grows, global competition is also intensifying. Foreign firms are expanding aggressively into new international markets, and home markets are no longer as rich in opportunity. Few industries are currently safe from foreign competition. If companies delay taking steps toward internationalising, they risk being shut out of growing markets in Western and Eastern Europe, China and the Pacific Rim, Russia, India, Brazil and elsewhere. Firms that stay at home to play it safe might not only lose their chances to enter other markets but also risk losing their home markets. Domestic companies that never thought about foreign competitors suddenly find these competitors in their own backyards.

Ironically, although the need for companies to go abroad is greater today than in the past, so are the risks. Companies that go global may face highly unstable governments and currencies, restrictive government policies and regulations, and high trade barriers. The recently dampened global economic environment has also created big global challenges. In addition, corruption is an increasing problem; officials in several countries often award business not to the best bidder but to the highest briber.

A **global firm** is one that, by operating in more than one country, gains marketing, production, research and development (R&D) and financial advantages that are not available to purely domestic competitors. Because the global company sees the world as one market, it minimises the importance of national boundaries and develops global brands. The global company raises capital, obtains materials and components, and manufactures and markets its goods wherever it can do the best job.

For example, US-based Otis Elevator, the world's largest elevator maker, is headquartered in Farmington, Connecticut. However, it offers products in more than 200 countries and achieves 83 per cent of its sales from outside the United States. It gets elevator door systems from France, small geared parts from Spain, electronics from Germany, and special motor drives from Japan. It operates manufacturing facilities in the Americas, Europe and Asia, and engineering and test centres in the United States, Austria, Brazil, China, Czech Republic, France, Germany, India, Italy, Japan, Korea and Spain. In turn, Otis Elevator is a wholly owned subsidiary of global commercial

Global firm—A firm that, by operating in more than one country, gains R&D, production, marketing and financial advantages in its costs and reputation that are not available to purely domestic competitors.

Figure 19.1 Major international marketing decisions

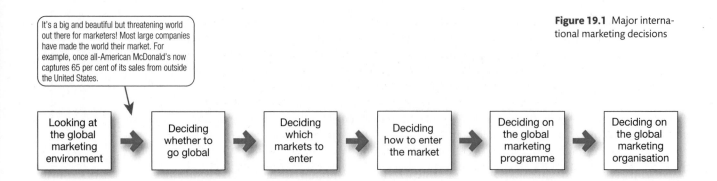

It's a big and beautiful but threatening world out there for marketers! Most large companies have made the world their market. For example, once all-American McDonald's now captures 65 per cent of its sales from outside the United States.

| Looking at the global marketing environment | Deciding whether to go global | Deciding which markets to enter | Deciding how to enter the market | Deciding on the global marketing programme | Deciding on the global marketing organisation |

and aerospace giant United Technologies Corporation.[5] Many of today's global corporations – both large and small – have become truly borderless.

This does not mean, however, that every firm must operate in a dozen countries to succeed. Smaller firms can practise global niching. But the world is becoming smaller, and every company operating in a global industry – whether large or small – must assess and establish its place in world markets.

The rapid move toward globalisation means that all companies will have to answer some basic questions: What market position should we try to establish in our country, in our economic region, and globally? Who will our global competitors be and what are their strategies and resources? Where should we produce or source our products? What strategic alliances should we form with other firms around the world?

As shown in Figure 19.1, a company faces six major decisions in international marketing. We discuss each decision in detail in this chapter.

LOOKING AT THE GLOBAL MARKETING ENVIRONMENT

Author comment

As if operating within a company's own borders wasn't difficult enough, going global adds many layers of complexities. For example, Coca-Cola markets its products in hundreds of countries around the globe. It must understand the varying trade, economic, cultural and political environments in each market.

Before deciding whether to operate internationally, a company must understand the international marketing environment. That environment has changed a great deal in recent decades, creating both new opportunities and new problems.

The international trade system

European companies looking abroad must start by understanding the international trade system. When selling to another country, a firm may face restrictions on trade between nations. Governments may charge *tariffs or duties*, taxes on certain imported products designed to raise revenue or protect domestic firms. Tariffs and duties are often used to force favourable trade behaviours from other nations.

For example, the European Union (EU) recently placed import duties on Chinese solar panels after determining that Chinese companies were selling the panels in EU countries at under-market prices. To retaliate, the very next day, the Chinese government placed duties on EU wine exports to China. The duties targeted the wines of Spain, France and Italy but spared Germany, which had taken China's side in the solar panel dispute. The disputes were resolved when Chinese solar panel producers agreed to a minimum price in Europe and Europe agreed to help China develop its own wine industry in return for promoting European wines there.[6]

Countries may set quotas, limits on the amount of foreign imports that they will accept in certain product categories. The purpose of a quota is to conserve on foreign exchange and protect local industry and employment. Firms may also encounter *exchange controls*, which limit the amount of foreign exchange and the exchange rate against other currencies.

A company also may face *non-tariff trade barriers*, such as biases against its bids, restrictive product standards or excessive host-country regulations or enforcement. For example, Walmart recently suspended its once-ambitious plans to expand into India's huge but fragmented retail market by opening hundreds of Walmart superstores there. Beyond difficult market conditions, such as spotty electricity and poor roads, India is notorious for throwing up non-tariff obstacles to protect the nation's own predominately mom-and-pop retailers, which control 96 per cent of India's €400 billion in retail sales. One such obstacle is a government regulation requiring foreign retailers in India to buy 30 per cent of the merchandise they sell from local small businesses. Such a requirement is nearly impossible for Walmart, because small suppliers can't produce the quantities of goods needed by the giant retailer. Further, India's few large domestic retailers are not bound by the same rule, making it difficult for Walmart to compete profitably. Walmart is now looking for a domestic partner that can help it crack the mammoth Indian market.[7]

At the same time, certain other forces can help trade between nations. Examples include the World Trade Organisation (WTO) and various regional free-trade agreements.

The World Trade Organisation

The General Agreement on Tariffs and Trade (GATT), established in 1947 and modified in 1994, was designed to promote world trade by reducing tariffs and other international trade barriers. It established the World Trade Organisation (WTO), which replaced GATT in 1995 and now oversees the original GATT provisions. WTO and GATT member nations (currently numbering 159) have met in eight rounds of negotiations to reassess trade barriers and establish new rules for international trade. The WTO also imposes international trade sanctions and mediates global trade disputes. Its actions have been productive. The first seven rounds of negotiations reduced the average worldwide tariffs on manufactured goods from 45 per cent to just 5 per cent.[8]

The most recently completed negotiations, dubbed the Uruguay Round, dragged on for seven long years before concluding in 1994. The benefits of the Uruguay Round will be felt for many years, as the accord promoted long-term global trade growth, reduced the world's remaining merchandise tariffs by 30 per cent, extended the WTO to cover trade in agriculture and a wide range of services, and toughened the international protection of copyrights, patents, trademarks and other intellectual property. A new round of global WTO trade talks, the Doha Round, began in Doha, Qatar, in late 2001 and was set to conclude in 2005; however, the discussions still continued through 2014.[9]

The EU represents one of the world's single largest markets.

Source: European Commission
© European Union, 2016

Regional free-trade zones

Certain countries have formed *free-trade zones* or **economic communities**. These are groups of nations organised to work toward common goals in the regulation of international trade. One such community is the European Union. Formed in 1957, the EU set out to create a single European market by reducing barriers to the free flow of products, services, finances and labour among member countries and developing policies on trade with non-member nations. Today, the EU represents one of the world's largest single markets.

Currently, it has 28 member countries containing more than half a billion consumers and accounting for almost 20 per cent of the world's exports.[10] The EU offers tremendous trade opportunities for US and other non-European firms.

Economic community—A group of nations organised to work toward common goals in the regulation of international trade.

Over the past decade and a half, 18 EU member nations have taken a significant step toward unification by adopting the euro as a common currency. Widespread adoption of the euro has decreased much of the currency risk associated with doing business in Europe, making member countries with previously weak currencies more attractive markets. However, the adoption of a common currency has also caused problems as European economic powers such as Germany and France have had to step in recently to prop up weaker economies such as those of Greece, Portugal and Cyprus. This recent 'euro crisis' has led some analysts to predict the possible break-up of the euro zone as it is now set up.[11]

It is unlikely that the EU will ever go against 2,000 years of tradition and become the 'United States of Europe'. A community with more than two-dozen different languages and cultures will always have difficulty coming together and acting as a single entity. Still, with a combined annual GDP of more than €12.5 trillion, the EU has become a potent economic force.[12]

In 1994, the North American Free Trade Agreement (NAFTA) established a free trade zone among the United States, Mexico and Canada. The agreement created a single market of 470 million people who produce and consume €15.2 trillion worth of goods and services annually. Over the past 20 years, NAFTA has eliminated trade barriers and investment restrictions among the three countries. Total trade among the NAFTA countries nearly tripled from €225 billion in 1993 to more than €0.8 trillion a year.[13]

Following the apparent success of NAFTA, in 2005 the Central American Free Trade Agreement (CAFTA-DR) established a free trade zone between the United States and Costa Rica, the Dominican Republic, El Salvador, Guatemala, Honduras and Nicaragua. Other free trade areas have formed in Latin America and South America. For example, the Union of South American Nations (UNASUR), modelled after the EU, was formed in 2004 and formalised by a constitutional treaty in 2008. Consisting of 12 countries, UNASUR makes up the largest trading bloc after NAFTA and the EU, with a population of more than 387 million and a combined economy of more than €3.6 trillion. Similar to NAFTA and the EU, UNASUR aims to eliminate all tariffs between nations by 2019.[14]

Each nation has unique features that must be understood. A nation's readiness for different products and services and its attractiveness as a market to foreign firms depend on its economic, political-legal and cultural environments.

Economic environment

The international marketer must study each country's economy. Two economic factors reflect the country's attractiveness as a market: its industrial structure and its income distribution.

The country's industrial structure shapes its product and service needs, income levels and employment levels. The four types of industrial structures are as follows:

- *Subsistence economies.* In a subsistence economy, the vast majority of people engage in simple agriculture. They consume most of their output and barter the rest for simple goods and services. These economies offer few market opportunities. Many African countries fall into this category.
- *Raw material exporting economies.* These economies are rich in one or more natural resources but poor in other ways. Much of their revenue comes from exporting these resources. Some examples are Chile (tin and copper) and the Democratic Republic of the Congo (copper, cobalt and coffee). These countries are good markets for large equipment, tools and supplies and trucks. If there are many foreign residents and a wealthy upper class, they are also a market for luxury goods.
- *Emerging economies (industrialising economies).* In an emerging economy, fast growth in manufacturing results in rapid overall economic growth. Examples include the BRIC countries – Brazil, Russia, India and China. As manufacturing increases, the country needs more imports of raw textile materials, steel and heavy machinery, and fewer imports of finished textiles, paper products and automobiles. Industrialisation typically creates a new rich class and a growing middle class, both demanding new types of imported goods. As more developed markets stagnate and become increasingly competitive, many marketers are now targeting growth opportunities in emerging markets.

- *Industrial economies.* Industrial economies are major exporters of manufactured goods, services and investment funds. They trade goods among themselves and also export them to other types of economies for raw materials and semi-finished goods. The varied manufacturing activities of these industrial nations and their large middle class make them rich markets for all sorts of goods. Examples include the United States, Japan and Norway

The second economic factor is the country's income distribution. Industrialised nations may have low-, medium- and high-income households. In contrast, countries with subsistence economies consist mostly of households with very low family incomes. Still other countries may have households with either very low or very high incomes. Even poor or emerging economies may be attractive markets for all kinds of goods. These days, companies in a wide range of industries – from cars to computers to food – are increasingly targeting even low and middle-income consumers in emerging economies.

For example, consider Brazil, now the world's sixth-largest economy. Thanks to historically low unemployment, rising wages and an influx of foreign direct investment, Brazil's consumer markets are soaring. Brazil's exploding middle class has grown by 40 million in just the past five years. Until recently, marketers have typically targeted consumers in Brazil's wealthiest, most-populated and easiest-to-reach areas, such as Sao Paulo, Brazil's richest state. However, as competition stiffens in more accessible and affluent regions, companies are now turning their attention to middle and lower-income consumers in other areas of the country.

Brazil's north-east region is its poorest, and many residents there lack access to basics such as roads and running water. With more mouths to feed in every household, north-eastern Brazilian consumers are also sticklers for low prices. But as it happens, north-east Brazil is also the region with the greatest growth in household income. So marketers are finding innovative ways to meet the distribution challenges in regions like the north-east to capture the growing potential there. Consider Nestlé:[15]

> To tap the potential in less developed regions of Brazil, Nestlé developed its *'Ate voce'* ('Reaching you') programme, by which its reps go door-to-door with push carts – a method residents find very appealing – selling 'kits' full of dairy products, cookies, yogurt and desserts. More than just selling products, these Nestlé vendors are trained to serve as nutrition consultants, helping customers to develop healthier diets. To serve consumers in north-east Brazil's Amazon River basin, which lacks a solid network of roads and highways, Nestlé has even launched a floating supermarket that takes goods directly to consumers. Setting sail from Belem, Brazil's biggest city along the Amazon, the boat serves 1.5 million consumers in 27 riverside towns with 300 different Nestlé products. It spends one day at each stop. Customers can check the floating store's schedule at nestleatevoce.com.br, call a toll-free number or text for more information and plan their shopping accordingly. This and other innovative Ate voce marketing initiatives are paying off for Nestlé. 'Demand for our products has more than doubled in the north and north-east compared to other Brazilian regions,' says Nestlé's marketing manager in Brazil.

Political-legal environment

Nations differ greatly in their political-legal environments. In considering whether to do business in a given country, a company should consider factors such as the country's attitudes toward international buying, government bureaucracy, political stability and monetary regulations.

Some nations are very receptive to foreign firms; others are less accommodating. For example, India has tended to bother foreign businesses with import quotas, currency restrictions, and other limitations that make operating there a challenge. In contrast, neighbouring Asian countries, such as Singapore and Thailand, court foreign investors and shower them with incentives and favourable operating conditions. Political and regulatory stability is another issue. For example, Russia is consumed by corruption and governmental red tape, which the government finds difficult to control, increasing the risk of doing business there. Although most international marketers still find the Russian market attractive, the corrupt climate will affect how they handle business and financial matters.[16]

Companies must also consider a country's monetary regulations. Sellers want to take their profits in a currency of value to them. Ideally, the buyer can pay in the seller's currency or in other world currencies. Short of this, sellers might accept a blocked currency – one whose removal from the country is restricted by the buyer's government – if they can buy other goods in that country that they need or can sell elsewhere for a needed currency. In addition to currency limits, a changing exchange rate also creates high risks for the seller.

Most international trade involves cash transactions. Yet many nations have too little hard currency to pay for their purchases from other countries. They may want to pay with other items instead of cash. Barter involves the direct exchange of goods or services. For example, Venezuela regularly barters oil, which it produces in surplus quantities, for food on the international market – rice from Guyana; coffee from El Salvador; sugar, coffee, meat and more from Nicaragua; and beans and pasta from the Dominican Republic. Venezuela has even struck a deal to supply oil to Cuba in exchange for Cuban doctors and medical care for Venezuelans.[17]

Cultural environment

Each country has its own folkways, norms and taboos. When designing global marketing strategies, companies must understand how culture affects consumer reactions in each of its world markets. In turn, they must also understand how their strategies affect local cultures.

The impact of culture on marketing strategy

Sellers must understand the ways that consumers in different countries think about and use certain products before planning a marketing programme. There are often surprises. For example, the average French man uses almost twice as many cosmetics and grooming aids as his wife. The Germans and the French eat more packaged, branded spaghetti than Italians do. Some 49 per cent of Chinese eat on the way to work. Most American women let down their hair and take off makeup at bedtime, whereas 15 per cent of Chinese women style their hair at bedtime and 11 per cent put on makeup.[18]

Companies that ignore cultural norms and differences can make some very expensive and embarrassing mistakes. Here are two examples:

Nike inadvertently offended Chinese officials when it ran an ad featuring LeBron James crushing a number of culturally revered Chinese figures in a kung fu themed television ad. The Chinese government found that the ad violated regulations to uphold national dignity and respect the 'motherland's culture' and yanked the multimillion-euro campaign. With egg on its face, Nike released a formal apology. Burger King made a similar mistake when it created in-store ads in Spain showing Hindu goddess Lakshmi atop a ham sandwich with the caption 'a snack that is sacred'. Cultural and religious groups worldwide objected strenuously – Hindus are vegetarian. Burger King apologised and pulled the ads.[19]

Business norms and behaviours also vary from country to country. For example, American executives like to get right down to business and engage in fast and tough face-to-face bargaining. However, Japanese and other Asian businesspeople often find this behaviour offensive. They prefer to start with polite conversation, and they rarely say no in face-to-face conversations. As another example, firm handshakes are a common and expected greeting in most Western

Overlooking cultural differences can result in embarrassing mistakes. China imposed a nationwide ban on this 'blasphemous' kung fu-themed television ad featuring LeBron James crushing a number of culturally revered Chinese figures.

Source: Mike Clarke/AFP/Getty Images

countries; in some Middle Eastern countries, however, handshakes might be refused if offered. Microsoft founder Bill Gates once set off a flurry of international controversy when he shook the hand of South Korea's president with his right hand while keeping his left hand in his pocket, something that Koreans consider highly disrespectful. In some countries, when being entertained at a meal, not finishing all the food implies that it was somehow substandard. In other countries, in contrast, wolfing down every last bite might be taken as a mild insult, suggesting that the host didn't supply enough.[20] Business executives need to understand these kinds of cultural nuances before conducting business in another country.

By the same token, companies that understand cultural nuances can use them to their advantage in the global markets. For example, furniture retailer IKEA's stores are a big draw for up-and-coming Chinese consumers. But IKEA has learned that customers in China want a lot more from its stores then just affordable Scandinavian-designed furniture:[21]

> In Chinese, IKEA is known as Yi Jia. Translated, it means 'comfortable home', a concept taken literally by the millions of consumers who visit one of IKEA's 15 huge Chinese stores each year. 'Customers come on family outings, hop into display beds and nap, pose for snapshots with the décor, and hang out for hours to enjoy the air conditioning and free soda refills,' notes one observer. On a typical Saturday afternoon, for example, display beds and other furniture in a huge Chinese IKEA store are occupied, with customers of all ages lounging or even fast asleep. One Chinese IKEA has even hosted several weddings. IKEA managers encourage such behaviour, figuring that familiarity with the store will result in later purchasing when shoppers' incomes eventually rise to match their aspirations. 'Maybe if you've been visiting IKEA, eating meatballs, hot dogs, or ice cream for ten years, then maybe you will consider IKEA when you get yourself a sofa,' says the company's Asia-Pacific president. Thanks to such cultural understandings, IKEA already captures about 7 per cent of the surging Chinese home-furnishings market, and its sales in China increased 17 per cent last year. What do Chinese consumers think of Swedish meatballs? 'They love them,' says IKEA China's marketing director.

Thus, understanding cultural traditions, preferences and behaviours can help companies not only avoid embarrassing mistakes but also take advantage of cross-cultural opportunities.

The impact of marketing strategy on cultures

Whereas marketers worry about the impact of global cultures on their marketing strategies, others may worry about the impact of marketing strategies on global cultures. For example, social critics contend that large American multinationals, such as McDonald's, Coca-Cola, Starbucks, Nike, Google, Disney and Facebook, aren't just globalising their brands; they are Americanising the world's cultures. Other elements of American culture have become pervasive worldwide:[22]

> There are now as many people studying English in China (or playing basketball, for that matter) as there are people in the United States. Seven of the ten most watched TV shows around the world are American, *Avatar* is the top-grossing film of all time in China, and the world is as fixated on US brands as ever, which is why US multinationals from McDonald's to Nike book more than half their revenues overseas. If you bring together teenagers from Nigeria, Sweden, South Korea and Argentina – to pick a random foursome – what binds these kids together in some kind of community is American culture – music, Hollywood fare, electronic games, Google and American consumer brands. The only thing they will likely have in common that doesn't revolve around the United States is an interest in soccer. The . . . rest of the world is becoming [ever more] like America – in ways good and bad.

'Today, globalisation often wears Mickey Mouse ears, eats Big Macs, drinks Coke or Pepsi, and does its computing with Windows,' says Thomas Friedman in his book *The Lexus and the Olive Tree: Understanding Globalization*. 'Some Chinese kids' first English word [is] Mickey,' notes another writer.[23]

Critics worry that, under such 'McDomination', countries around the globe are losing their individual cultural identities. Teens in India watch MTV and ask their parents for more Westernised clothes and other symbols of American pop culture and values. Grandmothers in small European villas no longer spend each morning visiting local meat, bread and produce markets to gather the ingredients for dinner. Instead, they now shop at American Supercentres. Women in Saudi Arabia see American films and question their societal roles. In China, most people didn't drink coffee before Starbucks entered the market. Now Chinese consumers rush to Starbucks stores 'because it's a symbol of a new kind of lifestyle'. Similarly, in China, where McDonald's operates more than 80 restaurants in Beijing alone, nearly half of all children identify the chain as a domestic brand.

Such concerns have sometimes led to a backlash against American globalisation. Well-known US brands have become the targets of boycotts and protests in some international markets. As symbols of American capitalism, companies such as Coca-Cola, McDonald's, Nike and KFC have been singled out by anti-globalisation protestors in hot spots around the world, especially when anti-American sentiment peaks.

Despite such problems, defenders of globalisation argue that concerns of Americanisation and the potential damage to American brands are overblown. US brands are doing very well internationally. In the most recent Millward Brown BrandZ brand value survey of global consumer brands, 20 of the top 25 global brands were American owned, including megabrands such as Google, Apple, IBM, Microsoft, McDonald's, Coca-Cola, GE, Amazon.com and Walmart.[24]

Many iconic American brands are soaring globally. For example, Chinese consumers appear to have an insatiable appetite for Apple iPhones and iPads. When Apple introduced its latest iPhone model in China recently, demand was so heavy that the company had to abandon sales in some Beijing stores to avert the threat of rioting by mobs of eager consumers. Similarly, many international markets covet American fast food. For instance, on the day that KFC introduced its outrageous Double Down sandwich – bacon, melted cheese and a 'secret sauce' between two deep-fried chicken patties – in one of its restaurants in Japan, fans formed long lines and slept on the sidewalks outside to get a taste. 'It was like the iPhone,' says the CMO of KFC International, 'people [were] crazy'. The US limited-time item generated substantial online buzz and has since become a runaway success worldwide, from Canada to Australia, the Philippines and Malaysia.[25] Iconic American drinks are also pervasive:

> It's lunchtime in Tehran's tiny northern suburbs, and around the crowded tables at Nayeb Restaurant, elegant Iranian women in Jackie O sunglasses and designer jeans let their table chatter glide effortlessly between French, English, and their native Farsi. The only visual clues that these lunching ladies aren't dining at some smart New York City eatery but in the heart of Washington's axis of evil are the expensive Hermès scarves covering their blonde-tipped hair in deference to the mullahs. And the drink of choice? This being revolutionary Iran, where alcohol is banned, the women are making do with Coca-Cola. Yes, Coca-Cola. It's a hard fact for some of Iran's theocrats to swallow. They want Iranians to shun 'Great Satan' brands like Coke and Pepsi, and the Iranian government has recently pressured Iranian soft drink companies to clarify their 'ties with the Zionist company Coca-Cola'. Yet Coke and Pepsi have grabbed about half the national soft drink sales in Iran, one of the Middle East's biggest drink markets. 'I joke with customers not to buy this stuff because it's American,' says a Tehran storekeeper, 'but they don't care. That only makes them want to buy it more.'[26]

More fundamentally, the cultural exchange goes both ways: America gets as well as gives cultural influence. True, Hollywood dominates the global movie market, but British TV originated the programming that was Americanised into such hits as *The Office*, *House of Cards*, *American Idol* and *Dancing with the Stars*. Although Chinese and Russian youth are donning NBA superstar jerseys, the increasing popularity of soccer in America has deep international roots. American kids are similarly wearing the football strips of Barcelona, Liverpool and Inter Milan. Even American childhood has been increasingly influenced by European and Asian cultural imports. Most kids know all about Hello Kitty, the Bakugan Battle Brawler, or any of a host of Nintendo or Sega game characters. And J. K. Rowling's so-very-British Harry Potter books have shaped the thinking of a generation of American youngsters, not to mention the millions of American oldsters who've fallen under their spell as well. For the moment, English remains the dominant language of the Internet, and having web access often means that third-world youth have greater exposure to American popular culture. Yet these same technologies let Eastern European students studying in the United States hear Webcast news and music from Poland, Romania or Belarus.

Thus, globalisation is a two-way street. If globalisation has Mickey Mouse ears, it is also wearing a French beret, talking on a Nokia mobile phone, buying furniture at IKEA, driving a Toyota Camry and watching England play cricket on a Samsung plasma TV.

DECIDING WHETHER TO GO GLOBAL

Not all companies need to venture into international markets to survive. For example, most local businesses need to market well only in their local marketplaces. Operating domestically is easier and safer. Managers don't need to learn another country's language and laws. They don't have to deal with unstable currencies, face political and legal uncertainties, or redesign their products to suit different customer expectations. However, companies that operate in global industries, where their strategic positions in specific markets are affected strongly by their overall global positions, must compete on a regional or worldwide basis to succeed.

Any of several factors might draw a company into the international arena. For example, global competitors might attack the company's home market by offering better products or lower prices. The company might want to counterattack these competitors in their home markets to tie up their resources. The company's customers might be expanding abroad and require international servicing. Or, most likely, international markets might simply provide better opportunities for growth. For example, as we discovered in the story at the start of the chapter, Coca-Cola has emphasised international growth in recent years to offset stagnant or declining US soft drink sales. Today, non-domestic sales account for 60 per cent of Coca-Cola's total revenues and 81 per cent of its earnings, and the company is making major pushes into 90 emerging markets, such as China, India and the entire African continent.[27]

Before going abroad, the company must weigh several risks and answer many questions about its ability to operate globally. Can the company learn to understand the preferences and buyer behaviour of consumers in other countries? Can it offer competitively attractive products? Will it be able to adapt to other countries' business cultures and deal effectively with foreign nationals? Do the company's managers have the necessary international experience? Has management considered the impact of regulations and the political environments of other countries?

Entering the Chinese market (the biggest toothpaste market) was central to P&G's strategy for the brand.
Source: Zhang Peng/LightRocket via Getty Images

DECIDING WHICH MARKETS TO ENTER

Before going abroad, the company should try to define its international marketing objectives and policies. It should decide what volume of foreign sales it wants. Most companies start small when they go abroad. Some plan to stay small, seeing international sales as a small part of their business. Other companies have bigger plans, however, seeing international business as equal to – or even more important than – their domestic business.

The company also needs to choose in how many countries it wants to market. Companies must be careful not to spread themselves too thin or expand beyond their capabilities by operating in too many countries too soon. Next, the company needs to decide on the types of countries to enter. A country's attractiveness depends on the product, geographical factors, income and population, political climate, among other considerations. In recent years, many major new markets have emerged, offering both substantial opportunities and daunting challenges.

After listing possible international markets, the company must carefully evaluate each one. It must consider many factors. For example, Netflix's decision to expand into European markets such as Germany, France, Italy and Spain seems like a no-brainer. Netflix needs to grow its subscriber base to cover rapidly rising content costs, and Europe offers huge opportunities. Western Europe boasts 134 million broadband homes, compared with 88 million in the United States. The as-yet-largely-untapped European video-services market is expected to grow by 67 per cent to more than €0.86 billion by 2017. Netflix has already entered the UK and the Nordic nations, and is the leading video service in Sweden after only two years.[28]

However, as Netflix considers expanding into new European markets, it must ask some important questions. Can it compete effectively on a country-by-country basis with local competitors? Can it master the varied cultural and buying differences of European consumers? Will it be able to meet environmental and regulatory hurdles in each country? For example, Netflix's expansion has been slow and difficult in Latin America, where e-commerce is less established.

In entering new European markets, Netflix will face many challenges. For example, Europe is now crowded with formidable competitors. More than a dozen local Netflix-like rivals have sprung up there during the past few years – services such as Snap in Germany, Infinity in Italy and CanalPlay in France have been busy locking in subscribers and content rights. And Amazon's Lovefilm is already the leading streaming service in Germany.

Content is another major consideration. Although Netflix is building its own portfolio of international content rights, European competitors already own exclusive in-country rights to many popular US and non-US shows. Netflix may also encounter local regulatory obstacles. Regulations in France, for instance, restrict services like Netflix from airing films until three years after they open nationally in theatres, and video services there are usually required to invest in film production in the country. Despite these challenges, however, Netflix CEO Reed Hastings seems unfazed. 'We can still build a very successful business [in these new markets],' he says. Wherever Netflix goes, 'I think the key is having unique content, a great reputation, a good value proposition,' things at which Netflix excels.

Possible global markets should be ranked on several factors, including market size, market growth, the cost of doing business, competitive advantage and risk level. The goal is to determine the potential of each market, using indicators such as those shown in Table 19.1. Then the marketer must decide which markets offer the greatest long-run return on investment.

Author comment

A company has many options for entering an international market, from simply exporting its products to working jointly with foreign companies to setting up its own foreign-based operations.

DECIDING HOW TO ENTER THE MARKET

Once a company has decided to sell in a foreign country, it must determine the best mode of entry. Its choices are *exporting, joint venturing* and *direct investment*. Figure 19.2 shows the three market entry strategies, along with the options each one offers. As the figure shows, each succeeding strategy involves more commitment and risk but also more control and potential profits.

Exporting

The simplest way to enter a foreign market is through exporting. The company may passively export its surpluses from time to time, or it may make an active commitment to expand exports to a particular market. In either case, the company produces all its goods in its home country. It

Table 19.1 Indicators of market potential

Demographic characteristics	Sociocultural factors
Education Population size and growth Population age composition	Consumer lifestyles, beliefs and values Business norms and approaches Cultural and social norms Languages
Geographic characteristics	**Political and legal factors**
Climate Country size Population density – urban, rural Transportation structure and market accessibility	National priorities Political stability Government attitudes toward global trade Government bureaucracy Monetary and trade regulations
Economic factors	
GDP size and growth Income distribution Industrial infrastructure Natural resources Financial and human resources	

Figure 19.2 Market entry strategies

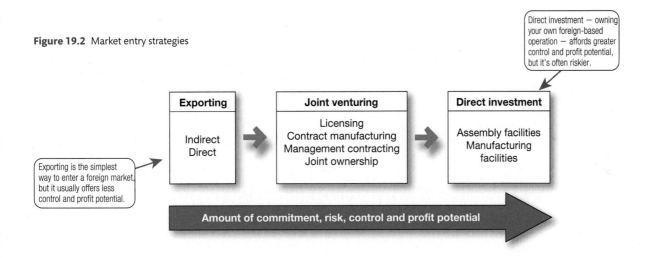

may or may not modify them for the export market. **Exporting** involves the least change in the company's product lines, organisation, investments or mission.

Companies typically start with *indirect exporting*, working through independent international marketing intermediaries. Indirect exporting involves less investment because the firm does not require an overseas marketing organisation or network. It also involves less risk. International marketing intermediaries bring know-how and services to the relationship, so the seller normally makes fewer mistakes. Sellers may eventually move into direct exporting, whereby they handle their own exports. The investment and risk are somewhat greater in this strategy, but so is the potential return.

Exporting—Entering foreign markets by selling goods produced in the company's home country, often with little modification.

Joint venturing

A second method of entering a foreign market is by **joint venturing** – joining with foreign companies to produce or market products or services. Joint venturing differs from exporting in that the company joins with a host country partner to sell or market abroad. It differs from direct investment in that an association is formed with someone in the foreign country. There are four types of joint ventures: *licensing, contract manufacturing, management contracting* and *joint ownership*.

Licensing

Licensing is a simple way for a manufacturer to enter international marketing. The company enters into an agreement with a licensee in the foreign market. For a fee or royalty payments, the licensee buys the right to use the company's manufacturing process, trademark, patent, trade secret or other item of value. The company thus gains entry into a foreign market at little risk; at the same time, the licensee gains production expertise or a well-known product or name without having to start from scratch.

In Japan, Budweiser beer flows from Kirin breweries, and Mizkan produces Sunkist lemon juice, drinks and dessert items. Tokyo Disney Resort is owned and operated by Oriental Land Company under license from The Walt Disney Company. The 45-year licence gives Disney licensing fees plus a percentage of admissions and food and merchandise sales. And Coca-Cola markets internationally by licensing bottlers around the world and supplying them with the syrup needed to produce the product. Its global bottling partners range from the Coca-Cola Bottling Company of Saudi Arabia to Europe-based Coca-Cola Hellenic, which bottles and markets 136 Coca-Cola brands to 585 million people in 28 countries, from Italy and Greece to Nigeria and Russia.[29]

Licensing has potential disadvantages, however. The firm has less control over the licensee than it would over its own operations. Furthermore, if the licensee is very successful, the firm has given up these profits, and if and when the contract ends, it may find it has created a competitor.

Contract manufacturing

Another option is **contract manufacturing**, in which the company makes agreements with manufacturers in the foreign market to produce its product or provide its service. For example, P&G serves 650 million consumers across India with the help of nine contract manufacturing sites there. And Volkswagen contracts with Russia's largest auto manufacturer, GAZ Group, to make Volkswagen Jettas for the Russian market, as well as its Škoda (VW's Czech Republic subsidiary) Octavia and Yeti models sold there.[30] The drawbacks of contract manufacturing are decreased control over the manufacturing process and loss of potential profits on manufacturing. The benefits are the chance to start faster, with less risk, and the later opportunity either to form a partnership with or buy out the local manufacturer. Contract manufacturing can also reduce plant investment, transportation and tariff costs, while at the same time helping to meet the host country's local manufacturing requirements.

Management contracting

Under **management contracting**, the domestic firm provides the management knowhow to a foreign company that supplies the capital. In other words, the domestic firm exports management services rather than products. Hilton uses this arrangement in managing hotels around the world. For example, the hotel chain operates DoubleTree by Hilton hotels in countries ranging from the UK and Italy to Peru and Costa Rica, to China, Russia and Tanzania. The properties are locally owned, but Hilton manages the hotels with its world-renowned hospitality expertise.[31]

Management contracting is a low-risk method of getting into a foreign market, and it yields income from the beginning. The arrangement is even more attractive if the contracting firm has an option to buy some share in the managed company later on. The arrangement is not sensible, however, if the company can put its scarce management talent to better uses or if it can make greater profits by undertaking the whole venture. Management contracting also prevents the company from setting up its own operations for a period of time.

Joint ownership

Joint ownership ventures consist of one company joining forces with foreign investors to create a local business in which they share possession and control. A company may buy an interest in a local firm, or the two parties may form a new business venture. Joint ownership may be needed for economic or political reasons. For example, the firm may lack the financial, physical or managerial resources to undertake the venture alone. Alternatively, a foreign government may require joint ownership as a condition for entry.

Often, companies form joint ownership ventures to merge their complementary strengths in developing a global marketing opportunity. For example, Chrysler's parent company, Fiat, recently formed a 50/50 joint venture with Chinese state-run Guangzhou Automobile Group (GAC) to produce Jeep vehicles in China. Jeep was one of the first Western auto brands sold in China, and the brand is well recognised and popular there. However, all of the Jeeps sold in China have been imported from the United States and are subject to steep 25 per cent import tariffs, driving Jeep prices to sky-high levels. For example, before the joint venture, a top-of-the-line Jeep Grand Cherokee sold for as much as €180,000 in China, more than triple its US price. Under the joint venture, once approved, Chrysler and GAC will partner to produce Jeeps in China, avoiding tariffs, reducing production costs and allowing competitive Jeep prices in the world's largest automotive market.[32]

Joint ownership has certain drawbacks, however. The partners may disagree over investment, marketing or other policies. Whereas many EU firms like to reinvest earnings for growth, local firms often prefer to take out these earnings; whereas EU firms emphasise the role of marketing, local investors may rely on selling.

Direct investment

The biggest involvement in a foreign market comes through **direct investment** – the development of foreign-based assembly or manufacturing facilities. For example, Ford has made more than €3.13 billion in direct investments in several Asian countries, including India, China and Thailand. It built its second facility in India, a €0.90 billion state-of-the-art manufacturing and engineering plant that will produce 240,000 cars a year, helping to satisfy Ford's burgeoning demand in India and other Asian and African markets. Similarly, Honda and Toyota have made substantial direct manufacturing investments in North America. For example, 90 per cent of the Honda and Acura models sold in the United States are made in North America. 'Our fundamental philosophy is to produce where we sell,' says a Honda executive.[33]

If a company has gained experience in exporting and if the foreign market is large enough, foreign production facilities offer many advantages. The firm may have lower costs in the form of cheaper labour or raw materials, foreign government investment incentives and freight savings. The firm may also improve its image in the host country because it creates jobs. Generally, a firm

Joint ownership—A cooperative venture in which a company creates a local business with investors in a foreign market, who share ownership and control.

Direct investment—Entering a foreign market by developing foreign-based assembly or manufacturing facilities.

Honda makes most of the cars it sells in the USA in North America.

Source: Peter Titmuss/Alamy Images

develops a deeper relationship with the government, customers, local suppliers and distributors, allowing it to adapt its products to the local market better. Finally, the firm keeps full control over the investment and therefore can develop manufacturing and marketing policies that serve its long-term international objectives.

The main disadvantage of direct investment is that the firm faces many risks, such as restricted or devalued currencies, falling markets, or government changes. In some cases, a firm has no choice but to accept these risks if it wants to operate in the host country.

DECIDING ON THE GLOBAL MARKETING PROGRAMME

Author comment

The major global marketing decision usually boils down to this: How much, if at all, should a company adapt its marketing strategy and programmes to local markets? How might the answer differ for Boeing versus McDonald's?

Companies that operate in one or more foreign markets must decide how much, if at all, to adapt their marketing strategies and programmes to local conditions. At one extreme are global companies that use **standardised global marketing**, essentially using the same marketing strategy approaches and marketing mix worldwide. At the other extreme is **adapted global marketing**. In this case, the producer adjusts the marketing strategy and mix elements to each target market, resulting in more costs but hopefully producing a larger market share and return.

The question of whether to adapt or standardise the marketing strategy and programme has been much debated over the years. On the one hand, some global marketers believe that technology is making the world a smaller place, and consumer needs around the world are becoming more similar. This paves the way for global brands and standardised global marketing. Global branding and standardisation, in turn, result in greater brand power and reduced costs from economies of scale.

Standardised global marketing—An international marketing strategy that basically uses the same marketing strategy and mix in all of the company's international markets.

Adapted global marketing—An international marketing approach that adjusts the marketing strategy and mix elements to each international target market, which creates more costs but hopefully produces a larger market share and return.

On the other hand, the marketing concept holds that marketing programmes will be more engaging if tailored to the unique needs of each targeted customer group. If this concept applies within a country, it should apply even more across international markets. Despite global convergence, consumers in different countries still have widely varied cultural backgrounds. They still differ significantly in their needs and wants, spending power, product preferences and shopping patterns. Because these differences are hard to change, most marketers today adapt their products, prices, channels and promotions to fit consumer desires in each country. However, global standardisation is not an all-or-nothing proposition. It's a matter of degree. Most international marketers suggest that companies should 'think globally but act locally'. They should seek a balance between standardisation and adaptation, leveraging global brand recognition but adapting their marketing, products and operations to specific markets. For example, cosmetics giant L'Oréal and its brands are truly global. But the company's outstanding international success comes from achieving a global–local balance that adapts and differentiates brands to make them responsive to local needs while integrating them across world markets to optimise their global impact.

Collectively, local brands still account for the overwhelming majority of consumer purchases. Most consumers, wherever they live, lead very local lives. So a global brand must engage consumers at a local level, respecting the culture and becoming a part of it. Starbucks operates this way. The company's overall brand strategy provides global strategic direction. Then regional or local units focus on adapting the strategy and brand to specific local markets. For example, when Starbucks entered China in 1998, given the strong local traditions and culture, a tailored approach was needed:[34]

Starbucks' success in China results from building on its global brand identity and values while at the same time adapting its brand strategy to the unique characteristics of Chinese consumers. Rather than forcing US products on the Chinese, Starbucks developed new flavours – such as green-tea-flavoured coffee drinks – that appeal to local tastes. Rather than just charging US-style premium prices in China, Starbucks boosted prices even higher, positioning the brand as a status symbol for the rapidly growing Chinese middle and upper classes. And rather than pushing take-out orders, which account for most of its US revenues, Starbucks promoted dine-in services – making its stores the perfect meeting place for Chinese professionals and their friends. Whereas US locations do about 70 per cent of their business before 10 am, China stores do more than 70 per cent of their business in the afternoon and evening. Under this adapted strategy, Starbucks China is thriving. China is now Starbucks' largest market outside of the United States, with more than 1,000 current stores and 1,600 stores in 70 cities planned by the end of 2015. 'We're trying to build a different kind of company in China and are mindful of how we grow while maintaining the heart and soul of what Starbucks stands for,' says the president of Starbucks China.

Product

Five strategies are used for adapting product and marketing communication strategies to a global market (see Figure 19.3).[35] We first discuss the three product strategies and then turn to the two communication strategies.

Straight product extension means marketing a product in a foreign market without making any changes to the product. Top management tells its marketing people, 'Take the product as is and find customers for it.' The first step, however, should be to find out whether foreign consumers use that product and what form they prefer.

Straight extension has been successful in some cases and disastrous in others. Apple iPads, Gillette razors and Bosch tools are all sold successfully in about the same form around the world. But when General Foods introduced its standard powdered JELL-O in the British market, it discovered that British consumers prefer a solid wafer or cake form. Likewise, Philips began to make a profit in Japan only after it reduced the size of its coffeemakers to fit into smaller Japanese kitchens and its shavers to fit smaller Japanese hands. And Panasonic's refrigerator sales in China surged ten-fold in a single year after it shaved the width of its appliances by 15 per cent to fit smaller Chinese kitchens.[36] Straight extension is tempting because it involves no additional product development costs, manufacturing changes or new promotion. But it can be costly in the long run if products fail to satisfy consumers in specific global markets.

Product adaptation involves changing the product to meet local requirements, conditions or wants. For example, McDonald's operates in 118 countries, with sometimes widely varying local food preferences. So although you'll find its signature burgers and fries in most locations around the world, the chain has added menu items that meet the unique taste buds of customers in local markets. McDonald's serves salmon burgers in Norway, mashed-potato burgers in China, shrimp burgers in Japan, a Samurai Pork Burger in Thailand, chicken porridge in Malaysia, and Spam and eggs in Hawaii. In a German McDonald's, you'll find the Nurnburger (three large bratwurst on a soft roll with lots of mustard, of course); in Israel, there's the McFalafel (chickpea fritters, tomatoes, cucumber and cheese topped with tahini and wrapped in lafa). And menus in Turkey feature a chocolate orange fried pie (Brazil adds banana, Egypt taro and Hawaii pineapple).

Straight product extension—
Marketing a product in a foreign market without making any changes to the product.

Product adaptation—
Adapting a product to meet local conditions or wants in foreign markets.

Figure 19.3 Five global product and communications strategies

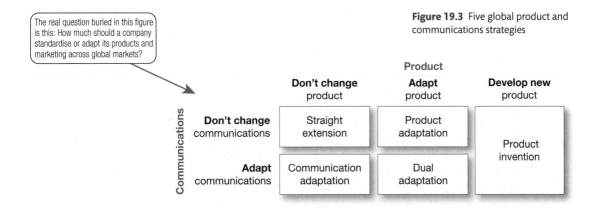

The real question buried in this figure is this: How much should a company standardise or adapt its products and marketing across global markets?

In many major global markets, McDonald's adapts more than just its menu. It also adjusts its restaurant design and operations. For example, McDonald's France has redefined itself as a French company that adapts to the needs and preferences of French consumers:[37]

> 'France – the land of haute cuisine, fine wine and cheese – would be the last place you would expect to find a thriving [McDonald's],' opines one observer. Yet the fast-food giant has turned France into its second-most profitable world market. Although a McDonald's in Paris might at first seem a lot like one in Chicago, McDonald's has carefully adapted its French operations to the preferences of local customers. At the most basic level, although a majority of revenues still come from burgers and fries, McDonald's France has changed its menu to please the French palate. For instance, it offers up burgers with French cheeses such as chevre, cantal and bleu, topped off with whole-grain French mustard sauce. And French consumers love baguettes, so McDonald's bakes them fresh in its restaurants and sells them in oh-so-French McBaguette sandwiches.

But perhaps the biggest difference isn't in the food, but in the design of the restaurants themselves, which have been adapted to suit French lifestyles. For example, French meal times tend to be longer, with more food consumed per sitting. So McDonald's has refined its restaurant interiors to create a comfortable, welcoming environment where customers want to linger and perhaps order an additional coffee or dessert. McDonald's even provides table-side service. As a result, the average French McDonald's customer spends about four times what an American customer spends per visit.

Product invention consists of creating something new to meet the needs of consumers in a given country. As markets have gone global, companies ranging from appliance manufacturers and carmakers to candy and soft drink producers have developed products that meet the special purchasing needs of low-income consumers in developing economies.

For example, Chinese appliance producer Haier developed sturdier washing machines for rural users in emerging markets, where it found that lighter-duty machines often became clogged with mud when farmers used them to clean vegetables as well as clothes. And solar lighting manufacturer d.light Solar has developed affordable solar-powered home lighting systems for the hundreds of millions of people in the developing world who don't have access to reliable power. d.light's hanging lamps and portable lanterns require no energy source other than the sun and can last up to 15 hours on one charge. The company has already reached 10 million users, is adding 1 million users per month, and plans to reach 100 million users by 2020.[38]

Product invention—Creating new products or services for foreign markets.

Promotion

Companies can either adopt the same communication strategy they use in the home market or change it for each local market. Consider advertising messages. Some global companies use a standardised advertising theme around the world. For example, Chevrolet recently swapped its previous, American-focused 'Chevy runs deep' positioning and advertising theme for a more global 'Find new roads' theme. The new theme is one 'that works in all markets,' says a GM marketing executive. 'The theme has meaning in mature markets like the US as well as emerging markets like Russia and India, where the potential for continued growth is the greatest.' The time is right for a more globally consistent Chevy brand message. Chevrolet sells cars in more than 140 countries, and nearly two-thirds of its sales are now outside the United States, compared with only about one-third a decade ago.[39]

Of course, even in highly standardised communications campaigns, some adjustments might be required for language and cultural differences. For example, ads for Pepsi's youthful 'Live for now' campaign have a similar look worldwide but are adapted in different global markets to feature local consumers, languages and events. Similarly, in Western markets, fast-casual clothing retailer H&M runs fashion ads with models showing liberal amounts of bare skin. But in the Middle East, where attitudes toward public nudity are more conservative, the retailer runs the same ads digitally adapted to better cover its models.

Global companies often have difficulty crossing the language barrier, with results ranging from mild embarrassment to outright failure. Seemingly innocuous brand names and advertising phrases can take on unintended or hidden meanings when translated into other languages. For example, Interbrand of London, the firm that created household names such as Prozac and Acura, recently developed a brand name 'hall of shame' list, which contained these and other foreign brand names you're never likely to see inside the local Kroger supermarket: Krapp toilet paper (Denmark), Plopp chocolate (Scandinavia), Crapsy Fruit cereal (France), Poo curry powder (Argentina) and Pschitt lemonade (France). Similarly, advertising themes often lose – or gain – something in the translation. In Chinese, the KFC slogan 'finger-lickin' good' came out as 'eat your fingers off'. And Motorola's Hellomoto ringtone sounds like 'Hello, Fatty' in India.

Marketers must be careful to avoid such mistakes, taking great care when localising their brand names and messages to specific global markets. In important but culturally different markets such as China, finding just the right name can make or break a brand.

Promotion should reflect the cultural differences of marketplaces.
Source: LILIAN WU/AFP/Getty Images

Communication adaptation—A global communication strategy of fully adapting advertising messages to local markets.

Rather than standardising their advertising globally, other companies follow a strategy of **communication adaptation**, fully adapting their advertising messages to local markets. For example, in the United States and most Western countries, where running is accepted as a positive, healthful activity, Nike advertising focuses on products and personal performance. In China, however, running is viewed as a boring sport, or even a punishment – something rigorous and painful. It's not something that most people in Asia's polluted cities choose to do, especially on streets jammed with pedestrians, bicycles, cars, and even rickshaws. 'The joke is that when there's a person running in the city (and it's often a Westerner), people turn to see who's chasing him,' quips one observer.

However, China is the largest footwear market in the world, offering huge untapped potential for Nike. So, in China, rather than pushing products and performance, Nike's advertising focuses on just trying to get more Chinese to put on running shoes. Ads and social media feature ordinary people who choose to run on city streets, letting them relate their reasons in their own words. 'I run to make the hidden visible,' says one young woman. 'I run to get lost,' says another. Salad – a stressed-out office worker who lives and runs in Shanghai – relates: 'The city is always noisy and busy. This adds even more pressure to my day. I guess for me, running is about shutting down the noise.' To make running a more social activity, Nike also sponsors night-time 'Lunar runs' in big cities like Beijing and marathons in Shanghai, featuring fitness instructors, live music and celebrities to introduce Chinese students and young professionals to running as a fun and rewarding after-class or after-work activity. The goal is to get more people to at least give running a try. But changing basic perceptions of the sport won't be easy. 'It's a very long road for us,' says a Nike China marketer.[40]

Media also need to be adapted internationally because media availability and regulations vary from country to country. TV advertising time is very limited in Europe, for instance, ranging from four hours a day in France to none in Scandinavian countries. Advertisers must buy time months in advance, and they have little control over airtimes. However, mobile phone ads are much more widely accepted in Europe and Asia than in the United States. Magazines also vary in effectiveness. For example, magazines are a major medium in Italy but a minor one in Austria. Newspapers are national in the United Kingdom but only local in Spain.[41]

Price

Companies also face many considerations in setting their international prices. For example, how might Makita price its power tools globally? It could set a uniform price globally, but this amount would be too high a price in poor countries and not high enough in rich ones. It could charge what consumers in each country would bear, but this strategy ignores differences in the actual costs from country to country. Finally, the company could use a standard mark-up of its costs everywhere, but this approach might price Makita out of the market in some countries where costs are high.

Regardless of how companies go about pricing their products, their foreign prices probably will be higher than their domestic prices for comparable products. An Apple iPad that sells for €350 in the United States goes for €480 in the United Kingdom. Why? Apple faces a *price escalation* problem. It must add the cost of transportation, tariffs, importer margin, wholesaler margin and retailer margin to its factory price. Depending on these added costs, a product may have to sell for two to five times as much in another country to make the same profit.

To overcome this problem when selling to less-affluent consumers in developing countries, many companies make simpler or smaller versions of their products that can be sold at lower prices. Others have introduced new, more affordable brands for global markets. For example, Google's Motorola division developed the ultra-cheap Moto G smartphone. Although not a flashy, high-tech gadget, the full-function device sells for only €140 in the United States with no contract. Google first introduced the phone in Brazil, one of the largest and fastest-growing emerging markets, then in other parts of South America, the Middle East, India and more of Asia. Intended primarily for emerging markets where consumers want low-cost phones, the Moto G may also sell well to cost-conscious consumers in major developed markets, such as the United States and Europe. Google's new phone puts pressure on Apple, which has focused on selling older models at reduced prices rather than developing cheaper models. 'The last few years have been about selling the top-of-the-line smartphones,' says one analyst. 'The next few years should be about selling a lower-cost version and welcoming in vast new numbers of subscribers.'[42]

Recent economic and technological forces have had an impact on global pricing. For example, the Internet is making global price differences more obvious. When firms sell their wares over the Internet, customers can see how much products sell for in different countries. They can even order a given product directly from the company location or dealer offering the lowest price. This is forcing companies toward more standardised international pricing.

Distribution channels

Whole-channel view—
Designing international channels that take into account the entire global supply chain and marketing channel, forging an effective global value delivery network.

An international company must take a **whole-channel view** of the problem of distributing products to final consumers. Figure 19.4 shows the two major links between the seller and the final buyer. The first link, *channels between nations*, moves company products from points of production to the borders of countries within which they are sold. The second link, *channels within nations*, moves products from their market entry points to the final consumers. The whole-channel view takes into account the entire global supply chain and marketing channel. It recognises that to compete well internationally, the company must effectively design and manage an entire *global value delivery network*.

Channels of distribution within countries vary greatly from nation to nation. There are large differences in the numbers and types of intermediaries serving each country market and in the transportation infrastructure serving these intermediaries. For example, whereas large-scale retail chains dominate the EU scene, most of the retailing in other countries is done by small, independent retailers. In India or Indonesia, millions of retailers operate tiny shops or sell in open markets.

Even in world markets containing similar types of sellers, retailing practices can vary widely. For example, you'll find plenty of Walmarts, Carrefours, Tescos and other retail superstores in major Chinese cities. But whereas consumer brands sold in such stores in Western markets rely largely on self-service, brands in China hire armies of uniformed in-store promoters – called 'promoter girls' or 'push girls' – to dispense samples and pitch their products person to person. In a Beijing Walmart, on any given weekend, you'll find 100 or more such promoters acquainting customers with products from Kraft, Unilever, P&G, Johnson & Johnson and a slew of local competitors. 'Chinese consumers know the brand name through media,' says the director of a Chinese retail marketing service, 'but they want to feel the product and get a detailed understanding before they make a purchase'.[43]

Figure 19.4 Whole-channel concept for international marketing

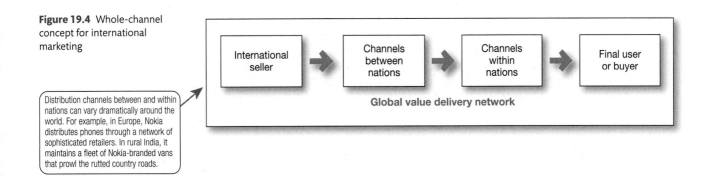

Distribution channels between and within nations can vary dramatically around the world. For example, in Europe, Nokia distributes phones through a network of sophisticated retailers. In rural India, it maintains a fleet of Nokia-branded vans that prowl the rutted country roads.

Global value delivery network

Similarly, as we learned in the chapter-opening story about its ventures in Africa, Coca-Cola adapts its distribution methods to meet local challenges in global markets. For example, in Montevideo, Uruguay, where larger vehicles are challenged by traffic, parking and pollution difficulties, Coca-Cola purchased 30 small, efficient, three-wheeled ZAP alternative transportation trucks. The little trucks average about one-fifth the fuel consumption and scoot around congested city streets with greater ease. In rural areas, Coca-Cola uses a manual delivery process. In China, an army of more than 10,000 Coca-Cola sales reps makes regular visits to small retailers, often on foot or bicycle. To reach the most isolated spots, the company even relies on teams of delivery donkeys. In Tanzania, 93 per cent of Coca-Cola's products are manually delivered via pushcarts and bicycles.[44]

DECIDING ON THE GLOBAL MARKETING ORGANISATION

Companies manage their international marketing activities in at least three different ways: most companies first organise an export department, then create an international division, and finally become a global organisation.

A firm normally gets into international marketing by simply shipping out its goods. If its international sales expand, the company will establish an *export department* with a sales manager and a few assistants. As sales increase, the export department can expand to include various marketing services so that it can actively go after business. If the firm moves into joint ventures or direct investment, the export department will no longer be adequate.

Many companies get involved in several international markets and ventures. A company may export to one country, license to another, have a joint ownership venture in a third and own a subsidiary in a fourth. Sooner or later it will create *international divisions* or subsidiaries to handle all its international activity.

International divisions are organised in a variety of ways. An international division's corporate staff consists of marketing, manufacturing, research, finance, planning and personnel specialists. It plans for and provides services to various operating units, which can be organised in one of three ways. They can be *geographical organisations*, with country managers who are responsible for salespeople, sales branches, distributors and licensees in their respective countries. Or the operating units can be *world product groups*, each responsible for worldwide sales of different product groups. Finally, operating units can be *international subsidiaries*, each responsible for their own sales and profits.

Many firms have passed beyond the international division stage and are truly *global organisations*. For example, consider Reckitt Benckiser (RB), a €11-billion European producer of household, health and personal care products and consumer goods with a stable full of familiar brands (Air Wick, Lysol, Woolite, Calgon, Mucinex, Clearasil, French's and many others – see www .rb.com):[45]

Author comment

Many large companies, regardless of their 'home country', now think of themselves as truly global organisations. They view the entire world as a single borderless market. For example, although headquartered in Chicago, Boeing is as comfortable selling planes to Lufthansa or Air China as to American Airlines.

RB products are sold in more than 200 markets across the world. Its top 400 managers represent 53 different nationalities. The company is headquartered in the United Kingdom and its CEO is Indian. Its US business is run by a Dutchman, its Russian business by an Italian, and its Australian business by a Brazilian. 'Most of our top managers . . . view themselves as global citizens rather than as citizens of any given nation,' says RB's chief executive officer.

RB recently relocated several of its operations to put key marketers in key countries within their regions. For example, it recently moved its Latin American headquarters from Miami to Sao Paulo, Brazil. The company has spent the past decade building a culture of global mobility because it thinks that's one of the best ways to generate new ideas and create global entrepreneurs. And it has paid off. Products launched in the past three years – all the result of global cross-fertilisation – account for 35–40 per cent of net revenue. Over the past few years, even during the economic downturn, the company has outperformed its rivals – P&G, Unilever and Colgate — in growth.

Global organisations don't think of themselves as national marketers that sell abroad but as global marketers. The top corporate management and staff plan worldwide manufacturing facilities, marketing policies, financial flows and logistical systems. The global operating units report directly to the chief executive or the executive committee of the organisation, not to the head of an international division. Executives are trained in worldwide operations, not just domestic *or* international operations. Global companies recruit management from many countries, buy components and supplies where they cost the least, and invest where the expected returns are greatest.

Today, major companies must become more global if they hope to compete. As foreign companies successfully invade their domestic markets, companies must move more aggressively into foreign markets. They will have to change from companies that treat their international operations as secondary to companies that view the entire world as a single borderless market.

OBJECTIVES REVIEW AND KEY TERMS

Companies today can no longer afford to pay attention only to their domestic market, regardless of its size. Many industries are global industries, and firms that operate globally achieve lower costs and higher brand awareness. At the same time, global marketing is risky because of variable exchange rates, unstable governments, tariffs and trade barriers, and several other factors. Given the potential gains and risks of international marketing, companies need a systematic way to make their global marketing decisions.

OBJECTIVE 1 Discuss how the international trade system and the economic, political–legal and cultural environments affect a company's international marketing decisions. (pp. 562–572)
A company must understand the *global marketing environment*, especially the international trade system. It should assess each foreign market's *economic*, *political-legal* and *cultural characteristics*. The company can then decide whether it wants to go abroad and consider the potential risks and benefits. It must decide on the volume of international sales it wants, how many countries it wants to market in, and which specific markets it wants to enter. These decisions call for weighing the probable returns against the level of risk.

OBJECTIVE 2 Describe three key approaches to entering international markets (pp. 572–576)
The company must decide how to enter each chosen market – whether through *exporting*, *joint venturing* or *direct investment*. Many companies start as exporters, move to joint ventures, and finally make a direct investment in foreign markets. In *exporting*, the company enters a foreign market by sending and selling products through international marketing intermediaries (indirect exporting) or the company's own department, branch or sales representatives or agents (direct exporting). When establishing a *joint venture*, a company enters foreign markets by joining with foreign companies to produce or market a product or service. In *licensing*, the company enters a foreign market by contracting with a licensee in the foreign market and offering the right to use a manufacturing process, trademark, patent, trade secret or other item of value for a fee or royalty.

OBJECTIVE 3 Explain how companies adapt their marketing strategies and mixes for international markets (pp. 576–581)
Companies must also decide how much their marketing strategies and their products, promotion, price and channels should be adapted for each foreign market. At one extreme, global

companies use *standardised global marketing* worldwide. Others use *adapted global marketing*, in which they adjust the marketing strategy and mix to each target market, bearing more costs but hoping for a larger market share and return. However, global standardisation is not an all-or-nothing proposition. It's a matter of degree. Most international marketers suggest that companies should 'think globally but act locally' – that they should seek a balance between globally standardised strategies and locally adapted marketing mix tactics.

OBJECTIVE 4 Identify the three major forms of international marketing organisation (pp. 581–582)
The company must develop an effective organisation for international marketing. Most firms start with an *export department* and graduate to an *international division*. A few become *global organisations*, with worldwide marketing planned and managed by the top officers of the company. Global organisations view the entire world as a single, borderless market.

NAVIGATING THE KEY TERMS

OBJECTIVE 1
Global firm (p. 563)
Economic community (p. 565)

OBJECTIVE 2
Exporting (p. 573)
Joint venturing (p. 574)
Licensing (p. 574)

Contract manufacturing (p. 574)
Management contracting (p. 574)
Joint ownership (p. 575)
Direct investment (p. 575)

OBJECTIVE 3
Standardised global marketing (p. 576)

Adapted global marketing (p. 576)
Straight product extension (p. 577)
Product adaptation (p. 577)
Product invention (p. 578)
Communication adaptation (p. 579)
Whole-channel view (p. 580)

DISCUSSION AND CRITICAL THINKING

Discussion questions

19-1 Explain what is meant by the term global firm and list the six major decisions involved in international marketing. (AACSB: Communication)

19-2 What is the World Trade Organisation? What is its purpose and what has it accomplished? (AACSB: Communication)

19-3 Name and define the four types of country industrial structures. (AACSB: Communication)

19-4 What factors do companies consider when deciding on possible global markets to enter? (AACSB: Communication; Reflective Thinking)

19-5 Discuss how companies manage their international marketing activities. (AACSB: Communication)

Critical-thinking exercises

19-6 Visit www.transparency.org and click on 'corruption perception index'. What is the most recent Corruption Perceptions Index (CPI) for the following countries:

Denmark, Jamaica, Malaysia, Myanmar, New Zealand, Somali and the United States? What are the implications of this index for European companies doing business in these countries? (AACSB: Communication; Use of IT; Reflective thinking)

19-7 What is a free trade zone? Give an example of a free trade zone and research how successful it has been. (AACSB: Communication; Reflective thinking)

19-8 One way to analyse the cultural differences among countries is to conduct a Hofstede analysis. Visit http://geert-hofstede.com/ to learn what this analysis considers. Develop a presentation explaining how three countries of your choice differ from the United States. (AACSB: Communication; Use of IT; Reflective thinking)

Mini-cases and applications

Online, mobile and social media: marketing Russian e-commerce

Russia is emerging as the next big e-commerce frontier with a population of 143 million, 60 million of whom are Internet users. Although online sales currently make up less than 2 per cent of retail sales in Russia, they are projected to increase to 5 per cent – that's €30 billion. That fact has caught the attention of global e-commerce firms such as Amazon and eBay, as well as China's equivalent of Amazon, Alibaba. The leading local online retailer in Russia is Ozon Group, often referred to as 'Russia's Amazon'. Ozon's sales last year were close to €450 million, an almost 70 per cent increase in just two years. There are obstacles to e-commerce in Russia, however. The majority of consumers do not have credit cards because many do not trust them to pay for purchases online or offline, making Russia a heavily cash-based marketplace. Delivery is another problem. To combat these barriers, Ozon developed its own courier system, and drivers not only collect cash payments, they even offer style advice on apparel orders when delivered. Russian consumers ordering items from international e-commerce sites such as Amazon may never receive their packages. In fact, officials at Moscow airport reported having 500 metric tons of unprocessed packages in one month alone. Seeing an opportunity for revenue, Russia's Customs Service is considering import duties on packages ordered from foreign websites.

19-9 What types of barriers are present in Russia that might slow the expansion of international e-commerce there? (AACSB: Communication; Reflective thinking)

19-10 What types of barriers are present in Russia that might slow the expansion of international e-commerce there? (AACSB: Communication; Reflective thinking)

19-11 Suggest the best ways companies such as eBay and Amazon can enter this market. (AACSB: Communication; Reflective thinking)

Marketing ethics: India's bitter pill

India's Supreme Court delivered what might be the final nail in the coffin of pharmaceutical innovation in India by rejecting Novaritis' attempt to win patent protection for a potentially life-saving drug. The ruling comes after more than six years of legal battles. Other multinational pharmaceutical companies have suffered setbacks related to patents as well. Bayer's patent for its expensive cancer drug was revoked after being challenged by an Indian generic drug manufacturer, and Bayer was even ordered to issue a licence to the Indian company so it could copy Bayer's drug and sell it for one-thirtieth the price Bayer charged. Roche also had a patent revoked after challenges from local companies and health organisations. India reluctantly agreed to offer patent protection after joining the World Trade Organisation in 1995, but it seems reluctant to grant or maintain patent protection to multinational pharmaceutical firms. India is a fast-growing market, with its pharmaceuticals demand expected to reach almost €45 billion by 2020, up substantially from its current €9.5 billion. However, this market is dominated by low-cost Indian generic drug producers, and India's government seems bent on protecting that industry. The Supreme Court ruling was praised by public-health advocacy groups, such as Medicins Sans Frontières (MSF), that see this as a way to get low-cost drugs in India and other developing nations, since India is the largest supplier of low-cost HIV and other drugs to these nations. Novaritis' drug, Glivec, costs almost €1,750 per month compared with €180 per month for comparable generic versions in India, which didn't help the company's case. However, the company claims that 95 per cent of 16,000 patients taking Glivec in India receive it free of charge through a company support programme.

19-12 Should pharmaceutical companies be granted patents in less developed countries? Debate both sides of this issue. (AACSB: Communication; Ethical reasoning)

19-13 Discuss another example of multinational companies having difficulty expanding into India. (AACSB: Communication; Reflective thinking)

Marketing by the numbers

A country's import/export activity is revealed in its balance-of-payments statement. This statement includes three accounts: the current account, the capital account, and the reserves account. The current account is most relevant to marketing because it is a record of all merchandise exported from and imported into a country. The latter two accounts record financial transactions. The Eurostat Key Indicators provides yearly and monthly figures on the country's trade in goods and services.

19-14 Visit epp.eurostat.ec.europa.eu/portal/page/portal/eurostat/home and find the international trade in goods and services for Europe for the most recent year available. What does that number mean? (AACSB: Communication; Use of IT; Reflective thinking)

19-15 Search the Internet for China's balance of trade information for the same year. How does it compare to that of Europe? (AACSB: Communication; Use of IT; Reflective thinking)

REFERENCES

1 Based on information from Monica Mark, 'Coca-Cola and Nestlé target new markets in Africa', *The Guardian*, 4 May 2012, www.guardian.co.uk/world/2012/may/04/coca-cola-nestle-marketsafrica; Duane Stanford, 'Africa: Coke's last frontier', *Bloomberg Businessweek*, 1 November 2010, pp. 54–61; Annaleigh Vallie, 'Coke turns 125 and has much life ahead', *Business Day*, 16 May 2011, www.businessday.co.za/articles/Content.aspx?id_142848; 'Coca-Cola makes big bets on Africa's future', *Trefis*, 25 May 2012, www.trefis.com/stock/ko/articles/123022/coca-cola-makesbig-bets-on-africas-future/2012–05–25; 'Deloitte on Africa', Deloitte, www.deloitte.com/assets/Dcom-SouthAfrica/Local%20Assets/Documents/rise_and_rise.pdf, accessed October 2015; Andrew Cave, 'Glaxo and Unilever take note: how General Electric and Coca-Cola are winning in Africa', *Forbes*, 2 April 2014, www.forbes.com/sites/andrewcave/2014/04/02/glaxo-and-unilever-takenote-how-general-electric-and-coca-cola-are-winning-in-africa/; and Coca-Cola annual reports and other information from www.thecoca-colacompany.com, accessed October 2015.

2 Data from '*Fortune 500*', *Fortune*, June 2014, http://money.cnn.com/magazines/fortune/fortune500/; Christopher Stolarski, 'The FDI effect', Marquette University Research and Scholarship 2011, www.marquette.edu/research/documents/discover-2011-FDIeffect.pdf; and 'List of countries by GDP: list by the CIA World Factbook', Wikipedia, http://en.wikipedia.org/wiki/List_of_countries_by_GDP_(nominal), accessed October 2015.

3 'Modest trade growth anticipated for 2014 and 2015 following two year slump', WTO Press Release, 14 April 2014, www.wto.org/english/news_e/pres14_e/pr721_e.htm.

4 Information from www.michelin.com/corporate/front/templates/affich.jsp?codeRubrique=1&lang=FR, www.jnj.com/connect, and www.mcdonalds.com/us/en/home.html, accessed October 2015; Huang Lijie, 'European brands shine in Asian hands', *The Straits Times*, 4 April 2011, http://www.asianewsnet.net/home/news.php?id=18287, accessed October 2015.

5 See www.otisworldwide.com/d1-about.html; and www.otisworldwide.com/pdf/Otis_Fact_Sheet_2012_with_milestones.pdf; and UTC Annual Report, http://2013ar.utc.com/assets/pdfs/UTCAR13_Full-Report.pdf, accessed October 2015.

6 Rob Schmitz, 'Trade spat between China and EU threatens exports of solar panels, wine', *Marketplace*, 6 June 2013, www.marketplace.org/topics/world/trade-spat-between-china-andeu-threatens-exports-solar-panels-wine; Jonathan Stearns, 'EU Nations approve pact with China on solar-panel imports', *Bloomberg*, 2 December 2013, www.bloomberg.com/news/2013-12-02/u-nations-approve-pact-with-china-on-solar-panel-trade.html; and Ben Blanchard and Francesco Guarascio, 'EU, China end wine dispute ahead of Xi's European tour', *Reuters*, 21 March 2014, www.reuters.com/article/idUSBREA2K0QE20140321.

7 Gardiner Harris, 'Wal-Mart drops ambitious expansion plan for India', *New York Times*, 10 October 2013, p. B3; and Paul Ausick, 'Walmart still struggles in India', *247wallst*, 8 April 2014, http://247wallst.com/retail/2014/04/08/walmart-still-struggles-in-india/.

8 'What is the WTO?', www.wto.org/english/thewto_e/whatis_e/what_we_do_e.htm, accessed October 2015.

9 See 'The Doha round', www.wto.org/english/tratop_e/dda_e/dda_e.htm, accessed October 2015.

10 'The EU at a glance', http://europa.eu/about-eu/index_en.htm; and 'EU statistics and opinion polls', http://europa.eu/documentation/statistics-polls/index_en.htm, accessed October 2015

11 'Economic and monetary affairs', http://europa.eu/pol/emu/index_en.htm, accessed October 2015; Dan O'Brien, 'Risk of Euro break-up now higher than ever before', *The Irish Times*, 5 April 2013, www.irishtimes.com/business/economy/europe/risk-of-euro-breakup-now-higher-than-ever-before-1.1349443; Jack Ewing, 'European banks feel heat in Crimea crisis, with Austria bearing brunt', *New York Times*, 28 March 2014, p. B6; and 'European Union: The Euro', http://europa.eu/about-eu/basic-information/money/euro/, accessed October 2015.

12 CIA, *The World Factbook*, www.cia.gov/library/publications/the-world-factbook, accessed October 2015.

13 Statistics and other information from CIA, *The World Factbook*; and Harold Meyerson, 'Free trade and the loss of US jobs', *Washington Post*, 14 January 2014, www.washingtonpost.com/opinions/harold-meyerson-free-trade-and-the-loss-of-us-jobs/2014/01/14/894f5750-7d59-11e3-93c1-0e888170b723_story.html.

14 See 'Explainer: what is UNASUR?' www.as-coa.org/articles/explainer-what-unasur, accessed November 2013; and http://en.wikipedia.org/wiki/Union_of_South_American_Nations, accessed October 2015.

15 See Kenneth Rapoza, 'Brazil's 'poor' middle class, and the poor that no longer serve them', *Forbes*, 22 January 2013, www.forbes.com/sites/kenrapoza/2013/01/22/brazils-poor-middleclass-and-the-poor-that-no-longer-serve-them/print/; Claudia Penteado, 'Brazil's Northeast goes from 'Land of Laziness' to Next China', *Advertising Age*, 13 June 2011, http://adage.com/print/228070/; Richard Wallace, 'Middle-classes on the up: why Brazil is growing', *IGD*, 15 September 2011, www.igd.com/ourexpertise/Retail/retail-outlook/4713/Middle-classes-on-the-upwhy-Brazil-is-growing/; and 'German retailers won't kick in Brazil', *German Retail Blog*, 7 May 2014, www.german-retail-blog.com/topic/past-blogs/German-retailers-wont-kick-in-Brazil-279.

16 See '2013 investment climate statement-Russia', US Bureau of Economic and Business Affairs, February 2013, www.state.gov/e/eb/rls/othr/ics/2013/204720.htm; and 'Welcome to the US Commercial Service in Russia', http://export.gov/russia/, accessed October 2015.

17 Laurent Belsie, 'What will Venezuela do with its oil?', *Christian Science Monitor*, 6 March 2013, www.csmonitor.com/Environment/2013/0307/What-will-Venezuela-do-with-its-oil-Top-five-energy-challenges-after-Chavez/Oil-bartering; John Paul Rathbone, 'Venezuela: in search of a solution', *Financial Times*, 2 March 2014, www.ft.com/intl/cms/s/2/45c3cae4-a049-11e3-8557-00144feab7de.html#axzz2xgjEix7Y; and International Reciprocal Trade Association, www.irta.com/index.php/about/modern-trade-barter, accessed October 2015.

18 For these and other examples, see Emma Hall, 'Do you know your rites? BBDO does', *Advertising Age*, 21 May 2007, p. 22.

19 Jamie Bryan, 'The Mintz Dynasty', *Fast Company*, April 2006, pp. 5661; Viji Sundaram, 'Offensive durga display dropped', *India-West*, February 2006, p. A1; and Emily Bryson York and Rupal Parekh, 'Burger King's MO: offend, earn media, apologize, repeat', *Advertising Age*, 8 July 2009, http://adage.com/print?article_id=137801; for other examples, see Ruth Manuel-Logan, 'Dunkin' Donuts apologizes for 'racist' blackface ad', *New One*, 3 September 2013, http://newsone.com/2709598/dunkindonuts-charcoal/; and Chris Isidore, 'Chevy pulls ad offensive to

Chinese', *CNNMoney*, 1 May 2013, money.cnn.com/2013/05/01/news/companies/offensive-chevy-ad/.

20 For these and other examples, see Bill Chappell, 'Bill Gates' handshake with South Korea's Park sparks debate', *NPR*, 23 April 2013, www.npr.org/blogs/thetwo-way/2013/04/23/178650537/bill-gates-handshake-with-south-koreas-park-sparks-debate; 'Managing quality across the (global) organization, its stakeholders, suppliers, and customers', Chartered Quality Institute, www.thecqi.org/Knowledge-Hub/Knowledge-portal/Corporate-strategy/Managing-quality-globally, accessed October 2015.

21 Quotes and other information found in David Pierson, 'Beijing loves IKEA – but not for shopping', *Los Angeles Times*, 25 August 2009, http://articles.latimes.com/2009/aug/25/business/fi-china-ikea25; Michael Wei, 'In IKEA's China stores, loitering is encouraged', *Bloomberg Businessweek*, i1 November 2010, pp. 22–23; and Pan Kwan Yuk, 'IKEA in China: turning gawkers into customers', *BeyondBrics*, 4 April 2013, http://blogs.ft.com/beyond-brics/2013/04/04/ikea-in-china-turning-gawkers-int oconsumers/?#axzz2SobYFh98; and 'A wedding in Aisle 3? Why IKEA encourages Chinese to make its stores their own', *Advertising Age*, 10 December 2013, http://adage.com/print/245573/.

22 Andres Martinez, 'The next American century', *Time*, 22 March 2010, p. 1.

23 Thomas L. Friedman, *The Lexus and the Olive Tree: Understanding Globalization* (New York: Anchor Books, 2000); and Michael Wei and Margaret Conley, 'Global brands: some Chinese kids' first word: Mickey', *Bloomberg Businessweek*, 19 June 2011, pp. 24–25.

24 'BrandZ top 100 most valuable global brands 2014', Millward Brown, www.millwardbrown.com/brandz/2014/Top100/Docs/2014_BrandZ_Top100_Chart.pdf.

25 See Kim-Mai Cutler, 'Apple's Chinese iPhone sales "mind-boggling", bring China revenues to $7.9 billion', *Tech Crunch*, 24 April 2012, http://techcrunch.com/2012/04/24/apples-iphone-sales-inchina-are-up-by-fivefold-from-a-year-ago/; and Rachael Tepper, 'Yum! Brands' international product strategy: how the Double Down went global', *Huffington Post*, 11 March 2013, www.huffington-post.com/2013/03/11/yum-brands-internationalproduct-strategy_n_2814360.html.

26 Eric Ellis, 'Iran's Cola war', *Fortune*, 5 March 2007, pp. 35–38; and 'Iran pressures firm over Coca-Cola links', 19 January 2009, *World News Network*, accessed at www.google.com/hostednews/afp/article/ALeqM5i0vWNjBSFX67GiiSk01zDDUwtY1w.

27 Kimberly Warren-Cohen, 'Coca-Cola sees market growth in non-soda and emerging markets', *Wall Street Cheat Sheet*, 16 April 2014, http://wallstcheatsheet.com/business/coca-cola-sees-growthin-non-soda-and-emerging-markets.html/?a=viewall; William J. Holstein, 'How Coca-Cola manages 90 emerging markets', *Strategy+Business*, 7November 2011, www.strategy-business.com/article/00093?pg=all; '2013 Annual Report', www.coca-colacompany.com/our-company/company-reports; annual reports and other financial and review data from www.coca-colacompany.com/our-company/, accessed October 2015.

28 This Netflix example is based on information found in Sam Schechner, 'Europe's media giants prep for Netflix landing', *Wall Street Journal*, 29 January 2014, http://online.wsj.com/news/articles/SB200014240527023 032777045793487741285485 20.

29 See www.olc.co.jp/en/ and www.coca-colahellenic.com/aboutus/, accessed October 2015.

30 See 'Škoda and Volkswagen Group Russia: one year of successful production in Nizhny Novgorod', 11 December 2013, www.volkswagenag.com/content/vwcorp/info_center/en/news/2013/12/Nizhny_Novgorod.html; and www.pg.com/en_IN/company/pgindia.shtml, accessed September 2014.

31 See http://en.wikipedia.org/wiki/Doubletree, accessed October 2015.

32 Mike Ramsey and Christina Rogers, 'Chrysler's Jeep faces uphill climb in China', *Wall Street Journal*, 10 May 2013, p. B4; and 'Fiat said near deal to start Jeep SUV production in China', *Bloomberg*, 4 December 2013, www.bloomberg.com/news/2013-12-03/fiat-said-near-deal-to-make-jeeps-in-china-with-plant-compromise.html.

33 Aradhana Aravindan, 'Ford looks to ride emerging market mini-SUV boom in India', *Reuters*, 17 June 2013, www.reuters.com/article/idUSBRE95G0RJ20130617; Alan Ohnsman, 'Major auto production at Toyota, Honda boosts US economy', 17 July 2012, www.autonews.com; www.india.ford.com/about, accessed October 2015; and www.hondainamerica.com/manufacturing, accessed October 2015.

34 'A tale of two countries: Starbucks in India and China', *Starbucks Newsroom*, 27 March 2014, http://news.starbucks.com/news/atale-of-two-countries-starbucks-growth-in-india-and-china; Anita Chong Beattie, 'Can Starbucks make China love Joe?' *Advertising Age*, 5 November 2012, pp. 20–21; and 'Starbucks unveils accelerated global growth plans', http://investor.starbucks.com/mobile.view?c=99518&v=203&d=1&id=1764541, accessed October 2015.

35 See Warren J. Keegan and Mark C. Green, *Global Marketing*, 7th ed. (Upper Saddle River, NJ: Prentice Hall, 2013), pp. 303–308.

36 Toshiro Wakayama, Junjiro Shintaku, and Tomofumi Amano, 'What Panasonic learned in China', *Harvard Business Review*, December 2012, pp. 109–113.

37 Information on McDonald's menus and operations found in Lucy Fancourt, Bredesen Lewis, and Nicholas Majka, 'Born in the USA, made in France: how McDonald's succeeds in the land of Michelin stars', Knowledge@Wharton, 3 January 2012, http://knowledge.wharton.upenn.edu/article.cfm?articleid=2906; Richard Vines and Caroline Connan, 'McDonald's wins over French chef with McBaguette Sandwich', *Bloomberg*, 15 January 2013, www.bloomberg.com/news/2013-01-15/mcdonald-s-wins-overfrench-chef-with-mcbaguette-sandwich.html; and 'McDonald's food you can't get here', *Chicago Tribune*, www.chicagotribune.com/business/ct-biz-mcdonalds-food-around-the-world,0,5168632.photogallery, accessed October 2015.

38 See Normandy Madden, 'In China, multinationals forgo adaptation for new-brand creation', *Advertising Age*, 17 January 2011, p. 10; Susan Adams, 'The 10 companies considered "best for the world"', *Forbes*, 31 March 2014, www.forbes.com/sites/susanadams/2014/03/31/10-companies-considered-best-forthe-world/; Meg Cichon, 'Solar making big strides to power the developing world', *Renewable Energy World*, 7 May 2014, www.renewableenergyworld.com/rea/news/article/2014/05/solarmaking-big-strides-to-power-the-developing-world; and www.dlightdesign.com/, accessed October 2015.

39 Jeffrey N. Ross, 'Chevrolet will "find new roads" as brand grows globally: aligns around the world behind singular vision', 8 January 2013, http://media.gm.com/media/us/en/gm/news.detail.html/content/Pages/news/us/en/2013/Jan/0107-findnew-roads.html; and Dale Buss, 'Chevy wins at Sochi by giving dimension to "find new roads"', *Forbes*, 24 February 2014, www.forbes.com/sites/dalebuss/2014/02/24/chevrolet-winsat-sochi-as-find-new-roads-theme-gets-traction/.

40 'Nike faces ultimate marketing challenge in China: make running cool', *Advertising Age*, 31 October 2011, pp. 1+; 'Firms help spur a running craze in China', *China Sports News*, 30 December 2013, www.chinasportsbeat.com/2013/12/firmshelp-spur-running-craze-in-china.html; and 'Nike faces tough competition in Europe and China', *Forbes*,

4 March 2014, www.forbes.com/sites/greatspeculations/2014/03/04/nike-facestough-competition-in-europe-and-china/.

[41] See George E. Belch and Michael A. Belch, *Advertising and Promotion: An Integrated Marketing Communications Perspective*, 8th ed. (New York: McGraw Hill, 2011), Chapter 20; Shintero Okazaki and Charles R. Taylor, 'What is SMS advertising and why do multinationals adopt it?', *Journal of Business Research*, January 2008, pp. 4–12; and Warren J. Keegan and Mark C. Green, *Global Marketing*, 7th ed. (Upper Saddle River, NJ: Prentice Hall, 2013), pp. 398–400.

[42] Information and quote from Alistar Barr and Edward C. Baig, 'Google targets low-end smartphone market with Moto G', *USA Today*, 13November 2013, www.usatoday.com/story/tech/2013/11/13/google-motorola-moto-g/3516039/; and Brian X. Chen, 'Motorolato offer Moto G smartphone aimed at emerging markets', *New York Times*, 14 November 2013, p. B5.

[43] Anita Chang Beattie, 'Catching the eye of a Chinese shopper', *Advertising Age*, 10 December 2013, pp. 20–21.

[44] See 'Coca-Cola rolls out new distribution model with ZAP', ZAP, 23 January 2008, www.marketwired.com/press-release/cocacola-rolls-out-new-distribution-model-with-zap-813288.htm; Jane Nelson, Eriko Ishikawa, and Alexis Geaneotes, 'Developing inclusive business models: a review of Coca-Cola's manual distribution centers in Ethiopia and Tanzania', Harvard Kennedy School, 2009, www.hks.harvard.edu/mrcbg/CSRI/publications/other_10_MDC_report.pdf; and 'How Coca-Cola's distribution system works', *Colalife*, 19 December 2010, www.colalife.org/2010/12/19/how-coca-colas-distribution-system-works. For some interesting photos of Coca-Cola distribution methods in third-world and emerging markets, see www.flickr.com/photos/73509998@N00/sets/72157594299144032, accessed October 2015

[45] Based on information found in Bart Becht, 'Building a company without borders', *Harvard Business Review*, April 2010, pp. 103–106; 'From Cincy to Singapore: why P&G, others are moving key HQs', *Advertising Age*, 10 June 2012, http://adage.com/print/235288; G. A. Chester, '3 things to love about Reckitt Benckiser', *Daily Finance*, 19 June 2013, www.dailyfinance.com/2013/06/19/3-things-to-love-about-reckitt-benckiser/; and www.rb.com/Investorsmedia/Investor-information, accessed October 2015.

COMPANY CASE

IKEA: making life better for the world's many people

Walmart may be the biggest retailer in the world, but IKEA is the largest furniture retailer. Last year, more than 684 million shoppers flocked to the Scandinavian retailer's 303 huge stores in 26 countries, generating revenues of more than €29 billion. That's an average of more than €95 million per store per year, about two-and-a-half times the average sales of a Walmart store. From Beijing to Cardiff to Barcelona, customers pour into IKEA's stores for simple, practical furniture at affordable prices. IKEA is big and getting bigger – its sales have doubled during the past decade. But it's also practical and methodical, growing by only 20 or so superstores each year.

Even these big numbers don't begin to illustrate the impact that IKEA has had on consumers all over the world. Far more than just a big furniture chain, IKEA has achieved global growth and success by connecting with consumers of all nationalities and cultures. IKEA has excelled as a curator of people's lifestyles. Consumers around the world shop at IKEA to signal that they have arrived, that they both have good taste and recognise value. In fact, without IKEA, many people in the world would have little access to affordable, contemporary products for their homes. IKEA's mission is to 'create a better everyday life for the many people'. It accomplishes this seemingly impossible mission by striking just the right balance between global brand standardisation and catering to the local cultural differences in global markets.

A standardised global brand

In the 1940s, Ingvar Kamprad developed what became known as the 'IKEA concept'. He was a native of Småland, Sweden, where the soil was poor and the people had a reputation for working hard, living frugally and making the most of limited resources. The IKEA Concept reflects those characteristics – 'offering a wide range of well-designed, functional home furnishing products at prices so low that as many people as possible will be able to afford them'.

Some aspects of IKEA's products are consistent in all markets. For starters, its products are rooted in Swedish contemporary design. The classic, simple lines of the IKEA design produce timeless products that few companies in any industry can match. For example, POANG – an upholstered chair based on a laminated, bentwood frame with only two front legs – was created in 1976 but remains one of the company's best-selling lines today. The same holds true for the BILLY bookcase. In fact, most of IKEA's best-selling products have been around for years. And that's how IKEA intends customers to enjoy them – for years.

Low price is another key common component of IKEA's products. The benchmark for every IKEA product is half the price of similar products from competitors. And with its relentless focus on cost-cutting, IKEA can keep the price of a product constant or even reduce it over time. Selling the same products in every market achieves scale, which also contributes to IKEA's low-cost structure. So does its 'flat pack' approach – designing furniture so that it can be packed and sold in pieces and assembled by customers at home.

IKEA stores around the world also share a standard design. For starters, they're huge. At an average size of 300,000 square feet, the average IKEA store exceeds the size of the average Carrefour store or Walmart Supercenter by 50 per cent. These large stores let IKEA achieve another aspect of its global brand concept – a one-stop home shopping experience that includes furniture, appliances and household goods for every room. Although such massive size may be overwhelming to some consumers, IKEA's stores are organised in three main sections. Its *showrooms* are set up in a series of rooms that not only show off each product, but also put products in an actual room context, giving customers ideas for how they might use the products in their homes. The *marketplace* section contains the small items – everything from desk lamps to kitchen utensils – also organised by area of the home. The *warehouse* allows customers to pull their own furniture items in flat pack boxes and cart them out. One main thoroughfare weaves its way clockwise through the store from one area to the next, a design that encourages customers to see the store in its entirety. Parents can drop their children in the Småland play area and the entire family can eat in the three-meal-a-day restaurant or the snack bar, making it easy to hang around and shop for hours.

Listening, understanding and adapting

Although most of IKEA's standardised formula works in every market, the company has learned that one size does not fit all when it comes to global customers. So IKEA tweaks its marketing mix in different markets to better meet local consumer needs. The retailer seeks constant feedback from customers in stores, and it visits thousands more each year though in-home visits, observing how consumers live and asking about their dreams and challenges.

When the first US IKEA store opened in Philadelphia in 1985, the beds that it carried were the same as those offered in its other world markets. But Americans weren't buying them, and sales suffered. As IKEA opened more US stores, it worked to figure out the American manner of sleeping. It learned that height, firmness and maximum size are key bed characteristics sought by US consumers. So IKEA altered the composition of its mattresses and added king size beds to the mix. Then it altered the presentation and promotion of these products so the concept was clear. Not surprisingly, its sleep product lines really took off.

A more recent change resulting from listening to consumers in European markets is offering more services. Whereas picking, pulling, hauling and assembling still works for most people, for others it was all just too much trouble. IKEA now offers flat-rate pricing on pulling orders and home delivery. It even maintains a list of contractors in each market that customers can call on to assemble the items in their homes.

Some markets have required more changes. As IKEA has expanded into Asia, for example, it has learned that customer needs vary substantially from those in Europe and North America. Take China, for example. With some of the largest cities in the world, China has no shortage of customers. But most of China's 1.3 billion people don't buy home furnishings. So IKEA focuses instead on China's exploding middle class – 'the many people' in growing urban populations who are more educated and fall into a 25- to 35-year-old age range. For this reason, IKEA stores in China are located closer to city centres, rather than in the suburbs, and are located near light-rail transportation lines.

Some of the changes for IKEA China are based on the fundamental principle of stocking products that people in a given area will buy. In China, for example, people love a good, hard mattress, so IKEA sells mostly firmer ones there. Whereas IKEA stores in China carry the same number of products as those in other parts of the world – most of them from the standard IKEA range – in China the company also stocks rice cookers and chopsticks. And when IKEA stocked 250,000 placemats commemorating the year of the rooster, they sold out in just weeks.

In massive city centres such as Beijing and Shanghai, home ownership among the middle class has gone from nearly zero to about 70 per cent in the past 15 years. Because virtually all new homeowners have little sense of how to furnish and decorate their homes, they are eager to learn from the West. However, not everything that works in more developed parts of the world works in China. For one thing, the average living space in China's crowded cities is much smaller than in Europe and North America. An average Chinese family lives in a small apartment in a high-rise building, often with multigenerational family members. So in China, IKEA focuses on products geared toward saving space and organising a household. And it helps consumers figure out how to live smart and organise in small living spaces.

Pricing in China is somewhat of a paradox. Chinese customers are attracted to IKEA's design and the comprehensive selection, so that's where IKEA puts its emphasis in terms of positioning. But at the same time, in emerging markets such as China, low prices are the norm, and IKEA must cut prices drastically to remain competitive. When it first opened its doors in China more than a decade ago, IKEA found that it was more expensive than local low-priced firms. Competitors began selling copies of IKEA's designs at a fraction of the price. Using its cost-cutting expertise, however, IKEA has reduced prices in China by more than 50 per cent over the past ten years. The classic Klippan sofa, for example, now costs only €129, a third of what it did a decade ago (the same sofa costs €378 in Sweden).

Another challenge in selling furniture in the world's most populated country is that there are significant differences across the country's many regions. For example, in some regions, apartments have smaller rooms. Thus, IKEA designs showrooms in those areas to reflect the smaller size. Apartment buildings throughout China have balconies. But in northern China, balconies are widely used for food storage, whereas in southern China, they double as laundries. IKEA showrooms in these regions reflect such differences and regional needs.

The Chinese market features another unusual characteristic–gawkers. IKEA stores in China boast more traffic than those in any other part of the world (the Beijing store pulls in 28,000 customers on a typical Saturday – a strong week's draw for a typical European IKEA). But the majority of visitors just hang out and look. Actually, many visitors are there just to enjoy the air conditioning, a cheap meal and a place to relax in comfort. People often lounge for extended periods in showrooms as they would in their own living rooms. Some even pull back the covers on an IKEA bed, take off their shoes and hunker down for a good nap. Whereas this kind of behaviour would get customers booted out of IKEAs in other markets, management recognises that with China's rapidly growing middle class, allowing such behaviour is an investment in the future.

IKEA plans to expand its number of stores in China from 15 to 40 during the next six years. But IKEA's China operations are just one example of IKEA's strategy throughout the world. The company also plans to double its number of stores in North America during the same period. And as IKEA continues to grow in existing markets, it is also eyeing new markets with vast, untapped potential, such as India, where it plans to open 25 stores. Having doubled sales in the past decade, IKEA plans to double them again by 2020. And that's based on the same methodical growth of 20 to 25 new stores per year. With its keen ability to understand the cultural differences of each market and to adapt its marketing accordingly, there seems to be little standing in IKEA's way.

Questions for discussion

1. Does IKEA have a truly global strategy, or just a series of regional strategies? Explain.
2. Discuss IKEA's global strategy in terms of the five global product and communications strategies.
3. If IKEA can sell a sofa in China for €140, why doesn't it sell the product at that low price in all of its markets?
4. Can competitors easily duplicate IKEA's strategy? Why or why not?
5. Should IKEA expand more rapidly than 20 to 25 stores per year? Explain.

Sources: Based on information from www.ikea.com/, accessed October 2015; also see Anna Ringstrom, 'IKEA turns the global local for Asia push', *Reuters*, 6 March 2013, www.reuters.com/article/2013/03/07/us-ikea-expansion-idUS-BRE92606220130307; Pan Kwan Yuk, '*IKEA* in China: turning gawkers into consumers', *Financial Times*, 4 April 2013, http://blogs.ft.com/beyond-brics/2013/04/04/ikea-in-china-turning-gawkers-into-consumers/?Authorised=false#axzz2VAi2u6c8; Jens Hansegard, 'IKEA taking China by storm', *Wall Street Journal*, 26 March 2012, http://online.wsj.com/article/SB10001424052702304636404577293083481821536.html; and Jens Hansegard and Niclas Rolander, 'IKEA's focus remains on its superstores', *Wall Street Journal*, 29 January 2014, p. B9.

CHAPTER TWENTY

Social responsibility and ethics

Chapter preview

In this final chapter, we'll examine the concepts of sustainable marketing: meeting the needs of consumers, businesses and society – now and in the future – through socially and environmentally responsible marketing actions. We'll start by defining sustainable marketing and then look at some common criticisms of marketing as it impacts individual consumers and actions that promote sustainable marketing. Finally, we'll see how companies themselves can benefit from proactively pursuing sustainable marketing practices that bring value not only to individual customers but also to society as a whole. Sustainable marketing actions are more than just the right thing to do; they're also good for business.

First, let's visit the concept of social responsibility in business. The Raspberry Pi computer in the UK follows the tradition of the 'One laptop per child' project originated in the US. The founders of the Raspberry Pi project have a goal of enhancing computer science teaching in schools and the programming skills of school children, and the Pi is an incredibly cheap and accessible programmable computer. The Pi is made and distributed by regular commercial companies operating in partnership with the Raspberry Pi Foundation, and paying licence fees per computer sold. The project is a great illustration of the pursuit of both social and business goals in a compatible and productive way – delivering social benefits and commercial value. Three years in to the project, the Raspberry Pi has sold around 5 million units to schoolchildren, hobbyists and businesses around the world.

Objectives Outline

➤ Objective 1 Define sustainable marketing and discuss its importance.
Sustainable marketing (pp. 593–594)

➤ Objective 2 Identify the major social criticisms of marketing.
Social criticisms of marketing (pp. 594–602)

➤ Objective 3 Define consumerism and environmentalism and explain how they affect marketing strategies.
Consumer actions to promote sustainable marketing (pp. 602–607)

➤ Objective 4 Describe the principles of sustainable marketing.
Business actions toward sustainable marketing (pp. 607–610)

➤ Objective 5 Explain the role of ethics in marketing.
Marketing ethics (pp. 610–613)
The sustainable company (p. 613)

The Raspberry Pi

The One Laptop Per Child (OLPC) programme started at MIT in the US and led to revolutionary change in the global laptop business – both directly through the OLPC innovation but importantly also indirectly through the impact of that innovation on the computer industry. The goal of producing a very low-price laptop for children in the emerging markets stimulated a major change among established manufacturers to produce very low-price laptops, improving accessibility to computing and the Internet for children around the world. The initiative has driven such innovations as the launch in India of the Aakash tablet computer ('sky' in Hindi) selling at $35 to support children in schools – and outpacing the OLPC equivalent at more than $200. The OLPC initiative has delivered social value – cheap laptops for schools in emerging markets – by its own efforts and the impact on business opportunities for others.

In a completely separate development, in February 2012, a team of computer scientists at Cambridge University in the UK launched the Raspberry Pi. In the first six months the Pi sold around 500,000 units. The Raspberry Pi is a credit card-sized computer designed to interest young people in computer programming. The Pi is modelled on the BBC Micro – a primitive device, the red and white keyboard of which introduced a generation of software entrepreneurs to programming, back in the 1980s. The Raspberry Pi could cost as little as £15–£22, depending on the model.

Thirty-four-year-old Eben Upton is one of the masterminds behind the Raspberry Pi. The business is structured as a charity, established in 2009 – all profits go to educational activities, and the project started with only one full-time employee – Upton's wife Liz, responsible for social media and marketing.

The Pi does not look good. It has no sleek case, but has an exposed green circuit board dotted with silicon chips – processor, video unit, connections and an Ethernet port soldered on. It plugs into a television – add a keyboard and mouse and you are ready to go. In fact, the graphics are better than some games players and it can play Blu-Ray quality films. The Pi uses the open-source Linux operating system.

The stripped-down computer is part of an effort to boost British children's programming skills and revive the 1980s when hundreds of thousands of schoolchildren learned to code at home on ZX Spectrums and Commodore 64 computers. Much of the UK's computer games industry was created by boys who started developing games on these types of devices in their bedrooms.

The Pi is not only cheap it is also flexible. It can be manipulated by amateurs to solve many practical problems. The Kenya Wildlife Service has used a batch of Raspberry Pi's as a low-cost way of controlling hidden cameras hat keep track of endangered animals. In South Wales a Raspberry Pi has been programmed to operate the test rig in a factory where the devices are made, because it is cheaper and faster than a PC. On top of this are thousands of 'hobbyists' experimenting and developing applications. For example, one user has installed a home-made, tweeting cat flap as a bit of fun with a Raspberry Pi computer – it takes a photo of the cat going in and out and posts a tweet singing her praises.

The main point of the initiative was that the creators hoped that they could encourage children to design their own apps – by giving them a low-cost computer they could own, and one where programming was the natural thing to do with it. The goal is to rejuvenate the teaching of computer science in schools. The Foundation originators hope that their project will eventually create 1,000 extra computer engineers in the UK each year. Upton says that now the venture has launched, he and his colleagues can go back to teaching people how to program.

The origins of the Raspberry Pi are that, as university computer science teachers faced with declining student interest and numbers, Upton and his colleagues decided to take action. This team became the Raspberry Pi Foundation. With a handful of local

The Pi does not look good. It has no sleek case, but has an exposed green circuit board dotted with silicon chips. The stripped down computer is part of an effort to boost British children's programming skills.

Source: gbimages/Alamy Stock Photo

investors they raised £126,000 to design a prototype successor to the BBC Micro. They had four criteria for the new machine: it had to be interesting for things other than programming; be robust; be as cheap as a textbook; and come with software. In fact, when they showed an early version to a BBC technology correspondent, the video went viral and got 800,000 views. They had accidentally promised 800,000 people they could have a computer!

The Foundation used its seed funding to pay for the manufacture of the first 10,000 Pi's. Demand went wild when they went on sale in February 2012 – orders were for ten times the available supply, distributors' websites crashed, orders had to be limited to one per person, and the Pi sold for thousands on eBay. The first batch sold out within hours of the launch.

The founders quickly decided to license the manufacture to Premier Farnell and RS Components, which make the computers in China. Egoman makes a version just for sale in China and Taiwan. Some manufacturing has since been re-located in Wales. The commercial partners pay a fee to the Foundation for every unit sold. The business model is a form of alliance between a not-for-profit charity supporting education, and for-profit manufacturers and distributors. Admittedly, the Foundation has been criticised by some for keeping the design secret – while the software is open-source, the hardware is not – to allow the manufacturers to recoup their investment by not opening the field to imitators.

Two-thirds of sales have gone to America and Europe and one-third to Africa and Asia, where families want a cheap computer they can plug into an ordinary television. A cheaper version of the Pi was launched later in 2012. By late 2013, the Pi had sold 1.8 million units.

Raspberry Pi was set up as a charity because the number of chips it wanted was small and deals could be done. As a for-profit venture Pi would have had to start much smaller or take a private equity stake – in either case ending up with a retail price of £60–£120. The innovation is not just the computer, but also the business model. The goal is to sell a million Pi's a year into education and a million a year to 'hobbyists'. Essentially, Raspberry Pi makes money by selling blueprints to manufacturers based on designs from Arm, the chip designer that is also based in Cambridge. It takes a roughly 10 per cent cut on licences sold, making £5.7 million from such trading activities in 2013.

November 2014 saw Raspberry Pi unveiling its tiniest and cheapest device so far – a $20 microcomputer that measures 6.5cm in length – as it continues to design cheaper and smaller products for techno-tinkerers, coding enthusiasts and anyone who wants to learn about computer hardware. The Model A+ is the latest effort by this Cambridge-based, non-profit tech group that designs stripped-down computers. Its products can be programmed by users to do anything from playing videos to running an attached sprinkler system.

As of 18 February 2015, over 5 million Raspberry Pi's had been sold. While already the fastest selling British personal computer, the Pi has in fact sold the second largest number of units, behind the Amstrad, the 'personal computer word processor', which sold 8 million units.

In early February 2015, the next-generation Raspberry Pi, Raspberry Pi 2, was released. Crucially, the Raspberry Pi 2 retains the same $35 price point of the model B, with the $20 model A+ remaining on sale.

The impact of the Raspberry Pi on the computer industry is following a similar pattern to the earlier impact of OLPC. December 2014 saw Imagination Technologies, better known for making iPhone chips, launch the MIPS Creator I20 to challenge the Raspberry Pi in the market for hobbyists and children. Early 2015 saw the BBC announcing it will give away 'micro bit' computers to every child starting secondary school in the UK as part of a drive to improve technology skills. The Micro Bit programmable devices are similar to the Raspberry Pi. Other open source hardware groups include Arduino, which sells programmable microcontrollers, and Kano, which enables users to build their own computers, and is powered by the Raspberry Pi.

A recent report by Gartner, the research group, labelled such ventures 'mavericks', and said they would produce the ideas for 50 per cent of connected devices on the market by 2017.[1]

Responsible marketers discover what consumers want and respond with market offerings that create value for buyers, to capture value in return. The marketing concept is a philosophy of customer value and mutual gain. Its practice leads the economy by an invisible hand to satisfy the many and changing needs of millions of consumers.

Not all marketers follow the marketing concept, however. In fact, some companies use questionable marketing practices that serve their own rather than consumers' interests. Moreover, even well-intentioned marketing actions that meet the current needs of some consumers may cause immediate or future harm to other consumers or the larger society and global community. Responsible marketers must consider whether their actions are sustainable in the longer run.

Consider the sale of four-wheel drive cars (4×4s). These large vehicles meet the immediate needs of many drivers in terms of capacity, power and utility, are great to drive and are in fact a heck of a lot of fun for the driver. However, to some consumers four-wheel drive vehicle sales involve larger questions of consumer safety and environmental responsibility. For example, environmental critics suggest that in accidents, four-wheel drive vehicles are more likely to kill both their own occupants and the occupants of other vehicles. Their research claims that four-wheel drive vehicle occupants are three times more likely to die from their vehicle rolling than are occupants of other cars. Moreover, environmentalists say gas-guzzling 4×4s use more than their fair share of the world's energy and other resources and contribute disproportionately to pollution and congestion problems, creating costs that must be borne by both current and future generations. Of course, it may also be that environmentalists just don't like car drivers having fun.

This chapter examines sustainable marketing and the social and environmental effects of private marketing practices. First, we address the question: What is sustainable marketing and why is it important?

> **Author comment**
>
> Marketers must think beyond immediate customer satisfaction and business performance towards sustainable strategies that preserve the world for future generations.

SUSTAINABLE MARKETING

Sustainable marketing calls for socially and environmentally responsible actions that meet the present needs of consumers and businesses, while also preserving or enhancing the ability of future generations to meet their needs. Figure 20.1 compares the sustainable marketing concept with marketing concepts we studied in earlier chapters.

The *marketing concept* recognises that organisations thrive by determining the current needs and wants of target group customers and fulfilling those needs and wants more effectively and efficiently than competitors do. It focuses on meeting the company's short-term sales, growth and profit needs by giving customers what they want now. However, satisfying consumers' immediate needs and desires doesn't always serve the future best interests of either customers or the business.

For example, fast-food giant McDonald's early decisions to market tasty but fat- and salt-laden fast foods created immediate satisfaction for customers and sales and profits for the company. However, critics assert that McDonald's and other fast-food chains contributed to a longer-term international obesity epidemic, damaging consumer health and burdening national health systems. In turn, many consumers began looking for healthier eating options, causing a slump in the sales and profits of the fast-food industry. Beyond issues of ethical behaviour and social welfare, McDonald's was also criticised for the sizable environmental footprint of its vast global operations, everything from wasteful packaging and solid waste creation to inefficient energy use in its stores. Thus, McDonald's strategy was not sustainable in terms of either consumer or company benefit.

> **Sustainable marketing—**
> Socially and environmentally responsible marketing that meets the present needs of consumers and businesses, while also preserving or enhancing the ability of future generations to meet their needs.

Figure 20.1 Sustainable marketing

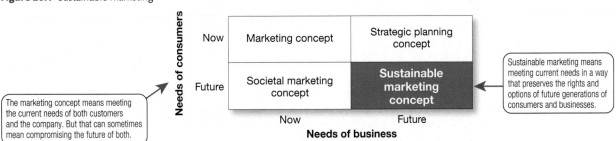

Whereas the *societal marketing concept* identified in Figure 20.1 considers the future welfare of consumers and the *strategic planning concept* considers future company needs, the *sustainable marketing concept* considers both. Sustainable marketing calls for socially and environmentally responsible actions that meet both the immediate and future needs of customers and the company.

For example, McDonald's has responded to these challenges in recent years with a more sustainable 'Plan to win' strategy of diversifying into salads, fruits, grilled chicken, low fat milk, and other healthier food. The company has also launched a major multi-faceted education campaign – called 'it's what I eat and what I do . . . I'm lovin' it' – to help consumers better understand the keys to living balanced, active lifestyles. And it recently announced a list of 'Commitments to offer improved nutrition choices', including a continuing commitment to children's well-being, with expanded and improved nutritionally balanced menu choices, and increased consumer and employee access to nutrition information. McDonald's points out that 80 per cent of the items on its menu fall into its 'favourites under 400 calories' category. Last year, the chain served 410 million cups of vegetables, 200 million cups of fruit and 420 million servings of whole grain in products such as Apple & Cherry Porridge and the Melon Fruit Bag for breakfast.

The McDonald's 'Plan to win' strategy also addresses environmental issues. For example, it calls for food-supply sustainability, reduced and environmentally sustainable packaging, reuse and recycling, and more responsible store designs. McDonald's has even developed an environmental scorecard that rates its suppliers' performance in areas such as water use, energy use and solid waste management. McDonald's more sustainable strategy is benefiting the company as well as its customers. Since announcing its 'Plan to win' strategy, McDonald's sales have increased by more than 60 per cent, and profits have almost tripled. Thus, McDonald's is well positioned for a sustainably profitable future.[2]

Truly sustainable marketing requires a smooth-functioning marketing system in which consumers, companies, public policy makers and others work together to ensure socially and environmentally responsible marketing actions. Unfortunately, however, the marketing system doesn't always work smoothly. The following sections examine several sustainability questions: What are the most frequent social criticisms of marketing? What steps have consumers taken to curb marketing ills? What steps have legislators and government agencies taken to promote sustainable marketing? What steps have enlightened companies taken to carry out socially responsible and ethical marketing that creates sustainable value for both individual customers and society as a whole?[3]

SOCIAL CRITICISMS OF MARKETING

Author comment

In most ways, we all benefit greatly from marketing activities. However, like most other human endeavours, marketing has its flaws. Here we present both sides of some of the most common criticisms of marketing.

Marketing receives much criticism. Some of this criticism is justified; much is not. Social critics claim that certain marketing practices hurt individual consumers, society as a whole and other business firms.

Marketing's impact on individual consumers

Consumers throughout the world have many concerns about how well the marketing system serves their interests. Surveys usually show that consumers hold mixed or even slightly unfavourable attitudes toward marketing practices. Consumer advocates, government agencies and other critics have accused marketing of harming consumers through high prices, deceptive practices, high-pressure selling, shoddy or unsafe products, planned obsolescence and poor service to disadvantaged consumers. Such questionable marketing practices are not sustainable in terms of long-term consumer or business welfare.

High prices

Many critics charge that marketing causes prices to be higher than they would be under more 'sensible' systems. Such high prices are hard to accept, especially when the economy takes a downturn. Critics point to three factors – *high costs of distribution*, *high advertising and promotion costs* and *excessive mark-ups*.

High costs of distribution

A long-standing charge is that greedy channel intermediaries mark up prices beyond the value of their services. As a result, distribution costs too much, and consumers pay for these excessive costs in the form of high prices. Critics claim that there are too many intermediaries, which are also inefficient and/or provide unnecessary or duplicate services. Resellers respond that that intermediaries do work that would otherwise have to be done by manufacturers or consumers. Their prices reflect the cost of services that consumers want – more convenience, larger stores and assortments, more service, longer store hours, returns policies, among others. In fact, they argue, retail competition is so intense that margins are actually quite low. If some resellers try to charge too much relative to the value they add, other resellers will step in with lower prices. Low-price stores such as Walmart, Tesco, Carrefour, Aldi, Lidl pressure their competitors to operate efficiently and keep their prices down. In fact, in the wake of economic downturn and recession, only the most efficient retailers have survived profitably.

High advertising and promotion costs

Modern marketing is also accused of pushing up prices to finance unneeded advertising, sales promotion and packaging. For example, a heavily promoted brand leader sells for much more than a virtually identical retailer branded own-label product – a pack of a heavily promoted brand of pain reliever with 28 tablets sells for the same price as 100 tablets of retailer brands. Differentiated products – cosmetics, detergents, toiletries – include promotion and packaging costs that can amount to 40 per cent or more of the manufacturer's price to the retailer. Critics claim that much of the packaging and promotion adds only psychological, not functional, value to the product.

Marketers respond that although advertising adds to product costs, it also adds value by informing potential buyers of the availability and merits of a brand. Brand name products may cost more, but branding gives buyers assurance of consistent quality. Moreover, consumers can usually buy functional versions of products at lower prices if they wish to do so. However, they *want* and are willing to pay more for products that also provide psychological benefits – that make them feel wealthy, attractive or special. Also, heavy advertising and promotion may be necessary for a firm to match competitors' efforts; the business would lose 'share of mind' if it did not match competitive spending.

At the same time, companies are cost conscious about promotion and try to spend their funds wisely. Today's increasingly more frugal consumers are demanding genuine value for the prices they pay. The continuing shift toward buying retailer own-brands and generics suggests that when it comes to value, consumers want action, not just talk.

High prices: a heavily promoted manufacturer brand sells for much more than a virtually identical non-branded or retailer-branded product. Critics charge that promotion adds only psychological value to the product rather than functional value.

Source: Lynne Sutherland/Alamy Images

Excessive mark-ups

Critics also charge that some companies mark up goods excessively. They point to the drug industry, where a pill costing a few pennies to make may cost the consumer £1 to buy. They point to the pricing tactics of funeral homes that prey on the confused emotions of bereaved relatives, and the high charges for car repairs and other services.

Marketers respond that most businesses try to deal fairly with consumers because they want to build customer relationships and repeat

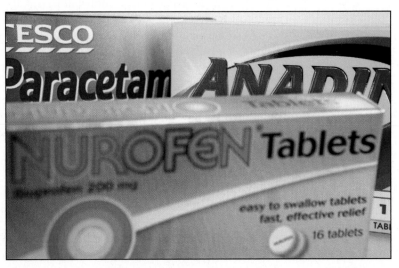

Deceptive practices: Ferrero recently settled a legal action claiming that ads for its Nuttella chocolate-hazelnut spread made deceptive claims that the product was 'healthy' and 'part of a balanced diet'.

Source: Stefano Rellandini/ Reuters

business, and that most consumer abuses are unintentional. Also, they respond that consumers often don't understand the reasons for high mark-ups. For example, pharmaceutical mark-ups must cover the costs of purchasing, promoting and distributing existing medicines plus the incredibly high R&D costs of formulating and testing new medicines. As pharmaceuticals company GlaxoSmithKline states in its ads, 'Today's medicines finance tomorrow's miracles'.

Deceptive practices

Marketers are sometimes accused of deceptive practices that lead consumers to believe they will get more value than they actually do. Deceptive practices fall into three groups: pricing, promotion and packaging. *Deceptive pricing* includes practices such as falsely advertising 'factory' or 'wholesale' prices or a large price reduction from a phoney high retail list price. *Deceptive promotion* includes practices such as misrepresenting the product's features or performance or luring customers to the store for a bargain that is out of stock. *Deceptive packaging* includes exaggerating package contents through subtle design, using misleading labelling, or describing size in misleading terms.

Deceptive practices have led to legislation and other consumer protection actions. Different countries have taken different approaches to deceptive practices through laws, regulation and voluntary codes of practice, but despite those expanding bodies of laws and regulations, some critics argue that deceptive claims are still the norm.

The toughest problem is defining what is 'deceptive'. For instance, an advertiser's claim that its chewing gum will 'rock your world' isn't intended to be taken literally. Instead, the advertiser might claim, it is 'puffery' – innocent exaggeration for effect. However, others claim that puffery and alluring imagery can harm consumers in subtle ways. Think about the popular and long-running MasterCard 'priceless' commercials that painted pictures of consumers fulfilling their priceless dreams despite the costs. The ads suggested that your credit card can make it happen. But critics charge that such imagery by credit card companies encouraged a spend-now-pay-later attitude that caused many consumers to overuse their cards. They point to statistics showing that consumers in the developed countries took on record amounts of credit card debt – often more than they could repay – contributing heavily to the international financial crisis of the early 2010s.

Marketers argue that most companies avoid deceptive practices. Because such practices harm a company's business in the long run, they simply aren't sustainable. Profitable customer relationships are built on a foundation of value and trust. If consumers do not get what they expect, they will switch to more reliable products. In addition, consumers usually protect themselves from deception. Most consumers recognise a marketer's selling intent and are careful when they buy, sometimes even to the point of not believing completely true product claims. The post-recession environment in Europe is characterised by a lack of trust in traditional marketing messages and marketers are having to rethink their approaches to more cynical, value-oriented consumers.

High-pressure selling

Salespeople are sometimes accused of high-pressure selling that persuades people to buy goods they had no intention of buying. It is often said that insurance, property and used cars are *sold*, not *bought*. Salespeople are trained to deliver smooth, scripted talks to entice purchase. They sell hard because sales contests and bonuses promise big rewards to those who sell the most. Similarly, some TV advertising uses crude 'yell and sell' presentations that create a sense of consumer urgency that only those with the strongest willpower can resist.

But in most cases, marketers have little to gain from high-pressure selling. Such tactics may work in one-time selling situations for short-term gain. However, most selling involves building long-term relationships with valued customers. High-pressure or deceptive selling can seriously damage such relationships. For example, imagine a P&G account manager trying to pressure a Tesco buyer or an IBM salesperson trying to browbeat an IT manager at GE. It simply wouldn't work.

Shoddy, harmful or unsafe products

Another criticism concerns poor product quality or function. One common complaint is that products/services are not made well and do not perform adequately. A second complaint concerns product safety. Product safety has been a problem for several reasons, including company indifference, increased product complexity and poor quality control. A third complaint is that many products deliver little benefit or that they might even be harmful.

For example, think about the soft drink industry – Coke, Pepsi, and all the rest. Many critics blame the plentiful supply of sugar-laden, high-calorie soft drinks for the rapidly growing global obesity epidemic. For example, in the US studies show that more than two-thirds of American adults are either obese or overweight and, one-third of American children are obese.[4] This obesity phenomenon continues despite repeated medical studies showing that excess weight brings increased risks for heart disease, diabetes and other maladies, even cancer. Critics are quick to attack what they see as greedy soft drinks marketers cashing in on vulnerable consumers, turning the world into 'big gulpers'. Throughout the world policy makers are looking for ways to reduce sugar consumption in the form of soft drinks and snacks through taxes and prohibitions.

But is the soft drink industry really being socially irresponsible by aggressively promoting overindulgence to ill-informed or unwary consumers? Or is it simply serving the wants of customers by offering products that appeal to consumer tastes, while letting consumers make their own consumption choices? Surely most places selling Coke also sell water if that's what the consumer wants? Since when has it been industry's job to police public tastes? As in many matters of social responsibility, what's right and wrong may be a matter of opinion. Whereas some analysts criticise the industry, others suggest that responsibility lies with consumers. 'Soft drinks have unfairly become the whipping boy of most anti-obesity campaigns,' suggests one business reporter. 'Maybe friends shouldn't give friends Big Gulps, but to my knowledge, no one's ever been forced to buy and drink one. There's an element of personal responsibility and control that [needs to be addressed].'[5]

Obesity is one of the greatest public health challenges of the twenty-first century and its prevalence has tripled in many countries of the European region since the 1980s. The numbers of those affected continue to rise at an alarming rate, particularly among children. Obesity is already responsible for 2–8 per cent of health costs and 10–13 per cent of deaths in different parts of the European region. Within Europe, the UK has the highest level of obesity. However, most manufacturers want to produce quality goods that do no harm to anyone. For example, drinks giant Heineken stopped selling two leading strong cider brands – White Lightening and Strongbow Black – even though the products were selling fast. Research showed these were the products of choice for problem drinkers, particularly street drinkers. Heineken now promotes lower strength and no-alcohol ciders. The company was prepared to sacrifice the profits because it took the view that 'We just weren't comfortable with the way those products were being used.'[6]

After all, the way a company deals with product quality and safety problems can make or break reputation. Companies selling poor-quality or unsafe products risk damaging conflicts with consumer groups and regulators. Unsafe products can result in product liability suits and large awards for damages. More fundamentally, consumers who are unhappy with a firm's products may avoid future purchases and talk other consumers into doing the same. In the modern world of social media and online reviews, word of poor quality can spread like wildfire. Thus, quality missteps are not consistent with sustainable marketing. Today's marketers know that good quality results in customer value and satisfaction, which in turn creates sustainable customer relationships.

Planned obsolescence

Critics also have charged that some companies practise *planned obsolescence*, causing their products to become obsolete before they actually should need replacement. They accuse some producers of using materials and components that will break, wear, rust or rot sooner than they should. And if the products themselves don't wear out fast enough, other companies are charged with *perceived obsolescence* – continually changing consumer concepts of acceptable styles to encourage more and earlier buying.[7] An obvious example is the fast fashion industry with its constantly changing clothing fashions, which some critics claim creates a wasteful disposable clothing culture. 'Too many garments end up in landfill sites,' bemoans one designer. 'They are deemed aesthetically redundant and get discarded at the end of the season when there are often years of wear left.'[8]

Still others are accused of introducing planned streams of new products that make older models obsolete, turning consumers into 'serial replacers'. Critics claim that this occurs all the time in the consumer electronics and computer industries. If you're like most people, you probably have a drawer full of yesterday's hottest technological gadgets – from mobile phones and cameras to iPods and flash drives – now reduced to the status of fossils. It seems that anything more than a year or two old is hopelessly out of date. For example, early iPods had non-removable batteries that failed in about 18 months, so that the whole iPod had to be replaced. It wasn't until unhappy owners filed a class action suit that Apple started offering replacement batteries. Also, rapid new product launches – as many as three in one 18-month period – made older iPod models obsolete.[9]

Marketers respond that consumers *like* style changes; they get tired of the old goods and want a new look in fashion. Or they *want* the latest high-tech innovations, even if older models still work. No one has to buy the new product, and if too few people like it, it will simply fail. Finally, most companies do not design their products to break down earlier because they do not want to lose customers to other brands. Instead, they seek constant improvement to ensure that products will consistently meet or exceed customer expectations. Much of the so-called planned obsolescence is the working of the competitive and technological forces in a free society – forces that lead to ever-improving goods and services.

Poor service to disadvantaged consumers

Finally, the marketing system has been accused of poorly serving disadvantaged consumers. For example, critics in the US claim that the urban poor of that country often have to shop in smaller stores that carry inferior goods and charge higher prices. The presence of large national chain stores in low-income neighbourhoods would help to keep prices down. However, the critics accuse major chain retailers of 'redlining', drawing a red line around disadvantaged neighbourhoods and avoiding placing stores there.

For example, in the US, poor areas have 30 per cent fewer supermarkets than affluent areas do. As a result, many low-income consumers find themselves in what one expert calls 'food deserts', which are awash with small markets offering fast food, confectionery and Cokes, but where fruits and vegetables or fresh fish or chicken are out of reach. 'In low-income areas, you can go for miles without being able to find a fresh apple or a piece of broccoli,' says the executive director of the Food Trust, a group that's trying to tackle the US problem. In turn, the lack of access to healthy, affordable fresh foods has a negative impact on the health of underserved consumers in these areas.[10] Indeed, many national chains, such as Walmart, Walgreens, SuperValu, and even Whole Foods Market, have recently agreed to open or expand more stores that bring nutritious and fresh foods to underserved communities. For example, Whole Foods has recently been opening stores in disadvantaged parts of cities such as Detroit, Chicago and New Orleans, 'trying to serve the needs of communities that others ignore completely'.[11]

Clearly, better marketing systems must be built to service disadvantaged consumers. In fact, many marketers profitably target such consumers with legitimate goods and services that create real value. In cases in which marketers do not step in to fill the void, it is likely governments will force them. There is also the growing potential for emerging market companies to bring their ways of doing business – successful with the poorest consumers in the world – to bear in Europe and the US and shut existing companies out from this market.

Marketing's impact on society as a whole

The marketing system has been accused of adding to several 'evils' in society at large, such as creating too much materialism, too few social goods and a glut of cultural pollution.

False wants and too much materialism

Critics have charged that the marketing system urges too much interest in material possessions, and the consumer's love affair with worldly possessions is not sustainable. Too often, people are judged by what they *own* rather than by who they *are*. These critics do not view this interest in material things as a natural state of mind but rather as a matter of false wants created by marketing. Marketers, they claim, stimulate people's desires for goods and create materialistic models of the good life. Thus, marketers have created an endless cycle of mass consumption based on a distorted interpretation of the human priorities.

> One sociologist attributes consumer overspending to a growing 'aspiration gap' – the gap between what we have and what we want, between the lifestyles we can afford and those to which we aspire. This aspiration gap results at least partly from a barrage of marketing that encourages people to focus on the acquisition and consumption of goods. Advertising encourages consumers to aspire to celebrity lifestyles, to keep up with the Joneses by acquiring more stuff. Some marketing-frenzied consumers will let nothing stand between them and their acquisitions. Recently, rumours of half-price clothes caused a riot among shoppers at Primark's new flagship store in London. A security guard was injured as eager shoppers surged into the Oxford Street store shoving other shoppers to the ground. It was reported that mounted police and the store security guards struggled to get control of the hundreds of shoppers, who were shouting and screaming. As the doors were opened the bargain-hunters, some of whom had been queuing for several hours, surged forward and the doors collapsed. The scenes of mayhem continued inside as shoppers were seen stripping down to their underwear to try on clothes. Staff at Primark said although they were prepared for a large number of customers, even they were amazed by the chaotic scenes.[12]

Thus, marketing is seen as creating false wants that benefit industry more than consumers. 'In the world of consumerism, marketing is there to promote consumption,' says one marketing critic. It is 'inevitable that marketing will promote over-consumption, and from this, a psychologically, as well as ecologically, unsustainable world'. Says another critic: 'For most of us, our basic material needs are satisfied, so we seek in ever-growing consumption the satisfaction of wants, which consumption cannot possibly deliver. More is not always better; it is often worse.'[13]

Some critics have taken their concerns to the public, via the web or even straight to the streets. For example, consumer activist Annie Leonard founded the 'Story of Stuff' project with a 20-minute web video about the social and environmental consequences of the consumerist society's love affair with stuff; the video has been viewed more than 10 million times online and in thousands of schools and community centres around the world (see http://www.storyofstuff.org/).[14]

Marketers respond that such criticisms overstate the power of business to create needs. People have strong defences against advertising and other marketing tools. Marketers are most effective when they appeal to existing wants rather than when they attempt to create new ones. Furthermore, people seek information when making important purchases and often do not rely on single sources. Even minor purchases that may be affected by advertising messages lead to repeat purchases only if the product delivers the promised customer value. Finally, the high failure rate of new products shows that companies are not able to control demand.

At a deeper level, human wants and values are influenced not only by marketers but also by family, peer groups, religion, cultural background and education. If Europeans and Americans are highly materialistic, these values arose out of basic socialisation processes that go much deeper than business and mass media could produce alone.

Moreover, consumption patterns and attitudes are also subject to larger forces, such as the economy. As discussed in Chapter 1, the economic downturn and recession put a damper on materialism and conspicuous spending. As a result, far from encouraging today's more frugal consumers to overspend their means, marketers are working to help them find greater value with less.[15]

An example is the 'shwopping' movement started by British retailing giant Marks & Spencer, in which it urges customers to drop off an old item of clothing, even if it's not from M&S, each time they buy something new. Shwopped items go to Oxfam International, a non-profit organisation that resells, recycles or forwards them to raise money and help people around the world overcome poverty. 'We hope to collect as many clothes as we sell and change the way we all shop forever,' says Marks & Spencer.[16]

Too few social goods

Business has been accused of overselling private goods at the expense of public goods. As private goods increase, they require more public services that are usually not forthcoming. For example, an increase in car ownership (private good) requires more roads, traffic control, parking spaces and police services (public goods). The overselling of private goods results in 'social costs'. For cars, some of the social costs include traffic congestion, fuel shortages and air pollution. Traffic congestion costs the European Union more than 1 per cent of gross domestic product – or over €100 billion per year.[17] In the United States, American travellers lose, on average, 38 hours a year in traffic jams, costing the country more than $120 billion annually – $820 per commuter, and in the process, they waste 2.9 billion gallons of fuel and emit millions of tons of greenhouse gases.[18]

A way must be found to restore a balance between private and public goods. One option is to make producers bear the full social costs of their operations. For example, the government is requiring car manufacturers to build vehicles with more efficient engines and better pollution-control systems. Car makers will then raise their prices to cover the extra costs. If buyers find the price of some cars too high, however, the producers of these cars will disappear, or the models will be discontinued. Demand will then move to those producers that can support the sum of the private and social costs.

A second option is to make consumers pay the social costs. For example, many cities around the world are now charging 'congestion tolls' in an effort to reduce traffic congestion. To unclog its streets, the city of London levies a congestion charge of £11.50 per day per car to drive in an eight-square-mile area of the city. The charge has not only stopped the growth in traffic congestion within the zone, and increased bicycling, but also raises money to shore up London's public transport system.[19]

Cultural pollution

Critics charge the marketing system with creating *cultural pollution*. Our senses are being constantly assaulted by marketing and advertising. Commercials interrupt serious programmes; pages of ads infest magazines; advertising inserts cascade from newspapers and magazines; advertising hoardings mar beautiful scenery; spam fills our inboxes; flashing display ads intrude on our online and mobile screens. These interruptions continually pollute people's minds with messages of materialism, sex, power or status. Research suggests that most consumers think there are too many TV ads, and some critics call for sweeping changes.[20]

Marketers answer the charges of 'commercial noise' with these arguments. First, they hope that their ads primarily reach the target audience. But because of mass-communication channels, some ads are bound to reach people who have no interest in the product and are therefore bored or annoyed. People who buy magazines addressed to their interests – such as *Vogue* or *Fortune* – rarely complain about the ads because the magazines advertise products of interest.

Second, because of ads, commercial television and radio, and many online and social media sites, are free to users. Ads also keep down the costs of magazines and newspapers. Many people think commercials are a small price to pay for these benefits. Consumers find many television commercials entertaining and seek them out; for example, by viewing them on YouTube and sharing with friends. Finally, today's consumers have alternatives. For example, they can zip or zap TV commercials on recorded programmes or avoid them altogether on many paid cable, satellite or online channels. Thus, to hold consumer attention, advertisers are making their ads more entertaining and informative.

Marketing's impact on other businesses

Critics also charge that a company's marketing practices can harm other companies and reduce competition. Three problems are involved: acquisition of competitors, marketing practices that create barriers to entry, and unfair competitive marketing practices.

Critics claim that firms are harmed and competition reduced when companies expand by acquiring competitors rather than by developing their own new products. The large number of acquisitions and the rapid pace of industry consolidation over the past several decades have caused concern that vigorous young competitors will be absorbed, so competition will be reduced. In virtually every major industry – retailing, entertainment, financial services, public utilities, transport, automotive, telecommunications, healthcare – the number of major competitors is shrinking.

Acquisition is a complex subject. Acquisitions can sometimes be good for society. The acquiring company may gain economies of scale that lead to lower costs and lower prices. A well-managed company may take over a poorly managed company and improve its efficiency. An industry that was not very competitive might become more competitive after the acquisition. But acquisitions can also be harmful and, therefore, are closely regulated by government and competition regulators.

Critics have also charged that marketing practices bar new companies from entering an industry. Large marketing companies can use patents and heavy promotion spending or tie up suppliers or dealers to keep out or drive out competitors. Those concerned with anti-monopoly regulation recognise that some barriers are the natural result of the economic advantages of doing business on a large scale. Existing and new laws can challenge other barriers. For example, some critics have proposed a progressive tax on advertising spending to reduce the role of selling costs as a major barrier to entry.

Finally, some firms have, in fact, used unfair competitive marketing practices with the intention of hurting or destroying other firms. They may set their prices below costs, threaten to cut off business with suppliers, or discourage the buying of a competitor's products. Various laws work to prevent such predatory competition. It is difficult, however, to prove that the intent or action was really predatory.

For example, in the UK over recent years, Tesco has been accused of trying to build a 'Tescopoly' or monopoly on British towns and cities. The retailer is accused of using predatory pricing and sheer market power in selected towns to drive smaller retailers out of business. Tesco has become a lightning rod for protests by people in many towns who worry that the dominant UK retailer's unfair practices will choke out local businesses – protestors have subverted Tesco's 'Every little helps'. slogan into 'Every little hurts' on their website (see www.everylittlehurts.co.uk/web/). However, whereas critics charge that Tesco's actions are predatory and an abuse of market power, others assert that its actions are just the healthy competition of a more efficient company against less efficient ones. Indeed, as a troubled Tesco now looks at loss of market share to deep discount firms like Aldi and Lidl it seems markets do, in fact, adjust to favour the most efficient.

Interestingly, in the US, when mass retailer Walmart began a programme to sell generic drugs at $4 a prescription, local pharmacists complained of predatory pricing. They charged that at those low prices, Walmart must be selling under cost to drive them out of business. But Walmart claimed that, given its substantial buying power and efficient operations, it could make a profit at those prices. The $4 pricing programme, the retailer claimed, was not aimed at putting competitors out of business. Rather, it was simply a good competitive move that served customers better and brought more of them in the door. Moreover, Walmart's programme drove down prescription prices at the pharmacies of other supermarkets and discount stores, again to the benefit of customers. Currently more than 300 prescription drugs are available for $4 at the various chains and Walmart claims that the programme has saved consumers more than $4.8 billion.[21]

CONSUMER ACTIONS TO PROMOTE SUSTAINABLE MARKETING

Author comment

Sustainable marketing isn't something that only businesses and governments can do. Through consumerism and environmentalism, consumers themselves can play an important role.

Sustainable marketing calls for more responsible actions by both businesses and consumers. Because some people view business as the cause of many economic and social ills, grassroots movements have arisen from time to time to keep companies in line. Two major movements have been *consumerism* and *environmentalism*.

Consumerism

Consumerism—An organised movement of citizens and government agencies designed to improve the rights and powers of buyers in relation to sellers.

Consumerism is an organised movement of citizens and government agencies to improve the rights and power of buyers in relation to sellers. Traditional *sellers' rights* include the following:

- The right to introduce any product in any size and style, provided it is not hazardous to personal health or safety, or, if it is, to include proper warnings and controls.
- The right to charge any price for the product, provided no discrimination exists among similar kinds of buyers.
- The right to spend any amount to promote the product, provided it is not defined as unfair competition.
- The right to use any product message, provided it is not misleading or dishonest in content or execution.
- The right to use buying incentive programmes, provided they are not unfair or misleading.

Traditional *buyers' rights* include the following:

- The right not to buy a product that is offered for sale.
- The right to expect the product to be safe.
- The right to expect the product to perform as claimed.

In comparing these rights, many believe that the balance of power lies on the seller's side. True, the buyer can refuse to buy. But critics feel that the buyer has too little information, education and protection to make wise decisions when facing sophisticated sellers, even though this view is somewhat patronising. Consumer advocates call for the following additional consumer rights:

- The right to be well informed about important aspects of the product.
- The right to be protected against questionable products and marketing practices.
- The right to influence products and marketing practices in ways that will improve 'quality of life'.
- The right to consume now in a way that will preserve the world for future generations of consumers.

Each proposed right has led to more specific proposals by consumerists, and consumer protection actions by governments and regulators. The right to be informed includes the right to know the true interest on a loan (truth in lending), the true cost per unit of a brand (unit pricing), the ingredients in a product (ingredient labelling), the nutritional value of foods (nutritional labelling), product freshness (sell-by dating), and the true benefits of a product (truth in advertising). Proposals related to consumer protection include strengthening consumer rights in cases of business fraud and financial protection, requiring greater product safety, ensuring information privacy, and giving more power to regulators. Proposals relating to quality of life include controlling the ingredients that go into certain products and packaging and reducing the level of advertising 'noise'. Proposals for preserving the world for future consumption include promoting the use of sustainable ingredients, recycling and reducing solid wastes, and managing energy consumption.

Sustainable marketing applies not only to consumers but also to businesses and governments. Consumers have not only the *right* but also the *responsibility* to protect themselves, instead of leaving this function to the government or someone else. Consumers who believe they got a bad deal have several remedies available, including contacting the company or the media; contacting compliance and enforcement authorities; and going to small-claims courts. Consumers should also make good consumption choices, rewarding companies that act responsibly while punishing those that don't. Ultimately, the move from irresponsible consumption to sustainable consumption is in the hands of consumers.

Environmentalism

Whereas consumerists consider whether the marketing system is efficiently serving consumer wants, environmentalists are concerned with marketing's effects on the environment and the environmental costs of serving consumer needs and wants. **Environmentalism** is an organised movement of concerned citizens, businesses and government agencies to protect and improve people's current and future living environment.

Most environmentalists are not against marketing and consumption (although some are); they usually just want people and organisations to operate with more care for the environment. 'Too often the environment is seen as one small piece of the economy,' says one activist. 'But it's not just one little thing, it's what every single thing in our life depends upon.'[22] The marketing system's goal, as asserted by environmentalists, should not be to maximise consumption, consumer choice or consumer satisfaction but rather maximise life quality. 'Life quality' means not only the quantity and quality of consumer goods and services but also the quality of the environment, now and for future generations.

Environmentalism is concerned with damage to the ecosystem caused by global warming, resource depletion, toxic and solid wastes, litter, the availability of fresh water, and other problems. Other issues include the loss of recreational areas and the increase in health problems caused by bad air, polluted water and chemically treated food.

Over the past several decades, such concerns have resulted in laws and regulations governing industrial commercial practices impacting on the environment. Some companies have strongly resented and resisted such environmental regulations, claiming that they are too costly and have made their industries less competitive. These companies responded to consumer environmental concerns by doing only what was required to avert new regulations or keep environmentalists quiet.

In recent years, however, most companies have accepted responsibility for doing no harm to the environment. They are shifting from protest to prevention and from regulation to responsibility. More and more

Environmentalism—An organised movement of concerned citizens, businesses and government agencies designed to protect and improve people's current and future living environment.

Environmental sustainability: as part of its Sustainable Living Plan, Unilever is working with its more than two billion customers worldwide to improve the social and environmental impact of its products in use. 'Small actions. Big difference.'
Source: Unilever PLC and group companies

Environmental sustainability—A management approach that involves developing strategies that both sustain the environment and produce profits for the company.

companies are adopting policies of **environmental sustainability**. Simply put, environmental sustainability is about generating profits while helping to save the planet. Today's enlightened companies are taking action not because someone is forcing them to or to reap short-run profits but because it's the right thing to do – because it's for their customers' well-being, the company's well-being, and the planet's environmental future. For example, consumer products giant Unilever has successfully built its core mission around environmental sustainability – its aim is to 'make sustainable living commonplace' (see company case at the end of the chapter).

Figure 20.2 shows a grid that companies can use to gauge their progress toward environmental sustainability. It includes both internal and external 'greening' activities that will pay off for the firm and environment in the short run, and 'beyond greening' activities that will pay off in the longer term. At the most basic level, a company can practise *pollution prevention*. This involves more than pollution control – cleaning up waste after it has been created. Pollution prevention means eliminating or minimising waste before it is created. Companies emphasising prevention have responded with internal 'green marketing' programmes – designing and developing ecologically safer products, recyclable and biodegradable packaging, better pollution controls and more energy-efficient operations.

For example, Burger King stopped using its Indonesian palm oil suppliers, because of concerns about environmental damage following Greenpeace allegations of rainforest destruction. Unilever, Nestlé and Kraft have broken off relationships with the same suppliers for the same reason. Swedish furniture company IKEA has bought German wind farms as part of its efforts to reduce the carbon footprint of its worldwide chain of flat-pack furniture stores, following a similar deal in France. In the UK, retailers are changing the practice of centralised buying to stock more local produce – Tesco is looking at sales of locally sourced goods reaching £1 billion, and Asda is achieving a 25 per cent annual growth in sales of local produce – supporting local farmers and reducing transport costs. Some of the world's largest clothing and footwear manufacturers and retailers have an eco-label to allow shirts, trousers and shoes sold globally to be labelled with tags, so consumers can see how much the items' production and use impacts on the environment – participants include Gap, Levi Strauss, Marks & Spencer, H&M and Li & Fung (a major textile supplier).[23]

The intensity of media and consumer scrutiny of these promises is more searching than ever before. If you do not make information about your products and supplies public, the chances are increasing that consumers will do it for you. For example, GoodGuide is an online database of information about the health, environmental and social impact of 65,000 common products, which consumers can access to trace the provenance of their products.[24] Nonetheless, sometimes companies get it wrong and suffer the consequences:

> Shoppers buying Polo mints at Poundworld's discount store in York might have expected them to come from the Nestlé factory a mile up the road. In fact, the mints have travelled 7,300 miles from Indonesia where Poundworld buys them at a cheaper price than they can get from the factory in York. Nestlé does not appear to think this is a problem. In 2011, supermarket Tesco was accused of stocking Britain's least sustainable tinned tuna by a study finding that hundreds of thousands of

Figure 20.2 The environmental sustainability portfolio

Source: adapted from Stuart L. Hart, 'Innovation, Creative Destruction and Surtainability', *Research Technology Management*, September–October 2005, pp. 21–27.

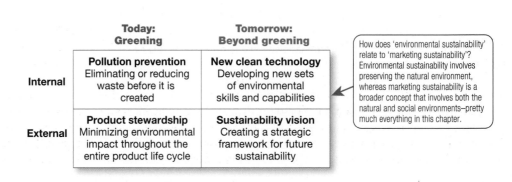

sharks, turtles, dolphins and other creatures are killed each year by its suppliers. The retailer quickly announced its intention to end all its links with these fisheries. Gingster's factory making pasties is next to a Tesco store in Cornwall, yet its pasties make a 250 mile journey to a distribution depot before returning to the store next to the factory – and neither company appeared to think there might be anything wrong with this regarding environmental impact.[25]

At the next level, companies can practise *product stewardship* – minimising not only pollution from production and product design but also all environmental impacts throughout the full product life cycle, while at the same time reducing costs. Many companies are adopting *design for environment (DFE)* and *cradle-to-cradle* practices. This involves thinking ahead to design products that are easier to recover, reuse, recycle or safely return to nature after usage, becoming part of the ecological cycle. Design for environment and cradle-to-cradle practices not only help to sustain the environment, they can also be highly profitable for the company.

For example, more than a decade ago, IBM started a business designed to reuse and recycle parts from its mainframe computers returned from lease – IBM Global Asset Recovery Services. Last year, IBM processed more than 19.1 million kilos of end-of-life products and product waste worldwide, stripping down old equipment to recover chips and valuable metals. Since 2002 it has processed more than 445 million kilos of machines, parts and material. IBM Global Asset Recovery Services finds uses for more than 99 per cent of what it takes in, sending less than 1 per cent to landfills and incineration facilities. What started out as an environmental effort has now grown into a multibillion-dollar IBM business that profitably recycles electronic equipment at 22 sites worldwide.[26] Today's 'greening' activities focus on improving what companies already do to protect the environment. The 'beyond greening' activities identified in Figure 20.2 look to the future. First, internally, companies can plan for *new clean technology*. Many organisations that have made good sustainability headway are still limited by existing technologies. To create fully sustainable strategies, they will need to develop innovative new technologies.

For example, Coca-Cola has committed by 2020 to be reclaiming and recycling the equivalent of all the packaging it uses around the world. It has also pledged to dramatically reduce its overall environmental footprint. To accomplish these goals, the company invests heavily in new clean technologies that address a host of environmental issues, such as recycling, resource usage and distribution:[27]

First, to attack the solid waste problem caused by its plastic bottles, Coca-Cola invested heavily to build the world's largest state-of-the-art plastic-bottle-to-bottle recycling plant. As a more permanent solution, Coke is researching and testing new bottles made from aluminium, corn or bioplastics. It has been steadily replacing its PET plastic bottles with PlantBottle packaging, which incorporates 30 per cent plant-based materials. The company is also designing more eco-friendly distribution alternatives. Currently, some 10 million vending machines and refrigerated coolers gobble up energy and use potent greenhouse gases called hydrofluorocarbons (HFCs) to keep Cokes cold. To eliminate them, the company invested \$40 million in research and began installing sleek new HFC-free coolers that use 30 to 40 per cent less energy – so far 1 million have been installed. Coca-Cola also aims to become 'water neutral' by researching ways to help its bottlers add back all the fresh water they extract during the production of Coca-Cola beverages.

Finally, companies can develop a *sustainability vision*, which serves as a guide to the future. It shows how the company's products and services, processes and policies must evolve and what new technologies must be developed to get there. This vision of sustainability provides a framework for pollution control, product stewardship and new environmental technology for the company and others to follow.

Most companies today focus on the upper-left quadrant of the grid in Figure 20.2, investing most heavily in pollution prevention. Some forward-looking companies practise product stewardship and are developing new environmental technologies. However, emphasising only one or two quadrants in the environmental sustainability grid can be shortsighted. Investing only in the left half of the grid puts a company in a good position today but leaves it vulnerable in the future.

In contrast, a heavy emphasis on the right half suggests that a company has good environmental vision but lacks the skills needed to implement it. Thus, companies should work at developing all four dimensions of environmental sustainability

We will see in the company case at the end of this chapter that Unilever is setting a high sustainability standard. In 2015 it continued to hold its place as one of the most sustainable corporations in the annual 'Global 100 most sustainable corporations in the world' ranking and has multiple programmes in place to manage the environmental impacts of its own operations and reduce the environmental impact of its products in use.[28]

Indeed, across the world, the food and agriculture sectors are at the forefront of efforts to involve the whole supply chain in sustainability. A recent comparison of the market share of sustainable commodities is revealing. Comparing 2008 and 2012 regarding the percentage of total production that is certified as sustainable: coffee has gone from 15 per cent in 2008 to 40 per cent in 2012; cocoa from 3 per cent to 22 per cent; palm oil from 2 per cent to 15 per cent; and tea from 6 per cent to 12 per cent. There is a long way still to go until whole supply chains meet sustainability goals, but the shift is already dramatic.[29]

Reflecting these priorities, *Fortune* magazine now evaluates the world's top eco-innovators. Top of the 2014 list was Elon Musk, CEO of Tesla Motors, leading electric car development, closely followed by Tony Fadell, CEO of NEST, pioneering a smart grid to manage home heating and cooling, saving money and scarce resources, and Lyndon and Peter Rive from Solar City, who have pioneered solar leasing programmes and energy storage systems. The world is watching closely how businesses are responding to the challenge of sustainability.[30]

Environmentalism creates some special challenges for global marketers. As international trade barriers come down and global markets expand, environmental issues are having an ever-greater impact on international trade. Countries in North America, the European Union and other developed regions are generating strict environmental standards. For example, over the past 30 years the EU has adopted a substantial and diverse range of environmental measures aimed at improving the quality of the environment for European citizens and providing them with a high quality of life. The European Union Forum of Judges for the Environment contributes to promoting the enforcement of national, European and international environmental law. To support the implementation and enforcement of Community environmental legislation, the Community has adopted the directive on environmental liability, the recommendation providing for minimum criteria for environmental inspections, and the directive on the protection of the environment through criminal law. In addition, the EU's Eco-Management and Audit Scheme (EMAS) provides guidelines for environmental self-regulation.[31]

However, environmental policies still vary widely from country to country. Countries such as Denmark, Germany, Japan and the United States have fully developed environmental policies and high public expectations. But major developing countries like the BRICs are only in the early stages of developing such policies. Moreover, environmental factors that motivate consumers in one country may have no impact on consumers in another. For example, PVC soft-drink bottles cannot be used in Switzerland or Germany. However, they are preferred in France, which has an extensive recycling process for them. Thus, international companies have found it difficult to develop standard environmental practices that work globally. Instead, they are creating general policies and then translating these policies into tailored programmes that meet local regulations and expectations.

From a sustainable marketing perspective environmental awareness stimulates innovation and creative approaches to business. For example, a chemist in India has developed a way of turning litter into roads. Grocery bags and other low-quality plastic litter are shredded, added to gravel and tar and used to provide a road surface. As chemistry professor and inventor of the process Rajagopalan Vasudevan says: 'What is the use to spend thousands of rupees when we can do it much more cheaply?' Cheaper roads that recycle waste shows how business can meet the challenges of environmentalism.[32] Even closer to home, Knowaste is a recycling firm specialising in 'absorbent hygiene waste' (mainly babies' disposable nappies) which is processed to be made into such products as plastic roof tiles. Entrepreneurial efforts provide many examples of sustainable strategies at work.[33]

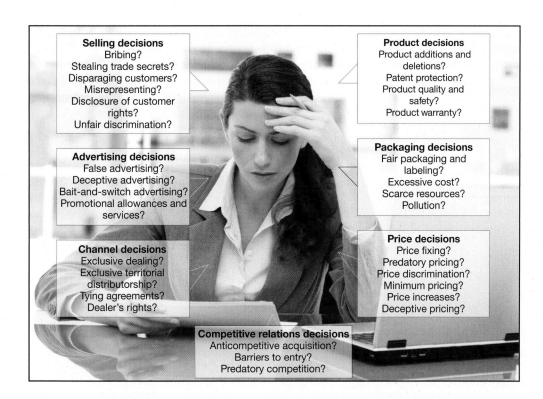

Figure 20.3 Major marketing decision areas that may be called into question under the law

Selling decisions
Bribing?
Stealing trade secrets?
Disparaging customers?
Misrepresenting?
Disclosure of customer rights?
Unfair discrimination?

Advertising decisions
False advertising?
Deceptive advertising?
Bait-and-switch advertising?
Promotional allowances and services?

Channel decisions
Exclusive dealing?
Exclusive territorial distributorship?
Tying agreements?
Dealer's rights?

Product decisions
Product additions and deletions?
Patent protection?
Product quality and safety?
Product warranty?

Packaging decisions
Fair packaging and labeling?
Excessive cost?
Scarce resources?
Pollution?

Price decisions
Price fixing?
Predatory pricing?
Price discrimination?
Minimum pricing?
Price increases?
Deceptive pricing?

Competitive relations decisions
Anticompetitive acquisition?
Barriers to entry?
Predatory competition?

Public actions to regulate marketing

Citizen concerns about marketing practices will usually lead to public attention and legislative proposals. Many of the laws that affect marketing were identified in Chapter 3. The task is to translate these laws into a language that marketing executives understand as they make decisions about competitive relations, products, price, promotion and distribution channels. Figure 20.3 illustrates the major legal issues facing marketing management.

BUSINESS ACTIONS TOWARDS SUSTAINABLE MARKETING

At first, many companies opposed consumerism, environmentalism and other elements of sustainable marketing. They thought the criticisms were either unfair or unimportant. But by now, most companies have grown to embrace sustainability marketing principles as a way to create greater immediate and future customer value and strengthen customer relationships.

Sustainable marketing principles

Under the sustainable marketing concept, a company's marketing should support the best long-run performance of the marketing system. It should be guided by five sustainable marketing principles: *consumer-oriented marketing*, *customer-value marketing*, *innovative marketing*, *sense-of-mission marketing* and *societal marketing*.

Consumer-oriented marketing

Consumer-oriented marketing means that the company should view and organise its marketing activities from the consumer's point of view. It should work hard to sense, serve and satisfy

Author comment

In the end, marketers themselves must take responsibility for sustainable marketing. That means operating in a responsible and ethical way to bring both immediate and future value to customers.

Consumer-oriented marketing—A company should view and organise its marketing activities from the consumer's point of view.

the needs of a defined group of customers – both now and in the future. The good marketing companies that we've discussed throughout this text have had this in common: an all-consuming passion for delivering superior value to carefully chosen customers. Only by seeing the world through its customers' eyes can the company build lasting and profitable customer relationships.

Customer-value marketing

Customer-value marketing—A company should put most of its resources into customer-value-building investments.

According to the principle of **customer-value marketing**, the company should put most of its resources into customer-value-building marketing investments. Many things marketers do – one-shot sales promotions, cosmetic packaging changes, direct-response advertising – may raise sales in the short run but add less *value* than would actual improvements in the product's quality, features or convenience. Enlightened marketing calls for building long-run consumer loyalty and relationships by continually improving the value consumers receive from the firm's market offering. By creating value *for* consumers, the company can capture value *from* consumers in return.[34]

Innovative marketing

Innovative marketing—A company should seek real product and marketing improvements.

The principle of **innovative marketing** requires that the company continuously seek real product and marketing improvements. The company that overlooks new and better ways to do things will eventually lose customers to another company that has found a better way. For example, remember the Nike story:[35]

> For nearly 50 years, through innovative marketing, Nike has built the ever-present swoosh into one of the world's best-known brand symbols. When sales languished in the late 1990s and new competitors made gains, Nike knew it had to reinvent itself via product and marketing innovation. 'One of my fears is being this big, slow, constipated, bureaucratic company that's happy with its success,' says Nike CEO Mark Parker. Instead, over the past few years, a hungry Nike has unleashed a number of highly successful new products. For example, with the new Nike Flyknit Racer, Nike has now reinvented the very way that shoes are manufactured. The featherweight Flyknit feels more like a sock with a sole. Woven not sewn, the Flyknit is super comfortable and durable, more affordable to make, and more environmentally friendly than traditional sneakers. Top off Nike's new products with a heavy investment in social media content and Nike remains the world's largest sports apparel company, an impressive 25 per cent larger than closest rival Adidas. Both *Forbes* and *Fast Company* recently anointed Nike as the world's number one most innovative company.

Sense-of-mission marketing

Sense-of-mission marketing—A principle of sustainable marketing that holds a company should define its mission in broad social terms rather than narrow products terms.

Sense-of-mission marketing means that the company should define its mission in broad *social* terms rather than narrow *product* terms. When a company defines a social mission, employees feel better about their work and have a clearer sense of direction. Brands linked with broader missions can serve the best long-run interests of both the brand and consumers.

> For example, Pedigree makes good dog food, but that's not what the brand is really all about. Instead, the brand came up with the tagline 'Dogs rule'. The tagline 'is the perfect encapsulation of everything we stand for', says a Pedigree marketer. 'Everything that we do is because we love dogs, because dogs rule. It's just so simple.' This mission-focused positioning drives everything the brand does – internally and externally. One look at a Pedigree ad or a visit to the Pedigree.com or UK.Pedigree.com website confirms that the people behind the Pedigree brand really do believe the 'Dogs rule' mission. An internal manifesto called 'Dogma' even encourages employees to take their dogs to work and on sales calls. To further fulfil the 'Dogs rule' brand promise, the company created the Pedigree Adoption Drive Foundation, which has raised millions of dollars for helping 'shelter dogs' find good homes. Sense-of-mission marketing has made Pedigree the world's number one dog food brand.[36]

Some companies define their overall corporate missions in broad societal terms. For example, defined in narrow product terms, the mission of the well-known US outdoor gear and apparel maker Patagonia might be 'to sell clothes and outdoor equipment'. However, Patagonia states its mission more broadly, as one of producing the highest quality products while doing the least harm to the environment. From the start, Patagonia has pursued a passionately held social responsibility mission:[37]

> For us at Patagonia, 'a love of wild and beautiful places demands participation in the fight to save them, and to help reverse the steep decline in the overall environmental health of our planet'. Our reason for being is to 'build the best product, cause no unnecessary harm, use business to inspire and implement solutions to the environmental crisis'. Yet we're keenly aware that everything we do as a business – or have done in our name – leaves its mark on the environment. As yet, there is no such thing as a sustainable business, but every day we take steps to lighten our footprint and do less harm. Each year since 1985, the company has given away 10 per cent of its pre-tax profits to support environmental causes. Today, 'we donate our time, services and at least 1 per cent of sales to hundreds of grassroots environmental groups all over the world who work to help reverse the environmental tide'.

However, having a 'double bottom line' of values and profits isn't easy. Over the years, companies such as Patagonia, Ben & Jerry's and The Body Shop – all known and respected for putting 'principles before profits' – have at times struggled with less-than-stellar financial returns. In recent years, however, a new generation of social entrepreneurs has emerged – well-trained business managers who know that to 'do good', they must first 'do well' in terms of profitable business operations. Moreover, today, socially responsible business is no longer the sole province of small, socially conscious entrepreneurs. Many large, established companies and brands have adopted substantial social and environmental responsibility missions.

Societal marketing

Following the principle of **societal marketing**, a company makes marketing decisions by considering consumers' wants, the company's requirements, consumers' long-run interests and society's long-run interests. Companies should be aware that neglecting consumer and societal long-run interests is a disservice to consumers and society. Alert companies view societal problems as opportunities.

Sustainable marketing calls for products that are not only pleasing but also beneficial. The difference is shown in Figure 20.4. Products can be classified according to their degree of immediate consumer satisfaction and long-run consumer benefit.

Sense-of-mission marketing: A for-profit company telling consumers to buy less sounds crazy. But its right on target with Patagonia's conscious-consumption mission, which urges consumers to buy only what they need and take only what the planet can replace.

Source: Property of Patagonia. Used with permission.

Societal marketing—A company should make marketing decisions by considering consumers' wants, the company's requirements, consumers' long-term interests and society's long-term interests.

Figure 20.4 Societal classification of products

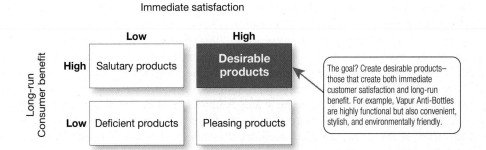

Deficient products—Products that have neither immediate appeal nor long-run benefits.

Pleasing products—Products that give high immediate satisfaction but may hurt consumers in the long run.

Salutary products–Products that have low immediate appeal but may benefit consumers in the long run.

Desirable products—Products that give both high immediate satisfaction and high long-run benefits.

Desirable products: Vapur Anti-Bottles' reusable, collapsible water bottles are highly functional and also more convenient, stylish and environmentally friendly than either the disposable plastic bottles or rigid water bottles they replace. The photo shows Laura Bylund - professional climber.

Source: Vapur/Laura Bylund - Professional Climber/Kev Steele/kevsteele.com

Deficient products, such as bad-tasting and ineffective medicine, have neither immediate appeal nor long-run benefits. **Pleasing products** give high immediate satisfaction but may hurt consumers in the long run. Examples include cigarettes, alcohol and junk food. **Salutary products** have low immediate appeal but may benefit consumers in the long run, for instance bicycle helmets or some insurance products. **Desirable products** give both high immediate satisfaction and high long-run benefits, such as a tasty *and* nutritious breakfast food.

Examples of desirable products abound. For example, Vapur makes a line of reusable, lightweight, collapsible water bottles that are highly functional and also more convenient, stylish and environmentally friendly than either the disposable plastic bottles or rigid water bottles they replace. When full, pliable Vapur Anti-Bottles can be easily stuffed in pockets or backpacks; when empty, they can be rolled, folded or flattened and easily tucked away. At the same time, the bottles require less energy to make and transport than rigid bottles, and unlike disposable plastic bottles, they don't clog landfills or require recycling. Vapur also donates portions of its sales to organisations such as Leave No Trace and The Conservation Alliance, and its Drops of Hope programme annually donates thousands of Vapur bottles to charitable organisations around the world.[38]

Companies should try to turn all of their products into desirable products. The challenge posed by pleasing products is that they sell very well but may end up hurting the consumer. The product opportunity, therefore, is to add long-run benefits without reducing the product's pleasing qualities. The challenge posed by salutary products is to add some pleasing qualities so that they will become more desirable in consumers' minds.

For example, PepsiCo recently hired a team of 'idealistic scientists', headed by a former director of the World Health Organisation to help the company create attractive new healthy product options while 'making the bad stuff less bad'.[39] The group of medical doctors, PhDs and other health advocates, under the direction of PepsiCo's vice president for global health policy, looks for healthier ingredients that can go into multiple products. For example, their efforts led to an all-natural zero-calorie sweetener now featured in several new PepsiCo brands, including the $100-million Trop50 brand, a Tropicana orange juice variation that contains no artificial sweeteners and half the sugar and calories.

MARKETING ETHICS

Good ethics are a cornerstone of sustainable marketing. In the long run, unethical marketing harms customers and society as a whole. Further, it eventually damages a company's reputation and effectiveness, jeopardising its very survival. Thus, the sustainable marketing goals of long-term consumer and business welfare can be achieved only through ethical marketing conduct.

Conscientious marketers face many moral dilemmas. The best thing to do is often unclear. Because not all managers have fine moral sensitivity, companies need to develop *corporate marketing ethics policies* – broad guidelines that everyone in the organisation must follow. These policies should cover distributor relations, advertising standards, customer service, pricing, product development and general ethical standards.

The finest guidelines cannot resolve all the difficult ethical situations the marketer faces. **Table 20.1** lists some difficult ethical issues marketers could face during their careers. If marketers choose immediate sales-producing actions in all these cases, their marketing behaviour might well be described as immoral or even amoral. If they refuse to go along with *any* of the actions, they might be ineffective as marketing managers and unhappy because of the constant moral tension. Managers need a set of principles that will help them figure out the moral importance of each situation and decide how far they can go in good conscience.

Table 20.1 Some morally difficult situations in marketing

Your R&D department has slightly changed one of your company's products. It is not really 'new and improved', but you know that putting this statement on the package and in advertising will increase sales. What would you do?

You have been asked to add a stripped-down model to your line that could be advertised to pull customers into the store. The product won't be very good, but salespeople will be able to switch buyers who come into the store up to higher-priced units. You are asked to give the green light for the stripped-down version. What would you do?

You are thinking of hiring a product manager who has just left a competitor's company. She would be more than happy to tell you all the competitor's plans for the coming year. What would you do?

One of your top dealers in an important territory recently has had family troubles, and his sales have slipped. It looks like it will take him a while to straighten out his family troubles. Meanwhile, you are losing many sales. Legally, on performance grounds, you can terminate the dealer's franchise and replace him. What would you do?

You have a chance to win a big account in another country that will mean a lot to you and your company. The purchasing agent hints that a 'gift' would influence the decision. Such gifts are common in that country, and some of your competitors will probably make one. What would you do?

You have heard that a competitor has a new product feature that will make a big difference in sales. The competitor will demonstrate the feature in a private dealer meeting at the annual trade show. You can easily send a snooper to this meeting to learn about the new feature. What would you do?

You have to choose between three advertising campaigns outlined by your agency. The first (a) is a soft-sell, honest, straight-information campaign. The second (b) uses sex-loaded emotional appeals and exaggerates the product's benefits. The third (c) involves a noisy, somewhat irritating commercial that is sure to gain audience attention. Pretests show that the campaigns are effective in the following order: c, b and a. What would you do?

You are interviewing a capable female applicant for a job as salesperson. She is better qualified than the men who have been interviewed. Nevertheless, you know that in your industry some important customers prefer dealing with men, and you will lose some sales if you hire her. What would you do?

But the question remains, *what* principle should guide companies and marketing managers on issues of ethics and social responsibility? One philosophy is that the free market and the legal system should decide such issues. Under this principle, companies and their managers are not responsible for making moral judgements. Companies can in good conscience do whatever the market and legal systems allow. However, history provides an endless list of examples of company actions that were legal but highly irresponsible.

A second philosophy puts responsibility not on the system but in the hands of individual companies and managers. This more enlightened philosophy suggests that a company should have a 'social conscience'. Companies and managers should apply high standards of ethics and morality when making corporate decisions, regardless of 'what the system allows'.

Each company and marketing manager must work out a philosophy of socially responsible and ethical behaviour. Under the societal marketing concept, each manager must look beyond what is legal and allowed and develop standards based on personal integrity, corporate conscience and long-run consumer welfare.

Dealing with issues of ethics and social responsibility in an open and forthright way helps to build strong customer relationships based on honesty and trust. In fact, many companies now routinely include consumers in the social responsibility process.

As with environmentalism, the issue of ethics presents special challenges for international marketers. Business standards and practices vary immensely from one country to the next. Countries like the UK and the US have stringent and actively enforced laws prohibiting bribery. For example, the 2011 Bribery Act in Britain creates a new offence of failure to prevent bribery by people working on behalf of a business, in addition to the existing criminal offence to give, promise or offer a bribe at home or abroad. Penalties for bribery are increased to ten years imprisonment and an unlimited fine. British anti-corruption law is now more sweeping than its American counterpart.[40]

Similarly, bribes and kickbacks are illegal for US firms. In addition, a variety of treaties against bribery and corruption have been signed and ratified by more than 60 countries. Yet these are still standard business practices in many countries.

The World Bank estimates that bribes totalling more than $1 trillion per year are paid out worldwide. One study showed that the most flagrant bribe-paying firms were from Indonesia, Mexico, China and Russia. Other countries where corruption is common include Sierra Leone, Kenya and Yemen. The least corrupt were companies from Australia, Denmark, Finland and Japan.[41] The question arises as to whether a company must lower its ethical standards to compete effectively in countries with lower standards. The answer is no. Companies should make a commitment to a common set of shared standards worldwide. The long-term risks in not doing so are simply too high. The global pharmaceutical industry faces huge problems in removing from its business model marketing practices which were conventional policies but are now seen as wholly unacceptable and subject to sanctions by governments – incentives to clinicians to prescribe drugs were once seen as legitimate sales promotion, but are now viewed as bribery and corruption, and guilty companies are subject to huge fines and legal action.

Many industrial and professional associations have suggested codes of ethics, and many companies are now adopting their own codes. One of the longest-established and widely accepted codes is the one produced by the American Marketing Association, the US association of marketing managers and scholars. A similar document concerning professional marketing standards has been produced by the Chartered Institute of Marketing in the UK.[42] The American Marketing Association code of ethics that calls on marketers to adopt the following ethical norms:[43]

- *Do no harm.* This means consciously avoiding harmful actions or omissions by embodying high ethical standards and adhering to all applicable laws and regulations in the choices we make.
- *Foster trust in the marketing system.* This means striving for good faith and fair dealing so as to contribute toward the efficacy of the exchange process as well as avoiding deception in product design, pricing, communication and delivery or distribution.
- *Embrace ethical values.* This means building relationships and enhancing consumer confidence in the integrity of marketing by affirming these core values: honesty, responsibility, fairness, respect, transparency and citizenship.

Companies are also developing their own programmes to teach managers about important ethical issues and help them find the proper responses. They hold ethics workshops and seminars and create ethics committees. Furthermore, many major international companies have appointed high-level ethics officers to champion ethical issues and help resolve ethics problems and concerns facing employees. Google is a good example.

Google's official 'Google Code of Conduct' is the mechanism by which the company puts its well-known 'Don't be evil' motto into practice. The detailed code's core message is simple: Google employees (know inside as 'Googlers') must earn users' faith and trust by holding themselves to the highest possible standards of ethical business conduct. The Google 'Code of Conduct' is 'about providing our users unbiased access to information, focusing on their needs, and giving them the best products and services that we can. But it's also about doing the right thing more generally – following the law, acting honourably, and treating each other with respect'.

Google requires all Googlers – from board members to the newest employee – to take personal responsibility for practising both the spirit and letter of the code and encouraging other Googlers to do the same. It urges employees to report violations to their managers, to human resources representatives, or using an Ethics & Compliance hotline. 'If you have a question or ever think that one of your fellow Googlers or the company as a whole may be falling short of our commitment, don't be silent,' states the code. 'We want – and need – to hear from you.'[44]

Still, written codes and ethics programmes do not ensure ethical behaviour. Ethics and social responsibility require a total corporate commitment. As the Google 'Code of Conduct' concludes: 'It's impossible to spell out every possible ethical scenario we might face. Instead, we rely on one another's good judgment to uphold a high standard of integrity for ourselves and our company. Remember . . . don't be evil. If you see something that isn't right, speak up!'

THE SUSTAINABLE COMPANY

At the foundation of marketing is the belief that companies that fulfil the needs and wants of customers will thrive. Companies that fail to meet customer needs or that intentionally or unintentionally harm customers, others in society, or future generations will decline. The Internet is accelerating the spread of a global consciousness – the 'conscience culture' and social responsibility is no longer an add-on but is intrinsic to all the functions of the business. Moreover, expertise in social responsibility may be a particular requirement of the marketing department.[45]

Importantly, initiatives like the Global Institute for Tomorrow, offering experiential education for executives, are changing the way people think about sustainability, overcoming complacency and providing executives with new insights into the role of business in the world.[46] Indeed, the move to link executive pay to sustainability targets has been underway for some time, with companies like TNT, DSM and Azco Nobel in the Netherlands leading the way.[47]

Says one observer, 'Sustainability is an emerging business megatrend, like electrification and mass production, that will profoundly affect companies' competitiveness and even their survival.'[48] Says another, 'increasingly, companies and leaders will be assessed not only on immediate results but also on . . . the ultimate effects their actions have on societal wellbeing. This trend has been coming in small ways for years but now is surging. So pick up your recycled cup of fair-trade coffee, and get ready'.[49]

Sustainable companies are those that create value for customers through socially, environmentally and ethically responsible actions. Sustainable marketing goes beyond caring for the needs and wants of today's customers. It means having concern for tomorrow's customers in assuring the survival and success of the business, shareholders, employees and the broader world in which they all live. It means pursuing the mission of a triple bottom line: people, planet and profits. Sustainable marketing provides the context in which companies can build profitable customer relationships by creating value *for* customers to capture value *from* customers in return – now and in the future.

OBJECTIVES REVIEW AND KEY TERMS

In this chapter, we addressed many of the important sustainable marketing concepts related to marketing's sweeping impact on individual consumers, other businesses and society as a whole. Sustainable marketing requires socially, environmentally and ethically responsible actions that bring value to not only present-day consumers and businesses but also future generations and society as a whole. Sustainable companies are those that act responsibly to create value for customers to capture value from customers in return – now and in the future.

OBJECTIVE 1 Define sustainable marketing and discuss its importance (pp. 593–594)

Sustainable marketing calls for meeting the present needs of consumers and businesses while preserving or enhancing the ability of future generations to meet their needs. Whereas the marketing concept recognises that companies thrive by fulfilling the day-to-day needs of customers, sustainable marketing calls for socially and environmentally responsible actions that meet both the immediate

and future needs of customers and the company. Truly sustainable marketing requires a smooth-functioning marketing system in which consumers, companies, public policymakers and others work together to ensure responsible marketing actions.

OBJECTIVE 2 Identify the major social criticisms of marketing (pp. 594–602)

Marketing's *impact on individual consumer welfare* has been criticised for high prices, deceptive practices, high-pressure selling, shoddy or unsafe products, planned obsolescence and poor service to disadvantaged consumers. Marketing's *impact on society* has been criticised for creating false wants and too much materialism, too few social goods and cultural pollution. Critics have also denounced marketing's *impact on other businesses* for harming competitors and reducing competition through acquisitions, practices that create barriers to entry, and unfair competitive marketing practices. Some of these concerns are justified; some are not.

OBJECTIVE 3 Define consumerism and environmentalism and explain how they affect marketing strategies (pp. 602–607)

Concerns about the marketing system have led to citizen action movements. *Consumerism* is an organised social movement intended to strengthen the rights and power of consumers relative to sellers. Alert marketers view it as an opportunity to serve consumers better by providing more consumer information, education and protection. *Environmentalism* is an organised social movement seeking to minimise the harm done to the environment and quality of life by marketing practices. The first wave of modern environmentalism was driven by environmental groups and concerned consumers; the second wave was driven by the federal government, which passed laws and regulations governing industrial practices impacting on the environment. Most companies are accepting responsibility for doing no environmental harm. They are adopting policies of *environmental sustainability* – developing strategies that both sustain the environment and produce profits for the company. Both consumerism and environmentalism are important components of sustainable marketing.

OBJECTIVE 4 Describe the principles of sustainable marketing (pp. 607–610)

Many companies originally resisted these social movements and laws, but most now recognise a need for positive consumer information, education and protection. Under the sustainable marketing concept, a company's marketing should support the best long-run performance of the marketing system. It should be guided by five sustainable marketing principles: *consumer-oriented marketing, customer-value marketing, innovative marketing, sense-of-mission marketing* and *societal marketing*.

OBJECTIVE 5 Explain the role of ethics in marketing (pp. 610–613)

Increasingly, companies are responding to the need to provide company policies and guidelines to help their managers deal with questions of *marketing ethics*. Of course, even the best guidelines cannot resolve all the difficult ethical decisions that individuals and firms must make. But there are some principles from which marketers can choose. One principle states that the free market and the legal system should decide such issues. A second and more enlightened principle puts responsibility not on the system but in the hands of individual companies and managers. Each firm and marketing manager must work out a philosophy of socially responsible and ethical behaviour. Under the sustainable marketing concept, managers must look beyond what is legal and allowable and develop standards based on personal integrity, corporate conscience, and long-term consumer welfare.

NAVIGATING THE KEY TERMS

OBJECTIVE 1
Sustainable marketing (p. 593)

OBJECTIVE 3
Consumerism (p. 602)
Environmentalism (p. 603**)**

Environmental sustainability (p. 604)

OBJECTIVE 4
Consumer-oriented marketing (p. 607)
Customer-value marketing (p. 608)
Innovative marketing (p. 608)

Sense-of-mission marketing (p. 608)
Societal marketing (p. 609)
Deficient products (p. 610)
Pleasing products (p. 610)
Salutary products (p. 610)
Desirable products (p. 610)

DISCUSSION AND CRITICAL THINKING

Discussion questions

20-1 What is sustainable marketing? Explain how the sustainable marketing concept differs from the marketing concept and the societal marketing concept. (AACSB: Communication)

20-2 What is planned obsolescence? How do marketers respond to this criticism? (AACSB: Communication; Reflective thinking)

20-3 How can marketers respond to the criticism that marketing creates false wants and encourages materialism? (AACSB: Communication)

20-4 What is consumerism? What rights do consumers have and why do some critics of marketing feel buyers need more protection? (AACSB: Communication)

20-5 What is environmental sustainability? How should companies gauge their progress towards achieving it? (AACSB: Communication)

Critical-thinking exercises

20-6 The chapter discusses how companies respond to social responsibility criticisms. Find other examples of how marketers have responded to social criticisms of their products or marketing practices. (AACSB: Communication; Reflective thinking)

20-7 Deceptive advertising hurts consumers and competitors alike. Discuss a recent example of a deceptive advertising complaint investigated by the regulators in a country of your choice and the advertising industry itself in the same country. (AACSB: Communication; Use of IT; Reflective thinking)

20-8 In a small group, discuss each one of the morally difficult situations in marketing discussed in the chapter, and examine the particular difficulties in resolving it for an international marketer. (AACSB: Communication; Ethical reasoning)

Mini-cases and applications

Online, mobile and social media marketing: teenagers and social media

Facebook recently announced that it will let teenagers' posts become public. Before the change, Facebook would only allow 13- to 17-year-old users' posts to be seen by their 'friends' and 'friends of friends'. Now, however, their posts can be seen by anyone on the network, if the teenager chooses to make their posts 'public'. Twitter, another social medium gaining popularity with teenagers, has always let users, including teenagers, share tweets publicly. But because of Facebook's vast reach, privacy advocates are very concerned about this latest development, particularly when it comes to children's safety. Online predators and bullying are real safety issues facing young people. Other criticisms of Facebook's decision boil down to money – some argue that this is just about monetising children. Facebook will be able to offer a younger demographic to advertisers wanting to reach them. Facebook defends its actions, saying the change in policy is due to teenagers wanting the ability to post publicly, primarily for fundraising and promoting extracurricular activities such as sports and other school student organisations. Facebook has added precautions, such as a pop-up warning before teenagers can post publicly and making 'seen only by friends' the default, that must be changed if the teenage user desires posts to be public.

20-9 Do you think Facebook is acting responsibly or merely trying to monetise children as critics claim? (AACSB: Communication; Ethical reasoning)

20-10 Come up with creative ways marketers can reach this demographic on Facebook without alienating their parents. (AACSB: Communication; Reflective thinking)

Marketing ethics: pricey deal?

Rent-to-own retailing originated in the UK and Europe in the 1930s and developed in the US in the 1950s and 1960s. However, Kmart recently introduced a new Lease-to-Own programme targeted to low-income consumers and is taking some heat over it. Rent-to-own is not new – chains such as Aaron's and Rent-A-Center have been around for years in the US – but it is new that a mainstream retailer is moving into this market. Kmart's parent corporation, Sears Holdings Corporation, launched a similar programme, and according to a company executive, it is satisfying the unmet needs of new customers. Some critics say that it is just encouraging instant gratification and exploiting disadvantaged consumers. These types of customers don't qualify for credit and don't have enough cash to purchase desired products outright, such as televisions and other big ticket items. However, a $300 TV purchased through Kmart's programme ends up costing consumers $415 if purchased at the end of the lease. If customers just make minimum payments over the course of the lease, one expert calculated, it is equivalent to charging a 117 per cent annual interest rate. Sears' spokespeople defend their service as being better for consumers compared to other rent-to-own options because the retailer does not mark up the price of the product beyond the normal retail mark-up and limits the lease period to 18 months, whereas other national rental chains' prices are much higher and leases can run two to four years.

20-11 Are rent-to-own retailers, like Sears and Kmart, exploiting disadvantaged consumers? Explain why or why not. (AACSB: Communication; Ethical reasoning)

20-12 Low-income consumers often don't have bank accounts and credit cards. Describe how some financial institutions are trying to meet the needs of these 'unbanked' consumers. (AACSB: Communication; Reflective thinking)

Marketing by the numbers: the cost of sustainability

In the United States, Kroger, the country's leading grocery-only chain, added a line of private label organic and natural foods call Simple Truth to its stores. If you've bought organic foods, you know they are more expensive. For example, a dozen conventionally farmed Grade-A eggs at Kroger costs consumers $1.70, whereas Simple Truth eggs are priced at $3.50 per dozen. One study found that, overall, the average price of organic foods is 85 per cent more than conventional foods. However, if prices get too high, consumers will not purchase the organic options. One element of sustainability is organic farming, which costs much more than conventional farming, and those higher costs are passed on to consumers. Suppose that a conventional egg farmer's average fixed costs per year for conventionally farmed eggs are $1 million per year, but an organic egg farmer's fixed costs are three times that amount. The organic farmer's variable costs of $1.80 per dozen are twice as much as a conventional farmer's variable costs. Refer to Appendix 2, Marketing by the numbers, to answer the following questions.

20-13 Most large egg farmers sell eggs directly to retailers. Using Kroger's prices, what is the farmer's price per dozen to the retailer for conventional and organic eggs if Kroger's margin is 20 per cent based on its retail price? (AACSB: Communication; Analytical reasoning)

20-14 How many dozen eggs does a conventional farmer need to sell to break even? How many does an organic farmer need to sell to break even? (AACSB: Communication; Analytical reasoning)

REFERENCES

[1] The sources for this case are: Oliver Shah, 'Geeks go mad for a bit of Pi – Raspberry Pi, the £15 computer', *The Sunday Times*, 2 September 2012, p. 1 & p. 9; Sean Poulter, '£22 App factory', *Daily Mail*, 1 March 2012, p. 31; Maija Palmer, 'Raspberry Pi minicomputer sells out', *Financial Times*, 1 March 2012, p. 2; Jonathan Moules, 'An unexpected slice of success', *Financial Times*, 2 October 2013, p. 14; Kate Bevan, 'How smart homes put a price on data', *Financial Times*, 17 May 2015; Mark Odell, 'BBC to give 1M computers to children', *Financial Times*, 12 March 2015' Sally Davies, 'Raspberry Pi launches its smallest, cheapest device yet', *Financial Times*, 10 November 2014.

[2] McDonald's financial information and other facts from www.aboutmcdonalds.com/mcd/investors.html and www.aboutmcdonalds.com/mcd, accessed September 2014.

[3] See, for example: Nigel F. Piercy and Nikala Lane, 'Corporate social responsibility: impacts on marketing and customer value', *The Marketing Review*, Vol. 9, No. 4, 2009, pp. 335–360; Nigel F. Piercy and Nikala lane, 'Corporate social responsiobility initiatives and strategic marketing imperatives', *Social Business*, Vol. 1, Winter, 2011, pp. 325–345.

[4] See 'Overweight and obesity in the US', FRAC, http://frac.org/initiatives/hunger-and-obesity/obesity-in-the-us/, accessed July 2014; and 'Overweight and obesity', Centers for Disease Control and Prevention, www.cdc.gov/obesity/data/index.html, accessed September 2014.

[5] Elena Ferretti, 'Soft drinks are the whipping boy of anti-obesity campaigns', Fox News, 1 June 2012, www.foxnews.com/leisure/2012/06/01/soda-ban/; also see Stephanie Strom, 'In ads, Coke confronts soda's link to obesity', *New York Times*, 14 January 2013; and Natalie Zmuda and others, 'Coca-Cola would like to teach the world to move', *Advertising Age*, 11 September 2013, http://adage.com/print/244077.

[6] Sarah Bridge, 'We were making money out of misery – so we dropped two leading brands', *Mail on Sunday*, 11 May 2014, p. 84.

[7] For more on perceived obsolescence, see Annie Leonard, *The Story of Stuff* (New York: Free Press, 2010), pp. 162–163; and www.storyofstuff.com, accessed April 2010.

[8] Brian Clark Howard, 'Planned obsolescence: 8 products designed to fail', *Popular Mechanics*, www.popularmechanics.com/technology/planned-obsolescence-460210#slide-5, accessed September 2014.

[9] See 'Law targets obsolete products', 22 April 2013, *The Connexion*, www.connexionfrance.com/Planned-obsolescence-obsoleteproducts-iPod-washing-machine-printers-14655-view-article.html.

[10] See Karen Auge, 'Planting seed in food deserts: neighborhood gardens, produce in corner stores', *Denver Post*, 18 April, 2010, p. 1; and 'Supermarket campaign: improving access to supermarkets in underserved communities', *The Food Trust*, www.thefoodtrust.org/php/programs/super.market.campaign.php, accessed July 2010.

[11] See Spence Cooper, 'National food chains join first lady to reach "food deserts"', *Friends Eat*, 25 July 2011, http://blog.friendseat.com/michelle-obama-program-reaches-food-deserts; 'Whole foods takes the high, low (priced) roads', *Adweek*, 3 June 2013, pp. 10–11; Matt Lerner, 'Do you live in a food desert?' *Walk Score*, 26 March 2014, http://blog.walkscore.com/2014/03/best-and-worst-u-s-food-deserts/; and US Department of Agriculture, 'Creating access to healthy, affordable food', http://apps.ams.usda.gov/fooddeserts, accessed September 2014.

[12] Leonard Stern, 'Aspiration gap behind downward cycle in US', *Calgary Herald* (Canada), 9 November 2008, p. A11; See www.metro.co.uk/news/44366-riot-at-new-london-primark-store#ixzz1nt5ze01L, accessed March 2012.

[13] Oliver James, 'It's more than enough to make you sick', *Marketing*, 23 January 2008, pp. 26–28; and Richard J. Varey, 'Marketing means and ends for a sustainable society: a welfare agenda for transformative change', *Journal of Macromarketing*, June 2010, pp. 112–126.

[14] See 'Overconsumption is costing us the earth and human happiness', *The Guardian*, 21 June 2010, accessed at www.guardian.co.uk/environment/2010/jun/21/overconsumption-environment-relationships-annie-leonard; and 'The story of stuff', www.storyofstuff.com, accessed July 2010.

[15] Conor Dougherty and Elizabeth Holmes, 'Consumer spending perks up economy', *Wall Street Journal*, 13 March 2010, p. A1.

[16] See www.marksandspencer.com/s/plan-a-shwopping, accessed September 2014.

[17] See www-07.ibm.com/innovation/my/exhibit/documents/pdf/2_The_Case_For_Smarter_Transportation.pdf, accessed 18 July 2015.

[18] See Texas Transportation Institute, 'Inconsistent traffic conditions forcing Texas commuters to allow even more extra time', http://d2dtl5nnlpfr0r.cloudfront.net/tti.tamu.edu/documents/tti-umr.pdf, accessed September 2014.

[19] See https://tfl.gov.uk/modes/driving/congestion-charge?cid=pp020, accessed July 13 2015.

[20] See 'Advertising in the U.S.: synovate global survey shows Internet, innovation and online privacy a must', 3 December 2009, www.synovate.com/news/article/2009/12/advertising-in-the-us-synovate-global-survey-shows-internet-innovation-and-online-privacy-a-must.html; and Katy Bachman, 'Survey: clutter causing TV ads to lack effectiveness', *MediaWeek*, 8 February 2010, www.mediaweek.com/mw/content_display/esearch/e3ief7f94880dc0982ebfa130c698f8d2e8?src=bchallenge.

[21] See 'Walmart launches national advertising campaign to show "The real Walmart"', 4 May 2013, http://news.walmart.com/news-archive/2013/05/04/walmart-launches-national-advertisingcampaign-to-show-the-real-walmart; and www.walmart.com/cp/PI-4-Prescriptions/1078664, accessed September 2014.

[22] 'Overconsumption is costing us the earth and human happiness', *The Guardian*, 21 June 2010, accessed at www.guardian.co.uk/environment/2010/jun/21/overconsumption-environment-relationships-annie-leonard.

[23] Examples taken from: Anthony Deutsch, 'Burger King axes palm oil supplier', *Financial Times*, 4/5 September 2010, p. 17; Andrew Ward and Mark Mulligan, 'Ikea buys six German wind farms', *Financial Times*, 9 September 2010, p. 23; Cecilie Rohwedder, 'Big UK chains tout local produce', *Wall Street Journal*, 17 March 2011, p. 25; Peter Marsh, 'Big names in clothing eco-label plan', *Financial Times*, 1 March 2011.

[24] Paul Tyrrel, 'Technology lets buyers unravel the ethics behind the label', *Financial Times*, 16 September 2010, p. 16.

[25] Jonathan Leake, 'Sea life massacred for Tesco tuna tins', *The Sunday Times*, 9 January 2011, S1, p. 13; 'Cornish pasty's 25-mile journey from the factory to the Tesco store next door', *Daily Mail*, 30 May 2010, p. 5; Chris Brooke, 'The Pound Shop Polo that went all round the qorld', *Daily Mail*, 2 September 2010, p. 5.

[26] See Alan S. Brown, 'The many shades of green', *Mechanical Engineering*, January 2009, http://memagazine.asme.org/Articles/2009/January/Many_Shades_Green.cfm; and www-03.ibm.com/financing/us/recovery/, accessed September 2014.

[27] Based on information from Simon Houpt, 'Beyond the bottle: Coke trumpets its green initiatives', *The Globe and Mail (Toronto)*, 13 January 2011; Marc Gunther, 'Coca-Cola's green crusader', *Fortune*, 28 April 2008, p. 150; 'Coca-Cola installs 1 millionth HFC-free cooler globally, preventing 5.25MM metric tons of CO2', 22 January 2014, www.coca-colacompany.com/press-center/press-releases/coca-co-la-installs-1-millionth-hfc-free-coolerglobally-preventing-525mm-metrics-tons-of-co2; 'Position statement on climate protection', 1 January 2012, www.coca-colacompany. com/stories/position-state-ment-on-climate-protection; and www.coca-cola.com/content-store/en_US/SC/PlantBottle/, accessed September 2014.

[28] See http://www.corporateknights.com/reports/global-100/2015-global-100-results/, acessed July 13 2015.

[29] Emiko Terazono, 'Sustainability creeps up the supply chain', *Financial Times*, 21 April 2015, p. 36.

[30] For the full list see: Brian Dumaine, 'The world's top 25 eco-innovators', *Fortune*, 19 May 2014, pp. 46–51.

[31] See http://ec.europa.eu/environment/legal/implementation_en.htm, , and 'What is EMAS?', http://ec.europa.eu/environment/emas/index_en.htm, accessed July 2015.

[32] Akash Kapur, 'It's a future highway', *Bloomberg BusinessWeek*, 10 July 2914, pp. 55–57.

[33] Kiki Loizou, 'I won't let babies mess up world', *The Sunday Times*, 19 September 2011, S3, p. 13.

[34] For example, see: Nigel F Piercy, *Market-Led Strategic Change: Transforming the Process of Going to Market*, 4th ed., Oxford: Elsevier, 2009, Chapter 4; and Nigel F Piercy and Nikala Lane, 'Corporate social responsibility initiatives and strategic marketing imperatives', *Social Business*, Vol. 1 Winter, 2011, pp. 325–345.

[35] See Austin Carr, 'Nike: The no. 1 most innovative company of 2013', *Fast Company*, March 2013, www.fastcompany.com/most-innovative-companies/2013/nike; and Haydn Shaughnessy, 'The world's most innovative companies, a new view', *Forbes*, 13 January 2014, www.forbes.com/sites/haydnshaughnessy/2014/01/13/anew-way-of-looking-at-the-worlds-most-innovative-companies/.

[36] Information from Eleftheria Parpis, 'Must love dogs', *Adweek*, 18 February 2008, accessed at www.adweek.com/aw/content_display/esearch/e3i14785206d4d123ec32476ca4ac7470d5; and 'The PEDIGREE® adoption drive partners with dog lover Carrie Underwood to help homeless dogs', 12 February 2010, accessed at www.mars.com/global/news-and-media/press-releases/news-releases.aspx?SiteId=94&Id=1767.

[37] See 'Our reason for being', www.patagonia.com/web/us/patagonia.go?slc=en_US&sct=US&assetid=2047, accessed November 2010.

[38] See http://vapur.us/about-vapur and http://vapur.us/cause, accessed September 2014. Vapur® and Anti-Bottle® are registered trademarks of Vapur, Inc.

[39] Nanette Byrnes, 'Pepsi brings in the health police', *Bloomberg Businessweek*, 25 January 2010, pp. 50–51; and www.pepsico.com/Purpose/Human-Sustainability/Product-Choices, accessed September 2014.

[40] Elliot Wilson, 'Britain goes to war on bribery', *Daily Mail*, 1 April 2011, p. 91; Dionne Searcey, 'U.K. bribes law has firms in a wweat', *Wall Street Journal*, 29 December 2010, p. 6.

[41] See Transparency International, 'Bribe Payers Index 2011', http://bpi.transparency.org/bpi2011; and 'Global Corruption Barometer 2013', www.transparency.org/gcb2013; also see Michael Montgomery, 'The cost of corruption', American RadioWorks, http://americanradioworks.publicradio.org/features/corruption/, accessed September 2014.

[42] See www.cim.co.uk/learning/marketing-standards/professional-marketing-standards/, accessed July 2015.

[43] See www.marketingpower.com/AboutAMA/Pages/Statement%20of%20Ethics.aspx, accessed September 2014.

[44] See http://investor.google.com/corporate/code-of-conduct.html#toc-VIII, accessed September 2014.

[45] Steve Overman, *The Conscience Economy: How A mass Movement for Good Is Great for Business*, Bibiomotion, 2014.

[46] Ben Bland, 'Executives shown a fresh perspective on sustainability', *Financial Times*, 13 January 2014, p. 10.

[47] Richard Milne, 'Drive to link pay to sustainability begins', *Financial Times*, 24 February 2010, p. 22.

[48] David A. Lubin and Daniel C. Esty, 'The sustainability imperative', *Harvard Business Review*, May 2010, pp. 41–50.

[49] David A. Lubin and Daniel C. Esty, 'The sustainability imperative', *Harvard Business Review*, May 2010, pp. 41–50; and Roasbeth Moss Kanter, 'It's time to take full responsibility', *Harvard Business Review*, October 2010, p. 42.

COMPANY CASE

Unilever: a prototype for tomorrow's company?

Unilever, the Anglo-Dutch consumer goods company, is a leading player in putting sustainability at the top of the corporate agenda. When Paul Polman took over as CEO a few years ago, the foods, home and personal care products company was a slumbering giant. Despite its stable of star-studded brands – including the likes of Dove, Axe (Lynx), Noxzema, Sunsilk, OMO, Hellmann's, Knorr, Lipton and Ben & Jerry's – Unilever had experienced a decade of stagnant sales and profits. The company needed renewed energy and purpose. 'To drag the world back to sanity, we need to know why we are here,' said Polman.

To answer the 'why are we here' question and find a more energising mission, Polman looked beyond the usual corporate goals of growing sales, profits and shareholder value. Instead, he asserted, growth results from accomplishing a broader social and environmental mission. Unilever exists 'for consumers, not shareholders,' he said. 'If we are in sync with consumer needs and the environment in which we operate, and take responsibility for our [societal impact], then the shareholder will also be rewarded.'

Polman stands alongside environmentalists who are not against marketing and consumption but simply want people and organisations to operate with more care for the environment. They call for doing away with what the Unilever CEO calls 'mindless consumption'. According to Polman, 'the road to well-being doesn't go via reduced consumption. It has to be done via more responsible consumption.'

Working on sustainability impact is nothing new at Unilever. Prior to Polman taking the reins, the company already had multiple programmes in place to manage the impact of its products and operations. But the existing programmes and results – while good – simply didn't go far enough for Polman.

So in late 2010 Unilever launched its Sustainable Living Plan – an aggressive long-term plan that takes capitalism to the next level. Under the plan, the company set out to 'create a better future every day for people around the world: the people who work for us, those we do business with, the billions of people who use our products, and future generations whose quality of life depends on the way we protect the environment today'. According to Polman, Unilever's long-run *commercial* success depends on how well it manages the *social* and *environmental* impact of its actions. Anyone who has followed corporate pronouncements in recent years should be fluent in sustainability, but Polman's opening phrases in announcing the Sustainable Living Plan to investors were about customers demanding that their goods be ethically sourced and that companies help preserve the environment. Sustainability requires that companies reduce their use of water, energy and packaging. This cuts costs and boosts profitability, so shareholders win too.

Unilever's Sustainable Living Plan sets out three major social and environmental objectives to be accomplished by 2020: '(1) to help more than one billion people take action to improve their health and well-being; (2) to halve the environmental footprint of the making and use of our products; and (3) to enhance the livelihoods of millions of people as we grow our business.'

The Sustainable Living Plan pulls together all of the work Unilever had already been doing and sets ambitious new sustainability goals. These goals span the entire value chain, from how the company sources raw materials to how consumers use and dispose of its products. 'Our aim is to make our activities more sustainable and also encourage our customers, suppliers, and others to do the same,' says the company.

On the 'upstream supply side', more than half of Unilever's raw materials come from agriculture, so the company is helping suppliers develop sustainable farming practices that meet its own high expectations for environmental and social impact. Unilever assesses suppliers against two sets of standards. The first is the Unilever Supplier Code, which calls for socially responsible actions regarding human rights, labour practices, product safety and care for the environment. Second, specifically for agricultural suppliers, the Unilever Sustainable Agriculture Code details Unilever's expectations for sustainable agriculture practices, so that it and its suppliers 'can commit to the sustainability journey together'.

But Unilever's Sustainable Living Plan goes far beyond simply creating more responsible supply and distribution chains. Approximately 68 per cent of the total greenhouse gas footprint of Unilever's products, and 50 per cent of the water footprint, occur during consumer use. So Unilever is also working with its consumers to improve the environmental impact of its products in use. Around 2 billion people in 190 markets worldwide use a Unilever product on any given day. Therefore, small everyday consumer actions can add up to a big difference. Unilever sums it up with this equation: 'Unilever brands × small everyday actions × billions of consumers = big difference.'

So, the Unilever briefing to the City on the Sustainable Living Plan began in familiar fashion. Consumers were increasingly turning to socially responsible brands, such as the company's Small & Mighty concentrated laundry detergent, which washes at lower temperatures. By 2020, Unilever's transport carbon dioxide emissions would be at or below current levels in spite of significantly higher volumes. Unilever would achieve this by reducing truck miles, using lower-emission vehicles and relying more on rail and ships.

But where were the figures on cost savings? Where were the promises about savings flowing to the bottom line? Someone asked: what will investors make of this? Mr Polman gave an unusual answer: 'Unilever has been around for 100-plus years. We want to be around for several hundred more years. So if you buy into this long-term value-creation model, which is equitable, which is shared, which is sustainable, then come and invest with us. If you don't buy into this, I respect you as a human being, but don't put your money in our company.'

But Unilever's tough stance on ethical behaviour and sustainability as a core social responsibility is more than promises, it turns into practical actions throughout its operations.

For a start, Unilever management believes there is a 'fortune at the bottom of the pyramid' – that companies can profit by selling cheap products to the poorest people in the world. Half of Unilever's sales are in emerging markets. For example, so notable is the drive to find adaptable products for the Indian mass market that it has a name, 'Indovation'. Recently, Unilever showed off Pureit, its low-cost water purifier. (At his London presentation Mr Polman had hoped to drink imported Mumbai water after putting it though the device. UK customs vetoed this, so he downed purified Thames water instead.)

Earlier, in Unilever's London headquarters, Gavin Neath, the consumer goods group's head of sustainability, took a plastic contraption out of its cardboard box and placed it on a table. It looks like a small and semi-transparent version of the vending machines that dispense drinks to office workers. This device is the Pureit – and it is a drinks dispensing machine of sorts. Developed by Hindustan Unilever, the company's Indian subsidiary, the Pureit provides drinking water from any source, however polluted, purifying it with a series of meshes, parasite and pesticide traps and a germ-killing battery kit, without the need for boiling and without the use of mains electricity.

The Pureit is an illustration of how multinationals like Unilever are trying to get to grips with the notion of sustainability. In the US and western Europe, the priorities are reducing the amount of packaging, cutting fuel consumption and providing for consumers who want to be sure that their purchases have been produced in an ethical or environmentally friendly fashion.

But in emerging markets, priorities are different. One high priority is to kill harmful germs that can lead to water-borne diseases like cholera and typhoid. In developing the market for Pureit, Hindustan Unilever had to come up with a product capable of competing with the usual method of purifying water for drinking – boiling it. Unilever's study of how to provide India with clean drinking water resulted in the production of Pureit. The cost of boiling water means that one rupee buys 2.5 litres. For those who can afford bottled water, one rupee buys 0.3 litres. The up-front cost of a Pureit is Rs1,800 (£23, €28), while the germ-killing battery has to be replaced at a cost of Rs300 after producing 1,500 litres of purified water. One rupee buys 3.5 litres of Pureit water, including the initial cost. The potential market for a low-cost machine providing drinkable water is

huge, and not just in India. 'China has appalling water problems,' Mr Neath points out.

And companies like Unilever say that focusing on sustainability also helps them develop new markets. A study by Unilever on how clothes are washed in India revealed that far more water was used in rinsing than in the washing itself. The result was Surf Excel, an 'easy rinse' detergent.

But there is far more to Unilever's approach to social responsibility strategy. Today, in the developing world, 3.5 million children under five die from diarrhoea and respiratory infections. Teaching children to wash their hands is a way of reducing this toll. The company sees opportunities to save lives and sell soap.

Not long ago, in south-west Uganda, the residents of Muko stood transfixed yet suspicious, arms crossed and frowning, as the strangers who arrived that morning danced on a stage they had erected from the back of a truck. With the aid of a sound system – rare enough to draw a crowd of 150 – three easygoing young visitors pumped out music and tried to strike up casual conversations with the villagers.

'How many people ate breakfast this morning?' one asks the audience, composed of women in kaleidoscopic shawls, men in sports shirts and children in blue school sweaters. The majority of hands are raised, but not all. 'And how many people washed their hands before eating?' About 30 people signal they did. And then: 'How many people used soap?' Two.

The result is familiar, which is why Unilever looks increasingly to emerging markets to drive sales growth, but finds antibacterial soaps a hard sell in parts of Africa. That is why its staff helped to write songs and skits for the show in Muko, which is delivering a message that washing hands with soap can eliminate the bugs that cause diarrhoea and respiratory infections – the two biggest killers of children in Africa after malaria. The event is a pilot for a government-backed country-wide campaign in which performers, decked out in 'Hands touch everywhere' T-shirts, will promote hand-washing in 11 languages. But two aspects of Unilever's involvement make it unusual.

First, the company does not coat it in the do-goody mantra of 'corporate social responsibility'. It states openly that it wants to make washing hands with soap a habit – especially after going to the toilet and before eating – in order to sell more bars of its Lifebuoy soap. Unilever sells around £700,000 of soap in Uganda each year and is third in the market behind local manufacturers Mukwano and Bidco. But a survey by the Steadman research group found that only 14 per cent of Ugandan adults used soap to wash their hands after going to the toilet. 'Imagine if we change behaviour, if every household starts to wash hands with soap,' says George Inholo, Unilever's head in Uganda. 'We'll be smiling all the way to the bank.'

The second novel feature of the campaign in Africa is that Unilever has gained several unlikely bedfellows: Unicef, USAid, the London School of Hygiene and Tropical Medicine, the Bill and Melinda Gates Foundation, and several non-governmental organisations. The institutions have formed a public-private partnership that is coordinated by the World Bank and replicated in Kenya, Tanzania, Senegal and Benin, where a total of $4.5 million will be spent on handwashing.

But even for Unilever, it is not always easy maintaining the high moral ground. Unilever built Dove into a multibillion pound brand with ads promoting women's self-esteem, emphasising the gentle, caring and accepting nature of the brand. But environmental activists at Greenpeace made parodies of the Unilever ads, which were big hits on YouTube, accusing the company of destroying Indonesian rainforests for palm oil, a key ingredient in its products. Greenpeace demonstrators, some dressed as orangutans, climbed on to balconies at Unilever's London headquarters and other company sites to protest at the alleged destruction of Indonesia's rainforests for palm oil. Unilever's response was not to fight with Greenpeace, but instead to reverse its purchasing policy to buy palm oil only from suppliers who can demonstrate they do not cut down forests. Unilever's smart response to this pressure was important to protecting its credibility on wider environmental issues.

Questions for discussion

1. Give as many examples as you can of how Unilever is defying common social criticisms of marketing.
2. Is Unilever successfully applying concepts of sustainability? What are the best examples of this?
3. Analyse Unilever's policies and developing strategies according to the environmental sustainability portfolio in Figure 20.2.
4. Are Unilever's sustainability initiatives truly practising enlightened marketing, or are these 'green' policies no more than vested self-interest and a marketing ploy? Give as many examples as you can to justify your answer.
5. Are sustainable strategies likely to provide greater profitability for Unilever compared to conventional approaches? Explain your answer.

Sources: Barney Jopson, 'Unilever looks to clean up in Africa', *Financial Times*, 15 November 2007, p. 20; Aaron O. Patrick, 'Turnabout at Unilever', *Wall Street Journal*, 2–4 May 2008, p. 6; Michael Skapinker, 'Virtue's reward? Companies make the business case for ethical initiatives', *Financial Times*, 27 April 2008, www.ft.com; Michael Skapinker, 'Long-term corporate plans may be lost in translation', *Financial Times*, 23 November 2010, p. 15; James Lamont, 'Indian innovators target nation's high demand', *Financial Times*, 19 January 2010, www.ft.com; Philip Kotler, 'Reinventing marketing to manage the environmental imperative', *Journal of Marketing*, July 2011, pp. 132–135; Kai Ryssdal, 'Unilever CEO: for sustainable business, go against "mindless consumption"', *Marketplace*, 11 June 2013, www.marketplace.org/topics/sustainability/consumed/unilever-ceo-paul-polman-sustainble-business; Andrew Saunders, 'Paul Polman of Unilever', *Management Today*, March 2011, pp. 42–47; Adi Ignatius, 'Captain Planet', *Harvard Business Review*, June 2012, pp. 2–8; Holly Ellyatt, 'Unilever profit beats, shares jump', CNBC, 21 January 2014, www.cnbc.com/id/101349908; 'Making progress, driving change', www.unilever.com/images/slp_Unilever-Sustainable-Living-Plan-2013_tcm13-388693 .pdf, accessed July 2014; and www.unilever.com/sustainable-living-2014/ and www.unilever.com/images/Unilever_AR13_tcm13-383757.pdf, accessed September 2014.

APPENDIX 1: Marketing plan

THE MARKETING PLAN: AN INTRODUCTION

As a marketer, you will need a good marketing plan to provide direction and focus for your brand, product or company. With a detailed plan, any business will be better prepared to launch a new product or build sales for existing products. Non-profit organisations also use marketing plans to guide their fundraising and outreach efforts. Even government agencies put together marketing plans for initiatives such as building public awareness of proper nutrition and stimulating area tourism.

The purpose and content of a marketing plan

Unlike a business plan, which offers a broad overview of the entire organisation's mission, objectives, strategy and resource allocation, a marketing plan has a more limited scope. It serves to document how the organisation's strategic objectives will be achieved through specific marketing strategies and tactics, with the customer as the starting point. It is also linked to the plans of other departments within the organization. Suppose, for example, a marketing plan calls for selling 200,000 units annually. The production department must gear up to make that many units, the finance department must arrange funding to cover the expenses, the human resources department must be ready to hire and train staff, and so on. Without the appropriate level of organisational support and resources, no marketing plan can succeed.

Although the exact length and layout will vary from company to company, a marketing plan usually contains the sections described in Chapter 2. Smaller businesses may create shorter or less formal marketing plans, whereas corporations frequently require highly structured marketing plans. To guide implementation effectively, every part of the plan must be described in considerable detail. Sometimes a company will post its marketing plans on an intranet site, which allows managers and employees in different locations to consult specific sections and collaborate on additions or changes.

The role of research

Marketing plans are not created in a vacuum. To develop successful strategies and action programmes, marketers need up-to-date information about the environment, the competition and the market segments to be served. Often, analysis of internal data is the starting point for assessing the current marketing situation, supplemented by marketing intelligence and research investigating the overall market, the competition, key issues, and threats and opportunities. As the plan is put into effect, marketers use a variety of research techniques to measure progress toward objectives and identify areas for improvement if results fall short of projections.

Finally, marketing research helps marketers learn more about their customers' requirements, expectations, perceptions and satisfaction levels. This deeper understanding provides a foundation for building competitive advantage through well-informed segmenting, targeting, differentiating and positioning decisions. Thus, the marketing plan should outline what marketing research will be conducted and how the findings will be applied.

The role of relationships

The marketing plan shows how the company will establish and maintain profitable customer relationships. In the process, however, it also shapes a number of internal and external relationships. First, it affects how marketing personnel work with each other and with other departments to deliver value and satisfy customers. Second, it affects how the company works with suppliers, distributors and strategic alliance partners to achieve the objectives listed in the plan. Third, it influences the company's dealings with other stakeholders, including government regulators, the media and the community at large. All of these relationships are important to the organisation's success, so they should be considered when a marketing plan is being developed.

From marketing plan to marketing action

Companies generally create yearly marketing plans, although some plans cover a longer period. Marketers start planning well in advance of the implementation date to allow time for marketing research, thorough analysis, management review and coordination between departments. Then, after each action programme begins, marketers monitor on-going results, compare them with projections, analyse any differences and take corrective steps as needed. Some marketers also prepare contingency plans for implementation if certain conditions emerge. Because of inevitable and sometimes unpredictable environmental changes, marketers must be ready to update and adapt marketing plans at any time.

For effective implementation and control, the marketing plan should define how progress toward objectives will be measured. Managers typically use budgets, schedules and performance standards for monitoring and evaluating results. With budgets, they can compare planned expenditures with actual expenditures for a given week, month, or other period. Schedules allow management to see when tasks were supposed to be completed–and when they were actually completed. Performance standards track the outcomes of marketing programmes to see whether the company is moving toward its objectives. Some examples of performance standards are market share, sales volume, product profitability and customer satisfaction.

SAMPLE MARKETING PLAN: CHILL BEVERAGE COMPANY

Executive summary

The Chill Beverage Company is preparing to launch a new line of vitamin-enhanced water called NutriWater. Although the bottled water market is maturing, the vitamin-enhanced water category is still growing. NutriWater will be positioned by the slogan 'Expect more' – indicating that the brand offers more in the way of desirable product features and benefits at a competitive price. Chill Beverage is taking advantage of its existing experience and brand equity among its loyal current customer base of Millennials who consume its Chill Soda soft drink. NutriWater will target similar Millennials who are maturing and looking for an alternative to soft drinks and high-calorie sugared beverages.

The primary marketing objective is to achieve first-year US sales of €35 million, roughly 2 per cent of the enhanced water market. Based on this market share goal, the company expects to sell more than 20 million units the first year and break even in the final period of the year.

Current marketing situation

Founded in 2005, the Chill Beverage Company found success primarily by distributing niche and emerging products in the beverage industry. Its Chill Soda soft drink brand hit the market with six unique flavours in glass bottles. A few years later, the Chill Soda brand introduced an energy drink as well as a line of natural juice drinks. The company now markets dozens of Chill Soda flavours, many unique to the brand. Chill Beverage has grown its business every year since it was founded. In the most recent year, it achieved €185 million in revenue and net profits of €14.5 million. As part of its future growth strategy, Chill Beverage is currently preparing to enter a new beverage category with a line of vitamin-enhanced waters.

As a beverage category, bottled water experienced tremendous growth during the 1990s and 2000s. Currently, the average person in the United States consumes more than 31 gallons of bottled water every year, a number that has increased 20-fold in just 30 years. Bottled water consumption is second only to soft drink consumption, ahead of milk, beer and coffee. Although bottled water growth has tapered off somewhat in recent years, it is still moderately strong at 3 to 4 per cent growth annually. Most other beverage categories have experienced declines. In the most recent year, 10.1 billion gallons of bottled water were sold in the United States with a value of approximately €12.3 billion.

Competition is more intense now than ever as demand slows, industry consolidation continues, and new types of bottled water emerge. The US market is dominated by three global corporations. With a portfolio of 12 brands (including Poland Spring, Nestlé Pure Life and Arrowhead), Nestlé leads the market for 'plain' bottled water. However, when all subcategories of bottled water are included (enhanced water, flavoured water, and so on), Coca-Cola leads the US market with a 22.9 per cent share. Nestlé markets only plain waters but is number two at 21.5 per cent of the total bottled water market. PepsiCo is third with 16.2 per cent of the market. To demonstrate the strength of the vitamin-enhanced water segment, Coca-Cola's Vitaminwater is the fourth-largest bottled water brand, behind plain water brands Nestlé Pure Life, Coca-Cola's Dasani and Pepsi's Aquafina.

To break into this market, dominated by huge global corporations and littered with dozens of other small players, Chill Beverage must carefully target specific segments with features and benefits valued by those segments.

Market description

The bottled water market consists of many different types of water. Varieties of plain water include spring, purified, mineral and distilled. Although these different types of water are sold as consumer products, they also serve as the core ingredient for other types of bottled waters including enhanced water, flavoured water, sparkling water, or any combination of those categories.

Although some consumers may not perceive much of a difference between brands, others are drawn to specific product features and benefits provided by different brands. For example, some consumers may perceive spring water as healthier than other types of water. Some may look for water that is optimised for hydration. Others seek additional nutritional benefits claimed by bottlers that enhance their brands with vitamins, minerals, herbs and other additives. Still other consumers make selections based on flavour. The industry as a whole has positioned bottled water of all kinds as a low-calorie, healthy alternative to soft drinks, sports drinks, energy drinks, and other types of beverages.

Bottled water brands also distinguish themselves by size and type of container, multipacks and refrigeration at point-of-sale. Chill Beverage's market for NutriWater consists of consumers of single-serving-sized bottled beverages who are looking for a healthy yet flavourful alternative. 'Healthy' in this context means both low-calorie and enhanced nutritional content. This market includes traditional soft drink consumers who want to improve their health as well as non-soft drink consumers who want an option other than plain bottled water. Specific segments that Chill Beverage will target during the first year include athletes, the health conscious, the socially responsible, and

Table A1.1 Segment needs and corresponding features/benefits of NutriWater

Targeted segment	Customer need	Corresponding features/benefits
Athletes	• Hydration and replenishment of essential minerals • Energy to maximise performance	• Electrolytes and carbohydrates • B vitamins, carbohydrates
Health conscious	• Maintain optimum weight • Optimise nutrition levels • Avoid harmful chemicals and additives • Desire to consume a tastier beverage than water	• Half the calories of fully sugared beverages • Higher levels of vitamins A, B, C, E, Zinc, chromium and folic acid than other products; vitamins unavailable in other products • All natural ingredients • Six new-age flavours
Socially conscious	• Support causes that help solve world's social problems	• 25 cent donation from each purchase to Vitamin Angels
Millennials	• Aversion to mass-media advertising/technologically savvy • Counter-culture attitude • Diet enhancement due to fast-paced lifestyle	• Less-invasive online and social networking promotional tactics • Small, privately held company • Full RDA levels of essential vitamins and minerals

Millennials who favour independent corporations. The Chill Soda brand has established a strong base of loyal customers, primarily among Millennials. This generational segment is becoming a prime target as it matures and seeks alternatives to full-calorie soft drinks.

Table A1.1 shows how NutriWater addresses the needs of targeted consumer segments.

Product review

Chill Beverage's new line of vitamin-enhanced water – called NutriWater – offers the following features:

- Six new-age flavours: Peach Mango, Berry Pomegranate, Kiwi Dragonfruit, Mandarin Orange, Blueberry Grape and Key Lime.
- Single-serving size, 20-ounce, PET recyclable bottles.
- Formulated for wellness, replenishment and optimum energy.
- Full Recommended Daily Allowance (RDA) of essential vitamins and minerals (including electrolytes).
- Higher vitamin concentration–vitamin levels are two to ten times higher than market-leading products, with more vitamins and minerals than any other brand.
- Additional vitamins–vitamins include A, E, and B2, as well as folic acid – none of which are contained in the market-leading products.
- All natural–no artificial flavours, colours or preservatives.
- Sweetened with pure cane sugar and Stevia, a natural zero-calorie sweetener.
- Twenty-five cents from each purchase will be donated to Vitamin Angels, a non-profit organisation with a mission to prevent vitamin deficiency in at-risk children.

Competitive review

As sales of bottled waters entered a strong growth phase in the 1990s, the category began to expand. In addition to the various types of plain water, new categories emerged. These included flavoured waters – such as Aquafina's Flavorsplash – as well as enhanced waters. Enhanced waters emerged to bridge the gap between soft drinks and waters, appealing to people who knew they should drink more water and less soft drinks but still wanted flavour. Development of brands for this product variation has occurred primarily in start-up and boutique beverage companies. In the 2000s, major beverage corporations acquired the most successful smaller brands, providing the bigger firms with a solid market position in this category and diversification in bottled waters in general. Currently, enhanced water sales account for approximately 18 per cent of the total bottled water market.

The fragmentation of this category, combined with domination by the market leaders, has created a severely competitive environment. Although there is indirect competition posed by all types of bottled waters and even other types of beverages (soft drinks, energy drinks, juices, teas), this competitive analysis focuses on direct competition from enhanced water brands. For the purposes of this analysis, enhanced water is bottled water with additives that are intended to provide health and wellness benefits. The most common additives include vitamins, minerals (including electrolytes) and herbs. Most commonly, enhanced waters are sweetened, flavoured and coloured. This definition distinguishes enhanced water from sports drinks that have the primary purpose of maximising hydration by replenishing electrolytes.

Enhanced water brands are typically sweetened with a combination of some kind of sugar and a zero-calorie sweetener, resulting in about half the sugar content, carbohydrates and calories of regular soft drinks and other sweetened beverages. The types of sweeteners used create a point of differentiation. Many brands, including the market leaders, sell both regular and zero-calorie varieties.

Pricing for this product is consistent across brands and varies by type of retail outlet, with convenience stores typically charging more than grocery stores. The price for a 20-ounce bottle ranges from €1.00 to €1.89, with some niche brands costing slightly more. Key competitors to Chill Beverage's NutriWater line include the following:

- *Vitaminwater*. Created in 2000 as a new product for Energy Brands' Glacéau, which was also the developer of Smartwater (distilled water with electrolytes). Coca-Cola purchased Energy Brands for €4.6 billion in 2007. Vitaminwater is sold in regular and zero-calorie versions. With 15 bottled varieties as well as availability in fountain form and drops, Vitaminwater offers more options than any brand on the market. Whereas Vitaminwater varieties are distinguished by flavour, they are named according to functional benefits such as Stur-D (healthy bones), Defence (strengthens immune system), Focus (mental clarity) and Restore (post-workout recovery). The brand's current slogan is 'Hydration for every occasion–morning, noon, and night'. Vitaminwater is vapour distilled, de-ionised and/or filtered and is sweetened with crystalline fructose (corn syrup) and erythritol all-natural sweetener. Together with Smartwater, Vitaminwater exceeds €1.1 billion in annual sales and commands 61 per cent of the enhanced waters market.

- *SoBe Lifewater*. PepsiCo bought SoBe in 2000. SoBe introduced Lifewater in 2008 with a hit Super Bowl ad as an answer to Coca-Cola's Vitaminwater. The Lifewater line includes 15 regular and zero-calorie varieties. Each bottle of Lifewater is designated by flavour and one of six different functional categories: Electrolytes, Lean Machine, B-Energy, C-Boost, Antioxidants and Pure. Each variety is infused with a formulation of vitamins, minerals and herbs designed to provide the claimed benefit. The most recent line–Pure–contains only water, a hint of flavour and electrolytes. Sweetened with a combination of sugar and erythritol, Lifewater makes the claim to be 'all natural'. It contains no artificial flavours or colours. However, some analysts debate the 'natural' designation for erythritol. Lifewater is sold in 20-ounce PET bottles and multipacks as well as 1-litre PET bottles. With more than €200 million in annual revenues, Lifewater is the number two enhanced water brand.

- *Propel Zero*. Gatorade created Propel in 2000, just one year prior to PepsiCo's purchase of this leading sports drink marketer. Originally marketed and labelled as 'fitness water', it is now available only as Propel Zero. Although the fitness water designation has been dropped, Propel Zero still leans toward that positioning, with the label stating 'REPLENISH + ENERGISE + PROTECT'. Propel Zero comes in seven flavours, each containing the same blend of B vitamins, vitamin C, vitamin E, antioxidants and electrolytes. It is sweetened with sucralose. Propel Zero is available in a wider variety of sizes, with 16.9-, 20- and 24-ounce PET bottles and multipacks. Propel Zero is also marketed in powder form and as a liquid enhancer to be added to bottled water. With €181 million in revenues, Propel Zero is the number three enhanced water brand with a 10 per cent share of the enhanced waters market.

- *RESCUE Water*. The Arizona Beverage Company is best known as the number one producer of ready-to-drink bottled teas. However, it also bottles a variety of other beverages including smoothies, sports drinks, energy drinks and juice blends. Its newest brand is RESCUE

Water, introduced to the US market in 2010. It sets itself apart from other enhanced waters with green tea extract added to a blend of vitamins and minerals. This provides a significant point of differentiation for those desiring green tea, but rules the brand out for the majority of customers who do not want it. It comes in five flavours, each with its own functional benefit. RESCUE Water touts other points of distinction as well, including branded Twinlab vitamins, all-natural ingredients, and a high-tech plastic bottle that resembles glass and maximizes freshness. Its Blueberry Coconut Hydrate variety contains real coconut water, an emerging alternative beverage category. Although RESCUE Water sales and market share figures are not yet known because of the product's newness, the Arizona Beverage Company is a multibillion-euro corporation with a long history of successful new product introductions.

- *Niche brands*. The market for enhanced waters includes at least four companies that market their wares on a small scale through independent retailers: Assure, Ex Aqua Vitamins, Ayala Herbal Water and Skinny Water. Some brands feature exotic additives and/or artistic glass bottles.

Despite the strong competition, NutriWater believes it can create a relevant brand image and gain recognition among the targeted segments. The brand offers strong points of differentiation with higher and unique vitamin content, all-natural ingredients, and support for a relevant social cause. With other strategic assets, Chill Beverage is confident that it can establish a competitive advantage that will allow NutriWater to grow in the market. Table A1.2 shows a sample of competing products.

Channels and logistics review

The purchase of Vitaminwater by Coca-Cola left a huge hole in the independent distributor system. NutriWater will be distributed through an independent distributor to a network of retailers in the United States. This strategy will avoid some of the head-on competition for shelf space with the Coca-Cola and PepsiCo brands and will also directly target likely NutriWater customers. As with the rollout of the core Chill Soda brand, this strategy will focus on placing coolers in retail locations that will exclusively hold NutriWater. These retailers include:

- *Grocery chains*. Regional grocery chains such as HyVee in the Midwest, Wegman's in the East and WinCo in the West.

- *Health and natural food stores*. Chains such as Whole Foods, as well as local health food co-ops.

- *Fitness centres*. National fitness centre chains such as 24 Hour Fitness, Gold's Gym and other regional chains.

Table A1.2   Sample of competitive products

Competitor	Brand	Features
Coca-Cola	Vitaminwater	Regular and zero-calorie versions; 15 varieties; each flavour provides a different function based on blend of vitamins and minerals; vapour distilled, de-ionised and/or filtered; sweetened with crystalline fructose and erythritol; 20-ounce single-serve or multi-pack, fountain and drops.
PepsiCo	SoBe Lifewater	Regular and zero-calorie versions; 15 varieties; six different functional categories; vitamins, minerals and herbs; Pure–mildly flavoured, unsweetened water; sweetened with sugar and erythritol; 'all natural'; 20-ounce single-serve and multi-packs as well as 1-litre bottles.
PepsiCo	Propel Zero	Zero-calorie only; seven flavours; fitness positioning based on 'REPLENISH + ENERGISE + PROTECT'; B vitamins, vitamin C, vitamin E, antioxidants and electrolytes; sweetened with sucralose; 16.9-ounce, 20-ounce and 24-ounce PET bottles and multipacks; powdered packets; liquid enhancer.
Arizona Beverage	RESCUE Water	Full calorie only; five flavours, each with its own blend of vitamins and minerals; green tea extract (caffeine included); only brand with coconut water; Twinlab branded vitamins; high-tech plastic bottle.

Table A1.3 NutriWater's strengths, weaknesses, opportunities and threats

Strengths	Weaknesses
Superior quality	Lack of brand awareness
Expertise in alternative beverage marketing	Limited budget
Social responsibility	
Anti-establishment image	
Opportunities	**Threats**
Growing market	Limited shelf space
Gap in the distribution network	Image of enhanced waters
Health trends	Environmental issues
Anti-establishment image	

As the brand gains acceptance, channels will expand into larger grocery chains, convenience stores and unique locations relevant to the target customer segment.

Strengths, weaknesses, opportunities and threat analysis

NutriWater has several powerful strengths on which to build, but its major weakness is lack of brand awareness and image. Major opportunities include a growing market and consumer trends targeted by NutriWater's product traits. Threats include barriers to entry posed by limited retail space, as well as image issues for the bottled water industry. Table A1.3 summarises NutriWater's main strengths, weaknesses, opportunities and threats.

Strengths

NutriWater can rely on the following important strengths:

1. *Superior quality.* NutriWater boasts the highest levels of added vitamins of any enhanced water, including full RDA levels of many vitamins. It is all natural with no artificial flavours, colours or preservatives. It is sweetened with both pure cane sugar and the natural zero-calorie sweetener, Stevia.

2. *Expertise in alternative beverage marketing.* The Chill Soda brand went from nothing to a successful and rapidly growing soft drink brand with fiercely loyal customers in a matter of only one decade. This success was achieved by starting small and focusing on gaps in the marketplace.

3. *Social responsibility.* Every customer will have the added benefit of helping malnourished children throughout the world. Although the price of NutriWater is in line with other competitors, low promotional costs allow for the substantial charitable donation of 25 cents per bottle while maintaining profitability.

4. *Anti-establishment image.* The big brands have decent products and strong distribution relationships. But they also carry the image of the large, corporate establishments. Chill Beverage has achieved success with an underdog image while remaining privately held. Vitaminwater and SoBe were built on this same image, but both are now owned by major multinational corporations.

Weaknesses

1. *Lack of brand awareness.* As an entirely new brand, NutriWater will enter the market with limited or no brand awareness. The affiliation with Chill Soda will be kept at a minimum in order to prevent associations between NutriWater and soft drinks. This issue will be addressed through promotion and distribution strategies.

2. *Limited budget.* As a smaller company, Chill Beverage has much smaller funds available for promotional and research activities.

Opportunities

1. *Growing market.* Although growth in the overall market for bottled water has slowed to some extent, its current rate of growth in the 3 per cent range is relatively strong among beverage categories. Of the top six beverage categories, soft drinks, beer, milk and fruit drinks experienced declines. The growth for coffee was less than 1 per cent. More important than the growth of bottled waters in general, the enhanced water category is experiencing growth in the high single and low double digits.

2. *Gap in the distribution network.* The market leaders distribute directly to retailers. This gives them an advantage in large national chains. However, no major enhanced water brands are currently being sold through independent distributors.

3. *Health trends.* Weight and nutrition continue to be issues for consumers in the United States. The country has the highest obesity rate for developed countries at 34 per cent, with well over 60 per cent of the population officially 'overweight'. Those numbers continue to rise. Additionally, Americans get 21 per cent of their daily calories from beverages, a number that has tripled in the last three decades. Consumers still desire flavoured beverages but look for lower calorie alternatives.

4. *Anti-establishment image.* Millennials (born between 1977 and 2000) maintain a higher aversion to mass marketing messages and global corporations than do Gen Xers and Baby Boomers.

Threats

1. *Limited shelf space.* Whereas competition is generally a threat for any type of product, competition in retail beverages is particularly high because of limited retail space. Carrying a new beverage product requires retailers to reduce shelf or cooler space already occupied by other brands.

2. *Image of enhanced waters.* The image of enhanced waters is currently in question as Coca-Cola recently fought a class-action lawsuit accusing it of violating FDA regulations by promoting the health benefits of Vitaminwater. The lawsuit exposed the number one bottled water brand as basically sugar water with minimal nutritional value.

3. *Environmental issues.* Environmental groups continue to educate the public on the environmental costs of bottled water, including landfill waste, carbon emissions from production and transportation, and harmful effects of chemicals in plastics.

Objectives and issues

Chill Beverage has set aggressive but achievable objectives for NutriWater for the first and second years of market entry.

First-year objectives

During the initial year on the market, Chill Beverage aims for NutriWater to achieve a 2 per cent share of the enhanced water market, or approximately €35 million in sales, with breakeven achieved in the final period of the year. With an average retail price of €1.69, that equates with a sales goal of 20,710,059 bottles.

Second-year objectives

During the second year, Chill Beverage will unveil additional NutriWater flavours, including zero-calorie varieties. The second-year objective is to double sales from the first year, to €70 million.

Issues

In launching this new brand, the main issue is the ability to establish brand awareness and a meaningful brand image based on positioning that is relevant to target customer segments. Chill Beverage will invest in non-traditional means of promotion to accomplish these goals and to spark word-of-mouth. Establishing distributor and retailer relationships will also be critical in order to make the product available and provide point-of-purchase communications. Brand awareness and knowledge will be measured in order to adjust marketing efforts as necessary.

Marketing strategy

NutriWater's marketing strategy will involve developing a 'more for the same' positioning based on extra benefits for the price. The brand will also establish channel differentiation, as it will be available in locations where major competing brands are not. The primary target segment is Millennials. This segment is comprised of tweens (ages 10 to 12), teens (13 to 18) and young adults (19 to 33). NutriWater will focus specifically on the young adult market. Subsets of this generational segment include athletes, the health conscious and the socially responsible.

Positioning

NutriWater will be positioned on an 'Expect more' value proposition. This will allow for differentiating the brand based on product features (expect more vitamin content and all natural ingredients), desirable benefits (expect greater nutritional benefits) and values (do more for a social cause). Marketing will focus on conveying that NutriWater is more than just a beverage: it gives customers much more for their money in a variety of ways.

Product strategy

NutriWater will be sold with all the features described in the Product Review section. As awareness takes hold and retail availability increases, more varieties will be made available. A zero-calorie version will be added to the product line, providing a solid fit with the health benefits sought by consumers. Chill Beverage's considerable experience in brand-building will be applied as an integral part of the product strategy for NutriWater. All aspects of the marketing mix will be consistent with the brand.

Pricing

There is little price variation in the enhanced waters category, particularly among leading brands. For this reason, NutriWater will follow a competition-based pricing strategy. Given that NutriWater claims superior quality, it must be careful not to position itself as a lower cost alternative. Manufacturers do not quote list prices on this type of beverage, and prices vary considerably based on type of retail outlet and whether or not the product is refrigerated. Regular prices for single 20-ounce bottles of competing products are as low as €1.00 in discount-retailer stores and as high as €1.89 in convenience stores. Because NutriWater will not be targeting discount retailers and convenience stores initially, this will allow Chill Beverage to set prices at the average to higher end of the range for similar products in the same outlets. For grocery chains, this should be approximately €1.49 per bottle, with that price rising to €1.89 at health food stores and fitness centres, where prices tend to be higher.

Distribution strategy

Based on the information in the Channels and Logistics Review, NutriWater will employ a selective distribution strategy with well-known regional grocers, health and natural food stores, and fitness centres. This distribution strategy will be executed through a network of independent beverage distributors, as there are no other major brands of enhanced water following this strategy. Chill Beverage gained success for its core Chill Soda soft drink line using this method. It also placed coolers with the brand logo in truly unique venues such as skate, surf and snowboarding shops; tattoo and piercing parlours; fashion stores; and music stores-places that would expose the brand to target customers. Then, the soft drink brand expanded by getting contracts with retailers such as Panera, Barnes & Noble, Target and Starbucks. This same approach will be taken with NutriWater by starting small, then expanding into larger chains. NutriWater will not target all the same stores used originally by Chill Soda, as many of those outlets were unique to the positioning and target customer for the Chill Soda soft drink brand.

Marketing communication strategy

As with the core Chill Soda brand, the marketing communication strategy for NutriWater will not follow a strategy based on traditional mass-communication advertising. Initially, there will be no broadcast or print advertising. Promotional resources for NutriWater will focus on three areas:

- *Online and mobile marketing.* The typical target customer for NutriWater spends more time online than with traditional media channels. A core component for this strategy will be building web and mobile brand sites and driving traffic to those sites by creating a presence on social networks, including Facebook, Google+ and Twitter. The NutriWater brand will also incorporate location-based services by Foursquare and Facebook to help drive traffic to retail locations. A mobile phone ad campaign will provide additional support to the online efforts.

- *Trade promotions.* Like the core Chill Soda brand, NutriWater's success will rely on relationships with retailers to create product availability. Primary incentives to retailers will include point-of-purchase displays, branded coolers, and volume incentives and contests. This push marketing strategy will combine with the other pull strategies.

- *Event marketing.* NutriWater will deploy teams in brand-labelled RVs to distribute product samples at events such as skiing and snowboarding competitions, golf tournaments and concerts.

Marketing research

To remain consistent with the online promotional approach, as well as using research methods that will effectively reach target customers, Chill Beverage will monitor online discussions via services such as Radian6. In this manner, the company will gauge customer perceptions of the brand, the products and general satisfaction. For future development of the product and new distribution outlets, crowdsourcing methods will be utilised.

Action programmes

NutriWater will be introduced in February. The following are summaries of action programmes that will be used during the first six months of the year to achieve the stated objectives.

- *January.* Chill Beverage representatives will work with both independent distributors and retailers to educate them on the trade promotional campaign, incentives and advantages for selling NutriWater. Representatives will also ensure that distributors and retailers are educated on product features and benefits as well as instructions for displaying point-of-purchase materials and coolers. The brand website and other sites such as Facebook will present teaser information about the product as well as availability dates and locations. Buzz will be enhanced by providing product samples to selected product reviewers, opinion leaders, influential bloggers and celebrities.

- *February*. On the date of availability, product coolers and point-of-purchase displays will be placed in retail locations. The full brand website and social network campaign will launch with full efforts on Facebook, Google+ and Twitter. This campaign will drive the 'Expect more' slogan, as well as illustrate the ways that NutriWater delivers more than expected on product features, desirable benefits and values by donating to Vitamin Angels and the social cause of battling vitamin deficiency in children.

- *March*. To enhance the online and social marketing campaign, location-based services Foursquare and Facebook Places will be employed to drive traffic to retailers. Point-of-purchase displays and signage will be updated to support these efforts and to continue supporting retailers. The message of this campaign will focus on all aspects of 'Expect more'.

- *April*. A mobile phone ad campaign will provide additional support, driving web traffic to the brand website and social network sites, as well as driving traffic to retailers.

- *May*. A trade sales contest will offer additional incentives and prizes to the distributors and retailers that sell the most NutriWater during a four-week period.

- *June*. An event marketing campaign will mobilise a team of NutriWater representatives in NutriWater RVs to concerts and sports events. This will provide additional visibility for the brand as well as giving customers and potential customers the opportunity to sample products.

Budgets

Chill Beverage has set a first-year retail sales goal of €35 million with a projected average retail price of €1.69 per unit for a total of 20,710,059 units sold. With an average wholesale price of 85 cents per unit, this provides revenues of €17.6 million. Chill Beverage expects to break even during the final period of the first year. A break-even analysis assumes per-unit wholesale revenue of 85 cents per unit, a variable cost per unit of 14 cents, and estimated first-year fixed costs of €12,500,000. Based on these assumptions, the break-even calculation is:

$$\frac{\$12,500,000}{\$0.85/\text{unit} - \$0.17/\text{unit}} = 17,605,634$$

Controls

Chill Beverage is planning tight control measures to closely monitor product quality, brand awareness, brand image, and customer satisfaction. This will enable the company to react quickly in correcting any problems that may occur. Other early warning signals that will be monitored for signs of deviation from the plan include monthly sales (by segment and channel) and monthly expenses. Given the market's volatility, contingency plans are also in place to address fast-moving environmental changes such as shifting consumer preferences, new products and new competition.

Sources: 'Channel Check', *Bevnet*, June 2014, p. 18; 'Channel Check', *Bevnet*, November/December 2013, p. 30; Chris Hogan, 'Bottled water trends for 2014', *Food Manufacturing*, January/February 2014, p. 38; Jeffrey Klineman, 'Restoring an icon', *Beverage Spectrum Magazine*, December 2010, pp. 16–18; Matt Casey, 'Enhanced options divide a category', *Beverage Spectrum Magazine*, December 2008, p. 74; and product and market information obtained from www.sobe.com, www.vitaminwater.com, www.nestle-waters.com, and www.drinkarizona.com, March 2015.

APPENDIX 2: Marketing by the numbers

Marketing managers are facing increased accountability for the financial implications of their actions. This appendix provides a basic introduction to measuring marketing financial performance. Such financial analysis guides marketers in making sound marketing decisions and in assessing the outcomes of those decisions.

This appendix is built around a hypothetical manufacturer of consumer electronics products – HD. The company is introducing a device that plays videos and television programming streamed over the Internet on multiple devices in a home, including high definition televisions, tablets and mobile phones. In this appendix, we will analyse the various decisions HD's marketing managers must make before and after the new-product launch.

The appendix is organised into *three sections*. The *first section* introduces pricing, break-even and margin analysis assessments that will guide the introduction of HD's new product. The *second section* discusses demand estimates, the marketing budget and marketing performance measures. It begins with a discussion of estimating market potential and company sales. It then introduces the marketing budget, as illustrated through a *pro forma* profit-and-loss statement followed by the actual profit-and-loss statement. Next, we discuss marketing performance measures, with a focus on helping marketing managers to better defend their decisions from a financial perspective. In the *third section*, we analyse the financial implications of various marketing tactics.

Each of the three sections ends with a set of quantitative exercises that provide you with an opportunity to apply the concepts you learned to situations beyond HD.

PRICING, BREAK-EVEN AND MARGIN ANALYSIS

Pricing considerations

Determining price is one of the most important marketing-mix decisions. The limiting factors are demand and costs. Demand factors, such as buyer-perceived value, set the price ceiling. The company's costs set the price floor. In between these two factors, marketers must consider competitors' prices and other factors such as reseller requirements, government regulations and company objectives.

Most current competing Internet streaming products sell at retail prices between €100 and €500. We first consider HD's pricing decision from a cost perspective. Then, we consider consumer value, the competitive environment and reseller requirements.

Determining costs

Fixed costs—Costs that do not vary with production or sales level.

Recall from Chapter 10 that there are different types of costs. **Fixed costs** do not vary with production or sales level and include costs such as rent, interest, depreciation, and clerical and management salaries. Regardless of the level of output, the company must pay these costs. Whereas total fixed costs remain constant as output increases, the fixed cost per unit (or average fixed cost) will decrease as output increases because the total fixed costs are spread across more units of output. **Variable costs** vary directly with the level of production and include costs related to the direct production of the product (such as costs of goods sold – COGS) and many of the marketing costs associated with selling it. Although these costs tend to be uniform for each unit produced, they are called variable because their total varies with the number of units produced. **Total costs** are the sum of the fixed and variable costs for any given level of production.

HD has invested €10 million in refurbishing an existing facility to manufacture the new video streaming product. Once production begins, the company estimates that it will incur fixed costs of €20 million per year. The variable cost to produce each device is estimated to be €125 and is expected to remain at that level for the output capacity of the facility.

Variable costs—Costs that vary directly with the level of production.

Total costs—The sum of the fixed and variable costs for any given level of production.

Setting price-based on costs

HD starts with the cost-based approach to pricing discussed in Chapter 10. Recall that the simplest method, **cost-plus pricing** (or **mark-up pricing**), simply adds a standard mark-up to the cost of the product. To use this method, however, HD must specify expected unit sales so that total unit costs can be determined. Unit variable costs will remain constant regardless of the output, but average unit fixed costs will decrease as output increases.

To illustrate this method, suppose HD has fixed costs of 20 million, variable costs of €125 per unit, and expects unit sales of 1 million players. Thus, the cost per unit is given by:

Cost-plus pricing (or mark-up pricing)—A standard mark-up to the cost of the product.

$$\text{unit cost} = \text{variable cost} + \frac{\text{fixed costs}}{\text{unit sales}} = \text{€}125 + \frac{\text{€}20{,}000{,}000}{1{,}000{,}000} = \text{€}145$$

Note that we do *not* include the initial investment of €10 million in the total fixed cost figure. It is not considered a fixed cost because it is not a *relevant* cost. **Relevant costs** are those that will occur in the future and that will vary across the alternatives being considered. HD's investment to refurbish the manufacturing facility was a one-time cost that will not reoccur in the future. Such past costs are *sunk costs* and should not be considered in future analyses.

Also notice that if HD sells its product for €145, the price is equal to the total cost per unit. This is the **break-even price** – the price at which unit revenue (price) equals unit cost and profit is zero.

Suppose HD does not want to merely break even but rather wants to earn a 25 per cent mark-up on sales. HD's mark-up price is:[1]

Relevant costs—Costs that will occur in the future and that will vary across the alternatives being considered.

Break-even price—The price at which total revenue equals total cost and profit is zero.

$$\text{Mark-up price} = \frac{\text{unit cost}}{(1 - \text{desired return on sales})} = \frac{\text{€}145}{1 - 0.25} = \text{€}193.33$$

This is the price at which HD would sell the product to resellers such as wholesalers or retailers to earn a 25 per cent profit on sales.

Another approach HD could use is called **return on investment (ROI) pricing** (or **target-return pricing**). In this case, the company would consider the initial €10 million investment, but only to determine the euro profit goal. Suppose the company wants a 30 per cent return on its investment. The price necessary to satisfy this requirement can be determined by:

Return on investment (ROI) pricing (or target-return pricing)—A cost-based pricing method that determines price based on a specified rate of return on investment.

$$\text{ROI price} = \text{unit cost} + \frac{\text{ROI} \times \text{investment}}{\text{unit sales}} = \text{€}145 + \frac{0.3 \times \text{€}10{,}000{,}000}{1{,}000{,}000} = \text{€}148$$

That is, if HD sells its product for €148, it will realise a 30 per cent return on its initial investment of €10 million.

In these pricing calculations, unit cost is a function of the expected sales, which were estimated to be 1 million units. But what if actual sales were lower? Then the unit cost would be higher because the fixed costs would be spread over fewer units, and the realised percentage mark-up on sales or ROI would be lower. Alternatively, if sales are higher than the estimated 1 million units, unit cost would be lower than €145, so a lower price would produce the desired mark-up on sales or ROI. It's important to note that these cost-based pricing methods are *internally* focused and do not consider demand, competitors' prices or reseller requirements. Because HD will be selling this product to consumers through wholesalers and retailers offering competing brands, the company must consider mark-up pricing from this perspective.

Setting price based on external factors

Whereas costs determine the price floor, HD also must consider external factors when setting price. HD does not have the final say concerning the final price of its product to consumers – retailers do. So it must start with its suggested retail price and work back. In doing so, HD must consider the mark-ups required by resellers that sell the product to consumers.

In general, a euro **mark-up** is the difference between a company's selling price for a product and its cost to manufacture or purchase it. For a retailer, then, the mark-up is the difference between the price it charges consumers and the cost the retailer must pay for the product. Thus, for any level of reseller:

$$\text{Euro mark-up} = \text{selling price} - \text{cost}$$

Mark-ups are usually expressed as a percentage, and there are two different ways to compute mark-ups – on *cost* or on *selling price*:

$$\text{Mark-up percentage on cost} = \frac{\text{dollar mark-up}}{\text{cost}}$$

$$\text{Mark-up percentage on selling price} = \frac{\text{dollar mark-up}}{\text{selling price}}$$

To apply reseller margin analysis, HD must first set the suggested retail price and then work back to the price at which it must sell the product to a wholesaler. Suppose retailers expect a 30 per cent margin and wholesalers want a 20% margin based on their respective selling prices. And suppose that HD sets a manufacturer's suggested retail price (MSRP) of €299.99 for its product.

HD selected the €299.99 MSRP because it is lower than most competitors' prices but is not so low that consumers might perceive it to be of poor quality. In addition, the company's research shows that it is below the threshold at which more consumers are willing to purchase the product. By using buyers' perceptions of value and not the seller's cost to determine the MSRP, HD is using **value-based pricing**. For simplicity, we will use an MSRP of €300 in further analyses.

To determine the price HD will charge wholesalers, we must first subtract the retailer's margin from the retail price to determine the retailer's cost (€300 − (€300 × 0.30) = €210). The retailer's cost is the wholesaler's price, so HD next subtracts the wholesaler's margin (€210 − (€210 × 0.20) = €168). Thus, the **mark-up chain** representing the sequence of mark-ups used by firms at each level in a channel for HD's new product is:

Suggested retail price:	€300
minus retail margin (30%):	− €90
Retailer's cost/wholesaler's price:	€210
minus wholesaler's margin (20%):	− €42
Wholesaler's cost/HD's price	€168

By deducting the mark-ups for each level in the mark-up chain, HD arrives at a price for the product to wholesalers of €168.

Break-even and margin analysis

The previous analyses derived a value-based price of €168 for HD's product. Although this price is higher than the break-even price of €145 and covers costs, that price assumed a demand of 1 million units. But how many units and what level of euro sales must HD achieve to break even at the €168 price? And what level of sales must be achieved to realise various profit goals? These questions can be answered through break-even and margin analysis.

Mark-up—The difference between a company's selling price for a product and its cost to manufacture or purchase it.

Value-based pricing—Offering just the right combination of quality and good service at a fair price.

Mark-up chain—The sequence of mark-ups used by firms at each level in a channel.

Determining break-even unit volume and euro sales

Based on an understanding of costs, consumer value, the competitive environment, and reseller requirements, HD has decided to set its price to wholesalers at €168. At that price, what sales level will be needed for HD to break even or make a profit on its product? **Break-even analysis** determines the unit volume and euro sales needed to be profitable given a particular price and cost structure. At the break-even point, total revenue equals total costs and profit is zero. Above this point, the company will make a profit; below it, the company will lose money. HD can calculate break-even volume using the following formula:

Break-even analysis— Analysis to determine the unit volume and euro sales needed to be profitable given a particular price and cost structure.

$$\text{Break-even volume} = \frac{\text{fixed costs}}{\text{price} - \text{variable cost}}$$

The denominator (price − unit variable cost) is called **unit contribution**. It represents the amount that each unit contributes to covering fixed costs. Break-even volume represents the level of output at which all (variable and fixed) costs are covered. In HD's case, break-even unit volume is:

Unit contribution—The amount that each unit contributes to covering fixed costs – the difference between price and variable costs.

$$\text{Break-even volume} = \frac{\text{fixed costs}}{\text{price} - \text{variable cost}} = \frac{€20,000,000}{€168 - €125} = 465,116.2 \text{ units}$$

Thus, at the given cost and pricing structure, HD will break even at 465,117 units.

To determine the break-even euro sales, simply multiply unit break-even volume by the selling price:

$$\text{BE sales} = \text{BE}_{vol}\,\text{price} = 465,117 \times €168 = €78,139,656$$

Another way to calculate euro break-even sales is to use the percentage contribution margin (hereafter referred to as **contribution margin**), which is the unit contribution divided by the selling price:

Contribution margin—The unit contribution divided by the selling price.

$$\text{Contribution margin} = \frac{\text{price} - \text{variable costs}}{\text{price}} = \frac{€168 - €125}{€168} = 0.256 \text{ or } 25.6$$

Then,

$$\text{Break-even sales} = \frac{\text{fixed costs}}{\text{contribution margin}} = \frac{€20,00,000}{0.256} = €78,125,000$$

Note that the difference between the two break-even sales calculations is due to rounding.

Such break-even analysis helps HD by showing the unit volume needed to cover costs. If production capacity cannot attain this level of output, then the company should not launch this product. However, the unit break-even volume is well within HD's capacity. Of course, the bigger question concerns whether HD can sell this volume at the €168 price. We'll address that issue a little later.

Understanding contribution margin is useful in other types of analyses as well, particularly if unit prices and unit variable costs are unknown or if a company (say, a retailer) sells many products at different prices and knows the percentage of total sales variable costs represent. Whereas unit contribution is the difference between unit price and unit variable costs, total contribution is the difference between total sales and total variable costs. The overall contribution margin can be calculated by:

$$\text{Contribution margin} = \frac{\text{total sales} - \text{total variable costs}}{\text{total sales}}$$

Regardless of the actual level of sales, if the company knows what percentage of sales is represented by variable costs, it can calculate contribution margin. For example, HD's unit variable cost is €125, or 74 per cent of the selling price (€125 ÷ €168 = 0.74). That means for every €1 of sales revenue for HD, €0.74 represents variable costs, and the difference (€0.26) represents contribution to fixed costs. But even if the company doesn't know its unit price and unit variable cost, it can calculate the contribution margin from total sales and total variable costs or from knowledge of the total cost structure. It can set total sales equal to 100 per cent regardless of the actual absolute amount and determine the contribution margin:

$$\text{Contribution margin} = \frac{100\% - 74\%}{100\%} = \frac{1 - 0.74}{1} = 1 - 0.74 = 0.26 \text{ or } 26\%$$

Note that this matches the percentage calculated from the unit price and unit variable cost information. This alternative calculation will be very useful later when analysing various marketing decisions.

Determining 'break even' for profit goals

Although it is useful to know the break-even point, most companies are more interested in making a profit. Assume HD would like to realise a €5 million profit in the first year. How many must it sell at the €168 price to cover fixed costs and produce this profit? To determine this, HD can simply add the profit figure to fixed costs and again divide by the unit contribution to determine unit sales:

$$\text{Unit volume} = \frac{\text{fixed costs} - \text{profit goal}}{\text{price} - \text{variable cost}} = \frac{€20,000,000 + €5,000,000}{€168 - €125} = 581,395.3 \text{ units}$$

Thus, to earn a €5 million profit, HD must sell 581,396 units. Multiply by the price to determine the euro sales needed to achieve a €5 million profit:

$$\text{Euro sales} = 581,396 \text{ units} \times €168 = €97,674,528$$

Or use the contribution margin:

$$\text{Sales} = \frac{\text{fixed costs} + \text{profit goal}}{\text{contribution margin}} = \frac{€20,000,000 + €5,000,000}{0.256} = €97,656,250$$

Again, note that the difference between the two break-even sales calculations is due to rounding.

As we saw previously, a profit goal can also be stated as a return on investment goal. For example, recall that HD wants a 30 per cent return on its €10 million investment. Thus, its absolute profit goal is €3 million (€10,000,000 × 0.30). This profit goal is treated the same way as in the previous example:[2]

$$\text{Unit volume} = \frac{\text{fixed costs} + \text{profit goal}}{\text{price} - \text{variable cost}} = \frac{€20,000,000 + €3,000,000}{€168 - €125} = 534,884 \text{ units}$$

$$\text{Euro sales} = 534,884 \text{ units} \times €168 = €89,860,512$$

Or:

$$\text{Euro sales} = \frac{\text{fixed costs} + \text{profit goal}}{\text{contribution margin}} = \frac{€20,000,000 + €3,000,000}{0.256} = €89,843,750$$

Finally, HD can express its profit goal as a percentage of sales, which we also saw in previous pricing analyses. Assume HD desires a 25 per cent return on sales. To determine the unit and sales volume necessary to achieve this goal, the calculation is a little different from the previous two examples. In this case, we incorporate the profit goal into the unit contribution as an additional variable cost. Look at it this way: if 25 per cent of each sale must go toward profits, that leaves only 75 per cent of the selling price to cover fixed costs. Thus, the equation becomes:

$$\text{Unit volume} = \frac{\text{fixed costs}}{\text{price} - \text{variable cost} - (0.25 \times \text{price})} \text{ or } \frac{\text{fixed costs}}{(0.75 \times \text{price}) - \text{variable cost}}$$

So,

$$\text{Unit volume} = \frac{€20,000,000}{(0.75 \times €168) - €125} = 20,000,000 \text{ units}$$

$$\text{Euro sales necessary} = 20,000,000 \text{ units} \times €168 = €3,360,000,000$$

Thus, HD would need more than €3 billion in sales to realise a 25 per cent return on sales given its current price and cost structure! Could it possibly achieve this level of sales? The major point is this: Although break-even analysis can be useful in determining the level of sales needed to cover costs or to achieve a stated profit goal, it does not tell the company whether it is *possible* to achieve that level of sales at the specified price. To address this issue, HD needs to estimate demand for this product.

Before moving on, however, let's stop here and practise applying the concepts covered so far. Now that you have seen pricing and break-even concepts in action as they relate to HD's new product, here are several exercises for you to apply what you have learned in other contexts.

Marketing by the numbers exercise set one

Now that you've studied pricing, break-even and margin analysis as they relate to HD's new-product launch, use the following exercises to apply these concepts in other contexts.

1. Elkins, a manufacturer of ice makers, realises a cost of €250 for every unit it produces.

   Its total fixed costs equal €5 million. If the company manufactures 500,000 units, compute the following:

   (a) unit cost

   (b) mark-up price if the company desires a 10 per cent return on sales

   (c) ROI price if the company desires a 25 per cent return on an investment of €1 million

2. A gift shop owner purchases items to sell in her store. She purchases a chair for €125 and sells it for €275. Determine the following:

   (a) euro mark-up

   (b) mark-up percentage on cost

   (c) mark-up percentage on selling price

3. A consumer purchases a coffee maker from a retailer for €90. The retailer's mark-up is 30 per cent, and the wholesaler's mark-up is 10 per cent, both based on selling price. For what price does the manufacturer sell the product to the wholesaler?

4. A lawn mower manufacturer has a unit cost of €140 and wishes to achieve a margin of 30 per cent based on selling price. If the manufacturer sells directly to a retailer who then adds a set margin of 40 per cent based on selling price, determine the retail price charged to consumers.

5. Advanced Electronics manufactures DVDs and sells them directly to retailers, who typically sell them for €20. Retailers take a 40 per cent margin based on the retail selling price. Advanced's cost information is as follows:

DVD package and disc	€2.50/DVD
Royalties	€2.25/DVD
Advertising and promotion	€500,000
Overhead	€200,000

   Calculate the following:
   (a) contribution per unit and contribution margin

   (b) break-even volume in DVD units and dollars

   (c) volume in DVD units and euro sales necessary if Advanced's profit goal is 20 per cent profit on sales

   (d) net profit if 5 million DVDs are sold

DEMAND ESTIMATES, THE MARKETING BUDGET AND MARKETING PERFORMANCE MEASURES

Market potential and sales estimates

HD has now calculated the sales needed to break even and to attain various profit goals on its new product. However, the company needs more information regarding demand in order to assess the feasibility of attaining the needed sales levels. This information is also needed for production and other decisions. For example, production schedules need to be developed and marketing tactics need to be planned.

Total market demand—The total volume that would be bought by a defined consumer group in a defined geographic area in a defined time period in a defined marketing environment under a defined level and mix of industry marketing effort.

The **total market demand** for a product or service is the total volume that would be bought by a defined consumer group in a defined geographic area in a defined time period in a defined marketing environment under a defined level and mix of industry marketing effort. Total market demand is not a fixed number but a function of the stated conditions. For example, next year's total market demand for this type of product will depend on how much other producers spend on marketing their brands. It also depends on many environmental factors, such as government regulations, economic conditions and the level of consumer confidence in a given market. The upper limit of market demand is called **market potential**.

Market potential—The upper limit of market demand.

One general but practical method that HD might use for estimating total market demand uses three variables: (1) the number of prospective buyers, (2) the quantity purchased by an average buyer per year, and (3) the price of an average unit. Using these numbers, HD can estimate total market demand as follows:

$$Q = n \times q \times p$$

where

Q = total market demand
n = number of buyers in the market
q = quantity purchased by an average buyer per year
p = price of an average unit

Chain ratio method—Estimating market demand by multiplying a base number by a chain of adjusting percentages.

A variation of this approach is the **chain ratio method**. This method involves multiplying a base number by a chain of adjusting percentages. For example, HD's product is designed to stream high-definition video on high-definition televisions as well as play other video content streamed from the Internet to multiple devices in a home. Thus, consumers who do not own a high-definition television will not be likely to purchase this player. Additionally, only households with broadband Internet access will be able to use the product. Finally, not all HDTV-owning Internet households will be willing and able to purchase this product. HD can estimate demand using a chain of calculations like the following:

Total number of households
× percentage of HDTV-owning households with broadband Internet access
× percentage of these households willing and able to buy this device

HD's research indicates that 60 per cent of households own at least one HDTV and have broadband Internet access. Finally, the company's research also revealed that 30 per cent of households possess the discretionary income needed and are willing to buy a product such as this. Then, the total number of households willing and able to purchase this product is:

115 million households × 0.60 × 0.30 = 20.7 million households

Households only need to purchase one device because it can stream content to other devices throughout the household. Assuming the average retail price across all brands is €350 for this product, the estimate of total market demand is as follows:

20.7 million households × 1 device per household × €350 = €7,245,000,000

This simple chain of calculations gives HD only a rough estimate of potential demand. However, more detailed chains involving additional segments and other qualifying factors would yield more accurate and refined estimates. Still, these are only estimates of market potential. They rely heavily on assumptions regarding adjusting percentages, average quantity and average price. Thus, HD must make certain that its assumptions are reasonable and defendable. As can be seen, the overall market potential in euro sales can vary widely given the average price used. For this reason, HD will use unit sales potential to determine its sales estimate for next year. Market potential in terms of units is 20.7 million (20.7 million households $\times$ 1 device per household).

Assuming that HD forecasts it will have a 3.6 per cent market share in the first year after launching this product, then it can forecast unit sales at 20.7 million units $\times$ 0.036 = 745,200 units. At a selling price of €168 per unit, this translates into sales of €125,193,600 (745,200 units $\times$ €168 per unit). For simplicity, further analyses will use forecasted sales of €125 million.

This unit volume estimate is well within HD's production capacity and exceeds not only the break-even estimate (465,117 units) calculated earlier, but also the volume necessary to realise a €5 million profit (581,396 units) or a 30 per cent return on investment (534,884 units). However, this forecast falls well short of the volume necessary to realise a 25 per cent return on sales (20 million units!) and may require that HD revise expectations.

To assess expected profits, we must now look at the budgeted expenses for launching this product. To do this, we will construct a pro forma profit-and-loss statement.

The profit-and-loss statement and marketing budget

All marketing managers must account for the profit impact of their marketing strategies. A major tool for projecting such profit impact is a **pro forma** (or **projected**) **profit-and-loss statement** (also called an **income statement** or **operating statement**). A pro forma statement shows projected revenues less budgeted expenses and estimates the projected net profit for an organisation, product or brand during a specific planning period, typically a year. It includes direct product production costs, marketing expenses budgeted to attain a given sales forecast, and overhead expenses assigned to the organisation or product. A profit-and-loss statement typically consists of several major components (see Table A2.1):

Pro forma (or projected) profit-and-loss statement (or income statement or operating statement)—A statement that shows projected revenues less budgeted expenses and estimates the projected net profit for an organisation, product or brand during a specific planning period, typically a year.

Table A2.1 Pro forma profit-and-loss statement for the 12-month period ended 31 December 2015

			% of sales
Net sales		€125,000,000	100
Cost of goods sold		62,500,000	50
Gross margin		€62,500,000	50
Marketing expenses			
Sales expenses	€17,500,000		
Promotion expenses	15,000,000		
Freight	12,500,000	45,000,000	36
General and administrative expenses			
Managerial salaries and expenses	€2,000,000		
Indirect overhead	3,000,000	5,000,000	4
Net profit before income tax		€12,500,000	10

- *Net sales.* Gross sales revenue minus returns and allowances (for example, trade, cash, quantity and promotion allowances). HD's net sales for 2015 are estimated to be €125 million, as determined in the previous analysis.
- *Cost of goods sold* (sometimes called *cost of sales*). The actual cost of the merchandise sold by a manufacturer or reseller. It includes the cost of inventory, purchases and other costs associated with making the goods. HD's cost of goods sold is estimated to be 50 per cent of net sales, or €62.5 million.
- *Gross margin (or gross profit).* The difference between net sales and cost of goods sold. HD's gross margin is estimated to be €62.5 million.
- *Operating expenses.* The expenses incurred while doing business. These include all other expenses beyond the cost of goods sold that are necessary to conduct business. Operating expenses can be presented in total or broken down in detail. Here, HD's estimated operating expenses include marketing expenses and general and administrative expenses.
- Marketing expenses include sales expenses, promotion expenses and distribution expenses. The new product will be sold through HD's sales force, so the company budgets €5 million for sales salaries. However, because sales representatives earn a 10 per cent commission on sales, HD must also add a variable component to sales expenses of €12.5 million (10 per cent of €125 million net sales), for a total budgeted sales expense of €17.5 million. HD sets its advertising and promotion to launch this product at €10 million. However, the company also budgets 4 per cent of sales, or €5 million, for cooperative advertising allowances to retailers who promote HD's new product in their advertising. Thus, the total budgeted advertising and promotion expenses are €15 million (€10 million for advertising plus €5 million in co-op allowances). Finally, HD budgets 10 per cent of net sales, or €12.5 million, for freight and delivery charges. In all, total marketing expenses are estimated to be €17.5 million + €15 million + €12.5 million = €45 million.
- General and administrative expenses are estimated at €5 million, broken down into €2 million for managerial salaries and expenses for the marketing function and €3 million of indirect overhead allocated to this product by the corporate accountants (such as depreciation, interest, maintenance and insurance). Total expenses for the year, then, are estimated to be €50 million (€45 million marketing expenses + €5 million in general and administrative expenses).
- *Net profit before taxes.* Profit earned after all costs are deducted. HD's estimated net profit before taxes is €12.5 million.
- In all, as Table A2.1 shows, HD expects to earn a profit on its new product of €12.5 million in 2015. Also note that the percentage of sales that each component of the profit-and-loss statement represents is given in the right-hand column. These percentages are determined by dividing the cost figure by net sales (that is, marketing expenses represent 36 per cent of net sales determined by €45 million ÷ €125 million). As can be seen, HD projects a net profit return on sales of 10 per cent in the first year after launching this product.

Marketing performance measures

Now let's fast-forward a year. HD's product has been on the market for one year and management wants to assess its sales and profit performance. One way to assess this performance is to compute performance ratios derived from HD's **profit-and-loss statement** (or **income statement** or **operating statement**).

Whereas the pro forma profit-and-loss statement shows projected financial performance, the statement given in Table A2.2 shows HD's *actual financial* performance based on actual sales, cost of goods sold, and expenses during the past year. By comparing the profit-and-loss statement from one period to the next, HD can gauge performance against goals, spot favourable or unfavourable trends, and take appropriate corrective action.

The profit-and-loss statement shows that HD lost €1 million rather than making the €12.5 million profit projected in the pro forma statement. Why? One obvious reason is that net sales fell €25 million short of estimated sales. Lower sales translated into lower variable costs associated

Profit-and-loss statement (or income statement or operating statement)—A statement that shows actual revenues less expenses and net profit for an organisation, product or brand during a specific planning period, typically a year.

with marketing the product. However, both fixed costs and the cost of goods sold as a percentage of sales exceeded expectations. Hence, the product's contribution margin was 21 per cent rather than the estimated 26 per cent. That is, variable costs represented 79 per cent of sales (55 per cent for cost of goods sold, 10 per cent for sales commissions, 10 per cent for freight, and 4 per cent for co-op allowances). Recall that contribution margin can be calculated by subtracting that fraction from one $(1 - 0.79 = 0.21)$. Total fixed costs were €22 million, €2 million more than estimated. Thus, the sales that HD needed to break even given this cost structure can be calculated as:

$$\text{Break-even sales} = \frac{\text{fixed costs}}{\text{contribution margin}} = \frac{\text{€22,000,000}}{0.21} = \text{€104,761,905}$$

If HD had achieved another €5 million in sales, it would have earned a profit.

Although HD's sales fell short of the forecasted sales, so did overall industry sales for this product. Overall industry sales were only €2.5 billion. That means that HD's **market share** was 4 per cent (€100 million ÷ €2.5 billion = 0.04 = 4%), which was higher than forecasted. Thus, HD attained a higher-than-expected market share but the overall market sales were not as high as estimated.

Market share—Company sales divided by market sales.

Analytic ratios

The profit-and-loss statement provides the figures needed to compute some crucial **operating ratios** – the ratios of selected operating statement items to net sales. These ratios let marketers compare the firm's performance in one year to that in previous years (or with industry standards and competitors' performance in that year). The most commonly used operating ratios are the gross margin percentage, the net profit percentage, and the operating expense percentage. The inventory turnover rate and return on investment (ROI) are often used to measure managerial effectiveness and efficiency.

Operating ratios—The ratios of selected operating statement items to net sales.

The **gross margin percentage** indicates the percentage of net sales remaining after cost of goods sold that can contribute to operating expenses and net profit before taxes. The higher this ratio, the more a firm has left to cover expenses and generate profit. HD's gross margin ratio was 45 per cent:

$$\text{Gross margin percentage} = \frac{\text{gross margin}}{\text{net sales}} = \frac{\text{€45,000,000}}{\text{€100,000,000}} = 0.45 = 45$$

Gross margin percentage—The percentage of net sales remaining after cost of goods sold – calculated by dividing gross margin by net sales.

Note that this percentage is lower than estimated, and this ratio is seen easily in the percentage of sales column in Table A2.2. Stating items in the profit-and-loss statement as a percentage of sales allows managers to quickly spot abnormal changes in costs over time. If there was previous history for this product and this ratio was declining, management should examine it more closely to determine why it has decreased (that is, because of a decrease in sales volume or price, an

Table A2.2 Profit-and-loss statement for the 12-month period ended 31 December 2015

			% of sales
Net sales		€100,000,000	100
Cost of goods sold		55,000,000	55
Gross margin		€45,000,000	45
Marketing expenses			
Sales expenses	€15,000,000		
Promotion expenses	14,000,000		
Freight	10,000,000	39,000,000	39
General and administrative expenses			
Managerial salaries and expenses	€2,000,000		
Indirect overhead	5,000,000	7,000,000	7
Net profit before income tax		−€1,000,000	−1

increase in costs, or a combination of these). In HD's case, net sales were €25 million lower than estimated, and cost of goods sold was higher than estimated (55 per cent rather than the estimated 50 per cent).

The **net profit percentage** shows the percentage of each sales euro going to profit. It is calculated by dividing net profits by net sales:

$$\text{Net profit percentage} = \frac{\text{net profit}}{\text{net sales}} = \frac{-€1,000,000}{€100,000,000} = -0.01 = -1.0$$

This ratio is easily seen in the percentage of sales column. HD's new product generated negative profits in the first year; this is not a good situation, given that before the product launch net profits before taxes were estimated at more than €12 million. Later in this appendix, we will discuss further analyses the marketing manager should conduct to defend the product.

The **operating expense percentage** indicates the portion of net sales going to operating expenses. Operating expenses include marketing and other expenses not directly related to marketing the product, such as indirect overhead assigned to this product. It is calculated by:

$$\text{Operating expense percentage} = \frac{\text{total expenses}}{\text{net sales}} = \frac{€46,000,000}{€100,000,000} = 0.46 = 46$$

This ratio can also be quickly determined from the percentage of sales column in the profit and-loss statement by adding the percentages for marketing expenses and general and administrative expenses (39% + 7%). Thus, 46 cents of every sales euro went for operations. Although HD wants this ratio to be as low as possible, and 46 per cent is not an alarming amount, it is of concern if it is increasing over time or if a loss is realised.

Another useful ratio is the **inventory turnover rate** (also called **stockturn rate** for resellers). The inventory turnover rate is the number of times an inventory turns over or is sold during a specified time period (often one year). This rate tells how quickly a business is moving inventory through the organisation. Higher rates indicate that lower investments in inventory are made, thus freeing up funds for other investments. It may be computed on a cost, selling price or unit basis. The formula based on cost is:

$$\text{Inventory turnover rate} = \frac{\text{cost of goods sold}}{\text{average inventory at cost}}$$

Assuming HD's beginning and ending inventories were €30 million and €20 million, respectively, the inventory turnover rate is:

$$\text{Inventory turnover rate} = \frac{€55,000,000}{(€30,000,000 + €20,000,000)/2} = \frac{€55,000,000}{€25,000,000} = 2.2$$

That is, HD's inventory turned over 2.2 times in 2015. Normally, the higher the turnover rate, the higher the management efficiency and company profitability. However, this rate should be compared to industry averages, competitors' rates and past performance to determine if HD is doing well. A competitor with similar sales but a higher inventory turnover rate will have fewer resources tied up in inventory, allowing it to invest in other areas of the business.

Companies frequently use **return on investment** (**ROI**) to measure managerial effectiveness and efficiency. For HD, ROI is the ratio of net profits to total investment required to manufacture the new product. This investment includes capital investments in land, buildings and equipment (here, the initial €10 million to refurbish the manufacturing facility) plus inventory costs (HD's average inventory totalled €25 million), for a total of €35 million. Thus, HD's ROI for this product is:

$$\text{Return on investment} = \frac{\text{net profit before taxes}}{\text{investment}} = \frac{-€1,000,000}{€35,000,000} = -0.286 = -2.86$$

ROI is often used to compare alternatives, and a positive ROI is desired. The alternative with the highest ROI is preferred to other alternatives. HD needs to be concerned with the ROI realised. One obvious way HD can increase ROI is to increase net profit by reducing expenses. Another way is to reduce its investment, perhaps by investing less in inventory and turning it over more frequently.

Net profit percentage—The percentage of each sales euro going to profit – calculated by dividing net profits by net sales.

Operating expense percentage—The portion of net sales going to operating expenses – calculated by dividing total expenses by net sales.

Inventory turnover rate (or stock turn rate)—The number of times an inventory turns over or is sold during a specified time period (often one year) – calculated based on costs, selling price or units.

Return on investment (ROI)—A measure of managerial effectiveness and efficiency – net profit before taxes divided by total investment.

Marketing profitability metrics

Given the previous financial results, you may be thinking that HD should drop this new product. But what arguments can marketers make for keeping or dropping it? The obvious arguments for dropping the product are that first-year sales were well below expected levels and the product lost money, resulting in a negative return on investment.

So what would happen if HD did drop this product? Surprisingly, if the company drops the product, the profits for the total organisation will decrease by €4 million! How can that be? Marketing managers need to look closely at the numbers in the profit-and-loss statement to determine the *net marketing contribution* for this product. In HD's case, the net marketing contribution for the product is €4 million, and if the company drops this product, that contribution will disappear as well. Let's look more closely at this concept to illustrate how marketing managers can better assess and defend their marketing strategies and programmes.

Net marketing contribution

Net marketing contribution (NMC), along with other marketing metrics derived from it, measures marketing profitability. It includes only components of profitability that are controlled by marketing. Whereas the previous calculation of net profit before taxes from the profit-and-loss statement includes operating expenses not under marketing's control, NMC does not. Referring back to HD's profit-and-loss statement given in Table A2.2, we can calculate net marketing contribution for the product as:

$$\text{NMC} = \text{net sales} - \text{cost of goods sold} - \text{marketing expenses}$$

$$= €100 \text{ million} - €55 \text{ million} - €41 \text{ million} = €4 \text{ million}$$

The marketing expenses include sales expenses (€15 million), promotion expenses (€14 million), freight expenses (€10 million), and the managerial salaries and expenses of the marketing function (€2 million), which total €41 million.

Thus, the product actually contributed €4 million to HD's profits. It was the €5 million of indirect overhead allocated to this product that caused the negative profit. Further, the amount allocated was €2 million more than estimated in the pro forma profit-and-loss statement. Indeed, if only the estimated amount had been allocated, the product would have earned a *profit* of €1 million rather than losing €1 million. If HD drops the product, the €5 million in fixed overhead expenses will not disappear – it will simply have to be allocated elsewhere. However, the €4 million in net marketing contribution *will* disappear.

Marketing return on sales and investment

To get an even deeper understanding of the profit impact of marketing strategy, we'll now examine two measures of marketing efficiency – *marketing return on sales* (marketing ROS) and marketing return on investment (marketing ROI).[3]

Marketing return on sales (or marketing ROS) shows the per cent of net sales attributable to the net marketing contribution. For our product, ROS is:

$$\text{Marketing ROS} = \frac{\text{net marketing contribution}}{\text{net sales}} = \frac{€4,000,000}{€100,000,000} = 0.04 = 4$$

Thus, out of every €100 of sales, the product returns €4 to HD's bottom line. A high marketing ROS is desirable. But to assess whether this is a good level of performance, HD must compare this figure to previous marketing ROS levels for the product, the ROSs of other products in the company's portfolio, and the ROSs of competing products.

Marketing return on investment (or marketing ROI) measures the marketing productivity of a marketing investment. In HD's case, the marketing investment is represented by €41 million of the total expenses. Thus, marketing ROI is:

Net marketing contribution (NMC)—A measure of marketing profit ability that includes only components of profitability controlled by marketing.

Marketing return on sales (or marketing ROS)—The percentage of net sales attributable to the net marketing contribution – calculated by dividing net marketing contribution by net sales.

$$\text{Marketing ROI} = \frac{\text{net marketing contribution}}{\text{marketing expenses}} = \frac{€4,000,000}{€41,000,000} = 0.0976 = 9.76$$

As with marketing ROS, a high value is desirable, but this figure should be compared with previous levels for the given product and with the marketing ROIs of competitors' products. Note from this equation that marketing ROI could be greater than 100 per cent. This can be achieved by attaining a higher net marketing contribution and/or a lower total marketing expense.

In this section, we estimated market potential and sales, developed profit-and-loss statements, and examined financial measures of performance. In the next section, we discuss methods for analysing the impact of various marketing tactics. However, before moving on to those analyses, here's another set of quantitative exercises to help you apply what you've learned to other situations.

Marketing by the numbers exercise set two

1. Determine the market potential for a product that has 20 million prospective buyers who purchase an average of 2 items per year in which the price averages €50. How many units must a company sell if it desires a 10 per cent share of this market?

2. Develop a profit-and-loss statement for the Westgate division of North Industries. This division manufactures light fixtures sold to consumers through home improvement and hardware stores. Cost of goods sold represents 40 per cent of net sales. Marketing expenses include selling expenses, promotion expenses and freight. Selling expenses include sales salaries totalling €3 million per year and sales commissions (5 per cent of sales). The company spent €3 million on advertising last year, and freight costs were 10 per cent of sales. Other costs include €2 million for managerial salaries and expenses for the marketing function and another €3 million for indirect overhead allocated to the division. Develop the profit-and-loss statement if net sales were €20 million last year. Develop the profit-and-loss statement if net sales were €40 million last year. Calculate Westgate's break-even sales.

3. Using the profit-and-loss statement you developed in question 2.2b, and assuming that Westgate's beginning inventory was €11 million, ending inventory was €7 million, and total investment was €20 million including inventory, determine the following:

   (a) gross margin percentage

   (b) net profit percentage

   (c) operating expense percentage

   (d) inventory turnover rate

   (e) return on investment (ROI)

   (f) net marketing contribution

   (g) marketing return on sales (marketing ROS)

   (h) marketing return on investment (marketing ROI)

   (i) Is the Westgate division doing well? Explain your answer.

FINANCIAL ANALYSIS OF MARKETING TACTICS

Although the first-year profit performance for HD's new product was less than desired, management feels that this attractive market has excellent growth opportunities. Although the sales of HD's product were lower than initially projected, they were not unreasonable given the size of the current market. Thus, HD wants to explore new marketing tactics to help grow the market for this product and increase sales for the company.

For example, the company could increase advertising to promote more awareness of the new product and its category. It could add salespeople to secure greater product distribution. HD could decrease prices so that more consumers could afford its product. Finally, to expand the market, HD could introduce a lower-priced model in addition to the higher-priced original offering. Before pursuing any of these tactics, HD must analyse the financial implications of each.

Increase advertising expenditures

HD is considering boosting its advertising to make more people aware of the benefits of this device in general and of its own brand in particular. What if HD's marketers recommend increasing national advertising by 50 per cent to €15 million (assume no change in the variable cooperative component of promotional expenditures)? This represents an increase in fixed costs of €5 million. What increase in sales will be needed to break even on this €5 million increase in fixed costs?

A quick way to answer this question is to divide the increase in fixed cost by the contribution margin, which we found in a previous analysis to be 21 per cent:

$$\text{Increase in sales} = \frac{\text{increase in fixed costs}}{\text{contribution margin}} = \frac{€5,000,000}{0.21} = €22,809,524$$

Thus, a 50 per cent increase in advertising expenditures must produce a sales increase of almost €24 million to just break even. That €24 million sales increase translates into an almost 1 percentage point increase in market share (1 per cent of the €2.5 billion overall market equals €25 million). That is, to break even on the increased advertising expenditure, HD would have to increase its market share from 4 per cent to 4.95 per cent (€123,809,524 ÷ €2.5 billion = 0.0495 or 4.95 per cent market share). All of this assumes that the total market will not grow, which might or might not be a reasonable assumption.

Increase distribution coverage

HD also wants to consider hiring more salespeople in order to call on new retailer accounts and increase distribution through more outlets. Even though HD sells directly to wholesalers, its sales representatives call on retail accounts to perform other functions in addition to selling, such as training retail salespeople. Currently, HD employs 60 sales reps who earn an average of €50,000 in salary plus 10 per cent commission on sales. The product is currently sold to consumers through 1,875 retail outlets. Suppose HD wants to increase that number of outlets to 2,500, an increase of 625 retail outlets. How many additional salespeople will HD need, and what sales will be necessary to break even on the increased cost?

One method for determining what size sales force HD will need is the **workload method**. The workload method uses the following formula to determine the sales force size:

$$NS = \frac{NC \times FC \times LC}{TA}$$

where

NS = number of salespeople
NC = number of customers
FC = average frequency of customer calls per customer
LC = average length of customer call
TA = time an average salesperson has available for selling per year

Workload method–An approach to determining sales force size based on the workload required and the time available for selling.

HD's sales reps typically call on accounts an average of 20 times per year for about 2 hours per call. Although each sales rep works 2,000 hours per year (50 weeks per year × 40 hours per week), they spend about 15 hours per week on non-selling activities such as administrative duties and travel. Thus, the average annual available selling time per sales rep per year is 1,250 hours (50 weeks × 25 hours per week). We can now calculate how many sales reps HD will need to cover the anticipated 2,500 retail outlets:

$$NS = \frac{2,500 \times 20 \times 2}{1,250} = 80 \text{ salespeople}$$

Therefore, HD will need to hire 20 more salespeople. The cost to hire these reps will be €1 million (20 salespeople × €50,000 salary per salesperson).

What increase in sales will be required to break even on this increase in fixed costs? The 10 per cent commission is already accounted for in the contribution margin, so the contribution margin remains unchanged at 21 per cent. Thus, the increase in sales needed to cover this increase in fixed costs can be calculated by:

$$\text{Increase in sales} = \frac{\text{Increae in fixed cost}}{\text{contribution margin}} = \frac{€1,000,000}{0.21} = €4,761,905$$

That is, HD's sales must increase almost €5 million to break even on this tactic. So, how many new retail outlets will the company need to secure to achieve this sales increase? The average revenue generated per current outlet is €53,333 (€100 million in sales divided by 1,875 outlets). To achieve the nearly €5 million sales increase needed to break even, HD would need about 90 new outlets (€4,761,905 ÷ €53,333 = 89.3 outlets), or about 4.5 outlets per new rep. Given that current reps cover about 31 outlets apiece (1,875 outlets ÷ 60 reps), this seems very reasonable.

Decrease price

HD is also considering lowering its price to increase sales revenue through increased volume. The company's research has shown that demand for most types of consumer electronics products is elastic – that is, the percentage increase in the quantity demanded is greater than the percentage decrease in price.

What increase in sales would be necessary to break even on a 10 per cent decrease in price? That is, what increase in sales will be needed to maintain the total contribution that HD realised at the higher price? The current total contribution can be determined by multiplying the contribution margin by total sales:[4]

$$\text{Current total contribution} = \text{contribution margin} \times \text{sales} = 0.21 \times €100 \text{ million}$$
$$= €21 \text{ million}$$

Price changes result in changes in unit contribution and contribution margin. Recall that the contribution margin of 21 per cent was based on variable costs representing 79 per cent of sales. Therefore, unit variable costs can be determined by multiplying the original price by this percentage: €168 × 0.79 = €132.72 per unit. If price is decreased by 10 per cent, the new price is €151.20. However, variable costs do not change just because price decreased, so the contribution and contribution margin decrease as follows:

	Old	New (reduced 10%)
Price	€168	€151.20
− Unit variable cost	€132.72	€132.72
= Unit contribution	€35.28	€18.48
Contribution margin	€35.28/€168 = 0.21 or 21%	€18.48/€151.20 = 0.12 or 12%

So, a 10% reduction in price results in a decrease in the contribution margin from 21 per cent to 12 per cent.[5] To determine the sales level needed to break even on this price reduction, we calculate the level of sales that must be attained at the new contribution margin to achieve the original total contribution of €21 million:

$$\text{New contribution margin} \times \text{new sales level} = \text{original total contribution}$$

So,

$$\text{New sales level} = \frac{\text{orginal contribution}}{\text{new orginal contribution}} = \frac{€21,000,000}{0.21} = €175,000,000$$

Thus, sales must increase by €75 million (€175 million − €100 million) just to break even on a 10 per cent price reduction. This means that HD must increase market share to 7 per cent

(€175 million ÷ €2.5 billion) to achieve the current level of profits (assuming no increase in the total market sales). The marketing manager must assess whether or not this is a reasonable goal.

Extend the product line

As a final option, HD is considering extending its product line by offering a lower-priced model. Of course, the new, lower-priced product would steal some sales from the higher-priced model. This is called **cannibalisation** – the situation in which one product sold by a company takes a portion of its sales from other company products. If the new product has a lower contribution than the original product, the company's total contribution will decrease on the cannibalised sales. However, if the new product can generate enough new volume, it is worth considering.

Cannibalisation—The situation in which one product sold by a company takes a portion of its sales from other company products.

To assess cannibalisation, HD must look at the incremental contribution gained by having both products available. Recall in the previous analysis that we determined unit variable costs were €132.72 and unit contribution was just over €35. Assuming costs remain the same next year, HD can expect to realise a contribution per unit of approximately €35 for every unit of the original product sold.

Assume that the first model offered by HD is called HD1 and the new, lower-priced model is called HD2. HD2 will retail for €250, and resellers will take the same mark-up percentages on price as they do with the higher-priced model. Therefore, HD2's price to wholesalers will be €140 as follows:

Retail price:	€250
minus retail margin (30%):	− €75
Retailer's cost/wholesaler's price:	€175
minus wholesaler's margin (20%):	− €35
Wholesaler's cost/HD's price	€140

If HD2's variable costs are estimated to be €120, then its contribution per unit will equal €20 (€140 − €120 = €20). That means for every unit that HD2 cannibalises from HD1, HD will lose €15 in contribution toward fixed costs and profit (that is, contribution HD2 − contribution HD1 = €20 − €35 = −€15). You might conclude that HD should not pursue this tactic because it appears as though the company will be worse off if it introduces the lower priced model. However, if HD2 captures enough additional sales, HD will be better off even though some HD1 sales are cannibalised. The company must examine what will happen to total contribution, which requires estimates of unit volume for both products.

Originally, HD estimated that next year's sales of HD1 would be 600,000 units. However, with the introduction of HD2, it now estimates that 200,000 of those sales will be cannibalised by the new model. If HD sells only 200,000 units of the new HD2 model (all cannibalised from HD1), the company would lose €3 million in total contribution (200,000 units × −€15 per cannibalised unit = −€3 million) − not a good outcome. However, HD estimates that HD2 will generate the 200,000 of cannibalised sales plus an additional 500,000 unit sales. Thus, the contribution on these additional HD2 units will be €10 million (i.e., 500,000 units × €20 per unit = €10 million). The net effect is that HD will gain €7 million in total contribution by introducing HD2.

The following table compares HD's total contribution with and without the introduction of HD2:

	HD1 Only	HD1 and HD2
HD1 contribution	600,000 units × €35 = €21,000,000 0	400,000 units × €35 = €14,000,000
HD2 contribution	0	700,000 units × €20 = €14,000,000
Total contribution	€21,000,000	€28,000,000

The difference in the total contribution is a net gain of €7 million (€28 million − €21 million). Based on this analysis, HD should introduce the HD2 model because it results in a positive incremental contribution. However, if fixed costs will increase by more than €7 million as a result of adding this model, then the net effect will be negative and HD should not pursue this tactic.

Now that you have seen these marketing tactic analysis concepts in action as they relate to HD's new product, here are several exercises for you to apply what you have learned in this section in other contexts.

Marketing by the numbers exercise set three

1. Alliance, Inc. sells gas lamps to consumers through retail outlets. Total industry sales for Alliance's relevant market last year were €100 million, with Alliance's sales representing 5 per cent of that total. Contribution margin is 25 per cent. Alliance's sales force calls on retail outlets and each sales rep earns €50,000 per year plus 1 per cent commission on all sales. Retailers receive a 40 per cent margin on selling price and generate average revenue of €10,000 per outlet for Alliance.

   (a) The marketing manager has suggested increasing consumer advertising by €200,000. By how much would euro sales need to increase to break even on this expenditure? What increase in overall market share does this represent?

   (b) Another suggestion is to hire two more sales representatives to gain new consumer retail accounts. How many new retail outlets would be necessary to break even on the increased cost of adding two sales reps?

   (c) A final suggestion is to make a 10 per cent across-the-board price reduction. By how much would euro sales need to increase to maintain Alliance's current contribution? (See endnote 5 to calculate the new contribution margin.)

   (d) Which suggestion do you think Alliance should implement? Explain your recommendation.

2. PepsiCo sells its soft drinks in approximately 400,000 retail establishments, such as supermarkets, discount stores, and convenience stores. Sales representatives call on each retail account weekly, which means each account is called on by a sales rep 52 times per year. The average length of a sales call is 75 minutes (or 1.25 hours). An average salesperson works 2,000 hours per year (50 weeks per year × 40 hours per week), but each spends 10 hours a week on non-selling activities, such as administrative tasks and travel. How many salespeople does PepsiCo need?

3. Hair Zone manufactures a brand of hair-styling gel. It is considering adding a modified version of the product – a foam that provides stronger hold. Hair Zone's variable costs and prices to wholesalers are:

	Current hair gel	New foam product
Unit selling price	2.00	2.25
Unit variable costs	0.85	1.25

   Hair Zone expects to sell 1 million units of the new styling foam in the first year after introduction, but it expects that 60 per cent of those sales will come from buyers who normally purchase Hair Zone's styling gel. Hair Zone estimates that it would sell 1.5 million units of the gel if it did not introduce the foam. If the fixed cost of launching the new foam will be €100,000 during the first year, should Hair Zone add the new product to its line? Why or why not?

REFERENCES

[1] This is derived by rearranging the following equation and solving for price: Percentage mark-up = (price − cost) ÷ price.

[2] Again, using the basic profit equation, we set profit equal to ROI × I: ROI × I = (P × Q) − TFC − (Q × UVC). Solving for Q gives Q = (TFC + (ROI × I)) ÷ (P − UVC).

[3] See Roger J. Best, *Market-Based Management*, 4th ed. (Upper Saddle River, NJ: Prentice Hall, 2005).

[4] Total contribution can also be determined from the unit contribution and unit volume: Total contribution = unit contribution × unit sales. Total units sold in 2015 were 595,238 units, which can be determined by dividing total sales by price per unit (€100 million ÷ €168). Total contribution = €35.28 contribution per unit × 595,238 units = €20,999,996.64 (difference due to rounding).

[5] Recall that the contribution margin of 21% was based on variable costs representing 79% of sales. Therefore, if we do not know price, we can set it equal to €1.00. If price equals €1.00, 79 cents represents variable costs and 21 cents represents unit contribution. If price is decreased by 10%, the new price is €0.90. However, variable costs do not change just because price decreased, so the unit contribution and contribution margin decrease as follows:

	Old	New (reduced 10%)
Price	€1.00	€0.90
− Unit variable cost	€0.79	€0.79
= Unit contribution	€0.21	€0.11
Contribution margin €0.21/€1.00	€0.21/€1.00 = 0.21 or 21%	€0.11/€0.90 = 0.12 or 12%

GLOSSARY

Action programmes–Action programmes should be coordinated with the resources and activities of other departments, including production, finance and purchasing.

Adapted global marketing–An international marketing strategy that adjusts the marketing strategy and mix elements to each international target market, bearing more costs but hoping for a larger market share and return.

Administered VMS–A vertical marketing system that coordinates successive stages of production and distribution, through the size and power of one of the parties.

Adoption process–The mental process through which an individual passes from first hearing about an innovation to final adoption.

Advertising agency–A marketing services firm that assists companies in planning, preparing, implementing and evaluating all or portions of their advertising programmes.

Advertising budget–The euros and other resources allocated to a product or a company advertising programme.

Advertising media–The vehicles through which advertising messages are delivered to their intended audiences.

Advertising objective–A specific communication *task* to be accomplished with a specific *target* audience during a specific period of *time*.

Advertising strategy–The strategy by which the company accomplishes its advertising objectives. It consists of two major elements: creating advertising messages and selecting advertising media.

Advertising–Any paid form of non-personal presentation and promotion of ideas, goods or services by an identified sponsor.

Affordable method–Setting the promotion budget at the level management thinks the company can afford.

Age and life-cycle segmentation–Dividing a market into different age and life-cycle groups.

Agent–A wholesaler who represents buyers or sellers on a relatively permanent basis, performs only a few functions and does not take the goods.

Allowance–Promotional money paid by manufacturers to retailers in return for an agreement to feature the manufacturer's products in some way.

Alternative evaluation–The stage of the buyer decision process in which the consumer uses information to evaluate alternative brands in the choice set.

Approach–A salesperson meets the customer for the first time.

Attitude–A person's consistently favourable or unfavourable evaluations, feelings and tendencies toward an object or idea.

Baby boomers–The 78 million people born during years following the Second World War and lasting until 1964.

Base-point pricing–A geographical pricing strategy in which the seller designates some city as a base point and charges all customers the freight cost from that city to the customer.

Behavioural segmentation–Dividing a market into segments based on consumer knowledge, attitudes, uses or responses to a product.

Behavioural targeting–Using online consumer tracking data to target advertisements and marketing offers to specific consumers.

Belief–A descriptive thought that a person holds about something.

Benchmarking–The process of comparing one company's products and processes to those of competitors or leading firms in other industries to identify best practices and find ways to improve quality and performance.

Benefit segmentation–Dividing the market into segments according to the different benefits that consumers seek from the product.

Big data–The huge and complex data sets generated by today's sophisticated information generation, collection, storage and analysis technologies.

Blogs–Online journals where people post their thoughts, usually on a narrowly defined topic.

Brand–A name, term, sign, symbol, design, or a combination of these, that identifies the products or services of one seller or group of sellers and differentiates them from those of competitors.

Brand equity–The differential effect that knowing the brand name has oncustomer response to the product or its marketing.

Brand extension–Extending an existing brand name to new product categories.

Brand value–The total financial value of a brand.

Branded community website–A website that presents brand content that engages consumers and creates customer community around a brand.

Break-even analysis–Analysis to determine the unit volume and euro sales needed to be profitable given a particular price and cost structure.

Break-even price–The price at which total revenue equals total cost and profit is zero.

Break-even pricing (target return pricing)—Setting price to break even on the costs of making and marketing a product or setting price to make a target return.

Broker—A wholesaler who does not take title to goods and whose function is to bring buyers and sellers together and assist in negotiation.

Budgets—Managers use budgets to project profitability and plan for each marketing programme's expenditures, scheduling and operations.

Business analysis—A review of the sales, costs and profit projections for a new product to find out whether these factors satisfy the company's objectives.

Business buyer behaviour—The buying behaviour of organisations that buy goods and services for use in the production of other products and services that are sold, rented or supplied to others.

Business buying process—The decision process by which business buyers determine which products and services their organisations need to purchase and then find, evaluate and choose among alternative suppliers and brands.

Business portfolio—The collection of businesses and products that make up the company.

Business promotions—Sales promotion tools used to generate business leads, stimulate purchases, reward customers and motivate salespeople.

Business-to-business (B-to-B) online marketing—Businesses using online marketing to reach new business customers, serve current customers more effectively and obtain buying efficiencies and better prices.

Business-to-consumer (B-to-C) online marketing—Businesses selling goods and services online to final consumers.

Buyer-readiness stages—The stages consumers normally pass through on their way to a purchase, including awareness, knowledge, liking, preference, conviction and, finally, the actual purchase.

Buyers—People in an organisation's buying centre who make an actual purchase.

Buying centre—All the individuals and units that play a role in the purchase decision-making process.

Buzz marketing—Cultivating opinion leaders and getting them to spread information about a product or a service to others in their communities.

By-product pricing—Setting a price for by-products to make the main product's price more competitive.

Cannibalisation—The situation in which one product sold by a company takes a portion of its sales from other company products.

Captive product pricing—Setting a price for products that must be used along with a main product, such as blades for a razor and games for a computer game console.

Catalogue marketing—Direct marketing through print, video or digital catalogues that are mailed to select customers, made available in stores, or presented online.

Category killer—A giant speciality store that carries a very deep assortment of a particular line and is staffed by knowledgeable employees.

Causal research—Marketing research to test hypotheses about cause-and-effect relationships.

Chain ratio method—Estimating market demand by multiplying a base number by a chain of adjusting percentages.

Chain stores—Two or more outlets that are commonly owned and controlled.

Channel conflict—Disagreement among marketing channel members on goals, roles and rewards – who should do what and for what rewards.

Channel level—A layer of intermediaries that performs some work in bringing the product and its ownership closer to the final buyer.

Click-and-mortar companies—Traditional brick-and-mortar companies that have added online marketing to their operations.

Click-only companies—The so-called dotcoms, which operate online only and have no brick-and-mortar market presence.

Closing—A salesperson asks the customer for an order.

Co-branding—The practice of using the established brand names of two different companies on the same product.

Cognitive dissonance—Buyer discomfort caused by postpurchase conflict.

Commercial online databases—Collections of information available from online commercial sources or accessible via the Internet.

Commercialisation—Introducing a new product into the market.

Communication adaptation—A global communication strategy of fully adapting advertising messages to local markets.

Competition-based pricing—Setting prices based on competitors' strategies, prices, costs and market offerings.

Competitive advantage—An advantage over competitors gained by offering greater customer value, either by having lower prices or providing more benefits that justify higher prices.

Competitive marketing intelligence—The systematic collection and analysis of publicly available information about consumers, competitors and developments in the marketing environment.

Competitive monitoring marketing strategies—Strategies that strongly position the company against competitors and give the company the strongest possible strategic advantage.

Competitive review—The purpose of a competitive review is to identify key competitors, describe their market positions and briefly discuss their strategies.

Competitive-parity method—Setting the promotion budget to match competitors' outlays.

Competitor analysis—The process of identifying key competitors; assessing their objectives, strategies, strengths and weaknesses, and reaction patterns; and selecting which competitors to attack or avoid.

Competitor-centred company—A company whose moves are mainly based on competitors' actions and reactions.

Complex buying behaviour—Consumer buying behaviour characterised by high consumer involvement in a purchase and significant perceived differences among brands.

Concentrated (niche) marketing—A market-coverage strategy in which a firm goes after a large share of one or a few segments or niches.

Concept testing—Testing new-product concepts with a group of target consumers to find out if the concepts have strong consumer appeal.

Consumer buyer behaviour—The buying behaviour of final consumers - individuals and households that buy goods and services for personal consumption.

Consumer market—All the individuals and households that buy or acquire goods and services for personal consumption.

Consumer product—A product bought by final consumers for personal consumption.

Consumer promotions—Sales promotion tools used to boost short-term customer buying and involvement or enhance long-term customer relationships.

Consumer-generated marketing—Brand exchanges created by consumers themselves - both invited and uninvited - by which consumers are playing an increasing role in shaping their own brand experiences and those of other consumers.

Consumerism—An organised movement of citizens and government agencies to improve the rights and power of buyers in relation to sellers.

Consumer-oriented marketing—A principle of sustainable marketing that holds a company should view and organise its marketing activities from the consumer's point of view.

Consumer-to-business (C-to-B) online marketing—Online exchanges in which consumers search out sellers, learn about their offers and initiate purchases, sometimes even driving transaction terms.

Consumer-to-consumer (C-to-C) online marketing—Online exchanges of goods and information between final consumers.

Content marketing—Creating, inspiring and sharing brand messages and conversations with and among consumers across a fluid mix of paid, owned, earned and shared channels.

Contract manufacturing—A joint venture in which a company contracts with manufacturers in a foreign market to produce a product or provide a service.

Contractual VMS—A vertical marketing system in which independent firms at different levels of production and distribution join together through contracts.

Contribution margin—The unit contribution divided by the selling price.

Convenience product—A consumer product that customers usually buy frequently, immediately and with minimal comparison and buying effort.

Convenience store—A small store, located near a residential area, that is open long hours seven days a week and carries a limited line of high-turnover convenience goods.

Conventional distribution channel—A channel consisting of one or more independent producers, wholesalers and retailers, each a separate business seeking to maximise its own profits, even at the expense of profits for the system as a whole.

Corporate (brand) website—A website designed to build customer goodwill, collect customer feedback and supplement other sales channels rather than sell the company's products directly.

Corporate chains (or multiples)—Two or more outlets that are commonly owned and controlled.

Corporate VMS—A vertical marketing system that combines successive stages of production and distribution under single ownership - channel leadership is established through common ownership.

Cost-based pricing—Setting prices based on the costs for producing, distributing and selling the product plus a fair rate of return for effort and risk.

Cost-plus pricing (or mark-up pricing)—A standard mark-up to the cost of the product.

Creative concept—The compelling 'big idea' that will bring the advertising message strategy to life in a distinctive and memorable way.

Crowdsourcing—Inviting broad communities of people - customers, employees, independent scientists and researchers and even the public at large - into the new-product innovation process.

Cultural environment—Institutions and other forces that affect society's basic values, perceptions, preferences and behaviours.

Culture—The set of basic values, perceptions, wants and behaviours learned by a member of society from family and other important institutions.

Customer (or market) sales force structure—A sales force organisation in which salespeople specialise in selling only to certain customers or industries.

Customer database—An organised collection of comprehensive data about individual customers or prospects, including geographic, demographic, psychographic and behavioural data.

Customer-engagement marketing—Making the brand a meaningful part of consumers' conversations and lives by fostering direct and continuous customer involvement in shaping brand conversations, experiences and community.

Customer equity—The total combined customer lifetime values of all of the company's customers.

Customer insights—Fresh understandings of customers and the marketplace derived from marketing information that become the basis for creating customer value and relationships.

Customer lifetime value—The value of the entire stream of purchases that the customer would make over a lifetime of patronage.

Customer relationship management (CRM)— The overall process of building and maintaining profitable customer relationships by delivering superior customer value and satisfaction.

Customer satisfaction—The extent to which a product's perceived performance matches a buyer's expectations.

Customer value analysis—An analysis conducted to determine what benefits target customers value and how they rate the relative value of various competitors' offers.

Customer value-based pricing—Setting price based on buyers' perceptions of value rather than on the seller's cost.

Customer-value marketing—A company should put most of its resources into customer-value-building investments.

Customer-centred company—A company that focuses on customer developments in designing its marketing strategies and delivering superior value to its target customers.

Customer-centred new-product development—New-product development that focuses on finding new ways to solve customer problems and create more customer-satisfying experiences.

Customer-managed relationships—Marketing relationships in which customers, empowered by today's new digital technologies, interact with companies and with each other to shape their relationships with brands.

Customer-perceived value—The customer's evaluation of the difference between all the benefits and all the costs of a marketing offer relative to those of competing offers.

Customer-value marketing—A principle of sustainable marketing that holds a company should put most of its resources into customer-value-building marketing investments.

Deciders—People in an organisation's buying centre who have formal or informal power to select or approve the final suppliers.

Decline stage—The PLC stage in which a product's sales decline.

Deficient products—Products that have neither immediate appeal nor long-term benefits.

Demand curve—A curve that shows the number of units the market will buy in a given time period, at different prices that might be charged.

Demands—Human wants that are backed by buying power.

Demographic segmentation—Dividing the market into segments based on variables such as age, gender, family size, family life cycle, income, occupation, education, religion, race, generation and nationality.

Demography—The study of human populations in terms of size, density, location, age, gender, race, occupation and other statistics.

Department store—A retail organisation that carries a wide variety of product lines – each line is operated as a separate department managed by specialist buyers or merchandisers.

Derived demand—Business demand that ultimately comes from (derives from) the demand for consumer goods.

Descriptive research—Marketing research to better describe marketing problems, situations or markets, such as the market potential for a product or the demographics and attitudes of consumers.

Desirable products—Products that give both high immediate satisfaction and high long-term benefits.

Differentiated (segmented) marketing—A market-coverage strategy in which a firm decides to target several market segments and designs separate offers for each.

Differentiation—Differentiating the market offering to create superior customer value.

Digital and social media marketing—Using digital marketing tools such as websites, social media, mobile apps and ads, online video, email and blogs that engage consumers anywhere, at any time, via their digital devices.

Direct investment—Entering a foreign market by developing foreign-based assembly or manufacturing facilities.

Direct and digital marketing—Engaging directly with carefully targeted individual consumers and customer communities to both obtain an immediate response and build lasting customer relationships.

Direct marketing channel—A marketing channel that has no intermediary levels.

Direct-mail marketing—Direct marketing by sending an offer, announcement, reminder or other item to a person at a particular physical or virtual address.

Direct-response television (DRTV) marketing—Direct marketing via television, including direct-response television advertising (or infomercials) and interactive television (ITV) advertising.

Discount—A straight reduction in price on purchases during a stated period of time or of larger quantities.

Discount store—A retail operation that sells standard merchandise at lower prices by accepting lower margins and selling at higher volume.

Disintermediation—The cutting out of marketing channel intermediaries by product or service producers or the displacement of traditional resellers by radical new types of intermediaries.

Dissonance-reducing buying behaviour—Consumer buying behaviour in situations characterised by high involvement but few perceived differences among brands.

Distribution centre—A large, highly automated warehouse designed to receive goods from various plants and suppliers, take orders, fill them efficiently and deliver goods to customers as quickly as possible.

Diversification—Company growth through starting up or acquiring businesses outside the company's current products and markets.

Downsizing—Reducing the business portfolio by eliminating products or business units that are not profitable or that no longer fit the company's overall strategy.

Dynamic pricing—Adjusting prices continually to meet the characteristics and needs of individual customers and situations.

Economic community—A group of nations organised to work toward common goals in the regulation of international trade.

Economic environment—Economic factors that affect consumer purchasing power and spending patterns.

E-mail marketing—Sending highly targeted, highly personalised, relationship-building marketing messages via e-mail.

Environmental sustainability—A management approach that involves developing strategies that both sustain the environment and produce profits for the company.

Environmentalism—An organised movement of concerned citizens and government agencies to protect and improve people's current and future living environment.

E-procurement—Purchasing through electronic connections between buyers and sellers – usually online.

Ethnographic research—A form of observational research that involves sending trained observers to watch and interact with consumers in their 'natural environments'.

Event marketing (or event sponsorships)—Creating a brand-marketing event or serving as a sole or participating sponsor of events created by others.

Exchange—The act of obtaining a desired object from someone by offering something in return.

Exclusive distribution—Giving a limited number of dealers the exclusive right to distribute the company's products in their territories.

Execution style—The approach, style, tone, words and format used for executing an advertising message.

Executive summary—This section of a marketing plan summarises and overviews the main goals, recommendations and points for senior managers who will read and approve the marketing plan. For management convenience, a table of contents usually follows this section.

Experience curve (learning curve)—The drop in the average per-unit production cost that comes with accumulated production experience.

Experimental research—Gathering primary data by selecting matched groups of subjects, giving them different treatments, controlling related factors and checking for differences in group responses.

Exploratory research—Marketing research to gather preliminary information that will help define problems and suggest hypotheses.

Exporting—Entering a foreign market by selling goods produced in a company's home country, often with little modification.

Factory outlet—An off-price retailing operation that is owned and operated by a manufacturer and normally carries the manufacturer's surplus, discontinued or irregular goods.

Fad—A temporary period of unusually high sales driven by consumer enthusiasm and immediate product or brand popularity.

Fashion—A currently accepted or popular style in a given field.

Fixed costs—Costs that do not vary with production or sales level.

FOB-origin pricing—A geographical pricing strategy in which goods are placed free on board a carrier; the customer pays the freight from the factory to the destination.

Focus group interviewing—Personal interviewing that involves inviting six to ten people to gather for a few hours with a trained interviewer to talk about a product, service or organisation. The interviewer 'focuses' the group discussion on important issues.

Follow up—The sales step in which a salesperson follows up after the sale to ensure customer satisfaction and repeat business.

Franchise organisation—A contractual vertical marketing system in which a channel member, called a franchisor, links several stages in the production–distribution process.

Franchise—A contractual association between a manufacturer, wholesaler or service organisation (a franchisor) and independent businesspeople (franchisees) who buy the right to own and operate one or more units in the franchise system.

Freight-absorption pricing—A geographical pricing strategy in which the seller absorbs all or part of the freight charges to get the desired business.

Gatekeepers—People in an organisation's buying centre who control the flow of information to others.

Gender segmentation—Dividing a market into different segments based on gender.

General need description—The stage in the business buying process in which a buyer describes the general characteristics and quantity of a needed item.

Generation X—The 45 million people born between 1965 and 1976 in the 'birth dearth' following the baby boom.

Generation Z—People born after 2000 (although many analysts include people born after 1995) who make up the 'kids, tweens and teens' markets.

Geographic segmentation—Dividing a market into different geographical units, such as nations, states, regions, counties, cities or even neighbourhoods.

Geographical pricing—Setting prices for customers located in different parts of the country or world.

Global firm—A firm that, by operating in more than one country, gains R&D, production, marketing and financial advantages in its costs and reputation that are not available to purely domestic competitors.

Good-value pricing—Offering the right combination of quality and good service at a fair price.

Government market—Governmental units that purchase or rent goods and services for carrying out the main functions of government.

Gross margin percentage—The percentage of net sales remaining after cost of goods sold – calculated by dividing gross margin by net sales.

Group—Two or more people who interact to accomplish individual or mutual goals.

Growth stage—The PLC stage in which a product's sales start climbing quickly.

Growth-share matrix—A portfolio-planning method that evaluates a company's SBUs in terms of its market growth rate and relative market share.

Habitual buying behaviour—Consumer buying behaviour characterised by low-consumer involvement and few significantly perceived brand differences.

Handling objections—A salesperson seeks out, clarifies and overcomes any customer objections to buying.

Horizontal marketing system—A channel arrangement in which two or more companies at one level join together to follow a new marketing opportunity.

Idea generation—The systematic search for new-product ideas.

Idea screening—Screening new-product ideas to spot good ideas and drop poor ones as soon as possible.

Income segmentation—Dividing a market into different income segments.

Independent off-price retailer—An off-price retailer that is either independently owned and run or is a division of a larger retail corporation.

Indirect marketing channel—Channel containing one or more intermediary levels.

Individual marketing—Tailoring products and marketing programmes to the needs and preferences of individual customers – also called *one-to-one marketing*, *customised marketing* and *markets-of-one marketing*.

Industrial product—A product bought by individuals and organisations for further processing or for use in conducting a business.

Influencers—People in an organisation's buying centre who affect the buying decision; they often help define specifications and also provide information for evaluating alternatives.

Information search—The stage of the buyer decision process in which the consumer is aroused to search for more information; the consumer may simply have heightened attention or may go into an active information search.

Innovative marketing—A principle of sustainable marketing that requires a company to seek real product and marketing improvements.

Inside sales force—Salespeople who conduct business from their offices via telephone, the Internet or visits from prospective buyers.

Institutional market—Schools, hospitals, nursing homes, prisons and other institutions that provide goods and services to people in their care.

Integrated logistics management—The logistics concept that emphasises teamwork – both inside the company and among all the marketing channel organisations – to maximise the performance of the entire distribution system.

Integrated marketing communications (IMC)—Carefully integrating and coordinating the company's many communications channels to deliver a clear, consistent and compelling message about an organisation and its products.

Intensive distribution—Stocking the product in as many outlets as possible.

Interactive marketing—Training service employees in the fine art of interacting with customers to satisfy their needs.

Intermarket segmentation (cross-market segmentation)—Forming segments of consumers who have similar needs and buying behaviour even though they are located in different countries.

Intermodal transportation—Combining two or more modes of transportation.

Internal databases—Electronic collections of consumer and market information obtained from data sources within the company network.

Internal marketing—Orienting and motivating customer contact employees and supporting service people to work as a team to provide customer satisfaction.

Internet—A vast public web of computer networks that connects users of all types around the world to each other and an amazingly large information repository.

Introduction stage—The PLC stage in which a new product is first distributed and made available for purchase.

Inventory turnover rate (or stockturn rate)—The number of times an inventory turns over or is sold during a specified time period (often one year) – calculated based on costs, selling price, or units.

Joint ownership—A joint venture in which a company joins investors in a foreign market to create a local business in which a company shares joint ownership and control.

Joint venturing—Entering foreign markets by joining with foreign companies to produce or market a product or a service.

Learning—Changes in an individual's behaviour arising from experience.

Licensing—A method of entering a foreign market in which a company enters into an agreement with a licensee in a foreign market.

Lifestyle—A person's pattern of living as expressed in his or her activities, interests and opinions.

Line extension—Extending an existing brand name to new forms, colours, sizes, ingredients or flavours of an existing product category.

Local marketing—Tailoring brands and promotions to the needs and wants of local customer segments – cities, neighbourhoods and even specific stores.

Macroenvironment—The larger societal forces that affect the microenvironment – demographic, economic, natural, technological, political and cultural forces.

Madison & Vine—A term that has come to represent the merging of advertising and entertainment in an effort to break through the clutter and create new avenues for reaching consumers with more engaging messages.

Management contracting—A joint venture in which a domestic firm supplies the management know-how to a foreign company that supplies the capital; the domestic firm exports management services rather than products.

Manufacturers' and retailers' branches and offices—Wholesaling by sellers or buyers themselves rather than through independent wholesalers.

Market challenger—A runner-up firm that is fighting hard to increase its market share in an industry.

Market description—Describes the targeted segments in detail and provides context for the marketing strategies and detailed action programmes.

Market development—Company growth by identifying and developing new market segments for current company products.

Market follower—A runner-up firm that wants to hold its share in an industry without rocking the boat.

Market leader—The firm in an industry with the largest market share.

Market nicher—A firm that serves small segments that the other firms in an industry overlook or ignore.

Market offerings—Some combination of products, services, information or experiences offered to a market to satisfy a need or want.

Market penetration—Company growth by increasing sales of current products to current market segments without changing the product.

Market potential—The upper limit of market demand.

Market segment—A group of consumers who respond in a similar way to a given set of marketing efforts.

Market segmentation—Dividing a market into distinct groups of buyers who have different needs, characteristics or behaviours, and who might require separate products or marketing programmes.

Market share—Company sales divided by market sales.

Market targeting—The process of evaluating each market segment's attractiveness and selecting one or more segments to enter.

Market—The set of all actual and potential buyers of a product or service.

Market-centred company—A company that pays balanced attention to both customers and competitors in designing its marketing strategies.

Marketing channel (or distribution channel)—A set of interdependent organisations that help make a product or service available for use or consumption by the consumer or business user.

Marketing channel design—Designing effective marketing channels by analysing customer needs, setting channel objectives, identifying major channel alternatives and evaluating those alternatives.

Marketing channel management—Selecting, managing and motivating individual channel members and evaluating their performance over time.

Marketing concept—A philosophy that holds that achieving organisational goals depends on knowing the needs and wants of target markets and delivering the desired satisfactions better than competitors do.

Marketing control—Measuring and evaluating the results of marketing strategies and plans and taking corrective action to ensure that the objectives are achieved.

Marketing environment—The actors and forces outside marketing that affect marketing management's ability to build and maintain successful relationships with target customers.

Marketing implementation—Turning marketing strategies and plans into marketing actions to accomplish strategic marketing objectives.

Marketing information system (MIS)—People and procedures for assessing information needs, developing the needed information, and helping decision makers to use the information to generate and validate actionable customer and market insights.

Marketing intermediaries—Firms that help the company to promote, sell and distribute its goods to final buyers.

Marketing logistics (or physical distribution)—Planning, implementing and controlling the physical flow of materials, final goods and related information from points of origin to points of consumption to meet customer requirements at a profit.

Marketing management—The art and science of choosing target markets and building profitable relationships with them.

Marketing mix—The set of tactical marketing tools – product, price, place and promotion – that the firm blends to produce the response it wants in the target market.

Marketing myopia—The mistake of paying more attention to the specific products a company offers than to the benefits and experiences produced by these products.

Marketing organisation—The marketing department may be organised by function, geography, product or customer (or some combination thereof).

Marketing research—The systematic design, collection, analysis and reporting of data relevant to a specific marketing situation facing an organisation.

Marketing return on investment (or marketing ROI)—A measure of the marketing productivity of a marketing investment – calculated by dividing net marketing contribution by marketing expenses.

Marketing return on sales (or marketing ROS)—The percent of net sales attributable to the net marketing contribution – calculated by dividing net marketing contribution by net sales.

Marketing strategy development—Designing an initial marketing strategy for a new product based on the product concept.

Marketing strategy—The marketing logic by which the company hopes to create customer value and achieve profitable customer relationships.

Marketing website—A website that engages consumers in interactions that will move them closer to a direct purchase or other marketing outcome.

Marketing—The process by which companies create value for customers and build strong customer relationships to capture value from customers in return.

Market-penetration pricing—Setting a low price for a new product to attract a large number of buyers and a large market share.

Market-skimming pricing (price skimming)—Setting a high price for a new product to skim maximum revenues layer by layer from the segments willing to pay the high price; the company makes fewer but more profitable sales.

Mark-up—The difference between a company's selling price for a product and its cost to manufacture or purchase it.

Mark-up chain—The sequence of mark-ups used by firms at each level in a channel.

Maturity stage—The PLC stage in which a product's sales growth slows or levels off.

Merchant wholesaler—An independently owned wholesale business that takes title to the merchandise it handles.

Microenvironment—The actors close to the company that affect its ability to serve its customers – the company, suppliers, marketing intermediaries, customer markets, competitors and publics.

Micromarketing—Tailoring products and marketing programmes to the needs and wants of specific individuals and local customer segments; It includes *local marketing* and *individual marketing*.

Millennials (or Generation Y)—The 83 million children of the baby boomers, born between 1977 and 2000.

Mission statement—A statement of the organisation's purpose – what it wants to accomplish in the larger environment.

Mobile marketing—Marketing messages, promotions and other content delivered to on-the-go consumers through mobile phones, smartphones, tablets and other mobile devices.

Modified rebuy—A business buying situation in which the buyer wants to modify product specifications, prices, terms or suppliers.

Motive (drive)—A need that is sufficiently pressing to direct the person to seek satisfaction of the need.

Multi-channel distribution system—A distribution system in which a single firm sets up two or more marketing channels to reach one or more customer segments.

Multichannel marketing—Marketing both through stores and other traditional offline channels and through digital, online, social media and mobile channels.

Multimodal transport—Combining two or more modes of transport.

Natural environment—Natural resources that are needed as inputs by marketers or that are affected by marketing activities.

Need recognition—The first stage of the buyer decision process, in which the consumer recognises a problem or need.

Needs—States of felt deprivation.

Net marketing contribution (NMC)—A measure of marketing profitability that includes only components of profitability controlled by marketing.

Net profit percentage—The percentage of each sales euro going to profit – calculated by dividing net profits by net sales.

New product—A good, service or idea that is perceived by some potential customers as new.

New task—A business buying situation in which the buyer purchases a product or service for the first time.

New-product development—The development of original products, product improvements, product modifications and new brands through the firm's own product development efforts.

Non-personal communication channels—Media that carry messages without personal contact or feedback, including major media, atmospheres and events.

Objective-and-task method—Developing the promotion budget by (1) defining specific promotion objectives, (2) determining the tasks needed to achieve these objectives and (3) estimating the costs of performing these tasks. The sum of these costs is the proposed promotion budget.

Observational research—Gathering primary data by observing relevant people, actions and situations.

Occasion segmentation—Dividing the market into segments according to occasions when buyers get the idea to buy, actually make their purchase or use the purchased item.

Off-price retailer—A retailer that buys at less-than-regular wholesale prices and sells at less than retail. Examples are factory outlets, independents and warehouse clubs.

Online advertising—Advertising that appears while consumers are browsing the Web, including display ads, search-related ads, online classifieds and other forms.

Online focus groups—Gathering a small group of people online with a trained moderator to chat about a product, service or organisation and gain qualitative insights about consumer attitudes and behaviour.

Online marketing research—Collecting primary data online through Internet surveys, online focus groups, Web-based experiments or tracking consumers' online behaviour.

Online marketing—Marketing via the Internet using company websites, online ads and promotions, e-mail, online video and blogs.

Online social networks—Online social communities – blogs, social networking websites or even virtual worlds – where people socialise or exchange information and opinions.

Operating expense percentage—The portion of net sales going to operating expenses – calculated by dividing total expenses by net sales.

Operating ratios—The ratios of selected operating statement items to net sales.

Opinion leader—A person within a reference group who, because of special skills, knowledge, personality or other characteristics, exerts social influence on others.

Opportunities—Opportunities are external elements that a company may be able to exploit to its advantage.

Optional product pricing—The pricing of optional or accessory products along with a main product.

Order-routine specification—The stage of the business buying process in which the buyer writes the final order with the chosen supplier(s), listing the technical specifications, quantity needed, expected time of delivery, return policies and warranties.

Outside sales force (or field sales force)—Salespeople who travel to call on customers in the field.

Packaging—The activities of designing and producing the container or wrapper for a product.

Partner relationship management—Working closely with partners in other company departments and outside the company to jointly bring greater value to customers.

Percentage-of-sales method—Setting the promotion budget at a certain percentage of current or forecasted sales or as a percentage of the unit sales price.

Perception—The process by which people select, organise and interpret information to form a meaningful picture of the world.

Performance review—The stage of the business buying process in which the buyer assesses the performance of the supplier and decides to continue, modify or drop the arrangement.

Personal communication channels—Channels through which two or more people communicate directly with each other, including face to face, on the phone, via mail or e-mail, or even through an Internet 'chat'.

Personal selling—Personal presentation by the firm's sales force for the purpose of making sales and building customer relationships.

Personality—The unique psychological characteristics that distinguish a person or group.

Pleasing products—Products that give high immediate satisfaction but may hurt consumers in the long term.

Political environment—Laws, government agencies and pressure groups that influence and limit various organisations and individuals in a given society.

Portfolio analysis—The process by which management evaluates the products and businesses that make up the company.

Positioning statement—A statement that summarises company or brand positioning. It takes this form: *To (target segment and need) our (brand) is (concept) that (point of difference)*.

Positioning—Arranging for a product to occupy a clear, distinctive and desirable place relative to competing products in the minds of target consumers. Positioning built on meaningful differentiation, supported by appropriate strategy and implementation, can help a company build competitive advantage.

Postpurchase behaviour—The stage of the buyer decision process in which consumers take further action after purchase based on their satisfaction or dissatisfaction with a purchase.

Preapproach—The sales step in which a salesperson learns as much as possible about a prospective customer before making a sales call.

Presentation—The sales step in which a salesperson tells the 'value story' to the buyer, showing how the company's offer solves the customer's problems.

Price elasticity of demand—A measure of the sensitivity of demand to changes in price.

Price—The amount of money charged for a product or a service; the sum of the values that customers exchange for the benefits of having or using the product or service.

Primary data—Information collected for the specific purpose at hand.

Pro forma (or projected) profit-and-loss statement (or income statement or operating statement)—A statement that shows projected revenues less budgeted expenses and estimates the projected net profit for an organisation, product or brand during a specific planning period, typically a year.

Problem recognition—The first stage of the business buying process in which someone in the company recognises a problem or need that can be met by acquiring a good or a service.

Product adaptation—Adapting a product to meet local conditions or wants in foreign markets.

Product bundle pricing—Combining several products and offering the bundle at a reduced price.

Product concept—The idea that consumers will favour products that offer the most quality, performance and features and that the organisation should therefore devote its energy to making continuous product improvements.

Product development–Developing the product concept into a physical product to ensure that the product idea can be turned into a workable market offering.

Product invention–Creating new products or services for foreign markets.

Product life cycle (PLC)–The course of a product's sales and profits over its lifetime. It involves five distinct stages: product development, introduction, growth, maturity and decline.

Product line pricing–Setting the price steps between various products in a product line based on cost differences between the products, customer evaluations of different features and competitors' prices.

Product line–A group of products that are closely related because they function in a similar manner, are sold to the same customer groups, are marketed through the same types of outlets, or fall within given price ranges.

Product mix (or product portfolio)–The set of all product lines and items that a particular seller offers for sale.

Product position–The way the product is defined by consumers on important attributes – the place the product occupies in consumers' minds relative to competing products.

Product quality–The characteristics of a product or service that bear on its ability to satisfy stated or implied customer needs.

Product review–The product review summarises the main features for all of a company's products, organised by product line, type of customer, market and/or order of product introduction.

Product sales force structure–A sales force organisation in which salespeople specialise in selling only a portion of the company's products or lines.

Product specification–The stage of the business buying process in which the buying organisation decides on and specifies the best technical product characteristics for a needed item.

Product–Anything that can be offered to a market for attention, acquisition, use or consumption that might satisfy a want or need.

Product/market expansion grid–A portfolio-planning tool for identifying company growth opportunities through market penetration, market development, product development or diversification.

Production concept–The idea that consumers will favour products that are available and highly affordable and that the organisation should therefore focus on improving production and distribution efficiency.

Profit-and-loss statement (or income statement or operating statement)–A statement that shows actual revenues less expenses and net profit for an organisation, product or brand during a specific planning period, typically a year.

Promotion mix (or marketing communications mix)–The specific blend of promotion tools that the company uses to persuasively communicate customer value and build customer relationships.

Promotional pricing–Temporarily pricing products below the list price, and sometimes even below cost, to increase short-term sales.

Proposal solicitation–The stage of the business buying process in which the buyer invites qualified suppliers to submit proposals.

Prospecting–A salesperson or company identifies qualified potential customers.

Psychographic segmentation–Dividing a market into different segments based on social class, lifestyle or personality characteristics.

Psychological pricing–Pricing that considers the psychology of prices, not simply the economics; the price says something about the product.

Public relations (PR)–Building good relations with the company's various publics by obtaining favourable publicity, building up a good corporate image, and handling or heading off unfavourable rumours, stories and events.

Public–Any group that has an actual or potential interest in or impact on an organisation's ability to achieve its objectives.

Pull strategy–A promotion strategy that calls for spending a lot on consumer advertising and promotion to induce final consumers to buy a particular product, creating a demand vacuum that 'pulls' a product through the channel.

Purchase decision–The buyer's decision about which brand to purchase.

Push strategy–A promotion strategy that calls for using the sales force and trade promotion to push a product through channels. A producer promotes a particular product to channel members, who in turn promote it to final consumers.

Reference prices–Prices that buyers carry in their minds and refer to when they look at a given product.

Relevant costs–Costs that will occur in the future and that will vary across the alternatives being considered.

Retailer–A business whose sales come *primarily* from retailing.

Retailing–All the activities involved in selling goods or services directly to final consumers for their personal, non-business use.

Return on advertising investment–The net return on advertising investment divided by the costs of the advertising investment.

Return on investment (ROI) pricing (or target-return pricing)–A cost-based pricing method that determines price based on a specified rate of return on investment.

Return on marketing investment (or marketing ROI)–The net return from a marketing investment divided by the costs of the marketing investment.

(ROI)–A measure of managerial effectiveness and efficiency – net profit before taxes divided by total investment.

Sales 2.0–The merging of innovative sales practices with Web 2.0 technologies to improve sales force effectiveness and efficiency.

Sales force management–Analysing, planning, implementing and controlling sales force activities.

Sales promotion–Short-term incentives to encourage the purchase or sale of a product or a service.

Sales quota–A standard that states the amount a salesperson should sell and how sales should be divided among the company's products.

Salesperson–An individual representing a company to customers by performing one or more of the following activities:

prospecting, communicating, selling, servicing, information gathering and relationship building.

Salutary products—Products that have low appeal but may benefit consumers in the long term.

Sample—A segment of the population selected for marketing research to represent the population as a whole.

Secondary data—Information that already exists somewhere, having been collected for another purpose.

Segmented pricing—Selling a product or service at two or more prices, where the difference in prices is not based on differences in costs.

Selective distribution—The use of more than one but fewer than all the intermediaries who are willing to carry the company's products.

Selling concept—The idea that consumers will not buy enough of the firm's products unless it undertakes a large-scale selling and promotion effort.

Selling process—The steps that salespeople follow when selling, which include prospecting and qualifying, pre-approaching, approaching, presenting and demonstrating, handling objections, closing and following up.

Sense-of-mission marketing—A principle of sustainable marketing that holds a company should define its mission in broad social terms rather than narrow product terms.

Service inseparability—Services are produced and consumed at the same time and cannot be separated from their providers.

Service intangibility—Services cannot be seen, tasted, felt, heard or smelled before they are bought.

Service perishability—Services cannot be stored for later sale or use.

Service profit chain—The chain that links service firm profits with employee and customer satisfaction.

Service retailer—A retailer whose product line is actually a service, including hotels, airlines, banks, colleges and many others.

Service variability—The quality of services may vary greatly depending on who provides them and when, where and how.

Service—An activity, benefit or satisfaction offered for sale that is essentially intangible and does not result in the ownership of anything.

Share of customer—The portion of the customer's purchasing that a company gets in its product categories.

Shopper marketing—Using in-store promotions and advertising to extend brand equity to 'the last mile' and encourage favourable in-store purchase decisions.

Shopping centre—A group of retail businesses built on a site that is planned, developed, owned and managed as a unit.

Shopping product—A consumer product that the customer, in the process of selecting and purchasing, usually compares on such attributes as suitability, quality, price and style.

Showrooming—The shopping practice of coming into retail store showrooms to check out merchandise and prices but instead buying from an online-only rival, sometimes while in the store.

Social class—Relatively permanent and ordered divisions in a society whose members share similar values, interests and behaviours.

Social marketing—The use of commercial marketing concepts and tools in programmes designed to influence individuals' behaviour to improve their well-being and that of society.

Social media—Independent and commercial online communities where people congregate, socialise and exchange views and information.

Social selling—Using online, mobile and social media to engage customers, build stronger customer relationships and augment sales performance.

Societal marketing concept—The idea that a company's marketing decisions should consider consumers' wants, the company's requirements, and the long-term interests of consumers and society.

Societal marketing—A principle of sustainable marketing that holds a company should make marketing decisions by considering consumers' wants, the company's requirements, consumers' long-run interests and society's long-run interests.

Spam—Unsolicited, unwanted commercial e-mail messages.

Speciality product—A consumer product with unique characteristics or brand identification for which a significant group of buyers is willing to make a special purchase effort.

Speciality store—A retail store that carries a narrow product line with a deep assortment within that line.

Standardised global marketing—An international marketing strategy that basically uses the same marketing strategy and mix in all of a company's international markets.

Store brand (or private brand)—A brand created and owned by a reseller of a product or service.

Straight product extension—Marketing a product in a foreign market without any changes to the product.

Straight rebuy—A business buying situation in which the buyer routinely reorders something without any modifications.

Strategic group—A group of firms in an industry following the same or a similar strategy.

Strategic planning—The process of developing and maintaining a strategic fit between the organisation's goals and capabilities and its changing marketing opportunities.

Strengths—Strengths are internal capabilities that can help a company reach its objectives.

Style—A basic and distinctive mode of expression.

Subculture—A group of people with shared value systems based on common life experiences and situations.

Supermarket—A large, low-cost, low-margin, high-volume, self-service store that carries a wide variety of grocery and household products.

Superstore—A store much larger than a regular supermarket that offers a large assortment of routinely purchased food products, non-food items and services.

Supplier development—Systematic development of networks of supplier-partners to ensure an appropriate and dependable supply of products and materials for use in making products or reselling them to others.

Supplier search—The stage of the business buying process in which the buyer tries to find the best vendors.

Supplier selection—The stage of the business buying process in which the buyer reviews proposals and selects a supplier or suppliers.

Supply chain management—Managing upstream and downstream value-added flows of materials, final goods and related information among suppliers, the company, resellers and final consumers.

Survey research—Gathering primary data by asking people questions about their knowledge, attitudes, preferences and buying behaviour.

Sustainable marketing—Socially and environmentally responsible marketing that meets the present needs of consumers and businesses while also preserving or enhancing the ability of future generations to meet their needs.

SWOT analysis—An overall evaluation of the company's strengths (S), weaknesses (W), opportunities (O) and threats (T).

Systems selling (or solutions selling)—Buying a packaged solution to a problem from a single seller, thus avoiding all the separate decisions involved in a complex buying situation.

Target costing—Pricing that starts with an ideal selling price and then targets costs that will ensure that the price is met.

Target market—A set of buyers sharing common needs or characteristics that the company decides to serve.

Team selling—Using teams of people from sales, marketing, engineering, finance, technical support and even upper management to service large, complex accounts.

Team-based new-product development—An approach to developing new products in which various company departments work closely together, overlapping the steps in the product development process to save time and increase effectiveness.

Technological environment—Forces that create new technologies, creating new product and market opportunities.

Telemarketing—Using the telephone to sell directly to customers.

Telephone marketing—Using the telephone to sell directly to customers.

Territorial sales force structure—A sales force organisation that assigns each salesperson to an exclusive geographic territory in which that salesperson sells the company's full line.

Test marketing—The stage of new-product development in which the product and its proposed marketing programme are tested in realistic market settings.

Third-party logistics (3PL) provider—An independent logistics provider that performs any or all of the functions required to get a client's product to market.

Threats—Threats are current or emerging external elements that could potentially challenge a company's performance.

Total costs—The sum of the fixed and variable costs for any given level of production.

Total market demand—The total volume that would be bought by a defined consumer group, in a defined geographic area, in a defined time period, in a defined marketing environment, under a defined level and mix of industry marketing effort.

Trade promotions—Sales promotion tools used to persuade resellers to carry a brand, give it shelf space and promote it in advertising.

Undifferentiated (mass) marketing—A market-coverage strategy in which a firm decides to ignore market segment differences and go after the whole market with one offer.

Uniform-delivered pricing—A geographical pricing strategy in which the company charges the same price plus freight to all customers, regardless of their location.

Unit contribution—The amount that each unit contributes to covering fixed costs – the difference between price and variable costs.

Unsought product—A consumer product that the consumer either does not know about or knows about but does not normally consider buying.

Users—Members of the buying organisation who will actually use the purchased product or service.

Value chain—The series of internal departments that carry out value-creating activities to design, produce, market, deliver and support a firm's products.

Value delivery network—A network composed of the company, suppliers, distributors and, ultimately, customers who 'partner' with each other to improve the performance of the entire system in delivering customer value.

Value proposition—The full positioning of a brand – the full mix of benefits on which it is positioned.

Value-added pricing—Attaching value-added features and services to differentiate a company's offers and charging higher prices.

Value-based pricing—Offering just the right combination of quality and good service at a fair price.

Variable costs—Costs that vary directly with the level of production.

Variety-seeking buying behaviour—Consumer buying behaviour characterised by low consumer involvement but significant perceived brand differences.

Vertical marketing system (VMS)—A distribution channel structure in which producers, wholesalers and retailers act as a unified system. One channel member owns the others, has contracts with them, or has so much power that they all cooperate.

Viral marketing—The Internet version of word-of-mouth marketing: websites, videos, e-mail messages or other marketing events that are so infectious that customers will want to pass them along to friends.

Wants—The form human needs take as they are shaped by culture and individual personality.

Warehouse club—An off-price retailer that sells a limited selection of brand name grocery items, appliances, clothing and a hodge-podge of other goods at deep discounts to members who pay annual membership fees.

Weaknesses—Weaknesses are internal elements that may interfere with a company's ability to achieve its objectives.

Wheel-of-retailing concept—A concept that states that new types of retailers usually begin as low-margin, low-price, low-status operations but later evolve into higher-priced, higher-service operations, eventually becoming like the conventional retailers they replaced.

Whole-channel view—Designing international channels that take into account the entire global supply chain and marketing channel, forging an effective global value delivery network.

Wholesaler—A firm engaged *primarily* in wholesaling activities.

Wholesaling—All the activities involved in selling goods and services to those buying for resale or business use.

Word-of-mouth influence—Personal communications about a product between target buyers and neighbours, friends, family members and associates.

Workload method—An approach to determining sales force size based on the workload required and the time available for selling.

Zone pricing—A geographical pricing strategy in which the company sets up two or more zones. All customers within a zone pay the same total price; the more distant the zone, the higher the price.

INDEX